WEST'S
BUSINESS
LAW

ALTERNATE UCC
COMPREHENSIVE
EDITION

WEST'S BUSINESS LAW

ALTERNATE
UCC
COMPREHENSIVE
EDITION

KENNETH W. CLARKSON
University of Miami School of Law

ROGER LeROY MILLER
University of Miami School of Business

STEPHEN A. CHAPLIN
University of Miami School of Law

BONNIE BLAIRE
Sparber, Shevin, Rosen, Shapo, and Heilbronner
Miami Florida

WEST PUBLISHING COMPANY
St. Paul   New York   Los Angeles   San Francisco

West's Business Law: Alternate, UCC, Comprehensive Edition is reprinted in part from *West's Business Law: Text and Cases*, Copyright © 1980 by West Publishing Co.

COPYRIGHT © 1981 By WEST PUBLISHING CO.
        50 West Kellogg Boulevard
        P.O. Box 3526
        St. Paul, Minnesota 55165

Library of Congress Cataloging in Publication Data

West's business law.
Edition for 1980 by K. W. Clarkson, R. L. Miller, and B. Blaire.
Bibliography: p.

Includes index.
1. Commercial law—United States—Cases.
2. Business law—United States.
I. Clarkson, Kenneth W.
II Clarkson, Kenneth W. West's business law.
III. West Publishing Company, St. Paul.
KF888.C55 1981   346.73'07   80-25189
ISBN 0-8299-0366-6

A study guide has been developed to assist you in mastering the concepts presented in this text. The study guide includes outlines, and fill-in-the-blanks and multiple choice questions with answers. This study guide is available from your local bookstore under the title *Study Guide to Accompany West's Business Law: Alternate, UCC, Comprehensive Edition* prepared by Barbara Behr.

If you cannot locate it in your bookstore, ask your bookstore manager to order it for you.

PREFACE

The average business man or woman is now, more than ever before, practically inundated with possible legal problems. So, too, is the average consumer. We are clearly witnessing a trend in American society in which the law is taking on more importance. It is with this underlying fact in mind that we have written this text. Familiarity with the legal process and specific laws can only benefit today's business student whether or not he or she continues a career in the world of commerce. We have written this text to present with maximum accuracy the legal realities facing business men and women of today.

While we cannot in any way dictate how business law should be taught, we can and have attempted to present a text that allows maximum flexibility to the instructor. To that end, you will find this text to be extremely comprehensive. Instructors can choose those areas of the law that they wish to emphasize rather than depending on our, the authors', personal preferences.

OTHER SPECIAL FEATURES OF THIS TEXT

In addition to being comprehensive and, we believe, accurate, our text provides some unique features for the student and the instructor.

1. **Cases fully integrated:** Cases follow the legal point that they either substantiate or illustrate rather than appearing at the back of each chapter.

2. **Cases have a unique format:** The case cite is fully presented in the margin. *Background and Facts*, followed by *Decision and Rationale* are presented in italics to differentiate them from the text. In most cases, the *Decision and Rationale* section ends with actual case excerpts.

3. **Vocabulary stressed:** Each time a new word of importance is introduced, it is presented in bold face. A further explanation of bold faced terms is given in a glossary at the end of the text.

4. **Easy to read and learn from:** The text is written in an easy-to-read manner that is liberally broken up with appropriate subheadings of four different levels. This greatly eases the learning process and allows for easier outlining by the student reader.

5. **Case questions and problems:** At the end of every chapter, there are approximately ten questions and case problems. The majority of these are taken out of important cases for which full and correct cites are given. Complete answers to these end-of-chapter problems and questions are given in a separate booklet which instructors may order to put on reserve in their libraries. The answers to these end-of-chapter problems and questions constitute a complete review of the law.

UNIQUE CHAPTERS

In keeping with the trends in today's law, we have added several unique chapters that we believe many professors will want to use. They cover **Limited Partnerships, Special Corporate Forms** (including subchapter S corporations), and **Private Franchises.** We have also added an entire unit on government regulation which includes chapters on **Regulation and Administrative Agencies, Consumer Protection, Environmental Law, Antitrust,** and **Trade Regulation.** Finally, since many students taking this course will use some of the law they have learned in their own personal lives, we have included a final chapter on **Wills, Trusts, and Estates.**

UCC APPENDIX

Because many students keep their text as a reference source, we have included a fully updated *Uniform Commercial Code* in the appendix.

SUPPLEMENTAL MATERIALS

We realize that most business law teachers face a difficult task in finding the time to teach all of the materials they are required to teach during each term. We have developed, with several colleagues, supplementary materials which will ease both the students' and instructors' jobs.

Study Guide

Professor Barbara Behr of Bloomsburg State College has put together what we believe to be the most comprehensive, informative, and helpful *Study Guide* for business law students that exists. It is directly aimed at allowing the student to comprehend not only "black letter" law but also some of the subtleties behind the legal process. Basically, though, it is designed to allow the student to comprehend each chapter in such a way that exam time will not be a moment of panic. The student workbook contains:

1. A "things to keep in mind" section.
2. An outline of the chapter.
3. A set of fill-in questions (a type of program learning device).
4. A set of multiple choice questions.
5. The answers to the fill-in and multiple choice questions.

Instructor's Manual and Test Banks

Testing is an inevitable part of teaching business law. With the help of William Auslen and Stephen Chaplin, we have put together approximately 600 multiple choice and 600 true and false questions that instructors can use to make up their exams. We have also included in the *Instructor's Manual* the answers to the end-of-chapter questions and case problems. As mentioned above, these answers also appear in a separately-bound booklet which can be put on reserve in your library. An alternate booklet of over 800 multiple choice and true and false questions is also available under the title *Alternate Test Items to Accompany West's Business Law.* Further, WESTEST, a computerized testing program is also available to qualified adopters.

Legal Business Forms

A separate booklet of approximately forty often used sample forms is also available.

ACKNOWLEDGEMENTS

Literally hundreds of individuals have participated in one way or another on this project. While it is impossible for us to mention all of them here, we would like to thank a number of individuals for the extraordinary jobs they have done in helping us. In particular, Barbara Behr of Bloomsburg State College, the author of the *Study Guide,* has been a consistent, never-tiring critic of our work. She read the second and third drafts of the manuscript and made extensive comments throughout, helping us refine our presentation and the correctness of the law. Stephen Chaplin, the co-author of the *Instructor's Manual* and also the author of the end-of-chapter questions and case problems, has worked with us well beyond the call of duty. He has made extensive comments at various stages of our project and has helped us immensely. We have had helpful research assistance from Joseph Krabacher, Andrew Caverly, Randy Chartash, Robert Staaf, and others at the University of Miami School of Law. We were also able to impose on other colleagues at the University of Miami School of Law without them complaining too loudly. In particular, we wish to thank Professors Daniel E. Murray, Richard A. Hausler, Irwin Stotzky, and Patrick O. Gudridge. Finally, we wish to acknowledge valuable secretarial assistance from Linda Craig and Mary Gilmore.

Since we firmly believe that this book should be the most accurate of any published, we have relied on in-house help from the staff at West Publishing Company. Additionally, we have had numerous reviewers throughout the country. They are: Robert D. McNutt, California State University, Northridge; Roger E. Meiners, Texas A & M University; James E. Moon, Meyer, Johnson & Moon, Minneapolis; William Auslen, San Francisco City College; Barbara Behr, Bloomsburg State College - Pennsylvania; Donald Cantwell, University of Texas at Arlington; Frank Forbes, University of Nebraska; Bob Garrett, American River College - California; Thomas Gossman, Western Michigan University; Charles Hartman, Wright State University, Ohio; Robert Jesperson, University of Houston; Susan Liebeler, Loyola University; Gerald S. Meisel, Bergen Community College - New Jersey; Bob Morgan, Eastern Michigan University; Arthur Southwick, University of Michigan; Raymond Mason Taylor, North Carolina State; Edwin Tucker, University of Connecticut; Gary Victor, Eastern Michigan University; Gary Watson, California State University, Los Angeles; Jeffrey E. Allen, University of Miami.

Needless to say, we do not hold any of the above-mentioned individuals responsible for any errors that might exist in this text. We do ask, however, that instructors who believe that they have found an error to write us about it. It is only through the help of concerned teachers of business law that we can continue to improve upon our product and make it even more well-suited for today's student of business law.

CONTENTS IN BRIEF

ix

CONTENTS

TABLE OF CASES

The principal cases are in italic type. Cases cited or discussed are in roman type.

WEST'S
BUSINESS
LAW
ALTERNATE UCC
COMPREHENSIVE
EDITION

UNIT I

The Legal Environment Of Business

1

Introduction
to the Law

WHAT IS THE LAW?

Oliver Wendell Holmes contended that the law was a set of rules that allowed one to predict how a court would resolve a particular dispute—"the prophecies of what the courts will do in fact, and nothing more pretentious, are what I mean by the law." Aristotle saw the law as a rule of conduct. Plato believed it was a form of social control. Cicero contended that it was the agreement of reason and nature, the distinction between the just and the unjust. The British jurist, Sir William Blackstone, described the law as "a rule of civil conduct prescribed by the supreme power in a state, commanding what is right, and prohibiting what is wrong."

There have been and will continue to be different definitions of the law. We can begin to understand something about the nature of law by looking at two different approaches to the study of it. The *traditional approach* sees the law as a body of principles and rules that courts apply in deciding disputes. The study of law is the study of these rules and the general principles of right and wrong on which the rules are based. Reason and logic tell how the rules should be applied in specific cases. The traditional approach is based on the idea that the principles of right and wrong are unchanging even though society changes. This approach fulfills one of the important functions of law—to provide stability and continuity so that people can be sure of how to order their affairs.

The *environmental approach* sees the law as only one part of the total environment of society. The law is the institution that specializes in social control, and other parts of society act upon and influence it. Studying the process by which the broader society shapes the rules is part of the study of law. In the legal world this approach is known as sociological juris-prudence. The environmentalist emphasizes how social change is accomplished by using the legal system and how the law functions to provide an orderly process for social change. The environmentalist believes that if the law fails to adapt to changes in technology, attitude, and organization, social change may become violent.

Most of the material in this book takes the traditional approach. It presents the rules of law that apply to the business world and the principles on which they are based. Remember, however, that outside forces in the environment *do* shape the rules. The interplay between logic and social pressure and the tension between stability and change act on the law and the courts.

SCHOOLS OF LEGAL, OR JURISPRUDENTIAL, THOUGHT

The court opinions in this book show that judges will often refer to custom, logic, history, or a philosophy of what is right in making a decision. Sometimes, however, they may seem to ignore custom and history, to stretch their logic to the breaking point, and to depart from previous notions of what is right. It would be easy to shrug one's shoulders, say "that's legal reasoning," and dismiss the majority of judges as scoundrels. However, there are reasons for deciding a case one way as opposed to another. Part of the study of law, or **jurisprudence,** is discovering what these reasons are.

All legal philosophers would agree that custom, history, logic, and ideals have influenced the development of the law in some way. They disagree, however, on the importance that each of these influences should have in shaping the law, and their disagreements have produced different schools or philosophies of jurisprudence.

The Natural Law School

The natural law philosopher assumes that there is an ideal state of being, either inherent in the nature of humanity or derived from a divine source. This ideal state, or *natural law*, presupposes a definite right and wrong. The purpose of a legal system is to order society toward the ideal of natural law. People do not create this natural law; they discover it through the use of reason and the knowledge of good and evil. The natural law school emphasizes ethics as the source of the law's authority. It uses basic philosophical values to make legal decisions. Documents such as the Magna Carta, the Declaration of Independence, the U.S. Constitution, and the U.N. Declaration of Human Rights reflect natural law ideals in phrases like: "We hold these truths to be self-evident, that all men are created equal, that they are endowed by their creator with certain inalienable rights. . . ."

The Historical School

The historical school emphasizes the evolutionary process of law. It concentrates on the origin and history of the legal system and looks to the past to discover what the principles of contemporary law should be. The legal principles that have withstood the passage of time—those that have worked in the past—should be used to shape present laws. Thus, law develops in and with the social environment. The law's legitimacy and authority come from adhering to the principles that historical development has shown to be workable.

The Analytical School

The analytical school uses logic to shape the law. A legal analyst examines the structure and subject matter of a legal code and uses logical analysis to extract the principles that underlie it. By analyzing cases and rules, analysts formulate general principles, and these principles become the starting points for legal reasoning. Individual laws are judged on the basis of whether they are in logical agreement with these starting points. The law's legitimacy and authority come from the fact that it is commanded and enforced by the legal institutions in society.

The Legal Realists

Legal realism is based on the idea that the law is shaped by social forces and is an instrument of social control. It stresses the pragmatic and empirical sides of the law. Legal realists see the law as a means to a social end, and they desire to predict and influence lawmaking. They believe that, despite moral law, historical development, and logical analysis, the same conclusion will not always follow from the same set of facts. A reviewing court may view facts differently than a lower court. For the legal realist, the legitimacy of law and of legal institutions is measured by how well they serve the needs of society.

HISTORY AND SOURCES OF AMERICAN LAW

Because of our colonial heritage, much of American law is based on the English legal system. Understanding this heritage is necessary to understanding the nature of our legal system today.

The Establishment of Courts of Law

In 1066 the Normans conquered England, and William the Conqueror and his successors began the process of unifying the country under their rule. One of the means they used to this end was the establishment of the *Curia Regis*, or king's court. Before the Conquest, disputes had been settled locally according to local custom. The king's court sought to establish a common or uniform set of customs for the whole country. The body of rules that evolved under the *Curia Regis* was the beginning of the **common law.** As the number of courts and cases increased, the more important decisions of each year were

gathered together and recorded in year books. Judges settling disputes similar to ones that had been decided before used the year books as the basis for their decisions. If a case was unique, judges had to create new laws, but they based their decisions on the general principles suggested in earlier cases. The body of judge-made law that developed under this system is still used today and is known as the common law.

Stare Decisis

The practice of deciding new cases with reference to former decisions eventually became a cornerstone of the English and American judicial systems. It forms a doctrine called **stare decisis** ("to stand on decided cases"). It means that judges will follow the *precedent* established by the decisions of the past.

The rule of *stare decisis* performs many useful functions. First, it helps the courts to be more efficient. It would be very time-consuming if each judge had to reason out the policies for deciding what the law should be for each case brought before a court. Instead, the judge can rely on precedent to help make a decision.

Second, *stare decisis* makes for a more just system. All courts follow precedent, and thus, different courts will use the same rule of law. There is no incentive to shop around for a favorable court. Also, the rule of precedent tends to neutralize the personal prejudices of individual judges. Whatever their personal feelings may be, judges are obligated to use precedent as the basis for their decision.

Third, the rule makes the law stable and predictable. Someone bringing a case to court can rely on the court to make a decision based on what the law has been.

Finally, *stare decisis* reflects the experience of the past and is based on the wisdom of the past.

Sometimes a court will depart from the rule of precedent because it has decided that the precedent is incorrect. Several factors can lead to such a decision. If changes in technology, business practice, or society's attitudes necessitate a change in the law, courts might depart from precedent. Judges are reluctant to overthrow precedent, and whether they do or not will depend on how strong the precedent is and how radical the change in society is.

Sometimes there is no precedent on which to base a decision, or there are conflicting precedents. In these situations, a court will: (1) refer to past decisions that may be similar to the current case and decide the case by reasoning through analogy; (2) look at social factors—changes in the status of women, for example—that might influence the issues involved; (3) examine historical trends that indicate a direction for a decision; and (4) consider the question of justice and what the fairest result would be.

Cases that overturn precedent often receive a lot of publicity, and it might seem that they are fairly common. In reality, the vast majority of cases are decided according to precedent by the rule of *stare decisis*.

SOURCES OF THE LAW TODAY

Much law has been made since the officials of the king's court made decisions with reference to the year books. Today, courts have sources other than precedent to consider when making their decisions.

Constitutions

The federal government and the states have constitutions that set forth the general organization, powers, and limits of government. The U.S. Constitution is the supreme law of the land. A law in violation of the Constitution, no matter what the source, will not be enforced by the courts. Similarly, the state constitutions are supreme within their respective borders.

The U.S. Constitution defines the powers and limitations of the federal government. All powers not retained by the federal government reside in the states or the people. For example, the Constitution gives the federal government the power to regulate *interstate* commerce. The states retain the power to regulate *intrastate*

commerce. The Constitution also delineates how federal powers are divided among the three government branches, establishing a system of checks and balances. Thus, the legislative power (power to make laws) is vested in the Congress; the executive power (power to see that laws are carried out) is vested in the president; and the judicial power (power to determine what the law is and whether laws are valid) is vested in the courts.[1]

The judiciary did not always have the power to decide whether a law was contrary to the mandates of the Constitution. The authority to make such determinations, known as *judicial review*, is of great importance in the system of checks and balances. It was first established in the famous case, Marbury v. Madison. The court determined that:

It is emphatically the province and duty of the Judicial Department to say what the law is. Those who apply the rule to a particular case, must of necessity expound and interpret that rule. If two laws conflict with each other, the courts must decide on the operation of each.

So if the law be in opposition to the Constitution, if both the law and the Constitution apply to a particular case, so that the court must either decide that case conformably to the law, disregarding the Constitution; or conformably to the Constitution, disregarding the law; the court must determine which of these conflicting rules governs the case. This is of the very essence of judicial duty.

If, then, the courts were to regard the Constitution and the Constitution is superior to any ordinary Act of the Legislature, the Constitution, and not such ordinary Act, must govern the case to which they both apply.[2]

In another famous case, United States v. Nixon, the court again exercised its authority to interpret the Constitution with respect to President Nixon's claim of executive privilege. In 1974, a grand jury indicted seven individuals for

---

1.   State governments are generally established and organized the same way as the federal government.

2.   5 U.S. (1 Cranch) 137, 2 L.Ed. 60 (1803). How to read case citations is explained at the end of Chapter 2.

obstruction of justice and conspiracy to defraud (among other things). President Nixon was ordered by the special prosecutor to produce tapes, memoranda, papers, and transcripts. The president attempted to avoid the subpoena on the ground of executive privilege, but this ground was denied him by the district court. The Supreme Court eventually heard the case, denied the claim of executive privilege that was the heart of the controversy, and affirmed the order of the district court. Among other things, the court pointed out that:

* * * The Sixth Amendment explicitly confers upon every defendant in a criminal trial the right "to be confronted with the witnesses against him" and "to have compulsory process for obtaining witnesses in his favor * * * " It is the manifest duty of the courts to vindicate those guarantees and to accomplish that it is essential that all relevant and admissible evidence be produced.

    * * * [T]he allowance of the privilege to withhold evidence that is demonstrably relevant in a criminal trial would cut deeply into the guarantee of due process of law and gravely impair the basic function of the courts. * * *[3]

Statutes and Ordinances

Another source of law in the United States is the statutes enacted by the Congress and the various state legislative bodies (statutory law). In addition, cities and counties pass ordinances, none of which can violate the U.S. Constitution or the relevant state constitution. Because the states retain many powers, Congress can pass only the legislation that falls within the range of power granted to it by the U.S. Constitution.[4] Today, legislative bodies and regulatory agencies have assumed an ever-increasing share of lawmaking. A large part of the work of modern courts is interpreting what the rulemakers meant when the law was passed and applying it to a present set of facts. In large part, statutory law has replaced the common law.

3.   418 U.S. 683, 94 S.Ct. 3090 (1974).
4.   Given in Article I, Section VIII; there are eighteen specific powers given to Congress. Amendment X gives all other powers to the states or to the people.

Administrative Agency Regulations

An administrative agency is created when the executive or legislative branch of the government delegates some of its authority to an appropriate group of persons. Administrative agencies exercise legislative, executive, and judicial power—in their rulemaking, they are using legislative power; in their regulation and supervision, they are using executive power; and in their adjudication procedures, they are wielding judicial power.

    Government agencies have proliferated in the United States. Federal agencies include the Federal Communications Commission, the Civil Aeronautics Board, the Federal Aviation Administration, the National Labor Relations Board, the Consumer Product Safety Commission, the Environmental Protection Agency, the National Highway Safety Transportation Administration, and the Interstate Commerce Commission. There are also state boards and agencies—for example, environmental agencies and state labor agencies.

    Administrative law is the branch of public law concerned with the executive power and actions of administrative agencies, their officials, and their workers. When an individual has a dispute with such an agency, administrative law comes into play. The scope of administrative law has expanded enormously in recent years, and the scope of administrative agencies has increased so much that their activities have come to be called administrative process, in contrast to judicial process. *Administrative process* involves the administration of law by nonjudicial agencies, whereas *judicial process* is the administration of law by judicial bodies (the courts). Because administrative bodies are quasi-judicial, appeals from their rulings can be taken directly to the courts after administrative remedies have been exhausted.

    Federal administrative agencies have expanded the number of their rulings at what appears to be an exponential rate. Some observers believe that the United States is in danger of having an overly bureaucratic government.

Case Law and Common Law

Case law comprises the rules of law announced in court decisions. It is sometimes called judge-made law. In most instances, case law is an interpretation of the other sources of law noted above. Once a court has interpreted a statute, a regulation, or a constitution, the interpretation becomes part of the authoritative law on the subject.

Much of the common law has been either included in legislation or changed by it, but there are still areas of law that legislation does not cover. In those areas, courts still refer to the common law. The history and circumstances of the various states differ, and this has given rise to differences in the common law in each state. Even where legislation has been substituted for common law, courts rely on common law rules to interpret the legislation and the judicial methodology used in making decisions has its origins in common law.

THE UNIFORM COMMERCIAL CODE

In the interests of uniformity and reform, the legal profession, under the leadership of the American Law Institute, has suggested comprehensive codes of laws to be adopted by the states. The most important of these to business students is the Uniform Commercial Code, which is the basis of many chapters in this book. Its origins will be briefly examined here.

Commercial Law

The body of laws that pertain to commercial dealings is commonly referred to as commercial law. It includes most of the topics in this text—partnerships, corporations, agency, and contracts, for example.

The Law Merchant

A system of mercantile courts existed in England well before the advent of the common law courts. These courts administered a law known as *Lex Mercatoria*, or the Law Merchant. This law was based on customs of the merchants, many of whom traveled from place to place to do business. The law merchant was important during the Middle Ages when the fair, or market, was an important commercial event. In fact, the Magna Carta made special provisions for merchants. Section 41, for example, states that all merchants should "have safe and secure conduct, to go out of, and to come into England, and to stay there, and to pass as well by lands as by water, for buying and selling by the ancient and allowed customs."

The Operation of Merchant Courts

From the very beginning, there was an attempt to get cases in and out of the merchant courts as quickly as possible. Law merchant courts operated from hour to hour. One of the most common types was called the piepoudre court. The words *pied* and *poudre* together mean dusty feet. In principle, justice was administered in such courts even before dust could fall from the litigant's feet. Piepoudre courts were courts of record (they kept a written record of their proceedings). They had jurisdiction over mercantile, or commercial, wrongs and minor offences that occurred at a particular fair or marketplace. Even in these early courts, there was an ideal that it was fairer to resolve disputes in the way they had been resolved before (*stare decisis*). The law merchant eventually became part of the common law and was incorporated into American law.

Codification of Commercial Law

The National Conference of Commissioners on Uniform State Laws started to meet in the late 1800s to draft uniform statutes. Once these uniform codes were drawn up, the commissioners urged each state legislature to adopt them. The first such code, or act, was the Negotiable Instruments Act, finally approved in 1896 and ultimately adopted in every state.

Afterwards, other acts were drawn up in a similar manner; they included the Uniform Sales Act, the Uniform Warehouse Receipts Act, the Uniform Bills of Lading Act, and the Uniform Stock Transfer Act. Recently, a Uniform Probate Code was prepared. The most ambitious uniform act of all, however, is the Uniform Commercial Code.

The Uniform Commercial Code (UCC)

The National Conference of Commissioners on Uniform State Laws and the American Law Institute sponsored and directed the preparation of the Uniform Commercial Code. These two organizations were assisted by literally hundreds of law professors, businesspersons, judges, and lawyers. The work on the UCC began in 1942, and the finished draft was completed in 1952. The complete text of the Code can be found in Appendix A in this book. All fifty states, the District of Columbia, and the Virgin Islands have adopted the Uniform Commercial Code.[5]

The UCC consists of ten articles:

1. General Provisions
2. Sales
3. Commercial Paper
4. Bank Deposits and Collections
5. Letters of Credit
6. Bulk Transfers
7. Documents of Title
8. Investment Securities
9. Secured Transactions
10. Effective Date and Repealer

When each of the states adopted the Code, it repealed numerous statutes, such as the Uniform Sales Act, the Uniform Bills of Lading Act, the Uniform Warehouse Receipts Act, the Uniform Negotiable Instruments Act, the Uniform Conditional Sales Act, the Uniform Trust Receipts Act, the Uniform Stock Transfer Act, the Bulk Sales Act, and the Factors Lien Act.

The Code does not change the basic principles of commercial law derived from the law merchant and common law but expands and codifies them in order to modernize, clarify, and liberalize the rules. The Code also helps state the legal relationship of the parties in modern commercial transactions. The Code is designed to help determine the intentions of the parties to a commercial contract and to give force and effect to their agreement.

CLASSIFICATION OF LAW

Much of the study of law involves the process of classification—taking the whole mass of law and putting it into categories in order to make sense of it. Different approaches to the law and the different sources of law have already been classified. This section will consider some other ways of classifying the law.

Substantive versus Procedural Law

Substantive law includes all those laws that define, regulate, and create legal rights and obligations. A rule stating that promises are enforced only where each party receives something of value from the other party is part of substantive law. So, too, is a rule stating that a person who injures another through negligence must pay damages.

Procedural law establishes the methods of enforcing the rights that are established by substantive law.[6] Questions about how a lawsuit should begin, what papers need to be filed, which court the suit should go to, which witnesses can be called, and so on are all questions of procedural law. In brief, substantive law tells us our *rights*; procedural law tells us *how to get the benefit of them.*

Exhibit 1-1 classifies law in terms of its subject matter, dividing it into law covering substantive issues and law covering procedural issues. Most of this text concerns substantive law.

---

5. Louisiana has adopted only Articles 1, 3, 4, and 5, however.

6. Sometimes procedural law is called adjective law.

EXHIBIT 1-1 SUBJECT MATTER DIVIDED
INTO SUBSTANTIVE AND PROCEDURAL[a]

SUBSTANTIVE	PROCEDURAL
Agency	Evidence
Commercial Paper	Civil Procedure
Contracts	Criminal Procedure
Corporation Law	Administrative Procedure
Property	Appellate Procedure
Torts	
Taxation	
Sales	
Real Property	
Personal Property	
Partnerships	
Trusts and Wills	
Criminal Law	
Constitutional Law	
Administrative Law	

Public versus Private Law

Public law affects the relationship between individuals and their government; *private law* involves direct dealings between individuals. Criminal, constitutional, and administrative law are generally called public law because they deal with individuals and their relationships to government. Criminal acts are acts that individuals commit against society as a whole. They are prohibited by the governments themselves. (The violation of a criminal law may also violate a private right.) Constitutional law involves questions of whether the government—federal, state or local—has the *power* to act. In other words, governments receive their power from the Constitution. Additionally, constitutional law limits the exercise of governmental power in certain ways usually designed to protect the life, liberty, or property of individuals from governmental action. Administrative law details the procedures that govern the activities of various government commissions and administrative agencies. Other areas

a. The importance of this distinction is more than academic; the *result* of a case may well depend upon the determination that a rule is substantive rather than procedural.

of the law, such as contract rights and duties, fall within the private law category. (See Chapters 5 through 14.)

Civil versus Criminal Law

Civil law spells out the duties that exist between individuals. Contract law, for example, is part of civil law. The whole body of tort law, which has to do with the infringement by one person of the legally recognized rights of another, is an area of civil law. (Tort law is treated in Chapter 3.)

Criminal law is concerned with a wrong committed against the public as a whole. Criminal acts are proscribed by local, state, or federal government by statute. (Criminal law is treated in Chapter 4.)

Remedies in Law versus Remedies in Equity

The distinction between law and equity is primarily of historical interest, but it has special relevance to students of business law. In the early king's courts, the kinds of *remedies* (legal means to recover a right or redress for a wrong) that the courts could grant were severely restricted. If one person wronged another in some way, the king's court could award one or more of the following: (1) land, (2) items of value, or (3) money as compensation. The courts that awarded these compensations became known as *courts of law.* The three remedies were called *remedies at law.* Such a system introduced uniformity in the settling of disputes, but when *plaintiffs* (parties suing) wanted a remedy other than economic compensation, the courts of law could do nothing, so "no remedy, no right."

GOING TO THE KING FOR RELIEF When individuals could not obtain their preferred remedy in a court of law, they petitioned the king for relief. Most of these petitions were decided by an adviser of the king called the chancellor. When the chancellor thought that the claim was a fair one, new and unique remedies were granted. Thus, a new body of chancery rules and reliefs, or remedies, came into being. Finally, formal chancery courts were established. These were known as *courts of equity.* Thus, two distinct systems were created, each having a different set of judges. There were two bodies of rules and remedies that existed at the same time, *remedies in law* and *remedies in equity.* Plaintiffs had to specify whether they were bringing an "action at law" or an "action in equity," and they chose their courts accordingly.

DECREES OF SPECIFIC PERFORMANCE A plaintiff might come into a court of equity asking it to order a defendant to perform within the terms of a contract. A *court of law* could not order specific performance because its remedies were limited to payment of money or property as compensation for damages. A *court of equity,* however, could issue a decree of *specific performance*—an order to perform what was promised.

INJUNCTIONS If a person wanted certain activity prevented, he would have to go to the chancellor in equity to ask that the person doing (or about to do) the wrongful act be ordered to stop. The order was called an *injunction*—a court order requiring that a person either do something or stop doing something.

Today the distinction between courts of law and courts of equity has largely disappeared. Trial courts normally can grant remedies in law or in equity. The distinction is important to the student of business law because of the types of remedies available.

WHAT IS TO FOLLOW

This introductory chapter is meant to give the reader a feel for the nature of law, its origins, and the way it is classified. The rest of this introductory unit will cover the courts and the judicial system in the United States today (Chapter 2); torts—wrongs committed against individuals that are not criminal acts (Chapter 3); and, finally, criminal law (Chapter 4).

QUESTIONS AND CASE PROBLEMS

1. What is the difference between common law and statutory law? Should judges have the same authority to overrule statutory law as they have to overrule common law?

2. What is the difference between common law and *stare decisis*? Should judges have the same power to change the common law as they do to depart from *stare decisis*?

3. The law draws a distinction between substantive law and procedural law. Is there any reason for this distinction?

4. Note that *evidence* is included in procedural law. What is evidence all about? One rule of evidence, called the *hearsay rule,* states that in a trial one cannot introduce second-hand evidence of statements or writings that were made outside the courtroom to prove the truth of the matter asserted. That is, evidence that does not proceed from the *personal* knowledge of the witness is not admitted. What is the reason for such a rule?

5. The concept of *equity* was mentioned in this chapter. Courts of equity tend to follow general rules or maxims rather than following the common law or *stare decisis* as courts of law do. Some of those maxims are: "He who seeks equity must do equity"; "For one to seek the aid of equity courts he must come to the court with 'clean hands,' "; and "Equity does not lie for one who sits on his laches" (that is, one who does not pursue a remedy within a reasonable time). Why would equity courts give more credence to such maxims than to a hard and fast body of law?

6. The United States Constitution is a document in which the people of the United States give up to the government the "power to govern." Yet the Constitution was written by a handful of men who represented the aristocracy of the time. Surprisingly, this group of aristocrats wrote a document giving more freedoms to common people than any other constitution in existence. Name some of the basic guarantees found in the Constitution.

7. The Uniform Commercial Code took years to develop and has only recently been adopted by all of the states (although Louisiana did not adopt all the articles). The UCC attempts to establish uniformity throughout the states in every conceivable area of commercial law. What are some of the advantages of such a document?

2

Courts
and Procedures

The United States has a dual court system that includes the various state systems and one federal system. This chapter will look at the state system first and the federal system second. Then it will follow a typical case from beginning to end. Using the courts is part of the process of adjudication, that is, determining which rules apply to the facts in the case. The rules can be substantive or procedural. They can come from several sources and can cover several areas of the law.

The word *court* comes from the Latin word *cors*, meaning an open space near the king's palace. This is where disputants came to have their differences adjudicated by the king or by his representatives. Today courts settle controversies between persons or between persons and the state. Note that throughout the legal literature, the term *court* frequently is used synonymously with the term *judge*.

JURISDICTION

Juris means "law"; *diction* means "to speak." Thus, the power to speak the law is the literal meaning of the term *jurisdiction*. Before a court can decide a case, it must have jurisdiction, the power to decide that case. Otherwise it cannot exercise any authority in the case. In order for a court to exercise valid authority, it must have both jurisdiction over the subject matter of the case and jurisdiction over the person against whom the suit is brought.

11

Subject Matter Jurisdiction

Subject matter jurisdiction is a limitation on types of cases a court can hear. For example, probate courts—courts that handle only matters relating to wills and estates—are a common example of limited subject matter jurisdiction. The subject matter jurisdiction of a court is usually defined in the statute or constitution creating the court. A court's subject matter jurisdiction can be limited by the amount of money in controversy, by whether a case is a felony or misdemeanor, or by whether the proceeding is a trial or an appeal.

Jurisdiction over the Person

In order to consider a case, a court must also have power over the person or, in some cases, the property of the person against whom a suit is brought. Jurisdiction over the person is known as *in personam* jurisdiction. Generally, a court's power is limited to the territorial boundaries of the state in which it is located. Therefore, a court has jurisdiction over the person of anyone who can be served with a summons within those boundaries. Additionally, if a person is a resident of the state or does business within the state, there will be *in personam* jurisdiction. Finally, in some cases where an individual has committed a wrong, such as an automobile injury or the sale of defective goods within the state, a court can exercise jurisdiction using the authority of a *long-arm statute* even if the individual is outside the state. A court can exercise *in personam* jurisdiction over a corporation in the state where it is incorporated, in the state where it has its main plant or office, and in any state where it does business.

If an individual owns property within a state, and the property is the subject of the suit, a court can exercise jurisdiction by virtue of its authority over property within the state even if the owner is outside the state. This is known as an action *in rem* as opposed to an action *in personam*. A court can also use property within a state to help satisfy a general debt. This is known as an action *quasi in rem*.

In all cases where a court exercises jurisdiction, the parties must be served either with actual notice that they are involved in a suit (usually by service of a summons) or, where the parties cannot be located, by publication of notice in a manner defined by statute.

Venue

Jurisdiction is concerned with whether a court has authority over a specific subject matter or individual. *Venue* is concerned with the particular geographic area within a judicial district where a suit should be brought.

Basically, the concept of venue reflects the policy that a court trying a suit should be in the neighborhood where the incident leading to the suit occurred or where the parties involved in the suit reside. That neighborhood is usually the county where the incident occurred or where the parties live. The correct venue for a suit is defined by statute.

THE STATE COURT SYSTEM

There are variations among the court systems of the several states, but there is a general pattern to the hierarchy of courts within each state. Exhibit 2-1 illustrates a hypothetical state judicial system with four levels of courts: (1) inferior or trial courts of limited jurisdiction, (2) trial courts of general jurisdiction, (3) intermediate reviewing courts, or appellate courts, and (4) a final appellate court, usually called the supreme court of the state. In many states there is no intervening appellate court. The appeal goes directly from the court of original jurisdiction to the highest court.

Inferior Trial Courts

Every state has some type of trial court that has limited jurisdiction of subject matter. Some typical inferior trial courts are domestic relations courts, which handle only divorce actions and child custody; local municipal courts, which handle mainly traffic cases; probate courts, which handle the execution of wills and estate settlement problems; and small claims and justice-of-the-peace courts. These are sometimes called inferior courts because they have limited, specialized jurisdiction.

Trial Courts of General Jurisdiction

Cases involving state law most often originate in the general jurisdiction trial courts of that state. These courts can hear all cases arising under state law except those assigned expressly by statute to the inferior courts discussed above. (Sometimes jurisdiction is concurrent.) Many important cases involving business originate in these general trial courts. Thus, cases involving corporate law, contract law, and criminal law will start here. They can be called district courts, common pleas courts, or, in a few locations, superior courts. (This is a misnomer

because they are clearly not at the top of the hierarchy of state courts. In New York, the general jurisdiction courts are called *supreme courts*, which is even more of a misnomer.) General jurisdiction courts typically exist in at least every county of every state. In some counties, because of the heavy demand, there is more than one court. Conversely, in lightly populated areas, a judge will serve several counties and be in one county only at stated times. General jurisdiction courts are also called courts of record because a written report of the proceedings, taken by a court stenographer, is kept.

Appellate Courts, or Courts of Appeal and Review

In each state, there is at least one court of review, or appellate court. The subject matter jurisdiction of these courts is limited to hearing

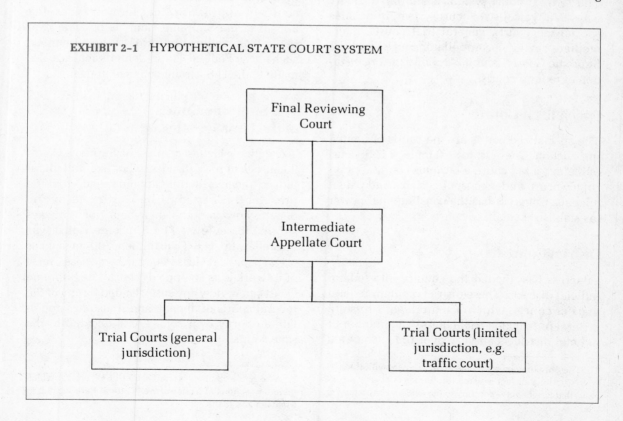

EXHIBIT 2–1   HYPOTHETICAL STATE COURT SYSTEM

Final Reviewing Court

Intermediate Appellate Court

Trial Courts (general jurisdiction)

Trial Courts (limited jurisdiction, e.g. traffic court)

appeals. In many states, there are intermediate reviewing courts and then one supreme court. The intermediate appellate, or review, court, is often called the court of appeals. The highest court of the state is normally called the supreme court (in New York it is called the Court of Appeals). Appellate courts do not try cases. They examine the record of the case on appeal and determine whether the trial court committed an error. They look at questions of law and procedure, not questions of fact.[1] The decisions of each state's highest court in all questions of state law are final. It is only when questions of federal law are involved that a state's highest court can be overruled by the Supreme Court of the United States.

THE FEDERAL COURT SYSTEM—CASES AND CONTROVERSIES

The federal court system is similar in many ways to a typical state court system. It includes specialized courts, general trial courts, intermediate review, or appellate, courts, and the Supreme Court. Exhibit 2-2 shows the organization of federal courts.

Specialized Courts

The specialized courts are the courts of limited jurisdiction. There is, for example, a U.S. court of claims, a tax court, a customs court, a bankruptcy court, and a court of customs and patent appeals. Congress has the constitutional power to establish specialized courts.

District Courts

Congress has divided the country into federal judicial districts. These districts contain federal district courts, which are analogous to state general jurisdiction trial courts. The number of judicial districts can vary over time. Congress

has established at least one in each state, but some states need, and have, more. Thus, an entire state can comprise a single district, or a state can be divided into several districts. With one exception, the districts do not cross state lines.[2] United States district courts are often called federal trial courts. Most federal cases originate in these courts. Whenever there are two or more district courts within a single state, there is limited geographical jurisdiction in each court. The state of Florida, for example, has district courts for northern, middle, and southern Florida.

Intermediate Courts of Review

The first level of review in the federal court system is the federal appellate courts, which are called U.S. circuit courts of appeal. Congress has established eleven judicial circuits that hear appeals from the district courts located within their respective circuits. The decisions of the courts of appeal are final in most cases, but appeal to the Supreme Court is possible. Appeals from federal administrative agencies, such as the Federal Trade Commission, are also made to the U.S. circuit courts of appeal.

The Supreme Court of the United States

The nation's highest court is the Supreme Court; it consists of nine justices, who, like all federal judges, receive lifetime appointments from the president. (They must be confirmed by the Senate, however, and their behavior is always subject to review.) The Supreme Court was created by the U.S. Constitution. Although it has original, or trial, jurisdiction in some cases, most of its work is as an appeals court. The Supreme Court can review any case decided by any of the federal courts of appeal, and it also has appellate authority over some cases decided in the state courts.

---

1. The only time an appellate court tampers with the trial courts findings of fact is when the finding is clearly erroneous, that is, when it is contrary to the evidence presented at trial.

2. The one exception is the District of Wyoming, which includes sections of Yellowstone National Park located in Montana and Idaho.

SUPREME COURT OF THE UNITED STATES

Original Jurisdiction
1. Cases in which a state, ambassador, public minister or consul is a party.

Appellate Jurisdiction
1. Cases from any federal court in which an act of Congress is held unconstitutional in a civil action to which the federal government or one of its employees is a party.
2. Cases from a federal court of appeals in which a state statute is held to be invalid because it violates a federal law.
3. Cases where the highest court of appeals of a state holds a federal law invalid or upholds a state law that has been challenged as violating the U.S. Constitution, or other federal law or treaty.
4. Appeals from certain orders of three judge courts.
5. Cases on writ of certiorari involving important federal questions.

COURT OF CUSTOMS AND PATENT APPEALS

Appellate Jurisdiction
1. Appeals from the Customs Court except where direct review may be had by the Supreme Court.
2. Appeals from the Patent and Trademark Office, and the Tariff Commission, and review of certain findings of the Secretary of Commerce (28 U.S.C.A. §1544) and the Secretary of Agriculture (7 U.S.C.A. §2461).

CUSTOMS COURT

COURT OF CLAIMS

Original Jurisdiction
1. Claims against the United States government except for tort claims.

Appellate Jurisdiction
1. Appeals from district court judgments in tort claims if the appellees consent.

COURTS OF THE TERRITORIES AND INSULAR POSSESSIONS

Canal Zone — Puerto Rico — Guam — Virgin Islands — Northern Marianas
Mixed local and federal jurisdiction.

COURTS OF APPEALS OF THE UNITED STATES AND THE DISTRICT OF COLUMBIA

Appellate Jurisdiction
1. Appeals from decisions of district courts except where direct review may be had by the Supreme Court.
2. Review of decisions and enforcement of orders of federal administrative agencies.

DISTRICT COURTS OF THE UNITED STATES

Original Jurisdiction
1. Federal questions (cases arising under the Constitution, laws, or treaties of the U.S.) where the amount in controversy exceeds $10,000.
2. Diversity of citizenship cases where the amount in controversy exceeds $10,000.
3. Other federal questions where Congress places no limit on the amount in controversy.
4. Federal crimes and criminal proceedings against federal officers.
5. Judicial review of actions of administrative agencies.
6. Admiralty and Maritime cases.

Appellate Jurisdiction
1. Cases appealed from the bankruptcy court unless (a) the circuit court has created a three judge bankruptcy panel to handle appeals or (b) both parties consent to take the appeal directly to the circuit court.

Three Judge District Courts
1. Actions required by Congress to be heard by a three judge court.

HIGHEST STATE COURTS

SPECIAL COURT REGIONAL RAIL REORGANIZATION
45 U.S.C.A. §§ 719, 743.

UNITED STATES COURT OF MILITARY APPEALS

Appellate Jurisdiction
1. All cases in which sentence affects a general or flag officer or extends to death.
2. All cases sent by the Judge Advocate General.
3. All cases in which review is granted.

U.S. TAX COURT

U.S. BANKRUPTCY COURT
11 U.S.C.A. §11

DEPARTMENTS, AGENCIES AND OFFICERS

Administrator of Environmental Protection Agency
Administrator of Federal Aviation Administration
Attorney General
Benefits Review Board
Civil Aeronautics Board
Civil Service Commission
Commissioner of Administration on Aging
Commissioner of Education
Commodity Futures Trading Commission
Consumer Product Safety Commission
Copyright Royalty Tribunal
Comptroller General
Federal Communications Commission
Federal Election Commission
Federal Deposit Insurance Corporation
Federal Energy Regulatory Commission
Federal Home Loan Bank Board
Federal Maritime Commission
Federal Mine Safety and Health Review Commission
Federal Reserve System, Board of Governors
Federal Savings and Loan Insurance Corporation
Federal Trade Commission
Foreign Trade Zones Board
Immigration and Naturalization Service
International Claims Commission
Interstate Commerce Commission
Law Enforcement Assistance Administration
Longshoremen's and Harbor Workers' Compensation
Maritime Administration
National Labor Relations Board
National Transportation Safety Board
Nuclear Regulatory Commission
Occupational Safety and Health Review Commission
Postal Services, Board of Governors
Railroad Retirement Board
Saint Lawrence Seaway Development Corporation
Secretary of the Army
Secretary of Agriculture
Secretary of Commerce
Secretary of Energy
Secretary of Health, Education and Welfare
Secretary of Labor
Secretary of Housing and Urban Development
Secretary of Transportation
Secretary of the Treasury
Securities and Exchange Commission
Small Business Administration
Subversive Activities Control Board

EXHIBIT 2-2   THE ORGANIZATION OF THE FEDERAL COURT SYSTEM

FEDERAL COURT JURISDICTION

Since the federal government is a government of limited powers, the jurisdiction of the federal courts is limited. Article III of the U.S. Constitution established the boundaries of federal judicial power:

Section 1. The judicial power of the United States shall be vested in one supreme Court and in such inferior Courts as the Congress may from time to time ordain and establish. * * *

Section 2. The judicial power shall extend to all Cases, in Law and Equity, arising under this Constitution, the Laws of the United States, and Treaties made, or which shall be made, under their Authority; —to all Cases affecting Ambassadors, other public Ministers and Consuls;—to all Cases of admiralty and maritime Jurisdiction;—to Controversies to which the United States shall be a Party;—to Controversies between two or more States; between a State and Citizens of another State;[3]—between Citizens of different States;—between Citizens of the same State claiming Lands under the Grants of different States, and between a State, or the Citizens thereof, and foreign States, Citizens or Subjects.

In all Cases affecting Ambassadors, other public Ministers and Consuls, and those in which a State shall be a Party, the supreme Court shall have original Jurisdiction. In all the other Cases before mentioned, the supreme Court shall have appellate Jurisdiction, both as to Law and Fact, with such Exceptions, and under such Regulations as the Congress shall make.

In line with the checks and balances system of the federal government, Congress has the power to control the number and kind of inferior courts in the federal system. Except in those cases where the Constitution gives the Supreme Court original jurisdiction, Congress can also regulate the jurisdiction of the Supreme Court. Therefore, although the Constitution sets the outer limits of federal judicial power, Congress can set other limits on federal jurisdiction. Furthermore, the courts themselves can promulgate rules that limit the types of cases they will hear.

3. Amendment XI, passed in 1798, prohibits any exercise of federal judicial power in cases brought against a state by citizens of another state.

Federal Questions

"The Judicial Power shall extend to all cases * * * arising under this Constitution, the laws of the United States and Treaties made * * * under their authority." Whenever a plaintiff's cause of action is based, at least in part, on the United States Constitution, a treaty, or a federal law, then a *federal question* arises, and the case comes under the judicial power of federal courts. People whose claims are based on rights granted by an act of Congress can sue in a federal court. People who claim that their constitutional rights have been violated can originate their suits in federal court. However, Title 28, Section 1331, of the United States Code limits the federal question jurisdiction of the district courts. Unless the suit is brought against the federal government or one of its employees, the amount in controversy in a federal question case must exceed $10,000, or else the district court will not have jurisdiction. Of course, if the suit does not meet the $10,000 requirement, the plaintiff can always begin the suit in a state court. There is no dollar amount requirement where federal courts have exclusive jurisdiction, that is, where the suit cannot be brought in a state court.

Diversity of Citizenship

Another basis for federal district court jurisdiction is *diversity of citizenship*. Diversity of citizenship cases involve (1) citizens of different states, (2) a foreign country as plaintiff and citizens of a state, or different states, and (3) citizens of a state and citizens or subjects of a foreign country. As in federal question suits, under Title 28, Section 1332, the amount in controversy must be $10,000 before a federal court can take jurisdiction. For purposes of diversity of citizenship jurisdiction, a corporation is a citizen of the state where it is incorporated and of the state where it has its principal place of business. Diversity cases starting out in a state court can be *removed*, or transferred, to a federal court if the defendant is not a citizen of the state where the case begins.

Diversity jurisdiction originated in 1789

with the authors of the Constitution, who felt that a state might be biased toward its own citizens. The option of moving to a federal court provided by diversity jurisdiction was thought to protect the out-of-state party. A large percentage of the 70,000 cases filed in federal courts each year are based on diversity of citizenship grounds. Consider some examples: Smith is driving from his home state, New York, to Florida. In Georgia, he runs into a car owned by Abel, a citizen of Georgia. Abel's new Mercedes is demolished, and he is out of work for six months; thus the case in question involves more than $10,000 worth of damages. Georgia gains *in personam* jurisdiction through a long arm statute, but Smith can have the suit removed to a federal district court on the basis of diversity of citizenship.

Jones, who resides in Texas, is owed $25,000 by Corporation XYZ, which is incorporated and has its principal place of business in Louisiana. XYZ does enough business in Texas to allow Texas courts to exercise *in personam* jurisdiction over it. Since, for purposes of diversity of citizenship jurisdiction, XYZ is a citizen of Louisiana, Jones can begin her suit in a federal district court in Texas.

Concurrent versus Exclusive Jurisdiction

Even though a case involves a federal question or diversity of citizenship, state courts can still hear the case. Federal jurisdiction is available, but it is not required. When both federal and state courts have the power to hear a case, jurisdiction is *concurrent*. When cases can be tried only in federal courts, jurisdiction is *exclusive*. Federal courts have exclusive jurisdiction in cases involving federal crimes, bankruptcy, patent, and copyright cases; in suits against the United States; and in some areas of admiralty law.

WHICH CASES REACH THE SUPREME COURT?

Many people are surprised to learn that in a typical case, there is no absolute right of appeal

to the United States Supreme Court. The Supreme Court is given original, or trial court, jurisdiction in a small number of situations. In all other cases, its jurisdiction is appellate "with such Exceptions, and under such Regulations as the Congress shall make." Today the exceptions and rules set by Congress and some rules that the court has set for itself are quite complex. Over 4,500 cases are filed with the Supreme Court each year; yet it hears an average of only 300.[4] There are basically two procedures for bringing a case before the Supreme Court: by *appeal* or by *writ of certiorari*.

Appeal

Under rules set out by Congress, the Supreme Court must review a decision (that is, an individual has a right to appeal) in the following situations:

1. When a federal court of appeals holds a state statute to be invalid because it violates federal law.
2. When the highest state court of appeals holds a federal law invalid or upholds a state law that has been challenged as violating federal law.
3. When a federal court holds an act of Congress unconstitutional and the federal government or one of its employees is a party.
4. When the hearing under appeal is for an injunction in a civil (as opposed to criminal) action that Congress requires a district court of three judges to determine.

Theoretically, the Supreme Court is required to hear any appeal that falls within one of these four categories, but it can decide which of these cases require full consideration, including written briefs from the lawyers and oral arguments before the Court. The Court will give full consideration only if four of the nine justices vote to do so. Otherwise the case will be

---

4.   There has been some discussion about establishing a new national appellate court to relieve the Supreme Court's workload. The new court would take cases that the Supreme Court felt it should not spend its time deciding so that it could take on more cases that had important public policy implications.

dismissed. A case can be dismissed because the Court agrees with the lower court's decision, because the federal question presented is not a substantial one, or on some other procedural ground. When a case is dismissed for reasons of substantive law—that is, when the higher court agrees with the lower court or when a substantial federal question is lacking—the Court's decision has value as precedent, and the dismissal can be cited in later cases.[5]

Writ of Certiorari

With a **writ of *certiorari*,** the Supreme Court orders a lower court to send it the record of a case for review. Parties whose cases do not fall into one of the appeal categories can petition the Supreme Court to issue a writ of *certiorari*, but whether the Court will issue one is entirely at its discretion. In no instance is the Court required to issue a writ of *certiorari*.

The following situations indicate when the Court can issue a writ, although they are not a limit on the Court's discretion:

1. When a state court has decided a substantial federal question that has not been determined by the Supreme Court before, or the state court has decided it in a way that is probably in disagreement with the trend of the Supreme Court's decisions.
2. When two federal courts of appeal are in disagreement with each other.
3. When a federal court of appeals has decided an important state question in conflict with state law, has decided an important federal question not yet addressed by the Court but which should be decided by the Court, has decided a federal question in conflict with applicable decisions of the Court, or has departed from the accepted and usual course of judicial proceedings.

Most petitions for writs of *certiorari* are denied. A denial is not a decision on the merits of a case; nor does it indicate agreement with

the lower court's opinion. Therefore, it has no value as precedent.[6] The court will not issue a writ unless at least four justices approve of it. This is called the "rule of four." Typically, only the petitions that raise the possibility of important constitutional questions are granted writs of *certiorari*.

JUDICIAL PROCEDURES— FOLLOWING A CASE THROUGH THE COURTS

American and English courts follow the *adversary system of justice*. The judge's role is viewed as nonbiased and mostly passive. The lawyer functions as the client's advocate, presenting the client's version of the facts in order to convince the judge or the jury (or both) that they are true. Judges do not have to be entirely passive. They are responsible for the appropriate application of the law. They do not have to accept the legal reasoning of the attorneys. They can base a ruling and a decision on a personal study of the law. Judges sometimes ask questions of witnesses and even suggest types of evidence to be presented. For example, if an indigent defendant chooses to act as his or her own counsel, the judge will often play less of a passive role and more of an advocate role, intervening during the trial proceedings to help the defendant.[7]

Procedure

Procedure involves the way disputes are handled in the courts. A large body of law, procedural law, establishes the rules and standards for determining disputes in courts. The rules are very complex, and they vary from court to court. There is a set of federal *rules of procedure*, and there are various sets of procedural rules in the state courts. Rules of procedure differ in criminal and civil cases.

We will now follow a civil case through the

---

5. Hicks v. Miranda, 422 U.S. 332, 95 S.Ct. 2281 (1975).

6. Singleton v. Commissioner of Internal Revenue, 439 U.S. 940, 99 S.Ct. 335 (1978).

7. See Faretta v. California, 422 U.S. 806, 95 S.Ct. 2525 (1975).

state courts. The case involves an automobile accident in which Jones, driving a Cadillac, has struck Adams, driving a Ford. The accident has occurred at an intersection in New York. Adams has suffered personal injuries, incurring medical and hospital expenses as well as four months of lost wages. Jones and Adams are unable to agree on a settlement, and Adams sues Jones. Adams is the *plaintiff,* and Jones is the *defendant.* Both have lawyers.

The Pleadings

Adams's suit or action against Jones will commence when her lawyer files a *complaint* (sometimes called a petition or declaration) with the clerk of the general trial court that has jurisdiction and venue. The complaint will contain: (1) a statement alleging the facts necessary for the court to take jurisdiction, (2) a short statement of the facts necessary to show that the plaintiff is entitled to a remedy, and (3) a statement of the remedy the plaintiff is seeking.

First, Adams's complaint will be filed with a court of general jurisdiction in the county where the accident has occurred. The complaint will state that Adams was driving her Ford through a green light at the specified intersection, exercising good driving habits and reasonable care, when Jones carelessly drove his Cadillac into the intersection from a cross street and struck Adams, causing serious personal injury and property damage. The complaint will go on to state that she is entitled to $85,000 to cover medical bills, $10,000 to cover lost wages, and $5,000 to cover property damage to the car.

After the complaint has been filed, the sheriff or a deputy of the county will serve a summons and a copy of the complaint on the defendant Jones. The *summons* notifies Jones that he is required to prepare an answer to the complaint and file a copy with both the court and the plaintiff's attorney within a specified time period (usually thirty days after the summons has been served). The summons also informs Jones that failure to answer will result in a judgment by default for the plaintiff. Rules governing the service of a summons vary, but

usually *service* is made by handing the summons to the defendant personally or by leaving it at the defendant's residence or place of business. In a few states, a summons can be served by mail. When the defendant cannot be reached, special rules sometimes permit serving the summons by leaving it with a designated person, such as the secretary of state.

Upon receiving the summons and complaint, the defendant must file a document with the court and with the plaintiff. The document either admits the statements set out in the complaint or denies them and sets out any defenses the defendant may have. Appropriately enough, this document is called an *answer.* If Jones admits all of Adams's allegations in his answer, judgment will be entered for Adams. If Jones denies Adams's allegations, the matter will proceed to trial. Jones can deny Adams's allegations and set forth his own claim that Adams was negligent and owes Jones money for damages to the Cadillac. This is called a *counterclaim.* If Jones files a counterclaim, Adams will have to answer it with a document that is normally called a *reply.* Jones can also admit the truth of Adams's complaint but raise *new* facts that will result in dismissal of the action. This is called raising an *affirmative defense.* For example, Jones can admit that he was negligent but plead that the time Adams had to raise the claim has passed and that her complaint must therefore be dismissed.

The complaint and answer (and the counterclaim and reply) taken together are called the *pleadings.* The pleadings inform each party of the claims of the other and specify the issues involved in the case. Pleadings remove the element of surprise from a case. They allow lawyers to prepare better arguments, and they increase the probability that a just and true result will be forthcoming from the trial.

Dismissals and Judgments before Trial

Many actions for which pleadings have been filed never come to trial. There are numerous procedural avenues for disposing of a case without a trial. Many of them involve one or the other party's attempts to get the case dismissed through the use of pretrial *motions*.

MOTION TO DISMISS, OR DEMURRER The defendant can present to the court a *motion to dismiss*, or *demurrer*, instead of an answer. (The rules of civil procedure in many states do not use the term *demurrer*; they use only *motion to dismiss*.) The motion to dismiss is an allegation that even if the facts presented in the complaint are true, their legal consequences are such that there is no reason to go further with the suit and no need for the defendant to present an answer. It is a contention that the defendant is not legally liable even if the facts are as the plaintiff alleges. If, for example, Adams's complaint alleges facts that exclude the possibility of negligence on Jones's part, Jones can move to dismiss, and he will not be required to answer because his motion will be granted.

If Adams wishes to discontinue the suit because, for example, an out-of-court settlement has been reached, she can likewise move for dismissal. The court can also dismiss on its own motion.

A MOTION FOR JUDGMENT ON THE PLEADINGS After the pleadings are closed—after the complaint, answer, and any counterclaim and reply have been filed—either of the parties can make a *motion for a judgment on the pleadings*. This motion is basically an argument that the court can decide the case just by looking at the pleadings without having to consider any evidence. A judgment on the pleadings will be granted if the complaint is insufficient to allow any remedy or if the answer admits the allegations of the complaint or fails to deny them and no affirmative defense is pleaded. If, for example, Jones admits all of the facts alleged in Adams's complaint—admits that, in fact, he was negligent—the court can grant a motion for judgment on the pleadings and grant Adams her remedy.

MOTION FOR SUMMARY JUDGMENT A lawsuit can be shortened or a trial can be avoided if there are no disagreements about the facts in a case and the only question is which laws apply to those facts. Both sides can agree to the facts and just ask the judge to apply the law to them. In this situation, it is appropriate for either party to move for *summary judgment*. Summary judgment will be granted when there are no genuine issues of fact in a trial and the only question is one of law. In a pretrial setting, one party can bring in a sworn statement that refutes the other party's claim. Unless the second party brings in affidavits of conflicting facts, the first party will receive summary judgment. Jones, for example, can bring in the sworn statement of a witness that Jones was in California at the time of the accident. Unless Adams can bring in other statements raising the possibility that Jones was at the scene of the accident, Jones will be entitled to dismissal on a motion for summary judgment. Motions for summary judgment can be made before or during a trial, but they will be granted only if it is plain that there are no factual disputes.

Discovery

Before a trial begins, the parties can use a number of procedural devices to obtain information and gather evidence about the case. Adams, for example, will want to know how fast Jones was driving, whether he had been drinking, whether he saw a red light, and so on. The process of obtaining information from the opposing party or from other witnesses is known as **discovery**. Discovery serves several purposes. It preserves evidence from witnesses who might not be available at the time of the trial or whose memories will fade as time passes. It can pave the way for summary judgment if it is found that both parties agree on all facts. It can lead to an out-of-court settlement if one party decides that the opponent's case is too strong to challenge. Even if the case does go to trial, discovery prevents surprises by giving parties access to evidence that might otherwise be hidden, and it serves to narrow the issues so that trial time is spent on the main questions in the case. The federal rules of civil procedure and similar rules in the states set down the guidelines for discovery activity. Discovery includes gaining access to witnesses, documents, records, and other types of evidence.

DEPOSITIONS AND INTERROGATORIES Discovery can involve the use of depositions or interrogatories, or both. *Depositions* are sworn testimony by the opposing party or any witness, recorded by a court official. The person deposed appears before a court officer and is sworn. That person then answers questions asked by the attorneys from both sides. The questions and answers are taken down, sworn to, and signed. These answers will, of course, help the attorneys prepare their cases. They can also be used in court to impeach a party or witness who changes testimony at the trial. Finally, they can be used as testimony if the witness is not available at trial. Depositions can also be taken with written questions from both sides prepared ahead of time.

Interrogatories are a series of written questions for which written answers are prepared and then signed under oath. The main difference between interrogatories and depositions for written questions is that the former are directed to a party, not to a witness, and the party can prepare answers with the aid of an attorney. The scope of interrogatories is broader because parties are obligated to answer questions even if the answer requires disclosing information from their records and files. Interrogatories are also less expensive than depositions.

REQUEST FOR ADMISSIONS A party can serve a written request to the other party for an admission of the truth of matters relating to the trial. Any matter admitted under such a request is conclusively established for the trial. For example, Adams can ask Jones to admit that he was driving at a speed of forty-five miles an hour. A request for admission saves time at trial because parties will not have to spend time proving facts on which they already agree.

DOCUMENTS, OBJECTS, AND ENTRY UPON LAND A party can gain access to documents and other items not in the party's possession in order to inspect and examine them. Likewise, the party can gain entry upon land to inspect the premises. Jones, for example, can gain permission to inspect and duplicate Adams's medical records and repair bills.

PHYSICAL AND MENTAL EXAMINATION Where the physical or mental condition of a party is in question, a party can ask the court to order a physical or mental examination. If the court is willing to make the order, the party can obtain the results of the examination. It is important to note that the court will make such an order only when the need for the information outweighs the right to privacy of the person to be examined.

The rules governing discovery are designed to make sure that a witness or party is not unduly harassed, that privileged material is safeguarded, and that only matters relevant to the case at hand are discoverable.

Pretrial Hearing

Either party or the court can request a pretrial conference or hearing. Usually the hearing consists of an informal discussion between the judge and the opposing attorneys after discovery has taken place. The purpose of the hearing is to identify the matters that are in dispute and to plan the course of the trial. The pretrial hearing is not intended to compel the parties to settle their case before trial, although judges may encourage them to settle out of court if circumstances suggest that a trial would be a waste of time.

Jury Trials

A trial can be held with or without a jury. If there is no jury, the judge decides the truth of the facts in the case. The Seventh Amendment guarantees the right to a jury trial for cases at law in federal courts. Most states have similar guarantees in their own constitutions, although many states put a minimum dollar amount restriction on the guarantee. For example, Iowa requires the dollar amount of damages to be at least $1,000 before there is a right to a jury trial.

The right to a trial by jury does not have to be exercised, and many cases are tried without one. In most states and in federal courts, one of the parties must request a jury or the right is presumed to be waived.

In the case between Adams and Jones, both parties want a jury trial. The jurors are questioned by the judge and by both attorneys to ensure that their judgment will be impartial. After the jurors are selected, they are sworn, and the trial is ready to begin.

The Trial

Both attorneys are allowed to make *opening statements* concerning the facts that they expect to prove during the trial. Since Adams is the plaintiff and has the burden of proving that her case is correct, Adams's attorney begins the case by calling the first witness for the plaintiff and examining (questioning) the witness. (For both attorneys, the type of question and the manner of asking are governed by the rules of evidence.) This examination is called *direct examination.* After Adams's attorney is finished, the witness will be questioned by Jones's attorney in *cross-examination.* After that, Adams's attorney has another opportunity to question the witness in *redirect examination,* and Jones's attorney can then follow with *recross-examination.* When both attorneys have finished with the first witness, Adams's attorney will call the succeeding witnesses in the plaintiff's case, each of whom is subject to cross-examination (and redirect and recross, if necessary).

At the conclusion of the plaintiff's case, the defendant's attorney has the opportunity to ask the judge to direct a verdict for the defendant on the ground that the plaintiff has presented no evidence that would justify the granting of the plaintiff's remedy. This is called a *motion for a directed verdict.* In considering the motion, the judge will look at the evidence in the light most favorable to the plaintiff and will grant the motion only if there is insufficient evidence to raise an issue of fact. Motions for directed verdicts are seldom granted. An experienced attorney will not take a case to court unless there is enough evidence to ensure the possibility of a favorable verdict.

The defendant's attorney will then present the evidence and witnesses for the defendant's case. Witnesses are called and examined. The plaintiff's attorney has a right to cross-examine them, and there is a redirect and recross if necessary. At the end of the defendant's case, either attorney can again move for a directed verdict, and the test will again be whether the jury can, under any reasonable interpretation of the evidence, find for the party against whom the motion is made.

After the defendant's attorney has finished the presentation of evidence, the plaintiff's attorney can present additional evidence to refute the defendant's case in a *rebuttal.* The defendant's attorney can meet that evidence in a *rejoinder.* After both sides have rested their cases, the attorneys each present a *closing argument,* urging a verdict in favor of their respective clients. The judge instructs the jury (assuming it is a jury trial) in the law that applies to the case. The instructions to the jury are often called *charges.* Then the jury retires to the jury room to deliberate a verdict. In a case like Adams v. Jones, the jury will not only decide for the plaintiff or for the defendant but will also make a finding on the amount of money to be paid to the plaintiff.

JUDGMENT N.O.V. (NOTWITHSTANDING THE VERDICT) If Adams wins, Jones's attorney can make a motion for a *judgment n.o.v. (notwithstanding the verdict).* In other words, Jones can state that even though the jury found for the plaintiff, none of the evidence presented at the trial supported such a verdict. If the judge finds this to be correct or decides that the law requires the opposite result, the motion will be granted. This occurrence is rare indeed. Assume here that this motion is set aside, and Jones appeals the case. (If Adams wins but receives a smaller money award than she sought she can appeal also.) These events are illustrated in Exhibit 2-3.

The Appeal

A notice of appeal is filed with the clerk of the trial court within the prescribed time. Jones then becomes the *appellant*. His attorney files in the reviewing court (or court of appeal) the record on appeal, which contains the following: (1) the pleadings, (2) a transcript of the testimony, (3) the judge's rulings on motions made by the parties, (4) the arguments of counsel, (5) the instructions to the jury, (6) the verdict, (7) the posttrial motions, and (8) the judgment order from which the appeal is taken.

Jones's attorney is required to prepare a condensation of the record, known as an *abstract*. The abstract, the brief, and the argument are filed with the reviewing court. The brief contains (1) a short statement of the facts, (2) a statement of the issues, (3) the rulings by the trial court that Jones contends are erroneous and prejudicial, (4) the grounds for reversal of the judgment, (5) a statement of the applicable law, and (6) an argument on Jones's behalf. The attorney for the *appellee*, Adams, must now file an answering brief and argument. Jones's attorney can now file a reply (although this is not required). The reviewing court then considers the case.

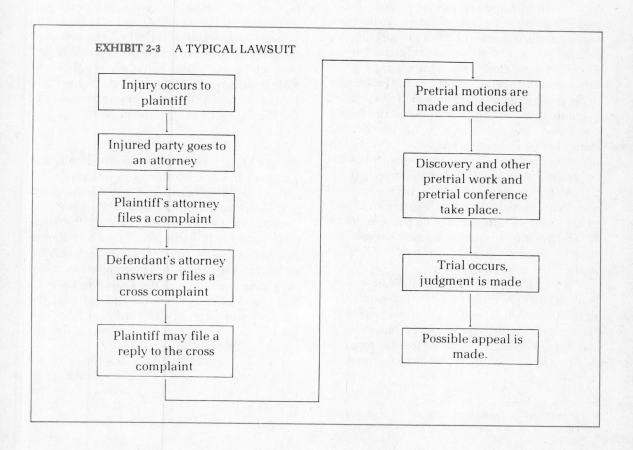

EXHIBIT 2-3   A TYPICAL LAWSUIT

Injury occurs to plaintiff

Injured party goes to an attorney

Plaintiff's attorney files a complaint

Defendant's attorney answers or files a cross complaint

Plaintiff may file a reply to the cross complaint

Pretrial motions are made and decided

Discovery and other pretrial work and pretrial conference take place.

Trial occurs, judgment is made

Possible appeal is made.

NO EVIDENCE HEARD Appeals courts do not hear any evidence. They take the case upon the abstracts, the record, and the briefs. The attorneys can present oral arguments, after which the case is taken under advisement. When the court has reached a decision, the decision is written. It contains the opinion (the court's reason for its decision), the rules of law that apply, and the judgment. If the reviewing court believes that the trial court was correct, it affirms the judgment. If the reviewing court believes that a reversible error was committed during the trial, the judgment will be reversed. Sometimes the case will be *remanded* (sent back) for a new trial.

HIGHER APPEALS COURTS If the reviewing court is an intermediate appellate court, the losing party (in that court) can seek a reversal of its decision by filing within the prescribed time period a petition for leave to appeal to the state supreme court.[8] Such a petition corresponds to a petition for a writ of *certiorari* in the United States Supreme Court. The winning party in the intermediate appellate court can file an answer to the petition for leave to appeal. If the petition is granted, the record is certified to the higher court, and new briefs must be filed before the state supreme court. Whenever the state supreme court concludes that the judgment of the intermediate appellate court is correct, it affirms. If it decides otherwise, it reverses the appellate court's decision and enters an appropriate order of remand. At this point, unless a federal question is at issue, the case has reached its end. If a new trial is ordered, it will start again at the court of origin.

It is important to know that the vast majority of disputes are settled out of court mainly due to the time and expense of trying a case. Furthermore, of those cases that go to trial, about 97 percent are decided at the trial level as relatively few trial court decisions are changed on appeal.

---

8. In some states, the appeal from the court of original jurisdiction to the state supreme court is a matter of right.

HOW TO FIND THE LAW

Most trial court decisions are not published. Except for the federal courts and New York and a few other states that publish selected opinions of their trial courts, decisions in trial courts are merely filed in the office of the clerk of the court, where they are available for public inspection.

On the other hand, the written decisions of appellate courts are published and distributed. Virtually all the cases in this book have been taken from these decisions. It is therefore important to understand the case reporting system.

The reported appellate decisions are published in volumes called *Reports*, which are numbered consecutively. State court decisions are found in the state reports of that particular state. Additionally, state reports appear in regional units of the *National Reporter System*, published by West Publishing Company. Most lawyers and libraries have the West reporters because they report cases more quickly and they are distributed more widely than the state-published reports. In fact, many states have eliminated their own reports in favor of the West's *National Reporter System*.

GEOGRAPHICAL AREAS West Publishing Company has divided the states into geographical areas: Atlantic (A. or A.2d), Southeastern (S.E. or S.E.2d), Southwestern (S.W. or S.W.2d), Northwestern (N.W. or N.W.2d), Northeastern (N.E. or N.E.2d), Southern (So. or So.2d), and Pacific (P. or P.2d). After appellate decisions are published, they are normally referred to (cited) by giving the name of the case; the volume, name, and page of the state report (if any), the volume and page of the National Reporter publication, and the year of filing of the appellate court decision.

Federal court decisions are found in the *Federal Reporter* (F. or F.2d), *Federal Supplement* (F.Supp.), *Federal Rules Decisions* (F.R.D.), *West's Bankruptcy Reporter* (B.R.), *United States Supreme Court Reports* (U.S.),

Supreme Court Reporter (S.Ct.), and the Lawyer's Edition (L.Ed.).

In reading the title of a case such as Adams v. Jones, the v. or vs. stands for versus, which means against. In the trial court, Adams was the plaintiff—the person who filed the suit. Jones was the defendant. When the case is appealed, however, the appellate court will sometimes place the name of the party appealing the decision first, so that the case will be called Jones v. Adams. Since some appellate courts retain the trial court order of names, it is not possible to distinguish between the plaintiff and the defendant from the title of a reported appellate court decision.

A SUPREME COURT CASE

The following summarizes an actual case heard by the Supreme Court of the United States. It is presented in the same way that cases throughout the rest of the book will be presented.

BACKGROUND AND FACTS *Vincent Chiarella, a printer, worked as a mark-up man for Pandick Press, which produced financial documents. In the course of his work, he handled five announcements of corporate takeover bids. When these documents were first delivered to the printer, blank spaces or false names concealed the identities of the acquiring and target corporations until the night of the final printing. Chiarella, however, was able to deduce the names of the target companies before the final printing from other information contained in the documents. Based on this special knowledge, he purchased stock in the target companies and sold his shares—at a $30,000 profit—immediately after the takeover attempts were made public. Chiarella was indicted on 17 counts of violating Securities and Exchange Commission Rule 10b-5. He was brought to trial and convicted on all counts. The Court of Appeals for the Second Circuit affirmed Chiarella's conviction.*

DECISION AND RATIONALE *The Supreme Court reversed Chiarella's conviction. Rule 10b-5 of the Securities and Exchange Commission makes it unlawful for any person to "employ any device, scheme, or artifice to defraud," or to "engage in any act, practice, or course of a business which operates or would operate as a fraud or a deceit upon any person, in connection with the purchase or sale of any security." Chiarella's use of the information that he obtained through his work as a printer would violate Rule 10b-5 only if he were under an affirmative duty to disclose such information before trading in the target company's securities. The Court of Appeals affirmed Chiarella's conviction by holding that no one—corporate insider or not—who regularly receives material, nonpublic information can use it to trade in securities unless the information is disclosed to the person with whom he or she is dealing. "[T]he element required to make silence fraudulent—a duty to disclose— is absent in this case. *** Section 10(b) is aptly described as a catchall provision, but what it catches must be fraud. When an allegation of fraud is based upon nondisclosure, there can be no fraud absent a duty to speak. We hold that a duty to disclose under Section 10(b) does not arise from the mere possession of nonpublic market information."*

CHIARELLA v. UNITED STATES
Supreme Court of the United States, 1980.
444 U.S. 895, 100 S. Ct. 1108.

1. The name of the case, also known as the *style*, is *Chiarella v. United States*. Vincent F. Chiarella and the United States were the parties involved, but one cannot tell, without reading the opinion closely, which was the plaintiff and which was the defendant at the trial court level. Generally, in actions in which the United States is a party, the United States is the plaintiff.

2. The court that heard this case was the Supreme Court, the highest court of appeals in the United States. This can be determined from the *citation*, discussed below.

3. Though it is not indicated, Mr. Justice Powell delivered the opinion of the Court. Justices Stevens and Brennan filed *concurring* opinions, and Chief Justice Berger, along with Justices Blackmun and Marshall, filed *dissenting* opinions.

    Members of the Supreme Court are known as justices. Persons who preside over other courts in the United States are known as judges. The Supreme Court has a total of nine members—a chief justice and eight associate justices. Often, not all the appellate justices hearing a case agree. Those who disagree are said to *dissent*. Those who agree with the results reached by the majority but disagree with some part of the majority's rationale (legal reasoning) can file *concurring* opinions. Each case is decided by majority vote.

4. The numbers and letters found below the case name or party names constitute the *citation*. This is what lawyers use to locate a case. The Chiarella case can be found in volume 100 of the *Supreme Court Reporter*, a West publication, on page 1108. The case may also be found in the *United States Supreme Court Reports*, usually published several months later than the *Supreme Court Reporter*, in volume 444, on page 895. The case was decided in 1980.

5. Court opinions usually begin with a recital of the facts followed by a discussion of the law. The cases in this text have been summarized and are presented in a similar manner, first the *background and facts* and then the *decision and rationale*. Included at the end of each *decision and rationale* is a quoted portion of the actual court opinion.

6. Triple asterisks (***) indicate that the authors of this book have deleted part of the quoted opinion.

7. The case came to the Supreme Court of the United States in the following way. Chiarella was charged by the United States government with *criminal* violations of the federal securities acts. (The Securities and Exchange Commission could have brought a *civil* suit against Chiarella, but he settled with the commission out of court.) Chiarella was tried and convicted in the United States District Court, which is a trial court. He then appealed his conviction to the Court of Appeals for the Second Circuit. Circuit courts of appeal are the intermediary courts in the federal court system. The circuit court *affirmed* the conviction, and Chiarella appealed to the United States Supreme Court on a *writ of certiorari*. The Supreme Court granted *cert*, meaning that it agreed to hear the case. Then it reversed the circuit court's decision.

QUESTIONS AND CASE PROBLEMS

1. The American system of government is unique in that it has essentially two sets of governments—state and federal. This is called the dual, or federal, system. One problem that arises in a federal system is that each government tends to duplicate the other's efforts. Can you see any way to avoid such problems of duplication?

2. How does the Constitution attempt to categorize the respective powers of the state and federal governments so that duplication of effort is avoided?

3. When a person commits an act that violates both state and federal law, quite often both the federal and the state government have jurisdiction. What problems do you see here?

4. The Constitution says that a person cannot be tried twice for the same crime. Does this problem arise when both the federal and the state government try the same person for the same crime? Explain.

5.   a.   Before two parties go to trial, there is an involved process called pleadings and discovery. Until recently, pleadings were very formal, and trials often turned on elements of surprise. For example, a plaintiff would not necessarily know until the trial what the defendant's defense was going to be. Does this seem like a fair way to conduct a trial?

  b.   Within the last twenty years, new rules of pleadings and discovery have substantially changed all this. Now, each attorney can discover practically all the evidence that the other will be presenting at trial. However, certain information is still not available to the parties—namely, each attorney's work product. *Work product* is not a clear concept. Basically, it includes all the attorney's thoughts on the case. Can you see any reason why such information should not be made available to the opposing attorney?

6.   Quite often, trials are concluded before they are ever begun. If the parties do not dispute what the facts are, they simply relate those facts to the judge, and then, through motions on the pleadings, they simply ask the judge to decide what the law is, given this basic set of facts. How is it possible that two parties can agree on the facts yet disagree that one party is liable to the other party?

7.   If a judge enters judgment on the pleadings, the losing party can usually appeal but cannot present evidence to the appellate court. Does this seem fair? Explain.

8.   Once a case is appealed, most appellate courts do not have the power to enter judgment or to award damages to a party who should have received them at trial. Thus, if the appellate court disagrees with the trial court's decision, it will reverse and remand, in effect, ordering the trial court judge to change the judgment. Why should an appellate court not take a judge's word as final?

9.   Sometimes on appeal there are questions of whether the facts presented in a trial support the conclusion reached by the judge or the jury. The appellate court will reverse on the basis of the facts only when so little evidence was presented at trial that no reasonable person could have reached the conclusion that the judge or jury reached. Appellate courts normally defer to a judge's decision with regard to the facts. Can you see any reason for this?

3

Torts

Part of doing business today and, indeed, part of everyday life is the risk of being involved in a lawsuit. A normal and ever-increasing business operating cost is the cost of liability insurance to protect against lawsuits. The list of possible circumstances in which businesspeople can be sued is long and varied. An employee injured on the job may attempt to sue the employer because of an unsafe working environment. The consumer who is injured while using a product may attempt to sue the manufacturer because of a defect in the product. The patient who has received negligent treatment may attempt to sue the doctor. The issue in all of these examples is alleged wrongful conduct by one person that causes injury to another. Such wrongful conduct is covered by the law of torts.

Tort law has its origin in early common law. Even today, when most other areas of the law have been codified in statutes, tort law is found primarily in the reports of court opinions. A **tort** can be simply defined as wrongful conduct by one individual that results in injury to another. However, this definition does not say much about the specific nature of torts, what wrongs are considered torts, and what injuries find a remedy in tort law. It is difficult to find a more exact definition because there are so many different torts, and torts cover such a broad area. Other areas of the law are more readily defined. Contract law, for example, covers the area of mutual promises and their enforcement. Criminal law deals with activities which contravene the rights of society as a whole. (Note, however, that a criminal act can also be a tort.) Tort law is a broad, almost all-encompassing area of law covering the whole range of human activity.

THE SCOPE
OF TORT LAW

Two notions serve as the basis of all torts: wrongs and compensation. The word *tort* is French for "wrong" and derives from the Latin for "twisted." Tort law recognizes that some acts are wrong because they cause injury to someone. The actor is to blame or bears the fault for these injuries. There are, of course, different types of wrongs. A crime involves conduct society has defined as wrongful, but a crime and a tort are not the same. A crime is an act so wrong that it is considered to be a wrong against the state or against society as a whole as well as a wrong against the individual victim. Therefore, the state prosecutes the criminal. A tort is a civil action in which one person brings a suit of a personal nature against another, and the state is not involved as a party to the suit. On the other hand, there are some acts which you or I might consider morally wrong that are not "wrongs" for purposes of tort law. You or I might consider it wrong to be rude or ungrateful or to shirk our responsibilities. Yet, this type of wrongful conduct does not constitute a tort.

Tort law also recognizes that the victims of wrongs should be compensated. Criminal law and the law of torts are both concerned with wrongful conduct, but criminal law punishes the culprit. The function of torts, on the other hand, is to provide the injured party with some remedy. The law of torts is used to decide when victims must bear the loss of their injuries themselves and when the responsibility belongs to someone else. One quick way of recognizing a tort is by asking whether the injury done is of the type that deserves compensation from another.

THE ELEMENTS
OF EVERY TORT

A tort has been committed when someone has suffered injury caused by the failure of another to live up to a required duty of care. There are three key elements in this definition: (1) injury, (2) causation, and (3) breach (failure) of duty of care.

Injury

In order for a tort to have been committed, there must be a recognizable injury to the plaintiff. The plaintiff must have suffered some loss, harm, wrong, or invasion of a protected interest to recover damages (that is, to receive compensation). The reason for the requirement of injury is obvious. Without an injury of some kind, there can be no compensation. Remember that the purpose of torts is to *compensate* for injuries resulting from wrongful acts, not to *punish* the act.

Tort law covers a broad variety of injuries. Society recognizes an interest in personal physical safety, and tort law provides a remedy for acts causing physical injury or interfering with physical security and freedom of movement. Society recognizes an interest in protecting personal property, and tort law provides a remedy for acts causing destruction or damage to property. Society recognizes other more intangible interests in such things as personal privacy, family relations, reputation, and dignity. Tort law provides a remedy for invasion of protected interests in these areas. Tort law is constantly changing and growing with society. Although many torts have their origin in the old common law, new torts protecting new interests develop in step with social change.

Causation

The second element necessary to a tort is causation. If a person fails in a duty of care and someone suffers injury, the wrongful activity must have caused the harm for a tort to have been committed. In deciding whether there is causation, the court must actually address two questions:

1. Is there factual causation?
2. Was the act the proximate cause of the injury?

FACTUAL CAUSATION Did the injury occur because of the defendant's act or would it have occurred anyway? If an injury would not have occurred without the defendant's act, then there is *factual causation*. If X carelessly leaves a campfire burning, and the fire burns down the rest of the forest, there is factual causation. If X carelessly leaves a campfire burning, but it burns out, and then lightning causes a fire that burns down the forest, there is no factual causation. In both cases there is a wrongful act and damage. In the second case, however, there is no causal connection and, thus, no liability. Factual causation can usually be determined by use of the *but for* test: But for the wrongful act, the injury would not have occurred.

In some cases, factual causation is difficult to determine. What if X's campfire did spread, but at the same time, lightning also started a fire. In this type of situation, the courts apply the *substantial factor* test. If X's conduct was a substantial factor in bringing about the damage, X will be held liable.

Determining factual causation involves examining the facts portrayed in evidence in a trial. The plaintiff has the burden of proving factual causation and other elements such as damages. The plaintiff need not prove factual causation beyond a reasonable doubt but must prove only that the causal connection is more likely than not.

PROXIMATE CAUSATION How far should a defendant's liability extend for a wrongful act that was a substantial factor in causing injury? For example, X's fire not only burns down the forest but also sets off an explosion in a nearby chemical plant that spills chemicals into a river, killing all the fish for a hundred miles downstream and ruining the economy of a tourist resort. Should X be liable to the resort owners? To the tourists whose vacation was ruined? These are questions about the limitation of liability, which is the second element in the general issue of causation. The courts use the term **proximate cause** (or sometimes legal cause) to describe this element. Proximate cause is a question not of fact but of law. The question is whether the connection between an act and an injury is strong enough to justify imposing liability. Probably the most cited case on proximate cause is the *Palsgraf* case.

PALSGRAF v. LONG ISLAND RAILROAD COMPANY
Court of Appeals of New York, 1928.
248 N.Y. 339, 162 N.E. 99.

BACKGROUND AND FACTS *The plaintiff, Palsgraf, was waiting for a train on the station platform. A man carrying a package was rushing to catch a train that was already moving away from a platform across the tracks from Palsgraf. As the man attempted to jump aboard the moving train, he seemed unsteady and about to fall. A railroad guard on the car reached forward to grab him, and another guard on the platform pushed him from behind to help him on the train. In the process, the man's package fell upon the railroad tracks and exploded because it contained fireworks. There was nothing about the package to indicate its contents. The repercussions of the explosion caused decorative scales to fall from the ceiling and walls around the train platform. One of these scales struck Palsgraf, causing injuries for which she sued the railroad company. At the trial, the jury found that the railroad guards were negligent in their conduct.*

DECISION AND RATIONALE *The railroad was not liable for the injuries that Palsgraf suffered. The question of whether the railroad's guards were negligent with respect to her turns on whether her injury was reasonably foreseeable. It is true that the guards may have acted negligently in helping the man to board the train and that this conduct may have resulted in injury to that man. However, this has no bearing on* the question of their negligence with respect to Palsgraf. This is not the same as a case where a person commits an act that is so potentially harmful (for example, firing a gun at a building) that he or she would be held responsible for any harm that resulted. According to the chief justice, "Here, by concession, there was nothing in the situation to suggest to the most cautious mind that the parcel wrapped in newspaper would spread wreckage through the station."

FORESEEABILITY Since the decision in the *Palsgraf* case, the courts have used *foreseeability* as the test for proximate cause. The railroad guards were negligent, but the railroad's duty of care did not extend to Palsgraf because she was an unforeseeable plaintiff. If the consequences of the harm done or the victim of the harm are unforeseeable, there is no proximate cause. Of course, it is foreseeable that people will stand on railroad platforms and that objects attached to the platforms will fall as the result of explosions nearby. However, this is not a chain of events against which a reasonable person will normally guard. It is difficult to predict when a court will say that something is foreseeable and when it will say that something is not. This difficulty stems from the fact that proximate cause is tied up with the notion of duty. (This point is obvious from Chief Justice Cardozo's opinion.) How far a court stretches foreseeability will be determined in part by how far the court stretches the defendant's duty of care.

Breach of Duty of Care

The final element in a tort can also be broken up into a two-part question:

1. Is there a duty of care?
2. Did the defendant's action breach (fail to live up to) that duty?

DUTY OF CARE Basically, the concept of duty arises from the notion that, if we are to live in society with other people, some actions can be tolerated and some cannot, some actions are right and some are wrong, and some actions are reasonable and some are not. The basic rule of

duty is that people are free to act as they please as long as their actions do not interfere with and infringe on the interests of others.

Tort law measures duty by a standard of reasonableness—the *reasonable person standard*. In determining whether a tort has been committed, the courts will ask how a reasonable person would have acted in the same circumstances. The reasonable person standard is objective. It is not necessarily how a particular person would act. It is society's judgment on how people should act. If the reasonable person existed, he or she would be the most careful, most conscientious, most even-tempered, and most honest of people.

BREACH OF DUTY When someone fails to live up to the standard of reasonableness, a tortious act has been committed (but not necessarily a completed tort since that will depend on whether there is damage and proximate cause). Failure to live up to the standard of care may be an act (setting fire to a building) or an omission (forgetting to put out a fire). It may be an intentional act, a careless act, or a careful but dangerous act that results in injury.

Whether or not a person's act or failure to act is unreasonable depends on the interaction of a number of factors. One factor is the nature of the act. Some actions—spitting on someone, for instance—are so outrageous that the actor should pay for what has been done regardless of physical damage. Other acts, like blasting with dynamite, are so dangerous that any damage they cause should be paid for. Another factor in determining whether damages should be paid is the manner in which an act is performed. Intentionally hitting someone on the back probably should be paid for; accidentally doing so probably should not be. A third factor is the nature of the injury—whether it is serious or slight, extraordinary, or simply part of everyday life. Two other factors are whether the activity causing the injury was socially useful and how easily the injury could have been guarded against. Finally, when all other factors hang in the balance, the determining factor may be the ability to suffer the loss. For instance, a large corporation can shoulder a loss more easily than an individual victim because the corporation will be able to spread the loss to all its customers by raising prices.

KINDS OF TORTS

Determining whether or not some action is a tort basically involves drawing a conclusion about the way that losses in an increasingly complex society should be allocated. As such, it is a decision on social policy, and it requires the balancing of many social factors. Legal commentators traditionally divide torts into three categories: intentional torts, negligence, and strict liability. Intentional torts, as the name implies, are concerned with intentional acts. Negligence concerns careless acts, and strict liability concerns liability without regard to fault.

INTENTIONAL TORTS: WRONGS AGAINST THE PERSON

An intentional tort is one in which the defendant wished to perform the tortious act or knew with substantial certainty that an injury would result. Note that it is intent with respect to the act that is important. The nature of the damage caused is irrelevant in determining whether there was intent. If I intentionally push you, and you fall to the ground and break your arm, it does not matter that I had no intention of breaking your arm. I did intend to push you, and that in itself is the tortious act for which I am liable for damages, including the injury to your arm.

Battery

A battery is harmful or offensive physical contact done with the intent of making the contact. If I intentionally punch someone in the nose, it is a battery. The interest this tort protects is the right to personal security and safety. The contact can be harmful, or it can merely be offensive. There is no necessity for actual physical injury. The contact can be to any part of the body or anything attached to it—for example, a hat or other clothing, a purse, a chair, or an automobile one is sitting in. Whether the contact is offensive or not is determined by the reasonable person standard. The contact can be made by the defendant or by some force that the defendant sets in motion—for example, a rock thrown, food poisoned, or a stick swung.

There is no need to prove special damages. If the plaintiff shows that there was a contact, and the jury agrees that the contact was offensive, that is enough to have a right to some compensation. Furthermore, there is no need to show that the defendant acted out of malice. He or she could have been joking or playing. The defendant's motive does not matter.

Assault

Any intentional act which creates a reasonable apprehension or fear of immediate harmful or offensive contact is an assault. The apprehension of contact must be a reasonable one, but apprehension is not the same as fear. The plaintiff may be unafraid, but if he or she believes the contact is coming, there is apprehension. At the same time, the apprehended contact must be such that a reasonable person would want to avoid it.

The interest protected in assault is the interest in being free from having to expect harmful or offensive contact. The arousal of the apprehension is enough to justify compensation. Of course, the *completion* of the act which threatens harm causing apprehension in another is a battery, discussed above. For example, A threatens B with a gun, then shoots him. The pointing of the gun at B is an assault, the firing of the gun is a battery.

DEFENSES TO ASSAULT AND BATTERY

Assault and battery have certain legally recognized defenses. A person who voluntarily signs up for a touch football team implicitly consents to the *normal* physical punishment that takes place during such activities. People who use reasonable force in attempting to remove intruders from their homes can use the excuse of **defense of property** to counter tort lawsuits for assault or battery or both. The same is true for people who are defending their lives or their physical well-being. This is called **self-defense.**

False Imprisonment

False imprisonment, sometimes called false arrest, is defined as the intentional confinement or restraint of another person. It involves interference with the freedom to move without restraint. The confinement can be accomplished through the use of physical barriers, physical restraint, or threats of physical force. Moral pressure or future threats are not a restraint sufficient to constitute false imprisonment. It is essential that the person being restrained not comply with the restraint willingly. On the other hand, a person is under no duty to risk personal harm in trying to escape.

Businesspeople are often confronted with suits for false imprisonment after they have attempted to confine a suspected shoplifter for questioning. Consider, for example, the case in which a store detective locks an alleged shoplifter in one of the store's offices. An hour later, the manager returns and is told of the act. If the customer can prove his or her innocence, the store can be sued for false imprisonment.

The loss to business from shoplifting is estimated to exceed 10 billion dollars a year. Almost all states have adopted so-called merchant protection legislation, which allows a merchant to detain any suspected shoplifter, provided that there is reasonable cause for suspicion and provided that the confinement is carried out in a reasonable way. However, the risk of real injury to an innocent person is great. Educational programs are often offered to all employees; these programs explain the exact procedures to be followed when a customer is suspected of shoplifting. Harm to reputation and the mental distress from a wrongful imprisonment are believed by the law to be so real that damages are presumed and need not be proven to make a case.

A merchant can use the defense of probable cause to justify delaying a suspected shoplifter, but the delay must be *reasonable*. The following case provides a good example.

BACKGROUND AND FACTS *Barbara Faulkenberry brought an action against her employer, Springs Mills, Inc., for false imprisonment. On two separate occasions, fellow employees had reported to supervisory personnel that Faulkenberry had been seen secreting cloth in her pocketbook. After the second report, her supervisors and some plant security guards delayed her for about fifteen minutes at the mill gatehouse as she attempted to leave work. The delay was to investigate whether she had any cloth in her possession.*

Faulkenberry refused to open her pocketbook at the request of her supervisors. After some discussion and her continued refusal to open her pocketbook to reveal its contents, she left the mill gatehouse without further hindrance. Subsequently, she filed this action for false imprisonment based upon the delay at the gatehouse.

The trial court found the employer guilty of false imprisonment.

DECISION AND RATIONALE *Springs Mills was not liable for false imprisonment of its employee because it had legal justification for stopping*

FAULKENBERRY v. SPRINGS MILLS, INC.
Supreme Court of South Carolina, 1978.
247 S.E.2d 445.

> *her to investigate reports that she was stealing. False imprisonment results when a person is deprived of liberty without lawful justification. Company officials did hold Faulkenberry against her will, but only after they had received two eyewitness reports that she was placing cloth in her purse. The court quoted 32 Am.Jur.2d, False Imprisonment, Section 74: "[W]here a person has reasonable grounds to believe that another is taking his property, he is justified in detaining the suspect for a reasonable length of time for the purpose of making an investigation in a reasonable manner."*

Infliction of Mental Distress

Recently the courts have begun to recognize an interest in freedom from mental distress as well as an interest in physical security. The tort of mental distress can be defined as an intentional act that amounts to extreme and outrageous conduct resulting in severe emotional distress to another. For example, a prankster telephones an individual and says that the individual's spouse has just been in a horrible accident. As a result, the individual suffers intense mental pain or anxiety. Extreme and outrageous conduct is defined as conduct that is outside the bounds of decency accepted by society. This test is measured by the reasonable person standard.

Defamation

The protection of a person's body is involved in the torts of assault, battery, and false imprisonment. **Defamation** of character involves wrongfully hurting a person's good reputation. The law has imposed a general duty on all persons to refrain from making defamatory, false statements about others. Breaching this duty orally involves the tort of **slander;** breaching it in writing involves the tort of **libel.**[1]

The basis of the tort is the publication of a statement or statements that hold an individual up to contempt, ridicule, or hatred. *Publication* here means that the defamatory statements are made to or within the hearing of persons other than the defamed party. If Thompson writes Andrews a letter accusing him of embezzling

_____
1. This distinction between oral and written defamation is becoming less meaningful.

funds, that does not constitute libel. If Peters calls Gordon dishonest, unattractive, and incompetent when no one else is around, that does not constitute slander. In neither case was the message communicated to a third party. Interestingly, the courts have generally held that dictating a letter to a secretary constitutes publication. Moreover, if a third party overhears defamatory statements by chance, the courts have generally held that this also constitutes publication. Note further that any individual who republishes or repeats defamatory statements is liable even if that person reveals the source of such statements. Most radio stations have instituted seven-second delays for live broadcasts such as talk shows to avoid this kind of liability.

Whenever libel is concerned, there is a presumption of damages unless the written statement is not defamatory on its face. On the other hand *slander* is not actionable (i. e., no grounds for a lawsuit) without proof of damages unless the statements can be classed as *defamatory per se.* The common law defines four types of false utterances that are torts per se:

1. A statement that another person has a loathsome communicable disease.
2. A statement that another person has committed improprieties while engaging in a profession or trade.
3. A statement that another person has committed or has been imprisoned for a serious crime.
4. A statement that an unmarried woman is unchaste.

DEFENSES AGAINST DEFAMATION Truth is normally an absolute defense against a defamation charge. Furthermore, there may be a privilege involved. For example, statements made by attorneys and judges during a trial have an *absolute privilege* against a defamation charge. Members of Congress making statements on the floor of Congress have an absolute privilege. Legislators have complete immunity from liability for false statements made in debate, even if they make such statements maliciously—that is, knowing them to be untrue. In general, false and defamatory statements that concern public figures and are published in the media are privileged if they are made without malice.[2] Under this rule of privilege, public figures are defined as those who "thrust" themselves into the forefront of public controversy. A plaintiff needs to show that the defendant either has actual knowledge of falsity or has engaged in a reckless disregard of the truth in order to show malice.

The tort law of slander and libel will continue to change as federal and state courts continue to expand or constrict the free speech guarantees of the federal and state constitutions.

Slander of Title and Disparagement of Goods

A tort that is related to defamation involves harm or injury resulting from false statements made about one's product, business, or title to property. Thus, any type of property interest that is legally protected can be the subject of disparagement, which can consist of false statements about leases, land, patents, or literary property. False statements can relate to the character of a business or a product. Again, publication is required for the tort of disparagement of goods to have occurred. Furthermore, actual damages must result. For example, if Myers owns a bakery and Smith falsely claims to a third party that Myers puts rat poison in the flour, Myers can sue for damages only if

2. New York Times Co. v. Sullivan, 376 U.S. 254, 84 S.Ct. 710 (1964).

the third party indeed no longer patronizes the shop.

Defamation by Computer

A computer can contain erroneous information about a person's credit standing or business reputation. When such information is given out, it can seriously damage the ability of that person to obtain credit in the future. Who is liable to the injured person under such circumstances—the data bank operator or the company that owns the information? Whichever one acted negligently is liable. (If both were negligent, both are liable.) The tort involved has been given the distinctive but misleading name of defamation by computer. Such liability can arise also under the federal Fair Credit Reporting Act of 1970 when the individual affected is a consumer. Furthermore, the federal Credit Card Act of 1970 gives further protection against defamation by computer.

Invasion of the Right to Privacy

A person's right to solitude and to freedom from prying public eyes is the interest protected by the tort of invasion of privacy. Four different acts qualify as an invasion of privacy:

1. The use of a person's name or picture for commercial purposes without permission.
2. Intrusion upon an individual's affairs or seclusion.
3. Publication of information that places a person in a false light. This could be a story attributing to the person ideas that are not held or actions that were not taken. (Publishing such a story could involve the tort of defamation as well.)
4. Public disclosure of private facts about an individual. The private facts that are made public must be facts that an ordinary person would find objectionable.

Misrepresentation (Fraud, Deceit)

The tort of misrepresentation involves the use of fraud and deceit for personal gain. It includes several elements:

1. Misrepresentation of facts or conditions with knowledge that they are false or with reckless disregard for the truth.

2. Intent to induce another to rely on the misrepresentation.

3. Justifiable reliance by the deceived party.

4. Damages suffered as a result of reliance.

5. Causal connection between the misrepresentation and the injury suffered.

In general, the reliance must be upon a statement of fact. Reliance on a statement of opinion is not justified unless the person making the statement has a superior knowledge of the subject matter. A lawyer's opinion of the law, for example, is an example of superior knowledge.

INTENTIONAL TORTS: WRONGS AGAINST PROPERTY

Wrongs against property include (1) trespass to land and to personal property, (2) conversion, and (3) nuisance. The wrong is against the individual who has legally recognized rights with regard to land or personal property.

Trespass to Land

Any time a person enters onto land that is owned by another, or causes anything to enter onto the land, or remains or permits anything to remain on it, such action constitutes a **trespass to land.** Note that *actual* harm to the land is not an essential element of this tort, because the tort is designed to protect the right of an owner to exclusive possession. Clearly, though, if no harm is done, usually only nominal damages (such as $1) can be recovered by the landowner. Examples of common types of trespass to land include walking or driving on the land, shooting across it with a gun, throwing rocks or spraying water on a building in the possession of another, building a dam across a river that causes water to back up on someone else's land, and placing part of one's building on the adjoining landowner's property.

DEFENSES AGAINST TRESPASS TO LAND

Trespass to land involves wrongful interference with another person's real property rights. But if one can show that the trespass was warranted, a complete defense is given. Another defense is to show that the purported owner did not actually have the right to the possession of the land in question.

Some situations carry a measure of damages for trespass to land, especially when the trespasser damages or wrongfully destroys items of value on the land. For example, land purchasers can recover the value of destroyed trees when avoidable errors caused construction crews to knock them down.

Trespass to Personal Property

Whenever any individual unlawfully injures the personal property of another or otherwise interferes with the personal property owner's right to exclusive possession and enjoyment of that property, **trespass to personalty** occurs. Trespass to personal property involves intentional meddling. If a fellow student takes your business law book as a practical joke and hides it so that you are unable to find it for several days prior to your final examination, the student has engaged in a trespass to personal property. (Today, this is called conversion, which is discussed below.)

DEFENSES AGAINST TRESPASS TO PERSONAL PROPERTY

If it can be shown that trespass to personal property was warranted, then a complete defense has been made. Many states, for example, allow hotel owners to retain the personal property of guests who refuse to pay for their lodgings.

Conversion

Whenever personal property is taken and kept from its rightful owner or possessor, the act of **conversion** has occurred. Conversion is the civil side of the crimes relating to stealing.[3] A bank

---

3. A theft is usually both a tort and a crime.

clerk who steals money from the bank commits a crime and a conversion at the same time. A person who unlawfully takes goods is liable for the tort of conversion even if the person mistakenly believed that he or she was entitled to them. In other words, good intentions are not a defense against conversion, and conversion can be an entirely innocent act. If I mistakenly deliver your groceries to someone else, and that person eats them, I have committed a conversion even though I did not intend to commit such an act. (The recipient of the groceries has also committed a conversion.)

Whoever suffers a conversion is generally entitled to recover the reasonable value of the goods that have been lost. If you enter a china shop, pick up a $500 vase, and drop it, you owe the store owner the value of the vase (and value can be different from price).

DEFENSES AGAINST CONVERSION If one can show that the purported owner has no superior title or right to possess, then that can be a successful defense against the charge of conversion.

Nuisance

It is possible to commit a tort and be liable because of unreasonable use of your own property. A **nuisance** is an improper activity that interferes with another's enjoyment or use of his or her property. Nuisances can be either public or private. A public nuisance disturbs or interferes with the public in general, whereas a private nuisance interferes with the property interest of only one individual. Reasonable limitations are placed on the use of the property in all situations. Such limitations prevent the owner from unreasonably interfering with the health and comfort of neighbors or with their right to enjoy their own private property. Those who suffer from nuisances can seek redress in the courts through an injunction, an equitable remedy whereby the undesirable activity is prohibited by court order.

BUSINESS TORTS

Many torts that have arisen in recent years can be classified as business torts. They involve the disparagement of goods and slander of title mentioned above as well as infringement on trademarks. A **trademark** is a word, name, device, or symbol used by a manufacturer or seller to distinguish his or her goods from those of others. Infringements of *patents* and *copyrights* are also business torts. The term *unfair competition* covers a variety of business torts. Such unlawful conduct is normally reported to various government agencies, such as the Federal Trade Commission.

Malicious injury to business is a tort that occurs when an individual engages in a business venture for the sole purpose of injuring an established business.[4]

---

4. The existence of a tort in this situation depends on the motive of the party.

BACKGROUND AND FACTS *The plaintiff, a barber, filed suit against the defendant for malicious interference with his business. The plaintiff had owned and operated a barbershop for the previous ten years and had been able to maintain himself and his family comfortably from the income of the business.*

The defendant was a banker in the same community. During the past twelve months, the defendant had "maliciously" established a competitive barbershop, employed a barber to carry on the business, and used his personal influence to attract customers from the plaintiff's barbershop. Apparently, the defendant had circulated false and malicious reports and accusations about the plaintiff and had personally solicited, urged,

TUTTLE v. BUCK
Supreme Court of Minnesota, 1909.
107 Minn. 145, 119 N.W. 946.

threatened, and otherwise persuaded many of the plaintiff's patrons to stop using the plaintiff's services and to use the defendant's shop instead. The plaintiff charged that the defendant undertook this entire plan with the sole design of injuring the plaintiff and destroying his business, not for serving any legitimate business interest or as fair competition.

DECISION AND RATIONALE *The defendant was guilty of maliciously interfering with the plaintiff's business. Based upon the facts presented, it was clear that the defendant's sole purpose in establishing the competing barber shop was to deprive plaintiff of his livelihood. The court was bound by precedent to preserve competition in the marketplace, but, at the same time, it was to guard against abusive practices. The line between the two is not easily drawn. However, when a person starts a competing business is motivated to drive a competitor out of business rather than to earn profits, that person is guilty of a tort and must answer for the harm done. "To call such conduct competition is a perversion of terms. It is simply the application of force without legal justification, which in its moral quality may be no better than highway robbery."*

Interference with Contractual Relations

Tort law relating to *intentional interference with contractual relations* has increased greatly in recent years. A landmark case in this area involved an opera singer, Joanna Wagner, who was under contract to sing for a man named Lumley for a specified period of years.[5] A man named Gye, who knew of this contract, nonetheless "enticed" Wagner to refuse to carry out the agreement, and Wagner began to sing for Gye. Gye's action constituted a tort because it interfered with the contractual relationship between Wagner and Lumley. In principle, any lawful contract can be the heart of an action for interference with contractual relations. The plaintiff must prove that the defendant actually induced a breach of contractual relationship, not merely that the defendant reaped the benefits of a broken contract. If Jones has a contract with Smith that calls for Smith to mow Jones's lawn every week for a year at a specified price, Jones cannot sue Miller when Smith breaches the contract merely because Miller now receives gardening services from Smith.

_____
5.   Lumley v. Gye, 118 Eng.Rep. 749 (1853).

NEGLIGENCE

Unlike intentional torts, negligence does not involve a mental state. In negligence, the actor neither wishes to bring about the consequences of the act nor believes that they will occur. The actor's conduct creates a *risk* of such consequences. Without the creation of a risk there can be no negligence, and the risk must be foreseeable; that is, it must be such that a reasonable person would be likely to anticipate it and guard against it. By the standard of the reasonable person, the negligent person should have foreseen the risk.

In examining a question of negligence, five questions should be asked:

1.   What did the person do (act)?
2.   Did the act create a foreseeable risk of harm (breach of duty of care)?
3.   Was harm done (damages)?
4.   Did the act cause the harm (causation in fact)?
5.   At what point should liability cease (proximate cause)?

Many of the actions discussed in the section on intentional torts would constitute negligence if they were done carelessly without intent. For instance, carelessly bumping into someone who falls and breaks an arm constitutes negligence. Likewise, carelessly, as opposed to intentionally, flooding someone's land constitutes negligence. In a sense, negligence is a way of committing a tort rather than a distinct category of torts.

Negligence involves the allocation of loss between an innocent plaintiff and an innocent, but careless, defendant. In all torts, but especially in negligent torts, the extent of duty and liability is determined by social policy—for example, by the extent to which the injurious activity is socially useful or by the extent to which the injuring party can spread the cost.

Defenses to Negligence

There are three basic defenses in negligence cases: (1) superseding, intervening forces; (2) assumption of risk; and (3) contributory and comparative negligence.

SUPERSEDING, INTERVENING FORCES A superseding, intervening force breaks the connection between a wrongful act and damage to another. It cancels out the original, wrongful act. For example, if I have a can of gasoline in the trunk of my car, this creates a foreseeable risk and is, thus, a negligent act. If lightning strikes my trunk, exploding the can and injuring passing pedestrians, the lightning supersedes my negligence as a cause of the damage if it was not foreseeable. This example illustrates that the doctrine of superseding forces is also a question of proximate cause and legal duty.

An act of God, such as a lightning bolt, if it is not foreseeable, is a superseding force. If one person creates a potentially dangerous condition, and the gross negligence of a second person causes the condition to result in damage, the second person's act can be a superseding force. Criminal acts or intentional torts by other persons, if not foreseeable, constitute superseding forces.

In other situations, the intervention of a force may not relieve liability. If medical maltreatment of an injury aggravates the injury, the person who orginally caused the injury by negligence is not relieved of liability. If subsequent disease or a subsequent accident is proximately caused by the original injury, the person who caused the *original* injury will be liable for the injury caused by the disease or subsequent accident. Where negligence endangers property, and the owner is injured in an attempt to protect the property, the negligent party will be liable for the injury. Finally, rescuers are considered a foreseeable intervening force, and a negligent party will be liable for injuries to them.

In negligence cases the negligent party will often attempt to show that some act has intervened after his or her action and that this second act was the proximate cause of injury. Typically, in cases where an individual takes a defensive action, such as attempting to escape by swerving or leaping from a vehicle, the original wrongdoer will not be relieved of liability even if the injury actually resulted from seeking to escape. The same is true under the so-called "rescue doctrine." Under this doctrine, if Smith commits an act that endangers Jones, and Brown sustains an injury trying to protect Jones, then Smith will be liable for Brown's injury. Rescuers can injure themselves, or the person rescued, or even a stranger, but the original wrongdoer will still be liable. The following case illustrates this doctrine.

BACKGROUND AND FACTS *This case arose out of an accident that killed three men and seriously injured five others. All were sewage treatment workers. After correcting a water leakage problem in a New York City sewer, one of the workers, Rooney, was fatally stricken by lethal gas present in the sewer when the oxygen-type protective mask he was wearing failed to operate properly. A companion worker shouted for*

GUARINO v. MINE SAFETY APPLIANCE CO.
Court of Appeals of New York, 1969.
25 N.Y.2d 460, 306 N.Y.S.2d 942, 255 N.E.2d 173.

help. Two other workers responded to the cries for help and were fatally stricken by the gas when they entered the sewer tunnel without masks.

The plaintiffs sued the manufacturer of the oxygen masks to recover damages for injuries they sustained in attempting to rescue a member of the sewer repair crew whose oxygen mask had malfunctioned.

DECISION AND RATIONALE *The defendant manufacturer was liable to the plaintiffs for the injuries they sustained in their attempted rescue. The fact that the rescuers were not users of the defectively manufactured masks is irrelevant. It is enough that they attempted to rescue others whose lives were imperiled as a result of the malfunctioning masks. The presiding judge quoted Justice Cardozo in rendering his opinion: "Danger invites rescue. The cry of distress is the summons to relief. *** The wrong that imperils life is a wrong to the imperilled victim; it is a wrong also to his rescuer."*

ASSUMPTION OF RISK A plaintiff who voluntarily enters into a risky situation knowing the risk involved will not be allowed to recover. This is the defense of **assumption of risk.** For example, a driver who enters a race knows that there is a risk of being killed or injured in a crash. The driver has assumed the risk of injury. The two requirements of this defense are: (1) knowledge of the risk and (2) voluntary assumption of the risk.

The risk can be assumed by express agreement, or the assumption of risk can be implied by the plaintiff's knowledge of the risk. Of course, the plaintiff does not assume a risk different from or greater than the risk normally carried by the activity. Risks are not deemed to be assumed in situations involving emergencies. Neither are they assumed where a statute protects a class of people from harm and a member of the class is injured by the harm.

CONTRIBUTORY AND COMPARATIVE NEG-LIGENCE All individuals are expected to exercise a reasonable degree of care in looking out for themselves. Failure to do so, combined with the negligence of another, which results in an injury, prevents either party from recovering for their injuries. Thus, recovery for negligence is barred by the defense of **contributory neg-ligence.** Each party has been negligent, and

their combined negligence has contributed to cause the injury. When one party sues the other in tort for damages for negligence, the defen-dant can claim contributory negligence, which is a complete defense under common law rules. (Contributory negligence is not, however, a defense to intentional torts or to suits based on strict liability, a topic that will be covered later.)

There is a trend toward narrowing the scope of the defense of contributory neglience. Instead of allowing contributory negligence to negate a cause of action *completely*, an increas-ing number of states allow recovery based on the doctrine of **comparative negligence.**[6] Comparative negligence is the proportional sharing between the plaintiff and the defendant of compensation for injuries based on the relative negligence of the two. In jurisdictions that follow the contributory negligence doc-trine, negligence on the part of the plaintiff will bar any recovery of damages. In comparative negligence jurisdictions, however, the plaintiff will be able to recover the percentage of damages that was due to the defendant's neg-ligence.

If a person has a last chance to avoid injury and could have avoided it by doing what a

_____
6. Comparative negligence has been adopted in about half the states.

reasonable person in the circumstances would have done, many jurisdictions will deny recovery to the injured party. This is known as the doctrine of *last clear chance*. There must be proof that the injured party discovered the situation and had the time to prevent the injury.

STRICT LIABILITY

The final category of torts is called **strict liability** or *liability without fault*. Intentional or negligent torts involve an act that departs from a reasonable standard of care and causes an injury. Under the theory of *strict liability*, liability for injury is imposed for reasons other than fault.

Abnormally Dangerous Activities

Strict liability for damages proximately caused by abnormally dangerous activities is one application of strict liability. Abnormally dangerous activities have three characteristics:

1.   The activity involves potential harm of a serious nature.
2.   The activity involves a high degree of risk that cannot be completely guarded against by reasonable care.
3.   The activity is not commonly performed in the community or area.

Strict liability is applied because of the extreme risk of the activity. Although the activity is performed with all reasonable care, there is still a risk of injury. Balancing that risk against the potential for harm, it is fair to ask the person engaged in the activity to pay for injury caused. Although there is no fault, there is still responsibility because of the nature of the activity.

BACKGROUND AND FACTS   *The Yommers operated a grocery store and gasoline station. In December 1967, their neighbors, the McKenzies, noticed a smell in their well water, which proved to be caused by gasoline in the well water. McKenzie complained to the Yommers, who arranged to have one of their underground storage tanks replaced. Nevertheless, the McKenzies were unable to use their water for cooking or bathing until they had a filter and water softener installed. At the time of the trial in December 1968, they were still bringing drinking water in from an outside source.*

The McKenzies sued the Yommers for nuisance and recovered damages of $3,500. The Yommers appealed the verdict on the grounds that the McKenzies did not prove that there was any negligence.

YOMMER v. McKENZIE
Court of Appeals of Maryland, 1969.
255 Md. 220, 257 A.2d 138.

DECISION AND RATIONALE   *The judgment against the Yommers was affirmed. There was no need for the McKenzies to prove negligence. Some wrongs are actionable in tort law even though they do not result from intentional wrongdoing or from negligence. Persons engaging in abnormally dangerous activities, that is, activities whose nature and location involve a high degree of risk to others, are held strictly liable for injuries caused by their acts. Judge Singley provided the following test for an abnormally dangerous activity:*

In determining whether an activity is abnormally dangerous, the following factors are to be considered:
(a)   Whether the activity involves a high degree of risk of some harm to the person, land or chattels [things] of others;

    (b)   Whether the gravity of the harm which may result from it is likely to be great;

    (c)   Whether the risk cannot be eliminated by the exercise of reasonable care;

    (d)   Whether the activity is not a matter of common usage;

    (e)   Whether the activity is inappropriate to the place where it is carried on; and

    (f)   The value of the activity to the community.

Other Applications of Strict Liability

There are other applications of the strict liability principle, most notably in the workmen's compensation acts and in the area of products liability. Liability here is a matter of social policy, and it is based on two factors: (1) the ability of the employer and manufacturer to better bear the cost of injury by spreading it out to society through an increase in the cost of goods and services and (2) the fact that the employer and manufacturer are making a profit from their activities and therefore should bear the cost of injury as an operating expense. Products liability will be considered in depth in Chapter 21.

QUESTIONS AND CASE PROBLEMS

1. Fisher was standing in line waiting to be served at a buffet luncheon when a waiter grabbed a plate from his hand, shouting that Negroes could not be served in that restaurant. The waiter never struck Fisher; nor did he threaten to strike him. Given that the definition of a battery is "the intentional unprivileged touching of another," decide whether a battery has been committed. [Fisher v. Carrousel Motor Hotel, Inc., 424 S.W.2d 627 (Texas 1967)]

2. A local department store caught fire and was ransacked by a number of people. Jones was suspected of having taken a pair of shoes from the store during the fire. The next night, Smith, a police officer, and two deputies went to Jones's house and told him that he was under arrest. Smith did not have a warrant for Jones's arrest. At first, Jones refused to go, but later he agreed. Smith then told Jones that if he would agree to come to town voluntarily the next day, he would not have to go with the police that night. Jones promised to do this, and the next day he went into town but was never indicted (charged) for the crime. Can Jones recover from Smith for false arrest? [Martin v. Houck, 141 N.C. 317, 54 S.E. 291 (1906)]

3. Hodgeden purchased a stove from Hubbard's warehouse in Montpelier, Vermont. Hubbard was not in the store at the time of the purchase. Hodgeden gave Hubbard's clerk a promissory note for the stove payable in six months. When Hubbard learned of the purchase and of Hodgeden's irresponsibility about paying his debts, he started in pursuit of Hodgeden and overtook him about two miles outside of Montpelier. Hodgeden refused at first to give back the stove, claiming that he had paid good money for it. Hubbard, who had brought an employee along with him, drew a knife, and his employee held Hodgeden back. Then Hubbard took the stove, put it into his own wagon and told his employee to let Hodgeden go. Hodgeden sued Hubbard for assault and battery. Hubbard claimed as a defense that since the goods were fraudulently purchased he could use such force as was necessary to recover them. Is he right? [Hodgeden v. Hubbard, 18 Vt. 504 (1846)]

4. Roger owned a large home in a residential area outside the city of New York. Roger's four children all left their toys scattered around the house, throughout the hallways, and on the stairways. On October 1, Steven, the youngest child, left his toy dump truck just inside the front door. Late that night, Dan the Man, a local cat burglar, gained entry into Roger's home by picking the lock on the front door. As Dan entered the home, he stepped on the cab of Steven's dump truck, slipped, fell, and suffered severe head injuries. Dan sued Roger. Can he recover?

5. a.   A father who was an avid golfer left one of his golf clubs in the backyard behind his home. Later that day, his five-year-old son picked up the golf club and swung it, hitting a neighbor. Is the father liable for the injury sustained by the neighbor on the grounds of negligence? Was the son's act foreseeable? [Lubitz v. Wells, 19 Conn.Sup. 322, 113 A.2d 147 (1955)]

   b.   Another time, a father left a loaded gun alongside a fence at the edge of his yard. Later that day, a boy who lived in the neighborhood picked up the gun and fired it, injuring Jones. The boy who picked up the gun had not known that it was loaded. Is the father liable in this case? Was the injury foreseeable? [Sullivan v. Creed, 2 Ir. R. 317 (K.B. 1904)]

6. Gulf sold a drum of gasoline to Williams for use in Williams's farm tractor. When Williams attempted to open the drum, he found that the bung hole cap was stuck because the threads were in disrepair. When Williams attempted to loosen the cap by banging on it, he produced a spark that caused an explosion and a fire. When Williams sued Gulf, Gulf admitted that it knew that the threads in the bung cap were in a state of disrepair because the drum had been used for a number of years, and bung caps had always been replaced by repeated hammering. Gulf claimed, however, that it should not be held liable for the injury sustained by Williams because it was so unusual that it was not reasonably foreseeable. Is Gulf correct? [Gulf Refining Company v. Williams, 183 Miss. 723, 185 So. 234 (1938)]

7. Hank Johnson, a frozen food delivery man, was employed by Clarkson and Company. Bubba Clarkson was both president and general manager of the company. On Tuesday morning, Clarkson sent Johnson out on a regular run to a local grocery store about six miles from Clarkson's warehouse, instructing him to take the regular route to the grocery store, which was straight up Hwy. 1. Clarkson knew that Johnson's girlfriend lived just half a mile off Hwy. 1 along the route to the grocery store, and he told Johnson to go directly to the grocery store, to return directly, and not to engage in any "funny business" along the way. On his return trip, since he was running a little bit ahead of schedule, Johnson turned off Hwy. 1 to visit his girlfriend. About halfway there, he negligently struck a young boy who was in the middle of the road. Most courts today hold employers liable for the negligent acts of their employees if the acts are committed within the "scope of the employee's employment." Employers are generally not held liable if the employee has gone on a "frolic of his own." Is Clarkson liable for Johnson's misconduct?

8. On a Friday evening at about dusk, Butterfield was riding his horse at a "swift rate of speed" down the road. Shortly before this, Forrester, who was making some repairs to his home, laid a long pole partially across the road. Because of the speed at which he was riding, Butterfield did not see the pole. The horse collided with it, and Butterfield was thrown many feet from his horse and injured. At trial, evidence showed that the pole could be seen from approximately a hundred yards away at that time of night. The facts also showed that Butterfield would have seen the pole and could have avoided hitting it if he had been riding at a normal rate of speed. If the court finds that both Butterfield and Forrester were negligent, can Butterfield collect any damages at all? [Butterfield v. Forrester, 11 East 60, 103 Eng.Rep. 926, Huntsey (1809)]

9. Fletcher owned and operated a mill that needed a large reservoir of water to operate. Fletcher dug a large surface reservoir and filled it with water. A number of mines operated within the general area of the reservoir. Eventually, water started to leak through the ground into an underground mine shaft owned and operated by Rylands. Rylands sued Fletcher for the damage that Fletcher's reservoir had caused to Rylands's mining operation. Rylands, however, did not allege that Fletcher had been negligent in constructing or in operating his reservoir or mill. Can Rylands sue Fletcher without claiming that Fletcher has been negligent in any way? [Rylands v. Fletcher, L.R. 3 H.L. 330 (1868)]

4

Criminal Law

Businesspeople are concerned with crimes for two reasons. First, businesses are often the target of criminals. The crimes of embezzlement, passing bad checks, shoplifting, and theft, for example, are costly for both businesses and consumers. Second, some criminal law applies directly to the activities of businesses and those who run them. For example, the Sherman Antitrust Act contains specific criminal sanctions. The Great Electrical Conspiracy of the 1960s resulted in several top officials from various electric companies serving time in jail for price fixing.

THE NATURE OF CRIME

Crimes are distinguished from other wrongful conduct in that they are offenses against society as a whole. Certain acts hurt not only the individual against whom they are committed but all other members of the community as well. For this reason, crimes are prosecuted by a public official and not by their victims.

    In addition, criminals are punished. Tort remedies are generally intended to compensate the injured, but criminal law is directly concerned with punishing the wrongdoer. The act of punishment is intended to accomplish four aims:

1.   Punishment is supposed to deter not only the wrongdoer in a particular instance but also all other members of society who might

commit a similar wrong.

2.   Punishment protects society by incapacitating the criminal through imprisonment.

3.   Punishment serves as a substitute for private vengeance.

4.   Punishment is supposed to rehabilitate criminals by showing them the error of their ways. Programs for treatment and education are part of the American penal system.

A final distinguishing factor is that the source of criminal law is primarily statutory. Both the acts that constitute crimes and the resulting punishments are formally set out in statutes. A **crime** can thus be defined as a wrong against society proclaimed in a statute and punishable by society if committed.

Classifications of Crimes

FELONIES AND MISDEMEANORS Crimes are classified as felonies or misdemeanors according to their seriousness. **Felonies** are more serious than misdemeanors and are punishable by death or by imprisonment in a federal or state penitentiary for more than a year. The definition of a felony derives from the common law crimes of arson, rape, grand larceny, and murder. Felonies can be divided into degrees of seriousness. The Model Penal Code, for example, provides for four degrees of felony: capital offenses where the maximum penalty is death, first degree felonies punishable by a maximum penalty of life imprisonment, second degree felonies punishable by a maximum of ten years imprisonment, and third degree felonies punishable by up to five years imprisonment. (It is important to note that these are maximum penalties. The actual sentence served can be less than the maximum.)

Misdemeanors are crimes punishable by a fine or by confinement for up to a year.[1] Misdemeanors are also sometimes defined as offenses where incarceration takes place in a local jail instead of in a penitentiary. In prac-

tice, the jail confinement is usually for no more than a year. Disorderly conduct and trespass are common misdemeanors. Some states have different classes of misdemeanors. For example, in Illinois there are Class A misdemeanors (confinement for up to a year), Class B (not more than six months), and Class C (not more than thirty days).

Whether a crime is a felony or a misdemeanor can determine whether the case is tried in a magistrate court or a general trial court.

Another kind of wrong is termed a petty offense and often is not classified as a crime. Petty offenses include traffic violations or violations of building codes. Even for petty offenses, a guilty party can be put in jail for a few days, or fined, or both.

MALA IN SE AND MALA PROHIBITA Crimes are also classified by whether they are inherently evil or wrong simply because the law says so. **Crimes *mala in se*** are immoral in themselves. Murder, arson, larceny, and any other acts involving moral turpitude are crimes *mala in se*. **Crimes *mala prohibita*** are acts that are wrong because they are prohibited by law, but they are not inherently evil. Parking in a no parking zone is an example. The distinction between the two types of crime is a very old one, but it can still be important today, especially where intent to harm is an element required for conviction.

Crimes *mala prohibita* change through time as laws change; and to a lesser extent, crimes *mala in se* change as social mores change. The fact that the definition of criminal conduct changes over time does not negate the continuity of criminal law. Virtually all societies have considered murder, theft, and treason as crimes, but the severity of the penalty and, indeed, the nature of the crime itself have varied. Today, in the United States, publishing criticism of the government does not constitute treason; but elsewhere in the world, it does.

FEDERAL AND STATE CRIMES   Criminal law is primarily the province of the states, but the

---

1.   The Constitution prohibits sending to jail an offender who cannot pay a fine. Tate v. Short, 401 U.S. 395, 91 S.Ct. 668, 28 L.Ed.2d 130 (1971). Williams v. Illinois, 399 U.S. 235, 90 S.Ct. 2018, 26 L.Ed.2d 586 (1970).

federal government also has a criminal code. Federal crimes relate to federal government functions or involve federal personnel or institutions. Counterfeiting, unlawful immigration, spying, robbing a federally insured bank, or assaulting a federal officer are examples of federal crimes. In other instances, the federal government can use its general regulatory powers to aid state law enforcement agencies in combating crimes that have a national impact. Transporation of stolen vehicles across state lines, kidnapping, and civil rights violations are areas that fall under federal criminal law.

CLASSIFICATION BY NATURE Crimes can be classified according to their nature. For example, there are crimes against property (theft, burglary, arson), crimes against the person (murder, assault, rape), and crimes against the government (perjury, bribery). These classifications are used to group crimes within a statutory code.

In addition, there are sociological classifications of crimes. These classifications may not have any legal consequence, but they are helpful in describing different types of crime. *Organized crime*, for example, is characterized by organization, continuity, a broad scope of operations, and the use of public corruption. It is involved in such activities as gambling, prostitution, labor rackets, and narcotics. In *victimless crime*, such as prostitution, gambling, and drug abuse, the participants consent to acts defined as criminal. They can also harm themselves, and their criminal acts can lead them to commit crimes against unwilling victims. For example, an addict may have to steal to support a habit. *White collar crime* refers to crimes committed in the course of business by employees (white collar workers). It includes crimes committed for the benefit of the business, such as price fixing, and crimes committed against the business, such as embezzlement.

THE ESSENTIALS OF CRIMINAL LIABILITY

Three elements are necessary for a person to be convicted of a crime: (1) the performance of a prohibited act, (2) a specified state of mind or intent on the part of the actor, and (3) the absence of circumstances that the law recognizes as excusing actions that would otherwise be criminal.

Prohibited Acts

Every criminal statute prohibits certain behavior, called the *actus reus*, or guilty act. Most crimes require an act of commission; that is, the criminal must do something. In some cases an act of omission can be a crime, but only if what is omitted is a legal duty. Failure to file a tax return is an example of an omission that is a crime.

The *guilty act* requirement is based on one of the premises of criminal law—that a person is punished for *harm done* to society. Thinking about killing someone or about stealing a car may be wrong, but these thoughts do no harm in themselves until they are translated into action. Of course, a person can be punished for attempting murder or robbery, but only if substantial steps toward the criminal objective have been taken.

Completion of the act will not complete the crime, however. A court must also find that the required state of mind was present.

State of Mind

In addition to the act, there is also a mental element called the *mens rea*, or evil intent, required for criminal liability. Without a wrongful mental element, the actor is not truly guilty. Both the *actus reus* and the *mens rea* vary from crime to crime. Thus, for murder, the *actus reus* is the taking of a life, and the *mens rea* is the intent to take life. For theft, the *actus reus* is the taking of another person's property, and the *mens rea* involves both the knowledge that the property belongs to another and the intent to deprive the owner of it. Without the mental state required by law, there can be no crime.

The *mens rea*, or mental state, in which a particular act is committed can vary in the degree of its wrongfulness. The same act— shooting someone—can be committed with varying mental states. It can be done coldly after premeditation. It can be done in the heat of passion or can be the result of negligence. In each of these situations, the law recognizes a different degree of wrongfulness, and the punishment varies accordingly.

The Model Penal Code recognizes four categories of *mens rea*: (1) purpose or intent, (2) knowledge (both formerly covered under the term *specific intent*), (3) recklessness, and (4) negligence (both formerly covered by the term *general intent*).

DEFENSES TO CRIMINAL LIABILITY

The law recognizes certain conditions that will relieve a defendant of criminal liability. These conditions are called defenses, and the most important of them are infancy, intoxication, insanity, mistake, consent, duress, entrapment, statute of limitations, and justifiable use of force. A criminal defendant can also gain immunity from prosecution.

Infancy

In the common law, children up to seven years of age were considered incapable of committing a crime because they did not have the moral sense to understand that they were doing wrong. Children between the ages of seven and fourteen were presumed to be incapable of committing a crime, but this presumption could be rebutted by showing that the child understood the wrongful nature of the act. Today, states vary in their approaches, but all retain the defense of infancy as a bar to criminal liability. Most states retain the common law approach, although age limits vary from state to state. Other states have rejected the rebuttable pre-

sumption and simply have a minimum age required for criminal responsibility. All states have juvenile court systems that handle children below the age of criminal responsibility who commit crimes. Their aim is reform rather than punishment. In states that retain the rebuttable presumption approach, children who are beyond the minimum age but are still juveniles can be turned over to the criminal courts if the juvenile court judges that they should be treated as adults.

Intoxication

The law recognizes two types of intoxication, whether from drugs or from alcohol: voluntary and involuntary. Involuntary intoxication occurs when a person is either physically forced to inject an intoxicating substance or is unaware that a substance contains drugs or alcohol. Involuntary intoxication is a defense to crime if its effect was to make a person either incapable of understanding that the act committed was wrong or incapable of obeying the law.

Voluntary intoxication is a defense where intoxication precludes having the required *mens rea*. Thus, if Johnson shoots Peters while too drunk to know what she is doing, she cannot be convicted of *murder* because she did not have the required intent to kill when she shot Peters. Voluntary intoxication, however, does not serve as a defense for crimes requiring recklessness or negligence. The law requires that people be aware that intoxication can make it impossible to behave as a reasonable person. Therefore, becoming intoxicated and committing a reckless or negligent act is a crime. In the example above, Johnson could be convicted of *manslaughter*.

BACKGROUND AND FACTS *Following fresh tire tracks in the snow from the scene of a break-in, police discovered White and some companions stuck in a snowbank. White and his companions were charged with burglary and tried before a jury. White contended that just prior to the alleged burglary he had drunk large quantities of beer. He claimed that his intoxication precluded him from forming the specific intent needed to commit burglary. The jury found him guilty, and he appealed.*

STATE v. WHITE
Supreme Court of
South Dakota, 1978.
269 N.W.2d 781.

DECISION AND RATIONALE *The jury was justified in convicting White. It was the jury's function to weigh the credibility of White's testimony against the evidence. The evidence showed that several persons had participated in the burglary, including White. White even admitted that he had been with the other accused persons several hours before the burglary. Most importantly, White violently resisted arrest. As Justice Porter said "This allows an inference that defendant was aware of his implication since ordinarily one being extricated from a car stuck in a snowbank in midwinter would have no reason to resist, particularly since he recognized the officers as police."*

Insanity

Just as a child is judged incapable of the state of mind required to commit a crime, so also is someone suffering from mental illness. Thus, insanity is a defense to a criminal charge. The law has had difficulty deciding what the test for legal insanity should be, and psychiatrists are critical of the tests used. Almost all federal courts and some states use the standard in the Model Penal Code:

A person is not responsible for criminal conduct if at the time of such conduct as a result of mental disease or defect he lacks substantial capacity either to appreciate the wrongfulness of his conduct or to conform his conduct to the requirements of the law.

Other states use the M'Naghten test, which excuses a criminal act if a mental defect makes a person incapable of appreciating the nature of the act or incapable of knowing that it was wrong. Some states that follow the M'Naghten rule have also adopted the irresistible impulse test. A person operating under an irresistible impulse may know that an act is wrong but may still be unable to keep from doing it. Even if a mental illness is not grave enough to serve as a complete defense, it may render a person legally incapable of certain crimes if the illness precludes the possibility of the required *mens rea.*

Mistakes

Everyone has heard the saying "ignorance of the law is no excuse." It may seem harsh to presume that everyone knows or should know the law, but imagine what the result of a different rule would be. Ordinarily, ignorance of the law or a mistake about what the law requires is not a valid defense. In some states, however, that rule has been modified. A person who claims that he or she honestly did not know that a law was being broken may have a valid defense if: (1) the law was not published or reasonably made known to the public or (2) the person relied on an official statement of the law that was erroneous. An official statement is a statute, judicial opinion, administrative order, or statement by someone responsible for administering, interpreting, or enforcing the law. Statements in newspapers or textbooks are not official statements.

A mistake of fact, as opposed to a mistake of law, will operate as a defense if it negates the required *mens rea.* If, for example, John Jones mistakenly drives off in Mary Thompson's car because he thinks that it is his, there is no theft. Theft requires knowledge that the property belongs to another.

Consent

What if a victim consents to a crime or even encourages a criminal to commit it? The law will allow consent as a defense if the consent cancels the harm that the law is designed to prevent. In each case, the question is whether the law forbids an act against the victim's will or forbids the act without regard to the victim's wish. The law forbids murder, prostitution, and drug use whether the victim consents to it or not.

Consent operates as a defense most successfully in crimes against property since one can always give away one's property. Of course, if the act operates to harm a third person who has not consented, there will be no escape from criminal liability. Consent or forgiveness given after a crime has been committed is not really a defense, though it can affect the likelihood of prosecution.

Duress

A person who is asked or instructed to commit a crime is not excused from criminal liability, but committing a crime under duress is a valid defense. The courts use a number of requirements to measure duress. First, the threat must be of serious bodily harm or death. A person who was threatened with failing a course or losing a job cannot plead duress as a defense. Second, the harm that is threatened must be greater than the harm that will be caused by the crime. A threat to shoot a woman's husband unless she robs a bank would be sufficient; a threat to hit her over the head would not be. The third requirement is that the threat must be immediate and inescapable. Finally, people who plead duress as a defense must have gotten into the situation through no fault of their own. If, for example, a person committing a burglary forces an accomplice to kill someone, the accomplice cannot use duress as an excuse. Participating in the burglary in the first place carries with it the possibility of being forced to commit a greater crime. The situation is the accomplice's fault.

The threat in a duress defense can be to the person under duress or to someone close to him or her, like a spouse. One crime that cannot be excused by duress is murder. It is difficult to justify taking a life even if the threat is to one's own life.

Justifiable Use of Force

Probably the most well-known defense to criminal liability is self-defense. But there are other situations that justify the use of force: the defense of one's dwelling, the defense of other property, and the prevention of a crime. In all of these situations, it is important to distinguish between the use of deadly and nondeadly force. Deadly force is likely to result in death or serious bodily harm. Nondeadly force is force that reasonably appears necessary to protect against the imminent use of criminal force.

Generally speaking, persons can use the amount of nondeadly force that seems necessary to protect themselves or their dwelling or other property or to prevent the commission of a crime. Deadly force can be used in self-defense if there is a reasonable belief that imminent death or grievous bodily harm will otherwise result, if the attacker is using unlawful force (e. g., not a police officer), and if the person has not initiated or provoked the attack. Deadly force can be used to defend a dwelling only if the unlawful entry is violent, and the person believes that deadly force is necessary to prevent imminent death, great bodily harm, or, in some jurisdictions, the person believes deadly force is necessary to prevent commission of a felony in the dwelling.

In defense of other property, the use of nondeadly force is justified to prevent or end the criminal's attempt to take away or otherwise interfere with the property. Deadly force usually is justifiable only when used in self-defense.

Force reasonably necessary to prevent a serious crime is permissible, but in the modern view, deadly force can be used to prevent only crimes that involve a substantial risk of death or great bodily harm.

Entrapment

Entrapment is a defense designed to prevent the police or other government agents from encouraging criminal acts in order to apprehend criminals. In the typical entrapment case, an undercover agent suggests that a crime be committed and somehow pressures or induces an individual to commit it. The agent then arrests the individual for the crime. Both the suggestion and the inducement must take place. The defense is not intended to prevent the police from setting a trap for an unwary criminal. It is intended to prevent them from pushing the criminal into it. The crucial issue is whether a criminal was predisposed to commit the crime or committed the crime because the agent induced it. This is often a question of fact.

Statute of Limitations

An individual can be excused from criminal liability by a statute of limitations. Such statutes provide that the state has only a certain amount of time to prosecute a crime. If it does not do so within the allotted time, it has lost its opportunity, and the suspect is free from prosecution. The idea behind these statutes is that people should not have to live under the threat of criminal prosecution indefinitely. Also, if prosecution is delayed for too long, it becomes difficult to find out what the truth is because witnesses die or disappear and evidence is destroyed.

Time limits vary from state to state. Felonies usually have a longer time period than misdemeanors, and there is no time limitation placed on murder. For all other crimes, the time limit runs from the time the crime is committed, unless it is a crime that is difficult to discover. In those cases, the time begins to run when the crime is discovered. A time limitation will be suspended, however, if the suspect leaves the state or hides. Normally, statutes will provide for subtraction of time if the suspect cannot be found or is not available to stand trial.

Immunity

At times, the state may wish to obtain information from a criminal. Criminals, of course, have an absolute right against self-incrimination and are understandably reluctant to give information if it will be used to prosecute them. In these cases, the state can grant immunity from prosecution or agree to prosecute for a less serious offense in exchange for the information.

CRIMINAL PROCEDURE

Our criminal justice system operates on the premise that it is far worse for an innocent person to be punished than for a guilty person to go free. A person is innocent until proven guilty, and guilt must be proven beyond a reasonable doubt. The procedure of the criminal law system is designed to protect the rights of the individual and preserve the presumption of innocence.

Constitutional Safeguards

Criminal law brings the weighty force of the state, with all its resources, to bear against the individual. Recognizing this fact, the Founding Fathers provided specific safeguards for the accused criminal in the Constitution. The Supreme Court has ruled that most of these safeguards apply not only in federal but also in state courts by virtue of the due process clause of the Fourteenth Amendment. The safeguards include:

1. Fourth Amendment protection from unreasonable searches and seizures.
2. Fourth Amendment requirement that no warrants for a search or an arrest can be issued without probable cause.
3. Fifth Amendment requirement that no one can be deprived of "life, liberty, or property without due process of law."
4. Fifth Amendment prohibition of double jeopardy, or trying someone twice for the same offense.
5. Sixth Amendment guarantees of a speedy trial, by jury, a public trial, the right to confront witnesses, and the right to a lawyer.
6. Eighth Amendment prohibitions against excessive bails and fines and cruel and unusual punishment.

In recent years, the Supreme Court has been active in interpreting these rights. Some of the cases are widely known. The *Miranda* decision, for example, established the rule that individuals who are arrested must be informed of their right to remain silent, of the fact that anything they say can be used against them in court, of their right to have a lawyer present, and of the duty of the state to provide lawyers if individuals cannot pay for them.[2] The following

case established the bounds of the Fourth Amendment protection against unreasonable searches and seizures.

_____

2.   Miranda v. Arizona, 384 U.S. 436, 86 S.Ct. 1602 (1966).

BACKGROUND AND FACTS *Katz was convicted of transmitting wagering information by telephone in violation of a federal statute. Over Katz's objection, the government introduced evidence of telephone conversations that he had had and that were overheard by FBI agents through an electronic device attached to the outside of a public telephone booth. Katz argued that this evidence should not be admissible as it violated his Fourth Amendment rights.*

KATZ v. UNITED STATES,
Supreme Court of
the United States, 1967.
389 U.S. 347, 88 S.Ct. 507.

DECISION AND RATIONALE   *The decision was reversed because the evidence should not have been admitted. It is true that the surveillance involved no physical penetration of the telephone booth. At one time, it was thought that the Fourth Amendment was limited to searches and seizures of personal property, which involved the necessity of physical intrusion. However, the amendment should be construed to protect people, not places, against unreasonable searches and seizures. "Once it is recognized that the Fourth Amendment protects people—and not simply areas—against unreasonable searches and seizures it becomes clear that the breach of that Amendment cannot turn upon the presence or absence of a physical intrusion into any given enclosure."*

Criminal Process

A criminal prosecution differs significantly from a civil case in several respects. These differences reflect the desire to safeguard the rights of the individual against the state.

ARREST   Before a warrant for arrest can be issued, there must be a finding that there is probable cause to believe that the individual has committed a crime. **Probable cause** can be defined as a substantial likelihood that the individual has committed or is about to commit a crime. Note that probable cause involves a likelihood, not just a possibility. Arrests are sometimes made without a warrant when there is no time to get one, but the action of the arresting officer is still judged by the standard of probable cause.

INDICTMENT   Individuals must be formally charged with specific crimes before they can be brought to trial. This is called an **indictment** if issued by a grand jury and an **information** if issued by a magistrate. Before a charge can be issued, the grand jury or the magistrate must determine that there is sufficient evidence to justify bringing the individual to trial. The standard used to make the judgment varies in different jurisdictions. Some courts use the probable cause standard. Others use the preponderance of evidence standard, which is a belief based on evidence provided by both sides that it is more likely than not that the individual committed the crime. Still another standard is the *prima facie* case standard, which is a belief based only on prosecution evidence that the individual is clearly guilty.

TRIAL   At the trial, the accused criminal does not have to prove anything. The entire burden of proof is on the prosecution (the state). Guilt is judged on the basis of the **reasonable doubt** test. The prosecution must show that, based on all the evidence, the defendant's guilt is established beyond all reasonable doubt. Note that a verdict of not guilty is not the same as a statement that the defendant is innocent. It merely means that there is not enough evidence to prove guilt beyond all reasonable doubt.

CRIMES INVOLVING AND AFFECTING BUSINESS

Forgery

The fraudulent marking or alteration of any writing that changes the legal liability of another is **forgery**. If Smith signs Brown's name to the back of a check made out to Brown, Smith has committed forgery. Forgery also includes changing trademarks, falsifying public records, counterfeiting, and, in fact, the alteration of any legal document.

Most states have a special statute, often called a *credit card statute*, to cover the illegal use of credit cards. Thus, the prosecuting attorney can prosecute a person who misuses a credit card for violating either the forgery statute or the special credit card statute.

Robbery

At common law, **robbery** is defined as forcefully and unlawfully taking personal property of any value from another. The use of force or fear is usually necessary for an act of theft to be considered a robbery. Thus, pickpocketing is not robbery because the action is unknown to the victim. Typically, states have more severe penalties for *aggravated* robbery—robbery by use of a deadly weapon.

Burglary

The common law defines **burglary** as breaking and entering a dwelling at night with the intent to commit a felony. Originally, the offense was aimed at protecting a person's home and its occupants. Most state statutes have eliminated the requirements of the common law definition. Thus, the time at which the breaking and entering occurs is usually immaterial, state statutes frequently omit the element of breaking, and some states do not require that the building be a dwelling. Aggravated burglary, which is defined as burglary with the use of a deadly weapon, or burglary of a dwelling or both incurs a greater penalty.

Larceny

The wrongful or fraudulent taking and carrying away by any person of the personal property of another is **larceny**. It includes the fraudulent intent to permanently deprive an owner of property. Many business-related crimes entail fraudulent conduct.

The place from which physical property is taken is generally immaterial. However, statutes usually prescribe a stiffer sentence for property taken from buildings such as banks or warehouses. Larceny is differentiated from robbery by the fact that the latter involves force or fear. Therefore, pickpocketing is larceny, not robbery.

DISTINGUISHING BETWEEN GRAND AND PETIT LARCENY   The common law distinction between grand and petit larceny depends on the value of the property taken. Many states have abolished this distinction, but in those that have not, grand larceny is a felony and petit larceny a misdemeanor.

WHAT CONSTITUTES PROPERTY?   As society has grown more complex, the definition of the property that is subject to statutes of larceny has been expanded. Stealing computer programs now constitutes larceny, even though they consist of magnetic impulses. Trade secrets can be subject to larceny statutes. Stealing the use of telephone wires by the device known as a "blue box" is subject to larceny statutes. So, too, is the theft of natural gas.

Embezzlement

The fraudulent conversion of property or money owned by one person but entrusted to another is **embezzlement**. Typically, it involves an employee who fraudulently appropriates money. Banks face this problem, and so do a number of businesses in which corporate officers or accountants "jimmy" the books to cover up the fraudulent conversion of money for their own benefit. Embezzlement is not a larceny because the wrongdoer does not physically take the property from the possession of another, and it is not a robbery because there is no taking by use of force or fear.

It does not matter whether the accused takes the money from the victim or from a third person. If, as the comptroller of a large corporation, Saunders pockets a certain number of checks from third parties that were given to her to deposit into the account of another company, Saunders has committed embezzlement.

MISAPPLICATION OF TRUST FUNDS Often the owner of property will remit money to a contractor specifically for the contractor to pay various persons who worked on the owner's building. The contractor who does not use the money for this purpose commits a special form of embezzlement called misapplication of trust funds. The funds were entrusted to the contractor for a specific purpose and that trust has been violated. The fact that the accused intended to return the embezzled property does not constitute a sufficient defense. Practically speaking, though, an embezzler who returns what has been taken will not ordinarily be prosecuted because the owner usually will not testify.

Arson

The willful and malicious burning of a building (and in some states personal property) owned by another is the crime of **arson**. At common law, arson applied only to burning down the dwelling house of another. Such law was designed to protect human life. Today, arson statutes apply to other kinds of buildings. Also, if someone is killed as a result of an arson fire, the act is murder by the application of the murder-felony rule. This rule states that any killing that is committed in the course of a dangerous felony is a first degree murder, whether it is intentional or not.

BURNING TO DEFRAUD INSURERS Every state has a special statute that covers burning a building in order to collect insurance. If Allison owns an apartment building that is falling apart and pays someone else to set fire to it, Allison is guilty of burning to defraud insurers.

Obtaining Goods by False Pretenses

It is a criminal act to obtain goods by means of false pretenses—for example, buying groceries with a check, knowing that there are insufficient funds to cover it. Statutes covering such illegal activities vary widely from state to state.

Receiving Stolen Goods

It is a crime to receive stolen goods when there is knowledge of that fact and there is intent to deprive the owner of those goods. It does not matter that a third party has presented the goods to the ultimate possessor. Moreover, it does not matter whether the ultimate receiver knows the true identity of the owner or the thief.

Use of the Mails to Defraud

It is a federal criminal act to use the mails to defraud the public. Illegal use of the mails must involve (1) mailing or causing someone else to mail a writing for the purpose of executing a scheme to defraud and (2) a contemplated or organized scheme to defraud by false pretenses. If, for example, Johnson advertises the sale of a cure for cancer that he knows to be fraudulent because it has no medical validity, he can be prosecuted for fraudulent use of the mails. Federal law also makes it a crime to use a telegram to defraud.

False Measures, Labels, and Weights

Numerous federal and state regulations have been adopted to prevent and prosecute those who cheat, defraud, or mislead the public by using false labels, false measures, or false weights.

Lotteries

In general, lotteries are illegal even if they appear to be a legitimate form of business or advertising or are called by some other name. There are three necessary elements for a lottery to exist: a prize, a lot by chance, and payment of something of value in order to have the opportunity to win. Often, contest advertisements will say that participants can send in either a box top (or label) or a facsimile. This keeps the contest from being a lottery because contestants can enter without paying anything.

Some Specialized Crimes

The list of specialized crimes is very long indeed. It includes (1) misrepresentation, which is defined as failing to disclose knowledge of the commission of a felony; (2) subornation of perjury, which is defined as inducing or knowingly permitting another to commit perjury; and (3) false pretenses, which is the obtaining of the title to the personal property of another by an intentional false statement of past or existing fact with intent to defraud the other.

Other Crimes Affecting Businesses

The list of crimes affecting businesses could be extended for many pages. It includes swindles and confidence games, counterfeiting, criminal libel, civil disorders, riots, the making of false credit statements, false advertising, and so on. Undoubtedly, the list will continue to grow as society continues to insist on greater protection in the marketplace.

Corporate Crimes

Corporations are "artificial" persons created by law. Clearly, they cannot harbor the criminal intent that is required for conviction of a crime, but their officers can. The modern tendency is to hold corporations criminally responsible for their acts or omissions if the penalty provided for is a fine and intent either is not an element of the crime or can be implied.

Obviously, a crime such as perjury cannot be committed by a corporation but can be committed by a natural person, such as an officer of the corporation. Furthermore, crimes punishable by imprisonment or corporal punishment cannot be committed by corporations. However, when a statute allows a fine in addition to, or in the place of, these penalties, a corporation can be convicted of that crime. If, for example, a statute requires that adequate safety equipment be installed on machines, and a corporation fails to do so—and if the result is the death of a worker—the corporation can be fined for committing criminal manslaughter. In addition, officers of the corporation can be jailed for their conduct.

STATE v. ICE AND FUEL CO.

Supreme Court of North Carolina, 1914. 166 N.C. 366, 81 S.E. 737.

BACKGROUND AND FACTS *A North Carolina statute made it a criminal offense for any person to obtain money by false pretenses in selling a product by giving an inaccurate weight measure. Both the defendant corporation, Salisbury Ice and Fuel Company, and its president, who directed the company's affairs, were convicted under this statute for selling a ton (2,000 pounds) of coal weighing only 1,750 pounds and charging the full price. The statute provided for punishment by both fine and imprisonment. The company appealed on the ground that a corporation has no capacity to commit a crime because a crime requires specific intent. The president appealed on the ground that he was not acting on his own behalf but rather as an agent for the company.*

DECISION AND RATIONALE *Both convictions were upheld. In this case, the president was the motivating force behind the company's wrongful acts. He directed the company's affairs, including the short-weight transaction for which the state brought charges. Hence, he was culpable of committing the crime for which he was convicted. In addition, the word* person *used in the statute includes artificial as well as natural persons, so the company was guilty, also. "In this present case the business of selling coal and ice is carried on by a corporation, and it violated the statute by the false pretense of selling a ton of coal when it delivered in fact only 1,750 pounds, intending to cheat, as fully as an individual could have done. It is true that, when the statute imposes a penalty of a fine or imprisonment, only the fine can be placed upon a corporation. But this is no reason why that should not be imposed. The corporation should not be wholly exempted from punishment, because it cannot be imprisoned. The remedy is that the officer or agent may be indicted jointly with the corporation as a coprincipal or accessory ***."*

QUESTIONS AND CASE PROBLEMS

1. Civil trials and criminal trials are conducted under essentially the same format. There are, however, several important differences. In criminal trials, the defendant must be proven guilty beyond all reasonable doubt, whereas in civil trials, the defendant need only be proven guilty by a preponderance of the evidence. Can you see any reason for this difference?

2. In a criminal trial, but not in a civil trial, the defendant has the right to remain silent. In both civil and criminal cases, the defendant has a right to a trial by jury; and in civil cases, the plaintiff has the same right. Can you see any reason for this?

3. Davis, who had been married for a number of years, suspected that his wife and a neighbor by the name of Noe were having an affair. In fact, the two had never been intimate, but Davis, acting under an insane delusion, murdered Noe. Even though Davis was under a delusion, the jury found that he was able to distinguish between right and wrong at the time he committed the murder. Can the defense of insanity be invoked when it has been sufficiently shown that Davis was acting under an insane delusion at the time he murdered Noe? [Davis v. State, 161 Tenn. 23, 28 S.W.2d 993 (1930)]

4. Faulkner was a seaman on the ship Zemindar. One night while on duty, Faulkner went in search of the rum that he knew the ship was carrying. He found it and opened one of the kegs, but because he was holding a match at the time, he inadvertently ignited the rum and set fire to the ship. Faulkner was criminally prosecuted for setting fire to the ship. At the trial, it was determined that even though he had not intended to set fire to the rum, he had been engaged in the unlawful act of stealing it. Does Faulkner's theft of the rum make him criminally liable for setting fire to the ship? [Regina v. Faulkner, 13 Cox C.C. 530 (Ireland 1877)]

5. In 1965, Rybicki failed to pay the complete amount of income tax he owed the federal government. Attempts by the IRS to collect the tax proved fruitless. Therefore, the IRS, through lawful means, obtained a tax lien on Rybicki's personal property, which included his truck. In October 1967, while sitting in his living room, Rybicki heard somebody slam the doors of his truck in the driveway. Rybicki went to his front door wielding a shotgun and told the two men who were attempting to take his truck that he would shoot them if they did not get off his property. Rybicki claimed that he did not know that the two men were IRS agents. Subsequently, the federal government indicted Rybicki for obstructing justice. Can Rybicki be held criminally liable if he did not know that the men were IRS agents performing their duty? [United States v. Rybicki, 403 F.2d 599 (6th Cir. 1968)]

6. Pennsylvania makes it unlawful for any person or his or her agent to sell liquor to minors. This statute does not require that the sales be made knowingly, willfully, or intentionally. Koczwara, who owned a bar in Pennsylvania, was accused of having sold liquor to minors. Although Koczwara owned the bar,

he had no knowledge of such sales; nor had he ever given his permission that liquor be sold to minors. Should Koczwara be held absolutely liable for the acts of the bartenders he employed? [Commonwealth v. Koczwara 397 Pa. 575, 155 A.2d 825 (1959)]

7. Kanan was accused of writing several checks on an account that had been closed for over a month. It was unclear whether Kanan knew that his bank account had been closed, since his bank statements had never been delivered to him. In a criminal prosecution for passing bad checks, the judge instructed the jury that when a person writes checks, the law presumes that he knows whether his checking account has sufficient funds to cover the checks. Is this a proper instruction? [People v. Kanan, 186 Colo. 255, 526 P.2d 1339 (1974)]

8. For several years Horrocks had loaned money to May. With each loan, however, Horrocks had required May to seek his father's signature as a cosigner on the note. In October, May sought a further loan of $4,000 from Horrocks. As usual, Horrocks requested that May have his father cosign the note. That evening May cosigned his father's name without ever showing his father the note. The next day Horrocks loaned May the $4,000. Several years later, the state of Idaho indicted May for forging the note with the intent to defraud. The state contended that intent to defraud need not be specifically proven in this case but can be inferred from the fact that May had the forged note in his possession and passed it to Horrocks. Is this sufficient to prove intent to defraud? [State v. May, 93 Idaho 343, 461 P.2d 126 (1969)]

9. Monroe sold a certain quantity of croton oil to Horn. Horn in turn placed some of the oil in a piece of candy and gave it to Barrett, who ate the candy and suffered a physical injury. The state of North Carolina charged Monroe with criminal assault and battery. At trial Monroe admitted that he sold the oil to Horn and that he knew Horn's reputation for playing practical jokes. Was there adequate intent to commit an assault and battery on Monroe's part for him to be found guilty? [State v. Monroe, 121 N.C. 677, 28 S.E. 547 (1897)]

10. The state of Illinois prohibits the attempt to practice barbering without a license. Paluch, while in a barbershop one morning, invited Pinkston into the shop. Paluch then put on a barber smock, walked over to the barber chair, and asked Pinkston if he wanted to sit down. Paluch was unaware that Pinkston was a member of the local barber's union. When Pinkston demanded to see Paluch's license, Paluch at first refused but then admitted that he did not have one. Paluch was later tried for practicing barbering without a license. At the trial, in addition to the above facts, the state also proved that Paluch had possession of certain barber tools and a key to the barbershop into which he had invited Pinkston. Paluch denied that he had ever engaged in barbering and contended that he had never serviced Pinkston. Paluch further claimed that he had only prepared to serve Pinkston but had never completed any act that could be considered illegal. Is Paluch's contention valid? [People v. Paluch, Appellate Court of Illinois, 78 Ill.App.2d 356, 222 N.E.2d 508 (1966)]

11. Pivowar agreed to loan Mills approximately $10,000, and Mills agreed to repay the loan and further agreed that the loan would be secured by two houses that he owned. Mills showed Pivowar the two houses but falsely represented that Pivowar was to get a first mortgage on the houses. Pivowar later learned that the mortgages he held were not on the two houses but on two vacant lots and, further, that the mortgages were second mortgages and not first mortgages, as Mills had promised. Can Mills be prosecuted criminally for false pretenses if he contends that he intended to pay back the loan and that Pivowar never demanded payment on the note? [State v. Mills, 96 Ariz. 377, 396 P.2d 5 (1964)]

UNIT II

Contracts

5

Contracts
Nature, Form, and Terminology

SOME PERSPECTIVES

Society could make all promises binding, but it does not. An example of a promise which is not legally binding is a social engagement. Suppose Laura invites Luke to dinner and a movie, but later breaks the date. Can Luke sue Laura for breach of contract? No. Society does not place enough importance on such promises to provide a legal remedy for their enforcement.

The law of contracts establishes when contracts are binding and when they are not as well as the parties' remedies in case of breach. Why do we need contracts? Countless commodities are regularly bought and sold by the use of contracts. People who rent apartments and open bank accounts all enter into contracts, even though the contracts are not all written or even explicit. In short, we could not order our daily activities without them.[1] They help us predict the future because they look to the future.

The types of promises that society makes binding (e.g., sales of goods, land, or services) are legally enforceable only if certain elements are present. These elements are the subject of the Chapters which follow.

---

1. The Soviet Union attempted to eliminate the need for contracts by dispensing with the private ordering of activities. The state required everyone to engage in certain specified activities—work, education, recreation—in the hope of redistributing wealth according to

The Function of Contracts

Contract law assures the parties to private agreements that the promises they make will be enforced. When a promise is kept, however, it is not necessarily because the **promisor** (the person making the promise) is conscious of the rules of contract law. People routinely keep social and business engagements because of a sense of duty and, perhaps more importantly, because it is to the mutual self-interest of the parties to go through with the deal and keep the goodwill of customers or suppliers. Nevertheless, the rules of contract law are often followed in an apparent attempt to avoid potential problems if and when a party does not live up to the promises.

Since contract law provides procedures for the enforcement of private agreements, it also provides an essential condition for the existence of a market economy. Without a framework for reasonably assured expectations within which to plan and venture, businesspersons would be able to rely only on the good faith of others. Duty and good faith are usually sufficient, but when price changes or adverse economic factors make it costly to comply with a promise, these elements are not enough. Contract law is necessary in order to assure compliance with a promise or to entitle the innocent party to some form of relief.

Contract law provides a foundation upon which more specialized areas of law are built. The sale of goods (Chapters 17 to 22); the transfer and negotiation of checks, notes, and drafts (Chapters 23 to 28); the giving of security in goods or land (Chapters 29 to 30); the rights of debtors and creditors (Chapter 31); the rights of agents, employees, and their employers (Chapters 33 to 35); the creation, operation, and

termination of partnerships and corporations (Chapters 36 to 46); the regulation of trade and monopolies (Chapters 47 to 51); and the transfer of property (Chapters 52 and 55) all require a basic understanding of contract law.

Contract law underlies virtually all business relationships. Knowledge of it is essential to avoid costly mistakes. Additionally, studying contract law introduces the student to lawyers and how they think. Since businesspersons must often deal with lawyers, this understanding is of great practical value.

Freedom of Contract and Freedom from Contract

Contract law recognizes almost everyone's ability to enter freely into contractual arrangements. This recognition is called *freedom of contract,* and this freedom is protected by the U.S. Constitution in Article I, Section 10. As the character of institutions and society changes, however, the functions of contract law and its enforcement must also change. This change can be perceived today in the fact that not all agreements are valid and enforceable. For example, illegal bargains, agreements in restraint of trade, and "adhesion contracts" made by parties who have inordinate amounts of bargaining power are not enforced. In addition, certain contracts with consumers, as well as certain clauses within those contracts, are not enforceable. (See Chapter 10 for details.) Public policy, fairness, and justice do not allow these contracts to be enforced. The law of contracts is moving to place new controls on the manner of contracting and on the allowable terms of agreements. These controls are referred to as *freedom from contract,* and they serve to protect certain members of society from the contracts they make.

The Elements of a Contract

In order to comprehend the many topics that follow in this unit on contracts, an understanding of the basic requirements of a contract and the process by which it is created is needed. The

---

administrative standards and norms. The experiment failed, and Lenin explicitly recognized this when he wrote in 1921, "The private market proved to be stronger than we [thought]. * * * We ended up with ordinary * * * trade." Ultimately, contracts were reintroduced, and contract law was codified along traditional lines. See Loeber, *"Plan and Contract Performance in Soviet Law",* reprinted in LaFave, *Law in the Soviet Society,* Wayne R. LaFave, ed. Urbana, University of Illinois Press (1965).

following list is a brief description of the elements of a contract. The full explanations of these elements will come in later chapters.

1. **Agreement:** An agreement includes an offer and an acceptance. A party must offer to enter into a legal agreement, and another party must assent to the terms of the offer.
2. **Consideration:** Any promises made by the parties must be supported by legally sufficient consideration—something of legal value.
3. **Contractual capacity:** Both parties entering into the contract must have the contractual capacity to do so; they must be recognized by contract law to possess characteristics qualifying them as competent parties.
4. **Legality:** The contract must be made to accomplish some goal that is legal.
5. **Reality of assent:** Apparent consent of both of the parties must be genuine.
6. **Form:** The contract must be in whatever form the law requires.

NATURE AND TYPES OF CONTRACTS

In order for the detailed elements of a contract to be understood, certain terms and certain types of contracts must be defined. When reading the following chapters, refer to the definitions given in this chapter. This effort will reinforce the understanding of the language of contract law.

Definition of a Contract

A **contract** is simply any agreement that can be enforced in a court of law or equity. It is formed by two or more parties who agree to perform or refrain from performing some act.[2] Essentially, a contract is a promise that must be fulfilled. A promise is an undertaking either that something shall happen or that something shall not happen in the future. (Courts sometimes enforce

2. As defined by the American Law Institute, a contract is "a promise or a set of promises for the breach of which the law gives a remedy, or the performance of which the law in some way recognizes as a duty." Restatement, Second, Contracts (tentative draft), Section 1.

promises that are *not* contracts.) If the promise is not fulfilled, the party who made it is subject to the sanctions of a court of law or equity. The party may be required to pay money damages for failing to perform or may be required to perform the promised act.

TYPES OF CONTRACTS EXPLAINED

This section will explain the various types of contracts by comparing them to each other. They are: (1) express versus implied; (2) bilateral versus unilateral; (3) executed versus executory; (4) valid versus void, voidable, and unenforceable; and (5) formal versus informal contracts.

Express versus Implied Contracts

An **express contract** is one in which the terms of the agreement are fully and explicitly stated in words, oral or written. A signed lease for an apartment or house is an express written contract.[3] If a classmate calls you on the phone and agrees to buy your textbooks from last semester for $50, an express oral contract has been made.

A contract that is implied from the conduct of the parties is called an **implied-in-fact contract,** or an implied contract. Implied-in-fact contracts differ from express contracts in that the conduct of the parties, rather than their words, creates and defines the terms of the contract. For example, suppose you need a tax consultant or an accountant to fill out your tax return this year. You look through the phone book and find both an accountant and a tax consultant at an office in your neighborhood, so you drop by to see them. You go into the office and explain your problem; and they tell you what their fees are. The next day you return, leaving the secretary all of the necessary information such as cancelled checks, W-2 copies, and so on. You say nothing expressly to the secretary; rather, you walk out the door. Nonetheless, you have entered into an implied-in-fact contract to pay the tax consultant and accountant their usual and reasonable fees for

3. Leases historically were not contracts, although they are in most places today.

their services. The contract is implied from your conduct and from the tax preparers' conduct. They expect to be paid for helping you file your tax return, and by bringing in all of the necessary records that will allow them to do so, you *appear* to be intending to pay them for their work.

OBJECTIVE THEORY OF CONTRACTS   In the above example, *apparent intentions* rather than personal or subjective intentions are the controlling factor. You may have been thinking to yourself, "I really don't want tax help; I'm just leaving off all my tax records at their office because I can't think of a better place to keep them." However, a theory that runs through all aspects of the law of contracts—the **objective theory of contracts**—is illustrated by the tax preparation example. The theory says that a party's intention to enter into a contract is judged by outward, objective facts rather than by the party's own secret, subjective intentions. Objective facts include: (1) what the party said when entering into the contract, (2) how the party acted or appeared, and (3) the circumstances surrounding the transaction.

Courts need verifiable evidence in order to determine whether a contract has been made, so they usually rely only on objective facts when passing judgment on a contract dispute. Using this approach, they often determine that the parties have entered into contracts that are *implied-in-fact*. In other words, courts examine all the objective facts, conduct, and circumstances surrounding a particular transaction in order to determine if the parties have made a contract.

BACKGROUND AND FACTS   *Shepard, a plumber, went to the Glick home to discuss the installation of a sewer connection. Both Mr. and Mrs. Glick were present. Shepard later brought in men and equipment and installed the sewer. Thereafter, Mr. Glick died, and Mrs. Glick refused to pay, claiming that the contract was with her husband, not with her.*

DECISION AND RATIONALE   *The court found that an implied contract existed between Mrs. Glick and Shepard even though nothing was evidenced in writing. The court relied on the fact that Mrs. Glick had been present at the time the job was discussed and must have been aware of the work being performed by Shepard's work crew. Quoting from a legal treatise on contract law, the court said: " 'Implied contract' is one dictated by reason and justice, and which the law presumes from the relation of the parties. *** An 'implied contract' is inferred from the conduct, situation, or mutual relations of the parties, and enforced by the law on the ground of justice."*

SHEPARD v. GLICK
Court of Appeals of Missouri, 1966.
404 S.W.2d 441.

Bilateral versus Unilateral Contracts

Every contract involves at least two parties. When one party promises to perform some act if the other party *actually performs* some act, a **unilateral contract** is formed. With a unilateral contract, only the party who makes the promise is bound to perform. Therefore, only that person can break the promise (that is, breach the contract). A **bilateral,** or **reciprocal, contract** binds both parties. Both parties expressly enter into mutual engagements. An unconditional promise is exchanged for an unconditional promise.

An important problem arises in unilateral contracts when the promisor attempts to revoke the promise after the promisee has begun performance. Since acceptance can occur only upon full performance and since offers are normally revocable until accepted, the question arises whether the promisor can revoke after the promisee has started performance. The modern view is that the offer becomes irrevocable once performance begins.

The classic illustration of a unilateral contract is the situation where A says to B, "If you walk across the Brooklyn Bridge, I'll give you $10." A *promises* to pay if B walks the entire span of the bridge. Only then does B accept A's offer to pay $10. If B does not walk, there are no legal consequences.

The distinction between bilateral and unilateral contracts shows which party to a contract is bound by a promise and which party is not bound (because no promise was made by that party). Beyond this, the distinction has no significant value. The Uniform Commercial Code and the Restatement, Second, Contracts avoid using the terms, since they doubt the utility of the distinction.[4]

Formal versus Informal Contracts

Formal contracts are contracts that require a special form or method of creation (formation) to be enforceable. They include: (1) contracts under seal, (2) recognizances, and (3) negotiable instruments and letters of credit. **Contracts under seal** are formalized writings with a special seal attached.[5] The significance of the seal has been almost entirely eroded, although about ten states require no consideration when a contract is under seal. (See Chapter 7 for details.) A **recognizance** is an acknowledgment in court by a person who agrees to pay a certain sum if a certain event occurs. The most common form of recognizance is the surety bond or criminal recognizance bonds. Negotiable in-

struments and letters of credit are special methods of payment that are designed for use in many commercial settings. **Negotiable instruments** include checks, notes, drafts, and certificates of deposit. **Letters of credit** are agreements to pay contingent on the purchaser's receipt of invoices and bills of lading. Negotiable instruments and letters of credit are discussed at length in subsequent chapters.

Informal contracts include all other contracts. (Such contracts are also called *simple contracts*.) No special form is generally required (unless the contract *must* be in writing), as the contracts are usually based on their substance rather than their form. Informal contracts can be written or oral, bilateral or unilateral, executory or executed.

Quasi-Contracts, or Contracts Implied-in-Law

Quasi-contracts, or **contracts implied-in-law,** should be distinguished from contracts *implied-in-fact*. Quasi-contracts are not really contracts at all. They arise in order to achieve justice rather than from a mutual agreement between the parties. A quasi-contract is imposed on the parties in order to avoid *unjust enrichment*. The doctrine of unjust enrichment holds that people should not be allowed to profit or enrich themselves inequitably at the expense of others. The doctrine is equitable rather than contractual in nature.

In contrast to quasi-contracts, a contract implied-in-fact is a true contract. The parties express their agreement to the terms of the contract by conduct. When a quasi-contract is imposed on the parties, it is imposed despite their actual or apparent intentions. Equity and fairness require one party to pay for benefit received from another party, even if the parties had no true or explicit contract. Under a quasi-contract, the party receiving the benefit is required to pay for the reasonable value of that benefit, usually equal to the fair market value of the benefit.

Suppose A enters into an oral agreement with B and agrees to work with B for two years

4. Section 12 of the Restatement, Second Contracts (tentative draft), was eliminated because of this doubt. See Reporter's Note, Restatement, Second (tentative draft), Contracts, Section 12.

5. A seal is usually an impression made on a thin wafer of wax firmly affixed to the writing. In some instances, the word *seal* or the letters *L.S.* appear at the end of the document. *L.S.* stands for *locus sigilli* and means "the place for the seal."

in developing a noise reduction turbine for fixed-wing commercial jets. B agrees to pay A a "fair share of the profit" derived from the sale of the device. After working six months on the project and making considerable headway, B tells A she will not pay her anything because the terms of the contract are too indefinite and the contract must be in writing. Assuming B is correct, A cannot sue on the contract itself, since there is no contract. Instead A sues on the theory of quasi-contract for the reasonable value of her services. Obviously, it would be unfair to allow B to pay nothing for A's work, so the court will imply a quasi-contract. Thus, B will be required to pay A a fair wage for the six months of work.

A Limitation on the Quasi-Contract

The principle underlying quasi-contractual obligations is based on the notion of "unjust enrichment." Nonetheless, there are situations in which the party obtaining the "unjust enrichment" is not liable. Basically, the quasi-contractual principle cannot be invoked by the party who has conferred a benefit on someone else unnecessarily or as a result of misconduct or negligence. Consider the following example. You take your car to the local car wash and ask to have it run through the washer and to have the gas tank filled. While it is being washed, you go to a nearby shopping center for two hours. In the meantime, one of the workers at the car wash has mistakenly believed that your car is the one that he is supposed to hand wax. When you come back, you are presented with a bill for a full tank of gas, a wash job, and a hand wax. Clearly, a benefit has been conferred on you. But this benefit has been conferred because of a mistake by the car wash employee. You have no liability. You have not received an *unjust* benefit under these circumstances. People cannot normally be forced to pay for benefits "thrust" upon them.

Also, the doctrine of quasi-contract cannot be used when there is a contract that covers the area in controversy. For example, X delivers a stove to a building project and does not get paid. Contractor Y goes bankrupt. X cannot collect from Z—the owner of the building—in quasi-contract because X has a contract with Y already.

Executed versus Executory Contracts

Contracts are also classified according to their stage of performance. A contract that has been fully performed on both sides is called an **executed contract.** (Strictly speaking, it is not a contract.) A contract that has not been *fully* performed on either side is called an **executory contract.** If one party has fully performed but the other has not, the contract is said to be executed on one side and executory on the other (and is still called an executory contract). For example, assume you agree to buy ten tons of coal from the Wheeling Coal Company. Further assume that Wheeling has delivered the coal to your steel mill, where it is now being burned. At this point, the contract is executed on the part of Wheeling and executory on your part. After you pay Wheeling for the coal, the contract will be executed on both sides.

Valid versus Void, Voidable, and Unenforceable Contracts

A valid contract is one that has all the necessary elements; it entitles the parties to enforcement of the contract in court. The elements necessary for a valid contract include an offer and an acceptance and legally sufficient consideration. These elements are discussed in detail in the following chapters.

A **void contract** is no contract at all. The terms *void* and *contract* are contradictory, since a void contract is one that never existed. It produces no legal obligations by any of the parties. A contract can be void because one of the parties was adjudged legally insane or because the purpose of the contract was illegal, for example.

A **voidable contract** is one in which one of the parties has the option of avoiding his or her legal obligations. The party having this option can elect either to avoid any duty to perform or to *ratify* the contract. If the contract is avoided, both parties are released from it. If it is ratified, both parties must fully perform their respective legal obligations.

As a general rule, and subject to many qualifications, contracts made by minors are voidable at the option of the minor. (See Chapter 8 for details.) Contracts entered into under fraudulent conditions are voidable at the option of the defrauded party. (See Chapter 10 for details.) In addition, some contracts entered into because of mistakes and all contracts entered into under legally defined duress are voidable.

An **unenforceable contract** is one that

cannot be enforced. It remains in existence, but certain legal defenses make enforcement impossible. Contracts barred by a statute of limitations, for example, are unenforceable contracts.[6] Likewise, oral contracts under the Statute of Frauds are unenforceable.[7] In brief, an unenforceable contract is one that satisfies all the requirements of a contract except at least one, and this makes it unenforceable.

---

6.   A statute of limitations prevents a party from suing on a contract after a certain period of time has elapsed.
7.   The Statute of Frauds requires certain contracts to be in writing in order to be enforceable.

QUESTIONS AND CASE PROBLEMS

1.   Suppose Felix, a local businessman, is a good friend of Miller, the owner of a local candy store. Every day at his lunch hour Felix goes into Miller's candy store and usually spends about five minutes looking at the candy. After examining Miller's candy and talking with Miller, Felix usually buys one or two candy bars. One afternoon, Felix goes into Miller's candy shop, looks at the candy, picks up a $1 candy bar, and, seeing that Miller is very busy at the time, waves the candy bar at Miller without saying a word and walks out. Is there a contract? If so, classify it within the categories presented in this chapter.

2.   Sosa Crisan, an eighty-seven-year-old widow of Roumanian origin, collapsed while shopping at a local grocery store. The Detroit police took her to the Detroit city hospital. She was admitted, and she remained there fourteen days. Then she was transferred to another hospital, where she died some eleven months later. Crisan had never regained consciousness after her collapse at the local grocery store. After she died, the city of Detroit sued her estate to recover the expenses of both the ambulance that took her to the hospital and the expenses of her hospital stay. Is there a contract between Sosa Crisan and the hospital? If so, how much can the Detroit hospital recover? [In Re Crisan Estate, 362 Mich. 569, 107 N.W.2d 907 (1961)]

3.   Air Advertising employed Red, a World War II

flying ace, to fly its advertisements above Long Island Sound beaches. Burger Baby restaurants engaged Air Advertising to fly an advertisement above the Connecticut beaches that offered $1,000 to any person who could swim from the Connecticut beaches to Long Island across Long Island Sound in less than a day. On Saturday, October 10, at 10:00 a.m., Red flew a sign above the Connecticut beaches that read: "Swim across the Sound and Burger Baby pays $1,000." Upon seeing the sign, Davison dove in. About four hours later, when he was about halfway across the Sound, Red flew another sign over the Sound that read: "Burger Baby revokes." Is there a contract between Davison and Burger Baby? Can Davison recover anything?

4.   Womack was a well-known gambler in Saline County. Judge Maner, a friend of Womack, not only knew of Womack's gambling enterprises, but approved of them. From time to time over a period of several years, Womack paid money to the judge to ensure that he would not be prosecuted. As a result of this long-standing agreement, Womack paid the judge a total of $1,675. Womack then claimed that the consideration for his paying the judge was void and unlawful at the time the contract was entered into as well as at the present time. Therefore, Womack sued Judge Maner to rescind the contract and to get back the $1,675 he had paid. Should Womack recover? [Womack v. Maner, 277 Ark. 786, 301 S.W.2d 438 (1957)]

5.   On April 1, 1969, McLouth Steel Corporation entered into a contract with Jewell Coal Company under which Jewell agreed to supply all McLouth's coal requirements for the next thirty years. The

contract mentioned no specific quantities. The price was set at $100 a ton for the first year and was subject to an "escalation clause" whereby each subsequent year the original price would be increased by the cost increases encountered by Jewell. Five years later Jewell found that even with the cost increases that it had added onto the price it charged McLouth, the price it could receive in the open market was far greater. Jewell stopped shipping coal, claiming that the contract was invalid because the price and quantity under the contract were too indefinite to be enforced. Jewell admitted in court, however, that it had performed under this agreement for the past five years. Is the contract executory or nonexecutory? Is the contract enforceable or unenforceable? [McLouth Steel Corp. v. Jewell Coal and Coke Co., United States Court of Appeals, Sixth Circuit (1978), 570 F.2d 594]

6

Contracts
Agreement

A contract is a legally enforceable *agreement* creating rights between two or more individuals. The agreement need not be in writing (unless required by statute), but each of the parties must assent to it.[1] The judicial system enforces contracts that are assented (agreed) to by the parties,[2] supported by legally sufficient consideration,[3] not illegal,[4] and entered into freely by parties with contractual capacity.[5]

MUTUAL ASSENT

Ordinarily, assent is established by an **offer** and an **acceptance.** In other words, one party offers a certain bargain to another party, who then accepts that bargain. The parties are required to manifest to each other their **mutual assent** to the same bargain.[6] Because words often fail to

---

1. Under early English and American law, many contracts were not enforced unless they complied with rigid legal standards requiring a writing and in many cases a seal or impression made on wax, which was firmly affixed to the writing. Today, some contracts must still be in writing (see Chapter 11). The seal has been almost entirely done away with. [UCC, Sec. 2-203]
2. See discussion *infra.*
3. See Chapter 7.
4. See Chapter 9.
5. See Chapter 8.
6. Restatement, Second, Contracts (tentative draft,) Section 22.

convey the precise meaning intended, the law of contracts generally adheres to the objective theory of contracts, as discussed in Chapter 5. Under this theory, a party's words and conduct are held to mean what a reasonable person would think they mean. The court will give words their usual meaning even if "it were proved by twenty bishops that [the] party * * * intended something else."[7]

REQUIREMENTS OF THE OFFER

Most contracts are formed by one party, the **offeror,** who makes an offer or proposal to another party, the **offeree.** An **offer** is a promise or commitment to do or refrain from doing some specified thing in the future. Three elements are necessary in order for an offer to be effective: (1) there must be an *intention* (or, under the objective theory of contracts, an appearance of an intention) to become bound by the offer; (2) the terms of the offer must be reasonably *certain* or definite, so that the parties and the court can ascertain the terms of the contract; and (3) the offer must be *communicated* to the offeree. Once an effective offer has been made, the offeree has the power to accept the offer. If the offeree does so, the offer is transformed into a binding legal agreement.

Intention

The first element of an effective offer, intention, can best be explained by distinguishing between offers and various kinds of non-offers. None of the following statements or actions—expressions of opinion; preliminary negotiations; statements of intention; or advertisements, catalogues, and circulars—are effective offers because they all fail to meet the legal requirement of intention.

EXPRESSIONS OF OPINION An expression of opinion is not an offer. It does not evidence an

intention to enter into a binding agreement. Hawkins took his son to McGee, a doctor, and asked McGee to operate on the son's hand. McGee said the boy would be in the hospital three or four days and that the hand would probably heal within a few days afterward. The son's hand did not heal for a month, but the father did not win a suit for breach of contract. The court held that McGee did not make an offer to heal the son's hand in three or four days. He merely expressed an opinion as to when the hand would heal.[8]

PRELIMINARY NEGOTIATIONS A request or invitation to negotiate is not an offer. It only expresses a willingness to discuss entering into a contract. Included are statements such as "Will you sell Blythe Estate?" or "I wouldn't sell my car for less than $1,000." A reasonable person would not conclude that these statements evidence an intention to enter into a binding obligation. Likewise, when construction work is done for the government and private firms, contractors are invited to submit bids. The *invitation* to submit bids is not an offer, and a contractor does not bind the government or private firm by submitting a bid. (The bids that the contractors submit *are* offers, however, and the government or private firm can bind the contractor by accepting the bid.)

STATEMENTS OF INTENTION If Henry says "I *plan* to sell my stock in Ryder Systems for $150 per share," a contract will not be created if Fred "accepts" and tenders the $150 per share for the stock. Henry has merely expressed his intention to enter into a future contract for the sale of the stock. No contract is formed because a reasonable person would conclude that Henry was only thinking about selling his stock, not promising to sell, even if Fred accepts and pays the $150 per share. Henry is stating a future contractual intent, not a present one. The next case further illustrates this point.

7. Learned Hand in Hotchkiss v. National City Bank of N.Y., 200 F. 287 (2nd Cir. 1911), aff'd 231 U.S. 50, 34 S.Ct. 20, 58 L.Ed. 115 (1913).

8. Hawkins v. McGee, 84 N.H. 114, 146 A. 641 (1929).

MELLEN v. JOHNSON

Supreme Judicial Court of
Massachusetts, Essex, 1948.
322 Mass. 236, 76 N.E. 2d 658.

BACKGROUND AND FACTS   *Johnson, who owned a small cottage, sent a letter to Mellen saying that he was putting the cottage on the market. Earlier, Mellen had expressed an interest in purchasing it. The letter indicated that several other people, who had also expressed an interest in purchasing the property, were being informed of its availability at the same time. Mellen, interpreting the letter as an offer, promptly accepted. Johnson sold the property to a higher bidder, and Mellen sued.*

DECISION AND RATIONALE   *The court found that the letter was not an offer because it merely expressed Johnson's desire to sell the property and because it announced that the same letter was being sent to several persons at the same time. The appellate court justice stated: "The recipient could not reasonably understand this to be more than an attempt at negotiation. It was a mere request or suggestion that an offer be made to the defendant."*

Essential Contract Terms

The second element of an effective offer is the definiteness of its terms. Certain terms are *essential* to the contract and must be either expressed or capable of reasonable implication from the agreement. These terms are: (1) identification of the parties; (2) subject matter—goods, services, money loaned, and so on; (3) the time for performance; and (4) the price. If these terms are expressly stated, the contract is definite and enforceable. If absolutely no mention is made of the terms, some courts today will often *imply* reasonable terms, as long as the terms are consistent with the parties' intentions. If the contract mentions the terms, but does so in a vague or ambiguous manner, the terms may not be implied, and the contract will fail for indefiniteness.

For example, assume Gaines agrees to sell tobacco leaves to R. J. Reynolds Company. The leaves are to be delivered at the beginning of the following month. If a price is mentioned, then the contract is reasonably definite and may be enforced in a court of law. If no price is mentioned in the contract, a court may imply a reasonable price, which ordinarily will be equal to the fair market value of the tobacco leaves. If the parties say the price will be "cost plus a fair profit," no price term may be implied, and the contract will fail for indefiniteness because no definite proportion of the cost to be added as profit is mentioned. "Cost plus 10 percent" would, however, be sufficiently definite.[9]

Uncertainty or indefiniteness of *incidental,* or *collateral, terms* will not cause the contract to be unenforceable. Incidental terms include all other terms besides: (1) the parties, (2) the subject matter of the contract, (3) the time for performance, and (4) the price. The reason for enforcing contracts with uncertain incidental terms is that a party should not be deprived of a bargain merely because some minor aspect is overlooked. This is especially important in extremely complex and detailed contracts. If the parties were required to spell out every last detail explicitly, the negotiations process would be slowed, and contracts would encumber business instead of aiding it.

ADVERTISEMENTS, CATALOGUES, AND CIRCULARS   In general, advertisements, mail order catalogues, price lists, and circular letters are not offers to contract but invitations to negotiate. Suppose Loeser & Co. advertises a used paving machine. The ad is mailed to

_____

9. Gaines & Sea, v. R. J. Reynolds Tobacco Co., 163 Ky. 716. 174 S.W. 482 (1915).

hundreds of firms and reads, "Used Case Construction Co. paving machine. Builds curbs and finishes cement work all in one process. Price $11,250 firm." If Star Paving calls Loeser and says, "We accept your offer," no contract is formed. No reasonable person would conclude that Loeser was promising to sell the paving machine; the conclusion would have to be that Loeser was attempting to solicit offers to buy it.

The same result occurs when a new car dealership advertises "New Lincoln Continentals; loaded with options; now only $13,899." The ad is intended to draw customers who will make offers. If Bill Weinberg goes to the dealership with a check for $13,899, the dealership is not legally bound to sell the Lincoln. (However, federal and state statutes prohibit "false and misleading advertising" that is intended only to draw customers to the retail outlet.)

Advertisements are not offers because the seller never has an unlimited supply of the goods. If advertisements were offers, then everyone who "accepted" after the retailer's supply was exhausted could sue for breach of

contract. Suppose you had put a "For Sale" sign on your home and seven people had called and "accepted" your "offer" before you could take it down. If the sign were an offer, you would be bound on seven contracts to sell your home. Since initial advertisements are treated as invitations to make offers, you would have had seven offers to choose from, and you could have accepted the best one without incurring any liability for the six you rejected. Moreover, your sign lacked an element of a successful offer— the identity of the offeree. (However, rewards can be offers even though there is no predetermined and specified offeree.)

Sometimes offers are worded such that they can be accepted only by performance, as opposed to verbal or written acceptance. A unilateral contract requires a person to accept by performing the requested acts. In the following case, the court had to decide whether a newspaper advertisement announcing a "special sale" in a department store should be construed as an offer, the acceptance of which would complete a contract.

BACKGROUND AND FACTS *Lefkowitz read a newspaper advertisement offering fur coats for sale on a first come, first served basis. He went to the store and was the first person to demand the merchandise at the sale price. The department store refused to sell him the coats, saying that the offer was intended for women only. The advertisement in question appeared as follows:*

LEFKOWITZ v. GREAT MINNEAPOLIS SURPLUS STORE, INC.
Supreme Court of Minnesota, 1957.
251 Minn. 188, 86 N.W. 2d 689.

"Saturday 9 A.M. Sharp
3 Brand New
Fur
Coats
Worth to $100.00
First Come
First Served
$1
Each"

DECISION AND RATIONALE *The department store's advertisement was a binding offer and not merely an invitation to make an offer because it was clear and definite and included all the terms of the contract. Since Lefkowitz was the first one present when the store opened and was* *ready, willing, and able to pay, this constituted a valid acceptance. The appellate court justice stated, "[W]hile an advertiser has the right at any time before acceptance to modify his offer, he does not have the right, after acceptance, to impose new or arbitrary conditions not contained in the published offer."*

OTHER NON-OFFER SITUATIONS In other cases, what appears to be an offer is not sufficient to serve as the basis for formation of a contract.

Auctions In an auction, a seller "offers" goods for sale through an auctioneer. This is not, however, an offer for purposes of contract. The seller is really only expressing a willingness to sell. He or she may withdraw the goods at any time before the auctioneer closes the sale and may even refuse the highest bid. There is no obligation to sell. The bidder is actually the offeror. The auctioneer accepts a bid and completes a contract by knocking the hammer. A bidder can retract an offer while the auctioneer sings "going once, going twice, third and last call." If the bid is not withdrawn and the hammer falls, the contract is formed.[10]

Social Affairs Invitations to attend social affairs are not offers. If a friend asks you to dinner, and you arrive at the specified time but no one is home, you cannot bring suit. The invitation created a social obligation, not a legal one.

Definiteness An offer must have reasonably definite terms so that a court can determine if a breach has occurred and can give an appropriate remedy.[11] An offer may invite an acceptance that supplies the necessary terms to make that contract reasonably definite. For example, assume D'Onfro contacts your corporation and offers to sell "from one to ten sheet metal presses for $1,750 each, state number desired in acceptance." Your corporation agrees to buy two presses. If the quantity had not been specified in the acceptance, the contract would be unenforceable because the terms of the contract would have been indefinite. But since the acceptance stated that your corporation wanted two presses, the contract is definite and capable of enforcement.

Will an employment contract that provides for a salary plus "a share of the profits" be too vague and indefinite for a court to enforce? The following case tells the plight of a plaintiff, Victor Petersen, who worked first as construction supervisor and then as manager for the Pilgrim Village Company, the defendant.

10. See UCC Sec. 2-328. At auctions announced as "without reserve," goods must be sold to the highest bidder.

11. Restatement, Second, Contracts (tentative draft), Section 32.

PETERSEN v. PILGRIM VILLAGE

Supreme Court of Wisconsin, 1950.
256 Wis. 621, 42 N.W. 2d 273.

BACKGROUND AND FACTS *Petersen was employed by Pilgrim under a contract providing that he was to be paid a stated salary. Petersen claimed (1) that Pilgrim told him when he began work that he would share in the profits of the corporation and (2) that Pilgrim repeatedly promised that he would be paid. Petersen and Pilgrim, however, never came to any definite agreement as to what the percentage of profits was to be.*

DECISION AND RATIONALE *Pilgrim had no contractual obligation to pay Petersen any percentage of the company's profits because no contract with respect to profits was ever formed. Pilgrim's offer was too* *indefinite for a court to determine its terms with any reasonable degree of certainty. In the opinion of the court, "An offer must be so definite in its terms, or require such definite terms in the acceptance, that the promises and performances to be rendered by each party are reasonably certain."*

RELAXATION OF DEFINITENESS UNDER THE UNIFORM COMMERCIAL CODE Contract law is designed to aid business, not to hinder it. Thus, the Uniform Commercial Code has liberalized the requirement of definiteness as to essential terms. Contract law, however, continues to be much stricter than the Uniform Commercial Code. The UCC allows such terms as "according to custom and usage" in order to fill in indefinite terms in an otherwise valid agreement. Following are a few ways in which the UCC fills in missing terms. Even though one or more terms are left open, a contract for sale does not fail for indefiniteness if the parties have intended to make a contract and there is a reasonably certain basis for giving an appropriate remedy [UCC Sec. 2-204]. If no price is stated, or if the price is left open to be agreed on, "the price is a reasonable price at the time for delivery" [UCC Sec. 2-305]. If no place of delivery is specified, then delivery is to occur at the seller's place of business [UCC Sec. 2-308(a)].[12] If the time for shipment or delivery is not provided for, then the time shall be a reasonable time after the contract is formed [UCC Sec. 2-309]. If the time for payment is not specified, then payment is due at the time and place of delivery [UCC Sec. 2-310(a)].

In addition, under the UCC, omitted terms may be supplied by custom and usage in trade

---

12. But if both parties know the goods are elsewhere when the contract is formed, then the place of delivery is the place where the goods are located.

and by prior dealings. If the parties have dealt with each other previously, their past conduct may be used to supply the omitted terms. For example, assume John's Poultry has purchased spring chickens from Robinson Farms for the last ten years, and the chickens have always been paid for on credit. John's Poultry then enters into a contract to buy 150 chickens, but no mention is made of the terms of payment. Due to prior dealings, John's may pay on credit, since the understandings of the past may be implied in the current contract.

Indefiniteness may be cured by *part performance*, that is, by performance that has already begun. Assume Brown-Crummer, Inc., agrees to buy beans at $4 per bushel from Arkansas Grains. Arkansas Grains, however, has four different grades of beans. This is an indefinite contract since its subject matter is insufficiently described. But if Arkansas Grains ships No. 3 beans and Brown-Crummer accepts them, the indefiniteness is cured. This contract becomes enforceable when Brown-Crummer accepts the beans because Brown-Crummer's acceptance (part performance) identifies the subject matter of the contract [UCC Sec. 2-606].

In the following case, when plaintiff bought "chicken," he meant broiling and frying chickens—not stewing chickens. The defendant contended that a chicken is a chicken. The following case illustrates how a federal district court applied New York law to decide the weighty question "What is a chicken?"

BACKGROUND AND FACTS *B.N.S. agreed to sell and Frigaliment to buy a stated quantity of frozen chicken. The subject of the contract was described only as "chicken." B.N.S. shipped a low grade chicken suitable only for stewing. Frigaliment claimed that B.N.S. was in breach of contract, asserting that the term chicken meant chicken suitable for broiling or frying.*

FRIGALIMENT IMPORTING CO. LTD. v. B.N.S. INTERNATIONAL SALES CORP.

United States District Court of New York, 1960. 190 F. Supp. 116.

DECISION AND RATIONALE *Since the word chicken standing alone was ambiguous, its meaning had to be determined from trade usage or, in the absence of trade usage, from the common objective meaning of the term. Frigaliment failed to prove that in trade usage chicken meant fryers and broilers. Since stewing chicken falls within the dictionary meaning of chicken B.N.S. fulfilled its contractual obligation. Frigaliment "ha[d] the burden of showing that chicken was used in the narrower rather than in the broader sense ***."*

OUTPUT AND REQUIREMENT CONTRACTS
The Uniform Commercial Code also validates output and requirements contracts.[13] **Output contracts** are agreements to sell all production during a specified period to a certain party. **Requirements contracts** are agreements to buy all production needs "or requirements" during a specified period from a certain party. These contracts do not specifically state the quantity of output or requirements, but the quantity is definitely ascertainable, within reasonable limits. The courts have a reasonably certain basis for giving an appropriate remedy if either type of contract is breached.

Communication

An effective offer must be *communicated* to the offeree because one cannot agree to a bargain without knowing that the bargain exists. Suppose Emerman advertises a reward for the capture of her lost dog. Baldwin, not knowing of the reward, finds the dog and returns it to Emerman. Baldwin cannot recover the reward because he did not know it was offered.[14]

REWARDS A reward is a special kind of contract, for it is unilateral. It can be accepted only by performance. Another element to the reward contract is that one who claims a reward must have known that it was offered. Otherwise there can be no contract. This rule follows because it is impossible to have an acceptance under contract law unless the offeree knows the existence of the offer. The following case is one of the classic "reward" cases in the common law.

13. Brown-Crummer Inv. Co. v. Arkansas City, 125 Kan. 768, 266 P. 60 (1928).
14. A few states will allow recovery of the reward but not on contract principles. Since Emerman wanted her dog returned, and Baldwin returned it, these few states allow Baldwin to recover. It would be unfair to deny him the reward just because he did not know about it.

GLOVER v. JEWISH WAR VETERANS OF THE UNITED STATES, POST NO. 58
Municipal Court of Appeals for the District of Columbia, 1949.
68 A.2d 233.

BACKGROUND AND FACTS *The Jewish War Veterans of the United States put in the newspaper an offer of a reward of $500 "to the person or persons furnishing information resulting in the apprehension and conviction of the persons guilty of the murder of Maurice L. Bernstein." Mrs. Glover gave police information that led to the arrest and conviction of the murderers, not knowing that a reward had been offered and not learning of it until several days afterward.*

DECISION AND RATIONALE *Mrs. Glover was not entitled to the $500 reward because she was not aware of it when she gave the police the information. Her act could not constitute an acceptance since she did not act in response to the offer. The Restatement of the Law of Contracts says, "It is impossible that there should be an acceptance unless the offeree knows of the existence of the offer."*

TERMINATION OF THE OFFER

The communication of an effective offer to an offeree creates a power in the offeree to transform the offer into a binding legal obligation (a contract). This power of acceptance, however, does not continue forever. It can terminate by operation of law or by an act of the parties. The power may be terminated by *operation of law* through: (1) lapse of time, (2) destruction of the subject matter of the contract, (3) death or incompetency of the offeror or offeree, and (4) supervening illegality of the proposed contract. The power may be generally terminated by *action of the parties* through: (1) revocation of the offer, (2) counter-offer by the offeree, and (3) rejection of the offer by the offeree.

Termination by Operation of Law

LAPSE OF TIME An offer terminates when the period of time specified in the offer has passed. For example, suppose A offers to sell his boat to B if B accepts within twenty days. B must accept within the twenty-day period or the offer will lapse (terminate). The period of time specified in an offer begins to run when the offer is *actually received* by the offeree, not when it is sent or drawn up. When the offer has been delayed, the period begins to run from the date the offeree *would have* received the offer, but only if the offeree knew or should have known the offer was delayed.[15] For example, if A had used improper postage when mailing the offer to B, but B knew A had used improper postage, the offer would lapse twenty days after the day B would ordinarily have received the offer had A used proper postage.

If no time for acceptance is specified in the offer, the offer terminates at the end of a *reasonable* period of time. In order to determine what a reasonable period of time is, the subject matter of the contract, business and market conditions, and other relevant circumstances must be taken into account. An offer to sell farm produce, for example, will terminate sooner than an offer to sell farm equipment because farm produce is perishable and subject to greater fluctuations in market value.

DESTRUCTION OF THE SUBJECT MATTER An offer is automatically terminated if the subject matter is destroyed before the offer is accepted. For example, if Watts offers to sell her race horse to Teagle, but the horse dies before Teagle can accept, the offer is automatically terminated. Likewise, an offer to sell a particular lathe is terminated if the lathe is destroyed in a fire before the offer is accepted.

DEATH OR INCOMPETENCY OF THE OFFEROR OR OFFEREE An offeree's power of acceptance is terminated when the offeror or offeree dies or is deprived of legal capacity to enter into the proposed contract.[16] An offer is personal to both parties and cannot pass to the decedent's heirs, guardian, or estate. Furthermore, this rule applies whether or not the other party had notice of the death or incompetency of the party. For example, on June 4, Manne offers to sell Clark a rowboat for $300, telling Clark that he, Manne, needs the answer by June 20. On June 10, Manne dies. On June 18, Clark informs the executor of Manne's will that he has accepted the offer. The executor can refuse to sell the rowboat because the death of the offeror has terminated the offer.

Termination by Action of the Parties

REVOCATION OF THE OFFER BY THE OFFEROR An offer may be terminated by the offeror if a revocation is communicated to the offeree *before* the offeree accepts. Revocation may be accomplished by expressly repudiating the offer (such as "I withdraw my previous offer of October 17") or by acts inconsistent with the

---

15. Restatement, Second, Contracts (tentative draft), Section 51.

16. Restatement, Second, Contracts (tentative draft), Section 48.

existence of the offer (where, for example, the offeree discovers the offeror has sold the property that was the subject matter of the offer).

The revocation must be communicated to the offeree before acceptance, or the revocation will be ineffective and a valid contract will be formed. The general rule followed by most states is that a revocation is effective only upon actual receipt by the offeree or that person's agent of the revocation. Therefore, a letter of revocation that is deposited in a mailbox on April 1 and that arrives at the offeree's residence or place of business on April 3 becomes effective on April 3. If the offeree accepts the offer on April 2, a valid contract will be formed, and the contract will be enforceable in a court of law.

Alternatively, communication to the offeree exists if the offeree indirectly discovers that the offer is revoked. This indirect discovery may be through a third person who tells the offeree that the offeror has revoked prior to offeree's acceptance. In addition, the revocation may be communicated indirectly where the offeree learns that the subject matter of the contract has been sold to a third party.

Offers made to the general public may be revoked by communicating the revocation in the same manner in which the offer was communicated. For example, suppose Macy's offers a $10,000 reward for anyone giving information leading to the apprehension of the persons who burglarized Macy's downtown store. The offer is published in three local papers and in four papers in neighboring communities. In order to revoke the offer, Macy's must publish the revocation in all seven papers for the same number of days as it published the offer. The revocation will then be accessible to the general public, even though some particular offeree did not know about it.

Option Contracts As a general rule, offerors may revoke their offers even if they expressly agreed to hold them open for a specified period of time. When an offeror promises to hold an offer open for a specified period of time, how-

ever, and the offeree pays for the promise (gives consideration), an **option contract** is created. An option contract takes away the offeror's power to revoke the offer for the period of time specified in the option. If no time is specified, then a reasonable period of time is implied, just as in offers.

For example, suppose Brennan offers to sell one hundred shares of stock in Texas Instruments to Columbus for $189 per share. Brennan promises to keep the offer open for thirty days. After fourteen days Brennan calls Columbus on the telephone and says that the offer is revoked. If Columbus has not given any consideration (say $25 in cash) for the offer, Brennan may revoke the offer even though he promised to keep it open for thirty days. If Columbus has given some consideration for the offer, Brennan cannot revoke the offer for thirty days, and his attempt to do so will be ineffective. In the latter case, even if Brennan attempted to revoke after fourteen days, Columbus could still accept the offer and force Brennan to sell the Texas Instruments stock for $189 per share. This particular option contract (for the purchase of common stock) is becoming increasingly popular, and similar options are traded publicly on the Chicago Board Options Exchange.

Death or Incompetency of Offeror or Offeree
When the offer is in the form of an option and the decedent was not required to perform an essential part of the contract, the offer survives the death or incompetency of the offeror.[17] For example, assume Vendrick executes an option to Carney entitling Carney to purchase Vendrick's hundred-acre ranch in Costa Rica. Carney pays $750 for the option, but before he can exercise it, Vendrick dies. Carney can still exercise the option against Vendrick's estate, since Vendrick is not required to perform the act of conveying the ranch to Carney personally. In sum, option contract rights and duties are not discharged by the death of either party unless performance is of a personal nature—that is, consists of personal services.

17. Restatement, Second, Contracts (tentative draft), Section 35A.

Firm Offers Under the Uniform Commercial Code, certain offers may be irrevocable even if no consideration is given. These are called **firm offers.**[18] If a merchant makes a written, signed offer to buy or sell goods and states that the offer is not revocable, the offer cannot be revoked regardless of the lack of consideration. The offer will remain open for the period of time specified in the offer, but the period of irrevocability cannot exceed three months. Note the various elements necessary for a firm offer: (1) the offer must be for the purchase or sale of goods; (2) the offer must be made by a merchant dealing in those goods; (3) the offer must be written and signed by the merchant; and (4) the offer must give assurance that it will be held open for some period of time. (If the offer makes such assurances but does not state a period of time, a reasonable period of time not in excess of three months is assumed.)

Detrimental Reliance on the Offer A growing number of courts are refusing to allow an offeror to revoke the offer when the offeree changes position in justifiable reliance on the offer. In such cases, revocation would be unjust to the offeree. Consider an example. Feinberg has worked for Pfeiffer for thirty-five years. Pfeiffer tells her that whenever she quits, she will be paid $150 a month for the rest of her life. There is no indication by Pfeiffer that she should quit now. In fact, she works for a couple more years. She quits and Pfeiffer starts sending her checks every month for $150. Five years later, Pfeiffer dies and his son takes over the business. The son says the $150 checks are ridiculous and attempts to avoid the promise. He will not be able to do so because Feinberg has been relying on the promise to pay her $150 a month. Had the promise not been made, she would have rearranged her affairs to obtain other retirement funds. This is a case of a detrimental reliance on a promise and therefore cannot be revoked.

Revocation of Offer for Unilateral Contract In a unilateral contract, the offer invites acceptance only by *full* performance or forbearance. The offer of a unilateral contract cannot be accepted by promising to perform; only full performance will suffice. Obviously, injustice can result if an offeree expends time and money in part performance and then the offeror revokes the offer before full performance is complete. Therefore, many courts will not allow the offeror to revoke after the offeree has performed some substantial part of his or her duties.[19] In effect, part performance changes the offer into an option, and the offeree has reasonable time to complete performance.

REJECTION OF THE OFFER BY THE OFFEREE The offer may be rejected by the offeree, in which case the offer is terminated and may not subsequently be accepted by the offeree. Any subsequent attempt to accept will be construed as a new offer, giving the original offeror (now the offeree) the power of acceptance. A rejection is ordinarily accomplished by words or conduct evidencing an intent to reject the offer.

As in the case of revocation of the offer, rejection is effective only when actually received by the offeror or the offeror's agent. (The only difference is the party to whom the communication is made.)

Suppose you offer to sell Procter & Gamble twenty-five tons of linseed oil at thirty-five cents per pound. Procter & Gamble could reject your offer by writing or telephoning you, expressly rejecting the offer (perhaps by saying, "We are sufficiently stocked in linseed oil and do not need any more"). Alternatively, the company could mail your offer back to you, evidencing an intent to reject the offer. Or it could offer to buy the oil at twenty-three cents per pound, which would operate as a counter-offer, necessarily rejecting the original offer.

COUNTER-OFFER BY THE OFFEREE A counter-offer—a change in one or more terms of the original offer—by the offeree will terminate the original offer. It is treated as a rejection. Suppose X offers to sell his home to Y for

---

18. Restatement, Second, Contracts (tentative draft), Section 24A.

19. UCC Sec. 2-205.

$70,000. Y then offers to buy the house for $65,000. Y's offer is termed a counter-offer and terminates X's original offer. At common law, the "mirror image" rule requires the offeree's acceptance to match the offeror's offer exactly—to mirror the offer. Any change in, or addition to, the terms of the original offer automatically terminates that offer and substitutes the counter-offer, which, of course, need not be accepted. The original offeror can, however, accept the terms of the counter-offer and create a valid contract.

In a contract for the sale of goods, now governed by the Uniform Commercial Code, an acceptance that varies from the terms of an offer does not always terminate that offer. An acceptance can add terms to the offer or change its terms.[20] Between merchants, the new or changed terms become part of the contract automatically unless: (1) the original offer expressly required acceptance of its terms, (2) the new or changed terms materially alter the contract, or (3) the offeror rejects the new or changed terms.

ACCEPTANCE

Acceptance is a voluntary act (either words or conduct) by the offeree that shows assent (agreement) to the terms of the offer. The acceptance must ordinarily be made in the manner requested by the offeror.[21] In addition, the acceptance must be unequivocal and communicated to the offeror.

Who Can Accept?

Ordinarily, only the person to whom the offer is made (the offeree) can accept the offer and create a binding contract. If the offer is an option contract, however, the right to exercise the option is generally considered a contract right and as such assignable or transferable to third persons (with exceptions—see Chapter

---

20. E.g., Sylvestre v. Minnesota, 289 Minn. 142, 214 N.W. 2d 658 (1973). See UCC, Sec. 2-207.
21. The UCC has changed the common law in this area. [UCC Sec. 2-206(1)(a)].

12). If the offeree is an agent for an undisclosed principal, the acceptance may be made by the principal and will bind both the principal and the offeror (see Chapter 34).

Suppose Black & Decker offers to sell John Rushmore a combination power saw/grinder for $335. If Rushmore has not given consideration for the offer, only he can accept it. He cannot let his neighbor, Sam Ullman, accept the offer because Black & Decker assented to sell the power saw/grinder to Rushmore only. If he has paid $5 for the option to buy the power saw/grinder during the next thirty days, he can accept the offer. Additionally, he can sell his option contract to Ullman which will entitle Ullman to accept the offer from Black & Decker. Suppose further that Rushmore is the agent of Janet Blackstone, an undisclosed principal. Here, Blackstone can direct Rushmore to accept, and Black & Decker will be bound on a valid contract with Blackstone.

Unequivocal Acceptance

In order to exercise the power of acceptance effectively, the offeree must accept unequivocally. If the acceptance is subject to new conditions, or the terms of the acceptance change the original offer, the acceptance may be a counter-offer, implicitly rejecting the original offer. An acceptance may be unequivocal even though the offeree expresses dissatisfaction with the contract. For example, "I accept the goods, but I wish I could have gotten a better price" will operate as an effective acceptance. So, too, will "I accept, but can you shave the price?" On the other hand, the statement "I accept the goods, but I want to pay on ninety days credit" is not an unequivocal acceptance and operates as a counter-offer, rejecting the original offer.

CONDITIONS Certain conditions, when added to an acceptance, will not qualify the acceptance sufficiently to reject the offer. Suppose Childs offers to sell her sixty-five-acre cotton farm to Sharif. Sharif replies, "I accept your offer to sell the farm, provided you can supply a good title." This condition (providing of good title) does not make the acceptance equivocal. A warranty of good title is normally implied in every offer for the sale of land, so the condition does not add any new or different terms to the offer.

Or suppose that in response to an offer to sell a motorcycle, the offeree replies, "I accept; please send written contract." This does not make the acceptance ineffective. The request for a writing is not necessary or conditioned upon the acceptance. Therefore, the acceptance is effective. However, if the offeree replies, "I accept *if* you send a written contract," the acceptance is *expressly* conditioned on the request for a writing, and the statement is not an acceptance but a counter-offer.

As noted above, under the Uniform Commercial Code, an acceptance that varies in insignificant ways from the terms of the offer, can, nonetheless, operate as an acceptance. The additional or changed terms are treated as proposals for *additions* to the contract.[22] If both parties are merchants, the proposals become part of the contract unless the offer expressly limits acceptance to the terms of that offer, or the proposals materially alter the contract, or the offeror objects to the proposals within a reasonable time. Terms treated as proposals for addition to a contract between persons when one or both are not merchants must be agreed to by the original offeror.

Silence as Acceptance

Ordinarily, silence cannot be acceptance, even if the offeror states, "By your silence and inaction you will be deemed to have accepted this offer." This general rule applies because an offeree should not be put under a burden to act affirmatively in order to reject the offer.

Silence can operate as an acceptance when, for example, an offeree takes the benefit of offered services with an opportunity to reject them and knowledge that they were offered with the expectation of compensation. Suppose Sarah Holmes watches while her daughter is given piano lessons. The piano instructor has not been requested to give the daughter lessons but plans to give a series of fifteen. Holmes knows the instructor plans to be paid but lets the lessons continue nonetheless. Here, her silence constitutes an acceptance, and she is bound to pay a reasonable value for the lessons. This rule applies only to services and goods if they are used by the offeree.

A second situation arises when the offeree, due to prior dealings with the offeror, notifies the offeror only if the offer is rejected. To illustrate: X, a salesman, has previously ordered goods from Y and paid without notifying Y of his acceptance. Whenever X receives a shipment from Y, he sells it and simply sends a check to Y. Only if the goods are defective does X notify Y. The last shipment, however, has been neither paid for nor rejected. Nonetheless, X is bound on a contract and must pay Y for this last shipment of goods.[23]

A third and final situation arises when an offeror sends goods to an offeree and the parties have had no prior dealings. Here, silence does not constitute an acceptance *unless* the receiver exercises control over the goods. The most common example of this is when books or magazines are sent to an individual through the mails. The individual did not order the books or magazines and is under no duty to reship them to the seller. Under the common law, if the individual uses the books or magazines he or she will have accepted them and must pay reasonable value for them. This common law rule of contract law has been chaged by statute. The Postal Reorganization Act of 1970 provides that unordered merchandise sent by mail may be retained, used, discarded, or disposed of in any manner deemed appropriate, without the individual incurring any obligation to the sender.[24] In addition, the mailing of unordered merchandise (except for free samples) constitutes an unfair trade practice and is not permitted. (Exceptions are mailings by charitable agencies and those made by mistake.)

22. Restatement, Second, Contracts (tentative draft), Section 52 and UCC Sec. 2-207.

23. Restatement, Second, Contracts (tentative draft), Section 72 and Illustration 1.

24. 39 USCA, Sec. 3009, and state statutes.

Communication of Acceptance

Whether the offeror must be notified of the acceptance depends on the nature of the contract. In a unilateral contract, notification or communication is not necessary. Since a unilateral contract calls for the *full* performance of some act, acceptance is not complete until the act has been fully performed. Therefore, notice of acceptance is unnecessary. To illustrate: Beta offers to pay Gamma $150 to paint Beta's garage. Gamma can accept only by painting the garage. Once the garage is completely painted (and hence the acceptance is complete), notification of the acceptance is superfluous. Certain exceptions do exist. When the offeror requests notice of acceptance or has no adequate means of determining whether the requested act has been performed, notice of acceptance is necessary.

In a bilateral contract, notification of acceptance is necessary because acceptance is in the form of a promise (not performance), and the contract is formed when the promise is made (rather than when the act is performed). The offeree must use reasonable efforts to communicate the acceptance to the offeror. In a bilateral contract, however, notification of acceptance is not necessary if the offer dispenses with the requirement. In addition, if the offer can be accepted by silence, no communication or notification is necessary.

Under the Uniform Commercial Code, an order or other offer to buy goods for prompt shipment may be accepted by either a promise to ship or by actual shipment.[25]

When an Acceptance Becomes Effective

The general rule is that an acceptance becomes effective when the offeree assents to the same terms as the offeror by way of a reasonable and appropriate communication. If an offeree accepts by mail, the acceptance is effective when the letter is dropped in the mailbox. This is the so-called "mailbox rule,"[26] and it applies to any situation where: (1) no means of acceptance is specified in the offer and (2) acceptance is made in the same manner as the offer was made. For example, if an offer is made by telegraph, then the acceptance is made when the offeree gives a message to a telegraph operator. If the acceptance is not properly dispatched, it will not be effective until it is actually received by the offeror. Note that this rule involves two separate elements.

First, the acceptance must be properly dispatched. When the mails are involved, this simply means that the letter must be properly addressed and have the correct postage. If the acceptance is not properly dispatched, it will not be effective until the offeror actually receives it.[27] If the letter is delayed in the mails, the offer may lapse or be revoked in the meantime.

Second, the acceptance must be made via a reasonable means of communication. At common law, this requires the offeree to use the particular means used by the offeror or some faster means. If the offer is conveyed by the mails, then the acceptance can be sent by mail, telegraph, or telephone. If the offer is conveyed by telegraph, the use of the mails to accept is not authorized (since the mails are usually much slower than the telegraph). Naturally, if the offeror requires the use of some particular means, that means has to be used or the acceptance will not become effective until the offeror actually receives it.

Recall that rejections or revocations of offers are not effective until actually received, and then study the following hypothetical situations:

1.   On January 1, A mails an offer to B. On January 2, A decides to revoke the offer and sends B a letter to that effect. On January 3, B receives the offer and accepts it, putting a letter of acceptance in the mail. On January 4, B receives the letter of revocation. On January 5,

---

25.   UCC Sec. 2-206(1)(b).

26.   Adams v. Lindsell, 106 Eng.Rep. 250 (K.B. 1818).
27.   Restatement, Second, Contracts (tentative draft), Section 68.

A receives the letter of acceptance. Has a valid contract been formed? Yes, because B's acceptance was effective when it was dropped in the mail (on January 3). The revocation cannot become effective until B actually receives it (on January 4), which in this case was subsequent to the acceptance.

2.   On January 1, A mails an offer to B. On January 2, B receives the offer and mails a rejection letter to A. On January 3, B changes his mind, wires A, and accepts the offer. On January 4, A receives the letter of rejection. Has a valid contract been formed? Yes. Since the rejection was not effective until received, and the offer was accepted (on January 3) prior to A's receipt of the rejection letter (on January 4), a valid contract has been formed. This is a special situation in which the contract is valid upon receipt, not mailing, because of intervening attempted rejection.

QUESTIONS AND CASE PROBLEMS

1.   McKittrick Co. employed Embry under a written contract at a fixed annual salary. Just before the contract expired, Embry approached McKittrick's president, seeking to have his employment contract extended another year. The president did not make any firm commitments to Embry, and Embry continued working. A week after his contract had run out, Embry again approached the president, this time threatening to quit if his contract was not extended. The president responded, "Go ahead, you're all right, and don't let that worry you." Two months later Embry was laid off. Can Embry recover his salary under the contract for the entire year? [Embry v. Hargadine, McKittrick Dry Goods Co., 127 Mo.App. 383, 105 S.W. 777 (1907)]

2.   Calan Imports advertised a 1964 Volvo station wagon for sale in the *Chicago Sun-Times*. The newspaper erroneously stated the price as $1,095. Calan had instructed the newspaper to advertise the price at $1,795. Upon reading the advertisement, O'Brien visited Calan's showroom and told one of the salesmen that he wished to purchase the car. At first the salesman agreed, but upon learning of the advertising error, he refused to sell the car at that price. Can O'Brien recover for breach of contract? [O'Keefe v. Lee Calan Imports, Inc., 128 Ill.App.2d 410, 262 N.E.2d 758 (1970)]

3.   A widow wrote to her daughter: "If you come and live with me on my farm and support me for the rest of my life you may have the use of the farm during my lifetime and the farm will be yours when I have passed away." Without responding to the letter, the daughter and her husband sold their home and moved across the country onto the widow's farm. The daughter and husband lived with the widow until she died. Before she died, the widow sold the farm to her son instead. Can the daughter claim the farm? [Brackenbury v. Hodgkin, 116 Me. 399, 102 A. 106 (1917)]

4.   Jones was an inventor. Pym held exclusive rights to the invention. Campbell, who desired to purchase Pym's rights to the invention, entered into negotiations with Pym. On the day set for contract negotiations Campbell told Pym that he, Campbell, would agree to buy the invention if his friend Abernathie, an engineer, gave a favorable opinion of it. Since Abernathie was not able to be present at the negotiations, it was proposed that Pym and Campbell draw up a contract and sign it. But if Abernathie did not approve the invention, the contract was to be ineffective. Subsequently, Abernathie disapproved the invention. Pym contended that the contract they signed was a valid agreement. Is he correct? [Pym v. Campbell Q.B. 1856, 6 Ellis & Blackburn 370]

5.   On October 28, 1891, Sanders submitted the following proposition to Pottlitzer Bros.: "We offer you ten car loads of apples, 175 to 200 barrels per car, to be shipped as follows: 1st car by December 15th, 2nd car by December 30th and one car each ten days after January 1." To this Pottlitzer Bros. replied: "We accept your proposition on apples, provided you will change it to read — car every eight days from January first, none in December." On the same day, Sanders responded that he could not accept Pottlitzer's changes and had to insist on the original offer. Several days later, Pottlitzer Bros. wrote a detailed letter to Sanders explaining why the requested changes were important and reiterating that it could not do business on Sanders's terms. Sanders then responded: "Letter received. Will accept conditions. If satisfactory, answer, and will forward contract." Pottlitzer Bros. replied by telegraph: "All right. Send

contract as stated in our message." Sanders sent the contract as modified by Pottlitzer Bros. But Pottlitzer refused to accept the contract unless it also included a provision that Sanders furnish stoves on the carrier to protect the apples from freezing. Can Sanders enforce the agreement as originally modified? [Sanders v. Pottlitzer Bros. Fruit Co., 144 N.Y. 209, 39 N.E. 75 (1894)]

6. John H. Surratt was one of John Wilkes Booth's alleged accomplices in the murder of President Lincoln. On April 20, 1865, the Secretary of War issued and caused to be published in newspapers the following proclamation: "$25,000 reward for the apprehension of John H. Surratt and liberal rewards for any information that leads to the arrest of John H. Surratt." On November 24, 1865, President Johnson revoked the reward and published the revocation in the newspapers. Shuey learned of the reward but left for Rome prior to its revocation. In Rome, Shuey discovered Surratt's whereabouts; and, in April of 1866, unaware that the reward had been revoked, he reported this information to United States officials. Pursuant to receiving this information, the officials were able to arrest Surratt. Should Shuey have gotten the reward? If so, was he entitled to the full $25,000? [Shuey v. United States, 92 U.S. 73, 23 L.Ed. 697 (1875)]

7. Dodds signed and delivered to Dickinson the following memorandum on Wednesday, June 10:

> "I hereby agree to sell to Mr. George Dickinson the whole of the dwelling houses, garden ground, stabling, and outbuildings these to belonging, situated at Croft, belonging to me, for the sum of £800. As witness my hand this tenth day of June, 1874.
> "£88 [signed] John Dodds."
> "P.S. this offer to be left over until Friday, 9 o'clock A.M. 12th June, 1874."
> [Signed] J. Dodds."

The next afternoon (Thursday) Dickinson learned that Dodds was negotiating with a man named Allan. That evening Dickinson went to the house of Dodds' mother-in-law and left her a written acceptance. This document never reached Dodds. The next morning, at 7 A.M., Dickinson's agent gave Dodds a copy of the acceptance. Dodds replied that it was too late as he had already sold the property. Was the memorandum signed by Dodds a binding contract? If it was merely an offer, was Dickinson's acceptance sufficient to form a binding contract? [Dickinson v. Dodds, 2 Div. 463 (1876)]

8. For about the past two weeks Wilfred, a tall, good-looking college fraternity man, has been trying to get a date for fraternity Greek night. Wilfred has had his heart set on Melinda from the first day he saw her. Every night at 8:30 Wilfred calls Melinda to ask her to Greek fraternity night. Every night Melinda tells Wilfred that she does not like him and does not want to go anywhere with him. On Thursday, the evening before Greek fraternity night, Wilfred again calls Melinda at the usual time. This time he pleads with Melinda, "I promise if you go with me I'll never bother you again." Melinda promises to go with him, but the next night she stands Wilfred up. Wilfred goes to his attorney, Schiester, and asks him to bring a lawsuit against Melinda. Is there a breach of contract?

7

Contracts
Consideration

In order to create a legally binding promise, one or more of the parties must give legally sufficient consideration. **Consideration** is something that is intentionally exchanged for something else and is required in nearly every contract. The courts will not enforce a promise against a breaching party unless the party seeking enforcement has resorted to a proper form of agreement or has given up a valuable legal right.

Two elements constitute consideration: (1) something must be given, and (2) there must be a bargained-for exchange. Essentially, the parties must bargain together and trade something for something, that is, a *quid pro quo*.

Suppose Earl says to his son, "In consideration of the fact that you are not as wealthy as your brothers, I will pay you $500." This promise is not enforceable because Earl's son has not given any consideration to support it.[1] Earl has simply stated his motive for giving his son a gift.

REQUIREMENTS OF CONSIDERATION

Legal Sufficiency

To create a binding contract, the consideration must exist, and it must be legally sufficient. In order to be **legally sufficient,** *consideration* for a

---

1. Fink v. Cox, 18 Johns 145, 9 Am. Dec. 191. (1820).

promise must be either legally *detrimental to the promisee* or legally *beneficial to the promisor*, or both.[2] (The promisor makes a promise; the promisee receives it.) Legal detriment is doing or promising to do something that there was no prior legal duty to do. It also includes refraining or promising to refrain from doing something that there was no prior legal duty to refrain from doing. Conversely, legal benefit is obtaining something that there was no prior legal right to obtain. *Legal* detriment or benefit is not synonymous with *actual* (economic) detriment or benefit. In most cases, the promisor's legal benefit is the same as the promisee's legal detriment. However, the existence of *either* a legal detriment or a legal benefit constitutes legally sufficient consideration.

Suppose Myers owns a brickhouse that causes considerable air pollution in and around his property. Myers is thinking about getting out of the brick-making business since he is not making much profit and his property is constantly enveloped in a thick layer of smoke. Bernard, his neighbor, is sick of the smoke and pollution and offers Myers $1,500 to stop making bricks (and thus stop the smoke). Myers

agrees. The consideration flowing from Myers to Bernard is the promise to refrain from doing an act that Myers is legally entitled to do, that is, to earn a living by making bricks. The consideration flowing from Bernard to Myers is the promise to pay a sum of money that is not otherwise legally required to be paid.

On the other hand, assume X owes Y $100 and Y promises to discharge the debt if X pays $50. Consideration is not legally sufficient in this example because X had a prior legal obligation to pay Y the $100. This is known as X's pre-existing duty, a subject that will be discussed later in the chapter.[3]

In one of the classic cases in contract law, the court found that refraining from certain behavior at the request of another was sufficient consideration to support a promise to pay a sum of money.

---

2. The whole concept of sufficient consideration is losing its force. Restatement, Second, Contracts (tentative draft) drops the idea. Basically, one either meets the requirements of consideration outlined in Section 75 or does not. Nothing additional is needed. The modern way seems to be to talk simply in terms of "bargained-for" consideration.

3. The reasoning is limited to obligations that are or can be reduced to specific dollar amounts.

HAMER v. SIDWAY
Court of Appeals of New York,
Second Division, 1891.
124 N.Y. 538, 27 N.E. 256.

BACKGROUND AND FACTS *William E. Story, Sr., was the uncle of William E. Story, II. In the presence of family members and guests invited to a family gathering, Story, Sr., promised to pay his nephew $5,000 if he would refrain from drinking, using tobacco, swearing, and playing cards or billiards for money until he became 21. The nephew agreed and fully performed his part of the bargain. When he reached 21, he wrote and told his uncle that he had kept his part of the agreement and was thereby entitled to $5,000. The uncle replied that he was pleased with his nephew's performance, writing, "I have no doubt but you have, for which you shall have five thousand dollars, as I promised you. I had the money in the bank the day you was twenty-one years old that I intend for you, and you shall have the money certain."*

The letter went on to describe how the uncle had worked hard to earn his money and how he hoped that his nephew, Willie, would make good use of the money and not squander it. The uncle also indicated that he had bought his nephew fifteen sheep twenty-one years before and that every four years the sheep were put out to pasture and doubled their numbers. Now, there were between five hundred and six hundred sheep.

They were worth quite a bit of money, and the uncle wanted his nephew to have these as well. He wrote, "You can consider this money on interest."

The nephew received his uncle's letter and thereafter consented that the money should remain with his uncle according to the terms and conditions of the letter. The uncle died about two years later without having paid his nephew any part of the $5,000 and interest. The executor of the uncle's estate (the defendant in this action) did not want to pay the $5,000 (with interest) to the nephew, claiming that there had been no valid consideration for the promise.

DECISION AND RATIONALE   The uncle's estate was obligated to pay the nephew the $5,000. All the elements of a contract existed. The uncle made a valid offer to his nephew. Since the offer was unilateral, the nephew could accept only by performing the conditions in the offer. Thus, the nephew's forebearance from drinking, using tobacco, swearing, and playing cards or billards constituted an acceptance. Finally, the contract was supported by a valid consideration in that the nephew refrained from doing things he otherwise had a right to do. Justice Parker quoted from the definition of "consideration" as follows: "In general a waiver of any legal right at the request of another party is a sufficient consideration for a promise."

"Good Consideration" and Legal Sufficiency

Sometimes people feel a moral obligation to make a promise to loved ones. A father may promise to pay $10,000 to his daughter "in consideration of the love and affection that I have for you." An employer may promise to give a sum of money to a trusted employee "in consideration of the many acts of kindness and thoughtfulness over the years" that the employee has performed. This is generally called "good consideration." It is founded on natural duty and affection or on a strong moral obligation. Good consideration is not legally sufficient consideration, however. Therefore, promises made in exchange for it are unenforceable.

Adequacy of Consideration

Adequacy of consideration refers to the fairness of the bargain. If B agrees to pay $2 for S's motorcycle, B's consideration is legally suf-ficient since B was under no prior legal duty to pay out the money. However, the consideration is far from adequate, since S is not getting a very fair bargain.

In general, a court of law will not question the adequacy of consideration if the consideration is legally sufficient. Under the doctrine of freedom of contract, parties are normally free to bargain as they wish. If people could sue merely because they entered into an unwise contract, the courts would be overloaded with frivolous suits. In extreme cases, a court may look to the amount or value (the adequacy) of the consideration because inadequate consideration can indicate fraud, duress, or undue influence. Suppose Lansky has a house worth $25,000, and he sells it for $5,000. The consideration would be legally sufficient but not very adequate. The $5,000 sale could indicate that the buyer pressured Lansky into selling or that Lansky was defrauded into selling at far below market value.

In an equity suit, courts will question the

adequacy of consideration. (Remember from Chapter 1 that actions at law allow for remedies that consist of some form of compensation. Actions at equity allow for remedies that involve a specific performance or an injunction.) The parties in an equity suit must show that the transaction was fair and that substantially equivalent consideration was exchanged. For example, a suit to compel specific performance is equitable and requires the losing party actually to perform the contract duties rather than pay damages for breach of contract. Assume McMichael agrees to sell land worth $45,000 to Price for only $7,500. After signing the contract,

McMichael refuses to deliver possession, and Price sues for specific performance. The court may now look at the relative values of the consideration exchanged and may refuse to allow specific performance since the consideration is inadequate. Today, law and equity cases are no longer handled by separate courts.

As a general principle of contract law, the courts will not ordinarily look into the adequacy of the consideration in an agreed exchange. However, in the following case, the court would not allow "peace of mind" and $1.05 to constitute adequate consideration for a $12,000 land sale.

ROSE v. LURVEY
Court of Appeals of Michigan,
1972.
40 Mich. App. 230, 198 N.W.2d
839.

BACKGROUND AND FACTS *Robert and Barbara Rose owned a house worth about $25,000. They were indebted under a mortgage loan for about $13,000 when they entered into a contract to sell the house to Lurvey. At the time, the Roses were behind in their payments and owed back taxes. Robert was worried that he might default on the loan. The parties executed the sales contract but failed to state a definite sales price. The only money mentioned was $1.05 recited as consideration.*

Robert Rose continued to occupy the house after the contract was executed. Lurvey served him with notice to vacate the premises, but Rose ignored the notice. A month or so later, Robert Rose entered the hospital. During the short time the house was unoccupied, Lurvey moved in and began remodeling the interior. The Roses sued to have the contract thrown out.

DECISION AND RATIONALE *The contract was not enforceable because the consideration was grossly inadequate. As a general rule, a court will not examine adequacy of consideration when scrutinizing an agreement, but it will grant relief when the consideration is glaringly inadequate. In the present case, the equity value of the house (market value less mortgage outstanding) was about $12,000. The sales contract, however, recited consideration of only $1.05. Any peace of mind the Roses received by selling the house was merely a motive for entering into the contract and not, as Lurvey argued, additional consideration. "The motive which prompts one to enter into a contract and the consideration for the contract are distinct and different things." The court could not, in good conscience, countenance such a contract when the disparity between the sales price and the value of the item sold was so extreme. The court concluded, "Inadequacy of price paid for real property is not sufficient alone to authorize a court of equity to set aside a deed of conveyance, unless it is so gross as to shock a conscientious person; but, if the inadequacy is so great as to shock a conscientious person, it alone may furnish sufficient ground for annulling the conveyance."*

SITUATIONS WHERE CONSIDERATION IS NOT PRESENT

The element of exchange is absent whenever: (1) a promise is given in exchange for a past occurrence or transaction, (2) there is a pre-existing duty, (3) there is a moral obligation, (4) an illegal act is involved, and (5) there is an illusory promise.

Past Consideration

Past consideration is not consideration. Therefore, a promise given for something that has already been done is not enforceable. Suppose a father tells his son, "In consideration of the fact that you named your son after me, I promise to pay you $1,000." The promise is unenforceable since no present consideration supports it. There was no exchange.

Suppose instead that the father tells his son, "In consideration of your promise to name your next child after me, I promise to pay you $1,000." The son's next child is named after the father. Here, there is an exchange. Hence, legally sufficient consideration supports the father's promise to pay $1,000. (Note that in some jurisdictions, past consideration may serve as consideration if in writing.)

A familiar legal maxim says, "Love and affection do not constitute sufficient consideration to support a contract." This rule takes into account the so-called moral consideration that occurs when there is no expectation on the part of either party at the time the promise is made that it will be carried out.[4]

Performing a Pre-existing Duty

Under most circumstances, a promise to do what one already has a legal duty to do is not legally sufficient consideration because no legal detriment or benefit has been incurred.[5] The

pre-existing legal duty may arise out of a previous contract or may be imposed by law. A sheriff cannot collect a reward for information leading to the capture of a criminal if the sheriff is under a duty to capture the criminal. Similarly, assume Healey agrees to hire Brewster for one year at $175 per week. Brewster begins working. After two months, Healey agrees orally to increase the wages to $195 per week. Healey's promise is unenforceable because it is not supported by legally sufficient consideration. Brewster was under a pre-existing duty to work for one year, and the performance of that duty cannot be consideration for the wage increase.

The harshness of the pre-existing duty rule is evident. In the examples above, the sheriff is denied a reward that anyone else could have received, and Brewster, the employee, can be denied his pay raise. Therefore, the courts are ready to find *any* legal detriment or benefit, no matter how small or insignificant, so that the promise will be enforceable. Hence, if Brewster was required to perform any *extra* duties, the promise modifying his employment contract would be enforceable.

Incurring a Moral Obligation

Promises based on moral duty or obligation are not enforceable because a moral obligation is not legally sufficient consideration. Suppose your friend is injured in a distant city and a grocer takes care of him during his injury. Thereafter, feeling a moral obligation to help your friend and aid the grocer, you promise the grocer to pay for your friend's expenses. The promise is unenforceable since it is supported only by your moral obligation, and a moral obligation cannot be legally sufficient consideration. Other examples of promises made out of a moral obligation include promises to pay the debts of one's parents or promises to pay for the care rendered to relatives one was under no duty to support. A minority of states enforce promises supported only by a moral obligation— but only to the extent of the actual obligation or

---

4. For an exception, see Restatement, Second, Contracts (tentative draft), Section 89A.

5. Foakes v. Beer, 9 App.Cas. 605.

of the services or care rendered. For an example, see California Civil Code, Sec. 1606.

Performing an Illegal Act

A promise to perform an illegal act is not legally sufficient consideration. If it were, then an illegal act could be enforced in a court of law. Public policy requires the consideration to be for the performance of a legal act.

Making an Illusory Promise

An illusory promise is actually no promise at all. It may sound like a promise, but close examination reveals that the promisor has actually agreed to do nothing. For example, if I promise to buy "whatever supplies I *may want* during August and September," I have not really *promised* to buy anything. Therefore, I suffer no legal detriment, and the promise is unenforceable. (Note the difference here between the above promise, which is unenforceable, and a promise to buy "all the supplies I will need," which is enforceable.)

Illusory contracts result in no obligation on either party. For example: In May, Y offers to sell grain for a specified price during the September harvest and X accepts by promising to buy all the grain that X "might wish." There is no contract. X is not bound to buy any grain and has thus incurred no detriment. X can choose to buy grain anywhere. If X decides in September that it is advantageous to buy at Y's price and places an order with Y, Y is not obliged to sell X the grain.[6]

SPECIAL CONSIDERATION QUESTIONS

Settlement of Debts

When a debt is disputed and the dispute has some merit, payment of part of the debt can be satisfaction of the whole debt. Courts view the

debtor's relinquishing of contentions (reasons for the dispute) as legally sufficient consideration, and the entire debt is thereby discharged or satisfied.

A **liquidated debt** is one in which the amount owing is not disputed and can be expressed as a certain sum of money. (The term "liquidated" means ascertained, fixed, settled, and determined.) An **unliquidated debt** cannot be expressed as a certain sum. The debt in question may be either liquidated or unliquidated and may involve a dispute as to the existence or amount of the debt.

When both parties agree to discharge a debt for a lesser amount, and part payment is accepted by the creditor as *payment in full,* the debt is discharged if it was disputed or unliquidated. This discharge is usually accomplished by the parties first reaching a settlement agreement, then by sending the creditor a check marked "payment in full." Suppose you hire a painter to paint your apartment at $10 an hour plus materials costs. He finishes the job and presents you with a bill for $1,000. You contend that the job is only worth $500. The painter agrees to settle for $700, and you write a check for $700. The painter cannot come back later and sue you to recover the difference between $700 and $1,000. Why? Because his acceptance of the $700 is an implied promise to release you from the debt. Your payment to the painter constitutes a detriment to you because you can no longer go to court to contend that the debt was only $500. The painter cannot obtain a ruling in his favor that the debt was not completely paid. This is particularly true if you write "payment in full" on the back of the check, and the check is cashed by the painter. If the debt is liquidated and not disputed, payment of part of the debt will *not* discharge the entire amount. This is due to the pre-existing legal duty to pay the full amount. (Under the Uniform Commercial Code no consideration is necessary to discharge a liquidated and undisputed debt.[7] The discharge can be accomplished by a written waiver or renunciation signed and delivered to the debtor.)

---

6. However, if Y's original offer is a standing offer to sell at the stated price or if X's order comes within a commercially reasonable time of the original offer, the order constitutes a valid acceptance of an offer that has not terminated and creates a contract that is enforceable.

7. UCC Sec. 1-107.

Construction Contracts

Suppose Bauman-Bache, Inc., begins construction on a seven-floor office building and after three months demands an extra $75,000 on its contract or it will stop working. The owner of the land, having no one else to complete construction, agrees to pay the extra $75,000. The agreement is not enforceable because it is not supported by legally sufficient consideration; Bauman-Bache was under a pre-existing duty to complete the building. Some courts, however, have held such a modifying agreement enforceable. The conflicting policies are two: (1) people should be able to modify their legal relations; and (2) modification in some cases will resemble duress, as in the Bauman-Bache example.

Most of the time, a promise to modify a construction contract will not be enforced, but in some cases it will be. In those minority of cases, courts have said that the original contract was rescinded and replaced with the new agreement.[8] Other courts have said the original consideration carries over into the new agreement.[9]

As was pointed out, a promise to do something that a party is already under a legal obligation to do is not valid consideration sufficient to support a contract. However, sometimes a party runs into some unforeseen or substantial difficulty in the performance of a contract that could not have been anticipated when the contract was entered into. If this casts an additional burden not contemplated by the parties, an additional promise to pay extra compensation will be valid consideration. Such is the situation in the following case.

_____

8.   Armour & Co. v. Celic, 294 F.2d 432 (2d Cir. 1961).
9.   Holly v. First Nat. Bank, 218 Wis. 259, 260 N.W. 429 (1935).

BACKGROUND AND FACTS   *Lange Brothers entered into a contract with the United States to construct a laundry building, including a laundry chute. At the time it signed the contract, Lange was unaware of the strict government specifications required for building the chute. To comply with them would cost far more than anticipated. (The original contract price was $347; to comply with specifications would cost $1,071.). After much discussion, the parties entered into a second contract that was practically identical to the original except that it provided for a higher price. A dispute over the validity of the second contract followed.*

LANGE v. UNITED STATES
United States Court of Appeals, Fourth Circuit, 1941.
120 F.2d 886.

DECISION AND RATIONALE   *The second contract was enforceable even though Lange agreed to do only what, technically, it was already obligated to do—install a laundry chute. Courts generally validate substitute agreements when the parties have entered into the second contract to avoid a dispute under the original. It is sound public policy for courts to lend their support to this means of resolving disputes.*

In the case at hand, the inadequacy of the original consideration was the fault of both Lange and the United States. The unforeseen expense of the government's specifications would have caused Lange to bear a greater burden than either party had anticipated, and thus the extra compensation under the second contract was supported by valid consideration. The court found that, "both parties were taken by a surprise which might have been avoided had either party taken the necessary precautions."

Output and Requirements Contracts

An output contract requires a seller to sell the entire amount of goods produced over a specified period to another party. A requirements contract obligates a party to purchase all requirements from another party. For example, if U.S. Steel agreed to sell all I-beams produced during March to Boeing Aircraft, an output contract would be made. If U.S. Steel agreed to buy all coal needed during March from West Virginia Coal Company, a requirements contract would be made. These promises are not illusory. They obligate U.S. Steel to sell all output or buy all requirements, whatever they may be.

The Uniform Commercial Code imposes a *good faith limitation* on output and requirements contracts. The quantity under such contracts is the amount of output or the amount of requirements that occur during a *normal production year*. Therefore, if U.S. Steel produced 1,500 tons of I-beams last March and required 4,500 tons of coal, it could not sell 10,000 tons of I-beams or purchase 15,000 tons of coal under the contracts. The actual quantity sold or purchased cannot be unreasonably disproportionate to normal or comparable prior output or requirements.

Exclusive Dealing Contracts

An **exclusive dealing contract** requires a buyer to carry only products made by the seller. Wood agrees to market fabrics, millinery, and dresses upon which Lucy, Lady Duff-Gordon, places her endorsement. Lady Duff-Gordon receives no promise that Wood will market any dresses, but she gives Wood an exclusive right to market whatever number is deemed appropriate. At first blush, Wood's promise appears illusory. He has not agreed to sell anything. However, as in the output and requirements contracts, Wood is under a duty to use his "best efforts" to market the dresses.[10] This duty or obligation is consideration for the promise to either supply or sell.

Consider another example, that of a real estate broker who has obtained a thirty-day exclusive contract from the seller of a house.

The broker has the duty to perform his or her best efforts in selling the house within thirty days and in dealing with a potential buyer.

Promises Enforceable Without Consideration

Certain promises, either by statute or court decision, can be fully or partially enforceable without consideration.

PROMISSORY ESTOPPEL   A promise given by a party that induces another party to act may be enforceable without consideration. When the promisor (the person making the promise) can reasonably expect the promisee (the person receiving the promise) to act on the promise, and injustice cannot be avoided any other way, the promise will be enforced.[11] Additionally, the promisee must act with justifiable reliance on the promise.

The promise is enforced by refusing to allow the promisor to set up the defense of no consideration. This is called estoppel. The promisor is estopped from asserting the lack of consideration. The estoppel arises from the promise, hence **promissory estoppel.** (This doctrine is *not* used in some jurisdictions.)

Imagine that your grandfather tells you, "I'll pay you $75 per week so you won't have to work anymore." Then you quit your job, and your grandfather refuses to pay. You can enforce the promise since you have justifiably relied on it.[12]

Traditionally, promissory estoppel has been applied only to gratuitous promises, that is, when the parties are not bargaining in a commercial setting. The trend, however, is to apply it in any situation if justice so requires (as shown in the next case).

---

10.   Wood v. Lucy, Lady Duff-Gordon, 222 N.Y. 88, 118 N.E. 214 (1917).

11.   See UCC Sec. 2-306. Also Restatement, Contracts, Section 90 provides: a promise which the promisor should reasonably expect to induce action or forbearance of a definite and substantial character on the part of the promisee and which does induce such action or forbearance is binding if injustice can be avoided only by enforcement of the promise.

12.   Ricketts v. Scothorn, 57 Neb. 51, 77 N.W. 365 (1898).

BACKGROUND AND FACTS   *Red Owl Stores, Inc., induced the Hoffmans to give up their current business and run a Red Owl franchise. The
Hoffmans did so in reliance on the representations of Red Owl, but the
deal ultimately fell through. Red Owl failed to keep its promise to allow
the Hoffmans to operate a franchised store even though they had
satisfied all of Red Owl's requirements.*

**HOFFMAN v. RED OWL
STORES, INC.**
Supreme Court of Wisconsin,
1965.
26 Wis. 2d 683, 133 N.W.2d 267.

DECISION AND RATIONALE   *Even though no contract was ever
signed, Red Owl was liable to the Hoffmans for the damages they
suffered. Red Owl made a number of promises and assurances, which the
Hoffmans relied and acted upon to their detriment. Since they acted
reasonably in relying on Red Owl, the law granted them some measure of
relief. Under the doctrine of promissory estoppel, Red Owl was bound by
the representations it made to the Hoffmans since these representations
were such that a reasonable person would have relied on them. The
presiding justice cited the following test for promissory estoppel:*
    *"(1) Was the promise one which the promisor should reasonably
expect to induce action or forbearance of a definite and substantial
character on the part of the promisee?*
    (2) Did the promise induce such action or forbearance?
    (3) Can injustice be avoided only by enforcement of the promise?"

Exceptions to Consideration Under the Uniform Commercial Code

The Uniform Commercial Code has expressly
eliminated the requirement of consideration in
several situations. The UCC is treated extensively in Unit IV, so only a brief review of
some salient points is given here.

FIRM OFFERS   A signed written offer by a
merchant to buy or sell goods is not revocable
for lack of consideration. The offer, termed a
firm offer (defined in the previous chapter), is
irrevocable for the time stated in the offer (but
for no longer than three months). If no time is
stated, the offer remains irrevocable for a
reasonable time (UCC Sec. 2-205). The law of
firm offers is analogous to the option contract,
but by statute the firm offer does not require
consideration.

WAIVER OR RENUNCIATION OF CLAIM
Any claim or right arising out of an alleged

breach can be discharged in whole or in part
without consideration by a written waiver or
renunciation signed and delivered by the aggrieved party (UCC Sec. 1-107). By the use of
such a waiver, the repayment of $50 on a $100
debt can discharge the entire debt, notwithstanding the pre-existing duty rule.

COMMERCIAL PAPER   Special rules apply to
commercial paper. For a detailed discussion,
see Chapter 26.

MODIFICATION   An agreement modifying a
contract for the sale of goods needs no consideration to be binding [UCC Sec. 2-209(1)].

LETTERS OF CREDIT   No consideration is
necessary to establish a letter of credit. In
addition, no consideration is necessary to
modify or enlarge the terms of a letter of credit
(UCC Sec. 5-105).

New Promises to Pay Barred Debts

DEBTS BARRED BY THE STATUTE OF LIMITATIONS Statutes of limitations in all states require a creditor to sue within a specified period to recover debts. If the creditor fails to sue in time, recovery of the debt is barred by the statute of limitations. A debtor who promises to pay a previous debt barred by the statute of limitations makes an enforceable promise. *The promise needs no consideration.* (Some states, however, require that it be in writing.) In effect, the promise extends the limitations period, and the creditor can sue to recover the entire debt. The promise can be implied if the debtor acknowledges the barred debt by making a partial payment.

Suppose you borrow $5,000 from First National Bank of San Jose. The loan is due in November 1980. You fail to pay, and the bank does not sue you until December 1985. If California's statute of limitations for this debt is five years, recovery of the debt is barred. If you then agree to pay the loan off, First National Bank can sue for the entire amount. This is an example of an express promise, which extends the limitations period. Likewise, you can make a monthly payment and implicitly acknowledge the existence of the debt. Again First National

Bank can sue you for the entire debt. This is an example of acknowledgment. Suppose instead that you expressly promise First National Bank to pay it $2,500. This promise is enforceable only to the extent of $2,500 (and usually must be in writing).

DEBTS DISCHARGED BY BANKRUPTCY A promise to pay a debt previously discharged by bankruptcy proceedings needs no consideration to be binding (but it must be in writing). The promise must be clear and definite. For example, if D says, "I promise to pay you what I can if I make some money this year," the promise is not enforceable because it is not a definite promise.

Unlike debts barred by the statute of limitations, part payment of a debt discharged in bankruptcy will not implicitly acknowledge the existence of the debt. Therefore, if you make a monthly payment on the loan received from First National after the loan has been discharged in bankruptcy, you are not liable for the entire amount of the loan.[13]

---

13. The revisions of the Bankruptcy Act recently passed by Congress, make revival of debts discharged in bankruptcy very difficult, and in the case of consumer loans, virtually impossible.

QUESTIONS AND CASE PROBLEMS

1. Gray is a special police officer in Atlantic City. Martino, who lost a significant amount of her jewelry during a burglary of her home, offered a reward for the recovery of the property. Incident to his job, Gray possessed certain knowledge concerning the theft of Martino's jewelry. When Gray informed Martino of his knowledge of the theft, Martino offered Gray $500 to help her recover her jewelry. As a result of police work, the diamonds and jewelry were recovered and returned to Martino. Gray sued Martino for the reward he claimed she promised him. Was there a valid contract between Gray and Martino? [Gray v. Martino, 91 N.J.L. 462, 103 A.24 (1918)]

2. McMichael agreed to furnish Price all the sand of various grades and qualities that Price could "sell for shipment to various and sundry points outside of the city of Tulsa." McMichael agreed to furnish the sand upon Price's written or oral request within a reasonable time after the request was made. At the time of the agreement, Price was not engaged in the business of selling sand. The agreement was to run for a ten-year period. After about five months, McMichael refused to deliver any more sand to Price. Was McMichael in breach of contract? [McMichael v. Price, 177 Okl. 186, 58 P.2d 549 (1936)]

3. Feinberg was secretary to the president of Pfeiffer Company. After she had worked there for eighteen years, the board of directors, in recognition of her "long and faithful service," passed a resolution whereunder she would be paid $200 a month for the rest of her life at any time she decided to retire. Shortly thereafter, Feinberg retired and for several years received the $200 per month as promised. The president of Pfeiffer eventually died and was suc-

ceeded by his son, who cut off all subsequent money to Feinberg. Feinberg sued Pfeiffer Company. Was she able to recover under contract theory? [Feinberg v. Pfeiffer Company, 322 S.W.2d 163 (Mo. App. 1959)]

4. Reynolds refused to pay Penhow the $500 he owed him, and Penhow sued. Prior to judgment, in an attempt to work out their differences, Reynolds and Penhow agreed that Reynolds could pay off the debt in full settlement for $400. Later, after the parties had already agreed to this arrangement, judgment was entered in favor of Penhow for the full $500. Instead of accepting $400 from Reynolds as full payment of the debt, Penhow insisted that Reynolds pay according to the full force of the judgment. Was the settlement agreement entered into between Penhow and Reynolds supported by adequate consideration? [Reynolds v. Penhow, Cro.Eliz. 429 (1595)]

5. Kirksey wrote a letter to his widowed sister-in-law, "Sister Antillico," inviting her to come live with him. The letter, in part, stated: "If you will come down and see me, I will let you have a place to raise your family." Within a month or two after receiving this letter, Sister Antillico abandoned her home and moved her family sixty miles to Kirksey's residence. She and her family lived with Kirksey for two years, when he notified her that she was to remove all her possessions and leave. Unenforceable gift or enforceable contract? [Kirksey v. Kirksey, 8 Ala. 131 (1845)]

6. Star Furniture Company manufactured summer lawn furniture. Its sole product consisted of webbed aluminum frame furniture used mainly on outdoor patios and on beaches. As of October[1], Star Furniture was heavily indebted to its three main suppliers— Aluminum Pole, Inc., Plastic Webbing, Ltd., and The Little Steel Rivet Company. Star owed each of these suppliers approximately $10,000. Star's president met individually with the presidents of each of the three suppliers to work out some arrangement whereby the company could avoid declaring bankruptcy. Since all the parties desired that Star Furniture not go bankrupt, the president of each supplier company agreed to accept $7,000 in full payment of all outstanding debts as of October[1]. Was this agreement enforceable?

7. Nees owned two parcels of land. One parcel, located on Atlantic Avenue, he held exclusively in trust for two of his children, Sophia and George. The other parcel, known as the Sackett Street property, passed to all four of Nees's children upon Nees's death. None of the children learned that only Sophia and George were to receive the Atlantic Avenue property until they were informed by Nees's attorney at the time the attorney opened Nees's strongbox. Sophia and George, seeing that their brothers and sisters were disappointed that none of them had gotten any interest in the Atlantic property, promised to give them their share in the Sackett Street property, "if you don't bother us on the Atlantic Avenue house." Was this promise enforceable against Sophia and George? [Springstead v. Nees, 125 App.Div. 230, 109 N.Y.S. 148 (1908)]

8. Wyman was suddenly taken ill on a voyage. Mills, a nurse, took him in since he had no money and no place to go. Mills cared for Wyman over a considerable period of time and expended substantial sums of money in reviving him. After all the expenses had been incurred, Wyman's mother wrote a letter to Mills thanking her for taking care of her son and promising to repay all the expenses Mills had incurred on his behalf. Later, Wyman's mother refused to repay the expenses. Was Mills able to recover? Was there adequate consideration? [Mills v. Wyman, 20 Mass. (3 Pick.) 207 (1825)]

9. In the early 1960s the city of Boston was engaged in extensive redevelopment. In October of 1961, the Boston Redevelopment Authority (BRA) agreed to pay the expenses of relocating Graphic Arts Finishers, a business displaced by the Government Center Urban Renewal Project. BRA's promise to pay Graphic Arts' total moving expenses was given in exchange for performance of certain promises by Graphic Arts. The company promised: (1) to depart the premises peacefully and expeditiously, without requiring the BRA to resort to legal actions; (2) to relocate its business elsewhere and not liquidate; and (3) to induce its landlord to consider wiring, plumbing, and other property as the plaintiff's personal property so that the landlord would not claim greater damages from the BRA. Graphic Arts' moving expenses amounted to approximately $130,000. The BRA refused to pay. Did Graphic Arts give any consideration for BRA's promise? [Graphic Arts Finishers, Inc. v. Boston Redevelopment Authority, 357 Mass. 40, 255 N.E.2d 793 (1970)]

8

Contracts
Contractual Capacity

Some people, like minors and the mentally impaired, lack the capacity to make an enforceable contract, regardless of whether they understand its terms.

MINORS

At common law, a minor was defined as a male who had not attained the age of twenty-one or a female who had not attained the age of eighteen. Today, in most states, the age of majority (when a person is no longer a minor) has been changed by statute usually to eighteen years for both sexes.[1] In addition, some states provide for the termination of minority upon marriage. Subject to certain exceptions, the contracts entered into by a minor are avoidable at the option of that minor. A **voidable contract** is one in which the minor may avoid legal obligations by exercising the option to disaffirm the contract. On the other hand, an adult who enters into a contract with a minor cannot avoid his or her contractual duties on the ground that the minor can do so. Unless the minor exercises the option to avoid the contract, the adult party is bound by it.

---

1. While the age of majority applicable in contracts has been changed to eighteen in many states, it may still be twenty-one for some purposes, including the purchase and consumption of alcohol. The word "infant" is used synonymously with the word "minor."

Minors' Rights to Disaffirm

A minor's contract is not entirely void, despite the option to avoid the contract. A minor exercising the power to avoid a contract *disaffirms* it and *releases* both parties from their legal duties. A minor's voidable contract can become binding, however, if the minor *ratifies* or approves it. However, ratification cannot occur before the minor attains majority, since ratification is also voidable.

DISAFFIRMANCE IN GENERAL In order for a minor to exercise the option to avoid a contract, he or she need only manifest an intention not to be bound by it. The infant "avoids" the contract by "disaffirming" it. The technical definition of *disaffirmance* is the legal avoidance, or setting aside, of a contractual obligation. Words or conduct may express this intent. Suppose James Caldwell, a seventeen-year-old, enters into a contract to sell his car to Joseph Reed, an adult. Caldwell can avoid the contract and avoid his legal duty to deliver possession of the car to Reed by either telling Reed that he refuses to abide by the contract or by selling the car to a third person. In other words, Caldwell can disaffirm the contract by expressing his intention in words or by acting inconsistently with his duties under the contract.

The contract can ordinarily be disaffirmed at any time during minority or for a reasonable time after the minor comes of age. However, an exception exists in the case of a contract for the sale of land by a minor. Here a minor cannot disaffirm the contract until he or she reaches majority.

If a minor fails to disaffirm a contract in a reasonable time after reaching majority, the contract can be deemed ratified due to the minor's failure to disaffirm. This is almost always true where the contract has been executed by the other party. For example, suppose Susan Taylor enters into a contract to buy a pool table from Snooker, Inc. She takes delivery of the table while she is a minor, and the contract is thereby executed by Snooker, Inc. By keeping the pool table when she reaches majority, Susan ratifies the contract and is bound to fulfill her legal duty to pay the full purchase price.

In some states, common law and statutes require minors to disaffirm their contracts within a reasonable time after reaching majority or they lose the right to avoid their legal duties. When the contract is executory—in other words, when neither party has fully performed their contractual obligations—some states require the minor to expressly affirm the contract. Other states deem the executory contract ratified for failure to disaffirm within a reasonable time after majority.

DUTY OF RESTORATION When a contract has been executed, minors cannot disaffirm without returning whatever they have received (or making an offer to do so). This is called the minor's *duty of restoration.* Although many states recognize this duty, most place certain limitations on it. Under the majority view, the minor need only return the goods (or other consideration), provided they are in the minor's possession or control. Suppose Pat Boland, another seventeen-year-old, purchases a used Ford Fairmont from Jane Crow, an adult. Boland is a bad driver and runs the car into a telephone pole on his grandfather's farm. The next day he returns the car to Crow and disaffirms the contract. Under the majority view, this return fulfills Boland's duty even though the auto is now wrecked.

On the other hand, a few states, either by statute or by court decision, have placed an additional duty on the minor—the *duty of restitution.* The theory is intended to return the adult to his or her position before the contract was made. The duty of restitution requires Boland to pay Crow for the damage done to the car in addition to returning it. Some states do not require full restitution. A minor must pay a "reasonable" amount for the use of the property or to compensate the adult for the reasonable wear and tear to the property.

A minor must disaffirm the *entire* contract. The minor cannot decide to keep part of the goods and return the remainder. When a minor disaffirms, all property that the minor has transferred can be recovered even if it is then in the hands of a third party. If the property itself cannot be returned, the other party must pay the minor its equivalent value. Under UCC Sec. 2-403, the rule about recovering property does not apply if the transfer was a sale subject to the provisions of the UCC and if the transfer was to a bona fide purchaser.[2] (Note that the sale of land continues to be governed by common law—which often has specific rules for real estate. Therefore, when a minor contracts to sell real estate and ultimately disaffirms the contract, even a bona fide purchaser will be required to return the land to the minor. For example, if Mary sells real estate to a broker who in turn sells it to Carol, Mary can disaffirm the contract and recover the land from Carol.)

In the following case, a minor's father brought an action to disaffirm the minor's purchase of an automobile and to recover the purchase price. The court reviewed the contract with the minor and took into account the fact that the seller knew the buyer was a minor when the contract was made.

2. Defined as "a purchaser for a valuable consideration paid or parted with in the belief that the vender had a right to sell, and without any suspicious circumstances to put him on inquiry." (Merritt v. Railroad Co., 12 Barb., N.Y. 605).

QUALITY MOTORS, INC. v. HAYS

Supreme Court of Arkansas, 1949.

216 Ark. 264, 225 S.W.2d 326.

BACKGROUND AND FACTS *Johnny Hays, a 16-year-old minor, went to Quality Motors, Inc., seeking to purchase a car. The salesman refused to sell the car unless the purchase was made by an adult. Shortly thereafter, Johnny returned with a young man of twenty-three whom Johnny had met that day for the first time. The salesman recommended a notary public who could prepare the necessary papers to transfer title from the young man to Johnny and then drove the two boys into town for this purpose. The young man transferred title to Johnny, and the salesman delivered the car to Johnny at his college. Johnny's father attempted to return the car to Quality Motors for a full refund, but Quality Motors refused it. The car was stored while Johnny's father sought to get Quality Motors to take it back, but Johnny found the keys and wrecked the car in an accident.*

DECISION AND RATIONALE *Johnny was able to disaffirm the contract and return the car. He was not liable for damages to the car. When goods—other than necessaries—are sold to a minor, the minor can disaffirm the contract of sale. Since the salesman aided Johnny in obtaining the car by selling it to an adult and by assisting in the transfer of title to Johnny, a minor, the sale was essentially made to Johnny. The loss which Quality Motors suffered was the result of its own act of not accepting the undamaged car when it should have. The presiding justice quoted the law as follows: "The law is well settled *** that an infant may disaffirm his contracts, except those made for necessaries, without being required to return the consideration received, except such part as may remain in specie in his hands."*

LIABILITY FOR NECESSARIES A minor who enters into a contract for "necessaries" may disaffirm the contract but does remain liable for the reasonable value of the goods. The legal duty to pay a reasonable value does not arise from the contract itself but is imposed by law on a theory of quasi-contract. The theory is that the minor should not be *unjustly* enriched and should therefore be liable for those things that fulfill basic needs, such as food, clothing, and shelter.

Note, though, that the minor is liable only for the reasonable value of the goods (because there is no contract and therefore no contract price to which the court can refer). Suppose Hank Olsen, a minor, purchases a suit that is list priced at $150. After wearing the suit for several weeks, Olsen wants to disaffirm his contract with the clothier. He can do so, but he is liable for the reasonable value of the suit. If the value is actually $115, then the clothier can recover only that amount, even if this deprives the clothier of all profit on the sale.

Necessaries include items absolutely necessary for the minor's existence, like food, clothing, shelter, medicine, and hospital care. In order to determine whether an item is a necessary, all the facts and circumstances must be taken into account. Therefore, a minor's station in life or financial and social status will be taken into account to determine if an item is a necessary. Necessaries may include services that are reasonably necessary to enable a minor to earn a living, such as an employment agency fee in obtaining a job.

BACKGROUND AND FACTS *Bobby Rogers was nineteen years old and married. He went to the office of Gastonia Personnel Corporation, an employment agency, and signed a contract for assistance in obtaining suitable employment. Thereafter, he refused to pay a service charge of $295.*

DECISION AND RATIONALE *Bobby Rogers could not disaffirm the contract since it involved necessaries. Necessaries include not only food, shelter, and clothing but also the services that are reasonably necessary to enable minors to provide the necessities of life for themselves and their families. "Society has a moral obligation to protect the interests of infants from overreaching adults. But this protection must not become a straight jacket, stifling the economic and social advancement of infants who have the need and maturity to contract. Nor should infants be allowed to turn that protective legal shield into a weapon to wield against fair-dealing adults."*

GASTONIA PERSONNEL CORPORATION v. ROGERS
Supreme Court of North Carolina, 1970.
276 N.C. 279, 172 S.E.2d 19.

THE EFFECT OF A MINOR'S MISREPRESENTATION OF AGE Suppose a minor tells a seller that she is twenty-one years old when she is actually only seventeen. Ordinarily, the minor can still disaffirm the contract, even though she has acted fraudulently. However, since the other party has been induced by the minor's fraudulent misrepresentation to enter into the contract, the other party also has the option to avoid the contract. (See Chapter 10 on lack of real assent.) In the above example, the seller can therefore disaffirm the contract. In addition, the seller has the option of electing to seek a remedy under a tort action.

In certain circumstances a minor can be bound by a contract when a misrepresentation of age has been made. First, several states have enacted statutes prohibiting minors from disaffirming contracts when they have made a false representation of age. Some of these statutes prohibit disaffirmance by a minor who has engaged in business as an adult.[3]

Second, some courts refuse to allow minors to disaffirm executed contracts unless they can return the consideration received. The combi-

---

3. See, for example, statutes in Iowa, Kansas, Utah, and Washington.

nation of misrepresentation by minors and the unjust enrichment if they are allowed to keep the property received, has persuaded several courts to estop (prevent) minors from asserting contractual incapacity.

Third, some courts allow a misrepresenting minor to disaffirm the contract but hold the minor liable for damages in tort. Here, the defrauded party may sue the minor for misrepresentation or fraud. A split in authority exists on this point, since some courts have recognized that allowing a suit in tort is equivalent to the indirect enforcement of the minor's contract.

In the following case, an Ohio appellate court reviewed the trial court's decision regarding a purported disaffirmation of a purchase contract by a minor. The court was impressed mainly by the fact that the contract had been induced by a false representation of the age of the minor in question.

HAYDOCY PONTIAC, INC. v. LEE

Court of Appeals of Ohio, Franklin County, 1969. 19 Ohio App.2d 217, 250 N.E.2d 898.

BACKGROUND AND FACTS *Jennifer Lee was twenty years old when she contracted to purchase an automobile from Haydocy Pontiac, Inc. However, she represented to the salesman that she was twenty-one years old. Lee financed most of the purchase price. Immediately following delivery of the automobile, she turned the car over to a third person. She made no further payments on the contract and attempted to rescind it. She made no offer to return the automobile.*

DECISION AND RATIONALE *Haydocy Pontiac, Inc., could recover the balance due under the financial agreement. Under these circumstances, Lee was estopped (precluded) from rescinding the contract on the ground of her infancy since she induced the sale by misrepresenting her age. In the words of the presiding judge: "Where [an] infant *** through falsehood and deceit enters into a contract with another who enters therein in honesty and good faith and, thereafter, the infant seeks to disaffirm the contract without tendering back the consideration, no right or interest of the infant exists which needs protection. The privilege given the infant thereupon becomes a weapon of injustice."*

INSURANCE AND LOANS Traditionally, insurance has not been viewed as a *necessary*, so minors can ordinarily disaffirm their contract and recover all premiums paid. However, some jurisdictions limit the right to disaffirm—for example, when minors contract for life or health insurance on their own lives. Other jurisdictions allow a minor to disaffirm but limit recovery to the value of premiums paid less the insurance company's actual cost of protecting the minor under the policy. Suppose Bob Berzak takes out an automobile insurance policy and pays $125 in premiums. Bob has an accident for which his insurance company, State Farm, pays a claim of $85. In states following the traditional rule, Bob's recovery upon disaffirmance will be $125, the full value of the premiums. In states limiting his recovery, Bob can recover only $40, the excess of the value of the premiums over State Farm's actual cost under the policy.

In and of itself, a loan is seldom viewed as a necessary, even if the minor spends the money on necessaries. However, if the lender makes a loan for the express purpose of enabling the minor to purchase necessaries, and the lender personally makes sure the money is so spent, the minor is normally obligated to repay the loan.

Ratification

Ratification is an act or expression of words by which a minor, upon reaching majority, indicates an intention to become bound by the contract. As noted above, ratification must necessarily occur after the individual comes of age, since any attempt to become legally bound prior to majority is no more effective than the original contractual promise. This protects the minor and is consistent with the theory that the contracts of a minor are voidable at his or her option.

EXPRESS RATIFICATION Suppose John Lawrence enters into a contract to sell a house to Carol Ogden. At the time of the contract Carol is a minor. Naturally, Carol can avoid her legal duty to pay for the house by disaffirming the contract. Imagine, instead, that Carol reaches majority and writes a letter to John stating that she still agrees to buy the house. Carol thus ratifies the contract and is legally bound. John can sue for breach of contract if Carol refuses to perform her part of the bargain. This is an example of *express* ratification.

IMPLIED RATIFICATION The contract can also be ratified by *conduct*. Suppose, after reaching majority, Carol lives in the house. This conduct evidences an intent to abide by the contract and is a form of *implied* ratification. Again, Carol is legally bound, and John can sue her for breach of contract if she fails to perform her duty to pay the purchase price. Another example of implied ratification occurs when an individual, after reaching majority, continues to use property purchased as a minor. The continued use is inconsistent with disaffirmance and implicitly indicates an intention to be bound by the contract.

In general, any act or conduct showing an intention to affirm the contract will be deemed to be ratification. However, silence alone after reaching the age of majority will not constitute ratification of an executory contract in most situations. If Carol had said nothing to John and had not entered into possession, she would not have ratified the contract, since she had expressed no intention to abide by it. On the other hand, the minor may have a duty to speak in some circumstances. Suppose that after coming

of age, a minor fails to act while purchaser makes improvements on property of which the minor was the vendor. If the vendor knows of the improvements being made and says nothing, the vendor cannot disaffirm the contract.

NONVOIDABLE CONTRACTS

Minors

Many states have passed statutes restricting the ability of minors to avoid certain contracts. Loans for education or medical care received by minors create binding legal duties that they cannot avoid.[4]

In addition, certain statutes specifically require minors to perform legal duties. Suppose James Dornan, a minor, wants to attach the property of Davis Snowden for default of a loan. In some states, Dornan is required to file a bond before the legal attachment can occur. After filing the bond, Dornan cannot avoid the obligations of the bonding agreement, since the bond is a legal duty imposed by state statute. In such situations, a minor cannot rely on the common law rule that the bonding contract is voidable. Similar legal duties are imposed on minors with respect to bank accounts and transfers of stocks.

Parents' Liability

As a general rule, parents are not liable for the contracts made by their minor children. Due to this fact, businesses will ordinarily require parents to sign any contract made with a minor. Parents who sign such contracts then become personally obligated to perform the conditions of the contract, even though their child can or actually does avoid liability.

If the parents have neglected their minor child, they will be liable for the reasonable value of necessaries supplied to the child, even if they do not expressly agree to pay for such products. In other words, if a child purchases shoes because his parents refuse to give him something to wear on his feet, the parents can be held liable for the reasonable value of the shoes.

4. New York Education Laws, Sec. 281; Pennsylvania, 35 Pa.S., Sec. 10101.

INTOXICATED PERSONS

A contract entered into by an intoxicated person can be either voidable or valid. If the person was drunk enough to be *non compos mentis*, then the transaction is voidable at the option of the intoxicated person even if the intoxication was purely voluntary. In order to be *non compos mentis*, all reason and judgment must be impaired, so that the intoxicated party does not realize he or she is entering into a valid contract. If a party is slightly intoxicated but still comprehends the legal consequences of entering into a contract, the contract will be valid and can be enforced by the other party. Simply because the terms of the contract are foolish or largely in favor of the other party does not mean that the contract is voidable (unless the other party fraudulently induced the person to become intoxicated). Problems often arise in determining whether a party was drunk enough to avoid legal duties. Many courts will not inquire into the intoxicated party's mental state in order to determine the degree of intoxication. Instead, they look at objective indications to determine whether the contract is voidable.

The following case shows an unusual business transaction in which boasts, brags, and dares "after a few drinks" resulted in a binding sale and purchase transaction.

LUCY v. ZEHMER
Supreme Court of Appeals of
Virginia, 1954.
196 Va. 493, 84 S.E.2d 516.

BACKGROUND AND FACTS   *Lucy and Zehmer had known each other for fifteen or twenty years. For the last eight years or so, Lucy had been anxious to buy Zehmer's farm. Zehmer had always told Lucy that he was not interested in selling. One night, Lucy stopped in to visit with the Zehmers in a restaurant that they operated. Lucy said to Zehmer, "I bet you wouldn't take $50,000 for that place." Zehmer replied, "Yes, I would too; you wouldn't give fifty." Thoughout the evening the conversation returned to the sale of the farm. At the same time, the parties were drinking whiskey. Eventually, Lucy convinced Zehmer to write up an agreement for sale of the farm. Zehmer wrote the agreement on the back of a restaurant check and asked his wife to sign it. She did. When Lucy subsequently tried to enforce the agreement, Zehmer argued that he was "high as a Georgia pine" at the time and that the offer had been made in jest; ". . . two doggoned drunks bluffing to see who could talk the biggest and say the most." Lucy said that, while he felt the drinks, he was not intoxicated and, from the way Zehmer handled the transaction, did not think he was either.*

DECISION AND RATIONALE   *The agreement to sell the farm was binding, and Zehmer could not rescind. The opinion of the court was that the evidence given about the nature of the conversation, the appearance and completeness of the agreement, and the signing all tended to show that a serious business transaction and not a casual jest was intended. The court had to look into the objective meaning of the words and acts of the Zehmers. "An agreement or mutual assent is of course essential to a valid contract, but the law imputes to a person an intention corresponding to the reasonable meaning of his words and acts. If his words and acts, judged by a reasonable standard, manifest an intention to agree, it is immaterial what may be the real but unexpressed state of mind."*

Avoidance of Ratification

If a contract is held to be voidable due to a person's intoxication, that person has the option of disaffirming (avoiding) it—the same options available to a minor. Like a minor, an intoxicated person may ratify expressly or implicitly. An example of implied ratification is where a person enters into a contract while drunk and fails to disaffirm the contract within a *reasonable* time of becoming sober. Also, acts or conduct inconsistent with an intent to disaffirm will ratify the contract—for example, where the person continues to use property purchased under a voidable contract.

In addition, contracts for necessaries are voidable (as in the case of minors), but the intoxicated person is liable in quasi-contract (implied-in-law contract) for the reasonable value of the consideration received. Restitution must also be made, and the courts tend to require it more often than in the case of minors. In fact, it is usually necessary for the intoxicated person to return the full consideration before being permitted to disaffirm an executed contract. For example, a person may agree to purchase a set of encyclopedias while drunk. If the books are delivered, the purchaser can disaffirm the executed contract only by returning the encyclopedias.

The lack of contractual capacity due to intoxication while the contract is being made must be distinguished from capacity (or the lack thereof) of an alcoholic. If a contract is made while an alcoholic is sober, there is no lack of capacity.[5]

INSANE PERSONS

The contracts made by insane persons can be either void, voidable, or valid. If a person has been adjudged insane by a court of law and a guardian has been appointed, any contract made by the insane person is void—no contract at all. Only the guardian can enter into binding legal duties on behalf of the insane person.

Insane persons not so adjudged by a court may enter into *voidable* contracts if they do not know they are entering into the contracts or if they lack the mental capacity to comprehend the subject matter, nature, and consequences of the contracts. In such situations, the contracts are avoidable at the option of the insane person, although the other party does not have this option.[6]

The contract may be disaffirmed or ratified. Ratification must occur after the person is mentally competent or after a guardian is appointed and ratifies the contract. As in the case of minors and intoxicated persons, insane persons are liable in quasi-contract for the reasonable value of necessaries they receive.

A contract entered into by an insane person may also be valid. If the person understands the nature and effect of entering into a contract, the contract will be valid. Of course, here the person is not really insane and therefore has the contractual capacity to make a binding agreement.

In some circumstances, a substantial number of states refuse to allow disaffirmance of a contract entered into by an insane person. If the contract is fair and reasonable and the other party had no knowledge or reason to believe the person was insane, the contract will be enforced. However, the majority of states allow disaffirmance even here, provided the insane person restores any consideration received and makes restitution to the other party.[7]

CONVICTS

Persons convicted of a major criminal offense (a felony or treason) often lack full contractual capacity. Laws pertaining to their ability to contract vary from state to state. In some states, the convicted felon can make a valid transfer of

---

5. Olsen v. Hawkins, 90 Idaho 28, 408 P.2d 462 (1965).

6. This applies to all voidable contracts.

7. Modern courts no longer require a person to be *legally* insane to disaffirm contracts. See Ortelere v. Teachers' Retirement Bd., 25 N.Y.2d 196, 303 N.Y.S.2d 362, 250 N.E.2d 460 (1969). The court sets out what the tests for mental incompetency are.

his or her property while in prison. In other states, the convicted felon is typically under partial or total disability to contract during the period of incarceration.

ALIENS

An alien is a citizen of another country who resides in this country. Generally, aliens who are legally in this country have the same contractual rights as U.S. citizens. They may be sued and they may sue in the courts in order to enforce their contractual rights. Some states restrict the right of an alien to own real property. In virtually all cases, an enemy alien during time of war will not be able to enforce a contract, although the contract can be held in abeyance until the war is over.

MARRIED WOMEN

At common law, a married woman could not make binding contracts even if she lived apart from her husband. In other words, married women's contracts were *void* rather than voidable. Even after the death of the husband, the married woman was incapable of ratifying a previously drawn up contract because that contract was invalid from the beginning. Virtually all states have abolished common law restrictions on the contractual capacity of married women.[8] A number of restrictions do remain in certain states, although many of them will be eliminated if the Equal Rights Amendment is passed.

_____

8. These statutes are normally called Married Women's Property Acts.

QUESTIONS AND CASE PROBLEMS

1. Robertson, a minor, entered into a conditional sales agreement whereby he purchased a pickup truck from Julian Pontiac Company for the agreed price of $1,743.85. Robertson traded in a passenger car for which he was given a credit of $723.85 on the purchase price, leaving a balance of $1,020, which he agreed to pay in twenty-three monthly installments. Robertson had already paid one of the installments when the pickup truck began to experience electrical wiring difficulties. Less than a month after the purchase of the truck, Robertson turned eighteen. About two weeks later, as a result of the electrical wiring defects, the truck caught fire and was practically destroyed. Robertson refused to make any further payments under the installment agreement. Julian Pontiac Company sued Robertson for the balance of the installments. Was it able to recover? [Robertson v. King, 225 Ark. 276, 280 S.W.2d 402 (1955)]

2. Kiefer, a minor, purchased an automobile from Howe Motors, Inc. in December 1968. At the time he made the purchase, he had been living away from his parents for about six months. Several months after the purchase, Kiefer attempted to rescind the deal by returning the automobile to Howe Motors and requesting the company to return the purchase price to him. Howe Motors refused. Kiefer sued the company to recover payments made on the purchase of the automobile. Was he able to recover? [Kiefer v. Fred Howe Motors, Inc., 39 Wis.2d 20, 158 N.W.2d 288 (1968)]

3. Stuhl was an entrepreneur at age seventeen. He had flown to seven major cities, all for the purpose of entering into profitable business deals. On each trip, Stuhl flew his favorite airline, Eastern Airlines. Stuhl liked Eastern because it always took his checks, even though his checks always bounced. About five months after Stuhl's twenty-first birthday, Eastern Airlines instituted an action to collect on Stuhl's dishonored checks. The action was instituted in the state of New York, where the majority age is twenty-one. In his response to the lawsuit filed by Eastern Airlines, Stuhl disaffirmed the contract he had made with Eastern. Was Eastern able to recover? [Eastern Airlines, Inc. v. Stuhl, 65 Misc. 2d 901, 318 N.Y.S.2d 996 (1970)]

4. Pankas was the owner and operator of a hair styling boutique in downtown Pittsburgh, Pennsylvania. He had maintained his shop in the same location for a number of years and had built up a substantial clientele. In October 1962, Pankas hired Bell, who was about twenty and one-half years old at the time. Part of Bell's employment included an agreement that he would not thereafter leave Pankas's employ and work at another beauty parlor within a ten-mile radius of downtown Pittsburgh. Shortly after his twenty-first birthday, Bell left

Pankas's employ and, along with another Pankas employee, opened a beauty shop only a few blocks away from Pankas's business. In addition, Bell advertised the fact that he and his partner were former employees of Pankas. Pankas sued Bell to enjoin him from further breach of their restrictive covenant. Bell claimed that as a minor he could rescind the agreement. Was he correct? [Pankas v. Bell, 413 Pa. 494, 198 A.2d 312 (1964)]

5. Peddy and Montgomery entered into a contract under which Montgomery agreed to sell a certain parcel of her land to Peddy. At the time of the transaction, Montgomery was a resident of the state of Alabama. Alabama, by statute, prohibited married women from selling real estate without the consent of their husbands. Montgomery's husband refused to consent to the deal, and Montgomery in turn refused to transfer the land to Peddy. Montgomery claimed that because of the statute she was not obligated under the contract since the contract was invalid from the beginning. Peddy responded that the statute violated the equal protection clause of the Constitution since it treated men and women differently with no reasonable basis for the difference in treatment. Was the contract between Montgomery and Peddy void or voidable? What do you think of the Constitutional claim? [Peddy v. Montgomery, 345 So. 2d 631 (Ala. 1977)]

6. Hale, age eighteen, was employed by Ghost Canyon Ranch as a "wrangler" for the summer of 1965. Ghost Canyon Ranch was located in South Dakota, where the age of majority is twenty-one. One of Hale's duties was to drive camp children on trips. On one of these trips Hale rounded a curve on the wrong side of the road and ran into an approaching car. The accident resulted in injuries to Friedhoff, who was a passenger in the car that Hale was driving. Immediately after the accident, Hale returned to his employer all the compensation the employer had paid him and disaffirmed the employment contract. About a month later, Friedhoff sued Hale to recover for the injuries he had suffered in the accident caused by Hale. Under South Dakota's guest statute, a passenger in a car cannot sue the driver for the driver's negligence *unless:* (1) the passenger pays compensation, and (2) the driver receives some benefit from the compensation. Hale claimed that because he rescinded the contract, he *received* no compensation from the passenger. Therefore, Hale argued, the guest statute effectively prevented Friedhoff from suing him. Was this argument valid? [Friedhoff v. Engberg, 82 S.D. 522, 149 N.W.2d 759 (1967)]

7. Gordon, a minor, loved exotic animals. In fact, he loved them so much that he paid Hogue $1,150 for a pair of chinchillas. A month later, he purchased a second pair of chinchillas from Hogue, this time for $700. The chinchillas, having nothing better to do, doubled in number within a year. About a year and a half after Gordon had purchased the original chinchillas, he attempted to disaffirm both purchase contracts by returning the remaining chinchillas to Hogue. At the time he attempted to return the chinchillas, two had died due to his negligence. Hogue refused to return the purchase price. Gordon sued. By the time the case came to trial, four more of the chinchillas had died, again due to Gordon's negligence. Was Gordon able to rescind? [Hogue v. Wilkinson, 291 S.W.2d 750 (Tex.Civ.App.1956)]

8. Spaulding, a minor, was married and living with his wife and child when he entered into a contract with New England Furniture Co. for the purchase of bedroom furniture. The purchase included a three-piece bedroom set that was priced significantly higher than most other three-piece bedroom sets. After making several payments on the new furniture, Spaulding defaulted, disaffirmed his contract, and allowed the company to remove all the furniture. New England Furniture, however, refused to return the money that Spaulding had already paid. Was Spaulding able to recover these payments? [Spaulding v. New England Furniture Co., 154 Me. 330, 147 A.2d 916 (1959)]

9. Mr. Mills died in an automobile accident. Thereafter a dispute arose as to who was the intended beneficiary under an insurance contract on Mr. Mills's life. The parties to the dispute, Mrs. Mills and Mary Kopf, entered into an agreement whereby they would share the proceeds of the insurance. Later, Mary Kopf attempted to rescind the contract, claiming that she was insane at the time she made it. At trial, Kopf produced an expert witness who testified to her insanity at the time she had entered into the agreement with Mrs. Mills. Mrs. Mills also produced an expert witness who testified that Mary Kopf had been sane. Did the judge have to accept the testimony of Mary Kopf's witness over the testimony of Mrs. Mills's witness? [Mills v. Kopf, 216 Cal.App. 2d 780, 31 Cal.Rptr. 80 (1963)]

10. In 1937, Hanks entered into an agreement whereby he sold to McNeil Coal Corp. a large tract of land for coal mining. Three years later he was adjudicated insane. About a year after this, his son brought a suit on his behalf to rescind the sale of the coal mining land. To support a claim of insanity at the time the transaction was entered into, Hanks's son

introduced evidence that Hanks had grown quite ill around the year 1937, that Hanks had joined several religious cults at about that time, and that Hanks had concocted an odd medicine for the cure of horse disease that contained powdered glass and was to be poured into the animals' ears. McNeil Coal Corp. introduced the testimony of several local business-men who had had dealings with Hanks around 1937. They testified that Hanks had acted rationally at all times and that there had been nothing unusual in the way he had conducted his business affairs. Was Hanks's son able to rescind on behalf of his father? [Hanks v. McNeil Coal Corp., 114 Colo. 578, 168 P.2d 256 (1946)]

9

Contracts
Legality

In order for a contract to be enforced in court, the contract must call for the performance of a legal act. A contract is illegal if either its formation or its performance is criminal, tortious, or otherwise opposed to public policy.[1] The first part of this chapter will consider what makes a bargain illegal—when the contract is contrary to state or federal statutes and when the contract is contrary to public policy. The second part will consider the *effects* of an illegal bargain. Such contracts are often void—that is, they really are not contracts.

CONTRACTS CONTRARY TO STATUTE

Usury

Every state has statutes that set the maximum rates of interest that can be charged for different types of transactions, including ordinary loans. A lender who makes a loan at an interest rate above the lawful maximum is guilty of **usury**. The maximum rate of interest varies from state to state but is usually between 10 and 15 percent.

In order to determine the amount of interest being charged on a loan, many states require service charges, credit insurance, and "points" to be

---

1. Restatement, Contracts, Section 512.

included in the calculation. For example, suppose you are charged $60 per year to borrow $1,000. In addition, the lender charges you $15 in service charges and requires you to take out credit insurance that costs another $15. The true annual rate of interest is then 9 percent (the total of $90 in charges divided by the principal amount of $1,000). A discount from the principal amount (points) is also included in the calculation. If you receive only $970 for the $1,000 loan, you are paying $30 in points. Points are prorated over the life of the loan and then added to the other charges to determine the true rate of interest. Paying $30 in points on your loan increases the true interest rate from 9 to 12 percent.

EXCEPTIONS   Because usury statutes place a ceiling on the allowable rates of interest, exceptions have been made in order to facilitate business transactions. For example, many states exempt corporate loans from the usury laws. In addition, almost all states have adopted special statutes allowing interest rates up to 36 percent on small loans. Such high rates of interest are allowed because many borrowers simply cannot get loans at interest rates below the lawful maximum and will otherwise be forced to turn to loan sharks.

INSTALLMENT SALES   Sales made on an installment basis, generally calling for payment for goods on a monthly basis, with interest rates of 1.5 percent per month, sometimes have been exempted from usury statutes by court decision or legislative enactment. For example, purchases on a revolving credit account or purchases made with Visa or Master Charge credit cards usually call for interest payments of 1.5 percent per month on the outstanding balance. Courts have interpreted these transactions as not being "loans of money" and therefore not subject to the usury laws. Some states have passed installment sales statutes that expressly permit such practices.

The effects of a usurious loan differ from state to state. A number of states allow the lender to recover the principal of a loan along with interest up to the legal maximum. In effect, the lender is denied recovery of the excess interest. In other states the lender can recover the principal amount of the loan but not the interest. In a few states, a usurious loan is a void transaction, and the lender cannot recover _either_ the principal _or_ the interest.

Gambling

In general, wagers, lotteries, and games of chance are illegal. All states have statutes that regulate gambling—defined as any scheme for the distribution of property by chance, among persons who have paid a valuable consideration for the opportunity to receive the property.[2] Gambling is the creation of risk for the purpose of assuming it. A few states do permit gambling as long as the prizes or winnings do not exceed $100 to $500.[3] In addition, a number of states have recognized the substantial revenues that can be obtained from gambling and have legalized state-operated lotteries and those for charitable purposes.

Often it is difficult to recognize a gambling contract. Suppose Adams takes out a life insurance policy on Ziegler, naming himself as beneficiary under the policy. At first blush, this may seem entirely legal; but further examination shows that Adams is simply gambling on how long Ziegler will live. In order to prevent this type of practice, insurance contracts can be entered into only by someone with an **insurable interest.** An insurable interest, discussed in Chapter 54, is a property or ownership right in the thing being insured. Adams cannot take out an insurance policy on Ziegler's home or auto because Adams does not have an insurable interest in Ziegler's property. But if Adams has a mortgage on Ziegler's house, he can take out an insurance policy because he has a property interest in the house.

Futures contracts, or contracts for the future purchase or sale of commodities such as

2.   See Wishing Well Club v. Akron, 112 N.E.2d 41 (1951).
3.   Iowa and Florida are two such states.

corn and wheat, are not illegal gambling contracts. It might appear that a person selling a futures contract is essentially gambling on the price of the commodity. However, since the seller can purchase the commodity elsewhere and deliver the commodity as required in the futures contract, courts have upheld the legality of such contracts.

Sunday Laws

Statutes in some states prohibit the formation or performance of certain contracts on a Sunday. (These are often called Sunday laws.) At common law, contracts entered into or contracts to be performed on a Sunday were illegal. The statutes today vary greatly in scope and applicability. Some make all contracts entered into on Sunday illegal. Others prohibit only the sale of merchandise, particularly alcoholic beverages, on a Sunday. (These are often called Blue laws.) A number of states have laws that forbid the carrying on of "all secular labor and business on 'The Lord's Day'." In such states, it would appear that all contracts made on a Sunday are illegal and unenforceable *as long as they remain executory.*

Exceptions to Sunday laws permit works of necessity and works of charity to be performed on Sundays. In addition, a contract entered into on a Sunday that has been fully performed (that is, an *executed* contract) cannot be rescinded or cancelled. Active enforcement of Sunday laws also varies from state to state and even among communities within a particular state. Many do not enforce the Sunday laws, and many such laws have been held to be unconstitutional.

Licensing Statutes

All states require members of certain professions or callings to obtain licenses allowing them to practice. Doctors, lawyers, real estate brokers, construction contractors, electricians, and stockbrokers are but a few of the people who must be licensed. Some licenses are obtained only after extensive schooling and examinations. Others require only that the particular person be of good moral character.

When a person enters into a contract with an unlicensed individual, the contract may or may not be enforceable. By looking at the statute itself, one can often tell if a contract is enforceable. Some statutes expressly provide that the failure to obtain a license will bar enforcement of any contracts entered into by the unlicensed individual. If the statute does not expressly state whether or not the contracts are enforceable, one must look to the underlying purpose of the licensing requirements. If the underlying purpose is to protect the public from unauthorized practitioners, then the contract will be illegal and unenforceable. For example, if you enter into a contract with an unlicensed chiropractor, the chiropractor cannot enforce the contract. The licensing of chiropractors is designed to protect the public from persons who are not capable (or who have not shown their capability) of practicing their trade. On the other hand, if the underlying purpose of the licensing statute is to raise revenues, contracts entered into with an unlicensed practitioner will be enforceable. The sanction instead will be a fine on the unlicensed practitioner.

Assume you live in a state where anybody can be a television repairman. The only requirement for a license is the payment of $15 a year. Since there are no restrictions on who can get a license, it obviously is used only to raise revenue. If Hyde has his television fixed in a reasonable manner by Jenkins and is charged a reasonable price, Hyde cannot escape his contractual liability to pay Jenkins simply because Jenkins does not have a valid license.

CONTRACTS CONTRARY TO PUBLIC POLICY

Although contracts are entered into by private parties, some are not enforceable because of the negative impact they would have on society. These contracts are said to be *contrary to public policy.* In the following case, a famous movie star is party to a most unusual suit brought to enforce an oral contract for property and support growing out of a nonmarital relationship.

MARVIN v. MARVIN
Supreme Court of California,
1976.
18 Cal.3d 660, 134 Cal.Rptr. 815,
557 P.2d 106.

BACKGROUND AND FACTS *Michelle Marvin and Lee Marvin lived together for seven years without benefit of marriage. Michelle claimed that she was entitled to half the property that was acquired in Lee's name during that period. She based her claim on an oral agreement between them.*

DECISION AND RATIONALE *Assuming that the oral agreement was in fact made, Michelle could recover only if the agreement were supported by consideration. If the agreement explicitly rested on sexual services, it would be unenforceable since meretricious sexual services are immoral and violate public policy. A promise to perform homemaking services, however, would be lawful and adequate consideration for a contract. In the opinion of the court: "The fact that a man and woman live together without marriage, and engage in a sexual relationship, does not in itself invalidate agreements between them relating to their earnings, property, or expenses. Neither is such an agreement invalid merely because the parties may have contemplated the creation or continuation of a nonmarital relationship when they entered into it. Agreements between nonmarital partners fail only to the extent that they rest upon a consideration of meretricious sexual services."*

Contracts in Restraint of Trade

An example of contracts that adversely affect the public are contracts in restraint of trade. Public policy favors competition in the economy. Contracts in restraint of trade usually violate one or more federal statutes.[4] However, prior to the adoption of these federal statutes, case law prohibiting certain contracts that had the effect of restraining trade had developed.

AGREEMENTS NOT TO COMPETE *Agreements not to compete* are often contained in contracts for the sale of an ongoing business. The seller agrees not to open up a new store within a certain geographical area surrounding the old store. When agreements not to compete are accompanied by the sale of an ongoing business, the agreements are usually upheld as legal if they are "reasonable." The seller has built up an established clientele, and the buyer

pays for this goodwill or reputation when purchasing the ongoing business. Thus the seller should not be able to open up a similar business right down the block and draw away the buyer's customers.

If the agreement not to compete is made without an accompanying sales agreement, it is void. When no business is being sold, there is no reason for a person to agree not to compete in a certain geographical area. Such an agreement tends to restrain trade and is contrary to public policy.

Even when ancillary to a primary agreement, agreements not to compete can be contrary to public policy if they are unreasonably broad or restrictive. Suppose Orian Capital sells its San Francisco loan and finance business to Bankers Life Company. If Orian Capital agrees not to open another business in the whole state of California, the agreement not to compete is unreasonably broad. After all, the threat of losing customers to Orian is not very severe in San Diego. On the other hand, if the agreement covers only the San Francisco Bay area, it will probably be upheld.

---

4. Some of these statutes are the Sherman Antitrust Act, the Clayton Act, and the Federal Trade Commission Act. Antitrust and contracts in restraint of trade are fully discussed in Chapters 50 and 51.

Ancillary agreements not to compete can also be held contrary to public policy if they last for an unreasonably long period of time. In the above example, if Orian agrees not to compete for a hundred years, the contract will be contrary to public policy. On the other hand, a five-year agreement is reasonable and enforceable.

Agreements not to compete can be ancillary to employment contracts. It is common for many middle and upper level management personnel to agree not to work for competitors or not to start a new business for a specified period of time after terminating employment. If such an agreement is not ancillary to an employment contract, it is illegal. If ancillary, it is legal if it is not excessive in scope or duration. (The courts are reluctant to enforce these contracts, however.)

RESALE PRICE MAINTENANCE AGREE-MENTS Another contract in restraint of trade is the resale price maintenance contract between a manufacturer and a dealer or a set of dealers. The dealer or dealers agree not to sell a product at a price below some specified minimum, thereby assuring a certain price level for the product. Between 1937 and 1977, manufacturers could require resale price maintenance on the part of dealers throughout the country (subject to state control). Today, however, such laws (called fair trade laws) are against public policy as expressed by federal statute. They are illegal.[5]

The reasonableness of a "restraint of trade" covenant was the subject of the court's opinion in the following case.

_____

5.   There are exceptions, however. The states can regulate the sale of alcoholic beverages in virtually any way they wish, and many have resale price maintenance for alcoholic beverages. Additionally, in certain instances, if state laws regarding resale price maintenance comply with the "state action" doctrine expressed in Parker v. Brown, 317 U.S. 341, 63 S. Ct. 307 (1942), then those laws are allowed to stand.

BACKGROUND AND FACTS *Budget Rent-A-Car is engaged in franchising operators of automobile rental businesses. Budget required Fein, a prospective franchise purchaser, to sign a standard agreement in which Fein agreed "not to enter into any daily discount automotive rental business in the western hemisphere for a period of two years" without Budget's written permission. In exchange for signing the agreement, Budget divulged confidential information regarding its operating techniques. Fein did not take over a Budget franchise, but later did take over a competing franchise. Budget brought action to enforce the agreement.*

DECISION AND RATIONALE *The agreement was unenforceable. Fein's "covenant not to compete" was in restraint of trade and against public policy because it was not reasonably necessary to protect Budget's legitimate business interests. "Before the law will foreclose economic opportunity to an individual for a long period of time because of a covenant exacted as a prelude to the consideration of whether a new relationship is to come into being, it is obvious that what is to be revealed has to be something which is of demonstrable value and deserving of protection. *** Nothing in this record met that test. *** Obviously this [covenant] has an anti-competitive effect since anyone talking to Budget is nailed down for two years—anywhere in the western hemisphere. Business necessities justifying such a consequence are not revealed in this record."*

BUDGET RENT-A-CAR CORPORATION OF AMERICA v. FEIN
United States Court of Appeals, Fifth Circuit, 1965.
342 F. 2d 509.

Unconscionable Contracts and Exculpatory Clauses

Ordinarily, a court will not look at the fairness or equity of a contract. Persons are assumed to be reasonably intelligent, and the courts will not come to their aid just because they have made an unwise or foolish bargain. In certain circumstances, however, bargains are so oppressive that the courts will relieve innocent parties of their duties. Such bargains are called **unconscionable contracts**.

Contracts attempting to absolve parties of negligence are often held to be unconscionable. For example, suppose Jones and Laughlin Steel Company hires a laborer and has him sign a contract stating:

Said employee hereby agrees with employer, in consideration of such employment, that he will take upon himself all risks incident to his position and will in no case hold the company liable for any injury or damage he may sustain, in his person or otherwise, by accidents or injuries in the factory, or which may result from defective machinery or carelessness or misconduct of himself or any other employee in service of the employer.

Such clauses, called **exculpatory clauses**, are defined as clauses that have one party free the other party of all liability in the event of monetary or physical injury no matter who is at fault. This contract provision attempts to remove Jones and Laughlin's potential liability for injuries occurring to the employee, and it can be contrary to public policy.[6]

Contracts entered into because of one party's vastly superior bargaining power are sometimes held to be unconscionable. For example, if every auto manufacturer inserts an exculpatory clause (a clause freeing the manufacturer from liability for personal or monetary damage) in contracts for the sale of autos,

consumers will have no chance to bargain for the elimination of the clause. Essentially, the consumer can take it or leave it. In order to combat such clauses, courts have recently held them to be unconscionable.[7] The consumer has no choice, so the contract is contrary to public policy.

Both the Uniform Commercial Code (UCC) and the Uniform Consumer Credit Code (UCCC) have embodied the unconscionability concept—the former with regard to the sale of goods[8] and the latter with regard to consumer loans and the waiver of rights.[9]

Contracts for the Commission of a Crime or Tort

Contracts that require either party to commit a crime are illegal. The courts will not come to the aid of someone who entered into a contract to commit a crime.[10]

In addition, contracts that require a party to commit a civil wrong or a tort are illegal. Remember that a *tort* is an act that is wrongful to another individual in a private sense, even though it may not necessarily be criminal in nature.

Contracts Injuring Public Service

Contracts that interfere with a public officer's duties are contrary to public policy. For example, contracts to pay legislators for favorable votes or judges for favorable rulings are obviously harmful to the public. Often, a fine line is drawn between lobbying efforts and

---

6. For a case with similar facts, see Little Rock & Ft. Smith Railway Company v. Eubanks, 48 Ark. 460, 3 S.W. 808 (1887).

7. See Henningsen v. Bloomfield Motors, Inc., 32 N.J. 358, 161 A. 2d 69 (1960)

8. See, for example, UCC Secs. 2-302 and 2-719.

9. See, for example, UCCC Secs. 5.108 and 1.107.

10. See, for example, McConnell v. Commonwealth Pictures Corp., 7 N.Y. 2d 465, 199 N.Y.S. 2d 483, 166 N.E.2d 494 (1960). In this famous case, the majority view and the dissent clearly showed two different ideas about illegality.

agreements to influence voting. When a lobby group provides certain factual information in order to influence the outcome of legislation, the lobby is not engaging in an illegal activity. But if the lobby enters into a contingency fee agreement, where the legislator receives a certain amount of money if a certain bill is passed or a certain contract is awarded, the agreement is illegal as contrary to public policy. In the United States, people are not entitled to buy and sell votes. Therefore, agreements having that effect are illegal.

Agreements that involve a *conflict of interest* are often illegal. Public officers cannot enter into contracts that cause conflict between the officers' duties as representatives of the people and the officers' private finances. Statutes require many public officers to liquidate their interests in private businesses before serving as elected representatives. Other statutes merely require them to put their businesses in blind trusts, so that private and public responsibilities remain separate.

Suppose Ladd is a county official in charge of selecting land for the building of a new courthouse. He makes a contract for the state to buy land that he happens to own. This is a conflict of interest. If the state discovers later that Ladd owned the land, it can normally use this information to show a conflict of interest and to void the contract.

Agreements Obstructing Legal Process

Any agreement that intends to delay, prevent, or obstruct the legal process is illegal. For example, an agreement to pay some specified amount if a criminal prosecution is terminated is illegal. Likewise, agreements to suppress evidence in a legal proceeding or to commit fraud upon a court are illegal. Tampering with a jury by offering jurors money in exchange for their votes is illegal.

In a trial, most witnesses (except expert witnesses) are paid a flat fee to compensate them for their expenses. Offering to pay one witness more than another is contrary to public policy, since the extra payment can provide an incentive for the witness to lie.

A promise to refrain from the prosecution of a criminal offense in return for a reward is voidable because it is against public policy. A reward given under the threat of arrest or prosecution is also voidable. In the following situation, in order to cover up an embezzlement, a promissory note was given for the amount embezzled in return for the promise that criminal prosecution would not be pursued. Such consideration was illegal and therefore insufficient to support the note. The Supreme Court of Utah explained the situation as it related to the defenses of duress and illegal consideration.

BACKGROUND AND FACTS *Frank Berryessa, son of W. F. Berryessa, misappropriated funds from his employer. A bonding company agent, acting on behalf of the employer, ordered the Berryessas to pay $2,000 in cash and sign a promissory note for $4,865.20, payable at the rate of $50 per month. In return, the bonding agent agreed that the son would not be prosecuted if both the father and son cosigned the note; otherwise the son would be prosecuted. Later, the Berryessas refused to make the monthly payments.*

DECISION AND RATIONALE *The promissory note was not enforceable. A note given in exchange for a promise to refrain from criminal prosecution is void as against public policy. Such a promise constitutes illegal consideration. According to the court, "It is well settled that a note given to suppress a criminal prosecution is against public policy and is not enforceable between the parties."*

GREAT AMERICAN
INDEMNITY CO. v.
BERRYESSA
Supreme Court of Utah, 1952.
122 Utah 243, 248 P.2d 367.

FORUM SELECTION AND ARBITRATION CLAUSES Agreements that do not obstruct the legal process include agreements for the preselection of a forum or agreements for the arbitration of a dispute. *Forum selection clauses* are often contained in contracts where the parties are large multinational firms. For example, a contract for the sale of construction machinery made between a French corporation and a Colombian corporation can provide for the resolution of disputes in London, England. Agreements to preselect a forum are usually upheld unless they are designed to discourage litigation (for example, where a consumer in Florida buys an auto from General Motors Corp. and the contract contains a forum selection clause requiring any lawsuit to be brought in Detroit, Michigan).

Arbitration is the negotiation of a dispute before a certain panel of arbitrators. Both sides present their stories, and the arbitrator makes the decision. Essentially, arbitration is similar to a trial, although formal rules of pleading, discovery, and evidence are not recognized. After arbitration, the losing party usually can appeal the arbitrator's decision to a court of law. **Arbitration clauses** (clauses in the contract calling for the settlement of disputes through arbitration) are generally upheld today, although courts previously invalidated such clauses as interfering with the jurisdiction of the court.

Discriminatory Contracts

Contracts providing that parties must discriminate in terms of color, race, religion, national origin, or sex are contrary to statute and contrary to public policy.[11] A contract stating that a property owner will not sell the property to a member of a particular race is unenforceable. Public policy underlying these prohibitions is very strong. People should be treated equally, and the courts are quick to invalidate discriminatory contracts.

EFFECT OF ILLEGALITY

In general, an illegal contract is void. That is, the contract is deemed never to have existed, and the courts will not aid either party. This holds true whether the contract is executory or executed. Suppose Sonatrach, Algeria's national oil company, contracts to sell oil to Tenneco. Algeria has a law that prohibits the export of oil without government approval. Therefore, the contract is illegal and unenforceable. If Tenneco sues to enforce delivery of the oil, the suit will be dismissed since the contract is void. Even if Tenneco has paid for some of the oil, the contract cannot be enforced. Tenneco cannot even get back the money it paid under the illegal contract. The courts take a hands off attitude toward illegal contracts in order to discourage future illegality. Under certain circumstances, however, an illegal contract can be enforced.

Severable Contracts

If a contract is severable into legal and illegal portions, and the illegal portion does not go to the essence of the bargain, the legal portion can be enforced.[12] A *severable contract* consists of distinct parts, performance of which can be accomplished in installments, with separate consideration provided for each portion.

Suppose Norman Harrington contracts to buy ten pounds of bluegrass seed for $25 and five gallons of herbicide for $30. At the time, Harrington does not know that the Food and Drug Administration has banned sale of the herbicide and that the contract for its sale is therefore illegal. Here, the contract is severable because a separate consideration was stated for the bluegrass seed ($25) and the herbicide ($30). Therefore, the portion of the contract for the sale of bluegrass seed is enforceable; the other portion is not.

11. Federal Civil Rights Act of 1964; 42 U.S.C.A., Sec. 2000, et seq.
12. Restatement, Contracts, Section 606.

QUESTIONS AND CASE PROBLEMS

1. During the time that Mr. and Mrs. Littlewood were legally married, Mr. Littlewood agreed to marry Millard. Millard did not know that Mr. Littlewood was married. Thereafter Mr. Littlewood informed Millard that he was married, and refused to keep his promise to marry her. Millard brought a suit for breach of contract against Mr. Littlewood, claiming as damages that she had not married another man since she believed that she would marry Mr. Littlewood. Could she collect damages? [Millard v. Littlewood, 5 Exchq. 755 (Eng.)]

2. In October 1928, Laude Sells entered into an agreement with her two sons to sell the Food Machinery Company, a family-owned business, to her sons, Augden Miller and Neil Sells. The main business of Food Machinery Company was the manufacture of corn husking machines. Part of the agreement between Mrs. Sells and her sons obligated the new owners to pay her $25 for each corn husking machine sold during her lifetime. Upon her death the same royalties were to be paid thereafter to her daughter, Dorothy, provided that she (Dorothy) did not remarry. About a year before Mrs. Sells's death, Dorothy remarried. Upon Mrs. Sells's death, the company refused to pay any royalties to Dorothy, since she had violated the remarriage clause of the agreement. Dorothy sued to have the agreement enforced. Was she able to recover? [Shackleton v. Food Machinery and Chemical Corp., 166 F.Supp. 636, C.D.Ill. (1958)]

3. Williams, a woman of limited education who was separated from her husband and living on welfare, entered into a series of installment contracts with Walker-Thomas Furniture Company. During the period 1957 to 1962 she purchased various items from Walker-Thomas, including curtains, rugs, chairs, mattresses, a washing machine, and a stereo set. With each purchase, she paid part in cash and signed an installment agreement for the balance. Included in the installment agreement was a paragraph, in extremely fine print, that provided that payments, after the first purchase, were to be prorated on all purchases then outstanding. In other words, each time Williams made an additional purchase from Walker-Thomas under an installment agreement, her payments were credited against the total of all outstanding installment purchases from the company. This had the effect of keeping a balance due on every item until the total bill was paid. Prior to her final purchase, Williams had reduced her outstanding balance to $164. The last purchase, a stereo, increased her balance due to $678. After making several more payments, Williams defaulted. Walker-Thomas attempted to enforce the installment provision allowing it to repossess all the goods previously purchased by Williams. Was this contract enforceable? [Williams v. Walker-Thomas Furniture Company, 198 A.2d 914 (D.C.App.1964)]

4. In 1970, Overbeck received a Sears credit card. In 1974, he charged several purchases on the credit card. If Overbeck had paid for each purchase within thirty days, no service charge would have been added to the outstanding balance. But he chose to let the account "revolve." Therefore, under the credit card agreement between Overbeck and Sears, a service charge of 1.5 percent (18 percent annually) was added each month. Overbeck claimed that the 18 percent annual interest was usurious and contrary to the laws of Indiana that set the maximum legal rate at 6 percent. Was Overbeck correct? [Overbeck v. Sears, Roebuck and Company, Ind. App. , 349 N.E.2d 286 (1976)]

5. In 1963, the Interstate Commerce Commission issued an order increasing the rates charged by railroad grain shippers by about 16 percent. Southern Railway Company, whose business was primarily dependent on grain shipping, stood to lose millions of dollars if the order were enforced. Southern Railway hired Troutman, an attorney, to fight the order. It knew that Troutman had little experience in Interstate Commerce Commission matters, but it hired him because of his political connections with President John F. Kennedy. Southern Railway anticipated that Troutman could use his influence to gain access to the president and persuade him to use his power to stop enforcement of the ICC's order. Troutman prevented the rate increase, but when he attempted to recover a legal fee, Southern Railway refused to pay. Was the contract between Troutman and Southern Railway in violation of public policy? [Troutman v. Southern Railway Company, 441 F.2d 586 (5th Cir. 1971)]

6. Mr. and Mrs. Fong entered into an agreement with Miller, who owned and operated a bar and restaurant known as The Gate Inn. Under the contract, the Fongs agreed to manage the restaurant for a five-year period in return for all the profits from the

restaurant plus a percentage of profits derived from certain "amusement machines" located near the bar. Essentially, these amusement machines were gambling devices. Gambling was illegal under California law. Shortly after the agreement was made, a dispute arose between Miller and the Fongs. Thereafter, Miller refused to allow the Fongs to operate the restaurant or to collect revenues under the agreement. Could the Fongs enforce this agreement? [Fong v. Miller, 105 Cal.App. 2d 411, 233 P.2d 606 (1951)]

7. Ferguson and Coleman entered into an agreement for the sale of land to be used for growing cotton. The agreement stated two alternative prices. The land was to be sold for $900 "if cotton should rise to 8¢ by the first of November . . ." If cotton did not rise to the price of 8¢, the selling price was to be $500. Before the first of November, cotton rose to 8½¢, but Coleman refused to pay $900 for the land. Was this an illegal gambling contract? Do you see any possible usury here? What if the contract had read: "Price of the land $500 if Russia lands a man on the moon by the first of November, otherwise price $900"? [Ferguson v. Coleman, 3 Rich. 99, 45 Am.Dec. 761.]

8. Roeber and Diamond Match Company were both engaged in the business of manufacturing matches. Diamond desired to purchase Roeber's business, which was quite lucrative and essentially national in scope. Pursuant to the sale agreement between Diamond and Roeber, Roeber agreed not to engage in the match business in any state in the United States other than Nevada and Montana for ninety-nine years. Was the contract enforceable? [Diamond Match Company v. Roeber, 106 N.Y. 473, 13 N.E. 419 (1801)]

9. Riggs Realty entered into a contract with Zalis to pay Zalis a finder's fee of $15,000 for Zalis's services in seeking a buyer for certain farmland. Riggs had received a $45,000 commission on the sale. Thereafter, Riggs refused to pay Zalis his finder's fee, claiming that since Zalis was acting as a real estate broker without a broker's license the contract was unenforceable. Could Zalis collect his finder's fee? [Zalis v. Blumenthal, 254 Md. 265, 254 A.2d 692 (1969)]

10. The Constitution provides for the separation of church and state. The government can in no way support or affiliate itself with any particular religion or group of religions. (Note that across-the-board legislation, such as tax exemptions for religious organizations, is not prohibited by this constitutional provision) Illinois enacted a law requiring all non-food retailers to remain closed on Sunday. A local retailer challenged the law as a violation of the constitutional provision calling for separation of church and state. Do you think such a "Sunday closing law" is unconstitutional?

10

Contracts
Genuineness of Assent

When there is no *genuine assent* to the terms of a contract because of the existence of a mistake, fraud, undue influence, or duress, the contract is voidable. The innocent party is able to rescind the contract and avoid the legal obligations it imposes.

MISTAKE

It is important to distinguish between mistakes *as to facts* and mistakes *in judgment as to value or quality*. Only the former have legal significance. Suppose Jane Simpson plans to buy ten acres of land in Montana. If she believes the land is worth $10,000, and it is worth only $4,000, her mistake is one of value or quality. However, if she believes the land is the ten acres owned by the Boyds of Helena, and it is actually the ten acres owned by the Deweys, her mistake is one of fact. Only a mistake as to fact allows a contract to be avoided.

Mistakes occur in two forms—*unilateral* and *mutual* or *bilateral*. A unilateral mistake is made by only one of the contracting parties; a mutual mistake is made by both.

Unilateral Mistake

A unilateral mistake involves some *material fact* that is important to the consideration of the contract. If the party had not made the mistake, the

113

contract would probably not have been formed. However, in general, a unilateral mistake does not afford the mistaken party any right to relief from the contract.[1] According to the objective theory of contracts, the subjective intent of the contracting parties is irrelevant. If a party mistakenly believes something a reasonable person would not believe, the contract is enforceable, except when the other party knows or should have known of the mistake.

For example, Odell Construction Co. made a bid to install the plumbing in a proposed apartment building. When Herbert Odell, the president, added up his costs, his secretary forgot to give him the figures for the pipe fittings. Because of the omission, Odell's bid was $6,500 below that of the other bidders. The prime contractor, Sunspan Inc., accepted Odell's bid. If Sunspan was not aware of Odell's mistake or could not reasonably have been aware of it, the contract would be enforceable, and Odell would be required to install the plumbing at the bid price. However, if Odell's secretary had mentioned her error to Sunspan, the contract could be rescinded because Sun-

span would have known of the mistake. Similarly, if Odell's bid was so far below the others' that, as a contractor, Sunspan should reasonably have known of a mistake, the contract could be rescinded. Sunspan would not be allowed to accept the offer knowing it was made by mistake.[2] The law of contracts protects only *reasonable* expectations.

Mutual Mistakes of Material Fact

When both parties are mistaken as to a material fact, the contract can be rescinded by either party.[3] The mistake must be about a material fact—that is, a fact that is important and central to the contract.

The classic case on mutual mistake of fact involved a ship named "Peerless" that was to sail from Bombay with certain cotton goods on board. However, more than one ship named "Peerless" sailed from Bombay that winter. The mistake was mutual, and it was about a material fact.

1. Restatement, Contracts, Section 503.

2. Peerless Glass Co. v. Pacific Crockery Co., 121 Cal. 641, 54 P. 101 (1898).
3. Restatement, Contracts, Section 502.

RAFFLES v. WICHELHAUS AND ANOTHER
2 H. & C. 908, 1864.

BACKGROUND AND FACTS *Wichelhaus purchased a shipment of cotton from Raffles "to arrive ex 'Peerless' from Bombay." Wichelhaus meant a ship called the Peerless sailing from Bombay in October. Raffles meant another ship called the Peerless sailing from Bombay in December. When the goods arrived on the December Peerless, Raffles delivered them to Wichelhaus. However, by that time, Wichelhaus was no longer willing to accept them.*

DECISION AND RATIONALE *Since the mistake was a mutual one— that is, one based on reasonable assumptions made by both parties—there was no contract. When both parties have contracted under the mistaken, but reasonable, belief that a certain fact is true from an objective viewpoint, neither will be bound by the contracts. The British court hearing the case stated, "There is nothing on the face of the contract to show that any particular ship called the 'Peerless' was meant."*

Two Common Types of Mutual Mistakes

A mutual mistake as to some incidental aspect of the contract does not entitle the parties to

rescission (cancellation) or reformation (a rewording of the contract). Mutual mistakes usually occur in two types of cases. In the first, the parties erroneously believe the contract can be performed when it actually cannot. For example, suppose Adams contracts to buy Bender's race horse, and the night before the sale, unknown to either, the horse dies. Since both parties mistakenly assumed the horse would be alive, either can rescind the contract.

The second type of mistake usually involves the identity of the subject matter of the contract. For example, suppose you are the purchasing agent for Estner Cosmetics. You visit Sandra Imports one day and see four boxes marked No. 4 Red Dye. You ask Sandra to ship them to your plant. However, when they arrive, you discover that blue dye has been delivered in red dye boxes. Since both you and Sandra Imports believed that the boxes contained red dye, the contract can be rescinded or reformed.

Distinguish carefully between a mistake in identity and a mistake in value. Suppose Daniel Murray looks at Beverly Beale's violin and buys it for $250. Later, Murray discovers that the violin is a Stradivarius, built in 1717. Here there is no mistake that will warrant rescission or reformation. Both parties knew what the subject matter of the contract was — the violin that Murray had seen. Both Murray and Beale mistook the value of that particular violin. Therefore, the contract cannot be rescinded.

Modern courts still apply the "Peerless" theory of mutual mistake in evaluating whether or not a contract exists. In the following case, the court applied the mutual mistake doctrine to a situation where a contract was cancelled and the cancellation accepted on the basis of a mutual mistake of fact.

BACKGROUND AND FACTS *Christine Boyd was beneficiary of a policy issued by Aetna Life Insurance Company that provided for payment in the event of her husband's permanent total disability. Although the couple had been separated for a while, Mrs. Boyd continued to pay the premiums. Later, she stopped paying the premiums and surrendered the policy. At that time, she did not know the whereabouts of her husband. Mrs. Boyd subsequently learned that her husband had become disabled six months before she had surrendered the policy. She then asked the court to rescind her surrender agreement with Aetna.*

BOYD v. AETNA LIFE INSURANCE CO.
Appellate Court of Illinois,
Fourth District, 1941.
310 Ill.App. 547, 35 N.E.2d 99.

DECISION AND RATIONALE *As a matter of equity, the surrender agreement had to be rescinded. Had Mrs. Boyd known the true facts at the time she surrendered the policy, she certainly would not have done so. Since her mistaken belief (that her husband was not disabled at the time) was a material mistake of fact, which was not a result of her neglect, her rescision was not effective. In the opinion of the court, "The supposed elements of doubt as to the health of Boyd never entered into the contemplation of either party, nor did it form any part of the consideration for the cancellation and surrender of the policy."*

FRAUD

The five elements of *fraud* are: (1) a *misrepresentation* of *material* facts, (2) the misrepresenting party's *knowledge* that the facts are false, (3) an *intent* to deceive, (4) the innocent party's justifiable *reliance* on the misrepresentation, and (5) *injury* to the innocent party.

When a party consents to a contract with fraudulent terms, the contract can be voided because the party has not voluntarily consented to its terms.[4] In addition, fraud entitles the innocent party to recover damages caused by

---

4. Restatement, Contracts, Section 476; when there is fraud in the execution of the contract, it is void.

the fraud. The party can either rescind the contract and be restored to his or her original position or can enforce the contract and seek damages for any injury incurred from the fraud.

Today, courts find fraud more easily. Also, government standards of fraud, such as those used by the Federal Trade Commission in its litigation, are much less stringent than those of the common law.

Misrepresentation

In order to prove fraud, the innocent party must first show that a past or present fact has been misrepresented. The misrepresentation can be words or actions. For example, the statement "This sculpture was made by Michelangelo" is an express misrepresentation of fact if the statue was made by a local artisan.

Suppose Quid contracts to buy a horse from Ray. The horse is blind in one eye, but when Ray shows the horse, he skillfully keeps its head turned so that Quid does not see the defect. The concealment constitutes fraud because of Ray's *conduct*. Likewise, if a salesperson shows a sample from the top of a large box, but does not show the inferior samples at the bottom, a misrepresentation *by conduct* has occurred if there is a marked difference in quality between the top and the bottom.

Representations of future facts (predictions) or statements of opinion are generally not subject to a claim of fraud. Every person must exercise care and judgment when entering into contracts, and the law will not come to the aid of one who simply makes an unwise bargain. For example, statements that "This land will be worth twice as much next year" or "This car will last for years and years" are statements of opinion, not fact. Hence, contracting parties should recognize them as such and not rely on them. An opinion is usually subject to contrary or conflicting views; a fact is objective and verifiable.

In certain cases, however, opinions as to value may entitle the innocent party to rescission or reformation. These cases always involve some sort of "expert" giving a naive purchaser some opinion, and they are decided on equitable grounds. The courts usually hold it to be unfair to allow an expert to take advantage of a novice, especially if the expert knows the novice is relying on the expert's opinion.

VOKES v. ARTHUR MURRAY, INC.

District Court of Appeal of Florida, Second District, 1968.
212 So.2d 906.

BACKGROUND AND FACTS *Audrey Vokes was a fifty-one-year-old widow. While she was attending a dance party at Davenport's School of Dancing, an instructor sold her eight half-hour dance lessons for the sum of $14.50. Thereafter, over a period of less than sixteen months, she was sold a total of fourteen dance courses, which amounted to 2,302 hours of dancing lessons for a total cash outlay of $31,090.45. All these lessons were sold to her by salespersons who continually assured her that she was very talented and had a promising career in dancing. She finally attempted to terminate her contract for unused dance lessons.*

DECISION AND RATIONALE *Vokes could avoid her contractual obligations since her agreement to purchase lessons from the studio was procured by false representations that she had a promising career in dancing. To be grounds for rescision of a contract, a misrepresentation must usually be one of fact rather than opinion, but there are exceptions to the rule. "A statement of a party having *** superior knowledge may be regarded as a statement of fact although it would be considered as opinion if the parties were dealing on equal terms. It could be reasonably supposed here that defendants had 'superior knowledge' as to whether plaintiff had 'dance potential' ***."*

MISREPRESENTATION OF LAW Misrepresentation of law does not ordinarily entitle the party to relief from a contract. For example, S has a parcel of property that she is trying to sell to B. S knows that a local ordinance prohibits building anything on the property higher than three stories. Nonetheless, S tells B, "You can build a condominium fifty stories high if you want to." B buys the land and later discovers that S's statement is false. Normally B cannot avoid the contract because at common law people are assumed to know state and local law where they reside. Additionally, a layperson should not rely upon a statement made by a nonlawyer about a point of law.

Exceptions to this rule occur when the misrepresenting party pursues a profession that requires greater knowledge of the law. The courts are recognizing an increasing number of persons whose clients can expect them to know the law in their specific area of expertise. For example, real estate brokers are expected to know the law governing real estate sales, land use, and so on. If S, in the example above, were a lawyer or a real estate broker, her misrepresentation of the area's zoning status would probably constitute fraud.

CONCEALMENT AND SILENCE Ordinarily, neither party to a contract has a duty to come forward and disclose facts. Therefore, a contract cannot be set aside because certain pertinent information is not volunteered. For example, assume that General Corporation is involved in a dispute with Henderson Air Conditioning. The two companies have been doing business for ten years, but General is not satisfied with Henderson's performance on one large contract. Finally, General and Henderson enter into a settlement agreement of their differences. Henderson believes that the long-standing business relationship with General will continue after the dispute is settled. General, on the other hand, has decided to do no further business with Henderson. If Henderson does not question General about this issue,

General has no duty to make a full statement of this material fact.

Certain exceptions to this rule exist. When a defect or potential problem exists that a buyer cannot reasonably be expected to discover, the seller often has a duty to speak. When a house is infested with termites, the owner/seller is obliged to disclose this fact to potential buyers (and this is usually spelled out in real estate contracts). When the foundation of a factory is cracked, creating a potential for water damage, the seller must reveal this fact. Likewise, when a city fails to disclose to bidders subsoil conditions that will cause great expense in constructing a sewer, the city is guilty of fraud.[5]

In addition, failure to disclose important facts will constitute fraud when the parties have a relationship of trust and confidence. In such a relationship, if one party knows any facts that materially affect the other's interests, they must be disclosed. For example, an attorney has a duty to disclose material facts to a client. Other such relationships include partners in a partnership, directors of corporations and the shareholders, and guardians and wards.

Knowledge of the Fact's Falsity

The second element of fraud is knowledge (*scienter*) on the part of the misrepresenting party that facts have been falsely represented.[6] Proof of such knowledge is not limited to direct testimony, but may be *inferred* from the circumstances surrounding the transaction. For example, suppose Roper has owned a 1976 Oldsmobile for two years and suddenly, for no apparent reason, quits driving it. Roper then puts the auto up for sale. Chipper asks Roper how the engine runs, and Roper says, "This

---

5. City of Salinas v. Souza & McCue Constr. Co., 66 Cal.2d 217, 57 Cal.Rptr. 337, 424 P.2d 921 (1967).

6. Note, however, that where fraud is inferred from silence (where there is a duty to disclose) proof of this type of knowledge is irrelevant. Rather, the focus will be upon the party's knowledge of a particular defect or problem regarding the subject matter of the contract, not on the fact that there was no disclosure of the problem.

Olds runs like a Swiss watch; there's nothing wrong with it." So Chipper buys the Olds, only to discover that the engine block is cracked. Here, a court can *infer* that Roper knew the block was cracked (at least in the absence of another explanation from Roper), since he suddenly quit driving the car and put it up for sale.

Some states do not require actual knowledge of falsity, but hold that statements made with a reckless disregard for the truth will satisfy the knowledge requirement. [7] For example, a salesman who tells a customer, "This air conditioner will cool your whole house," without knowing the size of the customer's house, is acting with reckless disregard. A real estate broker who assures a customer that a particular house is insulated, when the broker does not know if it is insulated or not, is acting with reckless disregard.

An Intent to Deceive

The third element of fraud is an intent to deceive. Since this intent is very difficult to prove directly, circumstances surrounding the transaction are usually used *to infer* the intent. Often, courts combine this element with the second element of fraud, knowledgeable misrepresentation, and conclude that the act of misrepresentation combined with the knowledge of its falsity constitute an intent to deceive.

INNOCENT MISREPRESENTATION   If a person makes a statement honestly, and it misrepresents material facts, that person is guilty not of fraud, but only of an *innocent misrepresentation*. When an innocent misrepresentation occurs, the aggrieved party can rescind the contract but usually cannot seek damages caused by the misrepresentation (because there was indeed a lack of knowledge).

Reliance on the Misrepresentation

Another element of fraud is reasonably *justified reliance* on the misrepresentation of fact. The

reliance must be justified but need not be the only reason for entering into the contract. As long as the innocent party relies on the misrepresentation, and the misrepresentation is a major factor inducing the party to enter into the contract, the requirement of reliance will be satisfied.

Reliance is not justified if the innocent party knows the true facts or relies on extremely extravagant statements. For example, suppose a used car dealer tells you, "This old Cadillac will get fifty miles to the gallon." You would not normally be justified in relying on the statement. Or suppose Phelps, a bank director, induces Scott, a co-director, into signing a guarantee that the bank's assets will satisfy its liabilities, stating, "We have plenty of assets to satisfy our creditors." If Scott knows the true facts he will not be justified in relying on Phelps's statement. However, if Scott does not know the true facts and has no way of finding them out, he will be justified in relying on the statement. The same rule applies to defects in property sold. If the defects are obvious, the buyer cannot justifiably rely on the seller's representations. If the defects are hidden or latent, however, the buyer can rely on the seller's statements.

Injury to the Innocent Party

The final element of fraud is injury to the innocent party. The courts are divided on this issue, and some do not require a showing of injury when the action is to rescind or cancel the contract. Since rescission returns the parties to the position they were in prior to the contract, showing injury to the innocent party has been held to be unnecessary. [8]

In an action to recover damages caused by the fraud, proof of an injury is universally required. The measure of damages is ordinarily equal to what the value of the property would have been if it had been delivered as represented, less the actual price paid for the property. In effect, this gives the innocent (nonbreaching) party the benefit of the bargain, rather than

7.   E. g., Sanders Inc. v. Chesmotel Lodge Inc., 300 S.W.2d 239 (Ky.1957).

8.   E. g., Kaufman v. Jaffee, 244 App.Div. 344, 279 N.Y.S. 392 (1935).

reestablishing the party's position prior to the contract.

In the next case, Hazel Gales applied for auto insurance, stating falsely that she had not been in an auto accident in the past five years and had not received a ticket for a moving violation in the past three years. The defendant, Plains Insurance Co., claimed that such false representations made her policy void from the very beginning (void *ab initio*). The company contended that it would not have sold the policy at the specified rate and perhaps would not have sold it at all if Gales had provided true information about her driving record. Thus, the insurance company did not engage in a genuine assent (that is, there was no reality of consent).

BACKGROUND AND FACTS *Daizy Miller perished in an automobile crash. The owner and driver of the automobile, Hazel Gales, was insured by Plains Insurance Company. Daizy's husband claimed $500 in medical expenses and $10,000 under the uninsured motorists provision. Plains Insurance Company attempted to avoid any obligation under the insurance contract on the ground that Mrs. Gales had represented to it that she had not been in an accident in the last five years and had not had a moving violation in the last three years, when in fact these statements were not true.*

MILLER v. PLAINS INSURANCE COMPANY
Springfield Court of Appeals, Missouri 1966.
409 S.W.2d 770.

DECISION AND RATIONALE *Plains Insurance Company did not have to pay the $10,000 uninsured motorists claim or the $500 medical expense coverage because of the material misrepresentations Hazel Gales made when she filled out the insurance application. When one contracting party misrepresents facts that are material to the other, the party relying on the misrepresentations never truly assents to the contract. Judge Titus defined material as follows: "[W]hether a misrepresentation is material in an application for an automobile insurance policy, is determined by whether the fact, if stated truthfully, might reasonably have influenced the insurance company to accept or reject the risk or to have charged a different premium, and not whether the insurer was actually influenced. *** It is a well-known fact insurance companies rely on expense, loss, and other statistical data to measure differences among risks and thus ascertain rates to be charged for individual risks in accordance with standards for measuring variations in hazards."*

UNDUE INFLUENCE— FIDUCIARY RELATIONSHIPS

A contract entered into under the excessive or **undue influence** of another is voidable.[9] Undue influence arises from special kinds of relationships in which one party can greatly influence another party. Minors and elderly people are often under the influence of guardians. If the guardian induces a young or elderly ward to enter into a contract that benefits the guardian, undue influence is likely being exerted. There is no genuine assent (reality of consent) to the terms of the contract if the contract is entered into because of another's excessive influence. Undue influence can arise from a number of fiduciary or confidential relationships: attorney-client; doctor-patient; guardian-ward; parent-child; husband-wife; or trustee-beneficiary. The essential feature of undue influence is that the party being taken advantage of does

---

9. Restatement, Contracts, Section 497.

not, in reality, exercise free will in entering into a contract.

In the final analysis, to determine undue influence, the court must ask to what extent the transaction was induced by influencing a competent judgment or by dominating the mind or emotions. The weakness or dependence of the person in question will often show to what extent the persuasion from an outside influence was "unfair".

Courts often presume that in legally challenged contracts between, for example, guardians and their wards, the advantage is taken by the guardians. Thus, the guardian has to rebut this presumption in such cases. To rebut successfully, the guardian has to show that full disclosure was made to the ward, that consideration was adequate, and that the ward received independent and competent advice before completing the transaction.

In cases where the relation is one of trust and competence, such as between an attorney and a client, the dominant party (the attorney) is held to extreme or utmost good faith in dealing with the subservient party. A long-time attorney for an elderly man who induces him to sign a contract for the sale of some of his assets to a friend of the attorney at below-market prices has engineered a voidable contract. The attorney has not upheld good faith in dealing with the man.

DURESS

Assent to the terms of a contract is not genuine if one of the parties is *forced* into agreement. Recognizing this, the courts allow that party to rescind the contract. Forcing a party to enter a contract under the fear of threats is legally defined as **duress**.[10] For example, if Pirranha Loan Co. threatens to harm you or your family unless you sign a promissory note, Pirranha is guilty of using duress. In addition, threatening blackmail or extortion to induce consent to a contract constitutes duress. Duress is both a defense to the enforcement of a contract and a

ground for rescission or cancellation. Therefore, the party upon whom the duress is exerted can choose to carry out the contract or to avoid the entire transaction. (This is true in most cases in which assent is not real.)

Generally, the threatened act must be wrongful or illegal. Therefore, a husband's nagging to get a new car does not constitute duress unless he pulls a gun and demands one. Threatening civil litigation does not constitute duress, but threatening a criminal suit does. Suppose that Donovan injures Jones in an auto accident. Donovan has no automobile insurance, but she has substantial assets. Jones is willing to settle the potential claim out of court for $3,000. Donovan refuses. After much arguing, Jones loses her patience and says, "If you don't pay me $3,000 right now, I'm going to sue you for $35,000." Donovan is frightened and gives Jones a check for $3,000. Later in the day she stops payment on the check. Jones comes back to sue her for the $3,000. Donovan argues that she was the victim of duress. However, the threat of a civil suit is normally not duress.

Suppose Nelson and Dice belong to a fashionable social club. Nelson watches Dice cheating in a game of bridge and threatens to expose him unless Dice agrees to sign a contract with Nelson. In fear of being expelled from the club, Dice signs. Since Nelson's actions are wrongful, the contract is entered into under duress.

Economic need is generally not sufficient to constitute duress, even though one party exacts a very high price for an item the other party needs. However, if the party exacting the price also creates the need, duress may be found. For example, the Internal Revenue Service assessed a large tax and penalty against Sam Thompson. Thompson retained Earl Eyman to resist the assessment. The last day before the deadline for filing a reply with the Internal Revenue Service, Eyman declined to represent Thompson unless he signed a very high contingency fee agreement. The agreement was unenforceable.[11] Although Eyman had threatened

---

10. Restatement, Contracts, Section 492.

11. Thompson Crane & Trucking Co. v. Eyman, 123 Cal. App.2d 904, 267 P.2d 1043 (1954).

only to withdraw his services, something that he was legally entitled to do, he was responsible for delaying the withdrawal until the last day. Since it would have been impossible to obtain adequate representation elsewhere, Thompson was forced into either signing the contract or losing his right to challenge the IRS assessment.

ADHESION CONTRACTS AND UNCONSCIONABILITY

Modern courts are beginning to strike down terms that are dictated by one of the parties with overwhelming bargaining power. **Adhesion contracts** arise when one party forces the other party to adhere to dictated terms or go without the commodity or service in question. Adhesion contracts usually contain copious amounts of fine print disclaiming the maker's liability for everything imaginable. Standard lease forms are often called adhesion contracts. Formerly, many automobile retailers used contracts containing several pages of fine print when selling a car. In the past, nearly every company excluded liability for personal injuries suffered as a result of using the product. The average consumer, out to buy a five or six thousand dollar car, was in no position to bargain for personal injury coverage. The consumer could either go without an automobile or take the auto risking personal injury.

Standard form contracts are used by a variety of businesses and include life insurance policies, residential leases, loan agreements, and employment agency contracts. In order to avoid enforcement of the contract or of a particular clause, the aggrieved party must show substantially unequal bargaining positions and show that enforcement would be "manifestly unfair" or "oppressive."[12] If the required showing is made, the contract or particular term is deemed *unconscionable* and not enforced. Technically, unconscionability under the Uniform Commercial Code applies only to contracts for the sale of goods. Many courts, however, have broadened the concept and applied it in a number of situations. For example, provisions disclaiming liability, confessing judgment in the event of a breach, and consenting to repossession for trivial breaches have been stricken as unconscionable.

Unconscionability is not a strict legal doctrine, but it enables courts to exercise great discretion in validating or striking down particular contract provisions. As a result, some states have not adopted the appropriate Section 2-302 of the Uniform Commercial Code. In some of those states, the legislature and the courts prefer to rely on traditional notions of fraud, undue influence, and duress. In one respect, this gives certainty to contractual relationships, since parties know they will be held to the exact terms of their contracts. But on the other hand, public policy can dictate that there be some limit on the power of individuals and businesses to dictate terms of a contract. At a minimum, individuals and certain businesses should not be allowed to dictate terms to "powerless" consumers.

12.   See UCC Sec. 2-302.

QUESTIONS AND CASE PROBLEMS

1.   Jones was a salesman for Cash Register Company. Over the years he had sold cash registers to a number of retail establishments. Jones approached Townsend, a retail merchant, to sell him a cash register. Jones told Townsend that he would save the full cost of a bookkeeper and half the cost of a sales clerk if he bought a machine. Relying on this, Townsend bought the cash register. After several months, he realized that the cash register was not bringing about the savings that Jones had promised. Can Townsend rescind the agreement? [See Cash Register Co. v. Townsend Grocery Store, 137 N.C. 652, 50 S.E. 306 (1905)]

2.   Pierce's home was equipped with a four-ton York air-conditioning system that had been installed by a York distributor. When the unit began to malfunction,

Pierce contacted Walters, whom he thought was a York serviceman. Walters said that he was no longer in the air-conditioning repair business and suggested that Pierce contact a man named Lawler. Walters told Pierce that Lawler was experienced in repairing York units. Subsequently, Lawler and Pierce negotiated a price for the replacement of the condenser in Pierce's unit. Neither party ever mentioned the brand that was to be used to replace the old condenser, and Lawler installed a new condenser that was not made by York. When Pierce learned this, he demanded that Lawler replace it. Lawler refused. Can Pierce rescind? [Ouachita Air Conditioning, Inc. v. Pierce, 270 So.2d 595 (La.App.1972)]

3. Granite Management Services leased ice-making machines. Don Poag, one of Granite's leasing agents, convinced Usry to lease several Granite machines. Before Usry signed the lease agreement, Poag asked him to sign a document stating that the machines would be serviced free of charge by B Manufacturing Company throughout the lease period. Usry later signed a lease agreement that did not provide for free services. The contract did state, however, that "this contract constitutes the entire agreement between the lessor and lessee and that no representation or statement made by any representative of the lessor or the supplier not stated herein shall be binding." Shortly after Usry received the machines, they broke down and failed to work properly thereafter. Granite never supplied free services for the machines as represented by Poag. Usry discontinued payments under the lease agreement. Can Granite sue? [Granite Management Services, Inc. v. Usry, 130 Ga.App. 667, 204 S.E.2d 362 (1974)]

4. Laemmar was an employee of J. Walter Thompson Co. During the years of his employment, he purchased shares of common stock from the company. Laemmar's stock was subject to repurchase by the company if Laemmar quit. The officers and directors of the company decided to increase their control and demanded that Laemmar and several other employees sell their stock back or lose their jobs. Although Laemmar did not wish to sell his stock, he did so to keep his job. The officers and directors never made any physical threats or suggestions of physical harm to Laemmar. Several years later Laemmar instituted a lawsuit to rescind his sale of the stock. Can Laemmar rescind? [Laemmar v. J. Walter Thompson Co., 435 F.2d 680 (7th Cir. 1970)]

5. Groening wanted to purchase Opsata's home, which was located half way up the side of a small, steep hill overlooking Lake Michigan. The lake came up to the very foot of the hill. Groening, concerned about erosion of the hill and possible damage to the residence, inquired whether the proximity of the house to the lake could result in damage to the home. Opsata responded, "You don't have to have no fear; it is perfectly safe." Groening later purchased the home. Shortly after the purchase, the bottom of the hill eroded completely as a result of the waves in Lake Michigan. Groening sought to rescind the sale on the basis of fraud. Can Groening rescind? [Groening v. Opsata, 323 Mich. 73, 34 N.W.2d 560 (1948)]

6. Rollins was an inmate in the State Prison of Rhode Island. During a prison riot, several of the institution's employees were taken hostage, and a number of demands were made to improve conditions. One of the final demands was that none of the inmates, including Rollins, be prosecuted for any of the illegal acts committed during the riot. Rollins was later prosecuted for holding prison personnel hostage. Rollins claimed that he had a binding contract with the Rhode Island attorney general promising him immunity from prosecution. Is Rollins's defense valid? [State v. Rollins, 116, R.I. 528, 359 A.2d 315 (1976)].

7. Howard, an archeologist and collector of ancient Greek treasures, purchased a vase from Take It or Leave It Antique Company. Take It or Leave It told Howard that the vase had been found in the tomb of a famous Egyptian king. In reality, Take It or Leave It had purchased the vase for $2 from a local resident. Take It or Leave It sold the vase to Howard for $9,000. Howard later discovered that the vase had not in fact belonged to a famous Egyptian king but was instead the work of the famous sculptor Juan Reynaldo, whose vases sold for over $10,000. Howard seeks to rescind the sale. Must Take It or Leave It return Howard's money?

8. W & B Realty Company owned and operated an apartment building in Chicago and rented one of the apartments to O'Callaghan. O'Callaghan signed a lease with a clause relieving W & B from all liability for any injuries that O'Callaghan might sustain anywhere on the premises of the apartment area, regardless of any negligence by W & B Realty. One evening, while crossing the courtyard, O'Callaghan fell because the pavement in the courtyard had been inproperly maintained. O'Callaghan sued W & B for her injuries. W & B claimed that it was not liable because of the exculpatory clause contained in the lease. Is W & B correct? [O'Callaghan v. Waller and Beckwith Realty Co., 15 Ill.2d 436, 155 N.E.2d 545 (1958)].

Contracts
Writing and Form

I agree to mow your lawn. You agree to pay me $25. I mow your lawn. You give me $15. I threaten to sue. After all, we did have an *oral* contract. Is it enforceable? In most cases, it is, but the party seeking to enforce it must establish the existence of the contract as well as its actual terms. Naturally, when the parties have no writing or memorandum about the contract, only oral testimony can be used in court to establish the existence of the terms of the contract. The problem with oral testimony is that parties are sometimes willing to perjure themselves in order to win lawsuits. At early common law, parties to a contract were not allowed, therefore, to testify. This led to the practice of hiring third party witnesses. As early as the seventeenth century, the English recognized this practice as a problem and enacted a statute to help deal with it. The statute was known as "An Act for the Prevention of Frauds and Perjuries."[1] The act required *certain* types of contracts to be in writing and signed by the party to be charged. By requiring a writing, the act prevented unscrupulous parties from committing fraud and giving perjured testimony.

CONTRACTS THAT MUST BE IN WRITING

Today, almost every state has a Statute of Frauds, modeled after the English act. The actual name of the Statute of Frauds is misleading since it

---

1.   The English Parliament passed the act in 1677.

neither applies to fraud nor invalidates any type of contract. Rather, it denies enforceability to contracts that do not comply with its requirements. Although the statutes vary slightly from state to state, they all require the following types of contracts to be in writing or evidenced by written memorandum:[2]

1. Contracts for the sale of land or any interest in land.
2. Contracts which cannot *by their terms* be performed within one year.
3. Promises to answer for the debt or duty of another.
4. Promises by the administrator or executor of an estate to pay a debt of the estate personally.
5. Promises made in consideration of marriage.
6. Contracts for the sale of goods above a specified dollar amount.

Contracts for the Sale of Interests in Land

A contract calling for the sale of land or for the sale of any interest in land will not be enforceable unless it is in writing. Land is real property and includes all physical objects that are permanently attached to the soil. Thus, land includes buildings, crops, trees, and the soil itself. The Statute of Frauds operates as a *defense* to the enforcement of an oral contract for the sale of an interest in land. Therefore, even if *both* parties acknowledge the existence of an oral contract for the sale of land, under many circumstances the contract will still not be enforced.[3] If S contracts orally to sell Blackacre to B but later decides not to sell, B cannot enforce the contract. Likewise, if B refuses to close the deal, S cannot force B to close by bringing a lawsuit. The Statute of Frauds is a

2. Restatement, Second, Contracts (tentative draft), Section 178.
3. However, the contract will be enforced if the parties admit to the existence of the oral contract in court or admit to its existence pursuant to discovery before trial.

defense to the enforcement of this type of oral contract.[4]

It is necessary to distinguish between real property, which is property affixed to the land, and personal property. Ordinarily a contract for the sale of land involves the entire interest in the real property including buildings, growing crops, vegetation, minerals, and anything else affixed to the land. Suppose Collins Pine agrees to sell land to Seabrook. If timber is still standing on the land, the timber is part of the real property and is part of the sale. If the timber crop has been cut and is awaiting shipment to the mill, it is personal property and not included in the sale of land. A sale of the cut timber could still fall under the Statute of Frauds, however.[5]

LIFE ESTATES   The Statute of Frauds requires written contracts for the sale of an interest in land. Interests in land include life estates, real estate mortgages, easements, and leases. A **life estate** is an interest in land that lasts for a person's lifetime. For example, if Sally Manne sells Edenfarm to Mary Johnson "for life, then

4. In the majority of cases, contracts are fully performed by both parties without any problems and it does not matter if the contract is in writing. Most people in business feel a moral duty to perform contracts, and the strength of their word is sufficient to assure that the contract will be performed. However, unforeseen problems do arise, and when they do, a written contract is an absolute necessity. So in order to provide the extra reassurance, a written contract is always advisable. Even when the contract is not within the Statute of Frauds, it is wise to write down its essential terms. If problems do arise, it is much easier to settle them in court.
5. Under UCC Sec. 2-201, a contract for the sale of goods worth $500 or more must be in writing. Note that under the Uniform Commercial Code a contract for the sale of minerals or the like (including gas and oil), or a contract for the sale of a structure or its materials to be removed from realty is a contract for the sale of goods *if the items are to be severed from the land by the seller.* [UCC Sec. 2-107 (1)] Until they are severed from the land, any sales contract for them is effective only as a contract to sell. A contract for the sale of growing crops, of timber to be cut, or of other things attached to realty and capable of being removed without material harm to the land, but not described in subsection (1) is a contract for the sale of goods whether they are to be severed by the buyer or by the seller even though the items form part of the realty at the time of the contract. [UCC Sec. 2-107(2)]

after Johnson's death, to Nancy Smole," Johnson has a life estate in the farm. When Johnson dies, Smole will have a full estate in the farm— that is, she will own it entirely.[6]

MORTGAGES   A real estate **mortgage** is a conveyance of an interest in land as a security for repayment of a loan. If Nancy Smole, now full

6.   Full ownership like Nancy Smole's, is called a fee simple absolute. See Chapter 52.

owner of Edenfarm, wants to borrow money from First National Bank, First National will require collateral for the loan. By giving conditional title of Edenfarm to the bank, Smole can get the loan.[7] When Smole pays off the debt, Edenfarm will be hers once again.

7.   Technically, only in "title" states will Nancy Smole be required to convey title to First National Bank. In "lien" states, she can enter into a mortgage giving the bank a lien against the farm. Today, all the distinctions between title states and lien states have essentially been eliminated.

BACKGROUND AND FACTS   *Home Federal Savings and Loan Association loaned Lambert $672,000 for apartment construction. The loan was evidenced by a one-year note combined with a deed in trust. At about the same time, Home Federal agreed to loan Lambert $2,910,000 for further construction, but this agreement was not reduced to writing. Lambert then claimed that, since Home Federal could use the trust deed as security for further loans, it was sufficient to meet Statute of Frauds requirements. The trust deed, by its terms, expired when the amount of $672,000 was repaid.*

DECISION AND RATIONALE   *The trust deed was not sufficient to satisfy the Statute of Frauds because it became void on the repayment of $672,000 and therefore could not possibly have supported the almost $3,000,000 loan. Since the deed did not mention the additional loan agreement, it could not satisfy the Statute of Frauds.*

   "The general rule is that the memorandum, in order to satisfy the statute, must contain the essential terms of the contract, expressed with such certainty that they may be understood from the memorandum itself or some other writing to which it refers or with which it is connected, without resorting to parol evidence. A memorandum disclosing merely that a contract had been made, without showing what the contract is, is not sufficient to satisfy the requirement of the Statute of Frauds that there be a memorandum in writing of the contract."

LAMBERT v. HOME FEDERAL SAVINGS AND LOAN ASSOCIATION
Supreme Court of Tennessee, 1972.
481 S.W.2d 770.

EASEMENTS   An **easement** is a legal right to use land without owning it. Easements are created expressly and implicitly. An express easement arises when the owner of land expressly allows another person to use the land, and it must be in writing. Implied easements can arise from the past conduct of the parties. For example, when a farmer has used a certain

path to reach the back forty acres of his farm for 21 years, and the path goes across a neighbor's property, the farmer has an *implied* easement across the neighbor's property. Implied easements need not be in writing and rarely are because of the way they are created. Another example of an implied easement involves the ownership of adjacent properties by one person.

The owner establishes an apparent and permanent use of, say, a road through one property to the other. He then sells that property without specifying the easement. It is implied nonetheless.

LEASES A **lease** is a conveyance of real property for a certain period of time.[8] Most states have statutes dealing specifically with leases apart from the Statute of Frauds and exempt leases of less than one year from the writing requirements. Thus, any lease lasting more than one year must be in writing. Some states extend this period. For example, Indiana allows leases to be oral for up to three years.

Contracts That Cannot Be Performed Within One Year

Contracts that cannot, by their own terms, be performed within one year must be in writing to be enforceable. Since disputes over such contracts are unlikely to occur until some time after the contracts are made, the disputes will be too difficult to decide if the contracts are oral.

In order for a particular contract to fall into this category, it must be possible (even if highly improbable) to perform it in less than one year. If so, it is not within the Statute of Frauds and need not be in writing. Suppose Bankers Life contracts to loan $40,000 to Janet Lawrence "as long as Lawrence and Associates operates its financial consulting firm in Omaha, Nebraska." Assume further that Lawrence has just opened up the firm and plans to operate the company for at least five years. The contract is not within the one-year provision of the Statute of Frauds, for Lawrence and Associates may go out of business in less than one year. If the firm ceases operations, the loan will come to an end, and the contract will be fully performed in less than

one year. Although this is quite unlikely, it could happen, and that possibility removes the contract from the Statute of Frauds.[9] On the other hand, suppose Bankers Life agrees to loan the money to Lawrence "for a period of two years." Lawrence and Associates may go out of business in less than one year, but the terms of the contract cannot be performed in less than one year, so it is subject to the Statute of Frauds and must be in writing. Next assume that the contract states that the loan will last for two years "terminable at the end of six months subject to review of Lawrence and Associates' financial condition." Here the contract is not subject to the Statute of Frauds because, by the terms of the contract, it can be fully performed (by termination) within one year.

The one-year period begins to run the day after the contract is made.[10] Suppose Shearson, Hayden Stone, Incorporated agrees on May 31 of year one to hire Paul Simpson for the summer of year two. Performance of the contract will take place over three months. Counting from the day following May 31 until the last day of performance, it is apparent that the contract will take over one year to perform. Therefore it must be in writing.

Suppose instead that Shearson, Hayden Stone, Incorporated contracts on May 31 to hire Paul Simpson for one year, effective immediately. This contract is not subject to the Statute of Frauds (and need not be in writing) because counting from the day following May 31 until the last day of performance, it will take exactly one year to perform.

The test under the one-year rule of the Statute of Frauds is not whether an agreement is *likely* to be performed within a year from the date of making the contract but whether performance within a year is *possible*. Conversely, when performance of an oral contract is *impossible* during a one-year period, this provision of the Statute of Frauds will bar recovery.

---

8. While a lease is technically a conveyance of an interest in land, it is usually accompanied by a contract. This contract, though loosely referred to as a "lease," is not really a lease at all but merely a contract entered into pursuant to a lease.

9. See Warner v. Texas & P. Railway Co., 164 U.S. 418, 17 S.Ct. 147, 41 L.Ed. 495 (1896).

10. 2 Corbin on Contracts, Sec. 444.

BACKGROUND AND FACTS *Thomas H. Adams, Jr., a certified public accountant, was employed by the accounting firm of Wilson and Robbins. After much discussion, the two partners, Wilson and Robbins, agreed to permit Adams to purchase a one-third interest in the partnership. The purchase arrangement was oral. Under it, Adams was to pay $30,000 for the one-third interest. Of that amount, $20,000 was to be paid immediately ($10,000 to Wilson and $10,000 to Robbins) and the remaining $10,000 was to be paid from Adams's earnings from the partnership in any fiscal year that the earnings exceeded $20,000. Later Adams and Robbins formed a new partnership, and Adams refused to pay any more money to Wilson. Adams testified in court to the agreement but claimed that recovery by Wilson was barred by the Statute of Frauds.*

DECISION AND RATIONALE *The oral agreement was enforceable on two grounds. First, Adams's admission in testimony to the existence of the agreement was sufficient to satisfy the Statute of Frauds. Second, notwithstanding this testimony, the agreement satisfied the statute because by its terms it was able to be completed within a year. "[I]n view of the finding that the oral contract in regard to the deferred payment of $10,000 was conditioned on [Adams's] share of the profits from the partnership exceeding $20,000 in any one year, the contract was within the meaning of Section IV, Clause 5 of the Statute of Frauds."*

ADAMS v. WILSON
Court of Appeals of Maryland, 1971.
264 Md. 1, 284 A.2d 434.

Promises to Answer
for the Debt or Duty of Another

Promises made by one person to pay the debts or discharge the duties of another if the latter fails to perform are subject to the Statute of Frauds and must be in writing. This rule applies only if the promise is made to a creditor or obligee by one who is not presently liable for the debt in order to discharge the present or future obligations of a third party. Suppose a vice-president of European Cavenham Limited says that if Occidental Petroleum will send 40,000 barrels of crude oil to Husky Oil Company, European will pay for the oil if Husky does not. If the promise to pay is not in writing, it is not enforceable. The nature of European's liability is *secondary.* That is, European is liable only if Husky Oil does not pay. Only when the promise creates secondary liability will it fall under this section of the Statute of Frauds.

Suppose instead that Husky Oil Company has already ordered the barrels of crude oil, and European Cavenham Limited says, "We will pay your debt to Occidental Petroleum." If the agreement is oral and supported by legally sufficient consideration, it is valid.[11] In this case, European's liability is *primary.* It is obligated to Husky Oil Company to pay Husky's debt to Occidental Petroleum.

This section of the Statute of Frauds is not applicable if the primary contract is between the party making the promise and the creditor or obligee (buyer). Suppose European Cavenham Limited tells Occidental Petroleum to "send 40,000 of crude oil to Husky Oil Company and send the bill to us." Now European Cavenham Limited has entered into a contract with Occidental Petroleum with Husky Oil Company as

11. Restatement, Second, Contracts (tentative draft), Section 184.

a third party beneficiary.[12] This contract is not subject to the Statute of Frauds and therefore need not be in writing to be enforced.

Another exception to the writing requirement is a contract where the promisors' main purpose in contracting to guarantee the obligation or debt of another is to obtain a benefit. This type of contract need not be in writing.[13] Suppose the General Contracting Corp. agrees to build a home for Oswald. General Contracting subcontracts part of the work to Ace Construction Company. After several weeks, Ace

refuses to supply further labor or materials because General is in a shaky financial condition, and Ace is worried about being paid. Orally, Oswald agrees to pay General's debts if General fails to pay. Oswald's oral promise is enforceable because the primary, or main, purpose in making the guarantee was to get the house built.[14]

The promise to answer for the debt of another requires a written document under the Statute of Frauds; however, in certain circumstances such a promise is "taken out" of the statute when the promisor gains some benefit from making the promise.

---

12. See Chapter 12 for a full discussion of third party beneficiaries.
13. Restatement, Second, Contracts (tentative draft), Section 184.

14. Kampman v. Pittsburgh Contracting and Engineering Company, 316 Pa. 502, 175 A. 396 (1934).

HILL v. GRAT

Supreme Judicial Court of Massachusetts, Worcester, 1923.
247 Mass. 25, 141 N.E. 593.

BACKGROUND AND FACTS *Hill lent $400 jointly to Rubenstein and to Grat. Grat went bankrupt but made an oral agreement with Hill that if she would release Rubenstein from the $400 debt, he (Grat) would see that she was repaid. Hill thus discharged and cancelled the debt as it applied to Rubenstein. Grat then refused to pay.*

DECISION AND RATIONALE *Grat's promise was enforceable even though it was oral. A promise to pay the debt of another is within the Statute of Frauds and must be in writing; but an original promise, even though it extinguishes the debt of a third person, need not be in writing. Because Grat's debt was discharged in bankruptcy, he no longer had a duty to pay. When he promised to pay regardless of the discharge, this was an original promise. In the opinion of the court, "The agreement not being repugnant to the statute, nor barred by the discharge [in bankruptcy] can be enforced in the present action."*

Promises Made in Consideration of Marriage

A unilateral promise to pay a sum of money or to give property in consideration of a promise to marry must be in writing. If Bill MacAdams promises $10,000 to Bruce Coby if Coby promises to marry Sally MacAdams, MacAdams's promise must be in writing. The same rule applies to *prenuptial agreements* (agreements made before marriage), which define the ownership rights of each partner in the other partner's property. For example, a

prospective husband may wish to limit the amount his prospective wife could obtain if the marriage ended in divorce. Prenuptial arrangements must be in writing to be enforceable, and there must be consideration. (Some states do not require consideration—Florida, for example.)

Promises by the Administrator or Executor of an Estate to Pay the Debts of the Estate Personally

The administrator (or executor) of an estate has the duty of paying the debts of the deceased and distributing any remainder to the deceased's heirs. The administrator can contract orally on behalf of the estate. A writing is required only when the administrator promises to pay the debts of the estate personally. Suppose Edward Post (administrator) contracts with Martha Lynch for legal services. If Post contracts on behalf of the estate, an oral contract is valid, and the estate is bound to pay Lynch for her legal services. But if Post agrees to pay Lynch's legal fees personally, the contract must be in writing. Otherwise it is not enforceable, and Lynch cannot recover.

CONTRACTS FOR THE SALE OF GOODS

The Uniform Commercial Code contains several Statute of Frauds provisions that require a writing in certain circumstances. Section 2-201 contains the major provision, which generally requires a writing or memorandum for the sale of goods priced at $500 or more.[15] A writing that will satisfy the Code requirement need only state the quantity term, and that need not be stated accurately. The contract will not be enforceable, however, for any quantity greater than that set forth in the writing. In addition, the writing must be signed by the person to be charged—that is, the person who refuses to perform. Beyond these two requirements, the writing need not designate the buyer or seller, the terms of payment, or the price.

[A] contract for the sale of goods for the price of $500 or more is not enforceable by way of action or defense unless there is some writing sufficient to indicate that a contract for sale has been made between the parties and been signed by the party against whom enforcement is sought. * * * A writing is not insufficient because it omits or incorrectly states a term agreed upon but the contract is not enforceable under this paragraph beyond the quantity of goods shown in the writing. * * *

A contract which does not satisfy the requirements of subsection (1) but which is valid in other respects is enforceable * * * with respect to goods for which payment has been made and accepted or which have been received and accepted.

---

15. UCC Sec. 2-201, reads in part:

Exceptions

There are four general exceptions to the writing requirements contained in Section 2-201. First, if the buyer pays the purchase price, the contract can be enforced even though it was not originally in writing. Second, if the goods are made for a particular buyer, if they are of a type not suitable for sale to others, and if the seller has started to manufacture them or has made commitments for procuring them, then no writing is required. Third, if the seller has delivered the goods to the buyer, the contract can be enforced even though it is not in writing. Fourth, if the party admits in pleading testimony or otherwise in court that the contract was for sale, then the contract is enforceable.

PARTIAL PERFORMANCE The Statute of Frauds provides that an oral contract will be enforceable to the extent a seller accepts payment or to the extent a buyer accepts part of the goods contracted for. For example, Windblown Sailboats makes an oral contract with Sunset Sails to have Sunset make 750 sails for Windblown's new nineteen-foot Day Sailer. Windblown repudiates the agreement after the sails have been made and after two dozen have been delivered. The contract will be enforceable to the extent of the two dozen sails accepted by Windblown.

GOODS MADE SPECIALLY TO ORDER Even if the seller has not completed the manufacture of the goods, the contract is enforceable to the extent that actions have been taken. In each situation the action must be completed before the seller learns that the buyer has repudiated the oral agreement. Thus, if Sunset Sails had ordered the material and cut the sailcloth but had not begun to put the sails together, the agreement would still have been enforceable to the extent of the work performed.

RECEIPT OF CONFIRMATION Oral contracts will be enforced between merchants if, within a reasonable time, either party sends a written confirmation of the contract. The party receiving the confirmation must have knowledge of its contents, and it must satisfy the requirements of Section 2-201. Under these circumstances, the contract will be enforced unless written notice of objection is given within ten days after the confirmation is received.

ADMISSIONS   If a party to a normal contract "admits" in "pleading testimony or otherwise in court that a contract for sale was made," the contract will be enforceable. Thus, if the president of Windblown Sailboats admits under testimony that an oral agreement was made, the agreement will be enforceable.

Other Provisions

The Uniform Commercial Code has three other Statute of Frauds provisions: (1) all contracts for the sale of securities (bonds, stocks) must be in writing to be enforceable regardless of amount [UCC Sec. 8-319]; (2) security agreements under Article 9 must be in writing—see Chapter 29 [UCC Sec. 9-203]; and (3) contracts for the sale of personal property that do not fall under the other categories must be in writing if over $5,000 [UCC Sec. 1-206(1)]. This provision applies mainly to sales of intangibles, such as rights to royalties, which are not covered by the "sale of goods" provision of the Uniform Commercial Code.

SUFFICIENCY OF THE WRITING

To be safe, all contracts should be fully set forth in a writing signed by all the parties. This assures that if any problems arise concerning performance of the contract, a written agreement that can be introduced into court is available. The Statute of Frauds and the Uniform Commercial Code require only a written contract or a written memorandum signed by the party to be charged. In other words, any confirmation, invoice, sales slip, check, or telegram can constitute a writing sufficient to satisfy the Statute of Frauds.[16] The

---

16.   Remember that even if the Statute of Frauds is satisfied, the existence and terms of the contract must be proven in court.

signature need not be placed at the end of the document. It can be in the body of the writing or can even be an initial identifying the person to be charged.

Since only the party to be charged need sign the writing, one party may be able to enforce a contract, while the other party cannot. Suppose AT&T negotiates via telephone with General Electric Corp. for the purchase of radio transistors for a telecommunications satellite. AT&T decides to buy the transistors, and its vice-president of purchasing signs a confirming telegram setting forth the terms of the agreement. Here General Electric can force AT&T to buy the transistors because AT&T is the party to be charged, and AT&T has signed the memorandum. AT&T cannot, however, force General Electric (the party to be charged) to sell because General Electric has signed no writing or memorandum.

A memorandum evidencing the contract need only contain the essential terms of the contract. Under the Uniform Commercial Code, the writing need only name the quantity term and be signed by the party to be charged. Under other provisions of the Statute of Frauds, the writing must ordinarily name the parties, subject matter, consideration, and quantity. Contracts for the sale of land are exceptions. The memorandum must state the *essential* terms of the contract with sufficient clarity to allow the terms to be determined from the memo itself, without reference to any outside sources.[17]

THE PAROL EVIDENCE RULE

The **parol evidence rule** prohibits the introduction of words (parol) that contradict or vary the terms of certain written contracts. The written contract is ordinarily assumed to be the complete embodiment of the parties' agreement. Courts are reluctant to allow oral or other written evidence of prior or contemporaneous agreements that conflict with the terms of the written agreement. If courts allow contradictory oral evidence, the utility of the Statute of Frauds will be lost. Parties will once again be encour-

---

17.   Rhodes v. Wilkins, 83 N.M. 782, 498 P.2d 311 (1972).

aged to commit frauds and perjuries in order to win their lawsuits. Therefore, courts assume that all prior negotiations and oral agreements are embodied in the written contract.

Due to the rigidity of the parol evidence rule, courts make several exceptions. First, when the parties modify the written agreement orally, evidence of the modification can be introduced into court. Since courts assume all prior negotiations and oral agreements are merged in the written contract, there is no reason to forbid changes in the written contract when they occur after the writing. Second, oral evidence can be introduced in all cases to show that the contract was voidable or void (for example, induced by mistake, fraud, or misrepresentation). In this case, one of the parties was tricked into agreeing to the terms of a written contract, so oral evidence attesting to fraud should not be excluded. Courts frown upon bad faith and are quick to allow such evidence when it establishes fraud. Third, when the terms of a written contract are ambiguous, oral evidence is admissible to show the meaning of the terms.

Fourth, oral evidence is admissible when the written contract is incomplete. Here not all the essential terms are included in the writing, so courts allow oral evidence to fill in the gaps. Fifth, under the Uniform Commercial Code, oral evidence can be introduced to explain or supplement a written contract by showing a prior course of dealing or usage of trade. When buyers and sellers deal with each other over extended periods of time, certain customary practices develop. They are often overlooked when writing the contract, so courts allow the introduction of oral evidence to show how the parties have acted in the past.

The parol evidence rule applies only to an "integrated" contract, that is, one in which the parties have indicated within the terms of the writing that the writing is the complete statement of the agreement between them. When there is such an *integration clause*—often called a merger clause—in an agreement, no parol evidence of any other agreement will be permitted to vary, change, alter, or modify any of the terms or provisions of that written agreement.

BACKGROUND AND FACTS *Masterson sold his ranch to Sine but reserved a ten-year option to repurchase the ranch for the same price plus a percentage of the cost of any improvements. The sales contract did not include an integration clause. Sometime after the sale, Masterson went bankrupt. His trustee in bankruptcy wished to exercise the option clause to repurchase the ranch in order to obtain funds to satisfy Masterson's debts. The trial court refused to allow Sine to introduce extrinsic evidence showing the meaning the parties attached to the option clause, specifically, that it was personal to Masterson; that is, only Masterson, not the trustee, could exercise it. Sine appealed.*

DECISION AND RATIONALE *Evidence concerning the personal nature of the repurchase option was admissible because the agreement contained no provision that the writing embodied all of the terms that Masterson and Sine agreed to; that is, the agreement contained no integration clause.*

One of the tests used to determine whether to exclude extrinsic evidence is set forth in the UCC. The court applied it by analogy to this case: "If the additional terms are such that, if agreed upon, they would certainly have been included in the document in the view of the court, then evidence of their alleged making must be kept from the trier of fact."

MASTERSON v. SINE

Supreme Court of California, 1968.

68 Cal.2d 222, 65 Cal.Rptr. 545, 436 P.2d 561.

QUESTIONS AND
CASE PROBLEMS

1. In December 1965, Kaplin ordered 11,000 yards of madras at seventy-five cents a yard from Reich. The order was made over the telephone. On January 9, 1966, Reich sent Kaplin a bill that included a statement of the quantity that Reich had sent Kaplin. On February 18, 1966, Kaplin wrote to Reich, stating:

Replying to your letter of the 18th, please be advised that we examined a few pieces of merchandise that were billed to us against your invoice No. 10203, and found that it was not up to our standard. We are, therefore, unable to accept this shipment. * * * Very truly yours, (signed) Isador Kaplin.

Reich sued Kaplin for payment owed under the contract. Kaplin defended on the grounds that the contract was entered into over the telephone and therefore failed to meet Statute of Frauds requirements. Is Kaplin's argument convincing? [Reich v. Helen Harper, Inc., 3 UCC Rep. 1048 (1966)]
2. After lengthy discussions by its board of directors, Holiday Inn decided to build a new sixteen-story motel on Key Largo, Florida. On April 1, 1979, Holiday Inn and Lyonel Construction Company reached an oral agreement that Lyonel would build the motel according to Holiday Inn specifications. Lyonel agreed to begin work on May 15, 1979, and finish by January 1, 1980. Holiday Inn promised to pay Lyonel $200,000 for the job. Are the parties bound under this oral agreement?
3. In October 1968, Bagby entered into an oral contract with Livestock Company under which he was to sell the company 2,000 head of cattle, all to be delivered by January 15, 1969. Bagby delivered only 222 of the 2,000 head and refused to deliver any more. Can Livestock Company enforce the rest of the agreement? [Bagby Land and Cattle Company v. California Livestock Commission Company, 439 F.2d 315 (Tex.1971)]
4. Wasatch Orchard Company entered into an oral agreement with Fabian to have him sell its canned asparagus for a three year period. Wasatch agreed to pay Fabian a 2.5 percent commission on all sales he made in the East. Within six months Fabian had secured orders totaling $30,000. Thereafter, Wasatch refused to honor its oral commitment. Can Fabian sue

under the oral agreement? What, if anything, can Fabian recover? [Fabian v. Wasatch Orchard Company, 41 Utah 404, 125 P. 860 (1912)]
5. On July 26, 1955, William Rowe was admitted to General Hospital, suffering from the effects of a severe gastric hemorrhage. On the day Rowe was admitted, Rowe's son informed an agent for the hospital that his father had no financial means but that he would pay for his father's medical services. Subsequently, the son stated, "Well, we want you to do everything you can to save his life, and we don't want you to spare any expense because whatever he needs, Doctor, you go ahead and get it, and I will pay you." After Rowe was discharged from the hospital, his son refused to pay the medical bills. Can the hospital enforce the son's oral promise? [Peterson v. Rowe, 63 N.M. 135, 314 P.2d 892 (1957)]
6. Hoadley and Peck entered into the following agreement with Hayden:
We, the said Hoadley and Peck, in consideration of the said Haydens having this day conveyed to us their farm * * * have this day conveyed to the Haydens certain land and premises situated on the westerly side of North Street * * * and for additional consideration for such exchange of properties, bind ourselves and agree to make, without expense to said Haydens, the following repairs * * *: straighten up and shingle the barn on said premises; repair and paint the roof, and paint the same back of said house; and install a pump in said house.
Hayden later sued Hoadley and Peck for noncompliance with their agreement. At the trial, Hoadley and Peck attempted to show that an oral agreement had been entered into at the same time as the written agreement by which all parties agreed that repairs were not to exceed $60. Is this oral agreement admissible at trial? [Hayden v. Hoadley, 94 Vt. 345, 111 A. 343 (1920)]
7. Butler Brothers were the main contractors for a highway construction project near Minneapolis. Butler hired another contractor, Ganley Brothers, to perform some of the highway construction work. At the time the contract was formed, Ganley made several false representations to Butler. If Butler had known Ganley's statements were fraudulent, Butler would never have entered into the contract. The written contract between Butler and Ganley included the following clause: "The contractor [Butler] has examined the said contracts * * * and is not relying upon any statement made by the company in respect thereto." In light of this clause, can Butler introduce

evidence of Ganley's fraudulent misstatements at trial? [Ganley Brothers, Inc. v. Butler Brothers Building Co., 170 Minn. 373, 212 N.W. 602 (1927)]

8.   Rimshot, director of a local basketball camp, wished to increase his business by advertising his camp. He discussed with Lyal, a local printer, the possibility of Lyal printing up flyers about the camp. Rimshot told Lyal that not only did he want Lyal to print the flyers, he wanted him to distribute them to local merchants. Lyal said that he usually distributed about 20 flyers to each one and charged a small publication fee. Subsequently Lyal and Rimshot entered into a written agreement under which Lyal agreed to print 1,000 flyers for Rimshot and to "publish the same locally." Lyal printed the flyers but distributed them to only four merchants, giving 250 to each. After the poorest turnout in his basketball camp's history, Rimshot sued Lyal for breach of contract. Can he introduce parol evidence concerning Lyal's statements about how he normally distributed flyers? [See Stoops v. Smith, 100 Mass. 63, 97 Am.Dec. 76 (1868)]

9.   Washington Tent and Awning Company entered into a contract with 818 Ranch, Inc., under which Washington Tent was to manufacture and install a canopy in front of Ranch's restaurant. After Washington made the canopy, it called Ranch to set up a date for installation. Ranch told Washington that not only did it not want the canopy installed, but it had not wanted the canopy in the first place. Washington sued Ranch for payment for the canopy. At the trial, Ranch attempted to introduce evidence that the installation of the canopy depended on the approval of Ranch's landlord and that this had been discussed with Washington. Should this evidence be admitted? [Washington Tent and Awning Company v. 818 Ranch, Inc., 248 A.2d 126 (D.C.App.1968)]

10.   Ramsey Corporation, a manufacturer, entered into negotiations with Williams & Associates, architects, to design a new factory for Ramsey. After several days of negotiations, Ramsey and Williams signed a contract under which Williams promised to design the factory. The contract was brief, containing a short description of the type of plant as well as the number of offices that Ramsey wanted. Over the next several months Williams drew up plans for a new factory that would cost about $500,000. Since this was about twice what Ramsey expected to pay, Ramsey officials changed their minds and refused to compensate Williams for his plans. Williams sued Ramsey to recover for his services. Ramsey wished to defend Williams's claim on the ground that Williams had not performed the contract as agreed to by the parties. Specifically, Ramsey wanted to introduce evidence about an oral agreement made before the written contract, which said that Williams would design a building costing about $250,000. Since the building Williams had actually designed would cost $500,000, Williams had breached his contract. Can Ramsey introduce this evidence? [Williams & Associates v. Ramsey Products Corporation, 19 N.C.App. 1,198 S.E.2d 67 (1973)]

12

Contracts
Third Party Rights

Once it has been determined that a valid and legally enforceable contract exists, attention can be turned to the rights and duties of the parties to the contract. Usually, two parties promise to perform certain acts. *Third parties* have no right to enforce the promises of either of the original parties except in two special situations. The first is a *third party beneficiary contract.* Here, the rights of a third party against the promisor arise from the original contract, and the parties to the original contract make it in order to benefit the third party. The second situation is an **assignment of rights** or **delegation** of duties. Here, one of the original parties transfers contractual rights or obligations to a third party.

THIRD PARTY BENEFICIARY CONTRACTS

In Exhibit 12-1, A offers to pave B's driveway if B promises to pay C $375. A is the promisee (since she has received B's promise); B is the promisor (since she has made the promise); and C is the third party beneficiary (since she is benefiting from B's promise).

In general, the law recognizes three types of beneficiaries—creditor, donee, and incidental.[1] The courts will usually uphold B's promise if C is a creditor or donee beneficiary but not if C is an incidental beneficiary. In order to determine whether the third party beneficiary contract is valid, the intent of Promisee A in the above diagram must be examined.

---

1. Restatement, Second, Contracts (tentative draft), Section 133. This is the traditional terminology used to describe the various types of third party beneficiaries. Under the Restatement of Contracts (tentative draft), the term, "intended beneficiary" replaces "creditor beneficiary" and "donee beneficiary." However, a majority of state courts still distinguish between donee and creditor beneficiaries, so the traditional terms will be used here, too.

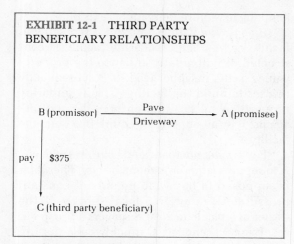

EXHIBIT 12-1   THIRD PARTY
BENEFICIARY RELATIONSHIPS

B (promissor) ———— Pave Driveway ————→ A (promisee)

pay | $375

C (third party beneficiary)

Creditor Beneficiaries

If a promisee's main purpose in making a contract is to discharge a duty he or she already owes to a third party, then the third party is a *creditor beneficiary.*[2] Suppose, for example, that several months ago, Duval Copper Company delivered 75,000 pounds of copper cathode to Pensoil Corporation. Pensoil still owes Duval $24,000, so Pensoil arranges to sell some of the copper cathode to Kennecott Copper Corp. Kennecott, in turn, agrees to pay the $24,000 purchase price to Duval. In terms of the diagram above, Pensoil (A) agrees to sell cathode to Kennecott (B) if Kennecott will pay the purchase price to Duval (C). Duval is a creditor beneficiary and can enforce payment of the $24,000 against Kennecott.

The following case is a classic illustration of third party beneficiary theory.

---

2.   Restatement, Contracts, Section 133 (1)(A).

BACKGROUND AND FACTS   *Holly owed $300 to Lawrence. At Fox's suggestion, Holly gave Fox the money, and Fox promised to take it to Lawrence to discharge Holly's debt. (Sufficient consideration was present to create a contract between Holly and Fox.) Fox failed to pay Lawrence, and Lawrence sued Fox as a third party beneficiary to the Holly-Fox contract.*

DECISION AND RATIONALE   *Lawrence could recover from Fox as a third party beneficiary of the contract between Holly and Fox. Generally, courts recognize the rights of third party beneficiaries in two situations: when the promisee intends to make a gift to a third party (donee beneficiary) and when the promisee owes a preexisting debt to the third party (creditor beneficiary). This case presents the latter situation. "In this case the defendant (Fox), upon ample consideration received from Holly, promised Holly to pay his debt to the plaintiff (Lawrence)."*

LAWRENCE v. FOX
Court of Appeals of New York,
1859. 20 N.Y. 268.

ASSUMPTION OF A MORTGAGE   The *assumption of a mortgage* is a very common type of third party beneficiary contract. Here one person buys real estate from another, and the real estate is encumbered by a mortgage. In the diagram above, suppose A is the original owner of a lawn and garden supply store. B wants to buy the store, which is subject to a mortgage held by C, City National Bank. When A and B make a contract for the sale of the store, A will agree to convey the store if B promises to pay A's debt to City National Bank. City National Bank is the creditor beneficiary of this third party beneficiary contract and can enforce payment against B.

Donee Beneficiaries

If a promisee's main purpose in making a contract is to confer a gift upon a third party, then the third party is a *donee beneficiary.*[3] A donee beneficiary can enforce the promise of a promisor (B in the diagram) just as a creditor beneficiary can. To illustrate: Suppose A goes to her attorney, B, and enters into a contract in which B promises to draft a will naming C as A's

---

3.   Restatement, Contracts, Section 133 (1)(B).

heir. C is a donee beneficiary, and if B does not prepare the will properly, C can sue B.[4] Or suppose A offers to paint B's house if B pays $750 to C. A does not owe C any money, but C is a close friend of A's, and A wants to give the money to C. Again, C is a donee beneficiary and can enforce B's promise to pay $750.

The most common third party beneficiary contract involving a donee beneficiary is a life insurance contract. A, the promisee, pays premiums to B, a life insurance company, and B promises to pay a certain amount of money upon A's death to anyone A designates as beneficiary. The beneficiary, C, is a donee beneficiary under the life insurance policy and can enforce payment against the insurance company upon A's death.

Incidental Beneficiaries

The benefit that an *incidental beneficiary* receives from a contract between A and B is unintentional. Therefore, an incidental beneficiary cannot enforce a contract against the promisor, B. Several factors must be examined to determine whether a party is an incidental beneficiary. The presence of one or more of the factors listed below strongly indicates an *intended* (rather than an incidental) benefit to the third party.

1. Performance rendered directly to the third party.
2. The rights of the third party to control the details of performance.
3. Express designation in the contract.

The following are examples of incidental beneficiaries. The third party has no rights in the contract and cannot enforce against the promisor.

1. B contracts with A to build a factory on A's land. B's plans specify that Ad Vest Company pipe fittings must be used in all plumbing. Ad Vest Company is an incidental beneficiary and cannot enforce the contract against B by at-

tempting to require B to purchase its pipe.
2. B contracts with A to build a recreational facility on A's land. Once the facility is constructed, it will greatly enhance the property values in the neighborhood. If B subsequently refuses to build the facility, C, a neighboring property owner, cannot enforce the contract against B by attempting to require B to build the facility.
3. B is a water company and contracts with city A to supply water throughout the city. The water is supposed to have 145 pounds of constant pressure. One day, in a local suburb, C, the owner of a pickle factory, discovers a fire in her receiving warehouse. C quickly calls the fire department, but because the water pressure is only 64 pounds, the fire hoses do not work correctly, and C's warehouse burns down. If C sues city A's water company, alleging that she is a third party beneficiary of the contract between the water company and the city, she will lose. She is an incidental beneficiary to the contract to supply water at a certain pressure level, so she cannot sue for breach of that contract in most courts.[5]

WHEN THE RIGHTS OF A THIRD PARTY VEST

Until the rights of a third party *vest*, the third party cannot enforce a contract against the original parties. The rights of a third party vest when the original parties cannot rescind or change the contract without the consent of the third party. Older cases distinguish between vesting in the case of a donee beneficiary and a creditor beneficiary, but modern courts no longer do so.[6]

The rights of a third party beneficiary (donee or creditor) vest (and the power of the

---

4. Lucas v. Hamm, 56 Cal.2d 583, 15 Cal.Rptr. 821, 364 P.2d 685 (1961); although the Lucas decision follows Restatement, Second, Contracts (tentative draft), it is not clear that all courts will agree.

5. The basis of liability can be in tort, and C can recover in tort, but the courts are split on this issue.
6. According to the original Restatement of Contracts as well as a number of courts (some of which make these distinctions), a donee beneficiary's rights vest immediately upon the creation of a contract, and knowledge or assent to the contract is unnecessary. Creditor beneficiaries, on the other hand, must have relied on a contract detrimentally or must bring suit upon the contract in order for their rights to vest.

original contracting parties to change, alter, or rescind the contract terminates) whenever one of the following three things happen:

1. The third party learns of and consents to the contract.[7]
2. The third party brings suit upon the contract.
3. The third party materially alters his position in detrimental reliance on the contract.

Suppose, for example, that C learns of B's intention to pay $375 to C after the driveway is paved. Before C agrees to accept the payment, however, B decides to make payment elsewhere. C's rights to the payment will not have been vested since C did not assent prior to the contract revision.

If the contract expressly reserves the right to cancel, rescind, or modify the contract, the third party takes his or her rights subject to such rights. In such a case, the vesting of the third party's rights will not terminate the power of the original contracting parties to alter their legal relationships.[8]

ASSIGNMENT OF RIGHTS AND DELEGATION OF DUTIES

Third parties can acquire rights or assume duties arising from a contract to which they were not parties. The rights are transferred to them by *assignment*. Duties are transferred by *delegation*. Assignment or delegation should be distinguished from third party beneficiary contracts. In a third party beneficiary contract, the rights of the third party arise from the original contract. Assignment, or delegation, occurs after the original contract is made, when one of the parties transfers an interest in the contract to another party.

A distinction must also be made between assignment, or delegation, and *novation* (see Chapter 13). A novation is an agreement entered into by *all* the parties whereby one party is substituted for another party. One party is completely dismissed from the contract, and another is substituted. The dismissed party is no longer liable under the original contract. In an assignment, or delegation, the original party remains liable on the contract.

Assignments

Every bilateral contract has corresponding rights and duties. One party has a *right* to require the other to perform some task, and the other has a *duty* to perform it. The transfer of rights to a third person is known as an *assignment*. When rights under a contract are assigned unconditionally, the rights of the assignor (the party making the assignment) are extinguished.[9] The third party (the assignee, or party receiving the assignment) has a right to demand performance from the other original party to the contract (the obligor, or buyer). This can best be illustrated by Exhibit 12-2.

Once A has assigned his or her rights under the original contract with B to C, C can enforce the contract against B if B fails to perform.

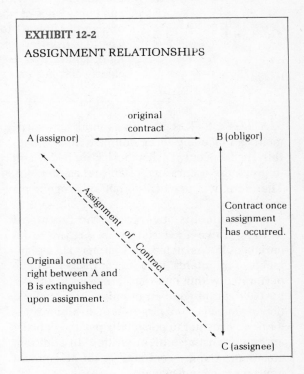

EXHIBIT 12-2

ASSIGNMENT RELATIONSHIPS

original contract

A (assignor) ←→ B (obligor)

Assignment of Contract

Contract once assignment has occurred.

Original contract right between A and B is extinguished upon assignment.

C (assignee)

---

7. Restatement, Second, Contracts (tentative draft), Section 142(3) says that the promisor and the promisee have to request assent.

8. Defenses raised against third party beneficiaries are given in Restatement, Second, Contracts (tentative draft), Section 140.

9. Restatement, Second, Contracts (tentative draft), Section 163.

NOLAN v.
WILLIAMSON MUSIC,
INC.
United States District Court,
Southern District of New York,
1969. 300 F.Supp. 1311.

BACKGROUND AND FACTS *Robert Nolan, the composer of "Tumbling Tumbleweeds," entered into an agreement with the Sam Fox Publishing Company (Sam Fox) whereby Nolan conveyed "all rights of every kind nature and description" in his song to Fox, "his successors and assigns." In consideration, Sam Fox agreed to pay Nolan certain royalties. Several years later, without formally ever notifying Nolan, Sam Fox assigned all of its rights and interest in the song to Williamson Music, Inc. In return, Williamson agreed to take on the duty of paying royalties. Nolan filed a suit to rescind the contract using as one argument that the contract was breached when Fox did not obtain Nolan's agreement to the assignment.*

DECISION AND RATIONALE *The court held that the assignment was not a breach of contract. Contracts that are personal in nature cannot be assigned without the consent of both parties, but Nolan could not show that his contract with Sam Fox involved such personal elements of trust and confidence as not to be assignable. The court found that "it was not a breach of contract for Sam Fox to assign the copyright to Williamson. The 1934 transfer from plaintiff [Nolan] to Sam Fox of 'all rights of every kind, nature and description' which plaintiff had in the copyright was clearly absolute on its face."*

STATUTE OF FRAUDS In general, an assignment can take any form, oral or written. Naturally, in the event of a dispute, it is more difficult to prove the occurrence of an oral assignment. Therefore, it is practical to put all assignments in writing.

Assignments covered by the Statute of Frauds, however, must be in writing to be enforceable. As noted in Chapter 11, assignments of an interest in land, contracts not to be performed within one year, promises to answer for the debts of another, promises in consideration of marriage, and promises of an administrator or an executor to personally pay the debts of an estate must also be in writing. In addition, most states require contracts for the assignment of wages to be in writing.[10]

CONSIDERATION An assignment need not be supported by *legally sufficient consideration* to be effective. A gratuitous assignment is just as effective as an assignment made for money.

However, the absence of consideration becomes significant when the assignor wants to revoke the assignment. If the assignment was made for consideration, the assignor cannot revoke it. If no consideration is involved, the assignor can revoke, thereby revoking the right of the third party to demand performance or to sue for failure to render that performance.[11] Gratuitous assignments can be revoked by:

1. The subsequent assignment of the same right to another third party.
2. The death of the assignor.
3. The bankruptcy of the assignor.
4. A notice of revocation given to the assignee.

WHAT RIGHTS CAN BE ASSIGNED Except in a few special situations, all rights can be assigned. If a state statute expressly prohibits assignment, the particular right in question cannot be assigned. If a contract stipulates that the rights cannot be assigned, then, ordinarily,

10. See, for example, California Labor Code Sec. 300.

11. Restatement, Second, Contracts (tentative draft), Section 164.

they cannot be assigned.[12] When a contract is personal in nature, the rights under the contract cannot be assigned. Finally, a right cannot be assigned if assignment will materially increase or alter the burdens of the obligor.

To illustrate these rules, recall the diagram showing A the assignor, B the obligor, and C the assignee. Suppose B owes A $50, and A assigns the right to receive the $50 to C. Here valid assignment of a debt exists, and B must pay the $50 to C, or C will be entitled to enforce payment in a court of law.

Next, suppose B agrees to build a house for A. The contract between A and B states: "The contract cannot be assigned by A. Any assignment renders this contract void and all rights hereunder will thereupon terminate." A then attempts to assign his rights to C. C cannot enforce the contract against B by trying to get B to build the house, since the contract expressly prohibits the assignment of rights.

Suppose B signs a contract to be a tutor for A's children. A then attempts to assign her right in B's services to C. C cannot enforce the contract against B because the contract called for the rendering of a personal service.[13]

Finally, assume A takes out an insurance policy on her hotel with B, an insurance company. The policy insures against fire, theft, floods, and vandalism. A then attempts to assign the insurance policy to C, who also owns a hotel. The assignment is ineffective because it alters B's *duty of performance* substantially. Insurance companies evaluate the particular risk of a certain party and tailor their policies to fit the exact risk of that party. If the policy is assigned to a third party, the insurance risk will be materially altered. Therefore, the assignment will not operate to give C any rights against B.

The following case illustrates the assignment of rights that materially changed the performance of obligations under the agreement.

---

12.   Several exceptions to this rule exist. First, a contract cannot prevent assignment of the right to receive money. This exception exists to encourage the free flow of money and credit in modern business settings. Second, the assignment of rights in real estate cannot be prohibited because this would be contrary to public policy. Such prohibitions are called *restraints against alienation.* Third, the assignment of negotiable instruments cannot be prohibited.

13.   Restatement, Second, Contracts (tentative draft), Section 149 and Section 150.

BACKGROUND AND FACTS   *Pizza Shop contracted with Virginia Coffee Services, Inc., for installation of vending machines. Thereafter, the Macke Company bought out Virginia Coffee Service. The purchase agreement included Virginia's assignment of its vending machine contracts to Macke. Later, Pizza Shop tried to rescind the contracts on the ground that the assignment was in breach of contract.*

MACKE COMPANY v. PIZZA OF GAITHERSBURG, INC.

Court of Appeals of Maryland, 1970.
259 Md. 479, 270 A.2d 645.

DECISION AND RATIONALE   *The contract between Virginia Coffee Service and Pizza Shop could validly be assigned. While one cannot delegate the obligation to provide personal services, the contract at issue here did not involve personal services. Even if Pizza Shop had claimed that it contracted with Virginia Coffee Service on the basis of that company's "skill and reputation," this would not prevent assignment of the contract unless there was a material change in the service Macke provided. According to the Restatement of Contracts: "Performance or offer of performance by a person delegated has the same legal effect as performance or offer of performance by the person named in the contract, unless, performance by the person delegated varies or would vary materially from performance by the person named in the contract as the one to perform, and there has been no *** assent to the delegation ***."*

ANTI-ASSIGNMENT CLAUSES As part of the terms of their agreement, parties can stipulate that the contract or certain rights under the contract are not assignable. However, anti-assignment clauses bring up public policy concerns. For example, when an anti-assignment clause restrains the alienation of property, courts will sometimes refuse to enforce it. Thus, anti-assignment clauses are subject to judicial review.

HANIGAN v. WHEELER
Court of Appeals of Arizona, Division 2, 1972.
19 Ariz.App. 49, 504 P.2d 972.

BACKGROUND AND FACTS *George Hanigan entered into a "Dairy Queen Store Agreement" with Eileen A. LeMoines. The contract contained a provision that read as follows: "Second party [LeMoines] shall not assign or transfer this agreement without the written approval of first party [Hanigan]." Subsequently, LeMoines entered into a contract to sell the franchise in question, as well as the real property located and built specifically for that franchise, to Wheeler. Hanigan refused to approve this sale, stating that Wheeler was inexperienced in business matters. Wheeler argued and the trial court agreed that the anti-assignment clause was an arbitrary and unreasonable restraint on the right to dispose of property and violated public policy since, theoretically, Hanigan could prevent LeMoines from ever selling the property.*

DECISION AND RATIONALE *Hanigan was able to prevent the sale of the franchise by his disapproval. Generally, contractual rights are assignable unless personal services are involved or unless the initial contract itself conditions assignment on the approval of one or both of the parties. The provision in the contract requiring Hanigan's approval prior to the sale of the franchise was valid and did not contravene public policy. The judge hearing the case stated: "We accept the fundamental principle that one of the primary incidents inherent in the ownership of property is the right of alienation or disposition. However, this right is not limitless. The right to make an assignment of property can be defeated where there is a clear stipulation to that effect [and] *** when the restraint is reasonably designed to attain or encourage accepted social or economic end."*

NOTICE OF THE ASSIGNMENT Once a valid assignment of rights has been made to a third party, the third party should notify the obligor (B in the diagram) of the assignment. This is not legally necessary because an assignment is effective immediately, whether or not notice is given, but it protects all of the parties. The following examples illustrate some of the problems that can arise when a third party fails to give notice of an assignment.

First, suppose A delivers eight ounces of high grade uranium to B, a nuclear energy cooperative. B is to pay a specified sum for the uranium. Before B pays, A assigns the right to receive payment for the uranium to C, one of A's suppliers in South Africa. C fails to notify B of the assignment, and B makes the payment to A. Since C failed to give notice of the assignment, C lost the right to collect the money from B. Before notice of the assignment, B is free to fulfill its obligation by paying A directly. If C had given notice of the assignment to B, B would have been required to pay C instead of A.

Second, suppose further that, after A assigned the right to receive payment to C, A also assigned the right to receive payment to D. Further assume that D then notified B of the second assignment. Many states will allow D to recover the money from B because of timely notification. Suppose several days after D notified B of the second assignment, C notified B of the first assignment. Here B is in a touchy situation, since it has received notice from two different people that payment is to be made to each. In this case, a majority of states will require payment to be made to D. D gave notice first and should be entitled to prevail over C, who was delinquent. However, some states would allow C to recover the money even though C failed to give notice before D.[14]

Delegation of Duties

Just as a party can transfer rights under a contract through an assignment, a party can also transfer duties. Duties are not assigned, however. They are "delegated." Normally, a delegation of duties does not relieve the party making the delegation of the obligation to perform in the event that the party who has been delegated the duty fails to perform.

FORM OF THE DELEGATION No special form is required to create a valid delegation of duties. As long as the delegator (the party delegating the duty) expresses a present intention to make the delegation, it will be effective. The delegator need not even use the word "delegate."

WHAT DUTIES CAN BE DELEGATED As a general rule, any duty can be delegated. How-

ever, when performance depends on the personal skill or talents of the obligor, or where special trust has been placed in the obligor, or when performance by a third party will vary materially from the expectancy of the obligee under the contract, the duty cannot be delegated.

Suppose B contracts with A to tutor A in the various aspects of financial underwriting and investment banking. B is an experienced businessman who is well known for his expertise in finance. Further, assume that B wants to delegate his duties to teach A to a third party, C. This delegation would be ineffective since B has contracted to render a service to A which is founded upon B's expertise. It is a change from A's expectancy under the contract. Therefore, C cannot perform B's duties.

Suppose B, an attorney, contracts with A, a bank, to advise A on a proposed merger with a savings and loan association. B wishes to delegate her duty to advise the bank to C, a law firm across town. Services of an attorney are personal in nature. B's delegation will be ineffective.

Finally, assume that B contracts with A to pick up and deliver heavy construction machinery to A's property. B then delegates this duty to C, who is in the business of delivering heavy machinery. The delegation is effective. The performance required is of a routine and nonpersonal nature and does not change A's expectancy under the contract. Exhibit 12-3 illustrates this relationship.

14. At common law, there were three different rules. The first rule was called the English rule. Second assignees prevailed in every case in which they had paid value, had taken the assignment without notice of the prior assignment, and had given the *obligor* notice of the assignment before the first assignee gave such notice. The next rule was called the New York rule: first in time, first in right. Finally, the third rule was the Massachusetts rule. The first assignee prevailed provided the first assignment was not revocable at the time the second assignment was made.

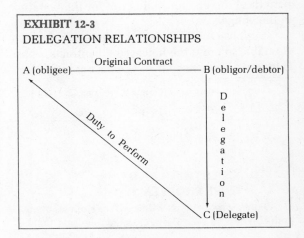

EXHIBIT 12-3
DELEGATION RELATIONSHIPS

A (obligee) —— Original Contract —— B (obligor/debtor)

Duty to Perform

Delegation

C (Delegate)

EFFECT OF A DELEGATION OF DUTIES

If a delegation of duties is legitimate, the obligee (A in the diagram) must accept performance from the delegate. The obligee can refuse performance from the delegate if the duty is one that may not be delegated. A valid delegation of duties does not relieve the delegator (B in the diagram) of obligations under the contract.[15] If the delegate (C in the diagram) fails to perform, the delegator is still liable to the obligee.

The liability of the delegate to the obligee depends on whether the agreement between delegate and delegator is interpreted as a "mere delegation" or a delegation plus an "assumption of duty" by the delegate. Where the delegate has made no promise to perform the duty *for the benefit of the obligee*, there is a "mere delegation." In these cases, the obligee cannot compel the delegate to perform or hold the delegate liable for non-performance. Common examples are cases where the delegate is an employee or a subcontractor of the obligor.

Where the delegate does make a promise to perform the duty for the benefit of the obligee, there is an "assumption of duty." The obligee is then in the position of third party creditor beneficiary and can hold the delegate liable for non-performance.

Suppose B contracts to build a house for A. B is the obligor. A is the obligee. B then contracts with C for C to supply the necessary construction materials. C fails to deliver. A can sue B, but cannot sue C. This is a clear case where C's promise to deliver the materials was for the benefit of the obligor, B, but not for the benefit of the obligee, A.

Suppose A and B have the same contract. B is unable to build the house so B contracts with C to build the house for A. C does not build the house. Here, the delegate, C, entered into a contract for the benefit of the obligee, A. A can sue both B and C.

When a party makes an assignment of a contract, the question of whether a delegation of duties and assumption of duties were not also intended will sometimes arise. For example, B assigns a contract with the words "I assign this contract to C." C has not expressly assumed any duties. Is C liable to perform the duties?

The traditional view was that under this assignment, C did not assume any duties. This view was based on the theory that the acceptance of the benefits of the contract was not sufficient to imply a promise to assume the duties of the contract. Modern authorities, however, take the view that the probable intention in using such general words was to create both an assignment of rights and an assumption of duties.[16] Therefore, when general words are used (e. g., "I assign the contract" or "all my rights under the contract") the contract is construed as implying both an assignment of rights and an assumption of duties. Naturally, this result occurs only when the parties have not expressly provided otherwise. When the agreement making the assignment and delegations specifically states that the delegate is not assuming the duties, the delegate cannot be sued for failure to perform those duties.

Suppose in the contract for the sale of B's boutique to C, it stated, "B does hereby sell, transfer, and assign to C all of B's rights with regard to the Honneywell Boutique." Under the traditional view, C would not be obligated to pay B's business debt to A. In the modern view, a promise to pay B's debt to A would be implied, and A could require C to pay.

---

15.   Crane Ice Cream Co. v. Terminal Freezing Co., 147 Md. 588, 128 A. 280 (1925).

16.   UCC Sec. 2-210 (where there is a general assignment of a contract for the sale of goods). Restatement, Second, Contracts (tentative draft), Section 160.

QUESTIONS AND CASE PROBLEMS

1.   Beman wrote out his wife's will as she was about to die. When he read the will to her, she said that it was not the way she wanted it and that she wanted to leave her house to her niece, Seaver. Beman offered to write her another will, but she said she was afraid she would not hold out long enough to sign it. Beman told her that if she would sign the will, he would leave Seaver the house in his will. When Beman died, no provision was made for Seaver to receive the house.

Seaver brought an action against Beman's estate, claiming a contract right in the house. What result? [Seaver v. Ransom, 224 N.Y. 233, 120 N.E. 639 (1918)]

2. Murray contracted with McDonald Construction Company to build an addition to a building Murray owned. Murray intended to rent part of the addition to Queen Anne News, and McDonald knew this. The terms of the contract between Murray and McDonald called for McDonald to complete the addition within 75 days. However, completion was delayed an additional 164 days. Queen Anne News sued McDonald for damages resulting from the delay in construction. Can Queen Anne recover? [McDonald Construction Company v. Murray, 5 Wash.App. 68, 485 P.2d 626 (1971)]

3. Isbrandtsen Company chartered a ship to transport paper pulp. Isbrandtsen hired Livano Shipping Company to unload the ship. After the ship was partially unloaded, the longshoremen's union, of which Livano's employees were members, went on strike in violation of their union contract. As a result, part of the pulp shipment was damaged. Isbrandtsen sued the longshoremen for breach of the union contract. Can Isbrandtsen recover? [Isbrandtsen Co. v Local 1291 Longshoremen, 204 F.2d 495 (3d Cir. 1953)]

4. Christopher wrote a letter to Daniel claiming that Daniel owed him $3,000 for the shipment of string bikinis that Christopher had sent him three months before. Daniel wrote back, saying that the bikinis were defective and that therefore he refused to pay. Christopher wrote back that his lawyer had advised him that it was questionable whether Daniel had informed him of the defect in time. Therefore Christopher felt that he might have a valid claim for the purchase price of $3,000. About a month later, Daniel wrote back to Christopher informing him that Jones, who owed Daniel $3,000 from a previous contract, had agreed with Daniel to make the payment to Christopher. Thereafter, Jones failed to make the payment to Christopher. Can Christopher sue Jones?

5. For several years, Eastern Company and Hudson Company had made a number of purchases and sales to each other on account. By January 1963, Eastern owed Hudson $2,200, and Hudson owed Eastern $1,300. Eastern assigned the accounts Hudson owed it to Home Factors Corporation. Home Factors attempted to collect the $1,300 debt from Hudson, but Hudson refused to pay because of the $2,200 debt Eastern owed it. Is this a valid defense? [Hudson Supply and Equipment Co. v. Home Factors Corp., 210 A.2d 837 (D.C.App.1965)]

6. Mrs. Jemison hired Tindall and two other men, Miller and Cohen, to help her sell her farm and agreed in writing to pay them a $300 commission. When the men procured the sale, Mrs. Jemison paid the $300 commission to Tindall, who was supposed to divide the money among the three. Tindall, however, concealed the commission from the other two men. When they learned of this fact, Miller and Cohen brought suit against Mrs. Jemison instead of against Tindall to recover the $200 owed them for their commissions. After she paid them the $200, Mrs. Jemison took back an oral assignment of their claims against Tindall. Mrs. Jemison then sued Tindall to recover the commissions of Cohen and Miller. Can she collect? [Jemison v. Tindall, 89 N.J. 429, 99 A. 408 (1916)]

7. D'Alassandro had an insurance policy with Bull Dog Insurance Company that protected against loss of an automobile by theft. On January 17, D'Alassandro's automobile was stolen and was never recovered. D'Alassandro's insurance policy provided that "no assignment of interest under this policy shall be or become binding upon the association unless the written consent of the attorney is endorsed thereon and an additional membership fee is paid." D'Alassandro assigned his claim under the policy to Ginsburg without complying with this policy provision. Ginsburg claimed D'Alassandro's insurance proceeds from BullDog Insurance Company. Bull Dog refused to pay Ginsburg, and Ginsburg sued. Can Ginsburg recover? [Ginsburg v. Bull Dog Auto Fire Insurance Association of Chicago, 328 Ill. 571, 160 N.E. 145 (1928)]

8. An obligor owed Tompkins $10,000. On January 1, Tompkins assigned his rights to the $10,000 to a bank. On January 10, Tompkins assigned the same rights to the $10,000 to an insurance company. On February 1, the insurance company notified the obligor of Tompkins's assignment. On February 15, the bank notified the obligor of Tompkins's assignment. On March 15, the obligation came due. Both the bank and the insurance company claimed the entire $10,000. Who wins? [Boulevard National Bank of Miami v. Air Metal Industries, Inc., 176 So.2d 94 (Fla1965)]

9. Southern Sports Corp., owned and operated by James Gardner, was the owner of the Cougar's Basketball Franchise. Cunningham had a four-year contract with Southern Sports to play with the Cougars. In 1971 Southern Sports assigned the basketball franchise, along with Cunningham's contract to play with the franchise, to Munchak. Cunningham thereafter refused to play, claiming that the assignment was invalid without his consent. Must Cunningham play for the new owners? [Munchak Corp. v. Cunningham, 457 F.2d 721 (4th Cir. 1972)]

10. Lea and Parkgate entered into a lease agreement whereby Lea rented certain wagons from Parkgate for a number of years. Part of the rental agreement provided that Parkgate would keep the wagons in good repair. During the term of the lease, Parkgate decided to liquidate its business. With several years left in the lease agreement, Parkgate assigned the rights and delegated the duties under its contract with Lea to British Wagon Company. When Lea learned of the transfer, it claimed that Parkgate had no right to sell the contract to British Wagon and that it did not have to accept services from British Wagon. Can British Wagon enforce the contract? [British Wagon Company v. Lea & Company, 5 Q.B. 149 (1880)]

Contracts
Performance and Discharge

The **discharge** (termination) of a contract is ordinarily accomplished when both of the contracting parties perform those acts promised in the contract. For example, the buyer of goods pays the seller for the goods, and the seller gives up possession to the buyer. Discharge can also occur in other ways. The parties can agree to terminate the contract, or one party can **breach** the contract—that is, fail to perform the acts promised in the contract. A breach discharges the duties of the nonbreaching party. In addition, the law can operate to terminate or discharge a contract. Finally, performance of the promised acts can be excused if the acts become impossible or extremely impractical to perform or if the purpose for which the contract was created is frustrated.

CONDITIONS

A condition is inserted into a contract for the protection of the promisor. A *condition* is any operative event, the occurrence or nonoccurrence of which modifies, limits, precludes, or must occur prior to the existence of a duty to be performed under a contract. The occurrence or nonoccurrence of a condition can also terminate an existing obligation under a contract. The more conditions attached to a promise, the less content the promise has. Thus, promises made by a person entering into a contract are either absolute or conditional. An absolute promise is one that must be performed, or the party promising the act will be in breach of contract. There is a fundamental distinction between the breach or performance of

145

an absolute promise and the failure or nonoccurrence of a condition. A breach of contract subjects the promisor to liability and can excuse performance of the other party's duty under the contract. The occurrence or nonoccurrence of a condition, on the other hand, prevents the promisee from acquiring a right or deprives the promisee of a right. It does not, however, subject the promisee to liability (unless he or she has promised that the condition will or will not happen).

For example, suppose you promise to buy a corn futures contract from Merrill Lynch if the price of No. 2 yellow corn reaches $2.25 per bushel. The condition to your promise to buy is that the price of No. 2 yellow corn will reach $2.25 per bushel. If there is a failure of that condition—if No. 2 yellow corn never reaches $2.25 per bushel and, therefore, you do not buy—the contract is not breached. However, once the price of corn does reach $2.25, your promise to buy becomes absolute, and if you do not buy, the contract is breached.

Types of Conditions

Three types of conditions can be present in any given contract—conditions *precedent,* conditions *subsequent,* and conditions *concurrent.*

CONDITIONS PRECEDENT   A condition that must be fulfilled before a party's promise becomes absolute is a **condition precedent.**[1] The condition precedes the absolute duty to perform. For example, if Craig promises to pay Davis $500 if Davis installs a tile roof on Craig's house, Craig's promise is subject to the condition precedent of Davis's installing the tile roof. Or if Fisher promises to contribute $1,000 to the Salvation Army if Calvin completes college, Fisher's promise is subject to the condition precedent of Calvin's completing college. Until the conditions are fulfilled or satisfied, Craig's promise to pay Davis and Fisher's promise to donate to charity do not become absolute.

CONDITIONS SUBSEQUENT   When a condition operates to terminate a party's absolute promise to perform, it is called a **condition subsequent.**[2] The condition follows, or is subsequent to, the absolute duty to perform. If the condition occurs, the party need not perform any further. For example, if Hartman promises to work for the San Pedro Company for one year unless he is called into military service, the absolute duty to work is conditioned upon not being drafted. Hartman's promise to work for San Pedro continues to be absolute until he is drafted or otherwise inducted. Once Hartman is drafted, the absolute duty to work for San Pedro ends, and Hartman is released from the contract.[3]

CONCURRENT CONDITIONS   Where each party's absolute duty to perform is conditioned on the other party's absolute duty to perform there are **concurrent conditions.** Concurrent conditions occur only when the parties are to perform their respective duties simultaneously. For example, if a buyer promises to pay for goods if they are delivered by the seller, each party's absolute duty to perform is conditioned upon the other party's absolute duty to perform. The buyer's duty to pay for the goods does not become absolute until the seller either delivers or tenders the goods.[4] Accordingly, the seller's duty to deliver the goods does not become absolute until the buyer tenders or actually makes payment.[5]

EXPRESS AND CONSTRUCTIVE CONDITIONS   Conditions can also be classified as: (1) express, (2) implied-in-fact, and (3) implied-

---

1.   Restatement, Contracts, Section 250(a).

2.   Restatement, Contracts, Section 250(b). It is possible that a condition may be subsequent in form but precedent in fact. Further, if there is any difference at all between the two, it is as to burdens of proof and pleading. For this reason, the draft of the Restatement, Second, Contracts drops the distinction between the two.

3.   Hartman v. San Pedro Commercial Co., 66 Cal.App.2d 935, 153 P.2d 212 (1945).

4.   Tender means offering to deliver the goods or making the goods available for the buyer to take delivery.

5.   This is in accord with UCC Secs. 2-503 and 2-511.

in-law. Express conditions are provided for by the parties' agreement. An express condition is usually prefaced by "if," "provided," "after," or "when." Conditions implied-in-fact are similar to expressed conditions because they are understood to be part of the agreement, but they are not expressly found in the language of the agreement. They can be inferred from the promise, however. Finally, implied-in-law, or constructive, conditions are imposed by the law in order to achieve justice and fairness. They are not contained in the language of the contract or even necessarily implied.[6] Suppose Silverman and Lyon enter into two agreements. The first states, "Silverman promises to pay Lyon $1,500 if Lyon delivers 100 cases of oranges to Silverman's business office. Lyon promises to deliver 100 cases of oranges to Silverman's business office if Silverman pays $1,500 for the oranges." The second agreement states, "Silverman promises to pay $1,500 for 100 cases of Lyon's oranges to be delivered at Silverman's business office." In the first agreement, Silverman's promise to pay is expressly conditioned on Lyon's promise to deliver. Also, Lyon's promise to deliver is expressly conditioned on Silverman's promise to pay. As noted above, these are *concurrent conditions*. In the second agreement, Silverman's promise to pay is *constructively* conditioned on Lyon's promise to deliver, and Lyon's promise to deliver is *constructively conditioned* on Silverman's promise to pay. The conditions are *implied* (the promises are construed as conditional) in order to achieve justice and fairness. The conditions are implied-in-fact because they are necessarily inferred from the promise contained in the contract. In other words, it is obvious from custom and context that the duties here are conditional.

Suppose neither Silverman nor Lyon perform their promises under the second agreement. If the promises were not constructively conditioned on the other party's performance, both parties could sue for breach of contract without attempting to perform themselves (since the promises would be absolute

and not subject to any conditions). By creating constructive conditions, this problem is eliminated. *In order to sue for breach of contract (that is, breach of an absolute promise to perform), the suing party must fulfill his or her respective condition(s) (or those conditional promises must be excused).*[7] Silverman must tender payment to Lyon before suing for breach of contract. Likewise, Lyon must tender delivery to Silverman before suing for breach of contract.

Now consider some examples of condition implied-in-law. A contract in which a builder is supposed to build a house for a buyer can leave silent when the buyer is supposed to pay the builder. Nonetheless, the court will infer an implied condition that the buyer is not obliged to pay the builder until the house is completed. This is done because the buyer should not be compelled to perform unless the builder has performed. (If the builder performs substantially, such as finishing everything except the hook-up for an outside water faucet, the court will allow the builder to recover the agreed price less the amount necessary to cover the cost of hooking up the outside water faucet.)

The following sections discuss some of the most important (and common) ways in which contracts are discharged.[8]

DISCHARGE BY PERFORMANCE

The great majority of contracts are discharged by performance. The contract comes to an end when both parties fulfill their respective duties by performing the acts they have promised to do. Performance can also be accomplished by tender. **Tender** is an unconditional offer to perform by one who is ready, willing and able to do so. Therefore, a seller who places goods at the disposal of a buyer has tendered delivery and can demand payment. A buyer who offers to pay for goods has tendered payment and can

---

6. Restatement, Contracts, Section 253.

7. See Kingston v. Preston, 2 Doug. 684 (K.B.) and followed in the Restatement, Contracts, Section 266.

8. Looking at all of them would take an entire book. For example, Restatement, Contracts, Section 385, presents twenty-five distinct ways a contract can be discharged.

demand delivery of the goods. Once performance has been tendered, the party making the tender has done everything possible to carry out the terms of the contract. If the other party then refuses to perform, the party making the tender can consider the duty discharged and sue for breach of contract.

The Degree of Performance Required

In most contracts, the parties will fulfill their respective duties completely. Sometimes, however, a party will fulfill most of the duties under the contract but not all of them. Or a party may complete all the duties but do so in a way that departs from the precise requirements of the contract. In order to determine whether all conditions have been fulfilled or whether the contract has been breached, the express and constructive conditions of the contract must be scrutinized.

EXPRESS CONDITIONS AND FULL PERFORMANCE Conditions that are expressly stated normally must be fully performed in all respects. For example, a contract stating that "Mason, the builder, will be paid $750 when he installs three-eighth inch DuPont asbestos covering on the welding work benches in Nie Company's Fort Lauderdale plant" expressly requires the installation of DuPont asbestos. If Mason installs Pennecott asbestos, he will not be fulfilling the express condition precedent to payment and will not be entitled to full payment.

BARNES v. EUSTER
Court of Appeals of Maryland,
1965.
240 Md. 603, 214 A.2d 807.

BACKGROUND AND FACTS *Euster contracted to sell Barnes a certain tract of land. The parties included in their contract a provision that "this sale is subject to the obtaining of necessary zoning for the erection of general offices for use of doctors within the next zoning application term [six months]." Barnes filed a zoning application in time, but the zoning board did not rezone "within the next rezoning application term." Euster notified Barnes that the contract was terminated and Barnes sued damages.*

DECISION AND RATIONALE *No damages were owed to Barnes since the contract of purchase was not breached. The contractual duty of both parties was subject to a condition precedent—namely, that the rezoning of the land would occur within a specified time. Since that condition did not occur, Euster's duty to sell never arose. In the words of the judge, "[W]here a contractual duty is subject to a condition precedent, whether express or implied, there is no duty of performance and there can be no breach by nonperformance until the condition precedent is either performed or excused."*

CONSTRUCTIVE CONDITIONS AND SUBSTANTIAL PERFORMANCE Conditions that are constructive (that is, imposed by law to achieve justice and fairness) can be fulfilled by *substantial performance* rather than full performance. In order to qualify as substantial, the performance must not vary greatly from the performance promised in the contract. If the performance is substantial, the constructive condition is satisfied and the other party's duty to perform becomes absolute.

Suppose you are a construction contractor and you contracted to build a meatpacking plant for Wilson & Company. Certain specifications for construction materials were set forth in the contract. One of them stated, "All wrought iron pipe must be well-galvanized, lap welded pipe of the grade known as 'standard pipe' of Reading Manufacture." After the plant was completed, Wilson & Company discovered that Cohose pipe was used and refused to pay anything for the plant, alleging that you had not fulfilled the constructive condition precedent of using Reading pipe. If you were required to use Reading pipe, you would not have fulfilled the condition, Wilson & Company's promise to pay would not become absolute, and you would not be paid. In order to avoid this harsh result, courts hold that substantial performance of a constructive condition precedent (or concurrent condition) is sufficient to satisfy or fulfill that condition.[9] Otherwise, Wilson & Company would be unjustly enriched, and you would forfeit all the time and expense put into building the meatpacking plant. However, if you installed Reading pipe, but the pipe was not galvanized and the seams were butt-welded, the performance would not be substantial. You would not be paid since the constructive condition precedent would not be satisfied or fulfilled.

Substantial performance does not operate to eliminate any breach of contract arising from less than full performance. *It operates only to satisfy or fulfill constructive (implied) conditions.* In the above example, if you installed Cohose pipe, Wilson & Company would still be entitled to recover damages caused by the less than full performance. If the meatpacking plant were worth $1,000 less because of the substitution of Cohose for Reading pipe, you, the builder would be allowed to recover the price of the building, less $1,000.

PERFORMANCE TO THE SATISFACTION OF ANOTHER

Contracts will often state that completed work must satisfy one of the parties or a third person. This satisfaction then becomes a condition precedent to the parties' duty to perform. The question that always arises is whether the performance must actually satisfy that person or whether performance that would satisfy a "reasonable" person will be sufficient.

When the subject matter of the contract is personal, contracts to be performed to the satisfaction of one of the parties must actually satisfy that party. For example, contracts for portraits, works of art, medical or dental work, and tailoring are considered personal. Therefore, only the personal satisfaction of the party will be sufficient to fulfill the condition. Suppose Williams agrees to paint a portrait of Hirshon's daughter for $500. The contract provides that Hirshon must be satisfied with the portrait. If Hirshon is not, she will not be required to pay for it. The only requirement imposed on Hirshon is that she act honestly. If she expresses dissatisfaction only to avoid paying for the portrait, the condition of satisfaction is excused, and her duty to pay becomes absolute.

Contracts that involve mechanical fitness, utility, or marketability need only be performed to the satisfaction of a reasonable person unless they expressly state otherwise. For example, construction contracts or manufacturing contracts are *not* considered to be personal, so the party's personal satisfaction is normally irrelevant. As long as the performance will satisfy a reasonable person, the condition is fulfilled. For example, assume Duplex Safety Boiler Company agrees to rebuild Garden's boiler "to Garden's satisfaction." After rebuilding the boiler, it operates properly, but Garden is dissatisfied and refuses to pay for the repair work. If a reasonable person would be satisfied with the boiler's operation, Duplex is entitled to be paid for the repair work.[10]

At times, contracts also require performance to the satisfaction of a third party (not a party to the contract). For example, assume you contract to pave several city streets. The contract provides that the work will be done "to the satisfaction of Phil Hopper, the supervising

---

9. For an excellent analysis of substantial performance see Judge Cardozo's opinion in Jacob & Youngs v. Kent, 230 N.Y. 239, 129 N.E. 889 (1921).

10. If, however, the contract specifically states that it is to be fulfilled to the "personal" satisfaction of one or more of the parties, and the parties so intended, the outcome will probably be different.

engineer." In this situation, the courts are divided. A minority of courts require the personal satisfaction of the third party, here Phil Hopper. If Hopper is not satisfied, you will not be paid, even if a reasonable person would be satisfied. Again, the personal judgment must be made honestly or the condition will be excused. A majority of courts require the work to be satisfactory to a reasonable person. So even if Hopper were dissatisfied with the cement work, you would be paid, as long as a reasonable supervising engineer would have been satisfied.

Time for Performance

If no time for performance is stated in the contract, a reasonable time is implied. If a specific time is stated, the parties must usually perform by that time. However, unless time is expressly stated to be vital, a delay in performance will not destroy the performing party's right to payment. When time is expressly stated to be vital, or when "time is of the essence," the time for performance must be strictly complied with. For example, a contract for the sale of soybeans without stating more, must be performed within a reasonable time. A contract for the sale of soybeans "on or before April 1" may be performed by April 2 or 3. (But the party rendering late performance will have to pay for any damages caused by the delay.) A contract for the sale of soybeans "on or before April 1— necessary for immediate shipment abroad on April 2" must be performed by April 1. Time is of the essence because the buyer plans on immediate resale. Delivery after April 1 will prevent the buyer from exporting the soybeans.

DISCHARGE BY AGREEMENT

Any contract can be discharged by agreement of the parties. The agreement can be contained in the original contract, or the parties can form a new contract for the express purpose of discharging the original contract.

Discharge by Rescission

Rescission is the process whereby the parties cancel the contract and return to the positions they occupied prior to forming it. In order to rescind a bargain, the parties must make another agreement, which must also satisfy the legal requirements for a contract. There must be an *offer,* an *acceptance,* and *consideration.* Ordinarily, if the parties agree to rescind the original contract, their promises not to perform those acts promised in the original contract will be legal consideration for the second contract.

Where one party has fully performed, however, an agreement to call off the original contract will not normally be enforceable. Because the performing party has received no consideration for the promise to call off the original bargain, additional consideration will be necessary. To illustrate: Suppose Beatrice Foods Company contracts to buy forty truckloads of oranges from Tropicana Products Inc. Later, representatives of Beatrice and Tropicana get together and decide to call off the deal or rescind the original contract. This agreement, without more, is enforceable since neither party has yet performed. The consideration for Tropicana calling off the deal is not having to perform that which it was legally bound to perform under the contract—that is, not having to deliver the forty truckloads of oranges. The consideration for Beatrice calling off the deal is not having to pay for the oranges, an obligation it otherwise had to honor. On the other hand, if Tropicana had already delivered the oranges, an agreement to call off the deal would not normally be enforceable. Since Tropicana had already performed, it had received no consideration for its promise to call off the deal. In sum, contracts that are *executory* on *both* sides (contracts where neither party has performed) can be rescinded by agreement without more.[11] But contracts that are *executed on one side* (contracts where one party has performed) can be rescinded only if the party who has performed receives consideration for the promise to call off the deal.

---

11. Note that certain sales made to consumers at their homes can be rescinded by the consumer within three days for no reason at all. This three-day "cooling-off" is designed to aid consumers who are susceptible to high-pressure door-to-door sales tactics. See Chapter 48 and 15 USC Sec. 1635(a).

Discharge by Novation or Substituted Agreement

The process of novation substitutes a new party for one of the original parties. Essentially, the parties to the original contract and one or more new parties all get together and agree to substitute the new party for one of the original parties. The requirements of novation are: (1) an agreement among all parties to discharge the original contract, (2) the substitution of a new party, and (3) a new contract that is valid. Suppose Union Carbide Corp. decides to sell its petrochemical business in Europe. Union Carbide contracts with British Petroleum Company to sell Bakelite Xylonite Ltd. stock to British Petroleum for $200 million in cash. The contract is signed by both parties. After British Petroleum consults its tax and securities experts, it decides to substitute BP Chemicals as the purchaser instead. In order to accomplish this, the parties agree to a novation. Union Carbide, British Petroleum, and BP Chemicals all get together and agree that BP Chemicals will buy the Bakelite Xylonite stock from Union Carbide. As long as the new contract is supported by consideration, the novation will discharge the original contract (between Union Carbide and British Petroleum) and replace it with the new contract (between Union Carbide and BP Chemicals).

A substituted agreement is a new contract that expressly or impliedly revokes and discharges a prior contract. The parties involved may simply want a new agreement with somewhat different terms. So they *expressly* state in a new contract that the old contract is now discharged. They can also make the new contract without expressly stating that the old contract is discharged. If the parties do not expressly discharge the old contract, it will be *impliedly* discharged due to the change or different terms of the new contract. For example, suppose Triangle Pacific Corp. contracts to sell its lumber manufacturing facilities in Slocan, British Columbia to a Canadian investor group for $7.9 million in cash and $800,000 in five-year subordinated debentures. Before the sale is closed, however, Triangle Pacific Corp. decides that it wants $6.9 million in cash and $1.8 million in five-year subordinated debentures. The Canadian investor group agrees, and the parties draw up a new contract with these terms of sale. If the second agreement states, "Our previous contract to accept payment of $7.9 million in cash, balance in five-year subordinated debentures is hereby revoked," the original contract will be expressly discharged by substitution. If the second agreement does not state this, the original contract will nevertheless be discharged by implication. Triangle Pacific Corp. cannot sell the same lumber manufacturing facilities under two different terms of payment. Since the terms are inconsistent, a court will enforce the terms that were decided upon most recently. In this case, the sale would be for $6.9 million in cash and $1.8 million in five-year subordinated debentures.

A compromise or settlement agreement that arises out of a bona fide dispute over the obligations under an existing contract will be recognized at law. Such an agreement will be substituted as a new contract, and it will either expressly or impliedly revoke and discharge the obligations under any prior contract. In the following case, a long history preceded an ultimate compromise settlement.

BACKGROUND AND FACTS *Jelco, Inc., was awarded a contract to do certain electrical work for a project in Colorado. Jelco in turn contracted with Stanspec Corp. to purchase hoists that it needed for the project. A dispute later arose over the price Jelco was to pay because Stanspec had estimated the price of the hoists on incomplete information supplied by the Colorado Highway Department. Actual highway department specifications increased the cost of the hoists significantly. Jelco and Stanspec entered into a modified contract under which Jelco agreed to pay a higher price. Subsequently, Jelco refused to pay the modified price.*

STANSPEC CORPORATION v. JELCO, INCORPORATED
United States Court of Appeals, Tenth Circuit, 1972.
464 F.2d 1184.

DECISION AND RATIONALE *Jelco was bound to pay the higher price under the modified agreement. Even though Stanspec was under a preexisting duty to supply the hoists at the original price, the modified agreement was supported by valid consideration because a bona fide dispute existed over the duties under the original contract. The circuit court judge stated: "An agreement which compromises a bona fide dispute as to the duties under an existing contract is of course enforceable and binding if the dispute as to those duties and obligations is not founded on bad faith. The law actively encourages compromise and settlement of disputes."*

Discharge by Accord and Satisfaction

For a contract to be discharged by accord and satisfaction, the parties must agree to accept performance different from the performance originally promised. An *accord* is defined as an executory contract (that is, one that has not yet been performed) to perform some act in satisfaction of an existing contractual duty.[12] The duty is not yet discharged. A *satisfaction* is the performance of the accord agreement. An **accord and satisfaction** discharge the original contractual obligation. However, an accord is not binding until the satisfaction is made. Thus, either party can revoke an accord before payment or performance has been made.

An accord can also be used to settle disputed debts. Suppose, for example, that Andrew Matthews obtains a judgment against Elizabeth

Brown for $3,000. Both parties agree that the judgment can be satisfied if Brown pays $2,000 in cash and transfers her automobile to Matthews in lieu of the $1,000 balance. Brown pays $2,000 in cash and then offers the car to Matthews, but he refuses it. The subsequent agreement for $2,000 in cash and the transfer of the automobile is the accord. However, the satisfaction does not occur, and the debt is not discharged until it is completed by both parties. As long as any part of the accord and satisfaction remains to be performed, it does not constitute payment of the debt.

Accord and satisfaction occur when the parties to a contract agree that a substitute performance will be rendered in satisfaction of the original obligation, and the substituted performance is accepted. A disputed amount and the consent to accept less must be involved before there can be an accord and satisfaction.

12. Restatement, Contracts, Section 417.

WIDMER v. GIBBLE OIL COMPANY
Supreme Court of Arkansas, 1967.
243 Ark. 735, 421 S.W.2d 886.

BACKGROUND AND FACTS *Widmer owed Gibble Oil Company $67.80 on his credit card account. Widmer sent a check for $9.01 and marked on it, "full payment of all accounts to date." Because Gibble cashed the check, Widmer contended that his debt was discharged.*

DECISION AND RATIONALE *Widmer's debt was not discharged. For the $9.01 check to satisfy Widmer's $67.80 debt to Gibble, the amount owed had to be in dispute, and Gibble had to consent to the lesser amount as full payment. This consent is known as an accord. For a debt to be discharged for a lessor amount, there must be both an accord and satisfaction.*

The judge stated: "It is not enough for the debtor merely to write on a voucher or on his check such words as "in full payment" or "to balance account," where there has been no such dispute or antecedent discussion as to give reasonable notice to the creditor that the check was being tendered as full satisfaction."

DISCHARGE BY OPERATION OF LAW

Alteration of the Contract

In order to discourage parties from altering written contracts, the law operates to discharge an innocent party when the other party has materially altered a written contract without consent. For example, contract terms such as quantity or price might be changed without the knowledge or consent of all parties. If so, the party who was unaware of the change can treat the contract as discharged or terminated.[13]

Statute of Limitations

Statutes of limitations limit the period of time during which a party can sue on a particular cause of action. A cause of action is a cause or reason for suing or bringing an action. After the applicable limitations period has passed, suit can no longer be brought in a court of law or equity. For example, the limitations period for oral contracts is usually two to three years; for written contracts, four to five years; for recovery of judgments, ten to twenty years. Technically, the running of a statute of limitations bars access only to *judicial* remedies; it does not extinguish the debt or the underlying obligation. The statute precludes access to the courts for collection. But if the party who owes the debt or obligation agrees to perform (that is, makes a new promise to perform) the cause of action barred by the statute of limitations will be revived. For example, suppose Burlington

---

13. The innocent party can also treat the contract as in effect, either on the original terms or on the terms as altered. A buyer who discovers that a seller altered the quantity of goods in a sales contract from 100 to 1,000 by secretly inserting a zero can purchase either 100 or 1,000 of the items.

Northern Railroad contracts for sixty-three new miles of track to be laid between Dalhart and Amarillo, Texas. Martin Marietta Corp. supplies four tons of cast iron railway for the project and is paid $22,000 of the $30,000 purchase price. Texas's statute of limitations for collection of this debt is five years, and Martin Marietta Corp. fails to collect the debt or sue for collection during that five-year period. Therefore, Martin Marietta Corp. can no longer sue. It is barred by the statute of limitations. But if Burlington Northern Railroad agrees, in writing, to pay the remaining $8,000, or if it actually pays part of the $8,000, Marietta Corp. can again sue to collect the debt. The statute of limitations is no longer a bar, and the cause of action for recovery of the debt is revived. (The Statute of Frauds in some states requires a writing here.)

Bankruptcy

Bankruptcy will ordinarily bar enforcement of a debtor's contract. (Bankruptcy is fully discussed in Chapter 32.) It can be entered into voluntarily or involuntarily. The essence of bankruptcy is that the debtor owes more than he or she owns, or is unable to pay debts as they come due. A proceeding in bankruptcy attempts to allocate the assets the debtor owns at bankruptcy to the creditors in a fair and equitable fashion. Once the assets are allocated, the bankrupt receives a **discharge in bankruptcy.** The discharge is not really a discharge of the debt but operates like a statute of limitations in barring a suit for collection of the debt. As with statutes of limitations, the debts of a bankrupt can be revived by a new promise to pay (that must be in writing). Partial payment of a debt barred by bankruptcy will not revive the entire debt (unlike partial payment of a debt barred by a statute of limitations).

DISCHARGE BY BREACH OF CONTRACT

Duties of the non-breaching party can be discharged by material breach of contract or by anticipatory repudiation of the contract by the other party.

Material Breach of Contract

A **breach of contract** is the nonperformance of a contractual duty. When the breach is *material,* the nonbreaching party is excused from the performance of contractual duties and has a cause of action to sue for damages caused by the breach. If the breach is *minor* (not material), the nonbreaching party's duty to perform can sometimes be suspended until the breach is remedied but is not entirely excused. Once the minor breach is cured, the nonbreaching party must then resume performance of the contractual obligations undertaken. Any breach entitles the nonbreaching party to sue for damages, but only a material breach discharges the nonbreaching party from the contract. The policy underlying these rules allows contracts to go forward when only minor problems occur but terminates them if major problems occur.

Suppose Raytheon Corp. contracts with the United States government to build an all-weather tactical strike force system and to test equipment for the Hawk missile system. Raytheon is to complete the project in two years and has certain schedules to meet for each stage of the production. Every six months Raytheon is to receive $3.8 million of the total $15.2 million contract price. If Raytheon is four months late in completing the first stage of production, the government will be entitled to treat the contract as discharged. Taking ten months to complete a stage that was scheduled for six months is a material breach of contract. In addition, the government can sue Raytheon for breach of contract and recover damages caused by the four-month delay. If, on the other hand, Raytheon is two days late in completing the first stage, the government will not be entitled to treat the contract as discharged. Two days is

only a minor breach. However, the government can sue Raytheon for damages caused by the minor delay.

A nonbreaching party need not treat a material breach as a discharge of the contract. Instead, the party can treat the contract as being in effect and sue for damages caused by the material breach. In the above example, if Raytheon delays four months on the first stage, the government can treat the contract as still being in effect and simply sue for damages caused by the delay.

Anticipatory Breach (Anticipatory Repudiation)

Before either party to a contract has performed, one of the parties may refuse to perform the contractual obligations. This is called **anticipatory breach,** or **repudiation.** For example, De La Tour made a contract with Hochester in March to employ Hochester as a courier for three months—June, July, and August. On April 1, De La Tour told Hochester, "I am going abroad this summer and will not need a courier." This is an anticipatory breach of the employment contract. Since De La Tour repudiated the contract, Hochester could treat the act as a present, material breach.[14] Furthermore, he could sue to recover damages *immediately,* without having to wait until June 1 to sue.[15]

There are two reasons for treating an anticipatory breach as a present, material breach:

1. The nonbreaching party should not be required to remain ready and willing to perform when the other party has already repudiated the contract.

---

14. Restatement, Contracts, Section 318, and UCC Sec. 2-610.

15. The doctrine of anticipatory breach first arose in the landmark case of Hochester v. De La Tour, 2 Ellis and Blackburn Reports 678 (1853) when the English court recognized the delay and expense inherent in a rule requiring a nonbreaching party to wait until the time for performance to sue on an anticipatory breach.

2. The nonbreaching party should have the opportunity to seek a similar contract elsewhere.

Hochester should not be required to remain ready to serve as De La Tour's courier until June 1 since that would be a waste of time. In the meantime, Hochester could be working elsewhere.

BACKGROUND AND FACTS *Reliance Cooperage Corporation agreed to buy 300,000 white oak bourbon staves at $450 per thousand from Treat. Before the delivery was due, the market price of oak staves rose sharply, and Treat informed Reliance that he would not supply the staves at the agreed-upon price. Treat stated that he would perform only if Reliance agreed to pay the market price.*

RELIANCE COOPERAGE CORP. v. TREAT
United States Court of Appeals, Eight Circuit, 1952.
195 F.2d 977.

DECISION AND RATIONALE *Treat's anticipatory repudiation constituted a breach of contract. When one party to an executory contract states that he or she "cannot" or "will not" perform prior to the date performance is due, the other party can treat the statement as an anticipatory repudiation.*

The measure of damages is the same as if Treat had breached the contract on the date performance was due.

According to the court: "The plaintiff [Reliance] would still have been entitled to recover what it had lost by reason of the defendant's [Treat's] failure to produce and deliver [on the delivery date] the staves contracted for, namely, the difference between the market price and the contract price of the staves on that date. The Comment in Restatement of the Law of Contracts, §338, Measure of Damages for Anticipatory Breach, contains the following statement ***: 'The fact that an anticipatory repudiation is a breach of contract *** does not cause the repudiated promise to be treated as if it were a promise to render performance on the date of the repudiation. Repudiation does not accelerate the time fixed for performance; nor does it change the damages to be awarded as the equivalent of the promised performances.' "

DISCHARGE BY IMPOSSIBILITY OF PERFORMANCE

After a contract has been made, performance may become impossible. One of the parties may die, the subject matter of the contract may be destroyed, or a change in law may make performance illegal. This is known as *impossibility of performance* and may discharge the contract.[16] It is necessary to distinguish between impossibility and a mistake. A mistake occurs if the

contract was always impossible to perform. Impossibility occurs if the contract was possible to perform when it was formed but became impossible to perform *at some later time.*

Normally, a duty to perform will be discharged when a change in circumstances makes performance impossible, impractical, or unreasonably expensive, provided the risk of loss due to impossibility has not already been allocated: (1) expressly by the contract, (2) by custom, or (3) due to one party's negligence. Thus, subject to these qualifications, impossibility where *no one* can possibly perform the

---

16. Restatement, Contracts, Section 457.

contractual duties will discharge the contract. Impossibility where someone can perform the contractual duties, but where the party who has promised to perform the duties cannot, will not normally discharge a contract. Examples of the latter type of impossibility include contracts to deliver goods that cannot be delivered on time due to freight car shortages[17] or contracts to pay money where the party cannot pay because the bank has closed.[18] In effect the party is saying "It is impossible for *me* to perform," not "It is impossible for anyone to perform." Accordingly, such excuses will not discharge the contract, and the nonperforming party will normally be held in breach of contract.

Three types of cases generally qualify as impossibility and discharge the contract: (1) where one of the parties to a personal service contract dies;[19] (2) where the subject matter of a contract is destroyed;[20] and (3) where a change in law makes performance illegal.[21] Here it is impossible for anyone to perform, and the contract is therefore discharged. Examples of the first type include contracts to paint portraits where the painter dies or contracts to perform in Broadway plays where the actor or actress dies. Examples of the second type include a contract to lease a building where the building is destroyed by fire or a contract to sell oil from a particular well where the well goes dry. Examples of the third type include a contract to loan money at 15 percent where the usury rate is changed to make loans in excess of 12 percent illegal or a contract to build an apartment building where the zoning laws are changed to prohibit the construction of residential rental property.

Temporary Impossibility

An occurrence or event that makes it temporarily impossible to perform the act for which a party has contracted will operate to suspend performance until the impossibility ceases. Then, ordinarily, the parties must perform the contract as originally planned. However, if the lapse of time and the change in circumstances surrounding the contract make it substantially more burdensome to perform the promised acts, the parties will be discharged. The leading case on this subject, Autry v. Republic Productions,[22] involved an actor who was drafted into the army in 1942. Being drafted rendered his contract temporarily impossible to perform, and it was suspended until the end of the war. When the actor got out of the army, the value of the dollar had so changed that performance of the contract would have been substantially burdensome for him. Therefore, the contract was discharged.

Commercial Impracticability

There is a growing trend of allowing parties to discharge contracts in which the performance that was originally contemplated turns out to be extremely different or more expensive than anticipated. This is known as the doctrine of commercial impracticability.[23]

In order to invoke this doctrine, the anticipated performance must become extremely difficult or costly. In a leading case, the California Supreme Court held that a contract was discharged because it would cost ten times more than the original estimate to excavate a certain amount of gravel.[24] In another case, commercial impracticability was not found where a carrier of goods was to deliver wheat from the West Coast of the United States to a safe port in Iran.[25] The Suez Canal, the usual route, was nationalized by Egypt and closed, forcing the carrier to travel around Africa and the Cape of Good Hope, through the Mediterranean and on to Iran. The added expense was approximately

17. Minneapolis v. Republic Creosoting Co., 161 Minn. 178, 201 N.W. 414 (1924).
18. Ingham Lumber Co. v. Ingersoll & Co., 93 Ark. 447, 125 S.W. 139 (1910).
19. Restatement, Contracts, Section 459.
20. Restatement, Contracts, Section 460.
21. Restatement, Contracts, Section 458.

22. 30 Cal.2d 144, 180 P.2d 888 (1947).
23. Restatement, Contracts, Section 454.
24. Mineral Park Land Co. v. Howard, 172 Cal. 289, 156 P. 458 (1916).
25. Transatlantic Financing Corp. v. United States, 363 F.2d 312 (D.C. Cir. 1966).

$42,000 above and beyond the contract price of $306,000, and the original journey of 10,000 miles was extended by an additional 3,000 miles. Nevertheless, the court held that the contract was not commercially impracticable to perform. Therefore, caution should be used when attempting to invoke commercial impracticability. The added burden of performing must be extreme—about ten times the original cost.

QUESTIONS AND CASE PROBLEMS

1. Miller, a general contractor, contracted with Village Apartments, Inc., to build a number of apartments. Miller hired a subcontractor, Mascioni, to construct certain walls and agreed to pay him $.55 per cubic foot for the walls. The contract between Miller and Mascioni contained the following clause: "Payments to be made as received from the owner." In compliance with his contract with Miller, Mascioni completed construction of the walls. However, the owner never paid Miller, and Miller therefore refused to pay Mascioni. Mascioni sued Miller. What judgment? [Mascioni v. I. B. Miller, Inc., 261 N.Y. 1, 184 N.E. 473 (1933)]

2. Beck Lithographing Company agreed in a contract with Colorado Milling Company to furnish 10,000 business cards and 5,000 checks, letterheads, noteheads, billheads, and envelopes bearing Colorado Milling's logo. Beck was to design and deliver these items to Colorado Milling within one year of the signing of the contract. Beck failed to tender or deliver the items contracted for until six or eight days after the expiration of the year. Colorado Milling refused to accept them and refused to pay any part of the contract price. Was Colorado Milling justified in doing this? [Beck and Pauli Lithographing Company v. Colorado Milling and Elevator Company, 52 F. 700 (10th Cir. 1892)]

3. Minweld, a steel producer, agreed to furnish McCloskey with the steel he needed for a hospital he had contracted to build. The contract between McCloskey and Minweld indicated that time was of the essence. After several letters were exchanged between McCloskey and Minweld concerning Minweld's shipment schedule, Minweld finally wrote to McCloskey explaining that it would have difficulty obtaining steel because of the war in Korea. Minweld also suggested to McCloskey that since the hospital was a state hospital, the state should attempt to use its influence to help Minweld obtain steel to fulfill its obligation under the contract. McCloskey felt that Minweld's letter to it constituted an anticipatory repudiation. Do you agree? [McCloskey and Company v. Minweld Steel Company, 220 F.2d 101 (3d Cir. 1955)]

4. Prince had been employed as a salesman by Sportswear, Inc., for over twenty-two years. Each year Prince and Sportswear entered into a one-year contract that described the way Prince would receive commissions for his sales. The last contract was dated January 2, 1962. Under it, Prince was allowed to employ persons to assist him, provided that their work was "consistent with the achievement of the result contracted for." Thus, Prince's obligation, if he hired an assistant, was in a supervisory capacity. At the beginning of the year, Prince hired Nadler as his sales assistant. Prince died on August 22, 1962. A dispute later arose over whether Prince's estate should receive the commissions on sales obtained prior to Prince's death and commissions on orders obtained by Nadler after Prince's death. What judgment? [Kowal v. Sportswear by Revere, Inc., 351 Mass. 541, 222 N.E.2d 778 (1967)]

5. Jones hired Haverty to install a plumbing and heating system in a building that Jones was constructing. Jones made a number of payments to Haverty during the period of construction, but when construction was completed, he still owed Haverty about $10,000. Jones refused to pay because Haverty had not completed his work according to the contract. Specifically, Haverty had used a number of inferior quality plumbing couplings and had substituted cheaper three-quarter-inch pipe for one-inch pipe in a few places. The damage to the building as a result of these and other deviations from the contract by Haverty amounted to about $2,000. Should Jones pay Haverty $8,000 or nothing at all? [Thomas Haverty Company v. Jones, 185 Cal. 285, 197 P. 105 (1921)]

6. Nicholson hired Howard Construction Company to build a building for use as a bridal salon. At the time, Nicholson had arranged that Honey's International would be the tenant. Once built, the building would be suitable only for a bridal salon. After Nicholson and Howard had entered into their contract but before construction had begun, Honey's International went bankrupt. Nicholson thereafter refused to pay Howard to go through with the contract

since Nicholson's intended tenant was no longer in existence. Howard sues Nicholson for breach of contract. Can Howard recover? [Howard v. Nicholson, 556 S.W.2d 477 (Mo.App.1977)]

7. The city of Fort Lauderdale hired La Gasse Pool Company to renovate a swimming pool owned and operated by the city. When La Gasse was about three-quarters finished, the pool was vandalized. The damage to the pool required La Gasse to redo part of its work. Thereafter, La Gasse completed the renovation project. Who should pay for the extra work caused by the vandalism? [La Gasse Pool Construction Company v. Fort Lauderdale, 288 So.2d 273 (Fla. App.1974)]

8. Persinger engaged Kichler to do certain interior decorating for Persinger's bedroom. Kichler was given the appropriate measurements for making a bedspread and was required to match this bedspread with valances and shades, which he was also supposed to supply. When Kichler delivered the bedspread, shade, and valances, several problems arose. First, the bedspread was two inches short. To remedy this, Kichler added a ruffle around the edge. In addition, the shades and valances did not match the bedspread. Persinger rejected Kichler's performance and demanded her money back. Kichler refused, claiming that he had substantially performed the contract. What result? [Kichler's Inc. v. Persinger, 24 Ohio App.2d 124, 53 O.O.2d 337, 265 N.E.2d 319 (1970)]

9. Peregoy owed Domestic Loan, Inc. a little over $500 on a promissory note. Peregoy refused to pay, and Domestic Loan brought an action and obtained a judgment for $509. Shortly thereafter, Peregoy voluntarily went into bankruptcy, and his obligation to Domestic Loan for $509 was extinguished. After Peregoy went bankrupt, the two parties entered into a revivor agreement in which Peregoy acknowledged the previous debt of $509 and agreed to pay $250. Peregoy failed and refused to pay Domestic Loan any money at all. What does Peregoy owe Domestic Loan—$509, $250, or nothing at all? [Domestic Loan, Inc. v. Peregoy, 116 Ohio App. 381, 22 O.O.2d 208, 184 N.E.2d 457 (1962)]

10. On June 10, 1927, Scoville sold certain shares of stock to Brooks. At the time of the sale, Scoville promised to repurchase the stock from Brooks at Brooks's request at any time within one year from the date of the purchase by Brooks. On November 1, Brooks notified Scoville that he wanted Scoville to repurchase the stock according to the terms of the agreement of June 10. On several occasions after November 1, Brooks again demanded that Scoville repurchase the stock. Each time Scoville agreed to repurchase the stock but failed to carry out his promise. Brooks claimed that each time he contacted Scoville, he was "ready and willing" to deliver the stock to Scoville. Brooks never made a *formal* tender of the stock. Is Scoville in breach of contract? [Brooks v. Scoville, 81 Utah 163, 17 P.2d 218 (1932)]

14

Contracts
Breach of Contract and Remedies

Whenever a party fails to perform part or all of the duties under a contract, that party is in *breach of contract*. Breach of contract is the failure to perform what a party is under an absolute duty to perform.[1] Once a party fails to perform or performs inadequately, the other party—the nonbreaching party—can choose one or more of several remedies. A *remedy* is the relief provided for an innocent party when the other party has breached the contract. It is the means employed to enforce a right or redress an injury. Strictly speaking, "remedy" is not a part of a lawsuit but the result thereof, the object for which the lawsuit is presented and the end to which all litigation is directed. The most common remedies available to a nonbreaching party include: (1) damages, (2) rescission and restitution, (3) specific performance, and (4) reformation.

DAMAGES

A breach of any contract entitles the nonbreaching party to sue for money damages. *Damages* are designed to compensate the nonbreaching party for the loss of the bargain. When a party loses the benefit of the bargain or contract, the breaching party must make up this loss to the nonbreaching party. Often, courts say that innocent parties are to be placed in the position they would have occupied had the contract been fully per-

---

1. Restatement, Contracts, Section 312.

159

formed. The nonbreaching party is entitled to the benefit of the bargain.[2]

Types of Damages

There are numerous types of damages. This chapter will discuss (1) compensatory, (2) consequential, (3) punitive, and (4) nominal damages.

COMPENSATORY DAMAGES Damages compensating the nonbreaching party for the loss of the bargain are known as **compensatory damages.** These damages compensate the injured party only for the injuries sustained. They simply make good or replace the loss caused by the wrong or injury. In a breach of contract, compensatory damages are usually the only damages recoverable. When a breach of contract places the innocent party in a *better* position, the party is not entitled to anything other than **nominal damages**—a trivial amount for the technical breach of the contract. For example, suppose that Jackson contracts to buy potatoes from Stanley at fifty cents a pound. Stanley breaches the contract and does not deliver the potatoes. If Jackson then buys the potatoes on the open market at half the price, he is clearly better off because of Stanley's breach.

Sale of Goods The standard or ordinary measure of damages depends on the type of contract involved. In a contract for the sale of goods the usual measure of damages is an amount equal to the difference between the contract price and the market price.[3] Suppose Chrysler Corporation contracts to buy ten model UTS 400 computer terminals from Sperry Rand Corporation for $8,000 apiece. If Sperry Rand fails to deliver the ten terminals, and their price rises to $8,150, Chrysler's measure of damages in this case is $1,500 (10 times $150).

Sale of Land The measure of damages in a contract for the sale of land is ordinarily the same as the measure in contracts for the sale of goods—that is, the difference between the contract price and the market price of the land. The majority of states follow this rule regardless of whether it is the buyer or the seller who breaches the contract. A minority of states, however, follow a different rule when the seller breaches the contract and the breach is not deliberate.[4] In such a case, these states allow the prospective purchaser to recover any down payment plus any expenses incurred (such as fees for title searches, attorneys, and escrows). This minority rule effectively places purchasers in the position they occupied *prior* to the sale. Purchasers do not get the benefit of their bargains as they would if the measure of damages equaled the difference between the contract price and the market price.

Construction Contracts The measure of damages in a building or construction contract varies depending upon which party breaches and at what stage the breach occurs. The owner can breach at three different stages of the construction: (1) before performance begins, (2) during performance, and (3) after performance is complete. If the owner breaches before performance begins, the contractor can recover only the profits that would have been made on the contract (that is, the total contract price less the cost of materials and labor). If the owner breaches after performance begins, the contractor can recover the profits plus the costs incurred in partially constructing the building. If the owner breaches after the construction is complete, the contractor can recover the entire contract price.[5] To illustrate: Goodyear Tire &

2. Restatement, Contracts, Section 329, and UCC Sec. 1-106(1).
3. At the time and place where the goods were to be delivered. See UCC Secs. 2-708 and 2-713.
4. A deliberate breach includes the vendor's failure to convey the land because the market price has gone up. A nondeliberate breach includes the vendor's failure to convey the land because an unknown easement rendered title unmarketable. See Chapter 52.
5. Actually, this is true for most contracts; the nonbreaching party is normally owed the contract profit plus the cost of performance.

Rubber Co. wants to build an international research center at its industrial and film products plant in Craigavon, Northern Ireland. Goodyear makes a contract for the 54,000-square-foot center with your corporation. The contract price is $5 million, and your company plans to spend $4.3 million in materials and labor. However, before construction begins, Goodyear's president calls you and unequivocally repudiates the contract. Your measure of damages is $700,000. Alternatively, assume you begin the work, but after you spend $1.2 million, Goodyear throws your crews off the land and refuses to allow any more construction to go on. Your measure of damages is $1.9 million ($700,000 of lost profit plus $1.2 million in costs). Next assume you are able to complete the research center, but Goodyear breaches the contract by refusing to pay. Your measure of damages is $5 million (the full contract price). Note that the result is ultimately the same in each example. You are able to recover the $700,000 profit and are reimbursed for your actual costs.

When the construction contractor breaches the contract by stopping halfway through the project, the measure of damages is the cost of completion. If the builder substantially performs, the courts may use the cost of completion formula, but only if there is no substantial economic waste in requiring completion.[6] If the

_____
6. Economic waste occurs when the cost of additional resources to finish the project exceeds any conceivable value placed on the additional work done. For example, if a contractor discovers that it will cost $10,000 to move a large coral rock eleven inches as specified in the contract, and the change in the rock's position will alter the appearance of the project only a trifle, full completion will involve an economic waste.

builder finishes late, the measure of damages will be the *loss of use*. As examples, assume three situations:

1. The builder of a house quits working after the foundation is built.
2. The builder of a house completes the construction, but the paneling is one-quarter-inch thick instead of five-sixteenths-inch thick.
3. The builder completes the house one week late.

In situation 1 the measure of damages equals the cost of getting another builder to complete the house. In situation 2 the cost to complete the house includes the cost of tearing out the walls and installing the thicker paneling. This additional cost is economic waste and a needless expense (which the owner probably would not incur anyway), so the courts will usually give the owner the difference between the value of the house as it is and the value of the house if it had been completed as promised. If the house is worth $2,000 less due to the thinner paneling, that will be the amount of damages recoverable. In situation 3 the measure of damages is the cost incurred by the owner to live elsewhere for a week.

Often, the party suing for compensatory damages has failed to perform completely his or her part of the bargain. Faced with this situation in the following case, two courts arrived at the same figure for damages but used different theories. The trial court used the theory of *substantial performance*; the appellate court insisted that the proper action was *quantum meruit* (recovery of fair value). In either event, a contractor who did not live up to the requirements of his contract was not entitled to full payment of the contract price.

_____

BACKGROUND AND FACTS   *Roper entered into an oral contract with Armstead Masonry Company under which Armstead agreed to do some brick veneer work on Roper's house for a price of $535.25. The contract required Armstead to match the new brick as closely as possible to the existing brick. Armstead failed to match the brick, although in all other respects his veneer work was of sound construction. Roper refused to pay the full contract price.*

REYNOLDS v. ARMSTEAD

Supreme Court of Colorado, 1968.
166 Colo. 372, 443 P.2d 990.

DECISION AND RATIONALE *Armstead failed to substantially perform his obligation under the contract. The agreement stipulated that Armstead's brick work be aesthetically, as well as functionally, acceptable. Since his performance deviated significantly from this requirement, his breach was a material breach. However, Armstead was only entitled to $267.62 for the value of his work. His breach of substantial performance deprived him of the right to the full contract price. The court concluded: "Armstead's failure to substantially perform his contract deprived him of the right to recover under the 'theory' of express contract. *** Upon a 'theory' of quantum meruit the plaintiff, under the evidence, was entitled to the judgment *** "*

CONSEQUENTIAL (SPECIAL) DAMAGES Damages resulting from a party's breach of contract are called *consequential damages.* They differ from compensatory damages in that they are caused by special circumstances beyond the contract itself. They flow only from the consequences or results of a breach. For example, if a seller fails to deliver goods that a buyer is planning to resell *immediately,* consequential damages will be awarded for the loss of profit from the planned resale. The buyer will also recover compensatory damages for the difference between the contract price and the market price of the goods.

In order to recover consequential damages, the breaching party must know (or have reason to know) that special circumstances will cause the nonbreaching party to suffer an additional loss. The rationale here is to give the nonbreaching party the whole benefit of the bargain, provided the breaching party knew of the special circumstances when the contract was made. For example, suppose Leed sends a vital part of her printing press to be repaired, and the part is properly repaired. Leed tells the shipper who is to return the part that she must receive it by Monday or she will not be able to print her paper and will lose $750. If the shipper is late, Leed can recover the consequential damages caused by the delay (that is, the $750 in lost profits). Likewise, when a bank wrongfully dishonors a check, and the drawer (the person writing the check) is arrested, the drawer can recover consequential damages (that is, damages from the harm to the drawer's reputation).[7] An ice company that is supposed to deliver ice to keep a butcher's meat cold can be held liable for meat spoilage if it does not deliver the ice on time.

A leading case on the necessity of giving notice of "consequential" circumstances is *Hadley v. Baxendale,* decided in 1854. The case involved a broken crankshaft used in a mill operation. In the mid-1800s, it was very common for large mills, such as the one the plaintiffs operated, to have more than one crankshaft in case the main one broke and had to be repaired, as it did in this case. Also, in those days it was common knowledge that flour mills had spares. It is against this background that the parties argued whether or not the damages resulting from lost profits while the crankshaft was out for repair were "too remote" to be recoverable.

---

7. Weaver v. Bank of America, 59 Cal.2d 428, 30 Cal.Rptr. 4, 380 P.2d 644 (1963). A checking account is a contractual arrangement.

HADLEY v. BAXENDALE
9 Exch. 341, 156 Eng.Rep. 145, 1854.

BACKGROUND AND FACTS *The plaintiffs owned a flour mill. A crankshaft in the mill's steam engine broke, causing the mill to shut down. The owners of the mill brought the shaft to the defendant, a common carrier, for shipment to another city, where a duplicate shaft* *was to be made. The defendant collected the freight charges and promised to deliver the shaft the following day. However, it was not delivered for several days, and the reopening of the mill was delayed. The owners sued the common carrier to recover the profits they lost while the mill was closed.*

DECISION AND RATIONALE   *The Court of Exchequer ordered a new trial. According to the court, the special circumstances that caused the loss of profits had never been sufficiently communicated by the plaintiffs to the defendants. In awarding damages, compensation is given only for those injuries that the defendant could reasonably have foreseen as a probable result of the usual course of events following a breach. If the injury is outside the usual and foreseeable cause of events, the plaintiffs must show specifically that the defendant had reason to know the facts and foresee the injury. "Where two parties have made a contract which one of them has broken, the damages which the other party ought to receive in respect of such breach of contract should be such as may fairly and reasonably be considered either arising naturally, i.e., according to the usual course of things, from such breach of contract itself, or such as may reasonably be supposed to have been in the contemplation of both parties, at the time they made the contract, as the probable result of the breach of it."*

PUNITIVE DAMAGES   Punitive, or exemplary, damages are generally not recoverable in a breach of contract action. *Punitive damages are designed to punish a guilty party and to make an example of the party in order to deter similar conduct in the future.* Such damages are also intended to give solace to the plaintiff from mental anguish, shame, and other aggravations of the original wrong. (These damages are also called "smart money.") Punitive damages have no real place in contract law since society does not punish a person for breaching a contract. Society compensates the other person for the loss of the bargain, no more and no less. In certain cases, however, punitive damages are available, but not on a contractual theory of recovery. Some breaches of contract are also torts (see Chapter 3) and the nonbreaching party may be able to recover compensatory and consequential damages for the breach of contract as well as punitive damages for the tort.[8]

NOMINAL DAMAGES   When no financial loss is involved because of a breach of contract, the court may award nominal damages to the innocent party. Nominal damage awards are often trifling, but they do establish that the defendant acted wrongfully.

Mitigation of Damages

Whenever a breach of contract occurs, the injured party should take reasonable steps to mitigate the damages. In a literal sense, the nonbreaching party is under no duty to mitigate damages, but a nonbreaching party who does not mitigate damages will recover less as a remedy. For example, if goods are in the process of manufacture, and the buyer repudiates the contract, the seller must stop production. The seller can recover only for the time, effort, and resources expended up to the time of repudiation. Similarly, an employee who is discharged before the end of an employment contract must

---

8.   For example, if a bus driver negligently swerves the bus so that a passenger is injured, the passenger can sue for breach of the contract for safe carriage and in tort for negligence.

seek similar employment elsewhere. A discharged employee is under no duty to accept dissimilar employment, but if he or she does, the pay received will be deducted from damages otherwise recoverable.

Liquidated Damages and Penalties

A **liquidated damages** provision in a contract specifies a certain amount to be paid in the event of a default or breach of contract. For example, a provision requiring a construction contractor to pay $100 for every day he is late in completing the construction is a liquidated damages provision. Liquidated damages differ from penalties. **Penalties** specify a certain amount to be paid in the event of a default or breach of contract and are designed to *penalize* the breaching party. Liquidated damage provisions are enforceable; penalty provisions are not. In order to determine if a particular provision is for liquidated damages or for a penalty, two questions must be answered. First, were the damages difficult to estimate when the contract was entered into? Second, was the amount set as damages a reasonable estimate and not excessive?[9] If both answers are yes, the provision will be enforced. If either answer is no, the provision will not be enforced. In a construction contract, it is difficult to estimate the amount of damages caused by a delay in completing construction, so liquidated damage clauses are often used. On the other hand, the damage caused by failure to pay rent is easily estimated, so in leases, liquidated damage clauses are not used. As to the reasonableness of the estimate, a liquidated damage provision that requires a construction contractor to pay $500 for every day's delay when the rental value of the property is $100 per day is clearly unreasonable and excessive. But if the provision requires the construction contractor to pay $110 or $90 per day, the provision is reasonable and not excessive.[10]

9.   Restatement, Contracts, Section 339.
10.   But to learn how inconsistent the courts are, see K. W. Clarkson, R. L. Miller, and T. J. Muris, "Liquidated Damages vs. Penalty: Sense or Nonsense?" *Wisconsin Law Review*, Spring 1978.

The amount that a nonbreaching party can recover from a breach of contract depends upon whether the provision is held to be a liquidated damage provision or a penalty. A liquidated damage provision is enforceable, and the nonbreaching party can recover the amount specified in the provision, even if the actual damages are less than the specified amount. If the provision is determined to be a penalty, it is not enforceable (no matter what it is called in the contract). Therefore, the nonbreaching party can recover only the actual damages. Actual damages are compensatory and consequential damages, as defined above.

RESCISSION AND RESTITUTION

Rescission is essentially an action to undo, or cancel a contract—to return the contracting parties to the places they occupied prior to the transaction.[11] Where fraud, a mistake, duress, or failure of consideration are present, rescission is available. (See Chapter 9.)[12] The failure of one party to perform entitles the other party to rescind the contract. The rescinding party must give prompt notice to the breaching party. In order to rescind a contract, both parties must make **restitution** to each other. Essentially, they must return whatever they have received under the contract. If the goods or property received can be restored *in specie*—that is, if the actual goods or property can be returned—they must be. If the goods or property have been consumed, restitution must be made in an equivalent amount of money.

SPECIFIC PERFORMANCE

The remedy of *specific performance* calls for the performance of the act promised in the

11.   The rescission discussed here refers to *unilateral* rescission where only one party wants to undo the contract. In mutual rescission, both parties agree to undo the contract. Mutual rescission discharges the contract; unilateral rescission is generally available as a remedy for breach of contract.
12.   States often have statutes allowing consumers to rescind unilaterally contracts made at home with door-to-door salespersons. Rescission is allowed within three days for any reason or for no reason at all. See, for example, California Civil Code, Sec. 1689.5.

contract. This remedy is quite attractive to the nonbreaching party since it provides the exact bargain promised in the contract. It also avoids some of the problems inherent in a suit for money damages. First, the nonbreaching party need not worry about collecting the judgment.[13] Second, the nonbreaching party need not look around for another contract. Third, the actual performance may be more valuable than the money damages.

Although the equitable remedy of specific performance is often preferable to other remedies, specific performance will not be granted unless the party's legal remedy (money damages) is inadequate. For example, contracts for the sale of goods rarely qualify for specific performance. The legal remedy, money damages, will ordinarily be adequate in such a situation because substantially identical goods can be bought or sold in the market. If the goods are unique, however, a court of equity will decree specific performance. For example, paintings, sculptures, or rare books are so unique that money damages will not enable a buyer to obtain substantially identical substitutes in the market.

Sale of Land

Specific performance is generally granted in a contract for the sale of land. The legal remedy for breach of a land sales contract is inadequate because every piece of land is considered to be unique. Money damages will not compensate a buyer adequately because the same land cannot be obtained elsewhere.

Contracts for Personal Services

Personal service contracts require one party to work personally for another party. Courts of law and equity uniformly refuse to grant specific performance of personal service contracts. The remedy at law may be adequate if substantially identical service is available from other persons (for example, if you hire someone to mow your lawn). On the other hand, it may be inadequate if no one of the same quality is available elsewhere (say, where a specific actress is to perform). In either event, courts are very hesitant to order specific performance by a party because public policy strongly discourages involuntary servitude.[14] Moreover, the courts do not want to have to monitor a continuing service contract.

Specific performance will be denied if it is impossible or impractical to enforce performance. Courts do not want to become entangled in complex business transactions and will not decree specific performance if supervision will be prolonged or difficult. For this reason, courts refuse to order specific performance that requires the exercise of personal judgment or talent. For example, if you contract with an eccentric artist for a portrait of your mother, and the artist refuses to paint it, a court will not compel the artist to do so. There is no way the court can assure meaningful performance. Similarly, courts refuse to order specific performance of a construction contract because they are not set up to operate as construction supervisors or engineers.

REFORMATION

Reformation is an equitable remedy used when the parties have *imperfectly* expressed their agreement in writing. Reformation allows the contract to be rewritten to reflect the parties' *true* intentions. It applies most often where fraud or mutual mistake is present. If B contracts to buy a certain piece of land from C, but both parties are mistaken about what piece of land is to be sold, a mutual mistake has occurred. Accordingly, a court of equity will reform the contract so that B and C can agree on which piece of land is being sold.

Reformation is frequently utilized to make use of another remedy. For example, a contract

---

13. Courts enter judgments as final dispositions of cases. The judgment, of course, must be collected. Collection, however, poses problems. For example, the judgment debtor may be broke or have only a very small net worth.

14. The Thirteenth Amendment to the United States Constitution prohibits involuntary servitude, but *negative* injunctions (i. e. prohibiting rather than ordering certain conduct) are possible.

for the sale of goods can be reformed in order for one of the parties to show that the contract has been breached. Or it can be reformed to show that one of the parties is entitled to rescission, restitution, or specific performance. Before a court will grant reformation, one or both of the parties must present clear and convincing evidence of either fraud or mutual mistake.

RECOVERY BASED ON QUASI-CONTRACT

As stated in Chapter 5, a quasi-contract is not a legal contract but an equitable theory *imposed* on the parties to obtain justice. Hence, a quasi-contract becomes an equitable basis for equitable relief. The contract arises because the law *implies* a promise to pay for benefits received by a party. Essentially, when one party has conferred a benefit on another party, justice requires the party receiving the benefit to pay the reasonable value of it. The party receiving the benefit should not be unjustly enriched at the other party's expense.

In order to recover on a quasi-contract, the party seeking recovery must show that: (1) a benefit has been conferred on the other party; (2) the benefit was conferred with the expectation of being paid; (3) the party seeking recovery did not act as a volunteer in conferring the benefit; and (4) retention of the benefit without being paid would result in unjust enrichment of the party receiving the benefit. Quasi-contractual recovery is useful where one party has *partially* performed under a contract that is unenforceable. It can be used as an alternative to a suit for damages and will allow the party to recover for the reasonable value of the partial performance. For example, suppose Abrams contracts to build two oil derricks for the Texas Gulf Sulfur Co. The derricks are to be built over a period of three years, but the parties do not make a written contract. Enforcement of the contract will therefore be barred by the Statute of Frauds.[15] If Abrams completes one derrick before Texas Gulf Sulfur tells him that the contract is unenforceable, Abrams can sue in quasi-contract.

First, a benefit has been conferred on Texas Gulf Sulfur, since one oil derrick has been built. Second, Abrams built the derrick (conferred the benefit) expecting to be paid. Third, Abrams did not volunteer to build the derrick; he built it under an unenforceable oral contract. Fourth, allowing Texas Gulf Sulfur to retain the derrick would enrich the company unjustly. Therefore, Abrams should be able to recover. Abrams is entitled to recover the reasonable value of the oil derrick (under the theory of *quantum meruit*). This is ordinarily equal to the fair market value of the derrick.

Benefits conferred as a result of fraud, mistake, or duress are recoverable by the use of the quasi-contractual theory of recovery. Quasi-contractual relief is generally available where some benefit has been conferred on a party and where the party conferring the benefit cannot sue on the contract itself.

Quasi-contractual relief and quasi-contractual liability are doctrines formulated and applied by the courts to prevent unjust enrichment. In the following situation, the plaintiff provided goods and services and was not paid. Although, as the court points out, the plaintiff sued the wrong defendant, the plaintiff's theory of recovery is a valid one.

---

15. Contracts which by their terms cannot be performed within one year must be in writing to be enforceable. See Chapter 11.

CALLANO v. OAKWOOD PARK HOMES CORP.
Superior Court of New Jersey, Appellate Division, 1965.
91 N.J.Super. 105, 219 A.2d 332.

BACKGROUND AND FACTS *Oakwood was engaged in the construction of a housing development and contracted to sell a certain house and lot to Pendergast. Before the house was completed, Callano, who operated a plant nursery, delivered and planted shrubbery pursuant to a contract with Pendergast. Pendergast died, and shortly thereafter his estate and Oakwood mutually agreed to cancel the contract of sale.*

Subsequently, Oakwood sold the Pendergast property, including the shrubbery located thereon, to a third party. Callano sought payment of the invoice price of the shrubbery from Oakwood.

DECISION AND RATIONALE *Since no express contract existed between Callano and Oakwood, Oakwood was not liable for the contract price. Nor was he obligated to pay for the reasonable value of the shrubbery on the theory of quasi-contract. Recovery under quasi-contract is granted only when a person stands to be unjustifiably enriched by the efforts of another and where the injured person has no other means of redress. In the opinion of the judge who heard the case: "Recovery on the theory of quasi-contract was developed under the law to provide a remedy where none existed. Here a remedy exists. Plaintiffs may bring their action against Pendergast's estate."*

COMMENTS *Note that in a lawsuit between Callano and Pendergast (or his estate), there would be a direct claim for damages based upon an underlying contract that had occurred between the parties. Hence, the theory of quasi-contract would be inapplicable in such a lawsuit.*

ELECTION OF REMEDIES

In many cases, a nonbreaching party will have several remedies available, and they may be inconsistent. The party must choose which remedy to pursue. For example, a person who buys a fradulently represented car can sue either to cancel (rescind) the sales contract or to recover damages. Obviously, these remedies are inconsistent. An action to rescind undoes the contract; an action for damages affirms it. The purpose of the *election of remedies* doctrine is to prevent double recovery. Suppose McCarthy agrees to sell his land to Tally. Then McCarthy changes her mind and repudiates the contract. Tally can sue for damages or for specific performance. If she receives damages caused by the breach, she should not be able to get specific performance of the sales contract, since failure to deliver possession of the land was the cause of the injury for which she received damages. If Tally could seek damages *and* specific performance, she would recover twice for the same breach of contract. The doctrine of election of remedies requires Tally to choose the remedy she wants, and it eliminates any possibility of double recovery.

Unfortunately, the doctrine has been applied in a rigid and technical manner, leading to some harsh results.[16] The nonbreaching party is required to choose a remedy fairly early in the lawsuit, and the choice is then irrevocable even if no prejudice will result to the other party from allowing the nonbreaching party to change remedies. The election can be made by conduct, and the party does not have to be aware that a certain remedy is being elected. Therefore, the doctrine of election of remedies has been eliminated in contracts for the sale of goods. The Uniform Commercial Code expressly rejects the doctrine. (See UCC Secs. 2-703 and 2-711.) Remedies under the UCC are essentially cumulative in nature and include all the available remedies for breach of contract. Whether

16. For example, in a Wisconsin case, Carpenter was fraudulently induced to buy a piece of land for $100. He spent $140 moving onto the land and then discovered the fraud. Instead of suing for damages, Carpenter sued to rescind the contract. The court denied recovery of the $140 because the seller, Mason, did not receive the $140 and was therefore not required to reimburse Carpenter for his moving expenses. So Carpenter suffered a net loss of $140 on the transaction. If Carpenter had sued for damages, he could have recovered the $100 and the $140. See Carpenter v. Mason, 181 Wis. 114, 193 N.W. 973 (1923).

the pursuit of one remedy bars another depends entirely on the facts of the individual case. In other words, if double recovery is possible, only one remedy can be chosen in the final analysis. However, this remedy need not be chosen until absolutely necessary to decide the case.

WAIVER OF BREACH

Under certain circumstances, a nonbreaching party may be willing to accept a defective performance of the contract. This knowing relinquishment of a legal right (that is, the right to require satisfactory and full performance) is called a **waiver.**[17] When a waiver of a breach of contract occurs, the party waiving the breach cannot take any later action on the theory that the contract was broken. In effect, the waiver erases the past breach; the contract continues as if the breach had never existed. Of course, the waiver of breach of contract extends only to the matter waived and not to the whole contract. Businesspersons often waive breaches of contract by the other party in order to get whatever benefit possible out of the contract.

Scope of a Waiver

Ordinarily the waiver by a contracting party will not operate to waive *subsequent* breaches of contract. This is always true when the subsequent breaches are unrelated to the first breach. For example, an owner who waives the right to sue for late completion of a stage of construction does not waive the right to sue for failure to comply with engineering specifications. However, subsequent breaches in the form of late performance can be waived by prior waivers.

Suppose the construction contract above was to be completed in six stages, each two months apart, spanning a period of one year. The question is whether the waiver of the right to object to lateness in stage 1 will operate as a waiver of the time requirements for stages 2 through 6. If only stage 1's time requirements have been waived, the waiver will not extend to the other five stages. However, if the first five

stages were all late (and the right to object to the lateness was always waived), the waivers will extend to stage 6.

A waiver will be extended to subsequent defective performance if a reasonable person would conclude that similar defective performance in the future will be satisfactory. Therefore, a *pattern of conduct* that waives a number of successive breaches will operate as a continued waiver. In order to change this result, the nonbreaching party should give notice to the breaching party that full performance will be required in the future. In the example above, the owner can simply notify the builder that each stage must be completed on time in the future.

A waiver of the right to full performance waives only the requirement of full performance. The party who has rendered defective or less than full performance remains liable for the damages caused by the breach of contract. In effect, the waiver operates to keep the contract going. The waiver prevents the nonbreaching party from calling the contract to an end or rescinding the contract. The contract continues, but the nonbreaching party can recover damages caused by defective or less than full performance.

CONTRACT PROVISIONS LIMITING REMEDIES

A contract can include provisions stating that no damages can be recovered for certain types of breaches or that damages must be limited to a maximum amount. In addition, the contract can provide that the only remedy for breach is replacement, repair, or refund of the purchase price. Provisions stating that no damages can be recovered are called *exculpatory clauses.* (See Chapter 3.) Provisions that affect the availability of certain remedies are called *limitation of liability clauses.*

Mutual Assent Required

Initially, a court must determine if the provision has been made a part of the contract by offer

---

17. Restatement, Contracts, Sections 297 and 298.

and acceptance. In order for a term or provision to become part of a contract, both parties must consent to it. Therefore, courts will analyze whether the provision was noticed by the parties—whether, for example, the provision was in fine print or on the back of a lengthy contract. If either party did not know about the provision, it will not be a part of the contract and will not be enforced. For example, motorists often park their cars in lots and receive a small ticket stub that excludes liability for damages to cars parked in the lot. If a reasonable person would have noticed such an exculpatory clause, it will be enforced. If the clause is not conspicuous and a reasonable person would not have noticed it, the clause will not be enforced, and the motorist can sue for damage caused to his or her car.[18]

Type of Breach Covered

Once it has been determined that the provision or clause is part of the contract, the analysis must focus on the type of breach that is exculpated. For example, a provision excluding liability for fraudulent or intentional injury will not be enforced. Likewise, a clause excluding liability for illegal acts or violations of law will not be enforced. On the other hand, a clause excluding liability for negligence will be enforced in appropriate cases. When an exculpatory clause for negligence is contained in a contract made between parties with roughly equal bargaining positions, the clause will be enforced.

For example, assume Delta Airways buys six DC-9s from Douglas Aircraft. In the contract for sale, a clause excludes liability for errors in design and construction of the aircraft. The clause will be upheld because both parties are large corporations with roughly equal bargaining positions. The equality of bargaining power assures that the exculpatory clause was not dictated by one of the parties and forced upon the other.

---

18. See California State Auto v. Barrett Garages, Inc., 257 Cal.App.2d 84, 64 Cal.Rptr. 699 (1967).

Limited Remedies

Under the Uniform Commercial Code, in a contract for the sale of goods, remedies can be limited, but rules different from those discussed above apply. First, in order to make a certain remedy the only remedy available, the contract must state that the remedy is exclusive. Suppose you buy an automobile, and the sales contract limits your remedy to repair or replacement of defective parts. Under the Uniform Commercial Code, the sales contract must also state that "the sole and exclusive remedy available to the buyer is repair and/or replacement of the defective parts." If the contract states that the remedy is exclusive, then the specified remedy will be the only one ordinarily available to the buyer (provided the contract is not unconscionable).

When circumstances cause an exclusive remedy to fail of its essential purpose, then it will not be exclusive. [See UCC Sec. 2-719(2).] In the above example, if your car breaks down several times, and the dealer is unable to fix or replace the defective parts, the exclusive remedy fails of its essential purpose. Then all the other remedies under the UCC become available.

Under the Uniform Commercial Code, a sales contract may limit or exclude consequential damages, provided the limitation is not *unconscionable*.[19] Where the buyer is a consumer, the limitation of liability for personal injury is *prima facie* unconscionable and will not normally be enforced. Where the buyer is not a consumer and the loss is commercial in nature, the limitation of liability for personal injuries is not necessarily unconscionable. In the above example, if the sales contract excludes all liability for personal injuries caused by defects in the design or the construction of the automobile, the provision will not be enforced because it is *prima facie* unconscionable. However, if you buy the car as a company car, the limitation will not necessarily be unconscionable, although if it were proven to be unconscionable, it would be unenforceable.

QUESTIONS AND CASE PROBLEMS

1. On July 1, 1946, Billetter and Posell entered into an oral contract whereby Posell employed Billetter as a designer for a period of one year commencing from the date of the contract. The salary agreed upon was $75 per week. On December 31, Posell fired Billetter without cause. Posell told Billetter that the company had decided to hire another designer and suggested that Billetter take a position as a floor lady at a salary of $55 per week. Billetter was unwilling to accept such a reduction in salary. For the remainder of the contract, Billetter was unable to find comparable employment, although she made a good faith effort to do so. During this period of unemployment, Billetter received payments from the state unemployment and compensation fund. In Billetter's suit against Posell, Posell defended on the ground that Billetter should have mitigated her damages by accepting the position as floor lady. Posell also argued that he should be allowed to deduct the unemployment payments Billetter received from her damages. What result? [Billetter v. Posell, 94 Cal.App.2d 858, 211 P.2d 621 (1949)]

2. The United States, acting through the Department of Agriculture, entered into a contract with Priebe and Sons for the purchase of dried eggs. The contract called for delivery by Priebe and Sons on May 18 or any day within a ten-day period thereafter at the option of the United States. Priebe and Sons was also required under the contract to have the eggs inspected prior to delivery. Finally, the contract contained a liquidated damage clause providing that "failure to have specified quantities of dried egg products inspected and ready for delivery by the date specified" will be cause for payment of liquidated damages. The contract between Priebe and Sons and the United States was entered into pursuant to the country's war effort. By May 18, the eggs had neither been delivered nor inspected. Inspection was completed on May 22. The United States did not call for delivery of the eggs until May 26. Priebe and Sons made timely shipments pursuant to this May 26 demand. The United States then attempted to sue Priebe and Sons under the liquidated damage clause for not having the eggs ready for shipment by the agreed upon date. Will the United States be successful in its suit? [Priebe and Sons v. United States, 332 U.S. 407, 68 S.Ct. 123, 92 L.Ed. 32 (1947)]

3. Avis Plumbing and Heating entered into a contract with McCormick to do plumbing and heating duct installation in McCormick Seminary. The contract expressly provided that if Avis breached its contract with McCormick, the general contractor could complete the work in any expedient manner. Thereafter, Avis did breach its contract, and the general contractor hired a subcontractor to complete Avis's work, relying on a subcontractor with whom it had had previous dealings. The general contractor made no attempt to select the lowest bidder to replace Avis. McCormick sued Avis Plumbing and Heating to recover the excess cost incurred in hiring a second subcontractor to complete Avis's work. Avis counterclaimed that McCormick's general contractor failed to mitigate damages. Is Avis's counterclaim correct? [Avis Plumbing and Heating Contractors Corp. v. McCormick Theological Seminary, 13 Ill.App.3d 484, 300 N.E.2d 542 (Ill.App.1973)]

4. Westinghouse entered into a contract with New Jersey Electric to manufacture and install a turbine generator for producing electricity. The contract price was over $10 million. The parties engaged in three years of negotiations and bargaining before they agreed on a suitable contract. The ultimate contract provided, among other things, that Westinghouse would not be liable for any injuries to the property belonging to the utility or to its customers or employees. Westinghouse warranted only that it would repair any defects in workmanship and materials appearing within one year of installation. After installation, part of New Jersey Electric's plant and several of its employees were injured because of a defect in the turbine. New Jersey Electric sued Westinghouse, claiming that Westinghouse was liable for the damages because the exculpatory provisions in the contract were unconscionable. What result? [Royal Indemnity Company v. Westinghouse Electric Corp., 385 F.Supp. 520 (D.C.N.Y.1974)]

5. Findlay College had employed Felch as a member of its faculty for a number of years. One of the provisions of Felch's employment contract was that Findlay College would not be allowed to dismiss Felch unless Felch were given an adequate hearing. In August 1961, Findlay College dismissed Felch without a hearing. Felch sought an injunction, requesting that the college be ordered to continue him as a member of its faculty. Should the court grant Felch the relief he requests? [Felch v. Findlay College, 119 Ohio App. 357, 200 N.E.2d 353 (1963)]

6. Bradley put his cow and 400 pounds of hay up for bid at an auction. The cow was present at the auction, but the hay was back at Bradley's farm. Minor

successfully bid $17 for the cow and the hay. He paid the $17, received the cow, and later demanded the hay. Bradley was unable to deliver the hay since it had already been used. Can Minor retain the cow but sue for the price of the hay? [Minor v. Bradley, 22 Pick. 457 (Mass.1839)]

7. Kerr Steamship Company delivered to RCA a twenty-nine-word coded message to be sent to Kerr's agent in Manila. The message included instructions on loading cargo onto one of Kerr's vessels. Kerr's profits on the carriage of the cargo were to be about $6,600. RCA mislaid the coded message, and it was never sent. Kerr sued RCA for the $6,600 in profits that it lost because RCA never sent the message. Can Kerr recover? [Kerr Steamship Company v. Radio Corp. of America, 245 N.Y. 284, 157 N.E. 140 (1927)]

8. Evergreen Amusement Corporation purchased a parcel of land for use as a drive-in movie theater. Evergreen contracted with Milstead to have the lot cleared and graded according to specifications that would make it adequate for a drive-in theater. Milstead was supposed to complete the work by June 1, and Evergreen planned to open the theater at about that time. However, Milstead did not finish clearing and grading the lot until the third week in August. Evergreen sued Milstead, claiming as damages the profits that it could have made on the drive-in theater had it been in operation. Are lost profits the proper measure of damages here? [Evergreen Amusement Corp. v. Milstead, 206 Md. 610, 112 A.2d 901 (1955)]

9. Chaplin was a contestant in the Miss America Beauty Contest. The bathing suit competition was to begin at 8:00 Sunday evening, August 5. Hicks, Chaplin's agent, inadvertently forgot to inform her that the bathing suit competition was to begin at that hour. As a result, Chaplin missed that competition. Twelve prizes were offered in the competition, and because Chaplin missed it, she lost all chance of winning any of the prizes. Chaplin sued Hicks for failing to inform her of the bathing suit segment of the competition, in breach of Hicks's contract. Can Chaplin recover anything? If so, how would a jury determine the amount of the award? [See Chaplin v. Hicks, 2 Kings Bench 786 (1911)]

10. Pareira and Wehner entered into a contract for the sale of land that Wehner intended to develop into a housing project. The contract called for payment in installments. Before Wehner took possession of the land, he drew up plans for the housing project. Shortly after the contract was formed, Wehner realized that the land was four acres smaller than Pareira had said. Because of this difference in size, Wehner was forced to hire a surveyor to replot the housing project. Wehner refused to make any further payments on the land. Pareira filed suit. What kinds of damages can Wehner claim in defending the suit by Pareira? [Pareira v. Wehner, 133 Vt. 74, 330 A.2d 84 (1974)]

UNIT III

Personal Property
and Bailments

15

Personal Property

Property is the legally protected rights and interests a person has in anything with an ascertainable value that is subject to ownership. Property would have little value (and the word would have little meaning) if the law did not define the right to use it, to sell it, and to prevent trespassing upon it. In the United States, the ownership of property receives unique protection under the law. The Bill of Rights states that "no person shall . . . (by any Act of Congress) be deprived of life, liberty, or property, without due process of law; nor shall private property be taken for public use, without just compensation." The Fourteenth Amendment provides that "no State shall . . . deprive any person of life, liberty, or property, without due process of law."

THE NATURE OF PERSONAL PROPERTY

Personal property is a right or interest in personal things that are moveable. Immovable property, like land or houses, is called *real property*. (See Chapters 52 & 53.) Personal property and real property differ significantly, so the law has developed different sets of rules to deal with their acquisition and the transfer of their ownership.

Personal property can be tangible or intangible. *Tangible personal property*, like a TV set, heavy construction equipment, or a car, has physical substance. *Intangible personal property* represents some set of rights and duties, but it has no real physical existence. Stocks and bonds are intangible personal property.

174

Attorneys sometimes refer to all personal property as **chattel**, a more comprehensive term than *goods* because it includes living as well as inanimate property. Often, instead of saying personal property, the law will refer to goods and chattel.

THE EXPANDING NATURE OF PERSONAL PROPERTY

In a dynamic society, the concept of personal property must expand to take account of new types of ownership rights. For example, gas, water, and telephone services are now considered property for the purpose of criminal prosecution when they are stolen or used without payment. Federal and state statutes protect against the copying of musical compositions.[1] It is a crime now to engage in "bootlegging"—illegal copying for resale—of records and tapes. The theft of computer programs is usually considered a theft of property.

ACQUIRING AND TRANSFERRING OWNERSHIP OF PERSONAL PROPERTY

Possession

The old saying, "possession is nine-tenths of the law," in certain respects is true. Possession is the most basic property right in personal property. It involves a certain amount of *control* over the property and the intention of excluding others from possession. It gives the possessor certain rights: (1) the right to enjoy the use of the property without interference from anyone except the true owner (if there is one) and (2) the right to recover the property if any person (except the true owner) wrongfully takes it. Of course, if the possessor is not the true owner, the latter can retrieve the property.

A third person cannot attempt to take personal property away by alleging that the possessor is not the true owner. Suppose Mary

---

1. Intangible property rights are generally protected by federal patent, trademark and copyright laws.

Bloomingthal has a Mack truck that she has been using in her hauling operation. One of her employees believes that the truck really belongs to his friend, Scott Lambert. The employee decides to take the truck and store it in his garage for Lambert. When he returns to work, his boss wants to know where the Mack truck is, and the employee says: "That truck is not yours. My friend, Scott Lambert, owns it. I am going to keep it for him." Bloomingthal immediately fires the employee and brings suit to recover the truck. Bloomingthal will recover the truck plus any damages she has sustained. The former employee will not prevail at trial unless Lambert comes in and proves that he owns the truck. It is not a defense to claim that a third person has *better* title than a possessor.

Purchase

Purchase is one of the most common means of acquiring and transferring ownership of personal property. The purchase or sale of personal property is covered in depth in Chapters 17 to 22 on the Uniform Commercial Code. The first step in solving problems with the purchase and sale of personal property is to determine which laws apply. Article 2 of the UCC governs the sale of goods. Intangible personal property like notes, checks, drafts, and certificates of deposit is governed by Articles 3 and 4. Other intangibles, such as stocks and other investment securities are dealt with in Article 8.

Production

Production—the fruits of labor—is another means of acquiring ownership of personal property. Nearly everyone in the United States today is involved in some sort of production. For example, writers, inventors, and manufacturers all produce personal property and thereby acquire title to it.

Gifts

A **gift** is another fairly common means of both acquiring and transferring ownership of real and personal property. A gift is essentially a *voluntary* transfer of property ownership. It need not be supported by legally sufficient consideration since the very essence of a gift is giving without consideration. A gift must be transferred in the present rather than in the future. For example, suppose your aunt tells you she is going to give you a new Mercedes Benz for your next birthday. This is simply a *promise* to make a gift. It is not enforceable unless you give some consideration for the promise. Then it becomes a binding contract.

THE REQUIREMENTS OF AN EFFECTIVE GIFT There are three requirements of an effective gift—delivery, donative intent, and acceptance by the donee.

Delivery Delivery is obvious in most cases, but some objects cannot be relinquished physically. Then the question of delivery depends upon the surrounding circumstances. When the physical object cannot be delivered, a symbolic or **constructive delivery** will be sufficient. Constructive delivery does not confer real possession of the object in question. It is a general term for all those acts that the law holds to be equivalent to acts of real delivery. Suppose you want to make a gift of various old rare coins that you have stored in a safety deposit box. You certainly cannot deliver the box itself to the donee, and you do not want to take the coins out of the bank. Instead, you can simply deliver the key to the box to your donee. This is symbolic, or constructive, delivery of the contents of the box.

Delivery of intangible personal property must be accomplished by symbolic or constructive delivery. Stocks and bonds are represented by certificates, and delivery of the certificate entitles the holder to income of dividends or interest. Other examples of intangible personal property that must be constructively delivered include insurance policies, contracts, promissory notes, and chattel mortgages.

An effective delivery also requires giving up *complete dominion and control* (ownership rights) over the subject matter of the gift. Cases often turn on the retaining or relinquishing of control over the subject matter of the gift. The Internal Revenue Service scrutinizes transactions between relatives when one relative has given away income-producing property. A relative who does not relinquish complete control over a piece of property will have to pay taxes on the income from the property. Under the tax laws, it is illegal to assign or give away income while retaining control over the property that produces the income.

Delivery can be accomplished by means of a third person. The third person may be the agent of the donor or the donee. If the person is the agent of the donor, the gift is effective when the agent delivers to the donee. If, on the other hand, the third person is the agent of the donee, the gift is effective when the donor delivers to the donee's agent.[2] Where there is doubt as to whose agent the third party is, he or she is generally presumed to be the agent of the donor. Naturally, no delivery is necessary if the gift is already in the hands of the donee. All that is necessary to complete the gift in such a case is the required intent and acceptance by the donee.

Donative Intent Donative intent is determined from the language of the donor and the surrounding circumstances. For example, when a gift is challenged in court, the court may look at the relationship between the parties and the size of the gift in relation to the donor's other assets. A gift to an arch enemy will be viewed with suspicion. Likewise, when people give away a large portion of their assets, the courts will scrutinize the transaction to determine whether there is any fraud or duress.

Acceptance The final requirement of a valid gift is acceptance by the donee. This rarely presents any problems since most donees readily accept their gifts. The courts generally assume acceptance unless shown otherwise.

---

2. Bickford v. Mattocks, 95 Me. 547, 50 A. 894 (1901).

In the following case, the Supreme Court of Mississippi dealt with an issue involving a certificate of deposit made payable to the order of two persons. Because the certificate was made payable *in the alternative*, the question arose whether it was actually the depositor's property at the time she died and therefore an asset of her estate or whether it was the property of the individual to whom it was payable in the alternative.

BACKGROUND AND FACTS *Mechanics' Bank of Water Valley issued a certificate of deposit in the amount of $14,000 payable to the order of Ruby Eubanks or Doyle Thomas. On two occasions during her lifetime, Eubanks stated to friends of hers that the proceeds represented by the certificate were the property of Thomas. When Eubanks died, the certificate of deposit was still in her possession. The following year, Thomas filed suit to gain possession of the note from Eubank's administratrix.*

DECISION AND RATIONALE *Doyle Thomas had no right to possession of the certificate even though there was evidence that at one time Eubanks considered the proceeds of the certificate to be his. In order for Eubanks to have made a valid gift of the property, she would have had to deliver the certificate to Thomas sometime during her life. As expressed by the court: "[O]ne of the essentials of a valid gift clausa mortis, as well as a gift inter vivos, is that the property must be delivered in such a manner that the donor retains no control or dominion over it."*

THOMAS v. ESTATE OF EUBANKS
Supreme Court of Mississippi, 1978. 358 So.2d 709.

INTER VIVOS GIFTS AND CAUSA MORTIS GIFTS **Inter vivos gifts** are made during one's lifetime.[3] **Causa mortis gifts** are made in contemplation of imminent death. *Causa mortis* gifts do not become absolute until the donor dies from the illness or disease that was contemplated. The donee must survive to take the gift, and the donor must not have revoked the gift prior to death. A *causa mortis gift* is revocable at any time up to the death of the donor and is automatically revoked if the donor recovers. Suppose Stevens is to be operated on for a serious tumor. Before the operation, he delivers an envelope to a close business associate. The envelope contains a letter saying "I realize my days are numbered and I want to give you this check for $1,000,000 in the event of my death from this operation." It also contains a check for $1,000,000. The surgeon begins the operation and decides not to remove the tumor. Stevens recovers from the operation but dies several months later. If Stevens's personal representative tries to recover the $1,000,000, she will succeed. The *causa mortis gift* is automatically revoked if the donor recovers. The specific event that was contemplated in making the gift was death from a particular operation. Since Stevens did not die, the gift is revoked and the $1,000,000 passes to Stevens's personal representative when Stevens dies.[4]

WILL OR INHERITANCE

Ownership of property can also be passed by *will* or under *inheritance laws.* Both methods

---

3. When a person dies and his or her will leaves property to anyone, there is technically no gift. Instead, the giving of the property is termed a bequest, devise, or inheritance.

4. Brind v. International Trust Co., 66 Colo. 60, 179 P. 148 (1919).

are statutory (property must be passed by will in accordance with specific statutory rules) and are discussed in Chapter 55.

ACCESSION

Literally, **accession** means "adding on" to something. *Accession* occurs when someone puts labor into a piece of property or adds materials to it. When a carpenter comes on an owner's land and builds a front porch with materials supplied by the owner, accession has occurred. There is usually no dispute about who owns the property after accession has occurred. The owner of the house in the example above can simply pay the carpenter for the improvements and leave it at that. However, disputes can arise over ownership of the property, especially when one party has expended a great deal of labor or materials. In general, whenever one party has wrongfully caused accession, that party is liable to the other party for the damage caused. For example, if Winkler wrongfully enters onto the land of Ames and makes improvements, Winkler cannot claim title to the property and is liable to Ames for any damage caused by the trespass.

In some situations the person making the addition or accession will be allowed to claim title to the property added to. For example, suppose Angelo is walking in a large field and discovers a huge marble stone that is shaped approximately like the Lone Ranger's horse, Silver. Angelo comes back for twenty-seven weeks and transforms the stone into an exact replica of Silver. Angelo's artist friends are very impressed and convince him to move the stone horse to a gallery. Subsequently, it is sold to an eccentric Arab, who wants to paint it red and put it in front of his Beverly Hills mansion. The owner of the field where Angelo found the stone now wants to claim title to it. Normally, the courts will give Angelo title to the stone because the changes he made caused it to increase in value. But Angelo will have to pay the owner of the field for the reasonable value of the stone before it was altered.

CONFUSION

When the personal property of two persons becomes intermingled, this is called **confusion**. Confusion is defined as the comingling of goods such that one person's property cannot be distinguished from another's. For example, if two farmers put their number 2 grade winter wheat in the same silo, confusion will occur. Under the confusion of goods doctrine, if one person wrongfully and willfully mixes goods with those of another in order to render them indistinguishable, the innocent party acquires title to the total.

On the other hand, the doctrine of confusion does not apply when confusion occurs by (1) agreement, (2) an honest mistake, or (3) the act of some third party. When one or more of those three events occurs, the owners all share ownership of the whole equally. Suppose you enter into a cooperative arrangement with six other farmers in your local community of Midway, Iowa. Each fall everyone harvests nearly the same amount of number 2 yellow corn. The corn is stored in silos that are held by the cooperative. Everyone owns one-sixth of the total corn in the silos.[5] If anything happens to the corn, each will bear the loss in equal proportions of one-sixth.

Often, though, each owner will not have an interest equal to the other owners. In such a case, the owners must keep careful records of their respective proportions. If a dispute over ownership arises, the courts will presume that everyone has an equal interest or proportion of the goods. So you must be prepared to prove that you own more than an equal part. As a practical matter, whenever you are dealing with goods that can easily be comingled, you should be aware of the special problems that can arise. Therefore, be sure to maintain accurate records of the goods you or your company owns. Suppose you own two-thirds of the corn in the Midway Co-op silos above. Further assume that the silos are partially damaged by a tornado and thunderstorm. How much have you lost of your total if one-half of the corn is blown away by the

5. As tenants-in-common. See Chapter 52.

storm? You have lost one-half of your two-thirds, or one-third. When corn is stored by several owners, each owning a different proportion of the total, any loss is suffered proportionally.

Intentional, or Negligent, Confusion

Confusion that results from intentional wrongdoing or negligent conduct creates a different problem. The person responsible for the comingling must bear the entire loss if any of the goods are lost, stolen, or destroyed. However, if the wrongdoer can show that no injury occurred and can show the specific portion contributed to the whole, then the wrongdoer can recover that portion.

Suppose you are the vice-president in charge of purchasing for a salad oil company. You buy 10,000 gallons of high grade salad oil and have it delivered to a field warehouse and company. The warehouse and company stores many grades of oil, and your oil is negligently mixed with a much lower grade of oil. The oil was worth $.64 per gallon before it was confused, but now it is worth only $.32 per gallon. Here you should be entitled to claim your 10,000 gallons of oil and sue the warehouse for damages caused by the negligent confusion. On the other hand, suppose the grades of oil were exactly the same but you wanted your oil stored in a separate bin? Here you have no reason to complain and you cannot recover any damage.[6]

MISLAID, LOST, AND ABANDONED PROPERTY

Mislaid Property

Property that has been placed somewhere by the owner voluntarily and then inadvertently forgotten is **mislaid property**. Suppose you go to the theater and leave your gloves on the concession stand. The gloves are mislaid property, and the theater owner is entrusted with the duty of reasonable care for the goods. Whenever mislaid property is found, the finder does not obtain title or possession to the goods.[7] Instead, the owner of the place where the property was mislaid becomes the caretaker of the property because it is highly likely that the true owner will return.[8]

Lost Property

Property that is *not* voluntarily left and forgotten is **lost property**. A finder of lost property can claim title to the property against the whole world, *except the true owner*. If the true owner demands that the lost property be returned, the finder must do so. However, a third party cannot fraudulently assert that title lies with another person in an attempt to take possession of the lost property from a finder. The finder is guilty of a tort, or civil wrong known as *conversion* (see Chapter 3), if he or she knows who the true owners of the property are and fails to return it to them. In addition, many states require the finder to make a reasonably diligent search to locate the true owner of lost property.

Suppose Arnolds works in a large library at night. In the courtyard on her way home, she finds a piece of gold jewelry that looks like it has several precious stones in it. Arnolds decides to take it to a jeweler to have it appraised. While pretending to weigh the jewelry, an employee of the jeweler removes several of the stones. If Arnolds brings an action to recover the stones from the jeweler, she will win because she found lost property and holds valid title against everyone *except the true owner*. Since the property was *lost* and not *mislaid*, the owner of the library is not the caretaker of the jewelry.

---

6. Unless, of course, you had a warehousing contract with a storage firm. Then you could sue for breach of contract, provided the contract required the warehouser to store in a separate bin. As a matter of commercial reality, very few, if any, warehouses contract for storage in separate facilities. If they did, many people would want separate facilities for fear of confusion. This would negate the savings in warehouse storage. Here we are really dealing with *fungible* goods.

7. The finder is an involuntary bailee. See Chapter 16.

8. He or she is a bailee with right of possession against all except the true owner. See Chapter 16.

Instead, Arnolds acquires title good against the whole world (except the true owner).[9]

ESTRAY STATUTES   Many states have **estray statutes** to encourage and facilitate the return of property to its true owner and then to reward a finder for honesty if the property remains unclaimed. Such statutes provide an incentive for finders to report their discoveries by making

---

9.   See Armory v. Delamire, 1 Strange 505. However, if Arnolds had found the jewelry during the course of her employment, her employer would be the involuntary bailee. Further, many courts now say that lost property recovered in a private place allows the owner of the place, *not* the finder, to become the bailee (even if the finder is not a trespasser).

it possible for them, after passage of a specified period of time, to acquire legal title to the property they have found. The statute usually requires the county clerk to advertise the property in an attempt to enhance the opportunity of the owner to recover what has been lost.

There are always some preliminary questions to be resolved before the estray statute can be employed. The item must be *lost property*, not merely mislaid or abandoned property. When the situation indicates that the property was probably lost, not mislaid or abandoned, as a matter of public policy loss is presumed and the estray statute applies. Such a situation occurs in the following case.

PASET v. OLD ORCHARD BANK & TRUST CO.

Appellate Court of Illinois, First District, Third Division, 1978.
62 Ill.App.3d 534, 19 Ill.Dec. 389, 378 N.E.2d 1264.

BACKGROUND AND FACTS   *On May 8, 1974, Bernice Paset found $6,325 on the seat of a chair just outside the safety deposit vault at Old Orchard Bank. Although the bank notified all persons who were in the vault on that day and on the preceding day, no one claimed the money. After a year passed, Paset claimed the money. The bank refused to give it to her.*

DECISION AND RATIONALE   *Since the money must be classified as lost property, Paset had a greater right to it than the bank, and the bank had to relinquish possession of it to her. The money was not abandoned property, since the owner obviously did not intend to relinquish all rights to it. Nor could it be deemed mislaid property, since someone who merely forgot the money would have been alerted by the bank's notice, or at least would have inquired about it within a year's time. The money was, therefore, lost property. According to the court, "The general rule is that the finder is entitled to possession of lost property against everyone except the true owner."*

Abandoned Property

Property that has been discarded by the true owner with no intention of claiming title to it is **abandoned property**. Someone who finds abandoned property acquires title to it, and such title is good against the whole world, *including the original owner.* If, however, a finder is trespassing and finds abandoned property, title does not become vested in the finder. This is also true of lost property.

Suppose C employs A and B to clean out a henhouse. C has recently purchased a home that previously had changed hands a number of times. A and B find a tin can full of gold buried in a corner of the henhouse. The can is extremely old and rusty, suggesting that it has been buried there for quite some time. C, the owner of the land, takes the coins from A and B and claims that they belong to her. A and B bring suit to recover the coins. A and B can recover the coins because they were lost articles found concealed in the earth. Such articles, commonly known as *treasure trove*, are usually coin, gold, or silver found hidden in the earth or other private place. In England, treasure trove belongs to the crown, but in the United States, it is treated like lost property and becomes the property of the finder, subject to the rights of the true owner. Note in this example that A and B are not trespassers. If they were trespassers, they would not be entitled to retain the title to the treasure trove.[10]

PATENTS

A patent is a grant from the government that conveys and secures to an inventor the exclusive right to make, use, and sell an invention for seventeen years. Patents are typically given for new articles, but *design patents* are given for manufactured articles that have been changed in a way that will enhance their sale. *Plant patents* are given to individuals who invent, discover, or reproduce a new variety of plant. Patent law has been evolving with respect to computer programs. Initially, computer programs could not be patented, but the commercial necessity of protecting them has led to a revised view.

TRADEMARKS

A trademark is a distinctive mark, model, device, or emblem that manufacturers stamp, print, or otherwise affix to the goods they produce so that the goods can be identified in the market and their origin can be vouched for. Federal statute allows a trademark to be registered by its owner or user. Exclusive use of the trademark can be perpetual. Protection depends on adoption and use; if the owner continues use, no one can infringe upon the trademark. International protection can also be

afforded by various registrations. Registration is made before using the trademark in most other countries.

A trademark must be distinctive in order to be registered. It is not enough to merely describe an article or to name a city. For example, it would be hard to register the trademark New York Clothes. Exceptions to this rule, of course, exist. When particular words have been used for such a long time that the public identifies them with a particular product and its origin, then those words can be registered as a trademark. The same holds for geographic terms that have acquired a meaning other than their location.

Trademarks can grow so common that they become generic names. For example, "Thermos" was originally a brand name for a thermal food-storage container. Now the term has become synonymous with such containers and therefore can no longer be used solely as one company's trademark.

COPYRIGHTS

A copyright is an intangible right granted by statute to the author or originator of certain literary or artistic productions. With a copyright, the owner is vested for a limited time period with the sole and exclusive privilege of reproducing copies of the work for publication and sale.

At common law, any author or compiler of data who prevented others from using the work without permission by keeping it secret had a common law copyright. Such a copyright ended when the work was published. (Publication meant any communication to others, not necessarily in written or printed form.) Federal statutes now govern virtually all copyright law in this country.

Copyright Law

On January 1, 1978, a new copyright law became effective, completely replacing Title 17 of the United States Code, which had been used since

---

10.   Danielson v. Roberts, 44 Or. 108, 74 P. 913 (1904). But the court will distinguish between finding "treasure" in the course of employment and finding it strictly in a private place. In the latter case, if the treasure trove is "embedded-in-the-soil", the landowner will normally prevail, *not* the finder.

1909. The new law is divided into eight different chapters, beginning with a discussion of the subject matter and scope of copyright. It includes chapters relating to copyright duration, notice, deposit and registration requirements, infringement, manufacturing requirements, administration, and the like. The new copyright law has four essential purposes:

1. To maximize the availability of creative works to the public.
2. To give creators of copyrighted works a fair return and to provide users of copyrighted works with a fair income.
3. To balance the interest of copyright users and owners.
4. To minimize any negative impact on industries regulated by change in the copyright law.

Copyright Duration

Works created after January 1, 1978, are given statutory copyright protection for the life of the author plus fifty years. Pseudonymous and anonymous publications, as well as those done "for hire" (ghosted) have a copyright term of seventy-five years from publication or one hundred years from creation, whichever is shorter. For those works already under copyright protection, their present term of twenty-eight years from date of first publication will remain. If a renewal is asked for, the second term will be increased to forty-seven years.

Exclusive Use of Copyright

The copyright holder is entitled to the exclusive use of all those materials that are copyrighted subject to a number of exceptions, such as fair use and library reproduction.

FAIR USE Some copying is allowed without payment of fees or permission of the copyright holder under the doctrine of "fair use". "Fair use" allows reproduction of copyrighted material without permission if the use of the material is reasonable and not harmful to the rights of the copyright owner. Section 107 of the new copyright law mentions permissible purposes such as criticism, comment, news reporting, teaching (including multiple copies for classroom use), scholarship, or research. Four criteria are used in considering whether a particular use is reasonable: (1) the purpose and character of the use, including whether it is of a nonprofit, educational nature or of a commercial nature; (2) the amount and importance of the material used in relation to the work as a whole; (3) the nature of the copyrighted work; and, (4) the effect of the use on the potential market or value of the copyrighted work.

LIBRARY REPRODUCTION Libraries and archives can reproduce single copies of certain copyrighted items for noncommercial purposes without violating the copyright law. Notice of copyright on the library or archive reproduction is necessary, however. Wholesale copying of periodicals is not permitted.

QUESTIONS AND CASE PROBLEMS

1. Ethel Yahuda had an extensive library of rare books and manuscripts. Several years before her death, Yahuda announced at a public luncheon attended by a head of state that she was donating her library to Hebrew University. Her public announcement was accompanied by the delivery of an itemized memorandum of the books and manuscripts contained in her library. Hebrew University Association accepted the list. No books were ever tendered by Yahuda to the university. Is there a completed gift? [Hebrew Univ. Assn. v. Nye (executors of estate of Ethel S. Yahuda), 26 Conn.Sup. 342, 223 A.2d 397 (1966)]

2. Waller dabbled for a number of years in the stock market, keeping most of his stocks in a safe deposit box to which there were two keys. On June 1, Waller gave one of these keys to his wife. On June 5, Waller died during an exploratory operation that had been scheduled on June 2. Is there a valid *causa mortis gift*

here? Is there a valid *inter vivos gift*? [Schilling v. Waller, 243 Md. 271, 220 A.2d 580 (1966)]

3. Lucille and Earl McVay were married in 1947, and their marriage ended in divorce. After the divorce, Earl took possession of the 1971 Buick automobile that he and Lucille owned jointly. Earl refused to return the automobile to Lucille and refused to pay her for her half of the value of the car. In an action by Lucille against her ex-husband for her share of the value of the car, she also claimed the value of the car's tires, which she herself had purchased. Assuming that Lucille presents adequate proof at trial that the tires were purchased with her own money, can she recover the full value of the tires in addition to half the value of the automobile? [McVay v. McVay, 318 So.2d 660 (La.App.1975)]

4. In 1963 the Rhoads Coal Company leased a large parcel of land and coal mining plant that it intended to take over for mining operations. The land was owned by Gilberton. As a result of Rhoads's mining operations, large piles of silt built up on various portions of the land. At one point during its coal mining operations, Rhoads sold a large amount of the silt to a zinc company. Thereafter, due to financial difficulties, Rhoads Coal Company ceased mining the parcel of land and vacated the premises. About a year later, in an attempt to collect back taxes owed by Rhoads, the United States government attempted to place a lien on the remaining piles of silt. Gilberton, the owner of the land, claimed that the piles of silt belonged to him since Rhoads had abandoned them. Was there an abandonment? [Gilberton Contracting Co. v. Hook (District Director of Internal Revenue), 255 F.Supp. 687 (D.C.Pa.1966)]

5. Dukes and Abernathy had been good friends for many years. Dukes, an elderly man who lived alone, died on November 8, 1966. Just before he died, and knowing that he did not have much time to live, he told a friend, Stewart, that he wished to give a number of his personal items to his good friend, Abernathy. Dukes instructed Stewart to place certain items in an envelope and deliver them to Abernathy. Stewart followed Dukes's instructions and delivered the items to Abernathy, who gratefully accepted them. After Dukes died, his heirs claimed the items in the envelope as part of their inheritance. In a suit between Abernathy and the heirs, who will win? [State v. Abernathy, 431 S.W.2d 359 (Tex.Civ.App. 1968)]

6. McAvoy owned a barbershop. Medina, a regular customer, spotted a pocketbook lying on one of the tables where McAvoy kept magazines for his cus-

tomers. Medina pointed out the pocketbook to McAvoy. McAvoy put the purse aside and told Medina that he would hold it until its owner returned. Several weeks passed, and no one claimed the pocketbook. Medina returned to the barbershop and claimed that, since the pocketbook was lost property and he was the finder, and since the owner had not reclaimed it, it was his. Who should get possession of the pocketbook—McAvoy or Medina? [McAvoy v. Medina, 93 Mass. (11 Allen) 548 (1866)]

7. Troop and Rust were partners in an oil and gas operation. Troop owned a three-fourths interest in the operation, and Rust owned a one-fourth interest. After eight years of operation, a dispute arose as to whether Rust had contributed his share of the expenses. As a result of the dispute, the partnership was dissolved. In attempting to divide up the oil, Rust learned that Troop had comingled the partnership's oil with oil from another lease that Troop owned. At trial, Troop was unable to show how much of the comingled oil had come from his other operation. How much of the oil should each of the parties receive? [Troop v. St. Louis Union Trust Co., 25 Ill. App.2d 143, 116 N.E.2d 116 (1960)]

8. Mark and Jeff Ellsworth and David Gibson, three small boys, entered Bishop's salvage yard without his permission and, while there, happened upon a bottle, partially embedded in the earth, which contained $12,590 in U.S. currency. The boys took the money to the police chief, who deposited it with the Canton State Bank. Bishop initiated suit against the three boys, claiming that since the boys found the money on his property, it was rightfully his. Who is entitled to the money? [Bishop v. Ellsworth, 91 Ill.App.2d 386, 234, N.E.2d 49 (1968)]

9. Hall Printing Company entered into a contract with Publishers' Typographic Service, Inc., in which Publishers' agreed to typeset some books that Hall wished to have printed. Hall requested that Publishers' keep its type intact for six months after the first publication of Hall's book. Publishers' refused to agree to this unless Hall would agree to supply all of the metal used in the typesetting. Thereafter, Hall agreed to supply twenty-five tons of metal for purposes of typesetting. The contract provided that all metal that was shipped to Publishers' was to remain Hall's property. The contract also explicitly required that Publishers' keep all the metal that Hall shipped to Publishers' separate and apart from Publishers' other property so that it could be identified as property belonging to Hall. In spite of this contractual obligation, Publishers' mixed Hall's metals with other

metals belonging to Publishers' and melted all of them down for reuse. About two years after the contract was entered into, Publishers' went into bankruptcy. Hall, knowing that Publishers' had 23,000 pounds of its metals, demanded the metals or their dollar value from the receiver in bankruptcy. The receiver refused to return either the metals or their dollar value to Hall since, in bankruptcy, all creditors divide up the bankrupt's total assets and each receives a share proportionate to the debt that the bankrupt owed it at the time of bankruptcy. Can Hall claim under the doctrine of confusion? [Baisch v. Publishers' Typographic Service, Inc., 70 N.J.Super. 340, 175 A.2d 485 (1961)]

16
Bailments

A **bailment** is an agreement in which the owner of personal property temporarily delivers it to another person for a particular purpose (loan, lease, storage, repair, or transportation). Later the property is returned to the owner or disposed of as directed. Some common bailments are lending a lawn mower to a neighbor, leasing a U-Haul, leaving clothes at the dry cleaner or tailor for repair, storing goods in a warehouse, and checking a coat at a restaurant. The owner of personal property who delivers the goods to another in a contract of bailment is the **bailor**. The person accepting temporary possession for a specific purpose is the **bailee**.

ELEMENTS OF A BAILMENT

Not all transactions involving the delivery of property from one person to another create bailments. The following sections will examine each of the general requirements necessary to create a bailment.

Personal Property Requirement

A bailment involves *personal* property. Bailments involving *tangible* items like jewelry, cattle, or automobiles are more frequent than bailments of *intangible* personal property like promissory notes and shares of corporate stock.

Delivery of Possession

Delivery of possession must transfer the possession of property to the bailee in such a way that: (1) the bailee is given *exclusive* possession and control over the property and (2) the bailee must *knowingly* accept the personal property.[1] Suppose, for example, that Stevenson is in a hurry to catch his plane. He has a package he wants to check at the airport. He arrives at the airport check-in office, but the man in charge has gone on a coffee break. Stevenson decides to leave the package in a corner. This does not constitute delivery, even though there has clearly been physical transfer of the package. The person in charge of the check-in station did not knowingly accept the personal property. Or consider a

woman checking a coat at a restaurant. In the coat pocket is a $20,000 diamond necklace. By accepting the coat, the bailee does not *knowingly* accept the necklace.

If either delivery of possession or knowing acceptance is lacking, there is no bailment relationship. To illustrate: Valet parking constitutes a bailment, but self-park parking does not. The difference is found in the control of the car keys. When a car owner is required to leave the car keys with the parking attendant, the owner transfers a sufficient amount of control over the car to the parking company to constitute a bailment. When the car is parked and locked and the keys retained by the owner, the parking garage is merely a *lessor* of space and the car owner a lessee. This distinction is illustrated in the next case.

1. We are dealing here with *voluntary* bailments.

CHALET FORD, INC. v. RED TOP PARKING, INC.

Court of Appeals of Illinois, 1978. 62 Ill. App.3d 270, 19 Ill. Dec. 573, 379 N.E. 2d 88.

BACKGROUND AND FACTS *Hall, sales manager for Chalet Ford, went to a hockey game at the Chicago Stadium and left his demonstrator car in a lot operated by the Red Top Parking Company. The sign at the lot read "Park and Lock, Attendant Not Authorized to Accept Keys." Hall pulled into the lot, left the motor running, and paid the attendant. The attendant parked the car. Hall had done this on numerous occasions over the preceding four years, as had many other Red Top patrons. That night, Hall's auto was stolen from the lot. Chalet Ford sued to recover the value of the car. Red Top Parking denied there was any bailment on which liability could be based.*

DECISION AND RATIONALE *Red Top Parking was liable for the loss as a bailee of Hall's auto. A bailment can arise by either express or implied agreement. In this case, the parking lot attendant, as the agent of Red Top, entered into an implied bailment agreement with Hall by accepting delivery of the auto and exercising control over it. In the opinion of the court: "Although a person dealing with an agent has the duty to use reasonable diligence to determine the scope of an agent's authority, it was reasonable under the circumstances here [the four year practice of turning cars over to attendants] for Hall to believe that the attendant's actions were authorized and that the signs were disregarded by those who ran the parking lot, as well as by its patrons."*

EXCLUSIVE POSSESSION A similar distinction is made between a restaurant patron who checks a coat with an attendant and the patron who hangs it on a coatrack. The coat given to the

attendant constitutes a bailment. The attendant (hence the restaurant) has exclusive possession and control over the retention and removal of the coat. By contrast, the self-hung coat can be removed at any time by the patron or anyone else so inclined. The restaurant does not have substantial control over the property and is not considered a bailee.

KNOWING ACCEPTANCE

A second aspect of the delivery of possession requirement is that the bailee knowingly accept the property. Consider this situation. An auto repair shop accepts a car for body work. The shop owner does not know, nor does the owner reveal, that some expensive jewelry is in the glove compartment. A contract for bailment exists for the car *but not for the valuables* in the glove compartment.

CONSTRUCTIVE DELIVERY

There are two further points that should be made about delivery of possession. First, *actual delivery* means the physical transfer of the property itself; however, *constructive delivery* can be sufficient to support a bailment. For example, X owns a boat that she loans to Y for the weekend. It is moored at a municipal marina. X gives Y the boat registration papers so that the harbor master will allow Y to board the boat. X has made constructive delivery of the boat to Y.

Second, there are certain unique situations in which a contract of bailment is found despite the apparent lack of the requisite elements of control or knowledge. In particular, safe deposit box rental is usually held to constitute a bailor-bailee relationship between the bank and its customer, despite the bank's lack of knowledge of the contents and its inability to have exclusive control of the property.[2]

_____

2. By statute or by express contract, however, a safe deposit box may be a lease of space or license depending on the jurisdiction or the facts or both.

BACKGROUND AND FACTS *Police arrested a robbery suspect who Capezzaro claimed had stolen his money. In the process, they seized money from the suspect's clothing, and the police department kept it as evidence. Later, charges were dropped against the suspect on the basis of medical opinion that said the suspect was unable to tell right from wrong at the time the crime was committed. The police returned the money to the suspect without notifying Capezzaro even though they knew of Capezzaro's claim to it. Capezzaro brought suit against the police department, claiming that the police were negligent in returning the money when they were aware of his claim to it.*

CAPEZZARO v. **WINFREY**

Superior Court of New Jersey, 1977.
153 N.J.Super. 267, 379 A.2d 493.

DECISION AND RATIONALE *Capezzaro was able to recover from the police. Even though he did not enter into an express agreement with the police, a bailment relationship existed. By operation of law, an ordinary bailment arose when the police seized the money, since they were holding it for their own benefit as well as for the rightful owner. In a bailment, the bailee (the police in this case) is held to a standard of reasonable care. In this case, the release of the suspect on medical grounds did not damage the credibility of Capezzaro's claim or establish the suspect's right to the money. Thus, the police were negligent in giving the money to the suspect without determining the validity of Capezzaro's claim. The court found "no error in the trial judge's *** instruct[ing] the jury on negligence, i.e., what a reasonable man would have done as custodian of the fund."*

The Bailment Agreement

A bailment agreement can be *express* or *implied*. Although a written agreement is not required (that is, the Statute of Frauds does not apply), it is a good idea to have one, especially when valuable property is involved. However, if there is a writing that appears to be *complete*, missing terms cannot be proven by parol evidence because of the parol evidence rule. (See Chapter 11.)

RETURN OF SPECIFIC PROPERTY AND THE FUNGIBLE GOODS EXCEPTION The bailment agreement presupposes that the bailee will return the *identical goods* originally given by the bailor. However, in bailment of *fungible goods*—uniform identical goods—or bailments with the option to purchase, only *equivalent* property must be returned.

Fungible goods are defined in UCC Sec. 1-201 as units of goods that are by nature equivalent to one another—for example, grain or gasoline. The UCC in Sec. 7-207(1) states clearly, "Fungible goods may be commingled." For example, Smith, Basen, and Kerlly each store 1,000 pounds of grain in Sam's Warehouse every year, and each receives receipts. When Smith returns to reclaim "his grain," Sam's Warehouse is obligated to give him 1,000 pounds of wheat grain—but not necessarily the particular kernels he originally deposited. Smith cannot claim that Sam's Warehouse is guilty of conversion in not returning him the exact wheat that he put into storage. As long as it returns goods of the same *type, grade,* and *quantity,* Sam's Warehouse—the bailee—has performed its obligation.

TYPES OF BAILMENTS

Bailments are either "ordinary" or "special" ("extraordinary"). There are three types of ordinary bailments. The distinguishing feature among them is *which party receives a benefit from the bailment.* Ultimately, the courts will use this factor to determine the standard of care owed by the bailee handling the goods or chattel (personal property), and this factor will dictate the rights and liabilities of the parties. However, modern courts tend to use reasonable standards of care regardless of the type of bailment arrangement in effect.

Bailments for the Sole Benefit of the Bailor (Gratuitous Bailments)

When one person holds something for safekeeping as a favor to another, a bailment for the sole benefit of the *bailor* is in effect. It is a *gratuitous bailment* for the convenience and *benefit* of the bailor. In such a situation, the bailee is expected to use *slight care* to preserve the bailed property. Consider an example. Michael is leaving for a two-week trip to Jamaica. He asks Susan if he can store his Ford Mustang II in her garage. He gives her the keys. She promises not to use the car for personal use. She is not paid any rent. One day, her children happen to be playing in the garage when Michael's car is there, and they accidentally dent its fender. When Michael returns, he complains that Susan should pay for the repair of the fender. She probably will not have to unless he can prove that she was guilty of gross negligence. Letting her children play in the garage would not normally be considered gross negligence.

Bailments for the Sole Benefit of the Bailee

The loan of an article to a person (the bailee) solely for that person's convenience and *benefit* is the essence of a *bailment for sole benefit of the bailee.* Under such circumstances, the bailee must use *great care* to preserve the bailed item from damage. If your best friend loans you a car so you can go out on a date, you must exercise great care in driving that car. If the car gets scratched because you parked it in a crowded parking lot, you will have trouble proving that you used great care, and, normally, you will be liable.

Bailments for the Mutual Benefit of the Bailee and the Bailor (Contractual Bailments)

Mutual benefit bailments are by far the most common kind, and they involve some form of compensation (although not necessarily money) between the bailee and the bailor for the service provided—for example, repair work, transporting goods, storing items, renting goods, or holding property.

A mutual benefit bailment need not involve the payment of a fee. All that is required is that both bailor and bailee receive a benefit. For example, many corporations provide locker and cloakroom facilities for their employees' personal belongings because employees are not permitted to bring these items into the work area. The employee (bailor) benefits by receiving storage facilities. The employer (bailee) benefits by keeping the work area uncluttered, thus decreasing the chances of minor accidents.

RIGHTS AND DUTIES OF A BAILEE (BAILEE'S RESPONSIBILITIES)

Rights of the Bailee

The bailee takes possession of personal property for a specified purpose after which that property is returned (in the same or prespecified altered form). Thus, implicit in the bailment contract is the right of the bailee to take possession, to utilize the property in accomplishing the purpose of the bailment, and to receive some form of compensation (unless the bailment is intended to be gratuitous). Depending upon the nature of the bailment and the terms of the bailment contract, these bailee rights are present (with some limitations) in varying degrees in all bailment transactions.

RIGHT OF POSSESSION Temporary control and possession of property that ultimately is to be returned to the owner is the hallmark of a bailment. The meaning of "temporary" depends upon the terms of the bailment. If a specified period is expressed, then the bailment is continuous for that time period. Earlier termination by the bailor is a breach of contract, and the bailee can recover damages from the bailor. If no duration is specified, the bailment ends when either the bailor or the bailee so demands.

A bailee's right of possession, even though temporary, permits the bailee to recover damages from any third persons for damage or loss to the property. For example, No Spot Dry Cleaners sends all suede leather garments to Cleanall Company for special processing. If Cleanall loses or damages any leather goods, No Spot has the right to recover against Cleanall. (The customer can also recover from No Spot.)

If goods or chattel are stolen from the bailee during the bailment, the bailee has a legal right to regain possession (recapture) of the goods or obtain damages from any third person who has wrongfully interfered with the bailee's possessory rights.

RIGHT TO USE BAILED PROPERTY Naturally, the extent to which bailees can use the goods or chattel entrusted to them depends upon the terms of the bailment contract. Where no provision is made, the extent of use depends upon how necessary it is to have the goods at the bailee's disposal in order to carry out the ordinary purpose of the bailment. For example, when leasing drilling machinery, the bailee is expected to use the equipment to drill. On the other hand, in long-term storage of a car, the bailee is not expected to use the car because the ordinary purpose of a storage bailment does not include use of the property.

RIGHT OF COMPENSATION In nonrental bailments, the bailor is expected to compensate the bailee for the safekeeping of or service to the property.[3] Most common nonrental bailments involve repair or transportation of goods and chattel. The amount of compensation is often expressed in the contract. For example, a moving company contract would ordinarily specify

---

3. In a rental bailment, the bailee pays the bailor for the use of the property—for example, rental of furniture or a car.

"moving and storage fees for 9,000 pounds of furniture loaded at point X and unloaded at point Y to be delivered on or about 30 days from this date . . . for $1,000." When the amount is not specified, the law provides that the bailee is entitled to "reasonable value for services rendered."

Duties of the Bailee

The bailee has two basic responsibilities: (1) to take proper care of the property and (2) to surrender the property at the end of the bailment. The bailee's duties are based on a mixture of tort law and contract law. The duty of care involves the standards and principles of tort law discussed in Chapter 3. A bailee's failure to exercise appropriate care in handling the bailor's property incurs tort liability for the bailee. The duty to relinquish the property at the end of the bailment is grounded in contract law principles. Failure to return the property is a breach of contract, and, with one exception, the bailee is liable for damages. The exception to this contractual liability exists when the obligation is excused because the goods or chattel have been lost or stolen through no fault of the bailee (or claimed by a third party with a superior claim).

DUTY OF CARE   Bailees must exercise proper care over the property in their possession to prevent its loss or damage. The three types of bailments demand different degrees of care, although the trend is toward a uniform standard of care. When a bailment exists for the sole benefit of the bailee, great care, or the highest level of care, is required. When the bailment exists for the mutual benefit of the bailor and the bailee, reasonable care is the standard. When the bailment exists for the sole benefit of the bailor, slight care, or something less than ordinary or reasonable care, is expected.

PRESUMPTION OF NEGLIGENCE   At the end of the bailment, a bailee has the duty to return the bailor's property in the condition it was received (allowing for ordinary wear and aging). In some cases, the bailor can sue the bailee in tort (as well as contract) for damages or lost goods on the theory of *negligence*. But often it is not possible for the bailor to discover and prove the specific acts of negligence committed by the bailee that caused damage to the property.[4] Thus, the law of bailments recognizes a rule whereby a bailor's proof that damage or loss to the property has occurred will, in and of itself, raise a presumption that the bailee is guilty of negligence. Once this is shown, the bailee must prove that he or she was *not* at fault. A bailee who is able to *rebut* (contradict) the presumption of negligence is not liable to the bailor. When damage to goods is normally of the type that results only from someone's negligence, and the bailee had full control of the goods, it is more likely than not that the damage was caused by the bailee's negligence. Therefore, the bailee's negligence is presumed.

Determining whether a bailee exercised an appropriate degree of care is usually a question of fact. This means that the trier-of-fact (a judge or a jury) weighs the facts of a particular situation and concludes that the bailee did or did not exercise the requisite degree of care at the time the loss or damage occurred. The failure to exercise appropriate care is *negligence,* and the bailee is liable for the loss or damage in tort. On the other hand, if the bailee has exercised sufficient care, then loss or damage to the property falls upon the bailor.

DUTY TO RELINQUISH PROPERTY   At the end of the bailment, the bailee normally must relinquish the identical undamaged property (unless it is fungible) to either the bailor or someone the bailor designates or otherwise dispose of it as directed. This is a *contractual* duty arising from the bailment agreement (contract). Failure to give up possession at the time the bailment ends is breach of a contract term.

As noted before, there are recognized exceptions from tort law that will *excuse* contract liability. If the bailee does not or cannot

---

4.   The basic formula for finding negligence requires proof that (1) a duty exists, (2) a breach of that duty occurred, and (3) the breach is the proximate cause of damage or loss.

return the property at the end of the bailment because it has been lost, stolen, or damaged *through no negligence* (fault) on the part of the bailee, then the contractual obligation to return the property is excused. (There are a number of exceptions to this rule that concern common carriers, public warehouse companies, and innkeepers. They are discussed below.) They usually cannot limit liability except as provided by statute because they have a higher duty of care. Also, if a third party with a superior claim takes the property, the bailee normally is not liable.

RIGHTS AND DUTIES OF A BAILOR

Rights of a Bailor

The bailor's rights are essentially a complement to each of the bailee's duties. A bailor has the right to expect the following:

1. The property will be protected with reasonable care while in the possession of the bailee.
2. The bailee will utilize the property as agreed in the bailment contract (or not at all).
3. The property will be relinquished at the conclusion of the bailment according to directions given by the bailor.
4. The bailee will not convert (alter) the goods.
5. In cases of rental or lease bailments, all agreed-upon payments will be made.
6. Repairs or service on the property will be completed without defective workmanship.

Many bailees attempt to contract against liability for negligence; for example, they disclaim liability on a claim check for any harm to property due to their negligence. Courts nonetheless often protect the rights of the bailor by considering disclaimer clauses as against public policy, especially where the clause is in very fine print or where there is great disparity in the relative bargaining strength of the parties.

Duties of a Bailor

A bailor has a single, all-encompassing duty to provide the bailee with goods or chattel that are free from hidden defects that could cause injury to the bailee. This duty translates into two rules:

1. In a *mutual benefit bailment*, the bailor must notify the bailee of all *known defects* and any *hidden defects* that the bailor could have discovered with reasonable diligence and proper inspection.
2. In *bailments for the sole benefit of the bailee*, the bailor must notify the bailee of all *known defects only*.

The bailor's duty to reveal defects is based on a negligence theory of tort law. A bailor who fails to give the appropriate notice is liable to the bailee and to any other person who might reasonably be expected to come into contact with the defective article. To illustrate: Rentco (bailor) leases four tractors to Hopkinson. Unknown to Rentco (but discoverable by reasonable inspection), the brake mechanism on one of the tractors is defective at the time the bailment is made. Hopkinson uses the defective tractor not knowing of the brake problem and injures herself and two other field workers when the tractor rolls out of control. Rentco is liable on a negligence theory for injuries sustained by Hopkinson and the two employees. This is the analysis: Rentco has a *duty* to notify Hopkinson of the discoverable brake defect. Rentco's failure to notify is the *proximate cause* of injuries to farm workers who might be expected to use or have contact with the tractor. Therefore, Rentco is *liable* for the resulting injuries. (Rentco normally could not escape liability by including a disclaimer in the rental contract. Disclaimers are normally unenforceable unless both parties are privy to the contract and are often unenforceable even with privity of contract because they are against public policy.)

A bailor can also incur *warranty liability* based on contract law for injuries resulting from bailment of defective articles. Property leased by a bailor must be *fit for the intended purpose of the bailment*. The bailor's knowledge or ability to discover any defects is immaterial. Warranties of fitness arise by law in sales contracts and by judicial interpretation in the case of bailments "for hire."

CINTRONE v. HERTZ TRUCK LEASING AND RENTAL SERVICE

Supreme Court of New Jersey, 1965.

45 N.J.Super. 434, 212 A.2d 769.

BACKGROUND AND FACTS *Contract Packers, Inc., leased trucks from Hertz for use in its business. Cintrone, an employee of Contract Packers, was injured when one of the truck's brakes failed. Cintrone appealed the trial court's decision that he must prove negligence to recover damages on the basis of implied warranty.*

DECISION AND RATIONALE *Hertz was liable for Cintrone's injuries under theories of breach of warranty and of strict liability in tort. When Contract Packers rented the truck from Hertz, not only did a bailor-bailee relationship arise, but a warranty relationship arose as well. In the words of the court: "A bailor for hire, such as a person in the [truck rental] business, puts motor vehicles in the stream of commerce in a fashion not unlike a manufacturer or retailer. *** Such a rental must be regarded as accompanied by a representation that the vehicle is fit for operation on the public highways."*

Exculpatory Clauses

Exculpatory clauses in contracts of bailment purport to "hold (one) absolutely harmless" from any and all risks of loss, damage, or injury. Courts regularly find them illegal and against public policy.

The classic illustration of an exculpatory clause is found on parking receipts: "We assume no risk for damage to or loss of automobile or its contents regardless of the cause. It is agreed that the vehicle owner assumes such risks." Whatever the language of such a clause, the result is normally the same—it is illegal and unenforceable. This is especially true in the case of bailees providing a quasi-public service. The "take it or leave it" message implicit in the exculpatory provision is normally located on the reverse side of a parking receipt, which most people are unaware of; and these clauses are generally in very fine print. The public policy violated, therefore, is one of *unfair surprise*.

Certain bailees can limit their liabilities by contract with the bailor, but such limitation must be brought to the bailor's attention. In particular, professional bailees, such as repair garages, are subject to this rule. A sign on Joe Brown's Garage indicating that the garage is "not responsible for anything that happens to any car left here" does not ordinarily come to the attention of the bailor. The bailee must show the writing to the bailor and inform the bailor that it limits or varies the bailee's liability. (The bailee is *not* required to read and interpret the limitation or variation to the bailor.)

Termination of Bailment

Bailments for a specific term end when the stated period lapses. When no duration is specified, the bailment can be terminated any time by the following events:

1. The mutual agreement of both parties.
2. A demand by either party.
3. The completion of the purpose of the bailment.
4. An act by the bailee that is inconsistent with the terms of the bailment.
5. The operation of law.

SPECIAL BAILMENTS

Most of this chapter has concerned itself with ordinary bailments. Special, or extraordinary, bailments include (1) common carriers, (2) warehouse companies, and (3) innkeepers or hotel keepers.

Common Carriers

Common carriers are publicly licensed to provide transportation services to the general public. They are distinguished from private carriers who operate transportation facilities for a select clientele. A private carrier is not bound to provide service to every person or company making a request. The common carrier, however, must arrange carriage for all who apply, within certain limitations.[5] The delivery of goods to a common carrier creates a *bailment relationship* between the shipper (bailor) and the common carrier (bailee). The common carrier contract of transportation creates a *mutual benefit bailment*. But, unlike ordinary mutual benefit bailments, the common carrier is held to a standard of care based on *strict liability* rather than reasonable care in protecting the bailed personal property. This means that the common carrier is absolutely liable for all loss or damage to goods except damage caused by one of the five common law exceptions: (1) an act of God, (2) an act of a public enemy, (3) an order of a public authority, (4) an act of the shipper, or (5) the inherent nature of the goods.

Common carriers are treated as if they were absolute insurers for the safe delivery of goods to the destination but really, they are not. They cannot contract away this liability for damaged goods, but, subject to government regulations, they are permitted to limit their dollar liability to an amount stated on the shipment contract.[6]

Except for the five exceptions given, any damage to goods in shipment, even that caused by the willful acts of third persons or sheer accident, do not relieve the common carrier from liability. Thus, a common carrier trucking company moving cargo is liable for acts of vandalism, mechanical defects in refrigeration units, or a dam bursting if any of these acts result in damage to the cargo. But damage caused by acts of God—earthquake or lightning striking, for example—are the shipper's loss.

There are many interesting cases concerning what constitutes an "act of God." The following extract is from a case in which a common carrier learned that a flood was *not* necessarily enough of an "act of God" to excuse liability:

The only acts of God that excuse common carriers from liability for loss or injury to goods in transit are those operations of the forces of nature that could not have been anticipated and provided against and that by their super human force unexpectedly injure or destroy goods in the custody or control of the carrier. Extreme weather conditions which operate to foil human obligations of duty are regarded as acts of God. However, every strong wind, snowstorm, or rainstorm cannot be termed an act of God merely because it is of unusual or more than average intensity. Ordinary, expectable, and gradual weather conditions are not regarded as acts of God even though they may have produced a disaster, because man had the opportunity to control their effects.[7]

SHIPPER'S LOSS The shipper bears any loss occurring through its own faulty or improper crating or packaging procedures. For example, if a bird dies because its crate was poorly ventilated, the shipper bears the loss, not the carrier.

CONNECTING CARRIERS Where connecting carriers are involved in transporting goods, the shipper can recover from the original carrier or any connecting carrier. In all cases of carrier liability, the shipper must prove that the cargo was in good condition at the time it was shipped. Normally, the *last* carrier is presumed to have received the goods in good condition.

5. A common carrier is not required to take any and all property anywhere in all instances. Public regulatory agencies, such as the Interstate Commerce Commission, govern commercial carriers, and carriers can be restricted to geographical areas. They can also be limited to carrying certain kinds of goods or to providing only special types of transportation equipment.

6. For example, federal laws and Interstate Commerce Commission regulations require common carriers to offer shippers the opportunity to obtain higher dollar limits for loss by paying a higher fee for the transport.

7. Southern Pacific Co. v. Loden, 508 P.2d 347 (Arizona App.1972)

Warehouse Companies

Warehousing is the business of providing storage of property for compensation. A warehouse company is a professional bailee whose responsibility differs from an ordinary bailee in two important aspects. First, a warehouse company is empowered to issue documents of title, in particular, warehouse receipts.[8] Second, warehouse companies are subject to an extraordinary network of state and federal statutes and Article 7 of the Uniform Commercial Code (as are carriers).

Like ordinary bailees, a warehouse company is liable for loss or damage to property and possession resulting from *negligence* (and therefore does not have the same liability as a common carrier). The duty is one of reasonable care to protect and preserve the goods. A warehouse company can limit the dollar amount of liability, but the bailor must be given the option of paying an increased storage rate for an increase in the liability limit.

A warehouse company accepts goods for storage and issues a warehouse receipt describing the property and the terms of the bailment contract. The warehouse receipt can be negotiable or nonnegotiable depending on how it is written. (Negotiable and nonnegotiable instruments are discussed in Chapter 24.) The warehouse receipt is negotiable if its terms provide that the warehouse company will deliver the goods "to the bearer" of the receipt, or "to the order of" a person named on the receipt.

The warehouse receipt serves multiple functions. It is a receipt for the goods stored; it is a contract of bailment; it also represents the goods (that is, it indicates title) and hence has value and utility in financing commercial transactions. Thus, Oakner, a rancher, delivers 6,000 head of buffalo to Abel, the owner of a warehouse. Abel issues a negotiable warehouse receipt payable "to bearer" and gives it to Oakner. Oakner goes to the ranchers' market and ultimately sells the entire herd of buffalo to Jones and Smith, buffalo investors. Oakner delivers the warehouse receipt to Jones and Smith. They are now the owners of the buffalo and have the right to obtain them from Abel. Jones and Smith present the warehouse receipt to Abel, who in return releases the 6,000 buffalo to them.

Most states have special laws relating to the warehousing industry. In addition, if the warehouse company operates in interstate commerce, federal regulations impose other controls on business operations. Article 7 of the Uniform Commercial Code is involved only with the rights and liabilities relating to documents of title.

Innkeepers

At common law, innkeepers, hotel owners, or similar operators were held to the same strict liability as common carriers with respect to bailed personal property. Now, only those who provide lodging to the public for compensation as a *regular* business are covered under this rule of strict liability. The rule further applies to those lodgers who are "guests". To be a guest, a person must be a traveler, not a permanent lodger. Courts and statutes are tending to reduce the strict liability of the common law.

STATUTORY CHANGES In many states, innkeepers can avoid strict liability for loss of guests' valuables and money by providing a safe in which to keep them. Each guest must be clearly notified of the availability of such a safe. Various statutes dictate the requirements for such notices. When articles are not kept in the safe, or when they are of such a nature that they are not normally kept in a safe, statutes will often limit innkeepers' liability.

Consider an example covering personal property that cannot be put in a safe. Jackson stays for a night at Hideaway Hotel. When he

---

8. Document of title is defined in UCC Sec. 1-201 (15) as any "document which in the regular course of business or financing is treated as adequately evidencing that the person in possession of it is entitled to receive, hold, and dispose of the document and the goods it covers. To be a document of title, a document must purport to be issued by or addressed to a bailee and purport to cover goods in the bailee's possession * * *."

returns from eating breakfast in the hotel restaurant, he discovers that the people in the room next door have forced the lock on the door between the two rooms and stolen his suitcase. Jackson claims that the hotel is liable for his loss. The hotel denies liability due to the lack of negligence on its part. At common law, innkeepers are actually insurers of the valuables of their guests. In states where this common law liability prevails, the hotel will be liable. In some states, though, the hotel will not be liable at all in the absence of negligence. In others, the liability of the hotel in the absence will be limited to a fairly small sum.

GUESTS' AUTOMOBILES Normally, the innkeeper assumes no responsibility for the safety of a guest's automobile because the guest usually retains possession and control. If, on the other hand, the innkeeper provides parking facilities, and the guest's car is entrusted to the innkeeper or to an employee, the innkeeper will be liable under the rules that pertain to parking lot bailees.

QUESTIONS AND CASE PROBLEMS

1. Pal lent his best friend, Penn, a crane that Penn intended to put to his own personal use. Penn tied the crane to the back of his truck with several chains. After he drove a short distance, he checked the chains. They were loose, and he tightened them. During the transport of the crane, Penn checked the chains two other times. Penn made several sharp turns with his truck between his last inspection of the chains and the truck's destination. Just before Penn reached his destination, the crane fell off the truck while he was driving down an interstate highway exit ramp. Even though the crane was extensively damaged, Penn claimed that he was not negligent. Can Pal recover for damage to his crane? [Great American Ins. Co. v. Penn, 275 So.2d 221 (La.App.1973)]

2. In the early 1970s, New York City was engaged in extensive urban renewal, and many people were forced to relocate. Phillips, a resident of a large apartment building that the city planned to tear down, was forced to move his belongings to an apartment that was not yet ready for occupancy. After Phillips had moved his belongings, but while he was staying with some friends, a number of his belongings were stolen. Phillips attempted to sue New York City for his lost property, but the trial court judge dismissed the case, stating that the city owed no duty to Phillips. Is the trial court judge correct? [Phillips v. City of New York, 71 Misc.2d 861, 337 N.Y.S.2d 303 (1972)]

3. The Mid-Top Restaurant, located in downtown Hartford, Connecticut, required its waitresses, as part of their work, to wear waitress uniforms. Mid-Top provided a rack and lockers adjacent to the waitresses' dining room in which they could change into their uniforms and get ready for work. On November 13, 1970, a fire destroyed most of the Mid-Top Restaurant. Sandra Grana, a waitress at the Mid-Top, sued the restaurant to recover for the destruction of the personal property that she had left in her locker. Mid-Top claimed that, since the locker room was always left unlocked, it was not holding Grana's personal property in storage and, therefore, was not a bailee. Is this argument convincing? [Grana v. Security Ins. Group, 72 Misc.2d 265, 339 N.Y.2d 34 (1972)]

4. During a dark November night in 1966, Adler and Sons, one of the largest jewelry stores in New Orleans, was burglarized. The burglars cut a hole in the roof and brought in special tools, including an acetylene torch, which they used to cut through the solid steel door on the vault. Even though an alarm system connected to the doors, windows, vents, and vault was activated by an employee before he left for the night, the burglars successfully completed their task and escaped without capture. One of the jewelry store's customers had left over $100,000 worth of jewelry with Adler for repair that morning. All of the customer's jewelry was stolen in the burglary. Can the customer recover from Adler? [Travelers Ins. Co. v. Coleman E. Adler, Inc., 285 So.2d 381 (La.App. 1973)]

5. Dunham owned and operated a business that included the selling of sand and gravel, which he obtained through a dredging operation. On July 20 Dunham informed his friend Roy Young, president of Roy Young, Inc., that the engine on one of Dunham's dredges had become inoperative. Dunham told Young that he wanted to borrow one of Young's engines for a few days until his own could be repaired. Young agreed to loan a diesel engine to

Dunham under the condition that Dunham would pay for repairs if the engine became damaged. The parties never agreed that any consideration would be paid for the use of the engine. When Dunham returned the engine to Young, it was damaged. Must Young prove that Dunham was negligent, or is Dunham presumed to have been negligent? [Roy Young, Inc. v. Delcambre, Inc., 233 So.2d 612 (La.App. 1970)]

6. Cook Company contracted with American Export Lines for American to carry certain cargo. Cook also contracted with McRoberts for McRoberts to provide storage and security for the cargo once it was placed in McRoberts's "safe room." American shipped the cargo belonging to Cook Company and unloaded it at the pier as provided in the contract. While the cargo was being unloaded, several of McRoberts's security guards were at the scene observing the operation. After the goods were unloaded onto the pier, but before they were transported into McRoberts's "safe room," the goods were stolen. In a suit by Cook Company against McRoberts, can Cook Company successfully claim that McRoberts was a bailee of the cargo? [Union Marine and General Ins. Co. v. American Export Lines, Inc., 274 F.Supp. 123 (D.C.N.Y. 1966)]

7. Ehrlich-Newmark Truck Company was a common carrier. It entered into a contract with David Crystal Inc. for the transportation of some garments from North Carolina to New York City. When Ehrlich-Newmark's truck arrived in New York, it was highjacked. All of the garments were stolen, and the truck was never retrieved. David Crystal sued Ehrlich-Newmark for the price of the garments. Ehrlich-Newmark conceded that there was a bailment, but defended on the grounds that the highjacking was the act of a "public enemy" and that therefore it was not responsible for the loss. Is this a valid defense? [David Crystal Inc. v. Ehrlich-Newmark Trucking Co., 64 Misc.2d 325, 314 N.Y.S.2d 559 (1970)]

8. Tire City, Inc., was in the business of whitewalling and recapping tires. Smith, a tire dealer, entered into a contract with Tire City to have four dozen of Smith's tires white-walled. Smith sent Tire City four dozen black-walls on May 1. On May 3, Tire City acknowledged receipt of the forty-eight tires. Soon thereafter, the tire business became somewhat deflated, and Tire City's financial situation steadily worsened. Shortly after Tire City received the ship-

ment from Smith, one of Tire City's creditors obtained a lien on Smith's four dozen tires. If Tire City does not object to its creditor taking possession of the tires, can Smith stop the creditor? [Nassar v. Smith, 21 Ill.App. 3d 462, 315 N.E.2d 692 (1974)]

9. Procter & Gamble was a distributor of soybean oils. Soybean oil production is seasonal, and Procter & Gamble's inventory was usually very high in the summer, decreasing gradually over the months that followed. The seasonal nature of oil production meant that Procter & Gamble had to store large quantities of oil for a long period of time. In 1962 the company began utilizing the storage facilities of Field Warehousing Corporation. Procter & Gamble shipped oil to Field Warehousing, which stored the oil in its own storage tanks. In exchange for the oil, Field Warehousing gave Procter & Gamble "warehousing receipts." This allowed Procter & Gamble to sell the oil by merely selling the receipt (which was evidence of title to the oil). Thus, Procter & Gamble did not have to ship any of the oil in order to make a sale. About six months after it began storing oil at Field Warehousing, Procter & Gamble sold a large number of its warehouse receipts to Allied Oil Refining Corp. When Allied attempted to get the oil, it found that the storage tanks were filled nine-tenths with water and one-tenth with oil. Allied rescinded its contract with Procter & Gamble, and Procter & Gamble in turn sued Field Warehousing. After a year-long investigation, neither Field Warehousing nor Procter & Gamble could determine how the oil disappeared. Who is liable for the missing oil? [Procter & Gamble Distributing Co. v. Lawrence American Field Warehousing Corp., 16 N.Y.2d 344, 266 N.Y.S.2d 785, 213 N.E.2d 873 (1965)]

10. Washington Toll Bridge Authority operated a ferry service in Port City, Washington. The ferry was docked at the far end of a pier several hundred feet in length. Tickets were sold by the Toll Bridge Authority at the near end of the pier. While waiting to buy a ticket to ride the Washington ferry, Zorotovich was struck by a vehicle being driven across the dock platform. Zorotovich sued Washington Toll Bridge Authority, claiming that the Toll Bridge Authority was liable to him as a passenger of the Washington ferry. Washington Toll Bridge Authority claimed that it was not liable. Who wins? [Zorotovich v. Washington Toll Bridge Authority, 80 Wash.2d 106, 491 P.2d 1295 (1971)]

UNIT IV

Commercial Transactions
and the
Uniform Commercial Code

17

Sales

Introduction to Sales Contracts and Their Formation

Every day of our lives we make purchases—the daily newspaper, groceries, clothes, textbooks, a stereo, a car, and so on. Most of our purchases are of "goods" rather than real property. Thus, studying the law of sales of goods is relevant to our daily lives.

The people from whom we buy our goods are, to us, "sellers." But our "sellers" are in turn "buyers" from their suppliers, who are in turn, "buyers" from manufacturers. The law of sales is the study of the rights and responsibilities of those in the purchase-and-sale of goods chain, from the original maker of the item to the ultimate user. A **sale** is a contract that, by its terms, transfers goods from a seller to a buyer for a price in current money (or a promise of payment).

HISTORICAL PERSPECTIVE

Today's law of sales originated centuries ago in the customs and traditions of merchants and traders. The *Lex Mercantoria* (Law Merchant) was a system of rules, customs, and usages self-imposed by early commercial traders and merchants to settle disputes and to enforce obligations among themselves. (See Chapter 2.)

By the end of the seventeenth century, the principles of the Law Merchant were widely accepted and quite naturally became part of the common law. From that time on, judges, not merchants, refined the principles of mercantile law into the modern commercial law of sales.

Numerous attempts were made in the United States to produce a uniform body of laws relating to commercial transactions. Two major enactments, the Uniform Negotiable Instruments Law (1896) and the Uniform Sales Act (1906), were followed by several other "uniform acts," none of which were widely adopted by the states. In the 1940's the need to integrate the half-dozen or so uniform acts covering commercial transactions into a single, comprehensive body of statutory law was recognized. Accordingly, the Uniform Commercial Code (UCC, or simply "the Code") was developed to serve that purpose.

THE UNIFORM COMMERCIAL CODE

The UCC is the single, most comprehensive codification of the broad spectrum of laws involved in a total commercial transaction. It views the entire "commercial transaction for the sale of and payment for goods" as a single legal occurrence having numerous facets. Consider a consumer who buys a refrigerator from an appliance store and agrees to pay for it on an installment plan. Article 2 of the Code treats the contract of sale. If a check is given as the down payment on the purchase price, it will be negotiated and ultimately passed through one or more banks for collection. This process is the subject matter of Article 3, Commercial Paper, and Article 4, Bank Deposits and Collections. The appliance store extends credit to the consumer through the intallment plan, and it retains a right in the refrigerator (collateral). This is the subject matter of Article 9, Secured Transactions. Suppose the appliance company must first obtain the refrigerator from its manufacturer's warehouse, after which it is to be delivered by common carrier to the consumer. The storage and shipment of goods is the subject matter of Article 7, Documents of Title. When the appliance company arranges to pay the manufacturer located in another state for the refrigerator supplied, a letter of credit, which is the subject matter of Article 5, may be used.

Every phase of commerce is involved in the seemingly simple sale of and payment for goods. The Code attempts to provide a consistent and integrated framework of rules to deal with all the phases *ordinarily arising* in a commercial sales transaction from start to finish.[1]

THE SCOPE OF ARTICLE 2: THE SALE OF GOODS

No body of law, and certainly not the Code, operates in a vacuum removed from other principles of jurisprudence. A sales contract is governed by the same common law principles applicable to all contracts—offer, acceptance, consideration, and capacity—and these principles should be re-examined when studying sales. The law of sales, found in Article 2 of the UCC, is a part of the law of contracts.

Two things should be kept in mind. First, Article 2 deals with the sale of *goods*, not real property (real estate), services, or intangible property such as stocks and bonds. Second, in some cases, the rules will vary quite a bit, depending upon whether the buyer or seller is a *merchant* or a consumer.

It is always a good idea to note the subject matter of a dispute and the kind of people involved. If the subject is goods, then the UCC will govern. If it is real estate or services, then the common law alone will apply. If one of the people involved is a merchant, certain rules apply. If both are, another rule applies. If neither is, still a different rule applies.

---

1. Two articles of the Uniform Commercial Code seemingly do not fit into the "ordinary" commercial sales transaction. Article 6, Bulk Transfers, involves merchants who sell off the major part of their inventory, (often pocketing the money and disappearing, leaving creditors unpaid). Since such "bulk sales" do not "ordinarily arise" in a commercial transaction for the sale of goods, they are treated separately. Article 8, Investment Securities, deals with negotiable securities (stocks and bonds), transactions that do not fall within the concept of sale of or payment for goods. However, the subject matter of Articles 6 and 8 was considered by the Code's drafters to be related closely enough to ordinary commercial transactions to warrant inclusion in the Uniform Commercial Code.

What Is a Sale?

Article 2 applies to the "sale of goods", but Section 2-102 states that Article 2 applies to "*transactions* in goods", indicating a broader scope that includes, for example, leases and gifts. However, for the purposes of this Chapter (and most authorities and courts will agree), Article 2 applies only to an actual *sale*.

The word "sale" is a shorthand way of saying "a sales contract which by its terms transfers goods from seller to buyer for a price." A sale is officially defined ". . . as the passing of title from the seller to the buyer for a price". [UCC Sec. 2-106(1)] The price may be payable in money or in other goods, services, or realty (real estate).

What Are Goods?

To be characterized as a *good*, an item must be *tangible*, and it must be *movable*.

A tangible item has physical existence—it can be touched or seen. Thus, intangible property such as corporate stocks and bonds, promissory notes, bank accounts, patents and copyrights, or ordinary contract rights have only conceptual existence and do not come under Article 2.

A *movable* item can be carried from place to place. Hence, real estate is excluded from Article 2. However, goods "*associated with real estate*" fall under Article 2. Section 2-107 provides the following rules:

1. A contract for the sale of minerals or the like (including oil and gas) or a structure (such as a building) is a contract for the sale of goods *if severance is to be made by the seller*. If the buyer is to sever them from the land, the contract is considered a sale of real estate governed by the principles of real property law, not the UCC. To illustrate: S agrees to sell B a quantity of oil that is located under S's property. If B is to drill the wells to remove the oil, the contract is a sale of real estate. If the agreement provides that S is to drill the wells to obtain the oil, the transaction is a sale of goods. Similarly, S agrees to sell B an old barn located on S's farm. If the agreement requires B to remove the barn, it is a contract for the sale of real estate. If S is to remove the barn, the contract is characterized as a sale of goods under UCC Article 2.

2. A sale of growing crops or timber to be cut is a contract for the sale of goods regardless of who severs them.

3. Other "things attached" to realty but capable of severance without material harm to the land are considered goods regardless of who severs them.[2] Examples of such things are a furnace or window air-conditioner in a house or counters and stools in a luncheonette. The test is whether removal will cause *material harm* to the realty to which the item is attached. Removal of a window air-conditioner would be a sale of goods, but removal of a central air-conditioning system or an in-ground swimming pool would probably do a great deal of damage and hence would be treated as a sale of real estate. When the parties do not envision any items being removed (severed) from the realty, such as in the sale of "ten acres of corn fields", then the transaction is characterized as the sale of real estate.

GOODS VERSUS SERVICES   Courts have disagreed over whether a particular transaction involves the sale of goods or the rendering of a service. For example, is the blood furnished to a patient during an operation a "sale of goods" or the "performance of a medical service"? Some courts say "a good"; some say "a service." The same kind of "mixed transaction" problem is encountered when a beautician applies hair dye to a customer in a beauty shop. The Code does not provide the answer, and court decisions are in conflict. The Code does stipulate, however, that serving food or drink to be consumed either on or off restaurant premises is the "sale of goods", at least for the purpose of an implied warranty of merchantability. [UCC Sec. 2-312(1)] Whether the transaction in question involves the sale of goods or services is important because the majority of courts treat services as being excluded by the UCC.

---

2.   The Code avoids using the word "fixtures" here because of the numerous definitions of this term. (See Chapter 52.)

SPECIAL CLASSIFICATIONS The Code refers to several special cases that it explicitly characterizes as "goods":

1. The unborn young of animals are goods.
2. Rare coins and other forms of money as a commodity are goods (but money as a form of payment is not).
3. Items specially manufactured for a particular buyer are goods. Even though the "special order" might be construed as a contract for "special services", the Code clearly categorizes these transactions as a sale of goods.

Who Is a Merchant?

Article 2 governs the sale of goods in general. It applies to sales transactions between all buyers and sellers. In a limited number of instances, however, the Code presumes that, in certain phases of sales transactions between *professional merchants*, special business standards ought to be imposed because of the merchants' degree of commercial expertise.[3] Such standards do not apply to the casual or inexperienced seller or buyer. Section 2-104 defines three ways that *merchant* status occurs:

1. A merchant is a person who *deals in goods of the kind* involved in the sales contract. Thus, a retailer, a wholesaler, or a manufacturer is a

---

3. The provisions that apply only to merchants deal with the Statute of Frauds, firm offers, confirmatory memoranda, warranties, and contract modification. These special rules reflect expedient business practice, commonly known to merchants in the commercial setting. They will be discussed in the materials presented later in this chapter on sales contract formation.

merchant of those goods sold in the business. A merchant for one type of goods is not necessarily a merchant for any other type. For example, a sporting equipment retailer is a merchant when buying tennis equipment but not when buying stereo equipment.
2. A merchant is a person who, by occupation, *holds himself or herself out as having knowledge and skill peculiar to the practices or goods involved in the transaction.* This is a broad definition that can include banks or universities as merchants.
3. A person who employs a merchant as a broker, agent, or other intermediary has the status of merchant in that transaction. Hence, if a "gentleman farmer" who ordinarily does not run the farm hires a broker to purchase livestock, the farmer is considered a merchant in the livestock transaction.

In summary, a person can be considered to have the professional status of "merchant" by having specialized knowledge of the business or the goods, by employing a merchant to conduct a particular transaction, or by holding him- or herself out to be a merchant. These provisions apply only when a merchant is acting in a mercantile capacity.

Is a farmer a merchant? The answer depends upon the particular goods involved, the transaction, and whether, in the particular situation, the farmer is held out as having special knowledge concerning the goods involved in the transaction. The following case illustrates how the courts decide whether or not a person is a merchant and therefore subject to the UCC version of the Statute of Frauds.

BACKGROUND AND FACTS *Urban, a wheat farmer, phoned the assistant manager of a grain-selling cooperative of which he was a member. The assistant manager claimed that Urban agreed over the phone to sell 10,000 bushels of wheat to the co-op at $2.86 per bushel. He further claimed that he sent a confirmation of the sale to Urban and that Urban never objected to it. As a member of the co-op, Urban was familiar with this sales procedure. Urban claimed that since there was no written agreement, the Statute of Frauds prevented recovery by the co-op. The co-op wanted possession of the grain at a price of $2.86 per bushel.*

DECATUR COOPERATIVE ASS'N. v. URBAN
Supreme Court of Kansas, 1976.
219 Kan. 171, 547 P.2d 323.

DECISION AND RATIONALE *The question raised for the appellate court was whether Urban was a "merchant" since, if he was, the Statute of Frauds defense would not apply to him under UCC Sec. 2-201(2). Noting that courts in other jurisdictions were divided on the issue of whether a farmer is a merchant, the Kansas court held that Urban was not a merchant as that term is used in Sec. 2-104. "The transaction in question here was the sale of wheat. Appellee as a farmer undoubtedly had special knowledge or skill in raising wheat. [Emphasis supplied.] But we do not think this factor, coupled with annual sales of a wheat crop and purchases of seed wheat, qualified him as a merchant in that field." However, since Urban could reasonably expect the co-op to rely on his promise, the court held that the doctrine of promissory estoppel prohibited application of the Statute of Frauds. "In order for the doctrine of promissory estoppel to be invoked the evidence must show that the promise was made under circumstances where the promisor intended and reasonably expected that the promise would be relied upon by the promisee and further that the promisee acted reasonably in relying upon the promise. Furthermore, promissory estoppel should be applied only if a refusal to enforce it would be virtually to sanction the perpetration of fraud or would result in other injustice."*

FORMATION OF A SALES CONTRACT

The policy of the Uniform Commercial Code is to recognize that the law of sales is part of the general law of contracts. The Code often restates general principles or is silent altogether. In those situations, the common law of contracts and applicable state statutes govern. The following sections summarize the ways that UCC provisions change the effect of the general law of contracts. Exhibit 17-1 summarizes the special rules for contracts of sale of goods and the Code section out of Article 2 that applies. All these rules will be treated in this chapter and in Chapters 18 through 22.

Offer

In general contract law, the moment a definite offer is met by an unqualified acceptance, a binding contract is formed. In commercial sales transactions, the verbal exchanges, the correspondence, and the actions of the parties may not reveal exactly when a binding contractual obligation arises. The Code states that an agreement sufficient to constitute a contract can exist even if the moment of its making is undetermined. [UCC Sec. 2-204]

OPEN TERMS According to contract law, an offer must be definite enough for the parties (and the courts) to ascertain its essential terms when it is accepted. The UCC states that a sales contract will not fail for indefiniteness even if one or more terms are left open as long as: (1) the parties intended to make a contract and (2) there is a reasonably certain basis for the court to grant an appropriate remedy.

The Code provides numerous *open term* provisions that can be used to fill in the gaps in a contract. Two factors should be kept in mind. The more terms left open, the less likely the courts will find that the parties *intended* to form a contract. As a general rule, if the *quantity* term is left open, the courts will have no basis for determining a remedy, and the sales contract will fail. If the contract is for all of one's needs, it is a requirements contract and is valid even though it has, in a sense, an open quantity term.

EXHIBIT 17-1   UCC RULES FOR CONTRACTS FOR THE SALE OF GOODS

	RULE	SECTION OF UCC
OFFER AND ACCEPTANCE	1. The acceptance of unilateral offers can be made by a promise to ship or by shipment itself.	2-206 (1) (b)
	2. Not all terms have to be included in negotiation for a contract to result.	2-204
	3. Particulars of performance can be left open.	2-311 (1)
	4. Firm written offers by *merchants* for three months or less cannot be revoked.	2-205
	5. Acceptance by performance requires notice within a reasonable time; otherwise the offer can be treated as lapsed.	2-206 (2)
	6. The price does not have to be included to have a contract.	2-205
	7. Variations in terms between the offer and the acceptance may not be a rejection but may be an acceptance.	2-207
	8. Acceptance can be made by any reasonable means of communication; it is effective when deposited.	2-206 (1) (a)
CONSIDERATION	1. A modification of a contract for the sale of goods does not require consideration.	2-209 (1)
	2. Adding a seal has no effect on the validity of the contract.	2-203
ILLEGALITY	1. Unconscionable bargains will not be enforced.	2-302
VOIDABLE CONTRACTS	1. Revocation of acceptance does not prevent a lawsuit for monetary damages.	2-721
	2. A person with voidable title has power to transfer a good title to a good faith purchaser for value.	
FORM OF THE AGREEMENT	1. The Statute of Frauds covers: (a) All sales of goods for a price in excess of $500. (b) Written confirmations between merchants. (c) Specially manufactured goods. (d) Memoranda that do not include all the agreement terms. (e) Goods for which payment has been made and accepted; goods which have been received and accepted. (f) Admission in pleadings or court proceedings that a contract for sale was made.	2-201
RIGHTS OF THIRD PARTIES	1. Delegation of duties is included when a contract, or the rights under a contract, are assigned.	2-210 (4)
PERFORMANCE OF CONTRACTS	1. Tender of payment is a condition precedent to a tender of delivery, unless a credit sale was agreed upon.	2-511
	2. Anticipatory breach cannot be withdrawn if the other party gives notice that it is final.	2-616, 2-611
	3. Claims and rights can be waived without consideration.	1-107
DISCHARGE	1. The statute of limitations is four years. Mutual agreement can reduce it to not less than one year.	2-725

Open Price Term If the parties have not agreed on a price, the court will determine "a reasonable price at the time for delivery." [UCC Sec. 2-305(1)] If either the buyer or the seller is to determine the price, it means a price fixed in good faith. [UCC Sec. 2-305(2)]

Sometimes the price fails to be fixed through the fault of one of the parties. In that case, the other party can treat the contract as cancelled or fix a reasonable price. For example, Axel and Beatty enter into a contract for the sale of goods and agree that Axel will fix the price. The agreement becomes economically burdensome to Axel, and Axel refuses to fix the price. Beatty can either treat the contract as cancelled, or he can set a reasonable price. [UCC Sec. 2-305(3)]

Although the UCC has radically changed the requirements for definiteness of essentials in contracts of sale, it has not obviated the common law requirement that the contract must at least be definite enough to allow the court to identify the agreement either for the purpose of enforcing it or for awarding appropriate damages if it is breached. In the following case, the language of the contract, even under the liberal standards of the UCC, was insufficient to identify the subject of the agreement of the parties.

ROYAL STORE FIXTURE CO. v. BUCCI
Pennsylvania County Court, 1969. 7 UCC Rep. Serv. 1193.

BACKGROUND AND FACTS *Bucci purchased a parcel of land with the intention of building a combination restaurant and delicatessen on it. Shortly thereafter, a representative of Royal Store Fixture Company offered to help Bucci set up the new store. In writing, Bucci agreed to purchase the necessary fixtures and refrigeration equipment for the store from Royal in consideration for Royal's assistance "at prices competitive with other manufacturers of similar equipment." Bucci later ignored the agreement and bought from one of Royal's competitors, and Royal brought suit.*

DECISION AND RATIONALE *No contract existed between Bucci and Royal Store Fixtures because the document Bucci signed was too vague and indefinite to be enforceable. Courts will enforce agreements with open price or quantity terms, but they cannot enforce agreements that so inadequately describe the subject matter as to make damages impossible to determine. According to the appellate court: "Nor do we believe that the price of the unspecified store fixtures and refrigeration equipment could ever be reduced to reasonable certainty. While Section 2-305 of the UCC dealing with 'open price terms' has been construed to call for a reasonable price, this may not necessarily be the same as the 'competitive prices' called for in the writing."*

Open Delivery Term When no delivery terms are specified, the buyer normally takes delivery at the seller's place of business. [UCC Sec. 2-308(a)] If the seller has no place of business, then the seller's residence is used. When goods are located in some other place and both parties know it, then delivery is made there. When the time for shipment or delivery has not been clearly specified in the sales contract, the court will infer a "reasonable" time under the circumstances for performance. [UCC Sec. 2-309(1)]

BACKGROUND AND FACTS *Wedner contracted to purchase 400 cartons of lettuce from Mendelson-Zeller to be delivered in time for the Monday morning market on January 22. Due to winter driving conditions, the goods arrived at 12:30 p.m. The produce was unloaded and was sold the next day. Wedner paid for the lettuce but deducted a certain amount as damages that it claimed to have suffered from the late delivery.*

MENDELSON-ZELLER CO., INC. v. JOSEPH WEDNER & SON CO.
U.S. Department of Agriculture, 1970.
7 UCC Rep. Serv. 1045.

DECISION AND RATIONALE *Wedner had to pay the entire contract price for the lettuce and could not deduct for damages. Since the lettuce was tendered by Mendelson-Zeller and accepted by Wedner, the only question remaining was whether delivery was at a reasonable time. In the opinion of the court: "Section 2-309(1) of the Uniform Commercial Code provides that the time for delivery in the absence of an agreed time shall be a reasonable time. *** Under the circumstances [the winter driving conditions] we are unable to say that delivery on January 23 was not within a reasonable time."*

Open Payment Term When parties do not specify payment terms, payment is due at the time and place at which the buyer is to receive the goods. Generally, cash, not credit, is used. [UCC Sec. 2-310(a)] The buyer can tender payment using any commercially normal or proper means, such as a check or credit terms. If the seller demands payment in cash, however, the buyer must be given a reasonable time to obtain it. [UCC Sec. 2-511(2)]

MERCHANT'S FIRM OFFER The merchant's firm offer is in the special category of rules applicable only to *merchants*. Under regular contract principles, an offer can be revoked any time before acceptance. The major common law exception is an option contract in which the offeree pays consideration for the offeror's irrevocable promise to keep the offer open for a stated period.

The UCC creates a second exception that applies only to *firm offers* for the sale of goods made by a merchant (regardless of whether or not the offeree is a merchant). If the merchant gives assurances in a signed writing that the offer will remain open for a stated period of time not to exceed three months, the *merchant's firm offer* is irrevocable without the necessity of consideration.[4] [UCC Sec. 2-205] To illustrate: Daniels, a used-car dealer, writes a letter to Peters on January 1 stating, "I have a 1974 Dodge Dart which I'll sell to you for $2,200 any time between now and the end of the month." By January 18, Daniels has heard nothing from Peters so he sells the Dodge Dart to another person. On January 23, Peters tenders $2,200 to Daniels and asks for the car. When Daniels tells him the car has already been sold, Peters claims that Daniels has breached a good contract. Peters is right. Since Daniels is a merchant of used cars, he is obligated to keep his offer open until the end of January. Since he has not done so, he is liable for breach.

It is necessary, however, that the offer be both *written and signed* by the offeror.[5] Where a firm offer is contained in a form contract prepared by the offeree, a *separate* firm offer

---

4. If the offeree pays consideration, then an *option contract* and not a *merchant's firm offer* is formed.
5. "Signed" includes any symbol executed or adopted by a party with present intention to authenticate a writing. [UCC Sec. 1-201(39)]

assurance must be signed in addition. The purpose of the merchant's firm offer rule is to give effect to a merchant's deliberate intent to be bound to a firm offer. If the firm offer is buried in one of the pages of the offeree's form contract amid copious language, the offeror might inadvertently sign the contract without realizing it, thus defeating the purpose of the rule.

Acceptance

METHODS OF ACCEPTANCE The general common law rule is that an offeror can specify a particular method of acceptance. This is still true under the Code. Where the offeror has said nothing about the manner in which acceptance must be made, however, the Code provides that acceptance can occur in any manner and by any means of communication reasonable under the circumstances. [UCC Sec. 2-206(1)]

For example, X phones Y to make an offer that X will keep open for five days. If Y telegraphs or mails an acceptance two days later, will there be a valid contract? The answer depends on which form of communication was commercially reasonable under the circumstances.

The UCC permits acceptance of an offer to buy goods for current or prompt shipment by either a promise to ship or prompt shipment of the goods to the buyer. The Code permits the seller to ship out "nonconforming goods" as an accommodation, as long as the seller notifies the buyer that the shipment is offered only as an accommodation. [UCC Sec. 2-206(1)(a)] For example, X orders 1,000 blue widgets from Y. Before the goods arrive, Y notifies X that black widgets have been sent as an accommodation instead of blue widgets. If accepted by X, the shipment is a counteroffer, and a valid contract for the purchase of black widgets will result.

If, however, Y has shipped 1,000 black widgets instead of blue, but does not notify X that the goods are being shipped *as an accommodation*, Y's shipment acts as both an acceptance of X's offer and a *breach* of the resulting contract. X may sue Y for any appropriate damages.

At common law, a unilateral contract invites acceptance by a performance. The offeree need not notify the offeror of performance unless the offeror would not otherwise know about it. The UCC is more stringent than common law, stating that "Where the beginning of requested performance is a reasonable mode of acceptance an offeror who is not notified of acceptance within a reasonable time may treat the offer as having lapsed before acceptance." [UCC Sec. 2-206(2)] To illustrate: Johnson writes the Scroll Bookstore on Monday, "Please send me a copy of *West's Book of Business Law* for $20, C.O.D., as soon as possible." Signed "Johnson." Scroll receives the request on Tuesday. The owner does nothing until the following month, when she ships the book for $20 C.O.D. Johnson receives the book and rejects it, indicating that the book has arrived too late to be of value. In this case, since Johnson heard nothing from Scroll for a month, he was justified in assuming that the store did not intend to deliver *West's Book of Business Law*. Johnson could consider that the offer lapsed due to the length of time.

ADDITIONAL TERMS Under traditional common law, if X makes an offer to Y and Y in turn accepts but adds some slight qualification, there is no contract. The so-called "mirror-image rule" of offer-to-acceptance makes Y's action a rejection of and a counteroffer to X's offer.

The UCC generally takes the position that if the offeree's response indicates a *definite* willingness to accept the offer, it will be recognized as an effective acceptance even if it includes terms in addition to or different from the original offer. [UCC Sec. 2-207(1)] The additional terms are construed as "proposals for addition" to the contract when ordinary buyers and sellers are involved. [UCC Sec. 2-207(1)] For example, X offers to sell his car to Y. Y replies, "I accept, but I would like you to put new tires on it". This is a contract. X is not bound to put new tires on the automobile. However, if Y says,

"I accept, but only on the condition that you put new tires on the car," there will be no contract unless X agrees to put on the new tires.

Rules Between Merchants The Code rule for additional terms in the acceptance is a little different when the transaction occurs *between merchants* (that is, when both buyer and seller are merchants). Additional terms do not become part of the contract between ordinary buyers and sellers—they are merely proposals. *Between merchants* the additional proposed terms *automatically* become part of the contract unless:

1. They materially alter the original contract.
2. The offer expressly states that no terms other than those in the offer will be accepted.
3. The offeror has already objected to the particular terms.

If the new terms make no material change and the offeror does not object to them, they will become part of the contract. [UCC Sec. 2-207] To illustrate: X and Y are merchants. X offers to sell 20,000 pens to Y at $10 each plus freight. Y responds: "I accept. Price is $10.01 each, including freight." There is a contract because the difference in total cost is only $200 out of a $200,000 contract. The change is probably not material and will automatically become part of the contract unless X objects. If X does object, there is a contract on X's original terms only. In the same situation, suppose Y replies: "Will take if you make the price $10.10 including freight." There is no contract here. This is merely a counteroffer since there is no definite expression of acceptance on the part of Y. Now suppose X offers to sell Y "20,000 pens at $10 each plus freight. No changes." Y replies: "I accept. Price is $10.10 each, including freight." There is no contract. The offer expressly limits Y's acceptance to the terms as stated. Finally, suppose that X offers to sell Y "20,000 pens at $10 each" and Y replies, "Accept. But I only need 10,000 pens at $10 each." There is no contract since Y's response materially alters X's offer.

In this next case, the court grapples with the question of whether a carpet manufacturer's written confirmation of a carpet dealer's oral orders for carpet was an "acceptance expressly conditioned on the buyer's consent to additional terms" (specifically, an arbitration provision), which would bring their situation within UCC Sec. 2-207(1), or whether the written confirmation between merchants automatically became part of the contract unless they "materially altered it", which would bring the action within the provisions of UCC Sec. 2-207(2).

DORTON v. COLLINS & AIKMAN CORP.

United States Court of Appeals, Sixth Circuit, 1972.
453 F.2d 1161.

BACKGROUND AND FACTS *The Carpet Mart, a carpet dealer, telephoned an order for carpet to Collins & Aikman Corp., a carpet manufacturer. Collins & Aikman then sent The Carpet Mart an acknowledgment form, which specified the quantity and price agreed to in the telephone conversation. The reverse side of the printed acknowledgment form stated that Collins & Aikman accepted subject to the buyer's agreement to submit all disputes to arbitration. The Carpet Mart and Collins & Aikman had never discussed arbitration. Thereafter, Collins & Aikman mailed the acknowledgment form and shipped the carpet to The Carpet Mart, which received all items without objection. A dispute later arose, and The Carpet Mart refused to be bound by the arbitration clause.*

DECISION AND RATIONALE *The Carpet Mart may or may not be bound by the arbitration clause. Although the use of the word "subject to" suggests some extent of conditional acceptance, it did not clearly signify* *that Collins & Aikman were unwilling to procede with the contract unless The Carpet Mart agreed to it. Because Collins & Aikman's acceptance was not expressly conditioned on The Carpet Mart's assent to the arbitration clause, there was a contract and the arbitration clause must be treated as a proposal for additional terms. This proposal would bind The Carpet Mart only if it does not materially alter the contract reached on the telephone. In the words of the appellate court: "We believe that the question of whether the arbitration provision materially altered the oral offer under Subsection 2-207(2)(b) is one which can be resolved only by the [trial court] on further findings of fact in the present case. If the arbitration provision did in fact materially alter The Carpet Mart's offer, it could not become a part of the contract unless expressly agreed to by The Carpet Mart."*

Consideration

The Uniform Commercial Code radically changes the common law rule that contract modification must be supported by new consideration. Section 2-209(1) of the UCC states that "an agreement modifying a contract needs no consideration to be binding." Of course, contract modification must be sought in good faith. [UCC Sec. 1-203] Modifications *extorted* from the other party are in bad faith and, therefore, unenforceable. For example, Hal agrees to manufacture and sell certain goods to Betty for a stated price. Subsequently, a sudden shift in the market makes it difficult for Hal to sell the items to Betty at the given price without suffering a loss. Hal tells Betty of the situation, and Betty agrees to pay an additional sum for the goods. Later Betty reconsiders and refuses to pay more than the original price. Under Section 2-209(1) of the UCC, Betty's promise to modify the contract needs no consideration to be binding. Hence, Betty is bound by the modified contract.

In the example above, a shift in the market provides an example of a *good faith* reason for contract modification. In fact, Section 1-203 states that "Every contract or duty within this act imposes an obligation of good faith in its performance or enforcement." Good faith in the case of a merchant is defined to mean honesty in fact and the observance of reasonable commercial standards of fair dealing in the trade. [UCC Sec.

2-103(1)(b)] But what if there really were no shift in the market, but Hal knew that Betty needed the goods immediately and refused to deliver unless Betty agreed to pay an additional sum of money? This sort of extortion of a modification without a legitimate commercial reason would be ineffective because it would violate the duty of good faith. Hal would not be permitted to enforce the higher price.

WHEN MODIFICATION WITHOUT CONSIDERATION REQUIRES WRITING There are situations in which modification without consideration must be written in order to be enforceable. According to Section 2-209(2), a contract that, by its terms, prohibits modification or rescission (cancellation) except by a signed writing, must be written in order to be enforceable. However, if a consumer (nonmerchant buyer) is dealing with a merchant, *and* the merchant supplies the form that contains a prohibition against oral modification, the consumer must sign a separate acknowledgment of such a clause.

Statute of Frauds

Section 2-201(1) of the UCC contains a Statute of Frauds provision that applies to contracts for the sale of goods. The provision requires a writing for the contract to be enforceable if the price is $500 or more. The parties can have an initial oral agreement, however, and satisy the Statute of Frauds by having a subsequent written memorandum of their oral agreement. In each case the writing must be signed by the party against whom enforcement is sought.

BETWEEN MERCHANTS—WRITTEN CONFIRMATION Once again the Uniform Commercial Code provides a special rule for a contract for the sale of goods between merchants. Merchants can satisfy the requirements of a writing for the Statute of Frauds if, after the parties have agreed orally, one of the merchants sends a signed written communication to the other merchant. The communication must indicate the terms of the agreement. The merchant receiving the confirmation must have reason to know of its contents, and, unless written notice of objection to its contents is given within ten days after receipt, the writing will be sufficient against the receiving merchant. (see *Decatur Cooperative Ass'n v. Urban,* page 283 above.)

RELAXED REQUIREMENTS The Uniform Commercial Code has greatly relaxed the requirements for the sufficiency of a writing to satisfy the Statute of Frauds. A written contract, a memorandum, or even an unsigned confirmation between merchants will be sufficient as long as all the essential terms of the agreement are reflected. The single term that must be included in the writing is the quantity (except in the case of output and requirements contracts). All other terms can be proved in court by oral testimony. Often, terms that are not agreed upon can be supplied by the open term provisions of Article 2 itself.

EXCEPTIONS Section 2-201 defines three exceptions to the Statute of Frauds requirement. A contract, if proved to exist, will be enforceable despite the absence of a writing and even if it involves a sale of goods for over $500 if:

1. *The oral contract is for specially manufactured goods for a particular buyer* and: (a) these goods are not suitable for resale to others in the ordinary course of the seller's business, and (b) the seller has substantially started to manufacture the goods or made commitments for the manufacture of the goods. In this situation, once the seller has taken action, the buyer cannot repudiate the agreement. To illustrate: Archer ordered a unique, strangely-styled cabinet from Collins, a cabinetmaker. The price of the cabinet is $1,000, and the contract is oral. Collins finishes the cabinet and tenders delivery to Archer. Archer refuses to pay for it even though the job is completed on time. Archer claims that he is not liable because the contract is oral. Clearly, if the style of the cabinet is so strange that Collins cannot find another buyer, or if it is not suitable for sale to Collins's ordinary customers, then Archer is liable to Collins. An oral contract for the manufacture of nonresalable goods is enforceable, even if the contract price is $500 or more, as long as the manufacturer has "made a substantial beginning of their manufacture. * * *"

2. *A party to a contract can admit in pleadings (written complaints), testimony, or other court proceedings that a contract for sale was made.* In this case the contract will be enforceable even though it was oral. To illustrate: By telephone Archer orders 50 gallons of gas from Collins for 75 cents a gallon. Collins agrees to deliver the next day, but Collins thinks that Archer has ordered 500 gallons of gas, and that is what he delivers. Archer refuses to accept or pay for *any* of the gas. Collins, who is certain that Archer ordered 500 gallons, sues Archer for breach of contract for the sale of 500 gallons. Archer's defense will be that he ordered only 50 gallons. Since Archer has admitted that he ordered 50 gallons only, that is the only damages that Collins can recover. The parties agree that a contract was made; therefore the contract is enforceable to the extent of the quantity of goods admitted by Archer, since there is no writing.

3. *An oral agreement will be enforceable to the extent that payment has been made and accepted or to the extent that goods have been received and accepted.* For example, suppose

that X orally agrees to sell Y ten chairs at $100 each. Before X delivers them, Y sends X a check for $500, which X accepts. X then attempts to dishonor the contract. Under the UCC, Y can enforce the oral contract to the extent of $500. Similarly, if Y had made no payment but X had made a partial shipment of five chairs that Y accepted, an oral contract against Y for $500, the price of five chairs, would be enforceable.

Parol Evidence

If the parties to a contract set forth its terms in a confirmatory memorandum (a writing expressing offer and acceptance of the deal) or in a writing intended as their final expression, the terms of the contract cannot be contradicted by evidence of any prior or contemporaneous oral or written agreements. Such terms, however, can be explained or supplemented by consistent additional terms, or by *course of dealing, usage of trade,* or *course of performance.*

CONSISTENT ADDITIONAL TERMS If the court finds an ambiguity in a writing that is supposed to be a complete and exclusive statement of the agreement between the parties, it may accept evidence of consistent additional terms to clarify and remove the ambiguity. The court will not, however, accept evidence of contradictory terms. This is the rule under both the Code and the common law of contracts.

COURSE OF DEALING AND USAGE OF TRADE In construing a commercial agreement, the court will assume that the course of prior dealing between the parties and the usage

of trade were taken into account when the agreement was phrased. [UCC Secs. 2-202 and 1-201(3)] The Code states, "A course of dealing between the parties and any usage of trade in the vocation or trade in which they are engaged or of which they are or should be aware give particular meaning to [the terms of an agreement] and supplement or qualify the terms of [the] agreement." [UCC Sec. 1-205(3)]

The Code has determined that the meaning of any agreement, evidenced by the language of the parties and by their action, must be interpreted in light of commercial practices and other surrounding circumstances.

Usage of trade is defined as any practice or method of dealing having such regularity of observance in a place, vocation, or trade as to justify an expectation that it will be observed with respect to the transaction in question. [UCC Sec. 1-205(2)] Further, the expressed terms of an agreement and an applicable course of dealing or usage of trade will be construed to be consistent with each other whenever reasonable. However, when such construction is unreasonable, the expressed terms in the agreement will prevail. [UCC Sec. 1-205(4)]

A *course of dealing* is a sequence of previous conduct between the parties to a particular transaction that establishes a common basis for their understanding. [UCC Sec. 1-205(1)] Course of dealing is restricted, literally, to the sequence of conduct between the parties that has occurred prior to the agreement in question.

In the following case, the court permitted the introduction of evidence of usage and custom in the trade to explain the meaning of quantity figures that the parties took for granted when the contract was formed.

HEGGBLADE-MARGULEAS-TENNECO, INC. v. SUNSHINE BISCUIT, INC.

Court of Appeals of California, 5th District, 1976. 59 Cal. App.3d 948, 131 Cal.Rptr. 183.

BACKGROUND AND FACTS *Heggblade-Marguleas-Tenneco (HMT) contracted with Sunshine Biscuit to supply potatoes to be used in the production of potato-snack foods. HMT had never marketed processing potatoes before. The quantity mentioned in their contract negotiations was 100,000 sacks of potatoes. It was agreed that the amount of potatoes to be supplied would vary somewhat with Sunshine Biscuit's needs. Subsequently, a decline in demand for Sunshine Biscuit's products severely reduced its need for potatoes, and it prorated the reduced* *demand among its suppliers, including HMT, as fairly as possible. Sunshine Biscuit was able to take only 60,105 sacks out of the 100,000 previously estimated. In HMT's suit for breach of contract, Sunshine Biscuit attempted to introduce evidence that it is customary in the potato-processing industry for the number of potatoes specified in sales contracts to be reasonable estimates rather than exact numbers that a buyer intends to purchase.*

DECISION AND RATIONALE   *The evidence of custom in the potato-processing trade was admissible. UCC Section 2-202 states that even though evidence of prior or contemporaneous agreements that contradict a written contract is inadmissible, evidence of course of dealing or of trade usage is admissible. The fact that specific numbers were used to designate quantities of potatoes that Sunshine Biscuit thought it needed does not dispose of the issue. In its statement that evidence of trade usage was admissible, the court quoted the UCC: "***[I]n order that the true understanding of the parties as to the agreement may be [reached, such] writings are to be read on the assumption that *** the usages of trade were taken for granted when the document was phrased. Unless carefully negated they have become an element of the meaning of the words used."*

COURSE OF PERFORMANCE   Course of performance is the conduct that occurs under the terms of a particular agreement. The course of performance actually undertaken is the best indication of what the parties to an agreement intended it to mean. Presumably, the parties themselves know best what they meant by their words, and their action under that agreement is the best indication of what they meant. [UCC Sec. 2-208]

To illustrate: Lumber Company A contracts with B to sell B a specified number of "2-by-4s". The lumber in fact does not measure 2 inches by 4 inches but rather $1\frac{7}{8}$ inches by $3\frac{3}{4}$ inches. If B objects to the lumber delivered, A can prove that "2-by-4s" are never exactly 2 inches by 4 inches by using usage of trade or course of prior dealings or both. A can show in previous transactions that B took $1\frac{7}{8}$ inch by $3\frac{3}{4}$ inch lumber without objection. In addition, A can show that, in the trade, 2-by-4s are commonly $1\frac{7}{8}$ inches by $3\frac{3}{4}$ inches. Both usage of trade and course of prior dealings are relevant in determining and explaining what the parties meant by 2-by-4s.

Using the same example, suppose that A agrees to deliver the lumber in five separate deliveries. The fact that B has accepted lumber without objection in three previous deliveries under the agreement (course of performance) is relevant in determining that the words 2-by-4 actually mean $1\frac{7}{8}$ by $3\frac{3}{4}$.

The Code provides *rules of construction.* Express terms, course of performance, course of dealing, and usage of trade are to be construed together whenever consistent with one another. When such construction is unreasonable, however, the following order of priority controls: (1) express terms, (2) course of performance, (3) course of dealing, and (4) usage of trade. [UCC Secs. 1-205(4) and 2-208(2)]

Unconscionability

An unconscionable contract is one that is so grossly unfair and one-sided that it would be unreasonable to enforce it. Section 2-302 allows the court to evaluate a contract or any clause in a contract, and if the court deems it to be unconscionable *at the time it was made,* the court can (1) refuse to enforce the contract, or (2) enforce the remainder of the contract without the unconscionable clause, or (3) limit the application of any unconscionable clauses to avoid an unconscionable result.

The court, in determining whether a contract or clause is unconscionable, uses a basic test that evaluates whether, in light of general commercial practice and the commercial needs of the particular trade involved, the clauses are so one-sided as to be unconscionable under the circumstances at the time the contract was made. In this day of consumer law, consumer sales contracts are increasingly coming under attack for unconscionability. Typical cases involve high pressure salespersons and uneducated consumers who may pay contract prices several times the market value of the goods. In general, the courts have concluded that unequal bargaining power, coupled with unscrupulous dealings by one party, will result in an unenforceable, unconscionable contract.

QUESTIONS AND CASE PROBLEMS

1. Article 2 of the Uniform Commercial Code applies to "transactions in goods." Which of the following transactions is covered by Article 2?

a. the contract for the sale of a large fishing boat
b. the sale of an aircraft
c. a contract between two private individuals for the sale of investment bonds
d. a contract for the sale and installment of tile by a professional tile setter
e. the sale of a laundry and dry cleaning business
f. the sale of a central heating and air-conditioning system in a home (pursuant to the sale of the home)

2. Pemberton went to Tradesmens Bank to secure a loan to buy a car. The bank would loan Pemberton the money only under the conditions that the car would serve as collateral for the loan, that the car would be insured, and that the car dealer who was to sell the car to Pemberton would guarantee payment of the loan if Pemberton defaulted. Both Pemberton and the car dealer agreed to these conditions, and Pemberton secured the loan and purchased the car. Shortly thereafter, Pemberton was involved in an accident. After the insurance company paid the claim, it cancelled his insurance policy. The bank, after learning that the insurance was cancelled, failed to notify the car dealer, even though it was the local business custom for banks to give such notice. Shortly thereafter, Pemberton was involved in another accident that totally wrecked the car. Pemberton's financial situation was such that he could not pay the balance of the loan. Therefore, the bank sued the car dealer based on the guarantee that the car dealer had given under the loan agreement. At trial, the car dealer defended on the grounds that it was not liable under the guarantee because the bank had failed to give the car dealer notice of the cancellation of the insurance. The bank claimed that it was under no obligation to give notice to the car dealer because such a term was not included in the written loan guarantee agreement. In light of the parol evidence rule, can the car dealer prove that there was an implied promise on the part of the bank to give notice of cancellation of insurance? [Provident Tradesmens Bank & Trust Co. v. Pemberton, 196 Pa. Super. 180, 173 A.2d 780 (1961)]

3. Frances and Burlington engaged in the purchase and sale of yarn for a number of years. Frances normally placed its orders for yarn over the telephone. Each time Burlington shipped yarn to Frances, it sent a contract along with the yarn. Included in the contract was a clause providing for arbitration of all disputes in New York. Frances was located in North Carolina. Frances never signed or returned any of these contracts but never rejected them or the yarn. After several years of uninterrupted dealings, Frances rejected one of Burlington's shipments, stating that the yarn was defective, and refused to pay for it. Burlington sought to enforce the arbitration clause contained in the contracts that it sent to Frances, but Frances said that it was not bound by the clause. Who is right? [Frances Hosiery Mills, Inc. v. Burlington Industries, Inc., 19 N.C. App. 678, 200 S.E.2d 668 (1973)]

4. After several weeks of negotiation, Valley Electric and Heating Service orally agreed to sell and install an air-conditioning system in a theater owned by Charlotte Theaters, Inc. Valley Electric then put the terms of the agreement in writing and sent two copies to Charlotte Theaters. Charlotte retained one copy for itself and returned the other copy to Valley Electric after inserting a clause calling for completion of the work by a specified date. Along with the copy of the contract, Charlotte Theaters also sent a cover

letter that mentioned the specified completion date. Valley Electric proceeded to install the air-conditioning system but was unable to complete work by the date specified by Charlotte Theaters. Is Valley Electric in breach of contract? [Gateway Co. v. Charlotte Theaters, Inc., 297 F.2d. 483 (1st Cir. 1961)]

5. For a period of years, Exchange National Bank lent money to Citrus Incorporated to finance Citrus's orange growing operations. Shortly after the beginning of the growing season, Citrus sold all of its crops then growing to Alturas Packing Company. After the sale, but before the orange crop was harvested, Exchange National Bank sued Citrus for nonpayment of several outstanding loans. Exchange National Bank obtained a judgment against Citrus and, pursuant to the judgment, obtained a levy on the citrus crops. Under the applicable state law, Exchange National's levy against the crops would fail if and only if the sale of the orange crop to Alturas was deemed a sale of real estate instead of a sale of goods. Was this a sale of goods within the meaning of Article 2? [Exchange Nat. Bank of Tampa v. Alturas Packing Co., 269 So.2d 733 (Fla. App. 1972)]

6. In 1961, Clark and American Sand & Gravel discussed the possibility of a purchase by Clark of 25,000 tons of sand at 45 cents per ton. Although both parties found the terms of the possible sale agreeable, no sale was ever made. About eighteen months later, Clark requested American Sand & Gravel to deliver 1,500 tons to one of Clark's construction sites. American Sand & Gravel made the delivery, but no purchase price was ever mentioned. Subsequently, American charged Clark 55 cents per ton for the sand. Is there a contract between American and Clark? If so, what price can American charge for the sand? [American Sand & Gravel, Inc. v. Clark and Fray Constr. Co., 2 Conn. Cir. 284, 198 A.2d 68 (1964)]

7. Loeb & Company entered into an oral agreement with Schreiner, a farmer, whereby Schreiner was to sell Loeb 150 bales of cotton. Shortly thereafter, Loeb sent Schreiner a letter confirming the terms of the oral contract. Schreiner neither acknowledged receipt of the letter nor objected to its terms. When delivery came due, Schreiner ignored the oral agreement and sold on the open market because the price of cotton had more than doubled (from 37 cents to 80 cents per bale) since the oral agreement was made. In a lawsuit by Loeb & Company against Schreiner, can Loeb & Company recover? [Loeb & Co. v. Schreiner, 294 Ala. 722, 321 So.2d. 199 (1975)]

8. Pittsburgh Brewing Company and Weilersbacher had a long-standing business arrangement under which Weilersbacher sold Pittsburgh Brewing the malt that Pittsburgh Brewing used in making beer. In 1963 Weilersbacher and Pittsburgh orally agreed to a particular price schedule based upon the varying qualities of malt sold. No agreement was made as to how long the price schedule would be in effect or how long the parties would be bound under the contract. About a year later, Weilersbacher informed Pittsburgh Brewing that it would no longer honor the oral agreement and thereafter refused to make any more shipments of malt. Can Pittsburgh Brewing force Weilersbacher to continue performing under the contract? [Weilersbacher, Distributor v. Pittsburgh Brewing Co., 421 Pa. 118, 218 A.2d 806 (1966)]

18

Sales
Title, Risk,
and Insurable Interest

The sale of goods transfers ownership from seller to buyer. Often a sales contract will be signed before the actual goods are available. For example, a sales contract for oranges is signed in May, but the oranges are not ready for picking and shipment until October. Any number of things can happen between the time that a sales contract is signed and the time that the goods are actually transferred to the buyer's possession. Fire, flood, or frost can destroy the orange groves. The oranges may be lost or damaged in transit. The parties may want to obtain casualty insurance on the goods. The government may levy a tax on the oranges.

Before the UCC, *title*—right of ownership—was the central concept in sales law, controlling all issues of rights and remedies of the parties to a sales contract. However, it was difficult to determine when title actually passed. Therefore, the UCC divorced the question of title as completely as possible from the question of the rights and obligations of buyers, sellers, or third persons (such as subsequent purchasers, creditors, or the tax collector).

In some situations title is still relevant under the Code, and the UCC has special rules for locating title. These rules will be discussed in the materials that follow. In most situations, however, the Code replaces the concept of title with three other concepts: (1) identification, (2) risk of loss, and (3) insurable interest.

PASSAGE OF TITLE

Sales Contracts and Contracts to Sell

A *sales contract* (or contract for sale) must pertain to specific goods already existing before any interest in them can pass. [UCC Sec. 2-105] *Contracts to sell* deal with future goods, such as crops not yet planted; but until the crops are actually growing, no title to them can pass to the buyer. [UCC Sec. 2-105(2)] Thus, the first condition to passage of title is that the goods be in existence.

Identification

A further condition for the passage of title is that the goods must be identified in a way that will distinguish the particular goods to be delivered under the sales contract from all other similar goods.[1] **Identification** is a designation of goods that are the subject matter of the sales contract. It is significant because it gives the buyer the right to obtain insurance (insurable interest) on the goods and the right to recover from third parties who damage the goods. In certain circumstances, identification allows the buyer to get the goods from the seller. In other words, the concept is easier to understand if one looks at the consequences of identification.

Parties can agree to when identification will take place in their contract; but if they do not specify, the following rules apply:

1. Identification takes place at the time the contract is made *if the contract calls for the sale of specific and ascertained goods already existing.*

2. If the sale involves unborn young animals that will be born within twelve months from the time of the contract, or if it involves crops to be harvested within twelve months (or the next harvest season occurring after contracting, whichever is longer), identification will take place, in the first case, when the young are conceived and, in the second case, when the crops are planted or begin to grow.

3. In other cases, identification takes place when the goods are marked, shipped, or somehow designated by the seller as the particular goods to pass under the contract. The seller can delegate the right to identify goods to the buyer.

When Title Passes

Once goods exist and are identified, the provisions of UCC Sec. 2-401 provide the rules relating to the passage of title.

BY AGREEMENT   Parties can expressly agree to the conditions under which title will pass to the buyer and to the time. In virtually all subsections of UCC Sec. 2-401, the words "unless otherwise explicitly agreed" appear, meaning that any explicit understanding between the buyer and the seller will determine when title passes.

WHEN THE SELLER COMPLETES THE DUTIES OF DELIVERY   Unless another agreement is explicitly made, title passes to the buyer at the time and the place the seller performs the *physical* delivery of the goods. [UCC Sec. 2-401(2)] The delivery arrangements determine when this occurs.

Shipment Contracts   Under shipment contracts, the seller is required only to deliver the goods into the hands of a carrier (like a trucking company), and title passes to the buyer at the time and place of shipment.

Destination Contracts   With destination contracts, the seller is required to deliver the goods

---

1. According to Section 2-104, each provision of Article 2 "with respect to the rights, obligations, and remedies of the seller, the buyer, purchasers or other third parties applies irrespective of title to the goods except where the provisions refer to such title." These provisions referring to title include: Section 2-312, warranty of title by seller; Section 2-326(3), consignment sales; Section 2-327(1)(a), sale on approval and "risk of loss"; Section 4-403(1), entrustment; Section 2-501(2), insurable interest in goods; and Section 2-722, who can sue third parties for injury to goods.

to a particular destination, usually directly to the buyer but sometimes to the buyer's designate. Title passes to the buyer when the goods are tendered at that destination.

Contracts Where Documents of Title Are Involved Where the contract of sale does not call for delivery the passage of title depends on whether the seller must deliver a document of title, such as a bill of lading or a warehouse receipt, to the buyer. When a document of title is required, title passes to the buyer *when and where the document is delivered.* Thus, if the goods are stored in a warehouse, title passes to the buyer when the appropriate documents are delivered. The goods never move. In fact, the buyer can choose to leave the goods at the same warehouse for a period of time, and the buyer's title to those goods will be unaffected.

Non-Document of Title Cases When no documents of title are required, and delivery is made without moving the goods, title passes at the time and place the sales contract was made, if the goods have already been identified. If the goods have not been identified, then title does not pass until identification occurs. Consider an example: Fein sells lumber to Ozo. It is agreed that Ozo will pick up the lumber at the yard. If the lumber has been identified (segregated, marked, or in any other way distinguished from all other lumber), title will pass to Ozo when the contract is signed. If the lumber is still in storage bins at the mill, however, title will not pass to Ozo until the particular pieces of lumber to be sold under this contract are identified.

RISK OF LOSS

Under the UCC, several concepts replace the concept of title in determining the rights and remedies of parties to a sales contract. The risk of loss does not necessarily pass with title. The question of who suffers a financial risk if goods are damaged, destroyed, or lost before or during shipment is resolved under Sections 2-509 and 2-319. Risk of loss depends on whether or not a

sales contract has been breached at the time of loss. [UCC Sec. 2-510]

Passage of Risk of Loss Absent a Breach of Contract

BY AGREEMENT Risk of loss can be assigned through an agreement between both parties, preferably in writing.

CARRIER CASES—SALES REQUIRING DELIVERY BY MOVEMENT OF GOODS Assuming that there is no specification in the agreement, the following rules will apply to so-called carrier cases.

Shipment Contracts In a shipment contract, the seller is required to ship the goods by carrier but is not required to deliver them to a particular destination. Risk of loss passes to the buyer when the goods are duly delivered to the carrier. [UCC Sec. 2-509(1)(b)] For example, a seller in New York sells 10,000 tons of sheet metal to a buyer in California, F.O.B. New York (free on board in New York—that is, buyer pays the transportation charges from New York). The contract authorizes a shipment by carrier; it does not require the seller to tender the metal in California. Risk passes to the buyer when the goods are placed in the possession of the carrier. If the goods are damaged in transit, the loss falls on the buyer. (Actually, buyers have recourse against carriers, subject to tariff rule limitations, and they usually insure the goods from the time they leave the seller.)

Destination Contracts In a destination contract, the seller is required to deliver the goods at a particular destination. The risk of loss passes to the buyer when the goods are tendered to the buyer at that destination. In the above example, if the contract had been F.O.B. California, risk of loss during transit to California would have fallen on the seller.

In the following case the court reviewed

UCC Sec. 2-509(1) as it relates to passage of the risk of loss. Under the Code, an F.O.B. term indicates whether the contract is a "shipment" contract or a "destination" contract, with the risk of loss passing at different times in each of these contracts. The F.O.B. terminology con-

trols. In the following case a "shipment" contract shifted the risk of loss to the buyer when the goods were delivered to a carrier. The fact that there was a "ship to" address had no significance in changing the UCC presumption that the contract was a "shipment" contract.

BACKGROUND AND FACTS   *Buyer and seller entered into various contracts for the manufacture and sale of electrical parts. Each contract was evidenced by a purchase order that the buyer sent to the seller. Each purchase order included instructions to the seller to "ship to" a particular destination. All of the contracts were made F.O.B. Norwalk, Connecticut, which was the location of the seller's place of business. Some of the goods that the seller manufactured and shipped were damaged in transit. The buyer sued for damages.*

ELECTRIC REGULATOR CORP. v. STERLING EXTRUDER CORP.

United States District Court
D. Connecticut, 1968.
280 F. Supp. 550.

DECISION AND RATIONALE   *The buyer could not recover because the risk of loss passed to it at the time the seller placed the goods in the hands of the common carrier. The "F.O.B (seller's place of business)" provision shifted the risk of loss to the buyer when the common carrier received the goods. The "ship to" provision in the purchase orders had no effect on the risk of loss. The court stated: "Here the term used was F.O.B. Norwalk, Connecticut, indicating that these contracts were "shipment" contracts, as opposed to "destination" contracts, with risk of loss passing when [seller] carried out the duties imposed upon it by *** Uniform Commercial Code §2-504."*

NON-CARRIER CASES—DELIVERY WITHOUT MOVEMENT OF GOODS   In non-carrier cases, goods are delivered without being moved. Sometimes the goods remain in the warehouse, or they are held by a bailee (the person to whom they are entrusted). [UCC Sec. 2-509(2)]

Merchant Seller   If the seller is a merchant, risk of loss passes to the buyer when the buyer actually takes physical possession of the goods. [UCC Sec. 2-509(3)] For example, a merchant sells goods to a buyer who is supposed to pick them up. Risk of loss does not pass to the buyer until the goods are actually picked up. (Tender is not enough.)

Non-Merchant Seller   If the seller is not a merchant, the risk of loss passes to the buyer *upon tender of delivery*. To illustrate: Suppose that

Jones and Farber negotiate a contract on May 1 concerning a pile of firewood that Jones has in his yard. At the time of their contract, Jones tells Farber that he can take the wood with him on that day if he wishes. Farber tells Jones to keep the wood until May 15, so that he, Farber, can arrange for a place to keep it after taking possession. The firewood burns up three days later through no fault of Jones's. Jones claims that Farber is obligated to pay for the wood, even though it has been destroyed. Jones is right. When goods are in the possession of a non-merchant seller, and they are not to be shipped by carrier, the risk of their loss passes when the seller tenders delivery, in the absence of any agreement to the contrary. Jones tendered delivery when he offered to let Farber take the wood with him on May 1. The question of tender of delivery arises in the following case.

LUMBER SALES, INC. v. BROWN

Court of Appeals of Tennessee, 1971.
63 Tenn. App. 189, 469 S.W.2d 888.

BACKGROUND AND FACTS   *Brown agreed to purchase five carloads of lumber from Lumber Sales, Inc. The terms of the contract did not include an F.O.B. provision but did require Lumber Sales to ship the lumber to the Nashville Railroad Company depot in Nashville. The lumber arrived early in the morning on the day before Thanksgiving. The railroad immediately phoned Brown to tell him he could pick up the five carloads of lumber any time. Even though unloading the lumber was only a four to five hour job, Brown was too busy to send anybody to get it until the day after Thanksgiving. When Brown arrived, one of the carloads was missing and apparently stolen. Brown refused to pay for it.*

DECISION AND RATIONALE   *Brown was liable for payment for all five carloads of lumber. Under UCC Sec. 2-509 (1) (b), Brown bore the risk of loss of theft, since Lumber Sales delivered the lumber to the Nashville depot and the railroad duly tendered the lumber to Brown. The court stated: "Counsel for defendant argues that the lumber in question was not duly 'so tendered as to enable the buyer to take delivery' as required by [UCC Sec. 2-509 (1) (b)]. However, this argument seems to be based upon the premise that it was not convenient for the defendant to unload the lumber on November 27th. *** To hold that the seller or the carrier should, under the circumstances existing in a case of this kind, continue to protect the goods until such time as the buyer may find it convenient to unload them would impose an undue burden upon the seller or the carrier and unnecessarily obstruct the channels of commerce."*

CASES INVOLVING BAILEES   When a bailee is holding goods for a person who has contracted to sell them, and the goods are to be delivered without being moved, the risk of loss passes to the buyer when: (1) the buyer receives a negotiable document of title for the goods, or (2) the bailee acknowledges the buyer's right to possess the goods, or (3) the bailee receives a non-negotiable document of title or other written direction to deliver the goods, unless the buyer objects within a reasonable period of time. [UCC Sec. 2-509(2) and Sec. 2-503(4)(b)] To illustrate, McKee stores goods in Hardy's warehouse and takes a negotiable warehouse receipt for them. On the following day, McKee endorses and sells the receipt to Byne for cash. The day after that, Hardy's warehouse burns down, and the goods are completely destroyed. At the time of the fire, Hardy had not been informed of the sale of the warehouse receipt.

The risk of loss is on Byne because it accompanies the negotiable warehouse receipt that gave him title to the goods.

SALE ON APPROVAL AND SALE OR RETURN CONTRACTS   Contracts for *sale on approval* or *sale or return* are distinct from other kinds of sales transactions. Under these contracts, the seller undertakes a particular business risk to enable the prospective buyer to obtain the goods on a trial basis.

Sale on Approval   If a buyer can return delivered goods even though they conform to the contract, the transaction is a "sale on approval" if the goods were originally delivered for use. [UCC Sec. 2-326(1)(a)] Goods held on approval are not subject to the claims of the buyer's creditors until acceptance.

A sale on approval contract can have a time limit. Both title and risk of loss are on the seller until "approval" or acceptance of the goods by the buyer. Upon approval, title passes to the buyer, who then becomes liable to the seller for the price of the goods.

Sale or Return   If a buyer can return delivered goods even though they conform to the contract, the transaction is a "sale or return" if the goods were originally delivered for resale. [UCC Sec. 2-326(1)(b)] Goods held on sale or return are subject to the claims of the buyer's creditors while they are in the buyer's possession. The risk of loss is on the buyer, who has title until the goods are returned. The return of the goods is at the buyer's risk and expense.

It is often difficult to determine from the facts of a particular transaction whether there is a sale on approval or a sale or return. The consequences are drastically different, though, with risk of loss and transfer of title. The Code states that (unless otherwise agreed) if the goods are for the buyer to use, the transaction is a sale on approval; if the goods are for the buyer to resell, the transaction is a sale or return.

Risk of Loss in a Breached Sales Contract

There are many ways to breach a sales contract; for example, the delivered goods may be defective. The transfer of risk operates differently, depending on whether the seller or the buyer breaches.

SELLER'S BREACH   If the goods are so defective that the buyer has the right to reject them, the risk of loss will not pass to the buyer until the defects are cured or until the buyer accepts the goods in spite of their defects (thus waiving the

right to reject). For example, a buyer orders blue widgets from a seller, F.O.B. seller's plant. The seller ships black widgets, giving the buyer the right to reject. The widgets are damaged in transit. The risk of loss falls on the seller, although the risk would have been on the buyer if blue widgets had been shipped under a shipment contract. [UCC Sec. 2-510]

If a buyer accepts a shipment of goods and later discovers a defect, acceptance can be revoked. For example, B orders $100,000 of frozen pies from S and insures them for $75,000. The pies are destroyed when the railroad carrying them loses its refrigeration, and B revokes his acceptance. B's insurance will cover $75,000, and S's insurance will cover the remaining $25,000. If B had no insurance, then S's insurance would cover the entire loss. Conversely, if B's insurance covered the entire value of the shipment, S's insurance company would not be liable at all. [UCC Sec. 2-510(2)]

BUYER'S BREACH   The general rule is that when a buyer breaches a contract, the loss *immediately* shifts to the buyer. There are three important limitations to this rule:

1.   The seller must have already identified the goods under the contract. (Regardless of the delivery arrangements, the risk will shift.)
2.   The buyer will bear the risk for only a *reasonable time* after the seller learns of the breach.
3.   The buyer will be liable only to the extent of any *deficiency* in the seller's insurance coverage. [UCC Sec. 2-510(3)]

The following case is a good example of the disastrous effect a buyer's breach can have when it results in a shift of the risk of loss for a shipment that becomes a total loss when fire destroys the seller's plant.

BACKGROUND AND FACTS *Multiplastics manufactured 40,000 pounds of plastic pellets under a contract with Arch Industries. When the delivery date arrived, Multiplastics requested shipping orders per the contract, but Arch Industries failed to tell Multiplastics where to deliver them. Despite repeated requests, Multiplastics did not issue the delivery*

MULTIPLASTICS INC. v. ARCH INDUSTRIES, INC.
Supreme Court of Connecticut, 1974.
166 Conn. 280, 348 A.2d 618.

orders. More than two months after manufacture, the pellets, which were still in the Multiplastics warehouse, were destroyed by a fire. Since Multiplastics did not have insurance to cover the loss, it sued Arch Industries to recover.

DECISION AND RATIONALE *Multiplastics was able to recover from Arch Industries under UCC Sec. 2-510 (3), which provides: "Where the buyer as to conforming goods already identified in the contract for sale repudiates or is otherwise in breach before risk of their loss has passed to him, the seller may to the extent of any deficiency in his effective insurance coverage treat the risk of loss as resting on the buyer for a commercially reasonable time.*

All of the requirements designated in this section of the UCC were met. The goods, which were specifically manufactured for Arch Industries, were "conforming goods." In addition, Arch Industries was in breach because it failed to accept delivery when acceptance became due. Finally, Multiplastics had repeatedly attempted to obtain delivery instructions, but Arch Industries had failed to provide them. The court concluded, "[T]he trial court found that the defendant repeatedly agreed to transmit delivery instructions.*** Under those circumstances, it was reasonable for [Multiplastics] to believe that the goods would soon be taken off its hands and so to forego procuring the needed insurance."

Bulk Transfers

Special problems arise when a major portion of a business's assets are transferred. This is the subject matter of Article 6, Bulk Transfers, which are defined as any large transfers of a major part of the material, supplies, merchandise, or other inventory not made in the ordinary course of the transferor's business. [UCC Sec. 6-102(1)] Problems arise, for example, when a business owing numerous creditors sells a substantial part of its equipment and inventories to third parties. [UCC Sec. 6-102(2)] If the merchant uses the proceeds to pay off debts, no problems arise. But what if the merchant spends the money on a trip around the world, leaving the creditors without payment? Can the creditors lay any claim to the goods that were transferred in bulk to the buyer? To prevent this problem from arising, Article 6 lays out certain requirements for bulk transfer:

1. Anyone engaging in a bulk transfer must furnish a list of creditors to the buyer. Both the buyer and the seller must prepare a list of the property to be sold. The buyer must notify the seller's creditors of the bulk sale at least ten days before taking possession or paying for the goods (whichever is first).
2. Any buyer who fails to comply with this advance notice requirement does not have effective claim to the purchased goods against the claims brought by the seller's extant creditors before (but not after) the sale takes place. Existing creditors, under such circumstances, can still treat the goods as belonging to the seller.
3. The buyer, on the other hand, can transfer good title to the goods to a bona fide purchaser. Existing creditors of the seller presumably cannot lay claim to the goods that are in the possession of a bona fide purchaser.

SALES BY NONOWNERS

Special problems arise when persons who acquire goods fraudulently attempt to resell them. UCC Sec. 2-403 governs the power to transfer, the good faith purchase of goods, and entrusting—all of which involve sales by non-owners.

Imperfect Title

VOID TITLE   A buyer acquires whatever title the seller has to the goods sold. A buyer may unknowingly purchase goods from a seller who is not the owner of the goods. If the seller is a thief, the seller's title is *void*—legally, there is no title at all. Thus, the buyer acquires no title, and the real owner can reclaim the goods from the buyer.

For example, if X steals goods owned by Y, X has *void title* (no legally recognized title) to those goods. If X sells the goods to B, Y can reclaim them from B even though B acted in good faith and honestly had no knowledge that the goods were stolen.

VOIDABLE TITLE   A seller will have a *voidable title* if goods are obtained by fraud; paid for with a check that is later dishonored; or purchased on credit, when the seller later learns that the buyer is insolvent. If a seller discovers that an insolvent buyer has received goods on credit, the seller will have only ten days from the time the buyer has received the goods to void the buyer's title and reclaim the goods. If the buyer, however, made a misrepresentation of solvency in writing to that owner within three months before delivery, then the ten-day limit to void the title and reclaim the goods does not apply. [UCC Sec. 2-702(2)] Purchasers of goods acquire all title that their transferors either had or had the power to transfer. However, a purchaser of a limited interest acquires rights only to the extent of the interest purchased. A seller with *voidable title* has power, nonetheless, to transfer a good title to a good faith purchaser for value. This means that the real owner cannot recover the goods from a good faith purchaser for value. [UCC Sec. 2-403(1)] If the buyer of the goods is not a good faith purchaser for value, then the actual owner of the goods can reclaim them from the buyer (or from the seller if the goods are still in the seller's possession).

The defendant in the following case had some warning that there was something suspicious about the transaction in which he was participating.

BACKGROUND AND FACTS   *Lane, who was engaged in the business of selling boats, sold a new boat and trailer to a person who represented himself as John W. Willis. The purchaser paid $6,285 for the boat and trailer with a check that was later dishonored. Two weeks later, representing himself as Garrett he sold the items to Honeycutt for $2,400. At the time of the sale, Garrett was unable to produce a document of title, substituting instead a permit issued by the North Carolina Wildlife Commission. Honeycutt made no objection. Subsequently, Lane sued to recover the boat and trailer from Honeycutt.*

DECISION AND RATIONALE   *Lane was able to recover from Honeycutt. This case is governed by UCC Sec. 2-403, which allows good faith purchasers to retain possession when they have purchased from persons with voidable titles. Garrett had voidable title since he purchased the boat and trailer with a check that bounced. Honeycutt, however, was not a good faith purchaser. He paid $2,400 for items valued at more than $6,000, and he accepted a document that was not an official certificate of title, "was sufficient to support the court's finding that the defendant was not a good faith purchaser."*

LANE v. HONEYCUTT
Court of Appeals of North Carolina, 1972.
14 N.C.App. 436, 188 S.E.2d 604.

ENTRUSTMENT According to Section 2-403(2), entrusting goods to a merchant *who deals in goods of that kind* gives the merchant the power to transfer all rights to a *buyer in the ordinary course of business. Entrusting* includes both delivering the goods to the merchant and leaving the purchased goods with the merchant for later delivery or pickup. [UCC Sec. 2-403(3)] A "buyer in the ordinary course" is a person who buys in good faith from another person, who deals in goods of the kind. The buyer cannot have knowledge that the sale violates the ownership rights of a third person. For example, X leaves her watch with a jeweler to be repaired. The jeweler sells the watch to Y, who does not know that the jeweler has no right to sell it. Y gets *good title* against X's claim of ownership.

The good faith buyer, however, obtains only those rights that the person entrusting the goods has. For example, X's watch is stolen by Z. Z leaves the watch with a jeweler for repairs. The jeweler sells the watch to L, who does not know that the jeweler has no right to sell it. L gets good title against Z, the entrustor, but not against X, who neither entrusted the watch to Z nor authorized Z to entrust it. Another example: X leaves a watch with a jeweler for repairs. The jeweler borrows money from a bank, using X's watch as collateral. X can recover the watch from the bank. The bank is not a buyer; it is a "purchaser," but the "entrusting" provision of Section 2-403 protects only the "buyer in the ordinary course." [UCC Secs. 1-201(9) and 1-201(33)]

SELLER'S RETENTION OF SOLD GOODS Ordinarily, sellers do not retain goods in their possession after the goods are sold. [UCC Sec. 2-402(1)] A seller who retained goods after they were sold could mislead creditors into believing that the seller's assets were more substantial than they really were.

The Code, in Section 2-402(2), recognizes that it is not necessarily a fraud upon creditors if a merchant seller retains possession in good faith for a "commercially reasonable time" in order to accomplish some legitimate purpose (for example, repairs or adjustments). In such situations, the seller's unsecured creditors cannot void the sale.

A seller can defraud creditors by selling items at something substantially less than "fair consideration," thereby depleting the seller's assets. This is fraud on the seller's creditors if the seller is insolvent at the time of the sale, is made insolvent by the sale, or actually intended to defraud or delay creditors. Assets sold at less than "fair consideration" often are sold to a friend or relative of the seller. Such sales are considered sham transactions used to conceal assets. For example, suppose that FL Boat Company is on the verge of bankruptcy. Many of the loans that FL's owner had taken out were personally secured by him, so his creditors can go after his personal assets to recover what he owes them. Knowing this, FL's owner sells several expensive cars to his father for only $3,000 apiece, and he sells his personal yacht to his brother-in-law for $10,000 (when it is worth $110,000). He has an implicit understanding with his father and his brother-in-law that he will retain control over these assets but that they will have title. At bankruptcy, if the creditors find out about the sham transactions, they can void the sales.

INSURABLE INTEREST

Buyers and sellers often obtain insurance policy coverage to protect against damage, loss, or destruction of goods. But any party purchasing insurance must have a "sufficient interest" in the insured item to obtain a valid policy. Insurance laws—not the Code—determine "sufficiency." (See Chapter 54.) However, the Code is helpful because it contains certain rules regarding a buyer's and a seller's insurable interest in goods on a sales contract.

Buyer's Insurable Interest

Buyers have an insurable interest in *identified* goods. This enables them to obtain necessary insurance coverage for goods that are the subject of a sales contract even before the risk of loss has passed. [UCC Sec. 2-501(1)] Consider an example: In March, a farmer sells a cotton crop he hopes to harvest in October to a buyer. After the crop is planted, the buyer insures it against hail damage. In September, a hailstorm ruins the crop. When the buyer files a claim under his insurance policy, the insurer refuses to pay the claim, asserting that the buyer has no insurable interest in the crop. The insurer is not correct. The buyer acquired an insurable interest in the crop when it was planted, since he had a contract to buy it. The rule in UCC Sec. 2-501(1)(c) indicates that a buyer obtains an insurable interest in the goods by identification, which occurs "when the crops are planted or otherwise become growing crops * * * if the contract is * * * for the sale of crops to be harvested within twelve months or the next normal harvest season after contracting, whichever is longer."

Seller's Insurable Interest

Sellers have an insurable interest in goods as long as they retain title to the goods. However, even after title passes to a buyer, a seller who has a "security interest" in the goods (a right to secure payment) still has an insurable interest and can insure the goods. [UCC Sec. 2-501(2)]

Hence, both a buyer and a seller can have an insurable interest in identical goods at the same time. In all cases, one must sustain an actual loss in order to have the right to recover from an insurance company.

QUESTIONS AND CASE PROBLEMS

1. In January 1961, James purchased an automobile from Hudiburg Chevrolet, Inc., an Oklahoma car dealer. Under the purchase contract, James was not to take the car outside the state of Oklahoma without the express permission of Hudiburg. James paid for the car with his personal check. Subsequently, the check was dishonored, and, when Hudiburg attempted to repossess the automobile, it found that James had taken it first to Georgia and then to Wisconsin. In both states James had obtained a certificate of title under a fictitious name. By the time Hudiburg caught up with the car, it was in the hands of Ponce, who had purchased it from a Milwaukee car dealer in good faith and for value. Who has title to the car? [Hudiburg Chevrolet, Inc. v. Ponce, 17 Wis.2d 281, 116 N.W.2d 252 (1962)]

2. Craig, interested in purchasing a chassis-cab combination vehicle, approached a salesman for Park County Implement Co. about ordering such a vehicle. Park's salesman told Craig that Park did not have the vehicle in stock but that it could purchase one for Craig from another dealer. The salesman then informed Craig that it would be cheaper for Craig to pick up the vehicle in Billings, Montana, than for it to be shipped to Wyoming, where Park was located. Subsequently, Craig did pick up the vehicle in Billings and brought it back to Wyoming, where he began installing a hoist and dump bed on it. Before Craig had finished installing this equipment, the vehicle was destroyed by fire. Craig refused to pay Park Company for the vehicle, claiming that, since he never received a certificate of title for the vehicle (none was ever issued), the sale was incomplete. Is Craig's argument valid? [Park County Implement Co. v. Craig, 397 P.2d. 800 (Wyo. 1964)]

3. Crump, a TV fanatic, purchased a TV antenna and antenna tower from Lair Company. The antenna was guaranteed to pick up any TV station within a 550-mile radius. Crump purchased the antenna and tower under a ten-year conditional sales contract that obligated him to make monthly payments. The sales contract provided that Lair Company would retain title until Crump had completed all payments under the contract. The purchase contract stated, among other things, that Crump was not to move or tamper with the antenna during the ten-year payment period. About a year later, lightning struck and destroyed Crump's new antenna. At Crump's request, Lair Company performed extensive repairs on the antenna. Crump refused to pay, claiming that risk of loss or damage resulting from the lightning should be borne by Lair Company. Will Lair be successful in a suit for the cost of its repairs? [Lair Distributing Co. v. Crump, 48 Ala. App. 72, 261 So.2d. 904 (1972)]

4. Dueitt, an industrial construction contractor, owned a large crane for his construction business.

Dueitt took the crane, which was badly in need of repair, to Small, who was in the business of both selling and repairing heavy duty equipment. Small told Dueitt that the repair work would take two months, but one week after Dueitt left the crane with Small, Small sold it to Lichfield, who, in good faith paid a reasonable price. Can Dueitt recover the crane from Lichfield? [Lichfield v. Dueitt, 245 So.2d. 190 (Miss. 1971)]

5. Consolidated Bottling Company agreed to purchase a used can-filling machine from Jaco Equipment. The contract provided that delivery of the machine was to be made "f.o.b. purchaser's truck." The parties agreed that Consolidated would send its truck to pick up the machine on the last day of June. On June 15 vandals broke into Jaco's warehouse where the machine was kept and did extensive damage to it. Who bears the risk of loss for the damage caused to the machine? [Consolidated Bottling Co. v. Jaco Equipment Corp., 442 F.2d. 660 (10th Cir. 1971)]

6. On August 15 Kaplan entered into an agreement with Odd Lot Corp. for the purchase and sale of 10,000 pieces of odd fabrics. Included in the contract between Kaplan and Odd Lot was the phrase "goods held at buyer's risk." Odd Lot, the seller, was to retain possession of the goods for fifteen days before Kaplan was to pick them up. During the fifteen-day period, while the goods were still in Odd Lot's possession, much of the material suffered water damage. Who must absorb the cost of the damage to the material—Kaplan or Odd Lot? [Kaplan v. Odd Lot Corp., 16 UCC Rptg. Serv. 704 (N.Y. 1975)]

7. S agreed to sell his car to B. The two arranged over the telephone to meet at B's place of business to complete the sales transaction. At the time agreed upon, S arrived at B's place of business, parked his car, and met with B to close the deal. S gave B the keys to the car along with an unnotarized certificate of title, and B paid S the full purchase price. Under local law, a certificate of title was not validly transferred until it was notarized, so the parties agreed to meet the next day and have the title officially transferred in front of a notary. That evening, on his way home, B injured a person while driving S's car. When the injured person attempted to sue B, B in turn sued S's insurance company, claiming that he was driving the car with S's permission, and it was therefore covered

under the "permission clause" included in S's policy. Has title passed to B so that S's insurance company is not liable under S's policy? [Semple v. State Farm Mutual Auto Ins. Co., 215 F.Supp. 645 (E.D. Pa. 1963)]

8. As one of the benefits of working with A&Z Motor Company, Knotts received a model car to use both for family and business purposes. Knotts was to be the sole user of the car, and A&Z retained the certificate of title. The car was insured by Safeco Insurance Company, and Knotts was named in the policy as the owner of the car. Several weeks after A&Z gave Knotts the use of the car, he had an accident. Knotts sued the insurance company to recover for damages, which were covered by the insurance policy. Safeco refused to pay, claiming that Knotts was not the owner of the car and that, since A&Z was the owner, the insurance policy necessarily ran in favor of it. Can Knotts recover from Safeco? [Knotts v. Safeco Ins. Co. of America, 78 N.M. 395, 432 P.2d. 106 (1967)]

9. In a patent infringement suit brought by a Delaware corporation against an Ohio corporation, the court, for purposes of determining where the suit should be brought, had to decide in what jurisdiction the Ohio corporation "sold" its goods. The court found that the Ohio corporation manufactured its goods in Ohio and shipped them to buyers in Michigan "F.O.B. Warren, Ohio." The court also found that the Ohio corporation had its main business office in Pennsylvania. This office controlled production policies and had the power to veto all sales. Where were the Ohio corporation's goods sold? [Welding Engineers, Inc. v. Aetna-Standard Engineering Co., 169 F.Supp. 146 (W.D. Pa. 1958)]

10. Jones purchased an automobile from Phillips Chevrolet in January 1978. Less than a year later, the car was stolen. After filling out the appropriate forms, Jones collected the full price of the car from his insurance company, Home Indemnity Company. When he was reimbursed, Jones assigned all his interest in the automobile to Home Indemnity. Subsequently, the thief sold Jones's car to an automobile wholesaler, who in turn sold it to a retail car dealer. Schrier purchased the automobile from the car dealer without knowledge of the theft. Home Indemnity Insurance Company sued Schrier to recover the car. Can Home Indemnity recover? [Schrier v. Home Indemnity Co., 273 A.2d. 248 (D.C. App. 1971)]

19

Sales
Performance and Obligation

DUTY OF GOOD FAITH AND
COMMERCIAL REASONABLENESS

The obligations of "good faith" and "commercial reasonableness" underlie every sales contract within the UCC. They are objective obligations,
and they can form the basis for a breach of contract suit later on. These
standards are read into every contract, and they provide a framework in
which the parties can specify particulars of performance. "Any such
specification must be made in good faith and within limits set by
commercial reasonableness." [UCC Sec. 2-311(1)]

The Code's "good faith" provision can never be disclaimed. "Every
contract or duty within this Act imposes an obligation of good faith in its
performance or enforcement." [UCC Sec. 1-203] "Good faith" in the case
of a merchant means honesty in fact *and* the observance of reasonable
commercial standards of fair dealing in the trade. [UCC Sec. 2-103(1)(b)]
Thus, when one party delays specifying particulars of performance for an
unreasonable period of time or fails to cooperate with the other party, the
innocent party is excused from any resulting delay in performance. In
addition, the innocent party can proceed to perform in any reasonable
manner. If the innocent party has performed as far as is reasonably
possible under the circumstances, then the other party's failure to specify
or lack of cooperation can be treated as a breach of contract.

Good faith can mean that one party must not take advantage of another party by manipulating contract terms. Good faith applies to both parties, even the nonbreaching party. The principle of good faith applies through both the performance and the enforcement of all agreements or duties within a contract. Good faith is a question of fact for the jury. In the following case, good faith was a major issue in determining the damages flowing from a breach of contract.

MASSACHUSETTS GAS & ELECTRIC LIGHT SUPPLY CORP. v. V-M CORP.
United States Court of Appeals, First Circuit, 1967.
387 F.2d 605.

BACKGROUND AND FACTS *Massachusetts Gas and Electric, a distributor of phonographs, tapes, records, and other appliances, entered into a written supply contract with V-M Corp., a manufacturer. Either party could cancel the agreement on thirty days written notice. When Massachusetts Gas and Electric learned that V-M was going to exercise the thirty-day cancellation option, it placed an order large enough to meet its estimated needs for six months. V-M refused to fill the order. This suit followed.*

DECISION AND RATIONALE *V-M was not obligated to fill Massachusetts Gas and Electric's extraordinarily large order. The contract at issue generally required V-M to stock Massachusetts Gas and Electric's tape and record inventory. Massachusetts Gas and Electric's last order far exceeded its normal inventory needs. The court concluded: "[T]he maximum *** order which defendant should have had to respect was to maintain an appropriate inventory through [the final month]. Plaintiff's order was not a good faith attempt to accomplish this but an effort to nullify the termination clause."*

PERFORMANCE OF A SALES CONTRACT

A *seller* has the basic obligation to *transfer and deliver conforming goods*. According to the terms of the sales contract, the *buyer* has the obligation to *accept and pay for the goods*. Overall performance of a sales contract is controlled by the agreement between the buyer and the seller. When the contract is unclear, or when terms are indefinite in certain respects and disputes arise, the Code provides built-in standards and rules for interpreting their agreement.

CONCURRENT CONDITIONS OF PERFORMANCE

The delivery of goods by the seller and the payment of the purchase price by the buyer are said to be *concurrent conditions*—those that are mutually dependent and are to be performed at the same time. The theoretical assumption is that delivery and payment can occur simultaneously. In reality this rarely, if ever, happens.

Section 2-301 of the Code provides that "the obligation of the seller is to transfer and deliver and that of the buyer is to accept and pay *in accordance with the contract.*" (Emphasis added.) If the contract expressly provides that the seller must first deliver the goods before receiving payment or that the buyer must pay before receiving the goods, then the terms of the contract control. However, where the agreement does not specifically provide, both the buyer and the seller can be "ready, willing, and able" to perform. But who goes first? The Code charges both parties with the duty to proceed. In other words, in order for either party to maintain an action against the other for breach, the party bringing suit must put the other party in default by performing. This is accomplished in one of three ways—through: (1) performance according to the contract, (2) tender of performance according to the contract, or (3) excuse from tender of performance.[1]

For example, Laval agrees to deliver goods to Boyd on September 1, and Boyd agrees to pay on September 15. If Laval fails to deliver the goods, Boyd can sue Laval on or after September 2. Since Laval is in default, Boyd can proceed without first tendering the purchase price.

SELLER'S OBLIGATION OF TENDER OF DELIVERY

Tender of Delivery

Tender of delivery requires that the seller have and hold *conforming* goods at the buyer's disposal and give the buyer whatever notification is reasonably necessary to enable the buyer to take delivery. [UCC Sec. 2-503(1)]

Tender must occur at a *reasonable hour* and in a *reasonable manner.* In other words, a seller cannot call the buyer at 2:00 A.M. and say, "The goods are ready. I'll give you twenty minutes to get them." Unless the parties have agreed otherwise, the goods must be tendered for delivery at a reasonable time and must be kept available for a reasonable period of time in order to enable the buyer to take possession of them. [UCC Sec. 2-503(1)(a)]

All goods called for by a contract must be tendered in a single delivery unless the parties agree otherwise [UCC Sec. 2-612] or the circumstances are such that either party can rightfully request delivery in lots. [UCC Sec. 2-307] Hence, an order for 1,000 shirts cannot be delivered two at a time. If seller and buyer contemplated, though, that the shirts would be delivered in four orders of 250 each as they are produced, for summer, winter, fall, and spring

stock, and the price can be apportioned accordingly, it may be commercially reasonable to do so.

Place of Delivery

NON-CARRIER CASES If the contract does not designate where the goods will be delivered, and the buyer is expected to pick them up, the place of delivery is the *seller's place of business* or, if the seller has none, the *seller's residence.* [UCC Sec. 2-308] If the contract involves the sale of *identified goods* (see Chapter 18 for a discussion of such goods), and the parties know when they enter into the contract that these goods are located somewhere other than at the seller's place of business (such as at a warehouse or in the possession of a bailee), then the *location of the goods* is the place for their delivery. [UCC Sec. 2-308] For example, Laval and Boyd live in San Francisco. In San Francisco, Laval contracts to sell to Boyd five used railroad dining cars, which both parties know are located in Atlanta. If nothing more is specified in the contract, the place of delivery for the railroad cars is Atlanta.

Assume further that the railroad cars are stored in a warehouse and that Boyd will need some type of document to show the warehouse (bailee) in Atlanta that Boyd is entitled to take possession of the five dining cars. The seller "tenders delivery" without moving the goods. The seller "delivers" either by giving the buyer a *negotiable document of title* or by obtaining the *bailee's* (warehouse's) *acknowledgment* that the buyer is entitled to possession.[2]

CARRIER CASES There are many instances, resulting either from attendant circumstances or from delivery terms contained in the contract, when it is apparent that the parties intended that a carrier be used to move the goods. There are two ways a seller can complete performance

---

1. To tender is to offer or make available money or property in pursuance of a contract in such a way that nothing further remains to be done to fulfill the obligation of the party tendering.

2. If the seller delivers a nonnegotiable document of title or merely writes instructions to the bailee to release the goods to the buyer without the bailee's *acknowledgment* of the buyer's rights, this will also be a sufficient tender, unless the buyer objects. [UCC Sec. 2-503(4)]

of the obligation to deliver the goods—through a shipment contract or a destination contract.

Shipment Contracts Under a shipment contract, the seller is authorized to send the goods to the buyer, but the contract does not obligate the seller to be responsible for the goods all the way to the buyer. [UCC Secs. 2-509 and 2-319] The seller must:

1. Put the goods into the hands of the carrier.
2. Make a contract for their transportation that is reasonable according to the nature of the goods and their value.
3. Obtain and promptly deliver for tender to the buyer any documents necessary to enable the buyer to obtain possession of the goods from the carrier.
4. Promptly notify the buyer that shipment has been made. [UCC Sec. 2-504]

If the seller fails to complete *any* of these requirements, and a *material loss* of the goods or a *delay* results, the buyer can reject the shipment. Of course, the parties can agree that a lesser amount of loss or a delay will be grounds for rejection.

Destination Contracts Under destination contracts, the seller agrees to see that the goods are actually delivered to the buyer at a particular destination. Once the goods arrive, the seller must tender the goods at a reasonable hour and hold conforming goods at the buyer's disposal for a reasonable length of time, giving appropriate notice. The seller must also provide the buyer with any documents of title necessary to enable the buyer to obtain delivery from the carrier. This is often done by tendering the documents through ordinary banking channels.

F.O.B. Contracts In contracts specifying that the goods, price, or delivery are F.O.B. to a particular point, the F.O.B. point is the delivery point. [UCC Sec. 2-319(1)]

If the F.O.B. point is the seller's place of shipment, then it is a *shipment contract,* and the

seller incurs only the risk and expense of putting the goods into the hands of the carrier under the four conditions described above. If the F.O.B. point is at a particular destination, then it is a *destination contract,* and the responsibilities to the seller are the same as those under any destination contract. [UCC Sec. 2-319]

If the vehicle of transportation at the F.O.B. point is referred to, then the seller must pay the expense of loading the goods on board the vehicle. For example, "F.O.B. car X23JM, Balt. RR yard, Baltimore" means that the seller transports the goods to the carrier (Baltimore Railroad) at the railroad yard in Baltimore and loads the goods onto car X23JM.

F.A.S. Contracts F.A.S. contracts involve transportation by ship or other seagoing vessel. In contracts specifying that the goods, price, or delivery are F.A.S. (free alongside ship), the seller must deliver the goods alongside the vessel, usually on a dock designated by the buyer. In effect, this is a *shipment contract.* The seller has no responsibility for loading the goods onto the vessel. The seller must obtain and tender a receipt, which is delivered to the buyer, ordinarily through banking channels. Once delivered, the F.A.S. contract is complete; the consigner (seller) is then relieved of any liability for the goods. [UCC Sec. 2-319(2)]

Ex-ship Contracts If the contract specifies ex-ship, then the seller is responsible for loading the goods onto the vessel. In effect, ex-ship, which means "from the carrying vessel," is a *destination contract,* and it includes the shipper's obligation to *unload the goods at the port of destination.* The words "ex-ship" do not constitute a condition of the contract but are inserted for the benefit of the seller.

C.I.F. Contracts Contracts specifying C.I.F. (a maritime term meaning "cost, insurance, and freight") indicate that the buyer's purchase price includes the *cost* of the goods, *insurance* during transit, and *freight* charges. If a contract is merely C&F, then only the cost and freight charges, not insurance, are included in the purchase price. Both C.I.F. and C&F contracts require the seller to load the goods on board the vessel, and in both cases the risk of loss in transit is borne by the buyer, who will be the insured under a C.I.F. contract. [UCC Secs. 2-320 and 2-321]

THE PERFECT TENDER RULE

As previously noted, the seller has an obligation to tender *conforming goods,* and this entitles the seller to acceptance by and payment from the buyer according to the terms of the contract. The so-called *perfect tender rule* of Section 2-601 of the UCC states that "if goods or tender of delivery fail, *in any respect,* to conform to the contract" the buyer is not obliged to accept them. (Emphasis added.) Such a rigid rule seems uncharacteristic of the Code's philosophy of finding and preserving a contract whenever possible.

Exceptions to the Perfect Tender Rule

AGREEMENT OF THE PARTIES If the parties have agreed, for example, that defective goods or parts will not be rejected if the seller is able to repair or replace them within a reasonable time, then the perfect tender rule does not apply.

CURE The term **cure** is not specifically defined in the Code, but it refers to the seller's right to repair, adjust, or replace defective or nonconforming goods. Some courts allow a money allocation to be sufficient cure—for example, when conforming goods are tendered after delivery is overdue—but a price allowance is made for late delivery. [UCC Sec. 2-508]

The seller's right to cure substantially restricts the buyer's right to reject. If the buyer refuses a tender of goods as nonconforming but does not disclose the nature of the defect to the seller, the buyer cannot later assert the defect as a defense if the defect is one that the seller could have cured. The buyer must act in good faith and state specific reasons for refusing to accept the goods. [UCC Sec. 2-605] When any tender or delivery is rejected because of *nonconforming goods* and the time for performance *has not yet expired,* the seller can notify the buyer promptly of the intention to cure and can then do so *within the contract time for performance.* [UCC Sec. 2-508] For example, Horn sells Gill a white refrigerator, to be delivered on or before September 15. Horn delivers a yellow refrigerator on September 10, and Gill rejects it. Horn can cure by notifying Gill that he intends to cure and by delivering a white refrigerator on or before September 15.

Once the time for performance under the contract has *expired,* the seller can still exercise the right to cure if the seller had *reasonable grounds to believe that the nonconforming tender would be acceptable to the buyer.* For example, Demsetz has been supplying auto body paint to Hall Body, an auto body paint shop, for several years. Demsetz and Hall have a contract for R-Z type paint. In the past, when Demsetz could not obtain R-Z type paint, he substituted R-Y type paint, and Hall accepted without any objection. Hall signs a new contract for R-Z type paint to be delivered on April 30. Demsetz realizes that, with the paint supply on hand, only half the order can be filled with R-Z type paint, so he completes the other half of the order with R-Y type paint. The order is delivered on April 30. Hall rejects. Demsetz, knowing from their prior course of dealing that R-Y had always been an acceptable substitute, has "reasonable grounds to believe" that R-Y will be acceptable. Therefore, Demsetz can cure within a reasonable time, even though conforming delivery will occur after the actual time for performance under the contract.

INAPPROPRIATE SHIPPING ARRANGEMENTS In a *shipment contract,* the seller's failure to make a reasonable contract of carriage for the particular goods with an appropriate carrier or the seller's failure to notify the buyer that the goods have been shipped is a *defect in tender*. This is grounds for a buyer to reject, but *only if material delay or loss results*. [UCC Sec. 2-504]

SUBSTITUTION OF CARRIERS Where an agreed manner of delivery (berthing, loading, or unloading facilities) becomes impracticable or unavailable through no fault of either party, but a commercially reasonable substitute is available, this substitute performance is sufficient tender to the buyer. [UCC Sec. 2-614(1)] For example, a sales contract calls for the delivery of a number of tons of oil "F.O.B. Stanley Steamer at New York." War breaks out, and the shipping line is prohibited from sailing to New York due to an embargo. The buyer will be entitled to make a reasonable substitute tender, perhaps by rail. Note that the seller here is responsible for any additional shipping costs, unless contrary arrangements have been made in the sales contract.

INSTALLMENT CONTRACTS An **installment contract** is a single contract that permits delivery in two or more separate lots to be accepted and paid for separately. In an installment contract, a buyer can reject an installment *only* if the *nonconformity substantially impairs the value of the installment and cannot be cured*. [UCC Secs. 2-612(2) and 2-307]

The entire installment contract is breached only when one or more nonconforming installments substantially impair the value of the *whole contract*. If the buyer subsequently accepts a nonconforming installment and fails to notify the seller of cancellation, then the contract is reinstated, however. Also, if the buyer brings an action with respect only to past installments or demands performance as to future installments, the aggrieved party has reinstated the contract. [UCC Sec. 2-612(3)]

GULF CHEM. & METALLURGICAL CORP. v. SYLVAN CHEM. CORP.

New Jersey Superior Court, 1973.
12 UCC Rep.Serv. 117.

BACKGROUND AND FACTS *Gulf and Sylvan entered into an installment contract that provided for goods to be delivered in three separate lots. Gulf delivered the first installment, but Sylvan failed to pay for it. Gulf refused to deliver the remaining goods, asserting that Sylvan's failure to pay impaired the value of the entire contract, thus relieving Gulf of its obligation to continue performing.*

DECISION AND RATIONALE *Gulf was obligated to continue to perform under the contract. The contract at issue was an installment contract within the meaning of the Uniform Commercial Code since it called for "the delivery of goods in separate lots ***." Therefore, Gulf was liable to Sylvan for non-delivery of the goods. The court hearing the case relied upon a New Jersey precedent: "[W]hen the seller has agreed to deliver the goods sold in installments, and the buyer has agreed to pay the price in installments which are proportioned to and payable on delivery of each installment of goods, then the default by either party with reference to any one installment will not, ordinarily, entitle the other party to abrogate the contract." The court concluded by saying: "In order for the seller [Gulf] to relieve itself of its obligation to continue the contract, there must be a showing . . . that the defendant's [Sylvan's] failure to pay for the first installment 'substantially impaired' the value of the whole contract. There is no such proof in this case. Furthermore there was never an overt cancellation of the entire contract by the seller."*

COMMERCIAL IMPRACTICABILITY Whenever unforeseen occurrences that neither party contemplated when the contract was made make performance commercially impracticable, the rule of perfect tender no longer holds. According to UCC Sec. 2-615(a), delay in delivery or nondelivery in whole or in part is not a breach when performance has been made impracticable "by the occurrence of a contingency the nonoccurrence of which was a basic assumption on which the contract was made * * *."

However, the seller must notify the buyer as soon as it is practicable to do so that there will be a delay or nondelivery.

The notion of commercial impracticability is derived from contract law theories of impossibility and frustration of purpose. Does a picket line at a job site cause a party's performance to become so "impracticable" that the excuse of "impossibility" becomes a valid defense to performance?

BACKGROUND AND FACTS *Mishara, a construction company, negotiated with Transit-Mixed Concrete Corp. (Transit) for the supply of ready-mixed concrete to be used on a housing project. Under the agreement, Transit was to supply all the necessary concrete for $13.25 a cubic yard, with deliveries to be made at the times and in the amount ordered by Mishara. Both parties performed under the contract for several months. Then labor difficulties arose on the project site and a picket line was maintained on the site until the project was completed in 1969. Throughout the period of labor difficulties, Transit made no shipments, claiming that the picket line made delivery commercially impracticable. After making numerous demands for shipment, Mishara notified Transit that it intended to purchase the rest of the concrete that it needed elsewhere. Mishara then sought damages to recover the higher price it had to pay for the replacement concrete.*

MISHARA CONSTR. CO., INC. v. TRANSIT-MIXED CONCRETE CORP.
Supreme Judicial Court of Massachusetts, 1974.
310 N.E.2d 363.

DECISION AND RATIONALE *Mishara could not recover for the additional expense of procuring concrete from another supplier. The jury decided that, under the facts of this case, the existence of the picket line excused Transit's performance. Mishara argued that, as a matter of law, "picket lines, strikes or labor differences" should never excuse the performance of a contract. In the opinion of the court: "This is too sweeping a statement of the law and we decline to adopt it. This question is a factual one for the jury. *** Rather than mechanically apply any fixed rule of law, where the parties themselves have not allocated responsibility, justice is better served by appraising all of the circumstances, the part the various parties played, and thereon determining liability."*

DESTRUCTION OF IDENTIFIED GOODS The Code provides that when a casualty occurs that totally destroys *identified goods* under a sales contract through no fault of either party and

*before risk passes to the buyer, the seller is excused from performance. [UCC Sec. 2-613(a)] However, if the goods are only *partially* destroyed, the buyer can inspect them and either treat the contract as voided or accept the damaged goods with an allowance off the contract price.

Mary Murphy contracts to sell lumber to Nancy Jones. If the lumber is destroyed by fire before identification and risk of loss pass to Jones, then Murphy must not only stand the loss of the fire, she must still perform by delivering the lumber to Jones. If the lumber is destroyed by fire *after risk of loss* has passed to Jones (for example, in a shipment contract when the lumber is already en route to Jones), then Jones must still pay because Murphy has completed performance (that is, she has put the lumber into the hands of the carrier). If the lumber is destroyed by fire *after* it has been identified and *before* risk of loss has passed to Jones (in a destination contract or in a shipment contract *before* lumber has been given to the carrier), then Murphy is excused from performance, but she must bear the fire loss.

BUYER'S OBLIGATIONS

Once the seller has adequately tendered delivery, the buyer is obligated to *accept* the goods and *pay* for them according to the terms of the contract. In the absence of any specific agreements, the buyer must:

1. Furnish facilities reasonably suited for receipt of the goods. [UCC Sec. 2-503(1)(b)]
2. Make payment at the time and place the buyer *receives* the goods even if the place of shipment is the place of delivery. [UCC Sec. 2-310(a)]

Payment

When a sale is made on credit, the buyer is obliged to pay according to credit terms (for example, 60, 90, or 120 days), *not* when the goods are received. The credit period begins on the *date of shipment.* [UCC Sec. 2-310(d)]

Payment can be made by any means agreed between the parties. Cash can be used, but the buyer can also use any other method generally acceptable in the commercial world. If the seller demands cash when the buyer offers a check, then the seller must permit the buyer reasonable time to obtain legal tender. [UCC Sec. 2-511]

Right of Inspection

The buyer's right to inspect the goods allows the buyer to verify before making payment that the goods tendered or delivered are what were contracted for or ordered. If the goods are *not* what the buyer ordered, there is no duty to pay. *An opportunity for inspection is therefore a condition precedent to the seller's right to enforce payment.* [UCC Sec. 2-513(1)]

C.O.D. SHIPMENTS If a seller ships goods to a buyer C.O.D. (collect on delivery), the buyer can rightfully refuse to accept them (unless the contract expressly provides for a C.O.D. shipment). Since C.O.D. does not permit inspection by the consignee, the effect is a denial of the buyer's right of inspection. It is a breach on the part of the seller to arrange shipment that will deprive the buyer of the right to inspect the goods. But when the buyer has agreed to a C.O.D. shipment in the contract or has agreed to pay for the goods upon the presentation of a bill of lading, no right of inspection exists because it was negated by the agreement. [UCC Sec. 2-513(3)]

PAYMENT DUE—DOCUMENTS OF TITLE Under certain contracts, payment is due on the receipt of the required documents of title even though the goods themselves may not have arrived at their destination. With C.I.F. and C&F contracts, payment is required upon receipt of the documents unless the parties have agreed to the contrary. Thus, payment is required prior to inspection, and it must be made unless the buyer knows that the goods are nonconforming. [UCC Secs. 2-310(b) and 2-513(3)]

Acceptance

The buyer can manifest assent to the delivered goods in different ways:

1. The buyer can expressly accept the shipment by words or conduct. For example, there is an acceptance if the buyer, after having reasonable opportunity to inspect, signifies agreement to the seller that either the goods are conforming or that they are acceptable despite their nonconformity. [UCC Sec. 2-606(1)(a)]

2. Acceptance will be presumed if the buyer has had a reasonable opportunity to inspect the goods and has failed to reject them within a reasonable period of time. [UCC Secs. 2-606(1)(b) and 2-602(1)]

3. The buyer accepts the goods by performing any act inconsistent with the seller's ownership. For example, any use or resale of the goods will generally constitute an acceptance. Limited use for the sole purpose of testing or inspecting the goods is not an acceptance, however. [UCC Sec. 2-606(1)(c)]

Revocation of Acceptance

A buyer who accepts goods and then fails to discover and notify the seller of any breach of contract within a reasonable time will be barred from any remedy. The burden is on the buyer to establish a breach of contract once the goods are accepted. [UCC Sec. 2-607(3)]

After a buyer accepts a lot or a commercial unit, acceptance can still be revoked if nonconformity substantially impairs the value of the goods and if acceptance was predicated on the reasonable assumption that the nonconformity would be cured, and it has not been cured within a reasonable period of time. [UCC Sec. 2-608(1)(a)] Acceptance can be revoked even if the buyer does not discover the nonconformity if acceptance was reasonably induced either by the difficulty of discovering the nonconformity before acceptance or by the seller's assurances. [UCC Sec. 2-608(1)(b)]

In the following case, the court made clear that "substantial impairment of the value to the buyer" is the test of whether revocation of purchased goods can occur once a buyer has "accepted" the goods.

BACKGROUND AND FACTS *Campbell contracted to purchase the contents of an automatic car wash facility from Bilotti, intending to remove the equipment and open a car wash of his own. Bilotti did not own the building, merely its contents. Bilotti told Campbell that the sale included "everything within the four walls of the building except the soft drink machine." As it turned out, the landlord of the building owned the boiler, hot air blowers, and fluorescent lighting. These items had become fixtures because they were attached to and legally part of the building. When Campbell was prevented from removing these items, he immediately demanded rescission of the contract. Bilotti refused to refund the purchase price, and Campbell brought suit.*

DECISION AND RATIONALE *Campbell was able to recover the purchase price of the car wash equipment because he properly revoked his acceptance. Under UCC Sec. 2-608, Campbell could revoke acceptance as long as the nonconformity of the car wash equipment substantially impaired its value to him and as long as he notified Bilotti within a*

CAMPBELL v. POLLACK
Supreme Court of Rhode Island, 1966.
101 R.I. 223, 221 A.2d 615.

*reasonable time after he learned of the nonconformity. Campbell's revocation was within a reasonable time. Additionally, the fact that all the equipment in the car wash was not included in the deal substantially impaired its value to him since Campbell had intended to open his own car wash. In the words of the court: "Here plaintiff expected to obtain everything within the four walls of the building and this he did not receive. *** [T]heir omission substantially impaired the value of the sale to the buyer."*

NOTICE OF REVOCATION REQUIRED Revocation of acceptance will not be effective until notice is given to the seller, and that must occur within a reasonable time after the buyer either discovers *or should have discovered* the grounds for revocation. The rule also provides that revocation must occur before the goods have undergone any substantial change that was not caused by their own defects (such as spoilage). [UCC Sec. 2-608(2)]

PARTIAL ACCEPTANCE If some of the goods delivered do not conform to the contract, and if the seller has failed to cure completely and part of the goods are still nonconforming, the buyer can make a *partial* acceptance. [UCC Sec. 2-601(c)] The same is true if the nonconformity was not reasonably discoverable before acceptance. A buyer cannot accept less than a single *commercial unit,* however. According to Section 2-105, "commercial unit" means a unit of goods that, by commercial usage, is viewed as a "single whole" for purposes of sale, division of which would materially impair the character of the unit, its market value, or its use. A commercial unit can be a single article (such as a machine), or a set of articles (such as a suite of furniture or an assortment of sizes), or a quantity (such as a bale, gross, or carload), or any other unit treated in the trade as a single whole.

Anticipatory Repudiation

The buyer and the seller have *concurrent* conditions of performance. But, what if before the time for either performance, one party clearly communicates to the other the intention not to perform? Such an action is a breach of the contract by *anticipatory repudiation.* When this occurs, the aggrieved party can, according to UCC Sec. 2-610:

1. For a commercially reasonable time await performance by the repudiating parties.
2. Resort to any remedy for breach even if the aggrieved party has notified the repudiating party that he or she awaits the latter's performance and has urged retraction.
3. In either case, *suspend performance* or proceed in accordance with the provisions of this Article on the seller's right to identify goods notwithstanding breach or to salvage unfinished goods. [Emphasis added.]

Sometimes the situation is unclear. One party may have reason to feel insecure about the other party's willingness or ability to perform when the time comes. Under these circumstances, a party who has a reasonable basis for feeling insecure can demand, in writing, to receive adequate assurance of due performance. Until such assurance is received, the insecure party can suspend any performance for which the agreed-upon return has not already been received, if it is commercially reasonable to do so. [UCC Sec. 2-609(1)] Failure to provide this assurance in response to a justified demand within a reasonable time not exceeding thirty days constitutes a repudiation of the contract. [UCC Sec. 2-609(4)]

QUESTIONS AND CASE PROBLEMS

1. Taunton entered into a contract to sell Allenberg Cotton Company three hundred bails of cotton. Taunton had not yet harvested the cotton but had planted it two months before. Both parties were aware that the cotton would be harvested at some later date. The contract specifically stated that the price of the cotton was $3.50 a bale, but it did not state either a time or a place for delivery. Subsequently, when the bottom dropped out of the cotton market, Allenberg attempted to avoid its contractual obligation. At the trial, Allenberg claimed that, since the contract failed to state a time or a place for performance, it was too indefinite and too vague to be enforced. Will Allenberg succeed in avoiding its liabilities under the contract? [Taunton v. Allenberg Cotton Co., Inc., 378 F.Supp. 34 (M.D.Ga. 1973)]

2. New York Window and Awning Company entered into a contract with Louisville Manufacturing Company to furnish Louisville with certain raw materials that Louisville needed for its window manufacturing operation. The agreement between the parties provided that New York Company would ship the raw materials "FOB New York." Pursuant to this agreement, New York Company prepared the raw materials and put them aboard a railroad car to Louisville. The railroad in turn gave New York Company the documents of title (bills of lading), and New York Company promptly mailed them to Louisville Company. Shortly after it mailed the documents, New York Company sent a telegram to Louisville Company informing it that the shipment had been made. When the goods arrived, the railroad notified Louisville Company. Louisville refused to accept the goods, claiming that New York Company was supposed to deliver the materials directly to Louisville Company's manufacturing plant. If Louisville Company refuses to pay, can New York Company recover? [Permalum Window and Awning Mfg. Co. v. Permalum Window Mfg. Corp., 412 S.W.2d 863 (Ky.App.1967)]

3. Riccardi needed a hearing aid and consulted his physician to determine the best model for his particular needs. After the doctor advised him that an R3 would be best, Riccardi contracted with Bartus to purchase one. Bartus placed an order for the R3 model but two weeks later received the R3X, an improved model of the R3. Bartus informed Riccardi that this was not the model that Riccardi had ordered, but it was an improved version. Bartus then proceeded to fit Riccardi with the new hearing aid. Shortly thereafter, Riccardi complained that the new model was noisy and gave him headaches. Bartus at this point offered to obtain the older model for Riccardi, but Riccardi neither consented to the offer nor refused it. About two weeks later, Riccardi returned the hearing aid and refused to make any further payments on it. Can Bartus recover the price of the hearing aid? [Bartus v. Riccardi, 55 Misc.2d 3, 284 N.Y.S.2d 222 (1967)]

4. Lynch, a candy distributor, ordered 100,000 cellophane bags from Paramount Paper Products. Lynch submitted a sample bag with his order, requesting that the 100,000 bags conform to the sample. The bags were delivered to Lynch's place of business while Lynch was out of town, and approximately 25,000 were used before he returned. Upon his return, Lynch discovered that the bags did not conform to the sample and stopped using them. Lynch immediately notified Paramount that the bags were unsuitable and that he wanted to return the unused ones. Must Paramount return the purchase price of the bags? If so, for how many of the bags must Paramount give Lynch a refund? [Paramount Paper Products Co. v. Lynch, 182 Pa. Super. 504, 128 A.2d 157 (1956)]

5. On October 1, Ingle purchased a combine to use on his farm from Marked Tree Equipment Company. The combine was delivered, and Ingle used it for about twelve days and then stopped. Later, during the month of November, Ingle attempted to use the combine approximately fifteen times. When Ingle's first payment came due on December 1, he told the salesperson that he would not pay until the machine worked. Marked Tree sued Ingle for the balance of the purchase price. Will Marked Tree recover? [Ingle v. Marked Tree Equipment Co., 244 Ark. 1166, 428 S.W.2d 286 (1968)]

6. Pursuant to its contract with General Foods Corporation, Bittinger Company made a large shipment of frozen corn to General Foods. Bittinger included in the shipment a copy of General Food's order, which was for six hundred pounds of grade A frozen cut corn. Unknown to General Foods, half the

corn was grade A and the other half was grade B. When the corn was unloaded and placed in General Food's freezers, however, all the grade A corn was placed in front, and all the grade B corn was placed in back. Four months after the delivery, General Foods opened and used the boxes containing grade B corn. Four months after that, General Foods notified Bittinger that the second half of the shipment had been grade B instead of grade A as General Foods had ordered. Must Bittinger return the purchase price paid by General Foods? [General Foods Corp. v. Bittinger Co., 31 D.&C.2d 282 (Pa. 1962)].

7. After lengthy telephone negotiations, Goldstein and Stainless Processing Company entered into an agreement whereby Stainless Processing agreed to sell Goldstein 20,000 pounds of nickle cathodes at $4.60 per pound. To secure the deal, Goldstein promised to send Stainless Processing a check for $20,000, which Stainless Processing was to hold in escrow until the nickle cathodes were ready for shipment. About a month later, Goldstein sent a letter confirming the oral negotiations and enclosed a $20,000 check as a "good faith deposit." Goldstein also indicated in his letter that the check was to be held in escrow awaiting preparation of the nickle cathodes. When Stainless Processing attempted to deposit Goldstein's $20,000 check in an escrow account, it was rejected by the bank because Goldstein had stopped payment on it. Stainless Processing immediately ceased production of the nickle cathodes. Subsequently, Goldstein purchased 20,000 pounds of nickle cathodes on the open market at a price substantially higher than the price it had contracted to pay Stainless Processing. Goldstein then sued to recover this difference in price. How can Stainless Processing defend against Goldstein's suit? [Goldstein v. Stainless Processing Co., 465 F.2d 392 (7th Cir. 1972)].

8. On October 2, 1956, the United States entered into a contract with Transatlantic under which Transatlantic promised to carry 10,000 tons of wheat from a port in the Gulf of Mexico to Iran. No route was specified in the contract. A month later, while en route to Iran, Transatlantic received notice that Egypt had just closed the Suez Canal. Transatlantic's anticipated route had been through the Suez, so it immediately changed its course and went to Iran by passing around the Cape of Good Hope. Transatlantic then sued the United States for the additional costs (15 percent) that it had incurred. The United States refused, claiming that no route was ever specified in the agreement between the parties. Can Transatlantic recover? [Transatlantic Financing Corp. v. United States, 363 F.2d 312 (D.C.Cir. 1966)].

9. Goddard and Ishikawajima Industries entered into a contract on December 1 under which Ishikawajima agreed to furnish Goddard with as many boats as Goddard would require. Over a period of several years, Goddard submitted numerous written orders to Ishikawajima requesting delivery of numerous boats of different sizes. Ishikawajima satisfactorily complied with all these orders. On January 28, 1965, Goddard sent a written order to Ishikawajima for three dozen boats. On February 17, 1965, just after Ishikawajima had begun manufacturing the boats, its plant was completely destroyed by fire. Goddard was therefore forced to purchase its boats on the open market at a far greater price than Ishikawajima had promised to charge. Is Ishikawajima liable to Goddard for the difference? [Goddard v. Ishikawajima-Harima Heavy Industries Co., 29 A.D.2d 754, 287 N.Y.S.2d 901 (1968)]

20

Sales
Introduction to
Sales Warranties

Until recently, *caveat emptor*—let the buyer beware—was the prevailing philosophy in sales contract law. In twentieth century America, however, this outlook has given way to a more enlightened consumer approach (although many sellers argue that today's standards of liability are unrealistic and excessive). This chapter will review the concept of product warranty as it occurs in a sales contract under the Uniform Commercial Code.

The concept of *warranty* is based upon the seller's assurance to the buyer that the goods will meet certain standards. The UCC designates five types of warranties that can arise in a sales contract:

1. Warranty of title. [UCC Sec. 2-312]
2. Implied warranty of merchantability. [UCC Sec. 2-314]
3. Implied warranty of fitness for particular purpose. [UCC Sec. 2-315]
4. Express warranty. [UCC Sec. 2-313]
5. Implied warranty arising from the course of dealing or trade usage. [UCC Sec. 2-314(3)]

In the law of sales, since a warranty imposes a duty upon the seller, a breach of warranty is a breach of the seller's promise, and a buyer can sue to recover damages against the seller. Also, a breach can allow the buyer to rescind the agreement.[1]

---

1. The word *rescind* carries two meanings. It can refer either to rejection of goods before acceptance or to revocation by the buyer after acceptance.

WARRANTY OF TITLE

The title warranty arises automatically in most sales contracts. Under Section 2-312, the Code imposes three types of warranties of title.

Good Title

In most cases, sellers warrant that they have good and valid title to the goods sold and that transfer of the title is rightful. [UCC Sec. 2-312(1)] For example, A steals goods from O and sells them to B, who does not know that they are stolen. If O discovers that B has the goods, then O has the right to reclaim them from B. Under this Code provision, however, B can then sue A for breach of warranty because a thief has no title to stolen goods and thus cannot give good title in a subsequent sale. Yet, under sales law, when A sold B the goods, A *automatically* warranted to B that the title conveyed was valid and that its transfer was rightful. Obviously this was not in fact the case, so A has breached the warranty of title imposed by UCC Sec. 2-312(1)(a).

No Liens

A second warranty of title provided by the Code protects buyers who are unaware of any encumbrances (claims or liens) against goods at the time of the contract. [UCC Sec. 2-312(1)(b)] This warranty protects buyers who, for example, unknowingly purchase goods that are subject to a creditor's security interest. (See Chapters 29 and 30.) If a creditor reclaims the goods from a buyer who *had no actual knowledge of the security interest*, then the buyer can recover from the seller. Of course, the buyer who has *actual knowledge* of a security interest has no recourse against the seller. Now consider an example: Henderson buys a used color TV from Sneed for cash. A month later Reynolds repossesses the set from Henderson, proving that she, Reynolds, has a valid security interest in it that was duly recorded with the proper county clerk and that Sneed had missed five payments on the set. Henderson demands his money back from Sneed after he gives the set to Reynolds. Under

Section 2-312(2)(b), Henderson will be able to recover because the seller of goods warrants that the goods shall be delivered free from any security interest or other lien of which the buyer has no knowledge.

No Infringements

A third, and special, category of title warranty is the warranty against infringement. A merchant is also deemed to warrant that the goods delivered are free from any patent, trademark, or copyright claims of a third person.[2] [UCC Sec. 2-312(3)] If this warranty is breached and the buyer is sued by a third person, the buyer *must notify the seller* of litigation within a reasonable time to enable the seller to decide whether to defend the lawsuit. If the seller decides to defend and agrees to bear all expenses, including that of an adverse judgment, then the buyer must let the seller undertake litigation; otherwise the buyer loses all rights against the seller if any infringement liability is established. [UCC Sec. 2-607(3)(b)] To illustrate: X buys a machine from Y, a manufacturer of such machines, for use in his factory. Three years later, Z sues X for damages for patent infringement. Z claims that he has a patent on the machine and that it cannot be used without his permission. At once, X informs Y of this suit and demands that Y take over the defense. Y refuses to do so, claiming that Z is crazy and has no case. X goes to court and loses. Z obtains a judgment against X, which X pays off. X now demands that Y reimburse him for the amount. Y must reimburse X because merchant sellers of goods warrant to buyers that the goods they regularly sell are free of infringement claims by third parties.

This infringement warranty does not apply to buyers who furnish specifications for the goods to be made in a particular way. In fact, it is the buyer who must hold the seller harmless (i. e., not liable) against any third person's claims

---

2. Recall from Chapter 17 that a *merchant* is defined in UCC Sec. 2-104(1) as a person who deals in goods of the kind involved in the sales contract or who, by occupation, holds himself or herself out as having knowledge or skill peculiar to the practices of goods involved in the transaction.

of infringement arising out of the goods manufactured to the buyer's specifications. [UCC Sec. 2-312(3)] The same requirements of notice apply to a seller who is sued for breach of an infringement warranty for which the buyer is answerable by virtue of the "hold harmless" agreement. [UCC Sec. 2-607(6)] To illustrate: X orders a custom-made machine from Y, who is a manufacturer of such machines. It is built strictly to X's specifications. While the machine is being built, Z files a suit against Y for patent infringement. Y immediately informs X in writing of this suit and demands that X take over the expense of the litigation. X refuses to do so. Y settles with Z out of court by paying Z modest damages. Y now wishes to be reimbursed by X. Y will be able to collect because a buyer who orders custom-built goods from a seller and who furnishes the seller with the specifications warrants to the seller that there are no patent infringements on the specifications.

DISCLAIMER OF TITLE WARRANTY   In an ordinary sales transaction, the title warranty can be disclaimed or modified only *by specific language* in a contract. For example, sellers assert that they are transferring only such rights, title, and interest as they have in the goods.

In certain cases, the circumstances of the sale are sufficient to indicate clearly to a buyer that no assurances as to title are being made. The classic example is a sheriff's sale, where buyers know goods have been seized to satisfy debts and it is apparent that the goods are not the property of the person who is selling them. [UCC Sec. 2-312(2)]

WARRANTIES OF QUALITY

Express Warranties

A seller can create an **express warranty** by making representations concerning the quality, condition, description, or performance potential of the goods. Under Section 2-313, express warranties arise when a seller indicates that:

1.   The goods will conform to any *affirmation or promise* of fact that the seller makes to the buyer about the goods. Such affirmations or promises are usually made during the bargaining process and can include such statements as "These drill bits will *easily* penetrate stainless steel—and without dulling"
2.   The goods will conform to any *description* of them. For example, "Crate contains one 150-horsepower diesel engine."
3.   The goods will conform to any *sample or model.*

BASIS OF THE BARGAIN   The Code requires that for any express warranty to be created, the affirmation, promise, description, or sample must become part of the "basis of the bargain." Just what constitutes the basis of the bargain is hard to say. The Code does not define the concept, and each case presents a question of fact to determine whether a representation came at such a time and in such a way that it induced the buyer to enter the contract.

A Federal court in Massachusetts held that a statement of fact made *after* title to the goods had passed to the buyer could not be construed as an express warranty relating back to the time of the sale, as illustrated in the next case.

BACKGROUND AND FACTS   *Maurice Smith Co., a manufacturer of boots and shoes, decided to make a boot using plastic instead of leather or rubber for the outer covering. No such product was on the market at the time. Smith ordered the plastic from Fisher Plastics Corp., but did not indicate the particular purpose for which it was intended. This was to guard the secrecy of the venture. Sometime after the agreement was concluded, but prior to delivery an officer of the Smith Co. asked a Fisher salesperson what temperature ranges the plastic would withstand. The salesman assured the officer that the plastic could withstand*

MAURICE C. SMITH CO. v. FISHER PLASTICS CORP.
District Court Massachusetts, 1948. 76 F.Supp. 641.

The salesman assured the officer that the plastic could withstand temperatures down to 50° below zero, Fahrenheit. The plastic was delivered, and the boots were manufactured and sold throughout the United States, primarily in the northern areas and Alaska. They proved totally unsatisfactory because their outer coverings cracked on exposure to cold temperatures. Smith was forced to recall all the boots. Smith then brought suit against Fisher using as one ground the argument that there was a breach of an express warranty since Fisher's salesperson had represented the goods as being able to withstand cold temperatures.

DECISION AND RATIONALE *The Smith Co. did not present legally sufficient grounds for recovery. Under Massachusetts law, title to the goods passed to Smith at the time the contract was made. In order to recover for breach of an express warranty, Smith would have to have shown that the representations of durability were made prior to the time the contract was entered into. In the opinion of the court, "A statement of fact made after the title to the goods has passed to the buyer cannot be construed as a warranty relating back to the time of the sale. The plaintiff has failed to sustain the burden of proving that the representations as to temperature were the inducing cause of the sale * * *."*

STATEMENTS OF OPINION AND VALUE— USE OF FORMAL WORDS NOT REQUIRED According to Section 2-313(2), "It is not necessary to the creation of an express warranty that the seller use formal words such as 'warrant' or 'guarantee' or that he has a specific intention to make a warranty * * *." It is necessary only that the buyer regard the representation as part of the basis of the bargain.

On the other hand, if the seller merely affirms that the value of the goods is such and such or makes a statement of opinion or recommendation about the goods, the seller is not creating an express warranty. [UCC Sec. 2-313(2)] For example, a seller claims, "This is the best used car to come along in years; it has four new tires, a 350-horsepower engine just rebuilt this year." The seller has made several *affirmations of fact* that can create a warranty: The automobile has an engine; it is a 350-horsepower engine; it was rebuilt this year; there are four tires on the automobile; the tires are new. But the seller's *opinion* that it is "the

best used car to come along in years" is known as "puffing" and creates no warranty. (Puffing is an expression of opinion by a seller that is not made as a representation of fact.) A statement relating to the value of the goods, such as "it's worth a fortune" or "anywhere else you'd pay $10,000 for it," will not normally create a warranty.

The ordinary seller can give an *opinion* that is not a warranty. However, if the seller is an expert and gives an opinion as an expert, then a warranty can be created. For example, S is an art dealer and an expert in seventeenth century painting. If S states to B, a purchaser, that a particular painting is definitely a Rembrandt, and B buys the painting, S has warranted the accuracy of his opinion.

Sometimes statements made by a seller cross the fine line between mere opinion and express warranty—for example, in the following case, where a dealer of secondhand automobiles assures a buyer that an automobile is in top mechanical condition.

BACKGROUND AND FACTS *Bradley purchased a used Buick from Wat Henry Pontiac. At the time of the sale, the salesperson assured Bradley that the automobile was in "A-1 mechanical condition" and that it would "take her anywhere she wanted to go." Bradley paid $890 for the car but ultimately spent $250 more in repairing and replacing parts. Bradley attempted to recover these expenditures on the ground that the salesperson's remarks constituted a warranty and that this warranty was breached.*

DECISION AND RATIONALE *Bradley was able to recover. The salesperson's representations constituted an express warranty of fitness because they were more an affirmation of the condition of the car than an expression of the salesperson's opinion. The court stated: "The rule is that to constitute an express warranty no particular form of words is necessary, and any affirmation of the quality or condition of the vehicle, not uttered as a matter of opinion or belief, made by a seller at the time of sale for the purpose of assuring the buyer of the truth of the fact and inducing the buyer to make the purchase, if so received and relied on by the buyer, is an express warranty. *** A decisive test is whether the vendor assumes to assert a fact of which the buyer is ignorant, or merely states an opinion, or his judgment, upon a matter of which the vendor has no special knowledge, and on which the buyer may also be expected to have an opinion and to exercise his judgment. In the former case there is a warranty; in the latter case there is not."*

WAT HENRY PONTIAC
CO. v BRADLEY
Supreme Court of Oklahoma,
1949. 202 Okl. 82, 210 P.2d 348.

MAGNUSON-MOSS WARRANTY ACT The Magnuson-Moss Warranty Act was designed to prevent deception in warranties by making them easier to understand.[3] The Magnuson-Moss Warranty Act is usually enforced by the Federal Trade Commission (FTC). Additionally, the attorney general or a consumer who has been injured can enforce the Act if informal procedures for settling disputes prove to be ineffective. The Magnuson-Moss Warranty Act modifies UCC warranty rules to some extent where personal sales transactions are involved. However, the UCC remains the primary codification of warranty rules for industrial and commercial transactions.

No seller is *required* to give a written warranty for consumer goods sold under the Warranty Act. But if a seller chooses to make an express written warranty, then it must be either a full or a limited warranty.

A *full warranty* binds the seller (but not others in the distribution chain) to meet rigid federal standards for certain types of products costing $10 or more. Full warranty requires free repair or replacement of any defective part; if it cannot be repaired within a reasonable time, the consumer has the choice of either a refund or a replacement without charge. The full warranty does not have a time limit on it. Any limitation on consequential damages must be *conspicuously* stated.

A *limited warranty* arises when the written warranty fails to meet one of the minimum requirements for a full warranty. The fact that a seller is giving only a limited warranty must be conspicuously designated. If it is only a time limitation that distinguishes a limited warranty from a full warranty, then the warranty act

---

3.   15 U.S.C.A. Secs. 2301-12.

allows the seller to indicate it by such language as "full 12-month warranty."

Creating an express warranty under the warranty act differs from creating one under the Uniform Commercial Code:[4]

1. An express warranty is *any written promise or affirmation of fact* made by the seller to a consumer indicating the quality or performance of the product and affirming or promising that the product is either free of defects or will meet a specific level of performance over a period of time. For example, "this watch will not lose more than one second a year."
2. An express warranty is a written agreement to refund, repair, or replace the product if it fails to meet written specifications. This is typically a service contract.

Implied warranties do not arise under the Magnuson-Moss Warranty Act. They continue to be created according to the Uniform Commercial Code provisions. In the case of an express warranty in a sales contract or a combined sales and service contract (where the service contract is undertaken within ninety days of the sale), the Magnuson-Moss Warranty Act prevents sellers from disclaiming or modifying the implied warranties of merchantability and fitness for a particular purpose. The time limit that a seller imposes on the duration of an implied warranty has to correspond with the duration stated in the express warranty.[5]

Implied Warranties

An *implied warranty* is one that *the law derives* by implication or inference from the nature of the transaction or the relative situation or circumstances of the parties. For example: Kaplan buys an axe at Enrique's Hardware

Store. The first time she chops wood with it, the axe handle breaks, and Kaplan is injured. She immediately notifies Enrique. Examination shows that the wood in the handle was rotten but that the rottenness could not have been noticed by either Enrique or Kaplan. Nonetheless, Kaplan notifies Enrique that she will hold him responsible for the medical bills. Enrique is responsible because a merchant seller of goods warrants that the goods he sells are fit for normal use. This axe was obviously not fit for normal use.

IMPLIED WARRANTY OF MERCHANTABILITY An **implied warranty of merchantability** arises in every sale of goods made *by a merchant* who deals in goods of the kind sold. [UCC Sec. 2-314] Thus, a retailer of ski equipment makes an implied warranty of merchantability every time she sells a pair of skis, but a neighbor selling skis at a garage sale does not.

Goods that are *merchantable* are "reasonably fit for the ordinary purposes for which such goods are used." They must be of at least average, fair, or medium-grade quality—not the finest quality and not the worst. The quality must be comparable to quality that will pass without objection in the trade or market for goods of the same description. Some examples of nonmerchantable goods include: light bulbs that explode when switched on, pajamas that burst into flames upon slight contact with a stove burner, high heeled shoes that break off under normal use, or shotgun shells that explode prematurely.

The implied warranty of merchantability imposes *absolute* liability for the safe performance of their product upon merchants when dealing in their line of goods. It makes no difference that the merchant did not know of a defect or could not have discovered it. (Of course, merchants are not absolute insurers against *all* accidents arising in connection with the goods. For example, a bar of soap will not be unmerchantable merely because a user can slip and fall by stepping on it.) In an action based on breach of warranty, it is necessary to show: (1) the existence of the warranty; (2) that the

4. For example, express warranties created by description or sample or model will continue to be governed under UCC provisions because only written promises or affirmations of fact are covered by the Magnuson-Moss Warranty Act.
5. The time limit on an implied warranty occurring by virtue of the seller's express warranty must, of course, be reasonable, conscionable, and set forth in clear and conspicuous language on the face of the warranty.

warranty was broken; and, (3) the breach of warranty was the proximate cause of the injury sustained.

The serving of food or drink on the premises of a restaurant is recognized by the UCC as a sale of goods subject to the warranty of merchantability. [UCC Sec. 2-314(1)] "Merchantable" food means food that is fit to eat.

BACKGROUND AND FACTS *Blue Ship Tea Room was located in Boston on the third floor of an old building on T wharf overlooking the ocean. Webster, who had been born and brought up in New England, entered the restaurant and ordered fish chowder. The chowder was milky in color. After three or four spoonfuls, she felt something lodged in her throat. As a result, she underwent two esophagoscopies; in the second, a fish bone was found and removed. Webster brought suit for breach of implied warranty of merchantability against the restaurant.*

DECISION AND RATIONALE *Webster could not recover against Blue Ship Tea Room because no breach of warranty had occurred. Under UCC Sec. 2-316 "a warranty that goods shall be merchantable is implied in a contract for their sale if the seller is a merchant with respect to goods of that kind. Under this section, the serving for value of food or drink to be consumed either on the premises or elsewhere is a sale. Goods to be merchantable must at least be *** fit for the ordinary purposes for which such goods are used ***." With regard to the chowder involved here, the question is whether a fish bone made the chowder unwholesome or unfit for eating. In the opinion of the judge: "We should be prepared to cope with the hazards of fish bones, the occasional presence of which in chowders is, it seems to us, to be anticipated, and which, in the light of a hallowed tradition, do not impair their fitness or merchantability."*

WEBSTER v. BLUE SHIP TEA ROOM
Supreme Judicial Court of Massachusetts, 1964.
347 Mass. 421, 198 N.E.2d 309.

IMPLIED WARRANTY OF FITNESS FOR A PARTICULAR PURPOSE The implied warranty of fitness for a particular purpose arises when *any seller* (merchant or non-merchant) knows the particular purpose for which a buyer will use the goods *and* knows that the buyer is relying upon the seller's skill and judgment to select suitable goods. [UCC Sec. 2-315]

A "particular purpose of the buyer" differs from the "ordinary purpose for which goods are used" (merchantability). Goods can be merchantable but still not fit for the buyer's particular purpose. For example, house paints suitable for ordinary walls are not suitable for painting over stucco walls. A contract can include both a warranty of merchantability *and* a warranty of fitness for a particular purpose,

which relates to the specific use or special situation in which a buyer intends to use the goods. For example, a seller recommends a particular pair of shoes, *knowing* that a customer is looking for mountain climbing shoes. The buyer purchases the shoes *relying* on the seller's judgment. If the shoes are found to be suitable only for walking, not for mountain climbing, the seller has breached the warranty of fitness for a particular purpose.

A seller does not need "actual knowledge" of the buyer's particular purpose. It is sufficient if a seller "has reason to know" the purpose. However, the buyer must have *relied* upon the seller's skill or judgment in selecting or furnishing suitable goods in order for an implied warranty to be created. For example, Josephs buys a shortwave radio from Radio Shack, telling the salesperson that she wants a set strong enough to pick up Radio Luxemburg. Radio Shack sells Josephs a Model XYZ set. The set works, but it will not pick up Radio Luxemburg. Josephs wants her money back. Here, since Radio Shack is guilty of a breach of implied warranty of fitness for the buyer's particular purpose, Josephs will be able to recover. The salesperson knew specifically that

she wanted a set that would pick up Radio Luxemburg. Furthermore, Josephs relied upon the salesperson to furnish a radio that would fulfill this purpose. Radio Shack did not do so. Therefore, the warranty was breached.

In the next case, a seller helped a buyer solve a painting problem and became the defendant in a lawsuit for breach of an implied warranty of fitness.

CATANIA v. BROWN
Circuit Court of Connecticut,
Appellate Division, 1967.
4 Conn.Cir. 344, 231 A.2d 668.

BACKGROUND AND FACTS *Catania asked Brown, a retail paint dealer, to recommend a paint to cover the exterior stucco wall of his house. Brown recommended and sold to Catania a brand of paint called "Pierce's Shingle and Shake" paint. Brown also advised Catania on how to mix the paint and how to prepare the walls before applying it. The paint, however, proved unsatisfactory. Catania brought an action against Brown alleging that a warranty of fitness was created when Brown recommended the paint as suitable for stucco and that this warranty had been breached.*

DECISION AND RATIONALE *Brown created a warranty of fitness when he recommended a particular brand to Catania for stucco walls and Catania relied upon his advice. This warranty was clearly breached. An implied warranty of fitness arises when a buyer tells a seller how goods will be used and then relies on the seller's skill and judgment to supply the proper articles. The court stated: "[T]he buyer, being ignorant of the fitness of the article being offered by the seller, justifiably relied on the superior information, skill, and judgment of the seller and not on his own knowledge or judgment, and under such circumstances an implied warranty of fitness could properly be claimed by the purchaser."*

Overlapping Warranties

Sometimes two or more warranties are made in a single transaction. An implied warranty of merchantability or of fitness for a particular purpose, or both, can exist in addition to an express warranty. For example, where a sales contract for a new car states that "this car engine is warranted to be free from defects for 12,000 miles or 12 months, whichever occurs first," there is an express warranty against all defects and an implied warranty that the car will be fit for normal use. The rule of Section 2-313 is that

express and implied warranties are construed as *cumulative* if they are consistent with one another. If the warranties are *inconsistent,* the courts will usually hold that: (1) *express* warranties will displace inconsistent *implied* warranties other than implied warranties of fitness for a particular purpose, (2) samples will take precedence over inconsistent general descriptions, and (3) technical specifications will displace inconsistent samples or general descriptions. [UCC Sec. 2-317] Say that when Josephs buys a shortwave radio at Radio Shack, the contract of sale states that the radio's maximum range is 4,000 miles. She tries to pick up Radio Luxemburg, which is 8,000 miles away, but the set cannot do it. Josephs claims that Radio Shack is guilty of breach of warranty of merchantability because the set is unfit for normal use. She does not have a good complaint because the contract contained an *express* warranty about the range of the set. This express warranty will take precedence over any implied warranty that a shortwave set would pick up any station anywhere in the world. On the other hand, if Josephs had specified to the salesperson that she wanted to pick up Radio Luxemburg, and if the salesperson had sold her that same radio, Josephs has a good claim. In a case of inconsistency between an express warranty and a warranty of fitness for buyer's particular purpose, the warranty of fitness for buyer's particular purpose prevails. [UCC Sec. 2-317(c)]

Warranty Disclaimers

Each warranty is created in a special way, and the manner in which each one can be disclaimed or qualified varies also.

EXPRESS WARRANTIES Any affirmation of fact or promise, description of the goods, or use of samples or models by a seller will create an express warranty. A seller can scarcely be expected to sell goods without somehow describing them, thereby affirming some fact about them—although selling goods without description is one way to exclude an express warranty under Section 2-316(1).

Express warranties can be excluded if the seller has carefully refrained from making any promise or affirmation of fact relating to the goods, or describing the goods, or selling by means of a sample model. [UCC Sec. 2-313] The seller can also disclaim an express warranty by clear, specific, and unambiguous language to that effect in the contract. [UCC Sec. 2-316(1)]

IMPLIED WARRANTIES Generally speaking, and unless circumstances indicate otherwise, implied warranties (merchantability and fit-

ness) are disclaimed by expressions like "as is," "with all faults," or other similar expressions that in common understanding call the buyer's attention to the fact that there are no implied warranties. [UCC Sec. 2-316(3)]

The fitness disclaimer must be in *writing* and *conspicuous*, but it can be a general statement. According to the Code, it is sufficient if, for example, the disclaimer states, "There are no warranties that extend beyond the description on the face hereof."

A *merchantability disclaimer* must be more specific; it must mention merchantability. It need not be written; but if it is, the writing must be *conspicuous*. According to UCC Sec. 2-201(10):

A term or clause is conspicuous when it is so written that a reasonable person against whom it is to operate ought to have noticed it. A printed heading in capitals is conspicuous. Language in the body of a form is conspicuous if it is in large or other contrasting type or color.

Consider the example used above. When Kaplan buys an axe from Enrique's Hardware Store, Enrique tells Kaplan that he (Enrique) is not responsible for any defects of the axe. The axe breaks when Kaplan uses it for the first time. Enrique is not liable because merchant sellers can orally disclaim the warranty of merchantability when they sell goods under an oral contract of sale. As long as Enrique uses words in the disclaimer that make it clear to a reasonable person that he is disclaiming all warranties as to the quality of the goods, the disclaimer is valid. Enrique has to make clear, though, that he is disclaiming the warranty of merchantability by using that specific word.

However, under UCC Sec. 2-316(2), "to exclude or modify any implied warranty of *fitness* the exclusion must be by a writing and conspicuous."

BUYER'S REFUSAL TO INSPECT If a buyer examines the goods (or a sample or model) as fully as desired before entering a contract or if the buyer *refuses* to examine the goods at all, *there is no implied warranty with respect to defects that a reasonable examination will reveal.* Suppose that the defect in Kaplan's axe could easily have been spotted by normal, careful inspection. Kaplan inspects the axe before buying it but somehow does not notice the defect. After being hurt by the defective axe, she will not be able to hold Enrique for breach of warranty of merchantability because she could have or should have spotted the defect during her inspection. [UCC Sec. 2-316(3)(b)]

Failing to examine the goods is not a refusal to examine them; it is not enough that the goods were merely available for inspection, and the buyer simply never did it. A "refusal" occurs when the seller makes a *demand* upon the buyer, *notifying* the buyer that the goods must be examined or the buyer will assume the risk of the defects that the examination might have revealed. Of course, the seller always remains liable for all latent (hidden) defects that ordinary inspection will not normally reveal. [UCC Sec. 2-316, Comment 8]

USAGE OF TRADE The Code recognizes in Section 2-314(3) that implied warranties can arise (or be excluded or modified) from course of dealing, course of performance, or usage of trade. [UCC Sec. 2-316(3)(c)] In the absence of evidence to the contrary, when both parties to a sales contract have knowledge of a well-recognized trade custom, the courts will infer that they both intended that custom to apply to their contract. For example, in the sale of a new car, where the industry-wide custom includes lubricating the car before delivery, a seller who fails to do so can be held liable to a buyer for resulting damages on a theory of breach of implied warranty.

Unconscionability and Warranty Disclaimers

The Code sections dealing with warranty disclaimers do not refer specifically to unconscionability as a factor. Eventually, however, the courts will test warranty disclaimers with reference to the unconscionability standards of Section 2-302. Such things as lack of bargaining position, "take it or leave it" choices, and failure of a buyer to understand a warranty disclaimer provision will become relevant to the issue of unconscionability. Note in the following landmark decision the court's recognition of the consumer's "bargaining" position with respect to large auto manufacturers.

HENNINGSEN v. BLOOMFIELD MOTORS, INC.
Supreme Court of New Jersey, 1960.
32 N.J. 358, 161 A.2d 69.

BACKGROUND AND FACTS *Henningsen purchased a new Chrysler from Bloomfield Motors for his wife. Subsequently, his wife suffered severe injuries as a result of defects in the manufacture of the car. The standard-form purchase order used in the transaction contained an express ninety-day/4,000-mile warranty. In addition, the purchase order contained a disclaimer in fine print, of any and all additional express or implied warranties. Thus, Bloomfield Motors refused to pay for Mrs. Henningsen's injuries, asserting that the sales contract, which warranted that Bloomfield would repair defects at no charge, disclaimed liabilities for injuries suffered because of negligent manufacture. A lawsuit followed.*

DECISION AND RATIONALE *The Henningsens can recover from Bloomfield Motors despite the disclaimer contained in the contract of sale. Bloomfield's liability rests upon an implied warranty of merchantability that arises under the Uniform Sales Act (now included in the UCC) on the sale of goods. A warranty of merchantability means that the goods sold must be reasonably fit for the general purpose for which they are manufactured or sold.*

A seller's liability for injuries resulting from breach of an implied warranty rests on strict liability rather than on finding of fault. The legislature's purpose in implying a warranty in the sale of goods was to protect consumers. In the opinion of the court: "The disclaimer of the implied warranty and exclusion of all obligations except those specifically assumed by the express warranty signify a studied effort to frustrate the protection. True, the Sales Act authorizes agreements between buyer and seller qualifying the warranty obligations. But quite obviously the Legislature contemplated lawful stipulations [which are determined by the circumstances of a particular case] arrived at freely by parties of relatively equal bargaining strength. The lawmakers did not authorize the automobile manufacturer to use its grossly disproportionate bargaining power [and the unfair surprise of fine print] to relieve itself from liability and to impose on the ordinary buyer, who in effect has no real freedom of choice, the grave danger of injury to himself and others that attends the sale of such a dangerous instrumentality as a defectively made automobile. In the framework of this case, illustrated as it is by the facts and the many decisions noted, we are of the opinion that Chrysler's attempted disclaimer of an implied warranty of merchantability and of the obligations arising therefrom is so inimical to the public good as to compel an adjudication of its invalidity."

QUESTIONS AND CASE PROBLEMS

1. While driving home from a fraternity dance, Peabody drove his 1979 Firebird off an embankment and into a tree, causing severe damage to the car. Peabody's insurance company, Motors Insurance Corp., paid Peabody under the insurance policy, and, in return, Peabody gave the insurance company title to the car. Motors Insurance then sold the car to John Street Auto Wrecking, a dealer in auto parts. John Street subsequently sold the car to Gullible, who hoped to restore the car to its original condition. About three weeks later, the police seized the car from Gullible as a stolen vehicle. Can Gullible recover from John Street? If so, can John Street in turn recover from Motors Insurance? [John Street Auto Wrecking v. Motors Ins. Corp., 56 Misc.2d 232, 288 N.Y.S.2d 281 (1968)]

2. Hanley and Herschel entered into a contract under which Herschel was to sell Hanley a used semitrailer. Hanley received the semitrailer and used it for sixteen months. Then it was impounded by the state police on the basis of a report that it had been stolen. Hanley immediately notified Herschel of the seizure and of his decision to rescind the contract. Shortly thereafter the police informed Hanley that the proper owner of the vehicle was unclear and that the person who claimed to be the owner had questionable title. Can Hanley still rescind his contract with Herschel instead of first going to court to determine rightful ownership? [American Container Corp. v. Hanley Trucking Corp., 111 N.J. Super. 322, 268 A.2d 313 (1970)]

3. Lattimer Foundry & Machine Company entered into a contract with Smith to manufacture and sell iron castings for use in Smith's manufacture of sausage-stuffing machines. Lattimer knew how the castings were to be used. Under the contract, the castings were to conform to samples that Lattimer had manufactured in accordance with blueprints drawn up by Smith. Before Lattimer started manufacturing the iron castings, it submitted the samples to Smith, and Smith approved them. Describe the warranties that resulted from the transaction between Lattimer and Smith. [John E. Smith's Sons Co. v. Lattimer Foundry & Machine Co., 19 F.R.D.379 (M.D. Pa. 1956)]

4. Carpenter entered Discount Drugs to purchase some hair dye. One of Discount's clerks told Carpenter that her personal favorite was Alberto. The clerk further stated that Carpenter "would get very fine results" with Alberto. When Carpenter used the hair dye, however, she suffered an adverse skin reaction. Carpenter sued both Discount Drugs and Alberto Culver Company for breach of warranty.

Carpenter also sued Discount Drugs for breach of the express warranties that Carpenter alleged that Discount's salesclerk had made to her. Were any express warranties made to Carpenter? [Carpenter v. Alberto Culver Co., 28 Mich.App. 399, 184 N.W.2d 547 (1970)]

5. In August 1961, McMeekin purchased a lawnmower from Gimbel Brothers. In June of the next year, while McMeekin was mowing his lawn, his son was struck in the eye by an unknown object and subsequently lost sight in the eye. In a suit filed by McMeekin on behalf of his son against Gimbels, McMeekin sought recovery on the theory that Gimbels had breached its warranty of merchantability. McMeekin claimed that "somehow, part of the lawnmower broke off and flew into my son's eye." Can McMeekin recover? [McMeekin v. Gimbel Brothers, Inc., 223 F. Supp. 896 (W.D. Pa. 1963)]

6. Montgomery Ward sold Vlases a number of one-day-old chicks. Vlases intended to raise them in his newly constructed chicken coop. Several weeks after Montgomery Ward sold the chickens to Vlases, they developed leukosis, and all of them died. Vlases demanded his money back from the company. Montgomery Ward refused, and Vlases brought suit, claiming breach of implied warranty of merchantability. Montgomery Ward claimed that it was not liable since no amount of knowledge, skill, or foresight on its part would have enabled it to detect the sickness. Assuming Montgomery Ward's claim is true, is this a valid defense? [Vlases v. Montgomery Ward Co., 377 F.2d 846 (3rd Cir. 1967)]

7. Tracy purchased a used car from Vinton Motors, Inc., on April 9. At the time of the purchase, one of Vinton's salespeople told Tracy that "this baby is good for years." Subsequently, Tracy paid cash for the car and signed a written contract that stated on its face that any express warranties accompanying the sale were effective for only thirty days or 1,000 miles, whichever came first. About six weeks later, Tracy noticed that the exterior paint on the car was peeling and demanded that Vinton Motors repaint it. Vinton Motors refused, and Tracy brought suit. What will be the result? [Tracy v. Vinton Motors, Inc., 130 Vt. 512, 296 A.2d 269 (1972)]

8. Maxwell Dynamometer Company sent the following purchase order to Marble Card Electric Corp.: "1 30/15 H.P. Induction Motor Drip Proof 3600/1800 RPM single winding, constant torque, 220 volt A.C. 60 cycle, 3 phase Frame 365. Shaft end to be tapered and threaded as per sketch forwarded to factory, Gladstone, Mich." Marble sent Maxwell the motor, but Maxwell failed to pay for it. Marble sued Maxwell to recover the purchase price of the motor. Maxwell defended on the ground that Marble breached its warranty of fitness for a particular purpose. Under the facts given, how valid is Maxwell's claim? [Marble Card Electric Corp. v. Maxwell Dynamometer Co., 10 Chest. 145 (Pa. 1961)]

9. Hunt, a fisherman, placed an order with Perkins Machine Company for a new engine for his fishing boat. When the engine arrived, Perkins called Hunt in to pick it up. Hunt paid cash for the engine and signed a written form contract from a pad of contracts as evidence of the sale. On the front of the contract was the following statement in boldface print: "Both this order and its acceptance are subject to 'terms and conditions' stated in this order." On the reverse side the words "terms and conditions" appeared at the top of the page. Below this was the following statement, also printed in boldface: "Seller makes no warranties including any warranties as to merchantability or fitness either express or implied." From about a week after Hunt purchased the new engine, it was in constant need of repair. Perkins made several attempts to repair it, but it still did not work properly, and Perkins refused to make further attempts to fix it. Hunt demanded his money back, but Perkins refused. In a lawsuit by Hunt against Perkins, can Hunt successfully claim that Perkins has committed breach of warranty? [Hunt v. Perkins Machinery Co., 352 Mass. 535, 226 N.E.2d 228 (1967)]

10. For the past twenty years Cardinale Trucking Corp. and Gindy Manufacturing Corp. have done business with each other, buying and selling semitrailers. It is customary in the semitrailer trade for sellers of semitrailers to assume responsibility for any manufacturing defects that might occur within a reasonable time after the sale. In July 1969, Gindy sold Cardinale twenty-five semitrailers, and Cardinale signed one of the written contracts supplied by Gindy. The contract stated that the new semitrailers were sold "as is." Shortly thereafter Cardinale learned that the semitrailers were defective and requested that Gindy repair them. Gindy refused, and Cardinale refused to pay for the trucks. In a suit by Gindy against Cardinale for the purchase price, what will be the result? [Gindy Mfg. Corp. v. Cardinale Trucking Corp., 111 N.J.Super. 383, 268 A.2d 345 (1970)]

21
Sales
Products Liability

As we learned in the previous chapter, retailers are liable to purchasers on express or implied warranties, even though the retailers do not always examine the goods prior to resale. Today, liability has been extended to manufacturers through the application of new principles of the law. Manufacturers and sellers of goods can be held liable to consumers, users, and bystanders for physical harm or property damage that is caused by the goods. This is called *products liability* and it encompasses tort theories of *strict liability* and *negligence* and the contract theory of *warranty*. It should be noted that these theories of recovery are *not* mutually exclusive.

WARRANTY THEORY

As we learned in Chapter 20, consumers and other purchasers of goods can recover *from any seller* for losses resulting from breach of implied or express warranty. Thus, since a manufacturer is a *seller*, a person who purchases goods from a retailer can recover either from the retailer or the manufacturer if the goods are not merchantable. This was not always the case. Until enactment of the UCC, *privity of contract* was required for a purchaser to bring an action for breach of warranty against a manufacturer.

Privity of Contract

Privity of contract is the connection or relationship that exists between two or more contracting parties because of the fact that they entered into a contract. Privity must exist between a plaintiff and a defendant with respect to the matter under dispute in order to maintain any action based upon a contract. At common law, the retailer making a sale was solely responsible to the consumer of defective goods. The UCC has broadened the basis of liability and therefore modified the notion of privity of contract as the basis for lawsuits.

Third-Party Beneficiaries of Warranties: Express or Implied

There is sharp disagreement over *how far* warranty liability should extend. In order to satisfy opposing views of the various states, the drafters of the Uniform Commercial Code proposed three alternatives for liability under UCC Sec. 2-318. Accordingly, some states have adopted alternative A; others, alternative B; and still others, alternative C. All three alternatives are intended to eliminate the privity requirement with respect to certain enumerated types of injuries (personal versus property) for certain beneficaries (e.g., household members, bystanders).

ALTERNATIVE A   All sellers' warranties (express or implied) extend to any *natural person* in the buyer's family or household or to anyone who is a guest in the home, when it is reasonable to expect that such persons will use, consume, or be affected by the goods or be personally injured because of a breach of the warranty. Consider an example. Anderson buys an electric washing machine from E-Z Appliances. One month after the purchase, Anderson's mother-in-law, who has been living with his family for a year, receives a severe electric shock from a defective wire while using the machine. Anderson's mother-in-law claims damages from E-Z Appliances for breach of warranty of merchantability. She can recover

because the defective wire made the washing machine unfit for normal use. Since she was living with Anderson's family, she naturally would use the washing machine if she helped with housekeeping chores. Anderson's mother-in-law therefore qualifies as a third-party beneficiary of the warranty. Note the restriction in this alternative—the guest has to be in the person's home. In one case, a federal court, applying Pennsylvania law, held that under the provision adopted in Pennsylvania, the warranty protection did not extend to a guest injured while riding in the purchaser's new automobile since it was not the buyer's home.[1]

ALTERNATIVE B   Alternative B extends the seller's warranty (express or implied) to any *natural person* who can reasonably be expected to use, consume, or be affected by the goods and who suffers personal injury because of the breach of warranty. This is a broader basis for liability than alternative A since protection is not limited to family or household members. Note the restrictions here. As with alternative A, the seller's warranty extends only to persons, not corporations. It also limits the right of recovery to personal injury damages and therefore eliminates the possibility of suing for property damages. A seller may not exclude or limit the warranties given under alternative A or B.

ALTERNATIVE C   Alternative C offers the broadest coverage of all. It extends to *any* person, and provides recovery for either personal or property injury. It does not allow the seller to exclude or limit the operation of liability for personal injury of an individual to whom the warranty extends.

LIABILITY BASED ON NEGLIGENCE

Chapter 3 defined *negligence* as omitting to do something that a reasonable person would do, guided by the considerations that ordinarily

---

1.   Thompson v. Reedman, 199 F. Supp. 120 (D.C. Pa. 1961).

regulate human affairs, or doing something that a reasonable and prudent person would not do. The failure to exercise reasonable care in the circumstances that cause an injury is the basis of liability for negligence. Thus, the manufacturer of a consumer product must exercise "due care" to make that product safe to be used as it was intended. Due care must be exercised in designing the product, in selecting the materials, in using the appropriate production process, in assembling and testing the product, and in placing adequate warnings on the label of dangers of which an ordinary person might not be aware. The duty of care extends to the inspection and testing of purchased products used in the final product sold by the manufacturer.

The opposite of due care is negligence. In the following case, the New York court dealt with the liability of a manufacturer who failed to use due care in manufacturing a finished product.

BACKGROUND AND FACTS *The MacPherson case is the classic products liability case. Its subject matter, defectively manufactured wooden wheels for automobiles, is dated, but the principles involved are not. MacPherson purchased a new Buick from a dealer of Buick Motor Company. Later, he was injured when the car ran into a ditch after one of its wheels collapsed because the spokes were made from defective wood. The wheel itself had been made by another manufacturer. MacPherson brought suit against Buick directly instead of against the retailer from whom he purchased the car. The evidence presented at the trial showed that the defects could have been discovered by reasonable inspection and that inspection had not been made.*

MACPHERSON v. BUICK MOTOR CO.
Court of Appeals of New York, 1916.
111 N.E. 1050, 217 N.Y. 382.

DECISION AND RATIONALE *MacPherson was able to recover for his injuries. Buick Motor Company's duty to exercise reasonable care extended to MacPherson even though MacPherson and the company were not in privity of contract. (The sales contract was between MacPherson and the retailer.) Buick Motor Company's duty of care lay in tort and extended to any person who could foreseeably be injured as a result of a defect in an automobile it manufactured. The duty arises because of the potential danger a defectively manufactured automobile poses to those who ride in it. In the words of Justice Cardozo, who heard the case:*

Beyond all question, the nature of an automobile gives warning of probable danger if its construction is defective. This automobile was designed to go fifty miles an hour. Unless its wheels were sound and strong, injury was almost certain. *** The defendant [Buick Motor Company] knew the danger. *** The maker of this car supplied it for the use of purchasers from the dealer ***. It is true that *** "an automobile is not an inherently dangerous vehicle." The meaning, however, is that danger is not to be expected when the vehicle is well constructed. *** If danger was to be expected as reasonably certain, there was a duty of vigilance, and this whether you call the danger inherent or imminent.

We think the defendant was not absolved from a duty of inspection because it bought the wheels from a reputable manufacturer. It was not merely a dealer in automobiles. It was responsible for the finished product. It was not at liberty to put the finished product on the market without subjecting the component parts to ordinary and simple tests. *** The obligation to inspect must vary with the nature of the thing to be inspected. The more probable the danger, the greater the need of caution.

PRIVITY OF CONTRACT NOT REQUIRED An action based upon negligence does not require privity of contract between the injured plaintiff and the negligent defendant-manufacturer. Section 395 of the Restatement, Second, Torts states:

A manufacturer who fails to exercise reasonable care in the manufacture of a chattel [movable good] which, unless carefully made, he should recognize as involving an unreasonable risk of causing substantial bodily harm to those who lawfully used it for a purpose for which it was manufactured and to those whom the supplier should expect to be in the vicinity of its probable use, is subject to liability for bodily harm caused to them by its lawful use in a manner and for a purpose for which it is manufactured.

Basis of Liability— Violation of Statutory Duty

Numerous federal and state laws impose duties upon manufacturers of cosmetics, drugs, foods, toxic substances, and flammable materials. These duties involve appropriate description of contents, labeling, branding, advertising, and selling. The statutes include the Federal Flammable Fabrics Act; the Federal Food, Drug, and Cosmetics Act; and the Federal Hazardous Substances Labeling Act. In a civil action for damages (tort), a violation of statutory duty is often held to constitute negligence per se. Consider an example: Jason Manufacturing Company produces pipe fittings for use in the construction of homes in Monroe County. The fittings do not comply with county building codes. One of the pipe fittings bursts in a home, allowing hot water to spray on the homeowner. The homeowner can bring a negligence action for personal damages on the ground that failure to comply with the building codes is a breach of the manufacturer's duty of reasonable care. Of course, the homeowner has to show proximate cause.

Fraudulent and Nonfraudulent Misrepresentation

When a fraudulent misrepresentation has been made to a user or consumer, and that misrepresentation ultimately results in an injury, the basis of liability may be the tort of **fraud.** Examples are the intentional mislabeling of packaged cosmetics or the intentional concealment of a product's defects. A more interesting basis of liability is nonfraudulent misrepresentation, when a merchant *innocently* misrepresents the character or quality of goods.

A famous example involved a drug manufacturer and a victim of addiction to a prescription medicine called Talwin. The manufacturer, Winthrop Laboratories, a division of Stirling Drug, Inc., innocently indicated to the medical profession that the drug was not physically addictive. Using this information, a physician prescribed the drug for his patient, who developed an addiction that turned out to be fatal.Even though the addiction was a highly unusual reaction resulting from the victim's highly unusual susceptibility to this product, the drug company was still held liable.[2]

THE DOCTRINE OF STRICT LIABILITY

A recent development of tort law is the revival of the old doctrine of strict liability, under which people are liable for the results of their acts regardless of their intentions or the degree of their negligence. For example, a company that uses dynamite to blast for a road is strictly liable for any damages that it causes, even if it takes reasonable and prudent precautions to prevent such damages. In essence, the blasting company becomes the insurer for any personal injuries it causes.

2. Crocker v. Winthrop Laboratories, Div. of Stirling Drugs, Inc., 514 S.W.2d 429 (Tex. 1974).

The English courts accepted the doctrine of strict liability for many years. Any persons whose conduct resulted in the injury of another were held liable for damages, even if they had not intended to injure anyone and had exercised reasonable or even great care. This approach was abandoned around 1800 in favor of the *fault* approach. An action was considered tortious only if it was wrongful or blameworthy in some respect. Strict liability was reapplied to manufactured goods in several landmark cases in the 1960s and has since become a common method of holding manufacturers liable. The purchaser of a product who is injured has a cause of action against the manufacturer simply by showing (1) that the product was defective, (2) that the defect made the product unreasonably dangerous, and (3) that the defect was the proximate cause of the injury.

The Restatement of Torts

The Restatement, Second, Torts designates how the doctrine of strict liability should be applied. It is a precise and widely accepted statement of the liabilities of sellers of goods (including manufacturers) and deserves close attention. Section 402A of Restatement, Second, Torts states:

(1)   One who sells any product in a defective condition unreasonably dangerous to the user or consumer or to his property is subject to liability for physical harm thereby caused to the ultimate user or consumer or to his property, if
   (a)   the seller is engaged in the business of selling such a product, and
   (b)   it is expected to and does reach the user or consumer without substantial change in the condition in which it is sold.
(2)   The rule stated in Subsection (1) applies although
   (a)   the seller has exercised all possible care in the preparation and sale of his product, and
   (b)   the user or consumer has not bought the product from or entered into any contractual relation with the seller.

Thus, liability is imposed by law as a matter of public policy. It does not depend on privity of contract or on proof of negligence. The manufacturer's liability to an injured party is virtually unlimited. The injured party does not have to be the buyer or a third-party beneficiary, as required under contract warranty theory. [UCC Sec. 2-318] Indeed, this liability in law is not governed by the provisions of the Uniform Commercial Code.

Requirements of Strict Liability

The five basic requirements of strict liability are:

1.   The defendant must sell the product in a defective condition.
2.   The defendant must normally be engaged in the business of selling that product.
3.   The product must be unreasonably dangerous to the user or consumer because of its defective condition.
4.   The plaintiff must incur physical harm to self or property by use or consumption of the product.
5.   The defective condition must be the proximate cause of the injury or damage.

Thus, in any action against a manufacturer or seller, the plaintiff does not have to show why or in what manner the product became defective. The plaintiff does, however, have to show that at the time the injury was sustained, the condition of the product was essentially the same as it was when it left the hands of the defendant manufacturer or seller.

Limitations on Recovery

Some courts have limited the application of the strict liability doctrine to cases in which personal injuries have occurred. Thus, when a defective product causes only *property damage*, the seller may or may not be liable under a theory of strict liability, depending on the law of the particular jurisdiction. Note, however, that recovery for *breach of warranty* may be available, depending upon the type of injury and which alternative section of UCC Sec. 2-318 is in effect. Finally, recovery under negligence theory may be possible, but negligence of the manufacturer may be difficult to prove.

Defenses

In some cases, manufacturers have proven as a defense that a product was being misused at the time of the injury or that it was used in a manner for which it was not made. Also, there have been recent legislative attempts to limit the application of the doctrine of strict liability to new goods.

Assumption of risk can be used as a defense in an action based on strict liability in tort. Whenever consumers or users use goods improperly under unreasonable circumstances, they assume the risk of injury. In order for such a defense to be established, the defendant must show (1) that the plaintiff voluntarily engaged in the risk while realizing the potential danger, (2) that the plaintiff knew and appreciated the risk created by the defect, and (3) that the plaintiff's decision to undertake the known risk was unreasonable.

Strict Liability to Bystanders

Some courts extend the strict liability of manufacturers and other sellers to injured bystanders, although the drafters of Restatement, Second, Torts, Section 402A did not take a position on bystanders. For example, the manufacturer of an automobile was held liable for injuries caused by the explosion of the car's motor while in traffic. A cloud of steam that resulted from the explosion caused multiple collisions because other drivers could not see well.[3]

Crash-worthiness Doctrine

Certain courts have adopted the doctrine of crash-worthiness, which imposes liability for defects in the design or construction of motor vehicles that increase the extent of injuries to passengers if an accident occurs. The doctrine holds even when the defects do not actually cause the accident.[4] By accepting the crash-worthiness doctrine, the courts reject the argument of automobile manufacturers that involving a car in a collision does not constitute "ordinary use" of a car. There are in fact, strong differences of opinion among the courts on this issue.

Strict Liability of Suppliers of Component Parts and Lessors

Under the rule of strict liability in tort, the basis of liability has been expanded to include suppliers of component parts and lessors of movable goods. Thus, if General Motors buys brake pads from a subcontractor and puts them in Chevrolets without changing their composition, and those pads are defective, both the supplier of the brake pads and General Motors will be held strictly liable for the damages caused by the defects.

Liability for personal injuries caused by defective goods extends to those who lease such goods. Section 408 of the Restatement, Second, Torts states that:

One who leases a chattel as safe for immediate use is subject to liability to those whom he should expect to use the chattel, or to be endangered by its probable use, for physical harm caused by its use in a manner for which and by a person for whose use it is leased, if the lessor fails to exercise reasonable care to make it safe for such use or to disclose its actual condition to those who may be expected to use it.

Some courts have held that a leasing agreement gives rise to a contractual *implied warranty* that the leased goods will be fit for the duration of the lease. Under this view, if Hertz Rent-a-Car leases a Chevrolet that has been improperly maintained, and a passenger is injured in an accident, the passenger can sue Hertz. (Liability is based on the contract theory of warranty, not tort.)

THE CONSUMER PRODUCT SAFETY ACT

One of the newest federal agencies designed to protect the consumer is the Consumer Product Safety Commission (CPSC). Established in 1972,

---

3. Giberson v. Ford Motor Co., 504 S.W.2d 8 (Mo.1974).

4. Turner v. General Motors Corp., 514 S.W.2d 497 (Texas Civ. App. 1974).

it was given sweeping powers to regulate the production and sale of potentially hazardous consumer products. The agency's staff will eventually be over a thousand, which will make it one of the major federal regulatory agencies for consumer protection.

Consumer product safety legislation began in 1953 with the enactment of the Flammable Fabrics Act. Between 1953 and 1972 Congress enacted legislation regulating specific classes rather than broad categories of consumer products. Finally, as a result of 1970 recommendations of the National Commission on Product Safety, the Consumer Product Safety Act was passed in 1972, creating the CPSC to regulate all potentially hazardous consumer products.

Products Subject to the Act

The 1972 Act states that "* * *any article, or component part thereof produced or distributed for sale to a consumer for use in or around a permanent or temporary household or residence, a school, in recreation or otherwise, or for the personal use, consumption or enjoyment of a consumer" shall be subject to regulation by the CPSC. As further evidence of how comprehensive the act is, the authority to administer other acts is transferred to the CPSC. These acts include the Federal Hazardous Substance Act, the Child Protection and Toy Safety Act, the Poison Prevention Packaging Act, the Flammable Fabrics Act, and the Refrigerator Safety Act.

Purposes of the Act

As stated in the act, the Consumer Product Safety Commission was created:

1. To protect the public against unreasonable risk of injury associated with consumer products.
2. To assist consumers in evaluating the comparative safety of consumer products.
3. To develop uniform safety standards for consumer products and to minimize conflicting state and local regulations.
4. To promote research and investigation into causes and prevention of product-related deaths, illnesses, and injuries.

Form and Functions of the CPSC

The commission was set up to conduct research on product safety and maintain a clearinghouse to "collect, investigate, analyze, and disseminate injury data, and information, relating to the causes and prevention of death, injury, and illness associated with consumer products * * *" To this end, the CPSC immediately started gathering data on the two hundred most hazardous consumer products in the nation. The commission required emergency wards to indicate the particular cause of any injury, illness, or death related to a consumer product. The initial CPSC survey found that the most hazardous consumer product was the bicycle. The CPSC hoped that the data obtained and the resulting hazard index for consumer products would move manufacturers to improve their most hazardous products voluntarily and to warn consumers about them.

Powers of the CPSC

Not only can the CPSC set safety standards for consumer products, it can also ban the manufacture and sale of any product deemed hazardous to consumers. The commission has the authority to remove from the market products that are deemed imminently hazardous. It can require manufacturers to report information about any products already sold or intended for sale that have proven hazardous.

Impact of the CPSC

Congress sought to create an agency with broad powers to regulate the sale and manufacture of all consumer products. The CPSC is likely to have increasingly profound effects upon the consumer products industry. At the very least, if it continues its present effectiveness, it will give consumers more information about the safety of the products that they buy.

CPSC regulations have resulted in safer but more expensive products. Recently, regulations for power mowers were challenged by certain government agencies because they would raise the price of the mowers too much. This involves the thorny problem of weighing the costs of safety against the benefits. In other words, how much safety do people want to pay for?

QUESTIONS AND CASE PROBLEMS

1. Howmedica, Inc., manufactured and distributed artificial replacements for human bones and joints. Hoffman, who was injured in a serious automobile accident, underwent surgery for repair to her injured hip. As part of the surgery, her doctor implanted a hip prosthesis. Several months later, Hoffman's hip fractured, causing serious injury. At trial, Howmedica, Inc., conceded that it had been negligent in manufacturing and testing the hip and that it had breached its warranty of merchantability. But Howmedica contended that it was not liable to Hoffman under UCC Sec. 2-318 (Alternative B) since Hoffman and Howmedica were not in privity of contract. Is this a sound argument? [Hoffman v. Howmedica, Inc., 364 N.E.2d 1215 (Mass.1977)].

2. While shopping in an Allied Supermarket store, Barker placed two bottles of soda in his shopping cart and thereafter paid for them. While Barker was pushing the cart out the exit door, one of the bottles exploded, and a sliver of glass flew into Barker's eye. Barker sued both Allied Supermarket and B&B Bottling Company, the manufacturer of the soda, but not until two years had passed, so he was no longer able to bring a tort action. Assuming Barker can prove breach of a warranty of merchantability, and assuming the jurisdiction in which he brings suit follows alternative A of UCC Sec. 2-318, can Barker recover against Allied Supermarket? Against B&B Bottling? [Barker v. Allied Supermarket, 20 U.C.C. Rptg. Serv. 6 (Okla. 1976)]

3. James Welding Company purchased from Delta Oxygen Company a cylinder filled with oxygen to be used in welding operations. Scott, who had worked for James Welding Company for a number of years, was attempting to connect the cylinder to an acetylene torch when a leak in the cylinder caused an explosion to occur. Scott was seriously burned and was hospitalized as a result of the explosion. In an action by Scott for breach of implied warranty against Delta Oxygen Company, Scott relied on UCC Sec. 2-318. What result? [Delta Oxygen Co. v. Scott, 238 Ark. 534, 383 S.W.2d 885 (1964)]

4. Miller purchased a vaporizer-humidifier from Rexall Drug Company. While she was using the humidifier in her home, it suddenly shot boiling water on her nephew. The incident resulted in the nephew's death. Miller's nephew did not live in Miller's home; he lived next door. Will an action brought against Rexall Drug Company on behalf of Miller's nephew be successful in a jurisdiction in which UCC Sec. 2-318 (alternative A) is in effect? [Miller v. Preitz, 422 Pa. 383, 221 A.2d. 320 (1966)]

5. Hardesty, the owner of an apartment building, contracted with a subcontractor to install a central air-conditioning system in the building. After the subcontractor had properly installed the air-conditioning system, it failed to work because the chiller unit of the system was defective. As a result of the defect and because the system failed to work, Hardesty was unable to rent many of the apartment units in his building. Hardesty sued the manufacturer of the units, from whom the subcontractor had purchased them, for damages for breach of warranty under UCC Sec. 2-318. Can he recover? [Hardesty v. Andro Corp.—Webster Div., 555 P.2d. 1030 (Okl. 1976)]

6. Downey owned a mechanical rug washer that he had purchased from a local retailer. The manufacturer was Moore's Time-Saving Equipment, Inc. While using the rug washer, Downey was struck in the eye and injured when the cam lift handle counter-rotated after Downey failed to turn it the required 180 degree arc. Downey was aware that such counter-rotation was common on these types of rug washers because he was experienced in the use of these machines. Downey wished to recover for his eye injury from Moore's Equipment, Inc., on a theory of strict liability. Can he recover? [Downey v. Moore's Time-Sav. Equipment, Inc., 432 F.2d. 1088 (C.A. Ind. 1970)]

7. Union Oil Company was engaged in drilling operations off the Alaskan coast. As a part of its operations, Union installed gas protection systems in its offshore drilling rigs. Over a period of less than a year, the salt water and spray caused the internal

parts of the detection system to corrode, resulting in a failure in the system. Subsequently, because of an undetected gas leak, an explosion killed one of Union's employees, Jones. Jones's representative sued Haragan, the manufacturer and seller of the gas detection system. Can Jones's representatives recover on a theory of strict liability? How would they argue that there was a defect? [Haragan v. Union Oil Co., 312 F.Supp. 1392 (D.C. Alaska, 1970)]

8. White, a bystander, was injured when a coal mining ram car with a defective steering valve struck an air line, which in turn struck White. Assuming that the steering mechanism was defective at the time the manufacturer sold it to the mining company, what problems will White have bringing suit under a theory of strict liability in tort? Look closely at the wording of Restatement, Second, Torts, Section 402A. [White v. Jeffrey Galion, Inc., 326 F.Supp. 751 (D.C. Ill. 1971)]

9. In July 1971, St. Regis Paper Corp. purchased a compressor from Norfolk Development Corp. for use in its paper-producing plant. Several weeks later the compressor exploded, resulting in a fire that caused extensive damage to the purchaser's manufacturing plant. The explosion was caused by a defect in the manufacture of the pistons. St. Regis sought to recover from Norfolk for damage done the plant and for the profits it lost while the plant was closed for repairs. What results? [Norfolk Dev. Corp. v. St. Regis Pulp and Paper Corp., 338 F.Supp. 1213 (D.C. Neb. 1972)]

10. Dreher purchased a plastic waste container from Maas for use in her home. After she brought the container home, she found that the lid had been improperly manufactured and did not fit on the top of the container. Dreher purposely hit the corner of the lid with her hand in an attempt to make it fit properly and suffered a deep gash in her hand when she hit the lid. She sought to recover for the injury from Maas, the seller, but Maas refused to compensate her. In a suit by Dreher against Maas, can Dreher successfully recover on a theory of strict liability? [Maas v. Dreher, 10 Ariz. App. 520, 460 P.2d. 191 (1969)]

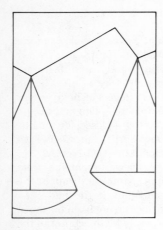

22

Sales
Remedies of Buyer and Seller
for Breach of Sales Contracts

When a sales contract is breached, remedies are provided to the non-breaching party not only for *damages* but also to enable the nonbreaching party to retain (or obtain) physical possession of the goods. [UCC Secs. 2-711 and 2-703] The general purpose of these remedies is to put the aggrieved party "in as good a position as if the other party had fully performed." [UCC Sec. 1-106(1)]

REMEDIES OF THE SELLER

The remedies available to an unpaid seller under the Uniform Commercial Code include: (1) the right to withhold delivery of the goods, (2) the right to stop a carrier or bailee from delivering goods to an insolvent buyer, (3) a limited right to reclaim goods in the possession of an insolvent buyer, (4) the right to identify and resell goods to the contract after the buyer has breached, (5) the right to recover the purchase price plus incidental damages, (6) the right to recover damages for the buyer's nonacceptance or repudiation of the contract, and (7) the right to cancel the sales contract.

Seller's Lien

In certain circumstances, a seller has a lien, or legal interest, in goods being sold. Technically, a lien is a right incident to the sale rather than a remedy for breach of contract. A lien enables the seller to retain possession of the goods until the buyer pays for them.

The seller's lien can be waived or lost by: (1) express agreement, (2) acts inconsistent with the lien's existence, (3) payment or tender of payment by the buyer, or (4) voluntary and unconditional delivery of the goods to a carrier or other bailee or to the buyer or an authorized agent of the buyer.

The seller's right to retain possession of the goods until the buyer pays the purchase price can be waived by express agreement in the sales contract. If the sales agreement provides for an extension of credit to the buyer, the seller has no lien on the goods, since the act of extending credit is inconsistent with the existence of the lien. The seller will have a lien on the goods, however, if the buyer becomes insolvent or if the credit period expires while the goods are still in the seller's possession. The tender of payment or the actual payment of the debt that the lien secures will ordinarily discharge the lien. This occurs when the buyer pays the full price for the goods and the seller gives up possession. When the buyer gives a promissory note, the lien will ordinarily *not* be discharged until the note is paid even if the seller relinquishes possession of the goods. Finally, sellers lose their liens when they voluntarily deliver possession of the goods to the buyer or to an authorized agent of the buyer. The lien is not lost, though, where delivery is qualified or where the buyer obtains possession fraudulently.

Consider the following illustration. Williams, the plaintiff, sold his Chevrolet sedan to the Greers, the defendants. The defendants paid $90 by check and $235 in cash. After the Greers received possession of the Chevy, they stopped payment on the check. Williams went to court to regain possession of the auto by enforcing his seller's lien. The court upheld his complaint, allowing him to regain possession of the auto and to keep it until the Greers paid the $90. Essentially, the Greers had obtained possession fraudulently; therefore, title had not passed to them. Since Williams had legal possession, he could validly enforce his lien.

The Right to Withhold Delivery of the Goods

In general, sellers can withhold or discontinue performance of their obligations under a sales contract when buyers breach. If a seller discovers that the buyer is insolvent, the seller can refuse to deliver the goods unless the buyer pays in cash. [UCC Sec. 2-702] If a buyer has wrongfully rejected, revoked acceptance, failed to make proper and timely payment, or repudiated a part of the contract, the seller can withhold delivery of the particular goods in question. Furthermore, the seller can withhold the entire undelivered balance of the goods if the buyer's breach is material. [UCC Sec. 2-703]

The Right to Stop a Carrier or Bailee from Delivering Goods to an Insolvent Buyer

An unpaid seller can stop a carrier from delivering goods in transit to a buyer whenever the seller learns of the buyer's insolvency. The seller can also stop delivery if the buyer repudiates or behaves in any other way that gives the seller the right to withhold or reclaim the goods when the quantity involved is at least a carload, a truckload, or a planeload. [UCC Sec. 2-705(1)]

Consider an example. On January 1, Beel orders a carload of onions from Sneed. Sneed is to ship them on January 8, and Beel is to pay for them on January 10. Sneed ships on time, but Beel does not pay. As soon as Sneed learns of this, she orders the carrier to stop the carload in transit. Since the carload is still on its way to Beel's city, the carrier stops shipment. Beel cannot claim that Sneed and the carrier have performed a wrongful act by stopping the shipment, for a seller can always stop a carload of goods in transit when a buyer commits some breach of contract that gives the seller the right to withhold or reclaim the goods.

In order to stop delivery, the seller must *timely notify* the carrier or other bailee that the goods are to be returned or held for the seller. If the carrier has sufficient time to stop delivery, then the goods must be held and delivered according to the instructions of the seller, who is liable to the carrier for any additional costs incurred. If the carrier fails to act properly, it will be liable to the seller for any loss. [UCC Sec. 2-705(3)]

The right of the seller to stop delivery is lost when: (1) the buyer obtains possession of the goods, (2) the carrier acknowledges the buyer's rights by reshipping or storing the goods for the buyer, (3) a bailee of the goods other than a carrier acknowledges that he or she is holding the goods for the buyer, or (4) a negotiable document of title covering the goods has been negotiated to the buyer. [UCC Sec. 2-705(2)]

The Right to Reclaim Goods in the Possession of an Insolvent Buyer

The seller can demand that an insolvent buyer return the goods if the demand is made within ten days after the buyer has received them. However, the seller can demand and reclaim the goods at any time if the buyer misrepresented his or her solvency in writing within three months prior to the delivery of the goods.

The seller's right to reclaim, however, is subject to the rights of a good faith purchaser or other buyer in the ordinary course of business who purchases the goods from the buyer before the seller reclaims.[1]

The Right to Identify Goods to the Contract after the Buyer Has Breached

Sometimes a buyer may breach or repudiate a sales contract while the seller is still in possession of some finished or partially manufactured goods. The seller can identify the conforming goods that are still in his or her possession or

1. *A buyer in the ordinary course of business* is a person who, in good faith and without knowledge that the sale violates the ownership rights or security interest of a third party, buys in ordinary course from a person (other than a pawnbroker) in the business of selling goods of that kind. [UCC Sec. 1-201(9)]

control even if they were not identified at the time of the breach. Then the seller can sue for the purchase price and resell the goods, holding the buyer liable for any loss.

Unfinished goods that were supposed to be used to fulfill a particular sales contract can be treated in two ways. First, the seller can cease manufacturing the goods and resell them for scrap or salvage value. [UCC Sec. 2-704] Second, the seller can complete the manufacture, identify the goods to the contract, and resell them, holding the buyer liable for any deficiency. In choosing between these two alternatives, the seller must exercise reasonable commercial judgment in order to mitigate the loss and obtain maximum realization of value from the unfinished goods. [UCC Sec. 2-704, Comment 2]

The Right to Resell the Goods

When buyers breach sales contracts by wrongfully rejecting goods, by revoking acceptance, by failing to pay, or by repudiating the contract, sellers can resell goods that remain in their possession or goods that they have reacquired, say, by stopping delivery. The resale must be made in good faith and in a commercially reasonable manner. The seller can recover any deficiency between the sales price and the contract price along with incidental damages. [UCC Sec. 2-706(1)] (The seller is *not* liable to the buyer for any profits made on the resale.) [UCC Sec. 2-706(6)] Consider an example. On Monday, S contracts to sell four thousand heads of romaine lettuce to B for thirty cents per head, delivery and payment to be due on Friday. On Wednesday, S has fourteen thousand heads of romaine lettuce in her inventory, but she has not yet identified the four thousand she means to sell to B. On that day, B telephones S to inform her that he will not accept or pay for the lettuce. B claims that, since the four thousand heads of romaine lettuce for his contract have not yet been identified, S cannot resell and recover damages from B. B is incorrect here. S has the right to identify the four thousand heads of romaine lettuce for B's contract. Under UCC

Sec. 2-704(1), S has the right to resell the lettuce at private sale and to recover damages of the contract price of thirty cents per head, less the resale price, plus expenses.

The resale can be private or public, and the goods can be sold as a unit or in parcels. A seller planning to use a private sale must give the original buyer reasonable notice of the intention to sell. If a public sale is anticipated, the seller must give the buyer reasonable notice unless the goods are perishable or will rapidly decline in value. [UCC Secs. 2-706(2) and 2-706(3)] A bona fide purchaser in a resale takes the goods free of any of the rights of the original buyer, even if the seller fails to comply with the requirements of the Uniform Commercial Code regarding resales. [UCC Sec. 2-706(5)]

The Right to Recover the Purchase Price Plus Incidental Damages

Before the Uniform Commercial Code was adopted, a seller could not sue for the purchase price of the goods unless title had passed to the buyer. Under the Code, an unpaid seller can bring an action to recover the purchase price and incidental damages in three situations: (1) when the buyer has accepted the goods and has not revoked acceptance, (2) when conforming goods have been lost or damaged after the risk of loss has passed to the buyer, and (3) when the buyer has breached after the goods have been identified to the contract and the seller is unable to resell at a reasonable price. [UCC Sec. 2-701(1)] This remedy is distinct from an action to recover damages for breach of the sales contract and is available to the seller only in the situations described above.

If sellers sue for the contract price of undelivered goods that they have been unable to resell, they must hold the goods for the buyer. The seller can resell at any time prior to the collection of the judgment from the buyer, but the net proceeds of the sale must be credited to the buyer. The following example illustrates these points. The Rubin Glass Company sells glass strips to the Clearview Window Corporation, which uses them in manufacturing jalousie windows. Part of the merchandise is delivered, and the purchase price for the delivered order is paid. When Rubin attempts to tender the remainder of the order to Clearview, the order is refused. Rubin has two alternatives. First, it can sell the remaining glass and sue for the difference between the contract price with Clearview and the price that the glass will bring on the open market. Second, it can keep the glass and sue for any difference between the contract price and the fair market value of the glass on the date of delivery. However, Rubin will be allowed to sue for recovery of the full contract price only if it is never able to sell the glass as scrap. [UCC Sec. 2-709(1)(b)]

If a buyer repudiates a contract or wrongfully refuses to accept the goods, a seller can maintain an action to recover the damages that were sustained. Ordinarily, the amount of damages will equal the difference between the contract price and the market price (at the time and place of tender of the goods). If the difference between the contract price and the market price is too small to place the seller in the position that he or she would have been in if the buyer had fully performed, the proper measure of damages is the seller's lost profits, including a reasonable allowance for overhead and other incidental expenses. [UCC Sec. 2-708(2)]

The Right to Cancel the Sales Contract

A seller can cancel a contract if the buyer wrongfully rejects or revokes acceptance of conforming goods, fails to make proper payment, or repudiates the contract in part or in whole. The contract can be canceled with respect to the goods directly involved, or the entire contract can be canceled if the breach is material. A material breach is one that substantially impairs the value of the entire contract. [UCC Sec. 2-703]

The seller must notify the buyer of the cancellation, and at that point, all remaining obligations of both the buyer and the seller are discharged. The seller, however, retains the right to a remedy for a breach on the part of the buyer if it occurred before the contract was canceled. [UCC Sec. 2-106(4)] If the seller's cancellation is not justified, then the seller is in breach of the contract, and the buyer can sue for appropriate damages.

In the following case, the seller attempted to cancel an installment sales contract because the buyer had been unreasonably slow in making payment. At the same time, the buyer sued the seller for damages in a cross-claim, which is the equivalent of a defendant's complaint. (See Chapter 2.) The buyer claimed that the seller's rescission (cancellation) was unjustified.

PLOTNICK v.
PENNSYLVANIA
SMELTING &
REFINING CO.

United States Court of Appeals,
Third Circuit, 1952.
194 F.2d 859.

BACKGROUND AND FACTS   *In an installment contract for the sale of battery lead, a buyer and a seller disputed over the timeliness of delivery and of payment. The first two of numerous anticipated shipments were satisfactorily completed and paid for, but the seller informed the buyer that it would not ship any more lead until the third shipment was fully paid for. The buyer, who had paid 75 percent of the price of the third shipment, suggested to the seller that it could use sight drafts to assure itself of payment for future shipments (that is, it could obtain the buyer's signature on a negotiable instrument). The seller rejected this idea, informing the buyer that it considered the entire contract at an end because it was uncertain that the buyer would be willing to make future payments. The buyer brought suit.*

DECISION AND RATIONALE   *Even though the buyer's failure to pay for the third shipment in full constituted a breach, it was not such a material breach that the seller could escape its duty under the balance of the contract. To justify rescission of an entire installment contract when only one installment has been breached requires that the single breach be significant enough to create a reasonable apprehension in the seller's mind concerning payment for future installments. Use of a sight draft presents a commercially reasonable approach to avoiding this apprehension. Thus, "[t]he clincher here is provided by the additional evidence concerning the possibility of delivery with sight draft attached."*

Repossession of Goods

An unpaid seller does not have any inherent right to repossess goods that are in the possession of a buyer.[2] In modern business practice, however, when goods are sold on an installment basis, a provision allowing the seller to repossess is ordinarily included in the security agreement. This enables the seller to retake the goods if the buyer defaults in payment. Security

agreements will be discussed in Chapters 29 and 30.

REMEDIES OF THE BUYER

Under the Uniform Commercial Code, the remedies available to the buyer include: (1) the right to reject nonconforming or improperly delivered goods, (2) the right to revoke acceptance of the goods, (3) the right of *cover*, (4) the right to recover damages for nondelivery or repudiation by the seller, (5) the right to recover

---

2. Except where the buyer is insolvent and the seller reclaims within ten days of delivery.

damages for breach in regard to accepted goods, (6) the right to recover identified goods upon the seller's insolvency, (7) the right to obtain specific performance, (8) the right to replevy the goods, (9) the right to retain and enforce a security interest in the goods, (10) the right to cancel the contract, and (11) remedies for fraud by the seller.

The Right to Reject Nonconforming or Improperly Delivered Goods

If either the goods or the seller's tender of the goods fail to conform to the contract in any respect, the buyer can reject the goods. If some of the goods conform to the contract, the buyer can keep them and reject the rest. [UCC Sec. 2-601]

TIMELINESS AND REASON FOR REJECTION REQUIRED Goods must be rejected in a reasonable time. Furthermore, the buyer must designate particular defects that are ascertainable by reasonable inspection. Failure to do so precludes the buyer from using an unstated defect to justify rejection or to establish breach when the seller could have cured the defect if it had been stated reasonably. [UCC Sec. 2-605] After rejecting the goods, the buyer cannot exercise any right of ownership over them. If the buyer acts inconsistently with the seller's ownership rights, the buyer will be deemed to have accepted the goods. [UCC Sec. 2-602]

The Right to Revoke Acceptance

A buyer who accepts goods can later revoke that acceptance, but only under limited circumstances. First, the defect in the goods must *substantially* impair their value to the buyer. Second, if the buyer accepted the goods without knowledge of the nonconformity (because the defect was not discoverable or because the seller assured the buyer that the goods were conforming), the buyer can revoke acceptance. Third, if the buyer accepted the goods knowing of their defect but reasonably believing that the seller would cure the problem, the buyer can revoke acceptance if the seller fails to cure.

In addition, the buyer must notify the seller of the revocation within a reasonable time after the defect is discovered or *should have been discovered.* If proper notice is given, the revocation of acceptance becomes effective, and the buyer need not make an immediate return of the goods. Ultimately, however, the buyer must return the goods to the seller. [UCC Sec. 2-608] (The right of a buyer to revoke acceptance is seldom used because the Code severely restricts buyers from claiming under it.)

Revocation after acceptance must be done within a reasonable time after delivery. Otherwise, failure to reject nonconforming goods will constitute an acceptance. The following case involves a dispute over whether and when a buyer has the right to revoke acceptance.

BACKGROUND AND FACTS *Lanners agreed to purchase an airplane from Whitney. An FAA mechanic inspected the airplane and told Lanners it was in airworthy condition. Within three weeks after its delivery, Lanners discovered that the airplane burned oil, overheated, and had abnormally high cylinder pressure. Shortly after discovering these defects, Lanners had an aircraft engineer inspect the plane. The engineer found that the plane was not airworthy. Within a week, Lanners informed Whitney of the substantial defects in the plane and requested that Whitney take it back. Whitney refused. Lanners sued for refund of the purchase price on the ground that he properly revoked his acceptance of the plane.*

LANNERS v. WHITNEY
Supreme Court of Oregon,
1967.
247 Or. 223, 428 P.2d 398.

DECISION AND RATIONALE *Lanners was able to recover the purchase price. This action involved a claim of revocation of acceptance* *rather than a claim of breach of warranty. (Under the latter claim, Lanners could recover only the difference between the value of the plane in its state of disrepair and the purchase price.) To prove that he had properly revoked his acceptance, Lanners had to show that the plane's nonconformity substantially impaired its value to him and that he was not able to discover defects in the plane due to Whitney's assurances that it was free from defects. Lanners also had to prove that he revoked within a reasonable time of the discovery of the defects (UCC Sec. 2-608). It is clear that the existing defects greatly diminished the plane's value to Lanners and that he was unable to discover how extensive the defects were for several weeks because of the FAA's assurances that the plane was airworthy. The court stated: "With respect to the question of reasonable notice, the evidence showed that *** Lanners notified defendant of the difficulty encountered with the [aircraft] and *** [o]ne week later *** inspection of the aircraft was made for Lanners by [an engineer]. *** Plaintiff was not required to notify the defendant of his intention to revoke his acceptance until he was reasonably certain that the nonconformity substantially impaired the value of the airplane to him. His mere suspicions prior to inspection were not sufficient to require notice."*

OPPORTUNITY FOR CURE REQUIRED Before a buyer can successfully revoke acceptance of the goods, the seller must be given a reasonable opportunity to *cure* the defects. Revocation of acceptance can be a hazardous remedy if done unsuccessfully. For example, B traded in his old car and purchased a new car from S. The car developed loud, thumping noises, and B returned it to S. S cured the defect in forty minutes, but B demanded a replacement auto or a refund. B left S's shop and refused to pay for the auto. The auto was repossessed. At trial the court held that B had improperly revoked acceptance and had entered into a valid contract. B's unsuccessful attempt to revoke acceptance lost him both his new car and his old one.[3] Therefore, this remedy should be used with caution.

The Right to Recover for Nondelivery or Repudiation

If a seller repudiates the sales contract or fails to deliver the goods, the buyer can sue for

damages. The measure of recovery is the difference between the contract price and the market price of the goods at the time that the buyer learned of the breach. The market price is determined at the place where the seller was supposed to deliver the goods. In appropriate cases, the buyer can also recover incidental and consequential damages less the expenses that were saved as a result of the seller's breach. [UCC Sec. 2-713] Note that the damages here are based upon the time and place a buyer would normally obtain cover.

THE RIGHT OF COVER In certain situations, buyers can protect themselves by obtaining *cover*, that is, by substituting goods for those that were due under the sales contract. This option is available to a buyer who has rightfully rejected goods or revoked acceptance. It is also available where the seller repudiates the contract or fails to deliver the goods. In obtaining cover, the buyer must act in good faith and without unreasonable delay. [UCC Sec. 2-712]

After purchasing substitute goods the buyer can recover from the seller the difference between the cost of cover and the contract price.

3. Rozmus v. Thompson's Lincoln-Mercury Co., 209 Pa. Super. 120, 224 A.2d 782 (1966).

The buyer can also recover incidental and consequential damages less the expenses that were saved as a result of the seller's breach. [UCC Secs. 2-712 and 2-715]

Consider the following illustration. Jefferson Island Salt Mining Company orders 5 million salt cartons made of a special moisture-proof cardboard from Empire Box Corporation. Empire delivers 1 million of the cartons but refuses to deliver the balance of the order. Jefferson purchases the remaining 4 million cartons in a distant market and sues Empire for the difference between the cover price—the price of purchasing the cartons in a distant market—and the contract price. The court will hold that Jefferson acted in good faith in purchasing the cartons in a distant market only if no close market was available in which it could fulfill its needs.

Buyers are not required to cover, and failure to do so will not bar them from using any other remedies that are available under the Uniform Commercial Code. [UCC Sec. 2-712(3)] But a buyer who fails to cover will not be able to recover the consequential damages that could have been avoided by purchasing substitute goods. [UCC Sec. 2-715(2)(a)] For example, if a wholesaler is supposed to supply a grocer with eggs, and the wholesaler is unable to deliver them, the grocer has the option of covering. If the grocer covers, he or she can recover any lost profits resulting from the wholesaler's breach of the contract. If the grocer does not cover, however, and has no eggs to sell, he or she cannot recover lost profits. The Code's remedies for buyers are designed to encourage them to cover since their recovery will normally be about the same whether they choose to cover or not.

The Right to Recover Damages for Breach in Regard to Accepted Goods

A buyer who has accepted nonconforming goods must notify the seller of the breach within a reasonable time after the defect was or should have been discovered. Otherwise, the buyer cannot complain about defects in the goods. [UCC Sec. 2-607(3)] In addition, the parties to a sales contract can insert a provision requiring the buyer to give notice of any defects in the goods within a certain prescribed period. Such a requirement is ordinarily binding on the parties.

MEASURE OF DAMAGES IF A WARRANTY IS BREACHED When the seller breaches a warranty, the measure of damages equals the difference between the value of the goods as accepted and their value if they had been delivered as warranted. The buyer can recover all damages resulting from the breach of warranty as well as incidental and consequential damages. [UCC Sec. 2-714] If the buyer is entitled to recover damages and the seller is notified, then the buyer can deduct the amount of the damages from the balance due on the sales contract. [UCC Sec. 2-717]

SUIT BY A BUYER'S CUSTOMER RESULTING FROM THE SELLER'S BREACH OF WARRANTY When a buyer resells defective goods that were originally sold by a breaching seller, the buyer's customer can sue the buyer. Under these circumstances the buyer has two alternatives:

1. The buyer can notify the seller of the pending litigation. The notice should state that the seller can come in and defend, and it should also state that the seller will be bound by the buyer's action if the seller does not come in and defend after reasonable receipt of the notice. [UCC Sec. 2-607(5)(a)]
2. The buyer can also defend against the customer's suit and later bring an action against the original seller. This situation arises most frequently where there is a manufacturer-dealer arrangement—for example, where a car dealer sells a defective automobile and the customer sues the dealer but not the manufacturer.

The Right to Recover Identified Goods from an Insolvent Seller

If a buyer pays for goods that remain in the possession of the seller, the buyer can recover the goods if the seller becomes insolvent within ten days after receiving the first payment as long as the goods are identified to the contract. To exercise this right, the buyer must tender to the seller any unpaid balance of the purchase price. [UCC Sec. 2-502]

The Right to Obtain Specific Performance

A buyer can obtain specific performance of a sales contract when the goods are unique or when the buyer's remedy at law is inadequate. [UCC Sec. 2-716(1)] Ordinarily, a suit for money damages will be sufficient to place a buyer in the position he or she would have occupied if the seller had fully performed. However, when the contract is for the purchase of a particular work of art, patent, copyright, or similarly unique item, money damages may not be sufficient. Under these circumstances, the equity side of the court will require the seller to perform exactly (a remedy of specific performance) by delivering the particular goods identified to the contract. To illustrate: Casey contracts to sell an antique car to Smith for $30,000, delivery and payment due on June 14. Smith tenders payment on June 14, but Casey refuses to deliver. Can Smith force delivery of the car? Probably she can because the antique car is unique. Therefore, Smith can obtain specific performance of the contract of the sale from Casey.

The Right to Replevy the Goods

Replevin is similar to specific performance. It is an action to recover specific goods in the hands of a breaching party who is unlawfully withholding them from the other party. The buyer can replevy goods identified to the contract if the seller has repudiated or breached the contract. Additionally, buyers must show that they were unable to cover for the goods after a reasonable effort.

Consider the following example. On July 1, S contracts to sell her tomato crop to B, delivery and payment due on August 10. By August 1, it is clear that the local tomato crop will be bad and that the price of tomatoes is going to rise. S therefore contracts to sell her tomato crop to X for a higher price and then informs B that she will not deliver on August 10 as agreed. B indicates that cover is unavailable and that he is therefore going to bring a replevin action against S to force her to deliver her tomatoes to B on August 10. This replevin action will succeed. Although a tomato crop is not unique, a buyer of scarce goods for which no cover is available has a right to a replevin. In a normal tomato year, cover would probably have been available. Under such circumstances, B would be limited to an action for damages.

The Right to Retain and Enforce a Security Interest in the Goods

Buyers who rightfully reject goods or who justifiably revoke acceptance of goods that remain in their possession or control have a security interest in the goods. The security interest encompasses any payments the buyer has made for the goods as well as any expenses incurred with regard to inspection, receipt, transportation, care, and custody of the goods. [UCC Sec. 2-711(3)] A buyer with a security interest in the goods is a "person in the position of a seller." This gives the buyer the same rights as an unpaid seller. Thus, the buyer can resell, withhold delivery, or stop delivery of the goods. A buyer who chooses to resell must account to the seller for any amounts received in excess of the security interest. [UCC Secs. 2-711(3) and 2-706]

The Right to Cancel the Contract

When a seller fails to make proper delivery or repudiates the contract, the buyer can cancel or rescind the contract. In addition, a buyer who has rightfully rejected or revoked acceptance of the goods can cancel or rescind. Under these circumstances, the buyer can cancel or rescind that portion of the contract directly involved in the breach. If the seller's breach is material and substantially impairs the value of the whole contract, the buyer can cancel or rescind the whole contract. Upon notice of cancellation, both parties are relieved of any further obligations under the contract. The buyer is entitled to a return of any part of the purchase price that was paid. The cancellation has no effect on the buyer's right to recover for any breach occurring prior to the cancellation. [UCC Sec. 2-711(1)]

(Recall the case of Plotnick v. Pennsylvania Smelting earlier in this chapter.)

The right to cancel or rescind a sales contract can be lost or waived if the buyer delays in exercising it. So too, a buyer who refuses to allow the seller to make repairs or one who acts inconsistently with the intent to cancel can lose or waive the right to rescind.

BACKGROUND AND FACTS   *The Wetterows entered into a contract to purchase the Kendrick Beer Tavern and Cafe from White. They paid part of the purchase price and took possession of the tavern. Within two months, they claimed to have learned of certain fraudulent misrepresentations about the business that had been made at the time of the transaction. Their attorney immediately notified White of their desire to rescind the sales contract and filed a lawsuit to rescind. However, after the suit was filed, the Wetterows continued to operate the business and made no effort to get the case disposed of. They did not make any payments on the contract nor did they try to turn the business back over to White or account for any profits. The suit to rescind finally came to trial on White's motion a year and eight months after the original filing.*

WETTEROW v. WHITE
Supreme Court of Idaho, 1951.
71 Idaho 372, 232 P.2d 973.

DECISION AND RATIONALE   *The Wetterows were not able to rescind after delaying for over a year. Rescission is an equitable remedy, and people who seek it must therefore do equity to their adversaries. Thus, the Wetterows were obligated to act promptly after discovering the grounds for rescission (that is, the misrepresentations). Even though they were prompt in informing White of their desire to rescind, they made no effort to get the case disposed of quickly. Since the Wetterows were in default, judgment was for the restoration of the business to White and the Wetterows forfeited the payments they had made to him. In the opinion of the court: "Having thus remained in the possession of the property and the business, operating it and treating it as their own during this period of nearly two years, the plaintiffs waived any right they had to rescission of the contract, or to a recovery of payments made."*

Remedies for Fraud of the Seller

Independent of any remedies provided by the Uniform Commercial Code, the buyer can sue the seller for fraud. This remedy can be asserted even if the buyer is barred from all other remedies under the Code. Since the general principles of law remain in force under the Code, sellers can also be held liable for the

fraudulent acts of their agents. This remedy, however, is not always the best solution for an aggrieved buyer, since fraud is generally difficult to prove.

STATUTE OF LIMITATIONS

In the case of breach of a sales contract, a statute of limitations limits the period of time during which an action can be brought. The interval depends upon the type of action, the jurisdiction, and the circumstances of the case.

Actions Brought under the Uniform Commercial Code

An action brought by a buyer or seller for breach of contract must be commenced under the Code *within four years after the cause of action accrues.* A cause of action accrues for breach of warranty when the seller makes tender of delivery. This is the rule even if the aggrieved party is unaware that the cause of action has accrued. [UCC Sec. 2-725(1)] In addition to filing suit within the four-year period, an aggrieved party must ordinarily notify the breaching party of a defect within a reasonable time. [UCC Sec. 2-607(3)(a)]

Future performance warranties (those that take effect in the future) are not breached until the time for performance begins. The statute of limitations also begins to run at that time. For example, B purchases a central air-conditioning unit for her restaurant. The unit is warranted to keep the temperature below a certain level. The unit is installed in the winter, but when summer comes, the restaurant does not stay cool. Therefore, this warranty was breached in the summer and not when the unit was delivered in the winter. The statute of limitations did not begin to run until the summer.

Actions Not Falling within the Uniform Commercial Code

When a buyer or seller brings suit on a legal theory unrelated to the Code, the limitations periods specified above do *not* apply, even though the claim relates to goods. For example, B buys tires for his automobile. The tires prove to have an inherently dangerous defect. Four years and one month after purchasing the tires, B loses control of the car and injures several passengers as well as himself. B can bring a suit against the tire manufacturer based on strict liability in tort. The suit will not be governed by the Code's statute of limitations, but rather by the state's tort statute of limitations.

CONTRACTUAL PROVISIONS AFFECTING REMEDIES

The parties to a sales contract can vary their respective rights and obligations by contractual agreement. Certain limitations are placed upon the ability of parties to contract around the requirements of the UCC, but the common provisions include: (1) the liquidation or limitation of damages, (2) the limitation of remedies, and (3) the waiver of defenses.

Liquidated Damages and Limitation of Damages

The parties to a sales contract can provide that a specified amount of damages will be paid in the event that either party breaches. These damages, called **liquidated damages,** must be reasonable in amount and approximately equal to the anticipated or actual loss caused by the breach. If the provision is valid, the aggrieved party is limited to recovering only that amount of damages. If the amount of liquidated damages is unreasonably large, the provision is void as a penalty. [UCC Sec. 2-718]

Consider as an example the sale of a car. S contracts with B to sell a car for $8,000. The contract contains a liquidated damages clause that holds the breaching party liable for $5,000 in case of a breach by either party. Payment and delivery of the car are due on January 1. B tenders payment on that date, but S refuses to deliver for no valid reason. Can B demand $5,000 in damages? If the car is an antique, B will probably be able to recover. S's breach might cause B a loss of $5,000. If the car can easily be acquired on the open market, B will probably not be able to recover $5,000. The normal measure of damages will be the market price of the car less the contract price. The liquidated damages clause would in essence be imposing a penalty upon S and therefore would be void. [UCC Sec. 2-718(1)]

A buyer often makes a down payment when a contract is executed. If the buyer defaults and the contract contains a liquidated damages provision, the buyer can recover only the amount by which the down payment exceeded the amount that was specified as liquidated damages. The buyer is entitled to this sum as restitution. If the contract contains no provision for liquidated damages, the seller's damages are deemed to be 20 percent of the purchase price or $500, whichever is less. [UCC Sec. 2-718(2)(b)] The amount by which the buyer's down payment exceeded this sum must be returned to the buyer. If the seller can prove that his or her actual damages are higher, the buyer can recover only the excess over the seller's actual damages.

For example, B pays $1,250 down on a $10,000 lathe. B then breaches, and S offers no proof of the actual damages. In the absence of a liquidated damages clause, B is entitled to restitution of $750 ($1,250 less $500). If B had put $350 down on a $500 lathe, she would be entitled to $250 ($350 less $100, which is 20 percent of the purchase price).

Limitation of Remedies

A seller and a buyer can expressly provide for remedies in addition to those provided in the Code. They can also provide remedies in lieu of those provided in the Code, or they can change the measure of damages. The seller can provide that the buyer's only remedy upon breach of warranty will be repair or replacement of the item, or the seller can limit the buyer's remedy to return of the goods and refund of the purchase price. A remedy that is so provided is in addition to remedies provided in the Code unless the parties expressly agree that the remedy is exclusive of all others.

If the parties state that a remedy is exclusive of all other remedies, then it is the sole remedy. [UCC Sec. 2-719(1)] But when circumstances cause an exclusive remedy to fail of its essential purpose, the remedy will no longer be exclusive. [UCC Sec. 2-719(2)] For example, a sales contract that limits the buyer's remedy to repair or replacement fails of its essential purpose if the item cannot be repaired and no replacements are available. This situation is illustrated in the next case.

BACKGROUND AND FACTS *Dale Steele, a western Kansas farmer who owned and operated a rather large wheat and barley farm, purchased three new combines manufactured by J. I. Case. The purchase order contained a printed warranty in which Case warranted the quality of its product. The warranty promised further that if the machine should contain a defect, the company would remedy it and that if the defect could not be remedied, Case had the option to replace the machine or refund the purchase price. But it stated that in the latter case, "no further claim shall be made." From the beginning, the combines failed to work properly. After repeated complaints from Steele, Case dispatched various employees and representatives in an effort to correct the defect. Because of the many delays resulting from the faulty performance of the combines, Steele's crops were harvested some ten to fourteen days later than normal. Steele instituted this action to recover consequential damages resulting from the delays. Case ultimately agreed to supply Steele with new combines, but not until the following year.*

STEELE v. J. I. CASE CO.
Supreme Court of Kansas, 1966.
197 Kan. 554, 419 P.2d 902.

DECISION AND RATIONALE *Under the particular facts of this case, Steele was able to recover consequential damages (damages resulting from delays in harvesting) even though Case's warranty explicitly* *excluded such damages. Case warranted that any defect in a combine would be repaired; and if not repairable, the machine would be replaced. Since Case's repairs were not successful and since it did not agree to replace the combine until a year later, it did not fulfill its warranty. In the opinion of the court: "[T]he question presented in this action is whether the limitation contained [in the warranty] *** precludes recovery of consequential damages of the character shown here, damages which, we hasten to add, we think must be within the contemplation of every person in harvesting equipment who is familiar with the exacting demands of a Kansas harvest. *** Under the conditions outlined, we conclude that it would be unfair and inequitable to give effect to the provisions of limitation encompassed in *** the warranty."*

LIMITING CONSEQUENTIAL DAMAGES A contract can limit or exclude consequential damages provided the limitation is not unconscionable. When the buyer is a consumer, the limitation of consequential damages for personal injuries resulting from a breach of warranty is *prima facie* unconscionable. The limitation of consequential damages is not necessarily unconscionable where the loss is commercial in nature—for example, lost profits and property damage.

Waiver of Defenses

A buyer can be precluded from objecting to a breach of warranty by a seller in certain situations. For example, when a buyer purchases on credit, the seller usually assigns the note or account to a financial institution in order to obtain ready cash. In order to facilitate the assignment of these notes or accounts, the seller will include a waiver of defense clause in the sales contract. By entering into the contract, the buyer agrees not to assert against the assignee defenses that may apply to the seller. In essence, the buyer must complain directly to the seller, and the buyer cannot withhold payment for breach of warranty. If the financial institution is a holder in due course of the buyer's note, no defenses can be asserted against the institution even if the contract contains no waiver of defense clause. In such a case buyers are in the same position they would be in if they had signed a waiver.

QUESTIONS AND CASE PROBLEMS

1. As a result of inquiries by Sumitomo, a steel manufacturer, Goodson supplied Sumitomo with a written statement of its solvency on February 7, 1968. On February 25, 1968, Goodson and Sumitomo entered into a contract for the sale of steel to be shipped from Japan. Goodson received the steel on June 24, 1968, about two months after Sumitomo had shipped it. On July 30, 1968, Sumitomo learned that Goodson was insolvent and had been insolvent for the entire month of February 1968. The same day, Sumitomo attempted to reclaim the steel from Goodson's trustee in bankruptcy. Will Sumitomo succeed? In the matter of Goodson Steel Corp., (citation omitted) (S.D. Tex. 1968).

2. Portal Gallaries, Inc., entered into a contract with Tomar Products to sell Tomar certain paintings. Pursuant to the contract, Portal delivered some of the paintings, worth $23,000, and Tomar made a partial payment for them. Portal withheld shipment of the remaining paintings until Tomar tendered the balance of the original payment. However, Tomar decided that it did not wish to purchase any more paintings and notified Portal of its desire to cancel the contract. After receiving notice of the cancellation, Portal resold the paintings at a public auction but did

not notify Tomar of the resale. Portal then claimed that Tomar owed it the balance due for the original shipment of paintings as well as the difference between the contract price and the price that the remaining paintings brought at auction. What damages is the court likely to award Portal Gallaries? [Portal Gallaries, Inc. v. Tomar Products, Inc., 60 Misc.2d 523, 302 N.Y.S.2d. 871 (1969)]

3. Jagger Brothers and Technical Textile Company entered into a contract for the purchase and sale of 20,000 pounds of yarn at $2.15 per pound. Delivery was to be made in a number of shipments and was to be completed by December 31, 1960. On August 12, 1960, the buyer, Technical Textile, repudiated the contract. On that date the market price for yarn was $2.35 per pound. Jagger Brothers immediately brought suit, but the case did not come to trial until nearly two years later. At the time of trial, the price of yarn was $2.80 per pound. Jagger Brothers had not manufactured any of the yarn at the time Technical Textile repudiated the contract. Therefore, Jagger Brothers claimed that Technical Textile owed it the difference between the contract price ($2.15 per pound) and the market price for yarn at the time of trial ($2.80 per pound). Technical Textile argued that it was liable only for the difference between the contract and the market price at the time and place of repudiation ($2.35 per pound). Who is correct? [Jagger Brothers, Inc. v. Technical Textile Co., 202 Pa. Super. 639, 198 A.2d. 888 (1964)]

4. Beco, Inc., entered into a contract with Minnechaug Golf Course to supply Minnechaug with certain restaurant equipment. Beco delivered the restaurant equipment to Minnechaug on June 24, 1966. After using it for two months, Minnechaug attempted to return the equipment, making a vague claim that it did not work properly. Beco repeatedly offered to cure any defects, and Minnechaug refused to accept any cure. Beco then demanded payment for the equipment, and Minnechaug refused. At trial, the issue arose as to whether damages should be based upon the difference between contract price and market price at the time and place of tender or whether Minnechaug should pay the purchase price. What is the proper measure here? [Beco, Inc. v. Minnechaug Golf Course, Inc., 5 Conn. Cir. 444, 256 A.2d. 522 (1968)]

5. Westmoreland Metal Manufacturing Company made school furniture. In 1955, Willred Company entered into a contract with Westmoreland to be the latter's exclusive distributor of school furniture in the metropolitan New York area. Under this contract, Westmoreland made a number of shipments of furniture to Willred, which Willred resold to the New York Board of Education. The distributorship contract between Willred and Westmoreland was to end in December 1957, but Westmoreland, without legal justification, terminated the contract in February 1956. Just before Westmoreland breached the contract, it made a large shipment of furniture to Willred that amounted to about half the furniture that Willred had just ordered from Westmoreland. Much of the furniture was shipped in damaged condition, requiring Willred to repair it extensively before it could be resold. In addition, Willred was forced to purchase a large quantity of school furniture on the open market to satisfy a current contract with the New York Board of Education. Finally, Willred had to rent a small amount of furniture in order to satisfy its contractual obligations to the New York Board of Education. Which of these expenditures, if any, can Willred recoup from Westmoreland? [Willred Co. v. Westmoreland Metal Mfg. Co., 200 F. Supp. 59 (E.D. Pa. 1961)]

6. Phillips, who was in the market for a new car, visited Union Motors, Inc., a local Dodge dealer. When Phillips saw some of the prices that the new cars were going for, he approached one of the salespersons and stated, "That's too darn much to spend on a new car. You got anything any cheaper?" Thereupon the salesperson showed Phillips what appeared to be a slightly used 1966 Dodge and stated that the car was a "demonstrator with 2,000 miles on it, that it was like a brand new one, and that it had been handled with kid gloves." Relying on this statement, Phillips purchased the car, but later he learned that the car had been in a bad accident and had been poorly repaired. Has there been any breach here? If so, what would be the proper measure of damages? [Union Motors, Inc. v. Phillips, 241 Ark. 857, 410 S.W.2d. 747 (1967)]

7. Lehigh Valley Mills, a producer of various types of seeds, sold several hundred pounds of grass seed to Ertag, Inc., a distributor to retail outlets and retail customers. Ertag sued Lehigh for breach of warranty, claiming that the grass seed was several years old and therefore would not germinate as warranted. Ertag proved at trial that a number of its customers were municipal golf courses. They had already done their spring planting, and they learned of the breach at a time that caused them to lose several weeks of business. While none of these golf courses had yet brought suit against Ertag, Ertag claimed as damages against Lehigh the projected losses that would result

from suits that might be brought by its customers. If the court is convinced that such lawsuits against Ertag are imminent, should it allow Ertag to recover against Lehigh for these damages? [Ertag, Inc. v. Lehigh Valley Mills, Inc., 29 Leh.L.J. 487 (Pa.1962)]

8. Erdman purchased a color television set from Johnson Brothers Radio and TV Company and experienced difficulties with it from the start. Erdman immediately called Johnson, and Johnson sent two repairmen to attempt to fix the set. Johnson's repairmen were unsuccessful on the first trip and on approximately twenty subsequent trips. Erdman continued to use the set during the four weeks that Johnson attempted to repair it. After it had been on for two hours one evening, the set began to smoke and spark. At first, Erdman ignored the smoke and sparks but later left the room to call Johnson again. While he was making the call, a fire began behind the TV set and subsequently destroyed his house. Erdman sued Johnson for breach of warranty of merchantability, claiming as consequential damages the destruction of his house. Can Erdman recover? [Erdman v. Johnson Brothers Radio and TV Co., Inc., 260 Md. 190, 271 A.2d 744 (1970)]

9. In a contract between Associated Metals and Minerals Corp. and Kaiser Trading Company, Associated promised to deliver to Kaiser 4,000 tons of cryolite over the next sixteen months. After Associated had delivered about one-eighth of the cryolite to Kaiser, it repudiated the contract. Kaiser sought to enforce the contract and requested the court to grant it specific performance against Associated. Kaiser presented convincing proof at trial that only a few hundred tons of cryolite were available on the open market and that Kaiser needed the 4,000 tons that Associated had promised to deliver in order for Kaiser to fulfill its contractual obligations to a number of other industrial companies. Should the court grant specific performance in this case? [Kaiser Trading Co. v. Associated Metals and Minerals Corp., 321 F. Supp. 923 (N.D. Cal. 1970)]

10. Denkin manufactured refrigeration equipment. Sterner entered into a contract with Denkin to purchase refrigeration equipment that was needed for a new grocery store. The contract included a clause allowing Denkin to retake all the goods that it had delivered to Sterner and to recover the entire price if Sterner breached the contract. Sterner signed the contract but later found that a number of other manufacturers could supply refrigeration equipment at far lower prices than Denkin. In a suit by Denkin against Sterner, can Denkin enforce the liquidated damages provisions stated above? [Denkin v. Sterner, 10 D.&C.2d. 203 (Pa. 1956)]

23

Commercial Paper
Basic Concepts of
Commercial Paper

Commercial paper can be defined as any written promise or order to pay a sum of money. Drafts, checks, and promissory notes are typical examples. Commercial paper is transferred more readily than ordinary contract rights, and persons who acquire it normally assume less risk than the ordinary assignee of a contract right.

FUNCTIONS AND PURPOSES OF COMMERCIAL PAPER

Commercial paper has two basic functions. It is a substitute for money, and it is a credit device.

A Substitute for Money

Commercial paper is used when a debt is paid by check. Debtors can use cash, but for convenience and safety, they use commercial paper. The substitute for money function of commercial paper developed in the Middle Ages. Merchants began to deposit their precious metal with bankers to avoid the dangers of loss or theft. When they needed funds to pay for the goods that they were buying, they gave the seller a written order addressed to the bank. This authorized the bank to deliver part of the precious metal to the seller. These orders were called *bills of exchange* and were sometimes used as a substitute for money. Today people use mainly checks, but they also use drafts and promissory notes that are payable either on demand or at some specified date in the future. That some commercial paper is a substitute for money is further indicated by the fact that the Federal Reserve's official definition of what is called the "narrow" money supply (M_1) is currency (dollar bills and coins) in the hands of the public and demand deposits (that is, checking account balances).

A Credit Device

Commercial paper creates credit. When a buyer gives a seller a promissory note by which the buyer agrees to pay in sixty days, the seller has essentially extended sixty days credit to the buyer. The credit aspect of commercial paper was also developed in the Middle Ages soon after bills of exchange began to be used as substitutes for money. Merchants were able to give to sellers bills of exchange that were not payable until a future date. Since the seller would wait until a maturity date to collect, this was a form of extending credit to the buyer.

DISCOUNTING The holder of a promissory note payable in sixty or ninety days who wishes to sell this instrument to a third party can do so for immediate cash in return. Typically, banks buy these instruments and wait until their maturity date to receive payment. In order to induce a bank to buy a promissory note, the holder of the instrument accepts a discount of, say, 5, 10, or 15 percent of the face amount. In effect, the bank pays less than the amount it will eventually collect as a way of charging interest.

The Law of Commercial Paper

Some historians believe that promissory notes were used more than two thousand years ago. In any event, by the thirteenth century, bills of exchange were used extensively, particularly in conducting foreign trade. In the earlier Middle Ages, English courts were not empowered to enforce commercial agreements. Therefore, merchants created their own methods for en-

forcing rights. Part of these methods were a form of the Law Merchant, discussed in Chapter 1.

By the eighteenth and nineteenth centuries, English and American courts recognized Law Merchant principles relating to commercial paper. In England in 1882, a Bills of Exchange Act that codified the common law on the subject was passed. In 1896, the Uniform Negotiable Instruments Law (NIL) was presented by the American Bar Association to the states, and all of them passed it eventually. Article 3 of the Uniform Commercial Code superseded the Uniform Negotiable Instruments Law. Every state has enacted Article 3, which is quite similar to the Uniform Negotiable Instruments Law.

TYPES OF COMMERCIAL PAPER

Section 3-104 of the Uniform Commercial Code specifies four types of instruments—drafts, checks, certificates of deposit, and notes.

Drafts

A draft, (or bill of exchange) is an unconditional written order. The party creating it (the *drawer*) orders another party (the *drawee*) to pay money to a third (the *payee*). Exhibit 23-1 shows a typical draft. The drawee must be obligated to the drawer either by agreement or through a debt relationship before acceptance can occur. (Acceptance occurs when the drawee signs the draft agreeing to honor it as presented.)

TIME AND SIGHT DRAFTS A time draft is a draft which is payable at a future time. A sight draft is payable on sight, that is, when the holder presents it for payment, or at a stated time after sight.

TRADE ACCEPTANCES The **trade acceptance** is a time draft that is ordinarily used in the sale of goods. The seller is both drawer and payee on this draft. Essentially, the draft orders the buyer to pay a specified sum of money to the seller at a stated time in the future. To illustrate: Good Yard Company sells $50,000 of fabric to Lane Dresses, Incorporated, each fall on terms requiring payment to be made in ninety days. One year Good Yard needs cash, so it draws a *trade acceptance* that orders Lane to pay $50,000 to the order of Good Yard Company ninety days hence. Good Yard presents the paper to Lane. Lane *accepts* by signing the face of the paper and returns it to Good Yard. Lane's acceptance creates an enforceable promise to pay the installment when it comes due in ninety days. Good Yard can sell the trade acceptance in the commercial money market more easily than it can assign the $50,000 account receivable. Thus, trade acceptances are the standard credit instruments in sales transactions. Exhibit 23-2 shows a trade acceptance.

EXHIBIT 23–1   TYPICAL DRAFT

F 501

Saint Paul, Minn. __January 16__ 19 80 $ 1,000.00 ------

__Ninety days after above date__ ------------ PAY TO THE ORDER OF **The First National Bank** 22-1
OF SAINT PAUL, MINNESOTA

------- One thousand and no/100 --- Dollars

VALUE RECEIVED AND CHARGE THE SAME TO ACCOUNT OF

To___ Bank of Warren   CANCELLED

Warren, Michigan   Stephen L. Eastman

EXHIBIT 23–2   TYPICAL TRADE ACCEPTANCE

Mytown, California   March 15   19 80

To ___ **The ABC Company**

On__ **June 15, 1980**   Pay to the order of __ **XYZ Corporation**

----- One thousand and no/100 -------------- Dollars ($ --- 1,000.00 -----)

The obligations of the acceptor hereof arise out of the purchase of goods from the drawer. The drawee may accept this bill payable at any bank or trust company in the United States which such drawee may designate.

Accepted at **Blackacre, N.Y.** on **March 15** 19 **79**
Payable at __ **Bank of Blackacre**
Blackacre, New York
Buyer's Signature ___ **ABC Company**
By Agent or Officer __ Tom Smith / V. Pres.

XYZ Corporation

By Jo Jones / pres.

TRADE ACCEPTANCE

BANK DRAFTS A bank draft is an instrument drawn by one bank upon another bank. Clearly, the first bank must have money on deposit with the drawee bank. The bank draft is often used for the same purpose as a cashier's check.

Checks

A **check** is a distinct type of draft, drawn on a bank and payable on demand. Checks are discussed more fully in Chapter 28. Note here, however, that on certain types of checks, the bank is both the drawer and the drawee. For example, cashier's checks drawn by the bank on itself are payable on demand when issued. Traveler's checks are drawn on the bank or on a financial institution, but they require the payee's authorized signature before becoming payable.

Promissory Notes

The **note** is the simplest form of commercial paper. It is a promise between two parties in which one person (the maker) promises to pay a sum of money to another person (the payee). Notes can be payable at a definite time or on demand. Note paper can name a payee or merely be payable to bearer. Whenever there are only two parties to the note it is commonly called a **promissory note.**

Notes are used to extend credit in business in many ways. For example, in real estate transactions, a buyer executes a promissory note for the unpaid balance on a house, secured by a mortgage on the property being purchased. This is called a *mortgage note*. A note which is secured by personal property is called a *collateral note*. A sample promissory note is shown in Exhibit 23-3.

Certificates of Deposit

A certificate of deposit is an acknowledgment by a bank of receipt of money with an engagement to repay it. [UCC Sec. 3-104(2)(c)] Certificates of deposit in small denominations are often sold by savings and loan associations, savings banks, and commercial banks. They are called small CDs and are for amounts up to $100,000. Certificates of deposit for amounts over $100,000 are called large CDs.[1] Exhibit 23-4 shows a typical small CD.

OTHER WAYS OF CLASSIFYING COMMERCIAL PAPER

The four-way classification of commercial paper presented above follows the language of the Uniform Commercial Code. There are numerous other ways in which to classify commercial paper, two of which are treated here.

Demand Instruments and Time Instruments

Commercial paper can be classified as demand instruments or as time instruments. A demand instrument is payable on demand, that is, whenever the holder—a possessor *to whom the instrument runs*—chooses to present it to the maker in the case of a note or the drawee in the case of a draft. (Instruments payable on demand include those payable on sight or on presentation, and in which no time for payment is stated.) [UCC Sec. 3-108] Time instruments are payable at a future date. All checks are demand instruments because, by definition, they must be payable on demand. Checking accounts are called demand deposits.

PARTIES TO COMMERCIAL PAPER

To review, notes have two original parties—the maker and the payee, and drafts or checks have three original parties—the drawer, the drawee, and the payee. Sometimes two of the parties to a draft can be the same person (drawer/drawee; drawer/payee). Once an instrument is issued, additional parties can become involved. The

---

1. Large CDs are included in certain definitions of the money supply because they are fully negotiable and because the interest they pay is not regulated by the Federal Reserve. Large CDs may, however, be subject to regulation by the state banking authority of the state in which they are issued.

following sections describe the various parties to commercial paper after the instrument has been issued.

Indorsers

The payee of a note or draft can transfer it by signing (indorsing) it and delivering it to another person. By doing this, the payee becomes an indorser. For example, Carol receives a graduation check for $25. She can transfer the check to her mother (or anyone) by signing it on the back. Carol is an indorser.

Indorsees

The person who receives the indorsed instrument is the indorsee. In the example above,

---

EXHIBIT 23-3   TYPICAL PROMISSORY NOTE

$ ---3,000.00 ---- Saint Paul, Minnesota   April 30 , 19 80   Due 6/20/80   NO.096-85-710

OFFICER Clark

-------- Sixty days -- after date,   BY RMD

for value received, the undersigned jointly and severally promise to pay to the order of THE FIRST NATIONAL BANK OF   ACCRUAL /

SAINT PAUL at its office in Saint Paul, Minnesota, $ --- Three Thousand and no/100 Dollars   ☑NEW ☐REN'L

with interest thereon from date hereof at the rate of - 15 per cent per annum (computed on the basis of actual days and   ☑SECURED

a year of 360 days) as indicated in No. 7 below.   ☐UNSECURED

☐ 7 INTEREST IS PAYABLE AT MATURITY
☐ 8 INTEREST IS PAID TO MATURITY
☐ 9 INTEREST IS PAYABLE _____ BEGINNING ON _____
☐

CANCELLED

The holder of this note may at its option without notice declare this note immediately due... [body text partially obscured]

SIGNATURE *Lawrence E. Roberts*   SIGNATURE *Margaret P. Roberts*

SIGNATURE _____   SIGNATURE _____

32-364 (8-71)

Left margin labels: ☐ OTHER ☐ SAVINGS ☐ INSURANCE ☑ SECURITIES SEC. AGREEMENT 1. INV. & ACCTS. 2. CONSUMER GOODS 3. EQUIP.

EXHIBIT 23-4   TYPICAL SMALL CD

THE FIRST NATIONAL BANK OF SAINT PAUL   22-1/960   Number 3999
NEGOTIABLE CERTIFICATE OF DEPOSIT

SAINT PAUL, MINNESOTA, February 15 , 19 80

THIS CERTIFIES to the deposit in this Bank of the sum of $ 5,000.00 -------

----- Five thousand and no/100 --------------------------------- DOLLARS

which is payable to bearer on the 15th day of July , 19 80 , against presentation and surrender of this certificate, and bears interest at the rate of 7 3/4 % per annum, to be computed (on the basis of 360 days and actual days elapsed) to, and payable at, maturity. No payment may be made prior to, and no interest runs after, that date. Payable at maturity in federal funds, and if desired, at Manufacturers Hanover Trust Company, New York.

THE FIRST NATIONAL BANK OF SAINT PAUL

BY *Paul* **CANCELLED** SIGNATURE

54-610

Carol's mother is the indorsee. She is entitled to the $25 payment by virtue of Carol's indorsement, and she can indorse the check to someone else or to a bank and thus become an indorser as well.

Holders

The term **holder** includes any person in possession of an instrument that runs to him or her, for example, named payees in possession of order instruments.[2] To illustrate: A check made to the order of John Doe in his possession makes John Doe a holder. So, too, if a promissory note written by Sam Smith promising to pay a sum of money to the order of Tom Jones, is in Jones's possession, then Jones is a holder. If Jones signs the back of the note and transfers (negotiates) it to Adam White, the note becomes bearer paper, and White becomes the holder.

The holder and the owner of negotiable paper can often be the same person, but not necessarily. For example, a thief who steals a bearer instrument is a *holder* under commercial law principles (but obviously the thief is not the owner). Nonetheless, the thief can legally transfer (negotiate) the bearer instrument to another person, who then becomes a *holder*.

HOLDER IN DUE COURSE Under UCC Sec. 3-302, a holder in due course (HDC) is a person who acquires an instrument for value in a good faith transaction without knowing it is defective. It is easier for an HDC to collect payment on an instrument than it is for an assignee of a non-negotiable contract to collect payment. The assignee is subject to all outstanding defenses of prior parties; the HDC is protected from all but a few defenses.[3]

---

2. UCC Sec. 1-201(17) defines *holder* as "a person who is in possession of a document of title or an instrument or an investment security drawn, issued, or indorsed to him or to his order or to bearer or in blank."

3. The HDC is subject to real defenses. These generally involve the validity of the instrument, for example, legal capacity or fraud. [UCC Sec. 3-305] An HDC is free from all personal defenses between prior parties, for example, breach of contract.

HOLDER THROUGH A HOLDER IN DUE COURSE An ordinary holder whose manner of acquisition fails to meet the requirements of a holder in due course can still be afforded HDC protection by proving that any prior holder qualified as a holder in due course. [UCC Sec. 3-201(1)]

Accommodation Parties

An accommodation party is a person who signs an instrument for the purpose of lending his or her name to another party to the instrument. [UCC Sec. 3-415 (1)]. The liability of an accommodation party depends on the capacity in which he or she signed. A person who signs on behalf of a maker or an indorser assumes the same liability as the maker or indorser. For example, Melinda Smith is the maker of a promissory note in which she promises to pay Ted Parker (the payee) $500 for Parker's car. Parker, however, is unsure of Smith's ability to pay and asks her to have her mother sign as an accommodation party. When the mother signs, she becomes an *accommodation maker* and is liable as a maker of the instrument.

Acceptor

A person who accepts an instrument (a draft) is known as an *acceptor*. An acceptance is a drawee's signed engagement or promise to honor a draft as presented. The mere signature of the drawee on the instrument is a sufficient acceptance. Customarily, the signature is written vertically across the face of the instrument, but since a drawee has no other reason to sign, the signature in any other place, even on the back of the instrument, is sufficient. [UCC Sec. 3-410 and comment 4]

Guarantor

A person who signs an instrument as a *guarantor* engages to pay it if it is not paid when due. Thus, a guarantor will not be liable unless the instrument is not paid. A guarantor who is required to pay can recover from the person who should have paid.

QUESTIONS AND
CASE PROBLEMS

1.   Adam Smith, a college student, wished to purchase a new component stereo system from John Locke Stereo, Inc. Since Smith did not have the cash to pay for the entire stereo system, he offered to sign a note promising to pay $150 per month for the next six months. Locke Stereo, anxious to sell the system to Smith, agreed to accept the promissory note as long as Smith had one of his professors sign it. Smith did this and tendered a note to John Locke Stereo that stated, "I, Adam Smith, promise to pay John Locke Stereo or its order the sum of $150 per month for the next six months." The note was signed by Adam Smith and his business law professor. About a week later, John Locke Stereo, which was badly in need of cash, signed the back of the note and sold it to Fidelity Bank. How are each of the four parties designated in commercial paper parlance?

2.   Larson and Adkins were partners in a law firm. Larson had just won a case for her client, Brown, against Bill Bucks. When Larson went to collect the judgment from Bucks, Bucks wrote out a check that read: "Pay to the order of Larson and Adkins $6,000,000. Signed Bill Bucks." On the top of the check were the words "Hanover Trust." When Larson went to deposit the check in the trust account that she had set up for her client, she signed the back of the check "L. Larson." How are each of these parties designated in commercial paper law?

3.   Negotiable instruments play an important part in commercial transactions. Different needs can be fulfilled by using different types of instruments in certain ways. For instance, many insurance companies use a form of draft instead of a check to remit insurance benefits. The insurance company is both the drawer and the drawee; the beneficiary (the person receiving the money) is the payee; and the draft is made payable through a named bank in which the insurance company maintains a large account. What are the advantages of using such a draft?

4.   Often when two parties to a sale are strangers to each other, and the sale is for a substantial amount of money, the selling party will insist that the purchaser make payment with a cashier's check. A cashier's check is a check for which the bank is both the drawer and the drawee. To purchase a cashier's check, a person goes to a bank teller, tenders the amount of money for which the check is to be payable, and supplies the teller with the name of the person who is to be the payee of the check. Once the payee's name is inscribed on the check, only the payee (or a person to whom the payee negotiates the check) will be able to receive money for the check. What problem might arise if a seller asks a prospective buyer of goods to make payment with a cashier's check, and the buyer purchases the check, naming the seller as the payee? How can this problem be avoided?

5.   A California statute makes possession of a check with intent to defraud a crime. Norwood had in his possession an instrument that had the following title in the upper right-hand corner: "AUDITOR CONTROLLER'S GENERAL WARRANT COUNTY OF LOS ANGELES." Below this the instrument stated, "The treasurer of the County of Los Angeles will pay to the order of John Norwood $5,000." At trial the district attorney proved that Norwood had intended to defraud the County of Los Angeles of $5,000 while in possession of the above instrument. You are Norwood's attorney, and you are now appealing the case. What arguments would you make to have Norwood's conviction overturned? [People v. Norwood, 26 Cal.3d 148, 103 Cal. Rptr. 7 (1972)]

24

Commercial Paper
Negotiability

This chapter will examine a special type of commercial paper—the negotiable instrument. The basic difference between a negotiable instrument and an ordinary contract is that negotiable instruments must have a specific form.

Whenever a dispute arises over the enforceability of an instrument, it is of vital importance to know whether it is negotiable. If it *is* negotiable, all disputes are resolved under Article 3 of the Uniform Commercial Code. If it is *not* negotiable, disputes must be resolved under ordinary contract law. The holder-in-due-course doctrine is recognized only under Article 3. Thus, anyone attempting to utilize this doctrine in enforcing an instrument must show that the instrument is negotiable.

Furthermore, commercial paper is relatively worthless as a substitute for money unless it is freely transferable—that is, unless a prospective purchaser is willing to accept it routinely.

THE REQUIREMENTS OF NEGOTIABILITY

Section 3-104(1) of the UCC specifies the requirements of negotiability. A negotiable instrument must:

1. Be in writing.
2. Be signed by the maker or drawer.
3. Be an unconditional promise or order.
4. Contain a specific sum of money.
5. Be payable on demand or at a definite time.
6. Be payable to order or to bearer.
7. Exclude any other promise, order, obligation, or power.[1]
8. Identify the drawee specifically if the instrument is a third-party instrument.

A Writing

Negotiable instruments must be in *written form*. Clearly, an oral promise can create the danger of fraud or make it difficult to assign liability. Negotiable instruments must possess the quality of certainty that only formal written expression can give.

PRACTICAL LIMITATIONS ON THE WRITING There are certain practical limitations concerning the writing and the substance on which it is placed.

1. The writing must be on material that will lend itself to *permanence*. Negotiable instruments have been written on the sides of cows, carved in blocks of ice, and recorded on other impermanent surfaces. However, these forms remain written for only a relatively short period of time. For example, if Mary writes in the sand, "I promise to pay $100 to the order of Tom," this is not a writing because it lacks permanence.
2. The writing must have *portability*. This is not a legal requirement, but if an instrument is not movable, it cannot meet the requirement that it be freely transferable. A promise to pay written on the side of a cow is formally correct, but a cow cannot easily be transferred in the ordinary course of business.

Signed by the Maker or the Drawer

For an instrument to be negotiable, it must be signed by the maker if it is a note or by the

drawer if it is a draft or check. [UCC Sec. 3-104(1)(a)] Extreme latitude is granted in determining what constitutes a signature. Section 1-201(39) of the UCC defines the word *signed* as "[including] any symbol executed or adopted by a party with present intention to authenticate a writing." Section 3-401(2) expands upon this: "A signature is made by use of name, including any trade or assumed name, upon an instrument, or by any word or mark used in lieu of a written signature." Thus, initials, an X, or a thumbprint will suffice. A trade name or an assumed name is sufficient even if it is false. Parol evidence is admissible in identifying the signer. When the signer is identified, the signature becomes effective. [UCC Sec. 3-104, Comment 2] Also, a rubber stamp bearing a person's name, when used by that person or an authorized agent, constitutes a signature.

PLACEMENT OF THE SIGNATURE The location of the signature on the document is unimportant. The usual place is the lower right-hand corner, but this is not required. A handwritten statement on the body of the instrument, such as "I, Mary Jones, promise to pay John Doe," is sufficient. [UCC Sec. 3-401, Comment 2]

There are virtually no limitations on the manner in which a signature can be made, but it is necessary to be careful when receiving an instrument that has been signed in an unusual way. The burden of proving the genuineness of a signature rests on the recipient. Furthermore, an unusual signature clearly decreases the marketability of an instrument because it creates uncertainty.

Unconditional Promise or Order

The terms of a promise or order have to be included in the writing on the face of a negotiable instrument and must not be conditioned upon the happening or failure to happen of some collateral agreement. [UCC Sec. 3-105(2)(a)]

PROMISE OR ORDER In order for an instrument to be negotiable, it must contain an

---

1. But see UCC Sec. 3-112.

express order or promise to pay. A mere acknowledgment of the debt, which might logically *imply* a promise, is not sufficient under the Uniform Commercial Code because the promise must be an *affirmative* undertaking. For example, the traditional I.O.U. is only an acknowledgment of indebtedness. Therefore, it is not a negotiable instrument. [UCC Sec. 3-102 Comment 2] But if such words as *to be paid on demand* or *due on demand* are added, the need for an affirmative promise is satisfied. For example, if a buyer executes a promissory note using the words, "I promise to pay $1,000 to the order of the seller for the purchase of goods X, Y, Z," then the requirement for a negotiable instrument is satisfied.

A certificate of deposit is different. Here, the requisite promise is satisfied because the bank's acknowledgment of the deposit and the other terms of the instrument clearly indicate a promise.

An order is usually associated with three-party instruments, such as trade acceptances, checks, and drafts. An order directs a third party to pay the instrument as drawn. The order is mandatory even if it is written in a courteous form with words like *please pay* or *kindly pay*. However, precise language must be used. An order stating, "I wish you would pay," does not fulfill the requirement of precision. [UCC Sec. 3-102(1)(b)] In addition to being precise, an effective order must specifically identify the drawee (the person who must pay). A bank's name printed on the face of a check, for example, sufficiently designates the bank as drawee.

UNCONDITIONAL

A negotiable instrument's utility as a substitute for money or as a credit device would be dramatically reduced if it had *conditional* promises attached to it. It would be expensive and time-consuming to investigate such conditional promises, and, therefore, the free transferability of negotiable instruments would be greatly reduced. There would be substantial administrative costs associated with processing conditional promises. Furthermore, the payee would risk the possibility of the condition not occurring. If X promises to pay Y

$10,000 only if a certain ship reaches port safely, anyone interested in purchasing the promissory note would have to investigate whether the ship arrived. Additionally, the facts that the investigation disclosed might be incorrect. To avoid such problems, the UCC provides that only unconditional promises or orders can be negotiable. [UCC Sec. 3-104(1)(b)] However, the Code expands the definition of *unconditional* in order to make sure that certain conditions do not render an otherwise negotiable instrument nonnegotiable.

FACTORS NOT AFFECTING NEGOTIABILITY

Many problems in interpreting unconditionality are resolved by Section 3-105 of the UCC:

A promise or order otherwise unconditional is not made conditional by the fact that the instrument (a) is subject to implied or constructive conditions; or (b) states its consideration * ** or the transaction which gave rise to the instrument * * *; or (c) refers to or states that it arises out of a separate agreement * * *; or * * * (e) states that it is secured, whether by mortgage reservation or title or otherwise; or (f) indicates a particular account to be debited or any other fund or source from which reimbursement is expected; or (g) is limited to payment out of a particular fund or the proceeds of a particular source, if the instrument is issued by a government or governmental agency unit; or, (h) is limited to payment out of the entire assets of a partnership, unincorporated association, trust or estate * * *.

Implied or Constructive Conditions Without the rule allowing implied or constructive conditions, no instrument could be negotiable. Implied conditions, such as good faith and commercial reasonableness appear in virtually every example of a negotiable instrument.

Statements of Consideration Many instruments state the terms of the underlying agreement as a matter of standard business practice. Somewhere on its face, the instrument refers to the transaction or agreement for which it is being used in payment. The policy of the Uniform Commercial Code is to integrate standard trade usages into its provisions. For example, the words *as per contract* or *this debt arises from the sale of goods X and Y* do not render an instrument nonnegotiable. If James Quinta writes, "On July 14, 1980, I promise to pay to the order of Louis Sneed $100 in full payment for the TV set that Louis Sneed will deliver to me on July 2, 1980, signed James Quinta," this can be a negotiable instrument. The statement concerning the TV set is not a condition. It describes the consideration for which the note is given.

Reference to Other Agreements The UCC provides that mere *reference* to another agreement does not affect negotiability. If, on the other hand, the instrument is *made subject* to the other agreement, it will be nonnegotiable. A reference to another agreement is normally inserted for the purpose of keeping a record or giving information to anyone who may be interested. Notes frequently refer to separate agreements that give special rights to a creditor for an acceleration of payment or to a debtor for prepayment. References to these rights do not destroy the negotiability of the instrument. For example, an instrument states, "On January 23, 1981, I promise to pay to the order of Patricia Senior $1,000, this note being secured under a security agreement and lien upon my 1974 Dodge Dart, noted upon the title certificate thereof, signed Henry Winn." This instrument is negotiable. A statement that an instrument's payment is secured by collateral will not render an otherwise negotiable instrument nonnegotiable. [UCC Sec. 3-105, Comment 5]

In the following case, a promissory note that incorporated and was made *subject to* another agreement was rendered nonnegotiable.

BACKGROUND AND FACTS *Holly Hill Acres was the maker of a promissory note that named Rogers and Blythe as payees. Holly Hill gave the note to Rogers and Blythe as payment for certain property, and they retained a mortgage (lien) on the property. The note stated in part: "This note is secured by a mortgage on real estate ***. The terms of said mortgage are by this reference made part hereof." Subsequently, Rogers and Blythe assigned the promissory note and the mortgage to Charter Bank of Gainesville. Holly Hill defaulted on the note, and, when the bank sued to recover, Holly Hill claimed that Rogers and Blythe had fraudulently induced it to purchase land. Holly Hill refused to pay on the note. The bank argued that it was a special type of assignee called a holder in due course because the promissory note was a negotiable instrument. This being so, the bank claimed an unhampered right to recover on the note despite any underlying disputes between Holly Hill and Rogers and Blythe. (A holder in due course takes a negotiable instrument free of most claims of other parties. This is the rule only when negotiable commercial paper is involved.)*

DECISION AND RATIONALE *Holly Hill Acres could assert fraud as a defense because the bank was not a holder in due course. For an assignee of a promissory to be a holder in due course, the note must first be negotiable. Since the promissory note is question incorporated the terms of the mortgage, it was non-negotiable. According to the court: "To be a negotiable instrument, [a writing] must *** contain an unconditional promise to pay ***. A promise or order is not unconditional if the instrument states that it is subject to or governed by any other agreement."*

HOLLY HILL ACRES, LTD. v. CHARTER BANK OF GAINESVILLE
District Court of Florida, 1975.
314 So.2d 209.

Secured by a Mortgage A simple statement in an otherwise negotiable note, indicating that the note is secured by a mortgage, does not destroy its negotiability. Actually, such a statement might make the note even more acceptable in commerce. Note that the statement that a note is secured by a mortgage does not stipulate that the maker's promise to pay is subject to the terms and conditions of the mortgage.

Indication of Particular Funds or Accounts If a particular fund out of which reimbursement is to be made or a particular account to be debited with the amount is indicated, this does not affect negotiability. Consider the following examples. A note dated March 3, 1979, reads, "Gilbert Corporation promises to pay to the order of the Miami Herald $150 on demand, charged to advertising expense, signed Harold Henry, Treasurer, Gilbert Corporation." This is negotiable. The phrase "charged to advertising expense" is merely a posting instruction to the corporation's accounting department. If a note states that "Jones plans to liquidate real estate to pay this obligation," the note is still considered negotiable.[2] On the other hand, if the instrument states that it is payable *only* from a particular fund or source, it then becomes conditional. For example, an instrument that states, "Payment of obligation only from a collection of accounts receivable," will be nonnegotiable. [UCC Sec. 3-105(2)(a)] The two exceptions to this rule are instruments issued by government agencies that are payable out of particular revenue funds and instruments limited to partnership, estate, or trust assets.

PROVISIONS NOT PERMITTED Subsection 2 of Section 3-105 lists two specific provisions that render a writing conditional and therefore nonnegotiable. A promise or order is conditional if the instrument states that (1) it is subject to or governed by any other agreement or (2) it is to be paid only out of a particular fund or source except as provided elsewhere in this section.

Instruments subject to other agreements have already been the subject of some of our discussion above. If the language indicates that promises or orders are subject to some other agreement, they are nonnegotiable. These instruments are typically unmarketable because prospective purchasers of such interest will not search out the other agreements to see what their actual provisions are.

Instruments payable only out of a specified fund are normally nonnegotiable. Such a promise or order is impliedly conditioned upon the fund being in existence on the date of maturity. Note, however, as discussed above that merely naming the fund from which payment is to be made, without use of such words as "only" do *not* render an instrument nonnegotiable.

Sum Certain in Money

Negotiable instruments must state the amount to be paid in a *sum certain of money*. This requirement promotes clarity and certainty in determining the value of the instrument. [UCC Sec. 3-104(1)(b)] Any promise to pay in the future is risky because the value of money (purchasing power) fluctuates. Nonetheless, the present value of such an instrument can still be estimated with a reasonable degree of accuracy by financial experts. If the instrument's value were stated in terms of goods or services, it would be too difficult to ascertain the value of those goods and services at the time the instrument was to be discounted.[3]

The UCC mandates that negotiable commercial paper be paid wholly in money. For example, a promise to pay $100 and deliver 10,000 chairs made out of wicker on January 1, 1982, is not a negotiable instrument; neither is a promise to perform 1,000 hours of skywriting.

---

2. Southern Baptist Hospital v. Williams, 89 So.2d 769 (La. App. 1956).

3. Discounting means transferring an instrument for which payment by the maker or drawer is not yet due to another party in exchange for face value of the instrument in cash, less some interest charge.

SUM CERTAIN   The term *sum certain* means an amount that is ascertainable from the instrument itself without reference to an outside source. A demand note payable with 8 percent interest meets the requirement of sum certain because its amount can be determined at the time it is payable. Section 3-106(1) of the UCC states that the sum is not rendered uncertain by the fact that it is to be paid

(a) with stated interest or by stated installments; or (b) with stated different rates of interest before or after default or a specified date; or (c) with a stated discount or addition if paid before or after the date fixed for payment; * * *

Thus, when the payee calls for payment and the amount due is certain, any such commercial paper will be freely transferable and commercially acceptable.

Instruments that provide for payment of interest at prevailing bank rates are generally nonnegotiable because bank rates fluctuate. In international trade, notes that are to be paid in another currency satisfy the "sum certain" requirement. If X promises to pay 1,000 French francs, this note meets the certainty requirement even though the parties must refer to exchange rates that are not embodied in the instrument. The Code, therefore, makes an exception to its own general rule because of the realities of international trade. [UCC Sec. 3-107]

Often, instruments have provisions authorizing court costs and attorneys' fees upon default. In Section 3-106(1)(e), the UCC indicates that an instrument with such provisions still meets the sum certain requirement and is therefore still negotiable. Providing for collection costs and attorneys' fees lessens some of the costs and risks that a bank (or other institution) dealing in commercial paper would otherwise incur. Note, though, that some states have invalidated such provisions either by statute or by judicial decision. In states where such provisions are legal, the fees must be reasonable, or the clause will be voided as against public policy.

The elements that determine negotiability must be present on the face of the instrument. In the following case, the amount of a finance charge was not apparent from the face of the note.

BACKGROUND AND FACTS   *Walls purchased a car from Morris Chevrolet and signed a promissory note and security agreement on the same piece of paper. The note stated the amount owed and the finance charge, but it did not state the amount that would be owed if the note was prepaid. This amount, however, could be determined from the security agreement, which was on the same paper. (The promissory note referred to the security agreement but did not incorporate its terms.) If Walls could show that the promissory note was negotiable, he could recover damages under a statute that prohibits acceptance of a negotiable instrument in conjunction with a consumer credit sale.*

DECISION AND RATIONALE   *Walls could not recover under the statute because the promissory note at issue was not a negotiable instrument. For an instrument to be negotiable, the sum payable must be a sum certain. This includes the sum payable when payment is accelerated. The court concluded as follows: "It is our opinion that a note cannot depend upon another agreement for elements of negotiability whether that agreement is attached to the note or separate from it ***. Negotiable notes are designed to be couriers without excess luggage under both the prior law*

WALLS v. MORRIS CHEVROLET, INC.
Court of Appeals of Oklahoma, 1973.
515 P.2d 1405.

and under the Code and so negotiability must be determined from the face of the note without regard to outside sources (with rare exceptions) so that the taker may know that he takes a negotiable instrument with the insurance of collectability provided by the Code and not an ordinary contract subject to the possibility of all defenses by the maker."

MONEY AND NO OTHER PROMISE The Uniform Commercial Code in Section 3-104(1)(b) provides that a sum certain is to be payable in "money and no other promise." The Code defines money as "a medium of exchange authorized or adopted by a domestic or foreign government as a part of its currency." [UCC Sec. 1-201(24)]

If, in consideration of a loan, Y promises to deliver fifty liters of 1964 Chateau Lafite, this is not sufficient for the instrument to be negotiable because the note is not payable in money. If Y then promises to pay $1,000 and deliver the wine, the instrument is still not negotiable because it is not payable *entirely* in money. X can promise to pay 50,000 Spanish pesetas in return for a loan because the instrument specifies a recognized foreign currency. The UCC has a special provision for such notes. [UCC Sec. 3-107(2)] Any instrument payable in the U.S. with a face amount stated in a foreign currency can be paid in the equivalent in U.S. dollars at the due date, unless the paper expressly requires payment in the foreign currency. Consider an instrument that is drafted in Guatemala City, is payable in Miami, Florida, and expressly calls for payment in 100 Guatemalan *quetzales*. The instrument will be deemed payable in money.

On the other hand, an instrument payable in U.S. government bonds or in shares of IBM stock is not negotiable because neither bonds nor stocks are a medium of exchange recognized by the U.S. government.

Payable on Demand or at a Definite Time

Section 3-104(1)(c) of the Uniform Commercial Code requires that a negotiable instrument "be payable on demand or at a definite time." Clearly, in order to ascertain the value of a negotiable instrument, it is necessary to know when the maker or acceptor can be compelled to pay. It is also necessary to know when the obligations of secondary parties—drawers, indorsers and guarantors—will arise. Finally, it is necessary to know the time during which the instrument will be valid before it expires by operation of the law, through the statute of limitations. With an interest-bearing instrument, it is necessary to know the exact interval during which the interest will accrue in order to determine the present value of the instrument.

PAYABLE ON DEMAND Instruments that are payable on demand usually contain the words *payable at sight* or *payable upon presentment*. No time for payment is specified, and the drawee must pay money for the instrument whenever it is tendered. [UCC Sec. 3-108]

PAYABLE AT A DEFINITE TIME To be negotiable, time instruments must be payable at a definite time that is specified on the face of the instrument. The maker or drawer is under no obligation to pay until the specified time has elapsed.

Many time instruments contain additional terms that seem to conflict with the definite time requirement. In Section 3-109, the Uniform Commercial Code attempts to clear up some of these potential problems:

(1) An instrument is payable at a definite time if by its terms it is payable
(a) on or before a stated date or at a fixed period after a stated date; or
(b) at a fixed period after sight; or
(c) at a definite time subject to any acceleration; or

(d) at a definite time subject to extension at the option of the holder, or to extension to a further definite time at the option of the maker or acceptor or automatically upon or after a specified act or event.

(2) An instrument which by its terms is otherwise payable only upon an act or event uncertain as to time of occurrence is not payable at a definite time even though the act or event has occurred.

Consider an example that relates to Subsection (2). An instrument is dated June 1, 1979, and states, "One year after the death of my grandfather, James Taylor, I promise to pay to the order of Henry Winkler $500. Signed Mary Taylor." This is nonnegotiable. Because the date of the grandfather's death is uncertain, the maturity date is uncertain.

Consider Subsections (a) and (b) of Section 3-109(1). When an instrument is payable on or before a stated date, it is clearly payable at a definite time, although the maker has the option of paying before the stated maturity date. This uncertainty does not violate the definite time requirement. If Lee gives Zenon an instrument dated May 1, 1981, which indicates on its face that it is payable on or before May 1, 1982, it satisfies the requirement. On the other hand, an instrument that is undated and made payable "one month after date" is clearly not negotiable. There is no way to determine the maturity date from the face of the instrument. Drafts stating that they are payable at a fixed period after sight are considered payable at a definite time. [UCC Sec. 3-109(1)(b)] The term *sight* means the moment that the draft is accepted by the drawee. The Code further requires that such instruments be presented for acceptance to the drawee in order to determine the maturity date. [UCC Sec. 3-501(1)(a)] Presenting an instrument for acceptance to the drawee establishes the sight and the time period, which runs from the date the instrument is presented.

ACCELERATION CLAUSES An **acceleration clause** is one which allows a payee or other holder of an instrument to demand payment of the entire amount due, with interest, if some event occurs, usually a default in payment or in

other performance. For example, X lends $1,000 to Y. Y makes a note promising to pay $100 per month for eleven months. The note can contain a provision that permits X to accelerate all of the payments plus interest if Y fails to pay in any given month. If, for example, Y fails to make the third payment, the note will be due and payable. If X accelerates the unpaid balance, Y will owe X the remaining principal plus interest.

Under Section 109(1)(c), instruments which include acceleration clauses are negotiable because the exact value of the instrument can be ascertained. The instrument will be absolutely payable on a fixed date, however, if the event allowing acceleration does not occur. Thus, the fixed date is the outside limit used to determine the value of the instrument. Furthermore, the payee or holder cannot accelerate the instrument even if it contains an acceleration clause unless it is done in good faith. Section 1-208 indicates that the acceleration clause "* * * shall be construed to mean that * * * [the holder of the instrument] shall have the power * * * [to accelerate] only if he in good faith believes that the prospect of payment or performance is impaired." But the burden of proving a lack of good faith is on the borrower—that is, the maker of the note.

EXTENSION CLAUSES The reverse of an acceleration clause is an extension clause, which allows the date of maturity to be extended into the future. To keep the instrument negotiable, the interval of the extension must be specified if the right to extend is given to the maker of the instrument. If, on the other hand, the holder of the instrument can extend it, the maturity date does not have to be specified. Consider some examples:

1. A note reads, "The maker [obligor] has the right to postpone the time of payment of this note beyond its definite maturity date of January 1, 1983. However, this extension shall be for no more than a reasonable time." Any note with this language is not negotiable because it does not satisfy the definite time requirement. The right to extend is the maker's, and the

maker has not indicated when the note will become due after the extension.

2. A note reads, "The holder of this note at the date of maturity, January 1, 1983, can extend the time of payment until the following June 1 or later, if the holder so wishes." This is a negotiable instrument. The length of the extension does not have to be specified because the option to extend is solely that of the holder.

Payable to Order or to Bearer

A negotiable instrument must clearly indicate that the maker or drawer intends the instrument to be fully transferable to someone other than the person to whom it was originally issued. Section 3-104(1)(d) states that the instrument must be "payable to order or to bearer." These are considered words of negotiability.

ORDER INSTRUMENT   Section 3-110(1) defines an instrument as an order to pay "when by its terms it is payable to the order * * * of any person therein specified with reasonable certainty * * *." This section goes on to state that an order instrument can be payable: (1) to the maker or the drawer; (2) to the drawee or a payee who is not a maker, drawer, or drawee; (3) to two or more payees together; (4) to the representative of an estate, trust, or fund; or (5) to a partnership or unincorporated association. Any time the words appear as "pay to the order of Jim Jones" or "pay to Sam Smith or order," the instrument is an order instrument. If the instrument states "pay John Smith," the Code provides that it can be *negotiated* (transferred from one party to another), but no holder of it can ever qualify as a holder in due course. (See Chapter 26 for details.)

BEARER INSTRUMENT   Section 3-111 defines a bearer instrument as one that does not designate a specific payee. The term *bearer* means the person in possession of an instrument that is

payable to bearer *or* indorsed in blank. [UCC Sec. 1-201(5)]

Any instrument containing the following terms is a bearer instrument: "Payable to the order of bearer," "Payable to Sam Sneed or bearer," "Payable to bearer," "Pay Cash," or "Pay to the order of cash." An instrument stating that it is "payable only to Mr. Smith" is not payable to bearer.

COMPARING ORDER INSTRUMENTS AND BEARER INSTRUMENTS

1. A check payable to cash is a bearer instrument. [UCC Sec. 3-111(c)]

2. A note payable to the order of Melinda Higgins, which has been indorsed and signed by Melinda Higgins, is a bearer instrument because it is an instrument indorsed in blank. A blank indorsement is made by merely signing the back of the instrument. [UCC Sec. 3-204(2)]

3. A note "payable to bearer" and indorsed "Pay to the order of Leroy Jones, signed by George Porsche," is an order instrument because the indorsement names the person to whom the instrument is being made payable. [UCC Sec. 3-204(1)] See Chapter 25 for a discussion of all types of indorsements.

OMISSIONS THAT DO NOT AFFECT NEGOTIABILITY

UCC Sec. 3-112 lists the following terms and omissions that do not affect negotiability:

1. The omission of a statement of any consideration.

2. The omission of the place where the instrument is drawn or payable.

3. The promise or power to maintain or protect collateral or to give additional collateral.

4. The term in a draft indicating that the payee, by indorsing or cashing the draft, acknowledges full satisfaction of the obligation of the drawer.

QUESTIONS AND CASE PROBLEMS

1. Between 1971 and 1974, a number of Oklahoma residents purchased homes from Jim Walter Homes, Inc. Each purchaser made a down payment and signed a promissory note promising to pay the balance in monthly installments over a number of years. The promissory notes were ordinary in every way, including the payment provisions, which named the exact sum due each month over a specified period of years. A number of persons who signed these notes brought a class action suit against Jim Walter Homes to recover certain credit and financing charges that they claimed were in violation of the Uniform Consumer Credit Code (UCCC). In order to win their case, the plaintiffs had to prove that the promissory notes were negotiable instruments. Jim Walter Homes contended that they were not negotiable because the UCCC allows all consumers to prepay loans such as those at issue here and to deduct from the balance due all proportional amounts of credit and finance charges associated with any prepayments made. The company argued that because of this statutory provision, the promissory notes were no longer for a sum certain as required by the UCC. Is this a valid argument? [Circle v. Jim Walter Homes, Inc., 535 F.2d. 583 (10th Cir. 1976)]

2. In December 1965, Joseph Smith drew a check on a bank payable on demand to his son, Edward Joseph Smith Gentilotti. Smith postdated the check by fifteen years; that is, he dated the check December 1, 1980. On the back of the check, Smith wrote, "For Edward Joseph Smith Gentilotti, my son, if I should pass away, the amount of $20,000 shall be taken from my estate at death." Joseph Smith signed and dated this indorsement. Is this a negotiable instrument? [Smith v. Gentilotti, 371 Mass. 839, 359 N.E.2d. 953 (1977)]

3. Ingel entered into a contract with Allied Aluminum Associates, Inc., to have aluminum siding put on his home. Ingel executed a promissory note naming Allied as payee, and, at the same time, both Ingel and the Allied representative signed a completion certificate that bound Allied to complete the job satisfactorily. The completion certificate was not mentioned in nor attached to the promissory note. Allied Aluminum Associates later negotiated the promissory note to Universal C.I.T. Credit Corp. Allied never finished the aluminum siding work and was never heard from again. In a suit by Universal to collect on the note, Ingel's defense turned on whether the promissory note was negotiable. Ingel contended that it was not negotiable since it was accompanied by a completion certificate that contained promises other than the promise merely to pay a sum certain in money. Will Ingel's argument succeed? [Universal C.I.T. Credit Corp. v. Ingel, 347 Mass. 119, 196 N.E.2d. 847 (1964)]

4. Robinson purchased forty-three $100 money orders from Nation-Wide Check Corp. The amount was stamped on each money order at the time of the purchase. The only other writing on the instrument was "payable to_____" and "from _____." Robinson was to fill in the names on the instrument later. Are money orders, such as the typical one presented above, negotiable instruments? [Nation-Wide Check Corp. v. Banks, 260 A.2d. 376 (D.C. App. Ct. 1969)]

5. Mason, a trucking company, owed to Blayton, a lessor, $3,000 for the rental of certain trucking equipment. Blayton informed the president of Mason that unless he issued his personal check for $3,000 immediately, Blayton would sue Mason. Blayton promised to hold onto the check for two weeks to allow Mason time to pay the arrearages, but when it received Mason's check, it negotiated it to another party. Mason claimed that the check was subject to a condition—Blayton's promise to hold onto the check—and that therefore the check was not negotiable. Assuming that Blayton's agreement not to cash the check was first made orally over the phone and later put in writing, will this affect the negotiability of the check issued by Mason's president? [Mason v. Blayton, 119 Ga. App. 203, 166 S.E. 2d. 601 (1969)]

6. Hotel Evans, Inc., issued two promissory notes, as maker, to A. Alport & Son, Inc., payee. One note contained a promise by Hotel Evans to pay Alport $1,600 "with interest at bank rates." The other note, for $900, had "bank rates" typed in after the printed word "interest." Are either of these promissory notes negotiable? [A. Alport & Son, Inc. v. Hotel Evans, Inc., 65 Misc. 2d. 374, 317 N.Y.S. 2d. 937 (1970)]

7. Zimmerman entered into a contract with Master Homecraft Company for the remodeling of Zimmerman's home. In payment for the remodeling, Zimmerman executed a promissory note in the amount of $9,747. The note contained unused blanks for installment payments. It did not contain a maturity date; nor did it indicate whether Zimmerman would be liable

for interest. Is this promissory note negotiable? [Master Homecraft Co. v. Zimmerman, 208 Pa. Super. 401, 222 A.2d. 440 (1966)]

8.   On May 25, 1963, John Sylvia executed the following note: "I, John Sylvia, promise to pay $3,000 to N. Ferri or his order, within ten years." Is this note payable at a definite time within the meaning of Section 3-109(1)(c)? When would Ferri have the right to collect on the note? [Ferri v. Sylvia, 100 R.I. 270, 214 A.2d. 470 (1965)]

9.   In October 1970, Hall issued a draft that included the following: "Pay to L. Westmoreland and B. Bridges or order $1,000 on demand." Before he handed it to Bridges, Hall scratched out the words *or order* with his pen. Does the fact that the draft is payable to two payees destroy its negotiability? Does the scratching out of the words *or order* destroy the draft's negotiability? [First Federal Sav. and Loan Ass'n v. Branch Banking and Trust Co., 282 N.C. 44, 191 S.E. 2d. 683 (N.C. 1972)]

25

Commercial Paper Transferability and Negotiation

Commercial paper must be freely transferable. Once a negotiable instrument circulates beyond the original parties, the commercial law principles of *negotiation* come into play.[1] The method of transfer that is used to pass a negotiable instrument from person to person determines the rights and duties that are passed with it.

ASSIGNMENT AND NEGOTIATION

Once issued, a negotiable instrument can be transferred by *assignment* or by *negotiation*.

Assignment

Recall from Chapter 12 that under general contract principles, a transfer by assignment to an assignee gives the assignee only those rights that the assignor possessed. Assignment is a transfer of rights under a contract. Any defenses that can be raised against an assignor can be raised against the assignee.

---

1. The first delivery of a negotiable instrument to a holder occurs when the maker or drawer "issues" the instrument. [UCC Sec. 3-102 (1) (a)] Since a payee is a holder, the issuance of a negotiable instrument is, strictly speaking, negotiation. However, in commercial practice, the term *negotiation* is used to identify those transfers occurring once an instrument has been issued.

Negotiation

Negotiation is the transfer of an instrument in such form that the transferee becomes a holder. [UCC Sec. 3-202 (1)] Under UCC principles, a transfer by negotiation creates a holder who, at the very least, receives the rights of the previous possessor. [UCC Sec. 3-201 (1)] Unlike an assignment, a transfer by negotiation can make it possible for a holder to receive more rights in the instrument than the prior possessor. [UCC Sec. 3-305] (A holder who receives greater rights is known as a *holder in due course*. See Chapter 26.)

NEGOTIATING ORDER PAPER There are two methods of negotiating an instrument so that the receiver becomes a holder. If the instrument is *order paper*, it is negotiated by delivery with any necessary indorsements. For example, the Transco Company issues a payroll check "To the Order of Jane Smith." Smith takes the check to the supermarket, signs her name on the back (an indorsement), gives it to the cashier (a delivery), and receives cash. Smith has negotiated the check to the supermarket. [UCC Sec. 3-202 (1)] Note that the payroll check, which began as *order* paper was converted to *bearer* paper when Smith indorsed it in blank.

NEGOTIATING BEARER PAPER If the instrument is payable to bearer, then it is negotiated by delivery — that is, by physically being handed into another person's possession. [UCC Sec. 3-202 (1)] The use of *bearer paper* involves more risk than the use of order paper. Assume Bob Brown writes a check "Payable to Cash" and hands it to Debbie Myers (a delivery). Brown has negotiated the check (as a bearer instrument) to Myers. Myers places the check in her billfold, which is subsequently stolen. The thief has possession of the check. At this point, negotiation has not occurred since delivery must be voluntary on the part of the transferor. If the thief "delivers" the check to an innocent third person, negotiation will be complete. All rights to the check will be passed *absolutely* to that third person, and Myers will lose all right to

recover the proceeds of the check from that third person. [UCC Sec. 3-305] Of course, she can recover her money from the thief if the thief can be found.

The method used for negotiation depends upon the character of the instrument at the time the negotiation takes place. For example, a check originally payable to "Cash", but subsequently indorsed "Pay to X", must be negotiated as order paper (by indorsement and delivery) even though it was previously bearer paper. [UCC Sec. 3-204 (1)]

INDORSEMENTS

Indorsements are made by the holder—that is, the person to whom the instrument is payable either as payee or by indorsement or the person in possession of bearer paper. An indorsement is a signature with or without additional words or statements. It is most often written on the back of the instrument itself. If there is no room on the instrument, indorsements can be written on a separate piece of paper called an **allonge**. The allonge must be "so firmly affixed" to the instrument "as to become a part thereof." [UCC Sec. 3-202(2)] Pins or paper clips will not suffice. Staples are preferable.

One purpose of an indorsement is to effect the negotiation of order paper. Sometimes the transferee of bearer paper will request the holder-transferor to indorse. This is done to impose contractual liability on the indorser. The liability of indorsers will be discussed later in Chapter 27.

Once an instrument qualifies as a negotiable instrument, the form of indorsement will have no effect on the character of the underlying instrument. Indorsement relates to the right of the holder to negotiate the paper and the manner in which it must be done.

Types of Indorsements

The following sections will examine three categories of indorsements: (1) blank versus special, (2) qualified versus unqualified, and (3) restrictive versus nonrestrictive.

BLANK INDORSEMENTS A blank indorsement specifies no particular indorsee and can consist of a mere signature. [UCC Sec. 3-204(2)] Hence, a check payable "To the Order of Rosemary White" can be indorsed in blank simply by having her signature written on the back of the check. Exhibit 25-1 shows a blank indorsement.

EXHIBIT 25-1 BLANK INDORSEMENT

> *Rosemary White*

An instrument payable to order and indorsed in blank becomes payable to bearer and can be negotiated by delivery alone. [UCC 3-204(2)] In other words, a blank indorsement converts an order instrument to a bearer instrument, which anybody can cash. If De Wert indorses a check payable to her order in blank and then loses it on the street, Jones can find it and sell it to Smith for value without indorsing it. This constitutes a negotiation because Jones makes delivery of a bearer instrument (which was an order instrument until it was indorsed).

SPECIAL INDORSEMENTS A **special indorsement** indicates the specific person to whom the indorser intends to make the instrument payable; that is, it names the indorsee. [UCC Sec. 3-204(1)] No special words of negotiation are needed. Words such as "Pay to the Order of Wilson" or "Pay to Wilson" followed by the signature of the indorser are sufficient.[2] When an instrument is indorsed in this way, it is order paper.

To avoid the risk of loss from theft one may convert a blank indorsement to a special indorsement. This returns the bearer paper to order paper. Section 3-204(3) allows that "the

holder may convert a blank indorsement into a special indorsement by writing over the signature of the indorser in blank any contract consistent with the character of the indorsement." For example, Ellen Gordon may wish to insert the words "pay to Ellen Gordon" over the signature of the indorser. Because Gordon is now identified as the indorsee, the check cannot be negotiated further without her indorsement. In this manner, Gordon converts a blank indorsement into a special indorsement. (Special indorsements are discussed below.)

EXHIBIT 25-2 SPECIAL INDORSEMENT

> *Pay to Wilson*
> *Arthur Engles*

QUALIFIED VERSUS UNQUALIFIED INDORSEMENTS Generally, an indorser, *merely by indorsing*, impliedly promises to pay the holder, or any subsequent indorser, the amount of the instrument in the event that the drawer or maker defaults on the payment. [UCC Sec. 3-414(1)] A **qualified indorsement** is used by an indorser to disclaim or limit this contractual liability on the instrument. In this form of indorsement, the notation *without recourse* is commonly used. A sample is shown in Exhibit 25-3.

EXHIBIT 25-3 QUALIFIED INDORSEMENT

> *Without recourse*
> *Arthur Engles*

A qualified indorsement is often used by persons acting in a representative capacity. For instance, insurance agents sometimes receive checks payable to them that are really intended as payment to the insurance company. The agent is merely indorsing the payment through to the principal and should not be required to

---

2. Had the words "Pay to Wilson" been used on the face of the instrument to indicate the payee, the instrument would not have been negotiable; it would only have been assignable.

make good on the check if it is later dishonored. The "without recourse" indorsement absolves the agent. If the instrument is dishonored the holder cannot obtain recovery from a person who has indorsed "without recourse" unless the indorser has breached one of the warranties listed in UCC Sec. 3-417(2). However, a person who indorses an instrument will be liable on the instrument in the absence of a qualified indorsement.

RESTRICTIVE VERSUS NONRESTRICTIVE INDORSEMENTS The **restrictive indorsement** requires indorsees to comply with certain instructions regarding the funds involved. Restrictive indorsements come in many forms. Section 3-205 categorizes four separate types.

Conditional Indorsements When payment is dependant on the occurrence of some specified event, the instrument has a conditional indorsement. [UCC Sec. 3-205(a)] For example, Ted Smith indorses a note to read:

EXHIBIT 25–4 CONDITIONAL INDORSEMENT

Pay to Bob Block, provided he complete renovations on building number 23 by September 1, 1982.

Ted Smith

The indorsement is enforceable (except against intermediary banks as defined below), but neither Bob Block nor any subsequent holder

has the right to enforce payment on the note before the condition is met. [UCC Sec. 3-206(3)] Read the example carefully and notice that Ted Smith is an *indorser*, not the maker of the note. Indorsers are permitted to condition rights of indorsees without affecting the negotiability of the instrument. However, if the conditional language had appeared on the face of the instrument, it would *not* have been negotiable because it would not have met the requirement of an unconditional order or promise to pay.

Indorsements Prohibiting Further Indorsement An indorsement such as, "Pay to Bill Jones Only, (signed) X," does not destroy negotiability. Jones can negotiate the paper to a holder just as if it had read "Pay to Bill Jones, (signed) X." [UCC Sec. 3-206(1)] This type of restrictive indorsement has the same legal effect as a special indorsement. It is rarely used. [UCC Sec. 3-205(b)]

Indorsement for Deposit or for Collection Indorsements that read "For Deposit Only" or "For Collection Only" have the effect of making the indorsee (almost always a bank) a collecting agent of the indorser. In particular, a "Pay Any Bank or Banker" indorsement has the effect of locking the instrument into the bank collection process. Only a bank can acquire rights of a holder following this indorsement unless it is specifically indorsed to a person and not to a bank. [UCC Sec. 4-201(2)]

Here again, the depositary bank has a special responsibility to act consistently with the restrictive indorsement, and the intermediary banks are not liable if the depositary bank fails to comply.

LAMSON v. COMMERCIAL CREDIT CORPORATION
Colorado Court of Appeals, 1974.
521 P.2d 785.

BACKGROUND AND FACTS *Defendant Commercial Credit Corporation issued two checks payable to the order of Rauch Motor Co. Rauch Motor, indorsed the checks in blank and deposited them in its account with University National Bank. University National stamped the checks "Pay Any Bank" and sent them through the collection process. The checks were subsequently returned to University National marked*

"Payment Stopped". Several months later University National assigned the checks to Lamson who sued Commercial Credit Corp. for the face amount of the checks.

DECISION AND RATIONALE *Lamson could not recover since he was not a holder of the checks. The Uniform Commercial Code defines a holder as "a person who is in possession of *** an instrument *** drawn, issued, or indorsed to him or to his order or to bearer or in blank." [UCC Sec. 1-201 (20)] When the bank stamped the checks "Pay Any Bank," this indorsement had the effect of locking the checks into the banking system. Thereafter, in the judgment of the court, only a bank could become a holder "*** [u]ntil the item has been returned to the customer initiating collection; or *** [u]ntil the item has been specially indorsed by a bank to a person not a bank. [UCC Sec. 4-201 (2)] Plaintiff is neither the customer initiating collection nor a bank, and the checks were not specially endorsed to him."*

Trust or Agency Indorsement Indorsements that are for the benefit of the indorsee or a third person are trust, or agency, indorsements. For example, "Pay to Ann North in Trust for Johnny North, (signed) R. P. North." Or, "Pay to Marge, as Agent of XXO, (signed) XXO." The indorsement results in legal title vesting in the original indorsee. To the extent that the original indorsee pays or applies the proceeds consistently with the indorsement (for example, "in Trust for Johnny. . ."), the indorsee is a holder and can become a holder in due course. (See Chapter 26). [UCC Secs. 3-205(d) and 3-206(4)]

The fiduciary restrictions on the instrument do not reach beyond the original indorsee.[3] Any subsequent purchaser can qualify as a holder in due course unless he or she has actual notice that the instrument was negotiated in breach of the fiduciary duty.[4]

Bank's Liability for Restrictive Indorsements Banks handling commercial paper in the nor-

mal course of *collection* are called intermediary banks [UCC Sec. 4-105(c)], and banks paying on commercial paper are called payor banks. [UCC Sec. 4-105(b)] Neither bank is bound by any restrictive indorsements of any person except the immediate holder who transfers or presents the instrument for payment. [UCC Sec. 3-206(2)] This means that only the first bank to which the item is presented for collection must pay in a manner consistent with any restrictive indorsement. [UCC Sec. 3-206(3)] This bank is called the depository bank. [UCC Sec. 4-105(a)] This is true even if the depository bank is also the payor bank (that is, where only one bank is involved).

To illustrate: Elliot writes a check on his New York bank account and sends it to Barton. Barton indorses the check with a restrictive indorsement that reads, "For Deposit into Account #4921 Only." A Miami bank is the first bank to which this check is presented for payment (the depository bank), and it must act consistently with the terms of the restrictive indorsement. Therefore, it must credit account #4921 with the money or be liable to Barton for conversion. Elliot's check leaves the Miami bank indorsed "For Collection." As the check moves through the collection network of intermediary banks to Elliot's New York bank for payment, each intermediary bank is only bound by the preceding bank's indorsement to collect.

---

3. Compare this to the rule governing conditional indorsements. A conditional indorsement binds all subsequent indorsers (except certain banks) and primary parties to see that the money is applied consistently with the condition. Agency or trust indorsements limit this responsibility only to the original indorsee. Subsequent parties are not encumbered with this restriction.

4. See Quantum Dev. v. Joy, 397 F. Supp. 329 (D.C. Virgin Is. 1975).

The division of responsibility between types of banks is necessary. Collecting banks process huge numbers of commercial instruments, and there is no practical way for them to examine and comply with the effect of each restrictive indorsement. Therefore, the only reasonable alternative is to charge the depositary bank with the responsibility of examining and complying with any restrictive indorsements.

Forged or Unauthorized Indorsements

People cannot be liable to pay on negotiable instruments unless their signatures appear on the instruments. Hence, a forged or *unauthorized signature* is wholly inoperative and will not bind the person whose name is forged.[5]

The forged indorsement rule of the Uniform Commercial Code places the burden of loss on the party who first accepted the forged indorsement, often the bank that cashes the instrument for the forger. In the following situations, the forged indorsement rule does not apply, and the loss resulting from forgery falls on the drawer or maker: (1) when the imposter induces the maker or drawer of an instrument to issue it to the imposter or to a confederate in the name of the payee or (2) when the imposter signs as or on behalf of a maker or drawer, intending that the payee will have no interest in the instrument, and an agent or employee of the maker or drawer has supplied the imposter with

the name of the payee, also intending the payee to have no such interest. [UCC Sec. 3-405(1)] These situations often involve an employee who wishes to swindle an employer by padding bills or payrolls.

An *unauthorized indorsement* of a payee's name can be as effective as if the real payee had signed. The *imposter rule* of Section 3-405 of the UCC provides that an imposter's indorsement will be effective — that is, not a "forgery." This occurs when an imposter induces the maker or drawer to issue an instrument in the name of an impersonated payee to the imposter or to an accomplice who is impersonating the payee. For example, an imposter goes to a bank, forges a withdrawal slip on X's account, and requests the bank to issue a check in X's name for the amount. The bank agrees, handing the imposter the check payable to X, thinking she really is X. When the imposter indorses X's name on the back of the check, the unauthorized indorsement will be effective to negotiate the check. Who bears the loss? In this case the drawer bank must bear the loss for being misled into delivering the check to an imposter.

The following case illustrates how a court applied the *imposter rule* which was later adopted in the Uniform Commercial Code.

5. On the other hand, a drawee is charged with knowledge of the *drawer's* signature, and the drawee cannot recover money paid out on a negotiable instrument bearing a forged drawee's signature.

GREENBERG v. A & D MOTOR SALES, INC.
Appellate Court of Illinois, 1950.
341 Ill.App. 85, 93 N.E.2d 90.

BACKGROUND AND FACTS *A person representing himself to be Wallace Gloss sold a car (which he did not own) to A & D Motor Sales. A & D issued a check to "Gloss," and "Gloss" indorsed and cashed it at a currency exchange operated by Greenberg. Before cashing the check, Greenberg called A & D and was told the check was good. Learning later of the fraud, A & D stopped payment on the check. The check was dishonored, and Greenberg sought to recover as a holder against A & D, the drawer. A & D claims that the signature was a forgery and, therefore, there is no right to enforce payment.*

DECISION AND RATIONALE *"Wallace Gloss's" signature was effective to pass title to Greenberg under the imposter rule, and therefore Greenberg had the right to enforce payment against the drawer, A & D.*

Generally, when a signature is forged, it is inoperative, and the person who receives it from the forger cannot enforce payment of it. However, since an imposter who presented himself as Wallace Gloss tricked A & D into issuing its check to him, the imposter rule makes the imposter's indorsement operative. It is not treated as a forgery. "The consequences of the mistake should fall upon the drawer rather the purchaser [of the instrument—Greenberg] since the mistake is primarily the former's, whether he has himself been deceived or has deliberately tried to shift the burden of identification by giving the imposter a negotiable instrument instead of cash. The fraud upon the drawer facilitiated a fraud upon the purchaser."

FURTHER EXAMPLES Assume that the Revco Company gives its bookkeeper, Sam Snyde, general authority to issue checks in the company name drawn on Second Federal Bank so that Snyde can pay employees and pay other corporate bills. Snyde decides to cheat Revco out of $10,000 by issuing a check payable to Fanny Freid, an old acquaintance of his. Snyde does not intend Freid to receive any of the money and Freid is not an employee or creditor of the company.

Snyde indorses the check in Freid's name, naming himself as indorsee. Snyde cashes the check with a local bank, which collects payment from the drawee bank, Second Federal. Second Federal then charges Revco's account $10,000.

Revco discovers the fraud and demands that its account be recredited. Who bears the loss? Neither the local bank that first accepted the check nor Second Federal are responsible. The rule of UCC Sec. 3-405 provides the answer. Since Snyde's indorsement in the name of a payee with no interest in the instrument is "effective," there is no "forgery." Hence, the collecting bank is protected in paying on the check, and the drawee bank is protected in charging Revco's account. It is the employer-drawer, Revco, that bears the loss.[6]

The Code makes no distinction in result when a dishonest employee does not actually sign the check, but merely supplies his employer with names of fictitious creditors or with true names of creditors having fictitious debts. For example, Ned Norris draws up the payroll list from which employee checks are written. Norris fraudulently adds the name Sue Swift (a fictitious person) to the payroll, thus causing checks to be issued to her. Again, it is the employer-drawer who bears the loss because the employer is in the best position to prevent such fraud.

Miscellaneous Indorsement Problems

NO STANDARD CATEGORY Sometimes an indorsement does not seem to fit into any of the standard categories. For example, the indorsement can read: "I hereby assign all my right and title and interest in this note, (signed) XXO." The signature is an effective indorsement despite the additional language of transfer. Use of the word *assign* does not change the negotiation into a mere assignment. Clearly XXO did not intend to limit the rights of the person to whom he was transferring the instrument. [UCC Sec. 3-202(4)]

CORRECTION OF NAME An indorsement should be identical to the name that appears on the instrument. The payee or indorsee whose name is misspelled can indorse with the misspelled name, or the correct name, or both. [UCC Sec. 3-203] For example, Susan Lock receives a check payable to the order of "Susan Locke." She can indorse the check either "Susan Locke" or "Susan Lock." The usual practice

---

6. May Dept. Stores Co. v. Pittsburgh Nat. Bank, 374F.2d 109 (3rd Cir. 1967).

is to indorse the name as it appears on the instrument and follow it by the correct name.[7]

BANK INDORSEMENTS When a customer deposits a check with a bank and fails to indorse it, the bank has the right to supply any necessary indorsement for its customer unless the instrument specifically prohibits it. For example, Bob Adams deposits his government check with First National Bank and forgets to indorse it. Since government checks typically state, "Payee's Indorsement Required," the bank will not supply the indorsement. The check will be returned to Adams for his signature.

Ordinarily, checks do not specifically require the payee's indorsement. The bank merely stamps or marks the check, indicating that it was deposited by the customer or credited to the customer's account. [UCC Sec. 4-205]

Commercial paper must move rapidly through banking channels. In the process of clearing through collection, a check can be transferred between banks using any agreed-upon method of indorsement that identifies the transferor bank. [UCC Sec. 4-206] For example, a bank can indorse using its Federal Reserve number instead of its name.

MULTIPLE PAYEES An instrument payable to two or more persons *in the alternative* (for example, "Pay to A or B") requires the indorsement of *either* payee. [UCC Sec. 3-116(a)]

7. Watertown Federal Sav. and Loan v. Spanks, 346 Mass. 398, 193 N.E.2d 333 (1963)

However, if an instrument is payable to two or more persons *jointly* (for example, "Pay C and D" or "Pay G, H"), then *both* indorsements are necessary for negotiation. [UCC Sec. 3-116(b)]

UNINDORSED ORDER PAPER If order paper is transferred without indorsement, it is a transfer by assignment, not by negotiation. The receiver is merely a transferee, not a holder, and can never qualify as a holder in due course. If, however, the transfer is made for value given, the unqualified indorsement of the transferor can be compelled by law unless the parties have agreed otherwise. The effect is the negotiation of the instrument. The transferee becomes a holder and can negotiate the instrument further. [UCC Sec. 3-201(3)]

The rule is a little different for banks. With one exception, a depositary bank receiving a check from its customer has the power to supply its customer's indorsement under UCC Sec. 4-205. Thus the bank is a holder and can negotiate the instrument.

AGENTS OR OFFICERS A negotiable instrument can be drawn payable to a legal entity such as an estate, a partnership, or an organization. For example, if a check reads "Pay to the Red Cross," an authorized representative of the Red Cross can negotiate it.

Similarly, negotiable paper can be payable to a public officer. For example, checks reading "Pay to the Order of the County Tax Collector," or "Pay to Larry White, Receiver of Taxes," can be negotiated by whoever holds the office. [UCC Sec. 3-110(1)(b)]

QUESTIONS AND CASE PROBLEMS

1. Graybar Electric Company and Marine Midland Bank had a long-standing agreement under which Marine Midland received checks payable to Graybar and transferred them to other parties, usually other banks. Graybar never saw the checks. They were made out to Graybar's order and delivered directly to Marine Midland. Marine Midland stamped the backs of the checks with Graybar's name and insignia and transferred them. Within the meaning of the UCC, is the act of sending checks to Marine Midland Bank a negotiation? Is Marine Midland's transfer of the checks to other parties a negotiation? [Marine Midland Bank-New York v. Graybar Electric Co., 41 N.Y. 2d 703, 363 N.E.2d. 1139 (1977)]

2. Wes-Con Development Company was a general contractor involved in building a large office building in San Francisco. Wes-Con hired Phillips as its plumbing subcontractor. As construction progressed, Phillips experienced financial difficulties, and

Phillips's plumbing supplier informed Wes-Con that it was hesitant to supply any more materials. Wes-Con therefore promised the supplier that the next allotment check to Phillips would be made out to the supplier and Phillips as joint payees. One month later, Wes-Con made out a joint check and gave it to Phillips. Phillips signed the back of the check and delivered it to another creditor. Was the check properly negotiated by Phillips? Why or why not? [Bank of West v. Wes-Con Dev. Co., Inc., 15 Wash. App. 238, 548 P.2d 563 (1976)]

3.   In May 1964, Northside Building and Investment Company issued a note, as maker, to the order of Citizens Bank. Citizens later indorsed the note to the order of Bankers Finance Company, and Bankers indorsed it to the order of Stockbridge. Several months later, Stockbridge gave the note to Finance Company of America as collateral for a loan. Is Finance Company of America a holder? [Northside Bldg. and Investment Co. v. Finance Co. of America, 119 Ga. App. 131, 166 S.E.2d. 608 (1969)]

4.   At one of the weekly auctions that Sweedler conducted, a purchaser bid for and received merchandise worth approximately $300. In return, the purchaser gave Sweedler a cashier's check that was payable to the purchaser. However, he failed to indorse the check, and Sweedler inadvertently failed to request the indorsement. Without the indorsement, the bank refused to pay Sweedler. The purchaser also refused to indorse the check because he was dissatisfied with the merchandise. If, at a trial between Sweedler and the bank, the purchaser admits that he gave Sweedler the cashier's check in exchange for certain merchandise, will Sweedler be allowed to recover against the bank? [Sweedler v. Oboler, 65 Misc. 2d 789, 319 N.Y.S. 2d 89 (1971)]

5.   Over several years, Vinson made a number of business investments for which he had to borrow substantial sums of money from his bank. As collateral for these loans, Vinson gave his bank several thousand shares of stock in XYZ company. Then, Vinson's business investments began to go sour, and XYZ company's stock dropped significantly in value. The bank therefore demanded that Vinson deliver additional collateral. Vinson gave the bank five $10,000 notes payable to his order. Instead of indorsing the notes on the back, Vinson made the indorsements on separate sheets of paper, which he then stapled securely to each note. Has Vinson made a proper negotiation of the notes to his bank? [Tallahassee Bank and Trust Co. v. Raines, 125 Ga. App. 623, 187 S.E. 2d. 320 (1972)]

6.   John Copeland owned a small apartment complex in Houston, Texas. Thelma Moore leased one of Copeland's apartments for a number of years. When the rent for March 1970 came due, Moore wrote out a check payable in the appropriate amount to "Mrs. Copeland" rather than "Mr. Copeland." If John Copeland later signs the check on the back "Mr. John Copeland" will this operate as a valid indorsement of the check? [Moore v. Copeland, 478 S.W. 2d. 573 (Tex. Civ. App. 1972)]

7.   Davis, student at Baltic University, often ran out of money and phoned his father to wire him extra cash. Davis's roommate watched Davis do this a number of times and later got very proficient at imitating Davis's voice over the phone. One night, the roommate phoned Davis's father and requested that he wire him $1,000 the next morning at 10:00. The father wired a money order at the prearranged hour to the Western Union office at Baltic University. The office wired back asking the father if he wished to have the person present in the office officially identified as his son. The father declined because he believed that it had been his son who had arranged to receive the money order. Later, when the father learned of the roommate's impersonation, he demanded his money back from Western Union. Western Union declined. Should the father recover? [Davis v. Western Union Telegraph Co., 4 D.&C. 2d. 264 (Pa. 1956)]

8.   During a two-year period, Young, an employee of General American Life Insurance Company, caused twenty checks to be drawn on First National Bank payable to the order of a fictitious policyholder. Young then took the checks, forged the policyholder's name, and cashed them. When General American learned of the fraud, it demanded that First National Bank reimburse its account. First National Bank refused, and a lawsuit followed. Who will prevail? [Delmar Bank v. Fidelity & Deposit Co., 300 F. Supp. 496 (E.D. Mo. 1969)]

9.   F. Mitchell, assistant treasurer of Travco Corporation, caused two checks payable to a fictitious company, L. and B. Distributors, to be drawn on the corporation's account. Mitchell took both checks to his personal bank, indorsed them "F. Mitchell," and gave them to the teller. The teller cashed them. When the bank attempted to collect from Travco, Travco refused to pay. The bank contended that, under the rule concerning fictitious payees and imposters, Mitchell's indorsement was valid and that, therefore, the bank should be allowed to collect. Is the bank's contention true? [Travco Corp. v. Citizens Federal Sav. & Loan Ass'n, 42 Mich. App. 291, 201 N.W.2d. 675 (1972)]

26

Commercial Paper
Holder in Due Course

Since commercial paper is not money itself, but payable in money, commercial paper litigation results when there is a dispute about who should be paid. Litigation issues usually turn on which party can obtain payment on an instrument when it is due or on whether some defense can be asserted to discharge or cancel liability on an instrument.

A holder in due course takes a negotiable instrument free of all claims of other parties. That means that the holder in due course has the right to collect payment on that instrument, and this right will take priority over the claims of other parties.[1]

CONTRACT LAW VERSUS
THE LAW OF COMMERCIAL PAPER

The basic principles of contract law govern when simple contract rights are assigned to a third party (assignee), when a nonnegotiable instrument is transferred to a third party (transferee), or when a negotiable instrument is improperly negotiated to a third party (transferee). The contract rights of assignees and transferees are burdened with every legal

---

1. UCC Sec. 3-505(2) specifically sets forth the very limited number of real *defenses* that defeat payment to a holder in due course. A holder in due course takes commercial paper free from personal (as opposed to real) defenses. These are discussed more thoroughly in Chapter 27.

defense that existed between prior parties regardless of the extent of their knowledge of them. Persons who transfer or assign contractual or nonnegotiable rights pass on only the rights that they had.

The body of rules contained in Article 3 of the UCC govern a party's right to payment of a check, draft, note, or certificate of deposit.[2] The third party is characterized as either an ordinary *holder* or a *holder in due course.* (The party can also be a transferee according to UCC Sec. 3-201.) Our discussion of holders in due course will primarily be concerned with *negotiable* instruments which have been negotiated.

HOLDER

A **holder** is a person who has possession of a negotiable instrument that is "drawn, issued, or indorsed" to that person or to that person's order, or to bearer, or in blank.[3] [UCC Sec. 1-201(20)] The holder is entitled to receive payment of the instrument. Either an original party or a third party can qualify as a holder. The manner in which possession of a negotiable instrument is acquired will determine whether or not a person qualifies as a *holder.* Negotiation is a special form of transfer in which the transferee becomes a *holder.* [UCC Sec. 3-202] (See Chapter 25.)

Order Paper

If the paper is an order instrument, the initial holder is the payee. Thus, Sam Smith is the holder of a check payable to him that is in his possession. If Smith indorses the check to Jane Brown and gives it to her, Brown will become the holder. Order paper is negotiated by delivery and indorsement. [UCC Sec. 3-202] The check payable to Sam Smith is issued when it is delivered to him. Smith's acts of indorsing and delivering the check into Brown's possession constitute negotiation to Brown.

Bearer Paper

If the paper is bearer paper, the holder is the person who is in physical possession of the instrument. Bearer paper can be negotiated only by delivery, but the transferor can indorse it. [UCC Sec. 3-202] Assume that a negotiable promissory note reads "Pay to Bearer the Sum of $100.00." Whoever the instrument is delivered to, whether or not that person is the real owner, is a holder.

Rights of a Holder

The holder of a negotiable instrument has the power to negotiate it to another party. The holder has the right to demand payment of the instrument in his or her own name. Similarly, with certain exceptions, a holder can cancel or discharge the obligation on an instrument whether or not he or she is the original owner. [UCC Sec. 3-301]

A holder has the status of an assignee of a contract right. A transferee of a negotiable instrument who is characterized merely as a holder (as opposed to a holder in due course) obtains only those rights that the predecessor-transferor had in the instrument. In the event that there is a conflicting, superior claim or defense to the instrument, an ordinary holder will not be able to collect payment.

HOLDER IN DUE COURSE

A holder in due course (HDC) is a special-status transferee of a negotiable instrument who, by meeting certain acquisition requirements, takes the instrument free of most defenses or adverse claims to it. Stated another way, an HDC can normally acquire a higher level of immunity to defenses against payment on the instrument or

---

2. The rights and liabilities on checks, drafts, notes, and certificates of deposit are determined under Article 3 of the Uniform Commercial Code. Other kinds of commercial paper, such as stock certificates or bills of lading and other documents of title, meet the requirements of negotiable instruments, but the rights and liabilities of the parties on these documents are covered by Articles 7 and 8 of the Code.

3. A holder, as the term is used in Article 3 of the Uniform Commercial Code, applies here only in the context of negotiable instruments.

claims of ownership to the instrument by other parties.

Requirements for Holder-In-Due-Course Status

The basic requirements for attaining HDC status are set forth in UCC Sec. 3-302. An HDC must first be a holder of a negotiable instrument. Then the holder must take the instrument (1) for value, (2) in good faith, and (3) without notice that it is overdue, or that it has been dishonored, or that any person has a defense against it or a claim to it.

The underlying requirement of "due course" status is that a person must first be a holder on that instrument. Review the qualifications of a holder because, regardless of other circumstances surrounding acquisition, only a holder has a chance to become an HDC.

Value

An HDC must have given *value* for the paper. [UCC Sec. 3-303] A person who receives an instrument as a gift or who inherits it has not met the requirement of value. In these situations, the person becomes an ordinary holder and does not possess the rights of an HDC.[4]

The concept of value in the law of negotiable instruments is not the same as the concept of consideration in the law of contracts. An executory promise (a promise to give value in the future) is clearly valid consideration to support a contract. [UCC Sec. 1-201(44)] However, an executory promise does not normally constitute the "value" (agreed consideration performed) that is necessary for holder-in-due-course status under UCC Sec. 3-303. If the holder plans to pay for the instrument later on or perform the required services at some future date, the holder has not yet given value.

Suppose Ted Green draws a $500 note payable to Roger Evans in payment for goods. Evans negotiates the note to Irene Franks, who promises to pay him for it in thirty days. During the next month, Franks learns that Evans breached the contract by delivering defective goods and that Green will not honor the $500 note. Franks can return the note to Evans. She has suffered no out-of-pocket loss because she has not given value. A purchaser of a note or draft who has merely promised to pay or to perform an act but has not yet done so can rescind the transaction and avoid it if he or she learns of a defense.[5]

Once a holder has given value, it may not be possible to rescind the deal. The holder in due course needs protection that permits recovery on the instrument from the primary party regardless of any personal defenses arising between the original parties. Reconsider the last example. Assume this time that Irene Franks pays Roger Evans for the note on the spot. Franks is a holder for value once the agreed consideration is performed. She has "paid" for holder-in-due-course protection. This means she is entitled to collect payment of the $500 note against Green regardless of any personal defenses that Green may have against Evans (for example, breach of contract). The rights between Irene and Ted on the note are governed by Article 3 of the UCC. The rights between Ted and Roger on the contract are governed by contract law and by Article 2.

The following case takes up the question of value. Donald Goldberg sold his interest in a corporation to Rothman and others for $7,500. Upon Goldberg's request the buyers made four promissory notes payable to Ethel Goldberg, his wife.

There is no apparent reason why Donald Goldberg designated the payee as his wife nor is there any indication that Ethel Goldberg received the notes for value as defined by UCC 3-303.

---

4. There is one way an ordinary holder who fails to meet the value requirement can qualify as a holder in due course. The "shelter provision" of the Code allows an ordinary holder to succeed to HDC status if any prior holder was an HDC. This exception is discussed later in the chapter. [UCC Sec. 3-201(1)]

---

5. Rescission is allowed under the theory that breach of warranty by the transferor is a defense. [UCC Sec. 3-417] Warranty liability is discussed in Chapter 27.

BACKGROUND AND FACTS *Donald Goldberg and six others were stockholders in a company known as 86th Street Bay 40th Corporation. In consideration for the sale of Donald Goldberg's interest in the corporation, the other six shareholders each issued a promissory note payable to Donald's wife, Ethyl. Ethyl Goldberg then brought suit to recover on the notes, because all six makers refused to pay. The six defendants counterclaimed that Ethyl should not recover because of certain debts that Donald owed them. These debts had no relation to the promissory notes.*

GOLDBERG v. **ROTHMAN**

Civil Court of the City of New York, 1971.
66 Misc.2d 981, 322 N.Y.S.2d 931.

DECISION AND RATIONALE *Ethyl was able to recover on the notes even though she was not a holder in due course. Ethyl had possession of the notes, and they were payable to her, but she did not give value for them. They were a gift from her husband. Therefore, she was merely a holder, since a holder in due course must give value. Nevertheless, the unrelated counterclaim that the defendants asserted could not be maintained against her. It is true that a maker can assert any defense against a mere holder. But a counterclaim is not a defense. The court stated: "Under §3-306, Uniform Commercial Code, plaintiff not having the rights of a holder in due course takes the instrument here, the notes in question, 'subject to *** all defenses of any party which would be available in an action on simple contract.' *** Defendants have not shown that any defenses exist against her in relation to the validity of the notes *** [emphasis added]."*

AGREED CONSIDERATION PERFORMED A holder takes an instrument for value to the extent that agreed consideration has been performed. In the typical situation, the holder is a purchaser for money. For example, Morris executes a $300 note payable to the order of Paulson. Paulson sells the note to a bank which pays Paulson $285 (a discount is usual). The bank has given value for Morris's note.

Performance of agreed consideration can also include an act such as the delivery of goods. Harper holds a note from Barton and agrees to negotiate the note to Thompson in payment for a purchase of goods. Delivery of the goods is Thompson's agreed performance, that is, the value given for the note.

Section 3-303(a) of the Code provides that a holder takes an instrument for value only to the extent that the agreed-upon consideration has been performed. For example, Arnolds negotiates a $1,000 note to Raymonds for a total price of $950 with $700 payable now and $250 due in thirty days. Raymonds is immediately an HDC to the extent of $700, and when she completes payment of $250, she will become an HDC for the full $1,000 face amount of the note.

Do not be confused when the value of the agreed consideration differs from the face amount of the instrument. When a time instrument is sold, it is usually discounted to allow for transfer costs, collection costs, and interest charges. Thus, a $1,000 note due in ninety days may be sold for $950 cash to a financial institution. The requirement of agreed consideration is satisfied by the $950 payment. If the discrepancy between the purchase and face value is great, however, it can be taken with other factors to indicate a lack of good faith on the part of the purchaser. The good faith element will be discussed later in the chapter.

A holder takes an instrument for value to the extent that the holder acquires a security interest or lien on the instrument.[6] Normally, an instrument is given as security for a loan or other obligation. If, for example, Norris issues a $1,000 note payable to Lomond, Lomond can use the note to secure a $700 loan from Hilton. (Lomond gets $700 cash, Hilton holds the note.) Hilton's $700 loan qualifies her as a holder for value. If Lomond does not repay the $700, Hilton can collect the note. But what if Norris has a personal defense against Lomond? Hilton, as an HDC, is free and clear of the defense, but *only to the extent of $700*. Hence, the rule is, "a purchaser of a limited interest can be a holder in due course only to the extent of the interest purchased." [UCC Sec. 3-302(4)]

ANTECEDENT CLAIM When an instrument is given in payment of an **antecedent claim** (or as security for an antecedent, or prior, debt), the value requirement is met.[7] [UCC Sec. 3-303(b)] Here, again, commercial law and contract law produce different results. An antecedent debt is not valid consideration under general contract law, but it does constitute value sufficient to satisfy the requirement for HDC status in commercial law.

Assume Cary owes Dwyer $2,000 on a past due account. If Cary negotiates a $2,000 note to Dwyer and Dwyer accepts it to discharge the overdue account balance, Dwyer has given value for the instrument.

---

6. A holder does not become an HDC of an instrument by purchasing it at a judicial sale or by taking it under legal process. [UCC Sec. 3-302(3)(a)]

7. The antecedent claim (or debt) discharged may be one against any person, not just the transferor of the instrument whether or not the claim is due.

NEGOTIABLE INSTRUMENT AS VALUE Merely promising to pay money or to perform an act in the future does not constitute giving value. However, if a purchaser's promise to pay money is made in the form of a negotiable instrument (for example, a check or an irrevocable letter of credit), the requirement of value is met. Section 3-303(c) of the Code provides that a holder takes the instrument for value "when he gives a negotiable instrument for it, or makes an irrevocable commitment to a third person." For example, Tillman writes a check to Samson for the purchase of a ninety-day note that Samson is holding. Tillman gives value when he issues the check to Samson.

A negotiable instrument has value when issued, not when the underlying money is finally paid. In the example above, if later that day but before the check is cashed, Tillman learns that the maker of the note has a personal defense against Samson, Tillman knows that he has the protection of HDC status. Commercial practicality requires this rule because a negotiable instrument, by its nature, carries with it the possibility that it might be negotiated to a holder in due course. If it is, the party that issued it cannot refuse to pay. [UCC Sec. 3-303]

A holder can also take for value by acquiring a lien on the instrument through an agreement rather than through operation of law. For example, a payee of a note pledges it to a bank as security for a loan. The terms of the pledge agreement give the bank a lien on the instrument. The bank is a holder for value to the extent of its lien.

There are various ways a holder can take a negotiable instrument for value and thus become a holder in due course. Section 3-303 of the Code includes within the definition of taking for value either taking an instrument in payment of or as security for an antecedent claim, or making an irrevocable commitment to a third person.

In the following case, the plaintiff tried to fall within the meaning of the definition of taking for value so that he could retain the proceeds of a check.

BACKGROUND AND FACTS *Bennett's mother, Mable, was the owner of a 1971 Datsun that Bennett used as his own. Bennett allowed his friend, Wilbur Prince, to borrow the car. While driving the car, Prince wrecked it. Prince's insurance company, Fidelity & Guaranty, issued a check payable to Mable and to Prince in settlement of the claim. Both indorsed the check to Bennett. He then deposited the check at his bank where he was told it would take a few days to clear. Waiting for the check to clear, he postdated a check of his own that he gave as payment for another car. In the meantime, Fidelity & Guaranty discovered that Prince's policy did not cover non-owned vehicles and stopped payment on the insurance check. Bennett claimed that he was entitled to the money as a holder in due course.*

DECISION AND RATIONALE *Bennett was not a holder in due course and was not entitled to the money. To qualify as a holder in due course, one must take the instrument in good faith, for value, and without knowledge of defenses against it. Bennett did not take for value.*

Bennett's first contention was that he took the check in payment of an antecedent claim against Prince, but the car was owned by Bennett's mother and, thus, Bennett had no claim against Prince. Bennett also claimed that he gave value because he made an irrevocable commitment to a third person in writing the check for a new car. The court rejected this argument also: "We are of the opinion that the wording of the statute contemplates a simultaneous transaction—a commitment to a third person made when the holder takes the instrument. We do not construe it to include a commitment made subsequent to the taking of the instrument. We hold, therefore, that plaintiff's subsequent reliance on the payment of the draft does not constitute a taking for value necessary to put plaintiff in the position of holder in due course."

BENNETT v. UNITED STATES FIDELITY AND GUAR. CO.
Court of Appeals of North Carolina, 1973.
19 N.C. App. 66, 198 S.E.2d 33.

CHECK DEPOSITS AND WITHDRAWALS Occasionally, a commercial bank can become an HDC when honoring other banks' checks for its own customers. Assume that Pat Stevens has $100 in her checking account at First National Bank. On Monday, after depositing her payroll check of $250 drawn on the Second National Bank, First National Bank cashes a check on her account for $150. The First National Bank has given value to Stevens for the check, making it an HDC to the extent of $50. The first $100 is presumed to come from the money already in Stevens' account—based on the Code's first-money-in, first-money-out approach. [UCC Sec. 4-208(2)]

Good Faith

The second requirement for HDC status is good faith. [UCC Sec. 3-302(1)(b)] The requirement of good faith means that the purchaser/holder acts honestly in the process of acquiring the instrument. **Good faith** is defined in UCC Sec. 1-201(19) as "honesty in fact in the conduct or transaction concerned."

The good faith requirement *applies only to the purchaser. It is immaterial whether the* transferor acted in good faith. Thus, a person who in good faith takes a negotiable instrument from a thief can be an HDC. The reason is simple. An inherent characteristic of negotiable paper is that any person in possession of an instrument that runs to him or her by its terms is a holder. Also, anyone can deal with the possessor as a holder.

The good faith requirement asks whether or not the purchaser, when acquiring the instrument, honestly believed the instrument was not defective. If a person purchases a $10,000 note for $100 from a stranger on a street corner, the issue of good faith can be raised on the grounds of the suspicious circumstances *and* the grossly inadequate consideration. The Code does not provide clear guidelines to determine good faith.

INDUSTRIAL NAT. BANK OF RHODE ISLAND v. LEO'S USED CAR EXCHANGE, INC.

Supreme Judicial Court of Massachusetts, 1973. 362 Mass. 797, 291 N.E.2d 603.

BACKGROUND AND FACTS *Leo's Used Car Exchange issued two checks to Frederick Villa in payment for two used automobiles that Leo's purchased at an auction. The checks were cashed (indorsed to the Industrial National Bank) and sent through the bank collection process. Later, Leo's issued a stop payment order when it learned that a third party claimed to hold a security interest in the cars. When Industrial National Bank brought suit to recover on the checks, Leo's argued that since the bank failed to follow its own management rule of having the teller obtain managerial approval before cashing the checks, it failed to exercise ordinary care. Leo's asserted that such failure to exercise ordinary care was tantamount to bad faith.*

DECISION AND RATIONALE *The bank's alleged negligence in this case did not constitute lack of good faith, and the bank thus qualified as a holder in due course. Consequently, Leo's could not assert its title-defense against it. In the judgment of the court: " 'Good faith' *** is defined [in UCC Sec. 1-201 (19)], as 'honesty in fact in the conduct or transaction concerned.' Nothing in the definition suggests that in addition to being honest, the holder must exercise due care to be in good faith."*

Notice

The third requirement for HDC status involves notice. [UCC Sec. 3-304] A person will not be afforded HDC protection if he or she acquires an instrument knowing, or having reason to know, that it is defective in any one of the following ways: [UCC Sec. 3-302(1)(c)]

1. It is overdue.
2. It has been dishonored.
3. There is a defense against it.
4. There is another claim to it.

The main provisions of UCC Sec. 3-304 spell out the common circumstances that, as a matter of law, constitute notice of a claim or defense and notice of an overdue instrument. In addition, Section 3-304(4) specifies certain facts that a purchaser might know about an instrument. These facts, in and of themselves, do not constitute notice of a defense or claim and do not disqualify the purchaser from HDC status.

NOTICE OF A FACT Notice of a fact involves (1) actual knowledge of it, or (2) receipt of a notice about it, or (3) reason to know that a fact exists, given all the facts and circumstances known at the time in question. [UCC Sec. 1-201(25)]

OVERDUE OR DISHONORED INSTRU-MENTS All negotiable paper is either payable at a definite time (time instrument) or payable on demand (demand instrument). What will constitute notice that an instrument is overdue or has been dishonored will vary depending upon whether a person takes demand or time paper.

Time Instruments A purchaser of a time instrument who takes the paper the day after its expressed due date is "on notice" that it is overdue. Nonpayment by the due date should indicate to any purchaser that the primary party has a defense to payment. Thus, a promissory note due on May 15 must be acquired before midnight on May 15. If it is purchased on May 16, the purchaser will be an ordinary holder, not an HDC.

Sometimes instruments read "payable in thirty days." A note dated December 1 payable in thirty days is due by midnight on December 31. But, what if the note were dated December 2 payable in thirty days? When is it due? If the payment date falls on a Sunday or holiday, the instrument is payable on the next business day so the note is due on January 2.

A large debt is often broken down into successive payments. The debt can be evidenced by a single, large-denomination note payable in installments, or there can be a series of notes in smaller denominations issued, each identified as part of the same indebtedness. In the case of an installment note, notice that the maker has defaulted on any installment of principal (but not interest payments) will prevent a purchaser from becoming an HDC. [UCC 3-304(3)(a)] The same result occurs when a series of notes, each with successive maturity dates, is issued at the same time for a single indebtedness. An uncured default in payment of any one note of the series will constitute

overdue notice for the entire series. Prospective purchasers then know that they cannot qualify as HDCs.

Suppose a note reads, "Payable May 15, but may be accelerated if the holder feels insecure." A purchaser, unaware that a prior holder has elected to accelerate the due date on the instrument, buys the instrument. In Section 3-304(3)(b), the Code indirectly provides that such a purchaser can be a holder in due course unless he or she has reason to know that the acceleration has occurred.

Demand Instruments A purchaser has notice that a demand instrument is overdue if he or she takes the instrument knowing that demand has been made or takes it an unreasonable length of time after its issue. "A reasonable time for a check drawn and payable within the states and territories of the United States and the District of Columbia is presumed to be 30 days." [UCC Sec. 3-304(3)(c)]

Naturally, there can be no notice if a purchaser honestly does not know and has no reason to know from the circumstances that an instrument is overdue or that it has been dishonored. For example, Burton holds a demand note dated March 1 on Kayto, Inc., a local business firm. On March 19, she demands payment, and Kayto refuses (that is, dishonors the instrument). On March 20, Burton negotiates the note to Reynolds, a purchaser who lives in another state. Reynolds does not know and has no reason to know that the note has been dishonored so Reynolds can become an HDC.

CLAIMS AGAINST OR DEFENSES TO AN INSTRUMENT Knowledge of claims or defenses can be imputed to the purchaser in certain situations because (1) they are apparent from an examination of the face of the instrument or (2) they are extraneous to the instrument but apparent from the facts surrounding the transaction.

Incomplete Instruments A purchaser cannot expect to become an HDC when an instrument is so incomplete on its face that an element of negotiability is lacking (for example, name of the payee on order paper is missing, or the amount is not filled in). Minor omissions are permissible because these do not call into question the validity of the instrument. For example, omission of connective words, such as the "on" in "pay to Smith on order," does not affect negotiability and neither does omission of the date from a check that has the month and year. [UCC Secs. 3-304(1)(a) and 3-114(1)]

When a person accepts an instrument without knowing that it is incomplete, then that person can take as an HDC and enforce the instrument as completed. To illustrate: Stuart Morgan asks Joan Nelson to buy a textbook for him when she goes to the campus bookstore. Morgan writes a check payable to the campus store, leaves the amount blank, and tells her to fill in the price of the textbook. Assume the textbook costs $15.50 in each of the following situations.

1. If Nelson gives the store the check with the amount entirely blank, the check is so incomplete that it is neither negotiable (no certain amount) nor enforceable.
2. If the cashier sees that the check is blank, watches Nelson complete the amount as $65.50, and then gives her $50 in change, the store will probably still be an HDC if the cashier is without notice that the filling in of the amount is improper. [UCC Sec. 3-304(4)(d), comment 10]
3. If Nelson fills in the check for $65.50 before she gets to the bookstore, the store sees only a properly completed instrument. Therefore it will take the check as an HDC and can enforce it for the full $65.50. The unauthorized completion is not a sufficient defense against the store in this situation. [UCC Secs. 3-407 and 3-115]

Irregular Instruments Any noticeable irregularity on the face of an instrument that should indicate to a purchaser that something is wrong with the paper will bar HDC status. For example, a note bearing a payee's signature that has been lined through with bold strokes with the second name penciled above it is highly irregular and will disqualify a taker from HDC status. [UCC 3-304 (1)(a)]

On the other hand, a note that is otherwise negotiable containing a notation "Payable at Newark" will not be the subject of inquiry because such notation does not raise questions essential to the terms, ownership, or validity of the note, nor does it create an ambiguity as to who is the party required to pay. [UCC Sec. 3-304(1)(a)]

Different handwriting used in the body of a check and in the signature will not normally make an instrument irregular. Postdating or antedating a check or stating the amount in digits but failing to write out the numbers will not make a check irregular. [UCC Sec. 3-114(2)] Visible evidence of forgery or alterations to material elements of negotiable paper will disqualify a purchaser from HDC status. Conversely, a careful forgery or alteration can go undetected by reasonable examination, and therefore, the purchaser can qualify as an HDC. [UCC Sec. 3-304(1)(a)] However, losses that result from careful forgeries usually fall on the party to whom the forger transferred the instrument (assuming, of course, that the forger cannot be found).

Voidable Obligations It stands to reason that a purchaser who knows that a party to an instrument has a defense that entitles that party to avoid the obligation in any way cannot be a holder in due course. At the very least, good faith requires honesty in fact of the purchaser in a transaction. For example, a potential purchaser who knows that the maker of a note has breached the underlying contract with the payee cannot thereafter purchase the note as an HDC. [UCC 3-304(1)(b)]

HOLDERS THROUGH A HOLDER IN DUE COURSE

A person who does not qualify as a holder in due course but who derives title through a holder in due course can acquire the rights and privileges of a holder in due course.

This has also been called the *shelter*

provision. This rule seems to detract from the basic holder-in-due-course philosophy. It is, however, in line with the concept of marketability and free transferability of commercial paper (as well as contract law, where assignees acquire the rights of assignors). The transfer rule extends the holder-in-due-course benefits, and it is designed to aid the HDC to dispose of the instrument readily. Since any instrument in the hands of an HDC is free from personal defenses (by definition), an HDC should reasonably have the privilege of transferring all rights in the instrument.

Consider an example: By fraud, Jensen induces Bonanza to write her a check payable to her order. Later Jensen negotiates the check to Gonzales, an HDC. Still later, Gonzales indorses it specially to Adams for value, but Adams knows of the original fraud. Adams is not an HDC but is a holder through an HDC and has the same rights as an HDC. Normally, a person who acquires an instrument from an HDC or from someone with HDC rights gets HDC rights on the principle that the transferee of an instrument gets at least the rights that the transferor had.

Limitations on the Shelter Provision

The second part of Section 3-201(1) explicitly indicates that persons who formerly held instruments cannot improve their positions by later reacquiring them from HDCs. An HDC should be able to market paper freely, but if a holder was a party to fraud or, as a prior holder, had notice of a claim or defense against an instrument, that holder should not be allowed to improve his or her status by repurchasing from a later HDC. In other words, a person is not allowed to "launder" the paper by passing it into the hands of an HDC and then buying it back. To illustrate: Bailey and Zopa collaborate to defraud Manor. Manor is induced to give Zopa a negotiable note payable to Zopa's order. Zopa then specially indorses the note for value to Adams, an HDC. Bailey and Zopa split the proceeds. Adams negotiates the note to Stanley, another HDC. Stanley then negotiates the note for value to Bailey. Bailey, even though he got the note through an HDC, is not a holder through an HDC, for he participated in the original fraud and can never acquire HDC rights in this note.

QUESTIONS AND CASE PROBLEMS

1. Murphy paid Stephens for some goods with a personal check. The check was drawn on the First National Bank of Pennsylvania. Stephens took the check to the Manufacturers and Traders Trust Company and exchanged it for a cashier's check made out to his order. Before Manufacturers Trust gave Stephens the cashier's check, one of its tellers called the First National Bank to make certain that there were sufficient funds to cover it. After it gave Stephens the cashier's check, Manufacturers Trust attempted to collect on Murphy's check. Since Murphy had a personal defense, he ordered his bank to stop payment on the check. Manufacturers Trust sued Murphy to recover. Murphy claimed that Manufacturers could not recover since it was not a holder in due course. Is Murphy correct? [Manufacturers and Traders Trust Co. v. Murphy, 369 F.Supp. 11 (W.D.Pa. 1974)]

2. Stephens was the maker of a promissory note in which Ford was named the payee. Ford placed the note with Bowie National Bank as his collection agent. For the first twelve months that the note was outstanding, Stephens made numerous late payments to which Ford never objected. Subsequently, Ford decided to foreclose on the note, and, at the bank's suggestion, he sold the note to the bank for the specific purpose of foreclosing on it. The bank knew about Stephens's late payments because it had been Ford's collection agent. After the bank became owner of the note, it gave the note over to its attorney for acceleration and foreclosure. Is Bowie National Bank a holder in due course? Is the bank's attorney a holder in due course? If Bowie National Bank is not a holder in due course, it takes as a transferee the rights of its transferor. What right might Bowie National Bank be prohibited from exercising? [Stephens v. Bowie Nat. Bank of Bowie, 517 S.W.2d 686 (Tex.Civ.App. 1974)]

3. Manchester Company entered into an executory

contract with Aryeh under which Aryeh was to perform certain construction services over a twelve- to fifteen-month period. Manchester issued a check to Aryeh in prepayment for the services. The check was postdated by fifteen months so that Aryeh could not cash it until he had performed under the contract. Aryeh immediately indorsed the check to Eastern International Finance Company. It soon became apparent to Manchester that Aryeh was not going to perform its part of the original contract properly. Manchester placed a stop order with its bank so that the check could not be cashed. A year and a half later, Eastern International tried to recover on the check. Is Eastern International a holder in due course? [Aryeh v. Eastern Int'l, 54 A.D.2d 850, 388 N.Y.S. 2d. 286, (1976)]

4.   Saka spent his first three months in America in the famed Sahara Motel. Each night Saka ordered a bottle of champagne and an expensive crystal drinking glass and had a nightcap. As was customary in his native Japan, Saka then threw his glass against the fireplace in his room and yelled "Hail to the Emperor" in Japanese. Since this ritual was customary, Saka assumed that when he paid for the champagne, the price of the crystal was included. When Saka checked out of the Sahara Motel after his three-month stay, he was handed a bill for $3,046 for the broken crystal. Saka refused to pay and immediately left the U.S. for Japan. The Sahara-Nevada Corporation demanded payment, but Saka refused. Later, however, Saka gave his agent a check made out to the Sahara-Nevada Corporation and signed by Saka to his agent. He instructed his agent to make the check out for $800 and give the cash to the Sahara Motel. Instead, the agent made the check payable for $3,046, the amount claimed by the motel, and delivered it to the motel's manager without mentioning the instructions. Is the Sahara Motel, the payee, a holder in due course? [Saka v. Sahara-Nevada Corp., 92 Nev. 703, 558 P.2d. 535 (1976)]

5.   By making several fraudulent misrepresentations, a builder induced several homeowners in Washington, D.C. to sign contracts authorizing home improvements. The homeowners obtained financing to pay the builder's fees from Jefferson Federal Savings and Loan Association, a local lending institution. In exchange for the financing, the homeowners each issued promissory notes to Jefferson. The builder's fees were exorbitant, and the promissory notes were issued by the homeowners in the exact amounts of the fees charged. In addition, it was the builder's agent who introduced the homeowners to the loan manager of Jefferson Savings and Loan. The loan manager was aware of the fact that this person was the builder's agent. About a month later, after the homeowners realized that the prices for the home improvements were exorbitant, they stopped payment on the notes held by Jefferson. If Jefferson qualifies as a holder in due course, it will have every right to payment. Does Jefferson qualify? [Slaughter v. Jefferson Federal Sav. and Loan Ass'n, 538 F.2d. 397 (D.C. Cir. 1976)]

6.   On May 23, 1971, Stewart signed an agreement to purchase a lot from Cochiss College Park, Inc. At the time of the sale, Stewart executed a promissory note and mortgage on the lot for $5,000. Cochiss was the named payee. Two days later Stewart rescinded the transaction as she was entitled to do under the Interstate Land Sales Full Disclosure Act. Under this act, a purchaser of land can rescind within forty-eight hours of the purchase. That same day, Cochiss sold the note to Thornton for $3,550, a one-third discount. Is Thornton a holder in due course? [Stewart v. Thornton, 116 Ariz. 107, 568 P.2d. 414 (1977)]

7.   Which of the following parties has given value such that the party would be deemed a holder in due course under the UCC: (a) A bank that takes a negotiable promissory note from a payee as collateral for a loan. [Millman v. State Nat. Bank, 323 A.2d. 723 (D.C. Ct. App. 1974)]; (b) A bank that receives a draft and then uses the draft to credit the transferor-customer's account toward advances previously made. [Lantz Int'l Corp. v. Industria Termotecnica Campana, S.P.A., 358 F. Supp. 510 (E.D.Pa. 1973)]; (c) A bank that takes a promissory note as security on an overdrawn account of one of it's customers; (d) A legatee who inherits a promissory note from his father? [Wyatt v. Mount Airy Cemetery, 209 Pa. Super. 250, 224 A.2d. 787 (1966)]?

8.   Jones signed a mortgage in order to obtain a note for $2,575 so that Bell Company would repair her home. Bell Company sold the note to United States Finance Company before it had finished repairs. When the work was eventually completed, it was inadequate. For example, in place of aluminum siding, Bell Company put tar paper on both sides of the house and sprayed it with aluminum paint. Over the previous two years, Bell had sold more than thirty such promissory notes to United States Finance Company. Jones wanted to avoid her obligation to pay on the promissory note. Can it be argued that United States Finance Company was not a holder in due course? [United States Finance Co. v. Jones, 285 Ala. 105, 229 So.2d. 495 (1969)]

9.   Anderson entered into a contract with Atlantic Storm Window Company for the installation of storm windows in his home. He signed a promissory note and a contract. They were stapled together, and neither had any dollar amounts filled in. Atlantic Storm Window had orally agreed with Anderson that the price would be $744, but later filled in both the contract and the promissory note for $895. Shortly thereafter, Atlantic sold the promissory note with the contract still attached to First National Bank. Atlantic failed to install any storm windows in Anderson's home. If First National Bank qualifies as a holder in due course, Anderson will be obligated on the promissory note. What result? [First Nat. Bank v. Anderson, 7 D. & C. 2d 661 (Pa. 1956)]

10.   Willman was the maker of four promissory notes naming Lucas the payee, each for $2,062.50. Lucas indorsed the notes to Wood and gave them to Wood as collateral for a $50,000 loan to Lucas. All but $458 of the loan was then repaid. Lucas refused to pay the balance, and Wood attempted to collect from Willman, the maker on the notes. Can Wood be considered a holder in due course of all four notes? [Wood v. Willman, 423 P.2d. 82 (Wyo. 1967)]

27

Commercial Paper
Liability, Defenses, and Discharge

Once issued, a negotiable instrument can be circulated from person to person. Consider what happens when a check is written to X, who indorses it to Y, who in turn indorses it to Z, who then deposits it in a bank for collection. If the check bounces, can Z recover from X, or must Z look only to Y for reimbursement? What can Z do if X's indorsement was forged by F? The material in this chapter will discuss the liability of drawers of checks and drafts, makers of notes, indorsers of negotiable instruments, accommodation parties, and guarantors of instruments. Since liability is not always absolute on a negotiable instrument, even for a holder in due course, the chapter will then consider the defenses available to prevent liability, and it will conclude by reviewing the various ways a person can be discharged from an obligation on a negotiable instrument. Note that the focus here is on liability *on the instrument itself* or *on warranties connected with transfer or present-ment of the instrument* as opposed to liability for the underlying contract.

LIABILITY BASED ON SIGNATURES

The key to liability on a negotiable instrument is a **signature** which is defined in UCC Sec. 3-401(2) as "any name, including any trade or assumed name, upon an instrument, or * * * any word or mark used in lieu of a written signature." [See also UCC Sec. 1-201 (39)] Signature has its origin in the Law Merchant and is based simply on the need to know whose obligation the instrument represents. The UCC in Section 3-401(1) states the general rule: "No person is liable on an instrument unless his [or her] signature appears thereon."

The few exceptions to the general rule are contained in UCC Sec. 3-404, covering unauthorized signatures:

1. Any unauthorized signature is wholly inoperative as that of the person whose name is signed *unless* that person ratifies it or is precluded from denying it. For example, a signature made by an agent exceeding the scope of either actual or apparent authority can be ratified by the principal. A Pennsylvania court held that a wife's acceptance and retention of benefits from a promissory note constituted ratification of an otherwise unauthorized signature made by her husband.[1] For example, a person who writes and signs a check, leaving blank the amount, or the payee, or both can be estopped (prevented) from denying liability for its payment. [UCC Secs. 3-115, 3-407, and 4-401(a)]
2. An unauthorized signature operates as the signature of the unauthorized signor in favor of an HDC. For example, a person who forges a check can be held personally liable to an HDC. [UCC Secs. 3-404 and 3-401(2)]

A signature can be handwritten, typed, or printed; or it can be made by mark, by thumbprint, or in virtually any manner. According to UCC Sec. 1-201(39), "signed" means any symbol executed or adopted by a party with the "present intention to authenticate a writing." A signature can be made in any name, including an alias, a trade name, or even a fictitious name. [UCC Sec. 3-401(2)] The critical element in a signature is a "present intention to authenticate a writing." Parol evidence can be used to identify the signor, and, once identified, the signature is effective against the signor no matter how it is made.

_____
1. Rehrig v. Fortunak, 39 D. & C.2d 20, (Pa. 1966).

Agent's Signatures

The general law of agency applies to negotiable instruments. Agents can sign negotiable instruments and thereby bind their principals (see Chapter 34). [UCC Sec. 3-403(1)] Without such a rule, all corporate commercial business would stop. As Chapter 44 will show, every corporation can and must act only through its agents. However, because of the critical function a signature plays in determining liability on a negotiable instrument, this chapter will go into some detail concerning the potential problems in agents' signatures.

Even an authorized agent will not normally bind a principal on the instrument unless the agent indicates that he or she is signing on behalf of a *clearly named* principal. The agent must write out the principal's name (by signature, mark, or some symbol) and his or her own, or the agent can supply only the principal's signature.[2]

If an authorized agent signs just his or her own name, the principal will not be bound on the instrument. The agent will be personally liable. In these situations, form prevails over intent.

Under Section 3-403(2)(a), when an agent carelessly signs just his or her own name, the agent is *personally* liable on the instrument even though the parties know of the agency relationship. The parol evidence rule precludes the introduction of evidence to establish that the signature was made for a principal (see Chapter 11).

Under Section 3-403(2)(b), two other situations in which an agent is held personally liable on a negotiable instrument can arise. If the instrument is signed in both the agent's name and the principal's name—"John Jones, Bob Smith"—but nothing on the instrument indicates the agency relationship, the agent cannot be distinguished from the principal. In such a case, the form of the signature binds the agent (and it can also bind the principal). Since

_____
2. If the agent signs the principal's name, the Code presumes that the signature is authorized and genuine. [UCC Sec. 3-307(1)(b)]

inclusion of both the agent's and the principal's names without indicating their relationship is ambiguous, parol evidence is admissable *as between the original parties* to prove the agency relationship and release the agent from personal liability.

Another situation envisioned under Section 3-403(2)(b) occurs when an agent signs a negotiable instrument and indicates agency status but fails to name the principal— for example, "Barry Scott, agent." Against any subsequent holder the agent is *personally* liable, but the unnamed principal cannot be held on the instrument. But, since the indications of agency status without naming the principal is ambiguous, parol evidence is admissable as between the original parties to prove the agency relationship, absolve the agent of liability and establish the liability of the unnamed principal. [UCC Sec. 3-403(2)(b)]

GRIFFIN v. ELLINGER
Supreme Court of Texas, 1976.
538 S.W.2d 97.

BACKGROUND AND FACTS *Griffin issued three checks to Ellinger, drawn on the account of the Greenway Building Company. Griffin, the president of the company, signed his name to the checks without revealing his representative capacity. The name of the company was on the face of each check. At the time the checks were issued, neither Ellinger (the payee) nor Griffin discussed who was responsible for paying the checks. Greenway Building Company went bankrupt, and Ellinger sought recovery from Griffin individually.*

DECISION AND RATIONALE *Under the facts of this case, Griffin was individually liable on the three checks. Under UCC Sec. 3-403: "An authorized representative who signs his own name to an instrument *** except as otherwise established between the immediate parties, is personally obligated if the instrument names the person represented but does not show that the representative signed in a representative capacity, or if the instrument does not name the person represented but does show that the representative signed in a representative capacity." In the three checks at issue, Greenway Building Company was named, but Griffin's representative capacity was not indicated. Thus, Griffin was individually liable (and the Greenway Building Company was also liable) unless parol evidence (that is, evidence not contained on the face of the check) showed that Ellinger and Griffin had established between themselves that Griffin would not be individually liable. The court stated: "Under Section 3-413, any person who signs a draft engages that, upon dishonor, he will pay the amount thereof to the holder. Indeed, under Section 3-404, the signer of a draft who has no authority to draw upon the account is nevertheless liable upon his contract as drawer to any person who takes the instrument in good faith for value."*

SAMPLE SIGNATURES Section 3-403 of the UCC applies only to the signature of a representative agent whose authority to sign for the principal has been established. It does not cover unauthorized signatures made by unauthorized agents. Assuming that Mary Night is a principal and Arthur King is her agent, a negotiable instrument can bear the following signatures (after each signature, the effect on each person is indicated):

1. "Mary Night, Incorporated." A signature in this form does not bind the agent, Arthur King, if the agent is authorized. [UCC Secs. 3-401 and 3-404]
2. "Arthur King." A signature written this way personally obligates the agent, and parol evidence will be inadmissible to undo the obligation on the instrument.
3. "Mary Night by Arthur King, agent." This is a clear, unambiguous signature indicating that Arthur King has signed on behalf of Mary Night. The named agent indicates the fact of agency and the name of the principal.
4. "Arthur King, agent." In some courts, an agent using this form of signature can introduce parol evidence *between immediate parties* to prove that the signature was rendered in a representative capacity.
5. "Mary Night, Arthur King." Again, as in (4) above, parol evidence can be admitted in litigations arising between the immediate parties on the instrument to prove that the agent signed in a representative capacity. Both (4) and (5) are covered under Section 3-403(2)(b). However, in either case, if the instrument has been negotiated the agent will be personally liable on the instrument.

When a negotiable instrument is signed in the name of an organization, and the organization's name is preceded or followed by the name and office of an authorized individual, the organization will be bound; the individual who has signed the instrument in the representative capacity will not be bound. [UCC Sec. 3-403(3)]

UNAUTHORIZED SIGNATURE   If a person's name is signed to a negotiable instrument by a person who has no authority to sign, that signature is wholly inoperative and does not bind the person named. Such a signing is a forgery. However, the signor can be held liable. For example, a thief steals Dana's checkbook and signs Dana's name to a check. Dana is not liable on the check because the thief had no authority to sign her name. The thief is liable because she signed Dana's check with "present intent to authenticate a writing." If the check is negotiat-

ed to an HDC, the thief is liable because the thief signed it. [UCC Secs. 3-404 and 3-401(2)]

Assume once again that Mary Night is the principal and Arthur King is her agent. Arthur King signs a note as follows: "Mary Night, Incorporated, by Arthur King, agent." This signature clearly binds Mary Night, Incorporated, if Arthur King is an authorized representative. However, if King's signature is unauthorized, is Mary Night, Incorporated, bound, or is Arthur King bound? The answer is found in Section 3-404 of the Code. Any unauthorized signature is wholly inoperative as that of the person whose name is signed (in this case, Mary Night, Incorporated) unless it is ratified by the person whose name is signed or that person is precluded from denying it. [UCC Sec. 3-406] The signature will operate as the signature of the unauthorized signor, Arthur King, in a lawsuit by an HDC. [UCC Sec. 3-404]

Contractual Liability

PRIMARY AND SECONDARY LIABILITY Every party to a negotiable instrument is either primarily or secondarily liable for payment of that instrument when it comes due. If a person is primarily liable on a negotiable instrument, then that person is absolutely required to pay the instrument, subject to certain real defenses. [UCC Sec. 3-305(a)] Only *makers* and *acceptors* are primarily liable. [UCC Sec. 3-413(1)]

The liability of a party who is secondarily liable on a negotiable instrument is similar to that of a surety in a simple contract. Drawers and indorsers have secondary liability. (See Chapter 30.) Secondary liability is "contingent liability." In the case of notes, an indorser's secondary liability does not arise until the maker who is primarily liable has defaulted on the instrument.[UCC Secs. 3-413(2) and 3-414] With regard to drafts and checks, a drawer's secondary liability does not arise until the drawee fails to pay. Note, however, that a drawee is *not* primarily liable. Makers of notes promise to pay, but drawees are ordered to pay. Therefore, the drawee is not primarily liable unless he or she promises to pay—for example, by certifying a check. Nor is a drawee even secondarily liable on an instrument. Unless the drawee *accepts*, its only obligation is to honor its drawer's orders.

Contract Theory The parties to a negotiable instrument are bound by all of the terms of the contract that are implied by their signatures by operation of law. Once it is established that a party signed the instrument (or that it was signed by that party's authorized agent), the Code defines the party's liability. The liability is contractual in the sense that each party voluntarily incurs it and can modify it by agreement. First, the liability of the primary parties to a negotiable instrument (makers of notes and acceptors of drafts or notes) will be examined. For purposes of this discussion, assume that no defenses against the holder can be asserted to prevent liability.

PRIMARY LIABILITY OF THE MAKER OR ACCEPTOR The maker of a note promises to pay the note. The words "I promise to pay" embody the maker's contract to pay the instrument according to the terms as written at the time of the signing. If the instrument is incomplete when the maker signs it, then the contract is to pay it as completed, assuming that the instrument is properly completed. [UCC Secs. 3-413(1) and 3-115]

A maker guarantees that certain facts are true by signing a promissory note. In particular, Section 3-413(3) specifies that a maker admits to all subsequent parties that the payee in fact exists and that the payee has current capacity to indorse the note (for example, the payee is not a minor at the time the note is signed).

The drawee/acceptor is in virtually the same contractual position as the maker of a note. [UCC Secs. 3-413(1) and (3)] A drawee owes a contractual duty to the drawer to pay in accordance with the drawer's orders, but a drawee owes no duty to either the payee or any holder.

For example, X buys goods costing $2,000 from Y. These goods will be shipped to arrive on

September 1. Instead of giving Y cash, X draws a draft on Finance Company for $2,000 payable to Y on September 1. At this point, Finance is not liable on the draft, and it will not become liable on that particular instrument unless and until it "accepts" the draft.

A check is a special type of draft that is drawn on a bank and is payable on demand. Acceptance of a check is called certification. Certification is not necessary on checks, and a bank is under no obligation to certify. (See Chapter 28 for details.)

A draft which is due on a certain date, or is payable a certain time after sight *may* be presented to the drawee for acceptance. A drawee who refuses to accept such a draft has dishonored the instrument. Similarly, a maker or drawee who refuses to pay an instrument when due (and presented for payment) has dishonored the instrument. Dishonor triggers the liability of secondary parties on the instrument—that is, the drawer, "unqualified indorsers" and accommodation indorsers.[3] The sections that follow will discuss secondary liability.

SECONDARY LIABILITY Secondary parties on a negotiable instrument promise to pay on that instrument only if:

1. The instrument is properly and timely presented.
2. The instrument is dishonored.
3. Notice of dishonor is timely given to the secondary party.[4]

These requirements must be satisfied in order for a secondary party to have contractual liability on a negotiable instrument, but they are not necessary to hold a secondary party to warranty liability (discussed in one of the following

---

3. A "qualified" indorser—one who indorses "without recourse," undertakes no obligation to pay. A qualified indorser merely assumes warranty liability which is discussed later in this chapter.

4. An instrument can be drafted to provide a waiver of the presentment, dishonor, and notice of dishonor requirements. Presume for simplicity's sake that such waivers have not been incorporated into the instruments described in this chapter.

sections). [UCC Secs. 3-414, 3-501, and 3-502]

Section 3-413(2) provides that "upon dishonor of the draft and any necessary notice of dishonor * * * [the drawer] will pay the amount of the draft to the holder or to any indorser who takes it up." For example, Nancy Jones writes a check on her account at Third National Bank payable to the order of Joel Andrews. If Third National does not pay the check when Andrews presents it for payment, then Jones is liable to Andrews on the basis of her secondary liability. Drawers are secondarily liable on drafts unless they disclaim their liability by drawing the instruments "without recourse." [UCC Sec. 3-413(2)] Since drawers are secondarily liable, their liability does not arise until presentment and notice of dishonor have been made properly and timely. If improperly made, however, the drawer is relieved of liability only when the drawee bank becomes insolvent. Since the days of the Great Depression, the insolvency of banks has become a rather rare phenomenon.

An unqualified indorser contracts that in the event of presentment, dishonor, and notice of dishonor, the indorser will pay the instrument. Thus, the liability of an indorser is much like that of a drawer, with one major exception: Indorsers are *relieved* of their liability to the holder of the instrument by (1) improper (late) presentment or (2) late notice or failure to notify the indorser of dishonor. [UCC Secs. 3-414, 3-501, and 3-502]

When an indorser has actively caused an instrument to be dishonored, the requirements of presentment and notice of dishonor are excused. [UCC Sec. 3-511(2)(b)]

ACCOMMODATION PARTY An **accommodation party** is one who signs an instrument for the purpose of lending his or her name to another party in credit to the instrument. [UCC Sec. 3-415(1)] Accommodation parties are one form of security against nonpayment on a negotiable instrument. For example, a bank about to lend money, a seller taking a large order for goods, or a creditor about to extend credit to a prospective debtor all want some reasonable assurance that the debts will be paid. A party's uncertain financial condition or the fact that the parties to a transaction are complete strangers can cause a creditor to be reluctant to rely solely on the prospective debtor's ability to pay. To reduce the risk of nonpayment, the creditor can require the joining of a third person as an accommodation party on the instrument.

If the accommodation party signs on behalf of a *maker,* he or she will be an *accommodation maker* and will be primarily liable on the instrument. If the accommodation party signs on behalf of a payee or other holder (usually to make the instrument more marketable), he or she will be an accommodation indorser and will be secondarily liable.

BACKGROUND AND FACTS *Herbert and Judith Applebaum issued several checks to United Refrigerator Company in their capacity as officers of the Economy Home Food Service, Inc. They signed the face of these checks as corporate officers. They also indorsed the back of the checks as individuals. Economy was unable to pay the checks. United Refrigerator sued the Applebaums. At trial, United Refrigerator moved for a judgment on the pleadings. That motion was denied and United Refrigerator appealed from that denial.*

UNITED REFRIGERATOR CO. v. **APPLEBAUM**
Supreme Court of Pennsylvania, 1963.
410 Pa. 210, 189 A.2d 253.

DECISION AND RATIONALE *The trial court was correct in denying the motion. There was an issue of fact to be determined. There was no question that the Applebaums were accommodation parties, but there was a question as to who they were accommodating. In their answer to*

United Refrigerator's complaint, they claimed that they had indorsed the checks solely for the benefit of United Refrigerator and did not receive any consideration whatsoever. Thus, if the Applebaums can prove they signed solely to accommodate United Refrigerator, they will not be liable since Section 3-145 (5) of the UCC provides that: "An accommodation party is not liable to the party accommodated."

Warranty Liability of Parties

In addition to the contractual liability discussed in the preceding sections, transferors make certain implied warranties regarding the instruments that they are negotiating. Liability under these warranties is not subject to the conditions of proper presentment, dishonor, and notice of dishonor. These warranties arise even when a transferor does not indorse the instrument (as in delivery of bearer paper). [UCC Sec. 3-417] Often it is more expedient to compel a transferor to take back an instrument on the basis of breach of warranty than it is to prove a case of contractual liability as a holder in due course against the maker or drawer. Warranties fall into two categories, those that arise upon the *transfer* of a negotiable instrument and those that arise upon *presentment*.

TRANSFER WARRANTIES The five *transfer warranties* are described in UCC Sec. 3-417(2). They provide that any person who indorses an instrument and receives consideration warrants to all subsequent transferees and holders who take the instrument in good faith that:

1. The transferor has good title to the instrument or is otherwise authorized to obtain payment or acceptance on behalf of one who does have good title.
2. All signatures are genuine or authorized.
3. The instrument has not been materially altered.
4. No defense of any party is good against the transferor.[5]

5. The transferor has no knowledge of any insolvency proceedings against the maker, the acceptor, or the drawer of an unaccepted instrument.

THE EXTENT OF TRANSFER WARRANTIES Finally, the manner of transfer and the negotiation that is used determine how far and to whom a transfer warranty will run. Transfer by indorsement and delivery of order paper extends warranty liability to any subsequent holder who takes the instrument in good faith. However, the warranties of a person who transfers without indorsement (by delivery of bearer paper) will extend only to the immediate transferee. [UCC Sec. 3-417(2)] For example, F takes a bearer note that is apparently made by M. F negotiates the note to G by delivery only. In turn, G negotiates the note by delivery to H. If M's signature turns out to be a forgery, H can hold G (the immediate transferor) liable for breach of warranty that all signatures are genuine. H cannot hold F, a prior transferor, liable. Hence, the distinction between transfer by indorsement and delivery of order paper and transfer by delivery of bearer paper is important. (It should be noted that if G must pay damages to H arising out of the breach of warranty action, G has the right to hold F liable because F's warranty runs to G.)

PRESENTMENT WARRANTY **Presentment warranties** arise when a person presents an instrument for payment or acceptance to a maker or drawee. This warranty operates to protect the person to whom the instrument is presented. As a general rule, when payment or acceptance of an instrument is made, it is final in favor of a holder in due dourse or any person who in good faith has changed a position in reliance on that payment. [UCC Sec. 3-418] This

---

5. A qualified indorser who indorses an instrument "without recourse" limits this fourth warranty to a warranty that he or she has "no knowledge" of such a defense. [UCC Sec. 3-417(3)]

general rule is subject to three exceptions, which are often referred to as the presentment warranties under Section 3-417(1). These warranties provide the following:

1.   The party presenting has good title to the instrument or is authorized to obtain payment or acceptance on behalf of a person who has good title.
2.   The party presenting has no knowledge that the signature of the maker or the drawer is unauthorized.
3.   The instrument has not been materially altered.

The second and third warranties do not apply in certain cases where the presenter is a holder in due course. It is assumed, for example, that a drawer or maker will recognize his or her own signature or that a maker or acceptor will recognize whether an instrument has been materially altered. Thus, the second and third warranties do not arise when an instrument is presented by a holder in due course acting in good faith.

Both transfer and presentment warranties attempt to shift liability back to a wrongdoer or to the person who dealt face to face with a wrongdoer and thus was in the best position to prevent the wrongdoing.

In the following case, the court had to settle a dispute between the holder of a note (the plaintiff) and a qualified indorser (the defendant) who transferred the instrument by qualified indorsement without recourse.

FAIR FINANCE CO. v. FOURCO, INC.

Court of Appeals of Ohio, 1968. 14 Ohio App.2d 145, 237 N.E.2d 406.

BACKGROUND AND FACTS   *Fourco, Inc. was the payee of a promissory note. In drawing up the note, the promissor used Fourco's printed form. The terms for computing interest on the note were part of the printed form. Fourco sold the note to Fair Finance Company and indorsed it "without recourse." In computing the price of the note, Fourco accidentally miscalculated the interest due and Fair Finance paid $1,361.96 more than the note was worth. Fair Finance discovered the mistake when it presented the note to the promissor for payment. It brought suit against Fourco to recover the overpayment.*

DECISION AND RATIONALE   *Fair Finance was able to recover the overpayment from Fourco. Under UCC Sec. 3-147, a party who transfers an instrument for consideration warrants that no defense of any party is good against him, but a party who transfers "without recourse" warrants only that he has no knowledge of such a defense. In this case, Fourco had no knowledge of the defense until after the attempt to obtain payment. However, the note was printed by Fourco, the terms were Fourco's handiwork, and Fourco was the party that computed the interest in setting the price for Fair Finance. Under these circumstances, the court held that Fourco had knowledge as a matter of law. "* * *[W]e believe that where an endorsement of a promissory note 'without recourse' is made by a vendor-payee, who computes the interest incorrectly . . . and where the form of note and terms thereof are those of the vendor-payee, such vendor-payee has knowledge of that wrongful computation, and the defense arising therefrom * * *."*

DEFENSES

Depending upon whether a holder or an HDC (or a holder through an HDC) makes the demand for payment, certain defenses will be effective to bar collection from persons who would otherwise be primarily or secondarily liable on an instrument.

Defenses fall into two general categories—personal defenses and real, or universal, defenses. Personal defenses are used to avoid payment to an *ordinary holder* of a negotiable instrument. [UCC Sec. 3-306] Real, or universal, defenses are used to avoid payment to all holders of a negotiable instrument (including an HDC or a holder through an HDC). [UCC Sec. 3-305(2)] (In all of these discussions, reference to an HDC includes a holder through an HDC.)

Personal Defenses

BREACH OF CONTRACT When there is a breach of the underlying contract for which the negotiable instrument was issued, the maker of a note can refuse to pay it or the drawer of a check can stop payment. Breach of the contract can be claimed as a defense to liability on the instrument. For example, P purchases several cases of imported wine from W. The wine is to be delivered in four weeks. P gives W a promissory note for $1,000, which is the price of the wine. The wine arrives; but many of the bottles are broken, and several bottles that are tested have turned to vinegar. P refuses to pay the note on the basis of breach of contract and breach of warranty. (Under sales law, a seller promises that the goods are at least merchantable; see Chapter 18.) If the note is no longer in the hands of the payee/seller but is presented for payment by an HDC, the maker/buyer will not be able to plead breach of contract as a defense against liability on the note.

FRAUD IN THE INDUCEMENT A person who issues a negotiable instrument based on false statements by the other party will want to avoid payment on that instrument. For example, P agrees to purchase S's slightly used tractor. S assures P that it is in complete working order, that the tires are new, and that it has been used for only one harvest. P issues a promissory note to S for the price of the tractor, but it turns out that the tractor is four years old and has been used in four harvests. P can refuse to pay the note if it is held by an ordinary holder; but if S has negotiated the note to an HDC, P must pay the HDC. Of course, P can then sue S directly.

BURCHETT v. ALLIED CONCORD FINANCIAL CORP.

Supreme Court of New Mexico, 1964.
74 N.M. 575, 396 P.2d 186.

BACKGROUND AND FACTS *Mr. and Mrs. Burchett contracted with Kelly for the installation of aluminum siding on their home. Kelly told the Burchetts that their house would serve as a show house for advertising purposes and that they would receive $100 credit on each contract sold in a specific area. The Burchetts agreed and signed certain papers tendered by Kelly. These papers included a contract and promissory note, neither of which mentioned the $100 credit. Kelly then indorsed the note to Allied Concord Financial Corp., which took it in good faith, for value, and without notice of Kelly's fraudulent scheme. The Burchetts then refused to pay Allied on the ground that they did not have reasonable opportunity to learn the contents of the papers they signed.*

DECISION AND RATIONALE *The Burchetts were liable on the note. Under UCC Sec. 3-305, a holder in due course takes free from most defenses. However, one defense that can be asserted is that the maker of an instrument signed it as a result of a misrepresentation and there was no reasonable opportunity for the maker to learn of the character or essential terms of the instrument. Such is not the case here. The Burchetts merely failed, by their own inadvertence, to read the contents of the papers that they signed. The court held as follows: "[G]enerally it is no defense to the enforcement of an obligation like the instant one to* *insist that a fraud has been wrought where the maker does not take the care to read the instrument being signed, inasmuch as such an omission generally constitutes negligence. If such were not the general rule, where a person is of average intelligence and is qualified to read, then every negotiable instrument would be clouded with the possible defense that the maker did not read the instrument prior to signing it."*

ILLEGALITY Certain types of illegality constitute personal defenses. Other types constitute real defenses; the latter will be explained below. Some transactions are prohibited under state statutes or ordinances, and some of these applicable statutes fail to provide that the prohibited transactions are void. If a statute provides that an illegal transaction is voidable, the defense is personal. If a statute makes an illegal transaction *void*, the defense is a *real* defense and can successfully be asserted against an HDC.

ORDINARY DURESS OR UNDUE INFLU- ENCE Duress involves threats of harm or force. Ordinary duress—for example, the threat of a boycott—is a personal defense. When the threat of force or harm becomes so violent and overwhelming that a person is deprived of his or her will (aggravated duress), it becomes a real, or universal, defense, good against all holders and all HDCs. [UCC Sec. 3-305, Comment 6]

MENTAL INCAPACITY There are various types and degrees of incapacity. Incapacity is ordinarily only a personal defense. If a maker or drawer is so extremely incapacitated that the transaction becomes a nullity, then the instrument is void. In that case, the defense becomes real, or universal, and it is good against an HDC as well. [UCC Sec. 3-305(2)(b)]

DISCHARGE BY PAYMENT OR CANCELL- ATION If commercial paper is paid before its maturity date, the maker will ordinarily request the return of the instrument itself or will note on the face of the instrument that payment has been made. Otherwise, it is possible for the instrument to continue circulating. If it comes into the hands of an HDC who demands payment at maturity, the defense of discharge by payment, which is merely a personal defense, will allow the maker to avoid paying a second time on the same note. [UCC Secs. 3-601(1)(a) and 3-602]

UNAUTHORIZED COMPLETION OF AN IN- COMPLETE INSTRUMENT It is unwise for a maker or drawer to sign any negotiable instrument that is not complete. For example, X signs a check, leaves the amount blank, and gives it to A, an employee, instructing A to make certain purchases and to complete the check "for not more than $500." A fills in the amount as $5,000 *contrary to instructions*. If X can stop payment in time, X *may* be able to assert the defense of unauthorized completion and avoid liability to an ordinary holder. However, if the check is negotiated to an HDC, the instrument is payable as completed. [UCC Secs. 3-115, 3-407, 3-304(4)(d), and 4-401(2)(b)]

NONDELIVERY If a bearer instrument is lost or stolen, the maker or drawer of the instrument has the defense of nondelivery against an ordinary holder. Recall that delivery means "voluntary transfer of possession." [UCC Sec. 1-201(14)] This defense, however, is not good against an HDC. [UCC Sec. 3-305. Compare UCC Sec. 3-306(c)]

Real, or Universal, Defenses

Real, or universal, defenses are valid against *all* holders.

FORGERY Forgery of a maker's or a drawer's signature cannot bind the person whose name is used (*unless* that person ratifies the signature or is precluded from denying it). [UCC Secs. 3-401 and 3-404(1)] Thus, when a person forges an instrument, the person whose name is used has no liability to pay any holder or any HDC the value of the forged instrument. In addition, a principal can assert the defense of unauthorized signature against any holder or HDC when an agent exceeds his or her authority to sign negotiable paper on behalf of the principal. [UCC Sec. 3-403] (Forgery is discussed in Chapter 25, and unauthorized signatures have been discussed earlier in this chapter in the section on liability.)

FRAUD IN THE EXECUTION (IN FACTUM) A person can sign a negotiable instrument because he or she is deceived about what the paper actually is. For example, a consumer unfamiliar with the English language signs a paper given by a salesperson who tells the consumer that it is merely a request for an estimate for roof repair. In fact, it is a promissory note. Even if the note is negotiated to an HDC, the consumer has a valid defense against payment. This defense cannot be raised, however, when a reasonable inquiry would have revealed the nature and terms of the instrument.[6]

MATERIAL ALTERATION An alteration is material if it changes the contract terms between the original parties in any way. Examples of material alterations are (1) a change in the number or relations of the parties, (2) the completion of an instrument in an unauthorized manner, or (3) adding to the writing as signed or removing any part of it. [UCC Sec. 3-407(1)] Thus, cutting off part of the paper of a negotiable instrument or any change in the amount, the date, or the rate of interest—even if the change is only one penny, one day, or 1 percent—is material. But it is not a material alteration to correct the maker's address, to have a red line drawn across the instrument to indicate that an auditor has checked it, or to correct the total final payment due when a mathematical error is discovered in the original computation. If the alteration is *not material*, any holder is entitled to enforce the instrument according to its original terms.

Material alteration is a *complete* defense against an ordinary holder but only a *partial* defense against an HDC. An ordinary holder can recover nothing on an instrument if it has been materially altered. An HDC can enforce the instrument according to its original terms *if* the alteration is so skillfully done that it is not readily apparent. [UCC Sec. 3-407(3)] If it is readily apparent, then obviously the holder has notice of some defect or defense, and such a holder cannot be an HDC. [UCC Secs. 3-302(1)(a) and 3-304(1)(a)]

DISCHARGE IN BANKRUPTCY Discharge in bankruptcy is an absolute defense on any instrument regardless of holder because the purpose of bankruptcy is to settle all of the insolvent party's debts *finally*. [UCC Sec. 3-305(2)(d)]

ILLEGALITY When the law declares that an instrument is *void* because it has been executed in connection with illegal conduct, then the defense is absolute against both an ordinary holder and an HDC. If the law merely makes it *voidable*, as in the personal defense of illegality discussed above, then it is still a defense against a holder, but not against an HDC. The courts are sometimes prone to treat the word *void* in a statute as meaning "voidable" in order to protect a holder in due course.[7]

MENTAL INCAPACITY If a person is adjudicated mentally incompetent by state proceedings, then any instrument that person issues is null and void. The instrument is *void ab initio* (from the beginning) and unenforceable by any holder or any HDC.

---

6. Burchett v. Allied Concord Financial Corp., 74 N.M. 575, 396 P.2d 186 (1964)

7. Hawkland, *Commercial Paper and Bank Deposits and Collections*, (Brooklyn: Foundation Press, 1979) p. 249.

EXTREME DURESS   When a person signs and issues a negotiable instrument under such extreme duress as an immediate threat of force or violence (for example, at gunpoint), the instrument is *void* and unenforceable by any holder or HDC. (Ordinary duress, discussed above, is only a personal defense.)

DISCHARGE

In addition to discharge by payment, discharge on a negotiable instrument can occur by cancellation, or it can result from a material alteration of the instrument. Discharge can also occur if a party reacquires an instrument, if a holder impairs another party's right of recourse, or if a holder surrenders collateral without consent. [UCC Sec. 3-601] When a party reacquires an instrument, all those who indorsed it between the holder's original and current possession are discharged.

Discharge by Payment

According to Sections 3-601(1)(a) and 3-603, all parties to a negotiable instrument will be discharged when the party primarily liable on it pays to a holder the amount due in full.[8] The same is true if the drawee of an unaccepted draft or check makes payment in good faith to the holder. In these situations, all parties on the instruments are usually discharged. By contrast, such payment made by any other party (for example, an indorser) will discharge only the

indorser and subsequent parties on the instrument. The party making such a payment still has the right to recover on the instrument from any prior parties.

INSTRUMENTS ACQUIRED BY THEFT OR RESTRICTIVELY INDORSED   A party will not be discharged when paying in bad faith to a holder who acquired the instrument by theft or who obtained the instrument from someone else who acquired it by theft (unless, of course, the person has the rights of a holder in due course). [UCC Sec. 3-603(1)(a)] Finally, a party who pays on a restrictively indorsed instrument cannot claim discharge if the payment is made in a manner inconsistent with the terms of the restrictive indorsement. [UCC Sec. 3-603(1)(b)]

Once payment or satisfaction is made to the holder in return for the surrender of the instrument, the liability of the maker or drawer is discharged and the transaction comes to an end. There are numerous acts by which makers or drawers can fulfill payment or satisfaction. In the following case, a dishonored check was satisfied when the purchaser returned to the seller the automobile for which the check had been given.

---

8.   This is true even if the payment is made "with knowledge of a claim of another person to the instrument unless prior to such payment or satisfaction the person making the claim either supplies indemnity deemed adequate by the party seeking the discharge or enjoins payment or satisfaction by order of a court of competent jurisdiction in an action in which the adverse claimant and the holder are parties." [UCC Sec. 3-603(1)]

BACKGROUND AND FACTS   *Senechal wished to purchase a 1959 Ford. He borrowed $500 from his credit union and gave the credit union a promissory note. The credit union issued a check in the amount of $500 payable jointly to the order of Senechal and American Auto Sales. Senechal indorsed and delivered the check to American Auto, and American Auto transferred ownership of the 1959 Ford to Senechal. (Neither American Auto nor the credit union had a security interest in the car.) When the credit union learned that Senechal had been fired from his job, it stopped payment on the check, and the check was later dishonored. Senechal returned the car, but did not return the bill of sale. American Auto claimed that it was entitled to payment on the check as a holder in due course because the return of the auto was not satisfaction.*

DUILIO v. SENECHAL

Massachusetts, 1969.
7 UCC Rep. Serv. 222.

DECISION AND RATIONALE *Regardless of whether American Auto Sales was a holder or a holder in due course, it was no longer entitled to payment of the check because the return of the car was sufficient satisfaction. Whether the return of the car satisfied Senechal's obligation to pay the check was a question of fact for the trial court to decide. The trial court properly found that American Auto's claim to payment was satisfied by the return of the auto. In the court's view: "It is provided by [UCC Sec. 3-603], that '(1) The liability of any party is discharged to the extent of his payment or satisfaction to the holder ***.' Whether the plaintiff is a holder in due course is inconsequential ***. It is enough that he is a holder, and that, as such, satisfaction was made with his consent, as the Uniform Commercial Code provides."*

Discharge by Cancellation

The holder of a negotiable instrument can discharge any party to the instrument by cancellation. Section 3-605(1)(a) of the UCC explains how cancellation can occur: "The holder of an instrument may even, without consideration, discharge any party in a manner apparent on the face of the instrument or the indorsement, as by intentionally cancelling the instrument or the party's signature by destruction or mutilation, or by striking out the party's signature." For example, to write the word *paid* across the face of an instrument constitutes cancellation. Tearing up a negotiable instrument cancels the instrument. Crossing out a party's indorsement cancels that party's liability and the liability of subsequent indorsers who have already indorsed the instrument, but not the liability of any prior parties.

Destruction or mutilation of a negotiable instrument is considered cancellation only if it is done with the intention of eliminating obligation on the instrument. [UCC Sec. 3-605(1)(a)]

Thus, if destruction or mutilation occurs by accident, the instrument is not discharged, and the original terms can be established by parol evidence. [UCC Sec. 3-804]

Discharge by Reacquisition

A person reacquiring an instrument that he or she held previously discharges all intervening indorsers against subsequent holders who do not qualify as holders in due course. [UCC Secs. 3-208 and 3-601(3)(a)]

Discharge by Impairment of Recourse of Collateral

Sometimes a party to an instrument will post or give collateral to secure that his or her performance will occur. When a holder surrenders that collateral without consent of the parties who would benefit from the collateral in the event of nonpayment, those parties to the instrument are discharged. [UCC Sec. 3-606(1)(b)]

QUESTIONS AND CASE PROBLEMS

1. G & J Wood Products Company had a long-standing relationship with its bank, American Bank. G & J's president, Emerick, and American Bank's president were personal friends. In October 1969,

Emerick obtained a loan from American Bank and in return signed a promissory note that provided for repayment in monthly installments over a ten-year period. The note was signed "G. Emerick." About a year later, American Bank sold the note to Commercial Savings Bank. Emerick subsequently resigned from G & J Wood Products and could not be located. Can the new holder of the promissory note, Commercial Savings Bank, enforce the note against G & J

Wood Products? [Commercial Sav. Bank v. G & J Wood Products Co., 46 Mich. App. 133, 207 N.W.2d. 401 (1973)]

2. P. J. Pansica, president of Pansica, Inc., signed two promissory notes as follows: "P. J. Pansica, president and agent for P. J. Pansica, Inc." Llobell, the payee of the note, then requested Pansica to sign the reverse sides of the notes but without specifying any representative capacity. Pansica complied, but only after Llobell assured him that Llobell would not seek payment from Pansica personally. Thereafter, P. J. Pansica, Inc., was liquidated in bankruptcy, and Llobell sought to enforce the promissory notes against Pansica personally. Is Pansica's personal signature on the reverse side of the note an indorsement? Will Pansica be allowed to introduce evidence of Llobell's promise not to seek payment from him? [P. J. Pansica, Inc., v. Llobell, 19 U.C.C. Rptg. Serv. 564 (N.Y. Sup. Ct. 1976)]

3. Sullivan County Dorms entered into a contract to purchase certain goods from Sullivan County Wholesalers, Inc. Dorms' president, James V. Holt, signed the note "J. Holt." On the face of the note, both at the top and at the bottom, appeared the name of Holt's company, Sullivan County Dorms, and the company's insignia. About two month later, Sullivan County Dorms went out of business. Sullivan County Wholesalers then attempted to collect from Holt personally. Can Holt present parol evidence that he signed the note only in his representative capacity and thus avoid liability? [Sullivan County Wholesalers, Inc. v. Sullivan County Dorms, 59 A.D.2d 628, 398 N.Y.S.2d 180 (1977)]

4. In January 1971, the law firm of Harkavy, Moxley, and Keane was dissolved. Keane left the firm, which continued under the names of the other two partners. Prior to its dissolution, the law firm maintained a business account at Pan American Bank in which the signature of any one of the partners was sufficient for the deposit or withdrawal of funds. After dissolution of the firm, the account was kept open to take care of the former firm's receivables. In May 1971, a check payable to Keane and Moxley in the amount of $16,500 was received by Harkavy for business carried on by the former firm. The check was deposited in the former firm's account after the bookkeeper had rubber-stamped the check with a facsimile of Harkavy's signature. The $16,500 was thereafter withdrawn by Harkavy and Moxley and deposited into the account of the new firm. If the stamping of the check is deemed to be an improper indorsement, then Keane can recover from Pan

American Bank. Can Keane recover? [Keane v. Pan American Bank, 309 So.2d. 579 (Fla. App. 1975)]

5. In June 1973, Hemmingway purchased a new home for which he made a small down payment and signed a promissory note and mortgage. The note provided for interest at the rate of 9¼ percent per year. On the face of the note were the words "post maturity rate" followed by a blank line. The seller of the house immediately transferred the note and mortgage to Fidelity Mortgage Investors. Later on, Fidelity wished to sell the note to Sterling National Bank. Before it did so, one of Fidelity's officers penciled in the notation "9¼" on the face of the promissory note to indicate that the postmaturity rate of interest was equal to the prematurity rate. This accorded with standard bank practices in that locality, and the person who made the notation reasonably believed that the holder would be entitled to this rate. Fidelity then sold the note and mortgage to Sterling. What effect did the notation of "9¼" have on each of the parties to the promissory note? [Sterling Nat. Bank and Trust Co. v. Fidelity Mortgage Investors, 510 F.2d. 870 (2d Cir. 1975)]

6. Daniel had a checking account in the Valley Bank of New York. Through no fault of his own, one of Daniel's checks was stolen by Theodore. Theodore made the check out for $333, payable to the Sound Galore Stereo Shop, and signed Daniel's name. Sound Galore then negotiated it to its bank, the Barnett Bank, which gave Sound Galore cash for the check. Barnett Bank obtained payment from Valley Bank, and Valley Bank debited Daniel's account. Daniel then learned of the whole episode and sought recovery. Who will recover from whom, and who will take the loss?

7. In January 1839, Canal Bank drew a check on the Bank of Albany payable to the order of E. Bently, Jr. Two months later, it was presented by the Bank of New York to the Bank of Albany for payment. At the time of presentment, the check appeared to contain the indorsements of Bently and another individual named Budd. The Bank of New York indorsed the check to the Bank of Albany, which paid it. The Bank of Albany then debited Canal Bank's account. Subsequently, it was learned that the indorsement purporting to be that of Bently was a forgery. Who will suffer the loss here, and why? [Canal v. Bank of Albany, 1 Hill 287 (Sup. Ct. N.Y. 1841)]

8. The LRZH Corporation loaned money to Arlington in exchange for Arlington's promissory note and a third mortgage on his property. LRZH also required Arlington to obtain the signature of a reputable party

to act as surety. Before LRZH loaned the money, Arlington had his friend Langeveld sign the face of the note as follows: "L. Langeveld, for the accommodation of Arlington." LRZH then advanced Arlington the money in exchange for the note and mortgage but failed to record the mortgage as required under state law. There were two prior mortgages in existence on the property at the time. Six months later, Arlington defaulted on the loan, and the same two mortgages were still outstanding. When the property was liquidated at foreclosure, the amount received was sufficient to cover only the first mortgage and a portion of the second. LRZH now seeks to recover from Langeveld. Can it recover? What defense does Langeveld have, if any? [Langeveld v. LRZH Corp., 130 N.J. Super. 486, 327 A.2d. 683 (1974)]

28

Commercial Paper
Checks and the
Banking System

The check is probably the most familiar variety of commercial paper. Checks, credit cards, and charge accounts have replaced cash as a means of payment in almost all transactions for goods and services. It is estimated that Americans write over 35 billion checks each year, transferring about $30 trillion of checkbook dollars around the nation.[1] This means that more than 100 million checks are issued every business day. Checks are more than a daily convenience; checkbook money is an integral part of the economic system.

This chapter will identify the legal characteristics of checks and the legal duties and liabilities that arise when a check is issued. Then it will consider the check deposit and collection process—that is, the actual procedure by which checkbook money moves through banking channels, causing the underlying cash dollars to be shifted from bank account to bank account.

CHECKS

A **check** is a special type of draft that is drawn on a bank, ordering it to pay a sum of money on demand. [UCC Sec. 3-104(2)(b)] The person who writes the check is called the drawer and is usually a depositor in the

1. Federal Reserve Bank of New York Publication Department, *The Story of Checks*, 6th ed. (New York: Federal Reserve Bank of New York, 1975), p. 13.

bank on which the check is drawn. The person to whom the check is payable is the payee. The bank or financial institution on which the check is drawn is the drawee. If Anne Gordon writes a check from her checking account to pay her school tuition, she is the *drawer*, her bank is the *drawee*, and her school is the *payee*.

The payee can indorse the check to another person, thereby making that receiver a holder. Recall from Chapter 26 that a holder is a person who is in possession of an instrument that is drawn to that person's order (or drawn to bearer) or that is indorsed to that person (or in blank). [UCC Sec. 1-201(20)] The *holder* of a check has the right to transfer or negotiate it or to demand its payment in his or her own name.

Negotiability

In order for checks to perform their credit function effectively, they must be freely transferable—that is, negotiable. Negotiability is solely a matter of form, which is determined by inspecting the face of the check. According to UCC Secs. 3-104(1) and (2)(b), in order for a check to meet the minimum requirements for negotiability it must:

1. Be signed by the drawer or someone duly authorized to sign on the account.

2. Contain an unconditional order to pay a sum certain in money.
3. Be payable on demand.
4. Be payable to order or to bearer.

Cashier's Checks

Checks are usually three-party instruments, but on certain types of checks, the bank can serve as both the drawer and the drawee. For example, when a bank draws a check upon itself, the check is called a **cashier's check**, and is a negotiable instrument upon issue (see Exhibit 28-1). In effect, with a cashier's check, the bank lends its credit to the purchaser of the check, thus making it available for immediate use in banking circles. (The drawee is treated like an acceptor.) A cashier's check is therefore an acknowledgment of a debt drawn by the bank upon itself.

Traveler's Checks

A traveler's check is always an instrument on which a financial institution is both the drawer and the drawee. (It is not always a check since a bank is not always the drawee.) On traveler's checks, however, there is an additional requirement that the payee must provide his or her authorized signature in order for it to become a

EXHIBIT 28-1   CASHIER'S CHECK

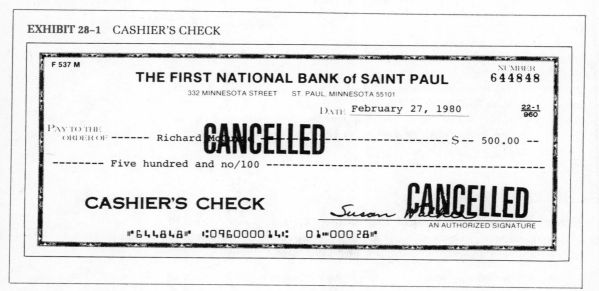

negotiable instrument. A traveler's check has the characteristics of a cashier's check from the issuing bank. It is drawn by the issuer upon itself. (See Exhibit 28-2.)

Certified Checks

A personal check is only as good as the credit of the drawer. When a person writes a check, it is assumed that he or she has money on deposit to cover that check when it is presented for payment. To insure against dishonor for insufficient funds, a check can be certified by the drawee bank. A **certified check** is recognized and accepted by a bank officer as a valid appropriation of the specified amount that is drawn against the funds held by the bank. (See Exhibit 28-3.) The usual method of certification is for the

EXHIBIT 28-2   TRAVELER'S CHECK

EXHIBIT 28-3   CERTIFIED CHECK

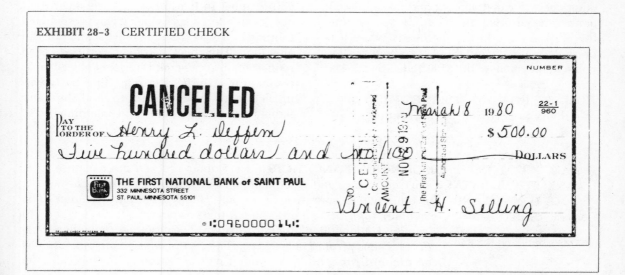

cashier or teller to write across the face of the check over the signature a statement that it is good when properly indorsed. The certification of a check prevents the bank from denying liability. It is a promise that sufficient funds are on deposit and *have been set aside* to cover the check. Certified checks are used in many business dealings, especially when the buyer and seller are strangers. Sometimes, certified checks are the required form of payment under state law—for example, in purchases at a sheriff's sale.

When a bank agrees to certification, it immediately charges the drawer's account with the amount of the check and transfers those funds to its own certified check account. In effect, the bank is agreeing in advance to accept that check when it is presented for payment and to make payment from those funds reserved in the certified check account. [UCC Sec. 3-411]

DRAWER'S REQUEST FOR CERTIFICATION

The legal liability of the drawer differs on the basis of whether the certification is requested by the drawer or the holder. The drawer who obtains certification remains *secondarily liable* on the instrument if for some reason the certifying bank cannot or does not honor the check when it is presented for payment. For example, Epstein buys Stiple's car for $500. Epstein writes out a check for that amount and takes it to the bank to be certified. In the unlikely event that the bank fails to honor the check when it is presented for payment, Stiple can hold Epstein liable for payment of the $500. [UCC Sec. 3-411]

HOLDER'S REQUEST FOR CERTIFICATION

If the check is certified at the request of the holder, then the drawer and any indorsers prior to certification are completely discharged. A holder's request for certification is viewed as an affirmative choice for the bank's promise to pay over the drawers and any indorsers. In this situation, the holder can look only to the bank for payment. In the example above, Epstein writes a $500 check to Stiple, but Stiple takes the check to the drawee bank for certification. At this point, Epstein is released from all liability, and Stiple can look only to the bank for his $500. [UCC Sec. 3-411(1)]

REVOCATION OF CERTIFICATION

The bank's ability to revoke certification is extremely limited. If a good faith holder has changed position in reliance on that certification, the bank cannot revoke. Furthermore, since certification constitutes acceptance of an instrument under the Uniform Commercial Code, a bank can never revoke certification against a HDC regardless of whether the HDC has changed position in reliance on the certification. [UCC Sec. 3-418]

ALTERATION OF A CERTIFIED CHECK

A bank will be liable for payment of an altered check only if the check was altered prior to certification. In the following case, a certified check was altered, and when it was presented to the bank, it was dishonored because of the alteration. The check had been certified at the request of the drawer and subsequently given in payment to a third party. The third party was unsuccessful in its attempt to hold the bank liable for the full amount of the instrument.

SAM GOODY, INC. v. FRANKLIN NAT. BANK OF LONG ISLAND

Supreme Court of New York, 1968.
57 Misc. 2d 193, 291 N.Y.S.2d 429.

BACKGROUND AND FACTS *A customer ordered merchandise from Sam Goody, Inc., and stated that he would secure a certified check from his employer drawn directly to Sam Goody to pay the balance. The customer then presented a check for $16 payable to Sam Goody to Franklin National Bank for certification. The customer then altered the certified check from $16 to $1,600. (The certification stamp did not show the amount for which the check was certified.) The next day he* *presented the check to Sam Goody. Franklin National Bank later dishonored the check. The bank asserted that it was responsible only for paying the instrument according to its tenor at the time of certification—$16. Sam Goody asserted that the bank should pay because it was negligent in not reflecting the amount in its certification stamp.*

DECISION AND RATIONALE *Franklin National Bank was liable only for the original tenor of the note—$16. When a bank certifies a check, it guarantees that the signature of the drawer is genuine and that the funds necessary to pay the check are on deposit with it. A bank is not liable for alterations made after the check is certified. The presiding judge stated: "[T]he controlling fact that alteration occurred after certification of the instrument is not disputed. The bank, in checking its records, discovered the alteration and refused payment. Under these circumstances, the negligence of the bank, if any, is not a substantial or proximate cause of the loss, and in accordance with the rules mentioned above, it is not liable to the plaintiff except for the amount for which the check was originally drawn."*

THE BANK-CUSTOMER RELATIONSHIP

The bank-customer relationship begins when the customer opens a checking account and deposits money that will be used to pay for checks written. The rights and duties of the bank and the customer are contractual and depend upon the nature of the transaction.

Article 4 of the UCC is a statement of the principal rules of modern bank deposit and collection procedures. It governs the relationship of banks with one another as they process checks for payment, and it establishes a framework for the deposit and checking agreement between a bank and its customer.

Article 3 of the UCC, dealing with the use of commercial paper, sets forth the requirements for negotiable instruments. The extent to which any party is either charged or discharged from liability on a check is established according to the provisions of Article 3. Note that a check can fall within the scope of Article 3 as a negotiable instrument and yet be subject to the provisions of Article 4 while it is in the course of collection. In the case of a conflict between Articles 3 and 4, Article 4 controls. [UCC Sec. 4-102(1)]

A creditor-debtor relationship is created between a customer and a bank when, for example, the customer makes cash deposits into a checking account or when final payment is received for checks drawn on other banks.

A principal-agent relationship underlies the check collection process. A check does not operate as an immediate legal assignment of funds between the drawer and the payee. [UCC Sec. 3-409] The money in the bank represented by that check does not move from the drawer's account to the payee's account; nor is any underlying debt discharged until the drawee bank honors the check and makes final payment. To transfer checkbook dollars among different banks, each bank acts as the agent of collection for its customer. [UCC Sec. 4-201(1)]

DUTIES OF THE BANK

A commercial bank serves its customers primarily in two ways:

1. Honoring checks for the withdrawal of funds on deposit in its customers' accounts.
2. Accepting deposits in U.S. currency and collecting checks written to or indorsed to its customers that are drawn on other banks.

Honoring Checks

When a commercial bank provides checking services, it agrees to honor the checks written by its customers with the usual stipulation that there be sufficient funds available in the account to pay each check. When a drawee bank wrongfully fails to honor a check, it is liable to its customer for damages resulting from its refusal to pay under breach of contract principles. [UCC Sec. 4-402] When the bank properly dishonors a check for insufficient funds, it has no liability to the customer. On the other hand, a bank may charge against a customer's account a check which is payable from that account even though the account contains insufficient funds to cover the check. The charging of overdrafts will be discussed later in this chapter.

The customer's agreement with the bank includes a general obligation to keep sufficient money on deposit to cover all checks written. The customer is liable to the payee or to the holder of a check in a civil suit if a check is not honored. If intent to defraud can be proved, the customer can also be subject to criminal prosecution for writing a bad check.

Once a bank makes special arrangements with its customer to accept overdrafts on an account, the payor bank can become liable to its customer for damages proximately caused by its wrongful dishonor of overdrafts.

KENDALL YACHT CORP. v. UNITED CALIFORNIA BANK
Court of Appeals of California, 1975.
50 Cal.3d 949, 123 Cal.Rptr. 848.

BACKGROUND AND FACTS *Lawrence and Linda Kendall were officers and principal shareholders of Kendall Yacht Corporation. Kendall Yacht had never issued stock and was under-capitalized. It had a payroll checking account and a general business checking account with United California Bank. Because the company was running into some financial problems, the bank agreed to honor overdrafts on the corporate accounts until, as the Kendall's claimed, the corporation was "out of the woods." Subsequently, the accounts became badly overdrawn, and the bank dishonored a number of their checks. The Kendalls brought suit against United California Bank, charging that a wrongful dishonor of checks that the bank had originally agreed to accept as overdrafts damaged the Kendalls' personal reputation and their credit rating.*

DECISION AND RATIONALE *The bank was liable to the Kendalls for attorneys' fees in the civil and criminal proceedings brought against them, as well as for the emotional distress and damage to reputation they suffered as a result of the bank's wrongful dishonor of the corporation's checks. Where wrongful dishonor is merely accidental, injury to reputation and emotional distress are more difficult to prove, and courts often award only nominal damages. Here, however, the bank had promised to honor the company's checks, and it was on this basis that the Kendalls continued to write the checks. Since sufficient evidence of emotional distress and damages to their reputation was presented (for example, several criminal prosecutions against them), the Kendalls were able to recover for them. The court stated: "[I]t was entirely foreseeable that the dishonoring of the Corporation's checks would reflect directly on the personal credit and reputation of the Kendalls and that they would suffer the adverse personal consequences which resulted when the Bank reneged on its commitments."*

Stale Checks

The bank's responsibility to honor its customers' checks is not absolute. A bank is not obliged to pay a noncertified check that is more than six months old. [UCC Sec. 4-404]. Commercial banking practice regards a check outstanding for longer than six months as *stale*. Section 4-404 of the UCC gives a bank the option of paying or not paying on a **stale check**. The usual banking practice is to consult the customer, but if a bank pays in good faith without consulting the customer, it has the right to charge the customer's account for the amount of the check.

BACKGROUND AND FACTS   *Five days after Granite Equipment Leasing Corporation issued a check to Overseas Equipment Company, the latter indicated that the check had not been received. Granite ordered payment stopped on the check and wired the funds to Overseas Equipment. Approximately one year later, the Hempstead Bank paid the check without making any inquiries of Granite Equipment Leasing. Granite Equipment Leasing sought to have the bank reimburse its account.*

GRANITE EQUIPMENT LEASING CORP. v. HEMPSTEAD BANK
Supreme Court of New York, 1971.
68 Misc.2d 350, 326 N.Y.S.2d 881.

DECISION AND RATIONALE   *Hempstead Bank was legally justified in paying the check when presented, and therefore it did not have to reimburse Granite's account. First, under the UCC Sec. 4-403, a customer's written stop order on a check is effective for only six months unless it is renewed. Since more than a year had passed, and the stop order had not been renewed, it was no longer effective. Second, Granite could not predicate a claim of liability upon the bank's payment of the check, even though the check was stale. The court stated, "The Bank does not have to pay a stale check, but it may pay one in 'good faith.' " UCC Sec. 1-201 (19) defines "good faith" as "honesty in fact in the conduct or transaction concerned." The court concluded: "In the absence of any facts which could justify a finding of dishonesty, bad faith, recklessness, or lack of ordinary care, in the face of circumstances actually known, or which should have been known, the Bank is not liable to Granite for its payment of the check drawn to Overseas."*

Death or Incompetence of a Customer

Section 4-405 of the UCC provides that if, at the time a check is issued or its collection has been undertaken, a bank does not know of an adjudication of incompetence, an item can be paid and the bank will not incur liability. Neither death nor incompetency revokes the bank's authority to pay an item until the bank knows of the situation and has had reasonable time to act. Even when a bank knows of the death of its customer, for ten days after the date of death, it can pay or certify checks drawn on or prior to the date of death unless a person claiming an interest in that account, such as an heir or an executor of the estate, orders the bank to stop all payment. Otherwise banks would constantly be required to verify the continued life and competency of their drawers.

Stop Payment Orders

Only a customer can order his or her bank to pay a check, and only a customer can order payment to be stopped. This right does not extend to holders—that is, payees or indorsees—because the drawee bank's contract is only with its drawers. A stop order must be received in reasonable time and in reasonable manner to permit the bank to act on it. [UCC Sec. 4-403] A stop order can be given orally, usually by phone, and it is binding on the bank for fourteen calendar days unless it has been confirmed in writing.[2] (See Exhibit 28-4.) Then it becomes effective for six months. A written stop order must be renewed every six months, or it will lapse. [UCC Sec. 4-403]

For example, Pat Davis orders one hundred used typewriters at $50 each from Jane Smith. Davis pays in advance for the goods with her check for $5,000. Later that day, Smith tells Davis that she is not going to deliver any typewriters. Davis immediately calls her bank and stops payment on the check. Two days later, in spite of this stop order, the bank inadvertently honors Davis's $5,000 check to Smith for the

undelivered typewriters. The bank will be liable to Davis for the full $5,000. The result would be different if Smith had delivered ninety-nine typewriters. Since Davis would have owed Smith $4,950 for the goods delivered, she would have been able to establish actual losses of only $50 due to the bank's payment over her stop order. The bank would be liable to Davis for only $50.

A stop payment order has its risks for a customer. The drawer must have a _valid legal ground_ for issuing a stop order; otherwise the holder can sue the drawer for payment. Moreover, defenses sufficient to refuse payment against a payee may not be valid grounds to prevent payment against a subsequent holder in due course. [UCC Sec. 3-305]

A person who wrongfully stops payment on a check will not only be liable to the payee for the amount of the check, but might also be liable for _special_ damages which result to the payee on account of the wrongful stop payment order. Special damages, however, must be separately pleaded and proven at trial.

_____

2. Some states do not recognize _oral_ stop payment orders.

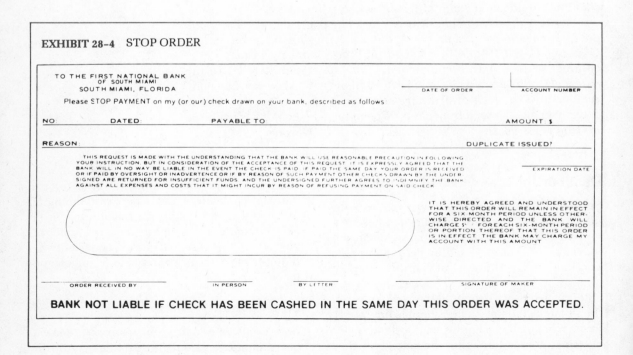

EXHIBIT 28-4   STOP ORDER

BACKGROUND AND FACTS *Sanford was fired from his job in a restaurant owned by Vickrey. Vickrey gave Sanford a number of checks for all wages due to him. Sanford had also paid $720 for stock in one of Vickrey's other businesses. Sanford told Vickrey that he needed the money to pay his bills and to get to Las Vegas where he could get another job. Vickrey gave him a check for $720 on which he wrote "Refund for stock deposit." After depositing the checks in his bank, Sanford returned to the restaurant where he cursed and threatened Vickrey and then set out for Las Vegas. Vickrey stopped payment on the $720 check. The bank got in touch with Sanford a few days later and asked him to sign a note for the $720. Sanford made two trips back to Texas to straighten out the matter. He sought to recover for the amount of the check and, as special damages, the expenses he incurred in making those trips.*

DECISION AND RATIONALE *The court decided that Vickrey was responsible for paying the $720 plus interest, but decided that there was insufficient evidence to show that the expenses Sanford claimed as special damages were reasonably necessary. Vickrey's stop order was wrongful. Vickrey claimed that there was no consideration given for the the check, but the court concluded that it was obvious to all parties that the check was given in consideration for cancellation of all of Sanford's rights to the stock. On the issue of the other expenses, the law is that special damages are recoverable if they "were within the contemplation of the parties at the time the contract was executed." To recover special damages, the party must show that they were reasonably necessary because of the breach of contract and that the amount of the damages is reasonable. The court assumed that it was within Vickrey's contemplation that a stop payment might cause Sanford expense in resolving the matter, but concluded that, "there was no evidence tending to show that the entire transaction with reference to Sanford signing the note to the bank could not have been handled by mail, thus rendering both of Sanford's trips to Texas unnecessary."*

VICKREY v. SANFORD

Court of Appeals of Texas, 1974.
506 S.W.2d 270.

Overdrafts

When the bank receives an item properly payable from its customer's checking account, but there are insufficient funds in the account to cover the amount of the check, the bank can either dishonor the item or pay it and charge the customer's account even though an overdraft is created. [UCC Sec. 4-401(11)] The bank can subtract the difference from the customer's next deposit because the check carries with it an enforceable implied promise to reimburse the bank.

When a check bounces, a holder can resubmit the check, hoping that at a later date sufficient funds will be available to pay it. The holder must notify any indorsers on the check of the first dishonor; otherwise they will be discharged from liability. A holder of a noncertified check cannot claim against the bank for dishonoring a check. A holder can sue only the drawer, and any unqualified indorser.

Payment on a Forged Signature of the Drawer

A forged signature on a check has no legal effect as the signature of a drawer. [UCC Sec. 4-404] Banks require signature cards from each customer who opens a checking account. The bank is responsible for determining whether the signature on a customer's check is genuine. The general rule is that the bank must recredit the customer's account when it pays on a forged signature. [UCC Sec. 4-401]

CUSTOMER NEGLIGENCE When the customer's negligence contributes to forgery, the bank will not normally be obliged to recredit the customer's account for the amount of the check. Suppose Axelrod Corporation uses a mechanical check-writing machine to write its payroll and business checks. Axelrod discovers that one of its employees used the machine to write himself a check for $10,000 and that the bank subsequently honored it. Axelrod requests the bank to recredit $10,000 to its account for incorrectly paying on a forged check. If the bank can show that Axelrod failed to take reasonable care in controlling access to the check-writing equipment, Axelrod cannot require the bank to recredit its account for the amount of the forged check. [UCC Sec. 3-406]

TIMELY EXAMINATION REQUIRED A customer has an *affirmative duty* to examine monthly statements and cancelled checks promptly and with reasonable care and to report any forged signatures promptly. [UCC Sec. 4-406(1)] A customer who fails to report a forged signature within one year from the date that the statement and cancelled checks containing the forgery were received loses the right to sue the bank for recredit. [UCC Sec. 4-406(4)

A customer who fails to examine and report any unauthorized signatures within fourteen calendar days of receipt of his or her bank statement and cancelled checks will be liable for subsequent forgeries made by the same wrongdoer. [UCC Sec. 4-406(2)(b)] When a series of forgeries are committed and a customer does not discover the initial forgery, he or she could lose more than the price of one forged check. Middletown Bank sends out monthly statements and checks on the last day of each month. Bradley, owner of a small store, received his April statement and cancelled checks on May 1. Bradley put the unopened envelope near his checkbook which he kept on top of his desk in the storage room. Unknown to Bradley, one of his salesmen, Harry, who had seen the checkbook lying around, had removed a check and forged Bradley's signature. Harry cashed check number 1 earlier that month. Harry forged check number 2 on May 5 and check number 3 on May 12 and cashed them at Middletown Bank. Bradley received his May statement and cancelled checks on June 1, but did not look at them. Meanwhile, Harry continued to forge Bradley's signature, cashing check number 4 on June 7 and check number 5 on June 15. On July 1 Bradley received another bank statement and cancelled checks for the month of June. On July 10, Bradley reviewed his statements and cancelled checks for the months of April, May, and June. He discovered the forgeries and notified the bank that same day.

Can Bradley demand the bank recredit his account for all five forged checks? Probably not. Bradley's deadline for reporting alterations or forgeries on the April checks (which includes forged check number 1) was fourteen days after receipt of his statement—May 15. Liability for any checks forged by Harry and honored by Middletown Bank after May 15 shifts from the bank to Bradley. Thus, the bank is not required to recredit Bradley on check numbers 4 and 5. Check numbers 1, 2, and 3 may be Middletown Bank's responsibility, since each of them was honored before the reasonable time period had elapsed. Note, however, that the bank may still deny liability on the basis of Bradley's failure to use reasonable care in securing his checkbook in a safe place. If the bank proves that Bradley's negligence substantially contributed to the forgery, Bradley—not the bank—will be liable on check numbers 1, 2, and 3. [UCC Secs. 4-406 and 3-406]

Payment on a Forged Instrument

A bank that pays a customer's check that bears a forged indorsement must recredit the customer's account or be liable to the customer-drawer for breach of contract. [UCC Sec. 4-401(1)] For example, B issues a $50 check "to the order of T." L steals the check, forges T's indorsement and cashes the check. When the check reaches B's bank the bank pays it and debits B's account. Under UCC Sec. 4-401, the bank must recredit B's account $50 because it failed to carry out B's order to pay "to the order of T." [B's bank will in turn recover from the bank which cashed the check under breach of warranty principles. See UCC Sec. 4-207(1)(a)].

By comparison, the bank has no right to recover from a holder who, without knowledge, cashes a check bearing a *forged drawer's signature*. The holder merely guarantees that he or she has no knowledge that the signature of the drawer is unauthorized. Unless the bank can prove such knowledge, its only recourse is against the forger. [UCC Secs. 3-417(1)(b) and 4-207(1)(b)]

CUSTOMER'S DUTY TO DISCOVER AND REPORT UNAUTHORIZED SIGNATURE OR ALTERATION The customer is never relieved of the duty to examine the returned checks and statements received from the bank and to report forged indorsements within a reasonable time. [UCC Sec. 4-406(1)] If carelessness that can be traced to the customer results in a loss to the bank, the loss will be borne by the customer. [UCC Sec. 4-406(2)(a)] Also, the customer has the duty to report any unauthorized signature or alteration within one year from the time he or she receives the bank statement and the items in question. Any unauthorized indorsement must be reported within three years. [UCC Sec. 4-406(4)] In the following case, the customer's duty to discover and report an unauthorized signature was at issue.

BACKGROUND AND FACTS *Costello hired Ussery as a night manager for Nu-Way. On occasion Costello signed and dated checks and filled in the name of the payee to pay for goods purchased by Nu-Way. The amount of the checks was left blank for Ussery to fill in when the cost of the goods was determined. On seven such checks, Ussery substituted his name as payee and cashed the checks. In addition, Ussery gained unauthorized access to Nu-Way's checkbook and removed forty-three blank checks. He made himself payee, forged Costello's signature, and cashed the checks. Mercantile Bank returned the forged checks and the altered checks to Nu-Way along with an itemized statement of account at the end of each month. Nu-Way's bookkeeper merely compared the amount of the checks with the statements, looking only for Mercantile's computation errors. When the scheme was later discovered, Costello informed Mercantile Bank, which thereafter cashed no more of the forged or altered checks and subsequently reimbursed Nu-Way for $231 to cover the amount of the first check that Ussery had altered. Nu-Way brought suit to recover for the rest of the forged and altered checks.*

NU-WAY SERVICES, INC. v. MERCANTILE TRUST CO. NAT. ASS'N
Missouri Court of Appeals, 1975. 530 S.W.2d 743.

DECISION AND RATIONALE *Based on the facts presented in this case, Nu-Way could recover for all of the altered checks but could not recover for the forged checks. UCC Sec. 4-406 disposes of the issue: "When a bank sends to its customer a statement of account accompanied by items paid in good faith in support of the debit entries or holds the statement and items pursuant to a request or instructions of its customer or* *otherwise in a reasonable manner makes the statement and items available to the customer, the customer must exercise reasonable care and promptness to examine the statement and items to discover his authorized signature or any alteration on an item and must notify the bank promptly after discovery thereof." Since the bank sent Nu-Way a monthly statement, and since Nu-Way failed to verify the signatures and amounts on the checks included in the statements, Nu-Way must suffer the losses unless it can show that the bank did not exercise ordinary care in paying the items. The facts show that the forgeries were adroitly done and that, even though bank officers compared most of the forged checks against Costello's signature card, no amount of comparison would have revealed them. Therefore, the bank was relieved of responsibility for the forged checks.*

With respect to the altered checks, the facts revealed that the alterations were sloppily performed and that ordinary care by the bank in inspecting the checks would have revealed them. "Whereas the forgeries were skillfully written, the alterations were maladroitly performed and the changes so egregious as to call for the reproval of the bank clerk. *** Thus there was substantial evidence to uphold the jury verdict *** on the alterations."

Payment on an Altered Check

The face amount of a check is the customer's instruction to the bank to pay an exact amount of dollars and cents to the holder. The bank must examine each check before making final payment. If it fails to detect an alteration, it is liable to its customer for the loss because it did not pay as the drawer-customer ordered. The loss is the difference between the original amount of the check and the amount actually paid. Suppose a check written for $11 is raised to $111. The customer's account will be charged $11 (the amount the customer ordered it to pay). The bank will be responsible for the $100 [UCC Sec. 4-401(2)(a)]

The bank is entitled to recover the amount of loss from the transferor who, by presenting the check for payment, warrants that the check has not been materially altered. No customer or collecting bank or other holder in due course who acts in good faith gives this warranty to: (1) the maker of a note, (2) the drawer of a draft, (3) the acceptor of an item with respect to an alteration made prior to the acceptance if the holder in due course took the item after the acceptance, or (4) the acceptor of an item with

respect to an alteration made after the acceptance. [UCC Sec. 4-207(1)(c) and 3-417(1)(c)]

A customer's negligence can shift the risk of loss. A common example occurs when a person carelessly writes a check, leaving large gaps around the numbers and words so that additional numbers and words can be inserted. (See, for example, Exhibit 28-5.)

Similarly, a person who signs a check and leaves the dollar amount for someone else to fill in is barred from protesting when the bank unknowingly and in good faith pays whatever amount is shown. [UCC Sec. 4-401(2)(b)] Finally, if the bank can trace its loss on successive altered checks to the customer's failure to discover the initial alteration, then the bank can alleviate its liability for reimbursing the customer's account.[3] [UCC Sec. 4-406]

In every situation involving a forged drawer's signature or alteration, a bank must observe reasonable commercial standards of

3. The bank's defense is the same whether successive payments were made on either a forged drawer's signature or an altered check. The bank must prove that prompt notice would have prevented its loss. For example, notification might have alerted it to stop paying further items or enabled the bank to catch the forger.

care in paying on a customer's checks. [UCC Sec. 4-406(3)] The customer's contributory negligence can be asserted only if the bank has exercised ordinary care.

ACCEPTING DEPOSITS

A second fundamental service a commercial bank provides for its checking account customers is to accept deposits of cash and checks. Cash deposits made in U.S. currency are received into the customer's account without being subject to further collection procedures. This section will focus on the check after it has been deposited. In the vast majority of cases, deposited checks are from parties who do business at different banks, but sometimes checks are written between customers of the same bank. Either situation brings into play the bank collection process as it operates within the statutory framework of Article 4 of the Uniform Commercial Code.

Definitions

The first bank to receive a check for payment is the **depository bank**.[4] When a person deposits his or her IRS tax refund check into a personal

---

4. All definitions in this section are found in UCC Sec. 4-105.

checking account at the local bank, the bank acts as a *depository* bank. The bank on which a check is drawn (the drawee bank) is also called the **payor bank**. Any bank except the payor bank and the depository bank handling a check during some phase of the collection process is a **collecting bank**. During the collection process, any bank can take on one or more of these roles.

Check Collection Process

A buyer in New York writes a check on her New York bank and sends it to a seller in San Francisco. The seller deposits the check in her San Francisco bank account. The seller's bank is both a *depository bank* and a *collecting bank*. The buyer's bank in New York is the *payor bank*. As the check travels from San Francisco to New York, any collecting bank (other than the depository bank and the payor bank) handling the item in the collection process is also called an **intermediary bank**.

CHECK COLLECTION BETWEEN CUSTOMERS OF THE SAME BANK An item that is payable by the depository bank that receives it is called an "on-us item." If the bank does not dishonor the check by the opening of the second banking day following its receipt, it is con-

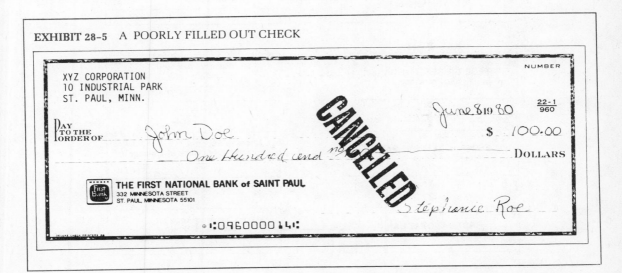

EXHIBIT 28–5   A POORLY FILLED OUT CHECK

sidered paid. [UCC Sec. 4-213(4)(b)] For example, Harriman and Goldsmith each have a checking account at First National Bank. On Monday morning, Goldsmith deposits into his own checking account a $300 check from Harriman. That same day, First National issues Goldsmith a "provisional credit" for $300. When the bank opens on Wednesday, Harriman's check is considered honored and Goldsmith's provisional credit becomes a final payment.

CHECK COLLECTION BETWEEN CUSTOMERS OF DIFFERENT BANKS Millions of checks circulate throughout the United States each day, and every check must be physically transported to its payor bank before final payment is made. Once a depository bank receives a check, it must arrange to present it either directly or through intermediary banks to the appropriate payor bank. Each bank in the collection chain must pass the check on before midnight of the next banking day following its receipt. [UCC Sec. 4-202]

The bank has a duty to use ordinary care in performing its collection functions. [UCC Sec. 4-202(1)] This duty requires banks to conform to general banking usage as established in the Uniform Commercial Code, Federal Reserve

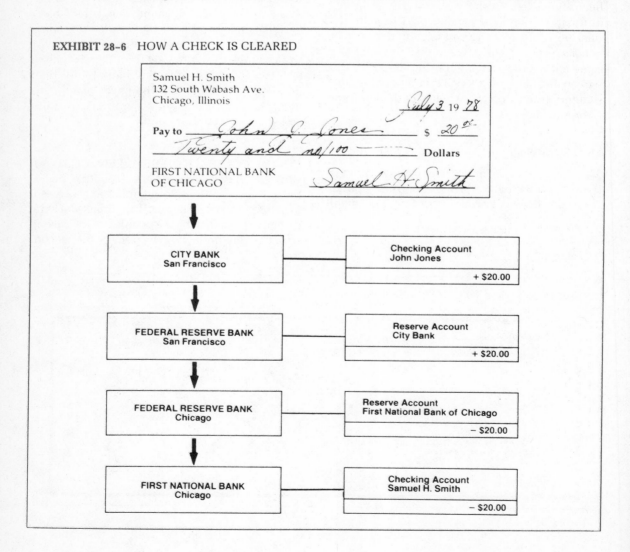

EXHIBIT 28-6   HOW A CHECK IS CLEARED

regulations, clearing house rules, and so on.[5] [UCC Sec. 4-103] Banks also have a duty to act seasonally. This means that a bank is generally required to take appropriate action before the midnight deadline following the receipt of a check, a notice, or a payment.[6] So, for example, a collecting bank that receives a check on Monday must forward it to the next collection bank prior to midnight on Tuesday.

_____

5. The Code is explicit that "the obligations of good faith, diligence, reasonableness and care * * * may not be disclaimed. * * *" [UCC Sec. 1-102(3)]
6. UCC Sec. 4-104(1)(h)

THE FEDERAL RESERVE SYSTEM CLEARS CHECKS The Federal Reserve System has greatly simplified the clearing of checks—that is, the method by which checks deposited in one bank are transferred to the banks on which they were written. Smith of Chicago writes a check to the Jones family in San Francisco. When the Joneses receive the check in the mail, they deposit it in their bank. Their bank then deposits the check in the Federal Reserve Bank of Chicago. That Federal Reserve Bank then sends the check to Smith's bank, where the amount of the check is deducted from Smith's account. Exhibit 28-6 illustrates this process.

QUESTIONS AND CASE PROBLEMS

1. Aetna Insurance Company received an insurance claim from Betty Johnson and drew a draft on itself payable to Johnson or her order. On the face of the draft appeared the words "payable through Traders National Bank and Trust." When she received the draft, Johnson negotiated it to Karen Bentley, her doctor. Bentley indorsed the draft "for deposit only, Karen Bentley," and gave it to her secretary, Mark Upton, to take to the bank. Upton took the check to the Elkstown Bank, which credited Bentley's savings account that evening and passed it on to the Federal Reserve Bank the next morning. Almost immediately, the Federal Reserve Bank transferred the draft to Traders National Bank and Trust. Pursuant to Aetna's instructions, Traders National paid the check from funds that Aetna kept in its account with Traders. What are each of the parties in the above transaction called under Article 4 of the UCC? [Aetna Cas. & Sur. Co. v. Traders Nat. Bank and Trust Co., 514 S.W.2d. 860 (Mo. Ct. App. 1974)]

2. Mr. and Mrs. Carney had a joint account in the Cambridge Trust Company. When they opened it, they both signed an agreement that allowed either of them to draw on the account individually and that stated that each would indemnify the bank against overdrafts made by the other. During a three-month period, Mr. Carney issued several large checks, each creating an overdraft in the account. Each time, Mrs. Carney reimbursed the account. Finally, Mrs. Carney instructed the bank that if any further large overdrafts were made, the bank was not to pay. Two weeks later, Mr. Carney again issued a check that overdrew the account by a large amount. The bank honored the check and then sought to recover for the overdraft from Mrs. Carney. Can the bank recover? [Cambridge Trust Company v. Carney, 115 N.H. 94, 333 A.2d. 442 (1975)]

3. On June 16, 1973, Max Schectman prepared a bank deposit of $5,669 in receipts from his business, Phillips Home Furnishings, Inc. He then proceeded to Continental Bank and properly placed his deposit in the bank's night depository safe. Five days later, not having received confirmation of his deposit, he phoned the bank, which informed him that it had no record of his deposit. In response to Schectman's inquiries, the Continental Bank showed him a copy of the "night deposit agreement" that he had signed in 1972, which placed the risk of loss on the bank's customers. Discuss whether such an agreement ought to be validated by the courts. [Phillips Home Furnishings, Inc. v. Continental Bank, 231 Pa. Super. 174, 331 A.2d. 840 (1974), rev'd 354 A.2d 542 (Pa. 1976)]

4. Security Trust was the holder of a check drawn on an account at the American National Bank. Security Trust forwarded the check for payment. It arrived on November 28, was processed manually, and was stamped "insufficient funds" on November 29. Notice of dishonor was not sent until December 3. Prior to the end of November, American National had used a manual system of bookkeeping, but a total conversion to computer bookkeeping was made during the last week of November and the first week of December. The last of the manual bookkeeping was done on about November 29. The next day, there

was a problem with the computer, and repairs were not completed for another forty-eight hours. When the repair delay became apparent, American National made use of another bank's computer and therefore was able to send notice of dishonor of the above check by December 3. What is the effect, if any, of the delay in giving the notice of dishonor? [Security Trust Co. v. First Nat. Bank, 79 Misc.2d 523, 358 N.Y.S. 2d. 943 (1974)]

5.   On July 12, 1968, Larsen drew a check for $10,000 on his account at Michigan National Bank and mailed it to the payee. The check was deposited in the account of a customer other than the payee by the Americal National Bank and Trust, which was the depository bank. American National then sent the check to the Federal Reserve Bank for collection. The check was presented for payment by the Federal Reserve Bank to Michigan National Bank and was paid on July 18. The payee notified Larsen in February 1970 that his check had never arrived. Larsen then examined his cancelled checks but did not notify Michigan National Bank of the possibly forged indorsement until August 1970, six months later. In January 1971, Michigan National Bank reimbursed Larsen and sued the Federal Reserve Bank on its warranty of good title and guarantee of prior indorsements. The Federal Reserve Bank filed a suit joining American National on the same grounds. Can the drawee bank, Michigan National, recover? Do you see any possible defenses that the collecting banks—American National and the Federal Reserve Bank—might assert against Michigan National Bank? [Michigan Nat. Bank v. American Nat. Bank and Trust Co., 34 Ill. App. 3d 30, 339 N.E.2d 375 (1975)]

6.   Rees Plumbing Company, Inc., and Weldon Douglas both maintained checking accounts at the Citizens Bank of Jonesboro. On August 19, 1966, Rees drew a check payable to Douglas in the amount of $1,000 and delivered it to Douglas. On that same day Douglas presented the check to Citizens Bank for deposit in his own checking account. Deposit slips were prepared, and a teller of the bank stamped the back of the check with the August 19 date, and a statement, "pay to any bank—prior indorsement guaranteed, Citizens Bank of Jonesboro, Jonesboro, Arkansas." On August 20, 1966, the bank dishonored the check because of insufficient funds and debited the amount of the check from Douglas's account. Did the bank, by stamping the indorsement upon the check deposited by Douglas and by delivering a deposit slip to Douglas, "accept" the check? Assume that instead of giving Douglas a provisional credit to

his account, the Citizens Bank had cashed the check. Could it then have debited Douglas's account upon dishonor of the check? [Douglas v. Citizens Bank of Jonesboro, 244 Ark. 168, 424 S.W.2d. 532 (1968)]

7.   Nancy Sims deposited a check for $756, drawn on an out-of-town bank, into her checking account with the Bank of Louisville Royal. In order to permit the check to clear, it was customary for the bank to delay crediting its customers' accounts for a period of three days. By mistake, however, one of the bank clerks posted a ten-day hold on this particular check. Thus, during a two-week period, Nancy Sims's checks were dishonored and returned with the notation "drawn against uncollected funds." Nancy Sims had some difficulty getting the whole matter straightened out and sued the Bank of Louisville for damages for wrongful dishonor of two small checks. She claimed as damages $1.50 for a telephone call, $130 for two weeks' lost wages, and $500 for "illness, harassment, embarrassment, and inconvenience." At trial she testified that she had been so embarrassed, humiliated, and mortified that the whole matter gave her a case of "nerves" resulting in her doctor advising her to take a two-week leave of absence from work, which she did. Can Nancy Sims recover for these damages? [Bank of Louisville Royal v. Sims, 435 S.W.2d. 57 (Ky. App. 1968)]

8.   Samples received a check drawn on the Trust Company of Georgia. He indorsed the check and received payment from another bank, which sent the check for collection to the Trust Company of Georgia and received payment. One week later, the Trust Company of Georgia discovered that the drawer of the check did not have an account with it. Apparently, Trust Company had mistaken the signature on the check for the signature of one of its customers with a similar name. The Trust Company of Georgia then sought to recover the amount paid on the check from Samples. Will it recover? Does Samples have any defense? [Samples v. Trust Co. of Georgia, 118 Ga. App. 307, 163 S.E.2d. 325 (1968)]

9.   Moon Over the Mountain, Ltd., was a resort in the mountains of upper New York State. It advertised luxurious rooms overlooking a crystal blue lake and seven moonlit evenings of dining and dancing for the low price of $500. The $500, however, had to be paid in advance and by cashier's check. Harvey, seeing this ad, rushed to his bank, the Marine Midland Bank, and gave the teller $500 cash in exchange for Marine Midland's cashier's check. The next week, Harvey went to the Moon Over the Mountain resort only to find a small rundown cottage overlooking Hudson

Bay. Harvey handed over his cashier's check when he arrived and spent the night but then decided that he had been taken. Harvey contacted Marine Midland Bank ten minutes after it opened the following morning and requested it to place a stop payment order on the check. Can Harvey order Marine Midland Bank to stop payment? [Moon Over the Mountain, Ltd. v. Marine Midland Bank, 87 Misc.2d. 918, 386 N.Y.S. 2d. 974 (1976)]

10. Northwest Shopping Center owned and operated a shopping center in Texas. Kaiser was one of its tenants. Pursuant to the rental agreement, Kaiser paid a monthly rent of $500 with a check that it mailed to Northwest. Northwest retained one of these rent checks for over nine months before presenting it to the bank for payment. If Northwest now presents to Kaiser's bank for payment, must the bank pay? If the bank refuses to pay, is Kaiser still liable? [Kaiser v. Northwest Shopping Center, 544 S.W.2d. 785 (Tex. Civ. App. 1976)]

29

Secured Transactions
Introduction

The concept of a secured transaction is as basic to modern business practice as the concept of credit. Few purchasers (manufacturers, wholesalers, retailers, consumers) have the resources to always pay cash for inventory. To a limited extent, consignment arrangements enable a retailer to maintain an adequate stock of goods without always advancing capital (cash), but credit is the most feasible and most common method used.

There are many credit devices available, such as securing credit with a chattel mortgage (tangible personal property) or a lien, giving a promissory note, or making an installment or time payment arrangement. Regardless of the credit method chosen, when the debtor-creditor relationship arises, the creditor often requires the debtor to provide some type of security beyond a mere promise that the debt will be paid. A credit transaction coupled with security is known as a **secured transaction.** The creditor has two major concerns if the debtor defaults on the obligation to repay:

1. Can the debt be satisfied from some *specific property offered as security* (collateral) by the debtor?
2. Will satisfaction of that particular debt from that collateral be given *priority* over the claims of other creditors?

These concerns form the basis for the law of secured transactions.

Virtually any transaction that is the subject of commercial financing when a security interest arises comes within the body of law known as "secured transactions." For example, secured transactions are often involved in the sale of goods when a retailer purchases goods for inventory on credit or when a business purchases equipment on credit or when a consumer buys merchandise on a credit plan. The law of secured transactions tends to favor the rights of creditors, but, to a lesser extent, it offers debtors some protection too.

THE LAW BEFORE THE UCC

Prior to the adoption of the UCC, the law relating to secured transactions was concerned with the person who had title to the property and with the form of the transaction. The law of secured transactions was mystifying, and the terminology was unwieldy because of the large number of methods of obtaining a security interest in goods. The methods most commonly used were chattel mortgages, trust receipts, conditional sales, and pledges.

ARTICLE 9 OF THE UCC

The UCC eliminated the distinctions among the various forms of financing outlined above and simplified the terminology. Article 9 of the UCC provides a framework for the law of secured transactions, and, regardless of the terms used in a security agreement (e.g. use of the term "chattel mortgage" instead of "security interest"), the creditor still has a "security interest" as defined by Article 9. The following sections will be concerned with the vocabulary of secured transactions. This terminology is unique to Article 9 of the Code and to secured transactions themselves.

DEFINITIONS

Under the UCC, not only has the terminology been simplified, but the particular credit devices used are irrelevant to determining the rules for establishing rights and priorities of creditors in the event of a default. The terminology used under the Code is now uniformly adopted in all documents drawn in a secured transaction situation:

1. **Security interest.** Every interest "in *personal property* or *fixtures* (emphasis added) which secures payment or performance of an obligation" is a security interest. [UCC Sec. 1-201(37)]
2. **Secured party.** A lender, seller, or any person in whose favor there is a security interest, including a person to whom accounts[1] or chattel paper[2] have been sold, is a secured party. [UCC Sec. 9-105(1)(m)]
3. **Debtor.** The party who owes payment or performance of the secured obligation, whether or not that party actually owns or has rights in the collateral, is a debtor. The term *debtor* includes sellers of accounts or chattel paper. When the debtor and owner of the collateral are not the same person, the term *debtor* refers to the actual owner of the collateral or describes the obligor on an obligation or *both*, depending upon the context in which the term is used. [UCC Sec. 9-105(1)(d)]
4. **Security agreement.** The agreement that creates or provides for a security interest between the debtor and a secured party is called a security agreement. [UCC Sec. 9-105(1)(l)]
5. **Collateral.** The property subject to a security interest, including accounts and chattel paper that have been sold, is collateral. [UCC Sec. 9-105(1)(c)]

There are four general *classifications of collateral* recognized in Article 9:

1. **Goods.** "All things which are *movable* at the time the security interest attaches or which are *fixtures*" (emphasis added) come under the general category of goods. Goods include standing timber that is to be cut and removed, the unborn young of animals, and growing crops. [UCC Sec. 9-105(1)(h)] They do not include money, documents, instruments, accounts, chattel paper, general intangibles, minerals before extraction, or the like. These fall into

---

1. *Account* refers to any right to payment for goods sold or leased or for services rendered; in effect, it is the ordinary commercial accounts receivable.
2. " 'Chattel paper' means a writing or writings which evidence both a monetary obligation and a security interest in or a lease of specific goods, * * *" [UCC Sec. 9-105(1)(b)]

other categories of collateral discussed in the items that follow.

Article 9 classifies "goods" as (a) consumer goods, (b) equipment, (c) farm products, and (d) inventory.

a. *Consumer goods.* Goods are consumer goods if they are used or bought for use primarily for personal, family, or household purposes—for example, household furniture. [UCC Sec. 9-109(1)]

b. *Equipment.* Goods are equipment if they are used or bought for use primarily in business—for example, a delivery truck. [UCC Sec. 9-109(2)]

c. *Farm products.* Crops or livestock or supplies used or produced in farming operations are farm products. Also the products of crops or livestock in their unmanufactured state (such as ginned cotton, maple syrup, milk, eggs) are farm products. Farm products must be in the possession of a debtor engaged in farming operations. [UCC Sec. 9-109(3)]

d. *Inventory.* Goods held for disposition (that is, for sale or lease) and materials used or consumed in the course of business (raw materials, for example) are all considered inventory. [UCC Sec. 9-109(4)]

2. **Chattel paper.** A writing that evidences both a *monetary obligation and a security interest* in specific goods or leased goods is chattel paper. For example, when a security agreement relates to specific equipment, it is called chattel paper. When any transaction is evidenced both by a security agreement and by instruments evidencing the debt obligation, the group of writings put together constitutes chattel paper. For example, a retail installment contract plus a signed note is chattel paper. [UCC Sec. 9-105(1)(b)]

3. **Accounts and general intangibles.** An *account* is any right to payment for goods sold or leased or for services rendered that is not evidenced by an instrument or chattel paper, whether or not it has been earned by performance. [UCC Sec. 9-106] For example, a retailer sells goods to a consumer on an open account. The consumer has sixty days in which to pay. The retailer can assign the account receivable

in an outright sale or use it to secure a loan. The transaction between the retailer and the lender based on this security is one type of *secured transaction.* The lender is the secured party, the retailer is the debtor, and the consumer is an account debtor.[3] The definition of **general intangibles** is "* * * any personal property (including things in action) other than goods, accounts, chattel paper, documents, instruments, and money." [UCC Sec. 9-106]

4. **Documents of title.** Documents of title include bills of lading, dock warrants, dock receipts, warehouse receipts, and any other documents that in the regular course of business or financing are treated as adequate evidence that the person in possession of them is entitled to receive, hold, and dispose of them and the goods they cover. [UCC Secs. 9-105(1)(f), 1-201(15) and 7-201]

5. **Financing statement.** A financing statement is a document that is filed with a state government office (usually the secretary of state) to give notice to the world that a security interest exists in particular collateral in the possession of the debtor. [UCC Sec. 9-402]

6. **Perfection.** Perfection refers to those procedures that are required under the UCC in order for a secured creditor to validly protect a security interest against other creditors. The sections that follow will discuss creating a security interest and the steps that must be taken to *perfect* that security interest.

CREATING A SECURITY INTEREST

The first concern in dealing with security interests is to determine whether the transaction falls within Article 9. Was there financing in the transaction? Did the parties intend to create a security interest? Are the collateral or the transaction items covered by Article 9? Article 9

---

3. The account debtor is the person who is obligated on the account, chattel paper, or general intangible. [UCC Sec. 9-105(1)(a)] So, for example, when the account of a third person (the user) is assigned to the bank, the dealer becomes a debtor, the bank is the secured party, and the third party is the account debtor.

applies to any transaction that is intended to create a security interest in personal property or fixtures. It also applies to any sale of accounts or chattel paper. Transactions that are excluded from Article 9 are real estate mortgages, landlords' liens, mechanics' liens, claims arising out of judicial proceedings, wage or salary claims, and so on. [UCC Sec. 9-104] In general, these transactions have been excluded because of their extensive treatment in other areas of the law. For example, landlords' liens against tenants who have defaulted are governed by rules of property law.

Purchase Money Security Interest

A **purchase money security interest** occurs when two things happen:

1.   The security interest is retained or taken by the seller of the collateral in order to secure part or all of its price; or
2.   The security interest is taken by a person who, by making advances or incurring an obligation, gives something of value that enables the debtor to acquire rights in the collateral or to use it. [UCC Sec. 9-107]

In either case, a lender or seller has essentially provided a buyer with the "purchase money" to buy goods. For example, Beasley borrows money from Frankel and uses it to purchase furniture. Beasley automatically has a security interest in the furniture. The security interest will last until the loan is repaid.

   The importance of the distinction between a purchase money security interest and other types of security interests will be discussed in Chapter 30. In short, a purchase money security interest ordinarily has priority over a nonpurchase money security interest.

Attachment

Assuming that the transaction comes within the scope of Article 9, a businessperson must meet three requirements in order to have an enforceable security interest. There must be an agreement in writing. The secured party must give value to the debtor. The debtor must have rights in the collateral. Once these requirements are met, the creditor's rights are said to "attach" to the collateral. This means that the creditor's security interest is *enforceable*. Attachment insures that the security interest between the debtor and the secured party is effective. [UCC Sec. 9-203]

WRITTEN AGREEMENT   Unless the collateral is in the possession of the secured party, there must be a *written security agreement* describing it and signed by the debtor. The security agreement creates or provides for a security interest. For example, it might read "Debtor hereby grants to secured party a security interest in the following goods. * * *" There are three requirements for the agreement to be valid:

1.   The agreement must be signed by the debtor.
2.   The agreement must contain a description of the collateral.
3.   The description must reasonably identify the collateral. [UCC Secs. 9-203(1) and 9-110]

VALUE GIVEN TO DEBTOR   The secured party must give *value*. According to UCC Sec. 1-201(44), value is any consideration that supports a simple contract. In addition, value can be security given for a preexisting (antecedent) obligation or any binding commitment to extend credit. Normally, the value given by a secured party is in the form of a direct loan, or it involves the sale of goods on credit.

DEBTOR HAS RIGHTS IN COLLATERAL   The debtor must have *rights* in the collateral; that is, the debtor must have some ownership interest or right to obtain possession of that collateral. The debtor's rights can represent either a current or a future legal interest in the collateral.

PERFECTING A SECURITY INTEREST

A creditor has two main concerns if the debtor defaults—satisfaction of the debt out of certain predesignated property and priority over other creditors. The concept of *attachment*, which establishes the criteria for creating an enforceable security interest, deals with the former concern; the concept of *perfection* deals with the latter. Even though a security interest has attached, the secured party *must* take steps in order to protect its claim to the collateral over claims that may exist in third parties, such as other secured creditors, general creditors, trustees in bankruptcy, and purchasers of the collateral that is the subject matter of the security agreement. Essentially, the security agreement binds the secured party to the debtor without the need for perfection. But the secured party must go through the process of perfection in order to protect his or her interest in the collateral against third parties, such as other creditors of the debtor. [UCC Sec. 9-301] Perfection represents the legal process by which a secured party protects itself against the claims of third parties who may wish to have their debts satisfied out of the collateral.

Methods of Perfection

There are basically three methods of perfection:

1. *By transfer of collateral.* The debtor can transfer possession of the collateral itself to the secured party. This occurs, for example, when the debtor gives the secured party stocks or bonds, or even a piece of jewelry, provided that it is collateral securing the debt. This type of transfer is called a **pledge.** [UCC Sec. 9-302(1)(a)]

2. *By purchase money security interest in consumer goods.* In certain circumstances, the security interest can be perfected automatically at the time of a credit sale—that is, at the time that the security interest is created under a written security agreement. Note that this *automatic perfection rule* with regard to purchase money security interests applies only when the goods are *consumer goods.* The seller in this situation need do nothing more to protect his or her interest. There are exceptions to this rule, however, that cover security interests in fixtures and in motor vehicles. [UCC Sec. 9-302(1)(d)]

3. *By filing.* The third and perhaps most common method of perfection is by filing a *financing statement.* The UCC requires a financing statement to have: (a) the signature of the debtor, (b) the addresses of both the debtor and the creditor, and (c) a description of the collateral by type or item.[4] [UCC Sec. 9-402(1)] Filing is the means of perfection to use in all cases unless, of course, the collateral is the kind that a secured party can merely take possession of in order to perfect (such as a money pledge), or unless the goods are of the consumer variety. Collateral does not have to be described as precisely in a financing statement as it does in a security agreement.

Both the security agreement and the financing statement must contain a description of the collateral which the secured party has a security interest in. The legal purposes for including a description in each of these documents differ. However, the description contained in each is usually the same. This is true because the secured party often merely files a copy of the security agreement with the secretary of state (in order to perfect). This practice of using a copy of the security agreement as the financing statement is generally valid.

The UCC requires that the security agreement include a description of the collateral because no security interest in goods could exist unless the parties agree on which goods are subject to the security interest and then describe these goods in writing. On the other hand, the purpose of including a description of

---

4. Certain types of collateral—crops, timber to be cut, minerals, accounts, or goods that are to become fixtures—require more than mere description. [UCC Secs. 9-402(1), 9-103(5), and 9-313]

collateral in a financing statement is to put persons who might later wish to lend to the debtor on notice that certain goods in the debtor's possession are already subject to a security interest. The following case demonstrates these different objectives for including a description of collateral in the security agreement and the financing statement.

BACKGROUND AND FACTS *Dugan purchased oil drilling equipment previously owned by Lucky Drilling Company at a sheriff's sale. Jones and Laughlin Supply claimed that it held a security interest in the property. However, although the security agreement between Lucky Drilling Company and Jones and Laughlin described numerous pieces of equipment, it did not include the equipment purchased by Dugan. Jones and Laughlin argued that it could prove that the security agreement was intended to include the equipment at issue by introducing into evidence a loan and mortgage agreement between Jones and Lucky Drilling Company.*

JONES & LAUGHLIN SUPPLY v. DUGAN PRODUCTION CORP.
Court of Appeals of New Mexico, 1973.
85 N.M. 51, 508 P.2d 1348.

DECISION AND RATIONALE *Since the security agreement did not include the equipment in question in its description of the collateral, Jones and Laughlin, the lien holder, was not entitled to assert a security interest in the equipment against the purchaser, Dugan. A security interest is not effective against third parties unless it contains a description of the collateral. Even though Jones presented extrinsic evidence showing that the security agreement was supposed to cover the equipment at issue, this evidence was inadmissible. The description of collateral must be included in the security agreement itself. "Plaintiff's security agreement neither refers to 'now owned equipment' or to 'all' equipment of Lucky Drilling Company. *** The disputed items cannot be included within the security agreement by the 'outside evidence' relied on by plaintiff because the disputed items are not described in the security agreement."*

THE RANGE OF PERFECTION AND THE FLOATING LIEN CONCEPT

A security agreement can cover various types of property in addition to collateral already in the debtor's possession—the proceeds of sale, after-acquired property, and future advances.

Proceeds

Proceeds include whatever is received when collateral is sold, exchanged, collected, or disposed of. Perfection of the proceeds of the sale of collateral is available automatically for ten days after the sale. One way to extend the ten-day automatic period is to provide for such coverage in the original security agreement. This is typically done when the collateral is the type that is likely to be sold. [UCC Sec. 9-306(3)(a)]

After-acquired Property

After-acquired property of the debtor is property acquired after the execution of the security agreement. The security agreement itself can provide for coverage of after-acquired property. [UCC Sec. 9-204] This is particularly useful for inventory financing arrangements. An after-acquired property clause normally does not allow for attachment of a security interest in consumer goods "unless the debtor acquires rights in them within 10 days after the secured party gives value." [UCC Sec. 9-204(2)] Presumably, this protects consumers from encumbering all their present and future property.

In the following case, a security agreement was executed to cover the sale of a guitar and an amplifier that were used by the buyer to perform in nightclubs. Hence they were not consumer goods. (Compare UCC Secs. 9-109(1) and (2).) The seller's perfection of the security interest required the filing of a security agreement and a financing statement. Imperfections in the security agreement did not trouble the court, but the absence of the seller's address on the financing statement was fatal.

STREVELL-PATERSON FINANCE CO. v. MAY

Supreme Court of New Mexico, 1967.
77 N.M. 331, 422 P.2d 366.

BACKGROUND AND FACTS *Strevell-Paterson Finance Company (Strevell) sold a guitar and amplifier to Chavez to be used primarily in the performance of nightclub acts. Strevell also financed the sale, thus taking a purchase money security interest in the items. In addition, Chavez and Strevell executed a security agreement and filed it at the appropriate county office. The security agreement, however, did not include Strevell's address. Chavez later defaulted on his payments and meanwhile pawned the guitar and amplifier to May, a pawnshop. May, in turn, sold the items to an unknown party. Strevell sought to recover from May for the value of the guitar and amplifier on a theory of conversion.*

DECISION AND RATIONALE *Strevell could not recover from May. If the guitar and amplifier had been consumer goods or if Strevell's address had appeared on the security agreement, the conclusion would have been in Strevell's favor. In both of these circumstances, Strevell would have had a perfected security interest.*

Strevell had a valid security interest in the equipment, but its interest was not perfected. (Under UCC Sec. 9-402, a purchase money security in consumer goods is automatically perfected. However, the guitar and amplifier were not to be put to consumer or household use, so this automatic perfection provision did not apply.) Under UCC Sec. 9-402, for a security interest to be properly perfected, the finance statement must include the address of the secured party. Strevell's security interest was not perfected because it failed to include an address. The court concluded: "If the secured party's address does not appear it would be an undue burden on the person seeking such information to find him. The filing system will perform its intended function only if [a] secured party substantially complies with the requirements of [UCC Sec.] 9-402 (1)."

The Floating Lien Concept

When a security agreement includes proceeds, after-acquired property, and future advances, it is typically called a **floating lien.** Floating liens generally arise in the financing of inventory. A creditor is not interested in specific pieces of inventory because they are constantly changing.

Exhibit 29-1 illustrates a typical floating lien, which involves future advances, after-acquired property, inventory, and proceeds.

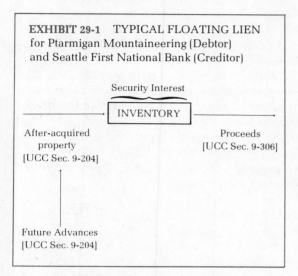

EXHIBIT 29-1   TYPICAL FLOATING LIEN
for Ptarmigan Mountaineering (Debtor)
and Seattle First National Bank (Creditor)

Security Interest

INVENTORY

After-acquired property
[UCC Sec. 9-204]

Proceeds
[UCC Sec. 9-306]

Future Advances
[UCC Sec. 9-204]

Suppose that Ptarmigan Mountaineering, a cross-country ski dealer, has a line of credit with Seattle First National Bank to finance an inventory of cross-country skis. Ptarmigan and Seattle First enter into a security agreement that provides for coverage of proceeds, after-acquired property, and future advances. One day, Ptarmigan sells a new pair of the latest nonwaxable cross-country skis, for which it receives a used pair in trade. That same day, it purchases two new pairs of skis from a local manufacturer with an additional amount of money obtained from Seattle First. Seattle First gets a perfected security interest in the used pair of cross-country skis under the proceeds clause, has a perfected security interest in the two new pairs of skis purchased from the local manufacturer under the after-acquired property clause, and has the new amount of money advanced to Ptarmigan secured by the future-advance clause. All of this is done under the original perfected security agreement. The various items in the inventory have changed, but Seattle First still has a perfected security interest in Ptarmigan's inventory, and hence it has a floating lien on the inventory.

The concept of a floating lien also applies to a shifting stock of goods. Under Section 9-205, the lien can start with raw materials and follow them as they become finished goods and inventories and as they are sold, turning into accounts receivable, chattel paper, or cash.

Collateral Moved to Another Jurisdiction

In general, collateral perfected in one jurisdiction that has been moved to another remains perfected for the time that it would have been perfected in the original jurisdiction or for four months, whichever expires first. [UCC Secs. 9-103(1)(d) and 9-103(3)(e)] The biggest problems here arise with automobiles. The general rule applies to automobiles with one difference. If either the new or the original jurisdiction requires a certificate of title as part of its perfection process, perfection does not automatically end after four months. Instead, it ceases as soon as the automobile is registered again after the end of the four-month period and a "clean" certificate of title is obtained.

The Effective Time of Perfection

A filing statement is effective for five years from the date of filing. [UCC Sec. 9-403(2)] If a continuation statement is filed within six months prior to the expiration date, the effectiveness of the original statement is continued for another five years, starting with the expiration date of the first five-year period. [UCC Sec. 9-403(3)] The effectiveness of the statement can be continued in the same manner indefinitely.

WHERE TO FILE   Depending upon the type of collateral, filing is done either with the secretary of state or with the county clerk or other official, according to state law. In general, financing statements for consumer goods or farm goods should be filed with the county clerk. Most other kinds of collateral require filing with the secretary of state. [UCC Sec. 9-401]

CAIN v. COUNTRY CLUB DELICATESSEN OF SAYBROOK, INC.

Superior Court of Connecticut, 1964.
25 Conn. Sup. 327, 203 A.2d 441.

BACKGROUND AND FACTS *On August 16, 1962, Country Club Delicatessen borrowed $35,000 from First Hartford Bank. On the previous day, First Hartford had filed a financing statement with the secretary of state. The statement covered "All goods, personal property, equipment, machinery, fixtures, etc. herein described and including all after-acquired property of like kind." (Attached was a schedule listing certain specific items included.) Approximately fifteen days later, Country Club purchased certain restaurant equipment from Hewitt. Hewitt executed a security agreement but failed to file a financing statement with the secretary of state. (It is unkown whether the equipment sold by Hewitt arrived before or after the sales contract was signed on August 30.) Country Club defaulted on its payments to both Hewitt and First Hartford, and these two secured parties then claimed priority in the same collateral—the restaurant equipment.*

DECISION AND RATIONALE *First Hartford had priority to all the restaurant equipment based on the after-acquired property clause in the financing statement that described the equipment. It is irrelevant that Hewitt executed a security agreement the same day it sold the equipment to Country Club. With respect to the UCC's filing requirements, First Hartford was first in time because it properly filed a financing statement describing the types of goods that Hewitt later sold to Country Club. The court stated: "The conditional sale contract of August 30, 1962, between [Country Club Corp.] and Hewitt created a security interest in favor of Hewitt which attached to the property thereby sold. [UCC Sec.] 9-204 (1) To perfect this security interest, a financing statement was required to be filed ***."*

CLASSIFICATION OF COLLATERAL DETERMINES WHERE TO FILE The classification of collateral is important in many situations. In determining the place of filing for goods, goods must be classified as consumer goods, equipment, farm products, or inventory. The classes of goods are mutually exclusive; *the same property cannot at the same time and to the same person be both equipment and inventory.* Is a physician's car equipment or a consumer good? Is a farmer's jeep equipment or a consumer good? The principal use to which the property is put determines its classification. If the physician uses the car primarily for personal use, then it is a consumer good; if it is used primarily for medical practice, then it is equipment. If a farmer's jeep is necessary for farming operations and is used primarily for that, then the jeep is classified as equipment. But the car and jeep can never be categorized as both equipment and inventory. [UCC Sec. 9-109]

Goods can fall into different classes at different times. For example, a CB radio is *inventory* when it is in the hands of a dealer. [UCC Sec. 9-109(4)] But when it is purchased by a consumer to use in a private car, it becomes a *consumer good.* [UCC Sec. 9-109(1)] When it is bought and then put in a patrol car, it is *equipment.* [UCC Sec. 9-109(2)] Under the Code, the classification and filing are based on the primary use being made of the collateral. According to Section 9-401, once the security agreement is properly filed, any change in the use of that collateral will not endanger the security interest of the secured party. State laws other than the UCC control where filing is done for each category of collateral.

OTHER WAYS TO PERFECT

Possession

When a creditor has possession of collateral, this is a form of security interest known under common law as a pledge. Possession gives rise to perfection of a security interest. The security interest is perfected from the time possession takes place and continues as long as possession continues. [UCC Sec. 9-305] The creditor can also maintain possession and, hence, perfect the security interest if the collateral is in the hands of a third party, such as a warehouse company. The creditor must inform the warehouse company of the security interest in the collateral, however. [UCC Sec. 9-305]

Consider an example. Ulster borrows $2,000 from Levine, giving Levine possession of three antique guns as collateral for the loan. Several months later, before Ulster has repaid the loan, a creditor obtains a judgment against Ulster. The creditor seeks to have the sheriff take the valuable antique guns away from Levine. Even though no financing statement has been filed, the creditor cannot touch the antique guns because Levine perfected his security interest in them when he took possession of them.

A security interest in *goods* can be perfected either by taking possession of the goods or by filing a financing statement, whereas a security interest in *negotiable instruments* can be perfected only by taking possession of them. The policy is to promote the free transferability of negotiable instruments by not requiring transferees of such instruments to search

through financing statements filed with the secretary of state before accepting them.

Automatic Perfection

Under some circumstances, perfection is automatic. One of them is the "purchase-money security interest" in consumer goods. [UCC Sec. 9-302(1)(d)] Otherwise, filing offices would be overwhelmed with financing statements because of the large number of such transactions. A security interest is also automatically perfected when the secured party takes possession of the collateral. A third instance of automatic perfection occurs when a person assigns a small portion of his or her accounts receivable—usually to a collecting agent known as a "factor." Perfection is automatic as long as the assignment does not by itself or in conjunction with other assignments to the same assignee constitute a transfer of a significant part of the outstanding accounts of the debtor. Other situations where perfection is automatic (but which are somewhat less important) are listed in UCC Sec. 9-302(1).

Temporary Automatic Perfection: Proceeds

If a debtor disposes of collateral, a creditor with a perfected security interest in that same collateral has an automatically perfected security interest in the proceeds of the sale of the collateral for ten days after the receipt of those proceeds by the debtor. [UCC Sec. 9-302(1)(b)] A creditor who wants a perfected security interest in those proceeds after ten days must (1) perfect the security interest before ten days, or (2) include coverage of the proceeds in the original financing statement that covered the original collateral. [UCC Sec. 9-306(3)]

QUESTIONS AND CASE PROBLEMS

1.   Canna loaned Diodato a sum of money for the purchase of an automobile. Diodato signed a promis-

sory note and procured a title certificate for the automobile. The title certificate included a typed notation designating Canna as a secured party. First County National Bank sued Diodato for money that Diodato owed the bank. The bank obtained a judgment against Diodato and attempted to levy execution upon the automobile. When it did, it became aware of Canna's claim of a prior lien. The bank then attempted to have Canna's lien set aside. Did Diodato and Canna create a valid security interest in the automobile in Canna's favor? [First County Nat. Bank and Trust Co. v. Canna, 124 N.J. Super. 154, 305 A.2d. 442 (1973)]

2.   Sabetta entered into an agreement with Industrial Leasing Corp., under which Industrial Leasing was to furnish Sabetta with certain machinery for a five-year period. The agreement provided for regular monthly payments by Sabetta and for all repair work to be provided free of charge by Industrial Leasing. At the end of the five-year term, the machinery was to be returned to Industrial Leasing. Industrial Leasing filed a copy of the agreement with Connecticut's secretary of state. The description of the equipment contained in the agreement was of "all presently owned and hereafter acquired tangible personal property." Does Industrial Leasing have a security interest in the machinery? [Industrial Leasing Corp. v. Sabetta, 16 U.C.C. Rptg. Serv. 195 (D. Conn. 1974)]

3.   Henry Reitz obtained a loan from National-Dime Bank in exchange for which he gave a security interest in a tractor and shovel that he owned. National-Dime drew a security agreement describing the collateral as "5/8 yd. shovel, diesel unit, booms, drag bucket." National-Dime then made a copy of the agreement, which both it and Reitz signed, and filed it with the secretary of state. National-Dime then procured Reitz's signature on the original security agreement and put it in its files without an officer of the bank ever signing it. Has National-Dime a security interest in the tractor and shovel attached (that is, is it enforceable)? Is it perfected? [National-Dime Bank v. Cleveland Brothers Equipment Co., 20 D.&C.2d. 511 (Pa. 1959)]

4.   Rutkin Electric Supply Company advanced money to Burdette Electronics, Inc., and received in exchange a promissory note secured by an assignment of an account receivable. As evidence of the security interest, the parties signed a financing statement and filed it with the secretary of state. Rutkin notified the account debtor of the arrangement he had made with Burdette. What is the state of Rutkin's security interest in the account receivable? Has it attached? Is it perfected? [Rutkin Electric Supply Co. v. Burdette Electronics, Inc., 98 N.J. Super. 378, 237 A.2d. 500 (1967)]

5.   Ford Motor Company shipped thirteen cars by common carrier to Lepley Ford with instructions to the common carrier not to deliver the cars to Lepley except for cash or certified check. The common carrier disregarded this order when it accepted an uncertified check by Lepley Ford that was subsequently dishonored. Ford now is attempting to recover the cars from a receiver in bankruptcy; it offers the following two arguments: Ford points to the written agreement between it and Lepley that provided that "title to each company product shall remain with Ford Motor Company until receipt by the company in cash of the full purchase price." The agreement also stated that Ford Motor Company "shall have the right to retake possession of and resell each company product until title to such product shall have passed to the dealer." Ford Motor Company claims that under the above agreement it still has title to the cars. Ford also argues that the above agreement constitutes an enforceable security agreement and that because cars are consumer goods, its security interest as a result of the agreement is automatically perfected. Discuss the validity of the two arguments made by Ford Motor Company. [Girard Trust Corn Exchange Bank v. Warren Lepley Ford, Inc., 12 D.&C.2d. 351 (Pa. 1957)]

6.   Goodyear sold several television sets to Redding on an installment basis, retaining a security interest in them. Redding quickly resold the sets to White-Sellie's, a pawnbroker shop, which sold the sets to customers. Goodyear never recorded its interest, and White-Sellie's had no knowledge of any such interest. Redding later defaulted on the installment contracts and left town. Under the law, if Goodyear can prove that it had a valid security interest in the televisions while they were in White-Sellie's hands, it can sue White-Sellie's for conversion. With what result? [White-Sellie's Jewelry Co. v. Goodyear Tire and Rubber Co., 477 S.W.2d. 658 (Tex. Civ. App. 1972)]

7.   Main National Bank made a loan to Cowley in the amount of $10,000. In return for the loan, Cowley signed a promissory note and entered into a security agreement whereby Main National Bank took a security interest in Cowley's assets, his accounts receivable, and two promissory notes payable to him. Main National Bank immediately filed a financing statement that described in detail all of the above items. Does Main National Bank have a perfected security interest in all of the above described items? [Bowles v. City Nat. Bank and Trust Co., 537 P.2d 1219 (Okl.Ct.App. 1975)]

8.   Block purchased shares of stock in Republic Corporation. These shares had not yet been issued, and there was a delay in their approval by the stock exchange. Before their issuance, Block assigned the

stock to Bergman as security for a loan. Is there any way for Bergman to perfect his security interest in the unissued shares of stock? What would your answer be if the shares of stock had already been issued? Do you think the manner of perfection would be different? [Heinicke Instruments Co. v. Republic Corp., 543 F.2d 700 (9th Cir. 1976)]

9.   A borrower executed a security agreement granting Waltman Appliance Buyers Credit Corporation a security interest in an automobile that he purchased. The borrower also obtained an insurance policy on the car. He later filed a voluntary petition in bankruptcy. Subsequently, his automobile was "totaled." The automobile insurer issued a check in settlement of the claim. Both the trustee in bankruptcy and Waltman claim the insurance proceeds. Waltman argues that since both the security agreement and the financing statement it filed give Waltman an interest in "any proceeds from the automobile," it is entitled to the insurance check. Is Waltman's argument a valid one? [In re Waltman Appliance Buyers Credit Corp. v. Stikes, 18 U.C.C.Rptg.Serv. 576 (S.D.Ala. 1975)]

10.   The Simplex Shoe Company borrowed $240,000 from Milwaukee Bank in return for which Simplex gave the bank its promissory note. Simplex also had two checking accounts with Milwaukee Bank. Prior to this loan, Commercial Discount Corporation made a large loan to Simplex and perfected a security interest in Simplex's "accounts receivable and all proceeds therefrom." When the bank loan came due, Simplex failed to pay, and the bank simply charged the amount of the loan against Simplex's checking accounts. Has Milwaukee Bank contravened Commercial Discount's security interest? [Commercial Discount Corp. v. Milwaukee Western Bank, 61 Wis.2d 671, 214 N.W.2d 33 (1974)]

30

Secured Transactions
Liens, Priorities, and Remedies

Under UCC Sec. 9-301, an unperfected security interest is not of much value when challenged by certain parties. Consider an example. James loans money to Ike, who gives James a written security agreement that gives James a security interest in Ike's antique car collection. James files no financing statement. Before Ike repays James, he files voluntary bankruptcy. The person in charge of Ike's bankruptcy (known as the trustee) claims that the antique cars are part of Ike's estate, free and clear of James's security interest. The trustee is right because James's security interest in the antique cars is unperfected.

PARTIES THAT PREVAIL OVER
THE UNPERFECTED SECURITY INTEREST

According to UCC Sec. 9-301, three categories of persons prevail over the unperfected security interest: (1) persons who have a perfected security interest in the same collateral; (2) lien creditors—that is, creditors who acquire a lien on property by attachment or levy (judicial process), including trustees in bankruptcy; and (3) buyers in the ordinary course. A *lien* is a claim against property for payment of some debt. Thus, a *lien creditor* is one whose debt or claim is secured by a lien on a particular property, as distinguished from a general creditor who has no such security. Buyers in the ordinary course are persons who purchase goods from a person in the business of selling goods of that kind (excluding pawnbrokers). But the purchasers must not know that their purchase *is in violation* of the ownership rights or security interest of another.

PRIORITIES

The consequences of perfection and nonperfection are important in determining priorities among parties having conflicting interests in the *same* collateral. As a general rule, perfection protects the interest of a secured party against all lien creditors of the debtor, against all unperfected secured parties, and against all *later* perfected, nonpurchase-money secured parties of that debtor. [UCC Sec. 9-312]

The first question is always whether an *enforceable* security agreement (that is, an agreement in writing, with value given, and with the debtor having interest in collateral) exists. The second question is to determine if and when the secured party's interest has been perfected. Assuming a party has an enforceable security interest, his or her priority will depend upon the time when the security interest attached (became enforceable) or the time when it became perfected or both, according to the following rules:

1. *Conflicting perfected security interest.* When two or more secured parties have perfected security interest in the same collateral, the first to perfect (file or take possession of collateral) wins.
2. *Conflicting unperfected security interest.* As long as conflicting security interests are unperfected, the first to attach has priority.

EXCEPTIONS TO PERFECTION PRIORITY RULES

Under certain circumstances, the perfection of a security interest will *not* protect a secured party against certain other third parties having claims to the collateral.

Buyers in the Ordinary Course of Business

Since buyers should not be required to find out if there is an outstanding security interest on a merchant's inventory, the Code provides that a person who buys "in the ordinary course of business" will take the goods free from any security interest in the merchant's inventory. [UCC Sec. 9-307] This is true even if the consumer knows at the time of purchase that there is a security interest in the inventory. Of course, if the buyer knows that the sale of goods is *in violation* of the specific terms of the security agreement, the sale is invalidated; but this is a very rare occurrence.

For example, R operates a furniture store, needs money, and seeks a loan from B Bank, using her inventory of furniture as security for the loan. B Bank makes the loan to R, perfecting its security interest in the furniture (collateral) by filing a financing statement with the secretary of state. Assume that a consumer purchases one of the pieces of furniture subject to the security interest. The consumer is a purchaser "in the ordinary course" and will take the property free of the bank's security interest unless he or she knows that the purchase violates a specific prohibition in the dealer's security agreement with the bank.

Secondhand Goods: Goods Sold by a Consumer *to* a Consumer

C is a consumer who purchases a refrigerator on credit because she cannot pay the full purchase price. The seller takes a "purchase money security interest" in the consumer goods under this type of credit plan. Further, the seller need not file a financing statement because, when a purchase money security interest is taken in consumer goods, perfection occurs automatically. [UCC Sec. 9-302(1)(d)] Later, C sells the refrigerator to her next door neighbor, N, who purchases it for home use without any knowledge of the credit arrangements between C and the original seller. Subsequently, C defaults on the credit payments to the seller. What are the seller's rights? The seller had a perfected purchase money security interest in the refrigerator when it was held by C. However, under Section 9-307(2), the perfection is not good against the next door neighbor.

Section 9-307(2) requires that the purchase take place *before* the secured party files a financing statement. In this case, recall that the seller took a purchase money security interest, which is perfected automatically. No filing was required. Hence, the next door neighbor purchased the refrigerator free and clear before the seller had filed a financing statement. The seller could have avoided this possibility simply by filing a financing statement, even though a purchase money security interest had been perfected.

In the following case, automobiles remained "consumer goods" in the hands of a dishonest consumer-purchaser who later resold them to other consumers. The subsequent buyers were protected by UCC Sec. 9-307(2) because the automobiles were deemed consumer goods both in their hands and in the hands of various sellers.

BALON v. CADILLAC AUTOMOBILE CO. OF BOSTON

Supreme Court of New Hampshire, 1973. 113 N.H. 108, 303 A.2d 194.

BACKGROUND AND FACTS *Saia fraudulently purchased two Cadillac automobiles from Cadillac Automobile Company of Boston. Saia told the salesman that he was purchasing the cars on behalf of two friends named Deluca and Russell when in fact Deluca and Russell were fictitious persons. The price of each car was $5,300. Saia paid $1,000 down on each car and had two friends posing as "Deluca" and "Russell" sign contracts for the balance. Shortly thereafter, Saia resold the cars (still new) to Gibert and Balon for $4,300 (cash) each. Only one payment was made to Cadillac Automobile Company. Neither Gibert nor Balon was aware of Saia's fraudulent scheme.*

Cadillac Automobile Company now sues to recover the cars from Gibert and Balon, claiming a purchase money security interest in them.

DECISION AND RATIONALE *Balon and Gibert were able to retain possession of the cars even though Cadillac Automobile Company had a perfected security interest in them. Under UCC Sec. 9-307 (2): "In the case of consumer goods *** a buyer takes free of a security interest even though perfected if he buys without knowledge of the security interest, for value and for his own personal, family or household purposes *** unless prior to the purchase the secured party has filed a financing statement covering such goods." Cadillac Automobile Company had a perfected security interest in the cars because it sold consumer goods under a purchase money arrangement. Since nothing was ever filed, however, such a security interest would not be good against Gibert and Balon if they were buyers of consumer goods. The court concluded: "The buyer protected under [UCC Sec.] 9-307 (2) is one who purchases goods for consumer use, that is, for personal, family or household purposes, from a consumer seller. In order to fall within the protection of this section the goods must be consumer goods in the hands of both the buyer and the seller *** [T]he trial court properly ruled that [Saia] was a dishonest consumer purchaser of these automobiles. We further hold that these cars remained consumer goods in his hands at the time of the sales to Balon and Gibert who were protected by UCC Section 9-307 (2) ***."*

Buyers of Chattel Paper

A third category of purchaser who is not subject to a secured party's interest despite perfection is the purchaser of chattel paper. This protection is provided by Section 9-308(a). Chattel paper is defined as a writing or writings that evidence both a monetary obligation and a security interest in specific goods. Chattel paper is a very important class of collateral used in financing arrangements, especially in automobile financing. When it is sold by a creditor, the creditor can deliver it over to the assignee, who is then responsible for collecting the debt directly from the debtor. This arrangement is known as "notification" or "direct collection." As an alternative, a creditor can sell chattel paper to an assignee with the understanding that the creditor will retain the chattel paper, make collections from the debtor, and then remit the money to the assignee. This kind of transaction is "nonnotification" or "indirect collection." The chattel paper is usually not delivered to the assignee. The widespread use of both methods of dealing with chattel paper is recognized by the Code, and hence the Code permits perfection of a chattel paper security interest either by filing or by taking possession.

Problems arise when perfection is made by filing only. If the chattel paper is thereafter sold to another purchaser who gives *new value* and takes possession of the paper in the ordinary course of business without knowledge that it is subject to a security interest, the new purchaser usually will have priority over the secured creditor.

THE RIGHTS AND DUTIES OF DEBTORS AND CREDITORS UNDER THE UCC

The security agreement itself determines most of the rights and duties of the debtor and the creditor. The UCC, however, imposes some rights and duties that are applicable in the absence of a security agreement to the contrary.

Information Request by Creditors

Under optional Section 9-407(1), a creditor making the filing can ask the filing officer to make a note of the file number, the date, and the hour of the original filing on a copy of the financing statement. The filing officer must send this copy to the person making the request. Under Section 9-407(2), a filing officer must also give information to a person who is contemplating obtaining a security interest for a prospective debtor. The filing officer must give a certificate that provides information on possible perfected financing statements with respect to the named debtor.

The Status of the Debt

During the time that the secured debt is outstanding, the debtor may wish to find out the status of the debt. To do so, he or she need only sign a statement that indicates the aggregate amount of the unpaid debt at a specific date (and perhaps a list of the collateral covered by the security agreement). The secured party must then approve or correct this statement in writing. [UCC Sec. 9-208] The creditor must comply with the request within two weeks of receipt; otherwise, the creditor is liable for any loss caused to the debtor by the failure to do so. One such request is allowed without charge every six months. For each additional request, the secured party can require a fee not exceeding $10 per request.

DEFAULT

Part 5 of Article 9 defines the rights and remedies of a secured party and the debtor. It encompasses alternatives that are available to secured lenders in the event of a default. It prescribes certain duties for a secured party to follow. Should the secured party fail to comply with its duties, the debtor is afforded particular rights and remedies. As mentioned before, while Article 9 tends to stress the rights of creditors, it also protects the rights of several kinds of purchasers of secured goods.

The topic of default is one that is of great concern to secured lenders and to the lawyers who draft security agreements. Default triggers the secured creditor's rights under part 5 of Article 9. However, what constitutes default is not always very clear. In fact, Article 9 does not define the term. Thus, parties are encouraged in practice and by the Code to include in their security agreements certain standards to be applied in the event that default actually comes about. Parties can stipulate the conditions that will constitute a default. [UCC Sec. 9-501(1)] Typically, because of the unusual disparity in the bargaining position between a debtor and creditor, these critical terms are shaped with exceeding breadth by the creditor to arrive at some sense of security. The ultimate terms, however, cannot run afoul of the limitations imposed by the good faith requirement of Section 1-208 and the unconscionability doctrine.

Common Events of Default

Default occurs most commonly when the debtor fails to meet the scheduled payments that the parties have agreed upon or when the debtor becomes bankrupt. If the security agreement covers equipment, the debtor may have warranted that he or she is the owner of the equipment or that no liens or other security interests are pending on that equipment. Breach of any of these representations can result in default.

Basic Remedies

According to Section 9-501, upon default, a secured creditor can reduce a claim to judgment, foreclose, or enforce a security interest by any available judicial process. Where the collateral consists of documents of title, a secured party can proceed against either the documents or the underlying goods.

A secured party's remedies can be divided into two basic categories:

1. A secured party can relinquish a security interest and proceed to judgment on the underlying debt, followed by execution and levy [UCC Sec. 9-501(1)] or
2. A secured party can take possession of the collateral covered by the security agreement. [UCC Sec. 9-503] Upon taking possession, the secured party can retain the collateral covered by the security agreement for satisfaction of the debt ("strict foreclosure") [UCC Sec. 9-505(2)] or can resell the goods and apply the proceeds toward the debt. [UCC Sec. 9-504]

The rights and remedies under Section 9-501(1) are cumulative; therefore, if a creditor is unsuccessful in enforcing rights by one method, another method can be pursued. The Uniform Commercial Code does not require election of remedies between an action on the obligation or repossession of the collateral.[1]

When a security agreement covers both real and personal property, the secured party can proceed against the personal property in accordance with the remedies of Part 5 of Article 9. On the other hand, the secured party can proceed against the entire collateral under procedures set down by local real estate law, in which case the Code does not apply. [UCC Sec. 9-501(4)] This situation occurs when the security interest on a corporate loan can apply to the manufacturing plant (real property) and also to the inventory (personal property). Determining whether a particular collateral is personal or real property can prove difficult, especially when dealing with fixtures—things affixed to real property. Under certain circumstances, the Code allows the removal of fixtures upon default; however, such removal is subject to the provisions of Part 5 of Article 9. [UCC Sec. 9-313]

The Secured Party's Right to Take Possession

The secured party has the right to take possession of the collateral upon default unless the

---

1. See White and Summers, *Uniform Commercial Code*, (St. Paul: West Publishing Co., 1972) pp. 964-968.

security agreement states otherwise. As long as there is no breach of the peace, the secured party can use self-help to repossess the collateral. Otherwise the secured party must resort to judicial process. [UCC Sec. 9-503]

What constitutes a breach of the peace is of prime importance to both parties, for such an act can open the secured party to liability under Section 9-507 and to tort liability. The Code does not define *breach of the peace*. Therefore, parties must resort to state law to determine it.

Generally, the creditor or the creditor's agent cannot enter a debtor's home, garage, or place of business without permission. Consider a situation where an automobile is collateral. If the repossessing party walks onto the debtor's premises, proceeds up the driveway, enters the vehicle without entering the garage, and drives off, it probably will not amount to a breach of the peace. However, in some states, an action for wrongful trespass could meet the threshold test and start a cause of action for breach of the peace. (Most car repossessions occur when the car is parked on a street or in a parking lot.)

REASONABLE CARE OF THE COLLATERAL REQUIRED Once the secured party comes into possession of the collateral after breach by repossession, or where the collateral has been pledged as security and is already in the possession of the secured party, there are certain rights, remedies, and duties provided by Section 9-207. The main requirement of that section calls for the secured party to exercise "reasonable care" in the custody and preservation of any collateral in its possession.

This duty cannot be disclaimed, and any exculpatory clause will be unenforceable. [UCC Sec. 1-201(3)] Reasonable limitations as to what will be required, however, can be agreed upon by the parties. Where the collateral is instruments or chattel paper, reasonable care extends to taking necessary steps to preserve rights against prior parties unless otherwise agreed. Should the secured party fail to meet its obligations as prescribed in Section 9-207, he or she will be liable for any damages occasioned by such failure. The secured party does not, however, lose the security interest for failure to exercise reasonable care.

Disposal of Collateral

Once default has occurred, the secured party is faced with several alternatives to secure payment of the debt. The party can, for example, retain the collateral in satisfaction of the debtor's obligation; this is called *strict foreclosure*. [UCC Sec. 9-505(2)] The party can also sell, lease, or otherwise dispose of the collateral in any commercially reasonable manner. [UCC Sec. 9-504(1)] Any sale is always subject to procedures established by state law. In addition, the UCC requires that notice be given before the collateral is sold.

BACKGROUND AND FACTS *In order to obtain floor plan financing for automobiles that Bob King, Inc., was selling, Irving Turk, Bob King, and Bob King, Inc., together executed a security agreement and a note for $35,000. St. Petersburg Bank and Trust Company took a security interest in the company's inventory of automobiles. Later, Turk ceased to be active in the corporation. The bank continued to advance money to the dealership until at one point its indebtedness reached $36,336. The bank became concerned for its collateral and advised Bob King, Inc., that it was going to take possession of the automobiles. The bank sold the automobiles for the sum of $17,881.52. At the time of repossession, the total outstanding indebtedness was $32,861. The bank sued Turk for the difference.*

TURK v. ST. PETERSBURG BANK & TRUST CO.
District Court of Appeal of Florida, 1973.
281 So.2d 534.

DECISION AND RATIONALE   *St. Petersburg Bank could not recover the deficiency from Turk because it seized the automobiles and sold them without giving Turk notice of the sale. In the words of the court: "The language [of the UCC] is clear that before a secured party (in this instance the bank) can obtain a deficiency against a debtor (in this instance Turk) the debtor must be given notice of what is about to occur. This is as it should be because the debtor, in this instance, Turk, could have done many things. He could have purchased the automobiles himself; he could have paid the extent of the liability, i.e., $20,000; he could have secured purchasers for the automobiles. He was not afforded the opportunity to do anything. If the bank in this instance wanted to dispose of the collateral without judicial process or notice to the debtor as the [UCC] provides, it may do so; but it is not then entitled to a deficiency against any debtor not so notified."*

RETENTION OF COLLATERAL BY SECURED PARTY AFTER DEFAULT   The Code recognizes that parties are often better off if they do not sell the collateral. Therefore, a secured party can retain collateral, but this general right is subject to several conditions. The secured party must send written notice of the proposal to the debtor if the debtor has not signed a statement renouncing or modifying his or her rights after default. With consumer goods, no other notice has to be given. In all other cases, notice must be sent to any other secured party from whom the secured party has received written notice of a claim of interest in the collateral in question. If within twenty-one days after the notice is sent the secured party receives an objection in writing from a person entitled to receive notification, then the secured party must dispose of the collateral under UCC Sec. 9-504. If no such written objection is forthcoming, the secured party can retain the collateral in satisfaction of the debtor's obligation. [UCC Sec. 9-505(2)]

CONSUMER GOODS   When the collateral is consumer goods and the debtor has paid more than 60 percent of the cash price, then the secured party must dispose of the collateral under Section 9-504 within ninety days. Failure to comply opens the secured party to an action for conversion or other liability under UCC Sec.

9-507(1) unless the consumer-debtor signed a written statement after default renouncing or modifying the right to demand the sale of the goods. [UCC Sec. 9-505(1)]

DISPOSITION PROCEDURES   A secured party who does not choose to retain the collateral, must resort to the disposition procedures prescribed under Section 9-504. The Code allows a great deal of flexibility with regard to disposition. The only real limitation is that it must be accomplished in a commercially reasonable manner. Section 9-507(2) supplies some examples of what does or does not meet the standard of commercial reasonableness:

(2) The fact that a better price could have been obtained by a sale at a different time or in a different method from that selected by the secured party is not of itself sufficient to establish that the sale was not made in a commercially reasonable manner. If the secured party either sells the collateral in the usual manner in any recognized market therefore or if he sells at the price currently in such a market at the time of sale or if he has otherwise sold in conformity with reasonable commercial practices among dealers in the type of property sold, he has sold in a commercially reasonable manner.

Any time before the secured party disposes of the collateral or enters into a contract for its disposition, or before the debtor's obligation has been discharged through the secured party's retention of the collateral, the debtor or any other secured party can exercise the right of *redemption* of the collateral. The debtor can do this by tendering performance of *all* obligations secured by the collateral, by paying the expenses reasonably incurred by the secured party, and by retaking the collateral and maintaining its care and custody. [UCC Sec. 9-506]

A secured party is not compelled to resort to public sale to dispose of the collateral. The party is given the latitude under the Code to seek out the best terms possible in a private sale. [UCC Sec. 9-504] Generally, no specific time requirements must be met; however, the time must ultimately meet the standard of commercial reasonableness.

Except when the collateral is perishable or threatens to decline speedily in value or is of a type customarily sold on a recognized market, notice must be sent by the secured party to the debtor if the debtor has not signed a statement renouncing or modifying the right to notification of sale after default. For consumer goods, no other notification need be sent. In all other cases, notification must be sent to any other secured party from whom the secured party has received written notice of a claim of an interest in the collateral. [UCC Sec. 9-504(3)]

PROCEEDS FROM DISPOSITION Proceeds from the disposition must be applied in a certain order:

1. Reasonable expenses stemming from the retaking, holding, or preparing for sale are covered first. Where authorized by law and if provided for in the agreement, this can include reasonable attorneys' fees and legal expenses.
2. The satisfaction of the debt is covered second.
3. Subordinate security interests whose written demand has been received prior to the completion of distribution of the proceeds are covered third. [UCC Sec. 9-504(1)]
4. Treatment of any surplus depends upon the nature of the underlying transaction and the existence of specified agreements between the parties. [UCC Sec. 9-504(2)]

TERMINATION

When a debt is paid, the secured party files a termination statement with the filing officer to whom the original financing statement was given. If the financing statement covers consumer goods, the termination statement must be filed within one month after the debt is paid. If, on the other hand, the debtor requests the termination statement in writing, it must be filed within ten days after the debt is paid. [UCC Sec. 9-404(1)] In all cases, the termination statement must be filed or furnished to the debtor within ten days after a written request is made by the debtor. Any failure by the secured party to comply with this rule makes the party liable for $100 and for any loss caused by the failure to provide the termination statement.

QUESTIONS AND CASE PROBLEMS

1. The city of Vermillion brought a declaratory judgment action to have a court determine to whom the city should pay the proceeds of a construction contract between the city and a bankrupt contractor. Shortly after the contract was formed, the contractor assigned its interest in the proceeds from the contract to the First National Bank as security for a loan. The contract was the contractor's sole account receivable. Subsequently, the IRS filed notice of a tax lien upon all property of the contractor. On January 15, 1970, the contractor filed for bankruptcy. The IRS renewed its tax lien, and the trustee in bankruptcy claimed all the contractor's assets. Does the First National Bank's claim to the proceeds from the construction contract have priority over either the IRS tax lien or the trustee in bankruptcy? [City of Vermillion v. Stan Houston Equipment Co., 341 F.Supp. 707 (D.C.S.D. 1972)]

2. On October 9, 1964, Schwab Brothers, Inc., purchased two trailers from L. B. Smith, Inc., under a

conditional sales contract. (Under a conditional sales contract, the seller retains title to the goods.) L. B. Smith failed to file a financing statement with respect to the two vehicles. Subsequently, Schwab Brothers defaulted on the contract. Shortly thereafter, the United States filed a tax lien against the two vehicles, and L. B. Smith attempted unsuccessfully to repossess them. Whose interest has priority in the vehicles? Would it make a difference if L. B. Smith had been successful in repossessing the trucks before the government filed its tax lien? [L. B. Smith, Inc. v. Foley, 341 F.Supp. 810 (W.D.N.Y. 1972)]

3. Chrysler Credit Corporation held a perfected security interest in the inventory of Local Chrysler Dealer (floor plan). Local owed Malone $10,000 and gave Malone a check for $5,000 as part payment. The same day, Malone returned to Local and indorsed the check back to Local in payment for an automobile in which Chrysler Credit held a security interest. Should Malone take free of Chrysler Credit's security interest? [Chrysler Credit Corp. v. Malone, 502 S.W.2d 910 (Tex.Civ.App. 1973)]

4. Schenectady Corp. financed the sale of mobile homes by NuTrend, a dealer, taking a security interest in NuTrend's inventory. Since Schenectady filed its security interest, it had a perfected security interest in each of the mobile homes in NuTrend's inventory. During the first week of March, NuTrend sold two mobile homes. The first it sold to Clothiers, who paid cash for it. When NuTrend later defaulted on its inventory loan with Schenectady, Schenectady sought to repossess the mobile home from Clothiers. NuTrend sold the second mobile home to Welch. The original buyer of this mobile home held the certificate of title, but the buyer had surrendered possession of the home to NuTrend due to default under a retail installment contract. Under the contract, the original buyer gave a promissory note to Schenectady and entered into a security agreement with Schenectady that Schenectady perfected. Upon the original buyer's default, Schenectady also sought to repossess this mobile home from Welch. Can Schenectady recover from Clothiers? Can it recover from Welch? [Black v. Schenectady Discount Corp., 31 Conn. Sup. 521, 324 A.2d 921 (1974)]

5. Rafferty purchased a truck under a retail installment contract from a local General Motors dealer. The contract was then assigned to General Motors Acceptance Corporation, which perfected a security interest in the truck. Rafferty took the truck to Colwell Diesel Service for repairs and was unable to pay the repair bill. Shortly thereafter, Rafferty also defaulted on his retail installment contract. General Motors Acceptance Corporation attempted to repossess the truck, but Colwell refused to give up possession until somebody paid the repair bill. Is Colwell legally justified in retaining possession? [General Motors Acceptance Corp. v. Colwell Diesel Service and Garage, Inc., 302 A.2d 595 (Me. 1973)]

6. Mr. and Mrs. Schramm operated a mobile home park. In 1968, Mr. Schramm agreed to allow John Applewhite to locate two mobile homes on his property for a fixed rental. In late 1969, the mobile homes remained unoccupied on Schramm's property. Schramm filed a "Notice of Intent to Hold Hotelkeepers' Lien" on these mobile homes for the amount of unpaid rentals. This notice was also sent to Bloomington National Bank, which was the holder of the perfected security interest in the two homes. (Applewhite had also failed to make payment to the bank.) In late 1970, one of the two homes was taken from the park by an agent of the bank without notice to Schramm. A few days later, several more of the bank's agents returned to the park to take away the remaining mobile home. When they did so, two of them assaulted Mrs. Schramm, who objected to the removal. If under local law, a hotelkeepers' lien has priority over a perfected security interest, what will the Schramms be allowed to recover from the bank? If hotelkeepers' liens are subordinate to perfected security interests, what can the Schramms recover? [Nicholson's Mobile Home Sales, Inc. v. Schramm, 330 N.E.2d 785 (Ind. Ct. App. 1975)]

7. In 1972, Borg-Warner executed a security agreement with David Brown Tractor Company to secure loans to David Brown for the purchase of inventory to be used in its business. Borg-Warner filed a financing statement with the secretary of state, describing the collateral as "all inventory." In January 1974, Wolfe City National Bank advanced money to David Brown Tractor Company for the purchase by David Brown of additional inventory. Wolfe City executed a security agreement covering the additional inventory, but it did not file a financing statement and did not give Borg-Warner notice of its security interest. When David Brown defaulted on its loan from Wolfe City, Wolfe City took possession of the inventory and sold it. Can Borg-Warner recover the proceeds of the sale? [Borg-Warner Acceptance Corp. v. Wolfe City Nat. Bank, 544 S.W.2d 947 (Tex. Civ. App. 1976)]

8. In March 1969 Kenworth sold to Sewell four trucks for which four separate security agreements were executed and perfected. In April 1971, First National Bank loaned Sewell money and took a security interest in all equipment owned or thereafter

acquired by Sewell. The security agreement was perfected by filing. About two months later, Sewell finished paying for the four trucks and thus was no longer in debt to Kenworth. A year later, Kenworth loaned more money to Sewell and took a security interest in the four trucks and other equipment belonging to Sewell. Kenworth also perfected this security interest. On Sewell's default to both Kenworth and First National Bank, who will recover the trucks? [Texas Kenworth Co. v. First Nat. Bank, 564 P.2d. 222 (Okl. 1977)]

9. In 1969, Wheeless purchased a car. In order to obtain the money, he executed a promissory note to the bank and gave the bank a security interest covering the automobile that the bank thereafter perfected by filing. About a year later, Wheeless defaulted on his loan, and the bank took possession of the car. At the time it repossessed the car, Wheeless asked the bank what it intended to do with it. An officer of the bank informed Wheeless that the bank intended to sell it. About two weeks later, the car was sold without Wheeless's knowledge. When Wheeless learned the price for which the bank had sold the car, he protested the sale. Does Wheeless have a legal right to protest? [Wheeless v. Eudora Bank, 256 Ark. 644, 509 S.W.2d. 532 (1974)]

10. In 1969, Jones and Percell executed a promissory note and a security agreement covering a converted military aircraft built in the 1950s. Upon default, the Bank of Nevada repossessed the aircraft. After providing the required notice, the bank placed advertisements in several trade journals as well as in major newspapers in several large cities. In addition, the bank sent 2,000 brochures to 240 sales organizations. A sales representative was hired to market the aircraft. The plane was later sold for $71,000 to an aircraft broker, who in turn resold it for $123,000 after spending $33,000 on modifications. Can Jones and Percell object to the bank's manner of resale? [Jones v. Bank of Nevada, 91 Nev. 368, 535 P.2d. 1279 (1975)]

UNIT V

Creditor's Rights
and Bankruptcy

31

Rights of
Debtors and Creditors

The law of debtor-creditor relations has undergone various changes over the years. Throughout history, debtors and their families have been subjected to terrible punishment for their inability to pay debts, including involuntary servitude, imprisonment, and dismemberment. The modern legal system has moved away from a punishment philosophy in dealing with debtors. In fact, many people say that it has moved too far in the other direction, to the detriment of creditors. Nonetheless, this area of consumerism and consumer protection is designed to aid and protect the debtor and the debtor's family.

This chapter deals with various rights and remedies available through statutory laws and under common law to assist the debtor and creditor in resolving their disputes. The next chapter discusses bankruptcy as one possible way to resolve debtor-creditor problems.

LAWS ASSISTING CREDITORS

Mechanic's Lien on Real Property

When a consumer contracts for labor, services, or material to be furnished for the purpose of making improvements on real property but does not immediately pay for the improvements, a special type of debt called a **mechanic's lien** is created. The real estate itself becomes the subject of security for the lien (debt). For example, a roofer repairs a leaky roof at the request of a homeowner. The homeowner owes the roofer the agreed price for the materials, labor, and services performed. If the homeowner cannot pay or pays only a portion of the charges, a mechanic's lien against the property is created. The roofer is the lienholder, and the real property is encumbered with a mechanic's lien for the amount owed. If the homeowner does not pay the lien, the property can be sold to satisfy the debt.

The procedures by which a mechanic's lien is created are controlled by state statutory law. Generally, the lienholder must file a written notice of lien against the particular property involved. The notice of lien must be filed within a specific time period, measured from the last date that materials or labor were provided (usually within 60 to 120 days). Failure to pay the debt entitles the lienholder to foreclose on the real estate where the improvements were made and sell it in order to satisfy the amount of the debt. Of course, the lienholder is required by statute to give notice to the owner of the property prior to foreclosure and sale. If there are any surplus proceeds after the debt and the costs of the legal proceedings are paid, the former owner receives them.

Artisan's Liens on Personal Property

An **artisan's lien** is a security device, created by statute, similar to a mechanic's lien but used to charge personal property with the payment of a debt for labor done, for value added, or for caring for the personal property (bailee or warehousing costs). For example, A leaves her watch at the jeweler's to be repaired and to have her initials engraved on the back. The jeweler can keep the watch if A fails to pay for the repairs and services that the jeweler provides. In that case, the jeweler can obtain a lien on A's watch for the amount of the bill and sell the watch in satisfaction of the lien. Money in excess of the debt and costs of the sale will be returned to A.

An artisan's lien is a *possessory lien*. The lienholder ordinarily must have retained possession of the property and have agreed to provide the services on a cash, not a credit, basis. Usually the lienholder retains possession of the property. When this occurs, the lien remains as long as the lienholder maintains possession and terminates once possession is voluntarily surrendered—unless the surrender is only temporary. If it is a temporary surrender, there must be an agreement that the property will be returned to the lienholder. Even with such an agreement, if a third party obtains rights in that property while it is out of the possession of the lienholder, the lien is lost. The only way a lienholder can protect a lien and surrender possession at the same time is to record notice of the lien in accordance with state lien and recording statutes.

Modern statutes permit the holder of an artisan's lien to foreclose and sell the property subject to the lien in order to satisfy payment of the debt. As with the mechanic's lien, the lienholder is required to give notice to the owner of the property prior to foreclosure and selling. If there are any surplus proceeds after the debt is satisfied and the costs of the sale are paid, the former owner of the property receives them.

Writ of Execution

A debt must be past due in order for a creditor to commence legal action against a debtor. If the creditor is successful, the court awards the creditor a judgment against the debtor (usually for the amount of the debt plus any interest and legal costs incurred in obtaining the judgment). If the debtor still does not or cannot pay the judgment, the creditor is entitled to go back to the court and obtain a **writ of execution.** This writ is an order, usually issued by the clerk of the court, directing the sheriff to seize (levy) and sell any of the debtor's nonexempt real or personal property that is within the court's geographic jurisdiction (usually the county in which the courthouse is located). The proceeds of the sale are used to pay off the judgment and costs of the sale. Any excess is paid to the debtor. The debtor can pay the judgment and redeem the nonexempt property any time before the sale takes place.

Attachment and Garnishment

Attachment is a court-ordered seizure and taking into custody of property that is in controversy over a debt. Attachment rights are created by state statutes. Attachment is normally a prejudgment remedy. It occurs either at the time of or immediately after the commencement of a lawsuit but before the entry of a final judgment. Under some statutes, the restrictions and requirements about when a creditor can attach before judgment are very specific. However, the statutory grounds for attachment before judgment are very limited. The Due Process Clause of the 14th Amendment to the Constitution limits courts' power to authorize seizure of debtors' property without notice to the debtor or a hearing of the facts. In recent years, a number of state attachment laws have been held to be unconstitutional.

In order to use attachment as a remedy, the creditor must follow certain procedures. He or she must file with the court an affidavit stating that the debtor is in default and stating the statutory grounds under which attachment is sought. A bond must be posted by the creditor to cover court costs, value of the loss of use of the good suffered by the debtor, and the value of the property attached. When the court is satisfied that all the requirements have been met, it issues a **writ of attachment.** This writ is similar to a writ of execution in that it directs the sheriff or other officer to seize nonexempt property. If the creditor prevails at trial, the seized property can be sold to satisfy the judgment.

The following case illustrates that because a writ of attachment operates against a debtor's property simply on the strength of the creditor's sworn statement that a debt is owed, strict compliance with every specific procedure established by the state's attachment statute is required before the property is subject to an enforceable writ of attachment.

JACK DEVELOPMENT, INC. v. HOWARD EALES, INC.

District of Columbia Court of Appeals, 1978. 399 A.2d 466.

BACKGROUND AND FACTS *Corcoran was the owner of a large building in Washington, D.C. In April 1976, Eales, a creditor of Corcoran, obtained a prejudgment "writ of attachment" from a Washington, D.C. court against the building. In June 1976, notice of the writ was posted on the building. In October 1976, Corcoran conveyed the building to Jack Development, Inc. Up to this time, Eales had been unable to serve notice on Corcoran as required by Washington D.C. statute. In the alternative, the statute allowed the notice requirement to be fulfilled by three week publication of the writ in a local newspaper. Eales first published notice of the writ in February 1977. Jack Development argued that it was the owner since title was transferred to it before the writ attached, that is, before the statutory notice requirements had been fulfilled. Eales argued that the writ attached when notice was posted on the building, and therefore Corcoran was unable to transfer clear title.*

DECISION AND RATIONALE *Jack Development was the owner since title was transferred to it before the writ attached. Eale's argued that the writ attached when notice was posted on the building and therefore Corcoran was unable to transfer clear title. The court concluded: "[W]e note that because a writ of attachment before judgment is a harsh and drastic remedy, strict compliance with procedures established by statute is required. In this case, the delivery of the writ of attachment before* *judgment to the marshall did create an inchoate [contingent] lien on the defendant's property. The mere posting of the property did not comply, however, with the notice procedures mandated by D.C. Code, 1971, §§16-502, 508."*

ENFORCEABLE RIGHT REQUIRED Attachment is one way that personal property in the debtor's possession that is capable of manual delivery can be taken into custody and held until the creditor's claim is adjudicated in a court of law. But not only must the creditor follow the statutory requirements, he or she must also have an enforceable right to payment of the debt under law. Otherwise, the creditor can be liable for damages for wrongful attachment with malice, as the following case illustrates.

BACKGROUND AND FACTS *Miller and Fox entered into a contract for the sale of several stud horses. Several years later, Miller sued Fox for the unpaid balance due on the contract. Miller also obtained a prejudgment writ of attachment against Fox's property. The trial court found that, due to Miller's own failure to produce stud papers for a particular horse involved in the sale, Fox never owed the money under the contract.*

MILLER v. FOX

Supreme Court of Montana,
1977.
174 Mont. 504, 571 P.2d 804.

DECISION AND RATIONALE *Miller wrongfully attached Fox's property because Fox did not owe Miller any money at the time the property was attached. In order for Fox to have a duty to pay Miller, Miller would be obligated to deliver stud registration papers to Fox. Delivery of the papers was a condition precedent to Fox's duty to pay. The court concluded: "[P]laintiff stated in his affidavit [sworn statement] for attachment that the action was on a 'contract for the direct payment of money now due,' and that the payment of the contract obligation 'has not been secured by any mortgage or lien upon real or personal property.' Plaintiff, however, knew when he filed the affidavit that the money was not 'now due' until he showed defendant the stud registration paper and that defendant's contract debt was 'secured' by plaintiff's retention of that registration paper."*

GARNISHMENT Garnishment is similar to attachment except that it is a collection remedy that is directed not at the debtor but at a third person. The third person, the garnishee, owes a debt to the debtor or has property that belongs to the debtor. The typical garnishee is an employer. The wages an employer owes to the debtor-employee are subject to garnishment. As will be discussed later, both state and federal laws, however, permit only a limited portion of the debtor's wages to be garnished.[1]

The legal proceeding for a garnishment action is governed by state law. As a result of a garnishment proceeding, the debtor's employer is ordered by the court to turn over a portion of

---

1. Some states (for example, Texas) do not permit garnishment of wages by private parties.

the debtor's wages to pay the debt. However, garnishment operates differently from state to state. According to the laws in some states, the judgment creditor needs to obtain only one order of garnishment that will then continuously apply to the judgment debtor's weekly wages until the entire debt is paid off. In other states, the judgment creditor must go back to court for a separate order of garnishment for each pay period. In the following case, the Colorado Supreme Court was asked to clarify whether, under its state statute, a writ of garnishment operated continuously or had to be renewed each pay period.

IN RE STONE
Supreme Court of Colorado, 1977.
573 P.2d 98.

BACKGROUND AND FACTS *The judgment creditor (plaintiff) obtained a judgment against the debtor (defendant) for $16,168.10. To collect on the judgment, plaintiff sought to garnishee the defendant's wages. The defendant received regular salary payments on the fifteenth and last day of each month. Plaintiff wanted the court to grant a single order allowing a continual garnishment of the defendant's wages until the entire debt was paid.*

DECISION AND RATIONALE *The plaintiff (judgment creditor) had to undertake separate garnishment proceedings against each payment of salary to the defendant (judgment debtor), even though the judgment debtor in this case received wages at regular intervals from his employer. This state's statutes do not provide for a Writ of Continuing Garnishment. The court stated:*

[The Colorado statute] provides for garnishment if "[t]he answer of the garnishee shows that he has *personal property* of any kind in his possession, or under his control, *belonging to the defendant* ***" and "if the answer shows that the garnishee *is indebted* to the defendant ***" [emphasis added]. It is well settled in this jurisdiction that garnishment is not available to reach debts that are not due and payable since the garnishee's liability is contingent. ***

Future earnings are contingent because they depend upon future performance. The employee cannot sue his employer for wages due before the employee has fulfilled his employment contract. At that stage, prospective earnings are hypothetical. Thus, future wages cannot be an indebtedness which is due.

FURTHER GARNISHMENT ISSUES The court must always be sure that it is the debtor's property that is actually being taken in a garnishment or attachment proceeding.

PETERSON v. PETERSON
Supreme Court of Utah, 1977.
571 P.2d 1360.

BACKGROUND AND FACTS *John and Patricia Peterson were divorced for several years, and John was remarried. John was delinquent in making child support payments, and Patricia obtained a judgment against him. Patricia then sought a writ of garnishment against funds deposited in a checking account that was solely in John's name (that is, the account was not a joint account between John and his present wife).*

John argued that the garnishment writ should be set aside because the funds in the garnished account belonged to his present wife. John had not worked since his divorce from Patricia, and the funds in the account were almost exclusively derived from his present wife's paychecks.

DECISION AND RATIONALE *In light of the fact that John had no equitable interest in the checking account, Patricia could not garnish that account to satisfy her judgment against him. In many jurisdictions, a judgment creditor cannot attach funds in which the judgment debtor has no equitable interest. The fact that the account was solely in John's name appeared to indicate that the funds were his alone, but this fact could be rebutted. The court concluded: "At the hearing on [John Peterson's] motion to set aside the garnishment execution, the evidence demonstrated that the garnished account was held in [John Peterson's] name; that only his name was on the bank's signature card and, therefore, only he was authorized to write checks against the account. However, [John Peterson] had not worked for over a year, and the funds in the account were almost exclusively derived from the paychecks of [his] present wife; and these checks were routinely endorsed to [him] by her and deposited by him. *** On the basis of these facts *** none of the money belonged to [John Peterson] and all of the funds remaining in the account belonged to [John Peterson's present] wife and were not subject to garnishment for [John Peterson's] debts."*

Guaranty and Suretyship

When one person becomes responsible for the debt of another, a relationship that insures that the debt will be paid to the creditor results. Such arrangements are of two types. One is called a contract of suretyship and the other a contract of guaranty.

SURETY A contract of suretyship is a promise made by a third person to be responsible for the debtor's obligation. Suretyship is an express contract between the surety and the creditor. The surety is *primarily* liable for the debt of the principal. The creditor can demand payment from the surety from the moment that the principal is in default. A suretyship is not a form of indemnity; that is, it is not merely a promise to make good any loss that a creditor may incur as a result of the debtor's failure to pay. A suretyship makes the surety liable to the creditor at any time the principal debtor defaults in perfor-

mance on the debt obligation. The creditor need not exhaust all legal remedies against the principal debtor before holding the surety responsible for payment. A surety agreement must always be in writing.

GUARANTY A guaranty contract is similar to a suretyship in that it includes a promise to answer for the debt or default of another. With suretyship, however, the surety is primarily liable for the debtor obligation of the principal. With a guaranty arrangement, the guarantor—the third person making the guarantee—is *secondarily liable*. The guarantor cannot be immediately required to pay the obligation after the debtor defaults. The creditor must first attempt to collect from the principal debtor.

RIGHTS OF THE SURETY A creditor must take care that certain actions that will release the surety from the obligation do not occur. Any material change that is made in the terms of the original contract between the principal debtor and the creditor, including the awarding of an extension of time for making payment without first obtaining the consent of the surety, will discharge the surety. When a creditor discharges the principal debtor (or debtors), discharge of any one of them releases the surety from any obligation unless the surety agrees to the discharge. Naturally, if the principal obligation is paid by the debtor or by another person on behalf of the debtor, the surety is discharged from obligation. Similarly, if valid tender of payment is made and the creditor for some reason rejects it, then the surety is also released from any obligation on the debt. Generally, any defenses available to a principal debtor can be used by the surety to avoid liability on the obligation to the creditor; the defenses that cannot be used are insolvency, bankruptcy, and the statute of limitations. The ability of the surety to assert any defenses the debtor may have against the creditor is the most important concept in suretyship, since the only defenses available to the surety are those of the debtor.

Mortgage Foreclosure on Real Property

A mortgage agreement provides that when the **mortgagor** (debtor/borrower) *defaults* in making payment in accordance with the terms of the agreement, the **mortgagee** (creditor/lender) can declare that the entire mortgage debt is due immediately. The mortgagee/creditor can enforce payment in full by a legal action called **foreclosure.**

In this action, the real estate that is covered by the mortgage is sold at a judicial sale.[2] If the proceeds of the sale are sufficient to cover both the costs of the foreclosure and the mortgaged debt, any surplus is paid over to the debtor. If, on the other hand, the sale proceeds are insuf-

ficient to cover the foreclosure costs and the mortgaged debt, the mortgagee can seek to recover the difference from the mortgagor by obtaining a *deficiency judgment.* This type of judgment represents the "deficiency amount"—that is, the difference between the mortgaged debt and the amount actually received from the proceeds of the foreclosure sale. A deficiency judgment is obtained in a separate legal action that is pursued subsequent to the foreclosure action. It entitles the creditor to recover from other property owned by the debtor. However, only nonexempt property can be used to satisfy a deficiency judgment.

For a period of time established by state law, prior to the sale of land, a mortgagor can redeem the property by paying the full amount of the debt plus any interest costs that have accrued. This right of the debtor is known as *equity of redemption.*

BULK SALES LAW— ARTICLE 6 OF THE UNIFORM COMMERCIAL CODE

A bulk transfer, or sale, is the sale of a substantial portion of the assets of a business. It usually includes sale of inventory, equipment, furniture, and fixtures used in the business. A bulk sale usually involves the entire assets of the business, but it can involve just the *major portion* of the business assets. In either case, the purpose of Article 6 of the Uniform Commercial Code is to protect the rights of creditors who have presumably extended credit on the strength of the inventory, equipment, furniture, fixtures, or other assets of the business. The business owner should not be permitted to sell all the assets, pocket the proceeds, and leave town, thereby avoiding paying creditors. By the same token, a purchaser should not be allowed to purchase a business and reincorporate, thereby leaving creditors of the prior corporation no recourse against the prior corporation's assets.

To avoid this situation, the Code imposes two basic requirements in the event of a bulk sale. First, Article 6 requires that the *seller* draw

2. This is true even if the property is the debtor's homestead. A mortgage is one debt that is *not* subject to the homestead statutory exemption that exempts the homestead from execution of any general debts of a householder or head of a family.

up a list of the property being sold and a list of all the creditors and that these lists be given to the potential buyer. Second, the buyer is given responsibility for notifying each of the seller's creditors of the proposed sale date. The notice and publication requirements are very specific. A potential purchaser must notify each of the seller's creditors individually and personally to inform them of the potential sale. Creditors must act within a specific time period to inform the potential buyer of the extent of their claims. If a potential buyer fails to follow the UCC procedures, the transfer will be ineffective, and creditors can use any appropriate remedy to collect the debt from the property purchased by the buyer. If the Code procedures have been followed, the transfer is effective, and creditors will lose any rights they failed to pursue at the time of notification. In that case, a purchaser who buys for value and in good faith can obtain the property free and clear of any claims of creditors.

PROTECTION OF THE DEBTOR

Exemptions

In most states, certain types of real and personal property are exempt from debts. Probably the most familiar of these exemptions is the **homestead exemption.** Commonly, state statutes provide that the family home of a debtor can be sold in order to satisfy a judgment debt. A specified amount of the sale price, however, will be exempt—that is, reserved for the debtor to provide money to obtain shelter for the family. For example, Daniels owes Carey $20,000. The debt is the subject of a lawsuit, and the court awards Carey a judgment of $20,000 against Daniels. To satisfy the **judgment debt,** Daniels's family home is sold at public auction for $20,000. Assume the homestead exemption is $5,000. The proceeds of the sale are distributed as follows:

1. Daniels is paid $5,000 as his homestead exemption.
2. Carey is paid $15,000 toward the judgment debt, leaving a $5,000 deficiency judgment (that

is, "leftover debt") that can be satisfied (paid) from any other nonexempt property (personal or real) that Daniels may have.

In many states, statutes permit the homestead exemption only if the judgment debtor has a family. The policy behind this type of statute is to protect the family. If a judgment debtor does not have a family, a creditor can be entitled to collect the full amount realized from the sale of the debtor's home.

State exemption statutes usually include both real and personal property. Personal property that is most often exempt from satisfaction of judgment debts includes:

1. Household furniture up to a specified dollar amount.
2. Clothing and certain personal possessions, such as family pictures or a Bible.
3. Pension or bonus monies based on military service and received from the government (also protected by federal statute).

Federal laws and state laws limit the amount of money that can be garnished from a debtor's weekly take-home pay. Typically, a garnishment judgment will be served on a person's employer so that part of the person's usual paycheck will be paid to the creditor. Federal law provides a minimal framework to protect debtors from losing all their income in order to pay judgment debts.[3] State laws also provide dollar exemptions, and these amounts are often larger than those provided by federal law. State and federal statutes can be applied together to help create a pool of funds sufficient to enable a debtor to continue to provide for family needs while also reducing the amount of the judgment debt in a reasonable way.

Garnishment of an employee's wages cannot be grounds for dismissal of an employee because federal law prohibits *any* employer from discharging an employee who has been involved in one garnishment proceeding.

_____

3. For example, the federal Consumer Credit Protection Act, 15 USCA 1601 et seq., provides that a debtor can retain either 75 percent of the disposable earnings per week or the sum equivalent to thirty hours of work paid at federal minimum wage rates, whichever is greater.

Consumer Credit Protection Act (CCPA)

The Consumer Credit Protection Act (CCPA) is commonly called the Truth-in-Lending Act. (It is discussed again in Chapter 48, which deals with consumer protection.) It is basically a "disclosure law," administered by the Federal Reserve Board, that requires sellers and lenders to disclose credit terms or loan terms so that a debtor can shop around for the best financing arrangements.

DISCLOSURE REQUIREMENTS UNDER THE TRUTH-IN-LENDING ACT The disclosure requirements of the Truth-in-Lending Act apply to any installment sales contract in which payment is to be made in more than four installments. The following is a breakdown of the disclosure requirements as they would apply to the sale of a stereo on such an installment plan:

1. The cash price of the stereo.
2. The down payment or trade-in allowance if any.
3. The unpaid cash price (cash price minus the down payment).
4. The finance charge, which includes interest, points, service charges, lender's fee, finder's fee, fee for investigation of credit, credit life insurance premium, accident insurance premium, and so on.
5. Charges not included as part of the finance charge.
6. The total amount to be financed.
7. The annual percentage rate of finance charge.
8. The date that the finance charge begins to accrue.
9. The number, amounts, and due dates of payments.
10. The penalties in case of delinquency or other late payment charges.
11. A description of the security interest (see Chapters 29 and 30).
12. A description of the prepayment penalty charge.
13. Sometimes a comparative index of credit costs to give the purchaser an idea of how much credit will cost on this account. [CCPA Sec. 127]

WHO IS SUBJECT TO TRUTH-IN-LENDING?
Only certain creditors or lenders and only certain types of transactions are subject to the Truth-in-Lending Act. It applies to persons who, in the ordinary course of their businesses, lend money or sell on credit or arrange for the extension of credit. For this reason, sales or loans made between two consumers do not come under the act. Only debtors who are *natural* persons are protected by this law; corporations or other legal entities are not. Transactions involving purchases of property (real or personal) for personal, family, household, or agricultural use come within the terms and provisions of the act if the price is less than $25,000. Transactions covered by the act typically include retail and installment sales and installment loans, car loans, home improvement loans, and certain real estate loans.

The act distinguishes between the information that must be disclosed in real estate loans and personal property loans. For example, in the latter case, a creditor must provide information about the amount financed, the finance charge (interest rate and all other charges), the annual percentage rate, and the amount and number of payments.

A creditor who fails to comply with the disclosure requirements may be liable to the consumer for twice the amount of the finance charge. In no event will that penalty be less than $100 or more than $1,000 for a violation against an individual consumer. The consumer has one year from the date of the violation to bring suit against a creditor who has failed to provide the disclosure statement or who has failed to discover and correct an error in the disclosure statement provided.

In the following case, a creditor furniture store failed to comply with several of the disclosure provisions of the Truth-in-Lending Act in its retail installment contracts. Within a year after making a credit purchase, the consumer-plaintiff sued on behalf of herself and all other persons who had entered into similar installment contracts with the defendant within the year. The plaintiff was permitted to proceed in a class action suit (a lawsuit initiated or defended by a person on behalf of all persons similarly situated and notified). If the defendant was found guilty, it would be liable to every person in the class for statutory damages.

BACKGROUND AND FACTS *Barber purchased certain merchandise from Kimbrell's, Inc., and signed an installment sales contract calling for repayment in twelve monthly installments. In accordance with Regulation Z, which sets out disclosure requirements for consumer credit purchases, the installment contract included a disclosure document. Regulation Z, however, also requires a detailing of the repayment schedule with the sum of payments due labeled as "total of payments." The installment contract instead referred to the sum as "total time balance." Barber and other individuals brought a class action suit for damages, claiming that the Truth in Lending Act (of which Regulation Z is part) had been violated.*

BARBER v. KIMBRELL'S, INC.

United States Court of Appeals, Fourth Circuit, 1978.
577 F.2d 216.

DECISION AND RATIONALE *Under the Truth in Lending Act, since a technical violation had occurred, Barber could recover damages and her attorney could recover reasonable attorney's fees. Had Barber sued as an individual, instead of bringing a class action, recovery would have amounted to her actual damages, "not to be less than $100 nor greater than $1,000" (plus attorney's fees). Since she brought a class action suit, no minimum recovery was allowed, and the maximum was $100,000 or 1 percent of Kimbrell's net worth, whichever was less. In the statement of the court:*

As an incentive to private enforcement, the [original version of the] Act allowed a successful plaintiff to recover statutory damages of twice the amount of the finance charge imposed in the transaction (but not less than $100 nor more than $1,000), plus reasonable attorneys' fees and court costs.

While the private enforcement scheme envisioned by the original Act worked well enough in individual suits, it soon became evident that the scheme was not equally well-suited to class actions. Since a class recovery consisted of simply an aggregation of individual statutory damages, with each class member being entitled to a minimum recovery of $100, courts soon recognized that a recovery of statutory damages by a large plaintiff class had the potential of visiting financial disaster upon a defendant creditor. As a consequence, courts became increasingly reluctant to certify class actions.

To strike an appropriate balance between the advantages of the class action as a vehicle of private enforcement and the need of creditors to avoid financial ruin, Congress in 1974 amended [the act] as it related to class recoveries of statutory damages. The amendment (1) eliminated any minimum recovery requirement as to individual class members, (2) placed a ceiling on the total class recovery so that a creditor's total liability for statutory damages would be no more than "the lesser of $100,000 or one per centum of the net worth of the creditor," and (3) made the award of statutory damages in the class context discretionary rather than a matter of right as it had been before the amendment and as it continued to be with regard to individual actions.

The Uniform Consumer Credit Code (UCCC)

Another legislative attempt to protect consumers by utilizing full disclosure of credit information to buyers is the Uniform Consumer Credit Code proposed in 1961. This code is a state statute and has been enacted in only a few states. Where it has been adopted, it applies to practically every transaction involving credit terms.

One of the focuses of the UCCC is to set ceilings on interest rates. In addition, the statute has detailed provisions regarding credit service charges, prepayments, delinquencies, deferrals, and other financing and refinancing costs. The provisions of the law are exceedingly detailed. The UCCC is, however, similar to the Truth-in-Lending Act in that it requires written disclosure of facts pertinent to the financing arrangements and it keys into the annual percentage rate that a buyer will be paying for the privilege of using a credit payment plan.

Some specific provisions of the Uniform Consumer Credit Code are discussed in Chapter 48, and these will not be reviewed here. Some of the remedy and penalty portions of the UCCC are, however, relevant to the subject matter of this chapter. For example, the code limits the amount of a debtor's take-home wages that can be subjected to garnishment. It prohibits garnishment *before* judgment has been rendered by a court of law, and it imposes stringent restrictions on deficiency judgments. Similar to the Truth-in-Lending Act, the UCCC prohibits an employer from discharging an employee merely because the employee is subject to a garnishment proceeding.

ALTERATION OF THE HOLDER-IN-DUE-COURSE DOCTRINE Historically, the holder-in-due-course doctrine barred a consumer from asserting most defenses against a third party who had purchased negotiable paper. In addition, many installment sales contracts contained provisions saying that if the contract was assigned to a third person, any defenses that might have been available to a debtor could not be used against that third person (referred to as "waiver of defense" clauses).[5] The result was that consumers were often required to pay for defective merchandise and then to seek remedy against the seller. For example, a consumer purchasing aluminum siding would enter a contract known as a **retail installment sales agreement**, which contained provisions whereby the consumer would make monthly installment payments until the entire sales price and financing charges were paid. Most sellers did not wait for the entire installment period to run its course to be paid. Instead, they sold the installment sales contract to others who paid them immediately. The consumer then had to make payments to the third party even if the aluminum siding was defective or never, in fact, installed by the original seller.

After a long history of substantial abuses inflicted upon consumers, many states enacted statutes that prohibit the use of contract clauses that cut off consumer defenses against a third party. Many states require that the words *consumer paper* be printed on the face of any contract or other paper that represents a consumer's indebtedness based upon the sale of consumer goods or services on credit between a retail seller and a retail buyer. In these situations, the paper is nonnegotiable as a matter of law. This means that any purchaser of the paper

_____
5.   UCC Sec. 9-206 accepts waiver of defense clauses whenever the assignee takes the assignment for value in good faith and without notice of a claim or defense "except as to defenses of a type which may be asserted against a holder-in-due-course of a negotiable instrument under the Article on Commercial Paper (Article 3)."

cannot become a holder in due course. Any defenses to payment the consumer has against the original retailer carry over and apply to any assignee of the contract.

Another alternative provided by some state laws is that the seller assigning the paper must give *written notice* of the assignment to the debtor. The consumer-debtor then has a period of time, usually three months, during which he or she can assert any defenses such as defective merchandise or nondelivery against the assignee-third party. Of course, once the statutory period passes, the consumer-debtor must then make payments. The consumer's only remedy thereafter is against the seller.

Credit Cards

In 1974, Congress passed an amendment to the Truth-in-Lending Act called the Fair Credit Billing Act.[6] Basically, under the rules set up pursuant to this act, a purchaser can withhold payment until a dispute over a faulty product that was purchased and paid for by credit card is resolved. It is up to the credit card issuer to intervene and attempt a settlement between the credit card user and the seller. A purchaser does not have an *unlimited* right to stop payment. Good faith effort to get satisfaction from the seller must first be exercised. The purchaser does not need to notify the credit card company that payment for that item is being cut off. The purchaser can wait for the issuer to act. It is probably a good idea, however, to advise the company.

Other provisions of this act relate to disputes over billing. If the debtor thinks there is an error in a bill, the credit card company must investigate and suspend payments until it does so. The card holder simply writes to the company within sixty days of receipt of the bill and briefly explains the circumstances and why he or she thinks there is an error. Under the law, the company must acknowledge the letter within thirty days and solve the dispute within ninety days. During that period, the debtor does

not have to pay the amount of the dispute or any minimum payment from the amount of dispute. The creditor cannot impose finance charges during that period for unpaid balances in dispute; nor can it close the account. However, if it turns out that there was no error, the creditor can then attempt to collect finance charges for the entire period for which payments were not made.

LOST OR STOLEN CREDIT CARDS The Truth-in-Lending Act contains two important provisions regarding credit cardholders. One provision limits the liability of a cardholder to $50 per card when the creditor has been notified that the credit card has been stolen or lost. The second prohibits a credit card company from billing a consumer for unauthorized charges, say if the company issues an unsolicited card.

Jones loses his Master Charge credit card in the street. Bilas finds it and buys $200 worth of goods with the card. The next day Jones informs Master Charge of his loss. Master Charge later bills Jones for the $200 worth of goods that Bilas bought. Clearly, Master Charge can collect only $50 (or nothing if Jones notified it of the loss before the card was used by Bilas) because that is the maximum liability imposed on the loser of a credit card.

Now consider that Master Charge mails a credit card to Farmer, who has not applied for a card or held one in the past. The envelope is stolen out of Farmer's mailbox, and the thief signs the card and buys $200 worth of goods. Master Charge bills Farmer for the $200. Farmer does not have to pay anything at all, not even $50, because Master Charge performed a prohibited act by sending an unsolicited card.

Credit Reports and Collection Practices

The Truth-in-Lending Act provides that consumers are entitled, upon request, to be informed of the nature and scope of a credit investigation, the kind of information that is

---

6.   15 USCA Sec. 1681.

being compiled, and the names of persons who will be receiving the report. They must make the request within specific time limits, however. Consumers have the right to require that any inaccurate or misleading material be reinvestigated and, if not verified, be removed from the file. If there is a dispute about the accuracy of certain parts of the reports, consumers have the right to include their own one hundred word statement in the file to set forth their position with regard to disputed matters. Such statements become part of the permanent record.

The law also provides for updating information that is obsolete. For example, any bankruptcy adjudication that has occurred more than fourteen years prior to the report can be removed. Lawsuits or judgments that are more than seven years old or for which the statute of limitations has expired (whichever is longer) can be removed. In general, any information unfavorable to consumers that is more than seven years old can also be removed.

Although the law provides that consumers have the right to be informed of the contents of their files, the Act limits that access for others. A person who wishes to obtain information contained in a consumer's credit file must have either a court order or a legitimate business need for the information or must have the permission of the consumer to obtain access to the information. Consumer reporting agencies must inform the consumer when an investigative report is being compiled and of the right to disclosure. A consumer credit reporting agency that fails to comply with the terms of the act can be held liable not only for actual damages but for punitive damages and attorneys' fees resulting from a lawsuit brought by the consumer.

DEBT COLLECTION Although debtors have always been able to use traditional tort law to protect themselves from creditor abuse, clearly the trend of the law, at the state and federal levels, is toward limiting abusive action by creditors in the debt collection process.[7]

Congressional concerns about improper debt collection practices led to the passage in 1977 of the Fair Debt Collection Practices Act. This act prohibits the following:

1.   Contacting the consumer at his or her place of employment if the employer objects.
2.   Contacting the consumer at inconvenient or unusual times, such as 3 o'clock in the morning, or contacting the consumer at all, if he or she is represented by an attorney.
3.   Contacting third parties other than parents, spouses, or financial advisers about the payment of a debt unless the court so authorizes.
4.   Using harassment and intimidation, such as abusive language, or using false or misleading information, such as posing as a policeman.
5.   Communicating with the consumer after receipt of notice that the consumer is refusing to pay the debt, except to advise the consumer of further action to be taken by the collection agency.

---

7.   Federal statutes also ban certain debt collection techniques. See 15 USCA Sec. 1692. The Federal Trade Commission prosecutes overly zealous debt collectors under federal regulations for unfair and deceptive trade practices.

QUESTIONS AND CASE PROBLEMS

1.   Reliable Work, Inc., a general contractor, entered into a contract with the owner of a building to do certain remodeling work. About a month later, pursuant to the contract, an electrical subcontractor proceeded to remove several light fixtures from one of the ceilings, cutting four holes in the ceiling and placing the removed light fixtures in the holes. Immediately after this work was begun, a new owner, Kate's, Inc., purchased the building. Several thousand dollars' worth of material and labor was expended before Kate's informed the general contractor that it did not wish to have the building remodeled. Can Reliable Work impose a mechanic's lien on the building even though the building contract was entered into with a different owner? [Kloster-Madsen, Inc. v. Tafi's, Inc., 303 Minn. 59, 226 N.W.2d. 603 (1975)]

2.   On Wednesday, Plunkett, who was in the towing

business, received two telephone calls. The first was from a policeman requesting Plunkett to tow a car from the scene of an accident. This towing was totally at the policeman's discretion, since the driver of the car was unconscious at the time. The second phone call requested Plunkett to tow a car from private property on which it had been parked. This call was made by the property owner. The owners of the two cars then wished to retrieve their cars, but Plunkett claimed that he had a lien on the cars and refused to give up possession unless the owners paid the towing charges. Does Plunkett have a lien on these two vehicles? [Younger v. Plunkett, 395 F. Supp. 702 (E.D. Pa. 1975)]

3. Jackson, the owner of a trailer with a refrigeration unit, brought the trailer to North Broadway Service Station for repairs. When the service station owner finished the repairs, Jackson was unable to pay. He pleaded with the owner to permit him to use the trailer to enable him to earn the money necessary to pay the repair bill. The owner kindheartedly returned the trailer to Jackson. Shortly thereafter, the trailer was repossessed by the Trailer Refrigeration Company, which held a mortgage on the trailer on which Jackson had defaulted. The service station owner then attempted to enforce an artisan's lien against the trailer, claiming priority over Trailer Refrigeration Company's mortgage. Will he succeed? What if the owner of the service station had obtained a written memorandum from Jackson at the time he released the trailer to him, stating that he retained an artisan's lien on the trailer and was releasing it only to enable Jackson to earn the money to pay the repair bill? Would the results be different? [Jackson v. Kusmer, 411 S.W.2d. 257 (Mo. App. 1967)]

4. One of the ways in which a plaintiff can collect a money judgment from a defendant is by garnishing a debt that is due from a garnishee to the defendant. Garnishment is allowed only where the debt due from the garnishee is unconditional. With this in mind, discuss the following situation. Cummings Company sued C & E Excavating Company. C & E had a contract with Volpe Construction Company to do certain excavating work for Volpe. Can Cummings garnish the money owed under this contract? What must be known about the contract in order to answer this question? [Cummings General Tire Co. v. Volpe Constr. Co., 230 A.2d. 712 (D.C. App. 1967)]

5. Asher entered into a contract with Herman for the sale of land. The contract provided that in the event that the vendors were unable to convey title, the vendors' sole liability would be to refund the purchaser's deposit. Subsequently, the contract fell through, but the escrow agent, who was holding the deposit made by the purchaser, embezzled the money. Under rules of escrow, the loss fell on the purchasers since it was their money. Can the purchasers argue that under the provision in the contract mentioned above the vendors could be deemed guarantors of the deposit money? Explain. [Asher v. Herman, 49 Misc. 2d. 475, 267 N.Y.S. 2d. 932 (1966)]

6. Evans Motors sold James Perry an automobile under an installment sales contract. The contract required the buyer of the automobile to procure and maintain insurance on it at all times. Evans then sold the installment contract to the American National Bank. Before the bank took the installment note, it required Evans to sign as an accommodation party (surety). Evans and American National had done business together for a number of years, and it was customary that if the bank received notice of cancellation of insurance on an automobile covered by an installment note, it would immediately notify Evans. Shortly after the bank purchased the installment note from Evans, it learned of cancellation of Perry's insurance. However, it failed to notify Evans of this fact, and it failed to make any other arrangements for insurance. Several months later, the automobile was totally destroyed in a collision. Since Perry was insolvent, American National Bank was unable to collect further payments from him and looked to Evans Motors as an accommodation party. Does Evans have any defense? [Evans v. American Nat. Bank and Trust Co. of Chattanooga, 116 Ga. App. 468, 157 S.E.2d. 816 (1967)]

7. Dunning Floor Covering, Inc., owed Raymond Darrah $7,500. In settlement of this debt, Dunning transferred about half of its floor covering inventory and some miscellaneous fixtures to Darrah. The items transferred had a value of $7,500. Darrah later resold the merchandise to a third party for $4,000. Glidden Company, one of Dunning's business creditors, claimed that since it had not received notice of the transfer of the merchandise, Article 6 of the UCC was violated. Is Glidden correct? Why? If Glidden's argument is correct, for what amount will Raymond Darrah be liable to Glidden? Will the third party to whom Darrah sold the goods be liable to Glidden? [Associated Creditors Agency v. Dunning Floor Covering, 265 Cal. App. 2d. 558, 71 Cal. Rptr. 494 (1968)]

8. In the summer of 1972, Robert Martin applied for and was issued an American Express credit card. Approximately three years later, in April 1975, Martin gave his card to a business associate named E. L. McBride and orally authorized McBride to

charge only up to $500 on the credit card. However, in June 1975, Martin received a statement from American Express indicating that the amount owed on his credit card account was approximately $5,300. Under the Truth-in-Lending Act, for how much will Martin be liable to American Express? [Martin v. American Express, Inc., 361 So.2d. 597 (Ala. Civ. App. 1978)]

9. GAC Finance Corporation was the holder of a promissory note in which Tom Burgess was the maker. When the note came due, Burgess refused to pay, and GAC brought suit against him. Burgess claimed that the note was in violation of the Truth-in-Lending Act since delinquent charges were designated in the note as .53 instead of $.53. Burgess contended that the amount of the delinquent charge was so unclear that it violated the act. He further contended that, regardless of whether he won or lost against GAC, GAC had to pay his attorney's fees. Discuss Burgess's contentions. [GAC Finance Corp. v. Burgess, 16 Wash. App. 758, 558 P.2d. 1386 (1977)]

32

Bankruptcies
and Reorganization

The U.S. Constitution provides that "The Congress shall have the power . . . to establish . . . uniform laws on the subject of bankruptcies throughout the United States." Bankruptcy proceedings are therefore rooted in federal laws; bankruptcy courts are special federal courts; and bankruptcy judges are federally appointed.

The original Bankruptcy Act was enacted in 1898 and was amended by the 1938 Chandler Act. A major overhaul of the federal bankruptcy law occurred in 1978 with the passage of the Bankruptcy Reform Act of 1978. The Bankruptcy Reform Act became effective on October 1, 1979 and governs all bankruptcy proceedings filed after that date.

GOALS OF BANKRUPTCY

Bankruptcy law is designed to accomplish two main goals. The first is to provide relief and protection to debtors who have gotten in "over their heads." The second major goal of bankruptcy is to provide a fair means of distributing a debtor's assets among all creditors.

Although the Bankruptcy Act is a federal law, state laws do play a role in a federal bankruptcy proceeding. For example, state laws on secured transactions, liens, judgments and exemptions all may affect a federal bankruptcy proceeding. Indeed, state insolvency laws and other state statutes may at times be utiltized to avoid federal bankruptcy.

THE BANKRUPTCY REFORM ACT OF 1978

The Bankruptcy Reform Act of 1978 (hereinafter the Code) is contained in Title 11 of the United States Code and has eight odd-numbered chapters. Chapters 1, 3, and 5 include general definitional provisions and provisions governing case administration, creditors, the debtor[1] and the estate. These three chapters apply generally to all kinds of bankruptcies. The next four chapters set forth the different types of bankruptcy relief that debtors or creditors may seek. Chapter 7 provides for liquidations. Chapter 9 governs the adjustment of debts of a municipality. Chapter 11 governs reorganizations and Chapter 13 provides for the adjustment of debts of individuals with regular income. The last chapter, Chapter 15, sets up a pilot United States trustee system.

The following sections deal with Chapter 7 liquidations, Chapter 11 reorganizations and Chapter 13 plans.

CHAPTER 7 LIQUIDATIONS

This is the most familiar type of bankruptcy proceeding and is often referred to as an ordinary or "straight" bankruptcy. Put simply, a debtor in a straight bankruptcy states his debts and turns his assets over to a trustee. The trustee sells the assets and distributes the proceeds to creditors. The balance of the debts are then discharged (extinguished) and the debtor is relieved from his obligation to pay the debts. Any "person" — defined as including individuals, partnerships and corporations[2] — may be a debtor under Chapter 7. Railroads, insurance companies, banks, savings and loan associations, and governmental units cannot be Chapter 7 debtors. Other chapters of the Code apply to them.

---

1. It is interesting to note that *bankrupts* no longer exist under the Code. Those who were formerly *bankrupts* under the old Bankruptcy Act are now merely *debtors* under the Code.
2. The definition of a *corporation* includes unincorporated companies and associations. It also covers labor unions.

Filing the Petition

A straight bankruptcy may be commenced by either the filing of a voluntary or involuntary petition.

VOLUNTARY BANKRUPTCY A voluntary petition is brought by the debtor, who files official forms that are designated for that purpose, in the bankruptcy court. The voluntary petition contains the following schedules: 1. A list of both secured and unsecured creditors, their addresses, and the amount of debt owed to each. 2. A statement of the financial affairs of the debtor. 3. A list of all property owned by the debtor, including property claimed by the debtor to be exempt.

The official forms must be completed accurately, sworn to under oath, and signed by the debtor. To conceal assets, or knowingly supply false information on these schedules is a crime under the bankruptcy laws. If the voluntary petition for bankruptcy is found to be proper, the filing of the petition itself will constitute an "order for relief."

INVOLUNTARY BANKRUPTCY An involuntary bankruptcy occurs when the debtor's creditors force the debtor into bankruptcy proceedings. An involuntary case cannot be commenced against a farmer[3] or a charitable institution. For an involuntary case to be filed, three or more creditors having unsecured claims aggregating at least $5,000 must join in the petition. If a debtor has fewer than twelve creditors, one or more creditor having such a claim of $5,000 may file.

If the debtor challenges the involuntary petition, a trial will be held and the bankruptcy court will enter an "order for relief" only if it finds that: 1. the debtor is generally not paying

---

3. The definition of *farmer* includes persons who receive more than 80 percent of their gross income from farming operations, such as tilling the soil, dairy farming, ranching, or the production or raising of crops, poultry or livestock. Corporations and partnerships can be "farmers".

debts as they become due[4]; or 2. a custodian was appointed or took possession of a portion of the debtor's property within 120 days before the filing of the petition for the purpose of enforcing a lien against such property. If the court grants an order for relief, the debtor will be required to supply the information in the bankruptcy schedules discussed above.

An involuntary petition should not be used as an everyday debt collection device and the Code provides penalties for the filing of frivolous petitions against debtors. Judgment may be granted against the petitioning creditors for the costs and attorney fees incurred by the debtor in defending against an involuntary petition which is dismissed by the court. If the petition is filed in bad faith, damages can be awarded for injury to the debtor's reputation. Punitive damages may also be awarded.

Automatic Stay

The filing of a petition, either voluntary or involuntary, operates as an automatic stay or suspension of virtually all litigation and other action by creditors against the debtor or the debtor's property. In other words, once a petition is filed, creditors cannot commence or continue legal action against the debtor to recover claims they have against him. Nor can creditors take any action to repossess property

_____

4. The inability to pay debts as they become due is known as *equitable* insolvency. A *balance sheet* insolvency, which exists when a debtor's liabilities exceed assets, is not the test. Thus, it is possible for debtors to be thrown into involuntary bankruptcy even though their assets far exceed their liabilities. This may occur when a debtor's cash flow problems become severe.

in the hands of the debtor. However, a secured creditor may request the bankruptcy court for relief from the automatic stay in certain circumstances.

Underlying the Code's automatic stay provision is a concept known as "adequate protection." The adequate protection doctrine protects secured creditors from losing their security as a result of the automatic stay. The bankruptcy court can provide adequate protection by requiring the debtor to make periodic cash payments (or provide additional or replacement liens) to the extent that the stay results in a decrease in the value of the property involved. Or the court may grant other relief which is the "indubitable equivalent" of the secured parties interest in the property. For example, suppose Speedy Express, a delivery service, owns three brand new delivery trucks in which First Bank has a security interest. Speedy Express has failed to make its monthly payments for two months. Speedy Express files a petition in bankruptcy and the automatic stay prevents First Bank from repossessing the trucks. Meanwhile, the trucks are depreciating at a rate of several hundred dollars a month. First Bank's inability to repossess and immediately resell the delivery trucks is harming First Bank to the extent of several hundred dollars per month. The bankruptcy court may prevent First Bank from being harmed by requiring Speedy Express to at least make cash payments (or provide additional or replacement liens) to the extent that the delivery trucks are depreciating in value. If the debtor is unable to provide adequate protection, the court may allow First Bank to repossess the trucks.

_____

BACKGROUND AND FACTS   *Epps, the owner of several parcels of real estate, was two years behind in mortgage payments on the property. The mortgagees' claims against Epps far exceeded the value of the real estate. On the eve of the foreclosure sale by the mortgagees, Epps filed a petition for relief under Chapter 13 of the Bankruptcy Code. The foreclosure sale was automatically stayed and Epps subsequently filed a repayment plan. The mortgagees then petitioned the court for relief from the stay on the ground that their mortgages were not being adequately protected. The*

FISHMAN v. EPPS
United States District Court,
Southern District of
New York, 1980.
3 Bankr. Rep. (CCH) ¶67, 438.

mortgagees asserted that since the property was worth less than their mortgage lien and since Epps was unable to pay overdue and future property taxes on the real estate, their position as secured creditors was eroding.

DECISION AND RATIONALE *Relief from the automatic stay was granted and the mortgagees proceeded with the foreclosure. A court can grant secured creditors (real estate mortgagees here) relief from an automatic stay whenever they can show that the debtor is unable to adequately protect their interest in the secured property. Here, the debtor's property was clearly worth less than the creditors' liens. In addition, the debtor failed to meet continuing obligations that directly affected the value of the real estate, such as property taxes and hazard insurance. In the words of the court: "[U]nless there is a concomitant increase in the value of the property, adequate protection at its minimum requires that the debtor must meet the accruing obligations. *** As a court of equity, the bankruptcy court must consider 'the impact of the stay on the parties and consider the balance of hurt in fashioning relief.' The evidence leads this court to conclude that continuance of the stay will hurt these mortgagees much more than vacating of the stay will impair the rights of the debtor."*

The Trustee

Promptly after the order for relief has been entered, an interim or provisional trustee is appointed to preside over the debtor's property until the first meeting of creditors. At the creditors' first meeting the debtor must appear and submit to examination under oath and a trustee must be elected. A permanent trustee is elected at the first meeting of creditors. The trustee's principle duty is to collect and reduce to money the "property of the estate" for which he serves, and to close up the estate as expeditiously as is compatible with the best interests of the parties.

Property of the Estate

Upon commencement of a Chapter 7 proceeding, an *estate in property* is created. The estate consists of all the debtor's legal and equitable interests in property, wherever located, together with community property, property transferred in a transaction voidable by the trustee, proceeds and profits from the property of the estate, and certain after-acquired property. Interests in certain property which the debtor acquires or becomes entitled to within 180 days after filing may also become part of the estate. Thus, the filing of a bankruptcy petition generally fixes a dividing line: property acquired prior to the petition becomes property of the estate and property acquired after the filing of the petition remains the debtor's.

Exemptions

An individual debtor is entitled to exempt certain property from the property of the estate. Prior to the enactment of the Code, state law exclusively governed the extent of the exemptions. However, the Code establishes a federal exemption scheme. An individual debtor now has the option of choosing between the exemptions provided under the applicable state law and the federal exemptions.[5] The Code exempts the following property:

---

5. Individual states are given the power to pass legislation precluding the use of the federal exemptions by debtors in their states. Some states have passed such legislation. In these states, only state exemptions are available.

1. Up to $7,500 in equity in a home and burial plot.
2. Interest in a motor vehicle up to $1,200.
3. Interest, up to $200 for any particular item, in household goods and furnishings, wearing apparel, appliances, books, animals, crops or musical instruments.
4. Interest in jewelry up to $500.
5. Any other property worth up to $400, plus any unused part of the $7,500 homestead exemption.
6. Up to $750 interest in any tools of the debtor's trade.
7. Any unmatured life insurance contract owned by the debtor.
8. Certain interests in accrued dividends or interest under life insurance contracts owned by the debtor.
9. Professionally prescribed health aids.
10. Debtor's right to receive social security and certain welfare benefits, alimony and support, and certain pension benefits.
11. Debtor's right to receive certain personal injury and other awards.

BACKGROUND AND FACTS   *On October 11, 1979, Levy filed a voluntary petition under Chapter 7 to the Bankruptcy Code. (His spouse did not file a bankruptcy petition.) As the code required, Levy also filed a schedule listing all his property. The schedule included his house, the land surrounding it, household furnishings, and the family's car. At the end of the schedule, Levy asserted that he and his wife owned this property as tenants by the entireties, and therefore, it should not be included as part of his bankruptcy estate.*

DECISION AND RATIONALE   *The property that Levy and his wife owned by the entireties was exempt from Levy's bankruptcy estate under Section 522 (b) (2) (B) of the Bankruptcy Code. The property that a debtor holds as a tenant by the entirety must initially be included in the estate [under Section 541 (a)] even though only one spouse is in bankruptcy. According to section 541 (a), the bankruptcy estate is comprised of "all legal or equitable interests of the debtor in property as of the commencement of the case." The interest of a tenant by the entirety is such a "legal interest." However, the property that Levy held as a tenant by the entirety was exempted from the estate under Section 522 (b) (2) (B). In this particular case, "the debtor's interest in entireties property is exempt from process by both his individual and joint creditors under [the laws of this state] ***."*

IN RE FORD, JR.
United States District Court of Maryland, 1980.
3 Bankr. Rep. (CCH) ¶67, 429.

Trustee's Powers

One of the objectives of a Chapter 7 liquidation is to distribute a debtor's assets equitably among all unsecured creditors. Secured creditors will receive their security as payment. Any excess becomes part of the debtor's estate. Any deficiency becomes an unsecured claim which shares in the debtor's estate with all other unsecured claims. In order to do this, the trustee has been given certain powers to recover or use property for the estate:

TURNOVER   Generally, anyone holding a debtor's property at the time of a filing may be required to deliver the property to the trustee.

VOIDABLE RIGHTS A trustee steps into the shoes of the debtor. Thus, any reason that a debtor can use to obtain return of his or her property can be used by the trustee as well. These grounds include fraud, duress, incapacity, and mutual mistake. For example, B sells his boat to F. F gives B a check, knowing that there are insufficient funds in the bank account to cover the check. F has committed fraud. B has the right to avoid that transfer and recover the boat from F. Once an order for relief has been entered for B, the trustee can exercise the same right to recover the boat from F.

PREFERENCES A debtor should not be permitted to transfer property or make a payment that favors one creditor over others. Thus, the trustee is allowed to recover payments made to one creditor in preference to another.

To constitute a preference that can be recovered, an insolvent debtor must have transferred property, for a pre-existing debt, within 90 days of the filing of the petition in bankruptcy. The transfer must give the creditor receiving it more than he or she would receive if the case were a Chapter 7 liquidation proceeding. Thus, not all transfers and conveyances are preferences. For example, if a creditor receives payment in the ordinary course of business or receives payment for a fully secured debt the payment cannot be recovered by the trustee in bankruptcy. If a preferred creditor has sold the property to an innocent third party, the property cannot be recovered from the party, but under certain circumstances the creditor can be held accountable for the value of the property.

LIENS ON DEBTOR'S PROPERTY The trustee is permitted to avoid the fixing of certain statutory liens on property of the debtor. Liens that first become effective on the bankruptcy or insolvency of the debtor are voidable by the trustee. Liens that are not perfected or enforceable on the date of the petition against a bona fide purchaser are voidable.

FRAUDULENT TRANSFERS The trustee may avoid fraudulent transfers or obligations if made within one year of the filing of the petition, if made with actual intent to hinder, delay, or defraud a creditor. Transfers made for less than a reasonable equivalent consideration are also vulnerable if the debtor thereby became insolvent, was engaged in business with an unreasonably small capital, or intended to incur debts that would be beyond his ability to pay.

Distribution of Property

Creditors are either *secured* or *unsecured*. (The rights of secured creditors were discussed in Chapter 30.) Basically, a secured creditor has a security interest in collateral that secures the debt. The secured creditor can enforce the security interest either by accepting the property in full satisfaction of the debt or by foreclosing on the collateral and using the proceeds to pay off the debt. If the secured creditor chooses to foreclose, and if the total value of the property is less than the amount of the debt, the secured creditor becomes an unsecured creditor for the difference. If the proceeds from the collateral exceed the value of the debt, the secured creditor is paid in full, and any excess is used by the trustee to satisfy the claims of unsecured creditors.

Bankruptcy law establishes an order or priority for classes of debts owed to *unsecured creditors,* and they are paid in the order of their priority. Each class of debt must be fully paid before the next class is entitled to any of the proceeds—if there are sufficient funds to pay the entire class. If not, the proceeds are distributed *proportionately* to each creditor in a class, and all classes lower in priority on the list receive nothing. The order of priority among classes of unsecured creditors is as follows:

1. All costs and expenses for preserving and administering the estate, including such items as court costs and trustee and attorney fees and costs incurred by the trustee during the administration of the estate, such as rental fees and appraisal fees.
2. Unsecured claims in an involuntary case arising in the ordinary course of the debtor's

business after commencement of the case but before the appointment of a trustee or the issue of an order for relief.

3. Claims for wages, salaries and commissions up to an amount of $2,000 per claimant, provided that they were earned within 90 days of the filing of the petition in bankruptcy. Any claims in excess of $2,000 are treated as the "claims of general creditors" (listed as number 7 below).

4. Unsecured claims for contributions to employee benefit plans arising under services rendered within 180 days before filing the petition and limited to the number of employees covered by the plan multiplied by $2,000.

5. Unsecured claims for money deposited (up to $900) with the debtor before the filing of the petition in connection with the purchase, lease or rental of property or services that were not delivered or provided.

6. Taxes legally due and owing within three years of the petition in bankruptcy.

7. Claims of general creditors. These debts have the lowest priority and are paid on a pro rata basis if and only if funds remain after all the debts having priority are paid in full.

8. Any remaining balance is returned to the debtor.

Discharge

From the debtor's point of view, the primary purpose of a Chapter 7 liquidation is to obtain a fresh start through the discharge of debts.[6] However, there are circumstances in which certain claims will not be discharged. There are also situations in which a discharge will be denied altogether.

EXCEPTIONS TO DISCHARGE Certain debts may not be discharged because of the nature of the claim or the conduct of the debtor. Claims that are not dischargeable include:

1. Claims for back taxes accruing within three years prior to bankruptcy.

2. Claims against property or money obtained by the debtor under false pretenses or by false representations.

3. Unscheduled claims.

4. Claims based on fraud or misuse of funds while acting in a fiduciary capacity, embezzlement or larceny.

5. Alimony and child support.

6. Claims based on willful or malicious injury by the debtor to another or to the property of another.

7. Certain fines and penalties payable to governmental units.

8. Certain student loans.

OBJECTIONS TO DISCHARGE As was stated above, there are certain situations in which a discharge will be denied. When a discharge is denied, the assets of the debtor are still distributed to the creditors, but the debtor remains liable for the unpaid portions of all claims. Some grounds for the denial of discharge include:

1. Debtor's concealment or destruction of property with the intent to hinder or delay or defraud a creditor.

2. Debtor's fraudulent concealment or destruction of records of his financial condition.

3. The commission of a bankruptcy crime.

4. Debtor's refusal to obey a lawful order of a bankruptcy court.

5. Debtor's failure to satisfactorily explain the loss of assets.

6. Grant of a discharge to debtor within six years of the filing of the petition.[7]

7. Debtor's written waiver of discharge approved by the court.

EFFECT OF DISCHARGE The primary effect of a discharge is to void any judgment on a discharged debt and enjoin any action to collect a discharged debt. A discharge does not affect the liability of a co-debtor.

---

6. Discharges are only granted to "individuals" who are debtors under Chapter 7.

7. A discharge under Chapter 13 of the Code within 6 years of the filing of the petition does not bar a subsequent Chapter 7 discharge where a good faith Chapter 13 plan paid at least 70 percent of all allowed unsecured claims.

Of course, a debtor may always choose to voluntarily pay off a discharged debt. However, the Code places restrictions on the formal reaffirmation of a debt. Such a reaffirmation must be approved by the court as being in the best interests of the debtor.

CHAPTER 11 REORGANIZATIONS

This is the type of bankruptcy proceeding used most commonly by a corporate debtor. Essentially, in a reorganization the creditors and the debtor formulate a plan under which the debtor pays a portion of his debts and is discharged of the remainder. The debtor is allowed to continue in business. Although this type of bankruptcy is commonly a corporate reorganization, any debtor who is eligible for Chapter 7 relief is eligible for Chapter 11 relief. Railroads are eligible for Chapter 11 relief.

The same principles that govern the filing of a Chapter 7 petition apply to Chapter 11 proceedings. The case may be brought either voluntarily or involuntarily. The same principles govern the entry of the order for relief. The automatic stay and adequate and protection provisions previously discussed are applicable in reorganizations. Recall that adequate protection of the creditors is required in a reorganization before a secured creditor can repossess collateral.

Debtor-in-Possession

Upon entry of the order for relief, the debtor continues to operate his business. He is called a "debtor-in-possession." However, the court may appoint a trustee to operate the debtor's business if gross mismanagement of the business is shown or if it is in the best interests of the estate. As soon as practicable after entry of the order for relief, a creditor's committee is appointed. The committee may consult with the trustee or the debtor in possession concerning the administration of the case or the formulation of the plan.

The Plan

FILING THE PLAN   Only the debtor may file a plan within the first 120 days after the date of the order for relief. However, if the debtor does not meet the 120 day deadline, or if the debtor fails to obtain the required consent within 180 days, any party in interest may propose a plan.

CONTENTS OF THE PLAN   A Chapter 11 plan must:
1. Designate classes of claims and interests under the plan.
2. Specify the treatment to be afforded the classes. The plan must provide the same treatment for each claim in a particular class.
3. Provide an adequate means for the plan's execution.

ACCEPTANCE OF THE PLAN It is not required that each creditor approve of a Chapter 11 plan in order for the plan to become effective. The plan must be approved by at least one "class" of claims. A class of claims has accepted the plan when a majority in number of creditors and two-thirds of the amount of the total claim vote to approve the plan.

CONFIRMATION OF THE PLAN   Even though all classes of claims accept the plan, the court may refuse to confirm it. The plan must be in the "best interests of the creditors." Even if only one class of claims has accepted the plan, the court may still confirm it under the Code's so-called "cram down" provision. The plan is binding upon confirmation. Upon confirmation the debtor is given a Chapter 11 discharge.

CHAPTER 13 PLANS

The former Bankruptcy Act provided for the formulation of "wage earner" plans as a means of allowing wage earners to pay off their debts free from the harassment of creditors. Under these plans, the wage earner avoided the stigma of being adjudicated a "bankrupt." Chapter 13 of the Bankruptcy Code provides for "Adjustment of Debts of an Individual with Regular Income."

Individuals with regular income who owe noncontingent, liquidated, unsecured debts of less than $100,000 or similar secured debts of $350,000 may take advantage of Chapter 13. This includes individual proprietors and individuals on welfare, social security, fixed pensions or investment income. Many small business debtors will have a choice of filing a plan either under Chapter 11 or 13. There are several advantages in filing a Chapter 13 plan when eligible. One of these advantages is that it is less expensive and less complicated than a Chapter 11 proceeding, or even a Chapter 7 liquidation.

Filing the Petition

A Chapter 13 case can only be initiated by the filing of a voluntary petition by the debtor. Certain Chapter 7 and 11 cases may be converted to Chapter 13 cases with the consent of the debtor.

Automatic Stay

Upon the filing of a Chapter 13 petition, the automatic stay previously discussed takes effect. Under Chapter 13, the stay also enjoins creditors from taking action against co-obligors of the debtor. The automatic stay applies to all or part of a consumer debt and does not apply to any business debt which may have been incurred by the debtor. A creditor has the right to seek relief from the automatic stay.

The Plan

FILING THE PLAN   Only the debtor may file a plan under Chapter 13. The debtor may propose a plan which either provides for the payment of all obligations in full or payment of an amount less than one hundred percent.

CONTENTS OF THE PLAN   A Chapter 13 plan must:
1.   Provide for the turnover of such future earnings or income of the debtor to the trustee as is necessary for execution of the plan.
2.   Provide for full payment in deferred cash payments of all claims entitled to priority.
3.   Provide for the same treatment of each claim within a particular class.

The time for payment under the plan may not exceed three years. With the approval of the court, however, it may be extended to as much as five years.

CONFIRMATION OF THE PLAN   After filing of the plan, the court holds a confirmation hearing at which interested parties may object to the plan. The court will confirm a plan with respect to each claim of a secured creditor 1. if the creditors have accepted the plan, 2. if the plan provides that creditors retain their liens and the value of the property to be distributed to them under the plan is not less than the secured portion of their claims, or 3. if the debtor surrenders the property securing the claim to the creditors. Unsecured creditors are protected only by the requirements that the plan be proposed "in good faith" and that they will receive at least as much under the plan as they would under a Chapter 7 liquidation. Unsecured creditors do not vote to accept or reject a Chapter 13 plan.

BACKGROUND AND FACTS   *William and Barbara Armstrong filed a petition and plan under Chapter 13 of the Bankruptcy Code. The plan provided that they would pay $200 per month for twenty-five months. This plan would provide unsecured creditors with 70 percent of their claims. The trustee questioned whether the plan was filed in good faith*

IN RE ARMSTRONG
United States District Court of Oregon, 1980.
3 Bankr. Rep. (CCH) ¶67, 421.

since the debtors could afford to pay 100 percent of the unsecured claims if the plan were extended to thirty-six months. No creditor objected to confirmation of the plan.

DECISION AND RATIONALE *The plan was filed in good faith, and therefore it was confirmed. Even though Section 1322 (c) provides that a Chapter 13 plan may continue for as long as three years, it does not require that all plans that provide for less than 100 percent payment to unsecured creditors must extend three years. The applicable provision of the Code 15 § 1325 (a) (3) which requires a finding that the plan has been filed in good faith is not defined. This requirement has been met. The court explained: "[T]here is no indication [in] § 1322 (c), or any other Section of the Code, that Congress intended that all plans which provide for less than 100% to unsecured creditors must continue for at least three years. This Section fixes maximum, not minimum, periods of time."*

Discharge

After completion of all payments under a Chapter 13 plan, the court grants a discharge of all debts provided for by the plan. The only exemptions to discharge are for certain long-term debts and for alimony and child support. In this respect the discharge is even greater than that provided for in a Chapter 7 liquidation.

Even if the debtor does not complete the plan, a "hardship" discharge may be granted if the failure to complete the plan was due to circumstances beyond the debtor's control and the property distributed with the plan was greater than would have been paid in a Chapter 7 liquidation.

QUESTIONS AND CASE PROBLEMS

1. Acme, Inc. filed a voluntary petition for reorganization under Chapter 11 of the Bankruptcy Code on April 1, 1980. On that date, Acme had five unsecured creditors. Acme owed creditor A $1,000, creditor B $2,000, creditor C $3,000, creditor D $4,000, and creditor E $5,000. Acme proposed a Chapter 11 plan providing for the payment of 50 percent on all general claims. Creditors A, D, and E accepted the plan. Can the bankruptcy court confirm the plan? Assume the bankruptcy court confirmed the plan despite the objections of creditors B and C. After Acme successfully completed all of the required payments under the plan, creditors B and C instituted suits to recover the 50 percent balance allegedly owed to them. Will they be successful in their suits? Assume that Acme was unable to make the required payments under the plan. Creditors A, B, C, D and E bring suits against Acme. What will be the recovery of each creditor in their respective suits?

2. Johnson had been drinking heavily one evening and was involved in an automobile accident while driving home. As a result of the accident, three of the passengers in the other automobile were seriously injured. Johnson was convicted of drunk driving in a criminal prosecution. Subsequently, all three of the injured passengers brought civil suits against Johnson. Judgments against Johnson were entered totalling $1,000,000. In an effort to have the debts created by the judgments discharged, Johnson filed for bankruptcy. Will those debts be discharged?

3. a. Edward Kline, owner of a small service station, went out of business on December 4, 1979. On that same date, Kline, who owed Clark Oil Company approximately $2,000, transferred the petroleum products remaining at his station (approximately $1,800 worth) to Clark Oil. On February 29, 1980,

Kline filed a voluntary petition in bankruptcy. Would a bankruptcy court deem this a preferential transfer?

b. Assume that Kline did not transfer the gas to Clark Oil but instead retained ownership and signed a security agreement that gave Clark Oil a security interest in the gas. Clark Oil then filed the security agreement, giving it a perfected security interest in Kline's gas on December 10, 1979. Is this a voidable transfer?

4. On June 8, 1980, Losner filed a voluntary petition in bankruptcy. Losner admitted that, about six months previously, he withdrew about $1,000 from his checking account and carried the money on his person, in cash. Subsequently, he used the money to purchase cashier's checks with which to pay several of his creditors. The payments to his creditors were made more than ninety days before filing the petition in bankruptcy. Losner also admitted that he withdrew the money and carried it on him because he knew he was about to go bankrupt and did not want all of the money attached through the bankruptcy action. Can any of Losner's creditors who were not paid with the $1,000 object to Losner's actions?

5. Kentile Floors, Inc. and Winham's Floor Coverings had a long-standing business relationship through which Kentile sold Winham floor covering goods. Kentile's sales were on a credit basis, and Winham made timely payments throughout the first several years of their business relationship. Beginning in 1965, however, Winham's payments became sporadic, and for the next year Winham had difficulty making payments. In January 1980, Kentile insisted that Winham supply it with a financial statement before Kentile would make further sales to Winham on credit. Before it received any financial statements from Winham, however, Kentile extended approximately $96,000 more in credit to Winham. The financial statements that Kentile finally received from Winham were false. Moreover, Winham's accounts payable on the financial statement were less than the $96,000 that it owed Kentile. Nevertheless, Kentile continued to extend credit to Winham. Shortly thereafter, Winham went into bankruptcy.

Kentile objected to being discharged in the bankruptcy because of the false financial statement. What will be the result?

6. Charles Edward & Associates, a partnership, had an order of relief entered against it in an involuntary proceeding. During the proceeding, it was revealed that the partners failed to keep records of their business transactions so that the bankruptcy court's administration of the bankrupt partnership was severely hindered. Should the partnership be granted a discharge in bankruptcy? Should the individuals who made up the partnership be granted a discharge in bankruptcy in their individual capacities?

7. On January 1, 1980, Mann conveyed his home to his three children. At the time, his home was worth $15,000 and was his only asset. At the same time, Mann's debt exceeded $30,000. Five months later, Mann filed a voluntary petition in bankruptcy. Will Mann's creditors be able to levy against the home? Would the answer be different if Mann's liabilities on January 1 had been only $5,000?

8. The XYZ Corporation went into bankruptcy with $100,000 in assets. Ten of its employees each claimed $5,000 in wages due. N claimed a judgment of $4,000 for injuries received because of XYZ's negligence. XYZ has two classes of stockholders — preferred and common. The preferred stockholders held $60,000 in preferred stock, and the common stockholders owned $500,000 worth of common stock. Costs of administering the estate totaled $20,000. Who will receive what from XYZ's estate?

9. Okamoto had liabilities of about $10,000, assets worth less than $1,000, and a total of nineteen creditors, each of which was unsecured. Okamoto owed Hornblower more than $6,000. Of the remaining eighteen creditors, eight were owed amounts less than $65 each, and none were owed more than $150. Hornblower filed an involuntary petition against Okamoto. Okamoto responded that, since he had more than twelve creditors, the petition could not be filed by only one creditor. Will Hornblower be successful if it argues that the other creditors should not be counted since the debt owed to it exceeds the total of all other debts owed by Okamoto?

UNIT VI

Agency and Employment

33

Agency and Employment
Creation and Termination of Agency Relationships

In **agency** relationships between two parties, one of the parties, called the agent, agrees to represent or act for the other, called the principal, subject to the principal's right to control the agent's conduct in matters entrusted to the agent. More formally, the Restatement, Agency, Second, defines *agency* as "the fiduciary relation which results from the manifestation of consent by one person to another that the other shall act in his behalf and subject to his control, and consent by the other so to act."[1] In general, the law of agency is based on the Latin maxim *qui facit per alium, facit per se* ("one acting by another is acting for himself"). Agency involves a person acting for and in the place of a principal.

THE NATURE OF AGENCY

Using agents, one individual can conduct multiple business operations simultaneously in various locations. Real estate brokers and corporate officers who serve in a representative capacity for their employers are familiar examples of agents.

Agency law is essential to the existence and operation of a corporate entity because only through its agents can a corporation function and enter into contracts. Partnership law is a special application of agency law—that is, mutual agency. Partnership and corporation law are discussed in Unit VII.

---

1. Restatement, Agency, Second, Section 1(1).

Purpose

An agency relationship can be created for any *legal* purpose. One created for a purpose which is illegal or is contrary to public policy is unenforceable. For example, it is illegal for medical doctors and other licensed professionals to contract unlicensed agents to perform professional actions.

Rights and Duties

The representative relationship created by agency law establishes certain *rights* and *duties*, which are similar to those that arise from the law of torts and contracts. Thus, when one individual acts on behalf of another, the legal impact can be felt in various ways.

DUTIES OF THE AGENT TO THE PRINCIPAL   Agents must act with reasonable care and exercise skill and knowledge typical to the place where they are to perform. In addition, they must exercise any particular skills that they possess. Failure to meet these standards allows a principal to bring an action against the agent in either tort or contract.

Generally, agents must act exclusively for the benefit of their principals in all matters within the scope of the agency. This duty obliges agents not to use unfairly any information or property that they have acquired by virtue of the agency.

DUTIES OF THE PRINCIPAL TO THE AGENT   The principal must pay the agent the agreed-upon compensation for the services that he or she has performed. The principal must also provide a suitable place for the agent to work and must use reasonable care to prevent injury to the agent.

KINDS OF AGENTS

The first step in analyzing an agency relationship is to determine whether or not such a relationship exists. Traditional analysis in the law of agency distinguishes three types of relationships: (1) principal and agent, (2) master and servant, and (3) employer and independent contractor.

Principal-Agent

In a principal-agent relationship, the parties have agreed that the agent will act *on behalf of and instead of* the principal in negotiating and transacting business with third persons. This relationship will affect the principal's rights and duties. Thus, an agent is empowered to perform legal acts that are binding on the principal. For example, an agent can bind a principal in a contract with a third person. An agent has *derivative authority* to use a degree of independent discretion in carrying out the principal's business.[2] For example, Earl is hired as a booking agent for a rock group—Harry and the Rockets. As the group's agent, Earl can negotiate and sign contracts for the rock group to appear at concerts. The contracts will be binding and thus legally enforceable against the group.

Master-Servant

Today's law defines *servant* as an agent employed by a master to perform services; the servant's physical conduct is controlled or is subject to the right to control by the master. Thus, a servant is a type of agent. However, the term *master-servant relationship* is anachronistic. Accountants, truck drivers, and business managers are not referred to as servants. For that matter, employers are not called masters. The more current terminology to describe a master-servant relationship is that of employer-employee.

The term *employee* held no significance to common law rules of agency. However, with the industrial revolution and recent social legislation, the term has come into prominence. An employee is an agent (other than an independent contractor) who has an appointment or contract for hire. In essence, only those agents

_____
2.   But an agent is not an independent contractor, described below.

or servants who work for pay can qualify as employees.

For example, Dana owns a dress shop. She employs Sandy, Sheila, and Sue as sales people. Dana is the employer/master; the women are the employees/servants. The key feature of the employer/employee relationship is that the employer controls, or at least has the right to control, the employee in the performance of the physical tasks involved in the employment. The employees do not have *independent* business discretion. The dress shop sales people can sell dresses, but they cannot sell the dress shop.

Independent Contractor

Independent contractors are not agents because they cannot make contracts with third persons for their employers, and they are not employees (servants) because their employers have no control over the details of their physical performance. The following factors are relevant in determining the status of independent contractors:

1.   What is the extent of control that the employer can exercise over the details of the work?
2.   Is the employed person engaged in an occupation or business distinct from that of the employer?
3.   Is the work usually done under the employer's direction, or is it done by a specialist without supervision?
4.   Does the employer supply the tools at the place of work?
5.   How long is the person employed?
6.   What is the method of payment—by time or at the completion of the job?
7.   What is the degree of skill required by the person employed?

Building contractors and subcontractors are independent contractors, and a property owner does not control the acts of either of these professionals. Truck drivers who own their equipment and hire out on an ad hoc basis are independent contractors; however, truck drivers who drive company trucks on a regular basis are usually employees (servants). A collection agency is another example of an independent contractor.

A TAX QUESTION   The federal government requires employers to deduct taxes from the wages of employees but not from the payments to independent contractors. In the following case, an insurance company paid taxes to the Internal Revenue Service but later attempted to characterize the particular employees as "independent contractors" and sought to recover the taxes it had paid to the government.

M.F.A. MUTUAL INS. Co. v. UNITED STATES

United States District Court, Western District of Missouri, Central District, 1970. 314 F.Supp. 590.

BACKGROUND AND FACTS   *M.F.A. Insurance Company had a special program for new agents called an "Agent Financing Agreement" whereby M.F.A. would guarantee each agent a monthly salary instead of a commission. The agreement specifically stated that these persons were "independent contractors." Persons under these agreements sold and serviced insurance contracts. They were specially supervised, they received instructions in training, and they were fully compensated for expenses incurred. M.F.A. took the position that it should not have to pay Social Security taxes on the ground that these "financed agents" were not employees within the meaning of the Internal Revenue Code definition, but rather were independent contractors.*

DECISION AND RATIONALE   *M.F.A.'s "financed agents" were employees as defined by the Internal Revenue Code despite their designation as independent contractors in the "Agent Financing Agreements."*

Therefore, M.F.A. was responsible for paying their Social Security taxes. "A financed agent was, in effect, given a guaranteed draw and the amount of money received was not related to the job performed. The money was paid to obtain the full time services of the financed agent ***. It should be understood, of course, that *** plaintiff's method of payment of its financed agents *** does not mean that we consider that factor to be controlling. We do not think that particular factor is a significant one *** because the method of payment involved in this case is highly inconsistent with the usual and familiar relationship of independent contractor."

Scope of Employment

The liability of an employer for the acts of an employee is limited to those acts performed within the scope of employment. The term *scope of employment* is not susceptible to any precise definition; nevertheless, two factors are usually present before it will be found in any given situation. First, the activity of the employee must be motivated at least in part by an intent to serve the employer's purpose rather than his or her own. Second, the manner, place, and time in which the act is performed must not vary substantially from that authorized or from that which is normal. In addition, the employer must have the right to control the activities of the employee. Taken together, an employer is liable only for those torts that would not have occurred except for the fact of the employer-employee relationship.

A very familiar agency relationship occurs in the real estate business. A real estate broker can hire several real estate salespersons who obtain listings, find buyers or sellers, and handle the actual sales transactions. In some states, only the broker obtains a license. Hence, the broker is identified as a principal, and the sales personnel are agents for the broker. In such a relationship, the broker is responsible for the acts of the sales agents.

ACTUAL VERSUS APPARENT AUTHORITY
The following case reviews the concepts of actual authority and apparent authority. A principal will be bound by all acts of a general agent whenever they come within the course and scope of the business entrusted to the agent. However, in some cases, the principal cannot be bound by the agent's acts, especially if they are beyond the ordinary and usual course of the business.

BACKGROUND AND FACTS *A husband and wife who had managed an apartment complex for several years devised a scheme of selling short-term savings certificates to the building's tenants. The husband and wife needed to raise money to pay off gambling debts. The certificates they issued were in the name of the apartment complex and bore the name of the manager as well as a fictitious name signed by the manager as treasurer. The owner of the apartments was not aware of the scheme. Eventually, the husband and wife were indicted and convicted of felonies. The tenants later sued the owners of the apartment complex to recover on the certificates under a theory of principal-agent relationship.*

GUNN v. SCHAEFFER
Court of Civil Appeals
of Texas, El Paso, 1978.
567 S.W.2d 30.

DECISION AND RATIONALE *The evidence showed that the apartment managers had neither actual nor apparent authority to issue the* *certificates of indebtedness. Therefore, the apartment complex owner was not liable on these certificates. As expressed in the words of the court: "When an apparent authority is claimed to arise from representations or conduct, the acts and statements of the principal must be looked to for the requisite foundation and not those of the agent; the former alone can give rise to authority of this character; the latter are never in themselves sufficient for that purpose ***. [A] manager has no power to borrow money in connection with the operation of the business or to issue negotiable instruments in the name of the principal, unless the business conducted is one involved in the borrowing of money or the issuing of negotiable instruments such as banking and other financial business."*

FORMATION OF THE AGENCY RELATIONSHIP

The following discussions will emphasize the usual form that an agency relationship takes. The contractual aspects of the formation and termination of agency are similar for employer-employee and independent contractor relationships. The distinctions among agent, employee, and independent contractor will become clearer in the chapter on liability.

The agency relationship is a *consensual* relationship; that is, it comes about by consent and agreement between the parties. The agreement need not be in writing, and consideration is not required.[3] The same basic rights and duties are involved whether it is a gratuitous agency or an agency for hire.

Generally, there are no formalities required to create an agency. The agency relationship can arise by acts of the parties in one of four ways: (1) by agreement, (2) by ratification, (3) by estoppel, or (4) by operation of law.

Agency by Agreement

As stated earlier, agency is a consensual relationship. It must be based on some *affirmative* indication between the principal and the agent that the agent agrees to act for the principal and the principal agrees to have the agent so act.

An agency agreement can take the form of an express written contract. For example, P enters into a sales agreement with A, a realtor, to sell P's house. An agency relationship exists between P and A for the sale of the house. Express agreements can be oral. For example, P asks B, a gardener, to care for her lawn on a regular basis. B agrees. An agency relationship exists between P and B for the lawn care.

An agency agreement can be implied from conduct. For example, a hotel allows Jack Andrews to park cars, but Andrews has no employment contract there. He can infer from the hotel's conduct that he has authority to act as a valet. It can be implied that he is an agent for the hotel. His purpose is to provide valet parking services for hotel guests.

Agency by Ratification

When a principal gives consent after his or her agent has acted, an agency is created by ratifica-

---

3. There are two main exceptions to oral agency agreements:
1. In many states, the Statute of Frauds requires that, whenever agency authority empowers the agent to enter into a contract that the Statute of Frauds requires to be in writing, then the agent's authority from the principal must likewise be in writing. This is known as the "Equal Dignity Rule." It occurs most frequently in contracts for the sale of an interest in land or contracts that cannot be performed within one year. The Statute of Frauds is discussed in Chapter 11.
2. A power of attorney is written authority conferred to an agent. It is conferred in a formal writing, usually acknowledged by a notary public, whose seal is attached to the formal document. A power of attorney can be general, giving the agent broad powers, or it can grant the agent only restricted authority.

tion. The effect is the same as if the consent were given before the action.

Ratification also occurs when the principal accepts the benefits of an agent's acts. For example, Alfred James, an employee of Anne Paul, contracts to purchase a tract of land in Paul's name without her authority to do so. Paul learns of James's actions and decides that the land is of great value and that she will go through with the sale. In this case, Paul has *ratified* James's acts, thereby creating an agency relationship between them. (Note that the creation of the agency "relates" to the time of James's unauthorized act.)

Agency by Estoppel

When a principal causes a third person to believe that another person is his or her agent, and the third person deals with the supposed agent, the principal is "estopped to deny" the agency relationship. In these situations, the principal's actions create the appearance of "apparent authority," which does not in fact exist. For example: M accompanies P to call on a customer, S, the proprietor of the General Store. M has done sales work but is not employed by P at this time. P boasts to S that he wishes he had three more assistants "just like M." S has reason to believe from P's statements that M is an agent for P. S then places seed orders with M. If P does not correct the impression that M is an agent, P will be bound to fill the orders just as if M were really P's agent. P's representation to S created the "apparent authority" in M to carry out the usual and necessary sales agent transactions for which P will be bound. Note, however, that this authority generally cannot be established by acts or declarations of the purported agent.

The theory of apparent authority does not extend to all acts under all circumstances. The third person must prove that he or she *reasonably* believed that the agent had authority. Facts and circumstances must show that an ordinary, prudent person who is familiar with business practice and custom would be justified in concluding that the agent had authority. The

law also is designed to protect third parties not privy to the original agreement.

Agency by Operation of Law

In some cases, the courts have found it desirable to find an agency relationship in the absence of either a formal agreement or the estoppel situation described above. This often occurs in family relationships. For example, suppose a wife purchases certain basic necessities and charges them to her husband's account. If the husband has not supplied these goods, the courts will often rule that the husband is liable for their payment because of a social policy of promoting the general welfare of the wife. Also, the husband has a legal duty to supply necessities for his wife and children. Sometimes agency by operation of law is created, giving an agent emergency power to act under unusual circumstances that are not covered by the agreement when failure to act would cause a principal substantial loss. If the agent is unable to contact the principal, the courts will often grant this emergency power.

LEGAL CAPACITY

A principal must have legal capacity to enter contracts. A person who cannot legally enter contracts directly should not be allowed to do it indirectly through an agent. An agent derives the authority to enter contracts from the principal, and a contract made by an agent is legally viewed as a contract of the principal. It is immaterial whether the agent personally has the legal capacity to make that contract. Thus, a minor can be an agent but cannot be a principal appointing an agent.[4] In the latter case, any resulting contracts will be voidable by the minor principal, but not by the adult third party.

Conversely, any person can be an agent, regardless of whether he or she has the capacity to contract. For example, newspaper delivery

---

4. Exceptions have been granted by some courts to allow a minor to appoint an agent for the limited purpose of contracting for the minor's necessities of life. Casey v. Kastel, 237 N.Y. 305, 142 N.E. 671 (1924).

boys and girls can enroll newspaper subscriptions. Even a person who is legally incompetent can be appointed an agent if that person is capable of performing the required functions.

AGENCY POWER COUPLED WITH AN INTEREST

An agency *coupled with an interest* is a relationship created for the benefit of the agent (or third person). The agent actually acquires a beneficial interest in the subject matter of the agency. Under these circumstances it is not equitable to permit a principal to terminate at will. Hence, this type of agency is "irrevocable."

For example, Sarah Roberts (principal) owns Blackacre. She needs some immediate cash, so she enters into an agreement with John Hartwell that Hartwell will lend her $10,000, and she will grant Hartwell a one-half interest in Blackacre and "the exclusive right to sell" it for $25,000 if she fails to repay the $10,000. The loan is to be repaid out of the sales proceeds. Hartwell's power to sell Blackacre is coupled with a beneficial interest of one-half ownership in Blackacre created at the time of the loan for the purpose of supporting it and securing its repayment. Hartwell's agency power is irrevocable.

An agency coupled with an interest should not be confused with situations in which the agent merely derives proceeds or profits from the sale of the subject matter. For example, an agent who merely receives a commission from the sale of real property does not have a beneficial interest in the property itself. Likewise, an attorney whose fee is a percentage of the recovery (a contingency fee) merely has an interest in the proceeds. These agency relationships are revocable by the principal, subject to any express contractual arrangements that the principal has with the agent.

Since, in an agency coupled with an interest, the interest is not created for the benefit of the principal, it is not really an agency power in the usual sense. Therefore, any attempt by the principal to revoke an agency normally has no legal force or effect. Finally, an agency coupled with an interest is not terminated by the death of either the principal or the agent.

TERMINATION OF AN AGENCY

Agency law is similar to contract law, and termination of agency occurs similarly to the termination of a contract—by act of the parties or by operation of law. Once the relationship between the principal and the agent has ended, the agent no longer has the right to bind the principal. However, third persons also need to be notified that the agency has been revoked.

Termination by Act of the Parties

LAPSE OF TIME An agency agreement may specify the time period during which the agency relationship will exist. The agency simply ends when that time expires. Of course, the parties can agree to continue the relationship, in which case the same terms will apply.

If no definite time is stated, then the agency continues for a reasonable time and can be terminated at will by either party. A "reasonable time" depends upon the circumstances and the nature of the agency relationship. For example, P asks A to sell P's car. After two years, if A has not sold P's car and there has been no communication between P and A, it is safe to assume that the agency relationship has terminated. A no longer has the authority to sell P's car.

PURPOSE ACHIEVED An agent can be employed to accomplish a particular objective such as the purchase of stock for a cattle rancher. The agency automatically ends upon the completion of the assignment—that is, after the cattle have been purchased.

If more than one agent is employed to accomplish the same purpose, such as the sale of real estate, the first agent to complete the sale terminates the agency relationship for all the others.

OCCURRENCE OF A SPECIFIC EVENT An agency can be created to terminate upon the happening of a certain event. For example, P appoints A to handle her business affairs while she is away. When P returns, the agency automatically terminates.

Sometimes an aspect of the agent's authority terminates on the occurrence of a particular event. For example, P, a banker, permits A, the credit manager, to grant a credit line of $1,000 to certain depositors who maintain $1,000 in a savings account. If any customer's savings account falls below $1,000, A can no longer continue making the credit line available to that customer. But A's right to extend credit to the other customers maintaining the minimum balance will continue.

MUTUAL AGREEMENT Recall from basic contract law that parties can cancel (rescind) a contract by mutually agreeing to terminate the contractual relationship. The same result occurs in agency law regardless of whether the agency agreement is in writing or whether it is for a specific duration. For example, P no longer wishes A to be his agent, and A does not want to work for P any more. Either party can communicate to the other the intent to terminate the relationship. Such communication effectively relieves each of the rights, duties, and powers inherent in the relationship.

The agent's act is said to be a renunciation of authority. The principal's act is a revocation of authority.

TERMINATION BY ONE PARTY As a general rule, either party can terminate the agency relationship; but although both parties may have the *power* to terminate, they may not each possess the *right*. Wrongful termination can subject the canceling party to a suit for damages.

For example, A has a one-year employment contract with P for $12,000. P can discharge A before the contract period expires (P has the *power* to breach the contract); however, P will be liable to A for money damages because P has no *right* to breach the contract.

The next case involves the premature termination of an agency relationship.

BACKGROUND AND FACTS *Davis hired McDonald as a real estate agent to find a buyer for his grocery store. The contract gave McDonald an exclusive right for six months to close a sale and provided that his commission was to be 10 percent of the sales price. One month after the contract was entered into, Davis wrote to McDonald requesting that he take the store off the market. McDonald sued for breach of an agency contract.*

McDONALD v. DAVIS
Court of Civil Appeals of
Texas, 1965.
389 S.W.2d 494.

DECISION AND RATIONALE *Davis was liable to McDonald for the profit that McDonald could have made on the sale of the store. (This may or may not have been equal to the 10 percent commission on the asking price, depending on other factors. The amount of damages was not at issue here.)*

*McDonald, as exclusive broker for Davis, was Davis's agent. This agency relationship was established in the contract that they both signed. A principal always has the power to revoke an agent's authority (so that the agent cannot thereafter bind an unwilling principal to an agreement with a third party). However, a principal does not have the right to revoke an agent's authority. As the court explained: "There is a distinction between his power to revoke and his right to revoke *** . [I]f* *he has no right to revoke it, he will be liable for damages suffered by the agent by reason of the wrongful revocation. Where, as here, there is a bilateral contract, the principal has no right to revoke to the prejudice of the agent."*

Termination by Operation of Law

DEATH OR INSANITY The general rule is that death or insanity of either the principal or the agent automatically and immediately terminates the ordinary agency relationship. Knowledge of the death is not required.[5] Some states, however, have changed this common law by statute. For example, P sends A to the Far East to purchase a rare book. Before A makes the purchase, P dies. A's agent status is terminated at the moment of death, even though A does not know that P had died.

Agent's transactions that occur after the death of the principal are not binding on the principal's estate. Assume A is hired by P to collect a debt from T (a third party). P dies, but A still collects the money from T, not knowing of P's death. T's payment to A is no longer legally sufficient to discharge T's debt to P because A no longer has P's authority to collect the money. If A absconds with the money, T must again pay the debt to P's estate. There are, however, limits to this rule. They are discussed in the section on partnerships in Chapter 34.

UNFORESEEN CIRCUMSTANCES

Impossibility When the subject matter of an agency is destroyed or lost, the agency terminates. For example, P employs A to sell P's house. Prior to any sale, the premises are destroyed by fire. A's authority to sell P's house terminates. When it is impossible for the agent to perform the agency lawfully, because of war, or because of a change in the law, the authority of the agent terminates.

Changed Circumstances When an event occurs that has such an unusual effect on the subject matter of the agency that the agent can reasonably infer that the principal will not want the agent to continue, the agency terminates. P hires A to sell a tract of land for $10,000. Subsequently, A learns that there is oil under the land and that the land is therefore worth $1 million. A's authority to sell the land for $10,000 is terminated. Note that the change in circumstances need not render performance impossible.

Bankruptcy Bankruptcy of the principal (or the agent) usually terminates the agency relationship.[6] Some situations, such as a serious financial loss, might indicate that future contracts should not be made.

Notice Required for Termination

When an agency terminates by operation of law due to death, insanity, or some other unforeseen circumstance, there is no duty to notify third persons.[7] However, if the parties themselves have terminated the agency, it is the principal's duty to inform any third parties who know of the existence of the agency that it has been terminated. Either the principal or another person can give the notice.

---

5. An exception to virtually all agency notice and termination rules occurs in an agency coupled with an interest, which is not automatically terminated by death or incapacity.

6. Insolvency, as distinguished from bankruptcy, will not necessarily terminate the relationship. Most states do not consider the appointment of a receiver grounds for terminating the agency.

7. There is an exception to this rule in banking. UCC Sec. 4-405 provides that the bank as the agent can continue to exercise specific types of authority even after the customer's death or insanity unless it has knowledge of the death or insanity. When it has knowledge of the customer's death, it has authority for ten days after the death to pay checks (but not notes or drafts) drawn by the customer unless the bank receives a stop payment order from someone who has an interest in the account, such as an heir. (This rule does not apply to insanity.)

An agent's authority continues until the agent receives some notice of termination. No particular *form* of notice is required. The principal can actually notify the agent, or the agent can learn of the termination through some occurrence that gives the agent reason to know of the termination. For example, Marshall bids on a shipment of steel, and Smith is hired to arrange transportation of the shipment. When Smith learns that Marshall has lost the bid, Smith's authority to make the transportation arrangement terminates.

Notice to third parties, however, follows the general rule that an agent's *apparent authority* continues until the third person is notified (from any source of information) that authority has been terminated.

The principal is expected to notify directly any third person whom the principal knows has relied upon the agency because that person has dealt with the agent. For third persons who have merely heard about the agency in general but have not dealt with the agent, constructive notice will be sufficient.

If the agent's authority is written, it must be revoked in writing and sent to all persons to whom the agent might have shown the writing that initially established the agency relationship. Sometimes a written authorization (like that granting power of attorney) contains an expiration date. The passage of the expiration date is sufficient notice of termination for third parties.

Death or incapacity of the principal automatically and immediately terminates the agent's apparent authority. Under these circumstances, no notice is required to third parties unless the agent's power is coupled with an interest.

QUESTIONS AND CASE PROBLEMS

1.   Lionberger's Auto Parts leased out automobile utility trailers. Lionberger was a member of Nationwide Trailer Rental System, an association of rental operators. Nationwide's leasing system operated as follows. Each member rented trailers that it owned. Trailers that were rented for a one-way trip were delivered at the point of destination to other members of Nationwide. The system was reciprocal in that members rented each other's trailers to customers. Uniformity in operation and administrative control was achieved through a system of rules implemented by Nationwide. A uniform lease agreement was used, and division of rental fees between the renter and the owner of one-way trailers was provided for in Nationwide's bylaws. When a trailer owned by Lionberger is rented out by another member of Nationwide, does a principal-agent relationship exist between Lionberger and the other member of Nationwide? Does a bailor-bailee relationship also exist? If so, does the latter relationship have any effect on the agency relationship? [Lionberger v. United States, 371 F.2d 831 (Ct. Cl. 1967)]

2.   Miller sold insurance for Massachusetts Mutual Life Insurance Company under a contract that he renewed annually. Miller derived his income almost exclusively from the efforts of agents who worked under him. In connection with his job, Miller borrowed and invested large sums of money to promote sales by his agents. He was free to vary the terms of the contracts he had with them in regard to their rates and commissions. In addition, he could hire and fire them without Massachusetts Mutual's approval. Miller received a commission from Massachusetts Mutual for all the sales that he or his agents made. Is Miller an employee of Massachusetts Mutual or an independent contractor? [Massachusetts Mutual Life Ins. Co. v. Central Penn Nat. Bank, 372 F.Supp. 1027 (E.D. Penn. 1974)]

3.   Holiday Inns operates its hotel chain on a franchise basis. Each hotel is owned by a franchisee who is responsible for operating and managing it. Holiday Inns, as franchisor, receives a small percentage of the profits of each franchised hotel. In exchange, each hotel uses the Holiday Inn name, follows certain business practices, and maintains certain standards set by the franchisor. Goynes was the night clerk in the Phenix City, Alabama, Holiday Inn. One evening, he was handed a Gulf Oil credit card by one of the hotel's customers. Noting that the card identification number was one that Gulf Oil had revoked, Goynes retained the card and refused to return it to the

customer. The customer wished to sue for conversion. Since Goynes had no money, the customer had to look to one of Goynes's principals. Does a principal-agent relationship exist between Goynes and Holiday Inn? between Goynes and the franchisor? [Wood v. Holiday Inns, Inc., 369 F.Supp. 82 (M.D. Ala. 1974)]

4. Roy Haven brought a medical malpractice action against his surgeon, Judson Randolph, M.D., and against the hospital where the surgery had been performed. Haven claimed that the doctor's negligence caused him to suffer paralysis as a result of minor surgery. Haven also wished to hold the hospital responsible as Randolph's principal. Randolph was not employed by the hospital, and any services that the hospital provided were at Randolph's direction. Would Randolph be deemed an agent of the hospital? [Haven v. Randolph, 342 F.Supp. 538 (D.C.D.C. 1972)]

5. Crittendon took his Chevrolet to a service station operated by Mendenhall and discussed the problem of its faulty wheel bearings with him. During their conversation, Mendenhall stated that he had previously worked at a Chevrolet garage and was familar with the repair of Chevrolets. The service station at which Mendenhall worked was owned by State Oil Company and displayed two signs, each containing only the word *State*. Mendenhall leased the service station from State but received neither a salary nor repair tools from State. Crittendon left his car for Mendenhall to repair. After Mendenhall repaired it, he took it out for a test drive, went off the road, and damaged it extensively. Crittendon wished to establish an agency relationship between State and Mendenhall so he could recover from State. Does Crittendon have any grounds to argue for the existence of a principal-agent relationship? [Crittendon v. State Oil Co., 78 Ill. App.2d 112, 222 N.E.2d 561 (1966)]

6. Robert and Esther Levine purchased two airline tickets through Comet Travel Agency for an overseas flight with British Overseas Airways. Subsequent to the purchase but prior to the flight, the Levines found that they would not be able to make the trip and therefore returned the tickets directly to British Overseas Airways for a refund. Instead of mailing the refund to the Levines, BOA mailed it to Comet Travel Agency. The manager of Comet absconded with the funds, and the Levines tried to recover from BOA, which claimed that it was justified in sending the refund to Comet since Comet was the Levine's authorized agent. What argument would allow the Levines to recover from British Overseas Airways? [Levine v. British Overseas Airways Corp., 66 Misc. 2d 766, 322 N.Y.S.2d 119 (1971)]

7. Pro Golf manufactured and marketed golf equipment both in the United States and abroad. In 1961, Robert Wynn became Pro Golf's sales representative in the Far East. Wynn and Pro Golf did not have a formal contract, but letters exchanged between them indicated the type of relationship they had. In a 1970 letter from Pro Golf to Wynn, Pro Golf stated, "You will continue to have the exclusive right to import and promote the sale of golf equipment in the Far East market. However, this is not an irrevocable right but would remain in effect only so long as you did a satisfactory business in this market." Several years later, Pro Golf terminated Wynn's exclusive right, but first it gave Wynn five months' notice of its desire to terminate. Was Pro Golf's termination proper? What if Pro Golf had given Wynn no notice? [First Flight Associates, Inc. v. Professional Golf Co., 527 F.2d 931 (6th Cir. 1975)]

8. On October 11, 1973, John Gray, owner of a 50 percent interest in a government oil and gas lease, assigned 10 percent of the operating rights and working interest to John Tylle in consideration of Tylle's payment of $10,000. The assignment was in writing and stated: "Until further notice assignee hereby appoints and designates assignor as agent and operator of the said lease for the purpose of development and management." A few weeks later, John Gray died unexpectedly. Tylle filed a claim against Gray's estate, seeking to recover the $10,000 he paid Gray. In order for Tylle to be successful, he must show that the agency relationship between him and Gray had been terminated. Will Tylle be successful? [In the matter of the estate of Gray, 37 Colo. App. 47, 541 P.2d 336 (1975)]

9. Selastomer, Inc., and P.S. & E. Inc. orally agreed in 1965 that P.S. & E. would become the exclusive selling agency for the seal rings and packing seals that Selastomer manufactured. P.S. & E. thereafter hired additional personnel, expended money for tooling, and used its staff to introduce Selastomer's products into the market. As a result, numerous prospective purchasers began to test and consider buying Selastomer's products. Shortly thereafter, Selastomer gave P.S. & E. notice that it intended to sell its products on its own; and three months after giving notice to P.S. & E., it began to invade P.S. & E.'s market. Is Selastomer in breach of the agency agreement? What damages, if any, should Selastomer pay P.S. & E.? [P.S. & E., Inc. v. Selastomer Detroit, Inc., 470 F.2d 125 (7th Cir. 1972)]

10. In 1970, the Moulton-Niguel Water District hired an independent contractor to construct a water tank for the district. During the construction process, one of the contractor's employees was injured. Those

in charge of the water district realized at the time they employed the independent contractor that construction of the water tank was particularly hazardous because of the type of construction and the tank's location. During construction, the contractor negligently failed to take certain precautions to protect its workers. Furthermore, the water district failed to demand that the contractor use certain safety precautions. Therefore, the contractor's employee was injured as a result of the contractor's negligence. Since the contractor was insolvent, the injured employee wants to sue the water district, but first he must prove a principal-agent relationship between himself and the water district. Will he succeed? [Stilson v. Moulton-Niguel Water District, 21 Cal. App. 3d. 928, 98 Cal. Rptr. 914 (1972)]

34

Agency and Employment
Duties of Agents and Principals

The principal-agent relationship is fiduciary—one of trust. In it, each party owes the other the duty to act with the utmost good faith. It is presumed that neither party will keep from the other information that has any bearing on their agency relationship. This chapter considers the duties that, in many cases, are simply specific applications of this general fiduciary obligation. It looks first at duties owed by the agent to the principal and then at duties owed by the principal to the agent.

THE AGENT'S DUTY TO THE PRINCIPAL

The duties that an agent owes to its principal are set out in the agency agreement, or they arise by operation of law. They are implied from the agency relationship whether or not the principal is known or disclosed to a third party. Chapter 35 will show the importance of whether or not the principal has been disclosed in its discussion of the liabilities of the agent and the principal.

Duty to Perform

An implied condition in every agency contract is the agent's agreement to use reasonable diligence and skill in performing the work. When an agent fails to perform his or her duties entirely, liability for breach of contract generally will occur. For example, an insurance agent who fails to obtain the insurance coverage requested by a principal is guilty of breach of contract. When an agent performs carelessly or negligently, the agent can be liable in tort as well.

In many situations, an agent who does not act for money (a gratuitous or free agent) can be subject to the same standards of care and duty to perform. A gratuitous agent cannot, however, be liable for breach of contract because there is no contract. A gratuitous agent is subject only to tort liability. However, once the agent has begun, the duty to continue to perform and to take care in rendering the performance is required. For example, Alex Paul's friend, Amy Foster, is a real estate broker. She (the agent) gratuitously offers to sell Paul's (the principal) farm, Black Acre. If she never attempts to sell Black Acre, Paul has no legal cause of action to force her to do so. But assume that Foster finds a buyer. She keeps promising the buyer to come up with the sales contract but fails to do so within a reasonable period of time. The buyer becomes disgruntled and seeks another property, and the sale ultimately falls through. Paul has a cause of action in tort for negligence—that is, failure to use the degree of care reasonably expected of real estate brokers.

Duty to Notify

A basic concept of agency law is that the agent is required to notify the principal of all matters that come to his or her attention concerning the subject matter of the agency. This means that *any facts disclosed to the agent are imputed to the principal*. It is not what the agent actually tells that is important; what the agent *should have told* is crucial. For example, A is P's agent for the purchase of certain property from X. In the course of dealing, A discovers that many years ago, Y obtained mineral rights to remove certain items from the subsurface. Thinking that this is unimportant, A neglects to tell P. The purchase of the land takes place subject to Y's right to mine on it. P does not have recourse against X; that is, P cannot rescind the sale or use the existence of Y's right to remove minerals as a defense to avoid going through with the

sale. A had the duty to notify P. The fact that he failed to do so and breached his fiduciary duty cannot be allowed to prejudice the rights of the innocent third party, X. P, however, does have recourse against A.

Duty of Loyalty

An agent has a duty not to compete with his or her principal unless the agent fully discloses the competitive actions and the principal consents. Thus, a salesperson representing Avon products cannot sell products of a competing line at the same time unless Avon consents.

Agreements not to compete after termination of employment, if validly drawn, are acceptable. Certain information is deemed so confidential, however, that even termination of the employment relationship will not permit an agent to disclose it. For example, an agent can never disclose trade secrets or confidential information acquired in the course of employment. An agent can, however, use the skills and basic knowledge that were acquired while working for the principal.

An agent's duty of loyalty does not require concealment of a principal's dishonest acts. For example, if a principal is cheating on contracts, an agent can tell a third party, and the third party can sue the principal for damages.

CONFLICTS OF INTEREST An agent cannot take a position adverse to its principal. Anything an agent obtains by virtue of the employment relationship belongs to the principal. It is a breach of an agent's fiduciary duty to secretly retain benefits or profits that, by right, belong to the principal. Courts in this case will imply a *constructive trust*: The agent actually holds the money on behalf of the principal, and the principal can recover it in a lawsuit. For example, Andrews, a purchasing agent, gets cash rebates from a customer. If Andrews keeps the rebates, he violates his fiduciary duty to his principal, Metcalf. Upon finding out about the cash rebates, Metcalf can sue Andrews and recover them.

Personal purchases operate the same way. The rules against self-purchase prohibit an agent from taking advantage of the agency relationship to obtain goods or property that the principal wants to purchase. For example, Peterson (the principal) wants to purchase property in the suburbs. Cox, Peterson's agent, learns that a valuable tract of land has just become available. Cox cannot buy the land for herself. Peterson gets the right of first refusal. If Cox purchases the land for her benefit, the courts will impose a constructive trust on the land; that is, the land will be held for and on behalf of the principal despite the fact that the agent attempted to buy it in her own name.

In the following case, a real estate agent was supposedly acting on behalf of a landowner for the sale of a piece of property. The agent was also in the business of buying and holding land for resale. When the agent realized that the land was increasing in value, he decided to purchase the real estate for himself. The landowner agreed to sell the land to the agent for an agreed-upon price. A sales contract was drawn up but never consummated because the land-owner later decided to sell the property to a third person. The agent attempted to sue the landowner for selling the property to the third party on the basis that the agent lost certain profits he would otherwise have made on the resale of the property. The trial court decided that the agent had no cause of action.

RAMSEY v. GORDON
Court of Civil Appeals of
Texas, Waco, 1978.
567 S.W.2d 868.

BACKGROUND AND FACTS *Ramsey, a licensed real estate broker, was an agent for Gordon, the owner of approximately 181 acres of land. Because the land was rapidly appreciating in value, Ramsey decided to purchase it himself, and Gordon agreed to sell it for $800 per acre. A contract of sale was drawn up, but before it could be completed, Gordon conveyed the property to a third party for the same price. Meanwhile, Ramsey had begun negotiating to resell the property to another customer for $1,250 per acre. When Ramsey learned that Gordon had conveyed the property to someone else, he sued Gordon for the profit he would have made on the resale.*

DECISION AND RATIONALE *Ramsey could not recover damages from Gordon because he breached the duty he owed as Gordon's agent. Ramsey was obliged to disclose to Gordon anything he knew that might affect Gordon. He knew that the value of the land far exceeded $800 per acre because he was in the midst of negotiating a resale to another purchaser for more than $1,000 per acre. Because Ramsey did not tell Gordon about the actual value of the land, agency law dictates that Gordon can void his contract with Ramsey. "Whenever an agent breaches his duty to his principal by becoming personally interested in an agency agreement, the contract is voidable at the election of the principal without full knowledge of all the facts surrounding the agent's interest."*

Duties Owed by Subagents

If Paul (the principal) authorizes Andy (the agent) to hire subagents, then the subagents have the same duties to Paul as the agent has.

(The principal's authorization is needed for the hiring of subagents, except in emergencies.) Additionally, the agent is responsible to the principal for any subagent's wrongdoing. Of course, the subagents owe Andy the same duties that Andy owes Paul. Thus, an agent can recover from a subagent for the subagent's improper performance.

UNAUTHORIZED SUBAGENTS If an agent hires a subagent without the principal's authority, then the subagent has no legal relationship to the principal. Since the subagent and the principal have no agency relationship to one another, no duties arise between them. A principal will not be liable to third parties for that subagent's acts. However, the agent who hires the subagent without authority will be liable to the principal if the subagent acts wrongfully, and the agent will bear the loss.

Duty to Account

Unless an agent and a principal agree otherwise, the agent has the duty to keep and make available to the principal an account of all property, money, and so on received and paid out on behalf of the principal. The agent has a duty to maintain separate accounts for the principal's funds and for personal funds, and no intermingling of them is allowed. Agents often violate this duty. When a professional, such as an attorney, violates the duty to account, he or she is subject to disciplinary proceedings by the Bar, as well as being liable to the principal.

Rights and Benefits Acquired during Employment

Every business interest (except small gifts) acquired during an employment relationship belongs to the principal, to be held for and on behalf of the principal. From this rule arises the duty of an agent to account to a principal.

An interesting question occurs when an employee invents a product and the employer claims a right to the invention or patent. The rules operate as follows. When an employee is hired to develop patents or inventions, then all rights to such developments belong to the employer, unless there is an agreement to the contrary. But when an employee is hired for other duties and, incidental to the employment, perfects a patent or invention, the property is not necessarily that of the employer. The **shop right doctrine** provides that if a patent or invention is perfected on the employer's time using the employer's materials *and* if it relates to the employer's business, then the employer has a right to it. The employer's right is irrevocable even after the employment relationship ends.

Principal's Right to Indemnification

A principal can be sued by a third party for an agent's negligent conduct, and in certain situations the principal can sue the agent for an equal amount of damages. This is called **indemnification.** The same holds true if the agent violates the principal's instructions. For example, Lewis (the principal) tells his agent, Moore, who is a used car salesman, to make no warranties about the used cars. Moore is anxious to make a sale to Walters, the third party, and makes warranties about the car's engine anyway. Lewis is not absolved from liability to Walters for engine failure, but if Walters sues Lewis, Lewis can then sue Moore for indemnification for violating his instructions.

In the following case, an insurance agent issued a binder policy knowing that the insurance company policy would not normally insure a boat of the type mentioned in the case without first inspecting it. When the boat was destroyed, the company was held liable, and it demanded that the agent (and the agency that hired the agent) indemnify the insurer for its losses.

BACKGROUND AND FACTS *An employee of Buckingham-Wheeler, an independent insurance agency, met with a boat owner, DiMicco, to discuss insuring a 13-year-old cruiser valued in excess of $5,000. The agent issued a binder policy on the boat despite his knowledge that the*

CRAWFORD v. DiMICCO
District Court of Appeals of Florida, Fourth District, 1968.
216 So.2d 769.

insurance company, Fidelity-Phenix Insurance Corporation (Fidelity) would not insure a boat having a value of $5,000 or greater or a boat that was over three years old without first inspecting it. A few weeks later, the boat was damaged in a storm and ultimately sank. The boat owner sought damages for the loss of his boat.

DECISION AND RATIONALE *DiMicco was able to recover from Fidelity, and Fidelity in turn could recover from its agent, Buckingham-Wheeler. Through its employee, Buckingham-Wheeler was an agent of Fidelity. As such it owed a duty not to exceed the authorization Fidelity had given it. This is particularly true where a principal has explicitly forbidden certain activities. In this case, Buckinham-Wheeler's employee knew that Fidelity did not wish to insure boats valued at greater than $5,000 or boats more than three years old without first inspecting them. According to the presiding judge: "Under the facts of the instant case and the settled law applicable thereto, unless and until the principal with full knowledge of all the applicable facts waived the breach of its instructions, ratified or adopted the agent's act as its own, or facts otherwise raising an estoppel against the principal, the agent became and remained liable to the principal for the damages incurred in acting without authority to the disadvantage of its principal. The facts herein reveal no adoption, ratification or estoppel on the part of the principal-insurer."*

LIMITS ON INDEMNIFICATION Sometimes it is difficult to distinguish between instructions of the principal that limit an agent's authority and those that are mere advice. For example, Willis (the principal) owns an office supply company; Jones (the agent) is the manager. Willis tells Jones, "Don't order any more supplies this month." Willis goes on vacation. A large order comes in from a local business, and the present inventory is insufficient to meet it. What is Jones to do? In this situation, Jones probably has the inherent power to order more supplies despite Willis' statement. It is unlikely that Jones would be required to indemnify Willis in the event that the local business subsequently cancelled the order.

PRINCIPAL'S REMEDIES FOR AGENT'S VIOLATION OF FIDUCIARY DUTY

A principal has contract remedies for breach of an agent's fiduciary duty and tort remedies for fraud committed by the agent. A principal can hold an agent accountable for damages proximately caused by the agent's actions. An agent can be required to give up secret profits or advantages obtained. If a principal can show malice or bad faith on the part of the agent, then punitive damages can also be awarded.

PRINCIPAL'S DUTIES TO AGENT

The principal's duties to an agent can be express, or they can be implied by law by virtue of the agency relationship.

Compensation and Reimbursement

Unless it is a gratuitous agency, the principal must pay agreed value (or reasonable value) for an agent's services. The principal must reimburse the agent for all expenses or losses involved in carrying out the agent's authorized duties. Most states have laws that regulate the payment of wages to employees. When the agent is a sales agent entitled to commission, the principal incurs liability once the offer is accepted, regardless of whether the contract is subsequently breached. In the case of subagents, a principal is liable to pay wages only if the agent was authorized to hire the additional employees. If not, the subagent must look to the agent who hired him or her for compensation.

Duty of Cooperation

A principal has a duty to both cooperate with and assist an agent in performing his or her duties and to do nothing to prevent such performance. For example, when a principal grants an agent an exclusive territory, the principal cannot compete with that agent in violation of the **exclusive agency.** To do so exposes the principal to liability for the agent's lost sales or profits.

Duty to Provide Safe Working Conditions

The common law requires a principal to provide safe premises, equipment, and conditions for all employees. The principal has a duty to inspect and warn employees of any defects. Today, the employer's liability is frequently covered by workmen's compensation acts, which are the primary remedy for an agent injured on the job.

AGENT REMEDIES AGAINST PRINCIPAL

Indemnification by Principal

Subject to the terms of the agency agreement, a principal has a duty to indemnify an agent for authorized payments or liabilities incurred because of authorized and lawful acts and transactions and also for losses suffered because of the principal's failure to perform any duties. Additionally, the principal must indemnify the agent for the value of benefits that the agent confers upon the principal unofficially.

The amount of indemnification is usually specified in the agency contract. If it is not, the courts will look to the nature of the business and the type of loss.

Authorized subagents can recover from either the principal or the agent who hires them, since the subagent is in a fiduciary relationship to both. If the authorized subagent gets indemnification from the agent who does the hiring, the agent can then seek indemnification from the principal.

Agent's Lien against Principal's Property

An agent can obtain a lien against property in the principal's possession up to the amount of compensation or indemnity owed. Similarly, a subagent can obtain a lien against the hiring agent for services and expenses and against the principal for property in the principal's possession to the extent of the agent's right in such property.

Other Remedies

An agent can (1) withhold further performance, (2) counterclaim if the principal sues, and (3) demand that the principal give an accounting. These contract remedies are all for damages. Since the principal-agent relationship is deemed to be consensual in nature, an agent has no right to specific performance in an ordinary agency contract. An agent can recover for past services and future damages but cannot force the principal to allow him or her to continue acting as an agent.

QUESTIONS AND CASE PROBLEMS

1. On April 15, 1965, Probert became a sales agent for American Gypsum Company. Although no formal contract was drawn up, one of American Gypsum's officers signed a memorandum to Probert indicating the amount of commission he would make on each sale and indicating that American Gypsum would reimburse him for his auto and travel expenses and that he would be sales agent for three states (including Washington). About a year later, and somewhat as

a result of Probert's efforts, American Gypsum made a large sale to a Washington-based lumber company. Probert claimed that American Gypsum owed him a commission on the sale even though he himself did not arrange the sale. Is Probert entitled to a commission? [Probert v. American Gypsum Div., 3 Wash. App. 112, 472 P.2d 604 (1970)]

2. Sam Kademenos was about to sell a $1 million life insurance policy to a prospective customer when he resigned from the company, Equitable Life. Before resigning, however, he had expended substantial company money and had utilized Equitable's medical examiners in order to procure the $1 million sale. After resigning, Kademenos joined a competitor, Jefferson Life Insurance Company, and made the sale through it. Has he breached any duty to Equitable? [Kademenos v. Equitable Life Assurance Society, 513 F.2d 1073 (3d Cir. 1975)]

3. HML Corporation and General Foods Corporation entered into an agreement under which General Foods agreed to buy for thirty-two months at least 85 percent of its salad dressing requirements in a designated area from HML. No minimum quantity was specified, and General Foods was to have exclusive rights to sell in the designated area. After attempting to promote HML's salad dressing for twelve months without success, General Foods informed HML that it would no longer require any salad dressing. What arguments based on agency law can HML assert to keep its contract with General Foods alive? Do you think HML will be successful? [HML Corp. v. General Foods Corp., 365 F.2d 77 (3d Cir. 1966)]

4. Walter T. Zumpe was employed by Chase and Sanborne from 1946 to 1964. Because Zumpe's work afforded him access to information that Chase and Sanborne considered confidential, Zumpe signed two agreements, one in 1959 and the other in 1964, which provided that he was not to disclose any of Chase and Sanborne's manufacturing processes and techniques to any of its competitors without Chase and Sanborne's express written permission. In 1964, Zumpe left Chase and Sanborne and joined one of its competitors. Chase and Sanborne sought to enjoin Zumpe from working for the competitor and from disclosing confidential information and trade secrets learned during his employment. Should a court issue such an injunction? [Standard Brands, Inc. v. Zumpe, 264 F.Supp. 254 (E.D. La. 1967)]

5. During the course of the administration of the estate of Baldwin M. Baldwin, it became necessary to sell a vast apartment complex owned by the estate,

known as "Baldwin Hills Village." Skyline Realty, a real estate broker, was commissioned to make the sale. A number of prospective purchasers were contacted, and they were present at the private sale of Baldwin Hills Village. Lemby, a real estate broker, was also present. On a number of prior occasions, he had indicated to the executors of Baldwin's estate that he was interested in purchasing the property. At the private sale, Lemby outbid all others and bought Baldwin Hills Village. Lemby then sought his commission on the sale from the Baldwin estate. Will anything in agency law prevent Lemby from recovering? [In re Estate of Baldwin, 34 Cal.App.3d 596, 110 Cal. Rptr. 189 (1973)]

6. On December 3, 1962, Dorin, acting in his capacity as soliciting agent for Occidental Life Insurance Company, submitted Milton Silverstein's application for a life insurance policy in the sum of $50,000. The application, signed by both Silverstein and Dorin, contained the following question and answer: "Has any company declined to issue or renew, postponed or cancelled, any life or accident and sickness insurance on your life? No." Notwithstanding his knowledge that Silverstein had been denied life insurance with the Equitable Life Assurance Society on the ground of ill health, Dorin failed to disclose this information to Occidental. On December 22, Occidental issued a life insurance policy for $50,000 as applied for by Silverstein. On June 30, 1963 Silverstein died, and an investigation by Occidental revealed the false statements contained in the application. Occidental then demanded that Dorin refund the $2,200 commission he had earned on that policy. Is Occidental entitled to a refund from Dorin? [Dorin v. Occidental Life Ins. Co., 132 Ill.App.2d 387, 270 N.E.2d 515 (1971)]

7. For seven years, Bertha Hecht did business with the brokerage firm of Harris, Upham and Company. Hecht gave Harris unfettered discretion to trade on the stock market with funds she supplied. Subsequently, she became dissatisfied with Harris, Upham and brought a suit to recover for losses resulting from bad investments it had made. Assuming the brokerage firm believed in good faith that the investments it had made were sound ones, can Hecht recover? [Hecht v. Harris, Upham and Co., 283 F.Supp. 417 (N.D. Cal. 1968)]

8. Diamantopoulos, known as "Barber Bill," was a barber of modest means in the city of Milwaukee. In 1961, he was in failing health and was frequently hospitalized. Because of his failing health, Barber Bill executed a power of attorney in favor of his godson,

Dakouras, that gave to Dakouras "full power and authority to do and perform all and every act and thing whatsoever required and necessary to be done as fully to all intents and purposes as I might or could do if personally present." At that time, Barber Bill had a bank account of $10,415. The bank book was delivered to Dakouras, and over the following ten-month period, Dakouras made four withdrawals, completely exhausting the account. None of this money was ever spent for Barber Bill's benefit. Has Dakouras breached any duty under agency law? [Alexopoulos v. Dakouras, 48 Wis.2d 32, 179 N.W.2d 836 (1970)]

9. Roger Simpson paid Larkin Travel Service $3,800 for a round trip airline ticket on Compagnie Nationale Air France. In addition to purchasing the ticket for Simpson, Larkin planned Simpson's itinerary for the trip and arranged for hotel accommodations and sight-seeing tours. Prior to the trip, Simpson became ill, informed Larkin that he wished to cancel his trip, and asked for a refund. Larkin responded that the travel agency had undergone voluntary bankruptcy and could not refund Simpson's money. Simpson then wished to recover from Air France; but first, he had to prove an agency relationship between Air France and Larkin Travel Service. Will Simpson be successful? [Simpson v. Compagnie Nationale Air France, 42 Ill.2d 496, 248 N.E. 2d 117 (1969)]

35

Agency and Employment
Liability of Principals and Agents

The first part of this chapter is concerned with the rights of third parties who contract with agents. Whether or not an agent's principal will be liable to the third party on a contract based on the agent's actions depends on a number of factors: (1) whether the agent had authority, (2) what kind of authority the agent had (that is, the source of the authority), and (3) how far that authority extended. If the agent lacked authority, it is necessary to determine whether the principal ratified the agent's acts. Once these issues are determined, the contractual duties of the principal and the agent can be established.

The second part of this chapter examines tort liability. Here the distinction between employer-employee, employer-independent contractor and principal-agent becomes important. Negligence liability usually arises in the employer-employee relationship based on the theory of *respondeat superior*. In the principal-agent relationship, the tort of misrepresentation is often the focus of lawsuits by third parties.

PRINCIPAL'S LIABILITY FOR CONTRACTS

A principal's liability based on a contract with a third party is rooted in the authority given to the agent to enter legally binding contracts on the principal's behalf. An agent's power to act comes from four sources: (1) actual authority, (2) apparent authority, (3) emergency, and (4) ratification.

Actual Authority

Actual authority is the power that the principal confers upon the agent to accomplish the purpose of the agency. The principal communicates actual authority directly to the agent, not to a third person. Actual authority can be *expressly* or *impliedly* conferred, but some manifestation from the principal must reach the agent and indicate that he or she is to act for the principal and is subject to the principal's command.

EXPRESS AUTHORITY   Express authority includes that which the principal has engaged the agent to do. It can be given orally or in writing. For example, giving an agent a power of attorney confers express authority.[1] The power of attorney is a written document and is usually notarized. Like all agency relationships, a power of attorney can be special—permitting the agent to do specified acts only—or it can be general—permitting the agent to transact all business dealings for the principal.

Equal dignity statutes in most states require that if the contract being executed is in writing, then the agent's authority must also be in writing.[2] Failure to comply with the equal dignity rule can make a contract voidable *at the option of the principal*. The law regards the contract at that point as a mere offer. If the principal decides to accept the offer, acceptance must be ratified in writing. For example, Palmer (the principal) asks Larkins (the agent) to sell a ranch that Palmer owns. Larkins finds a buyer and signs a sales contract on behalf of Palmer to sell the ranch. The buyer cannot enforce the contract unless Palmer subsequently ratifies Larkins' agency status *in writing*. Once ratified, either party can enforce rights under the contract.

The equal dignity rule does not apply when

an agent acts in the presence of a principal or when the agent's act of signing is merely perfunctory. For example, Lucas (the principal) negotiates a contract, but the day it is to be signed, Lucas is called out of town. Lucas authorizes Hilton to sign the contract. In that case, oral authorization is sufficient.

IMPLIED AUTHORITY   Implied authority is either conferred by custom or inferred by the principal's conduct if it leads the agent to believe that he or she possesses authority to act as an agent or authority reasonably necessary to carry out express authority. For example, Lester, a secretary (the agent), has purchased office supplies for years, and Henry (the principal) has always paid for them without any objection. Lester has implied authority to continue the purchases.

Mistakes can make agents out of the unwary. For example, Shaffer (the principal) goes to a stockbroker's office looking for Powell. Shaffer leaves a note on McPherson's desk, thinking it is Powell's desk. The note says, "I authorize you to sell my 100 shares of IBM stock at market price, signed Shaffer." Even though Shaffer intended the authorization for Powell, McPherson can act with valid authority to sell the stock.

Apparent Authority—Estoppel

Apparent authority is given when the principal tells *a third person* that a particular person is the principal's agent but does not tell the actual agent. If the third person reasonably believes and relies on the statements and deals with the purported agent, the principal will be bound to honor any contracts made by the agent. For example, Jones, a traveling salesman for ABC Company, has in his possession many samples of the company's goods. Any reasonable potential buyer will believe that ABC Company authorizes Jones to sell the goods. By allowing Jones to have the goods in his car, the company confers apparent authority on him. If the company tells Jones that some of the goods are defective and all should be returned, a potential

---

1.   An agent who holds the power of attorney is called an attorney-in-fact for the principal.
2.   An exception to the equal dignity rule exists in modern business practice. An executive officer of a corporation, when acting for the corporation in an ordinary business situation, is not required to obtain written authority from the corporation.

buyer will have no way of knowing that Jones's actual authority has been expressly limited. Here ABC Company is liable for any defective goods Jones sells after the company expressly limits his authority. The basis of ABC's liability is not Jones's actual authority; it is Jones's apparent authority.

In some cases, it is not reasonable for a third person to believe or rely on the statements made by an agent. In fact, apparent authority can never be created by statements of the agent alone. This is especially true when a contract contains language indicating that it must be approved by the home office. When such information is disclosed, as in the following case, the agent's own statements or assurances will not overcome the express restriction on the agent's authority.

MID-STATE HOMES, INC. v. BERRY

Court of Civil Appeals of Alabama, 1978.
359 So.2d 401.

BACKGROUND AND FACTS Berry signed a contract for the purchase of a show house from Mid-State Homes. The contract specifically stated that the purchase was "subject to the approval of Herb Clarkson, in Tampa." Nevertheless, on the assurance of an employee of Mid-State, Berry proceeded to make certain repairs and improvements on the house while awaiting approval of the sales contract. Subsequently, the sale was disapproved, and the house was destroyed by fire. Berry claimed damages for breach of contract for failure to complete the sale of the home after Mid-State's employee had assured Berry that the sale would go through.

DECISION AND RATIONALE Berry could not recover damages for breach of the sales contract since the contract was explicitly conditioned on the approval of a third party (Herb Clarkson), and the approval did not come through. Berry's claim that Mid-State was bound to complete the sale because of its agent's assurances was unfounded. "We have carefully examined the evidence and discern no authority, apparent or otherwise, shown to have been possessed by the sales representative to enter into such a contract as that claimed by the plaintiffs. The record is very clear that the representative expressly was without authority to execute a contract of sale of the property. That authority was expressly reserved to Herb Clarkson of the Tampa office by the written contract signed by the plaintiffs. * * * An agent cannot negative by his own representation the express restriction of his authority known to the third party."

FURTHER COMMENTS ON APPARENT AUTHORITY Sometimes a principal will go beyond merely making statements or performing actions that create the impression in a third party that a person is the agent for a particular purpose. If, for example, the principal has "clothed the agent" with both possession and apparent ownership of the principal's property, the agent will have very broad powers. The purported agent can deal with the property as if he or she were the true owner. For example, to deceive certain creditors, Baker (the principal) and Hunter (the agent) agree verbally that Hunter will hold certain stock certificates for Baker. Hunter's possession and apparent ownership of the stock certificates are such strong indications of ownership that a reasonable person would conclude that Hunter was the actual owner. If Hunter negotiates the stock certificates to a third person, Baker will be estopped from denying Hunter's authority to transfer the stock.

Where land is involved, courts have held that possession alone is not a sufficient indication of ownership. A reasonable person should realize that the possessor might be only a tenant or an adverse possessor. (See Chapter 52 for details.) However, if the agent also possesses the deed to the property and sells the property to an unsuspecting buyer, the principal cannot cancel the sale or assert a claim to title. Of course, the principal has a right to recover from the agent for violation of a fiduciary duty. The next case illustrates the operation of apparent authority to bind a principal.

WINEGARDNER v. BURNS
Supreme Court of Alabama, 1978. 361 So.2d 1054.

BACKGROUND AND FACTS *Winegardner, the owner of a vacant town house motel, hired Burns Patrol Service (Burns) to provide security for the building. Winegardner dealt solely with Burns's operations supervisor, Hancock. Hancock prepared the written agreement that Winegardner signed and later, Hancock orally agreed that, in addition to general security surveillance, Burns would periodically inspect the boiler room and pipes to see that proper pressure was maintained. Subsequently, the pipes froze and burst, and Winegardner sought to recover from Burns.*

DECISION AND RATIONALE *Winegardner could recover from Burns despite Burns's claim that Hancock did not have "actual" authority to bind Burns to any contract. Burns's liability was based upon Hancock's apparent authority to contract with third parties. Winegardner reasonably believed that Hancock had the authority to bind Burns since Hancock had been solely responsible for the contents of the original written agreement between Burns and Winegardner. Because Burns never objected to this written contract, and in fact proceeded to operate under it, Burns essentially held Hancock out as its authorized agent. The court concluded, "[i]f in fact Hancock did not have actual authority to contract for the Agency, then clearly under these circumstances he had apparent authority."*

Emergency Powers

An unforeseen emergency, where the agent is unable to communicate with the principal for some reason, gives rise to an agent's emergency power. The agent has the authority to do whatever is necessary to protect or preserve the property and rights of the principal.

For example, Fisher (the agent) is a brakeman on Pacific Railroad (the principal). While Fisher is acting within the scope of his employment, he falls under the train many miles from home and is severely injured. Davis, the conductor (also an agent), directs Thompson, a doctor, to give medical aid to Fisher. There is no express authority in Davis to bind Pacific Railroad for the services of Thompson. Yet, because of the emergency situation, the law recognizes this authority.

Ratification

In general, ratification is the affirmation of a previously unauthorized contract or act. Generally, only a principal can ratify. The principal must be aware of all material facts; otherwise, the ratification is not effective. Ratification binds the principal to the agent's acts and treats the acts or contracts as if they had been authorized by the principal *from the outset*. If the principal does not ratify, there is no contract, and the third party agreement with the agent is viewed merely as an unaccepted offer. The principal's acceptance (that is, the ratification) is binding only if the principal knows the terms of the contract accurately. If not, the principal can thereafter rescind ratification unless, of course, the third party has proceeded to change position in reliance on the contract.

For example, without authority, an agent contracts with a third person on behalf of a principal for repair work to the principal's office building. The principal learns of the contract from the agent and agrees to "some repair work," thinking that it will involve only patching and painting the exterior of the building. In fact, the contract includes resurfacing the parking lot, which the principal does not want done. Upon learning of the additional provision, the principal rescinds the contract. If the third party has made no preparations to do the work (such as purchasing materials, hiring additional workers, or renting equipment), then the principal can still rescind. But if the third party has, to his or her detriment, relied on the principal's ratification by making preparations, the principal must reimburse the third party for the cost of the preparations.

Two important points must be stressed. First, it is immaterial whether the principal's lack of knowledge results from the agent's fraud or is simply a mistake on the principal's part. If the third party has not changed position in reliance on the principal, the principal can repudiate the ratification. The unauthorized contract remains an offer, and the principal's acceptance is not valid because contract law provides that one cannot accept terms one does not know about. Second, the whole transaction must be ratified; a principal cannot affirm the desirable parts of a contract and reject the undesirable parts.

EXPRESS RATIFICATION If a principal's statements or conduct express an intent to be bound, the prior unauthorized act will be ratified, and the principal will become a party to the contract. For example, Smith (the agent) negotiates the sale of a shipment of oranges to World Markets without the authorization of Samuelson (the principal). Samuelson sees the completed paperwork and tells Smith to go ahead with it. Samuelson thus ratifies the sale and is now bound to the terms of the sales contract.

IMPLIED RATIFICATION Implied ratification occurs most commonly when a principal decides to accept the benefits of a previously unauthorized transaction. In the example above, if Samuelson accepts World Market's check in payment for the oranges, he ratifies the contract and is bound to its terms.

Ratification can be implied under certain circumstances. If Samuelson knows of the unauthorized acts and fails to repudiate or object to them within a reasonable time, the contract will be ratified.

A partnership is a special type of agency in which each partner is the agent of all the others. Therefore, the act of each partner (agent) is binding on all the others. In the following case, one of the partners in a Texas partnership executed a contract on behalf of the partnership for certain goods and services. Among the various provisions in the contract was an arbitration clause that required the partnership to go into arbitration over any contract dispute and not sue in a court of law. The partnership argued that the act of the individual partner who executed the contract on behalf of the partnership was unauthorized. Therefore, the binding arbitration agreement should not apply to them. However, since the partnership had already accepted and paid for the goods and services covered by the other provisions of the contract, the court held that the partnership could not affirm the desirable and reject the undesirable parts of the contract—that is, the arbitration provision.

BACKGROUND AND FACTS *Wydel Associates, a partnership, entered into a contract with Thermasol for the delivery, installation, and maintenance of twenty-eight steam bath units. The contract was executed by only one of Wydel's partners. Subsequently, Wydel sought to recover for Thermasol's alleged breach of contract and breach of warranty. Thermasol argued that Wydel had no right to be in a court of law because the contract contained a provision requiring disputes to proceed to arbitration before proceeding to court. Wydel argued that since the contract was not executed by all the partners, its arbitration clause was not binding upon the partnership because the executing partner exceeded his authority in executing that portion of the contract.*

DECISION AND RATIONALE *Wydel and Thermasol were bound by all the provisions of the contract, including the arbitration provision. In effect, Wydel's instituting a lawsuit on the contract ratified its partner's authority to enter into the contract. Therefore, Wydel had to assume the burdens as well as the benefits of the contract that the partner made. "A contract cannot be adopted in part and rejected in part because the act of ratification extends to the entire contract."*

WYDEL ASSOCIATES v. THERMASOL, LTD.
United States District Court, Western District of Texas, 1978. 452 F.Supp. 739.

AGENT'S LIABILITY FOR CONTRACTS

Normally, an agent is not party to a contract that he or she makes with a third party on behalf of a disclosed principal because the contract is between the third person and the principal. The agent is not liable for the nonperformance of either party. However, an agent who gives a personal promise to perform will normally be liable. Whether or not the agent is considered to have made a personal promise depends on the interpretation of the transaction that is based on writings in connection with it and its background, including the knowledge of the other party about the relationship between the agent and the principal. Thus, an agent becomes personally liable to third parties when he or she (1) enters into a contract on behalf of an undisclosed or partially disclosed principal, (2) acts without authority or exceeds the scope of authority granted by the principal, or (3) personally guarantees performance by the principal. Whenever the agent lacks authority or exceeds the scope of authority, the agent's liability is

based on the theory of breach of implied warranty of authority, not on breach of the contract itself.[3]

The agent's implied warranty of authority can be breached intentionally or by good faith mistake.[4] The agent's liability remains, *as long as a third party has relied on agency status.* Conversely, where the third party *knows* at the time of the contract that the agent is mistaken, or the agent indicates to the third party *uncertainty* about the extent of authority, the agent is not personally liable for breach of warranty.

Agent's Authorized Acts

An agent's acts are *authorized* if they are either within the scope of the agent's authority or subsequently ratified by the principal. However, the rules of liability differ on the basis of

---

3. The agent's liability is not on the contract because the agent was never personally intended as a party to the contract.
4. If the agent intentionally misrepresents his or her authority, then the agent can also be liable in tort for misrepresentation.

whether the principal's identity is disclosed or undisclosed to the third party.

UNDISCLOSED PRINCIPAL

UNDISCLOSED PRINCIPAL   When neither the fact of agency nor the identity of the principal is disclosed, a third party is deemed to be dealing with the agent personally, and the agent is liable as a party on the contract. For example, in a contract for the sale of a horse, a third party knows only that Scammon (the agent) wants to purchase the horse. The third party does not know that Scammon is actually negotiating for Johnson (the principal). Scammon signs a written contract in her own name, never indicating any agency relationship. She delivers the horse to Johnson, who is in fact the principal, but Johnson refuses to pay her. Scammon tries to return the horse to the third party, who refuses to take it. The third party is entitled to hold Scammon liable for payment. The agent's subjective intent is not relevant. The third party contracted with the agent on the basis of the *agent's* credit and reputation, not the undisclosed principal's. Therefore, the agent is liable.

However, in the example above, Scammon (the agent) has two possible means of recouping her losses. First, she can sue Johnson (the principal) for **indemnification.** There is an implied promise inherent in the agency relationship that the principal will perform any contract that the agent is authorized to enter on the principal's behalf.[5] Second, if Scammon can establish *actual* authority, once the principal's identity is revealed, the third party can hold either the principal or the agent liable on the contract.[6] Of course, the third party can obtain payment only once.

As a general rule, if a person is damaged by the negligence of an agent, that person can sue the agent and the principal in the same lawsuit or in separate lawsuits. A recovery or a judgment against one will not bar separate suit against the other. In the following case, the plaintiff chose to proceed against the agent and did not name the principal as a party to the lawsuit.

---

5. If A is a gratuitous agent, and P accepts the benefits of A's contract with a third party, then P will be liable to A on the theory of quasi-contract.

6.   The agent can never establish apparent authority because the principal has not previously been revealed and cannot, therefore, have informed the third party of an agency relationship.

ROSEN v. DEPORTER-BUTTERWORTH TOURS, INC.

Appellate Court of Illinois, 1978. 62 Ill.App.3d 762, 19 Ill. Dec. 743, 379 N.E.2d 407.

BACKGROUND AND FACTS   *Rosen purchased a package tour for an African safari from the Deporter-Butterworth Travel Bureau. Deporter-Butterworth failed to disclose that it was in fact a special agent for the tour's sponsor, World Trek. Rosen had direct contact with Deporter-Butterworth but not with World Trek. During the course of the trip, the itinerary had to be changed. Deporter-Butterworth failed to notify Rosen, leaving him stranded in Egypt for a week. Rosen sought to recover from both World Trek and Deporter-Butterworth for his inconvenience.*

DECISION AND RATIONALE   *The evidence was conclusive that Deporter-Butterworth acted negligently in not informing Rosen of the schedule change in the tour. The record also revealed that Deporter-Butterworth neglected to inform World Trek of Rosen's whereabouts so that World Trek could contact him. Deporter-Butterworth argued that only World Trek should be held liable since World Trek was the principal and Deporter-Butterworth acted only as its agent. Though generally the principal is held responsible for the acts of its agent, such liability will not apply where the agency relationship is undisclosed.*

*Therefore, Deporter-Butterworth, and not World Trek, was liable to
Rosen. The court concluded: "The legal principle that an agent is liable as
a principal [to] a third party in the case of an undisclosed agency
relationship is well established and needs no citation for authority. * * *
[I]f an agent does not disclose the existence of an agency relationship and
the identity of his principal, he binds himself to the third party with
whom he acts as if he, himself, were the principal."*

Negotiable Instruments The agency rule for
negotiable instruments is controlled by the
Uniform Commercial Code, not agency law.
The governing principles, however, are the
same. UCC Sec. 3-401 provides that only the
signer of negotiable paper can be held liable.
Extrinsic evidence to show an agency relationship is not admissible. Therefore, if an agent
signs an instrument using his or her own name
and not indicating any agency status, the agent
is personally liable. For examples of proper
signature form indicating agency, see UCC Sec.
3-403.

**The Third Party's Right to an Agent's Personal
Performance** In certain instances involving
undisclosed principals, the duties involved
cannot be delegated under contract law. The
third party can refuse to permit the principal's
performance and can hold the agent liable for
personal performance. Typical examples involve extensions of credit or highly personal
service contracts.

Partially Disclosed Principals

In some cases, an agent discloses his or her
agency status, but the principal goes unnamed.
When the principal is partially disclosed, the
principal and agent can both be parties to a
contract, or only one of them can be, depending
on the agreement of the parties. The burden of

proof is on the one who seeks to hold the agent
as a party to the contract. In the absence of
evidence otherwise, however, an agent for a
partially disclosed principal is inferred as a
party to a contract. In a contract where the agent
has written his or her name plus the word *agent*,
parol evidence can be introduced to show the
intent of the parties. Consider an example.
Casper, a manufacturer's representative, purchases supplies from a third party who knows
that Casper is an agent but who does not know
the identity of the manufacturer. Casper is a
party to the contract. In many situations, she can
be held personally liable to the third party. The
third party intended to contract with Casper on
the basis of her credit and reputation, not that of
the undisclosed, unknown principal.

The unknown principal, *once revealed*,
can obtain contract rights and be liable on the
contract, subject to the same exceptions noted
above for an undisclosed principal. Similarly, if
a third party actually knows the principal's
identity (perhaps through independent investigation), then even though the contract is made
with the agent, the principal can be held as a
party on the contract.

THE PRINCIPAL'S LIABILITY FOR TORTS OF AN AGENT

In general, a principal is liable for the tortious
acts committed by his or her agents while acting
within the scope of their authority. In general,
an agent is personally liable for wrongful acts
that injure or damage third parties whether or
not these acts are authorized by the principal
and whether or not the principal is liable. The
following sections take up several broad head-

---

7. If Short's powers were coupled with an interest, the third
party would not have a right to rescind. (See Chapter 33).
Short's powers coupled with an interest would be irrevocable, and his beneficial interest would be paramount over
Knight, since the benefit of the agency relationship would
really be for Short.

ings of tort liability, including misrepresentation and negligence.

Misrepresentation

A principal is exposed to tort liability whenever a third person sustains loss due to the agent's misrepresentation. The key to a principal's liability is whether or not the agent was actually or apparently authorized to make representations at all.

Assume Lewis is a demonstrator for Moore's products. Moore sends Lewis to a home show to demonstrate the products and answer questions from consumers. Moore has given Lewis authority to make statements about the products. If Lewis makes only true representations, all is fine; but if he makes false claims, Moore will be liable for any injuries or damages sustained by third parties in reliance on Lewis's false representations.

To hold a principal liable, the injured party must establish only that the agent had the principal's authority to make statements about the subject matter involved. In the case of written contracts, a principal can insert a disclaimer clause—for example, "Representations not contained in this written contract are not part of the agreement and have no effect." This avoids a principal's tort liability by limiting the agent's *actual authority* to make representations (other than those included in the written contract). However, a third party will retain basic contract remedies such as avoiding the contract if it is not performed or receiving money damages for losses sustained. (See Chapter 14 for details.)

An interesting series of cases have arisen on the theory that when a principal has placed an agent in a position to defraud a third party, the principal is liable for the agent's illegal acts. For example, Pratt is a loan officer at First Security Bank. In the ordinary course of the job, Pratt approves and services loans and has access to the credit records of all customers. Pratt falsely represents to a borrower, McMillan, that the bank feels insecure about McMillan's loan and intends to call it in unless McMillan provides additional collateral such as stocks and bonds. McMillan gives Pratt numerous stock certificates that Pratt keeps in his own possession, later using them to make personal investments. The bank is liable to McMillan for losses sustained on the stocks even though the bank had no direct role or knowledge of the fraudulent scheme.

The theory is that the agent's position conveys to third persons the impression that the agent has the authority to make statements and perform acts that are consistent with the ordinary duties that are within the scope of the position. When an agent appears to be acting within the scope of the authority that the position of agency confers but is actually taking advantage of a third party, the principal who placed the agent in that position is liable. In the example above, if a bank teller or security guard had told McMillan that the bank required additional security for a loan, McMillan would not be justified in relying on either person's authority to make that representation. However, McMillan could reasonably expect that the loan officer was telling the truth.

Negligence: Personal Injury

An employer (master) is liable for the physical harm caused by an employee (servant) who is acting within the scope of employment, because the employer has a legal right to control all the details of that physical performance. If a principal has the legal right to control the details of the physical performance of an agent, the principal becomes an employer (master). The principal-employer is liable for the physical harm of the agent-employee that occurs in the scope of the principal's authority and in furtherance of the principal's business.

THE DOCTRINE OF RESPONDEAT SUPERIOR The theory of liability based on *respondeat superior* is that it imposes vicarious liability on the principal (that is, liability without regard to the personal fault of the master for torts committed by a servant in the course of employment).[8]

At early common law, a servant (employee) was viewed as the master's (employer's) property. The master was deemed to have absolute control over the servant's acts and was held strictly liable for them no matter how carefully the master supervised the servant. The rationale for the doctrine of *respondeat superior* is based on the principle of social duty. Every person shall manage his or her own affairs, whether alone or through agents or servants, so as not to injure another. Liability is imposed on employers or principals because they are deemed to be in better financial positions to bear the loss. The superior financial position carries with it the duty to be responsible for damages. Normally, the loss is shifted to the public by a price increase or covered by liability insurance.

Today the doctrine continues, but employers carry liability insurance and spread the cost of risk over the entire business enterprise. Public policy requires that an injured person be afforded effective relief, and recovery from the business enterprise is far more effective than recovery from an individual employee. Since liability rights exist under law and public policy for the protection of third parties, a master (employer) cannot contract with a servant (employee) to disclaim responsibilities for injuries resulting from the servant's acts. Such disclaimer provisions will not normally be effective because they are against public policy.[9]

SUBSERVANTS If an agent is authorized to hire subservants (employees) for the employer, then the employer is liable for their acts. There

is a slight difference in result if the agent hires for an undisclosed employer. In such a case, the agent is responsible for the employee in contract law for such things as wages. However, the undisclosed employer is generally held to be liable for tort injuries. The doctrine of *respondeat superior* imposes liability on the *true* master.

An agent's unauthorized hiring of a subagent or employee generally will not create any legal relationship between the principal and the subagent. However, an agent can use emergency power to hire a subagent where it is impossible to contact the principal and the situation requires immediate action to preserve the principal's property or interest. Here again, the principal can be held liable for negligent actions of the subagent in carrying out the job.

BORROWED SERVANTS Employers can lend the services of their employees to other employers. Suppose employer 1 (general employer) leases ground moving equipment to employer 2 (special employer) and sends along an employee to operate the machinery. Who is liable for injuries caused by the employee's negligent actions at the job site? Liability turns on which employer had the right to control the employee at the time. In general, employer 1 (the general employer), who rents the equipment, is presumed to retain control of the employee. However, if the rental is for a long period of time, control may be deemed to pass to employer 2. Naturally, if employer 2 specifically directs the employee in the performance of specific acts, then employer 2 assumes liability for the employee. However, the division of control over the employee may be such that the employers are jointly liable.

INDEPENDENT CONTRACTORS The doctrine of *respondeat superior* is limited to master-servant (employer-employee) and principal-agent relationships. Thus, the general rule concerning liability for the acts of an independent contractor is that the employer is

---

8. The doctrine of *respondeat superior* applies not only to master-servant relationships but also to principal-agent relationships as long as there is the right of control by the principal over the agent. The theory of *respondeat superior* is similar to the theory of strict liability covered in Chapter 21.
9. This doctrine of *respondeat superior* may not apply if the principal or employer has sovereign or charitable organization immunity.

not liable for physical harm caused to a third person by the negligent act of an independent contractor in the performance of the contract. An employer who has no legal right to control the details of the physical performance of a contract cannot be held liable. Here again the test is the *right to control*. Since an employer bargains with an independent contractor only for results and retains no control over the manner in which those results are achieved, the employer is generally not expected to bear the responsibility of torts committed by an independent contractor. A collection agency is a typical example of an independent contractor relationship. The creditor is generally not liable for the acts of the collection agency because collection is a distinct business occupation.

Scope of Employment

Once the master-servant (employer-employee) relationship is established, the tortious act must have been committed within the course and scope of employment in order for the employer to be held liable under the theory of *respondeat superior*.[10]

"FROLIC" BY AN EMPLOYEE The act causing injury must have occurred as part of the employee's regular duties in employment. For example, Sutton (the agent) is a delivery driver for Schwartz (the principal). Schwartz provides Sutton with a vehicle and instructs him to use it for making company deliveries. Nevertheless, one day Sutton drives his own car instead of the company vehicle and negligently injures Walker. Even though Sutton's act (driving the car) was unauthorized, the negligence occurred as part of Sutton's regular duties of employment (making deliveries). Hence, Schwartz is still liable to Walker for the injuries caused by Sutton, even though Sutton used his own car contrary to Schwartz's instructions. Only if Sutton's acts exceed the scope of employment duties in a way that the employer would not reasonably expect to happen will Schwartz be relieved of liability.

An employee going to and from work or to and from meals is usually considered outside the scope of employment. All travel time of a traveling salesperson, however, is normally considered within the scope of employment for the duration of the business trip, including the return trip home.

When an employee goes on a frolic of his or her own—that is, departs from the employer's business to take care of personal affairs—is the employer liable? It depends. If the employee's activity is a substantial departure akin to an utter abandonment of the employer's business, then the employer is not liable.

For example, Susan is on an errand for Mary. Susan's house is a few blocks away. On the way back from the errand, Susan decides to drive home for a minute (that is, she takes a detour). On the way home, she negligently injures David. Susan's activity is probably not a substantial departure from Mary's business activity. Thus, Mary will be liable.

Assume, however, that Mary schedules Susan for a delivery route from Washington to New York City. The trip is expected to take two days. Susan departs; but instead of heading north, she decides to drive south to North Carolina to check out some property she wishes to buy there. Susan's plan is to call Mary with a false report of mechanical difficulties two days later to cover her extended absence. On the highway to North Carolina, Susan negligently collides with another vehicle, injuring James. Mary will probably not be liable for Susan's acts since Susan had substantially abandoned Mary's business purpose to pursue her own personal business.

---

10. The Restatement, Second, Agency, Section 229 indicates the general factors that courts will consider in determining whether or not a particular act occurred within the course and scope of employment. They are (1) whether the act was authorized by the master; (2) the time, place, and purpose of the act; (3) whether the act was one commonly performed by employees on behalf of their employers; (4) the extent to which the employer's interest was advanced by the act; (5) the extent to which the private interests of the employee were involved; (6) whether the employer furnished the means or instrumentality (for example, a truck or a machine) by which the injury was inflicted; (7) whether the employer had reason to know that the employee would do the act in question and whether the employee had ever done it before; and (8) whether the act involved the commission of a serious crime.

The Restatement, Second, Agency, Section 235 gives two illustrations of the concept of an agent's frolic:

While delivering gasoline for a principal, an agent lights a pipe and negligently throws the blazing match into a pool of gasoline that has dripped on the ground during the delivery process. The gasoline ignites, and the principal is subject to liability for the resulting harm.

While chauffeuring a principal, an agent negligently throws a lighted cigarette from the window of the car into a passing load of hay. The agent does not intend to ignite the hay, but is careless about where the cigarette falls. The principal is not liable for this act.

The difference in result between these two situations is that, in the former case, the negligence of the employee relates directly to the manner of conducting the business of delivering goods for which the employee was hired. On the other hand, the negligence of the chauffeur is unrelated to the management or control of the car the chauffeur is driving.

Fellow-Servant Injuries

A key exception to *respondeat superior* is the fellow-servant rule: an employer is not liable for injuries inflicted by one employee upon another while both are engaged in the same general enterprise.

Traditionally, employees were expected to assume the risk of injury by fellow employees, and an employee was deemed as capable as an employer of self-protection from such danger on the job. So except in cases where the employer was negligent in hiring irresponsible personnel or where a supervisor injured a worker, the employer was held blameless.

Today, broad coverage is provided for on-the-job injuries for industrial workers under workmen's compensation statutes. These statutes broadly define the scope of employment and provide fixed compensation to insured workers who are injured in industrial accidents. Workmen's compensation statutes create an absolute liability on the part of the employer at the sacrifice of all common law defenses. The employer can benefit because the employee cannot recover common law damages. Thus, workmen's compensation statutes eliminate contributory or comparative negligence and the fellow-servant rule, reducing the common law defenses based on risk taking.

Workmen's compensation, however, leaves large numbers of people in the labor force unprotected. For example, domestic workers, laborers, and independent contractors are not protected. Some industrial companies have very few employees who are covered. Finally, workmen's compensation will not cover injuries caused by willful misconduct of either the employer or a fellow employee. In these cases, the fellow-servant rule is still significant.

EMPLOYER'S LIABILITY FOR EMPLOYEE'S INTENTIONAL TORTS

Under *respondeat superior*, the employer is liable for intentional torts of the employee within the scope of employment, just as the employer is liable for negligence. For example, an employer is liable for an employee's assault and battery or an employee's false imprisonment within the scope of employment. Also, an employer is liable for permitting an employee to engage in reckless acts that can injure others. For example, an employer observes an employee smoking while filling containerized trucks with highly flammable liquids. Failure to stop the employee will cause the employer to be liable for any injuries that result.

An innocent employee acting at the employer's direction can nonetheless be liable as a tortfeasor along with the employer for committing the tortious act. For example, an employer directs an employee to burn out a field of crops. The employee does so, assuming that the field belongs to the employer, although the latter never said so. Both can be found liable to the owner of the field for damages.

EMPLOYER HAS A DUTY OF CARE IN HIRING EMPLOYEES An employer who knows or should know that an employee has a propensity for committing tortious acts is liable for the employee's acts even if they would not ordinarily be considered within the scope of employment. For example, the Blue Moon employs Joe

Green as a bouncer, knowing that he has a history of assault and battery. While he is working one night within the scope of his employment, he viciously attacks a patron who "looks at him funny." The Blue Moon will bear the responsibility for Green's acts because it knew that he had a propensity toward committing tortious acts.

NOTICE OF DANGEROUS CONDITIONS The employer is charged with knowledge of all facts discovered by an employee and pertinent to the employment situation. To illustrate, a maintenance employee in M's apartment notices a lead pipe protruding from the ground. The employee neglects either to fix it or to inform the employer of the danger. X falls on the pipe and is injured. The employer is charged with knowledge of the dangerous condition regardless of whether or not the employee actually informed the employer. That knowledge is imputed to the employer by virtue of the agency relationship.

QUESTIONS AND CASE PROBLEMS

1. Under the Fair Housing Act, racial discrimination in housing practices (including the renting of apartments) is prohibited. Leach owned two apartment complexes in Columbus, Mississippi, and employed Jenkins as office manager of the apartments. For the entire time that she managed the apartments, Jenkins did not rent to any blacks, even though blacks make up about 37 percent of the local population. The United States Attorney General brought suit against Leach for violations of the Fair Housing Act. Leach contended that Jenkins did all the renting and made all the decisions as to whom she rented the apartments. Will the government win its case against Leach? [United States v. Real Estate Development Corp., 347 F.Supp. 776 (N.D. Miss. 1972)]

2. Rausch hired Jones as a special agent and gave him the authority to negotiate a surety agreement on Rausch's behalf. Rausch's hiring of Jones was with the explicit understanding that Jones would not have to draw up the agreement unless Rausch qualified for a second mortgage from Citizens State Bank. If he did qualify, Jones was to draw up an agreement under which certain shares of stock owned by Rausch would be pledged to Citizens Bank. Jones thereafter negotiated an agreement with Citizens Bank that purported to make Citizens a pledgee of Rausch's stock. Rausch failed to qualify for the second mortgage, but Citizens Bank claimed that it was a pledgee of Rausch's stock under the agreement negotiated by Rausch's agent, Jones. Did Jones have the authority to make Citizens Bank a pledgee of Rausch's stock?

[Citizens State Bank v. Rausch, 9 Ill.App.3d 1004, 292 N.E.2d 678 (1973)]

3. Hohenberg Brothers was a Memphis-based cotton merchandiser, and Killebrew was a Mississippi cotton farmer. Both parties were represented by D. T. Syle, Jr., a cotton agent. In February 1973, Killebrew signed and delivered to Syle a one-page purchase and sales agreement form covering the sale of Killebrew's 1973 cotton crop. All of the blanks in this document were completed, except for the name and signature of the purchaser, who was still unknown. On March 2, Syle secured an oral commitment that Hohenberg would purchase Killebrew's crop at the prices set forth in the one-page contract. Hohenberg immediately sent Syle its standard three-page purchase and sales agreement, the terms of which were identical to Syle's one-page document. Syle signed Killebrew's name and returned it to Hohenberg. Has Syle acted beyond the scope of his agency in signing Killebrew's name? [Hohenberg Brothers Co. v. Killebrew, 505 F.2d 643 (5th Cir. 1974)]

4. U-Vend Corporation was engaged in the business of leasing and servicing vending machines. Mel Williams was the manager of a local Radio Shack store, a retailer of electrical goods. On November 12, U-Vend delivered at Williams's request a hot drink machine and a soda dispensing machine to the Radio Shack that Williams managed. Williams signed a receipt for them as manager. Monthly lease payments were made by check to U-Vend, and the checks were signed either by Williams or by other Radio Shack employees. Williams's authority as manager of the local store was limited. He could not make purchases of stock or of any other items used in the store. He could not write checks for Radio Shack, and he did not have a Radio Shack checkbook in his possession. No payments on the lease were ever made by Radio

Shack, and it knew nothing of the lease until Mel Williams left his position about seven months after he signed the contract with U-Vend. U-Vend wished to enforce the five-year lease agreement that Williams had signed. What authority, if any, can U-Vend argue that Williams had to bind Radio Shack? [Fairfield Lease Corp. v. Radio Shack Corp., 5 Conn. Cir. 460, 256 A.2d 690 (1968)]

5.   Lederer, a homeowner in the Chicago suburbs, hired Novera to care for the grounds around his home. One day Lederer mentioned to Novera that one of the maple trees in the backyard was in need of care and asked Novera to recommend someone for the job and to have that person talk to Lederer's wife. Three weeks later, Lederer and his wife left for vacation, and Novera brought in Wing's Tree Experts, which did extensive work pruning, clipping, and cutting down dead trees in Lederer's yard. When Lederer returned from vacation, he was presented with a bill by Wing. Must Lederer pay the bill? [Wing v. Lederer, 77 Ill.App.2d 413, 222 N.E.2d 535 (1966)]

6.   Roland "Cookie" Gomez began doing business as Cookie's Auto Sales in 1954 and continued operating as a sole proprietorship until May 29, 1963, at which time Cookie's Auto Sales became Cookie's Auto Sales, Inc. John Prevost did business with Cookie Gomez in a number of different capacities from the mid 1950s through the early 1970s. Prevost began working for University Volkswagen Inc. in January 1968, and in July of the same year, Gomez began sending automobiles from his place of business to University Volkswagen for body work. Prevost handled Volkswagen accounts. Because of his long-time friendship with Gomez, Prevost made arrangements so that Gomez would not have to pay for work done by University Volkswagen until thirty days after the work was performed. Several years later, Gomez defaulted on his payments to University Volkswagen. The company wished to hold Gomez personally liable for the money that Gomez owed it. Gomez pointed out that since his business was incorporated, he could not be held personally liable because he was acting as an agent for "Cookie's Auto Sales, Inc." Gomez also argued that Prevost should have realized that Cookie's Auto Sales was incorporated because all Gomez's ads were in the name of "Cookie's Auto Sales, Inc." Should Gomez be held personally liable? [Prevost v. Gomez, 251 So.2d 470 (La. App. 1971)]

7.   McQuade Travel Agency, Inc., agreed to sell two tickets for a European cruise aboard "HMS Riviera" to Harry and Viola Domeck. The Domecks paid McQuade Travel directly, and McQuade in turn sent the money, less the travel agent's 10 percent commission, to Caribbean Cruise Lines, Inc., which owned HMS Riviera and which employed McQuade Travel as its agent. Later the Domecks learned that their cruise was permanently cancelled because Caribbean Cruise Lines was in bankruptcy. The Domecks demanded their money back from McQuade, but McQuade defended on the ground that it was only an agent of Caribbean Cruise Lines and that the Domecks had to recover from it. McQuade also argued that the Domecks should have known that it was acting only as an agent of Caribbean Cruise Lines, even though it did not disclose the exact name of the principal, because it disclosed the name of Caribbean's ship. McQuade also argued that, in any event, it must have been obvious to the Domecks that McQuade could not afford to own a ship. Will the Domecks recover from McQuade Travel Agency? [E.A. McQuade Travel Agency, Inc. v. Domeck, 190 So.2d.3 (Fla. App. 1966)]

8.   Dinkler Management Corporation engaged the Stein Printing Company, a partnership, to print menus for a Bahamian hotel company. Dinkler failed to disclose the name of the Bahamian company, but the name did appear on the menus. When Stein sought payment for the printing work done through Dinkler, Dinkler insisted that the Bahamian hotel owed the money. Can Stein recover from Dinkler? Can Stein recover from the Bahamian hotel? Can it recover from both? [Dinkler Management Corp. v. Stein, 115 Ga.App. 586, 155 S.E.2d. 442 (1967)]

9.   For many years, Abell Company, publisher of the Sun newspaper in Baltimore City, ran advertisements for Warner and Company, a long-established and well-known haberdashery located in Baltimore City. Each February, two contracts were entered into; they provided that morning, evening, and Sunday editions would advertise the clothing store's merchandise. Skeen, Warner's advertising manager, was responsible for procuring the advertisements, and he always signed the contracts with his name followed by the words "Warner & Co." When Warner and Company went bankrupt, Abell argued that Skeen was personally responsible for the advertising debt owed by the company. Abell contended that the use of the name "Warner & Co." was not sufficient to indicate the corporate status of Warner, and thus Skeen should be held personally liable. Will Skeen be liable? [Abell Co. v. Skeen, 265 Md. 53, 288 A.2d 596 (1972)]

10.   Moore was employed by the federal government as an electronics engineer and was assigned to Edwards Air Force Base. He was ordered to travel

from his base to another army base for certain electronics testings, and he was authorized to travel by commercial carrier or by his privately owned automobile. Travel by private automobile was "authorized between Edwards Air Force Base, California and El Centro, California, and return, only" and was to be reimbursed at the rate of $.10 per mile. While on his return trip, Moore negligently drove off the road and hit a pedestrian. Assuming that the accident occurred while Moore was utilizing the most direct route from El Centro to Edwards Air Force Base, can the injured party hold the federal government liable? What if Moore had deviated about a mile from the most direct route in order to visit a friend who lived just a short distance from Edwards Air Force Base? What if Moore had deviated more than ten miles? [United States v. Romitti, 363 F.2d 662 (9th Cir. 1966)]

UNIT VII

Business Organizations

36

Forms of Business Organization

There are basically three types of business organizations—sole proprietorships, partnerships, and corporations. Additionally, there are two types of partnerships—limited partnerships and unlimited, or general, partnerships—and various classifications of corporations, such as closely-held corporations and Subchapter S corporations. There are also joint stock companies, business trusts, joint ventures, and syndicates or investment groups. This chapter will first describe the form of these business organizations. Then it will compare a partnership with a corporation in more detail, for a person starting out in business most often chooses between these two forms when deciding how a business should be organized.

SOLE PROPRIETORSHIP

The simplest form of business is a sole proprietorship. The owner is the business. This form is used by anyone who does business without creating an organization. One usually associates a sole proprietorship with small enterprises, although this is not necessarily the case. The owner's personal estate is liable for his or her business debts.

PARTNERSHIP

A partnership arises from an agreement—express or implied—between two or more persons to carry on a business for profit. Partners are co-owners of the business and have joint control over its operation and the right to share in its profits. Partnership agreements are not always formal, although it is often desirable that they be formal. The Uniform Partnership Act (UPA), now adopted by most states, sets out the rules of operation of a partnership in the absence of any formal agreement and also includes areas not covered by formal agreements. Partnerships are typically not separate legal entities in most states, and therefore the personal property of partners is subject to partnership obligations. Chapter 37 treats in detail the creation and termination of partnerships. Chapter 39 treats the duties of the partners.

Limited Partnerships

The most widely used form of a partnership is the limited partnership, which is comprised of at least one general partner and one or more limited partners. The law treats the general partner exactly the same as a partner in any ordinary partnership, but the limited partner is treated as an investor only. The limited partner contributes capital, but not management or control. Thus, a limited partner's personal property is not liable for partnership obligations beyond the capital invested. Limited partnerships are discussed in Chapter 39.

BUSINESS CORPORATIONS

The most important form of business organization is the corporation. A corporation comes into existence by an act of the state, and therefore it is a legal entity. It typically has perpetual existence. One of the key features of a corporation is that the liability of its owners is limited to their investments. Their personal property is usually not subject to the obligations of the corporation.

Corporations consist of shareholders, who are the owners of the business. A board of directors, elected by the shareholders, manages the business. The board of directors normally employs officers to oversee day-to-day operations.

OTHER FORMS OF BUSINESS ORGANIZATION

There are a number of other, less common forms of business organization. They include joint ventures, syndicates or investment groups, joint stock companies, and business trusts.

Joint Ventures

When two or more persons combine their interest in a particular business enterprise and agree to share in losses or profits jointly or in proportion to their contribution, they are engaged in a joint venture. The joint venture (also referred to as *joint adventure*), a less formal association than the partnership, is created in contemplation of a limited activity or a single transaction.

A joint venture is normally not a legal entity and therefore cannot be sued as such, but its members can be sued individually. Usually joint ventures are taxed like partnerships.

Joint Stock Company

A joint stock company or association resembles a corporation but is normally treated like a partnership. Ownership is evidenced by shares of transferable stock. Each shareholder is liable for the joint stock company's obligations as if he or she were a partner in a partnership. A modern example is the American Express Company, which was a joint stock association until 1965.

THE ADVANTAGES AND DISADVANTAGES OF A SOLE PROPRIETORSHIP

Advantages

One advantage of a sole proprietorship is that the proprietor receives all the profits because he or she takes all the risk. In addition, the problem of reaching agreement among a number of directors and managers is avoided. The sole proprietor is also free from corporate income taxes, paying only personal income taxes on profits. Depending upon the propietorship's income, taxes could be higher or lower than those paid by a corporation.

Disadvantages

As sole owner, the proprietor bears the entire risk of loss. In addition, the proprietor's opportunity to raise capital is limited to personal funds and the funds of those who are willing to make loans. Additionally, and perhaps more importantly for many potential entrepreneurs, the sole proprietor has unlimited liability (legal responsibility) for all obligations incurred in doing business.

EXHIBIT 36-1 COMPARING A PARTNERSHIP WITH A CORPORATION

CHARACTERISTIC	PARTNERSHIP	CORPORATION
1. Method Of Creation	Created by agreement of the parties.	Charter issued by state—created by statutory authorization.
2. Legal Position	Not a separate legal entity in many states.	Always a legal entity separate and distinct from its owners—a legal fiction for the purposes of owning property and being party to litigation.
3. Liability	Unlimited liability (except for limited partners in a limited partnership).	Limited liability of shareholders—shareholders are not liable for the debts of the corporation.
4. Duration	Terminated by agreement of the partners, by the death of one or more of the partners, by withdrawal of a partner, or by bankruptcy.	Can have perpetual existence.
5. Transferability Of Interest	Although partnership interest can be assigned, assignee does not have full rights of a partner.	Shares of stock can be transferred.
6. Management	Each general partner has a direct and equal voice in management unless expressly agreed otherwise in the partnership agreement. (Limited partner has no rights in management in a limited partnership.)	Shareholders elect directors who set policy and appoint officers.
7. Taxation	Each partner pays pro rata share of income taxes on net profits, whether or not they are distributed.	Double taxation—corporation pays income tax on net profits, with no deduction for dividends, and shareholders pay income tax on disbursed dividends they receive.
8. Organizational Fees, Annual License Fees, And Annual Reports	None.	All required.
9. Transaction Of Business In Other States	Generally no limitation.[a]	Normally must qualify to do business and obtain certificate of authority.

[a]A few states have enacted statutes requiring that foreign partnerships qualify to do businesss there—for example, 3 N.H. Rev. Stat. Ann. Chapter 305-A in New Hampshire.

COMPARING A PARTNERSHIP WITH A CORPORATION

Exhibit 36-1 is an abbreviated comparison between a partnership and a corporation, giving the essential advantages and disadvantages of each.

Other Points of Comparison

LIABILITY OF OWNERS The form of organization—whether a sole proprietorship, partnership, or corporation—does not always determine the issue of owners' liability. For example, banks may be unwilling to lend money to small

---

EXHIBIT 36-2 PARTNERSHIP VERSUS CORPORATION—TAX CONSIDERATIONS

TAX ASPECT	PARTNERSHIP	CORPORATION
1. Federal Income Tax	Partner is taxed on proportionate share of partnership income, even if not distributed; the partnership files information returns only.	Income of the corporation is taxed; stockholders are also taxed on distributed dividends. Must file corporate income tax forms.
2. Accumulation	Partners taxed on accumulated as well as distributed earnings.	Corporate stockholders not taxed on accumulated earnings. There is, however, a penalty tax, in some instances, that the corporation must pay for accumulations of income.
3. Capital Gains And Losses	All partners taxed on their proportionate share of capital gains and losses.	Corporation taxed on capital gains and losses. There is no special deduction to reduce taxes for any excess of long-term gains over short-term losses, but there is a special rate.
4. Exempt Interest	Partners are not taxed on exempt interest received from the firm.	Any exempt interest distributed by a corporation is fully taxable income to the stockholders. Exempt interest can come, for example, from municipal bonds.
5. Pension Plan	Partners are not eligible for an exempt pension trust. The firm cannot deduct payments for partners except under what is called a Keogh Plan.	Employees and officers who are also stockholders can be beneficiaries of a pension trust. The corporation can deduct its payments to the trust.
6. Social Security	Partners do not pay social security tax, but often must pay a self-employment tax.	All compensation to officers and employee stockholders subject to social security taxation up to the maximum.
7. Death Benefits (excluding those provided by insurance)	There is no exemption for payments to partners' beneficiaries.	Benefits up to $5,000 can be received tax-free by stockholders' and employees' beneficiaries.
8. State Taxes	In many states, the partnership is not subject to state income taxes.	The corporation is subject to state income taxes (although these taxes can be deducted on federal returns).

corporations with few shareholders, unless the owners agree to be personally liable for the loan. John Janks and several of his brothers own a small dry cleaning store. They have formed a corporation, and they now wish to start two more stores in a neighboring city. The local bank may require that each of them sign a note and be personally liable for the increased debt (often as a guarantor). The corporate form of business does not prevent them from having personal liability in such a case because they have assumed the liability voluntarily.

NEED FOR CAPITAL   One of the most common reasons for changing from a sole proprietorship or partnership to a corporation is the need for additional capital to finance expansion. A sole proprietor can seek partners. They will bring capital with them, and in some instances the partnership will be able to secure more funds than the sole proprietor could. But when a firm wants to expand greatly, simply increasing the number of partners can lead to too many partners for the firm to operate efficiently. Therefore, the corporation is the most logical choice for an expanding business organization. There are almost limitless possibilities for obtaining more capital by issuing shares of stock. The original owners find that their share of the company is reduced, but they are able to expand at a much more rapid rate by selling shares in the company.

TAX CONSIDERATIONS   Different tax treatments that accompany the various forms of doing business are considered by some the most important factor in determining the optimal business form. The various tax considerations that must be taken into account when comparing a partnership with a corporation are listed in Exhibit 36-2.

QUESTIONS AND CASE PROBLEMS

1.   Suppose A, B, and C are college graduates, and A has come up with an idea for a new product that she believes could make the three of them very rich. Her idea is to manufacture beer dispensers for home use, and her goal is to market them to consumers throughout the Midwest. A's personal experience qualifies her to be both first line supervisor and general manager of the new firm. B is a born salesperson. C has little interest in sales or management but would like to invest a large sum of money that she has inherited from her aunt. What should A, B, and C consider in deciding which form of business organization to operate under?

2.   The limited liability aspect of the corporation is one of the most important reasons that firms choose to organize as corporations rather than as partnerships or sole proprietorships. Limited liability means that if a corporation is not able to meet its obligations with corporate assets, creditors will not be allowed to look to the owners (stockholders) of the corporation to satisfy their claims. Assume that A and B (from problem 1) do not have a wealthy friend like C who wishes to go into business with them and that there-

fore they must borrow money to start their business. A and B decide to incorporate. What do you think a lender will ask them when they seek a loan? What effect does this have on the "advantage" of limited liability under incorporation?

3.   Assume A and B have incorporated and have successfully operated their beer dispenser manufacturing firm for nine months. They employ twenty-five persons. One of the employees severs a finger while working with a metal bending machine, and a jury awards him $300,000. Total assets of the corporation are $275,000. If the employee sues the corporation, who will pay the difference?

4.   Assume that A and B have been in business for several years and are very successful. Seeing how successful they are, C now wishes to join the firm. A and B agree to sell C a one-third interest in the firm so that all three have an equal say in management. B and C both agree that manufacturing beer dispensers is not enough and that the firm should expand its operations to include manufacturing and distributing bar accessories. A vehemently disagrees, arguing that the market is already flooded with such items and that most companies that manufacture them are only marginally profitable. B and C outvote A with their two-thirds share and expand the business. How could this have been avoided if the business had been incorporated? Could it have been avoided if the firm had operated as a partnership? Explain.

37

Partnerships
Creation and Termination

To a great extent, partnership law derives from agency law. Each partner is considered an agent of every other partner. Thus, the agency concepts of imputing knowledge and responsibility for acts done within the scope of the partnership relationship will apply.

Partnership law is distinct from agency law in an important way. A partnership is based upon a voluntary contract between two or more competent persons who agree to place some or all of their money, effects, labor, and skill in business with the understanding that there will be a proportional sharing of the profits and losses between them. An agent can be compensated from business profits but does not agree to bear the ordinary business losses and has no ownership interest in the business.

The *Uniform Partnership Act (UPA)*, which has been adopted in most states, replaces the body of common law principles dealing with partnerships.[1]

In the past, attempts to formulate a concrete definition of the term *partnership* caused endless controversy among judges, lawyers, and members of the business community. **Partnership** is defined by the UPA as "an association of two or more persons to carry on as co-owners a business for profit."[2] Therefore, two essential elements of a partnership are (1) a common ownership interest in a business, and (2) sharing of the profits and losses of the business.

---

1. The UPA was first passed in 1914 by Pennsylvania. To date, Louisiana, Georgia, and Mississippi have not adopted it.
2. UPA Sec. 6(1).

CHARACTERISTICS OF A PARTNERSHIP

A partnership is sometimes called a *firm*, a term that connotes an entity separate and apart from its aggregate members. Sometimes the law of partnership recognizes the independent entity, but for certain other purposes, the law treats it as an aggregate of individual partners. At common law, a partnership is never treated as a separate legal entity. Thus, a common law suit can never be brought by or against the firm in its own name; each individual partner has to sue or be sued. The UPA, on the other hand, recognizes a partnership as an entity (apart from its individual members) for limited purposes, including the capacity to sue or be sued, to collect judgments against the partnership in its own name, to proceed in federal bankruptcy courts, and to convey property.

Partnership as an Entity

LEGAL CAPACITY States vary on how a partnership is viewed as a party in a legal suit. Some permit a partnership to sue and be sued in the firm name; others allow a partnership to be sued as an entity but not to sue others in its firm name (that is, the partnership must use the names of the individual partners). Federal courts recognize the partnership as an entity that can sue or be sued when a federal constitutional question is involved. Otherwise, federal courts follow the practice adopted by the state in which the federal court is located.

JUDGMENTS Partnership liability is first paid out of partnership assets when a judgment is rendered *against the firm name*. In a general partnership, the personal assets of the individual members are subject to liability if the partnership's assets are inadequate. Even in limited partnerships, at least one of the partners—called a general partner—subjects his or her personal assets to liability for the partnership's obligations. Good legal practice dictates that where state law permits a firm to be sued,

the partners should be joined as parties to the suit. This insures that a wide range of assets will be available for paying the judgment.

The general rule is that a judgment creditor of a partnership can execute the judgment against either partnership or individual property. [UPA Sec. 15] In some states, the judgment creditor must, however, exhaust the remedies against partnership property before proceeding to execute against the individual property of the partners.[3]

BANKRUPTCY In federal court, an adjudication of bankruptcy *in the firm name* applies only to the partnership entity. It does not constitute personal bankruptcy for the partners. Similarly, the personal bankruptcy of an individual partner does not bring the partnership entity or its assets into bankruptcy.

CONVEYANCE OF PROPERTY The title to real or personal property can be held in the firm name. This means that the partnership as an entity can own property apart from that owned by its individual members. As such, the property can be conveyed (transferred) without having each individual partner join in the transaction.

Under common law, title to real estate could not be held in a partnership's firm name. Each partner was regarded as a co-owner (known in legal terminology as a *tenant in partnership*). Each partner had to join in all conveyancing. Although the modern rule of partnership property ownership disregards the need for aggregate action in conveyancing, there are some practical difficulties to consider. Most states do not require public records to keep lists of members of a partnership, although other states have statutes that require the filing of a certificate of copartnership. Hence, in determining the validity of a conveyance in a partnership name, it may be impossible to tell whether the person executing the deed is ac-

---

3. Under the doctrine of marshaling assets, this is the ranking, or arrangement, of assets in due order of administration. Marshaling of assets allows the proper application of the assets to various claims.

tually a partner and has authority to convey. Some states have passed laws requiring firms to file a statement of partnership. This list names members of the firm authorized to execute conveyances on behalf of the firm.

Aggregate Theory of Partnership

When the partnership is not regarded as a separate legal entity, it is treated as an *aggregate* of the individual partners. For example, for federal income tax purposes, a partnership is *not* a tax-paying entity. The income or losses incurred by it are "passed through" the partnership framework and attributed to the partners on their individual tax returns. The partnership as an entity has no tax identity or liability. It merely files an informational return with the IRS, indicating the profit and loss that each partner will report on his or her individual tax return.

FORMATION OF A PARTNERSHIP

A partnership is ordinarily formed by an explicit agreement among the parties. The law also recognizes another form of partnership —*partnership by estoppel.* This form arises when persons who are not partners represent themselves as partners when dealing with third parties. The liability of partners by estoppel is covered later in the chapter.

This section will describe the requirements for the creation of a true partnership, including references to the liability of "alleged partners." The next section will deal with the process by which partnerships are terminated.

A partnership is a voluntary association of individuals. As such, a *true partnership* is generally based on agreement among the parties that reflects their intention to create a partnership, contribute capital, share profits, and participate in management. The partnership relationship involves a high degree of trust and reliance.

Parties cannot avoid partnership liability, even by *expressly* designating themselves as some other business form, if the evidence establishes the essential elements of a partnership. In the following case, a physician purchased an interest in a medical center along with numerous other doctors. The amount of money each doctor received for practicing at the center was based upon the billing for the services that each performed. The bills were collected in the name of the center. From the total billing, a percentage was deducted to cover expenses and profit sharing. The center's method of allocating expenses to the doctors bore no direct relationship to their actual expenses.

BACKGROUND AND FACTS   *After working at the Overland Medical Center for a short time, Dr. Stuart, a dermatologist, was approached by Dr. Yanow about purchasing a portion of the center. An unwritten arrangement was entered into whereby Dr. Stuart would purchase a 4 percent interest in the center over a five-year period. Also, each doctor was to bill his or her patients through the center and to pay the center 10 percent of the amount received as a collection fee. Further, the doctors were to share the expenses of the center (for such things as lab tests) as a ratio of each individual doctor's earnings divided by the earnings of the center as a whole. Subsequently, Dr. Stuart left the center and terminated the agreement. When he claimed that a portion of the profits from the center were due him, the other doctors refused to pay. Dr. Stuart brought suit.*

STUART v. OVERLAND MEDICAL CENTER
Missouri Court of Appeals, 1978. 510 S.W.2d 494.

DECISION AND RATIONALE   *Dr. Stuart was able to recover the portion of profits received by the center up to the time he left, less any expenses he owed. Dr. Stuart was a partner with the other doctors in the center. As such, he was entitled to his share of the center's profits and was liable for his share of its expenses. In the opinion of the court: "The contract creating the partnership need not be written, but may be expressed orally or implied from the acts and conduct of the parties. The primary consideration in determining the existence of a partnership is whether the parties intended to carry on as co-owners a business for profit. *** Under these facts and circumstances, combined with the defendant's failure to prove that no partnership relation was intended *** the professional arrangement between the plaintiff and defendants was a partnership."*

Formalities

As a general rule, agreements to form a partnership can be oral, written, or implied by contract. Some partnership agreements, however, must be in writing to be legally enforceable within the Statute of Frauds. (See Chapter 11.) For example, a partnership agreement that, by its terms, is to continue for more than one year or one that authorizes the partners to deal in real property transfers must be evidenced by a sufficient writing.

Practically speaking, it is far better to set out the provisions of any partnership agreement in writing. It is much harder to prove exactly what the terms of an oral agreement are because a court must evaluate oral testimony given by persons with an interest in the eventual decision. In addition, the drafting of a written agreement enables the partners to anticipate problems that they might not otherwise foresee if the agreement is made orally. For instance, Tomkins and Fredericks plan to enter into a partnership agreement to sell tires. Among the provisions to be included is that Tomkins is to provide two-thirds of the capital to start up the business and is to receive two-thirds of the profit in return. The agreement is made orally. Tomkins now sues because Fredericks claims that one-half the profits should be his. Without a writing, Tomkins may have a hard time overcoming the presumption that he is entitled to only one-half the profits of a two-person partnership.[4] A partnership agreement, called *articles of partnership*, usually specifies each partner's share of the profits and is binding regardless of how uneven the distribution appears to be.

Duration of Partnership

The partnership agreement can specify the duration of the partnership in terms of a specific date or with respect to the completion of a particular project. This is called a *partnership for term*. A dissolution without the consent of all the partners prior to the expiration of the partnership term constitutes a breach of the agreement, and the responsible partner can be liable for any losses resulting from it.

If no fixed duration is specified, the partnership is a *partnership at will*. This type of partnership can be dissolved any time by any partner without violating the agreement or incurring liability for resulting losses to other partners.

Capacity

Any person having the capacity to enter a contract can become a partner. A partnership contract entered into with a minor as a partner is

---

4. The law assumes that members of a partnership share profits and losses equally unless a partnership agreement provides otherwise.

voidable and can be disaffirmed by the minor. (See Chapter 8.)

Lack of legal capacity due to insanity at the time of the agreement likewise allows the purported partner either to avoid the agreement or to enforce it. If a partner becomes insane and is adjudicated mentally incompetent during the course of the partnership, the partnership is not automatically dissolved.

The Corporation as Partner

Traditionally, there has been some disagreement as to whether a corporation can become a partner. A corporation is a legal entity authorized to engage in activities set out in its articles of incorporation and its bylaws, subject to general corporation statutes. One view is that a corporation cannot be a partner unless the corporation's articles of incorporation specifically empower it to enter into a partnership as a partner. The opposite view, which appears to prevail today, is contained in the Model Business Corporate Act. Basically, the capacity of corporations to contract is a question of corporation law. Many states have restrictions on corporations becoming partners, though such restrictions have become less common over the years. Many decisions in jurisdictions that do not permit corporate partners nevertheless validate the arrangements by characterizing them as joint ventures rather than partnerships.

Mutual Consent

A partnership is a voluntary association of co-owners. It cannot be forced upon anyone. The *intent* to associate is a key element of a partnership, and one cannot join a partnership unless *all* other partners consent.

Indications of Partnership

Parties commonly find themselves in conflict over whether their business enterprise is a legal partnership, especially in the absence of a formal written contract. To answer this question, the courts have developed broad guidelines for interpreting partnership status. The strongest indication of a partnership relationship is the presence of profit sharing. However, its existence is not the sole reason for the business relationship and should not be confused with profit sharing in the form of bonus or employee wages, rents, annuity payments, interest, or consideration for the sale of goodwill in a business.

Other indications that a partnership relationship is intended are more persuasive. They include contributing capital to the enterprise, joint ownership of property, and sharing of gross income. None of these factors alone is conclusive in proving that a partnership relationship exists. In the following case, a widow attempted to persuade the court that she and her late husband were business partners.

BACKGROUND AND FACTS   *In 1959, Philip and Isabelle Miller were married, and Isabelle gave up her low-paying job to move south with her new husband and help run a nursery business. Isabelle did not make any capital contributions to the business. However, she held a mangement position, did some physical labor, kept the firm's books and hired and fired employees.*

After her husband died, Isabelle attempted to prove for tax reasons that the business had been a partnership. In addition to describing the work she did, Isabelle testified that her husband had told her that she was "the best partner he ever had." Other evidence, however, included tax forms and schedules that listed the business as a sole proprietorship and Isabelle's occupation as a housewife. A Michigan business activities form also indicated a sole proprietorship. Furthermore, in an application for a

MILLER v. CITY BANK & TRUST CO., N.A.
Court of Appeals of Michigan, 1978.
82 Mich.App. 120, 266 N.W.2d 687.

self-employment and pension and profit-sharing plan, Philip Miller had stated that his business was a sole proprietorship.

DECISION AND RATIONALE *Mr. and Mrs. Miller were not partners in the nursery business. Rather, their business relationship was more one of employer-employee. The burden of proving a partnership is on the one alleging its existence, in this case, Isabelle Miller. Mutual control is one element of a partnership, and Isabelle's power to hire and fire employees, as well as her responsibility for the firm's books, demonstrated this control. However, the intention of the parties to enter into a partnership is the controlling issue. The evidence indicated that Philip had not intended to form a legal partnership with his wife. As the court summarized the evidence: "First, there is no written agreement and there is only plaintiff's testimony in support of an oral one. The income tax returns and schedules listed the business as a sole proprietorship, listing Mr. Miller's income as wages and Mrs. Miller's occupation as a housewife. *** All the capital contributions came from Mr. Miller and the property remained in his name (or his and his wife's name), and none was transferred to the partnership. *** After reviewing the entire record *** [we find] that [Isabelle] failed to carry her burden of proof."*

Partnership by Estoppel

Parties who are not partners but hold themselves out as partners and make representations that third persons rely on in dealing with them are estopped from denying that a partnership exists. The law of partnership imposes liability on the alleged partner or partners, but it does not confer any partnership rights on these persons.

There are two aspects of liability. The person representing to be a partner in an actual or alleged partnership is liable to any third person who extends credit in good faith reliance on such representations. Similarly, a person who expressly or impliedly consents to such misrepresentation of an alleged partnership relationship is also liable to third persons who extend credit in good faith reliance.

For example, Moore owns a small shop. Knowing that the Midland Bank will not make a loan on his credit alone, Moore represents that Lewis, a financially secure businesswoman, is a partner in Moore's business. Lewis knows of Moore's misrepresentation but fails to correct the bank's information. Midland Bank, relying on the strength of Lewis's reputation and credit, extends a loan to Moore. Moore will be liable to the bank for the loan repayment. Furthermore, in many states, Lewis would also be held liable to the bank in such a loan transaction. Lewis will normally be estopped from denying that Moore is her partner and will be regarded as if she were in fact a partner in Moore's business to the extent that this loan is concerned since she knowingly acquiesced in Moore's misrepresentation.

When a real partnership exists, and a partner represents that a nonpartner is a member of the firm, the nonpartner is regarded as an agent whose acts are binding on the partner. Middle Earth Movers has three partners—Johnson, Mathews, and Huntington. Mathews represents to the business community that Thompson is a partner. If Thompson negotiates a contract in Middle Earth Movers' name, the contract will be binding on Mathews, but normally not on Johnson and Huntington (unless, of course, Johnson and Huntington knew and consented to Mathews's representation).

PARTNERSHIP PROPERTY RIGHTS

For financial and credit reasons it is frequently necessary to distinguish between property belonging to the firm and property belonging to each individual partner, particularly in bankruptcy proceedings. A partnership can own any real or personal property, unless the partnership agreement contains some prohibition or limitation on what it can acquire. Holding property in the firm name can be merely a convenience, so *title alone is not conclusive* in establishing that a particular asset belongs to the partnership.

Factors Indicating Partnership Property

UPA Sec. 8(1) provides that "all property originally brought into the partnership's stock or subsequently acquired, by purchase or otherwise, *on account of the partnership,* is partnership property." (Emphasis added.) Indications that the asset was acquired with the intention that it be a partnership asset is the heart of the phrase *on account of the partnership.* Thus, the more closely an asset is associated with the business operations of the partnership, the more likely it is to be a partnership asset. Moreover, when such an asset is purchased with partnership funds, it will belong to the partnership unless a contrary intention is shown.

PROPERTY RIGHTS OF PARTNERS

A partner has three property rights delineated in UPA Sec. 24: a right to specific partnership property, a right to an interest in the partnership, and a right to participation in the management of the partnership.

Rights to Specific Partnership Property

Each partner holds partnership property as a *tenant in partnership* with all the other partners. Tenancy of ownership has several important effects. If a partner dies, the surviving partners have the right of survivorship. Because of principles of property law discussed in Chapter 52, the right of survivorship prevents the partnership's property from passing into the estate of the decedent. Surviving partners are entitled to possession, but they have a duty to account to the decedent's estate for the *value* of the deceased partner's interest in the partnership.

Rights to an Interest in the Partnership

A partner's interest in the partnership is his or her share of the profits and surplus. It is viewed under the UPA as personal property.[5] A partner can assign the right to receive profits and capital to an assignee. This action neither dissolves the partnership nor creates any management rights in the assignee. After assignment, the partner (assignor) remains personally liable on all partnership debts and remains a partner.

Creditor Rights against a Partnership

A partner's personal debts are not the debts of the partnership. A creditor cannot attach or execute against true partnership assets to satisfy a partner's personal debts. Depending on state laws, a creditor can obtain a judgment against the partner and afterwards be granted a "charging order" against the partner's interest in the partnership. When this occurs, the creditor holds a lien against the partnership and is entitled to any future distribution of profits and assets ordinarily belonging to the debtor/partner until the judgment is satisfied. A firm's creditor, on the other hand, has rights to partnership property.

---

5. For inheritance purposes, the distinction between personal and real property can be significant. This is especially important because even if the firm's assets are real property, the value of the interest paid to the estate is received and treated as personal property.

LIMITED PARTNERSHIPS

The limited partnership is a creature of statute. Most states have adopted some form of the Uniform Limited Partnership Act (ULPA), which codifies the law of limited partnerships. Limited partnerships are used most frequently in the context of commercial investment. A person willing to purchase the financial interest in a business might not want any management responsibility or personal liability for partnership debts. The limited partnership form meets this need, since only one general partner (who has unlimited liability) is necessary. In this case, the *general partner* assumes management responsibility of the partnership and takes full personal liability for all its debts. A *limited partner* contributes cash (or other property) and owns an interest in the firm but undertakes no management responsibilities and is not personally liable for partnership debts beyond the amount of his or her investment. This topic is treated in detail in Chapter 38.

TERMINATION

Introduction

Any change in the relations of the partners that demonstrates unwillingness or inability to carry on partnership business terminates the partnership. If any of the partners wish to continue the business, they are free to reorganize into a *new* partnership.

The termination of a partnership has two stages—dissolution and winding up. Both must take place before termination is complete.

Dissolution occurs when any partner (or partners) indicates an intention to disassociate from the partnership. *Winding up* is the actual process of collecting and distributing the partnership's assets.

Dissolution is the principal remedy of a partner against copartners. Events causing the dissolution can be grouped into three basic categories: (1) acts by partners, (2) operation of law, and (3) court decree. Dissolution terminates the right of a partnership to exist as a going concern, but the partnership continues to exist

long enough to wind up its affairs. When winding up is complete, the partnership's *legal* existence is terminated.

Dissolution by Acts of the Partners

BY AGREEMENT A partnership can be dissolved if certain events stipulated in the partnership agreement occur. For example, when a partnership agreement expresses a fixed term or a particular business objective to be accomplished, the passing of the date or the accomplishment of the project dissolves the partnership. However, partners do not have to abide by the stipulations in the agreement. They can mutually agree to dissolve the partnership early or to extend it. If they agree to continue in the partnership, they become *partners at will,* with all the rights and duties remaining as originally agreed.

PARTNER'S POWER TO WITHDRAW A partnership is a personal legal relationship among co-owners. No person can be compelled either to be a partner or to remain one. Implicit in a partnership is each partner's *power* to disassociate from the partnership at any time. A and C form a partnership with no definite term or particular undertaking specified—that is, a partnership at will. Both A and C have the power and the right to withdraw from the partnership. The partnership continues for three years, until one day C announces that she no longer wishes to continue in the partnership. Assuming that C's sudden withdrawal will not do irreparable damage to the firm, her act is sufficient to begin the process of dissolution.

It is expected that a partner will attempt to dissolve in good faith. Bad faith is evidenced, for example, when a partner's election of dissolution is prompted by hopes of personal gain from a business opportunity that ordinarily would go to the partnership. In such a case, the partner will still have the *power* to withdraw and dissolve the partnership but will not have the *right* and therefore may be liable for resulting losses.

ADMISSION OF NEW PARTNERS Any change in the composition of the partnership, whether by withdrawal of a partner or by *admission of a new partner*, results in dissolution. In practice, this result is usually modified by providing that the remaining or new partners continue in the firm's business. Nonetheless, a new partnership arises. The new partnership carries over the debts of the dissolved partnership. Creditors of the prior partnership become creditors of the one that is continuing the business. [UPA Sec. 41]

TRANSFER OF A PARTNER'S INTEREST The UPA provides that voluntary transfer [6] or involuntary sale of a partner's interest for the benefit of creditors does not alone operate to dissolve the partnership. [UPA Sec. 28] However, either occurrence can ultimately lead to judicial dissolution of the partnership, as discussed below.

Dissolution by Operation of Law

DEATH A partnership is dissolved upon the death of any partner, even if the partnership agreement provides for carrying on the business with the executor of the decedent's estate. Any change in the composition among partners results in a new partnership. (But there is always

---

6. UPA Sec. 27. A single partner cannot transfer his or her interest to another person and *make* that person a partner in the firm.

the possibility of a reformation of the partnership upon the death of a partner.)

BANKRUPTCY Because a partner's credit reputation is an intrinsic part of his or her contribution to a partnership, the bankruptcy of a partner will dissolve a partnership in most cases. Insolvency alone will not result in dissolution. Naturally, bankruptcy of the firm itself will result in dissolution.

ILLEGALITY Any event that makes it unlawful for the partnership to continue its business or for any partner to carry on in the partnership will result in dissolution. Even if the illegality of the partnership business is a cause for dissolution, the partners can decide to change the nature of their business and continue in the partnership. For example, A and B enter a partnership agreement to run a tuna fishing business. Subsequently a maritime law prohibiting tuna fishing by private concerns is passed. A and B do not necessarily have to dissolve their partnership. They can choose to remain partners and fish for something that is not prohibited.

When the illegality applies to an individual partner, then dissolution *must* occur. For example, the state legislature passes a law making it illegal for magistrate judges to engage in the practice of law. Once an attorney in a law firm is appointed a magistrate, the partnership must be dissolved. The next case deals with dissolution of a partnership due to illegality.

BACKGROUND AND FACTS *Williams and Burrus entered into a partnership agreement whereby they jointly owned and operated a restaurant and cocktail lounge. Part of the agreement provided for the purchase and operation of the restaurant under Burrus's name only, without revealing Williams's interest in the business. At the time, both parties knew that Williams would be unacceptable to the Washington State Liquor Control Board as a licensee. Williams later sued to dissolve the partnership and to receive an accounting (that is, his share of the business.)*

WILLIAMS v. BURRUS
Court of Appeals of Washington, Division 1, 1978. 20 Wash. App. 494, 581 P.2d 164.

DECISION AND RATIONALE *The partnership contract between Williams and Burrus was illegal. Therefore, the courts would hear neither a* *suit to enforce it nor one to dissolve it. In the words of the court: "Courts will not assist in the dissolution of an illegal partnership or entertain an action for an accounting or distribution of its assets. *** Under the general rule that the courts will not aid either party to an illegal agreement where a partnership is formed to carry out an illegal business or to conduct a lawful business in an illegal manner, the courts will refuse to aid any of the parties thereto in an action against the other."*

Dissolution by Judicial Decree

Dissolution of a partnership can result from judicial decree. UPA Sec. 32 provides the following situations in which a court can dissolve a firm.

INSANITY A partnership can obtain judicial declaration of dissolution where a partner is adjudicated insane or is shown to be of unsound mind. This action often involves a series of complex tests and standards.

INCAPACITY When it appears that a partner has become incapable of performing his or her duties under the partnership agreement, a decree of dissolution may be obtained. It must appear that the incapacity is permanent and will substantially affect the partner's ability to discharge his or her duties to the firm.

BUSINESS IMPRACTICALITY When it becomes obvious that the firm's business can be operated only at a loss, judicial dissolution may be ordered.

IMPROPER CONDUCT A partner's impropriety involving partnership business (for example, fraud perpetrated upon the other partners) or improper behavior reflecting unfavorably upon the firm (for example, habitual drunkenness) will provide grounds for a judicial decree of dissolution.

Dissolution may also be granted when personal dissension between partners becomes so persistent and harmful as to undermine the confidence and cooperation necessary to carry on the firm's business. (In general, courts are reluctant to allow partners to sue each other except for dissolution.) This type of dissension is illustrated by the next case.

FIRST WESTERN MORTGAGE CO. v. HOTEL GEARHART, INC.
Supreme Court of Oregon, 1971.
260 Or. 196, 488 P.2d 450.

BACKGROUND AND FACTS *First Western Mortgage Company and Hotel Gearhart, Inc., agreed to purchase a certain parcel of land. Hotel Gearhart was to operate a motel and restaurant already located on part of the property, and condominiums were to be built on another part. Shortly after the condominiums were completed, dissension began: First Western charged Hotel Gearhart with comingling partnership funds with its own funds and with failure to pay taxes. Hotel Gearhart charged First Western with failure to provide a full accounting of the first condominium project and with charging improper expenses, including excessive interest, against the income from the first project. First Western sued to dissolve the business venture.*

DECISION AND RATIONALE *Even though the parties were engaged in a joint venture, partnership law applied, and under partnership principles, First Western was entitled to a decree of dissolution. The* *agreement between the parties specified no duration—it was to last until the condominiums were completed and sold. Since no duration was established, either party to the agreement could terminate it, with reasonable notice to the other, at any time. Also, one of the parties could bring a suit for dissolution by judicial decree. In the conclusion of the court: "In such event, a court of equity may decree a dissolution because of any circumstances which render such dissolution just and equitable or where the interests of the partners will be best served by a dissolution. While a court of equity will not decree dissolution because of trifling disputes among the partners, dissolution will be granted where the dissensions are so serious and persistent as to make continuance impracticable, or where all confidence and cooperation between the parties have been destroyed. *** The evidence definitely establishes that serious disharmony exists between the parties. This fact is not disputed, and both parties want a termination of their joint venture."*

Notice of Dissolution

Dissolution ends the partnership as a going concern. Thereafter, it remains viable only for the purpose of winding up its affairs. In some circumstances, however, a partnership or a withdrawing partner can become bound to a contract made after dissolution has begun but before winding up is complete.

NOTICE TO PARTNERS The intent to dissolve or withdraw from a firm must be communicated *clearly*. All partners will share liability for the acts of any partner who continues conducting business for the firm without knowing the partnership has been dissolved. For example, A, B, and C have a partnership. A tells B of her intent to withdraw. Before C learns of A's intentions, C enters a contract with a third party. The contract is equally binding on A, B, and C. Unless the other partners have notice, the withdrawing partner will continue to be bound as a partner to all contracts created for the firm.

NOTICE TO THIRD PARTIES Dissolution of a partnership by the act of a partner requires notice to all affected third persons. The manner of giving notice depends upon the third person's relationship to the firm. Any third person who has dealt with the firm must receive *actual*

notice. For all others, a newspaper posting or similar public notice is sufficient.

Dissolution resulting from operation of law requires *no notice* to third parties. However, surviving partners can be bound by communications sent to a deceased partner from a client who did not know of the partner's death.[7]

Winding Up

Once dissolution occurs and partners have been notified, they cannot create new obligations on behalf of the partnership. Their only authority is to complete transactions begun but not finished at the time of dissolution and to wind up the business of the partnership. Winding up includes collecting and preserving partnership assets, discharging liabilities (paying debts), and accounting to each partner for the value of his or her interest in the partnership.

Where dissolution is caused by a partner's act that violates the partnership agreement, the innocent partners may have rights to damages resulting from the dissolution. Also, the innocent partners have the right to buy out the offending partner and continue the business instead of winding up the partnership.

Dissolution resulting from the death of a partner vests all partnership assets in the sur-

_____

7. Childers v. United States, 442 F.2d 1299 (5th Cir. 1971).

viving partners. The surviving partners act as a fiduciary in settling partnership affairs as quickly as practicable and in accounting to the estate of the deceased partner for the value of the decedent's interest in the partnership. The surviving partners are entitled to payment for their services in winding up the partnership as well as to reimbursement for any costs incurred in the process. [UPA Sec. 18(f)]

Distribution of Assets

Both creditors of the partnership and creditors of the individual partners can make claims on the partnership's assets. In general, creditors of the partnership have priority over creditors of individual partners in the distribution of partnership assets; the converse priority is usually followed in the distribution of individual partner assets.

The distribution of partners' assets is made after third party debts are paid. The priorities are as follows:

1.   Refund of advances made to or for the firm by a partner.
2.   Return of capital contribution to a partnership.
3.   Distribution of the balance, if any, to partners in accordance with their respective interest in the partnership.

QUESTIONS AND CASE PROBLEMS

1.   In April 1970, Harber, Pittman, and Calvert entered into an oral agreement to build and sell 235 houses. Following their agreement, Harber withdrew $6,000 in partnership funds and purchased three lots on which houses were to be built. The lots were purchased in his name, and after the homes were constructed, title was also in his name. When Harber sells the houses (at a profit) can he retain the proceeds for himself? [Davis v. Pioneer Bank and Trust Co., 272 So.2d 430 (La.App. 1973)]
2.   Prior to 1964, Dr. Cook was engaged in the practice of pathology in the city of Lake Charles. He owned a laboratory and worked at several local hospitals. Dr. Stevens, who had been practicing only a short time, moved to Lake Charles and entered into an agreement with Dr. Cook. The agreement provided that the two were to operate as partners. Dr. Cook agreed to furnish the use of his laboratory and equipment, which would remain in his own name; and each doctor agreed to devote his full working time to the partnership. Also, both agreed to perform, as nearly as feasible, 50 percent of the work of the partnership. Neither doctor transferred ownership of any money or property, including medical equipment, to the partnership. The agreement also provided that all partnership assets would belong to Dr. Cook upon termination of the partnership. Is there a partnership? [Stevens v. Cook and Stevens, 245 So.2d 798 (La.App. 1971)]

3.   Altman entered into an agreement with Young Lumber Company whereby Altman was to act as superintendent for a particular job that Young Lumber wished to contract as a subcontractor. The agreement also provided that Altman would estimate the job for Young Lumber and that he would receive 50 percent of the profits as his pay. There was no understanding, however, as to the sharing of losses. In addition, once work commenced, all necessary contracts were signed and all bills were paid in the name of Young Lumber. Is there a partnership between Altman and Young Lumber? [United States v. Young Lumber Co., 376 F.Supp. 1290 (D.C.S.C. 1974)]
4.   Everett H. Johnson was a home builder. He had operated under the trade name of "Everett H. Johnson & Son" since 1952, when his son, Everett R., was in his early teens. Not long after Everett R. returned from the Korean War, he became an employee of his father. Less than a year later, Everett H. Johnson entered into a contract with Mr. and Mrs. Bragg. Most of the discussions about contract negotiations were held in the presence of both Johnson and his son. In addition, the contract was typed on stationery bearing the name "Everett H. Johnson & Son." When Johnson and his son talked to the Braggs, it became apparent to the Braggs that Everett R. was a neophyte in the business and was just learning the trade. At no time did the father state to the Braggs that his son was a partner. As a result of a subsequent dispute, the Braggs asserted that they believed that Johnson and his son were partners and that their final decision to enter into the contract was based upon their belief that the son was a partner. Would a court infer a

partnership by estoppel under these circumstances? [Bragg v. Johnson, 229 A.2d 497 (Del.Super.Ct. 1966)]

5. In April 1964, Campbell and Miller agreed to go into the meat packing and processing business as a partnership. Campbell, who had experience in the meat packing business, promised Miller, who had experience in the construction business, that if Miller would plan and construct a meat packing building and draw a salary during the building's construction of only $75 per week, upon completion of the building the two would operate the business as a partnership, sharing profits and losses on a 50/50 basis. The building was to be built with both parties' funds, and upon its completion, Miller was to retain ownership and lease the building to the partnership. Just prior to the completion of the building, Campbell backed out of the partnership. Can Miller recover from Campbell for breach of partnership agreement? [Campbell v. Miller, 274 N.C. 143, 161 S.E.2d 546 (1968)]

6. In 1969, Simon, Genia, and Ury Rapoport entered into an agreement with Morton, Gerome, and Burton Parnes to form the partnership known as 55 Perry Company. Each of the families owned 50 percent of the partnership interests. In December 1974, Simon and Genia Rapoport assigned a 10 percent interest of their share in the partnership to their adult children, Daniel and Kalia. An amended partnership certificate was filed in the county clerk's office, as required by law, indicating the addition of Daniel and Kalia as partners. However, when the Rapoports requested the Parneses to execute an amended partnership agreement reflecting this change in the partnership, the Parneses refused. In a court action by the Rapoports to force the Parnes to execute the amended partnership agreement, what will be the result? What interest in the partnership, if any, can Daniel and Kalia Rapoport take without the Parneses' consent? [Rapoport v. 55 Perry Co., 50 A.D.2d 54, 376 N.Y.S.2d 147 (1975)]

7. Lynne, Ernest, and Stanley Timmermann established a partnership in 1965 for the purpose of engaging in farming activities. In January 1969, Lynne stated to the other two partners that he no longer wished to be involved in the partnership. It was not until August 31, 1970, however, that Lynne ceased to participate in the farming activities of the partnership. In January 1972, Lynne attempted to bring about a forced liquidation of the partnership through a lawsuit. In January 1969, the value of the partnership was approximately $50,000. On August 31, 1970, the value of the partnership was slightly less than $10,000; and in January 1972, the value of the partnership was in excess of $300,000. Assuming Lynne had a one-third interest in the partnership, approximately how much should he receive when he withdraws? Explain your answer. [Timmermann v. Timmermann, 272 Or. 613, 538 P.2d 1254 (1975)]

8. On September 28, 1958, Reid and three others entered into a written partnership agreement for the purpose of leasing for profit certain real property located in Montgomery County, Pennsylvania. Reid was to manage the property, and the others were to perform the physical labor necessary to maintain the premises in good condition. One year later, Reid notified the others that she was dissolving the partnership and requested that the partnership assets be liquidated as soon as possible. Has dissolution occurred? Assuming dissolution has occurred, can the other partners recover damages for breach of partnership agreement on the ground that the partnership was a partnership for a particular undertaking and hence not terminable at will? [Girard Bank v. Haley, 460 Pa. 237, 332 A.2d 443 (1975)]

9. A partnership, known as Mac Coal Company, was formed by Thomas Eddy and Carlo Teodori in 1964. Shortly thereafter, the partnership purchased a coal mine from North Star Coal Company, one-fourth of which was paid for with partnership funds and three-fourths of which was paid for with a mortgaged bank loan. One year later, Teodori withdrew from the partnership. Mortgage payments are due over the next nine years. Can Eddy, the remaining partner, continue paying the mortgage in the name of Mac Coal Company? [North Star Coal Co. v. Eddy, 442 Pa. 583, 277 A.2d 154 (1971)]

10. Respass and Sharp were partners who owned and managed a racing stable. In addition, they were engaged in bookmaking. At the time Sharp died, $4,724, representing the undistributed profits of the bookmaking business, was on deposit in Sharp's personal bank account. Respass, arguing that Sharp's death resulted in dissolution of the partnership, sought to recover one-half of the profits from the bookmaking business. What result? [Central Trust and Safe Co. v. Respass, 112 Ky. 606, 66 S.W. 421 (1902)]

38

Partnerships
Operation and Duties

The rights and duties of partners are governed largely by the specific terms of their partnership agreement. In the absence of provisions to the contrary in the partnership agreement, the law imposes the rights and duties discussed in this chapter. The character and nature of the partnership business generally influence the application of these rights and duties.

RIGHTS AMONG PARTNERS

Management

"All partners have equal rights in the management and conduct of partnership business." [UPA Sec. 18(c)] Management rights belong to all partners in an ordinary partnership.[1] Each partner has one vote in management matters *regardless of the proportional size of his or her interest in the firm*. Often, partners will agree to delegate daily management responsibilities to a management committee made up of one or more partners.

---

1. Compare the management rights of general and limited partners in limited partnerships. The absence of management responsibility and the concomitant liability limitations are distinguishing characteristics of such partnerships. See the discussion on limited partnership in Chapter 39.

The majority rule controls decisions in ordinary matters connected with partnership business. However, unanimous consent of the partners is required to bind the firm in any of the following actions:

1. To alter the essential nature of the firm's business as expressed in the partnership agreement or to alter the capital structure of the partnership. [UPA Sec. 18(h)]
2. To admit new partners or enter a wholly new business.
3. To assign partnership property into a trust for the benefit of creditors.
4. To dispose of the partnership's goodwill.
5. To confess judgment against the partnership or submit partnership claims to arbitration.
6. To undertake any act that would make further conduct of partnership business impossible. [UPA Sec. 9(3)]

Each of these matters significantly affects the nature of the partnership.

INTEREST IN THE PARTNERSHIP Each partner is entitled to the proportion of business profits and losses that is designated in the partnership agreement. If the agreement does not apportion profits and losses, the partners share in them equally. For example, Browning and Lewis form a partnership. Browning contributes 60 percent of the capital and Lewis 40 percent. Unless their agreement reflects a 60-40 distribution, they will each obtain a 50 percent interest in the firm and share equally in both profits and losses. This point is raised in the following case.

BACKGROUND AND FACTS *Waagen and Gerde ran a commercial fishing business. When they first began their business, they jointly purchased a fishing vessel. The two partners operated the vessel alternately every six months, fishing mainly for tuna and salmon. During Gerde's six-month turn, he conceived an idea to fish for soupfin shark and bought some secondhand nets and began experimenting with them. Gerde wrote Waagen about his idea. Waagen received the letter (as well as a second letter), and, although he never expressly agreed to the purchase of the nets, he never objected. After overcoming some initial difficulty with torn nets, and after expending several thousand dollars (none of which were contributed by Waagen), Gerde earned over $23,000 from shark fishing. Later, when the partnership was dissolved, Gerde refused to share the profits from shark fishing with Waagen, claiming that the shark fishing was a separate venture from the commercial fishing business in which the two were partners.*

WAAGEN v. GERDE
Supreme Court of Washington, 1950.
36 Wash. 2d 563, 219 P. 2d 595.

DECISION AND RATIONALE *Waagen was entitled to share the profits from Gerde's shark fishing enterprise even though the success of the venture was almost solely due to Gerde's efforts. Gerde admitted that the two were partners for all other enterprises involving the fishing vessel that they had purchased. This admission was inconsistent with Gerde's claim that the partnership did not exist during the months when Gerde was shark fishing. "The general rule is clear that one partner is not entitled to extra compensation from the partnership, in the absence of an express or an implied agreement therefor. *** While [Gerde's] ingenuity and industry were largely responsible for the success of the Princess in shark fishing, we cannot find anything in the record from which an* *agreement to pay him special compensation could be implied. [Gerde] did inform [Waagen] that he was busy getting the nets ready and that it would be 'lots of work to fix' them, but never at any time did he inform [Waagen] what the work actually entailed or that he expected any compensation for it. Since [Waagen] had so little knowledge of the conduct of the net operations, there could not be any implied agreement for compensation."*

Compensation

A partner's time, skill, and energy on behalf of partnership business is a duty and generally not a compensable service. Partners can, of course, agree otherwise. For example, the managing partner of a law firm often receives a salary in addition to his share of profits for performing special administrative duties in office and personnel management. UPA Sec. 18(s) provides that a surviving partner is entitled to compensation for services in winding up partnership affairs (and reimbursement for expenses incurred in the process) above and apart from his or her share in the partnership profits.

Each partner impliedly promises to devote full time and render exclusive service to the partnership. Assume that Hunter, Brooks, and Palmer enter a partnership. Palmer undertakes independent consulting for an outside firm without the consent of Hunter and Brooks. Palmer's compensation from the outside firm is considered partnership income. A partner cannot engage in any independent competitive or even noncompetitive activities that involve the partnership's time. If Palmer engages in an activity that competes with the partnership, then Palmer has breached the fiduciary duty that he owes it. Even with a noncompetitive activity, Palmer can breach his fiduciary duty if the partnership suffers from the loss of his efforts. Of course, the partnership agreement or unanimous consent of the partners can permit a partner to engage in any activity.

Inspection of Books

Partnership books and records must be kept equally accessible to all partners. Each partner has the right to examine (and each partner has the corresponding duty to produce) full and complete information concerning the conduct of all aspects of partnership business. [UPA Sec. 20] Each firm retains books in which to record and secure such information. Partners contribute the information, and a bookkeeper typically has the duty to preserve it. The books must be kept at the firm's principal business office and cannot be removed without the consent of all the partners. [UPA Sec. 19] Every partner, whether active or inactive, is entitled to inspect all books and records upon demand and can make copies of the materials.

Accounting

An accounting of partnership assets or profits is done to determine the value of each partner's proportionate share in the partnership. An accounting can be performed voluntarily, or it can be compelled by order of a court in equity.[2] Formal accounting occurs by right in connection with dissolution proceedings, but a partner also has the right to a formal accounting in the following situations:

1. When the partnership agreement provides for a formal accounting.
2. When a partner is wrongfully excluded from the business, from access to the books, or both.

---

2. The principal remedy of a partner against copartners is an equity suit for dissolution, an accounting, or both. With minor exceptions, a partner cannot maintain an action against other firm members for damages until partnership affairs are settled and an accounting is done. This rule is necessary because legal disputes between partners invariably involve conflicting claims to shares in the partnership. Logically, the value of each partner's share must first be determined by an accountant.

3.   When any partner is withholding profits or benefits belonging to the partnership in breach of the fiduciary duty.
4.   When circumstances "render it just and reasonable." [UPA Sec. 22]

Property Rights

There is an important legal distinction between a partner's rights in specific property belonging to the firm to be used for business purposes and a partner's right to share in the firm's earned profits to the extent of the partner's interest in the firm. No individual partner has a right to specific property of the firm. Chapter 37 discussed the factors that the courts use in determining property rights of partners in partnerships and the rights of creditors. A judgment creditor of an individual partner has no right to execute or attach specific partnership property, but he or she can obtain the partner's share of profits. A creditor of the firm can levy directly upon partnership property (discussed below).

PARTNER'S INTEREST IN THE FIRM   A partner's interest in the firm is a personal asset consisting of a proportionate share of the profits earned and a return of capital after dissolution and winding up.

A partner's interest is susceptible to assignment or to a judgment creditor's lien. Neither an assignment nor a court's charging order entitling a creditor to receive a share of the partner's money will cause dissolution of the firm.

PARTNERSHIP PROPERTY   Partners are "tenants in partnership" of all firm property. A partner has no right to sell, assign, or in any way deal with a particular item of partnership property as an exclusive owner. Nor is a partner's personal credit related to partnership property; creditors cannot use it to satisfy the personal debts of a partner. Partnership property is available only to satisfy partnership debts, to enhance the firm's credit, or to achieve other business purposes.

Every partner is a co-owner with all other partners of specific partnership property such as office equipment, paper supplies, and vehicles. Each partner has equal rights to possess partnership property for business purposes or in satisfaction of firm debts, but not for any other purpose without the consent of all the other partners. These principles are aptly illustrated by the next case.

BACKGROUND AND FACTS   *The plaintiff and the defendant were partners in a real estate business. The partnership agreement called for each partner to share 50 percent of profits and losses. The defendant made a down payment on a piece of property in his own name and reimbursed himself out of the partnership checking account. The property was carried on the books of the partnership. When the partnership was later dissolved by mutual agreement, the defendant refused to share the property that was in his name, or the profits from it.*

DECISION AND RATIONALE   *The plaintiff was entitled to his share of the property and the profits derived from it in accordance with the partnership agreement. That the property was in the defendant's name and not in the name of the partnership was evidence of who owned the property, but it was not dispositive. When a partner is reimbursed for the purchase price of a piece of property out of partnership funds, and the property is carried on the partnership books, the law imposes a trust on the property and views the defendant as holding it in trust for the partnership. The judge cited partnership law in giving his opinion: "An*

STAUTH v. STAUTH
Court of Appeals of Kansas, 1978. 2 Kan. App. 2d 512, 582 P.2d 1160.

agreement that certain real estate should be part of the firm assets may be implied from the acts and conduct of the partners; the agreement need not be express. *** Partnership books may also be considered to determine the question, as, for example, how the property was entered and carried on the books of the company. The manner in which the accounts are kept, whether the purchase money is severally charged to the members of the firm, or whether the accounts treat it the same as other firm property, may be controlling circumstances in determining such intention, and from these circumstances the agreement of the parties may be inferred."

DUTIES AND POWERS OF PARTNERS

Fiduciary Duty

Partners stand in a fiduciary relationship to one another the way that principals and agents do. (See Chapter 34.) It is a relationship of extraordinary trust and loyalty. The fiduciary duty imposes a responsibility upon each partner to act in good faith for the benefit of the partnership. It requires that each partner subordinate his or her personal interests in the event of conflict and consider the mutual welfare of all partners in partnership activities.

This fiduciary duty underlies the entire body of law pertaining to partnership and to agency. From it, certain other duties are commonly implied. Thus, a partner must account to the partnership for any personal profits or benefits derived without consent of all of the partners in any partnership transaction.[3] These include transactions among partners or with third parties connected with the formation, conduct, or liquidation of the partnership, or with any use of partnership property. [UPA Sec. 21]

Upon the death of a partner, the surviving partner is under a fiduciary duty to liquidate partnership assets without delay and credit the estate of the deceased partner for the value of the decedent's interest in the partnership. The fiduciary duty arises by implication in the personal representative of the deceased partner's estate as well. The principles of fiduciary duty and property rights are illustrated in the next case.

---

3.   In this sense, "to account" to the partnership means not only to divulge the information but also to determine the value of any benefits or profits derived and to hold that money or property in trust on behalf of the partnership.

ESTATE OF WITLIN
California Court of Appeal, 1978.
83 Cal. App. 3d 167, 147 Cal. Rptr. 723.

BACKGROUND AND FACTS   *About forty-five doctors, including Dr. Witlin, owned and operated a health center as partners. When Dr. Witlin died, the other doctors, in accordance with the partnership agreement, purchased his share of the center, paying his widow $65,228.*

The partnership agreement provided that, on a partner's death, a management committee of the partnership was required to make a good faith determination of the fair market value of the deceased partner's share. The partnership had the option to offer this amount to the deceased partner's spouse. The $65,228 offer, however, was based on the book value of the partnership's assets. Furthermore, the partnership was bargaining to sell the health center at a price that would double Dr. Witlin's widow's proportionate share, but the partnership did not inform *her of that fact. Mrs. Witlin therefore sought a greater amount for her husband's share, even though she had accepted the partnership's offer.*

DECISION AND RATIONALE   *Mrs. Witlin was entitled to a greater amount for her deceased husband's share in the medical center since the partnership had breached its duty of good faith in determining the market value of Dr. Witlin's share. The partnership agreement explicitly provided that a management committee of the partnership determine the fair market value of Dr. Witlin's share "in good faith." "Yet the management committee never revealed to [Mrs. Witlin] *** that the basic value in their formula for determining the fair market value of the partnership was book value alone. Likewise, as already noted, the management committee did not mention to [Mrs. Witlin's attorney] the possibility that the hospital might be shortly sold ***. Given this situation, how could their offer *** have been a good faith determination *** of the fair market value of the partnership?"*

General Agency Powers

Each partner is an *agent* of every other partner and acts as both a principal and an agent in any business transaction within the scope of the partnership agreement. Each partner is a general agent of the partnership to carry on the usual business of the firm. Thus, every partner's act in every contract and in every contract signed in the partnership name that furthers partnership business binds the firm. [UPA Sec. 9(1)]

The UPA affirms general principles of agency law that pertain to the authority of a partner to bind a partnership in contract or tort. When a partner is apparently carrying on partnership business with third persons in the usual way, both the partner and the firm share liability. It is only when third persons *know* that the partner has no such authority that the partnership is not liable. For example, P, a partner in Firm X, applies for a loan on behalf of the partnership without authorization from the other partners. The bank manager knows P has no authority. If the bank manager grants the loan, P will be personally bound, but the firm will not be liable.

JOINT LIABILITY   Partners have only joint liability on all partnership debts and contracts.

[UPA Sec. 15(b)] Partners are jointly and severally liable for tort actions and breaches of trust to third persons. [UPA Sec. 15(a)]

Joint liability means that the group of partners wins or loses as a group. One partner cannot be singled out to be sued. Every partner's name must be listed in the suit, and the individual assets of each partner are equally exposed to potential liability (although the actual contribution in the event of a judgment is calculated on each partner's proportionate share of the firm). If the court awards the claimant a judgment, the claimant is barred from further suits against the partners and against the firm, once satisfaction (that is, payment) of the judgment is made.

In states that allow a firm to be sued in its own name, a contract claimant or a creditor claimant can sue the firm as an *entity* without joining each partner. A judgment against the partnership binds only partnership assets. In such states, the better practice is to sue both the firm as an *entity* and all partners *jointly*. Then, judgment is enforceable against the assets of the partnership and the assets of the individual partners. The judgment rendered in such a case must be internally consistent. For example, if C sues Firm X and all its partners jointly for breach of contract and the court finds the firm liable, then it must hold the partners liable (and vice versa).

Joint and several liability means that a claimant can sue one partner without joining the others. Moreover, regardless of the outcome of the suit against the first partner, **res judicata** (a matter or thing settled by judgment in the courts) does not protect the other partners in subsequent suits filed against them.

Agency concepts relating to apparent authority, actual authority, and ratification are also applicable to partnerships. The extent of *implied authority* is generally broader for partners than for ordinary agents. The character and scope of the partnership business and the customary nature of the particular business operation determine the scope of implied powers. For example, the usual course of business in a trading or commercial partnership involves buying and selling commodities. Consequently, each partner in a trading firm has a wide range of implied powers to borrow money in the firm name and to extend the firm's credit in issuing or indorsing negotiable instruments.

In an ordinary partnership, firm members can exercise all implied powers reasonably necessary and customary to carry on that particular business. Some customarily implied powers include the authority to make warranties on goods in the sales business, the power to convey real property in the firm name where such conveyances are part of the ordinary course of partnership business, the power to enter contracts consistent with the firm's regular course of business, and the power to make admissions and representations concerning partnership affairs. [UPA Sec. 11]

Like the law of agency, the law of partnership imputes one partner's knowledge to all other partners because members of a partnership stand in a fiduciary relationship to one another. Such a relationship assumes that each partner willfully discloses to every other partner all relevant information pertaining to the business of the partnership. The same rule applies to members of a joint venture.

MOBIL OIL CORP. v. HURWITZ

Appellate Court of Illinois, 1978.

63 Ill. App. 3d 430, 20 Ill. Dec. 372, 380 N.E. 2d 49.

BACKGROUND AND FACTS   *Prehn, the owner of a certain parcel of land, subleased part of the land to Mobil Oil Company. Mobil insisted that the lease restrict the sale of petroleum products on property adjoining the leased premises or within a thousand feet of Mobil's service station. Thereafter, Sapp and Hurwitz, as partners, leased an adjoining portion of the land from Prehn. At the time, Sapp knew about the restriction on the use of the land but Hurwitz did not. Hurwitz later attempted to operate a hotel and service station on the premises. Mobil sued to enjoin (prohibit) operation of this service station.*

DECISION AND RATIONALE   *Hurwitz was enjoined from operating a service station adjacent to the land leased by Mobil because Hurwitz could be said to have had constructive knowledge of the restrictions on the land at the time he signed the lease. Sapp and Hurwitz were partners when they signed the lease, and Sapp knew about the restriction on the use of the land. The court quoted Section 12 of the Uniform Partnership Act: "Notice to any partner of any matter relating to partnership affairs, and the knowledge of the partner acting in the particular matter, acquired while a partner or then present to his mind, and the knowledge of any other partner who reasonably could and should have communicated it to the acting partner, operate as notice to or knowledge of the partnership, except in the case of a fraud on the partnership committed by or with the consent of that partner."*

QUESTIONS AND CASE PROBLEMS

1. A partnership agreement states the following: "The said partners have contributed to the partnership in the following proportions to-wit: John E. Craig, party of the first part, equipment, technical knowledge, skill, and experience in the proportion of 50 percent, Raymond L. Carney, party of the second part, equipment, technical knowledge, skill, and experience in the proportion of 50 percent, and John A. Hamilton, party of the third part, the sum of $20,000 cash to commence the business. It is agreed that the sum actually contributed by the party of the third part shall bear interest at the rate of 6 percent per annum." What proportion of profits or losses should be attributed to each of the partners? Would it make any difference if John Hamilton did not work in the business but the other two partners did? [Craig v. Hamilton, 213 Kan. 665, 518 P.2d 539 (1974)]

2. James and Edmund Bickett and William O'Brien entered into a written partnership agreement. Its express purpose was to buy a specific tract of timber land at a specific price. Contrary to this agreement, O'Brien purchased the land in his own name and with his own money. Can the Bicketts force O'Brien to convey the property to the partnership? Can they force O'Brien to convey two-thirds of the property to them personally? [O'Brien v. Bickett, 419 S.W.2d 726 (Ky. App. 1967)]

3. A and B were brothers operating a dairy farm in North Carolina. In 1963, their assets were worth $100,000, and they had accumulated profits of $12,000. That year, C joined the partnership and contributed a $200,000 farm that he owned. In 1973, the partnership was dissolved. At that time, the assets were valued at $500,000, and accumulated profits totaled $12,000. How much is each partner entitled to upon dissolution? [Halsey v. Choate, 27 N.C. App. 49, 217 S.E.2d 740 (1975)]

4. Summers, a partner in a two-person partnership, approached the other partner, Dooley, about hiring an additional employee. Dooley refused, stating that he did not believe the additional employee was needed. Nevertheless, Summers hired him. Dooley, who handled the payroll, objected to the hiring and refused to pay for the new employee out of partnership funds. After two months, Summers was finally forced to pay the man out of his own personal funds, and the man quit. Summers then sought reimbursement from the partnership. Can he recover? [Summers v. Dooley, 94 Idaho 87, 481 P.2d.318 (1971)]

5. David Bell and Fred Herzog were partners in a real estate partnership. The partnership operated from August 1968 until August 1969, when Herzog notified Bell that he, Herzog, considered Bell's failure to devote his time and efforts to the real estate business and his failure to make payments required by the partnership agreement a breach of the agreement and that he was therefore terminating the partnership. Bell in turn wrote to Herzog, stating that he considered Herzog's letter to be the "last straw" and that he, Bell, was therefore terminating the partnership. Bell then sought an accounting of all the partnership's assets and liabilities. Herzog objected on the ground that Bell's failure to contribute to the management of the partnership constituted a breach of fiduciary duty, a breach of the partnership agreement, and a breach of the Uniform Partnership Act. Should Bell's demand for an accounting be denied? [Bell v. Herzog, 39 A.D.2d 813, 322 N.Y.S.2d. 501 (1972)]

6. Frances, Henry, and Reuben Barthuly were partners in a somewhat unsuccessful partnership. Frances and Henry together owned a one-half interest, and Reuben owned the other half. Under the partnership agreement, Henry had the authority to hire employees and to fix their salaries. The partnership was dissolved in 1966, but the winding up process took approximately four years. During that period, Henry hired Frances as the firm's bookkeeper. Reuben became aware that Frances was drawing a salary from the partnership and that Henry had approved the salary so Reuben demanded an accounting. He objected to Frances's having collected a salary and demanded that she repay it into the partnership funds before the partnership's assets were divided. Can Frances keep the salary that she received? [Barthuly v. Barthuly, 192 Neb. 610, 223 N.W.2d 429 (1974)]

7. Harestad and Weitzel entered into an oral agreement in August 1970 to be "partners in a real estate and building business," and each contributed equal amounts to the partnership. In October 1970, Weitzel purchased an apartment project in his own name with his own funds. Over the next two years, he oversaw the development and consummated the sale of the apartment project for a handsome profit. Upon voluntary dissolution of the partnership by both parties, Harestad sought half the profit that Weitzel had made from his apartment project deal. Can she

recover? [Harestad v. Weitzel, 272 Or. 199, 536 P.2d 522 (1975)]

8.   A patient sued a physician for medical malpractice and successfully recovered a money judgment. The patient did not sue the partnership to which the physician belonged and made no allegation against the partnership. Injury to the patient occurred in the course of partnership business. Can the physician now recover from his copartners for damages that he paid out of his personal funds? [Flynn v. Reaves, 135 Ga. App. 651, 218 S.E.2d 661 (1975)]

9.   Harris and Phillips were co-partners doing business as Dan's Used Cars. On his way home from work one evening, Harris struck Cook with his automobile, causing extensive injuries to Cook and damages to Cook's automobile. At the time, Harris was using a partnership car and was headed home on the most direct route from the partnership lot to his home. Harris testified that he had no set working hours and that he frequently traveled to and from his home and the used car lot. In addition, Harris stated that he was constantly on call by Phillips or his customers while at home. Can Cook recover from Dan's Used Cars in addition to recovering from Harris individually? [Phillips v. Cook, 239 Md. 215, 210 A.2d 743 (1965)]

10.   Walsh and O'Connor were copartners in a general partnership. Barneson joined them and contributed $10,000. Later, Barneson realized that the partnership had been insolvent when he joined and that the copartners, Walsh and O'Connor, were $20,000 in debt to their various creditors. The creditors all obtained judgments against the partnership of Walsh, O'Connor, and Barneson and wished to levy against Barneson's $10,000 contribution. Can the creditors reach this money? Since the $10,000 would be insufficient to satisfy the creditors, they also wish to levy against Barneson's personal assets. Can they reach these assets? [Ellingson v. Walsh, O'Connor and Barneson, 15 Cal. 2d 673, 104 P.2d 507 (1940)]

39

Partnerships
Limited Partnerships

This chapter will look in detail at the management, formation, and termination of limited partnerships. It will also look at some other, highly specialized forms of partnerships, such as limited partnership associations, mining partnerships, and subpartnerships.

DEFINITION OF
LIMITED PARTNERSHIP

Limited partnerships are formed by compliance with statutory requirements. They consist of at least one general partner and one or more limited partners. The general partner (or partners) assumes management responsibility of the partnership and as such has full personal liability for all debts of the partnership. The limited partner (or partners) contributes cash (or other property) and owns an interest in the firm but does not undertake any management responsibilities and is not personally liable for partnership debts beyond the amount of his or her investment. A limited partner can forfeit limited liability by taking part in managing the business. In many respects, limited partnerships are like general partnerships, discussed in Chapter 37. They are sometimes referred to as special partnerships, in contrast to general partnerships.

HISTORY OF
LIMITED PARTNERSHIPS

Business employs services and capital. A need therefore exists for a form of organization that permits capital investment without responsibility for management and without liability for losses beyond the initial investment. Such an organization should also allow the right to share in the profits with limited liability for losses. During the Middle Ages, this kind of organization was called a *commenda*.[1] In a commenda, the *commendator* supplied money to the *tractator* and received a major portion of the profits but was not liable for losses. If the tractator lost the capital investment, the commendator was liable only if proven negligent. This particular institution was sanctioned by the French Commercial Code in 1707, Sections 23-28. Over a century later, the first limited partnership acts were adopted in Connecticut and Pennsylvania in 1836 and in New York in 1882.

Limited Partnership
Statutes—Early Versions

All states have enacted limited partnership statutes. The earlier versions of such acts displayed an obvious hostility toward limited liability that derived from the common law. Courts imposed full liability on limited partners when there were only trivial failures to comply with the law.

The Uniform
Limited Partnership Act

The Uniform Limited Partnership Act was promulgated in 1916. It has been adopted by forty-eight states (not Delaware or Louisiana) and by the District of Columbia and the Virgin Islands. The great virtue of the ULPA is that it expressly provides protection against technical defects if there has been a good faith attempt at

compliance. [ULPA Secs. 2(2), 6, and 11] Under the ULPA, a limited partnership can conduct any business that can be carried on by a general partnership unless there is an exception in the state statutes. The most predominant exceptions are banking and insurance.

The Revised Uniform
Limited Partnership Act

On August 5, 1976, the National Conference of Commissioners on Uniform State Laws approved a Revised Uniform Limited Partnership Act. It contains eleven articles and sixty-four sections,and it was made available to state legislatures in 1977. The articles are:

1. General Provisions.
2. Formation; Certificate of Limited Partnership.
3. Limited Partners.
4. General Partners.
5. Finance.
6. Distributions and Withdrawal.
7. Assignment of Partnership Interest.
8. Dissolution.
9. Foreign Limited Partnerships.
10. Derivative Actions.
11. Miscellaneous.

FORMATION

The creation of a limited partnership is a public and formal proceeding that must follow statutory requirements. Contrast this with the informal, private, and voluntary agreement that usually suffices for a general partnership as described in Chapter 37. There must be two or more partners, and they must sign a certificate that sets forth, at a minimum, the following information:

1. Firm name.
2. Character of the business.
3. Location of the principal place of business.
4. Name and place of residence of each member and whether each is a general or a limited partner.

---

1. W. Holdsworth, *History of English Law*, 195, Methuen and Co. Ltd., London (1956).

5. Duration of the partnership.
6. Amount of cash and a description and agreed-upon valuation of any other property contributed by each limited partner.
7. Additional contributions (if any) to be made by each limited partner and the times at which they are to be made.
8. Methods for changes in personnel (if any) and subsequent continuance of the business.
9. Share of profits or other compensation that each limited partner is entitled to receive.

In essence, the content of the certificate and the method of filing it resemble those of the corporate charter. Often, there are private, informal agreements covering matters that do not have to be stated in the certificate, such as the profit shares of the general partners.

Where to File Certificates

The certificate must be filed with the designated state official. It is usually open to public inspection. The official is normally in the county where the principal business of the firm will be carried on. Some states require multiple filings if business is carried on in numerous counties. Others require only one filing, usually at the state capital. Constructive notice (by reason of law) does not usually exist for a certificate filed in another state. Thus, if a limited partnership chooses to do business where a certificate is not filed, a court can rule that its failure to file locally makes it a general partnership. This is similar to the qualification rules for foreign corporations. Some states require newspaper publication of certificates, or at least a summary of them, in addition to a filing.

NUMBER OF LIMITED PARTNERS Originally, limited partnerships were conceived to accommodate only a few limited partners. There seems, however, to be no statutory limit to their numbers, and in some cases, very large groups have been assembled. In a 1966 case, the limited partners of a real estate syndicate brought a class action suit against the general partners and some outsiders.[2] The limited partners numbered several hundred.

The Role of the Limited Partner and Liability

General partners conduct a business as if it were a general partnership. They are personally liable to the creditors; thus at least one general partner is necessary so that someone has personal liability. This policy can, nonetheless, be circumvented in states where a corporation can be the general partner in a partnership. Since the corporation has limited liability by virtue of corporate laws, no one in the limited partnership actually has personal liability.

Limited Partners Cannot Participate in Management

The exemptions and personal liability of the limited partners rest on their not participating in management. In other words, the contribution of a limited partner cannot be in services—it has to be in cash or other property. Also, the surname of a limited partner cannot be included in the partnership name. A violation of either of these provisions renders the limited partner just as liable as a general partner to any creditor who does not know that he or she is a limited partner. Note that no law expressly bars the participation of limited partners in the management of the partnership. Rather, the threat of personal liability deters their participation. How much actual review and advisement a limited partner can engage in before being exposed to liability is an unsettled question.[3]
The issue of the degree of control of the limited partner comes up in the following case.

_____

2. Lichtyger v. Franchard Corp., 18 N.Y.2d 528, 223 N.E. 2d 869 (1966).
3. See Plasteel Products Corp. v. Helman, 271 F.2d 354 (1st Cir. 1959) (interpreting Massachusetts law).

HOLZMAN v. DE ESCAMILLA

District Court of Appeal, 4th District, 1948.
86 Cal. App.2d 858, 195 P.2d 833.

BACKGROUND AND FACTS *In 1943, Hacienda Farms, Ltd., was organized as a limited partnership. Ricardo de Escamilla was the general partner, and James Russell and H. W. Andrews were limited partners. Except for the farm's first crop, no crop was ever planted without the concurrence of Russell and Andrews. In fact, when Escamilla thought it was unwise to plant peppers, eggplant, and watermelons, Russell and Andrews overruled him. After the partnership became insolvent, the trustee in bankruptcy brought suit to determine whether Russell and Andrews should be held liable for partnership debts as general partners.*

DECISION AND RATIONALE *Because of their involvement in the operation of Hacienda Farms, Russell and Andrews were liable as general partners. It is unimportant that they organized the firm as a limited partnership since the control they exercised outweighed the mere claim that they were only limited partners. The court concluded,"[Russell and Andrews] were active in dictating the crops to be planted, some of them against the wish of Escamilla. This clearly shows they took part in the control of the business of the partnership and thus became liable as general partners."*

LIABILITY TO CREDITORS   A limited partner is liable to creditors to the extent of any contribution that had been promised to the firm but not made and to the extent of any part of a contribution that was withdrawn from the firm.[4] If the firm is defectively organized, and the limited partner fails to renunciate (withdraw from the partnership) on discovery of the defect, the partner can be held liable to the firm's creditors. Note, though, that the ULPA and the Revised ULPA allow people to remain limited partners regardless of whether they comply with statutory technicalities. Liability for false statements in a partnership certificate runs in favor of persons relying on them and against members who sign the certificate knowing of the falsity.[5] A limited partnership is formed by good faith compliance with requirements for signing and filing the certificate even if it is incomplete or defective. When a limited partner discovers a defect in the formation of the limited partnership, he or she can obtain shelter from liability by renouncing an interest in the profits of the partnership.

Liability of Limited Partners   The liability of a limited partner is limited to the capital that he or she contributes or agrees to contribute to the partnership. By contrast, the liability of a general partner for partnership indebtedness is virtually unlimited.

4.   See Kittredge v. Langley, 252 N.Y. 405, 169 N.E. 626 (1930).

5.   See Walraven v. Ramsay, 335 Mich. 331, 55 N.W.2d 853 (1953).

CHEMICAL BANK OF ROCHESTER v. ASHENBURG

Supreme Court of Monroe County, 1978.
94 Misc. 2d 64, 405 N.Y.S.2d 175.

BACKGROUND AND FACTS *Stanndco Developers, a construction company, formed a partnership with eighteen others for the purpose of marketing apartments that Stanndco had constructed. Stanndco was the sole general partner, the others were limited partners. All the limited partners executed personal promissory notes to the partnership to pay* *for their "share" in the partnership. Several years later, Stanndco, on its own, sought to borrow $101,000 from Chemical Bank using the partnership notes as collateral. As general partner, Stanndco indorsed the notes to itself without the consent of the limited partners. The bank then sought to collect on the notes from the limited partners.*

DECISION AND RATIONALE *Chemical Bank could not collect from the limited partners because it knew that Stanndco was negotiating the instruments in a transaction for its own benefit, without authority, and in breach of its duty as a fiduciary. A general partner owes a fiduciary duty to the limited partners in a partnership to protect their interests and investments. "[Chemical Bank's] conduct permitted the diversion of the partnership assets and it should not profit from its own wrongdoing.Under these circumstances it would be unconscionable not to permit the [limited partners] to assert their claim as a defense against [the bank]."*

RESTRICTIONS ON WHAT THE LIMITED PARTNER CAN DO As already mentioned, the limited partner cannot take control of the firm, cannot contribute services and cannot allow his or her name to appear in the firm name. Additionally, the limited partner has no authority to bind the firm, even though, in some sense, he or she is a "member" of it.

RIGHTS OF THE LIMITED PARTNER Subject to these limitations, limited partners have essentially the same rights as general partners: the right of access to partnership books, the right to an accounting of partnership business, and the right to participate in the dissolution winding up and distribution of partnership assets. They are entitled to a return of their contributions in accordance with the partnership certificate. They can also assign their interests subject to specific clauses in the certificate.

LIMITED PARTNER'S RIGHT TO SUE In jurisdictions that have considered the matter, courts seem to recognize fully the limited partner's right to sue, either individually or on behalf of the firm, for economic injury to the firm by the general partners or by outsiders. In addition, investor protection legislation, such as security laws (discussed in Chapter 43) may give some protection to limited partners.

THE USE OF A LIMITED PARTNERSHIP

The limited partnership is a less effective liability shield than the corporation. In many respects, the corporation is more flexible, and its charter does not require the frequent amendments that a limited partnership certificate does. The conclusion that one might draw is that limited partnerships have little utility, except for special reasons.

Before World War II, limited partnerships were used sparingly, but during and after the war, their number increased, largely because of high federal income tax rates, particularly on corporations. A limited partnership allows the limited partners to deduct expenses or losses against other income directly and to be protected from personal liability. These features make limited partnerships profitable for high income, high tax bracket individuals who invest in particularly high-risk enterprises, such as oil and gas drilling, Broadway plays, and the like. These advantages, combined with other tax benefits, such as deductions for intangible drilling expenses and percentage depletion in oil and gas ventures or accelerated depreciation in construction, make limited partnerships appealing.

DISSOLUTION

A limited partnership is dissolved in the same way as an ordinary partnership. The retirement, death, or insanity of a general partner can dissolve the partnership, but such circumstances do not do so if the business can be continued by one or more of the other general partners in accordance with their certificate or with the consent of all members. The death or assignment of interest of a limited partner does not dissolve the limited partnership. With respect to dissolution, limited partnerships resemble corporations more closely than they do general partnerships. This follows from the fact that there are public filings, passive investors, and limited liability, all of which are also features of corporations.

Causes of Dissolution

A limited partnership is dissolved by the expiration of its term or the completion of its undertaking. When there is no definite term or undertaking, the express will of any general partner will usually dissolve the partnership. Limited partners do not have the power to dissolve unless they have rightfully, but unsuccessfully demanded return of their contribution. (See ULPA Sec. 16) If, however, the general partners dissolve the partnership without the consent of the limited partners before the end of the term fixed by the certificate, this dissolution is considered a breach.

Illegality, expulsion, and bankruptcy dissolve a limited partnership, except that the bankruptcy of a limited partner does not dissolve the partnership unless it causes the bankruptcy of the firm.

The retirement of a general partner causes a dissolution unless the members consent to a continuation by the remaining general partners or unless this contingency is provided for in the certificate.

Consequences of Dissolution

The consequences of the dissolution of general partnerships apply to limited partnerships (see Chapter 37). Therefore, the firm continues in operation while winding up. The general partners of a limited partnership have the authority to wind up, as in an ordinary partnership. The representatives of general partners, not the limited partners, succeed the general partners. Limited partners have the right to obtain dissolution and winding up by a court decree.[6]

Assuming that the general partners continue the business, the limited partners generally have the right to be paid the value of their interests at dissolution, plus profits or interest on that value from dissolution until payment.

PRIORITIES IN DISTRIBUTION OF ASSETS

Upon dissolution, creditors' rights to distribution of assets precede partners' rights, and limited partners' rights precede general partners' rights. Limited partners take both their share of profits and of contributed capital before general partners receive anything.

LIMITED PARTNERSHIP ASSOCIATIONS

Certain states allow the formation of limited partnership associations. They are legal hybrids that actually resemble corporations, although they are called partnership associations in some states. They originated in Pennsylvania in 1874, and the capital that was subscribed to the association was made the sole source responsible for its debts. In 1966, the Pennsylvania Act was repealed except for professions not permitted to incorporate. Three other states have similar laws: Michigan, New Jersey, and Ohio. (Virginia had one from 1874 to 1918.) This organization is seldom seen outside Pennsylvania and Michigan.

---

6. Klebanow v. New York Produce Exchange, 344 F.2d 294 (2d Cir. 1965).

The organizational document is publicly filed and can be changed by amendment. It fixes the capital of the association, and there is no maximum or minimum amount. Each member contributes a designated part of the capital.

The association's life is restricted—usually to twenty years. There must be at least three members, and Ohio has established a maximum of twenty-five. The word *limited* must be the last word in the association's name, and it must be conspicuously used on advertisements, signs, and stationery. Dissolution of the limited part-nership association occurs when the prescribed term expires or by a majority vote of the members.

An important difference between this type of association and corporations involves the transfer of shares. The shares are freely transferable, but the new transferee does not become a member in the association unless duly elected by the other members. When membership is refused, however, the transferee can recover the value of his or her shares from the association.

QUESTIONS AND CASE PROBLEMS

1. A, B, C, and D entered into an oral partnership agreement under which A and B were to manage the firm and C and D were to contribute the funds necessary to start it up. The four also orally agreed that C and D would be limited partners. The partnership was formed in Pennsylvania, and under Pennsylvania's Uniform Partnership Act there is no requirement that a partnership agreement be in writing. Under Pennsylvania's Limited Partnership Act, however, limited partnerships must record a certificate of their establishment in the county clerk's office. A, B, C, and D failed to file such a certificate but operated as a limited partnership in that C and D exercised no control over management of the firm. Thereafter, one of the partnership's creditors sued, and, since the assets of the partnership were not sufficient to satisfy the partnership's debt, the creditor wished to attach C's and D's personal assets. Can he? [Ruth v. Crane, 392 F. Supp. 724 (E.D.Pa. 1975)]

2. The Ponderosa Land Company was a properly established limited partnership whose members were Harold Brown, Walter Brown, and W. D. Blaster. The Browns were general partners, and Blaster was the sole limited partner. His only contribution to the firm was providing it with start-up capital of $50,000. After a number of years of successful operation, Blaster decided to withdraw from the firm since he was badly in need of cash. He requested that the partnership return his capital contribution. Is the partnership dissolved? [Brown v. Brown, 15 Ariz. App. 333, 488 P.2d 689 (1971)]

3. Patricia Allen was a limited partner in a rather large firm that had been formed for the purpose of "ownership and promotion for development of a tract of land." A number of the general partners decided that it might be more profitable to mortgage the land owned by the partnership and make loans to small businesses. Thereafter the land was mortgaged, and the proceeds were loaned to numerous borrowers. In most cases the loans were unsecured. Patricia Allen objected to all of this but felt that, since she was merely a limited partner, her only option was to sell her investment and withdraw. Is any other recourse available to her? [Allen v. Steinberg, 244 Md. 119, 223 A.2d 240 (1966)]

4. Diversified Properties was a limited partnership that owned and operated several garden apartments and other real estate located mostly in Maryland. Weil was the only general partner; all the others were limited partners. The partnership was not well-managed and improvised from crisis to crisis. Kaye and Snider, two of the limited partners, took more and more of an interest in the affairs of the partnership as the partnership's financial condition worsened. On several occasions, both men gave Weil advice and suggestions on how to run the firm. In addition, Snider and Kaye often conferred between themselves and with Weil in attempts to salvage the enterprise and continue operations. Upon learning this, one of the partnership's creditors attempted to attach Snider's and Kaye's personal assets, claiming that their activities made them general partners. Do the facts support this claim? [Weil v. Diversified Properties, 319 F.Supp. 778 (D.C. D.C. 1970)]

5. Thirty-one limited partners with $202,000 invested in a real estate syndicate, River View Associates, brought suit against the managers and general

partners of River View for breach of trust and breach of fiduciary duty. The limited partners alleged that the partnership built and leased a hotel to Sheridan Corporation. Sheridan managed the hotel, and the general partners of River View assumed the ownership responsibilities of the hotel. Initially, the hotel had been leased to another corporation, and rental from the lease was $590,000 a year. This gave the limited partners an 11 percent return on their investment. In 1963, however, the managing partners of River View decided to lease the hotel to Sheridan Corporation. Under the new lease, the rental was reduced by approximately $157,000 a year, leaving the limited partners with an 8 percent return on their investment. The rent, however, was "guaranteed" under a bond procured by Sheridan. Can the limited partners interfere with the decision of the general partners to enter into a new lease with Sheridan? [Lichtyger v. Franchard Corp., 18 N.Y.2d 528, 277 N.Y.S.2d 377, 223 N.E.2d 869 (1966)]

6.   In 1970, John J. McMullen Associates was organized as a limited partnership with eight limited partners and one general partner for the purpose of managing and developing techniques and uses for liquefied natural gas. Several of the limited partners had technical skills and training with respect to natural gas uses. On occasion, one or more of the limited partners would appear at the various job sites where the partnership operated and would discuss technical problems that arose in the course of the firm's work. Often, the limited partners would give advice, but the final decision always rested with the project manager (general partner). Will such activities cause a limited partner to be deemed a general partner? [Gast v. Petsinger, 228 Pa. Super. 394, 323 A.2d 371 (1974)]

7.   Fidelity Lease Limited, a limited partnership, had over twenty limited partners and one general partner. The general partner was a corporation, Interlease Corporation, and was managed by Sanders, Kahn, and Crombie, all three of whom happened to be limited partners of Fidelity Lease Limited. Assuming that in Texas, where this partnership was established, corporations are allowed to be partners in a partnership, what will the liability of Sanders, Kahn, and Crombie be in a suit against Fidelity Lease Limited? Will their liability be limited? [Delaney v. Fidelity Lease Limited, 517 S.W.2d 420 (Tex. Civ. App. 1974)]

40

Corporations
Nature and Formation

A BRIEF HISTORY OF THE CORPORATION

The corporation is the most widely used form of business organization. It can be owned by a single person, or it can have hundreds, even thousands, of shareholders. The shareholder form of business organization developed in Europe at the end of the seventeenth century. The firms were called joint stock companies, and they frequently collapsed because their organizers absconded with the funds or proved incompetent. The most famous collapse involved the South Sea Company, which assumed England's national debt in 1711 and obtained in return a monopoly over British trade with the South Sea Islands in South America plus an annual interest payment. The shares of the company were driven up by speculation, fraud was exposed, and a collapse followed. The event came to be known as the South Sea Bubble, and it led to the Bubble Act of 1720, a law that curtailed the use of joint stock companies in England for over a hundred years. Because of this history of fraud and collapse, organizations resembling corporations were regarded with suspicion in the United States during its early years.

In the eighteenth century, a typical American corporation was a municipality. Although several business corporations were formed after the Revolutionary War, it was not until the nineteenth century that the corporation came into common use for private business. In 1811, New York passed a general incorporation law allowing businesses to incorporate. Incorporation was permissible by five or more persons for the manufacture of textiles, glass, metals, and paint. The corporation could have capital of only $100,000 and a life of twenty years.

The significance of the New York law was that it allowed voluntary incorporation using standard bureaucratic procedures rather than special acts of the legislature, which were usually available only to businesspersons with political influence. By the mid-nineteenth century, railroads predominated among corporations. After the Civil War, manufacturing corporations became numerous.

The Corporation as a Creature of Statute

The corporation is a creature of statute. Its existence depends generally upon state law, although some corporations, especially public organizations, can be created under federal law. Each state has its own body of corporate law, and these laws are not entirely uniform. The Model Business Corporation Act (often called the Model Act) is a codification of modern corporation law. It enunciates principles of corporate law that have been adopted to some degree or another by every state.

The key distinctions among the various organizational forms available to business involve: (1) the relationships among members of the organization, (2) the personal financial liability of members of the organization, (3) the control and continuity of the organization, (4) the establishment of credit and the acquisition of capital for the organization, and (5) the tax implications of the chosen organizational form.

THE NATURE OF A CORPORATION

The Corporation as a Legal "Person"

A **corporation** is a legal entity created and recognized by state law. It can consist of one or more *natural* persons identified under a common name. It is recognized under state and federal law as a "person," and it enjoys many, but not all, of the same rights and privileges that U.S. citizens enjoy.

The Bill of Rights guarantees citizens certain protections, and corporations are considered citizens in most instances. For example, a corporation has the same right as a natural person to "equal protection" of the law under the Fourteenth Amendment. It has the right of access to the courts as an entity that can sue or be sued. It also has the right of due process before denial of life, liberty, or property as well as the freedom from unreasonable search and seizures and from double jeopardy.

Characteristics of the Corporate Entity

A corporation is an artificial person, with its own corporate name, owned by individual shareholders. It is a legal entity with rights and responsibilities. The corporation substitutes itself for its shareholders in conducting corporate business and in incurring liability. Its authority to act and the liability for its actions are separate and apart from the individuals who own it, although in certain limited situations, the "corporate veil" can be pierced (that is, liability for the corporation's obligations can be extended to shareholders). In some instances, shareholders can voluntarily make themselves personally liable for some or all of the debts of the corporation. This is particularly true with smaller corporations that attempt to obtain financing.

Responsibility for overall management of the corporation is entrusted to the board of directors, which is elected by shareholders. Corporate officers and other employees are hired by the board of directors to run the daily business operations of the corporation.

SHAREHOLDERS The acquisition of a share of stock makes a person an owner or shareholder in a corporation. Unlike the members in a partnership, the body of shareholders can change constantly without affecting the continued existence of the corporation. Thus, a corporation is not affected by the death of a shareholder, whereas the death of a partner would dissolve a partnership.

As a general rule, a shareholder is not personally liable for the corporation's business debts; nor is the corporation responsible for a shareholder's personal debts. Each shareholder's liability is limited to the amount of the investment (that is, the money actually paid when the stock was acquired). Thus, if Paul Ginsberg purchases one hundred shares of Ace Manufacturing stock at $1 per share, and Ace Manufacturing goes bankrupt owing creditors millions of dollars, Ginsberg's loss is limited to the $100 purchase price that he originally paid for the shares. The converse is also true. If Ginsberg declares bankruptcy and owes creditors thousands of dollars, the Ace Manufacturing Company is not liable, and the creditors can claim only the one hundred shares of stock.

Shareholders have no legal title to corporate property vested in the corporation, such as buildings and equipment. They have only an *equitable* interest in the corporation. In a partnership, each general partner is a tenant in the partnership property. (See discussions in Chapter 39.) A limited partner, however, is like a shareholder in this regard—neither has ownership rights in business property.

A shareholder can sue the corporation, and the corporation can sue a shareholder. The shareholder's derivative suit and the special responsibility of majority shareholders of the corporation will be discussed in Chapter 41.

Shareholders are owners without direct control over the management of the corporation's business. Only through the election of the board of directors can they exercise influence over corporate policy. They are neither managers nor agents of the corporation. In a partnership, on the other hand, general partners have control and responsibility for the management of the business, and each partner is an agent who can bind all other partners in the course of business.

BOARD OF DIRECTORS A general rule in corporate law says, "Directors must direct the corporate business affairs." The board of directors is elected by shareholders and is periodically accountable to them for reelection.

The board is responsible for making deci-

sions about overall policy. Directors declare dividends, authorize major corporate contracts, appoint or remove officers and set their salaries, issue authorized shares of stock, and recommend changes in the corporate charter. They delegate the day-to-day operation of corporate affairs to the officers and other employees of the corporation. The board can organize itself into executive committees and delegate these committees particular responsibilities to act on behalf of the entire board or to report back to it. Then, it acts as a unit.

OFFICERS AND OTHER EMPLOYEES Officers are agents of the corporation. They answer to the board of directors rather than to the shareholders directly, and they can be removed at any time by the board.

TAX CONSIDERATIONS Since a corporation is a separate legal entity, corporate profits are taxed to the corporation (that is, before they are distributed to shareholders and taxed a second time as dividends). Corporations can do one of two things with corporate profits—retain them or pass them on to shareholders in the form of dividends. The corporation receives no tax deduction for dividends distributed to shareholders. When dividends are money payments, they are again taxable (except when they represent distributions of capital) as ordinary nonservice income to the shareholder receiving them. This double taxation feature of the corporate organization is one of its major disadvantages. On the other hand, retained earnings, if invested properly, will yield higher corporate profits in the future and thus cause the price of the company's stock to rise. Individual shareholders can then reap the benefits of these retained earnings in the gains they receive when they sell their shares. These gains are treated for tax purposes as capital gains. For many individuals, capital gains tax rates are lower than the tax rates applied to ordinary income.

Classification of Corporations

Corporations can be classified by location, sources of funds, objectives, corporate activities, and ownership arrangements. Some special corporate forms are discussed in the next chapter.

DOMESTIC AND FOREIGN CORPORATIONS

A corporation must be incorporated in a particular state. The corporation is referred to as a *domestic* corporation by its home state (the state in which it incorporates). When a corporation does business outside the state in which it is incorporated, it is referred to in these other states as a *foreign* corporation. This chapter is not concerned with international corporations, so the terms *domestic* and *foreign* apply only to status within the United States.

PUBLIC AND PRIVATE CORPORATIONS A

public corporation is one formed by the government to meet some political or governmental purpose. Cities and towns that incorporate are common examples. In addition, many federal government organizations, such as the post office and Amtrak, are public corporations.

Private corporations are created either wholly or in part for private benefit. Most corporations are private, and it is these corporations that the chapter discusses. Private corporations can serve a public purpose, such as a public utility does, but they are nonetheless owned by private persons rather than the government.

NONPROFIT CORPORATIONS A familiar

form of nonprofit corporation is the religious, charitable, or educational corporation. Its purpose is not to make a profit, but it is permitted to do so if the profit is left within the corporation. Nonprofit corporations are organized under state statutes that usually provide for different formation and operation policies. Such corporations can issue shares of stock but cannot pay out dividends to shareowners. Most nonprofit corporations are private.

PROFESSIONAL CORPORATIONS Profes-

sional corporations are relatively new in corporate law. Most of them are private corporations involving practitioners of professions such as law, accounting, or medicine. The professional corporation has become extremely popular because its tax benefits (pension plan, medical benefits, and so forth) are often more beneficial than those provided by a partnership form of organization.

CLOSE CORPORATIONS The "close corpora-

tion," or closely-held corporation is typically one in which the shares of stock are held either by a single shareholder or by a few shareholders (the actual number is usually controlled by state law). Close corporation shareholders manage the firm directly. The closely-held corporation is discussed more extensively in Chapter 42.

FORMATION OF A CORPORATION

Promoters' Activities

Before the corporation can become a reality, people must invest in it as original subscribers to stock. Specialized promoters often carry out the creation of corporations, taking the preliminary steps for corporate organization, issuing a prospectus, procuring subscriptions for stock, and arranging for the charter or articles of incorporation. In short, they analyze the economic feasibility of a proposed corporation and then set out to bring together the necessary resources and personnel.

It is not unusual for a promoter to purchase or lease property with a view to selling it to the corporation to be organized. In addition, the promoter enters into contracts with attorneys, accountants, architects, or other professionals whose services will be needed in planning for the proposed corporation. Finally, a promoter induces people to purchase stock in the corporation.

Some interesting legal questions arise in regard to the promoter's activities. The most important is whether the promoter is personally liable for contracts made on behalf of a corporation that does not yet have any legal existence. Moreover, once the corporation is formed, does it assume liability on these contracts, or is the promoter still personally liable? As a general rule, a promoter is held personally liable on pre-incorporation contracts. The courts have frequently found that promoters are not agents of a corporation to be formed. They are liable upon any contracts made for the proposed corporation unless the party with whom they have contracted agrees to hold only the corporation liable.

Obviously, promoters who make agreements in their own names without referring to the proposed corporation continue to be liable after incorporation unless the third party releases them. Even in cases where the third party has made the agreement in the name of or with reference to the proposed corporation, a number of courts still hold promoters personally liable after incorporation unless the third party clearly indicated at the time of signing the agreement an intent to release them after the formation of the corporation. Basically, the reasoning is that the promoter is acting as an agent for a nonexistent principal.

The promoter can be held personally liable for all contracts that he or she signs if the proposed corporation is not formed or if it is formed but does not adopt the promoter's signed agreements. There are exceptions, however. For example, the third party can release the promoter from liability. The agreement can also expressly release the promoter from liability in the event that the corporation is not formed or does not accept the agreement. Finally, if, on evidence, the court believes that the third party and the promoter entered into an agreement that would not hold the promoter personally liable should the corporation not come into being, then the promoter will not be held personally liable. Since there are substantial risks of personal liability, promoters should see an attorney before signing any pre-incorporation agreements.

In the following case, a corporation offered to purchase land. Its offer was signed by the promoter as president before the corporation came into existence. The sellers agreed to accept the offer under the erroneous belief that a corporation existed. When they learned that there was no corporation, the sellers withdrew their acceptance prior to the time the corporation became incorporated. The corporation then sought to have the contract for the sale of the land enforced.

BACKGROUND AND FACTS *An offer to purchase a forty-eight-acre parcel of land from Ramey was signed as follows:*

MACY CORP. v. RAMEY
Court of Common Pleas of
Ohio, 1957.
144 N.E.2d 698.

> "Macy Corporation
> by B. Ruben, Pres.
> Macy T. Block."

Ruben was the promoter of the Macy Corporation, which, at the time of the offer, had not yet been formed. Ramey accepted the offer, but later, he and his wife repudiated. Macy's articles of incorporation were not filed until six days after Ruben recived Ramey's letter of repudiation. After receiving the repudiation, Macy Corporation twice notified the Rameys that it was ready, willing, and able to proceed according to the terms of the contract for sale. When they refused to go through with the sale, Macy instituted this suit for specific performance.

DECISION AND RATIONALE *Macy Corporation cannot force the Ramey's to sell it the land with a suit for specific performance because no contract for the purchase and sale of the land ever existed. A valid*

> *contract requires two or more parties with the capacity to contract. Here, Macy Corporation, did not yet exist at the time of the purported contract. "[T]he Rameys had withdrawn from the arrangement and had so notified Mr. Ruben, Mr. Block and their embryo corporation, at least one week before the corporation came to life and made its attempt to accept the promise of the Rameys to sell their land at a certain price. Consequently, [Macy's attempted] acceptance was too late to effect a contract between the Rameys and the Macy Corporation."*

Subscribers and Subscriptions

Prior to the actual formation of the corporation, the promoter can contact potential individual investors and they can agree to purchase capital stock in the future corporation. This agreement is often called a subscription agreement, and the potential investor is called a subscriber. Subscribers become shareholders as soon as the corporation is formed. Thus, if the XYZ Corporation becomes insolvent, the trustee in bankruptcy can collect the consideration for any unpaid stock from a pre-incorporation subscriber.

Many courts view the pre-incorporation subscriptions as continuing offers to purchase corporate stock. On or after its formation the corporation can choose to accept the offer to purchase. In addition, the pre-incorporation subscriber can revoke the offer to purchase before acceptance. On the other hand, a majority of courts treat a subscription as a contract between the subscribers. It is therefore irrevocable except with the consent of *all* of the subscribers. Under Section 17 of the Model Act, a subscription can be revoked for a period of six months unless otherwise provided in the subscription agreement or unless all the subscribers agree to the revocation of the subscription.

There are various ways that a promoter can avoid the problem of revocation. One way is to set up a trust with the promoter as trustee and the corporation as beneficiary (under the law of trusts, a beneficiary need not exist at the creation of the trust). The promoter/trustee enters a contract with the subscriber. By the terms of the contract, the subscriber promises to buy the stock. If the subscriber fails to subscribe or fails to pay, he or she is liable to the promoter/trustee for breach of contract.

A typical problem in pre-incorporation subscription agreement cases is that the corporation actually formed differs from the corporation that the subscriber originally agreed to invest in. The rule of thumb is that if the departure is minimal (for example, merely a change in name), the agreement is likely to be upheld. But if the change is material (such as entering a different business entirely), the agreement will not be enforced against an unwilling investor. More important problems arise, however, when the corporation is not formed or it fails after formation.

Incorporation

Exact procedures for incorporation differ among states, but the basic requirements are relatively similar.

STATE CHARTERING   Since state incorporation laws differ, individuals have found some advantage in looking for the states that offer the most advantageous tax or incorporation provisions. Delaware has historically had the least restrictive laws. Consequently, a significant number of corporations, including a number of the largest, have incorporated there. Delaware's statutes permit firms to incorporate in Delaware and carry out business and locate operating headquarters elsewhere. (Most other states now permit this.) On the other hand, closely-held corporations, particularly those of a professional nature, generally incorporate in the state where their principal stockholders live and work. In recent years, a number of policy-makers have suggested that differences among state corporation statutes have led to some undesirable consequences. This has prompted various proposals, including a proposal for federal chartering with a more standardized and restrictive incorporation process.[1]

ARTICLES OF INCORPORATION
The primary document needed to begin this phase of the incorporation process is called the charter, the articles, or the certificate of incorporation. The articles include basic information about the corporation and serve as a primary source of authority for its future organizational and business functioning.

CORPORATE NAME
Choice of a corporate name is subject to state approval to insure against duplication or deception. Fictitious name statutes usually require that the secretary of state run a check on the proposed name in the state of incorporation. Once cleared, a name can be reserved for a short time, pending the completion of the articles of incorporation. All corporate statutes require the corporation name to include the word *Corporation, Incorporated, Co., Corp.,* or *Inc.*

Some states require that the name of the corporation be expressed in English letters or characters. States usually require that a corporate name not be the same as or deceptively similar to the name of an existing corporation doing business within the state. For example, if an existing corporation is named General Dynamics, the state will not allow another corporation to be called General Dynamic. The corporate goodwill established by the original name might go in part to the second corporation because the similarity of its name might confuse people.

---

1. See, for example, Symposium, Federal Chartering of Corporations, 61 Geo. L.J. 71 (1972); Carey, Federalism and Corporate Law: Reflections upon Delaware, 83 Yale L.J. 663 (1974).

GENERAL NATURE AND PURPOSE
The intended business activities of the corporation must be specified in the articles, and naturally, they must be lawful. A general statement of corporate purpose is usually sufficient to give rise to all of the powers necessary or convenient to the purpose of the organization. The corporate charter can state, for example, that the corporation is organized "to engage in the production and sale of agricultural products."

Some states have prohibitions against the incorporation of certain professionals, such as doctors or lawyers, except pursuant to a professional incorporation statute. In some states, certain industries, such as banks, insurance companies, or public utilities, cannot be operated in the general corporate form and are governed by special incorporation statutes.

DURATION
A corporation can have perpetual existence under most state corporate statutes. However, a few states prescribe a maximum duration after which the corporation must formally renew its existence.

CAPITAL STRUCTURE
The capital structure of the corporation is generally set forth in the articles. A few state statutes require a minimum capital investment for ordinary business corporations, while those engaged in insurance or banking can be required to have a greater capital investment. The number of shares of stock authorized for issuance, their par value, the various types or classes of stock authorized for issuance, and other relevant information concerning equity, capital, and credit must be outlined in those provisions of the articles. The range of possibilities is discussed in Chapter 43.

INTERNAL ORGANIZATION
Whatever the internal management structure of the corporation, it should be described in the articles, although it can be included in bylaws adopted after the corporation is formed. The bylaws should not be confused with the articles of incorporation, which state the name of the

corporation, its address, duration, purpose, number of shares, and so forth. The articles of incorporation commence the corporation; the bylaws are formed after commencement. Bylaws are subject to and cannot conflict with the incorporation statute or the corporation's charter. Section 27 of the Model Act provides that "the power to alter, amend, or repeal the bylaws or adopt new bylaws shall be vested in the board of directors unless reserved to the shareholders by the articles of incorporation." That section further indicates that the bylaws must be consistent with the articles of incorporation. Typical bylaw provisions describe the quorum and voting requirements for shareholders, the election of the board of directors, the methods of replacing directors, and the manner and time of fixing shareholder and board meetings.

A PRINCIPAL OFFICE AND REGISTERED AGENT The corporation must indicate the location and address of its principal office within the state. It must give the name and address of a specific person designated as *agent* to receive legal documents on behalf of the corporation.

INCORPORATORS Each incorporator must be listed by name and must indicate an address. An incorporator is a person (or persons) who applies to the state on behalf of the corporation to obtain its corporate charter. The incorporator need not be a subscriber and need not have any interest at all in the corporation. States vary on the required number of incorporators; it can be as few as one or as many as three. Incorporators *must* sign the articles of incorporation when they are submitted to the state; often this is their

only duty. In some states, they participate at the first organizational meeting of the corporation.

FIRST ORGANIZATIONAL MEETING The first organizational meeting is provided for in the articles of incorporation but is held after the charter is actually granted. At this meeting, the incorporators elect the first board of directors and complete the routine business of incorporation (pass bylaws, issue stock, and so forth). Sometimes, the meeting is held after the election of the board of directors, and the business to be transacted depends upon the requirements of the state's incorporation statute, the nature of the business, the provisions made in the articles, and the desires of the promoters.

Adoption of bylaws is probably the most important purpose of the first organizational meeting. The bylaws are the internal rules of management for the corporation. The shareholders, directors, and officers must abide by them in conducting corporate business. Unless they have knowledge of the bylaws, corporation employees and third persons dealing with the corporation are not bound by them.

CORPORATE CHARTER Once the articles of incorporation have been prepared, signed, and authenticated by the incorporators, they are sent to the appropriate state official, usually the secretary of state, along with the appropriate filing fee. In many states, the secretary of state then issues a *certificate of incorporation* representing the state's authorization for the corporation to conduct business. The certificate and a copy of the articles are returned to the incorporators, who then hold the initial organizational meeting that completes the details of incorporation. As the following case illustrates, the existence of the corporation depends upon the issuance of a certificate of incorporation.

ROBERTSON v. LEVY
United States Court of Appeals,
District of Columbia, 1964.
197 A.2d 443.

BACKGROUND AND FACTS *Levy, who contracted to buy a small business from Robertson, issued a note to Robertson providing for installment payments. The note was signed "Penn. Ave. Record Shack, Inc. by Eugene Levy, President." At the time the note was issued, the certificate of incorporation for Levy's business had not been issued. Subsequently, it* *was issued, and the newly formed corporation made one installment payment on the note. Six months later, the corporation became insolvent, and Robertson attempted to recover on the note from Levy individually.*

DECISION AND RATIONALE   *Under the Model Business Corporation Act, Levy was personally liable on the note even though he did not sign it as an individual. The Act eliminates such concepts as de facto corporations and corpations by estoppel. The sole factor in determining whether a corporation will be recognized is whether the certificate of incorporation has been issued. "No longer must courts inquire into the equities of a case to determine whether there has been 'colorable compliance' with the statute ***. [Thus,] Robertson [cannot be] estopped from denying the existence of the corporation [merely] because after the certificate was issued he accepted one payment on the note."*

IMPROPER INCORPORATION The procedures for incorporation are very specific, and sometimes errors are made that form the basis for challenging the existence of the corporation. This can become important when, for example, a third person attempts to enforce a contract or bring suit for a tort injury and fortuitously learns of the defective incorporation. The plaintiff then seeks to make the would-be shareholders personally liable. The situation can also arise when the corporation seeks to enforce a contract against a defaulting party who learns of the defective incorporation and seeks to avoid liability on that ground. Courts have developed three theories to prevent the windfall that would occur in giving a contracting party the benefit of the stockholders' personal liability. The theories are *de jure* corporation, *de facto* corporation, and corporation by estoppel.

DE JURE CORPORATION   If there is at least substantial compliance with all conditions precedent to incorporation, the corporation is said to have *de jure* existence in law. This means that the corporation is properly formed, and neither the state nor a third party can attack its existence. To illustrate, Brown Motor Company, Inc., a domestic corporation, is being sued by a customer, Fred Muris, for an injury sustained at Brown's headquarters. Muris wants to challenge Brown's corporate status because he knows that the personal assets of the owners, Gary and Edward Brown, far exceed the company's assets. Muris discovers that the address of one of the incorporators is incorrectly listed in the articles and argues that this error means that the corporation was improperly formed. Hence it is not a duly authorized corporation and Gary and Edward Brown are personally liable. The law disregards such inconsequential procedural defects as long as there has been substantial compliance with the state's corporation laws. A court will uphold the *de jure* status of Brown Motor Company. Fred Muris can sue only Brown Motor Company as a corporate entity.

DE FACTO CORPORATIONS   In some situations, there is a serious defect of compliance with statutory mandates—for example, the expiration of the corporation charter. In certain circumstances, the corporation is held to have *de facto* status, and its existence cannot be challenged by third persons (except for the State). The following elements are required for *de facto* status:

1.   There must be a state statute under which the corporation can be incorporated validly.
2.   The parties must have made a good faith attempt to comply with the statute.

3. The enterprise must have already undertaken to do business as a corporation.

Practically speaking, the concept of *de facto* status has limited utility in modern corporate law. The Model Act and most state statutes agree that the issuance of a certificate of incorporation (charter) by the secretary of state is *prima facie* evidence of corporate status (that is, *de jure* corporation). However, the right of the state to command a corporation to correct irregularities in corporate formation can be enforced under the *de facto* doctrine.

CORPORATION BY ESTOPPEL Sometimes a corporation has neither *de jure* nor *de facto* status. When justice requires, the courts treat an alleged corporation as if it were an actual corporation for the purpose of determining the rights and liabilities involved in that particular situation. Corporation by estoppel is thus determined by the situation. It does not extend recognition of corporate status beyond the resolution of the problem at hand.

If an association which is neither an actual corporation nor a *de facto* or *de jure* corporation holds itself out as being a corporation, it will be estopped from denying corporate status in a lawsuit by such third party. This usually occurs when a third party contracts with an association which claims to be a corporation, but does not hold a certificate of incorporation. When the third party brings suit naming the "corporation" as the defendant, the association may not escape from liability on the ground that no corporation exists.

DISREGARDING THE CORPORATE ENTITY

Sometimes, a corporate entity is used by its owners to perpetrate a fraud, circumvent the law, or in some other way accomplish an illegitimate objective. In these cases, the court will ignore the corporate structure by "piercing the corporate veil" and will expose the shareholders to personal liability.

Adequate Capitalization

In other typical cases, a corporation may have insufficient capital at the time it is formed to meet its prospective debts or potential liabilities. Such "thin capitalization" is exacerbated when a corporation fails to obtain the amount of insurance that any reasonable business can be expected to have in the interest of public responsibility. Hence, victims who are injured may be able to reach the personal assets of stockholders to satisfy their claims.

MINTON v. CAVANEY
Supreme Court of California, 1961.
56 Cal. 2d 576, 15 Cal. Rptr. 641, 364 P.2d 473.

BACKGROUND AND FACTS *Minton's daughter drowned in a public swimming pool operated by Seminole Hot Springs Corporation (Seminole). Cavaney was a director and the secretary-treasurer of Seminole and was active in controlling the company's business. In response to the Mintons' suit to recover for Seminole's negligent management of the pool, Cavaney stated that Seminole had never had any assets and that, in fact, its lease on the pool was forfeited for non-payment of rent. The Mintons therefore sought to recover from Cavaney individually.*

DECISION AND RATIONALE *Cavaney was individually liable to the Mintons for the death of their daughter. He was not insulated by the shield of incorporation. The owners and directors of a corporation are personally liable if they actively participate in operating a corporation for which they have provided inadequate capitalization. The presiding* *justice stated: "In the instant case the evidence is undisputed that there was no attempt to provide adequate capitalization. Seminole never had any substantial assets. It leased the pool that it operated, and the lease was forfeited for failure to pay the rent. Its capital was trifling compared with the business to be done and the risks of loss."*

SEPARATION OF PERSONAL AND CORPORATE INTEREST

Often, corporations are formed according to law by a single person or by a few family members. The corporate entity and the sole stockholder (or family member stockholders) must carefully preserve the separate status of the corporation and its owners. Certain practices indicate potential trouble for the one-person or family-owned corporation—the commingling of corporate and personal funds, the failure to hold and record minutes of board of directors' meetings, or the shareholders' continuous, personal use of corporate property (for example vehicles). When the corporate privilege is abused for personal benefit and the corporate business is treated in such a careless manner that the corporation and the shareholder in control are no longer separate entities, the court will require an owner to assume personal liability to creditors for the corporation's debts.

In short, where the facts show that great injustice would result from use of a corporation to avoid individual responsibility, a court of equity will look behind the corporate structure to the individual stockholder.

General corporation law has no specific prohibition against a shareholder lawfully lending money to his or her corporation. However, when an officer or director lends money and takes back security in the form of corporate assets, the courts will scrutinize the transaction closely. Any such transaction must be made in good faith and for fair value.

In the following case, two shareholders made a lawful loan of money to a corporation (which later became insolvent) and in return took a security interest in certain pieces of corporate property. When the corporation became insolvent, some creditors charged that the shareholders' loan transaction was not made in good faith and therefore that their security interest should be set aside.

BACKGROUND AND FACTS *Langley and Clayton, fifteen percent shareholders in Olympic Homes Systems, Inc., loaned the corporation $42,500. In return, they took a promissory note at 8½ percent interest and a security interest in certain corporate property. Thereafter, the company became insolvent, and the general creditors sought to set aside the priority of Langley's and Clayton's security interest in the corporation's assets.*

INTERTHERM, INC. v. **OLYMPIC HOMES SYSTEMS, INC.**
Court of Appeals of Tennessee, 1978.
569 S.W.2d 467.

DECISION AND RATIONALE *Even though they were Olympic shareholders, Langley and Clayton could legitimately loan money to their company and thereby take security interests in some of its assets as long as the entire transaction was exercised with the utmost good faith. Since the terms of the loan and the security interest appeared to be reasonable, the transaction was in good faith. The court concluded: "It is * * * generally held * * * that courts will closely scrutinize the transactions of a majority, dominant, or controlling shareholder with his corporation, and will place the burden of proof upon the shareholder when the good faith* *and fairness of such a transaction is challenged. *** We hold that the instant transaction should not be subjected to close scrutiny, and that the burden of proof should not be on [Langley and Clayton] because plaintiffs have offered no evidence from which we could conclude that defendants owned a majority of Olympic's stock or otherwise dominated it in such a way as to justify imposing fiduciary responsibilities on them."*

QUESTIONS AND CASE PROBLEMS

1. During the early months of 1971, a number of persons began to organize a company later known as Timberjack of Alabama, Inc. On June 8, 1971, a day before the company was formally incorporated, it was assigned certain rights in collateral that was held by Eaton Yale, Ltd. On June 8, Timberjack repossessed the collateral, and on June 9, Timberjack was formally incorporated. Eaton then demanded that Timberjack return the collateral since the right to repossess it was in Timberjack, Inc., and Timberjack, Inc. did not exist on the day repossession took place. Can Eaton reclaim the goods? [In re Wilco Forest Machinery, Inc., 491 F.2d 1041 (5th Cir. 1974)]

2. Johnson, Linder, and Green were promoters for a venture that was to own and operate an outdoor theater. It was agreed that they were to receive 75 percent of the stock of the new firm for performing the necessary work to open the theater, and Nychyk was to invest $60,000 for the remaining 25 percent. Nychyk's investment was to cover the cost of capital improvements for the theater. Green, who performed much of the design work and labor for the theater, paid himself a salary of $9,000 from the $60,000 as a salary to cover his living expenses, although there was never any agreement for Green to use any of these funds for his living expenses. When the venture failed, Nychyk sought to recover the $9,000 used by Green. Can Nychyk recover? [Johnson v. Nychyk, 21 Ariz. App. 186, 517 P.2d 1079 (1974)]

3. Watchie, an entrepreneur, acquired the rights to buy certain property that was later to be developed into a large shopping center. Watchie interested a group of Seattle investors, known as the Seattle Syndicate, in purchasing the land. Over the next two years, Watchie was the promoter of a corporation whose investors contributed approximately $1.5 million for the purchase of the land sold to the Seattle Syndicate. Watchie then convinced the Seattle

Syndicate to sell the land to the newly formed corporation for $1,458,000 and convinced the investors that this was a good price. The Seattle Syndicate made a handsome profit on the sale, but Watchie shared in none of it. He was, however, paid a commission of $162,000 on the sale by the Seattle Syndicate. He failed to report this amount to the investors of the newly formed corporation. Can he retain it? [Park City Corp. v. Watchie, 249 Or. 493, 439 P.2d 587 (1968)]

4. In December 1971, Hartmann and Daffern contacted Jones, an architect, about designing a lodge and restaurant building that Hartmann and Daffern wanted to construct. At this meeting, architects' fees and the general financing of the project were discussed. At the request of Hartmann and Daffern, Jones began work on schematic drawings. After each segment of work that he completed, he sent a bill to Hartmann. Hartmann paid the bills with personal checks. Jones was aware that Hartmann and Daffern intended to incorporate at some point but never inquired as to when the incorporation was to take place. At about the same time that Hartmann and Daffern became D.H.F. Corporation, Jones informed Hartmann that he was beginning the next phase of the project, the working drawings. Hartmann consented. Neither Hartmann nor Daffern informed Jones that the two had incorporated. Later, D.H.F. Corporation became insolvent, and Jones sought to recover for his work on the working drawings from Hartmann and Daffern individually. Are Hartmann and Daffern liable? [Jones v. Hartmann, 541 P.2d 123 (Colo. App. 1975)]

5. Vodopich, a registered real estate broker, participated in a transaction involving the sale of land from Naples Bay Industries, Inc. to Basil F. Mulley. For his services, Vodopich was entitled to a 10 percent commission, but he subsequently agreed to forego his rights to the commission in consideration for the exclusive right to resell the property. This agreement was reached orally between Vodopich and Mulley and other persons who were promoting

the creation of a corporation that was to become Collier County Development, Inc. At the time the agreement was made, Vodopich was aware that the corporation did not yet exist. Subsequently, Collier County Development, Inc. was duly incorporated, but neither it nor Mulley lived up to the agreement with Vodopich concerning the exclusive resale rights. Who will be the successful party in a lawsuit between Vodopich and Mulley and between Vodopich and Collier County Development, Inc.? [Vodopich v. Collier County Development, Inc., 319 So.2d 43 (Fla. App. 1975)]

6. Wesley Philpot and his wife engaged the services of Bob Childs Realty Company, Inc. to sell a tract of real estate. Childs Realty sold the property and demanded a commission from the Philpots. The Philpots refused to pay on the ground that Childs Realty had not complied with the Arkansas brokers' law, which required brokers to be incorporated before they could be licensed. Childs Realty argued that it should be deemed a corporation since its president had signed articles of incorporation, and it held itself out as a corporation by use of the designation "Inc." Has Bob Childs Realty Company complied with the Arkansas statute requiring licensed real estate brokers to be incorporated? [Childs v. Philpot, 253 Ark. 589, 487 S.W.2d 637 (1972)]

7. New Liberty Medical and Hospital Corporation entered into an agreement with New Liberty Hospital District under which the hospital district agreed to purchase the hospital's debentures under the sole condition that the debentures be legally issued. The district then attempted to avoid its obligation under the agreement with the hospital claiming that, even though the hospital held a proper certificate of incorporation issued by the secretary of state of Missouri, it did not properly comply with all of the statutory requirements of nonprofit corporations. In a suit by the hospital against the district to enforce the agreement, can the district raise this defense? Explain. [New Liberty Medical and Hospital Corp. v. E.F.Hutton and Co., 474 S.W.2d 1 (Mo. 1971)]

8. In a proceeding initiated by the Internal Revenue Service to seize certain records from Theodore Accounting Service, P.A., Charles Theodore, the company's vice-president, refused to turn over the records. He argued that since Theodore Accounting Service, P.A., never filed the articles of association required by South Carolina law, the partnership never became a valid corporation. The requested records, therefore, were the personal property of Charles Theodore and entitled to Fifth Amendment protection. Theodore Accounting Service had used the notation "P.A." on its federal tax returns and had claimed tax status as a corporation for the past three years. Can the IRS seize the records it seeks? [United States v. Theodore, 479 F.2d 749 (4th Cir. 1973)]

9. Slowek and Zamparelli are doing business under the assumed name of "New York Office of Consumer Interest" pursuant to a certificate duly filed in the Albany county clerk's office. Their firm is engaged in the business of soliciting advertising from contractors and home repair and improvement businesses for the purpose of publishing a booklet offering the prices of these advertisers. The booklet is called "Consumers' Home Improvement Guide." Should the attorney general for the state of New York take any action against Slowek and Zamparelli? [Lefkowitz v. Slowek, 79 Misc. 2d 1098, 362 N.Y.S.2d 110 (1974)]

10. Rosenbloom was the promoter for a new corporation that was to be known as Multinational Opportunities Investments. In order to finance the corporation, Rosenbloom sought out Thomas and Dorothy Howett as investors. The Howetts subscribed to one hundred shares of International Diversified stock at a price of $10 a share. This pre-incorporation subscription was signed and delivered to Rosenbloom on March 1, 1973. One month later, Multinational Opportunities Investments was duly incorporated under the laws of Delaware, but the articles of incorporation authorized only fifty shares of stock. Multinational Opportunities Investments became a highly successful company, and the Howetts wished to recover damages for the fifty shares of stock they never received. Can they recover? [Hidell v. International Diversified Investments, 520 F.2d 529 (7th Cir. 1975)]

41

Corporations
Corporate Powers and Management

CORPORATE POWERS

Express Powers

The express powers of a corporation are found in its articles of incorporation, in the law of the state of incorporation, and in the state and federal constitutions. The order of priority used when conflicts arise among documents involving corporations is: (1) the United States Constitution, (2) state constitutions, (3) state statutes, (4) the certificate of incorporation (charter), (5) bylaws, and (6) resolutions of the board of directors.

It is important to keep in mind that the corporation is a "legal person." Under modern law, except as limited by charter, statutes, or constitution, a corporation can engage in all acts and enter into any contract available to a natural person *in order to accomplish the purposes for which it was created.*

Implied Powers

Certain inherent powers attach when a corporation is created. Barring express constitutional, statutory, or charter prohibitions, the corporation has the implied power to do all acts reasonably appropriate and necessary to accomplish its corporate purpose. For this reason, a corporation has the implied power to borrow money within certain limits, to lend money or extend credit to those with whom it has a legal or contractual relationship, and to make charitable contributions.[1]

---

1. The right of a corporation to make political contributions in federal elections is prohibited by the Federal Elections Campaign Act. [18 USC Sec. 321]

To borrow money, the corporation acts through its board of directors to authorize the execution of negotiable paper. Most often, the president or chief executive officer of the corporation will execute the necessary papers on behalf of the corporation. In so doing, corporate officers have the implied power to bind the corporation in matters directly connected with the ordinary business affairs of the enterprise. This is the issue in the next case.

BACKGROUND AND FACTS   *Bentall loaned $5,000 to Koenig Brothers, a corporation. Through it president, Poulsen, Koenig Brothers executed a promissory note. Koenig Brothers had hired Poulsen under an agreement with its stockholders that Poulsen have an option to purchase Koenig stock and that he have as well "full management and control of the affairs of said corporation." Subsequently, however, Koenig Brothers refused to pay the note, claiming that Poulsen's status as president was not enough to give him the authority to bind the corporation on a promissory note.*

F. M. BENTALL v. KOENIG BROTHERS, INC.
Supreme Court of Montana, 1962.
140 Mont. 339, 372 P.2d 91.

DECISION AND RATIONALE   *Koenig Brothers was liable on the note to Bentall. It is true that the president of a corporation does not have the power, merely be virtue of the office alone, to execute negotiable instruments in the name of the corporation. "Where, however, such power is specially conferred upon him [president] *** by the corporate charter or by a resolution or by-law of the board of directors, or, where such power exists, by implication from the nature of the agency or by reason of his *** being held out by custom or course of dealing as having such authority, or being intrusted with the conduct and management of the corporate affairs, which requires the use of such instruments in the ordinary course of the business, the president *** may bind the corporation by the execution *** of negotiable papers ***."*

Ultra Vires Doctrine

The term *ultra vires* means "beyond the powers." In corporate law, acts of a corporation that are beyond the authority given to it under its charter or under the statutes by which it was incorporated are *ultra vires* acts.

Ultra vires acts can be understood only within the context of the particular purpose for which the corporation was organized. Acts in furtherance of the corporation's expressed purposes are within the corporate power; acts beyond the scope of corporate business as described in the charter are *ultra vires*.

The majority of cases dealing with *ultra vires* acts have involved contracts made for unauthorized purposes. For example, it is hard to know how a contract made by a plumbing company for the purchase of six thousand cases of vodka is reasonably related to the conduct and furtherance of the corporation's main purpose of providing plumbing installation and services. Hence, such a contract would probably be held *ultra vires*.

Corporate acts can be *ultra vires* simply in the sense of being beyond corporate powers. Such acts are not necessarily illegal; however, all illegal acts are inherently *ultra vires*.

In certain cases, the law recognizes the right of a shareholder to sue the board of directors for its alleged wrongful exercise of business judgment on behalf of the corporation. A stockholder can bring what is called a *derivative suit* against the corporation by first demanding that the directors correct the wrong. Failing that, the stockholder can ask the court to enforce the corporate right.

Certain acts of the board of directors can be unauthorized at the time they first occur but ratified later by a majority vote of the stockholders. Such ratification of the board of directors' actions by a majority of shareholders will ordinarily cure an otherwise voidable wrong. However, certain acts, such as waste of corporate assets, will usually require unanimous shareholder action for ratifying or condoning the wrong.

The Model Business Corporation Act essentially abolishes the *ultra vires* doctrine. Under Section 7 of the act, the doctrine cannot be asserted by the corporation as a means of avoiding its contractual obligations except in three very limited circumstances.

MICHELSON v. DUNCAN

Court of Chancery Delaware, 1978. 386 A.2d 1144.

BACKGROUND AND FACTS   In 1966, HFC, Inc., instituted an employee stock option plan as a means of retaining the services of valued employees as well as obtaining the services of new employees. In April 1974, due to a drop in the market price of HFC stock, the board of directors adopted a resolution canceling the 1966 plan and replacing it with one that allowed employees to purchase HFC's stock for a lower price. This was done to maintain the incentive value of the stock option plan. Michelson, a stockholder, brought a derivative suit against the board of directors and against the corporation alleging that the board of directors violated its fiduciary duties to the corporation and its stockholders by unauthorized modification of the stock option plan. Prior to the trial, the board's action was ratified by a majority of HFC's stockholders. The ratification, however, was not unanimous.

DECISION AND RATIONALE   The directors of HFC did not breach their fiduciary duty in modifying the stock option plan. Generally, stock option plans are an acceptable means by which corporations gain the services of valued employees. Even though the board of directors was not authorized to modify such a plan, ratification by the majority of the stockholders bound the corporation.

With his derivative suit, Michelson sought to have the board of directors reimburse the corporation for its alleged waste of corporate assets. Michelson was not seeking recovery for himself personally. But, as stated above, HFC was not entitled to recover from its board of directors because, in the opinion of the court, "the acts of the individual defendants in modifying the Stock Option Plan were subsequently ratified by an overwhelming vote of approval by the stockholders. If the ratification process was proper, in the absence of any allegation or showing of a gift or waste of corporate assets the ratification disposes of the allegations of Michelson."

When officers or directors breach their duty to the corporation, the corporation has a claim against the wrongdoers and can seek damages for breach of duty. Since the corporation can act only through its officers and directors, it is unlikely that the wrongdoers will cause the corporation to bring suit against themselves. In certain instances, a shareholder has the right to bring suit on behalf of the corporation. This suit is called a derivative suit,[2] and any recovery from it goes to the corporation.[3]

Before a derivative action can be filed, a stockholder must make a demand to the directors that the corporation bring suit. This gives management a chance to investigate the claim, after which management can have the corporation file suit on its own behalf.[4]

Judicial Treatment of *Ultra Vires*

The courts have treated *ultra vires* in a variety of ways. One treatment is based upon the common law principle of agency whereby an unauthorized contract made by an agent is void—no rights or duties arise for either party. Early decisions often held that *ultra vires* contracts were void.

The more modern approach is to uphold the validity of contracts that have been performed by all sides. In some states, when a contract is entirely executory, neither party having performed, a defense of *ultra vires* can be used by either party to prevent enforcement of the contract. The current trend in dealing with *ultra vires* contracts is embodied in statutory enactments similar to Section 7 of the Model Act, which upholds the validity and enforceability of an *ultra vires* contract as between the parties involved. However, the right of shareholders on behalf of the corporation, the right of the corporation itself to recover damages from the officers and directors who caused the transaction, and the right of the attorney general of the state to institute an injunction against the transaction or to institute

dissolution proceedings against the corporation for *ultra vires* acts have been upheld.

BROAD STATEMENT OF PURPOSE Corporations are increasingly aware of the benefit of adopting a very broad statement of purpose to include virtually all conceivable activities. Corporate statutes in many states permit the expression "any lawful purpose" to be a legally sufficient stated purpose in the articles of incorporation.

Torts and Criminal Acts

A corporation is liable for the torts committed by its agents or officers within the course and scope of their employment. A corporation can act only through its agents and servants. This principle applies to a corporation exactly as it applies to the ordinary agency relationships discussed in Chapter 35. It follows the doctrine of *respondeat superior.*

At common law, a corporation could not be held liable for a crime, particularly one that required intent. However, under modern criminal law, a corporation can sometimes be held liable for the criminal acts of its agents and employees, provided the punishment can be applied to the corporation.

CORPORATE MANAGEMENT: SHAREHOLDERS

Shareholders' Position in the Corporation

SHAREHOLDER POWERS Shareholders must approve fundamental changes affecting the corporation. Hence, shareholders are empowered to amend the articles of incorporation (charter) and bylaws, merger, consolidation, dissolution, and the sale of all or substantially all of the corporation's assets *outside the ordinary course of business.*

Election and removal of the board of directors are accomplished by vote of the share-

---

2. A derivative suit is different from a shareholder's individual suit, in which the plaintiff-shareholder claims that the wrongdoing directly injured a group of shareholders.
3. In the rare instances where recovery to the corporation would result in a windfall to a third party or to the wrongdoers, a court will award minority shareholders individual *pro rata* recovery. See Perlman v. Feldmann, 219 F.2d 173 [2d Cir., cert denied 349 U.S. 952, 75 S.Ct. 880 (1955)].
4. In certain limited circumstances, a demand on the board will be excused. For example, if the alleged wrongdoers constituted a majority of the board of directors, a demand would be futile.

holders. The first board of directors is either named in the articles of incorporation or chosen by the incorporators to serve until the first shareholders' meeting. From that time on, selection and retention of directors are exclusively a shareholder function.

Directors usually serve their full term. If they are unsatisfactory, they are simply not reelected. Shareholders have the inherent power to remove a director from office *for cause* (breach of duty or misconduct) by a majority vote.[5] Some state statutes permit removal of directors without cause by the vote of a majority of the holders of outstanding shares entitled to vote.[6] Some corporate charters expressly provide that shareholders, by majority vote or larger than majority vote, can remove a director at any time *without cause.*

---

5. A director can demand court review of removal for cause.
6. Some states provide for cumulative voting for directors. In states in which voting for directors is by cumulative ballot, a director cannot be removed without cause over the negative vote which would be sufficient to elect that director in the first place. See, for example, California Corporate Code, Sec. 303A.

GRACE v. GRACE INSTITUTE

Court of Appeals of New York, 1967.
19 N.Y.2d 307, 279 N.Y.S.2d 721, 226 N.E.2d 531.

BACKGROUND AND FACTS *The Grace Institute was incorporated in the state of New York as a charitable corporation. Michael P. Grace was a life member of the board of trustees of the Institute. As a result of a series of unsuccessful lawsuits that he brought against Grace Institute, the other trustees drew up charges against him, and a hearing was held. Michael was removed as a trustee and life member of the Institute despite the fact that neither the incorporating statute nor the bylaws of the corporation provided for the removal of a life member. Michael sued for reinstatement.*

DECISION AND RATIONALE *Michael had no legal right to reinstatement. The court stated: "It has been the consistent policy of the courts of this State to avoid interference with the internal management and operation of corporations. *** [T]he evidence clearly supported the finding of the trustees that Michael had embarked on a course of conduct designed to involve the Institute in endless and costly litigation and that the suits were undertaken for the purpose of harassing the Institute and its members. Under these circumstances, courts should not substitute their judgment for the judgment of those charged by the Legislature with the responsibility of running the corporation and seeing to it that it fulfills the purpose for which it was created."*

THE RELATIONSHIP BETWEEN THE SHAREHOLDER AND THE CORPORATION As a general rule, shareholders have no responsibility for the daily management of the corporation, but they are ultimately responsible for choosing the board of directors, which does have such control. Ordinarily, corporate officers and other employees owe no direct duty to individual stockholders. Their duty is to the corporation as a whole. However, a director is in a fiduciary relationship to the corporation and therefore serves the interests of the shareholders as a whole.

Generally, there is no legal relationship between shareholders and creditors of the corporation. Shareholders can, in fact, be creditors of the corporation and have the same rights of recovery against the corporation as any other creditor. The rights and liabilities of creditors and shareholders are discussed in Chapter 44.

SHAREHOLDERS' FORUM

Commonly, shareholders' meetings occur annually, but special meetings can be called to take care of urgent matters. Since it is not practical for most small shareholders of publicly-traded corporations to attend the shareholders' meetings, they normally give third persons a written authorization to vote their shares at the meeting. This authorization, called a proxy, is often solicited by management.

Shareholders in a corporation enjoy both common law and statutory inspection rights. Shareholders at common law enjoyed qualified rights to inspect corporate books and records, such as the bylaws and minutes of the board of directors' executive committee, and shareholders' meetings, as well as any other documents, such as contracts, correspondence, and tax returns. They even had the right to inspect the corporate headquarters.

The shareholders' common law inspection rights exist concurrently with any rights created by statute. However, corporate statutes do not usually deal with shareholders' right to inspect the minutes of the board of directors' or shareholders' meetings, the bylaws, or other records. The shareholders' common law right of inspection operates in these cases.

Notice of Meetings

The notice and time of meetings, including the day and the hour, is announced in writing to each shareholder a reasonable time [7] prior to the date of the shareholder meeting.[8] Special meeting notices must include a statement of the purpose of the meeting; business transacted at a special meeting is limited to that purpose.

Shareholder Voting

In order for shareholders to act, a minimum number of them (in terms of number of shares held) must be present at a meeting. This minimum number, called a **quorum,** is generally more than 50 percent. Corporate business matters are presented in the form of *resolutions*, which shareholders vote to approve or disapprove. Some state statutes have set forth voting limits, and corporations, articles, or bylaws must remain within the statutory limitations. Some states provide that the unanimous written consent of shareholders is a permissible alternative to holding a shareholders' meeting.

Once a quorum is present, a majority vote of the shares represented at the meeting is usually required to pass resolutions. Assume that Midwestern Supply, Inc., has 10,000 outstanding shares of voting stock. Its articles set the quorum at 50 percent of outstanding shares and provide that a majority vote of shares present is necessary to pass on ordinary matters. At the shareholders' meeting a *quorum* of stockholders representing 5,000 outstanding shares must be present to conduct business, and a *vote* of at least 2,501 of those shares represented at the meeting is needed to pass ordinary resolutions. If more than 5,000 are present, a larger vote will be needed.

At times, a larger than majority vote will be required either by statute or by corporation charter. Extraordinary corporate matters such as merger, consolidation, or dissolution of the corporation will require a higher percentage of the representatives of *all* corporate stock shares entitled to vote, not just a portion of those present at that particular meeting.

Voting Lists

Voting lists are prepared by the corporation prior to each shareholder meeting. Persons whose names appear on the corporation's stockholder records as the record owners of the shares are the persons ordinarily entitled to vote.[9] The voting list contains the name and

---

7. The shareholder can waive the requirement of written notice by signing a waiver form. A shareholder who did not receive written notice, but who learned of the meeting and attended without protesting the lack of notice, is said to have waived notice by such conduct.

8. State statutes and the bylaws typically set forth a minimum allowance notice requirement.

9. Where the legal owner is deceased, bankrupt, incompetent, or in some other way under a legal disability, his or her vote can be cast by a person designated by law to control and manage the owner's property.

address of each shareholder as shown on the corporate records on a given cutoff date (record date). It also includes the number of voting shares held by each owner. The list is usually kept at the corporate headquarters and is available for shareholder inspection.

Voting Techniques Some states permit or require shareholders to elect directors by *cumulative voting,* a method of voting designed to insure minority representation on the board of directors.[10] Under cumulative voting, stockholders are permitted to accumulate their votes and cast them for one or more nominees for director. All nominees stand for election at the same time. To illustrate, Scott owns 100 shares of stock in White Machinery Corporation. There are two director positions to be filled at the annual shareholders' meeting. Three candidates—Joseph White, Bryan Field, and Debbee Marshall—are running for these two positions. Under ordinary voting procedures, Scott would cast one vote per share, or 100 votes for each directorship to be filled. Under the cumulative voting method, Scott is permitted to cast the total number of votes to which he is entitled for all positions to be filled in the election (200 votes) and to distribute these votes among the candidates in any way he chooses. Thus, Scott can give all 200 votes to Joseph White, or he can give 190 votes to White and 10 votes to Field, or he can even give 50 votes to Field and 100 votes to Marshall and not vote 50 shares.

Cumulative voting is permitted by nearly every corporate statute if it is provided for in the corporation's charter. It is a mandatory method of voting for directors in a few states. In corporations not having cumulative voting, the entire board can be elected by stockholders voting a majority of those shares at the meeting.

VOTING TRUST Shareholders can enter an agreement (a trust contract) whereby legal title (record ownership on the corporate books) is transferred to a trustee who is responsible for voting the shares. The agreement can specify how the trustee is to vote, or it can allow the trustee to use his or her discretion. The trustee takes physical possession of the actual stock certificate and in return gives the shareholder a "voting trust certificate." The shareholder retains all rights of ownership (for example, the right to receive dividend payments) except the power to vote.[11]

CORPORATE MANAGEMENT: DIRECTORS

Position

Every corporation is governed by directors. Subject to statutory limitations, the number of directors is set forth in the corporation's articles or bylaws. Historically, the minimum number of directors has been three, but today many states permit fewer.

Few qualifications are legally required of directors. Only a handful of states retain minimum age and residency requirements. A director is sometimes a shareholder, but this is not a necessary qualification unless, of course, statutory provisions, corporate articles, or bylaws require ownership.

Compensation for directors is ordinarily specified in the corporate articles or bylaws. Because directors are in a *fiduciary* relationship to the shareholders and to the corporation, an express agreement or provision for compensation is necessary for them to receive money from the funds they control or for which they have responsibilities.

The first board of directors is normally appointed by the incorporators upon the creation of the corporation, or directors are named by the corporation itself in the articles. The first board serves until the first annual shareholders' meeting. Subsequent directors are elected by majority vote of the shareholders.

The term of office for a director is one

---

10. See, for example, the California Corporate Code, Sec. 708.

11. Under Section 34 of the Model Act, the term of a voting trust cannot exceed ten years.

year—from annual meeting to annual meeting. Longer and staggered terms are permissible under most state statutes. A board of directors can be divided into categories. A common practice is to have three classes, so that one-third of the board is elected each year for a three-year term. In this way, there is greater management continuity.[12]

Sometimes the board of directors itself can be empowered by the corporate articles or bylaws to remove a director *for cause*—even though it can *never* remove without cause. The board's action is subject to review by the shareholders.

When vacancies occur on the board of directors due to death or resignation, or when a new position is created through amendment of the articles or bylaws, either the shareholders or the board itself can fill the position, depending on state law or the provisions of the bylaws.

Management Responsibilities

Directors have responsibility for all policy-making decisions necessary to the management of all corporate affairs. Just as shareholders cannot act individually to bind the corporation, the directors must act as a body in carrying out routine corporate business. One director has one vote, and generally the majority rules.

The general areas of responsibility of the board of directors include:

1. Declaration and payment of corporate dividends to shareholders.
2. Authorization for major corporate policy decisions—for example, the initiation of proceedings for the sale or lease of corporate assets outside the regular course of business, the determination of new product lines, and the overseeing of major contract negotiations and major management-labor negotiations.
3. Appointment, supervision and removal of corporate officers and other managerial employees and the determination of their compensation.

4. Financial decisions involving such things as the issuance of authorized shares or bonds.

Directors' Liability

Honest mistakes of judgment and poor business actions on the part of the directors do not make them liable to the corporation for damages sustained. After all, directors are not insurers of the business success of the corporation. They must be loyal, honest, and reasonably careful, however. If directors (and officers) hire employees carefully, they are not personally liable for the willful wrongs and negligent acts of such employees; rather, the corporation is liable.

When, however, a director never attends board meetings nor examines records and books, he or she can be held liable for losses resulting from unsupervised acts of officers and employees. Also, when directors (and officers) allow the assets of the corporation to be diverted to objectives outside the charter or statutory powers, they may be held liable for damages to the corporation, to a trustee appointed for the corporation, or to the shareholders in a derivative suit.

The Board of Directors' Forum

The board of directors conducts business by holding formal meetings with recorded minutes.[13] The date upon which regular meetings are held is usually established in the articles and bylaws or by board resolution, and no further notice is customarily required. Special meetings can be called with notice sent to all directors.

Quorum requirements can vary among jurisdictions. Many states leave the decision to the corporate articles or bylaws. Voting is done *in person* (unlike voting at shareholders' meetings, which can be done by proxy).[14] The rule is one vote per director. Ordinary matters generally require a majority vote; certain extraordinary issues can require a larger than majority vote.

---

12. Of course, staggered boards defeat the purpose of cumulative voting.

13. Michigan now has a corporate statute authorizing conference phone calls for a board of directors' meeting.

14. Except in Louisiana, where a director can vote by proxy under certain circumstances.

Delegation of Board of Directors' Powers

The board of directors can delegate some of its functions to an executive committee or to corporate officers. In doing so, the board does not avoid its responsibility for directing the affairs of the corporation. Rather, the daily responsibilities of corporate management are given over to corporate officers and managerial personnel, who are empowered to make decisions relating to *ordinary corporate affairs* within *well-defined guidelines*.

Executive Committee   Most states permit the board of directors to elect an executive committee from among the directors to handle the interim management decisions between board of directors' meetings as provided in the bylaws. The *executive committee* is limited to making management decisions about ordinary business matters.

Corporate Officers   The officers and other executive employees are hired by the board of directors or, in rare instances, by the shareholders. In addition to the duties that are articulated in the bylaws, corporate and managerial officers are agents of the corporation, and the ordinary rules of agency apply or have been applied to their employment (unlike the board of directors, whose powers are conferred by the state). Qualifications are determined, in the main, at the discretion of the corporation and are included in the articles or bylaws. In most states, a person can hold more than one office. Corporate officers can be removed by the board of directors at any time with or without cause and regardless of the terms of the employment contract, although the corporation can still be liable for breach of contract damages.

QUESTIONS AND CASE PROBLEMS

1.   Woods, the president of Pecos Valley Gas Company, signed a contract with Greenspon Iron and Steel Company for the purchase of forty-five miles of gas pipe for sixty-one cents per foot. The board of directors of Pecos Valley, however, had instructed Woods not to sign the contract, and Pecos Valley refused to accept delivery of the pipe. Greenspon sued Pecos Valley for breach of contract, and Pecos Valley defended on the ground that Woods was not acting within the usual scope of his office, that in the past he had never had the authority to sign contracts for the company unless the board of directors approved. Greenspon had never done business with Pecos Valley before. Will Greenspon recover? [Joseph Greenspon's Sons Iron and Steel Co. v. Pecos Valley Gas Co., 156 A. 350 (Del. Super. Ct. 1931)]

2.   Harris Lumber Company was a corporation organized under the law of the state of Arkansas. Harris was the president of the corporation; Nelson was its secretary and treasurer; and Jones was its remaining director and shareholder. Several years after its incorporation, Harris Lumber owed Merchants and Farmers Bank $4,500. A promissory note was executed for the amount of the debt, and a mortgage was executed on certain personal property owned by Harris Lumber to secure payment. Nelson, who at the time was general manager of Harris Lumber, signed both the note and the mortgage. Payments amounting to $2,150 were made over the next two and one-half years on the promissory note. At that point payment ceased, and Merchants Bank brought this suit to recover the balance of the sum owed. Harris Lumber Company never objected to the execution of the mortgage or the note or to any of the payments under the note until Merchants Bank filed this suit. However, at that point, Harris Lumber claimed that Nelson did not have the authority to sign promissory notes or to execute mortgages on behalf of Harris Lumber. In fact, neither the corporate charter nor any of the board of directors' resolutions vested the general manager with any authority to bind the corporation. Will Merchants Bank be successful in its suit against Harris Lumber Company? [Merchants and Farmers Bank v. Harris Lumber Co., 103 Ark. 283, 146 S.W. 508 (1912)]

3.   Capital Electric Power Association, a utility, had 10,000 shares of stock authorized, issued, and outstanding. Capital's articles of incorporation provided that voters holding 50 percent of its outstanding shares constituted a quorum. At a shareholders'

meeting, only two shareholders appeared. Each held exactly 2,000 shares, but one also had the proxies of 600 shareholders. Can any official action be undertaken at the shareholders' meeting? [McNair v. Capital Electric Ass'n., 324 So.2d. 234, (Miss. 1975)]

4. Monaghan Land Co. was organized by a number of incorporators to "buy, hold and sell" a one-half interest in a piece of land known as the Sicily Island Tract. A majority of the stockholders of Monaghan entered into a voting trust agreement under which trustees were given the right to vote all of the majority shares at all meetings and in all proceedings where stockholder consent was required by law. At a subsequent stockholders' meeting, the trustees voted to sell the Sicily Island Tract, which constituted substantially all of Monaghan's assets. Can the stockholders who parted with their voting rights object? [Clarke Memorial College v. Monaghan Land Co., 257 A.2d. 234 (Del. Ch. 1969)]

5. Edward Beresth, Gershon Weil, Nathan Weil, and Raymond Harrison comprised all the directors of Self Service Sales Corporation and were holders of a majority of its stock. On August 27, the above stockholders entered into a voting agreement under which they agreed to call a meeting to approve the following amendments to the bylaws: (1) that three directors would constitute a quorum and (2) that the stockholders would not thereafter vote to amend the bylaws "so adopted" without consent of all four of the signatories to the agreement. Thereafter, in an attempt to squeeze out Nathan Weil, the other three directors voted to *repeal* the bylaw that provided that three directors constituted a quorum and *replace* it with a bylaw establishing that two directors would constitute a quorum. Can Nathan Weil legally stop this? [Weil v. Beresth, 154 Conn. 12, 220 A.2d. 456 (1966)]

6. The capital stock of G.S.P. Corporation was owned by Plodzik, Ricketts, and Westbury, who were also the sole directors of the corporation. In 1965, Plodzik and Ricketts agreed to sell their company to Star Corporation. Since Plodzik and Ricketts constituted two-thirds of the shareholders of G.S.P. Corporation, as well as a majority of the board of directors, they took this action without consulting Westbury. Have Plodzik and Ricketts exceeded their authority? [Star Corp. v. General Screw Products Co., 501 S.W.2d 374 (Tex. Civ. App. 1973)]

7. Orloff was both secretary and director of the Stott Realty Company. The majority of Stott Realty's board of directors directed the secretary to sign certain mortgage papers. Orloff refused, both as secretary

and director, to sign them. Shortly thereafter, at a full meeting of the board of directors, she was removed from both offices, and T. P. Danahey was appointed to fill both vacancies. Was the board of directors' action proper? [Stott v. Stott Realty Co., 246 Mich. 267, 224 N.W.623 (1929)]

8. Scott N. Brown, the president of First Trust Company, was also president or controlling shareholder in a number of other companies. As president of First Trust, Brown authorized a number of loans to the companies that he dominated. The directors of First Trust knew of the loans and also knew that most were unsecured, but they never objected to any of the loans made by First Trust to Brown's companies; nor did they examine the companies' financial reports. In fact, the directors virtually turned the entire management of First Trust over to Brown because of their faith in him as an entrepreneur. First Trust later became insolvent in large measure due to the loans that it had made to several of Brown's other companies. The trustee in bankruptcy of First Trust, representing First Trust's creditors, wished to recover from the directors of First Trust for the damages sustained as a result of the loans. Are the directors of First Trust liable? [Neese v. Brown, 218 Tenn. 686, 405 S.W.2d. 577 (1964)]

9. Free For All Missionary Baptist Church, Inc., by and through its pastors (who were also its president and secretary), leased from Southeastern Beverage and Ice Equipment Company, Inc., certain liquor dispensary equipment for use in an establishment known as Soul On Top of Peachtree. The church made an initial payment of $1,575 and then defaulted on the monthly rental payments. Southeastern brought suit against the church corporation, seeking damages for the balance of the lease. The shareholders of the church corporation defended on the ground that the action by its president and secretary and by the church were all *ultra vires*. Is this a valid defense? [Free For All Missionary Baptist Church, Inc. v. Southeastern Beverage and Ice Equipment Co., Inc., 135 Ga. App. 498, 218 S.E.2d. 169 (1975)]

10. On July 1, 1924, Ralston Purina Company hired Harker under the terms of a five-year employment contract. The contract provided that Ralston was to sell Harker 290 shares of its capital stock immediately at $25 per share, which was substantially less than the actual value of the stock. The contract further provided that if Harker stopped working at Ralston for any reason other than his death within the next five years, Ralston would have the power to repurchase the stock from Harker at the price Harker paid. Prior to April

15, 1928, Harker completed payment of the purchase price of the stock, and on that date his employment for some reason came to an end. Ralston Purina wished to enforce the contract and repurchase the stock from Harker. Harker argued that such a repurchase would be *ultra vires* since a corporation could not enter into an agreement to repurchase its own stock from an employee. Is Harker's argument sound? [Harker v. Ralston Purina Co., 45 F.2d. 929 (7th Cir. 1930)]

42

Corporations
Special Corporate Forms
and Benefits of Incorporating

Chapter 36 mentioned several specialized classifications of corporations, such as Subchapter S corporations, closely-held corporations, and professional corporations. This chapter will examine certain of these classifications in more detail. The last part of the chapter will look briefly at the costs and benefits of starting a corporation.

THE SUBCHAPTER S CORPORATION

Certain corporations can choose to qualify under Subchapter S of the Internal Revenue Code to avoid the imposition of income taxes at the corporate level while retaining all the advantages of a corporation, particularly limited legal liability. A Subchapter S corporation is sometimes known as a *tax option* corporation. Basically, it elects to be taxed in a manner similar to that of a partnership—to file only an informational return that allocates income among the shareholders regardless of dividend distributions. This is the way corporate taxes can be avoided. While the Subchapter S corporation has the advantages of the corporate form without the double taxation of income (corporate income is not taxed separately), it does have some disadvantages. One of the most important disadvantages relates to the amount of income that can be placed in pension plans that permit corporate shareholders to shelter income from personal federal income taxes.

Requirements for Subchapter S Qualification

There are numerous requirements for Subchapter S qualification. The following are some of the more important:

1.   The corporation must be a domestic corporation.
2.   The corporation must not be a member of an affiliated group of corporations.
3.   The shareholders of the corporation must be either individuals, estates, or certain trusts that are treated as owned by the grantor. Corporations and partnerships cannot be shareholders.
4.   For taxable years beginning after 1978, the corporation must have fifteen or fewer shareholders.
5.   The corporation can have only one class of stock; all shareholders have the same voting rights.
6.   The corporation must not derive more than 20 percent of its gross receipts from passive investment income.
7.   The corporation cannot derive more than 80 percent of its gross receipts from outside the United States.
8.   No shareholder of the corporation can be a nonresident alien.

Benefits of Electing Subchapter S

At times, it is beneficial for a regular corporation to elect Subchapter S status. Below are checklists of situations where Subchapter S election can be beneficial.

1.   When the corporation has losses, the Subchapter S election allows the shareholders to use them to offset other income.
2.   Whenever the stockholders are in a lower tax bracket than the corporation, the Subchapter S election causes their entire income to be taxed in the shareholders' bracket, whether or not it is distributed. This is particularly attractive when the corporation wants to accumulate earnings for some future business purpose.
3.   Taxable income of a Subchapter S corporation is taxable only to those who are shareholders at the end of the corporate year when that income is distributed.
4.   The Subchapter S corporation can choose a fiscal year that will permit it to defer some of its shareholders' taxes. This is important because undistributed earnings are not taxed to the shareholder until after the corporation's (not the shareholder's) year.
5.   The shareholder in a Subchapter S corporation can give some of his or her stock to other members of the family who are in a lower tax bracket.
6.   A Subchapter S corporation can still offer some tax-free corporate benefits. These fringe benefits can mean federal tax savings to the shareholders.

CLOSE CORPORATIONS

This section deals with close corporations—sometimes called closed corporations, closely-held corporations, family corporations, or privately-held corporations. A close corporation is one whose shares are closely held by members of a family or by relatively few persons. Usually, the members of the small group that is involved in a close corporation are personally known to each other. Because there is such a small number of shareholders, there is no trading market for the shares.

In practice, a close corporation is often operated like a partnership. A few states recognize this in the special statutory provisions that cover close corporations. Under these statutes, a number of the formalities and mechanics required of a regular corporation are waived. Under Maryland statute, for example, the close corporation can elect to eliminate the board of directors.

Close Corporation Statutes

In order to be eligible for close corporation status, a corporation has to have a limited number of shareholders, the transfer of corporation stock must be subject to certain restrictions, and the corporation must not make any public offering of its securities.[1] Close corporation statutes provide greater flexibility by expressly permitting electing corporations to vary significantly from traditional corporation law.[2]

Management

The close corporation has a single shareholder or a closely-knit group of shareholders who usually hold the positions of directors and officers. The management of a close corporation resembles that of a sole proprietorship or a partnership. In the eyes of the law, however, it is still a corporation and must meet the same legal requirements as other corporations subject to the special statutes mentioned above. In states where special statutes have not been enacted, close corporations have sometimes had to circumvent the law.

Consider an example where a state law requires that a corporation have two directors, and a close corporation has only one shareholder. In the articles of incorporation, the number of directors can be set at two, but the corporation can operate with a permanent vacancy on the board of directors. Alternatively, a disinterested person, usually a friend, or the incorporators' attorney, can be convinced to put his or her name down as director.

1. See, for example, 8 Del. Code Annotated, Sec. 342. This section provides that electing corporations must have a maximum limitation on the number of shareholders, not exceeding thirty.
2. For example, in some states, the close corporation need not have a board of directors.

Transfer of Shares

Since, by definition, a close corporation has a small number of shareholders, the transfer of shares of one shareholder to someone else can cause serious management problems. In other words, the other shareholders can find themselves required to share control with someone they either do not know or do not like. To avoid this problem, it is usually advisable for the close corporation with several shareholders to specify restrictions on the transferability of stock in its articles of incorporation.

Consider an example. Tom, Dick, and Harry Smith are the only shareholders of Smith Boat Company. Tom and Dick Smith do not want Harry to sell his shares to someone they do not know. The articles of incorporation might therefore restrict the transferability of shares to outside persons. For example, the restriction might require shareholders to offer their shares to the corporation or other shareholders first before going to an outside purchaser.

Another way that control of a close corporation can be stabilized is through the use of a shareholder agreement. Agreements among shareholders to vote their stock in a particular way are generally upheld. Shareholder agreements can also provide that when one of the original shareholders dies, his or her shares of stock in the corporation are divided in such a way that the proportionate holdings of the survivors, and thus their porportionate control, be maintained.

BACKGROUND AND FACTS *Benjamin and Isadore Galler were brothers and 50 percent shareholders in a wholesale drug business that was incorporated under Illinois law as the Galler Drug Company. Benjamin and Isadore and their wives entered into a written agreement providing that, in the event of the death of either brother, the corporation would provide income for the support and maintenance of his immediate family. In addition, the family of the deceased brother would have equal control of the corporation. Benjamin died and his wife, Emma, sought specific performance of the agreement. Isadore refused to comply, asserting that the agreement was void as against public policy.*

GALLER v. GALLER
Supreme Court of Illinois, 1965.
32 Ill.2d 16, 203 N.E.2d 577.

DECISION AND RATIONALE *Since the Galler Drug Company was a close corporation the provision for continuing family control and for supporting family owners after the death of the head of the household was not invalid. A close corporation is one where a few persons (or families) hold ownership and where stock is rarely bought or sold. In such corporations, agreements that provide for continuity of ownership do not violate public policy. "Obviously, there is no evil inherent in a contract entered into for the reason that the persons originating the terms desired to so arrange their property as to provide post-death support for those dependent upon them. Nor does the fact that the subject property is corporate stock alter the situation so long as there exists no detriment to minority stock interests, creditors or other public injury."*

PROFESSIONAL SERVICE ASSOCIATIONS— PROFESSIONAL CORPORATIONS

In the past, professional persons such as physicians, lawyers, dentists, and accountants could not incorporate. Today they can, and their corporations are typically called professional service associations or professional corporations. They can be identified by the letters S.C. (service corporation), P.C. (professional corporation), Inc. (incorporated), or P.A. (professional association). In general, a professional corporation is formed like an ordinary business corporation.

The Liability of Members of a Professional Corporation

Subject to certain exceptions, the shareholders of a professional corporation have limited liability.

MALPRACTICE OF AN ASSOCIATE The liability of a shareholder in a professional service association for the malpractice of another member is not clear. In a partnership, dentists X, Y, and Z are each unlimitedly liable for whatever malpractice liability is incurred by the others within the scope of the partnership. If the three formed a professional corporation, the orthodox corporate law rule would apply, and none of the dentists would be liable for the malpractice of the others. As far as statutory

reference to malpractice liability is concerned, a conservative court might interpret the statutory preservation of malpractice liability, thus causing the individual shareholder in a professional association to be liable for the acts of his or her associates as if the professional corporation were a partnership.

ORDINARY TORT Torts that are not related to malpractice are often treated differently from malpractice. A shareholder in a professional corporation is protected from the liability imposed because of torts committed by other members. If a secretary has been sent from the office to pick up tax forms from the IRS and, in the process, runs into another car, both the corporation and the secretary will be held liable. Ordinarily, the shareholder in a professional corporation will not be personally liable.

THE SHAREHOLDER CREATES LIABILITY Any shareholder of a professional corporation who engages in a negligent action and who is guilty of malpractice is *personally* liable for the damage caused. Basically, this is the same rule of law that applies to ordinary business corporations.

Tax Benefits of the Professional Corporation

The tax benefits of the professional corporation are basically those that apply to all corporations.

One of the major benefits involves a pension and profit-sharing plan that can be set up. This is discussed under the subheading "Benefits of Incorporating."[3]

FOREIGN CORPORATIONS

As indicated earlier, a corporation is referred to as a *domestic corporation* by its home state; a corporation organized in any other state is called a *foreign corporation*. Thus, a corporation holding a Washington state charter is a domestic corporation in Washington but a foreign corporation in all other states (and nations). Whether or not a corporation is domestic is determined by the state in which it is chartered, not by the state of residence of its shareholders and incorporators or the state in which it conducts its business.

Status and Rights of Foreign Corporations

A corporation incorporated in one state typically must obtain a certificate to do business as a foreign corporation within another state. Once this has occurred, the powers conferred upon a corporation by its home state can be exercised in the other state. Numerous states have specific local laws that are designed to regulate foreign corporations. Sometimes, local statutes relating to corporations in general will also apply to foreign corporations. When these statutes relate to internal corporate affairs, they normally do not apply to foreign corporations.

POSTING A BOND Often a foreign corporation must comply with standards of financial responsibility before a certificate of authority to transact business will be issued. Some jurisdictions require that a foreign corporation post a bond to insure performance of its contracts.

JURISDICTION OVER FOREIGN CORPORATIONS Before a state court can hear a dispute in which a foreign corporation is the defendant, the state court must have *jurisdiction* over the defendant. A state court only has jurisdiction over foreign corporations which have sufficient *contacts* with the state. A foreign corporation which has its home office within the state or has manufacturing plants in the state meets this "contacts" requirement. A foreign corporation whose only contact with the state is that one of its directors resides there does not have sufficient contact with the state for the state court to exercise jurisdiction over it.

In the following case, the defendant was a foreign corporation that manufactured a defective component part for a forklift vehicle that injured the plaintiff. The Florida court had to determine whether or not the foreign corporation had sufficient legal presence in the state of Florida to permit it to be the subject of a lawsuit in Florida.

---

3. See also R. A. Anderson, *Running a Professional Corporation* (Philadelphia, Pa.: Littoral Development Company, 1971).

BACKGROUND AND FACTS *Norfolk was injured when the arm of a defective forklift owned by Case fell. Harlo, a foreign corporation with its principal base of business in Grandville, Michigan, had manufactured the defective component. Harlo was not licensed to do business in Florida, and it did not engage in business there. Its only contact with Florida occurred when the forklifts containing a component it had manufactured found their way into the state. Case attempted to bring Harlo to court in Florida to answer for Norfolk's personal injury claim. Harlo denied that Florida courts had jurisdiction over it.*

DECISION AND RATIONALE *Harlo was correct. For a state to have jurisdiction over a corporation (or other person), the corporation must be*

HARLO PRODUCTS CORP. v. J.I. CASE CO.
District Court of Appeals of Florida, First District, 1978.
360 So.2d 1328.

doing business in the state where jurisidction is sought. In other words, the corporation must have minimum contacts with the state—contacts sufficient to satisfy the fairness requirements of due process. The court concluded: "The statements in Harlo's affidavit that it was a Michigan corporation not licensed to do business in Florida, that it did not engage in business in Florida and that it maintained no offices, agents, employees, bank accounts, books, records, telephone listings or other business activities in Florida, are unrefuted by Case. There are no allegations showing that Harlo purposely availed itself of the privilege of carrying on business activities in Florida nor that it had minimum contacts with Florida."

CORPORATE FORMATION AND ITS COSTS

This section will discuss the desirability of an individual's incorporating as a close corporation, a professional corporation, or a Subchapter S corporation. Incorporation for individuals with regular jobs is limited to those who also have substantial outside, "moonlighting" income that can be funneled through the corporation. This income cannot be salaried income; it must be in the form of payments that can go directly into a corporation. (Any checks that the individual receives from which social security and federal withholding taxes are deducted generally cannot be deposited into the corporation as corporate income.) A family cannot incorporate simply because it is a family; it must be engaged in a bona fide business from which it receives nonsalaried income.

The Costs of Incorporating

Just about anyone in any state can start a corporation. There are, however, numerous expenses associated with starting and running such a venture. Below is a list of the possible expenses:

1. *Lawyers' fees.* These can range from a minimum of $250 to as much as $3,000.
2. *Accountants' fees.* It can cost several hundred dollars to establish a bookkeeping system for a corporation.
3. *Fees to the state.* The state can require an annual corporate fee ranging from a few dollars to several hundred dollars.
4. *Unemployment insurance taxes.* Even if

the corporation has only one employee, and it is clearly set up for tax reasons only, it must still pay unemployment insurance taxes, either to the state in which it is registered or to the federal government.
5. *Employer's contribution to social security.* Even if a person is a salaried employee of some other company, as an employee of his or her own corporation, he or she must pay an employer's "contribution" to social security. This "contribution" is nonrefundable and seems to be on the rise.
6. *Annual legal and accounting fees.* Many forms must be filed for corporations in different states. In addition, corporate records and minute books must be maintained. Typically, an accountant or a lawyer does this. Annual fees for such services can run into many hundreds of dollars. Numerous forms must be filled out every year for retirement funds in particular.

The Benefits of Incorporating

One of the major benefits of incorporating is the tax benefit of starting a pension or profit-sharing plan and the tax-related benefits associated with fringe benefits.

PENSION AND PROFIT-SHARING PLANS
The IRS routinely allows pension plans consisting of two parts—a 10 percent retirement plan and a 15 percent profit-sharing plan. The 10 percent and 15 percent numbers refer to the percentage of the gross salary paid to the corporation's individual employees in any one year. Assume that Leed has $50,000 of his

income funneled through his close corporation and that he pays himself that $50,000 in salary. Leed could contribute $5,000 to his corporate pension plan and $7,500 to his corporate profit-sharing plan.

THE BENEFIT OF PENSION AND PROFIT-SHARING PLANS—A DIGRESSION The tax-sheltered pension or profit-sharing plan allows the individual to save before taxes as opposed to saving after-tax dollars. If the individual is in the 50 percent tax bracket, for example, a pension tax shelter will allow him or her to save twice as many before-tax dollars as after-tax dollars.

A tax-exempt savings plan does not, however, allow the individual to avoid paying taxes indefinitely on the savings put into the plan. Eventually, the individual will have to pay taxes, but they will be paid as they are taken out of the plan. Thus, the individual saves on taxes because he or she is usually in a lower tax bracket after retirement. Moreover, the individual puts off having to pay those taxes, allowing savings to grow at compounded rates. This is a key aspect of tax-exempt pension and

profit-sharing plans. By deferring taxes until a future date, interest can be earned on those deferred taxes while they are not being paid (and the taxes on those earnings are deferred). In other words, the government loans the individual the taxes owed for a number of years and does not charge interest on the loan. It must be repaid, generally at retirement, but in the meantime, extra income can be earned. A simple numerical example follows to illustrate the point.

Compare two possibilities—a regular savings program in which the individual puts, say, $100 in a savings and loan account each year and another program in which the individual sets up a retirement pension plan containing money that is not currently taxed. To simplify the arithmetic, assume that the individual is in the 50 percent tax bracket; thus, this individual can have the same after-tax income to spend during the year by placing $200 in the tax-exempt pension plan. Assume further that the same rate of return is earned in the pension plan as in the savings and loan association.

As Exhibit 42-1 indicates, the individual with the pension plan will have more retire-

EXHIBIT 42-1 THE BENEFITS OF A TAX-SHELTERED SAVINGS PLAN

	YEAR 1	YEAR 2	YEAR 3	YEAR 4	YEAR 5
PLAN 1—Not Tax Sheltered					
Principal	$100.00	$102.50	$105.06	$107.69	$110.382
Interest	5.00	5.125	5.253	5.384	5.519
Taxes	−2.50	−2.5625	−2.627	−2.692	−2.7596
After-tax total	$102.50	$105.06	$107.69	$110.38	$113.14

Net after-tax savings, end of 5 years = $113.14

PLAN 2—Tax Sheltered					
Principal	$200.00	$210.00	$220.50	$231.525	$242.826
Interest	10.00	10.50	11.025	11.57625	12.1413
Total	$210.00	$220.50	$231.53	$242.83	$254.97

Taxes paid at 50% at end of year 5 = 0.5 x $254.97 = 127.48
Net after-tax savings at end of 5 years = $254.97 − $127.48 = $127.49

ment dollars to spend than the individual without it, although they both have the same after-tax income during their working years. In the example, the tax-exempt savings plan would have yielded $14.34 more than the other plan after five years. This does not sound like much, but it is equivalent to an increase in total savings of 12.7 percent. That percentage figure would increase dramatically in a comparison of a tax-sheltered plan over a thirty-year period to a plan that is not a tax shelter. Moreover, even 12.7 percent represents quite a difference if the sums of money involved are large. And they certainly would be greater than those in our example for the average retirement plan. Again, the benefit of the pension plan is that the payment of taxes is deferred until some later date. Moreover, a person with a tax-exempt pension plan does not pay taxes on the interest earned until it is distributed later on.

Fringe Benefits

An individual who starts a corporation can take advantage of a number of fringe benefits that provide items that might otherwise have to be bought with after-tax dollars.

TERM LIFE INSURANCE An individual, through his or her own corporation, can purchase up to $50,000 of term life insurance every year with dollars out of the corporation. Because these dollars are a cost to the corporation, they are not taxable. If the person is in the 50 percent tax bracket, for example, that means that he or she is buying $50,000 of term insurance for "fifty-cent dollars." In this example, the cost of that insurance is essentially one-half what it would have been if it had been purchased outside the corporate structure.

A MEDICAL PLAN An individual can set up a completely comprehensive medical plan to cover virtually all kinds of medical expenses. Thus, the corporation can reimburse the individual with before-tax dollars for any payments made for medical insurance. The corporation can pay for all medicines, dental work, and anything that relates to physical well-being. For someone with a large family, this comprehensive medical plan can mean substantial savings every year. If, in general, an individual spends $2,000 more each year in medical expenses than his or her medical insurance covers and if the individual is in the 50 percent tax bracket, he or she gets a "kickback" of $1,000.

The benefit of a medical plan is reduced by the availability of medical deductions that the individual could have taken off his or her income before figuring federal income taxes. Part of the person's medical insurance plus any medical expenses exceeding 3 percent of the adjusted gross income can be itemized as specific deductions on his or her personal federal income tax return. Essentially, then, a medical plan within the corporation for the individual and dependents eliminates the medical expenses that generally are not deductible.

The Revenue Act of 1978 requires that a medical plan not discriminate among employees. In other words, if it is made available for the president of the corporation, it must also be made available for all employees in the corporation.

DISABILITY INSURANCE An individual can purchase, with before-tax dollars, long-term disability insurance through the corporation. In other words, a person can buy a salary continuation policy with before-tax dollars that might otherwise have to be bought with after-tax dollars. Such policies pay a certain amount of money every month if the person becomes disabled and is unable to work.

QUESTIONS AND CASE PROBLEMS

1. Life Carpet and Tile Company, Inc. is incorporated in Florida and does all of its business in that state. Pace Carpet Mills, Inc. is a foreign corporation. Life Carpet filed a lawsuit against Pace Carpet Mills in a Florida court. In its complaint, it alleged that Pace carried on its Florida business through a local distributor and that Pace exercised almost complete control over the distributor. Can the lawsuit be

brought in Florida? [Pace Carpet Mills, Inc. v. Life Carpet and Tile Co., Inc., 365 So.2d. 445 (Fla. App. 1978)]

2. In Illinois, foreign corporations are subject to the Illinois Attachment Act. Under this act, a corporation that is not a state resident subjects its property in Illinois to court supervision during any lawsuits that are pending against it. Vinylweld, Inc., an Illinois corporation, brought suit in Illinois against Metropolitan Greetings, Inc., a Massachusetts corporation. Prior to the suit, Metropolitan Greetings had complied with the registration provisions of Illinois's statutes that license corporations to do business in Illinois. Should Metropolitan Greetings be subject to Illinois's attachment statute? [Vinylweld, Inc. v. Metropolitan Greetings, Inc., 360 F.Supp. 1360 (N.D. Ill. 1973)]

3. Arthur B. and Eleanor L. Clemens, husband and wife, were the stockholders of Clemens Company, Inc., which was incorporated under the laws of California. After two years of fairly unsuccessful operation, the company finally began turning a profit. Arthur Clemens then filed with the IRS for treatment as a Subchapter S corporation because of the tax advantages. His wife, Eleanor, who was a 50 percent stockholder of the company, objected, but the firm began filing tax returns as a Subchapter S corporation in spite of her objection. Has Clemens Company properly become a Subchapter S corporation? [Clemens v. Commissioner of Internal Revenue, 453 F.2d. 869 (9th Cir. 1971)]

4. Shelborne Enterprises, Inc., a Florida corporation, had done business for a number of years before its shareholders unanimously decided to elect for Subchapter S tax treatment. The corporation's stock was divided into four categories, each having an unequal number of shares and each entitled to elect one director. Shelborne conducted its business and filed tax returns for the next three years as a Subchapter S corporation. The commissioner of the Internal Revenue Service then sought to recover past taxes beginning with the year that Shelborne first filed as a Subchapter S corporation. The IRS claimed that Shelborne improperly elected Subchapter S status. What result? [Pollack v. Commissioner of Internal Revenue, 392 F.2d. 409 (5th Cir. 1968)]

5. The Valley Loan Association was engaged in the financing of retail installment sales of consumer goods by loans and by purchase of retail installment sales contracts. Valley Loan elected for treatment as a Subchapter S corporation. The commissioner of the Internal Revenue Service, however, challenged Valley Loan's election on the ground that Section 1372(e)(5) of Subchapter S denies the right of election to small business corporations whose gross receipts from dividends, interest, and so forth exceed 20 percent of their total gross receipts. Would it be a fair result to deny Valley Loan Association the right to elect under Subchapter S of the Internal Revenue Code? [Valley Loan Ass'n. v. United States, 258 F.Supp. 673 (D. Colo. 1966)]

6. Paul Hessler was the president of Hessler, Inc., a family corporation. Hessler controlled approximately 80 percent of the corporation's stock and completely dominated the management of its business. Matters of business, contracts, hiring, and firing were carried on by the president without action or approval of the directors. Farrel was employed by Hessler for forty years as Hessler's outdoor advertising business manager. During Farrel's employment, the firm's president repeatedly assured Farrel that upon retirement he would receive some kind of retirement benefits. Relying on this assurance, Farrel, over a course of years, declined several attractive offers of employment with other businesses. Farrel retired about five years after Hessler. Hessler, Inc., by and through its directors, refused to pay Farrel any retirement benefits, arguing that the board of directors never approved such benefits. Can Farrel recover? [Hessler, Inc. v. Farrel, 226 A.2d. 708 (Del. 1967)]

7. Shirley Botwin owned 25 percent of the stock of Central Structural Steel Company, Inc. Central was a closed corporation. Botwin's husband, along with two other persons, owned the remaining stock. When the Botwins decided to divorce, Shirley Botwin wished to examine corporate records in order to plan a divorce settlement. She was denied all information about the affairs of the corporation. Can she force Central to allow her to examine the corporate records? [Botwin v. Central Structural Steel Co., 28 A.D.2d 522, 279 N.Y.S.2d. 741 (1967)]

8. Donald McCallum, John Gray, and Lee Evans entered into a pre-incorporation agreement that provided: (1) the three-named persons would cause a corporation to be organized under the laws of Oregon with an authorized capital of a thousand shares, (2) each would receive one-third of the shares, and (3) no shareholder would sell, transfer, or in any way dispose of his shares unless and until he offered to sell the shares to the other shareholders. Subsequently, Lee Evans wished to withdraw from the corporation and offered his shares to both McCallum and Gray. Gray declined, but McCallum agreed to purchase all the shares. Thereafter, at a stockholders' meeting with McCallum and Gray both present,

McCallum voted, over Gray's objections, to amend the bylaws allowing an additional thousand shares to be issued. Since Gray had no money to invest at the time, the shares would be purchased by outsiders. Gray objected to the dilution of his interest in the company. Does Gray have any legal grounds to object to McCallum's action? [McCallum v. Gray, 273 Or. 617, 542 P.2d. 1025 (1975)]

43

Corporations
Corporate Financing
and Securities Regulation

In order to obtain financing, corporations issue **securities**—evidence of the obligation to pay money or of the right to participate in earnings and the distribution of corporate trusts and other property. The principal method of long-term and initial corporate financing is the issuance of stocks—**equity**—and bonds—**debt**—both of which are sold to investors. Stocks, or **equity securities,** represent the purchase of ownership in the business firm. Bonds (debentures), or **debt securities,** represent the lending of money by firms (and governments).[1]

CHARACTERISTICS OF BONDS

Bonds are issued by business firms and by government at all levels as evidence of the funds they are borrowing from investors. Bonds almost always have a designated maturity date—the date when the principal or face amount of the bond (or loan) is returned to the investor. Bonds are sometimes referred to as *fixed income securities* because their owners receive a fixed dollar interest payment during the period of time until maturity.

In the bond trade, the word *bond* refers specifically to a debenture

---

1. The term *bonds* is often used to describe both secured and unsecured obligations. Technically, however, bonds are secured by a lien or other security interest and debentures are unsecured.

with a face value of $1,000. Bonds can be sold below their face value at a *discount* or above their face value at a *premium*. Bonds sold at premiums have yields that are less than their coupon, or stated, rates; those sold at a discount have yields that are greater.

Corporate Bonds

The characteristics of corporate bonds vary widely, in part because corporations differ greatly in their ability to generate the earnings and cash flow necessary to make interest payments and to repay the principal amount of the bonds at maturity. Furthermore, corporate bonds are only part of the total debt and overall financial structure of corporate business.

Because debt financing represents a legal obligation on the part of the corporation, various features and terms of a particular bond issue are specified in a lending agreement called a **bond indenture.** A corporate trustee, often a commercial bank trust department, represents the collective well-being of all bondholders in insuring that the terms of the bond issue are met by the corporation. The bond indenture specifies the maturity date of the bond and the pattern of interest payments until maturity. Most corporate bonds pay semiannually a coupon rate of interest on the $1,000 face amount of the bond. For example, the owner of a 6 percent corporate bond would receive $30 interest every six months. The indenture indicates whether any portion of the bond is to be retired each year in a series of *sinking fund payments,* and it specifies any collateral for the bond issue, such as buildings or equipment. Additionally, the indenture indicates how the bondholder (and other creditors of the business firm) will fare if the firm gets into serious financial difficulty and is unable to meet all its legal obligations.

DEBENTURES No specific assets of the corporation are pledged as backing for debentures. Rather, they are backed by the general credit rating of the corporation, plus any assets that can be seized if the corporation allows the debentures to go into default.

MORTGAGE BONDS Mortgage bonds are secured by a mortgage on all or part of the corporate-owned real property. There are a variety of mortgage bonds, including first, second, and even third mortgage types. The first mortgage bonds are "senior" securities. Their owners have first claim to the mortgaged assets of the company if it defaults.

EQUIPMENT TRUST BONDS The collateral for the equipment trust bond (loan) is a specific piece of equipment. The title of the equipment is vested in a trustee, who holds it for the benefit of the bond owners.

COLLATERAL TRUST BONDS Collateral trust bonds are secured by intangibles. They can be shares of stock in another corporation or accounts receivable.

CONVERTIBLE BONDS Convertible bonds can be exchanged for a specified number of shares of common stock when and if the bondholder so desires. The rate of conversion is determined when the convertible bond is issued.

CALLABLE BONDS Callable bonds, which may be debentures or any other kind of bonds, may be called in and the principal repaid at any time. The callable provision is put into the bond when it is issued.

CHARACTERISTICS OF STOCKS

Issuing stocks is another way corporations obtain financing. Stocks represent ownership in a business firm; bonds represent borrowing by the firm. Government does not issue stocks because there is no ownership of government. Stocks are important because private enterprise society rests upon the concept of private ownership of the business organizations that produce and distribute the countless products and services purchased by consumers, business units, government, and other organizations.

A 1975 survey revealed that 25,270,000 individuals, representing 11.8 percent of the total United States population, owned corporate stock. The two major types of stock are preferred stock and common stock.

Preferred Stock

Preferred stock is "preferred" in the sense that its owners must be paid their dividends before common shareholders are paid theirs. Also, preferred shareholders generally have a higher claim on the assets of the corporation if the firm is liquidated. Preferred stock shareholders may or may not have the right to vote. There are a number of different types of preferred stock, which are defined below.

From an investment standpoint, preferred stock is more like bonds than like common stock. It is not included among the liabilities of a business because it is equity. Like all equity securities, preferred shares have no fixed maturity time when they must be retired by the firm. Occasionally, firms do retire preferred stock, but they are not legally obligated to do so. Preferred shareholders receive periodic dividend payments, usually established as a fixed percentage of the face amount of each preferred share. A 7 percent preferred stock with a face amount of $100 per share would pay its owner a $7 dividend each year. This is not a legal obligation on the part of the firm, but the interest payments due to bondholders are legal obligations.

CUMULATIVE PREFERRED STOCK Any dividend payment on cumulative preferred stock not made in a given year must be paid before any dividends can be paid to owners of common stock. In other words, the corporation is liable to the preferred shareholders for past dividends not yet paid (called dividend arrearages). If, for example, a corporation fails to pay dividends for three years on a stock with a $100 par value and a $5 annual dividend preference, then the company must pay the cumulative preferred stockholders $15 per share at the end of the three years before any dividends can be paid to common stockholders. Sometimes there are limits as to how far back dividends have to be paid—for example, there may be three- or five-year cumulative limits.

PARTICIPATING PREFERRED STOCK With participating preferred stock, the owner can share to some extent in additional dividends that are paid by the firm. Usually, the preferred stockholders are paid their agreed-upon rate of, say, $5 per share (the dividend preference), and then common stockholders are paid an equal percentage rate, after which any additional dividends declared by the board of directors are distributed equally among preferred and common stockholders.

CONVERTIBLE PREFERRED STOCK The owner of shares of convertible preferred stock has an option of converting each share into a specified number of common shares. Sometimes convertible preferred stock can be exchanged for common stock in another company. In any event, the exchange ratio is determined when the convertible preferred shares of stock are issued. Hence, if there is an increase in the market value of the corporation's common stock, the market value of the convertible preferred stock also rises.

REDEEMABLE OR CALLABLE PREFERRED STOCK Redeemable or callable preferred stock is issued by a corporation under the express condition that the corporation has the right to buy back the shares of stock from the preferred stockholders at some future time. The terms of such a buy-back arrangement are specified when the preferred stock is issued. Corporations issue callable preferred so that they can call in the higher-cost preferred stock and reissue lower-cost shares if interest rates fall in the future.

THE CAUTIOUS POSITION OF THE PREFERRED SHAREHOLDER Preferred shareholders are investors who have assumed a rather cautious position in their relationship to the corporation. They have a stronger position than common shareholders with respect to dividends and claims on assets, but as a result, they will not share in the full prosperity of the firm if it grows successfully over time. A preferred shareholder receives fixed dividends periodically, and there may be changes in the market price of the shares. The return and the risk for a share of preferred stock lie somewhere between those of bonds and common stock. As a result, preferred stock is often categorized with corporate bonds as a fixed income security even though the legal status is not the same. Some experts even contend that preferred stock is more like bonds than like common stocks, even though preferred stock appears in the ownership section of the firm's balance sheet (financial statements).

Common Stock

Common stock represents the true ownership of a corporation. Typically, each investor in a particular firm is entitled to one vote per common share held. Voting rights in a corporation apply to election of the firm's board of directors and to any proposed changes in the ownership structure of the firm.[2] For example, a common shareholder generally has the right to vote in a decision on a proposed merger, since mergers can change the proportion of ownership. Many small investors in giant corporations probably feel, and rightly so, that their small number of votes has little impact on the business firm—particularly when incumbent management owns or obtains right-to-vote shares by proxy and thus has a significant and often controlling proportion of the total votes. Still, voting rights are an important characteristic of common stock and one that some investors take seriously.

There is no obligation to return a principal amount per share to each common stock shareholder. No firm can insure that the market price per share of its common stock will not go down over time. Neither does the issuing firm guarantee a dividend; indeed, some business firms

never pay dividends. Considering these negative aspects, why would an individual even consider investing in common stock? The answer, of course, is that all owners are entitled to their proportional share of the corporation's after-tax earnings. If Janet Gray owns 100 shares (0.01 percent of 1 million shares outstanding) of a firm that earns $3 million after taxes, she will receive a proportional share of those earnings totaling $300. Earnings are the key to the benefits that an investor receives from common stock.

Either the earnings of a corporation are paid out in the form of cash dividends to shareholders, or they are retained in the business for the express purpose of enhancing future earnings. If the board of directors of Janet Gray's firm (and it is *her* firm because she is a common shareholder) declares a dividend of $1.20 per share, then $120 of her $300 earnings is received now as a tangible benefit, with the other $180 retained. Her other tangible benefit is the market price per share that she will receive if and when she ultimately sells part or all of her 100 common shares. But market price depends, among other things, on the recent earnings (and dividends) of the firm and, more importantly, on expectations for future earnings and dividends, as well as on the overall economic well-being of the country.

Common shareholders, then, are a group of investors who assume the *residual* position in the overall financial structure of a business. In terms of receiving payment for their investment, they are last in line. The earnings to which they are entitled also depend on all the other groups—suppliers, employees, managers, bankers, governments, bondholders, and preferred shareholders—being paid what is due them first. Once those groups are paid, however, common shareholders are entitled to *all* the remaining earnings. (But the board of directors is not normally under any duty to declare the remaining earnings as dividends.) This is the central feature of ownership in any business, be it a corner newsstand, a retail store, an architectural firm, or a giant international oil corporation. In each instance, the common stock

---

2. State corporation law specifies the types of issues on which shareholder approval must be obtained.

owners occupy the riskiest position, but they can expect a correspondingly greater return on their investment. Again, it can be seen why the return and risk pattern holds. As one moves from savings accounts and U.S. government bonds to corporate bonds with different ratings to preferred stock and, finally, to common stock, expected returns increase to compensate for the higher risks that are undertaken. Exhibit 43-1 is a comparison of stocks and bonds.

DIVIDENDS

A dividend is a distribution of property. It can be shares of stock or cash paid to the shareholders in proportion to their interests. In most cases, dividends are paid in cash. The sources of dividends are (1) retained earnings, (2) net profits (current earnings), or (3) surplus. Dividends are payable from limited funds as prescribed by various state statutes:

1. *Retained earnings.* All states allow dividends to be paid from the undistributed net profits earned by the corporation, including capital gains from the sale of fixed assets. The undistributed net profits are called earned surplus or retained earnings.

2. *Net profits.* A few state statutes allow dividends to be issued from current net profits without regard to deficits in prior years.

3. *Surplus.* A number of state statutes allow dividends to be paid out of any kind of surplus.

Limitations on Dividends

All states prohibit the payment of dividends when a corporation is or will become insolvent if it pays them (that is, if its liabilities exceed its assets or if the corporation is unable to pay its debts as they mature). Other states prohibit dividends if they impair the capital of the corporation. Various federal statutes (to be described below) place further limitations.

General principles of accounting are often relevant to the discussion of some of the legal rules governing the distribution of dividends. Many modern corporate statutes define the accounting terms used in their provisions. In short, the question of whether or not to declare and distribute a dividend is within the discretion of the board of directors, but the question of which account to use to make the payment is a question to be settled under the corporation law of the state.

EXHIBIT 43–1   HOW DO STOCKS AND BONDS DIFFER?

Common Stocks	Bonds
1. Stocks represent ownership.	1. Bonds represent owed debt.
2. Stocks (common) do not have a fixed dividend rate.	2. Interest on bonds must always be paid, whether or not any profit is earned.
3. Stockholders can elect a board of directors, which control the corporation.	3. Bondholders usually have no voice in or control over management of the corporation.
4. Stocks do not have a maturity date; the corporation does not usually repay the stockholder.	4. Bonds have a maturity date when the bondholder is to be repaid the face value of the bond.
5. All corporations issue or offer to sell stocks. This is the usual definition of a corporation.	5. Corporations do not necessarily issue bonds.
6. Stockholders have a claim against the property and income of a corporation after all creditors' claims have been met.	6. Bondholders have a claim against the property and income of a corporation that must be met before the claims of stockholders.

UNITED STATES v.
RIELY

Circuit Court of Appeals,
Fourth Circuit, 1948.
169 F.2d 542.

BACKGROUND AND FACTS *Pierce Oil Corporation was organized in 1913 under the laws of the state of Virginia. By 1937, it had a deficit of $1,150,000. In 1938, it had net earnings and profits of $86,000. Although none of this was distributed as dividends, the IRS taxed the company's income. Pierce Oil protested, claiming that, since it still had a deficit, its earnings could not be taxed as profits.*

DECISION AND RATIONALE *Pierce Oil's earnings for 1938 could be taxed because, under Virginia statutes, dividends can be paid out of net earnings or out of net assets in excess of capital. "[T]he term 'net earnings' is ordinarily used to refer to the earnings of a particular period such as a year rather than to earnings accumulated from corporate organization. *** We think that the Virginia Statute did not forbid the taxpayer from paying dividends during the year in question. The taxpayer, accordingly, is not entitled to a refund of the taxes paid under protest."*

Who Declares and Who Receives Dividends

Generally, dividends are declared at the discretion of the board of directors. Unless there has been bad faith or an obvious abuse of discretion, shareholders cannot compel distribution of dividends no matter how large the surplus in the corporation.

Cash dividends belong to the shareholders "of record," as declared by the board of directors. The corporation can, for example, make the cash dividend payable to those who will be holders of record on a later date.

FEDERAL SECURITIES REGULATIONS

The sale and transfer of securities is heavily regulated by federal and state statutes and by government agencies. This is a complex area of the law, and the rest of this chapter will outline the nature of federal security regulations and their effect on the business world.

The most important federal security regulations are the Securities Act of 1933 and the Federal Securities Exchange Act of 1934. These acts and others are administered by the Securities and Exchange Commission.

Securities and Exchange Commission

Congress has delegated to the Securities and Exchange Commission (SEC) the responsibility of administering all federal securities laws. The SEC acts as an interpreter of federal statutes and as a rule maker. It also investigates alleged infractions of the laws. Violation of federal securities law involves both criminal and civil liability. The U.S. Attorney General, the Securities and Exchange Commission, and, in certain circumstances, the purchaser or seller of stock can bring suit. The SEC has regulatory authority over brokers, dealers, and stock exchanges.

The Securities Act of 1933

The Securities Act of 1933 was passed to avoid another stock market crash like the one of 1929.[3] The act was designed to prohibit various forms of fraud and to stabilize the securities industry by requiring that all essential information concerning the issuance of stocks be made available to the investing public. The 1933 law

3. 15 USCA, Secs. 77A-77AA (1976) For a survey of the various provisions of the 1933 act, see David L. Ratner, *Securities Regulation in a Nutshell* (St. Paul: West Publishing Co., 1978) and Blumenthal, *Securities Law in Perspective* (1977).

requires that a registration statement be filed with the SEC when certain securities are to be publicly offered. The public offering and sale of securities is generally accomplished with the aid of professional underwriters—investment bankers specializing in the sale and distribution of securities. Corporate management and the underwriters usually retain attorneys specializing in securities law to assist them in complying with the law.

The 1933 act is basically a disclosure statute. It permits a corporation to sell junk to the public as long as appropriate disclosures are made. This is in contrast to several state securities statutes, which permit the registration (and sale) of only those securities offerings that are fair or equitable.

SOME REQUIREMENTS OF THE REGISTRATION STATEMENT
The registration statement must include the following:

1. A description of the significant provisions of the security offered for sale, including the relationship between that security and the other capital securities of the registrant. Also, the corporation must disclose how it intends to use the proceeds of the sale.
2. A description of the registrant's properties and business.
3. A description of the management of the registrant, its security holdings, remuneration, and other benefits, including pensions and stock options. There must be disclosure of the interest of directors or officers in any material transactions with the corporation.
4. A financial statement certified by an independent public accounting firm.
5. A description of threatened or pending lawsuits.

EXEMPTIONS
A corporation can avoid the high cost and complicated procedures associated with registration by taking advantage of certain exemptions. Transactions are exempt if they do not involve a public offering. Some exempt transactions are private offerings to a limited number of persons, offerings to an institution that has access to the required infor-

mation,[4] and offerings restricted to residents of the state in which the issuing company is organized and doing business (but these are still subject to state law).[5] The SEC also has the power to exempt small issues under $500,000 from the registration requirement.[6]

The Securities Act of 1933 deals primarily with the initial distribution of securities by an issuer. It has two main parts, the registration and prospectus requirements and the antifraud provisions.

Under the registration and prospectus requirements, no security can be sold or offered for sale through the mails or through interstate commerce without filing a registration statement unless either the security is exempt or the transaction falls within one of the exempt categories.[7] The registration statement becomes a matter of public record, and the information it contains furnishes the basis for drawing up a prospectus that must be given to each purchaser or prospective purchaser of the securities.

The antifraud provisions of the 1933 act apply if either interstate commerce or the mails are involved in the offer or sale of corporate securities. Even though a security may fall into an exempt category, or the transaction may otherwise be exempt from registration, the civil and criminal liabilities for misrepresentation and fraud still apply.

A registration statement is first filed with the SEC. Then, a public selling campaign begins, making use of the written preliminary prospectus. However, the securities cannot be sold until after the effective date of the registration statement.[8] Federal legislation provides

---

4. Securities Act, Sec. 4(2), 15 USCA Sec. 77d(2).
5. Securities Act, Sec. 3(a)(11), 15 USCA Sec. 77c(a)(11).
6. Securities Act, Sec. 3(b), 15 USCA Sec. 77(b). For issues of less than $500,000, the commission has adopted a simplified registration process under Regulation A.
7. Not surprisingly, certain types of securities are exempted from the registration provisions, including securities issued by nonprofit corporations and securities issued by the federal government or state governments.
8. As a practical matter, the registration statement does not become effective until its effectiveness is ordered by the SEC. Theoretically, a registration statement becomes effective twenty days after the filing of the most recent amendment.

severe sanctions for engaging in transactions in securities that should have been registered and for making any false statements or material omissions in a registration statement or prospectus. Liability for false statements and omissions extends to every director of the issuer at the time of registration, every person who has signed the registration statement, every expert who provided expert information incorporated into the statement or prospectus, every underwriter, every person named as one who is about to become a director, and, of course, the issuer.

The Securities Exchange Act of 1934

The Securities Exchange Act provides for the regulation and registration of security exchanges, brokers, dealers, and national securities associations (such as NASD). It regulates the markets in which securities are traded by maintaining a continuous disclosure system for all corporations with securities on the security exchanges and for those companies that have assets in excess of $1 million and five hundred or more shareholders. These corporations are referred to as Section 12 companies, since they are required to register their securities under Section 12 of the 1934 act. The act regulates proxy solicitation for voting, and it allows the SEC to engage in market surveillance to regulate undesirable market practices such as fraud, market manipulation, misrepresentation, and stabilization. ("Stabilization" is a kind of market manipulating technique whereby securities underwriters bid for securities to stabilize their price during their issuance. See Rules 10b-6, 7, and 8.)

INSIDER TRADING   One of the most important parts of the 1934 act relates to so-called insider trading. Because of their positions, corporate directors and officers often obtain advance inside information that can affect the future market value of the corporate stock. Obviously, their position can give them a trading advantage over the general public and shareholders. The 1934 Securities Exchange Act defines and extends liability to officers and directors in their personal transactions for taking advantage of such information when they know it is unavailable to the person with whom they are dealing. In addition, in order to deter the use of inside information, the 1934 act requires officers, directors, and certain large shareholders to turn over to the corporation all short-term profits realized on the purchase and sale of corporate stock.

SEC RULE 10b-5   Section 10(b) of the 1934 act and SEC Rule 10b-5 cover not only corporate officers, directors, and majority shareholders but also any persons having access to or receiving information of a nonpublic nature on which trading is based. Those persons to whom the material information is transmitted are known as *tippees*.

DISCLOSURE UNDER RULE 10b-5   Any material omission or misrepresentation of material facts in connection with the purchase or sale of a security may violate Section 10(b) and Rule 10b-5. The key to liability under this rule is whether the insider's information is "material."

Following are some examples of material facts calling for a disclosure under the rule:

1.   A new ore discovery.
2.   Fraudulent trading in the company stock by a broker/dealer.
3.   A dividend change (whether up or down).
4.   A contract for the sale of corporate assets.
5.   A new discovery (process or product).
6.   A significant change in the firm's financial condition.

WHEN MUST DISCLOSURE UNDER RULE 10b-5 BE MADE?   Courts have struggled with the problem of when information becomes public knowledge. Clearly, when inside information becomes public knowledge, all insiders should be allowed to trade without disclosure. The courts have suggested that insiders should refrain from trading for a "reasonable waiting period" when the news is not readily translatable into investment action. Presumably, this gives the news time to filter down and to be evaluated by the investing public. What a reasonable waiting period is is not at all clear.

The following is one of the landmark cases interpreting Rule 10b-5. The SEC sued Texas Gulf Sulphur for issuing a misleading press release. The release underestimated the magni-

tude and value of a mineral discovery. The SEC also sued several of Texas Gulf Sulphur's directors, officers, and employees under Rule 10b-5 after these persons had purchased large amounts of the corporate stock prior to the announcement of the corporation's rich ore discovery.

BACKGROUND AND FACTS   *The Texas Gulf Sulphur Company (TGS) drilled a hole on November 12, 1963 that appeared to yield a core with an exceedingly high mineral content. TGS kept secret the results of the core sample. Officers and employees of the company made substantial purchases of TGS's stock after learning of the ore discovery even though further drilling was necessary to establish whether there was enough ore to be mined commercially. The SEC brought suit against the officers and employees of TGS for violating the insider trading prohibition of Rule 10b-5. The officers and employees, however, argued that the probhibition did not apply because the information on which they had traded was not material since the mine had not been commercially proven. They pointed out that the SEC's own rules under Regulation A prohibited a company from making any statement about the discovery of ore unless it was sufficiently tested to be properly classified as "proven" or "provable."*

DECISION AND RATIONALE   *Notwithstanding the prohibitions in Regulation A regarding premature statements about provable ore deposits, the employees and officers violated Rule 10b-5's prohibition against insider trading. For Rule 10b-5, the test of materiality is not whether a company would be permitted to disclose the information if it were selling securities (which is what Regulation A deals with). Rather, the test is whether the information would affect the judgment of reasonable investors. Reasonable investors includes speculative as well as conservative investors. "[A] major factor in determining whether the *** discovery [of the ore] was a material fact is the importance attached to the drilling results by those who knew about it. *** [T]he timing by those who knew of it of their stock purchases and their purchases of short-term calls—purchases in some cases by individuals who had never before purchased calls or even TGS stock—virtually compels the inference that the insiders were influenced by the drilling results."*

SECURITIES AND EXCHANGE COMM. v. **TEXAS GULF SULPHUR CO.**
United States Court of Appeals, Second Circuit, 1968.
401 F.2d 833.

WHEN DOES RULE 10b-5 APPLY?   Rule 10b-5 applies in virtually all cases concerning the trading of securities, whether on organized exchanges, in over-the-counter markets, or in private transactions. The rule covers notes, bonds, certificates of interest and participation

in any profit-sharing agreement, agreements to form a corporation, and joint venture agreements; in short, it covers just about any form of security. It is immaterial whether a firm has securities registered under the 1933 act for the 1934 act to apply.

Rule 10b-5 is applicable only when the requisites of federal jurisdiction, such as the use of the mails, of stock exchange facilities, or of any instrumentality of interstate commerce, are present. However, virtually no commercial transaction can be completed without such contact. In addition, the states have corporate securities laws, many of which include provisions similar to Rule 10b-5.

INSIDER REPORTING AND TRADING— SECTION 16 (b) Officers, directors, and certain large stockholders[9] of Section 12 corporations are required to file reports with the SEC concerning their ownership and trading of the corporation's securities.[10] In order to discourage

such insiders from using nonpublic information about their company to their personal benefit in the stock market, Section 16(b) of the 1934 act provides for the recapture by the corporation of all profits realized by the insider on any purchase and sale or sale and purchase of the corporation's stock within any six-month period.[11] It is irrelevant whether the insider actually used inside information; all profits must be returned to the corporation.

Section 16(b) applies not only to stock but to warrants, options, and securities convertible into stock. In addition, the courts have fashioned complex rules for determining profits. Corporate insiders are well advised to seek competent counsel prior to trading in the

---

9. Those stockholders owning 10 percent of the class of equity securities registered under Section 12 of the 1934 act.
10. 1934 Act, Sec. 16(a), 15 USCA Sec. 78.

11. In a declining stock market, one can realize profits by selling at a high price and repurchasing at a later time at a lower price.

EXHIBIT 43—2 COMPARISON OF COVERAGE APPLICATION AND LIABILITIES UNDER 10b-5 AND SECTION 16 (b)

	RULE 10-b-5	SECTION 16 (b)
1. Subject matter of transaction	Any security (does not have to be registered).	Any security (does not have to be registered).
2. Transactions covered	Purchase or sale.	Short swing purchase and sale or short swing sale and purchase.
3. Who is subject to liability?	Virtually anyone with inside information— including officers, directors, controlling stockholders, and tippees.	Officers, directors, and certain 10 percent stockholders.
4. Is omission, scheme or misrepresentation necessary for liability?	Yes.	No.
5. Any exempt transactions?	No.	Yes, there are a variety of exemptions.
6. Is direct dealing with the party necessary?	No.	No.
7. Who can bring an action?	A person transacting with an insider or the SEC or a purchaser or a seller damaged by a wrongful act.	Corporation and shareholder by derivative action.

corporation's stock. Exhibit 43-2 compares the effects of Rule 10b-5 and Section 16b.

PROXY STATEMENTS Section 14(a) of the Securities and Exchange Act of 1934 regulates the solicitation of proxies from shareholders of Section 12 companies. The SEC regulates the content of proxy statements sent to shareholders by corporate managers who are requesting authority to vote on behalf of the shareholders in a particular election on specified issues. Whoever solicits a proxy must fully and accurately disclose all facts that are pertinent to the matter to be voted on. SEC Rule 14a-9 is similar to the antifraud provisions of Rule 10b-5. Remedies for violation are extensive, ranging from injunctions to preventing a vote from being taken, to monetary damages.

Other Federal Securities Laws

There are numerous other federal securities laws, and they are briefly listed here:

1. The Public Utility Holding Company Act of 1935.
2. The Trust Indenture Act of 1939.
3. The Investment Company Act of 1940.
4. The Investment Advisors Act of 1940.
5. The Security Investors Protection Act of 1970.

In addition, miscellaneous federal statutes regulate the issue of securities. For example, the Interstate Commerce Commission regulates motor and rail carriers, the Federal Home Loan Bank Board regulates federal saving and loan associations, and the Comptroller of the Currency regulates national banks.

STATE SECURITIES LAWS

Today, all states have their own corporate securities laws that regulate the offer and sale of securities within individual state borders.[12] Often referred to as *blue sky laws,* they are designed to prevent "speculative schemes which have no more basis than so many feet of blue sky."

Since the adoption of the 1933 and 1934 securities acts, the state and federal governments have regulated securities concurrently. Indeed, both acts specifically preserve state securities laws. There are certain common features in the state blue sky laws. They have antifraud provisions, many of which are patterned after Rule 10b-5. Also, most state corporate securities laws regulate securities brokers and dealers.

Typically, these laws also provide for the registration or qualification of securities offered or issued for sale within the state. Unless an applicable exemption from registration is found, issuers must register or qualify their stock with the appropriate state official, often called a corporations commissioner. There is a difference in philosophy in the state statutes. Many are like the Securities Act of 1933 and mandate certain disclosures before registration is effective and a permit to sell the securities is issued. Others have fairness standards that a corporation must meet in order to offer or sell stock in the state. The Uniform Securities Act, which has been adopted in part by several states, was drafted to be acceptable to states with differing regulatory philosophies.

---

12. These laws are catalogued and annotated in CCH, *Blue Sky Law Reporter,* a loose-leaf service.

QUESTIONS AND CASE PROBLEMS

1. Maresh, an experienced geologist, owned certain oil and gas leases covering land in Nebraska. To raise money for the drilling of a test well, he undertook to sell fractional interests in the leases. He approached Garfield, a man with whom he had done business in the past. Garfield had mentioned that he would be interested in investing in some of Maresh's future oil ventures. Garfield had wide business experience in the stock market and in oil stocks. He felt that the investment in Maresh's gas leases could be lucrative. Based on Garfield's promise to wire the money promptly, Maresh began drilling. Soon after, when

Maresh realized that the land was dry, Garfield refused to pay his share of the investment. Garfield claimed that he could rescind the agreement to invest since the investment offered by Maresh was a security within the meaning of the Securities Act of 1933, and it had not been registered. Did Maresh offer a security within the meaning of the 1933 act? [Garfield v. Strain, 320 F.2d 116 (10th Cir. 1963)]

2. The Howey Company owned large tracts of citrus acreage in Lake County, Florida. For several years, it planted about five hundred acres annually, keeping half of the groves itself and offering the other half to the public to help finance additional development. Howey-in-the-Hills Service, Inc. was a service company engaged in cultivating and developing these groves, including the harvesting and marketing of the crops. Each prospective customer was offered both a land sales contract and a service contract after being told that it was not feasible to invest in a grove unless service arrangements were made. Of the acreage sold by Howey, 85 percent was sold with a service contract with Howey-in-the-Hills Service, Inc. Must Howey register the sales of these parcels of citrus groves with the Securities and Exchange Commission? [Securities and Exchange Comm. v. W. J. Howey Co., 328 U.S. 293, 66 S.Ct. 1100 (1946)]

3. Zabriskie purchased certain notes from Lewis in connection with a real estate venture that Lewis was trying to establish. The notes bore a maturity date of eight months after the date of purchase. The Securities Act of 1933 excludes from its definition of securities any note that has a maturity date not exceeding nine months at the time of issue. Knowing that the Securities Act is an attempt to control the sales of *investment* securities, can a better test be devised than this strict nine-month rule? [Zabriskie v. Lewis, 507 F.2d 546 (10th Cir. 1974)]

4. Children's Hospital offered and sold a number of 8 percent mortgage bonds in order to raise enough money to begin operation. Its promoters solicited purchasers mainly through the mails and through local newspaper advertisements. Children's Hospital was to be a nonprofit medical organization established mainly to serve the needs of children in the local community. The promoters, however, expected to earn large profits from organizing the hospital. Must the promoters of Children's Hospital register the sale of the mortgage bonds with the Securities and Exchange Commission? [Securities and Exchange Comm. v. Children's Hospital, 214 F.Supp. 883 (D. Ariz. 1963)]

5. On September 1, 1971, the Ecological Science Corporation issued a press release stating, in part, that it had renegotiated the terms of approximately $14 million in loans from its prime lender and that, under the renegotiated agreement, $4 million was due upon demand and the remainder on a specified date. The press release, however, failed to mention that, on the same date as the renegotiated loan agreement, an insurance and annuity association had refused to provide the corporation with the $4 million loan that it had planned to use to repay the demand loan. Moreover, while discussing its European prospects in the press release, Ecological Science Corporation failed to mention the proposed transfer of voting control among its European subsidiaries. Has Ecological Science Corporation violated any of the provisions of the Securities Act of 1934? [Securities and Exchange Comm. v. Koenig, 469 F.2d. 198 (2d Cir. 1972)]

6. Vincent Chiarella was employed by a printing house that specialized in printing financial statements for public companies. Chiarella thus had access to information about certain companies before the information was released to the general public. While doing some typesetting for the XYZ Corporation, Chiarella came across some information about XYZ that led him to conclude that its stock would be a worthwhile investment. Chiarella purchased several thousand shares of XZY Corporation stock and within nine months had made a profit of $30,000. Has Chiarella violated Rule 10b-5 of the 1934 securities act? [United States v. Chiarella, 588 F.2d 1358 (2nd Cir. 1978)]

7. Emerson Electric Company owned 13.2 percent of Dodge Manufacturing Company's stock. Within six months of the purchase of this stock, Emerson sold enough shares to a broker to reduce its holding to 9.96 percent. One week later (but still less than six months after Emerson's initial purchase), Emerson sold its remaining shares of Dodge stock. The sole purpose of Emerson's initial sale of just over 3 percent of its Dodge stock was to avoid liability under Section 16 of the Securities Act of 1934, which prohibits short-swing trading. Assuming Emerson made no profit on the initial sale of stock but made substantial profits when it sold the remaining 9.96 percent of Dodge stock, must it disgorge the profits it made on the sale? [Reliance Electric Co. v. Emerson Electric Co., 404 U.S. 418, 92 S.Ct. 596 (1972)]

8. Repide owned three-quarters of the stock of the Philippine Sugar Estates Development Company, which in turn owned one-half of what were known as the "Friar Lands" in the Philippine Islands. The

government wished to purchase the Friar Lands and made an offer to purchase them for approximately $6 million. Since the Philippine Sugar Company owned one-half the lands and the remaining lands were fractionally owned, the company had a strong say in whether or not the owners would jointly accept the government's offer. Repide, acting on behalf of the company, rejected the government's offer and informed the government that he believed the lands to be worth over $13 million. In fact, Repide knew that the lands were almost worthless, except for the fact that the government wanted to buy them. Meanwhile, Repide sought to purchase the remaining 25 percent of the outstanding shares of the Philippine Sugar Company from their owner, Strong. Instead of negotiating with Strong directly, Repide began negotiations with her agent, Jones, whom he knew was in possession of the stock. Repide never informed Jones or Strong of the government's offers for the Friar Lands and thereafter purchased Strong's shares for a very small amount. In fact, the purchase price was lower than Strong would have received if the government's original offer for the Friar Lands had been accepted. Subsequently, the government paid almost $8 million for the Friar Lands. What liability does Repide have to Strong, if any? [Strong v. Repide, 213 U.S. 419, 29 S.Ct. 521 (1909)]

9.   Leston Nay owned 90 percent of the stock of First Securities Company. Between the years 1942 and 1966, Hochfelder sent large sums of money to Nay to be invested in escrow accounts of First Securities. The whole investment scheme was a fraud, and Nay converted the money sent by Hochfelder to his own use. Hochfelder then sued Ernst & Ernst, First Securities' auditor, for failing to use proper auditing procedures and thus negligently failing to discover the fraudulent scheme. Will Ernst & Ernst be found guilty of violating Section 10(b) and Rule 10b-5 of the 1934 Securities Act? [Ernst & Ernst v. Hochfelder, 425 U.S. 185, 96 S.Ct. 1375 (1976)]

10.   Lakeside Plastics and Engraving Company was a close corporation incorporated in Minnesota. The company suffered losses from the time it was incorporated in 1946. Of its four shareholders, only one was involved in management of the firm. Notwithstanding its earlier difficulties, by 1954, it was apparent that the firm was about to become profitable. Without informing the other shareholders of this fact, the shareholder-manager bought out the remaining shareholders. He accomplished this by making numerous misrepresentations to them. Assuming the shareholder-manager used none of the instrumentalities of interstate commerce, including the mails or the telephone, in making these misrepresentations, can the remaining shareholders bring an action under Section 10(b) of the Securities Act of 1934? If not, do the remaining shareholders have any legal recourse? [Myzel v. Fields, 386 F.2d 718 (8th Cir. 1967)]

44

Corporations
Rights and Duties of Directors, Managers, and Shareholders

The corporation combines the efforts and resources of a large number of individuals to jointly produce greater returns than the individuals could obtain outside the corporation. Sometimes, actions that benefit the corporation as a whole do not coincide with the interests of the individual. This chapter focuses on the rights and duties of directors, managers, and shareholders and the resolution of conflicts among them.

THE ROLE OF OFFICERS AND DIRECTORS

Directors occupy a position of responsibility unlike that of other corporate personnel. Directors are sometimes inappropriately characterized as *agents* because they act for and on behalf of the corporation. However, no individual director can act as an agent to bind the corporation, and, as a group, directors collectively control the corporation in a way no agent can control a principal. Directors are often incorrectly characterized as *trustees* because they occupy positions of trust and control over the corporation. However, unlike trustees, they do not own or hold title to property for the use and benefit of others.

    Directors manage the corporation through the officers who are selected by the board; these officers are agents of the corporation. Directors and officers are deemed *fiduciaries* of the corporation. Their relationship with the corporation and its shareholders is one of trust and confidence. The fiduciary duties of the directors and officers include the duty of care and the duty of loyalty.

The Duty of Care

Directors are obligated to be honest and reasonably careful to use prudent business judgment in the conduct of corporate affairs. The so-called business judgment rule does not require directors to insure the success of every venture that the corporation undertakes. The test is objective—the directors must exercise the same degree of care that reasonably prudent people use in the conduct of their own personal business affairs. Thus, corporate losses resulting merely from poor business judgment or an honest mistake of judgment will not normally result in the imposition of legal liability on directors.

BREACH OF THE DUTY OF CARE   Directors can be held answerable to the corporation and to the shareholders for breach of their duty of care. When directors delegate work to corporate officers and employees, they are expected to use a reasonable amount of supervision. Otherwise, they will be held liable for *negligence* or *mismanagement* of corporate personnel. For example, a corporate bank director failed to attend any board of directors' meetings in five and a half years and never inspected any of the corporate books or records. Meanwhile, the bank president made various improper loans and permitted large overdrafts. The corporate director was held liable to the corporation for losses of nearly $20,000 resulting from the unsupervised actions of the bank president and the loan committee.

The standard of due care has been variously described and codified in many corporation codes.[1] The impact of the standard is to require that directors carry out their responsibility in an informed, business-like manner.

---

1.   See, for example, Section 36 of the Model Business Corporation Act, which provides that "a director shall perform his duties as a director, including his duties as a member of any committee of the board upon which he may serve, in good faith, in any manner he reasonably believes to be in the best interest of the corporation, and with such care as an ordinarily prudent person in a like position would use under similar circumstances."

The standard also varies by the nature of the business. Directors and officers are often expected to act carefully in light of their own actual knowledge and training.

It is expected that directors attend board of directors' meetings and have their votes entered into the minutes of corporate meetings. Directors are also expected to keep themselves well informed on corporate matters and to familiarize themselves with corporate financial statements. Furthermore, they are expected to understand the legal advice rendered by corporate counsel. A director who is unable to carry out such responsibilities must resign. Even when the required duty of care has not been exercised, directors and officers are liable only for the damages caused to the corporation by their negligence.

Duty of Loyalty

The essence of the fiduciary duty requires subordination of self-interest to the interest of the entity to which the duty is owed. It presumes constant loyalty to the corporation on the part of the directors and officers. In general, the duty of loyalty prohibits directors from using corporate funds or confidential corporate information for personal advantage. It requires officers and directors to fully disclose any corporate opportunity or any possible conflict of interest that might occur in a transaction involving the directors and the corporation.

Cases dealing with fiduciary duty typically involve one or more of the following: (1) competing with the corporation, (2) usurping a corporate opportunity, (3) having an interest that conflicts with the interest of the corporation, (4) engaging in insider trading, (5) authorizing some corporate transaction that is detrimental to minority shareholders, and (6) sale of control of the corporation.

In the following case, the Alabama court reviewed a situation in which officers, directors, and shareholders attempted to secure advantages for themselves at the expense of the corporation.

**MORAD v.
COUPOUNAS**
Supreme Court of Alabama,
1978. 361 So.2d 6.

BACKGROUND AND FACTS *Morad, Thomson, and Morad's wife were officers, directors and shareholders of Bio-Lab, Inc. Coupounas was also a shareholder. While serving as officers and directors of Bio-Lab, Morad, Thomson, and Morad's wife incorporated and operated a competing business, Med-Lab, Inc. Thereupon, Coupounas sued individually and derivatively, alleging that the directors of Bio-Lab had breached their fiduciary duty to him and to Bio-Lab by opening the competing business.*

DECISION AND RATIONALE *The directors of Bio-Lab were guilty of misappropriating a corporate opportunity from the company. Officers and directors of a corporation may in some instances seize upon an opportunity that they discover as a result of their positions. However, if the opportunity is available both to the corporate officer or director personally and to the corporation, the officer or director must make others in the company aware of the opportunity and may not surreptitiously exploit it. The court concluded: "It is well settled that directors and other governing members of a coproration are so far agents of the corporation that in their dealings respecting corporate interests, they are subject to the rules which apply generally to persons standing in fiduciary relations and which forbid such persons to secure an advantage for themselves which fidelity to the trust reposed in them would carry to others whose interests they ought to represent."*

Conflicts of Interest

Corporate directors often have many business affiliations, and they can even sit on the board of more than one corporation. Of course, they are precluded from entering into or supporting any business that operates in direct competition with the corporation. The fiduciary duty requires them to make full disclosure of any potential *conflicts of interest* that might arise in any corporate transaction.

Contracts between Director and Corporation

Sometimes the corporation will enter into a contract or engage in a transaction in which an officer or director has a material interest. The director or officer must make full disclosure of that interest and should abstain from voting on the proposed transaction.

For example, Pacific Business Corporation needs office space. Louis Allen, one of its five directors, owns the building adjoining the corporation. He negotiates a lease with Pacific Business for the space, making full disclosure to Pacific Business and the other four board directors. The lease arrangement is fair and reasonable, and it is unanimously approved by the corporation's board of directors. In such a case, the contract is valid. The rule is one of reason; otherwise directors would be prevented from ever giving financial assistance to the corporations they serve. The various state statutes contain different standards, but a contract will generally not be voidable if (1) it was fair and reasonable to the corporation at the time it was entered into, (2) there is full disclosure of the interest of the officers or directors in the transaction, and (3) the contract is approved by a majority of the disinterested directors or shareholders.

Contracts between Corporations Having Common Directors

Often, contracts are negotiated between corporations having one or more directors who are members of both boards. Care should be taken in these situations because they are often severely scrutinized by courts.

LIABILITIES OF CORPORATE OFFICERS

The duties of corporate officers are the same as the duties of directors because their respective corporate positions involve both of them in decision making and place them in similar control positions. Hence, they are viewed as having the same fiduciary duty of care and loyalty in their conduct of corporate affairs. Officers are subject to the same obligations concerning corporate opportunities and conflict of interest as are directors. Corporate officers and other high-level managers are employees of the company, and their rights and duties are defined by employment contracts. Employee rights are outlined in Chapter 34.

DUTIES AND LIABILITIES OF MAJOR SHAREHOLDERS

In some cases, a majority shareholder is regarded as having a fiduciary duty to the corporation and to the minority shareholders. This occurs when a single shareholder (or a few acting in concert) own a sufficient number of shares to exercise de facto control over the corporation.

RIGHTS OF DIRECTORS

Right of Participation

A corporate director must have certain rights in order to function properly in the position—the main one being the right to be notified of board of director meetings and to participate in them.

Right of Inspection

A director must have access to all corporate books and records in order to make decisions and exercise the necessary supervision. This right is virtually absolute and cannot be restricted.

Right of Indemnification

It is not unusual for corporate directors to become involved in lawsuits by virtue of their position and their actions as directors. Under certain circumstances, most states (and the Model Act) permit a corporation to indemnify a director for legal costs, fees, and judgments involved in defending corporation related suits. The common law, however, has restricted the right to reimbursement of costs, even in successful litigation, without explicit insurance or the agreement of the corporation.

Right of Compensation

Historically, directors have had no inherent right to compensation for their services as directors. Officers receive compensation, and nominal sums are often paid as honoraria to directors. In many cases, directors are also chief corporate officers and receive compensation in their managerial positions. Most directors, however, gain through indirect benefits, such as business contacts, prestige, and other rewards.

There is a growing trend toward providing more than nominal compensation for directors, especially in large corporations where directorships can be enormous burdens in terms of time, work, effort, and risk. Many states permit the corporate articles or bylaws to authorize compensation for directors, and in some cases the board can set its own compensation unless the articles or bylaws provide otherwise.

SHAREHOLDER RIGHTS

Shareholders own the corporation. Their rights are established in the articles of incorporation and under the state's general incorporation law.

The Right to a Stock Certificate

A stock certificate evidences ownership, and shareholders have the right to demand that the corporation issue a certificate and record their names and addresses in the corporate stock record books. Stock is *intangible* personal property—the ownership right exists independently of the certificate itself. A stock certificate may be lost or destroyed, but ownership is not destroyed with it. Corporate records reflect ownership, although they do not determine it.

A new certificate can be issued to replace one that has been lost or destroyed.[2] Notice of shareholder meetings, dividends, and operational and financial reports are all distributed according to the recorded ownership listed in the corporation's books, not on the basis of possession of the certificate. Assume that Betty Anderson's corporate stock in Chrysler Corporation is destroyed in a fire on September 1. The corporation declares a dividend on September 5. According to corporate records, Betty Anderson is the "record owner" and receives the dividend even though she no longer has the certificate.

Of course, to sell or otherwise transfer the shares, indorsement and delivery of the actual certificate to the transferee are required.

Preemptive Rights

Preemption is a preference given to a shareholder over all other purchasers to subscribe to or purchase a prorated share of a new issue so the shareholder can maintain his or her portion of control, voting power, or financial interest in the corporation. Preemptive rights exist only if permitted by state statute, and they can be denied or limited by corporate articles. Generally, preemptive rights apply only to additional stock sold for cash. For example, Paula Smith purchases one hundred shares of National Clothing Corporation stock. A total of one thousand shares of that issue are outstanding. Subsequently, National Clothing decides to issue another thousand shares to increase its capital stock to a total of two thousand shares. If preemptive rights have been provided, Smith can purchase one additional share of the new stock being issued for each share currently owned—or one hundred additional shares. Thus she can own two hundred of the two thousand shares outstanding, and her relative position as a shareholder will be maintained. If preemptive rights are not reserved, her proportionate control and voting power will be diluted from that of a 10 percent shareholder to that of a 5 percent shareholder because of the issuance of the additional one thousand shares.

Preemptive rights are far more significant in a close corporation because of the relatively few number of shares and the substantial interest each shareholder controls.

Stock Warrants

When preemptive rights exist and a corporation is issuing additional shares, each shareholder is usually given *stock warrants*. A **stock warrant** entitles each shareholder to buy a given number of shares within a limited time period (usually two weeks) at a stated price.

Dividend Rights

A dividend is a distribution of corporate profits *ordered by the directors* and paid to the shareholders in proportion to their respective shares in the corporation. Dividends can be paid in cash, property, stock of the corporation that is paying the dividends, or stock of other corporations.[3]

State laws vary, but every state controls the general legal requirements under which dividends are paid. Once declared, a dividend

---

2. To have a lost or destroyed certificate reissued, a shareholder is normally required to furnish an indemnity bond to protect the corporation against potential loss should the original certificate reappear at some future time in the hands of a bona fide purchaser. [UCC Secs. 8-302 and 8-405(2)]

3. Technically, dividends paid in stock are not dividends. They maintain each shareholder's proportional interest in the corporation. On one occasion a distillery declared and paid a "dividend" in bonded whiskey.

becomes a corporate debt enforceable at law like any other debt.[4]

When directors fail to declare a dividend, shareholders can ask a court of equity for an injunction to compel the directors to meet and to declare a dividend. It must be shown that the directors have acted so unreasonably in withholding the dividend that their conduct is an abuse of discretion. Often, large money reserves

---

4. State laws prescribe the circumstances under which dividends can be paid. An insolvent corporation cannot declare a dividend. State laws also control the sources of revenue to be used. Only certain funds are legally available for paying dividends.

are accumulated for a bona fide purpose such as expansion, research, and other legitimate corporate goals. The mere fact that sufficient corporate earnings or surplus are available to pay a dividend will not be enough to compel directors to distribute funds that, in the board's opinion, should not be paid. The courts are circumspect about interfering with corporate operations and will not compel directors to declare dividends unless abuse of discretion is clearly shown. Directors are not ordinarily required to declare dividends to shareholders. A striking exception to this rule is exemplified by the following case.

BACKGROUND AND FACTS   *Henry Ford was the president and major shareholder of Ford Motor Company. In the company's early years, business expanded rapidly, and, in addition to regular quarterly dividends, special dividends were often paid. By 1916 surplus above capital was still $111,960,907. That year, however, Henry Ford declared that the company would no longer pay special dividends, but would put back into the business all the earnings of the company above the regular dividend of 5 percent. The court quoted Ford: "My ambition," declared Mr. Ford, "is to employ still more men; to spread the benefits of this industrial system to the greatest possible number, to help them build up their lives and their homes. To do this, we are putting the greatest share of our profits back into the business." The minority shareholders of Ford (who owned 10 percent of the stock) brought suit to force the declaration of a dividend.*

DODGE v. FORD MOTOR CO.

Supreme Court of Michigan, 1919.
204 Mich. 459, 170 N.W. 668.

DECISION AND RATIONALE   *Because of the special circumstances of this case, the court compelled Ford to pay a dividend. The undisputed facts were that Ford had a surplus of $112 million—approximately $54 million in cash on hand. It had made profits of $59 million in the past year and expected to make $60 million in the coming year. The board of directors gave no reason to justify withholding a dividend. Thus, the doing so violated the stated purpose of the corporation's existence. "Courts of equity will not interfere in the management of the directors unless it is clearly made to appear that they are guilty of fraud or misappropriation of the corporate funds, or refuse to declare a dividend when the corporation has a surplus of net profits which it can, without detriment to its business, divide among its stockholders, and when a refusal to do so would amount to such an abuse of discretion as would constitute a fraud, or breach of that good faith which they are bound to exercise towards the stockholders."*

Right to Vote

Shareholders exercise ownership control through the power of their vote. In the early development of corporate law, each shareholder was entitled to one vote per share. This rule still holds today, but the voting techniques discussed in Chapter 43 (pooling agreements, voting trusts, cumulative voting methods, and so on) all enhance the power of the shareholder's vote.

Inspection Rights

Shareholders have the right to inspect and copy certain corporate books and records for any *proper purpose*, provided they make the request in advance. Either the shareholder can inspect in person, or an attorney, agent, accountant, or other assistant can do so.

The power of inspection is fraught with potential abuses, and the corporation is allowed to protect itself from them. For example, a shareholder can properly be denied access to corporate records to prevent harassment or to protect trade secrets or other confidential corporate information. Section 52 of the Model Act imposes various standard requirements on the shareholder's inspection right:

Any person who shall have been a holder of record shares * * * at least six months immediately preceding his [or her] demand or [who is] * * * the holder of * * * at least 5 percent of all the outstanding shares of the corporation, upon written demand stating the purpose thereof, shall have the right to examine, in person, or by agent or attorney, at any reasonable time or times, for any proper purpose its relevant books and records of accounts, minutes, and record of shareholders and to make extracts therefrom.

However, a corporation's improper refusal to allow access to its records can result in severe and costly liability to the corporation. Under Section 52 of the Model Act, the penalty is 10 percent the value of the shares owned by the shareholder who has been denied access to the books.

SKOURAS v. ADMIRALTY ENTERPRISES, INC.

Court of Chancery of Delaware, 1978.
386 A.2d 674.

BACKGROUND AND FACTS *Skouras owned 5 percent of the shares of Admiralty Enterprises, Inc., a closely held family corporation. Skouras demanded an inspection of the corporate books and records so that he could substantiate his fears of mismanagement and determine whether some of the directors were using corporate funds improperly for such things as club memberships. Admiralty Enterprises contended that Skouras's motive was merely harassment. Skouras sued, claiming that his desire to inspect the books was in good faith.*

DECISION AND RATIONALE *Because the court was convinced that Skouras's motives were in good faith, he had the right, as a minority shareholder, to inspect Admiralty's books and records. The court will not allow minority shareholders to inspect company books if their sole motive is harassment. The court gave the following explanation: "A proper purpose [for inspecting corporate books and records] is defined in [the Delaware statutes] as one which is '*** reasonably related to such person's interest as a stockholder ***' and it is clearly proper for a stockholder to ask leave to examine corporate books and records to follow up his suspicions of corporate mismanagement, thereby acting not only on his own behalf but on that of the corporation and its other stockholders."*

Right to Transfer Shares

Corporate stock represents an ownership right in intangible personal property. The law generally recognizes the right of an owner to transfer property to another person unless there are valid restrictions on its transferability. Although stock certificates are negotiable instruments and freely transferable by indorsement and delivery, transfer of stock in closely-held corporations is generally restricted by contract, the bylaws, or a restriction stamped on the stock certificate. The existence of any restrictions on transferability should always be noted on the face of the stock certificate.

CLOSELY-HELD CORPORATIONS Sometimes, corporations impose restrictions on transfer. In a closely-held corporation, for example, the shareholders often actively manage and are intimately involved in the daily business operations of the corporation. Hence, a restriction on transfer of shares to third persons is a general practice.

RIGHT OF FIRST REFUSAL Sometimes, corporations or their shareholders restrict transferability by reserving the option to purchase any shares offered for resale by a shareholder. The option remains with the corporation or the shareholders only for a specified or reasonable time limit. Variations on the purchase option are possible. For example, a shareholder might be required to offer the shares to other shareholders or the corporation first.

CORPORATE RECORDS When shares are transferred, a new entry is made in the corporate stock book to indicate the new owner. Until the corporation is notified and the entry is complete, voting rights, notice of shareholder meetings, dividend distribution, and so forth are all held by the current record owner.

Rights upon Dissolution

When a corporation is dissolved and its outstanding debts and the claims of its creditors have been satisfied, the remaining assets are distributed pro rata among the shareholders. Certain classes of preferred stock can be given priority to the extent of their contractual preference. If no preferences to distribution of assets upon liquidation are given to any class of stock, then the stockholders share the remaining assets.

COMPELLING RECEIVERSHIP A minority shareholder does not simply have to watch the board of directors mishandle or waste corporate assets or to permit a deadlock to threaten or irreparably injure the corporation's finances. A minority shareholder can petition a court to appoint a receiver and to liquidate the business assets of the corporation. The Model Act, Section 97, permits any shareholder to institute such an action when it appears that (1) the directors are deadlocked in the management of corporate affairs, shareholders are unable to break that deadlock, and irreparable injury to the corporation is being suffered or threatened; (2) the acts of the directors or those in control of the corporation are illegal, oppressive, or fraudulent; or (3) corporate assets are being misapplied or wasted.

SHAREHOLDER LIABILITIES

One of the hallmarks of the corporate organization is that shareholders are not personally liable for the debts of the corporation. If the corporation fails, shareholders can lose their investment, but that is generally the limit of liability. In certain instances of fraud, undercapitalization, or careless observance of corporate formalities, a court will pierce the corporate veil (disregard the corporate entity) and hold the shareholders individually liable. But these situations are the exception, not the rule.

Illegal Dividends

Whenever a dividend is paid while the corporation is *insolvent*, it is automatically an illegal dividend, and shareholders can be liable for returning the payment to the corporation or its creditors.

Dividends are generally required by statute to be distributed only from certain authorized corporate accounts representing profits. Sometimes dividends are improperly paid from an unauthorized account, or their payment causes the corporation to become insolvent. Generally, shareholders must return illegal dividends only if they knew that the dividends were illegal when they received them.

In all cases of illegal and improper dividends, the board of directors can be held personally liable for the amount of the payment. However, when directors can show that a shareholder *knew* a dividend was illegal when it was received, they can recover their loss of that amount from the shareholder.

QUESTIONS AND CASE PROBLEMS

1. Alex, Brown and Sons was a Pennsylvania stockbroker that purchased and sold stock and owned stock in its own name for a number of companies, including Latrobe Steel Company. Upon learning that a large corporation was about to make a tender offer (that is, an offer to purchase stock from shareholders) to Latrobe's shareholders, Alex, Brown sought permission to inspect and obtain a copy of Latrobe's list of shareholders. Alex, Brown stood to make a substantial profit by way of commission for shares it could secure in conjunction with the tender offer. Should Alex, Brown be allowed to inspect and obtain the shareholder list from Latrobe? [Alex, Brown and Sons v. Latrobe Steel Co., 376 F.Supp. 1373 (W.D. Pa. 1974)]

2. Robertson and Tedder were directors and officers of the Plantation Golf Club. Together they made up the majority of shareholders in the company. Coleman was a minority shareholder. For the previous three years, Robertson and Tedder had fixed their own compensation for their services as officers of the corporation. Coleman felt that the salaries were excessive. Can he now object? [Coleman v. Plantation Golf Club, Inc., 212 So.2d. 806 (Fla. Dist. Ct. App. 1968)]

3. Grant and Martin were directors of Lincoln Stores, Inc. Both had worked for Lincoln Stores in other capacities—as store manager and as general manager, respectively. Hayley was one of the managers of the very successful Lincoln store that was located in Norwich, Connecticut. The Reid and Hughes Company owned a store several buildings down from the Lincoln store in Norwich. Reid and Hughes presented little competition to Lincoln. On April 27, Grant, Martin, and Hayley agreed to purchase the Reid and Hughes store, and Hayley resigned from Lincoln's employ to take charge of it. Before he left, however, Hayley obtained certain confidential information that he later used to assist him in setting up operations at the Reid and Hughes store. Grant and Martin, desiring to continue in Lincoln's employ, concealed their ownership of the new store and continued as directors at Lincoln. Thereafter, the Reid and Hughes store became quite successful and competitive with Lincoln. Lincoln Stores then sued Grant, Martin, and Hayley for their breach of loyalty. Should it recover? If so, what should Lincoln be awarded as damages: lost profits? ownership of the competing store? [Lincoln Stores v. Grant, 309 Mass. 417, 34 N.E.2d. 704 (1941)]

4. Barnes-King Development Company, a Montana corporation, was voluntarily dissolved by order of the court on December 16, 1925. On December 20, 1968, some 43 years later, the trustee of Barnes-King filed a petition for distribution of the company's assets. The petition showed that, in 1968, the assets amounted to $42,000. At the time of dissolution in 1925, there were 400,000 shares of stock outstanding. At the time of distribution in 1970, only 185,000 shares of the assets of Barnes-King had been proportionately distributed to shareholders. These shareholders claimed that the remaining unclaimed shares had been abandoned and therefore should go to them. Under common law, abandoned property escheats to the state. Who gets the unclaimed assets? [Barnes-King Development Co. v. Corette, 156 Mont. 202, 478 P.2d. 868 (1971)]

5. Crothers, Williams, and Ross were the sole shareholders of Ross Transport, Inc. Each held approximately one-third of the company's stock. Without contacting Crothers, Williams and Ross, who were the directors of the company, had the company

issue additional shares to themselves. Crothers sued, claiming that both his voting power and his right to share in dividends had been lessened. What theory should Crothers assert to be successful against Williams, Ross, and Ross Transport? [Ross Transport, Inc. v. Crothers, 185 Md. 573, 45 A.2d 267 (1946)].

6. Shubin and Surchin were codirectors of Approved Business Machines Company, Inc. Each owned a 20 percent interest in the company. The remaining 60 percent was owned by four persons, each owning 15 percent. For a year, there was serious internal dissension between the two major shareholders, Shubin and Surchin. The corporation was a closed corporation, and the remaining shareholders were evenly divided in their support of one of the two directors. Surchin applied to the courts for a dissolution of the firm, since he felt that the disagreement among the shareholders was irreconcilable. Should a judge grant Surchin's request? [Application of Surchin, 55 Misc.2d 888, 286 N.Y.S.2d 580 (1967)]

7. Engdahl was a 10 percent stockholder, a director, and the treasurer of Aero Drapery, Inc. In May of 1967 several Aero employees expressed to Engdahl their dissatisfaction with their employment with Aero. Later that month, at Engdahl's suggestion, Engdahl met with the employees and suggested that they join together and form a new enterprise. In early June they decided to go into the custom-drapery business in direct competition with Aero. Later that month the new business associates decided upon a location for the new business, contacted suppliers, and secured an advertisement in the Yellow Pages. In July, 1967, Engdahl tendered his resignation as Director and Treasurer of Aero Drapery, Inc. Has Engdahl breached any duty to Aero Drapery, Inc.? Would your answer be different if Engdahl had resigned early in May of 1967? (What additional fact do you need to know to answer the latter question?) Aero Drapery of Kentucky, Inc. v. Engdahl, 507 S.W. 2d 166 (Ky. App. 1974).

8. Hartung, Odle and Burke were architects. In 1971 they organized as a corporation. Their association, however, was riddled with dissent from the start. As it became apparent that the corporate turmoil would eventually result in reorganization of the corporation, Hartung began conferring with several clients of the firm informing them that he was willing to continue as their architect after his withdrawal from the corporation. The corporation was later dissolved, and several of its clients continued to do business with Hartung. Do Odle and Burke have any recourse against Hartung for his activities? Hartung vs. Architects Hartung/Odle/Burke, Inc., 301 N.E.2nd 240 (Ind. App. 1973).

45

Corporations
Merger, Consolidation,
and Termination

Corporations increase their holdings for a number of reasons. They may wish to enlarge their physical plants, increase their property or investment holdings, or acquire the assets, know-how, or goodwill of another corporation. Sometimes acquisition is motivated by a desire to eliminate a competitor, to accomplish diversification, or to insure adequate resources and markets for the acquiring corporation's product. Whatever the reason, the corporation typically extends its operations by combining with another corporation through (1) merger, (2) consolidation, (3) purchase of assets, or (4) purchase of a controlling interest of the other corporation.

This chapter will examine the various ways that merger or consolidation alters the fundamental structure of the corporation. The terms *merger* and *consolidation* are often used interchangeably, but they refer to two legally distinct proceedings. Whether a combination is in fact a merger or a consolidation, the rights and liabilities of shareholders, the corporation, and its creditors are the same.

Dissolution and liquidation are the combined processes by which a corporation terminates its existence. The last part of this chapter will discuss the typical reasons and methods for terminating a corporation.

MERGERS AND CONSOLIDATION

Mergers

A **merger** involves the legal combination of two or more corporations. After a merger, only one of the corporations continues to exist (the **surviving corporation**), and all the others cease to exist (disappearing corporations). For example, Corporation A and Corporation B decide to merge. It is agreed that A will absorb B, so, upon merger, B ceases to exist as a separate entity and A continues as the *surviving corporation.*

A merger can be represented symbolically as A + B = A. After the merger, A is recognized as a single corporation, possessing all the rights, privileges, and powers of itself and B. A automatically acquires all of B's property and assets without the necessity of formal transfer or deed. A becomes liable for all B's debts and obligations. Finally, A's articles of incorporation are deemed *amended* to include any changes that are stated in the articles of merger.

Consolidation

In the case of a **consolidation**, two or more corporations combine so that each corporation ceases to exist and a new one emerges. Corporation A and Corporation B consolidate to form an entirely new organization, Corporation C. In the process, A and B both terminate. C comes into existence as an entirely new entity.

A symbolic representation of consolidation, then, is A + B = C. The results of consolidation are essentially the same as the results of merger. C is recognized as a new corporation and a single entity; A and B cease to exist. C accedes to all the rights, privileges, and powers previously held by A and B. Title to any property and assets owned by A and B passes to C without formal transfer. C assumes liability for all debts and obligations owed by A and B. The articles of consolidation *take the place of* A's and B's original corporate articles and are thereafter regarded as C's corporate articles.

In both merger and consolidation, the surviving or newly formed corporation takes over the assets of the former corporations and assumes their liabilities. Further, the surviving or newly formed corporation issues new shares or pays some fair consideration to shareholders in exchange for the stock of the corporations that have ceased to exist.

In a merger, the surviving corporation is vested with the disappearing corporation's preexisting legal rights and obligations. For example, if the disappearing corporation had a right of action against a third party, after the merger, the surviving corporation could then bring suit to recover for the disappearing corporation's damages. The corporation statutes of many states provide that a successor (surviving) corporation inherit a *chose in action* (a right to sue for a debt or sum of money) from a merging corporation as a matter of law. So, too, the common law rule recognizes that a chose in action to enforce a property right upon merger will vest with the successor (surviving) corporation, and no right of action will remain with the disappearing corporation.

BACKGROUND AND FACTS *OMR, Inc. owned an easement (right of way) to a pipe line across certain property. Altes, the owner of the property, operated a rock quarry on the land. Altes warned his workers not to conduct the quarrying operation in the area where the pipeline was buried. Nevertheless, one of his employees negligently punctured it.*

OMR, Inc. merged with Sun Pipe Line Company (Sun), and Sun was the surviving firm. Sun sued Altes to recover for the damage to the pipeline that his negligent employee had caused. Altes defended on the ground that OMR and not Sun had suffered the damage, and therefore Sun could not sue.

SUN PIPE LINE CO. v. ALTES

United States Court of Appeals, Eight Circuit, 1975.
511 F.2d 280.

DECISION AND RATIONALE   *Sun could recover. State statute determines a corporation's capacity to sue or be sued. The statutes of the state where this case was tried provided that when two or more firms merge, all the assets and liabilities of the merging firms, including choses in action, vest in the survivor. "[T]his Court has stated that statutes such as [this state's], which provide that a successor corporation inherits a chose in action from a merging corporation as a matter of law merely serve to codify the common law rule 'which recognizes that a chose in action to enforce a property right upon merger vests in the successor corporation and no right of action remains in the merging corporation.' "*

The Procedure

All states have statutes authorizing mergers and consolidations for *domestic* corporations, and most allow the combination of domestic (in-state) and foreign (out-of-state) corporations. Although the procedures vary somewhat among jurisdictions, they all contain the basic requirements outlined below:

1.   The board of directors of *each* corporation involved must approve a merger or consolidation plan.
2.   The shareholders of *each* corporation must vote approval of the plan at a shareholders' meeting. Most state statutes require approval of a majority or two-thirds of the outstanding shares of voting stock. Frequently, statutes require that each class of stock approve the merger; thus, the holders of nonvoting stock must also approve the merger.
3.   Once approved by *all* the boards of directors and the shareholders, the plan is filed, usually with the secretary of state.
4.   When state formalities are satisfied, the state issues a certificate of merger (to the surviving corporation) or a certificate of consolidation (to the newly consolidated corporation).

Short-Form Merger Statutes (or Parent-Subsidy Mergers)

The Model Act in most states provides a simplified procedure for the merger of a substantially owned subsidiary corporation into its parent corporation. Under these provisions, a short-form merger can be accomplished *without*

approval of the shareholders of either corporation.

The **short-form merger** can be utilized only when the parent corporation owns at least 90 to 95 percent of the outstanding shares of each class of stock of the subsidiary corporation. The simplified procedure requires that a plan for the merger be approved by the board of directors of the parent corporation before it is filed with the state.

Appraisal Rights

What if a shareholder disapproves of the merger or consolidation, but is outvoted by the other shareholders? The law recognizes that a dissenting shareholder should not be forced to become an unwilling shareholder in a corporation that is new or different from the one in which the shareholder originally invested. The shareholder has the right to dissent and is entitled to be paid fair value for the number of shares held on the date of the merger or consolidation.

A dissenting shareholder must protect his or her right to payment by adhering strictly to statutory procedures, which vary from state to state.

Valuation of shares is often a point of contention between the dissenting shareholder and the corporation. The Model Act provides that the "fair value of shares" is the value on the day prior to the date on which the vote was taken.[1] The corporation must make a written

---

1.   Section 81 of the Model Act provides for excluding any appreciation or depreciation of the stock in anticipation of the approval.

offer to purchase a dissenting shareholder's stock, accompanying the offer with a current balance sheet and income statement for the applicable (appropriate) corporation. If the shareholder and the corporation do not agree on the fair value, a court will determine it.

Shareholder Approval

Shareholders invest in a corporate enterprise with the expectation that the board of directors will manage the enterprise and will approve ordinary business matters. Actions taken on extraordinary matters must be authorized by the board of directors and the shareholders. Often, modern statutes will require that certain types of extraordinary matters be approved by a prescribed voter consent of the shareholders. Typically, matters requiring shareholder ap-

proval include sale, lease, or exchange of all or substantially all corporate assets outside of the corporation's regular course of business. Other examples include amendments to the articles of incorporation, transactions concerning merger or consolidation, and dissolution.

Hence, when any extraordinary matter arises, the corporation must proceed as authorized by law to obtain shareholder and board of director approval. Sometimes, a transaction can be characterized in such a way as not to require shareholder approval, but a court will use its equity powers to require such approval. In order to determine the nature of the transaction, the courts will look not only to the details of the transaction but also to its consequences. In the following case, a "reorganization agreement" seemed to be a guise for a merger.

BACKGROUND AND FACTS *Farris filed suit to enjoin Glen Alden Corp. and the List Corporation from carrying out a proposed reorganization agreement that would, in effect, transform Glen Alden into a diversified holding company. Under the agreement, Glen Alden, the smaller company, purchased the assets of the List Corporation, the larger company, in exchange for a larger amount of Glen Alden stock. The book value of List's shares was $7.50 per share, but under the reorganization, List's shareholders would receive shares with a book value of $21 per share. In addition, Glen Alden, which was primarily a mining company, would be transformed into a conglomerate of more than twice its present size with holdings ranging from the motion picture industry to textiles.*

FARRIS v. GLEN ALDEN CORP.
Supreme Court of
Pennsylvania, 1958.
393 Pa. 427, 143 A.2d 25.

DECISION AND RATIONALE *List Industries was not permitted to carry out the proposed reorganization agreement without granting shareholders appraisal rights because the reorganization was a merger not a sale of assets. Shareholders must approve a merger, and, if it is approved, dissenting shareholders must be reimbursed for the value of their stock.*

Determining whether a particular transaction is a merger or a sale of assets is not simple. The facts showed that Glen Alden, which was a mining company, would become a large conglomerate as a result of the reorganization. Also, Farris's proportional interest in the conglomerate would be much smaller than his interest in Glen Alden. "[W]hen a corporation combines with another so as to lose its essential nature and alter the original fundamental relationships of the shareholders among themselves and to the corporation, a shareholder who does not wish to continue his membership therein may treat his membership in the original corporation as terminated and have the value of his shares paid to him."

Purchase of Assets

When a corporation acquires all or substantially all of the assets of another corporation by direct purchase, the purchasing or *acquiring* corporation simply extends its ownership and control over more physical assets. Since no change in the legal entity occurs, the *acquiring corporation* is not required to obtain shareholder approval for the purchase.[2]

Although the acquiring corporation may not be required to obtain shareholder approval for an acquisition, the Department of Justice has issued guidelines that significantly constrain and often prohibit mergers for any acquisition, including takeover bids (discussed in the next section). These guidelines are part of the federal

---

2. If the acquiring corporation plans to pay for the assets with its own corporate stock and not enough authorized unissued shares are available, the shareholders must vote to approve issuance of additional shares by amendment of the corporate articles. Also, acquiring corporations whose stock is traded in a national stock exchange can be required to obtain their own shareholders' approval if they plan to issue a significant number of shares, such as 20 percent or more of the outstanding shares.

antitrust laws to enforce Section 7 of the Clayton Act (discussed in Chapters 50 and 51). The Department of Justice merger guidelines are given in Exhibit 45-1. A horizontal merger involves two firms in the same industry. A vertical merger involves two firms in different industries, where one supplies the other (such as an electricity company and a coal company). A conglomerate merger involves totally unrelated firms.

The corporation that is *selling* all its assets is substantially changing its business position and perhaps its ability to carry out its corporate purposes. For that reason, the corporation whose assets are *acquired* must obtain both board of director and shareholder approval. In some states, a dissenting shareholder of the selling corporation can demand appraisal rights.

A dissenting shareholder's appraisal remedy is essentially a statutory creation. Depending on the jurisdiction, the appraisal remedy will often apply to mergers, consolidations, and sales of substantially all corporate assets other than those made in the regular course of business.

CAMPBELL v. VOSE
United States Court of Appeals,
Tenth Circuit, 1975.
515 F2d 256.

BACKGROUND AND FACTS *The Southwestern Cotton Oil Company created a wholly-owned subsidiary called Machine Works and transferred substantially all its assets to the subsidiary. Campbell, a minority shareholder in Southwestern, objected to the transaction and demanded the company give him dissenters' appraisal rights—that is, the fair market value of his shares. Southwestern refused, and this suit followed.*

DECISION AND RATIONALE *Campbell was entitled to appraisal rights. Under the statutes of the state where this case was tried, any "sale, lease, exchange or other disposition of all or substantially all" of a corporation's assets requires the corporation to give any dissenting shareholders appraisal rights. In this case, Southwestern, the parent company, had transferred substantially all its assets to Machine Works, its subsidiary. "An exchange for stock and for evidence of indebtedness was made, and the indicia of ownership were held by the subsidiary. We must hold that the transaction did bring into play the statutory rights of dissenting shareholders. ***"*

EXHIBIT 45-1   DEPARTMENT OF JUSTICE MERGER GUIDELINES

HORIZONTAL
MERGERS

1. When the share of sales of the four largest firms in a market amounts to approximately 75 percent or more of industry sales, a merger will ordinarily be challenged between two firms with the following shares of the market:

Acquiring Firm	Acquired Firm
4% or more	4% or more
10% or more	2% or more
15% or more	1% or more

2. When the share of sales of the four largest firms in a market, amounts to less than approximately 75 percent of industry sales, a merger will ordinarily be challenged between two firms with the following shares of the market:

Acquiring Firm	Acquired Firm
5% or more	5% or more
10% or more	4% or more
15% or more	3% or more
20% or more	2% or more
25% or more	1% or more

3. Mergers occurring in a market in which there is a significant trend toward increased concentration are also likely to be challenged. The trend toward concentration is considered present when the market share of two of eight of the largest firms in that market has increased by 7 percent or more in the five or ten years prior to the merger. An acquisition by any of the eight largest firms of another firm that has a market share of approximately 2 percent or more will ordinarily be challenged.

VERTICAL MERGERS

1. When the supplying firm accounts for 10 percent or more of the sales in its market, and the purchasing firm accounts for 6 percent or more of the purchases in that market, the merger will ordinarily be challenged.

2. When the purchasing firm accounts for 6 percent or more of the purchases in the market and the supplying firm accounts for 10 percent or more of the sales in that market, the merger will ordinarily be challenged.

3. In some situations, mergers outside the above limits will be challenged.

CONGLOMERATE
MERGERS

1. When one of the firms: (1) has approximately 25 percent or more of the market, (2) is one of the two largest firms in a market where the two largest firms have a market share of 50 percent or more, (3) is one of the four largest firms in a market where the eight largest firms have a market share of approximately 75 percent or more and the acquired firm has a 10 percent market share, or (4) is one of the market's eight largest firms and the eight have a combined market share of approximately 75 percent, the merger will ordinarily be challenged.

2. When there is a danger that reciprocal buying might result, the merger will ordinarily be challenged.

3. When the acquisition might raise barriers to entry or increase the acquiring firm's market power, the merger will ordinarily be challenged.

Purchase of Stock

An alternative to the purchase of another corporation's assets is the purchase of a substantial number of the voting shares of its stock. This enables the acquiring corporation to control the acquired, or *target* corporation. The acquiring corporation deals directly with the shareholders in seeking to purchase the shares they hold.

A so-called "take-over bid" is subject to state and federal securities regulations. When the acquiring corporation makes a public offer to all shareholders of the target corporation, it is called a *tender offer* (an offer that is publicly advertised and addressed to all shareholders of the would-be target company). A tender offer is sometimes made when the acquiring firm believes that the target company is poorly managed. For this reason, the offer price is generally higher than the market price of the target stock prior to the announcement of the tender offer. The higher price induces shareholders to tender their shares to the acquiring firm. The tender offer can be conditional upon the receipt of a specified number of outstanding shares by a specified date. The offering corporation can make an *exchange* tender offer in which it offers target stockholders its own securities in exchange for their target stock. In a cash tender offer, the offering corporation offers the target stockholders cash in exchange for their target stock.

Federal securities laws strictly control the terms, duration, and circumstances under which most tender offers are made. In addition, over thirty states have passed "take-over" statutes that impose additional regulations on tender offers.

The use of the tender offer as a method of gaining corporate control began in the mid-1960s. Highly contested legal battles and enormous expenses involved in complying with federal and state regulations have worked to discourage the use of tender offers as a vehicle for obtaining control of a corporation through stock purchase.

TERMINATION

Termination of a corporate life, like termination of a partnership, has two phases—liquidation and dissolution. **Liquidation** is the process by which corporate assets are converted into cash and distributed among creditors and shareholders according to specific rules of preference.[3] **Dissolution** is the legal death of the artificial "person" of the corporation.

Dissolution can be brought about in any of the following ways: (1) an act of a legislature in the state of incorporation; (2) the expiration of the time provided in the certificate of incorporation; (3) the voluntary approval of the shareholders and the board of directors; (4) unanimous action by all shareholders; or (5) court decree brought about by the attorney general of the state of incorporation for any of the following reasons— failure to comply with administrative requirements (for example, failure to pay annual franchise taxes or to submit an annual report or to have a designated registered agent), the procurement of a corporate charter through fraud or misrepresentation upon the state, the abuse of corporate powers (*ultra vires* acts), the violation of the state criminal code after the demand to discontinue has been made by the secretary of state, the failure to commence business operations, or the abandonment of operations before starting up.

3. Upon dissolution, the liquidated assets are first used to pay creditors. Any remaining assets are distributed to shareholders according to their respective stock rights; preferred stock has priority over common stock.

GRUENBERG v. GOLDMINE PLANTATION, INC.

Court of Appeal of Louisiana, Fourth Circuit, 1978. 360 So.2d 884.

BACKGROUND AND FACTS *Goldmine Plantation, Inc. (Goldmine) was a Louisiana corporation. Its principal asset was a nine hundred acre tract of land fronting the bank of the Mississippi River. In 1941 this land was acquired for $65,000. In 1975 the property was appraised at $3,000* *per acre and various industrial enterprises offered as much as $3,600 per acre. The majority shareholders, however, declined all offers. As a result, Gruenberg, a 40 percent shareholder, brought suit to force dissolution claiming that, since the firm's sugar cane business had made profits of less than one-half of one percent over the past ten years, the majority shareholders were misdirecting the corporation in not selling the land.*

DECISION AND RATIONALE   *Gruenberg was not entitled to a court-ordered dissolution even though the majority shareholders of Goldmine Plantation appeared to be making an unwise business decision in not selling the land. The fact that the majority wished to speculate on increases in the profitability of the sugar business or on a future increase in the land's value was a decision entirely up to the company and one in which a court cannot interfere. "[T]o warrant the interposition of a court in favor of the minority shareholders in a corporation, as against the contemplated action of the majority, where such action is within the corporate powers, a case must be made out which plainly shows that such action is so far opposed to the true interests of the corporation itself as to lead to the clear inference that no one thus acting could have been influenced by any honest desire to secure such interests, but that he must have acted with an intent to subserve some outside purpose, regardless of the consequences to the company and in a manner inconsistent with its interests."*

QUESTIONS AND CASE PROBLEMS

1.   Some of the stockholders of the Gulf Company, who were also shareholders of the Warrior Company, wished to have the former sell all its assets to the latter. Both the bylaws and the certificate of incorporation of the Gulf Company were silent on the matter of the sale of company assets, so the shareholders needed to find out how to proceed with the sale of assets. What three steps must they take? [Finch v. Warrior Cement Co., 16 Del. Ch. 44, 141 A. 54 (1928)]

2.   For many years, Bellanca Corporation had been in the business of manufacturing airplanes, although in recent years it had engaged in no business operations, had been delisted by the American Stock Exchange, and had in fact become an "empty shell." In 1961, through a series of agreements, the majority shareholder of Bellanca agreed to purchase all the stock of seven California corporations engaged in the egg business and in turn agreed to sell his majority share in Bellanca to Dean and Glen Olson. Orzeck, a minority shareholder of Bellanca, objected to the entire transaction, but it was carried through in spite of her objections. Orzeck felt that she should have been given dissenting shareholders' appraisal rights, which are available when a minority shareholder objects to a company's merger. Should Orzeck be granted dissenters' appraisal rights? [Orzeck v. Englehart, 41 Del. Ch. 361, 195 A.2d 375 (1963)]

3.   The Delaware Racing Association owned 95 percent of the shares of Delaware Steeplechase Association. Pursuant to the Model Business Corporation Act, the Delaware Racing Association proceeded to merge with Steeplechase. The owner of the 5 percent remaining shares of Steeplechase objected to the merger and filed a petition with the court to prevent it. Can he prevent the merger? [Application of Delaware Racing Ass'n, 213 A.2d 203 (Del. 1965)]

4.   Assume in Question 3 above that the 5 percent shareholder elected to take cash for his shares instead of exchanging them for shares of the parent corporation. Should valuation be based on the liquidation value of Steeplechase, since Steeplechase will no longer exist after merging into Delaware Racing Association? On the other hand, should the minority

shareholder be given the "going concern" value of his stock since he himself chose to withdraw from a going concern?

5. A owned two-thirds of the outstanding shares of United States Distributing Corporation, a Virginia corporation. B owned the remaining one-third. In United States Distributing's charter and on each of its stock certificates was the following provision: "In case of the liquidation or dissolution of this corporation, or a distribution of its assets, the assets of this corporation shall first be applied toward paying the holders of its stock all accrued and unpaid dividends thereon." The accumulative unpaid dividends on United States Distributing's stock amounted to $84 per share. At a shareholders' meeting, A voted in favor of a merger with Pittston Company, a Delaware corporation, and B dissented. After filing the proper written notice of his dissent, B demanded dissenting shareholders' appraisal rights. B argued that these rights included payment by the surviving corporation, the Pittston Company, of accumulated dividends out of the assets received from United States Distributing as provided in United States Distributing's charter. What result? [Adams v. United States Distributing Corp., 184 Va. 134, 34 S.E.2d 244 (1945)]

6. Nevada Land and Mortgage Company was engaged in a variety of property transactions. Prior to 1965, it had suffered financial reverses causing its board of directors to contemplate merger or consolidation with or sale of assets to the Leroy Corporation. Lamb was a creditor of Nevada Land and Mortgage. If the two corporations merge, and Leroy is the surviving corporation, will Leroy be liable to Lamb? If the two consolidate, will the resulting corporation be liable to Lamb? If Leroy purchases the assets of Nevada Land and Mortgage, will it then be liable to Lamb? [Lamb v. Leroy Corp., 85 Nev. 276, 454 P.2d 24 (1969)]

7. Arthur Gerth owned 53 percent of the XYZ Corporation's common stock and half of its preferred stock. His brother, Harry, owned 1 percent of its common stock, and Kruger owned the remainder of its common and preferred stock. The XYZ Corporation was in the retail lumber business. Of the three shareholders, Gerth was the only employee of the corporation. As its president, he paid himself a combined salary and bonus of approximately $15,000 annually. This left less than $2,000 in profits to be distributed as dividends. Kruger brought suit to have XYZ Corporation dissolved on the ground that Gerth was drawing an excessive salary and bonus and was thus wasting corporate assets and leaving an insufficient amount available for dividends. Under Gerth's leadership, the XYZ Corporation had become quite successful, and Gerth claimed that he deserved the salary and bonus because of his efforts. Should XYZ be dissolved? [Kruger v. Gerth, 22 A.D.2d 916, 255 N.Y.S.2d 498 (1964)]

8. Vulcan Manufacturing Company had been engaged in the manufacture of automobile jacks but went out of business in 1965. Vulcan's assets were auctioned off at a sheriff's sale about six months later. The bulk of the assets came into the hands of Great Lakes Distributing Company. Subsequently, Great Lakes rented the building in which Vulcan had previously conducted its business and began manufacturing and repairing automobile jacks. Comstock, who had been injured by one of the defective jacks manufactured by Vulcan in 1963, obtained a judgment against Vulcan that same year. Can Great Lakes Distributing Company be held liable on the judgment that Comstock obtained against Vulcan? Are there any additional facts that might make Great Lakes liable? [Comstock v. Great Lakes Distibuting Co., 209 Kan. 306, 496 P.2d 1308 (1973)]

9. Parker Laundry Company was an Illinois corporation owned and operated by Paul A. Parker. Its offices were in the city of Rock Island. In 1954, Parker, as sole director of Parker Laundry, filed the appropriate petition with the court for dissolution and dissolved the company. At the time, Parker Laundry's assets totaled $2,000, and its liabilities totaled approximately $4,000. Parker notified all the company's creditors except for the city of Rock Island, to which the company owed taxes of approximately $1,000. Two years later, after the city realized that the company had dissolved, it filed suit against Paul A. Parker personally for the $1,000 that Parker Laundry had owed in back taxes at the time of its dissolution. Can Paul Parker be held personally liable? If so, for how much? [People v. Parker, 30 Ill.2d 486, 197 N.E.2d 30 (1964)]

46

Corporations
Private Franchises

The Federal Trade Commission has defined *franchise* as "an arrangement in which the owner of a trademark, a trade name, or a copyright licenses others, under specified conditions or limitations, to use the trademark, trade name, or copyright in purveying goods or services." The franchise system has also been described as an organization composed of distributive units established and administered by a supplier as a medium for expanding and controlling the market of its products. Each franchise dealer is a legally independent but economically dependent unit of the integrated business system. The individual *franchisee* (the holder of the franchise) can operate as an independent business; yet it can obtain the advantages of a regional or national organizational affiliation to supply products, advertising, and other services.

The franchise system also provides the consumer public with an opportunity to obtain uniform products at numerous distribution points from small independent contractors. The system therefore seems good for the businessperson, good for the consumer, and good for the economy.

The use of franchises has expanded rapidly in recent years. The system began in the early part of the century. Between 1910 and 1940, early applications of franchising appeared in the automobile industry, sports, and the soft drink bottling industry. Franchises now account for about 25 percent of all retail sales and over 13 percent of gross national product in the United States. The franchise pattern of business development is a particularly appealing form of capitalistic enterprise. It has the advantage of enabling groups of individuals with small amounts of capital to become entrepreneurs.

THE LAW OF FRANCHISING

The growth in franchise operations has outdistanced the law of franchising. There has yet to be developed a solid body of appellate decisions under federal or state laws relating to franchise law. Because of the absence of law precisely addressed to franchising, the courts tend to apply general common law principles and the federal or state statutory definitions where they are applicable. The franchise relationship has characteristics associated with agency law, employment law, and independent contracting; yet it really does not fit into any of these traditional classifications.

About fifteen states currently have statutes dealing with franchise law. Although there is no real uniformity among the states' statutes, the following definition was adopted by two states to provide for a basic definition of franchising:

"Franchise" means a written agreement for a definite or indefinite period, in which a person grants to another person a license to use a trade name, trademark, service mark, or related characteristics, and in which there is a community of interest in the marketing of goods or services at wholesale, retail, by lease, agreement, or otherwise.[1]

TYPES OF FRANCHISES

There are three types of franchises: distributorships, chain-style businesses, and manufacturing or processing plants.

1. A *distributorship* relationship occurs where a manufacturing concern (franchisor) licenses a dealer (franchisee) to sell its product. Often, a distributorship covers an exclusive territory.
2. A *chain-style business* operation occurs when a franchisee operates under a franchisor's trade name and is identified as a member of a

1.   N.J. Rev. Stat. Sec. 56:10-3 (Supp.1972). Wash. Rev. Code Ann. Sec. 19.100.010 (Supp.1972).

select group of dealers who engage in the franchisor's business. The franchisee is generally required to follow standardized or prescribed methods of operations. Often, the franchisor requires that minimum prices and standards of operation be maintained. In addition, sometimes the franchisee is obligated to deal exclusively with the franchisor to obtain materials and supplies.
3. A *manufacturing or processing plant arrangement* is one in which the franchisor transmits to the franchisee the essential ingredients or formula to make a particular product. The franchisee then markets it either at wholesale or at retail in accordance with the franchisor's standards.

ADVANTAGES OF THE FRANCHISE SYSTEM

A system of franchises allows a highly effective means of gaining rapid market expansion and exposure with a minimum of capital outlay by the franchisor. Because franchisees make their own investments in order to undertake business operations, they have a strong incentive to make a profit. In most cases, the contract is written so that both the franchisee and the franchisor make a profit.

The franchisee gets the benefit of all of the franchisor's trade names and trademarks. In addition, the franchise carries with it goodwill and customer acceptance as well as the benefits of the franchisor's national advertising. The franchisee can obtain guidance from an experienced organization in areas such as site selection, operational know-how, and bookkeeping. For the franchisee, a moderate investment can develop into a prosperous business.

In short, the franchisee pledges money and service; the franchisor pledges aid and protection. In an economic context, franchising systems are clearly desirable for both parties. But there are some shortcomings—especially for the franchisee. The following sections will attempt to outline some of the problems that have arisen in the franchise arrangement. Most problems occur *after* the franchise agreement has been entered into. Because there are usually a number of potential franchisees for every franchise operation, typical contract provisions favor the franchisor. The courts, hampered by a lack of case law or statutory law, have been very slow to protect the rights of the franchisee.

THE FRANCHISE AGREEMENT

The franchise relationship is defined by a contract between the franchisor and the franchisee. Each franchise relationship and each industry has its own characteristics, so it is difficult to describe the broad range of details a franchising contract will include. The following sections, however, will define the essential characteristics of the franchise relationship.

Entering the Franchise Relationship

Prospective franchisees must initially decide on the type of business they wish to undertake. Then, they must obtain information about the business from the franchisor. Usually, franchisors will have numerous statistics and market studies available for prospective franchisees to examine. Of course, people who acquire franchised businesses differ greatly in their grasp of business operations. Some purchasers are experienced businesspersons with a firm grasp of the economic realities of how to operate a franchise. Others want to own a business but have never had business experience. In the latter situation, the franchisee must rely heavily on the franchisor in evaluating and setting up the initial business organization.

Payment for Franchise

The franchisee ordinarily pays an initial fee for the franchise license (the privilege of being granted a franchise). This fee is separate from the various products that the franchisee purchases from or through the franchisor. In some industries, the franchisor relies heavily on the initial sale of the franchise for realizing a profit.

In other industries, the continued dealing between the parties brings profit to both.

In most situations, the franchisor will receive a stated percentage of the annual sales or annual volume of business done by the franchisee. The franchise agreement may also require the franchisee to pay a percentage of advertising costs and certain administrative expenses incurred throughout the franchise arrangement.

Location and Business Organization

Typically, the franchisor will determine the territory to be served. The franchise agreement can specify whether the premises for the business must be leased or purchased outright. In some cases, construction of a building is necessary to meet the terms of the franchise agreement. In addition, the agreement will specify whether the franchisor supplies equipment and furnishings for the premises or whether this is the responsibility of the franchisee. When the franchise is a service operation such as a motel, the contract often provides that the franchisor will establish certain standards for the facility and will make inspections to insure that the standards are being maintained in order to protect the franchise name and reputation.

The business organization of the franchisee is of great concern to the franchisor. Depending on the terms of the franchise agreement, the franchisor may specify particular requirements for the form and capital structure of the business. The franchise agreement can provide that standards of operation such as sales quotas, quality standards, or record keeping, be conducted by the franchisor. Furthermore, a franchisor may wish to retain stringent control over the training of personnel involved in the operation and over administrative aspects of the business. Although the day-to-day operation of the franchise business is normally left up to the franchisee, the franchise agreement can provide for whatever amount of supervision and control the parties agree upon.

Price and Quality Controls

Franchises provide the franchisor with an outlet for the firm's goods and services. Depending upon the nature of the business, the franchisor may require the franchisee to purchase products from the franchisor at an established price. Of course, without explicit statutory authorization, such as fair trade laws or their equivalent, a franchisor cannot set the prices at which the franchisee will resell the goods. A franchisor can suggest retail prices but cannot coerce the franchisee into selling at that particular price.

A franchisor can require franchisees to purchase supplies from it. In fact, in certain franchise arrangements there may be an obligation to deal exclusively with the franchisor. However, requiring a franchisee to purchase *exclusively* from the franchisor may violate federal antitrust laws. The implications of antitrust violations on territorial restrictions, restrictions on products sold, resale price fixing, and price discrimination will be discussed later.

As a general rule, there is no question of the validity of a franchise agreement provision that permits the franchisor to maintain certain quality standards. Since the franchisor has a legitimate interest in maintaining the quality of the product or service in order to protect its name and reputation, it can exercise greater control in this area than would otherwise be tolerated.

Termination of the Franchise Arrangement

The duration of the franchise is a matter to be determined between the parties. Generally, a franchise will start out for a short period, such as a year, so that the franchisee and the franchisor can determine whether they want to stay in business with one another. Usually the franchise agreement will specify that termination must be "for cause" such as death or disability of the franchisee, insolvency of the franchisee, breach of the franchise agreement, or failure to meet specified sales quotas. Most franchise contracts provide that notice of termination must be given. If no set time for termination is given, then a reasonable time with notice will be implied. A franchisee must be given reasonable time to wind up the business—that is, to do the accounting and return the copyright or trademark or any other property of the franchisor.

Much franchise litigation has arisen over termination provisions. Since the franchise agreement is normally a form contract drawn and prepared by the franchisor, and since in reality there is very little equality of bargaining power between the franchisee and the franchisor, the termination provisions of contracts are generally more favorable to the franchisor. The lack of statutory law and case law is felt most harshly by the franchisee in this area. In some states automobile dealer and gasoline station franchises have some statutory protection.

The franchisee normally invests a substantial amount of time and money in the franchise operation to make it successful. Despite this fact, the franchisee may receive little or nothing for the business upon termination. The franchisor owns the trademark and hence the business. The courts have often struggled to offer a terminated franchisee some kind of relief, as is illustrated in the next case.

ATLANTIC RICHFIELD CO. v. RAZUMIC

Supreme Court of Pennsylvania, 1978.
480 Pa. 366, 390 A.2d 736.

BACKGROUND AND FACTS   *Atlantic Richfield Co. (Arco) leased a service station to Razumic for three years. The agreement provided, among other things, for Arco's signs and trade name to be prominently displayed at the service station and for gasoline and other related products to be sold. The agreement detailed other aspects of the parties' business relationship, including Razumic's obligation to "operate the service station in such a manner as to reflect favorably on Atlantic's goodwill*

***.*" After one year, Arco attempted to terminate the lease claiming that since the agreement did not provide any guidelines for termination, it could be terminated at will. Razumic resisted, and this suit followed.*

DECISION AND RATIONALE *The agreement between Razumic and Arco was a franchise agreement. Arco could not terminate it at will. The fact that the agreement was labeled a "lease agreement" and that it referred to the parties as lessor and lessee were not conclusive. "Unlike a tenant pursuing his own interests while occupying a landlord's property, a franchisee such as Razumic builds the goodwill of both his own business and Arco. In exchange, an Arco dealer such as Razumic can justifiably expect that his time, effort, and other investments promoting the goodwill of Arco will not be destroyed as a result of Arco's arbitrary decision to terminate their franchise relationship. *** Arco cannot arbitrarily sever its franchise relationship with Razumic. A contrary conclusion would allow Arco to reap the benefits of its franchisees' efforts in promoting the goodwill of its name without regard for the franchisees' interests."*

DETERMINATION OF RELIEF The courts and legal commentators have tried to apply many theories to protect a franchisee's rights upon termination. Some courts have held that every contract contains an implied covenant of good faith and fair dealing. Others have held that if a franchise investment is substantial and the relationship has been established for an indefinite duration, it cannot be terminated until after a reasonable period of time has elapsed. What a reasonable time is will depend upon the circumstances in each case. Some of the circumstances that the courts consider are: (1) the amount of preliminary and promotional expenditures made, (2) the length of time the franchise has been in operation before notice of termination was given, (3) the prospects for forfeiture of profits, and (4) whether or not the franchise has been proven profitable during its actual operation.

If contract provisions allow for termination, even though they may be unfair to the franchisee, no cause of action can be found. The Uniform Commercial Code Sec. 2-302 has been used by some courts to find that termination provisions dispensing with notification are invalid if their effect is unconscionable. The courts have generally refused to find that franchises terminable by notice at any time or at the end of a specific time are unconscionable *per se.*

BACKGROUND AND FACTS *Marinello entered a lease and dealer agreement with the Shell Oil Company in 1959. The agreement provided that Marinello could terminate at any time upon ninety days notice and that Shell could terminate upon ten days notice. Their agreement was to run for three years and was renewable for one year periods. Just before the end of three years, Shell terminated the agreement (giving approximately thirty days notice). Marinello objected to the termination on the ground that it was arbitrary and without cause and that, even though the agreement made no provision with respect to grounds for termination, "good cause" was required by implication.*

SHELL OIL COMPANY v. MARINELLO
Supreme Court of New Jersey, 1973. 63 N.J. 402, 307 A.2d 598.

DECISION AND RATIONALE *Shell could not terminate the franchise agreement with Marinello without good cause. It was true that the only requirement for termination under the written agreement between Shell and Marinello was that Shell give ten days notice. However, because of the inequality of bargaining power between the two parties, termination at will would violate public policy. "Where there is grossly disproportionate bargaining power, the principle of freedom to contract is nonexistent and unilateral terms result. In such a situation courts will not hesitate to declare void as against public policy grossly unfair contractual provisions which clearly tend to the injury of the public in some way."*

MEASURE OF DAMAGES The courts have also struggled to determine how best to measure damages to prevent injustice or unfairness when misconduct occurs in a franchise relationship. Since franchising is a rather peculiar form of capitalist enterprise, serious franchising problems warrant legislative attention. Congress enacted statutory requirements under the Automobile Dealers' Day in Court Act (15 USCA Sec. 1221). Thus, in some cases, a franchisee need not rely on common law principles to obtain protection in the courts from franchisor abuses.

CONSUMER AND FRANCHISEE PROTECTION The consumer protection movement and pressures from certain industries (primarily car dealers) have resulted in the passage of numerous statutes to protect franchisees from bad faith termination of their franchise contracts. For example, the Automobile Dealers' Day in Court Act (15 USCA Sec. 1221) allows an

auto dealer who contends that the franchisor did not act in good faith and without coercion in terminating the franchise to take the matter to court for a judicial termination. Moreover, various states have passed laws in recent years that spell out certain conditions and circumstances under which a franchise can be terminated. However, these laws are subject to serious constitutional challenges under the impairment of contracts clause, the due process clause, and the interstate commerce clause of the U.S. Constitution.

The realities of the franchise industry demonstrate a need for uniform regulation. Common law theories and existing statutory remedies are really not very helpful in their application to franchising problems. The franchise system is a complex and unique business enterprise. It is growing so fast that it seems almost impossible that any regulatory scheme designed can be both comprehensive and flexible enough to meet the needs of franchises.

REA AND 22 FORD, INC. v. FORD MOTOR CO.
United States Court of Appeals, Third Circuit, 1977. 560 F.2d 554.

BACKGROUND AND FACTS *In February 1964, Rea was given a franchise for a Ford dealership in Pennsylvania. At the time, he was already a principal stockholder of a nearby Oldsmobile dealership. Ford informed Rea that it would withhold the Ford franchise unless Rea liquidated the competing Oldsmobile franchise. Rea gave up his interest in the Oldsmobile franchise, keeping part of its assets for use in operating the Ford franchise and selling the rest. Subsequently, Rea claimed that Ford's "coercive" action violated the Automobile Dealer's Day in Court Act, which requires auto franchisers to act in good faith in complying with the terms of a franchise agreement.*

DECISION AND RATIONALE *Ford was liable to Rea for violating the Automobile Dealer's Day in Court Act. Ford argued that the act required good faith compliance only with regard to the specific terms of a franchise agreement. However, the court did not agree: "[T]he evidence in this case *** is sufficient to support the jury's finding that Ford breached its duty to act in good faith by threatening to stop supplying cars to Edward C. Rea, Inc., unless Rea Oldsmobile resigned its Oldsmobile franchise."*

REGULATION OF THE FRANCHISING INDUSTRY

Any industry that expands rapidly without a uniform regulatory scheme is likely to engage in certain abusive and destructive practices. The franchising industry is no exception. The Federal Trade Commission has recently begun investigations to determine whether illegal methods have been used to compel restaurant franchisees to purchase goods and services at artificially inflated prices. Other abusive practices have been discovered in the form of hidden markups on the capital assets and equipment that must be purchased by a franchisee either from the franchisor or from approved vendors. Cases of misrepresentation occur in the initial sale of many franchises. More than a few unsuspecting franchisees have learned after entering into the franchise contract that in order to operate the business and meet the established sales quotas they must work an inordinate number of hours a week.

The franchise relationship grows out of a contract. But because of the nature of the franchise system, the common law remedies that have been applied to contract and sales contract situations do not provide adequate relief. Furthermore, only about fifteen states have enacted statutory laws to govern franchise relationships. Thus, what is permissible in one state may not be permissible in another. Such lack of uniformity places a great hardship on franchise arrangements, especially when they are operated on a national scale. Within the last ten years, regulation of the franchise industry has finally begun at the federal level. Most federal remedies deal with violations of anti-

trust laws. Attempts at control using the federal securities laws have been less effective. The courts, the state legislatures, and the Congress are all attempting to develop uniform regulations for the franchising industry.

The Franchise Contract: Disclosure Protection

A franchise purchaser can suffer substantial loss if the franchisor has not provided full and complete information regarding the franchisor-franchisee relationship as well as the details of the contract under which the business will be operated. When misrepresentation permeates the initial sale of a franchise operation, the common law remedy of fraud in the inducement provides inadequate relief. In most cases, the franchisee has already paid the franchise purchase price and may also have incurred substantial losses in the initial operating phases of the business. The elements of fraud are exceedingly difficult to prove. Even the tort of intentional misstatement or misrepresentation of a material fact upon which the franchisee relied places a great burden on the franchisee to show that the franchisor's original offer was misleading or fraudulent.

Only a few of the states that have enacted legislation concerning franchising have included disclosure provisions. California was the first state to enact a franchise disclosure law, and it has served as a model for other disclosure statutes. The California Franchise Investment Law sets out twenty-two items that must be disclosed in a registration filed with the state. Some of the items of disclosure include: (1) the name and business address of the franchisor, (2) the business experience of any persons affiliated with the franchisor, (3) whether any person associated with the franchisor has been convicted of a felony, (4) a recent financial statement, (5) a typical franchise agreement, (6) a statement of all fees that the franchisee is required to pay, and (7) other information that the commissioner of corporations may reasonably require.[2]

Some courts have attempted to apply the Securities Act of 1933 and various state blue sky laws to franchise agreements. This has met with limited success. The franchise agreement could possibly be considered an "investment contract" within the meaning of blue sky laws and the 1933 Securities Act. Thus, it would be subject to the registration and disclosure requirements of the securities laws. It has been argued that a franchise arrangement is an investment contract that is a security under the Securities Act. This theory, however, has not met with much success on the federal level. The United States Supreme Court has defined an investment contract as "a contract, transaction or scheme whereby a person invests his (or her) money in a common enterprise and is led to expect profits solely from the efforts of the promoter or third party."[3] The typical franchise agreement fails this test for determining "investment contracts" because a franchisee must make an effort to make money. Thus, franchise agreements are usually not considered securities under the Securities Act.

Federal law prohibits mail fraud. According to 18 USCA Sec. 1341, the U.S. mails cannot be used to further a scheme to defraud. Like

Section 5 of the FTC Act, the mail fraud provision penalizes misrepresentations made by use of the mails. In reality, this is not a very effective means for preventing fraud or misrepresentation in a franchisor's negotiations with a potential franchisee because it affords only an after the fact remedy. Similarly, the Federal Trade Commission, under Section 5 of the FTC Act, gives the FTC power to stop unfair or deceptive practices in commerce and to prohibit deceptive advertising. Both the FTC provisions and the mail fraud provisions lack the affirmative protection that disclosure laws would afford a potential purchaser of a franchise.

The FTC Franchise Rule

The FTC franchise rule was promulgated in response to widespread evidence of deception and unfair practices in connection with the resale of franchises and business opportunity ventures. This rule requires that, within a specified time, franchisors and franchise brokers furnish the information that prospective franchisees need in order to make an informed decision about entering into a franchise relationship. The rule sets forth the circumstances under which a franchisor or broker can make claims about the projected sales income or profits of existing or potential outlets. The rule also imposes requirements that concern the establishment of the franchise relationship.

Franchisee's Relationship to Franchisor: Agent or Independent Contractor?

The mere licensing of a trade name does not create an agency relationship. However, the courts have determined that certain factors in the franchisor-franchisee relationship do indicate an agency relationship:

1.   The terms of the agreement create an agency relationship.
2.   The franchisor exercises a high degree of control over the franchisee's activities.

---

2.   Cal. Corp. Code Sec. 31001 (West Supp.1975). The California Franchise Investment Law provides: "California franchisees have suffered substantial losses where the franchisor or his (or her) representative has not provided full and complete information regarding the franchisor-franchisee relationship, the details of the contract between the franchisor and the franchisee, and the prior business experience of the franchisor." It is the intent of this law to provide each prospective franchisee with the information necessary to make an intelligent decision regarding the franchise being offered. Cal. Corp. Code Section 31001 (West Supp.1975). As cited in 59 Minn. Law Rev. 1027 (1975). Casenote: Franchise Regulation.

3.   SEC v. W.J. Howey Co., 328 U.S. 293, 66 S.Ct. 1100 (1946).

3. A third person looking at the relationship between the franchisor and the franchisee would reasonably believe that there is an agency relationship.

4. The franchisor derives an especially great benefit from the franchisee's activities. The greater the benefit, the more likely an agency relationship will be found.[4]

If these factors show a very close relationship between the franchisor and the franchisee, then their relationship will be deemed to be that of an employer-employee or principal-agent. If the factors show a high degree of independence between the franchisee and franchisor, then the franchisee will be deemed an independent contractor. The characterization of the relationship has tax implications and implications for the regulatory treatment of the business organization. In addition, if an agency relationship is found, the franchisor is liable for the franchisee's improper actions or injuries to third parties both in tort and in contract.

4. See Kuchta v. Allied Builders Corp., 21 Cal. App. 3d 541, 98 Cal. Rptr. 588 (1971).

QUESTIONS AND CASE PROBLEMS

1. Joseph and Gertrude Kuchta entered into a contract with Ralph Weiner under which Weiner was to build an outdoor patio and living area in the back yard of the Kuchta's home. The relationship between Weiner and his franchisor, Allied Builders, was such that Weiner performed all construction work and Allied controlled construction standards and approved the design and utility of all of Weiner's construction plans. Weiner drew up plans for the outdoor living area and submitted them to the Orange County Building and Safety Department. The plans were not approved since they violated certain zoning ordinances. Nevertheless, without informing the Kuchtas, Weiner proceeded with the construction. After the work was completed, the Kuchtas received a notice from the Orange County Building and Safety Department advising them that the roof and other improvements violated the code and ordering their removal. The Kuchtas sought to recover both from Allied Builders and from Weiner. Since Weiner was insolvent, the Kuchtas' recovery depended upon their ability to sue Allied Builders. Can the Kuchtas sue Allied? Why or why not? [Kuchta v. Allied Builders Corp., 21 Cal. App. 3d 541, 98 Cal. Rptr. 588 (1971)]

2. Paul Rubenfeld and Mobil Oil Corporation signed a written agreement providing, among other things, that Rubenfeld had the right to use and occupy a service station owned by Mobil. Mobil required Rubenfeld to undergo a certain period of dealer training and granted him the right to use the Mobil trademark. In addition, Mobil had representatives visit Rubenfeld's service station to encourage the sale of Mobil's products, to inspect the station, and to make recommendations concerning the price at which Rubenfeld should sell his gasoline. Rubenfeld's rent and profits were both dependent upon the amount of gasoline he sold. Is the agreement between Rubenfeld and Mobil Oil Corporation one of lessor-lessee or franchisor-franchisee? [Mobil Oil Corp. v. Rubenfeld, 72 Misc. 2d 392, 339 N.Y.S. 2d 623 (1972)]

3. Ger-Ro-Mar, Inc. was a manufacturer and distributor of lingerie and swimwear. Through its multi-level marketing program, Ger-Ro-Mar enlisted the services of men and women throughout the country to sell its products at wholesale and retail. Under the selling arrangement, franchisees were required to buy an inventory before they could participate in the program. A prospective franchisee could enter at any of three levels—key distributor, senior key, or supervisor. Entry at a particular level was based on the amount of inventory initially purchased by the franchisee. To induce individuals to become franchisees, Ger-Ro-Mar distributed various promotional materials that described the marketing system and illustrated how an individual could earn large sums of money by building a large personal group of salespeople through recruitment. The illustration in Ger-Ro-Mar's brochures promised that district managers could earn up to $56,000 and regional managers up to $90,000 yearly. Of the regional manager position, Ger-Ro-Mar's promotional brochure promised, "ANY ONE CAN ACHIEVE THIS LEVEL." An investigation by the FTC revealed that the success promised in the brochure was dependent upon the franchisee's recruitment of salespersons who in turn would recruit salespersons

under them. Is there anything wrong with Ger-Ro-Mar's franchising scheme? Why might the FTC wish to order Ger-Ro-Mar to cease and desist distribution of its promotional brochure? [Ger-Ro-Mar, Inc. v. FTC, 518 F.2d 33 (2nd Cir. 1975)]

4. In June 1963, Econo-Car granted Carl Taute a franchise to operate a rent-a-car business in Billings, Montana. Burko, an Econo-Car agent, told Taute at the time that as a result of a study for Burko, Econo-Car knew the three best locations for a rent-a-car business in Billings, that Burko would send three men to Billings to help Taute during his first few weeks, and that the entire franchise fee paid by Taute would be spent for three pages of newspaper advertisements during the grand opening. In August 1963, while the contract was still in its early stages of performance and very little time or money had been spent by either party, Taute learned that Burko's statements were false. Nevertheless, Taute continued with his preparations to go into business and, in fact, conducted business for about six months. Thereafter, Taute sued Econo-Car to rescind the franchise agreement, claiming that Econo-Car's agent fraudulently induced him into becoming a franchisee. Will Taute be successful in rescinding the franchise agreement? [Taute v. Econo-Car Int'l, Inc., 414 F.2d 828 (9th Cir. 1969)]

5. Arthur Murray, Inc., was engaged in the business of licensing persons to operate dance studios using its registered trade name "Arthur Murray" along with the Arthur Murray method of dancing. A franchise agreement was entered into between Burkin, Inc., and Arthur Murray, Inc., granting Burkin a franchise to conduct a dance studio in San Diego, California. Under the franchise agreement, Burkin received the right to use the Arthur Murray name and method of dancing. Arthur Murray, Inc., had the right to control Burkin's employment practices, to fix the minimum tuition rates to be charged, to select the financial institution handling all pupil installment contracts, and to designate the location, layout, and decoration of Burkin's dance studio. Gertrude Nichols signed up for several dozen dancing lessons, all of which she paid for in advance. Shortly thereafter, Burkin became insolvent and closed its dance studio franchise. Can Nichols recover from Arthur Murray, Inc.? Would she be able to recover if none of the signs in Burkin's franchised studio and none of the contracts that she signed indicated that such a company as Arthur Murray, Inc., existed? [Nichols v. Arthur Murray, Inc., 248 Cal. App. 2d 610, 56 Cal. Rptr. 728 (1967)]

6. Terry Wilson owned a small stereo store in Eugene, Oregon. Charles Zimmerman was an agent for Soundarama Marketing Company. Zimmerman approached Wilson, offering to sell Wilson a Soundarama franchise under which Wilson would be allowed to sell Soundarama products and advertise its service. Wilson was unwilling to purchase a Soundarama franchise unless Soundarama's equipment was certified. Zimmerman assured Wilson that the equipment was certified by Underwriters Laboratory. It was unlawful to sell stereo equipment in Oregon unless it was certified. After purchasing the franchise from Zimmerman, Wilson learned that the Soundarama equipment was not certified by Underwriters Laboratory. Wilson informed Soundarama of his dissatisfaction and told them that if certification was not obtained within two weeks, he would rescind the franchise contract. Since Soundarama was a California corporation, it informed Wilson that it would be simpler for him to obtain certification and that it was his duty to have the equipment certified. When two weeks passed and Soundarama's equipment remained uncertified, Wilson brought suit to rescind the franchise agreement. Will he succeed? [Wilson v. Zimmerman, 261 Or. 528, 495 P.2d 713 (1972)]

7. Geraldine Yarborough owned the Tastee Freeze Company. She entered into a contract with Roger Harkey under which Harkey was granted a ten-year franchise to operate a Tastee Freeze in the city of Roswell, New Mexico. Harkey agreed to sell "on certain premises only the franchised products, or other such products as the franchise owner might approve." In addition, the franchise agreement provided that when Harkey ceased to sell the franchised products, the agreement would terminate. After three years, Harkey ceased selling Tastee Freeze products, removed all indication of the Tastee Freeze name and trademark, and began selling the product of a competitor. Can Yarborough stop Harkey from selling a competitor's product? (Hint: Consider what is the most commercially reasonable construction of the provisions of the franchise contract.) [Yarborough v. Harkey, 67 N.M. 204, 354 P.2d 137 (1960)]

8. E.T. Runyan and Pacific Air Industries, Inc. entered into a written franchise agreement whereby, in consideration of Runyan's payment of $25,000, he was awarded an exclusive photogrammetric franchise for four southern California counties. Under the agreement, Pacific was obligated to train Runyan in the rudiments of photogrammetry, including twenty-

five hours of sales and technical assistance for an initial period. In the meantime, Runyan resigned his position with Tidewater Oil Company. Since Runyan was entering a technical field in which he had no experience, he relied on Pacific's promise. Pacific's training program proved to be entirely inadequate. Runyan nevertheless attempted to operate his franchise, but when he realized that he was unable to do so, he attempted to rescind. Can Runyan rescind the franchise agreement? [Runyan v. Pacific Air Industries, Inc., 2 Cal. 3d 304, 85 Cal. Rptr. 138, 466 P.2d 682 (1970)]

9. A franchise agreement entered into between Shakey's Incorporated, as franchisor, and Charles Martin, as franchisee, included the following provision: "Upon termination of this agreement, for a period of one year thereafter, the franchisee shall not engage in the production or sale of pizza products in a location within a radius of thirty miles from the franchised premises." After operating a Shakey's pizza franchise for several years, Martin ceased doing business as Shakey's, removed all indications of Shakey's trade name from the premises, and proceeded to do business as "Martin's Pizza Parlor." Has Martin violated his agreement not to compete? What protectable business interest does Shakey's have, if any? Is the agreement not to compete a reasonable one? [Shakey's Incorporated v. Martin, 91 Idaho 758, 430 P.2d 504 (1967)]

10. Earl Lovelace was the owner of an H & R Block franchise. The franchise agreement between Lovelace and H & R Block included a covenant not to compete, which provided that "if Lovelace shall terminate or breach the franchise agreement, he shall not enter into competition directly or indirectly with H & R Block for a period of five years thereafter." Is this covenant reasonable? [H & R Block, Inc. v. Lovelace, 208 Kan. 538, 493 P.2d 205 (1972)]

UNIT VIII

Government Regulation

47

Government Regulation
Regulation and
Administrative Agencies

Regulation of private business activities was relatively minimal in the United States until the 1930s. The Great Depression was associated with many major changes in individuals' lives, one of which was the increased regulation of private activities. There was even talk about socializing all industrial activity. Regulation has always increased during major conflicts, such as World Wars I and II. However, in the last decade or so, business regulations have shifted from rules primarily evolved from the common law and from judicial interpretation of statutory regulations to more direct controls.

Furthermore, until recently, the functions and authority of many government agencies were primarily ministerial. Their actions were generally limited to carrying out specific activities mandated by legislatures. Thus, social security offices gave information and advice to individuals filing for benefits but possessed relatively few discretionary powers. Starting in the late 1960s, an increasing number of new rules and regulations were established along with new federal regulatory agencies. Probably, the current constraints placed on business transactions by regulatory authorities have more impact on the economy than those that stem from the common law and the courts. For example, seven new regulatory agencies, including the Occupational Safety and Health Administration (OSHA), the Consumer Product Safety Commission (CPSC), and the Environmental Protection Agency (EPA), were created in the early 1970s. The first four years of the 1970s saw a doubling of the number of pages in the Federal Register, the primary document for notification of federal rules and regulations.

INCREASING REGULATIONS

The scope of regulation has also expanded, going beyond the traditional judicial regulation of commerce, employment, transportation, health, and financial markets. For example, the Clean Air Act amendments of 1970 provide for setting air quality standards,[1] and the Consumer Product Safety Commission Act of 1972 establishes a commission with the power to set safety standards for consumer products and ban products with undue risk of injury.[2] The early 1970s also saw extensive controls over petroleum manufacturers emerge with the Emergency Petroleum Allocation Act of 1973.

Existing agencies have also expanded their activities. For example, Exhibit 47-1 shows that, by fiscal year (FY) 1979, the administrative costs of forty-one regulatory agencies are expected to be more than double what they were in FY 1974. In FY 1974, these agencies' costs were $2.2

_____

1. 42 USCA Sec. 7401 (1977)
2. 15 USCA Sec. 2051 et seq.

billion. They are estimated to be $4.8 billion in FY 1979. Administrative costs, however, are very much smaller than the costs of compliance by business. In 1976, for example, the estimated total cost to business of federal regulation was approximately $65.5 billion; administrative costs represented only $3.2 billion, less than 5 percent of the total costs.

An important distinction between regulation created formally by government agencies and regulation that is established informally through the judicial system arises in the creation, promulgation, and enforcement of regulations. Administrative agencies possess a mixture of legislative and judicial authority as well as executive powers. In addition, procedural differences combined with the broader discretionary authority given to government agencies yield regulations that often differ significantly from those developed in the legislative and judicial process.[3] This chapter will investigate the general scope of regulatory actions and the activities that are subject to their control. In addition, it will emphasize regulatory powers and procedures and review the regulation process.

_____

3. Murray Weidenbaum, "On Estimating Regulatory Costs," *Regulation* (May/June 1978): 14-17.

EXHIBIT 47-1   ADMINISTRATIVE COSTS OF FORTY-ONE FEDERAL REGULATORY AGENCIES (FISCAL YEARS, DOLLARS IN MILLIONS)

Year	1974	1975	1976	1977	1978 (revised)	1979 (proposed)	Increase 1974-79
Consumer Safety and Health	$1,302	$1,463	$1,613	$1,985	$2,582	$2,671	105%
Job Safety and other Working Conditions	310	379	446	492	562	626	102%
Energy and Environment	347	527	682	870	989	1,116	222%
Industry-Specific	245	269	270	309	340	341	39%
Financial Reporting, etc.	36	45	53	58	70	69	92%
Total	2,240	2,683	3,064	3,714	4,543	4,823	115%

Source: Murray Weidenbaum, "On Estimating Regulatory Costs," *Regulation* (May/June 1978): 15. Copyright 1978 American Enterprise Institute for Public Policy Research. Reprinted with permission.

ADMINISTRATIVE AGENCIES

Administrative agencies are the primary interpreters and enforcers of many legislative statutes that focus on business regulation. Sometimes, these agencies are part of a traditional administrative branch of the government. For example, the Justice Department enforces the Sherman Act, the Clayton Act, and other antitrust laws. The National Highway Traffic Safety Administration and the Department of Transportation enforce regulations regarding safety, emissions, controls, and fuel economy of automobiles. In other cases, Congress has established administrative agencies that are independent of the executive branch. For example, the Interstate Commerce Commission regulates most service transportation within the United States as well as the service transportation of foreign countries that takes place within the boundaries of the United States. Other independent agencies include the Federal Aviation Administration, the Civil Aeronautics Board, the Commodity Futures Trading Commission, the Equal Employment Opportunity Commission, the Export-Import Bank of the United States, the Federal Communications Commission, the Federal Energy Administration, the Federal Home Loan Bank Board, the Federal Maritime Commission, the Federal Power Commission, the Federal Trade Commission, the International Trade Commission, the National Labor Relations Board, the Securities and Exchange Commission, and the Small Business Administration.

REGULATORY POWERS AND PROCEDURES

Administrative agencies combine the duties and responsibilities of the judicial, executive, and legislative branches of the government. Heads of administrative agencies are generally appointed by the president with the consent of two-thirds of the Congress. Because Congress has delegated certain powers to agencies, they are able to combine the legislative and judicial powers that are traditionally separated under the Constitution. Thus, agencies are able to promulgate rules, and they have policing powers to insure compliance. They are also able to render judgments and impose penalties or remedies as prescribed by law if violations have occurred. Administrative decisions can be appealed to the courts, but since the subject matter is generally very specialized or technical in nature (and the agency has been given broad discretionary powers initially), the courts will not generally reverse agency actions unless they are arbitrary and capricious, or they are not supported by the record or not in accordance with legal precedent (or the law).

It is the province and duty of the judiciary to interpret the law, and it is the province of Congress to formulate legislative policy, to mandate programs and projects, and to establish their relative priority for the nation. Once Congress has exercised its legislative power and decided the order of priorities in a given area, the executive branch administers the law, and the courts (the judiciary) interpret and enforce it when enforcement is sought.

At times, Congress provides funds and authorizes programs for purposes that conflict with one another. In the following case, a conflict arose between the completion and operation of a federal dam project by the Tennessee Valley Authority and the explicit provision of the Endangered Species Act of 1973 that prohibited the operation of that dam because it would destroy the only known population of the snail darter, an endangered species. In such a case, the judiciary is called upon not to question the legislative policies, programs, and projects of Congress but to determine what the law is and to enforce it as necessary.

TENNESSEE VALLEY AUTHORITY v. HILL
Supreme Court of the United States, 1978. 437 U.S. 153, 98 S. Ct. 2297.

BACKGROUND AND FACTS *Environmental groups and others brought an action under the Endangered Species Act of 1973 to enjoin the Tennessee Valley Authority from completing a dam and impounding a section of land on the Little Tennessee River. The dam was virtually* completed when the injunction was sought, and Congress continued to appropriate large sums of public money for the project even after congressional appropriations committees were advised of the project's apparent impact upon the survival of the snail darter, an endangered species.

DECISION AND RATIONALE Further construction of the dam had to be stopped even though it was virtually completed, and large sums of public money have been appropriated for the project. The evidence presented at the trial demonstrated that the dam would either eradicate the known population of the snail darters or destroy their habitat. Chief Justice Burger explained the court's ruling as follows: "It may seem curious to some that the survival of a relatively small number of three-inch fish among all the countless millions of species extant would require the permanent halting of a virtually completed dam for which Congress has expended more than $100 million. *** [But] [t]he plain intent of Congress in enacting this statute was to halt and reverse the trend toward species extinction, whatever the cost. This is reflected not only in the stated policies of the Act, but in literally every section of the statute."

Ministerial Powers

The legislative powers of administrators have grown considerably over time. Initially, their actions were more ministerial than legislative and were often explicitly specified by statute. Thus, administrators had the power to issue or renew licenses. Sometimes statutes required an administrator to accept or reject a commodity based on a congressionally established standard. Over the years, as society has become more complex, Congress has authorized administrators to formulate rules and guidelines under general authority granted to administrative agencies. Thus the safety and health administrator is authorized to make rules that protect the safety and health of individuals in certain circumstances, such as places of employment. The discretion given administrators effectively transmits legislative power to them. For example, they have been given the power to prohibit unfair methods of competition, to grant licenses "as public interest, convenience, or necessity requires," and to prevent or promote other generally specified goals.

Investigatory Powers

A number of administrative agencies generally have the power to investigate the records, practices, or premises of business organizations. For example, OSHA inspectors can obtain a warrant and enter a place of employment to determine if a violation of safety or health has occurred. In addition, Section 6B of the Federal Trade Commission Act grants the FTC broad investigatory powers to require the inspection of records, the completion of questionnaires, or other assistance to the commission in supplying information prior to a specific rule, complaint, or adjudicative action. Witnesses can also be subpoenaed and examined under oath by the agency.

Complaints

Complaints (or charges) can be initiated by private parties, including individuals and corporations, or by employees of the administrative agency. After a complaint is served on an alleged wrongdoer, the party is given an opportunity to answer. Eventually, the complaint is heard by an administrator appointed by the agency. The administrator makes a final decision and enters an order directing the party to cease (or engage) in certain acts if the party has engaged in misconduct as defined by the agency. Otherwise, the complaint is dismissed. Compliance with the order is usually enforced by a separate division of the administrative agency, and failure to comply can result in fines and other penalties. After the final hearing, the affected party can appeal to the courts. In some cases, the party can engage in an informal settlement process or agree to a **consent decree**—an agreement by the parties that carries the sanction of the court.

Rule-making Powers

General rule-making powers have been established by statute for a number of administrative agencies. Rule making often derives from evidence or facts obtained from investigatory activities. The process formally begins with notification, which can be in the form of a complaint to the party specifying the alleged misconduct. Usually the recipient of the complaint is given an opportunity to file an answer. In the case of general rules, notification is made through public announcement (in the Federal Register if the rule is promulgated by one of the federal administrative agencies). The second stage of rule making involves a hearing. Then the administrator makes a decision and, in the case of an individual complaint, either enters an order or dismisses it. In some cases, the administrator has a right to alter actions prior to the hearing, provided certain conditions are met. At any time, of course, there can be an informal settlement with a stipulation, consent decree, or other agreement.

Compliance and Enforcement Powers

All final orders carry the weight of statutory law with prescribed penalties for violations unless invalidated by the courts, and failure to comply

is treated like any other violation of the law. In most cases, violations are considered civil matters so that money damages must be paid or specific actions taken (such as the installation of pollution control equipment). In recent years, however, there has been a trend toward including criminal penalties as well. Thus, violators, including corporate officers, can be subject to jail sentences. For example, the Energy Policy and Conservation Act of 1976 makes the failure of any manufacturer to comply with any average fuel economy standard unlawful conduct.

Adjudicative Powers

Most final actions and orders of administrative agencies can be appealed to the courts. Judicial review is often provided to interpret the enabling statute or the validity of administrative agency procedures. The review, however, is generally limited and does not require a full-fledged rehearing to establish the validity of the facts. As noted earlier, unless the decision is a definite abuse, an arbitrary or capricious use of discretionary powers, or a question of law, review will often be denied. This has given administrators tremendous discretionary powers.

In the case of general rules, the administrative hearing can involve extensive presentations of evidence by employees of the administrative agency, by parties who are directly affected, and by the general public.[4] Economic evidence bearing on the potential consequences of the rule can be presented, and testimony can be given about the costs and benefits of the rule. For example, evidence on the prices of eyeglasses in localities with and without restrictions on price advertising was examined in the FTC hearings on ophthalmic goods.

In the case of a complaint, the agency enters, files an order, or dismisses the action. Agreement usually specifies the action that must be taken or stopped as well as penalties for

---

4. The trend in recent years has been to provide funds to the general public for participation at administrative hearings involving rule making.

not carrying out the provisions of the order. For general rules, the agency often modifies its initial policies to incorporate information obtained in the hearing. In individual complaints and general rule making, public record of the agreement or issued rule is necessary.

In some cases, rule making can preempt state law. In 1978, the FTC adopted the final rule on the advertising of ophthalmic goods and services. This rule states that it is an unfair practice for states to enforce restrictions against advertising unless the ads are deceptive.

A reviewing agency or court is generally bound by the findings of fact reached during the initial administrative hearing. In general, the courts have ruled that administrators are presumed to have based their final orders on reasonable grounds, and the courts will not attempt to second guess the agency on questions with which the agency is more familiar.[5] The courts will not infer a basis other than that articulated and will not enforce an order on any ground not stated.

_____

5. Kesler and Sons Constr. Co. v. Utah State Div. of Health, 30 Utah 2d 90, 513 P.2d 1017 (1973).

BACKGROUND AND FACTS   *The Federal Trade Commission issued a cease and desist order to Moog Industries, Inc., to stop illegal price discrimination. Moog argued that the order should not go into effect until its competitors, who were using the same practices, were also ordered to stop. Otherwise, the firm would have to go out of business. Moog appealed after the commission rejected this argument.*

MOOG INDUSTRIES INC. v. FEDERAL TRADE COMM.
Supreme Court of the United States, 1958.
355 U.S. 411, 78 S.Ct. 377.

DECISION AND RATIONALE   *There was no question that Moog Industries had engaged in illegal price discrimination. Therefore it had to obey the FTC's cease and desist order even though some of its competitors were still engaged in similar illegal practices. The court concluded: "[A]lthough an allegedly illegal practice may appear to be operative throughout an industry, whether such appearances reflect fact and whether all firms in the industry should be dealt with in a single proceeding or should receive individualized treatment are questions that call for discretionary determination by the administrative agency. *** [T]he Commission alone is empowered to develop that enforcement policy best calculated to achieve the ends contemplated by Congress and to allocate its available funds and personnel in such a way as to execute its policy efficiently and economically."*

OVERLAPPING REGULATION

Regulations originate in a large number of independent authorities that have overlapping jurisdiction, making the precise rule difficult, if not impossible, to interpret. Exhibit 47–2 shows more than a dozen agencies that have jurisdiction regarding the use of energy. In each case, some of the more important activities are listed along with their estimated expenditures in fiscal year 1979. The interstate transportation of petroleum is governed by regulations of the Department of Energy, the Department of the Interior, the Interstate Commerce Commission, and several other agencies, including the Internal Revenue Service.

TYPES OF REGULATION
Profit Regulation

One of the most important forms of regulation concerns the direct or indirect control of profits.

EXHIBIT 47–2 AGENCIES HAVING JURISDICTION OVER THE USE OF ENERGY

AGENCY	FUNCTION	ESTIMATED FY 1980 EXPENDITURES (MILLIONS OF DOLLARS)
Department of Energy	Energy information, regulation, and policy.	$1,003.0
Federal Energy Regulatory Commission	Oil, gas, hydro, and multiresource regulation.	73.9
Department of the Interior	Energy and minerals management, including leasing of offshore oil and gas and public land leasing for oil, gas, and coal fields.	92.1
Interstate Commerce Commission	Compliance, enforcement, and tariff examination. Includes regulation of oil and coal, slurry pipeline rates, and routes.	33.8
Environmental Protection Agency	Pollution abatement and control programs and their enforcement. Includes standards for vehicle and smokestack emissions.	814.0
Department of Transportation	Grants to state agencies to help fund gas pipeline safety programs.	2.8
Nuclear Regulatory Commission	Licensing of nuclear energy plants and control of nuclear fuel export.	57.0
Department of Commerce	Control of tanker construction and safety and establishment of marine sanctuaries.	112.5[a]
U.S. Coast Guard (Department of Transportation)	Inspection and monitoring of tankers and liquid natural gas carriers.	20.5[a]
National Highway Traffic Safety Administration (Department of Transportation)	Automotive fuel economy and consumer information.	12.5
Occupational Safety and Health Administration (Department of Labor)	Promulgation and enforcement of safety and health standards (includes energy related substances).	122.1
Consumer Product Safety Commission	Control of home structural products, including home insulation.	7.8
Federal Trade Commission	Litigation involving the energy industry.	—[b]
Department of Justice	Antitrust regulation.	43.6
Internal Revenue Service (Department of the Treasury)	Tax regulations affecting energy users and producers.	—[b]
Federal Trade Commission	Relief from import injury, including tariffs and quotas on energy imports.	—[b]

[a]FY 1979.
[b]Not available.
Source: Computed from Executive Office of the President, *Budget of the U.S. Government, Fiscal Year 1979 and 1980* (Washington D.C.: Government Printing Office, 1979), appendix.

Traditionally, profits have generally been unregulated. Not until the middle of the nineteenth century was the traditional **laissez-faire** doctrine challenged. Today, in addition to federal, state, and local taxation, the most important profit regulations arise where the government has granted exclusive rights to produce a commodity. Most electric and water public utilities fall into this category. In such situations, the regulatory form usually chosen is **rate making**. Rather than regulate profits directly, regulatory commissions or their equivalent set a rate of return on capital.

Price Regulation

A closely related form of regulation involves control of the actual prices that sellers can charge. Price regulation can take the form of a maximum, minimum, or uniform price. New York City, for example, establishes the maximum price that certain apartment owners can charge their tenants. The interstate movement of natural gas is also subject to a maximum price based on geographic location. Minimum prices are often established as floors for certain agricultural products, such as wheat. Price regulations can have substantial effects on the number of units sold, the quality of goods or associated services, and other terms of business transactions. For example, producers who find that the profit rates on price-controlled products are too low may decide to no longer produce the products. They will sell their existing supplies and cut out that particular line of production from their businesses. Sometimes, all prices (including those paid to workers) are controlled by national laws. In the early 1970s, for example, all wages and prices were controlled by the federal government.

Advertising

Restrictions on professional advertising have survived many constitutional challenges in the past, but they appear to be weakening today. The Supreme Court has held that commercial speech is entitled to certain protections under the First Amendment. A familiar phrase for all consumers is "truth in advertising." But beyond government concern for disclosure of information, consumers have a right to information that is helpful, and in many ways indispensable, to the formation of an intelligent decision on important private matters.

The public's right to become informed about the availability of legal services has been of particular concern in recent years. Each state individually controls its legal profession, defining professional and unprofessional conduct. The latter subjects attorneys to monetary penalties or the suspension or revocation of their licenses. For years, state statutes have effectively prevented advertising by members of the legal profession. In addition, the American Bar Association's code of professional responsibility prohibits advertising on ethical grounds. Advertising was always felt to have an adverse effect on professionalism because it suggests that a lawyer might be motivated merely by profit rather than by commitment to a client's welfare.

In the 1970s, the restraint upon attorney advertising was challenged on constitutional grounds as a violation of First Amendment rights and on the ground that it limited competition in violation of the Sherman Antitrust Act. The Supreme Court ultimately ruled that restraints on attorney advertising did not tend to limit competition. However, in a landmark decision, the Court held that price advertising of legal services was permissible within certain limitations, under the protection of the First Amendment.

BACKGROUND AND FACTS *Several attorneys who were members of the Arizona State Bar were charged by the state bar association with violating a professional disciplinary rule that prohibited attorneys from advertising in newspapers or other media. The attorneys had placed a newspaper advertisement for their "legal clinic," stating that they were*

BATES v. STATE BAR OF ARIZONA
Supreme Court of the United States, 1977.
433 U.S. 350, 97 S.Ct. 2691.

offering "legal services at very reasonable fees." They listed their fees for certain services—in particular, uncontested divorces, uncontested adoptions, simple personal bankruptcies, and changes of name.

DECISION AND RATIONALE   *Reasonable professional advertisements, such as those presented in this case, cannot be interfered with. The First Amendment protects freedom of all kinds of speech including commercial speech. Despite this constitutional right, the Arizona State Bar asserts numerous arguments against lawyers advertising, including the adverse effect on professionalism, the inherently misleading nature of attorney advertising, the adverse effect on the administration of justice, and the undesirable economic effects of advertising. Not only do these arguments ignore the constitutional right of free speech, but they ignore the great benefits that advertising—which is a traditional mechanism in a free market economy—can have on the legal community. Justice Blackmun gave the opinion of the court: "In holding that advertising by attorneys may not be subjected to blanket supression, and that the advertisement at issue is protected, we, of course, do not hold that advertising by attorneys may not be regulated in any way. *** Advertising that is false, deceptive, or misleading of course is subject to restraint."*

Quotas and Duties

Another form of regulation is the establishment of quotas or duties on specific levels of production, imports, or sales. Petroleum companies, for example, are limited in the amount of petroleum products that they can bring into the country. In other cases, explicit import duties or taxes are applied to various products. Unlike price regulation, quotas establish a fixed level of output for sales, so their effects are often more stringent than those associated with duties and other price regulation. Both quotas and duties are often established to protect domestic industries from competition.

Licensing and Allocating Rights

Through their exercise of licensing power, agencies control entry into given economic activities. Thus, no rail, motor, or water carrier can extend its routes without a license from the Interstate Commerce Commission. The Federal Power Commission has similar authority over utilities, the Federal Communications Commis-

sion over radio and television broadcasters, and the Securities and Exchange Commission over the investment business. In recent years, there has been a trend toward deregulation, which limits the licensing power of agencies. For example, the Civil Aeronautics Board no longer has the power to license routes.

Standard Setting

Another form of regulation involves standard setting. The U.S. Department of Agriculture establishes a large number of standards for food products. It grades beef and issues standards for other meat and poultry products, for example. Such grading helps consumers in evaluating alternative selections of beef, although sometimes the labeling standards are difficult to understand. For example, food products that are labeled "beef with gravy" must contain at least 50 percent cooked beef, but if the ingredients are reversed so that the label reads "gravy with beef," only 35 percent of the contents must be beef.

Disclosure Requirements

In recent years, regulatory authorities have instituted a number of measures that require sellers to disclose certain information prior to the completion of a sale. In some cases, disclosures must be made in alternative forms. For example, if Martin Pontiac advertises on local television that a 1980 Pontiac can be paid for over the next thirty-six months, the down payment, the amount of monthly payment, and the annual percentage rate of interest must also be specified in the ad. Another disclosure requirement that was recently proposed concerns sales by used car dealers. If enacted, the regulations would require the disclosure of the nature and type of repairs performed on all used cars prior to resale.

Materials and Process Regulations

Regulatory agencies can also specify the type of material that can be used in the manufacture of certain goods. The Food and Drug Administration (FDA), for example, has prohibited the use of red dye #2 in food and cosmetics. In other cases, regulatory action specifies the form of manufacturing or prohibits certain processes. The FDA also prohibits the use of a U-shaped assembly line in the manufacturing of pharmaceutical products. Firms must use an assembly line that has no bends.[6]

REGULATED ACTIVITIES

Virtually every economic activity is subject to some regulation at one stage or another in the process of manufacturing, wholesaling, retailing, or other activity. A few of those activities are discussed below.

Transportation

Virtually all forms of transportation—surface, air, and water—are subject to a multitude of government regulations. The commerce clause of the Constitution gives the federal government the power to regulate commerce and interstate trade. The Interstate Commerce Commission (ICC), created by the Act to Regulate Commerce in 1887, has regulated freight service transportation throughout the United States since that time. The major form of regulation concerns the rates that can be charged for different commodities as well as distance traveled.[7] In addition to rate regulation, the ICC prohibits carriers from carrying freight on back hauls (return trips) in a number of situations. Such prohibitions decrease the options of shippers, thereby generating higher prices for all shipping.

The ICC also regulates the lease rates on railroad freight cars and other rolling stock. In recent years, the price has not been permitted to rise, so individual firms have found that rail cars have become a cheaper means of storing merchandise. A significant shortage of railroad cars has been the main result of this regulation.

In some cases, the ICC's regulatory powers exceed those of other government agencies. For example, in United States v. Interstate Commerce Comm., the Justice Department attempted to block the commission's approval of the merger of the Great Northern Railway Company and the Northern Pacific Railway Company.[8] The department argued that the ICC failed to give sufficient weight to the diminution of competition between the lines and failed to balance antitrust objections and national transportation goals properly. By supporting the commission, the Court gave the ICC the right to approve mergers when the cost savings outweighed the anticompetitive consequences of the merger.

Communications

The most prominent form of regulation of communications is concerned with the right to

6.   21 CFR 211.42

7.   Thomas Gail Moore, "Freight Transportation Regulation: Service Freight and the Interstate Commerce Commission," AEI (1972).

8.   396 U.S. 491, 90 S.Ct. 708 (1970).

transmit or broadcast signals in the electromagnetic spectrum. Various regulatory agencies, including the Department of Defense and the Federal Communications Commission, have the right to allocate the air waves. Licenses are generally granted for specific periods of time, and they regulate the mixture of programming that the station can offer its audience. Licenses also specify the station's maximum and minimum wattage power for transmission without interference. Despite these regulations, broadcast rights represent significant assets, so firms often devote considerable effort to obtaining them. Licensing renewal is sometimes affected by a station's record in hiring or promoting members of minority groups.

Consumer Products

Ultimately, consumer products are subject to a large number of regulations, since virtually every regulation has its final impact on the price of the commodity in the market. Some regulations, however, are more direct. The Consumer Product Safety Commission (CPSC) has jurisdiction over more than ten thousand products. The agency has been given the authority to establish mandatory safety standards, to require warnings by manufacturers, to require producers to give rebates to consumers, and to ban or recall products without a court hearing. In addition, it can impose criminal penalties so that executives in firms with violations can face jail sentences.[9]

Health and Safety

In 1970, Congress passed a comprehensive act to regulate occupational safety and health.[10] In response, the Department of Labor has issued various detailed rules and regulations specifying safety standards for almost every industry. There are standards that apply to fire extinguishers, electrical groundings, exits from buildings, guards for machines, and other

9. Consumer Product Safety Act, Public Law 92-573. 42 USCA Sec. 3142-1, 29 USCA Sec. 661.

10. Occupational Safety and Health Act of 1970,

resources or activities generally affecting production in industry. In addition, certain rules apply to particular work activities. For example, regulations can specify the times and locations when construction personnel must wear hard hats. The law imposes numerous recordkeeping requirements concerning accidental injuries and job-related health problems.

Inspections must comply with statutory procedures. No examination that amounts to a warrantless search is permitted. The Constitution protects all citizens, including corporations, from unreasonable searches. Hence, health and safety inspections must meet constitutional requirements. This does not mean that surprise inspections cannot take place. It merely means that unless the agency conducting the inspection has obtained *consent* to inspect, an inspection cannot be made without a search warrant.

Employment

A number of regulations govern wage levels, hiring practices, pensions, and other conditions of employment. In most industries, employers are required to pay a minimum wage specified by Congress in the Fair Labor Standards Act. In 1980, the minimum wage for nonagricultural workers was $3.10. The act also prohibits the employment of children under the age of fourteen years, sets maximum hours, and specifies overtime pay provisions. Employers must also make a number of mandatory payments on behalf of employees. These include payments to social security for retirement (OASI), disability income (DI), unemployment compensation, and workmen's compensation (for work-related accidents).

A number of additional regulations govern hiring, promotion, and procedures for handling disputes between labor and management. Employers cannot, for example, discriminate against individuals because of age, race, sex, color, national origin, or religious beliefs. Since 1964, under Title VII of the Civil Rights Act, the Supreme Court has increasingly defined the limits of employment discrimination.

One of the objectives of Congress in enacting the Civil Rights Act was to achieve equality of employment opportunity and to remove barriers that operated in the past to favor identifiable groups of white employees over other employees. The Supreme Court has enforced the provisions of the Civil Rights Act pertaining to employment opportunities to prevent various employment practices that operated to disqualify minorities from advancement opportunities. The Civil Rights Act has been used to prohibit educational requirements from being invoked as a bar to promotion and transfer opportunities for minority employees when these requirements have no relationship to job performance. Even where employment practices are neutral on their face, but their impact is to maintain the status quo of prior discriminatory employment practices, the Civil Rights Act is a method for removing such barriers.

BACKGROUND AND FACTS *The defendant, Duke Power Company, was sued by a number of its black employees for practicing racial discrimination in hiring and assigning employees at its Dan River plant. The plant was organized into five operating departments: (1) labor, (2) coal handling, (3) operation, (4) maintenance, and (5) laboratory test. Blacks were employed only in the labor department, where the highest paying jobs paid less than the lowest paying jobs in the other four departments (which employed only whites). Promotions were normally made within each department on the basis of seniority. Transferees into a department usually began at the lowest position.*

In 1955, the company began to require a high school education for an initial assignment into any department except the labor department. In addition, it required a high school education for any transfer from the coal handling department to any inside department (operations, maintenance, or laboratory). For ten years, this company-wide policy was enforced.

In 1965, when the company abandoned its policy of restricting blacks to the labor department, a high school diploma or equivalency tests was nevertheless made a prerequisite to transfer from the labor department into any other department.

The test rendered a markedly disproportionate number of blacks ineligible for employment advancement in the company.

GRIGGS v. DUKE POWER CO.

Supreme Court of the United States, 1971.

401 U.S. 424, 91 S.Ct. 849.

DECISION AND RATIONALE *Duke Power's requirements respecting high school diplomas and equivalency tests violated the Civil Right Act. Ordinarily, requiring a high school education or the passing of a general intellegence test as a condition of employment does not violate a person's civil rights. However, when such requirements bear no relation to job performance, and they operate to disqualify racial minorities at a substantially higher rate than white applicants, they amount to illegal barriers in violation of the Civil Rights Act. This is true even though Duke Power Company imposed the requirements without discriminatory intent. The court explained its interpretation of the law as follows: "Congress directed the thrust of the Act to the consequences of employment practices, not simply the motivation. *** Nothing in the Act* *precludes the use of testing or measuring procedures; obviously they are useful. What the Congress has forbidden is giving these devices and mechanisms controlling force unless they are demonstrably a reasonable measure of job performance."*

Innovation

Many federal regulations indirectly affect investment and innovation. In some industries, however, the regulations are more closely applied to innovative actions and to the research and developmental process. For example, the 1962 Kefauver-Harris amendments to the Food, Drug and Cosmetic Act of 1938 effectively eliminated the time constraint for the Food and Drug Administration's approval of a new drug application. After 1962, the FDA could withhold a drug from the market indefinitely until the agency was satisfied that the drug was both safe and effective for its intended use. Currently, the FDA views its role as requiring the manufacturer to prove a drug safe, rather than requiring the agency to prove it unsafe. As a consequence, approval times for new drugs have gone from an average of six months to more than six years in many cases.

Energy

Energy is regulated by a large number of independent agencies, each of which promulgates numerous rules and regulations. More importantly, numerous studies have shown that these organizations have been extremely effective in altering economic activity in energy and related industries. For example, the Federal Power Commission (FPC) has regulated the price of natural gas for many years. The FPC uses a geographic area rate regulation procedure that is based on average regional accounting costs for establishing maximum prices. It set initial price ceilings close to market prices so the regulation had little or no effect. Throughout the 1960s, the FPC, in its determination to hold the line against increases in natural gas prices, failed to increase regional maximum prices to reflect real increases in demand and inflation-

ary pressures. As a consequence, shortages appeared; in some cases, they represented extreme problems by the 1970s.[11]

Patent and Copyright

The Constitution delegates powers "to promote the progress of science and useful arts, by securing limited times to authors and inventors concerning the exclusive right to their respective writings and discoveries * * *." As early as 1790, a number of statutes implementing this power were passed. The patent laws exclude others for a period of seventeen years from making, using, or selling inventions that are claimed and determined to be patentable. Patent laws are unique in that they permit a number of practices that are considered to be anticompetitive. For example, the owner of a patent can fix prices to at least one licensee—a per se violation of antitrust laws in the absence of a patent. Thus, the patent law deviates from the general policy of preventing monopolies in order to encourage the development and production of goods and services by offering economic protection for a limited period of time. In a similar manner, authors or their estates hold exclusive rights to the authors' published or unpublished works for life plus fifty years. For works that are anonymous or pseudonymous, protection is given for a minimum of seventy-five years from publication or one hundred years from creation.

Trademarks

Under common law, merchants acquire legal rights in the words or symbols they use to

11. Paul MacAvoy, "The Regulated Induced Shortage of Natural Gas," *Journal of Law and Economics* (April 1971): 167-200.

distinguish their goods from others by adoption and use. Congress, acting under the commerce clause of the Constitution, enacted legislation long ago to facilitate the acquisition and enforcement of trademark rights. In 1946, the Lanham Act permitted registration of any distinctive mark indicative of its source or origin. (Trademarks include "any word, name, symbol, or device, or any combination thereof adopted and used by the manufacturer [or] merchant to identify its goods and distinguish them from those manufactured or sold by others.") Existing law, however, has determined that if the trademark becomes associated as a generic term for the commodities and loses its association with a particular producer, then it is no longer valid. The trademarks linoleum and aspirin, for example, were lost when they became generally accepted as the generic name of the goods.

Financing

Many regulations have extensive impact on banking and other financial activities. For example, the Federal Reserve Board of Governors limits the maximum interest that banks can offer on checking and savings accounts.[12] This causes a significant differential between the amount that individuals can receive on checking and savings accounts relative to other forms of savings, especially during periods of extensive inflation. In addition, there are regulations regarding entry into banking promulgated by the Federal Reserve System and Federal Deposit Insurance Corporation. Among other things, these regulations require proof that there is sufficient need in the community for a new bank. Other government organizations, such as the Federal Housing Administration (FHA), also

govern financial transactions. For example, the FHA has requirements concerning the extension of mortgage credit as a condition of underwriting loans.

PUBLIC REVIEW OF REGULATION

In recent years, there has been growing recognition of the broad discretionary powers given to administrative agencies. In response, the Federal government has attempted to impose new constraints on agencies as a means of limiting the number of ineffective or potentially harmful rules. For example, in 1978, President Carter issued an order requiring agencies to determine the possible economic impacts of regulations that have substantial economic effects.[13] The order required agencies that wished to promulgate rules that were expected to have major consequences to prepare a clear statement of the problem requiring action and an analysis of the economic consequences of the proposed regulation, along with alternative solutions to the problem. Congress has also begun to hold hearings on the costs of complying with regulations. In 1973, for example, Congress held hearings focusing just on the burden of federal paperwork. Furthermore, a 1979 study of forty-eight manufacturing firms by the Business Roundtable found that government regulations account for 10 percent of total capital expenditures.

Finally, the public can seek specific statutory override of administrative powers through the U.S. Congress and other legislative bodies. For example, Congress significantly limited the Civil Aeronautics Board's ability to regulate air fares in the Airline Deregulation Act of 1978.

_____

12. Regulation Q. 12 CFR § 217 (1979).

13. Improving Government Regulations, Executive Order #12044.

QUESTIONS AND CASE PROBLEMS

1. Article III of the Constitution provides that the judicial power shall reside in the Supreme Court of

the United States and such inferior courts as the Congress shall from time to time create. Judicial power is the power to resolve disputes and includes the power to determine whether an individual has committed certain acts and whether the commission of such acts constitutes the breach of a duty owed to another or to society as a whole. Administrative agencies have the power to determine whether a person is guilty or innocent of violating agency rules and regulations. Does this contradict the mandate of Article III?

2. While courts have the power to review all agency decisions, they generally defer to the agency's findings of fact (especially where agency expertise is involved) but examine carefully the agency's findings of law. This, of course, is because courts deem *themselves* the experts on the law. Even in cases where agency expertise is not important, courts generally defer to the facts as found by the agency. For example, in a patent-related case investigated by the Federal Trade Commission, the commission made a certain finding of fact with respect to the testimony of Lidoff. The commission would not have made the finding if it had not found Lidoff to be a credible witness. Why might the reviewing court be unwilling to question the agency's determination with regard to Lidoff's credibility? [Charles Pfizer and Co. v. Federal Trade Comm., 401 F.2d 574 (6th Cir. 1968)]

3. Administrative agencies act in the capacities of both lawmaker and judge, or fact finder. Under the Constitution, these two roles are distinctly divided between the legislature and the courts. What advantages are there in combining the functions within an administrative agency? What disadvantages?

4. All actions taken by an administrative agency, whether legislative or judicial, are subject to review by the courts. The relevant test for review is whether the agency acted in an "arbitrary or capricious" manner in promulgating the rule. The Secretary of Commerce issued a flammability standard that required all mattresses, including crib mattresses, to pass a test that involved bringing the mattress in contact with a burning cigarette. The manufacturers of crib mattresses petitioned the court, asking it to hold that the flammability standard should not apply to crib mattresses. The manufacturers said that applying such a rule to crib mattresses would not only be unreasonable but arbitrary and capricious since infants do not smoke. How should the court rule? [Bunny Bear, Inc. v. Peterson, 473 F.2d 1002 (5th Cir. 1973)]

5. If an administrative agency acts arbitrarily or capriciously, the reviewing court will strike down its rule. Agencies, however, are given wide latitude or discretion in formulating agency rules. Only when an agency abuses this discretion will a reviewing court reverse it. In Question 4 above, the administrative agency promulgated a single flammability standard for more than one type of mattress. If the crib mattress

manufacturer had clearly demonstrated by proof that a flammability test used on infant mattresses in Europe was equally as satisfactory as the "cigarette test" and had been used with good results for years in Europe, would the Secretary of Commerce have abused his discretion in adopting the cigarette test? What if the crib mattress manufacturer proved that the flammability test used in Europe was better than the cigarette test? Would the Secretary of Commerce have abused his discretion?

6. The standard of review that applies to administrative adjudicatory procedures is somewhat higher than the one applied to the rule-making process. When an administrative agency decides whether an agency rule or regulation has been violated, it conducts a hearing somewhat similar to a nonjury trial. Why do courts require stronger support for agencies' adjudicatory decisions than for their rule-making decisions?

7. Reviewing courts readily support rules promulgated by administrative agencies, but they require that the adjudicative findings of an agency be supported by "substantial evidence on the record." When an administrative agency conducts an adjudicative hearing, a record is made of all the evidence and testimony presented at the hearing. If the finding of the hearing is supported by the evidence contained in the record, a reviewing court will uphold the agency's finding. The Adolph Coors Company was accused by the FTC of engaging in certain price-fixing agreements in violation of the Sherman Antitrust Act. After a complete adjudicative hearing, the commission concluded that Coors had in fact engaged in illegal price-fixing. Substantial evidence was presented at the hearing in support of the commission's findings. But Coors also presented substantial evidence that it had never entered into any price-fixing arrangements. Should a reviewing court uphold the FTC's findings? [Adolph Coors Co. v. Federal Trade Comm., 497 F.2d 1178 (10th Cir. 1974)]

8. Mary Burke Sprogis was employed by United Airlines as a stewardess. On June 19, 1966, she was discharged for violating a current company policy that required stewardesses to be unmarried. This rule had never been applied to any male employee. Sprogis sued United Airlines under Title 7 of the Civil Rights Acts of 1964, which prohibits, among other things, discrimination based on sex. Must United Airlines reinstate Sprogis? [Sprogis v. United Airlines, Inc. 444 F.2d 1194 (7th Cir. 1971)]

9. Johnson & Johnson's trademark "shower to

shower" was used as the label on body powder that it manufactured. The Colgate-Palmolive Company later adopted a similar trademark, "hour after hour," which it applied to its line of aerosol deodorants and antiperspirants. Johnson & Johnson sought to prevent Colgate-Palmolive from using the phrase "hour after hour" on the ground that it violated Johnson & Johnson's trademark. In determining whether one has adopted a phrase or name that violates another's trademark rights, courts look to the Lanham Trademark Act. The act provides that a product name violates another's trademark rights when the names are so similar that they are likely to deceive or confuse buyers. Under this test, has Colgate-Palmolive's "hour after hour" violated Johnson & Johnson's "shower to shower" trademark? [Johnson & Johnson v. Colgate-Palmolive Co., 345 F.Supp. 1216 (D.C.N.J. 1972)]

48

Government Regulation
Consumer Protection

Consumer protection arises from three distinct sources—from common law through judicial rulings; from simplification and codification of common law through federal, state, and local statutes, including the Uniform Commercial Code; and from administrative law through rule making and enforcement activities, such as the Federal Trade Commission's rule allowing consumers to keep unsolicited merchandise received through the mails.

Since parties who make contracts are generally given the right to specify the terms, consumer protection under the common law is sometimes limited. As Chapter 9 and Chapter 11 illustrated, the interests of consumers have often been important in judicial decisions. For example, the unconscionability doctrine (which deals with contracts that would be grossly unfair to enforce) protects consumers from certain pricing techniques for goods that are sold on credit. Consider the example of Williams, who made a series of purchases from Walker-Thomas Furniture Company from 1957 to 1962. Each of the time payment contracts that she signed contained the clause that all payments would be credited pro rata on all outstanding accounts. In 1962 she purchased furniture for $164, bringing her total purchases since 1957 to $1,800. The pro rata claim, however, meant that she still owed money on all items despite the fact that she had paid a total of $1,400 through 1962. A court found this clause to be unconscionable and unenforceable.[1]

---

1. Williams v. Walker-Thomas Furniture Co., 198 A.2d 914 (D.C.App. 1964).

CONSUMER PROTECTION SOURCES

A number of federal laws—such as the Consumer Credit Protection Act, the Uniform Consumer Sales Practices Act, and the Magnuson-Moss Warranty Act—have been passed to provide more explicit direction on the duty of sellers and the rights of consumers. In recent years, the pressure on Congress to enact further laws to protect consumers has increased. New regulations in this area are likely to be drafted in the future.

State Statutes

Various provisions of the Uniform Commercial Code provide consumer protection in commercial sales transactions.[2] A number of statutes in California, Florida, New York, and other states provide explicit protection to consumers. For example, the California Civil Code permits consumers to keep unsolicited goods. If they are billed for the goods, they can seek an injunction to stop billing, and they can collect reasonable attorneys' fees.[3] In New York, consumers who purchase goods at home must be made aware of their rights to cancel the transaction prior to midnight of the third business day after the transaction.[4]

Administrative Agencies

Administrative agencies provide an important form of consumer protection. For example, the Federal Trade Commission will spend approximately 46 percent of its estimated $66.5 million budget for fiscal year 1979 for consumer protection activities. The FTC, which is headed by five commissioners appointed by the president for terms of seven years, has been given extensive enforcement responsibilities in a number of statutes, some of which are discussed below.

The most important authority, however, is Section 5 of the original Federal Trade Commission Act of 1914 as amended in 1938. It permits the commission to stop "unfair or deceptive acts or practices" that influence, inhibit, or restrict consumers unfairly in their purchasing decisions. Many of these practices are prohibited by industry guidelines or trade regulation rules. Violations are punishable by law and can occur in two circumstances. A company can engage in a practice prohibited by a trade regulation, or it can violate a known cease and desist order issued against another party. For example, if the FTC issues a cease and desist order to Ford Motor Company that prohibits the advertising of fuel economy levels achieved when the automobiles are driven by professional drivers without disclosing that information, the FTC can impose civil penalties against another automobile producer if it advertises mileage tests without the disclosure.[5] The commission can also bring actions for consumers who have been injured. Other agencies of the federal government, such as the Department of Housing and Urban Development, are also engaged in consumer protection activities. HUD, for example, enforces provisions of the National Mobile Home Construction and Safety Standards Act of 1974, which require that periodic inspections and investigations be conducted to enforce federal standards. It also enforces the Interstate Land Sale Full Disclosure Act, which requires that sellers of subdivided lots provide certain statements of record that must include a legal description of the land, who has title to the land, and the present condition of the land.

The Courts

Finally, consumers themselves can use the courts to obtain remedies for their grievances. Since the time, embarrassment, and cost to consumers of private lawsuits can be prohibitive, various mechanisms have been developed to remove these barriers. They include prelegal services, small claims courts, and recovery of

---

2. The UCC is discussed more fully in the sections on sales and commercial transactions.

3. Section 1584.5

4. N.Y. Business Corporation Law, Sec. 1101 (McKinney 1964).

---

5. FTC Improvements Act of 1975.

attorneys' fees in class actions. Attorneys' fees, however, are generally recoverable only when there is an express statutory authorization.[6] Class actions have become a relatively more common form of addressing consumer grievances, but these actions are subject to certain rules and limits that make them difficult to pursue, particularly by individuals.

ADVERTISING

The basic protection afforded consumers against deceptive advertising derives more from statutory and administrative sources than from common law. Common law protection is based on fraud and requires proof of intent to misrepresent facts and other criteria. On the other hand, the statutory law and administrative

_____

6. See Alyeska Pipeline Service Co. v. The Wilderness Society, 421 U.S. 240, 95 S.Ct. 1612 (1975).

regulations focus on whether the advertising is likely to be misleading, regardless of intent. Behind this approach is the notion that the purpose of prohibiting false advertising through legislation is to protect the consumer rather than to punish the seller or advertiser.

The Federal Trade Commission Act empowers the FTC to determine what constitutes a deceptive practice within the meaning of Section 5 of the act. The FTC's judgment can be appealed to a court, but it is accorded great weight by the reviewing court. When the commission renders an opinion or issues an order, appeal can be taken through judicial channels. The commission is responsible for enforcing the legislative policy of the act it administers, and the courts will recognize that the administrative agency that deals continually with cases in the area is often in a better position than the courts are to determine when a practice is deceptive within the meaning of the act.

FEDERAL TRADE COMM. v. COLGATE-PALMOLIVE CO.
Supreme Court of the United States, 1965.
380 U.S. 374, 85 S.Ct. 1035.

BACKGROUND AND FACTS *The Federal Trade Commission issued a complaint against Colgate-Palmolive Company and Ted Bates & Company, Inc., an advertising agency, for using commercials that misrepresented the characteristics of Colgate's Rapid Shave. Bates had prepared TV commercials that showed how Rapid Shave could soften something as tough as sandpaper. In the commercial, Rapid Shave was applied to something that looked like sandpaper, and shortly thereafter a razor shaved it clean. Unknown to the viewers, the "sandpaper" was actually a piece of plexiglass with sand on it.*

DECISION AND RATIONALE *The court affirmed the Commission's interpretation that the television commercial was deceptive. Leading the viewer to believe that sandpaper was being used in the ads, when in fact it was plexiglass, constituted a materially deceptive advertising practice. "[W]hen the commercial not only makes a claim, but also invites the viewer to rely on his own perception for demonstrative proof of the claim, the [advertisers] will be aware that the use of undisclosed props in strategic places might be a material deception."*

Bait and Switch

In some cases, the Federal Trade Commission has promulgated specific rules to govern advertising. One of its more important rules is called

"Guides on Bait Advertising,"[7] and it is designed to prohibit advertisements that specify a very low price for a particular item. The low price is

_____

7. 16 CFR 238 §(1968).

the bait to lure the consumer into the store. Then, the salesperson tries to switch the consumer to some other, more expensive item. According to the FTC guidelines, bait advertising occurs if the seller refuses to show the advertised item, fails to have adequate quantities of it available, fails to promise or deliver the advertised item within a reasonable time, or discourages employees from selling the item.

Numerous techniques fall into the bait and switch category. In the following case, sales personnel not only were directed to engage in certain baiting practices but were rewarded for doing so.

BACKGROUND AND FACTS *All-State Industries, a producer of residential aluminum siding, storm windows, and other products, used a bait and switch sales technique in selling its products. The "ADV" lower-cost grade of aluminum was featured in the company's ads, but salespersons, following the training manual, attempted to actually sell the "PRO" grade after contacting the customers. The Federal Trade Commission found this practice to be an "unfair and deceptive" practice under 5(b) of the FTC act and issued a cease and desist order. All-State Industries appealed.*

ALL-STATE INDUSTRIES OF NORTH CAROLINA, INC. v. FEDERAL TRADE COMM.
United States Court of Appeals, Fourth Cir., 1970.
423 F.2d 423.

DECISION AND RATIONALE *All-State Industries had to change its selling tactics. Bait and switch tactics have long been found to be unfair and deceptive. The sales techniques at issue clearly fell within this category of deceptive practices. The judge concluded: "This 'bait and switch' artifice, the Examiner discovered, was fully set forth in the sales force's training manual and was employed generally."*

Corrective Advertising

If the Federal Trade Commission rules that a seller has made a false or deceptive advertising statement, the commission can require the seller to make additional advertisements that correct it. (Former statements are contradicted, and the correct statement is presented in the new ads.) For example, the FTC filed a complaint against Warner Lambert stating that the firm had misrepresented its product, Listerine, by advertising that it would prevent and cure colds and sore throats. After determining through expert medical testimony that Listerine would neither cure nor prevent colds and that similar relief could be obtained through the use of warm salt water, the commission concluded that the firm had made deceptive statements about the medical benefits of its product. The commission then ordered corrective advertising. In addition to the actual corrective advertisement, the FTC can require that the statement "THIS ADVERTISEMENT IS PUBLISHED PURSUANT TO THE ORDER OF THE FEDERAL TRADE COMMISSION" in large capital letters be placed in the ad.

CERTIFICATION

Many products have one or more of their attributes tested against predetermined standards and certified if the standards are met. For example, a toaster might be tested by Underwriters Laboratory, a private laboratory that tests manufactured products for electrical safety.[8] Statements about certification are often included in advertisements, displayed on the product, noted by sales personnel, or included in the brochures that accompany the product.

---

8. Underwriters Laboratory also investigates fire and other safety characteristics associated with the product.

Sometimes, the entire product is approved by some independent organization. Certification represents a seal of approval, which means that the product will satisfy the demands of ordinary use.

Third party certification permits an independent body that is better qualified than the consumer and that does not have a direct interest in the sale of the product to examine the commodity. In some cases, such organizations are indirectly funded by manufacturers through testing associations. For example, many gas appliances are tested by the American Gas Association. On the other hand, some organizations, such as Consumers Union and Consumers' Research, do not certify or approve products but choose particular tests and report their findings to the consumer in monthly magazines and annual volumes.[9]

Guaranteed Third Party Approval

Approval by third parties can be limited to testing and certification, but some third party approval mechanisms include remedies as well. For example, Good Housekeeping Approval means that the magazine will refund the purchase price or replace the purchased article if it should prove defective. Good Housekeeping Approval, however, is limited to the products that are advertised in the magazine and are tested to determine if the advertising statements are correct.

Guaranteed third party approval is generally limited to actual replacement of the product or refund of the money that was paid. Thus, Good Housekeeping Approval does not extend to damages incurred by using the product. Zayda Hanberry purchased shoes produced by Victor B. Handal and Brothers, Inc., from Akron, a retail store. The shoes were advertised as meeting the "Good Housekeeping Consumers' Guarantee Seal," which contains the promise, "If the product or performance is defective, Good Housekeeping guarantees replacement or refund to consumer." The day

she bought the shoes, Hanberry slipped and fell on the vinyl floor of her kitchen. The shoes were defective because they had a low coefficient of friction on vinyl and certain other floor coverings until they were broken in. Despite this defect, the court found that *liability* for individually defective items cannot be extended through warranty or strict liability theories to a general endorser who has made no representation that each item has been examined and tested. Thus, Good Housekeeping was not liable for damages by endorsing the shoes.[10]

Labeling and Packaging

A number of federal and state laws that govern labeling and packaging have been passed to provide the consumer with accurate information or warnings about the use or possible misuse of the product. For example, the Fur Products Labeling Act, the Wool Products Labeling Act, the Cigarette Labeling and Advertising Act, the Food, Drug and Cosmetic Act, the Flammable Fabrics Act, the Fair Packaging and Labeling Act, and others have been enacted in part to reduce the amount of incorrect labeling and packaging in consumer products. In general, labels must be accurate, which means that they must use words as they are ordinarily understood by consumers. For example, a regular size box of cereal cannot be labeled "giant" if it would tend to exaggerate the amount of cereal. Labels often must specify the raw materials used in the product, such as the percent of cotton, nylon, or other fibers used in a shirt. The Fair Packaging Act requires that consumer goods have labels that identify the product, the manufacturer, the packer or distributor and its place of business, the net quantity of contents, and the quantity of each serving if the number of servings is stated.[11] The statute also includes additional authority to add requirements governing words that are used to describe packages, terms that are associated with savings claims, information disclosure for

9. Consumers Union produces *Consumer Reports*, and Consumers' Research produces *Consumer Bulletin*.

10. Hanberry v. Hearst Corp., 276 Cal.App.2d 680, 81 Cal.Rptr. 519 (1969).

11. 15 USCA Sec. 1451 et seq.

ingredients in nonfood products, and standards for partial filling of packages. The provisions are enforced by the Federal Trade Commission and the Department of Health, Education, and Welfare.

SALES

A number of statutes that protect the consumer in sales transactions concern the disclosure of certain terms in sales, rules governing home or door-to-door sales, mail order transactions, and referral sales. For example, the Federal Reserve Board of Governors has issued Regulation Z, which governs credit provisions associated with sales contracts, and numerous states have passed laws governing the remedies available to consumers in home sales. Furthermore, states have adopted a number of provisions as they have incorporated the UCC and the UCCC into their statutory codes. In 1968, Congress passed the first of a series of statutes regarding the content of information contained in written and oral messages. If, for example, certain credit terms are used in an advertisement, other credit information is also required. Thus, if Prolific Pontiac Sales states in a newspaper advertisement that individuals have thirty-six months to pay, the firm must also include the cash price of the automobiles, the down payment, the amount of each periodic payment, and the annual percentage rate of interest.

Door-to-Door Sales

Door-to-door sales have often been singled out for special treatment in the laws of most states. The special treatment stems in part from the nature of the sales transaction if the salesperson is able to gain entrance. A door-to-door seller usually has a captive audience because many individuals are actually immobilized at home. Since repeat purchases are not as likely as they are in stores, the seller has little incentive to establish goodwill with the purchaser. Furthermore, the seller is unlikely to present alternative products and their prices. Thus, a number of states have passed statutes that permit the

buyers of goods sold door-to-door to cancel their contracts within a specified period of time, usually two to three days after the sale. In addition, a Federal Trade Commission regulation makes it a Section 5 violation for door-to-door sellers to fail to give consumers three days to cancel any sale. This rule applies in addition to state statutes so that consumers are given the most favorable benefits of the FTC rule and their own state statute. In addition, the FTC rule requires that the notification be given in Spanish if the oral negotiation was in that language.

Mail Order Transactions

Consumers buying from mail order houses have typically been given less protection than when they purchase in stores. Many mail order houses are outside the state, and it is more costly to seek redress for grievances in that situation. In addition to the federal statute that prevents the use of mails to defraud individuals, several states have passed statutes governing certain practices by sellers, including insurance companies, that solicit through the mails. The state statutes parallel the federal statutes governing mail fraud.

In some cases, the courts have found that transactions between consumers of one state and merchants who have offices located and organized under the law of another state can be regulated by the state where the transaction occurs. United Life Insurance Company, for example, was incorporated and maintained its offices outside California. The firm solicited sales of insurance policies by mail to California residents. The court held that the transactions made in California would be subject to the California Insurance Code.[12]

CREDIT

One of the more important areas of consumer protection concerns the rights of consumers in

_____

12. People v. United Nat. Life Ins., 66 Cal.2d 577, 58 Cal.Rptr. 599, 427 P.2d 199.

credit transactions. Credit has become the American way of life; nearly all major purchases are financed by some form of credit. Most consumer installment credit is extended by commercial banks and finance companies, although credit unions, retail outlets, and various miscellaneous lenders also provide credit to employees and customers.[13] Of course, a large percentage of credit, especially for automobile sales, originates with retailers but is subsequently sold to banks and finance companies. Perhaps the most important new form of credit issued by commercial banks is the credit card

(such as Master Charge or Visa). Holders of credit cards have open end accounts that can be used at thousands of stores and businesses throughout the world.

The credit industry is highly regulated and often subject to numerous state and federal licensing requirements. Nevertheless, state and federal legislators have found it necessary to pass laws governing those aspects of credit that have created the most significant consumer grievances.

In enacting the Truth in Lending Act, Congress provided that a credit card holder would be liable for a maximum of $50 in charges resulting from the unauthorized use of the card. The credit card holder must, of course, comply with the conditions set forth in the Truth in Lending Act in order to limit liability to $50. In the following case, the Alabama Court illustrates how this provision of the Truth in Lending Act applies when a "friend" abuses the credit card privilege.

---

13. Installment credit refers to all credit scheduled to be repaid in more than four payments and represents the predominant form of credit. The so-called Four Installment Rule has been codified into the Code of Federal Regulations under the designation Regulation Z, pursuant to the delegated powers under the Truth in Lending Act. The Four Installment Rule removes the creditor's incentive to bury credit charges. Consumer obligations that are payable in more than four installments require the disclosure of credit information even if no interest is being charged.

MARTIN v. AMERICAN EXPRESS, INC.

Court of Civil Appeals of Alabama, 1978.
361 So.2d 597.

BACKGROUND AND FACTS   *In 1975, Martin gave his credit card to a business associate, McBride. McBride was supposed to use the card to make purchases for a business venture in which the two men were engaged. Martin orally authorized McBride to charge up to $500 on the credit card. Martin also sent a letter to American Express prior to giving his card to McBride. In this letter, he asked American Express not to allow the total charges on his account to exceed $1,000. Martin received a statement from American Express indicating that the amount owed on his credit card account was $5,300. Martin refused to pay. American Express filed suit against Martin to obtain the money.*

DECISION AND RATIONALE   *The $50 liability limit for unauthorized use of a credit card under the Truth and Lending Act did not apply in this case. Martin voluntarily lent his card to McBride and was under no compulsion (by fraud or duress) to do so. Therefore, McBride's use of the card was not unauthorized. In the words of the presiding judge: "We believe Congress clearly indicated that 'unauthorized use' of a card would occur only where there was no 'actual, implied or apparent authority' for such use by the cardholder. *** McBride was actually authorized by Martin to use the latter's card. Martin admitted this fact. And the authority to use it, if not actual, remained apparent even after McBride ignored Martin's directions by charging over $500 to Martin's credit card account. *** Nor are we aware of any requirement, either by*

*statute, contract or trade usage, which would compel a credit card issuer
to undertake a policy whereby the issuer would see to it that charges on a
cardholder's account do not exceed a specified amount. Such a policy
would place a difficult and potentially disastrous burden on the issuer."*

The Uniform Consumer Credit Code

In 1968, the National Conference of Commissioners on the Uniform State Laws promulgated
the Uniform Consumer Credit Code (UCCC).
The UCCC has been controversial, but it has
been adopted in approximately 25 percent of
the states.[14] The UCCC is an attempt to promulgate a comprehensive body of rules governing
the most important aspects of consumer credit.
Sections of the UCCC, for example, focus on
truth in lending, maximum credit ceilings,
door-to-door sales, and referral sales. The
UCCC is also concerned with materials contained in fine print clauses and various provisions of creditor remedies, including deficiency
judgments (personal judgments for the amount
of debt that is not secured by property) and
garnishments (proceedings where property,
money, or wages controlled by a third person
are transferred to the court to satisfy a judgment). (See Chapter 31 for details.) For example,
the UCCC limits creditor remedies to either
repossession or suit for default if the purchase
price is $1,000 or less; purchases over $1,000 are
unaffected by the limitations of credit remedies.
The UCCC applies to most types of sales,
including real estate. It also replaces existing
state consumer credit laws as well as installment loan, usury, and retail installment sale
acts.

Since the UCCC prohibits a seller in consumer credit sales or leases from taking negotiable instruments, except checks, it places limits
on holders in due course. Cooling off periods for
door-to-door sales are also specified in the code.
Some provisions, such as those governing interest rates, differ from the provisions of other
statutes. For example, the UCCC establishes

interest rate ceilings of 18 percent per year on
unpaid balances of the principal rather than
having mandatory disclosure requirements.

Consumer Credit Reports

Nearly every credit transaction is accompanied
by a consumer report or an investigated report
for the creditor. The former is more common
and is largely concerned with the amount and
location of individual bank accounts, savings
accounts, and other assets. In addition, information on existing credit liabilities, such as charge
accounts and mortgages, is included in consumer credit reports. Information on the consumer's credit background, bill paying habits,
previous judgments, tax liens, bankruptcies,
and other related areas can also be provided. In
some cases, these reports contain income,
marital status, occupation, employment history,
legal difficulties, and other personal information.

Investigative reports, on the other hand, are
far more personalized than consumer reports
and are usually used for either employment or
insurance decisions. Extensive interviews with
business associates, neighbors, and other contacts are usually included in such reports. Prior
to the Fair Credit Reporting Act, consumers who
applied for credit had relatively little access to
the contents of the reports, and those who were
denied credit had no right to know why. If the
information in the reports was obsolete or
wrong, the consumer could not change it.

The Fair Credit Reporting Act specifies that
a consumer must be notified when an investigative report will be made. Upon request, the
consumer can obtain the substance of all information in the consumer reporting agency's files,
as well as the sources and recipients of information. The latter, however, is subject to certain

---

14. By 1974 the UCCC had undergone six redrafts. Furthermore, in those jurisdictions where the law has been adopted,
it is not uniform among them.

time limits. Reports by one business to a credit reporting agency or to another business that relate only to that business's experience with the consumer do not constitute a consumer report.

More importantly, if the consumer disagrees with the information in the agency's file, the agency must reinvestigate, unless the complaint is unfounded. Inaccurate information must be deleted from the agency's file, and the consumer can submit a statement concerning any unresolved disputes. Other information usually stays in the file for seven years.[15] The Federal Trade Commission has been given the responsibility for administering and enforcing provisions of the Fair Credit Reporting Act.

DISCLOSURE Perhaps the most important consumer protection law concerning disclosure is Title I of the Consumer Credit Protection Act, which is often referred to as the Truth-in-Lending Act. The act was instituted as a means of comparing different credit offers. For example, one creditor may offer a rate of 1.5 percent per month. Another creditor may specify the finance charges as an add-on so that the consumer will pay $8 per $100 borrowed for thirty months. Still another creditor may take the finance charges from the initial amount of the loan so that the proceeds to the consumer will be the face amount of the loan less interest deductions. A uniform method of presenting these alternatives, such as that specified in Title I, lowers the cost to consumers of choosing among alternative loan options.

The Truth-in-Lending Act covers a number of factors, including the amount and purpose of the credit, the status of the debtor, and the business of the creditor. But the most important provisions govern (1) the time of disclosure, (2) the finance charges, and (3) the annual percentage rate. Disclosure in a closed end credit transaction (that is, one that applies to the current purchase only) must be made before the credit is extended. For example, Mountain View Mortgage Company must provide Janet Martin with the cost of financing and the interest rate for the purchase of a home before

the time of closing (the time the purchase is finalized). Disclosure must be made early enough that Martin can shop around. In addition, the consumer must be told of the nature of the finance charges, including interest, service on other transaction activity charges, loan fees, points, finders' fees, investigation or credit report fees, and other charges. Buried finance charges must also be revealed. The finance charge then becomes the difference between the installment prices and the cash price. For example, a stereo can be sold for $600 payable in ten monthly installments of $60, or $500 cash. The $100 is really a finance charge and must be disclosed.

The final significant form of disclosure regards the "annual percentage rate," a method of reducing all finance charges to a common comparable finance charge per unit of time. In general, unless items are explicitly tied to particular clauses of the credit contract (such as a fee for the credit report) and are reported in the disclosure statement, their price must be included in the calculation of the annual percentage rate. Thus, when Colonial Bank, which handled the financing for Ron Starks's purchase of a used automobile, failed to disclose a sales fee separately or to include its value in the annual percentage rate, a violation of Regulation Z of the Truth-in-Lending Act was found. The sales fee in this case was included on the sales order form and represented the costs of title and license registration. The figure, however, was not separately itemized or listed as part of the finance charge on the disclosure statement.[16]

OPEN END CREDIT The key features to open end credit are (1) a plan by which the customer and the creditor enter into a series of consumer credit transactions and (2) discretion in the consumer to either pay in installments or pay the balance in full. American Express, Master Charge, Visa, and the typical department store revolving account are all examples of open end credit.

In contrast to open end credit, closed end

---

15. 15 USCA Sec. 1681 et seq. (1972).

16. Starks v. Orleans Motors, Inc., 500 F.2d 1182 (5th Cir. 1974).

credit is extended for a specific period of time. The total amounts, number of payments, and due dates are generally agreed upon by the creditor and the customer at the time of the transaction. Common examples of closed end credit include most consumer loans from finance companies; credit sales of large items such as cars, furniture, and major appliances; and real estate transactions. A typical statement includes the outstanding balance at the start of the billing period, amounts credited during the billing cycle, the amount of any finance charge, the periodic rate of interest, the annual percentage rate, the unpaid balance on which the finance charge was computed, the closing date of the billing cycle, and the outstanding balance, as well as the statement of the period in which payment must be made in order to avoid finance charges. Disclosure requirements also apply to real estate transactions.

RATE REGULATION

Laws regulating the maximum cost of credit, often referred to as usury laws, date back to the period when it was considered immoral to charge a borrower interest. Initially, regulated rates applied to all loans, but it became clear that since the typical consumer loan was much smaller than the commercial loan, the cost of extending credit to consumers was considerably higher per dollar of the loan. This substantially restricted credit and prompted a model consumer loan law in 1916. The law specified a maximum 3.5 percent per month interest rate, a rate approximately seven times larger than the prevailing commercial rate.[17] Usually compensation or other benefits received by the lender are classified as interest unless a specific charge is made to reimburse or compensate the seller for services other than extending credit. For example, expenses involved in opening a loan and closing expenses for appraising or recording fees can be excluded. Furthermore, charges paid by the debtor on default or prepayment penalties are not considered finance charges when computing the interest rate for usury statute purposes.[18]

17. The Uniform Small Loan Law.
18. Glaire v. La Lanne-Parris-Health Spa, Inc., 12 Cal.3d 915, 117 Cal.Rptr. 541, 528 P.2d 357 (1975).

COLLECTION AND REPOSSESSION

Repossession of goods and collection procedures have been the subject of a large number of consumer grievances in the past. A number of regulations and court decisions have been instituted to reduce the more serious problems facing consumers in these areas.

In 1965 (with amendments in 1968) the Federal Trade Commission established "Guides against Deceptive Debt Collection" in order to prevent the scare tactics used in the collection of debts. In addition, state statutes often prohibit bills or letters that give the consumer the impression that a lawsuit has actually been initiated. Threatening telephone calls to the consumer or to relatives can also be unlawful if they exceed all reasonable bounds of decency.

In 1977, Congress passed the Fair Debt Collection Practices Act. The purpose of the act is to regulate the debt collection practices of persons who collect debts from consumers arising out of purchases that are primarily for personal, family, or household purposes.

Billing errors have long represented problems to consumers, especially with credit cards and other open end installment credit options. Prior to 1975, a consumer who was billed incorrectly on a credit card statement might have received a series of computer-written letters threatening a bad credit rating in response to the consumer's letters asking that the statement be corrected. The Fair Credit Billing Act of 1975 establishes certain procedures for consumers who complain about billing errors and requires that creditors explain or correct the mistakes within thirty days.

For various reasons, debtors do not always make the required payments, and creditors seek judicial action. Collection of debts through the judicial system is usually dependent on the initial filing of legal action. In some cases, collection can be begun prior to judgment through the use of garnishment. Thus, if California Credit brings an action against Linda MacDonald to collect a debt and learns that Homestead Mortgage holds her property, California Credit can garnish this property. If California Credit is successful in its legal action against MacDonald, the judgment can be satisfied by MacDonald's property held by Homestead Mortgage. Furthermore, if Homestead Mortgage disposes of the property, California Credit can recover from Homestead directly. Some states have statutes that exempt certain property from the collection process, for example, personal property up to $750. Other states have homestead laws that protect the real property of the debtor. Purchase money mortgages and security interest are generally not protected by the homestead statute in most states.

Title 3 of the Consumer Credit Protection Act limits garnishment to either 25 percent of a person's disposable earnings or the amount that the disposable earnings exceed thirty times the minimum federal hourly wage, whichever is smaller. Creditors are also limited in their ability to repossess secured property without notice in some form of adversary hearing.

WARRANTIES

Warranties that accompany the sale of consumer products are governed by the Uniform Commercial Code in all states except Louisiana. Under the UCC, express and implied warranties of merchantability and fitness are given. If a car dealer states that an automobile is new, this constitutes an express warranty and need not be in writing, although the statement must be an affirmation of fact or promise.[19] Every sale of goods by a merchant seller carries an implied warranty of merchantability, which means that the goods must be fit for the ordinary purposes for which goods are used. For example, there is an implied warranty of merchantability that hand lotion will not burn the skin.[20] Implied warranties of fitness arise whenever buyers rely on the merchant's skill and judgment to select suitable goods. For example, if a customer wants to see ski boats, and the boat dealer sells the customer an outboard that has insufficient power to pull a water skier, a breach of warranty has probably occurred. Other provisions regarding disclosure of warranties are also governed by the UCC.

In response to a perceived problem in consumer warranty protection, Congress passed the Magnuson-Moss Warranty Act of 1975. The act was designed to simplify warranty protection so that the average consumer could understand the limitations or inclusions of warranty protection. The statute governs disclosure of warranty. Under its provisions, manufacturers and sellers are not required to make express warranties. However, if a warranty is given, it must comply with the disclosure requirements of the act. For the most part, warranties must now be designated either *full* or *limited*. A full warranty means that the seller warrants *at least* the minimum federal standards set forth in Section 104 of the Act (e.g., the warrantor must remedy any defect within a reasonable time and without charge). A limited warranty means that the warranties listed in Section 104 are *not all* included.[21]

---

19. Additional actions that are likely to result in express warranties are covered by Section 2-313 of the UCC; they are described in Chapter 21.

20. Section 2-314 covers additional implied warranties of merchantability; it too is discussed in Chapter 21.
21. See Chapter 21.

QUESTIONS AND CASE PROBLEMS

1. Norman's Health Club, Inc., was a chain of recreation centers located in St. Louis, Missouri. The health clubs sold lifetime memberships for $360; the fee could be paid either in full or in twenty-four installments of $15 each. The vast majority of persons joining the health clubs chose the installment plan. Under this plan, Norman's Health Club had prospective members sign installment notes, which in turn were sold to finance companies at discounts of between $85 and $165. Club members who paid cash were charged about 10 percent less than those who paid under the installment plan. Assuming that no disclosures about finance charges were made on the installment notes signed by the prospective club members, has Norman's Health Club violated the

disclosure requirements of the Truth-in-Lending Act? Has there been any violation by the finance companies that purchased the notes? [Joseph v. Norman's Health Club, Inc., 532 F.2d 86 (8th Cir. 1976)]

2. In 1969, a door-to-door salesman for Family Publications Services, Inc., sold Leila Mourning a five-year subscription to four magazines. Mourning agreed to pay $3.95 immediately and to remit a similar amount monthly for thirty months. She also signed a form contract that contained a clause stating that the subscriptions could not be cancelled and providing that any default in an installment payment would render the entire balance due. The contract made no reference to service or finance charges. Mourning thereafter defaulted on one of her payments, and Family Publications threatened to bring suit for the balance due. Mourning defended on the ground that Family Publications failed to disclose the nature and amount of the finance charges in its installment contract. Family Publications contended that since no finance charges were involved, no disclosure was necessary. Assuming no finance charges were involved in the installment plan, has Family Publications Services, Inc. violated the Truth-in-Lending Act? [Mourning v. Family Publications Services Inc., 411 U.S. 356, 93 S.Ct. 1652 (1973)]

3. On July 16, Polly Ann Barber entered into a retail installment contract with Kimbrell's, Inc., for the purchase of various items of household furniture totaling $592. Barber later sued Kimbrell's for violating the Truth-in-Lending Act because Kimbrell's used the term *total time balance* in its disclosure document rather than *total of payments* as the act required. At the same time, Barber sued Furniture Distributors, Inc., claiming that it too was liable as a creditor under the act. Furniture Distributors, Inc. participated in the development and preparation of the standard contract form and distributed it for use in all the retail stores in the Kimbrell's chain. It was also the parent company of Kimbrell's and had extensive knowledge of the credit terms for all the consumer credit sales that Kimbrell's made. Each time one of the Kimbrell's stores made a consumer credit sale, the installment contract was sent to Furniture Distributors for review. If Kimbrell's is in violation of the Truth-in-Lending Act, can Barber also hold Furniture Distributors liable? [Barber v. Kimbrell's, Inc., 577 F.2d 216 (4th Cir. 1978)]

4. The W. T. Grant Company (Grants), a retailer, sold both on a cash basis and under Grants credit plans. A customer who entered into a credit contract with Grants was offered the opportunity to take out credit life insurance, health and accident insurance, and property insurance. The election of insurance coverage was purely voluntary and was evidenced by the customer's signature on the contract within the blocked-off "Insurance Agreement" segment. The insurance charges became part of the unpaid balance upon which the finance charge was computed. Must the insurance charges be disclosed as finance charges? [Welmaker v. W. T. Grant Co., 365 F.Supp. 531 (N.D.Ga. 1972)]

5. Under Georgia law, promissory notes signed by consumers must be notarized. Generally, a small fee is charged by notaries for their signatures. American Finance Company was engaged in the business of making consumer loans. The loan contracts complied with all of the requirements of the Truth-in-Lending Act but failed to mention that customers would be charged a fee for notarization. Buford brought suit against American Finance Company. He had signed one of American's promissory notes and claimed in the suit that failure to disclose the notary fee constituted a violation of the Truth-in-Lending Act. Is he correct? American Finance Company argued that Buford was incorrect and further argued that even if Buford was right, American Finance should not be held liable since the charge was a minimal one and was left off inadvertently. Assuming that American Finance did not intentionally omit the charge, is this a valid defense? [Buford v. American Finance Co., 333 F.Supp. 1243 (N.D.Ga. 1971)]

6. Roseman was employed as a debit agent for the John Hancock Insurance Company. He resigned, following accusations that he had been dishonest with his company expense account. Before his resignation he reimbursed the account. Part of the information concerning Roseman's resignation was contained in a credit report held by the Retail Credit Company, Inc. Subsequently, Roseman was denied a position with another insurance company after it consulted the Retail Credit Company's report. Assuming that the information held by the Retail Credit Company was accurate, was its circulation of such information illegal?

Roseman felt that he was slighted by Retail Credit Company because there were two sides to the story of his resignation, and his side was not included in the company's files. He complained that Retail Credit Company should have informed him that it had such information, and he claimed further that he had the right to include a statement in the files setting forth his version of the circumstances surrounding his resignation. Is Roseman correct? [Roseman v. Retail Credit Co., Inc., 428 F.Supp. 643 (E.D.Pa. 1977)]

7. Harold Grey signed an installment contract as

payment for membership in a European Health Spas Club. The disclosure documents that accompanied the installment loan contract were printed in regular type, with the exception of the words: "FINANCE CHARGE," "ANNUAL PERCENTAGE RATE," and "MEMBER ACKNOWLEDGES THAT HE HAS READ AND RECEIVED A FILLED-IN SIGNED COPY OF THIS AGREEMENT." In addition, at the top of the disclosure statement, the words "NOTICE TO BUYER" were printed. Under federal truth-in-lending regulations, the words *finance charge* and *annual percentage rate* must be printed conspicuously in the truth-in-lending disclosure statements. Otherwise, the creditor is deemed in violation of the act. Has the requirement of conspicuousness been met? [Grey v. European Health Spas Inc., 428 F.Supp. 841 (D.C.Conn. 1977)]

8. Roger Gonzalez purchased a Ford from Schmerler Ford on credit. The installment credit agreement that Gonzalez signed named Ford Motor Credit Corporation as the payee of the loan. Nowhere on the loan form or the disclosure documents did the name Schmerler Ford appear. Schmerler Ford, however, helped Gonzalez fill out the loan forms and then forwarded them to Ford Motor Credit Corporation. Schmerler lacked the authority to negotiate the interest rate charged on the loan and lacked the ability to approve Gonzalez's loan. Gonzalez's loan was made solely by Ford Motor Credit Corporation. Later it was discovered that the loan forms failed to disclose all of the relevant information that was required under the Truth-in-Lending Act. Who can be held liable as having violated the act—Schmerler Ford, Ford Motor Credit Corporation, or both? [Gonzalez v. Schmerler Ford, 397 F.Supp. 323 (N.D.Ill. 1975)]

9. On December 7, 1973, Jerry Reed and his wife executed an installment sales contract for the purchase of a new 1974 mobile home from Washington Trailer Sales, Inc. The Reeds made a cash down payment of $863 and were to pay the balance on an installment basis. On December 13, 1973, Washington Trailer Sales assigned the sales contract to Commerce Union Bank, a bank with which it did business on an irregular basis. In fact, this was the first contract that Washington Trailer Sales had assigned to the bank within the last seven months. Commerce Union Bank played no part in the arranging for and extending of credit to the Reeds. Subsequently, the Reeds brought an action against Washington Trailer Sales and Commerce Union Bank on the ground that certain statements contained in the installment sales contract disclosure form were not conspicuous, as required by the Truth-in-Lending Act. If the technical violation of the act that the Reeds allege could not have been discerned by Commerce Union Bank after a reasonable inspection of the installment contract and disclosure form, would Commerce Union Bank be liable? [Reed v. Washington Trailer Sales, Inc., 393 F.Supp. 886 (M.D.Tenn. 1974)]

10. A garnishment proceeding was brought by Sterling Finance Company against Lawrence Thornhill pursuant to a judgment that Sterling Finance had against Thornhill. Under the Truth-in-Lending Act, which limits garnishment to 25 percent of the garnishee's disposable earnings, Sterling Finance could have obtained $66.25 from Thornhill. Under the law of Ohio, where the garnishment proceeding was brought, Sterling Finance was entitled to $192.52. How much of Thornhill's pay can Sterling Finance Company garnish? [Sterling Finance Co. v. Thornhill, 263 N.E.2d 925 (Mun.Ct. 1970)]

49

Government Regulation
Environmental Law

HISTORICAL BACKGROUND

In one sense, concerns about the environment are not new. The English Parliament, for example, passed a number of acts that regulated the burning of soft coal in medieval England. Moreover, through common law nuisance statutes, property owners were given relief from pollution in situations where the individual could identify a distinct harm separate from that affecting the general public. Thus, if a factory polluted the air and killed a farmer's crops, the farmer could seek an injunction against the factory.

Needless to say, nuisance suits that granted specific relief for individuals were inadequate when the harm from pollution could not be identified with groups separate from the public at large. Under the common law, citizens were denied *standing* (access to the courts) unless specific harm could be shown. Thus, a group of citizens who wished to stop a new development that would cause significant water pollution would be denied access to the courts on the ground that the harm to them did not differ from the harm borne by the general public.[1] A public authority, however, could sue for public nuisance.

---

1. Save the Bay Committee, Inc. v. Mayor, etc., of the City of Savannah, 227 Ga. 436, 181 S.E.2d 351 (1971).

The common law also limited relief from pollution in situations where the harm was caused by two or more independent sources. For example, if a number of firms were polluting the air, a harmed individual could sue any individual firm; however, until early in the twentieth century, the plaintiff was not able to sue all of the factories simultaneously. Thus, specific proof of damages and individual actions was often impossible. These difficulties in seeking relief in pollution cases, along with the forces creating additional pollution, have been largely responsible for the development of statutory regulations of environmental quality.

ENVIRONMENTAL PROTECTION AGENCY

The Environmental Protection Agency (EPA) is a primary administrative organization for dealing with federal regulations concerning the environment. It employs approximately ten thousand individuals who carry out the directives of the numerous and complex regulations of federal statutes affecting the environment, including those described above.

Environmental Impact Statements

One of the important responsibilities of the EPA is seeing that all federal actions, including proposed legislation, affecting the quality of the human environment have their impact on the environment analyzed. The environmental impact statement has become an important instrument used by private citizens, consumer interests, businesses, and federal agencies in shaping the final outcome of regulatory actions. Even if an agency believes that the impact statement is unnecessary, a statement supporting this conclusion must be filed.[2]

_____

2.   Arizona Public Service Co. v. Federal Power Comm., 483 F.2d 1275 (D.C.Cir. 1973).

NATURAL RESOURCES DEFENSE COUNCIL INC. v. MORTON

United States Court of Appeals, District of Columbia Circuit, 1972.
458 F.2d 827.

BACKGROUND AND FACTS   *The director of the Bureau of Land Management prepared an environmental impact statement in connection with the proposed sale of offshore oil lands by the Department of the Interior. Adjacent to the area in question was the greatest coastal marsh complex in the United States, encompassing almost eight million acres and providing food and spawning ground vital to fish and other wildlife. The environmental impact statement acknowledged that both short- and long-term effects on the environment could be expected from the sale of the lands, especially resulting from oil spillages. However, they omitted discussion of several alternatives listed in the statement, such as development of tar roads, coal liquification, nuclear energy and elimination of oil import quotas, on the ground that they were beyond the scope of the Department of the Interior.*

DECISION AND RATIONALE   *The environmental impact statement did not meet the requirements of the National Environmental Policy Act. To meet the requirements of the act, a statement must furnish sufficient information about the alternatives to a proposed policy to permit a reasoned choice among these alternatives to be made. The fact that the Department of the Interior does not have the authority on its own to pursue each alternative is irrelevant. "While the Department of the Interior does not have the authority to eliminate or reduce oil import quotas, such action is within the purview of both Congress and the*

President, to whom the impact statement goes. The impact statement is not only for the exposition of the thinking of the agency, but also for the guidance of these ultimate decision-makers, and must provide them with the environmental effects of both the proposal and the alternatives, for their consideration along with the various other elements of the public interest."

WHO PREPARES THE STATEMENT Environmental impact statements are prepared by the agency with the responsibility for carrying out the project. Anything that will potentially affect the environment—such as urban renewal projects, new construction, or the introduction of new technology—requires an environmental impact statement.[3] Among other requirements, environmental impact statements must (1) identify the environmental impact of the proposed action, (2) discuss alternatives to it, (3) identify differences between short-term and long-term impacts, (4) identify unavoidable impacts of the proposed action, and (5) indicate all irreversible uses of resources.

The Environmental Protection Agency is also responsible for the primary enforcement of statutory regulations concerning the environment, and it is likely that the number of regulations enforced by the agency will continue to increase in the future.

PRIVATE LITIGATION

Private parties will continue to recover damages or obtain injunctions for environmental harms under a combination of statutory and common law provisions. The Clean Air Act Amendments of 1972, the Water Pollution and Prevention Control Act of 1972, and the Noise Control Act of 1972, for example, authorize private lawsuits for violations of air, water, and noise pollution standards. Furthermore, some courts have held that organizations can have standing in representing members' interests even if there is no direct organizational interest in the dispute.[4] On the other hand, some federal statutes give the government exclusive rights to lawsuits for violations of environmental protection regulations. For example, the Environmental Protection Agency is given the exclusive right to bring suits involving the violation of the Federal Water Pollution Control Act.

AIR POLLUTION

Federal involvement with air pollution goes back to the 1950s, when Congress authorized funds for air pollution research. In 1963, the federal government passed the Clean Air Act, which focused on multistate air pollution and provided assistance to states. Various amendments, particularly in 1970 and 1977,[5] strengthened the government's authority to regulate the quality of air. In total, these acts provide the regulatory basis for promulgating standards to control pollution, primarily automobile and stationary sources.

Automobile Pollution

Regulations governing air pollution from automobiles and other mobile sources specify pollution standards and time schedules. For example, the 1970 Clean Air Act required a reduction of 90 percent in the amount of carbon monoxide and hydrocarbons emitted from automobiles by 1975.[6] Additional regulations that control air pollution indirectly focus on

---

3. Loveless v. Yantis, 82 Wash.2d 754, 513 P.2d 1023 (1973).
4. Undergraduate Student Ass'n v. Peltason, 359 F.Supp. 320 (N.D.Ill. 1973).

5. Clean Air Act Amendments of 1970, 42 USC Sec. 7521, Clean Air Act Amendments of 1977, 42 USC Secs. 7521-25, 7541-51.
6. Carbon monoxide, a colorless, odorless gas, can reduce mental performance and result in death if inhaled in sufficient quantities. Hydrocarbons are unburned fuel, one of the principal ingredients that generate smog.

improved gas mileage for new automobiles and gasoline additives such as lead. Similar regulations for aircraft are administered by the Federal Aviation Administration. The Environmental Protection Agency also sets national air quality standards for major pollutants throughout the United States.

The 1977 amendments to the Clean Air Act establish multilevel standards by preventing the deterioration of air quality in areas where the existing quality exceeds that required by federal law. These air quality standards cover carbon monoxide, nitrogen dioxide, hydrocarbons, sulfur dioxide, and other harmful materials. Standards are specified at two levels. The highest, which is designed to protect human health, has general guidelines for protecting vegetation, climate, visibility, and certain economic conditions. The Department of Health, Education, and Welfare has divided the country into atmospheric areas for the purpose of preparing these controls, and each area is required to institute a plan for meeting the standards.

ETHYL CORP. v. ENVIRONMENTAL PROTECTION AGENCY
United States Court of Appeals, District of Columbia Circuit, 1976.541 F.2d 1.

BACKGROUND AND FACTS *Ethyl Corporation, a leading producer of "antiknock" compounds for increasing gasoline octane ratings, filed for review of the Environmental Protection Agency order that required annual reductions in the lead content of gasoline. The Clean Air Act authorized the agency to regulate gasoline additives that are a danger to public health or welfare.*

DECISION AND RATIONALE *The Environmental Protection Agency did not abuse its discretion in requiring the Ethyl Corp. to reduce the lead compounds in its gasoline. The record in this case was massive—over 10,000 pages. The EPA relied on this evidence in its decision, and, although the evidence was not wholly unassailable, it did provide a reasonable basis on which to base a decision. The court defined the scope of the court's review as follows: "Our scope *** requires us to strike 'agency action, findings, and conclusions' [only if] we find [them] to be 'arbitrary, capricious, an abuse of discretion, or otherwise not in accordance with law.' This standard of review is a highly deferential one. It presumes agency action to be valid. Moreover, it forbids the court's substituting its judgment for that of the agency ***".*

WATER POLLUTION

Federal regulations governing the pollution of water can be traced back nearly a century to the River and Harbor Act of 1886 as amended in 1899.[7] These regulations required a permit for discharging or depositing refuse in navigable waterways. The courts have even determined that hot water can be considered refuse.[8] In 1965, Congress passed the Federal Water Pollution Control Act, which strengthened the Environmental Protection Agency's enforcement powers.

---

7. 33 USC Sec. 407.

8. 33 USC Sec. 1254(t).

Clean Water Regulation

Perhaps the most important regulations that govern the quality of water were instituted in 1972 by Congress. These regulations establish goals to (1) make waters safe for swimming, (2) protect fish and wildlife, and (3) eliminate the discharge of pollutants into the water. They set forth specific time schedules, which were extended by amendment in 1977. The 1972 Clean Water Act also specifies a number of regulations with time schedules for controlling industrial water pollution. Regulations for the most part specify that the best available technology be installed. Further, the act requires both municipal and industrial dischargers to apply for permits before they discharge wastes into the nation's navigable waters. Finally, the act establishes standing for citizens (or organizations) whose interests have been affected against parties who violate EPA or state standards and orders. Both injunctive relief and damages can be sought through claims under the act.

Other Regulations

In 1972, through the Marine Protection Research and Sanctuaries Act, Congress established a system of permits that regulate the discharge and introduction of materials into coastal waters and continuous marine areas. The Safe Drinking Water Act of 1974 established additional regulations governing drinking water standards. The rules, which are similar to those under the Clean Water Act, provide that states assume the primary responsibility for complying with national standards. The federal government assumes responsibility where states fail to institute or enforce drinking water standards. In most cases, explicit penalties are imposed on parties that pollute the water. The polluting party can also be required to clean up pollution or pay for the cost of doing so.

BACKGROUND AND FACTS *A number of oil companies, including Atlantic Richfield Company and Gulf Oil Co., were assessed monetary penalties that included paying for the cost of cleaning up oil discharges. Atlantic Richfield argued that the imposition of such penalties in an accidental oil spill when the reporting and cleaning requirements had been satisfied constituted a criminal action. Therefore, the defendants believed that they had the right to a jury trial. The court had to determine whether these penalties denied due process.*

UNITED STATES OF AMERICA v. ATLANTIC RICHFIELD CO.

Eastern District of Pennsylvania, 1977.
429 F.Supp. 830.

DECISION AND RATIONALE *Even though the defendant oil companies were not negligent in their handling of the oil spills, they were still subject to the statutory penalties. The statute does not make negligence an element in imposing the penalty. Negligence is merely one of several factors to be considered. The defendants claimed that "no regulatory purpose would be served by imposing a *** penalty, an argument we reject because it proceeds from a faulty premise. *** First, *** the principal goal of [the fines] is to deter spills. Second, the Congressional purpose here was to impose a standard of conduct higher than that related just to economic efficiency."*

NOISE POLLUTION

In 1972, Congress prescribed standards and regulations for the control of aircraft noise, including sonic booms, and for the control of emissions of railroad and motor vehicles involved in interstate commerce. The Noise Control Acts of 1970 and 1972 established the goal of creating an environment free from noise that is injurious to the health and welfare of the public. The courts have ruled that local control of noise is preempted when state regulations conflict with those established by federal statutes.[9]

Regulations promulgated by the noise control acts are administrated by the Federal Aviation Administration, the Environmental Protection Agency, and the Department of Transportation. The EPA, for example, is authorized to establish noise emission levels for equipment, motors, and engines. It also reviews production processes, verifies reports for compliance with the law, conducts audit tests, and makes inspections of manufacturer records.

TOXIC SUBSTANCES

The Toxic Substances Control Act was passed in 1976 to regulate chemicals and chemical compounds that are known to be toxic and to introduce procedures for investigating harmful effects from new chemical compounds. The regulations authorize the Environmental Protection Agency to insure that manufacturers, processors, and other organizations using chemicals determine their effect on human health and the environment before they are used by the public. The EPA also has the authority to regulate substances that potentially create a hazard or an unreasonable risk of injury.

PESTICIDE CONTROL

The use of chemical pesticides to kill insects and weeds has significantly increased agricultural productivity. On the other hand, there is a growing body of evidence that residuals from these chemicals have not been absorbed by the environment. In some cases, build-ups of residuals have killed animals, and some potential long-term effects detrimental to the public have also been identified. The original regulations governing pesticides were established by the Federal Insecticide, Fungicide and Rodenticide Act of 1947, as amended in 1972.[10] The Environmental Protection Agency has been given the authority to control the introduction of pesticides. Pesticides must be (1) registered before they can be sold, (2) certified and used only for approved applications, and (3) used in amounts that meet established limits when they are applied to crops that provide food for animals or people. The EPA also has the right to inspect manufacturing establishments. In some situations, the supply of pesticides is controlled to keep hazardous chemicals off the market. Those substances that have been identified as harmful are subject to suspension and cancellation of registration.

WASTE DISPOSAL

Waste disposal can occur on land, in the water, or in the air; thus regulations protecting these resources from pollution also apply to waste disposal. In 1970, Congress passed the Materials Policy Act, an act designed to reduce solid waste disposal by encouraging the recycling of waste and the reuse of materials by society. The Act also provides for pilot waste disposal projects utilizing modern technology. For example, the development and use of technology that converts garbage into useful products has been greatly encouraged by the solid waste programs

9. Burbank v. Lockheed Air Terminal Inc., 411 U.S. 624, 93 S.Ct. 1854 (1973).

10. Federal Environmental Pesticide Control Act of 1972.

of the Environmental Protection Agency. The EPA also carries out the provisions of the Resource Conservation and Recovery Act of 1976, which governs EPA studies and recommendations of solid waste disposal ranging from glass and plastic waste to airport landfill. The EPA is primarily concerned with issuing federal facility permits and reviewing the state permit system for the use of certain equipment. It conducts on-site inspections of hazardous waste generators and cites violators. The Solid Waste Disposal Act gives each state the power to enact its own hazardous waste standards.

Federal statutes also attempt to generate state and local community initiative for solving solid waste disposal problems by providing monies and expert guidance for state and local studies. A number of states have sought to reduce the problem of solid waste disposal by requiring recycling or reuse of various products.

AMERICAN CAN CO. v. OREGON LIQUOR CONTROL COMM.

Supreme Court of Oregon, 1974.
15 Or.App. 618, 517 P.2d 691.

BACKGROUND AND FACTS *The State of Oregon adopted a law prohibiting the use of nonreturnable containers for beer and carbonated beverages. It also prohibited the sale of metal beverage containers that used detachable pull-top opening devices. The American Can Company instituted an action against the Oregon Liquor Control Commission as well as other administrative bodies of the State of Oregon.*

DECISION AND RATIONALE *Oregon's bottle bill was a legitimate exercise of that state's police power. Although the beverage industry had to bear increased costs as a result of the bottle bill, this was not a basis on which a court could justify overturning a statute. The question, rather, was whether the state of Oregon had a legitimate governmental purpose in passing the bottle bill. The purpose of the bill was to reduce litter and solid waste in Oregon and reduce injuries to people from discarded pull tops. In the court's opinion: "The Oregon legislature was persuaded that the economic benefit to the beverage industry [of nonreturnable containers] brought with it deleterious consequences to the environment and additional cost to the public. The aggravation of the problems of litter in public places and solid waste disposal and the attendant economic and esthetic burden to the public outweighed the narrower economic benefit to the industry. Thus the legislature enacted the bottle bill over the articulate opposition of the industries represented by plaintiffs. As with every change of circumstances in the market place, there are gainers and there are losers."*

JUDICIAL LIMITS

In the first half of the 1970s, federal and state legislators enacted many statutes that regulate environmental quality. Judicial interpretations of these statutes have generally given the administrative agencies that carry out their directives broad discretionary powers. Beginning in the mid 1970s, however, the courts began to place stricter limits on administrative discretion. Recent court decisions that impose a cost-benefit standard on administrative decisions are likely to limit discretion in the environmental area as well.

In American Petroleum v. Occupational Safety and Health Administration, an OSHA regulation limiting benzine exposure in the workplace was invalidated by the Fifth Circuit Court of Appeals.[11] In 1977, OSHA promulgated

---

11.   581 F.2d 493 (5th Cir. 1978).

regulations reducing permissible exposure by 90 percent from the 1971 standard. This action was based primarily on the results of three studies that showed an increased risk of leukemia in workers who had been exposed to benzine at levels in excess of one hundred times the 1977 permissible levels. The court interpreted the "reasonably necessary" language of the Occupational Safety and Health Act to require an estimate of the expected benefits of the regulation "in order to determine whether the benefits bear a reasonable relationship to the standard's demonstrably high costs."

QUESTIONS AND CASE PROBLEMS

1.   In April 1973, virtually all of the nation's railroads requested ICC authority for a rate increase of 5 percent. After an environmental study was completed, the ICC determined that the rate increase would not have a significant environmental impact. Thus, instead of publishing a complete environmental impact statement, the ICC published only a short statement giving its conclusions that no significant adverse environmental impact would result from the rate increase and giving the reasons for its determination. A number of interested parties brought suit to enjoin the rate increase on the ground that it would lead to higher costs for recycling materials and therefore have a significant adverse impact on the environment, since recycled materials would be priced out of the market. The ICC's published decision not to prepare a complete environmental impact statement documented the alleged effects of the rate increases on recyclable materials. Did the ICC comply with the Environmental Policy Act when it published an abbreviated statement? [Asphalt Roofing Mfg. Ass'n v. ICC, 567 F.2d 994 (D.C. Cir. 1977)]

2.   Citizens against Toxic Sprays, Inc. was an organization established to challenge the use of toxic sprays in places where they could be harmful to humans, animals, or vegetation. The group sought to enjoin the

United States Forest Service from using the herbicide TCDD because of its hazardous effect on people who breathed it. TCDD was used only in national forests, not in any residential areas. Citizens against Toxic Sprays alleged that some of its members were affected by the use of TCDD in two of the national forests because they lived near them, worked in them, or used them for recreational activities. Does Citizens against Toxic Sprays have *standing* to sue the United States Forest Service? [Citizens Against Toxic Sprays, Inc. v. Bergland, 428 F.Supp. 908 (D.C.Or. 1977)]

3.   Virginia Dalsis, the proprietor of a small store in the city of Olean, New York, brought a suit to enjoin the construction of a mall because of its projected size. Dalsis alleged that the large size of the shopping center would have an adverse environmental effect on the downtown area, causing economic blight and deterioration to the section in which her business was located. Dalsis, however, did not bring the suit until three months after construction of the shopping mall had begun even though she was aware of the mall's potential size almost a year before construction started. Should Dalsis be allowed to enjoin the construction of the shopping mall? [Dalsis v. Hills, 424 F.Supp. 784 (W.D.N.Y. 1976)]

4.   The Government Services Administration (GSA) entered into an agreement with a private individual under which the individual was to construct a building to GSA's specifications and lease it to the GSA. Under the contemplated lease provision, GSA would have use of the entire building for a five-year (renew-

able) period. As many as 2,300 government employees would be assigned to the building, and most would commute by automobile. Cost of the lease was approximately $11 million. GSA proceeded with its plans for the building without preparing any environmental impact statement. Was a statement necessary? [S.W. Neighborhood Assembly v. Eckard, 445 F.Supp. 1195 (D.C.D.C. 1978)]

50

Government Regulation
Antitrust

Competition is the socially desired state of market organization in the
United States today. Antitrust laws have been enacted keep markets
competitive. The next two chapters will look at the important developments in the field of antitrust law and how they affect business today.
Chapter 50 will discuss those statutes that are enforced by the Department
of Justice. Chapter 51 will investigate the enforcement of other statutes,
such as the Robinson-Patman Act.

COMMON LAW ACTIONS

Today's antitrust laws are direct descendants of common law actions intended to limit restraints of trade. That is not to say, however, that a neat
classification of trade restraints can be found in the common law.

The first recorded case concerning trade restraints in the common
law involved a man named John Dyer and has become known as Dyer's
Case.[1] Dyer had agreed not to "use his art of a dyer's craft within the town
* * * for half a year." The court denied the plaintiff the ability to collect on
a bond for Dyer's breach of his agreement. The effect of the agreement
was to restrain trade, according to the common law. At that time, restraint
of trade was defined as the failure to promote "fair" commercial activity.

---

1.   Y.B. Pasch. 2 Hen. 5 f. 5, PL. 26 (1414).

The same issue arose on numerous occasions. A celebrated case occurred in 1711 when a man named Mitchell leased a baking shop for five years, subject to the condition that the lessor, Reynolds, who was also a baker, would not practice the baking art in the immediate area for the term of the lease. Thus, Mitchell was actually buying the use of a baking shop *and* the trade that went with it. The court rejected Mitchell's argument and ruled in favor of Reynolds.[2] This case is so celebrated because the court's opinion systematically classified trade restraints into those that were good and those that were bad. Lord Parker, who rendered the opinion, distinguished between general and particular restraints, the former being invalid and the latter valid. *General restraints* were used for the purpose of limiting competition. On the other hand, certain *particular restraints* that were supported by "good consideration" were acceptable. These *partial,* or *ancillary, restraints*, as they became known, were generally upheld if limited in time and place. Thus Mitchell v. Reynolds provided the basis for the modern formulation of the so-called "rule of reason" in which the court determines whether the restraint in question is reasonable. Since Mitchell v. Reynolds, the rule of reason has played an important role in antitrust litigation in this country. In order to find out whether a partial restraint is reasonable (i.e. legal), the courts inquire into its purpose and its probable effect.

Price Fixing Takes Over

The phrase *laissez-faire* refers to an economic philosophy that government should leave the economy strictly alone. In England in the nineteenth century, as *laissez-faire* ideas became dominant, the courts expanded the concept of the rule of reason. They began to suggest, for example, that what was reasonable could best be judged by those involved in a contract, not by outsiders. Ultimately, *laissez-faire* theory gained such ascendancy that courts began to accept agreements among traders to

divide territories or to sell only at agreed-upon prices. By the second half of the nineteenth century, such transactions were generally held to be lawful where no element of coercion was involved.[3]

Common Law in the United States

Common law in the United States was not as receptive to restraints in trade as English law. In U.S. v. Addyston Pipe & Steel Co.,[4] Circuit Judge William Howard Taft concluded that apart from "reasonable" ancillary (partial) restraints, the common law condemned all other restraints of trade. Thus, contrary to the English rule, American courts did not apply a reasonableness test to certain forms of anticompetitive activity like price fixing, territorial divisions, or concerted refusals to deal. This view of the common law was adopted by the Supreme Court in its first interpretations of the Sherman Act, the mainstay of American antitrust law.

THE BEGINNING OF ANTITRUST LAW IN AMERICA

With the growth of national markets after the Civil War, a number of small companies were combined to form large companies, and they started to engage in practices that were seen as monopolistic. Reported abusive practices by corporate giants in the second half of the nineteenth century finally led to legislation restricting the power of these so-called trusts. The first piece of legislation was the Interstate Commerce Act of 1887, and in 1890, the Sherman Act was passed. These acts were designed to prevent trusts from acting against the public interest.

The Formation of Trusts

Interestingly, *trusts* were a legal innovation that John D. Rockefeller's Standard Oil Company

---

2. 1 P. Wms. 181, 24 Eng. Rep 347 (1711).

3. See, for example, Mogul Steamship Co. v. McGregor Gow & Co. [1892] A.C. 25 (1891).
4. 85 F. 271 (6th Cir. 1898) modified and affirmed 175 U.S. 211, 20 S.Ct. 10 (1899).

created. Standard's attorneys established an arrangement whereby owners of stock in several companies could transfer their stock to a group of trustees. In return, the owners received consideration in the form of certificates entitling them to a specified share in the pooled earnings of the jointly managed companies. In the late 1800s, the term *trust* was randomly applied to all forms of suspicious business combinations. There were trusts in oil, sugar, cotton, linseed oil, whiskey, and other industries, and the trusts seemed to absorb new enterprises at an expanding rate. Furthermore, it was felt that the process of consolidation was achieved by *predatory* tactics. Predatory business tactics advance the competitive position of one business by threatening to drive another business out of the market. In fact, the activities of the Standard Oil Company are given as the prime example of such tactics. Because of its size, Standard Oil was able to sell kerosene at a price below its cost. Standard's lower prices forced many competitors to sell or close down. As total industry output declined, Standard Oil raised the price and presumably obtained monopoly power.[5]

The 1890 Sherman Act was the response, and its purpose was to promote competition within the U.S. economy.[6] The author of the legislation, Senator Sherman, told Congress that the Sherman Act "does not announce a new principle of law, but applies old and well-recognized principles of the common law."[7] However, the common law was never very clear, and, indeed, it was certainly not very familiar to the legislators of the Fifty-first Congress of the United States. Actually, it appears that the Sherman Act was an attempt by Congress to get the federal courts to create a common body of federal antitrust law.

---

5. Not everyone agrees with this rendition of the facts. See, for example, John S. McGee, "Predatory Price Cutting: The Standard Oil (New Jersey) Case," *Journal of Law and Economics* 1 (1958). McGee finds that the facts are consistent with a competitive market with increased supply.

6. 26 Stat 209 (1890) as amended 15 USC Secs. 1-7.

7. 21 Congressional Record 2456 (1890).

The Main Provisions of the Sherman Antitrust Act

Sections I and II contain the main provisions of the Sherman Act. They are:

§ I: Every contract, combination in the form of trust or otherwise, or conspiracy, in restraint of trade or commerce among the several States, or with foreign nations, is hereby declared to be illegal [and is a misdemeanor punishable by fine and/or imprisonment]. * * *

§ II: Every person who shall monopolize, or attempt to monopolize, or combine or conspire with any other person or persons, to monopolize any part of the trade or commerce among the several States, or with foreign nations, shall be deemed guilty of a misdemeanor [and is similarly punishable]. * * *

Sections I and II Compared

The two main sections of the Sherman Act are quite different. Section I requires two or more persons, since a person cannot combine or conspire alone. Thus, the essence of the illegal activity is *the act of joining together*. Section II applies to both an individual person and several people because it states that "every person who * * *." Thus, unilateral conduct can result in a violation of Section II. The cases brought to court under Section I of the Sherman Act differ from those brought under Section II. Section I cases are often concerned with finding an agreement (written or oral) that leads to a restraint of trade. Section II cases deal with the structure of a monopoly that exists in the marketplace. Thus, Section I focuses on agreements that are restrictive—that is, agreements that have a wrongful purpose. Section II looks at the so-called misuse of monopoly power in the marketplace. However, both sections seek to curtail market industrial practices that result in undesired monopoly pricing and output behavior. Any case brought under Section II, however, must be one in which the "threshold" or "necessary" amount of monopoly power already exists.

Section II: Monopolies and Monopolization

The government rarely brings actions under Section II any more because of the complex nature of such actions. As seen in the following case, the government must prove the existence (or potential existence) of monopoly power in the relevant markets.

UNITED STATES v E.I. DUPONT DeNEMOURS AND COMPANY

Supreme Court of the United States, 1956. 351 U.S. 377, 76 S.Ct. 994.

BACKGROUND AND FACTS   *DuPont produced almost 75 percent of the cellophane sold in the United States. Cellophane competed with other flexible packaging materials such as aluminum foil, waxed paper, saran wrap, and polyethylene. With these goods included in the product market, duPont's market share was less than 20 percent. The United States brought a suit under Section 2 of the Sherman Act charging that duPont had illegally exercised monopoly power in the cellophane market.*

DECISION AND RATIONALE   *DuPont did not violate Section 2 because it did not possess the requisite monopoly power to do so. The monopolization prohibition of Section 2 is violated when a company that has monopoly power exercises that power unfairly to injure competitors. In measuring monopoly power, courts must look at both the relevant geographic market and the relevant product market. Here, the geographic market was the entire United States, but the product market was in dispute. Clearly, if the product market included all flexible packaging materials, duPont's 20 percent market share was insufficient to constitute monopoly power. The court explained its position thusly: "Determination of the competitive market for commodities depends on how different from one another are the offered commodities in character or use, how far buyers will go to substitute one commodity for another. *** [D]espite cellophane's advantages it has to meet competition from other materials in every one of its uses. *** Moreover a very considerable degree of functional interchangeability exists between these products."*

The Proscriptive Nature of the Sherman Act

The Sherman Act does not tell businesses how they should act. It tells them how they should *not* act. In this sense, the act is *proscriptive* rather than *prescriptive*. It is the basis for *policing* rather than *regulating* business conduct.

Other Aspects of the Sherman Act

JURISDICTION   The Sherman Act applies only to restraints that have a significant impact on commerce. In principle, only interstate commerce is affected because Congress can regulate only interstate commerce. If, however, a practice has a significant anticompetitive effect on commerce, the courts have construed the meaning of *interstate* more and more broadly. In principle, state regulation of anticompetitive practices covers purely local restraints on competition.

The Sherman Act extends to U.S. nationals abroad who are engaged in activities that will affect U.S. foreign commerce. It was applied, for example, in Continental Ore Co. v. Union Carbide and Carbon Corp.[8] In that case, the defendant, Union Carbide, tried to monopolize the Canadian market in Canada by excluding competitors. It did this by having its Canadian subsidiary, Electro-Met, initiate political action that resulted in the Canadian Metals Controller granting it an exclusive market in vanadium products. This effectively prohibited the U.S. plaintiff, Continental Ore Company, from entering Canadian markets.

STANDING The Department of Justice is not the only entity that can file suit under the Sherman Act. Some private parties can also sue for damages or other remedies. The courts have determined that the test of ability to sue depends on the directness of the injury suffered by the purported plaintiff. Thus, a person wishing to sue under the Sherman Act must prove that (1) the antitrust violation either directly caused or was at least a substantial factor in causing the injury that was suffered, and (2) the unlawful actions of the purported defendant affected business activities of the plaintiff that were protected by the antitrust laws.

One of the unique features of the Sherman Antitrust Act is that it allows any person injured as a result of violations of the Act to bring a suit for treble damages against the defendants in addition to reasonable attorneys' fees. In the 1960s, General Electric Company, along with other major electrical equipment manufacturers, paid over $200 million in treble damage claims. Certain of the corporate officers were fined, and some of them even went to jail.

8. 370 U.S. 690, 82 S.Ct. 1404 (1962).

REMEDIES AND SANCTIONS Any person found guilty of violating either Section I or Section II of the Sherman Act is subject to criminal prosecution for a misdemeanor. Currently, upon conviction, a person can be fined up to $100,000 or imprisoned for three years, or both. A corporation can be fined $1 million. The Department of Justice can simultaneously institute civil proceedings to restrain the conduct that is in violation of the act.

The various remedies that the Justice Department has asked the court to impose include divestiture, dissolution, and divorcement, or making a company give up one of its operating functions. A group of meat packers, for example, can be forced to divorce themselves from controlling or owning butcher shops.

The Courts' Initial Reaction to the Sherman Act

Initially, the Sherman Act was stripped of any effectiveness because the courts interpreted it so narrowly. For example, five years after passage of the act, the Supreme Court refused to apply the Sherman Act to a sugar trust.[9] The Court held that the law did not extend to restraints affecting *just* the manufacture of commodities. According to the Court, "commerce secedes to manufacturer, and is not a part of it." In other words, the manufacturer of a commodity does not control commerce and therefore cannot violate the Sherman Act.

Then the Court swung the other way. In essence, it significantly modified antitrust legislation by allowing no opportunity to adjust its decisions to practical necessities. In a series of opinions beginning with U.S. v. Trans-Missouri Freight Assn., the Court declared illegal certain price-fixing agreements and territorial divisions because Section I of the Sherman Act condemned *every* restraint of trade.[10] This absolute position clearly could not

9. United States v. E. C. Knight Co., 156 U.S. 1, 15 S.Ct. 249 (1895).

10. 166 U.S. 290, 17 S.Ct. 540 (1897).

hold for long. The Court then retreated once again. It first condemned direct restraints.[11] It then came to the conclusion that restraints that were lawful at common law might not be prohibited by the Sherman Act.[12]

One of the great political victories, at least from President Theodore Roosevelt's and President William Howard Taft's points of view, was the ruling of the Supreme Court that *holding companies* were not exempt from the Sherman Act. The case in point was Northern Securities Co. v. United States.[13] The court deemed the merger of two competing railroads an illegal restraint of trade. Two famous financiers, James J. Hill and J. P. Morgan, were successfully challenged by the judicial system.

In Standard Oil Company v. United States,[14] the Supreme Court ruled that only those restraints whose character was *unreasonably* anticompetitive were outlawed by the Sherman Act. Critics of that decision contended that conservative federal judges would reduce the act to insignificance again. Other critics contended that if the court was to interpret the act as applying only to unreasonable restraints, then businesses should be told in advance which restraints were lawful.

THE DEVELOPMENT OF *PER SE* VIOLATIONS

According to the rule of reason, only unreasonable restraints were illegal at common law.

11. Hopkins v. United States, 171 U.S. 578, 19 S.Ct. 40 (1898).
12. United States v. Joint Traffic Ass'n, 171 U.S. 505, 19 S.Ct. 25 (1898).
13. 193 U.S. 197, 24 S.Ct. 436 (1904).
14. 221 U.S. 1, 31 S.Ct. 502 (1911).

Clearly, the rule was applied in the Standard Oil case. However, there really is no rule of reason explicitly stated in Section I of the Sherman Act. It does not matter, according to Section I, whether the guilty party was successful in fixing prices, dividing markets or restraining trade in any other way. Section I states very clearly that any *attempt* to restrain trade is illegal. Thus, certain kinds of restrictive contracts will be deemed inherently anticompetitive—that is, in restraint of trade *as a matter of law*. In such *per se violations* of Section I, there is no need to examine any other facts. Recall that in United States v. Trans-Missouri Freight Ass'n., the Court held that Section I condemned *every* restraint of trade. In 1897, the Court recognized no exceptions. The defendants in the case contended that they were exempt from the Sherman Act because they were regulated by the Interstate Commerce Act. Thus, the fixing of rates was legal because it was reasonable and therefore valid under common law. To the Court, the railroads were engaging in a per se violation of Section I of the Sherman Act.

The following case involved six leading producers of cast iron pipe who agreed among themselves to divide the southern and western markets into what turned out to be regional monopolies. The six companies instituted a complex system of fixed prices for each territory. According to the evidence, the prices fixed by these companies were sufficiently low to discourage entry by eastern manufacturers. The defense contended (1) that the arrangement was not a monopoly but the avoidance of ruinous price competition and (2) that the prices at which pipes were sold in each region were reasonable.

UNITED STATES v. ADDYSTON PIPE & STEEL CO.
Sixth Circuit, 1898.
29 C.C.A. 141, 85 F. 271.

BACKGROUND AND FACTS *Six producers of pipe and steel formed an association to organize sales in their industry. Their reason was to alleviate the ruinous price competition that existed in the market and that had driven numerous companies out of business. The association divided up its selling market into regional territories and instituted a complex price scheme. The prices that members of the association* *charged were in all respects reasonable and stability was restored to the steel industry. The United States, however, brought suit to break up the association accusing its members of price fixing in violation of Section 1 of the Sherman Act.*

DECISION AND RATIONALE *The price fixing engaged in by the members of the pipe and steel association constituted a per se violation of Section 1 of the Sherman Act. The Sherman Act makes illegal every unreasonable restraint of trade. Furthermore, any tampering with prices by a group of competitors is considered per se unreasonable and in violation of the act. "[W]e can have no doubt that the association of the defendants, however reasonable the prices they fixed, however great the competition they had to encounter, and however great the necessity for curbing themselves by joint agreement from committing financial suicide by ill-advised competition, was void *** because in restraint of trade, and tending to a monopoly."*

The Effect of the Depression on *Per Se* Standards

During the Great Depression of the 1930s, a number of decisions tempered the Court's effort to establish per se violations. Prices fell dramatically during the depression, and a number of companies attempted to fix prices to prevent ruin. For example, when the price of bituminous coal fell 25 percent from 1929 to 1933, over 130 coal companies in the Appalachian region formed a new company that served as the exclusive selling agent for member firms. The agent was supposed to get the best price obtainable. If it could not sell all the output of all of the firms at that price, it allocated output to each firm in an orderly fashion. Thus, it was acting as a sales cartel, or a central sales agency, and clearly was in violation of the Sherman Act as interpreted prior to the depression. Nonetheless, the Supreme Court, in Appalachian Coals, Inc. v. United States, decided that the Sherman Act was to prevent "undue" restraints on interstate commerce.[15] With this decision, the Court returned to a rule of reason, even though it was using price-fixing language. Basically, the Court

held that the issue of legality ultimately rested on the effect of the agreement on competition.

But the Court's return to the rule of reason did not survive the depression. In United States v. Socony Vacuum Oil Co. [310 U.S. 150, 60 S. Ct. 811 (1940)], the Supreme Court returned to the rigid *per se* standard, condemning all price-fixing arrangements.

Additional *Per Se* Violations

In addition to the price-fixing agreements that violate Section I of the Sherman Act, two other types of violations are per se illegal.

HORIZONTAL MARKET DIVISIONS Dividing a territory for the sale of a specific product into two or more divisions allocated specifically to individual companies is also a per se violation of the Sherman Act. If two cement companies normally sell cement throughout the entire state of California, they cannot enter into an agreement in which one of them sells only in southern California and the other sells only in northern California. As a matter of law, this is illegal, even if it might seem "reasonable."

---

15.   288 U.S. 344, 53 S.Ct. 471 (1933).

JOINT REFUSALS TO DEAL, OR GROUP BOYCOTTS If a group of manufacturers or wholesalers of goods refuses to sell to a potential buyer or group of buyers, this is usually deemed a group boycott and is a per se violation of the antitrust laws. In a leading case, the Fashion Originators Guild attempted to eliminate illegal "style piracy" in their industry by refusing to deal with retailers who sold pirated fashions.

BACKGROUND AND FACTS *Members of a women's garment manufacturing guild attempted to stop the practice of "style piracy" by jointly refusing to sell to retailers who sold garments copied from a guild member's designs. (Style piracy is the practice by manufacturers of copying designs and selling these copies at much lower prices.) The guild also imposed restraints on advertising, regulation of sales days, and limits on allowable discounts to its members. The Federal Trade Commission brought suit alleging that the guild's concerted activities constituted a violation of Section 1 of the Sherman Act.*

DECISION AND RATIONALE *The guild's agreement constituted a concerted action in violation of the Sherman Act as an unreasonable restraint of trade. It is irrelevant that the guild's main purpose was eliminating the evils of style piracy, even though style piracy is illegal. Any time two or more persons join together and agree not to deal with a third person, their conduct will be questioned under the Sherman Act. "The purpose and object of this combination, its potential power, its tendency to monopoly, the coercion it could and did practice upon a rival method of competition, all brought it within the policy of the prohibition declared by the Sherman and Clayton Acts."*

FASHION ORIGINATOR'S GUILD OF AMERICA, INC. v. FEDERAL TRADE COMMISSION.

Supreme Court of the United States, 1951. 312 U.S. 457, 61 S.Ct. 703.

THE CLAYTON ACT

In 1914, Congress attempted to strengthen federal antitrust laws by adopting the Clayton Act, which was aimed at specific monopolistic practices. The important sections of the Clayton Act are sections 2, 3, 7, 8.

Section 2: [It is illegal to] discriminate in price between different purchasers [except in cases where the differences are due to differences in selling or transportation costs].
Section 3: [Producers cannot sell] on the condition, agreement or understanding that the * * * purchaser thereof shall not use or deal in the goods * * * of a competitor or competitors of the seller.
Section 7: [Corporations cannot hold stock in another company] where the effect * * * may be to substantially lessen competition.

Section 8: * * * no person at the same time shall be a director in any two or more corporations, any one of which has capital, surplus, and undivided profits aggregating more than $1 million, engaged in whole or in part in commerce, other than banks, banking associations, trust companies, and common carriers.

The Clayton Act outlaws price discrimination, exclusive dealing and tying contracts, the purchase of enough stock in a competing corporation to reduce competition, and interlocking directorates (discussed in Chapter 51).

Enforcement of the Clayton Act

Enforcement of the Clayton Act is carried out simultaneously by the Department of Justice and the Federal Trade Commission. Those portions of the Clayton Act that strengthen Sections 1 and 8 of the Sherman Act are enforced primarily by the Justice Department, as are exclusive dealings, tying contracts, and sections 7 and 8 of the Clayton Act. There is, however, some overlap between the two. For example, Section 7 of the Clayton Act, which involves mergers, is also enforced by the FTC. Other portions, such as Section 2 of the Clayton Act, fall almost exclusively under the jurisdiction of the FTC.

AGREEMENTS WHICH ARE NOT *PER SE* ILLEGAL

Price fixing and group boycotts are *per se* unreasonable under Section 1 of the Sherman Act, but other agreements that may be in restraint of trade might not be *per se* unreasonable. Suppose a group of manufacturers divides up the market by designating the areas in which each manufacturer may sell. This constitutes a horizontal territorial market allocation (horizontal because the agreement is among businesses at the same level of production, the manufacturing level), and it is per se unreasonable. On the other hand, the Supreme Court has recently held that vertical restraints that do not involve price fixing are not *per se* unreasonable under the Sherman Act. Such restrictions may still be unreasonable, but their reasonableness must be judged by looking at all the facts and circumstances of each individual case.

CONTINENTAL T.V., INC. v. GTE SYLVANIA, INC.

Supreme Court of the United States, 1977. 433 U.S. 36, 97 S.Ct. 2549.

BACKGROUND AND FACTS *GTE Sylvania, Inc., a manufacturer of television sets, adopted a franchise plan limiting the number of franchises granted in any given geographic area and requiring each franchise to sell Sylvania products only from the location or locations at which they were franchised. No price restraints were imposed on the franchisees. Continental T.V., Inc., was a retailer under Sylvania's franchise plan. Shortly after Sylvania proposed a new franchise that would compete with Continental, Continental brought an antitrust suit against Sylvania charging that its vertically restrictive franchise system violated Section 1 of the Sherman Act.*

DECISION AND RATIONALE *Sylvania's vertical, nonprice, restrictive system did not constitute a per se violation of Section 1 of the Sherman Act. The fact that Sylvania restricted franchise retailers in their locations, even though title in the televisions had passed to the retailers, was a violation of the Sherman Act only if the facts and circumstances indicated that the restrictions were unreasonable. Two facts militated against a per se rule here. The restrictions were between a manufacturer and retailer instead of between two entities on the same level (for example, two retailers or two manufacturers), and no price restrictions were involved. If price restrictions had been involved, Sylvania would have been guilty of a per se violation of the Sherman Act. Clearly, vertical restrictions can stimulate competition because they provide incentives to persons who wish to distribute competitive brands of a product in the market. Among these is the incentive for a new manufacturer to use restrictive systems "in order to induce competent and aggressive retailers to make the kind of investment of capital and labor that is often required in the distribution of products unknown to the consumer."*

EXEMPTIONS FROM ANTITRUST LAWS

In a sense, Congress's attention to the antitrust laws since the Clayton Act has focused primarily on writing *exceptions* to the coverage of the Sherman Act. The Clayton Act itself sought unsuccessfully to exempt unions from the antitrust law. The National Labor Relations Act of 1935 further protected them from antitrust legislation. Today, therefore, unions can lawfully engage in actions that are normally prohibited as long as they act in their self-interest and do not conspire or combine with nonlabor groups to accomplish their goals.

Labor and Agriculture

Labor and agricultural organizations are exempted from the Sherman Antitrust Act by Section 6 of the Clayton Act. Agriculture's exemption from antitrust legislation is further extended by the Capper-Volstead Act (1922), the Cooperative Marketing Act (1926), and certain provisions of the Robinson-Patman Act. Labor's exemption was strengthened by the Norris-La Guardia Act of 1932.

Sports

Most commercial activities are subject to the antitrust laws, but there are exceptions. For example, baseball remains untouched by the antitrust laws; it was not thought to be commerce in the Sherman Act's original contemplation and is thus not commerce today. Baseball's exemption is anomalous, especially since no other professional sport receives such treatment.

Professionals

A current controversial topic in antitrust law is the regulation of professionals, such as lawyers and doctors. Professional organizations are no longer exempt from antitrust enforcement. They cannot establish minimum fee schedules or prohibit competitive bidding in any way. The traditional incantations about the maintenance of high quality no longer shield professionals from the antitrust laws.

Insurance

The McCarran-Ferguson Act exempts from the antitrust laws all activities that are in the "business of insurance." The primary element of the insurance business is the spreading and underwriting of policyholder risk. Thus, any such activity can be exempt from the antitrust laws by the McCarran-Ferguson Act if it is regulated by state law.

Government Action

Government actions that hinder competition are exempt from antitrust laws. In Parker v. Brown, the Supreme Court upheld the activities of a California agency that fixed raisin production and prices, even though this was done at the request of and with the concurrence of a majority of growers.[16] The state regulation was not a burden on interstate commerce since it coincided with federal agricultural policy. Moreover, the Sherman Act's prohibition of contracts in restraint of trade by "any person" applied to private businesses, not government agencies.

---

16.   317 U.S. 341, 63 S.Ct. 307 (1943).

QUESTIONS AND CASE PROBLEMS

1.   Meister Brau, Inc., was engaged in the business of brewing beers, malts, and ales. It acquired the Berger

Meister Beer Company through a purchase of the latter's common stock. Berger Meister sold the beer it brewed through distributors who operated as individual businesses separate from Berger Meister. Soon after Meister Brau acquired Berger Meister, it terminated some of Berger Meister's distributors. The distributors handled the products of a number of other breweries, but they complained that the reduced sales volume that would result from their being terminated by Meister Brau would drive them out of business. The distributors thus brought suit against Meister Brau, alleging that its agreement with its new subsidiary, Berger Meister, to terminate the distributors constituted a conspiracy in restraint of trade in violation of Section I of the Sherman Act. The distributors alleged that the terminations would reduce competition in a market that was already tending toward concentration. Has Meister Brau violated Section I of the Sherman Act? [Ricchetti v. Meister Brau, Inc., 431 F.2d 1211 (9th Cir. 1970)]

2. Since 1946, Bay Distributors, Inc., a Florida corporation located in the Tampa Bay area, had been engaged in the wholesale distribution and sale of various brands of wines and distilled spirits in approximately a thirteen-county area of the west coast of Florida. The wines that Bay sold included a line produced by United Vintners, Inc., most of which was marketed under the trade name "Italian Swiss Colony." Bay was the exclusive distributor in the Florida west coast area of United Vintners' wines. Between March 1965 and May 1970, Cal Distributing Company acted as Bay's subdistributor in the Sarasota area, which included two of the thirteen counties mentioned above. Cal sold no wine outside the Sarasota area. Although customers in the Sarasota area could have purchased United Vintners' products from either Cal or Bay, neither actually solicited customers from the other. About May 5, 1970, Bay notified Cal that it would no longer sell Cal United Vintners' wines. It would, however, continue to sell Cal all other wines for which Bay was the exclusive distributor. After Bay refused to sell United Vintners' products to Cal as a subdistributor, Bay started selling them directly to the retail businesses to which Cal had been selling them. Using these facts, along with the other facts given below, answer the following questions. [Cal Distributing Co. v. Bay Distributors, Inc., 337 F.Supp. 1154 (M.D.Fla. 1971)]

a. Which, if any, of the antitrust statutes discussed in this chapter might Bay have violated when it terminated Cal as its subdistributor? Be specific.

b. In order to establish a claim for relief from monopolization, Bay must be shown to possess *monopoly power* in the relevant market. In determining the relevant market, the court must determine the relevant *geographic* market and the relevant *product* market. Both before and after Bay's termination of Cal, at least six other companies distributed wine at wholesale in the Sarasota area from warehouses located in Tampa. Each of these competitors supplied wine along the entire west coast of Florida, including the Sarasota area, from offices and warehouses located in Tampa. The cost of transporting wine to retailers throughout the Florida west coast area is not such as to prevent wholesale distributors from supplying this area from Tampa. The "relevant geographic market" is the area that Bay would have to monopolize if it were to be deemed in violation of the antitrust laws. Is the relevant geographic market in this case the city of Sarasota, the west coast of Florida, the entire state of Florida, or some other area?

c. In determining whether Bay's act of discontinuing Cal shows monopoly power, the "relevant product market" must be determined. This involves analyzing the commodities reasonably interchangeable by consumers for the same purposes. For example, in one case, the Supreme Court held that even though the DuPont Company produced approximately 75 percent of the cellophane sold nationwide, the competition between cellophane and other flexible packaging materials was sufficient to prevent cellophane from constituting a separate relevant product market in itself. Using the DuPont case as an analogy, what is the relevant product market in this case—all United Vintners wines, all wines, all alcoholic beverages, or something else?

d. Gallo Wines provides the primary competition to United Vintners. However, both Gallo and United Vintners face direct competition from all other wines. This competition prevents Bay from raising its prices without losing business. The competition provided by Gallo was described by Calvin LaHurd, the president of Cal Distributing Company, as "very, very vigorous." In fact, sales of Gallo Wines at wholesale have exceeded Bay's sales of United Vintners continuously for each month since December 1968. In addition, since December 1968, the monthly sales of United Vintners have never exceeded 22 percent of the total volume of wine sold to retailers in the relevant geographic area. By way of comparison, the monthly sales of Gallo Wines by Tampa Wholesale Liquor Company, one of the area distributors, have averaged over 22 percent of monthly wholesale wine sales in the relevant geographic area during the same period. In order to be deemed in violation of the antitrust laws, Bay Distributors must be shown to possess the power to control prices or exclude competition in the relevant market. In order to establish this, Cal must show that there exists a dangerous probability of monopoly power over prices and competition within the relevant market, coupled with a specific intent to monopolize. On the basis of all the facts given, can Cal establish that Bay possessed the necessary *monopoly power* just described?

3.   On August 5, 1969, at a hearing held before the Arizona Corporation Commission, the Arizona Water Company, a private corporation, sought and was granted the right to deliver water in a specified geographic area. Subsequently, the State of Arizona issued the company a "certificate of convenience and necessity," which confirmed the company's exclusive right to sell water in the specified area. In light of antitrust laws that prohibit the exercise of monopoly powers, should Arizona Water Company be granted this exclusive right? Under what conditions should the State of Arizona be allowed to withdraw the "certificate of convenience and necessity" that it awarded Arizona Water Company? [Fernandez v. Arizona Water Co., 21 Ariz.App. 107, 516 P.2d 49 (1974)]

4.   Buckeye and Lamb were competing to be the first to obtain a natural monopoly in the cable TV business in Toledo. To be first in obtaining a completed facility was crucial because in the cable TV business—like that of the electric, gas, and telephone utilities—it is not feasible to compete house-to-house for customers in the same area. Buckeye arranged construction of its cable TV facilities first, whereupon Lamb claimed that this violated the antitrust laws. In order to beat Lamb, Buckeye had to be the first to convince Bell Telephone to assist in the construction of a cable TV system along its telephone lines. Lamb objected to the contract between Bell Telephone and Buckeye, claiming that it was "an agreement in restraint of trade." What result? [Lamb Enterprises, Inc. v. Toledo Blade Co., 461 F.2d 506 (6th Cir. 1972)]

5.   The Professional Golfers Association of America (PGA) was founded in 1916 as a voluntary, unincorporated, nonprofit association. It has some 4,300 members and sponsors or cosponsors substantially all of the professional golf tournaments held in the United States. In order to compete in these tournaments, a player must be either a member of the PGA, an approved tournament player, or one of a limited number of participants designated or invited by the local sponsor of the tournament. Because of the increasing popularity of professional tournament golf, some means had to be found to limit the number of golfers who could enter these tournaments. PGA rules limiting entry to the categories of persons named above and defining the qualifications necessary for nonmember entrance were intended to accomplish this purpose. PGA gives official recognition to many tournaments that it neither sponsors nor cosponsors. These "approved tournaments" are free from any PGA control; yet PGA plans its schedule around them and counts them in determining its official standings. Herbert C. Deesen was a professional golfer who competed for several years in PGA-sponsored tournaments. Deesen sued the PGA, alleging that its sheer size and vast control over professional golf tournaments in the United States amounted to monopoly control in violation of Section II of the Sherman Antitrust Act. Do the PGA's activities violate the Sherman Act? If so, how? [Deesen v. Professional Golfers Ass'n of America, 358 F.2d 165 (9th Cir. 1966)]

6.   American Oil Company was a producer and distributor of oil, gas, and related products. Olson's was engaged in bulk distribution and retail sales of oil products. Early in 1967, American decided to acquire control of Olson's bulk distribution operations, and it purchased substantially all of Olson's assets. Thereafter, American negotiated a contract with Lawrence McMullen under which McMullen was to assume control of the Olson operation. Under the agreement, McMullen was to take charge of the Olson plant and was to be paid on a commission basis for the bulk petroleum sales that he procured. In addition, the contract between American and McMullen imposed certain territorial limitations and price restrictions on sales by the operations that McMullen was to control. Could the agreement between McMullen and American Oil imposing price restrictions and territorial controls on the operations of which McMullen took charge constitute a violation of Section I of the Sherman Antitrust Act? Explain. [American Oil Co. v. McMullen, 508 F.2d 1345 (10th Cir. 1975)]

7.   A relatively small number of companies are engaged in the manufacturing of corrugated containers in the United States. Corrugated containers are a fungible product for which demand is relatively inelastic. That is, changes in the price charged for the containers significantly affect demand for them. The dominant sellers in the corrugated container business agreed to give each other, on request, information about their most recent prices charged or quoted. This agreement stabilized corrugated container prices. At no time did the sellers agree to sell at fixed prices. Has a violation of the antitrust laws occurred? [United States v. Container Corp. of America, 393 U.S. 333, 89 S.Ct. 510 (1969)]

8.   Klor's was a retail establishment that sold appliances. Broadway-Hale, a retail chain of depart-

ment stores, operated a store next door that competed with Klor's in the sale of appliances. At Broadway-Hale's request, several manufacturers and distributors of the major brands of appliances agreed either not to sell to Klor's or to sell to it only at higher than normal prices. All the participants in this agreement admitted its existence. However, they justified their actions by stating that their participation in the agreement was the result of a private quarrel between Broadway-Hale and Klor's. Later, when Klor's sued both Broadway-Hale and these manufacturers and distributors, alleging that they participated in a "group boycott" against Klor's, the manufacturers and distributors asserted that Klor's was "just one small retailer" and therefore their actions could not be deemed in restraint of competition. Have the manufacturers and distributors presented any defense to the charge of group boycott that would stand up in court? [Klor's, Inc. v. Broadway-Hale Stores, Inc., 359 U.S. 207, 79 S.Ct. 705 (1959)]

51

Government Regulation
The Federal Trade Commission
and Trade Regulation

This chapter is concerned with business regulation as it is prescribed by various federal statutes, and it will concentrate on the activities associated with the Federal Trade Commission. It is difficult to divide the activities of the Justice Department that regulate business activities from those of the FTC along any accepted theoretical grounds. Nevertheless, the activities of the commission do, in general, differ from those of the antitrust division of the Justice Department.

COMMISSION RESOURCES AND AUTHORITY

The estimated budget of the Federal Trade Commission for fiscal year (FY) 1980 is nearly $70 million, and total staff is estimated at about 1,800 individuals.[1] In addition to the consumer protection activities discussed in Chapter 48, the commission spends about half its total budget in efforts designed to maintain the competitive nature of the U.S. economy. This effort involves enforcing federal statutes that include, but are not limited to, the Federal Trade Commission Act,[2] Sections 2, 3, 7, and 8 of the Clayton Act[3] as amended by the Celler-Kefauver and Robinson-Patman Acts,[4] the Export Trade Act,[5] the Emergency Petroleum Allocation Act,[6]

1. *Budget of the U.S. Government, Fiscal Year 1980* (Washington, D.C.: Government Printing Office, 1979), appendix, p. 910.
2. 15 USCA Secs. 41-58.
3. 15 USCA Secs. 12-27, as amended.
4. 15 USCA Secs. 18, 21, 13c.
5. 15 USCA Secs. 61-65.
6. 15 USCA Sec. 755.

the Federal Trade Commission Improvement Act,[7] and the Hart-Scott-Rodino Antitrust Improvement Act.[8]

The Federal
Trade Commission Act

In 1914, Congress passed the Federal Trade Commission Act, which created a bipartisan administrative agency headed by five commissioners, no more than three of whom could be of the same political party.[9] Section 5 of the act gives the FTC broad powers to prevent "unfair methods of competition in commerce and unfair or deceptive acts or practices in commerce." Amendments, particularly in 1975, have broadened the commission's powers.[10] The FTC also has the authority to conduct investigations relating to alleged violations of antitrust statutes and to make reports and recommendations to Congress regarding legislation. More importantly, the FTC can promulgate interpretive rules and general statements of policy with respect to unfair or deceptive acts or practices. It can also promulgate trade regulation rules, which *define* particular unfair or deceptive acts or practices including requirements for the purpose of preventing such acts or practices. The commission has issued guidelines defining unfair practices, but these guidelines are very broad, and many seemingly unfair practices are allowed.[11]

The FTC initiates most of its investigations because of oral or written communications from the general public and private business firms. The primary enforcement mechanism of the FTC is **cease and desist orders** (orders to stop certain activities or practices) against violations of the Federal Trade Commission Act. Furthermore, businesses that violate these orders are subject to fines of up to $10,000 per day for each

day of continued violation. Cease and desist orders can be appealed to the courts. Unlike the Sherman Act, treble damage actions cannot be brought under Section 5 of the FTC Act.

Beginning in the early 1960s, the FTC issued a number of **trade regulation rules**. These rules define acceptable and unacceptable practices for various industries. For example, the FTC has promulgated trade regulation rules governing the pricing of eyeglasses and funerals. The commission considers a number of proposed trade regulation rules covering a wide range of industry practices each year. Violations of trade regulation rules, like violations of cease and desist orders, are subject to potential fines of up to $10,000 per day.

Additional Authority

Section 5 of the Federal Trade Commission Act overlaps a number of other antitrust statutes, including the Sherman Act, the Clayton Act, and other laws designed to reduce unfair methods of competition. The FTC initiates investigations and issues cease and desist orders particularly for violations of Sections 2, 3, 7, and 8 of the Clayton Act as amended by Celler-Kefauver, the Robinson-Patman, and other acts.

PRICE DISCRIMINATION One of the more important activities of the Federal Trade Commission has been the detection and prohibition of **price discrimination** (that is, charging different prices to different purchasers for identical goods) when such discrimination lessens competition or tends to create a monopoly.

Subsequent judicial interpretation and responses by businesses effectively circumvented the original intent of Section 1 of the Clayton Act, so by 1936 Congress responded by enacting the Robinson-Patman Act. This act tightened the prohibition against price discrimination so that if goods of similar grade and quality were sold at different prices, and these differences could not be justified by differences in production costs, the practice would violate the Robinson-Patman Act. In addition, the act prohibited sellers from cutting prices to levels

7.   15 USCA Sec. 230 *et seq.*
8.   15 USCA Sec. 18a.
9.   15 USCA Secs. 41-51 (1914)
10.   Magnuson-Moss FTC Improvements Act of 1975.
11.   The commission, for example, has indicated that a practice is "unfair" if it offends public policy or is immoral, unethical, oppressive, unscrupulous, or causes substantial injury to consumers.

substantially below those charged by their competitors.[12]

In the following antitrust action, the plaintiff was a local company engaged in selling

_____
12.   Robinson-Patman Act, Subsection B.

frozen pies. The defendant was one of several national companies also engaged in selling frozen pies. The defendant cut the price of its frozen pies in a local market so that the price was below cost. The practice was found to be a violation of the Robinson-Patman Act.

BACKGROUND AND FACTS   *Utah Pie was organized in the 1920s and in 1957 decided to enter the frozen pie business. From 1957 through 1961, Utah Pie baked and sold frozen pies in the Salt Lake City area. Utah Pie was not large, but it had a large, steadily increasing share of the Salt Lake City market (approximately 50 percent). The price of Utah Pie's frozen pies to grocers was just over $3 per dozen. During a substantial part of the relevant period, Continental Baking, whose nearest plant was in California, sold pies in the Salt Lake City area for $2.85 per dozen—far less than the price for which it sold frozen pies in the rest of the country. Utah Pie sought to recover damages from Continental Baking for price discrimination in violation of the Robinson-Patman Act.*

DECISION AND RATIONALE   *Sufficient evidence was presented to support a jury verdict that Continental Pie committed predatory price discrimination without justification, in violation of the Robinson-Patman Act. Utah Pie was somewhat weaker financially than Continental Baking, and therefore, in the long run, it could not compete with a serious price cutting effort by Continental. Justice White delivered the majority opinion: "Section 2(a) [of the Robinson-Patman Act] does not forbid price competition which will probably injure or lessen competition by eliminating competitors, discouraging entry into the market or enhancing the market shares of the dominant sellers. But Congress has established some ground rules for the game. Sellers may not sell like goods to different purchasers at different prices if the result may be to injure competition in either the sellers' or the buyers' market unless such discriminations are justified as permitted by the Act."*

UTAH PIE CO. v. CONTINENTAL BAKING CO.
Supreme Court of the United States, 1967.
386 U.S. 685, 87 S.Ct. 1326.

EXCLUSIVE DEALINGS   Section 3 of the Clayton Act as amended prohibits exclusive dealing contracts when the effect of these contracts would be "to substantially lessen competition or tend to create a monopoly."[13]
Exclusive dealing contracts arise when a seller or manufacturer requires the buyer to *not* purchase the products of competitive sellers. Section 3 has also been interpreted by the courts

_____
13.   15 USCA Sec. 14 (1914).

to prohibit *tying contracts* where the seller of a commodity agrees to provide the commodity on the condition that the buyer purchase one or more other commodities offered by the seller. Thus, an auto dealer is not allowed to require that a customer purchase insurance from the firm.

INTERLOCKING DIRECTORATES   *Interlocking directorates* occur when substantially the same people serve as officers and board members of different corporations. Section 8 of the Clayton Act prohibits *interlocking directorates* when elimination of competition among firms with such directorates would constitute a violation of the antitrust laws. (Corporations with capital, surplus, and undivided profits totaling less than $1 million are exempt.)

A number of statutes deal directly with *potential* competition in the economy. For example, the FTC is responsible for registering the articles of association or incorporation for associations that are organized under the Export Trade Act. It is also responsible for receiving and monitoring regulations governing mandatory allocations of crude oil, residual fuel oil, and refined petroleum products under the Emergency Petroleum Act of 1973. And it is responsible for working with the Justice Department in developing voluntary agreements under the International Energy Program. The Energy Policy and Conservation Act also creates responsibilities relating to automobile fuel economy, appliance efficiencies, and recycled oil.

FTC ACTIVITIES

The Federal Trade Commission organizes its trade regulation activities into the three general categories of competition, consumer protection, and economic activities rather than along specific lines of enforcing explicit statutes. Most FTC investigation and trade regulation activities can be put into the main categories shown in Exhibit 51-1, which also gives the percentage of resources spent in maintaining competition for each of these major categories.

Energy

The major activity in the energy area concerns the Exxon investigation, the single largest enforcement activity in the history of the Federal Trade Commission. Beginning with a 1973 complaint, it now involves eight major petroleum refining companies. The commission believes that these companies are monopolizing domestic petroleum refining and that they maintain anticompetitive market conditions in petroleum products in certain portions of the

---

EXHIBIT 51-1 MAJOR FTC MAINTAINING COMPETITION MISSIONS AND PERCENT OF DIRECT TOTAL EFFORT

PROGRAM	PERCENT OF FISCAL YEAR 1979 RESOURCE ESTIMATES
Energy and petroleum industries	21.2
Health care	11.8
Food industries: Producer, manufacturer, distributor, and retailer	11.6
Transportation industries	11.0
Horizontal restraints	12.5
Mergers and joint ventures	8.4
Distributional restraints	7.2
Industry-wide matters	3.5
Compliance with competitive orders	4.3
Other	8.5
Total	100.0

Source: Federal Trade Commission, *Zero-Based Program Budget, FY1979* (Washington, D.C.: Government Printing Offices, 1978).

country. It hopes to determine whether there is access to petroleum supplies and facilities by independent producers and, if necessary, to seek remedies to enhance product or price competition. The commission is also investigating various methods of conducting and financing business operations in other energy-producing firms, including barriers to the development of new sources of fuel, delivery of existing energy supplies, or characteristics that can impede investment, exploration, development, production, transportation, or other aspects of conducting business in energy-producing firms.

A number of other industries are subject to FTC trade regulation rules, but they are generally categorized under particular forms of activity rather than by the services or goods they provide. Once the FTC has found a practice to be unacceptable, it is irrelevant whether the practice is permissible by state law. In the following case, the FTC ruled that advertisements used by a weight loss clinic were unacceptable, even though they had been reviewed by the attorney general of the state in accordance with a state health plan act and the attorney general had not disapproved of them.

Food

FTC food programs concern all stages of agricultural production and marketing. The commission is investigating the organization of the industry as well as existing regulations that include quotas, subsidies, support programs, or other methods of modifying market conditions. The investigation extends to the manufacturer-processor levels, where it is concentrating on barriers to entry that lessen competition. Similar activities are conducted at the distribution and retailing level.

Transportation

Regulatory activities of the commission are also concerned with the transportation service and equipment industries to the extent that high profits in those industries reflect anticompetitive conditions. Factors that can impede development of major innovations are also under the scrutiny of the commission.

Health Care

A major activity of the commission is the ongoing investigation of health care facilities, including professional health services and suppliers of hospital services, drugs, and medical products. Potential practices that impede competition— such as accreditation of professional schools, licensing, codes of professional ethics, minimum fee schedules, joint practice clinics, malpractice and other insurance costs, and other factors that directly or indirectly influence the provision of professional health services— are under continued investigation. The commission is also investigating the institutions and practices that determine the prices for prescription drugs, patent medicines, and medical supplies.

BACKGROUND AND FACTS   *The Federal Trade Commission entered a cease and desist order prohibiting Simeon Management, a weight loss clinic, from using an advertisement that failed to indicate one of the drugs it used was new and had not been approved by the Food and Drug Administration. The FDA found no substantial evidence that the drug was safe or effective, and the FTC adopted the FDA's conclusions in its cease and desist order. Simeon challenged the FTC's order on the ground that, under California law, the California Attorney General's approval was adequate to allow the advertising.*

SIMEON MANAGEMENT CORP. v. FEDERAL TRADE COMM.
United States Court of Appeals, Ninth Circuit, 1978. 579 F.2d 1137.

DECISION AND RATIONALE   *Since the FDA test results that the FTC adopted showed that Simeon's claims about the drug were unfounded, the cease and desist order was validly issued. The California Attorney General's failure to disapprove Simeon's advertisements had no legal effect on action taken by the FTC. The court concluded: "The Commission found that some consumers will reasonably believe that the government exercises control over the promotion and use of prescription drugs *** and [that] the representations may therefore reasonably lead consumers into the mistaken belief that the claims of safety and effectiveness are based, not on the advertiser's own opinion, but on a determination by the FDA. *** The need for the courts to defer to the Commission's judgment results in part from the statutory scheme and in part from the weight of accumulated agency expertise."*

VERTICAL RESTRAINTS

FTC activities involving vertical restraints include resale price maintenance, mergers, price discrimination, and other practices among firms at various levels of production, distribution, or sales that can result in anticompetitive outcomes. Investigations into resale price maintenance, the establishment of uniform retail prices by producers, are likely to become less important by the repeal of the federal statute authorizing states to adopt fair trade laws.[14]

Vertical Mergers

Vertical mergers occur when a company at one stage of production acquires a company at a higher or lower stage of production. Thus, the acquisition of a tire plant by an automobile manufacturer would constitute a backward vertical integration, while acquisition of a car-renting agency would constitute a forward vertical integration. The FTC's approach to vertical mergers depends on a number of factors, including definition of the relevant product in geographic markets as well as the characteristics identified as impeding competition. For example, the commission will attack any vertical merger that keeps competitors of either party from the segment of the market that otherwise would be open to them. Thus, in *Ashgrove Cement Co.* v. *Federal Trade Comm.*,[15] the commission found that "foreclosure manifests a particularly anticompetitive character when it occurs as part of a trend toward forward integration in a concentrated market."[16]

Both the FTC and the U.S. Attorney General may bring suit to enjoin a merger. The following case brought by the United States, involved both vertical and horizontal mergers. Only the vertical aspect of the merger was challenged on appeal.

14.   See the discussion of the Miller-Tydings Act in Chapter 50.

15.   85 FTC 1123, 519 F.2d. 934 (C.A.D.C., 1975).
16.   The law's current theory of injury to competition in vertical mergers is contained in the concept of foreclosure. For example, a manufacturer can acquire a retailer and force the new retail subsidiary to sell the manufacturer's parent product. This would "foreclose" rival manufacturers from the market.

**BROWN SHOE v.
UNITED STATES**
Supreme Court of the United
States, 1962.
370 U.S. 294, 82 S.Ct. 1502.

BACKGROUND AND FACTS   *Brown and Kinney were both manufacturers and retail distributors of men's and women's shoes. After determining that their respective operations could be run more efficiently and profitably by combining, the two companies drew up a merger agreement. The United States, however, objected to the merger on several grounds, and brought suit under Section 7 of the Clayton Act to prevent it. The government asserted that Brown was the fourth largest* *manufacturer and Kinney the eighth largest retailer of shoes in the nation. Therefore, the merger would substantially lessen competition in the marketplace.*

DECISION AND RATIONALE *The Brown-Kinney merger violated Section 7 of the Clayton Act. Under Section 7, one corporation cannot acquire another if the acquisition will substantially lessen competition in any "line of commerce." The government did not object to the merger of the two companies in their capacity as manufacturers since Brown and Kinney were two of nearly 900 shoe manufacturers in the United States. Rather, the adverse impact that the government feared was that the "vertical merger" was likely to close Kinney's retail outlets to a substantial number of other shoe manufacturers. Brown's president even admitted in testimony that he hoped to use the ownership of Kinney to introduce Brown Shoes into Kinney's stores. The likely result, of course, would be that other shoe manufacturers would no longer be able to sell to Kinney, the nation's eighth largest retailer. In the court's opinion: "Of course, some of the results of large integrated or chain operations are beneficial to consumers. Their expansion is not rendered unlawful by the mere fact that small independent stores may be adversely affected. It is competition, not competitors that the Act protects."*

Other Vertical Restraints

The commission also investigates other vertical restraints that promote unfair practices or impede competition. These restraints include, but are not limited to, long-term requirements contracts, territorial and customer restrictions, vertical price fixing, and tying requirements, in which the seller ties the purchase of one commodity to another commodity supplied by the seller. The commission determined that requirements to buy all products of a seller (full-output purchase requirements) seriously reduce competition in suppliers' markets. Accordingly, it attacked a series of full-output purchase requirement contracts to purchase petroleum coke (a by-product of the refining process) that Great Lakes Carbon had with various refiners.[17] The initial terms of these contracts ranged from seven to twenty years, with extensions for five-year minimum periods. The commission also determined that territorial restrictions are illegal when the firm also attempts to fix prices. Thus, in *Coors*,[18] the commission found that territorial restrictions on

Coors distributors with simultaneous wholesale and retail minimum prices reduced competition in the beer industry.

The commission has ruled that certain other exclusionary practices, such as tying arrangements and **reciprocal buying,** are unlawful. Reciprocal arrangements exist when the seller of one good is required to purchase one or more goods provided by the buyer of the initial good. Thus, if an automobile manufacturer sells to a leasing company, the leasing firm cannot require that employees of the automobile manufacturer rent cars from the firm.

HORIZONTAL RESTRAINTS

In addition to mergers, horizontal restraints include all practices that potentially limit the competition among firms selling products of similar characteristics: industry practices, such as basing-point or delivered pricing schemes, cooperative associations that engage in price fixing, restrictions on advertising and price competition, and other restraints on trade.

Horizontal Mergers

The statutory authority for enforcing anticompetitive mergers is Section 6 of the Clayton Act.

17. 2582 FTC 1529 (1973).
18. 83 FTC 32 (1973).

This section was introduced because it was feared that concentration would potentially facilitate collusion among sellers in the market, and that such collusion would be difficult to detect. In general, the commission determines the legality of **horizontal mergers** by looking at the degree of concentration or market shares of merging firms, although the Court has indicated that it would look at the likely effects of the merger as well. Thus, if a merger facilitates horizontal collusion without increasing production or marketing efficiencies, it will be declared unlawful. Mergers will be permitted when they enhance consumer welfare by increasing efficiency if they do not increase the probability of horizontal collusion. Furthermore, mergers that facilitate and increase efficiency must be evaluated on the relative magnitude of the two facts. For example, in *Philadelphia National Bank*,[19] the Commission held that even in situations with low entry barriers, there may be a loss of actual competition. Thus, mergers can be declared illegal even where entry is relatively easy.

Other Horizontal Restraints

Over the years, the traditional methods for fixing prices by allocating territories or boycotting competitors have been rapidly disappearing. Consequently, the commission has revised its enforcement approach to focus more on the hidden forms of restricting competition. These may, for example, concern the exchange of information on prices or other characteristics as a means of enforcing a hidden restrictive agreement. Thus, the commission has paid particular attention to trade associations that disseminate trade information among producers and potential clients. It is argued that this can

provide a mechanism for enforcing informal agreements. The FTC has, for example, charged a lettuce produce cooperative with price fixing.[20] More importantly, the commission has turned to activities or practices that can constitute restraints on competition. For example, in the early 1970s, it began the first of a number of cases attacking shopping center leases that give major tenants a veto over other tenants. For example, in *Tysons Corner*,[21] the three major department stores were given lease arrangements that permitted them to disapprove prospective tenants who wished to rent space in the center. These clauses were ruled as prima facie evidence of unreasonable restraint of trade. The commission in this case ruled that agreements that create approval rights as broad as those involved in the *Tysons Corner* case are per se illegal and amount to an agreement to fix prices.

CONGLOMERATE MERGERS

Conglomerate mergers often extend product lines at the retail level, particularly among products that are complementary, although mergers can also occur among firms using similar suppliers.

A large number of conglomerate mergers, however, occur where the merging firms have no direct functional business link. In such mergers there are no changes in market structure, market shares, or concentration ratios. In many cases, conglomerate mergers serve to reduce overhead costs by spreading them over a larger range of output and reducing advertising and other promotional costs.

19. FTC Docket No. 8986.

20. California Lettuce Producers Cooperative, FTC Docket No. 8970.
21. Tysons Corner Regional Shopping Center 85 FTC 970 (1975).

FEDERAL TRADE COMM. v. PROCTER & GAMBLE CO.
Supreme Court of the United States, 1967.
386 U.S. 568, 87 S.Ct. 1224

BACKGROUND AND FACTS *Procter & Gamble sought to acquire Clorox Chemical Company. At the time of the merger, Clorox was the leading manufacturer of household bleach (49 percent of the national market), and Procter & Gamble had over half the national detergent market. The Federal Trade Commission brought this action to prevent the merger on the ground that it violated Section 7 of the Clayton Act. The FTC argued* *that the merger would prevent other bleach producers from entering the market, thereby eliminating potential competitors.*

DECISION AND RATIONALE   *The merger between Procter & Gamble and Clorox violated Section 7. Procter & Gamble had sought to expand its product line by adding household bleach to it. It is important to note that the markets for the products of each of the companies were concentrated markets. That is, they were already dominated by a few companies. Thus, barriers to entry by potential competitors were already high, and competition was at a minimum. Justice Douglas gave the majority opinion: "In the marketing of soaps, detergents and cleansers, as in the marketing of household liquid bleach, advertising and sales promotion are vital. *** [T]he substitution of Procter with its huge assets and advertising advantages for the already dominant Clorox would dissuade new entrants and discourage active competition from the firms already in the industry due to fear of retaliation by Procter."*

INDUSTRY-WIDE MATTERS

The Federal Trade Commission investigates and enforces regulations in the context of industry-wide matters. Industry-wide problems may be indicated by high prices, profits, lack of product innovation, or the absence of entry by new firms. In such cases, the exact cause of reduced performance may not be readily identifiable. Determining the problem and selecting the appropriate remedy require a more extensive analysis than is necessary in other FTC investigations. Industry-wide matters include investigations of the petroleum and automobile industries as well as breakfast cereals as part of the food program investigation. Other matters under FTC investigation in the 1970s include the household detergent and appliance industries.[22] A typical investigation, such as that concerning the household detergent industry, might involve an initial specification that the industry is highly concentrated, has high profits, lacks price competition, and maintains high entry barriers that are caused by advertising and brand proliferation. In such cases, the commission remedy is likely to be diversification, although neither major violations nor specific remedies have been determined.

---

22.   In addition, the commission has investigated office copiers, automobile crash parts, title insurance, and automobile rental industries.

QUESTIONS AND CASE PROBLEMS

1.   In December 1964, Graflex, Inc. quoted a price to International Film Center, Inc. of $324 apiece for the sale of thirty-two sound projectors. International was to use the quoted price in its bid to supply projectors to the local school board. Graflex knew of International's intention to use its quoted price in its bid to the school board. Graflex also quoted a price of $275 to Rosenfeld for the same projectors. The school board accepted Rosenfeld's low bid to sell it projectors. International Film Center, learning of the difference between the two bids, complained to Graflex and was advised by letter that the difference had been inadvertent. In addition, Graflex apologized for the mistake and assured International that it would never happen again. It did not happen thereafter. International Film Center subsequently charged Graflex with price discrimination and brought a lawsuit against it for damages. Will it succeed? [International Film Center, Inc. v. Graflex, Inc., 427 F.2d 334 (3rd Cir. 1970)]

2.   Richard Carroll was a commercial fisherman. Several years ago, he brought a personal injury action

against his employer, a commercial fishing vessel owner. Because he brought the personal injury action, Carroll was blacklisted by the Protection Maritime Insurance Company and consequently denied employment. Protection Maritime informed other companies of Carroll's personal injury suit, and Carroll was unable to buy insurance except at very high rates. Since commercial fishing vessels are required to insure their employees, Carroll found it impossible to obtain employment. Carroll believed that Protection Maritime Insurance committed "price discrimination" in violation of federal laws by charging him only the highest rates. Will Carroll's claim stand up in court? [Carroll v. Protection Maritime Ins. Co., Ltd., 512 F. 2d 4 (1st Cir. 1975)]

3. Febco, Inc., manufactured lawn and turf equipment. The Colorado Pump and Supply Company was a wholesale distributor of such equipment in the Colorado area. An important item that Colorado Pump distributed was a control device for sprinkling systems. Although Febco manufactured one of the better sprinkler controls, a number of other manufacturers competed in the field with competitive and satisfactory substitutes for the Febco controllers. In an agreement between Febco and Colorado Pump under which Colorado Pump was given the right to distribute Febco products, Colorado Pump was required to stock a complete line of Febco products. Industry data proved that, in this line of goods, it was important for distributors to protect the "goodwill" of manufacturers by carrying a complete line of a manufacturer's goods or none at all. Does the requirement by Febco that Colorado Pump stock an entire line of Febco products constitute an illegal tying arrangement? [Colorado Pump and Supply Co. v. Febco, Inc., 472 F.2d 637 (10th Cir. 1973)]

4. In 1972, the Federal Maritime Commission approved an agreement under which the world's two largest containership operators—Sea Land Service, Inc. and United States Lines, Inc.—would become subsidiaries of the same corporate parent—R. J. Reynolds Tobacco Company. The commission approved the acquisition agreement on condition that the subsidiaries would remain independent companies in competition with each other. The Federal Maritime Commission, however, does not have the power to immunize companies from the antitrust laws. Knowing this, does the agreement described above violate any of the antitrust statutes discussed in this chapter? [American Mail Line Limited v. Federal Maritime Comm., 503 F.2d 157 (D.C. Cir. 1974)]

5. Fedders Corporation was a manufacturer of air-conditioners and air-conditioning systems. Fedders claimed in its advertising that its air-conditioners were unique because they had "reserved cooling power," a term that Fedders admitted was intended to imply "an unusual ability to produce cold air under extreme conditions of heat and humidity." In fact, however, Fedders air-conditioners had no technical advantage over the equipment manufactured by its competitors. Accordingly, the Federal Trade Commission concluded that Fedders was engaging in misrepresentations in its advertising in violation of Section 5 of the Federal Trade Commission Act. Was the Federal Trade Commission's conclusion correct? [Fedders Corp. v. Federal Trade Comm., 529 F.2d 1398 (2nd Cir. 1976)]

6. Double Eagle Lubricants, Inc., was engaged in the business of marketing motor oil re-refined from previously used oil. It sold the oil in quart cans of the type normally used in the oil trade. The brand name appeared on the front panel, and the side panel contained the required statement disclosing the source of the oil. The cans were intended for display with the front panel facing the prospective customer. The Federal Trade Commission held a hearing to determine whether Double Eagle labeling was deceptive. At the hearing, Double Eagle produced an array of so-called public witnesses, who testified in effect that the labeling did not deceive them. No effort was made by the commission to counter this testimony. Nevertheless, the commission found that placing the information that the oil was re-refined on the side panel was deceptive. Such information should have been included on the front panel. Was the FTC's finding correct? Would the finding made without the support of testimony of public witnesses withstand the scrutiny of a reviewing court? [Double Eagle Lubricants, Inc. v. Federal Trade Comm., 360 F.2d 268 (10th Cir. 1965)]

7. Tampa Electric is a public utility that serves a large area on the west coast of Florida. It entered into a contract with Nashville Coal Company under which it agreed to purchase all of the coal it would require over a twenty-year period for its station in Tampa. In addition, the agreement stated that Tampa Electric would purchase any additional coal it would require for other stations it might build during the term of the contract. Nashville Coal Company competed with approximately seven hundred producers in the "peninsular Florida" area. It was estimated that Tampa Electric would require 2.25 million tons of coal a year from Nashville Coal Company, an amount that would constitute 0.77 percent of the coal sold in

peninsular Florida. Nashville Coal Company subsequently notified Tampa Electric that it could not perform as agreed since the contract was in violation of Section 3 of the Clayton Act. Is the contract enforceable? [Tampa Electric v. Nashville Coal Co., 365 U.S. 320, 81 S.Ct. 623 (1961)]

8. The Phillipsburg Bank and the Second National Bank both conducted business as full-service banks in the town of Phillipsburg. Five other full-service banks operated in the Lehigh Valley area, which encompasses Phillipsburg and half a dozen other cities. Phillipsburg Bank and the Second National Bank merged, leaving only two banks in Phillipsburg. In determining whether a violation of Section 7 of the Clayton Act had occurred, the key issue is whether the "relevant geographic market" was the town of Phillipsburg or the entire Lehigh Valley. If it can be determined that the merger lessened competition in the "relevant geographic market" then the merger will be held to violate Section 7. What is the "relevant geographic market" in this case? (Consider where people will most likely go to do their banking after the merger.) [United States v. Phillipsburg Nat. Bank, 399 U.S. 350, 90 S.Ct. 2035 (1970)]

UNIT IX

Protection of Property
and Other Interests

52

Nature and Ownership of Real Property

Real property is land and the buildings and plants, trees, and crops it contains. Real property, also called real estate or realty, is immovable, whereas personal property is movable.

From earliest times, property has provided a means for survival. Primitive peoples lived off the fruits of the land, eating the vegetation and wildlife. Later, as the wildlife was domesticated and the vegetation cultivated, property provided pasturage and farmland. In the twelfth and thirteenth centuries, land was a symbol of the power of feudal lords. The more land they held, the more powerful they were. After the age of feudalism passed, property continued to be an indicator of family wealth and social position.

NATURE OF REAL PROPERTY

Real property usually means land, but there are other aspects of it that must be considered, such as subsurface and air rights, plant life and vegetation, and fixtures.

Land

Land includes the soil on the surface of the earth and natural or artificial structures that are attached to it. Land also includes all the waters contained on or under the surface and all the air space above it. The exterior boundaries of land extend straight down to the center of the earth and straight up to the farthest reaches of the atmosphere (subject to certain qualifications).

Subsurface and Air Rights

The owner of real property has relatively exclusive rights to the air space above the land as well as the soil and minerals underneath it. Until fifty years ago, the right to use air space was not too significant, but today, commercial airlines and high rise office buildings and apartments use the air space regularly. Early cases involving air rights dealt with matters such as the right to run a telephone wire across a person's property when the wire did not touch any of the property[1] and whether a bullet shot over the person's land constituted trespass.[2] Today, cases involving air rights present questions such as the right of commercial and private planes to fly over property or the right of individuals to seed clouds and produce artificial rain. Flights over private land do not normally violate the property owners' rights unless they are low and frequent, causing a direct interference with the enjoyment and use of the land.[3] Likewise, if cloud seeding activities interfere with the enjoyment and use of the land, the property owner can sue to stop them. The owner of land is entitled to use the property without others causing unreasonable noise, pollution, or vibrations.

The property owner also owns all the subsurface of the land. The boundaries of the land extend straight down to the center of the earth. Any oil, minerals, and treasure found under the surface of the land belong to the landowner. Any intrusion into the subsurface of the land violates the rights of its owner. For

example, suppose Homestake Mining Company has a mine directly adjoining Redland Company's land. Homestake digs a shaft several hundred feet deep and hits a rich vein of ore. Homestake begins mining operations and follows the vein up and across into Redland's property. Although Homestake does not intend to mine any of Redland's ore, it is still liable to Redland for trespass. Redland can recover damages for the ore taken from below the surface of its land.

Any limitations on either air rights or subsurface rights have to be indicated on the deed transferring title at the time of purchase. Where no such encumbrances are noted, a purchaser can expect unfettered right to possession of the property. If any preexisting covenant unknown to the purchaser interferes with these rights, the purchaser can sue for breach of warranty of title. However, most state statutes limit the time period in which the purchaser can sue. An alternative lawsuit is for breach of the covenant of quiet enjoyment. There is a limit on the time for bringing such a suit, but it does not begin to run until after the discovery of the breach.

Plant Life and Vegetation

Plant life, both natural and cultivated, is also considered to be real property. When a parcel of land is sold and the land has growing crops on it, the sale includes the crops, unless otherwise specified in the sales contract. When crops are sold by themselves, they are considered to be personal property or goods. Consequently, the sale of crops (whether they are severed by the buyer or the seller) is a sale of goods, and it is governed by the Uniform Commercial Code rather than by real property law. [UCC Sec. 2-107]

Fixtures

Certain personal property can become so closely associated with the real property to which it is attached that the law views it as real property. Such property is known as a **fixture.** For proper-

1.   Butler v. Frontier Telephone Co., 186 N.Y. 486, 79 N.E. 716 (1906). Stringing a wire across someone's property violates the air rights of that person. Leaning walls, buildings, projecting eave spouts and roofs also violate the air rights of the property owner.
2.   Herrin v. Sutherland, 74 Mont. 587, 241 P. 328 (1925). Shooting over a person's land constitutes trespass.
3.   United States v. Causby, 328 U.S. 256, 66 S.Ct. 1062 (1946).

ty to be deemed a fixture, two elements must exist: *annexation* and *intention*.

ANNEXATION   A thing is *annexed* to realty when it is attached to it by roots, embedded in it, or permanently attached by means of cement, plaster, bolts, nails, or screws. The fixture can be physically attached to real property, be attached to another fixture, or even be without any actual physical attachment to the land, as long as the owner *intends* the property to be a fixture.

INTENTION   In order to determine whether or not a certain item is a fixture, the *intention* of the party who placed the fixture must be examined. If the person intended the item to be a fixture, then it will be a fixture. To illustrate: Suppose the owner of a house buys a workbench for the garage. The workbench is not bolted to the wall, but it cannot easily be removed. If the owner intended the workbench to become a fixture—part of the garage—then it is a fixture. If the owner plans to remove it after a couple of months, then it is not a fixture. The objective intention of the owner will control. For instance, certain items can only be attached to property permanently; such items are fixtures. The owner must have intended them to be since they had to be permanently attached to the property. A tile floor, cabinets, and carpeting are good examples of this type of fixture. Objectively, any persons seeing the owner install such items would assume that the owner intended them to become part of the property. When a piece of property is custom-made for installation on real property, such as storm windows, the property is usually classified as a fixture. Again, any objective observer would assume that the owner intended the piece of property to become part of the real property.

Fixtures are included in the sale of land if the sales contract does not provide otherwise. The sale of a house includes the land and the house and garage on it as well as the cabinets, plumbing, and windows. Since these are permanently affixed to the property, they are

considered a part of it. However, unless otherwise agreed, the curtains and throw rugs are not included. Items such as drapes and window-unit air-conditioners are difficult to classify. Thus, a contract for the sale of a house or commercial realty should indicate which items of this sort are included in the sale.

TRADE FIXTURES   A **trade fixture** is any article placed in or attached to a rented building by the tenant in order to pursue the trade or business for which the tenant occupies the premises. Trade fixtures are generally removable without material alteration to the premises. Indeed, they are not fixtures at all, since the person who installs them intends to remove them eventually. In many cases, the item would be a fixture if the owner had installed it but not if the lessee installed it. For example, suppose Helen Getty rents a small structure located on a main highway and installs gas pumps and a storage tank. The pumps and tanks are trade fixtures, and Getty can remove them when the lease ends. Naturally, if any damages occur to the property when Getty removes the trade fixtures, she must pay the landlord for the damage.

OWNERSHIP INTEREST IN REAL PROPERTY— ESTATES IN LAND

Ownership of property is an abstract concept that cannot exist independent of the legal system. No one can actually possess or *hold* a piece of land, the air above, the earth below, and all the water contained on it. The legal system therefore recognizes certain rights and duties that constitute the ownership interest in real property.

Freehold Estates

Rights of ownership in real property, called **estates,** are classified according to their nature, quantity, and extent. Two major categories of estates are freehold estates, which are held indefinitely and less than freehold estates, which are held for a predetermined time. There are two kinds of freehold estates—estates in fee, and life estates.

THE FEE SIMPLE ABSOLUTE   The **fee simple absolute,** or fee simple, is the largest estate known to the law. It is limited absolutely to a person and his or her heirs and is assigned forever without limitation or condition. In a fee simple, the owner has the greatest aggregation of rights, privileges, and powers possible. The rights that accompany a fee simple include the right to use the land for whatever purpose the owner sees fit, subject to laws that prevent the owner from unreasonably interfering with another person's land. A fee simple is potentially infinite in duration and can be disposed of by will or by deed (by selling or giving it away). When the owner of a fee simple dies without a will, the fee simple passes to the owner's legal heirs. The owner of a fee simple absolute also has the rights of *exclusive* possession and waste. *Waste* means that the owner can use the land without replenishing what is used. If Albert Samuelson has fee simple absolute ownership of fifteen acres in the mountains, he can mine any ore on that land without replacing it. The term *waste* refers to injury done to the land by one rightfully in possession of the land.

At early common law, a fee simple absolute could be conveyed only by stating that the conveyance was "to A and his heirs." The words "and his heirs" denoted the fee simple as infinite in duration and distinguished it from other estates such as the *fee simple defeasible* (which is defined below). In the United States today, these so-called words of limitation have been eliminated and a conveyance "to A" as well as "to A and his heirs" will convey a fee simple.

THE FEE SIMPLE DEFEASIBLE   A **fee simple defeasible**[4] encompasses a number of estates

that *almost* constitute absolute ownership.[5] Essentially, a fee simple defeasible is a fee simple that can end if a specified condition or event occurs. For example, a conveyance "to A and his heirs as long as the land is used for charitable purposes" creates a fee simple defeasible. In this type of conveyance the original owner retains a *partial* ownership interest. As long as the condition does not occur, A has full ownership rights, but if the specified condition does occur (for example, if the land ceases to be used for charitable purposes), then the land reverts, or returns, to the original owner.[6] The interest that the original owner retains is called a *future interest* since, if it arises, it will arise in the future.[7]

Consider another example. Simon deeds some land to XYZ Church "for as long as this land is used for church purposes and no longer." For two years, the land is used by the church for a playground for the children going to Sunday School. The church then sells the land to Smith, who intends to build an apartment building on it. As soon as Simon learns of the sale to Smith, he begins a court action to have himself declared the owner of the land.[8] Since Simon deeded a fee simple determinable to XYZ Church, he will succeed in his court action. The church has absolute ownership of the land as long as it is used for church purposes. XYZ Church can even sell the land or otherwise dispose of it to those who will also use it for church purposes. However, as soon as the

---

4.   The word *defeasible* refers to an owner's ability to lose ownership of property, whether the loss is voluntary or involuntary.

5.   The term *fee simple defeasible* encompasses the fee simple determinable, the fee simple subject to special limitation, the fee simple subject to condition subsequent, and the fee simple subject to an executory interest.

6.   If the original owner is not living at the time, the land passes to his or her heirs. In other words, once the condition occurs, A is divested of rights regardless of whether the original owner to (or through) whom the land reverts is alive.

7.   In the specific example given in the text, the future interest that the owner holds is known as a *possibility of reverter.* In the conveyance "to A, but if the premises are ever used for the sale of alcoholic beverages then to B," the original owner has conveyed the entire interest. The owner has conveyed a fee simple defeasible to A and all future interest to B.

8.   Note that the instant the condition is broken, legal ownership automatically vests in Simon.

land stops being used for the specified purpose, the fee simple determinable terminates and ownership reverts to Simon.

THE LIFE ESTATE   A **life estate** is an estate that lasts for the life of some specified individual. A conveyance "to A for his life" creates a life estate.[9] Estates for life can be created by an act of law or by an act of the parties. In a life estate, the life tenant has fewer rights of ownership than the holder of a fee simple defeasible. The life tenant has the right to use the land provided no waste (injury to the land) is committed. In other words, the life tenant cannot injure the land in a manner that would adversely affect the owner of the future interest in it. The life tenant can use the land to harvest crops or, if mines and oil wells are already on the land, can extract minerals and oil from it. But the life tenant cannot exploit the land by creating new wells or mines.

Consider some examples. Michaelson deeds land to Hitchcock for life. Oil is found under that land. Agents of Mobil Oil Company negotiate an oil and gas lease with Hitchcock, but Mobil never contacts Michaelson. It merely starts drilling an oil well. When Michaelson learns of this, he demands that Mobil stop drilling or negotiate a lease with him. Michaelson can enforce his demand because a life tenant alone cannot make a binding oil and gas lease upon the property if no drilling was taking place at the time the life estate was created. By the same token, Hitchcock cannot sell any of the timber that is on the land without Michaelson's approval, because the removal of standing timber will reduce the value of the land.

The life tenant has the right to mortgage the life estate and create liens, easements, and leases; but none can extend beyond the life of the tenant. In addition, the owner of a life estate has exclusive right of possession during his or her life. Exclusive possession, however, is

subject to the rights of the future interest holder to come onto the land and protect the future interest.

Along with these rights, the life tenant also has some *duties*—to keep the property in repair and to pay property taxes. In short, the owner of the life estate has the same rights as a fee simple owner except that the future interest of the land must be kept intact for the person who eventually will receive possession.

Nonfreehold Estates

The **less than freehold estates** are generally considered to be personal rather than real property. They are covered in this chapter for the sake of convenience because they relate to ownership of an interest in land. These estates include (1) the tenancy for years, (2) the tenancy from period to period, (3) the tenancy at will, and (4) the tenancy by sufferance. All involve the transfer of the right to possession for *a specified period of time*. The owner or lessor (landlord) conveys the property to the lessee (tenant) for a certain period of time. In every nonfreehold estate, the tenant has a *qualified* right to exclusive possession (qualified by the right of the landlord to enter upon the premises to assure that no waste is being committed). The tenant can use the land, for example, by harvesting crops, but cannot injure the land by such activities as cutting down timber for sale or extracting oil.

TENANCY FOR YEARS   A **tenancy for years** is created by express contract (which can sometimes be oral) by leasing the property for a specified period of time. For example, signing a lease to rent an apartment creates a tenancy for years. At the end of the period specified in the lease, the lease ends (without notice) and possession of the land returns to the lessor. If the tenant dies during the period of the lease, the lease passes to the tenant's heirs as personal property. Often, leases include renewal or extension provisions.

---

9.   A less common type of life estate is created by the conveyance "to A for the life of B." This is known as an estate *pur autre vie*, or an estate for the life of another.

TENANCY FROM PERIOD TO PERIOD A **tenancy from period to period** is created by a lease that does not specify how long it is to last but does specify that rent is to be paid at certain intervals. For example, a tenancy from period to period is created by a lease that states, "Rent is due on the tenth day of every month." This is a tenancy from month to month. This type of tenancy can also be from week to week or from year to year. A tenancy from period to period sometimes arises when a landlord allows a tenant under a tenancy for years to hold over and continue paying monthly or weekly rent. At common law, in order to terminate a tenancy from period to period, the landlord or tenant must give one period's notice to the other party. If the tenancy is month to month, one month's notice must be given. If the tenancy is week to week, one week's notice must be given. State statutes often define the required notice of termination in a tenancy from period to period. Therefore, the particular statute in question should be referred to in order to determine the proper time for notice of termination.

As long as a tenancy exists, a landlord can collect rent in full regardless of whether the premises are actually occupied by the tenant. Thus, when a tenant wrongfully abandons the premises and refuses to pay rent, the landlord can either permit the premises to remain vacant or refuse to recognize the attempted surrender by the tenant and bring a lawsuit to collect the rent as it comes due. A tenant who wrongfully abandons the premises and refuses to pay rent cannot try to shift the burden onto the landlord to find someone to take the tenant's place. The issue of termination of tenancy is examined in the following case.

BACKGROUND AND FACTS *Hodsdon wished to rent apartment 51 in a building owned and operated by the Richards Company. Since it was occupied, Hodsdon and Richards orally agreed that Hodsdon would stay in apartment 2 until apartment 51 became vacant. On the day apartment 51 became available, Hodsdon vacated apartment 2 without notice and left the building for good. Richards cleaned apartment 2 and readied it for a new tenant, but eight months passed before she succeeded in renting it even though, during that period, she showed it to a number of prospective tenants. Therefore, Richards sued Hodsdon to recover rent for the eight month period.*

DECISION AND RATIONALE *Richards could not recover eight months of rent from Hodsdon even though Hodsdon vacated without notice. When Hodsdon wrongfully abandoned the premises and refused to pay rent, Richards, had two options. She could permit the apartment to remain vacant and sue to recover rent as it came due, or she could attempt to rent the premises to another tenant. She could not do both. The court explained its position as follows: "Mrs. Richards *** found fault because she had not been given a month's notice; but at the same time gave no intimation that she intended to hold Mrs. Hodsdon as a tenant. The key was left on the office desk. Mrs. Richards took the key, entered the apartment, cleaned it, made it ready for a new tenant and showed it to prospective tenants from time to time. Her conduct was unequivocal; she made no attempt to qualify it. Every act done is inconsistent with the present claim that the tenancy of Mrs. Hodson continued."*

ENOCH C. RICHARDS CO. v. LIBBY

Supreme Judicial Court of Maine, 1940.
136 Me. 376, 10 A.2d 609.

TENANCY AT WILL Suppose L, the landlord, rents an apartment to T "for as long as L wishes." In such a case, T receives a leasehold estate known as a **tenancy at will.** At common law, either party can terminate the tenancy without notice. This type of estate usually arises when a tenant who has been under a tenancy for years retains possession after the termination date of that tenancy with the landlord's consent. (This is called holding over.) Before the tenancy has been converted into a tenancy from period to period (by the periodic payment of rent), it is a tenancy at will terminable by either party without notice. The death of either party or the voluntary commission of waste by the tenant will terminate a tenancy at will.

TENANCY BY SUFFERANCE A **tenancy by sufferance** is not a tenancy at all. It is the mere possession of land without right. A tenancy by sufferance is not an estate, since it is created by a tenant *wrongfully* holding over. Whenever a life estate, tenancy for years, tenancy from period to period, or tenancy at will ends, and the tenant continues to retain possession of the premises without the owner's permission, a tenancy by sufferance is created. A tenancy by sufferance can be converted into a leasehold if a landlord accepts rent from the tenant. If the landlord does not accept rent and ultimately evicts the tenant, the tenant is liable to the landlord as if he or she were a trespasser.

RELATIONSHIP OF LANDLORD AND TENANT

Much real property is used by those who do not own it. A **lease** is a contract by which the owner—the landlord—grants the tenant an exclusive right to use and possess the land for an ascertainable period of time. The basic characteristic of this particular estate is that it continues for the ascertainable term and carries with it the obligation by the tenant to pay rent to the landlord. Usually, the creation of the leasehold estate by contract for terms longer than a

year (or three years in some jurisdictions) must be in writing.

Duties and Warranties of the Landlord

When a landlord leases premises to a tenant, a *warranty of possession* and a *covenant of quiet enjoyment* are implied by law. Under the warranty of possession, the landlord warrants that the premises have been leased only to one tenant, but he does not have an obligation to actually deliver possession to the tenant. It is the new tenant's responsibility to evict a former tenant who wrongfully holds over.

Under the covenant of quiet enjoyment, a landlord essentially warrants that he or she will not *evict* the tenant. Generally, questions regarding breach of a covenant of quiet enjoyment arise not when a landlord actually evicts a tenant, but rather when the landlord's action (or inaction) affects the tenant's use and enjoyment of the premises in a way that constitutes a *constructive eviction*. For example, suppose Smith, a quiet minister, rents half of a duplex from Lawson. Lawson rents the other half of the duplex to three members of a rock band. The band rehearses in the duplex every night from about 11:00 in the evening to 5:00 in the morning. Smith complains to Lawson that strange people are constantly entering and leaving the premises and that the noise is unbearable. If Lawson fails to take any action, he has breached his covenant of quiet enjoyment to Smith and has *constructively evicted* him from the premises. Smith can probably rescind the rental agreement.

Under the common law, a landlord was under no duty to repair the premises rented by a tenant or to warrant that the premises were habitable or suitable for the particular purpose for which they were rented. An exception to this common law rule existed for furnished premises that were rented for short periods of time. Under most state statutes today, and under judicial decisions, a landlord of residential premises impliedly warrants that the premises are habitable and cannot disclaim this warranty unless the landlord and the tenant are of equal bargaining power. Additionally, a landlord is under an affirmative duty to repair and maintain the structure and all its *common areas* and fixtures. The landlord will be held liable for injuries resulting from negligent failure to maintain the rented premises.

Duties Owed by the Tenant

TENANT'S OBLIGATION TO PAY   The tenant has an implied obligation to pay reasonable rent to the landlord. Most lease contracts contain an express promise, known as a covenant, that indicates that the tenant is to pay a specific amount at specified times. Generally, if the express promise is not in the lease agreement, then the tenant is obliged only to pay rent that is reasonable and only at the end of the term.

TERMINATING THE TENANT'S OBLIGATION TO PAY RENT   Whenever a tenant assigns his or her rights under a lease, the implied obligation to pay reasonable rent goes to the assignee. When there is an express agreement (a contract) for the tenant to pay rent of a specified sum at specified intervals, the tenant remains liable under this contract, even if he or she has assigned the leasehold estate to another. Note, however, that even though the assignee of the lease is bound to pay rent, the original tenant is not released from the contractual obligation to pay rent. Thus, whenever the assignee fails to pay, the landlord can look to the original tenant for compensation.

Many leases require that the right of assignment have the landlord's written consent, and an assignment that lacks consent can be avoided by the landlord. A landlord who knowingly accepts rent from the assignee, however, will be held to have waived the requirement. Once waived, it cannot later be revised.

Subleasing   Subleasing involves a partial transfer of the original tenant's rights to the lease. An assignment can read that the original tenant assigns all rights, title, and interest in the lease to another person for a stated sum of money. If, however, the assignment indicates that the original tenant can reenter the premises whenever the assignee fails to pay the rent, most courts will then label such an agreement a sublease. This is because the original tenant has reserved the right of reentry and has, therefore, transferred less than the whole interest in the lease. By subleasing, the original tenant is not relieved of any obligations to the landlord under the lease. The lease may prohibit subleasing without the landlord's consent.

DESTRUCTION OF THE PREMISES AND THE OBLIGATION TO PAY RENT   Under common law, destruction by fire or flood of a whole building leased by a tenant did not relieve the tenant of the obligation to pay rent or permit the termination of the lease. The reasoning behind the common law rule was that the tenant's obligation to pay rent was an exchange for the *estate* in the land. At common law, the concept of estate was divorced from any economic benefits that went with it. Presumably, destruction of the leased building destroyed only part of the benefit. The tenant retained a nonfreehold interest in the land on which the building was constructed.

Today, state statutes have altered the common law rule. In most states, tenants who occupy only a portion of the building will not be covered under the rule. Thus, if the building burns down, apartment dwellers in most states are not continuously liable to the landlord for the payment of rent. Many leases contain clauses covering destruction of the building. For example, a clause can indicate that the landlord will repair and restore the building, and the tenant's obligation to pay rent will be suspended until the premises are restored, but only if the premises are wholly unsuitable for habitation.

CONCURRENT OWNERSHIP

Property owned by one person is said to be held severally. When two or more persons own property, it is said to be held concurrently. There are several types of **concurrent estates,** including tenancy in common, joint tenancy, and tenancy by entirety.

Tenancy in Common

The most common type of concurrent estate is a **tenancy in common.** Suppose Y conveys land "to A and B and C." This conveyance creates a tenancy in common among A, B, and C, whereby each takes a one-third interest. In a tenancy in common, each tenant has the right to convey his or her interest in the property. When one of the tenants dies, that tenant's interest passes to his or her heirs (or, by will, to someone else). Essentially, tenants in a tenancy in common each own an undivided fractional share of the property.

Joint Tenancy

In a **joint tenancy,** each tenant owns an undivided whole interest in the property. Thus, when one tenant dies, the others' interests "swallow up" the deceased's share and no property passes to the heirs of the deceased (even by will). Instead, all property of the deceased passes to the other joint tenants. This characteristic, which differs from tenancy in common, is known as *survivorship*.

A joint tenancy is transformed into a tenancy in common when one of the joint tenants transfers his or her interest to another party. A joint tenancy can also be transferred by *partition*; that is, the tenants can physically divide the property in equal parts. Since a joint tenant's interest is capable of being conveyed without the consent of the other joint tenants, it can be levied against by the tenant's creditors. This is also true of the tenancy in common.

Tenancy by the Entirety

A final type of concurrent estate is the **tenancy by the entirety**—a joint tenancy between a husband and wife. At common law, a tenancy by the entirety could be created in a husband

and wife only where the conveyance was to, say, "Harriet and Daniel Campbell, husband and wife, and their heirs and assigns." A tenancy by the entirety differs from a joint tenancy and tenancy in common in that neither spouse can convey his or her interest without the express consent of the other. Since neither can voluntarily convey his or her interest, the creditors of one spouse cannot levy on the property. (However, if the spouses are jointly liable to the creditors, then the creditors can usually levy on the tenancy.) Divorce terminates a tenancy by the entirety and, in most states, creates a tenancy in common. The tenancy by the entirety is not recognized in many states.[10]

Condominiums ("Real Estate in the Sky")

A condominium involves a form of ownership that combines elements of both individual and concurrent ownership. Prior to the 1960s, the condominium ownership form was virtually unknown in Anglo-American law. The National Housing Act of 1961 helped create incentives for this form of ownership by authorizing FHA mortgage insurance on single-family units in multi-family structures. Soon after this, state legislation paved the way for rapid development of condominiums. In a condominium, each unit is individually owned. The units vary from the size of a one or two bedroom apartment to the size of a very large home. (Condominiums are sometimes offices in commercial buildings.) Each owner has an undivided interest (tenancy in common) in the "common areas" of the condominium, including stairways, halls, elevators, recreational facilities, courtyards, and parking lots. Each owner pays an annual fee for the upkeep of these areas.

Several advantages accompany condominium ownership. First, it can provide tax deductions for interest on the mortgage and taxes that

---

10. See Dorf v. Tuscarora Pipeline Co., 48 N.J.Super. 26, 136 A.2d 778 (1957) and Lindenfelser v. Lindenfelser 396 Pa. 530, 153 A.2d 901 (1959). Some of the states that recognize tenancy by the entirety require express language to create it, thereby modifying the common law rule.

previously were available only to *owners* of real estate, not to tenants. Second, condominiums can be constructed in areas that previously were available only for apartment buildings. This gives the condominium owner greater flexibility in choosing where to live, since in some locations only apartment buildings are economically feasible. Third, condominiums generally provide greater security, since a large number of units are located on one parcel of land. Fourth, the normal upkeep of a house is eliminated, and the owners need pay only a small annual fee for upkeep of the common areas. Fifth, a condominium can amass large sums of money to spend on the common areas. There are also many disadvantages to condominiums; one is that there is no guarantee against escalation of upkeep fees.

TRANSFER OF OWNERSHIP

There are a number of ways ownership of real property can pass from one person to another. They include deed, will, eminent domain, adverse possession, and inheritance. Conveyance by deed includes transfer by sale and by gift.

Conveyance by Deed

Possession and title to land are passed from person to person by means of a **deed**—the instrument of conveyance of real property. Deeds are writings signed by the owner of property by which title to it is transferred to another. They must meet certain requirements. Exhibit 52-1 shows a deed.

REQUIREMENTS OF A VALID DEED Unlike contracts, a deed does not have to be supported by legally sufficient consideration. Gifts of real property are common, and they require deeds even though there is no consideration for the gift. The necessary requirements for a valid deed are: (1) the names of the buyer (grantee) and seller (grantor), (2) words evidencing an intent to convey (for example, "I hereby bargain, sell, grant, or give"), (3) a legally sufficient

description of the land, (4) the grantor's (and usually the spouse's) signature, and (5) delivery of the deed.

Types of Deeds

GENERAL WARRANTY DEED General warranty deeds warrant the greatest number of things. In most states, special language is required to make a general warranty deed. If the deed states that the seller is providing the "usual covenants," most courts will imply all of the following covenants (warranties) of title:

1. *A covenant of seisin and a covenant of the right to convey* warrant that the seller has title and the power to convey the estate that the deed describes. For example, if A, the owner of a life estate in Whiteacre, attempts to convey a fee simple to B, A's covenant of seisin will be breached. If B is damaged by A's breach, then B is entitled to recover from A.

2. *A covenant against encumbrances* guarantees that the property being sold or conveyed is not subject to any outstanding rights or interests that will diminish the value of the land, except as stated. Examples of common encumbrances include mortgages, liens, profits, easements, and private deed restrictions on the use of land. Unless the deed expressly states that the conveyance is subject to a particular encumbrance, a covenant against encumbrances will be breached if the buyer discovers an undisclosed encumbrance. Again, as in the case of a covenant of seisin, the buyer is entitled to recover for any damage caused by the breach of this covenant.

3. *A covenant for quiet enjoyment* guarantees that the grantee or buyer will not be disturbed in his or her possession of the land by the grantor or any third persons. For example, suppose Nancy Thomas sells her two-acre lot and office building by general warranty deed. Subsequently, a third person shows better title than Nancy had and proceeds to evict the buyer. Here the covenant for quiet enjoyment has been breached, and the buyer can recover the purchase price of the land plus any other damages incurred in being evicted.

EXHIBIT 52-1

A TYPICAL DEED

Warranty Deed

This Indenture, Made the   day of   , A.D. 19
BETWEEN

of the County of   , and State of   , of the first part, and

*whose permanent address is   , of the County of
, and State of   , of the second part,*
Witnesseth, *That, the said part   of the first part, for and in consideration of the sum of
Dollars,
lawful money of the United States of America, to   in hand paid by the said part
of the second part, at or before the enlealing and delivery of these presents, the receipt whereof is
hereby acknowledged,   granted, bargained, sold, aliened, remised, released, conveyed
and confirmed, and by these presents do   grant, bargain, sell alien, remise, release, convey
and confirm unto the said part   of the second part, and   heirs and assigns
forever, all the following piece , parcel or tract of land, situate, lying and being in the
County of   , State of   , and more
particularly described as follows:*

Together *with all and singular the tenements, hereditaments and appurtenances thereunto
belonging or in anywise appertaining, and the reversion and reversions, remainder and remainders,
rents, issues and profits thereof, and also all the estate, right, title, interest, dower and right of
dower, separate estate, property, possession, claim and demand whatsoever, as well as in equity,
of the said part   of the first part, of, in and to the same, and every part and parcel
thereof, with the appurtenances.*

To Have and To Hold   *the above granted, bargained and described premises, with the
appurtenances, unto the said part   of the second part,   heirs and
assigns, to   own proper use, benefit and behoof forever.
     And the said part   of the first part, for   and for   heirs, executors
and administrators, do   covenant, promise and agree to and with the said part   of
the second part,   heirs and assigns, that the said part   of the first part, at the
time of the enlealing and delivery of these presents,   lawfully seized of and in all
and singular the above granted, bargained and described premises, with the appurtenances, and
              good right, full power and lawful authority to grant, bargain, sell and convey
the same in manner and form aforesaid. And the said part   of the second part,
heirs and assigns, shall and may at all times hereafter peaceably and quietly have, hold, use,
occupy, possess and enjoy the above granted premises and every part and parcel thereof, with
the appurtenances, without any let, suit, trouble, molestation, eviction or disturbance of the said
part   of the first part,   heirs or assigns, or of any other person or persons lawfully
claiming or to claim the same, by, through and under the grantor   herein.*

BROWN v. LOBER

Court of Appeals of Illinois,
1978.
63 Ill.App.3d 727, 20 Ill.Dec.
286, 379 N.E.2d 1354.

BACKGROUND AND FACTS Brown purchased land from Bost in 1957.
*The warranty deed mentioned no encumbrances. In 1974 Brown sold
mineral rights in the land to Consolidated Coal Company. In 1976 it was
discovered that Brown did not own the subsurface mineral rights free
and clear as indicated by the warranty deed of 1957. Consolidated
refused (rightly so) to pay the balance due on its purchase of the mineral
rights, and Brown filed suit against Bost for breach of covenant against
encumbrances. Bost defended on the ground that the statute of limitations for breach of covenant against encumbrances was ten years, and
therefore Brown was barred from bringing suit.*

And the said part   of the first part, for,   and for   heirs, warrants the above described and hereby granted and released premises, and every part and parcel thereof, with the appurtenances, unto the said part   of the second part,
heirs and assigns, against the said part   of the first part,   heirs, and against all and every person or persons whomsoever lawfully claiming or to claim the same, by, through and under the grantor   herein, shall and will warrant and by these presents forever defend.

In Witness Whereof. The said part   of the first part   hereunto set hand   and seal   the day and year first above written.

Signed, sealed and delivered in presence of us:

_____   _____(Seal)

_____   _____(Seal)

State of Florida.   } ss.
County of _____

On this day personally appeared before me,
                              to me well known and known to me to be the individual   described in and who executed the foregoing deed of conveyance, and acknowledged that   executed the same for the purpose therein expressed, whereupon it is prayed that the same may be recorded.

In Witness Whereof, I have hereunto affixed my hand and official seal, this day of   , A.D. 19   .

(Seal)   _____
                                            NOTARY PUBLIC

My commission expires: _____

State of Florida.   } ss.
County of _____

I,   , a
in and for said County and State, do certify that on the   day of   , A.D. 19   , personally appeared before me,
                              and
his wife, to me well known, and known to me to be the individual   described in and who executed the foregoing deed, and severally acknowledged that   executed the same for the purposes therein mentioned, and the said
                      , upon a separate and private examination, made separate and apart from her husband, then and there acknowledged before me that she executed the said deed for the purpose of conveying and relinquishing her dower and right of dower, homestead and separate estate in and to the land therein described, and also in token of having consented to the alienation of said described lands, and that she did the same freely and voluntarily, and without any constraint, apprehension, fear or compulsion of or from her said husband.

Given under my hand and official seal at   in said County and State, on this   day of   , A.D. 19   .

My commission expires: _____   _____
                                            NOTARY PUBLIC

DECISION AND RATIONALE   Brown was not barred by the statute of limitations from suing for breach of covenant against encumbrances. The statute of limitations provides that any suit for breach of covenant against encumbrances must be brought within ten years of the time the action accrues. Some states hold that the action accrues at the time the deed is delivered (since the covenant is either broken or not at that point). However, the court took the position that the statute begins to run when the landowner begins to suffer substantial damages because of the breach of the covenant. "[E]ven though the deed was made some 19 years previous to the suit, there was nothing done by the owner of the

> two-thirds coal interest to interfere with the grantee's rights. So far as the agreed state of facts shows no one attempted to assert paramount title to the underlying coal until 1976. It was not until then that the plaintiffs had any right to bring suit against the grantor on his covenant of warranty."

SPECIAL WARRANTY DEED The general warranty deed gives all the covenants of title listed above, but the special warranty deed (also known as deed with covenant against grantor's acts) warrants only that the grantor or seller has not previously done anything to lessen the value of the real estate. If the special warranty deed discloses all liens or other encumbrances, the seller will not be liable to the buyer if a third person subsequently interferes with the buyer's ownership. However, if the third person's claim arises out of, or is related to, some act of the seller, the seller will be liable to the buyer for damages. Both the special warranty deed and the general warranty deed warrant that the seller has "marketable" title. Common defects that may render a title unmarketable include variations in the names of grantors and grantees, breaks in the chain of title, outstanding liens, and defectively executed deeds in the chain of title.

QUIT CLAIM DEED A **quit claim** deed warrants less than any other deed. Essentially, it simply conveys to the grantee whatever interest the grantor had. In other words, if the grantor had nothing, then the grantee receives nothing. Naturally, if the grantor had a defective title, or no title at all, a conveyance by general warranty deed or special warranty deed will not cure the defects. However, such deeds will give the buyer a cause of action to sue the seller. A quit claim deed gives no cause of action. The buyer is simply left with whatever the seller had.

Quit claim deeds are often used to clear up past defects in the title. Suppose H and W own a parcel of land as tenants by the entirety.[11] They decide to sell it, and H makes out a deed in his name only. B, the buyer, keeps the property for several years and then wishes to sell it to C. C's

attorney, while examining the title, notices that the deed from H and W was signed by H alone. Therefore, W has an outstanding interest in the property that creates a "cloud" over C's title. C's attorney induces W to convey any interest she may have by quit claim deed to either C or B before advising his client to make the purchase. Thus, the quit claim deed removes the cloud over the title, and C, after purchasing the land from B, becomes the fee simple owner of the land. Quit claims are often used among tenants in common where one tenant "releases" interest to another.

Recording the Deed

Deeds are recorded in the presence of a notary public in the county where the property is located. Most statutes require that the deed be signed by the grantor in the presence of two attesting witnesses before it can be recorded. The grantor is then required to *acknowledge* the deed in the presence of a notary public. The purpose of recording the deed is to give notice to the world that a certain person is now the owner of a certain parcel of real estate. Putting everyone on notice as to the true owner means that the previous owners cannot fraudulently convey the land to a subsequent purchaser.

At common law, priorities as to titles were governed by a *first in time, first in right* rule. To illustrate: Suppose J sells Shady Acres to A. A receives the deed from J and is considered the true owner. If J subsequently attempts to convey the property to B, B will receive nothing, since A is the true owner.

Today this rule generally governs. However, in the example above, if B is a bona fide purchaser, he may prevail over A unless A has recorded the deed. A *bona fide purchaser* is a person who pays valuable consideration for the land, who acts in good faith, and who has no notice of a previous conveyance or sale.

---

11. An estate held in tenancy by the entirety cannot be conveyed unless both spouses sign the sales contract and deed.

Notice is accomplished by recording, so virtually every state has statutes defining the requirements of recording. Once the deed to Shady Acres is recorded, the records serve as notice to the whole world that A is the true owner. B cannot then be a bona fide purchaser, since the records give him *constructive* notice of the true owner. Before purchasing real estate, everyone is required to check the county records.

Warranty of Habitability

Under the common law the purchaser of a home was entitled to certain warranties with respect to title of the property purchased. However, the common law rule of *caveat emptor* ("let the buyer beware") held that the seller of a home made no warranties with respect to the soundness or fitness of the home unless such a warranty was specifically included in the deed or contract of sale. While *caveat emptor* is still the rule of law in many states, there is currently a strong trend against it and in favor of an implied warranty of habitability. Under this new approach, the courts hold that the seller of a new house warrants that it will be fit for human habitation regardless of whether any such warranty is included in the deed or contract of sale. Essentially, under an implied warranty of habitability, the seller warrants that the house is in reasonable working order and is of reasonably sound construction.

Historically, the protection afforded a new home buyer under the doctrine of *caveat emptor* has not been satisfactory since the buyer of a new home would only recover for defective workmanship if he or she could prove that the seller (builder) of the home was *negligent* in constructing the home. Recall from the chapter on torts that proof of negligence requires a plaintiff to prove the existence of a certain standard of care, and the unreasonable violation of that standard. Such facts are not easily proved in a court of law. Under an implied warranty of habitability, the purchser is only required to prove that the home he or she has purchased was somehow defective and to prove the damages which the defect caused. Thus,

under warranty of habitability theory, the seller of a new home is in effect a guarantor of the home's fitness.

Sale of Real Estate

Most transfers of ownership interest in real property are accomplished by means of a sale. The sale of real estate is similar to the sale of goods. It involves a transfer of ownership, often with certain warranties. However, in the sale of real estate, certain formalities are observed that are not required in the sale of goods. To meet the requirements of law, a deed must be signed and delivered.[12] In most states, the deed must also be recorded. In order to illustrate how a transfer of ownership in real property is accomplished, a typical real estate transaction is outlined below.

A Typical Procedure in the Sale of Real Estate

Suppose Janet Parker owns a parcel of real estate—a two-acre lot with an office building. Since her company is expanding to a new location, she has decided to sell the property. The first thing she will do is to attempt to locate a buyer. This can be accomplished in different ways. She can put the property up for sale herself, or she can employ a real estate broker or agent to help her locate a buyer.

LOCATING A BUYER Brokers generally find buyers because they can make a commission or percentage of the selling price. The broker can put Parker's property on an *open listing*. This means that the broker must produce a buyer who is ready, willing, and able to purchase the real estate. The broker who is the first to produce such a buyer is entitled to the commission. Alternatively, Parker can have an *exclusive agency* with the broker. In this type of arrangement, the broker has the exclusive right as an agent to sell the property, although Parker can employ another broker. If she does, the first

---

12. The phrase *signed, sealed, and delivered* used to refer to the requirements for transferring title to real property by deed. The seal has fallen from use, but signature and delivery are still required.

**EXHIBIT 52-2
A TYPICAL
CONTRACT**

SEEK THE SERVICE OF YOUR ATTORNEY PRIOR TO SIGNING

CONTRACT FOR SALE AND PURCHASE

PARTIES: __John Seller and Jane Seller, his wife_____, as "SELLER,"
of __Miami, Florida_____ (Phone _____).
and __Tom Buyer and Tess Buyer, his wife_____, as "BUYER,"
of __Decatur, Georgia_____ (Phone _____).
hereby agree that the Seller shall sell and the Buyer shall buy the following property upon the terms and conditions hereinafter set forth (INCLUDING THE STANDARDS ON THE REVERSE SIDE HEREOF), to-wit:

1. (a) Legal description of real estate located in _____Dade_____ County, Florida, to-wit:

> Lot 1 of Block 3 of Happy Acres according to the plat thereof recorded in Plat Book 4, page 65, of the Public Records of Dade County, Florida, together with one G. E. refrigerator, Serial Number xxx, and one Fedders air conditioner, Serial Number xxxx, located therein. The purchase price includes $500 for the refrigerator and air conditioner.

(b) Personal property included, to-wit: one G. E. Refrigerator and one Fedders air conditioner

(c) Street address, if any, of the property being conveyed __1000 Underwater Drive, Juno, Florida__

II. PURCHASE PRICE .... $ __21,500.00__
   PAYMENT:
   (a) Deposit to be held in trust by _____Real Tor_____ in the amount of ...... $ __2,000.00__
   (b) Subject to AND assumption of Mortgage in favor of ____Ace Federal____
      bearing interest at __7½__ % per annum and payable as to principal and interest $ __144.00__ per month
      having an approximate present principal balance of .... $ __15,300.00__
   (c) Purchase money mortgage and note bearing interest at __8__ % on terms set forth hereinbelow
      in the principal amount of .... $ __3,000.00__
   (d) Other .... $ _____
   (e) Balance to close (excluding deposit) subject to adjustments and prorations ...... $ __1,200.00__
                                                                   TOTAL $ __21,500.00__

III. EVIDENCE OF TITLE: In the event a base abstract to the subject property exists then the same shall be brought current as otherwise provided herein, but if such abstract does not exist then within __15__ days from the date of this Contract, the Seller shall, at his expense, deliver to the Buyer or his attorney, in accordance with Standard "A" on reverse side either (CHECK) ☒ (1) OR ☐ (2) (1) Abstract or (2) title guarantee commitment with fee owner's title policy premium payable by Seller at closing.

IV. TIME FOR ACCEPTANCE: If this Contract is not executed by both of the parties hereto on or before __September 1, 1974__, the aforesaid deposit shall be at the option of the Buyer, returned to him and this agreement shall thereafter be null and void. The date of Contract shall be the date when the last one of the Seller and Buyer has signed this Contract.

V. CLOSING DATE: This transaction shall be closed and the deed and other closing papers delivered on the __10th__ day of __November__ 19__74__ unless extended by other provisions of this Contract.

VI. RESTRICTIONS, EASEMENTS, LIMITATIONS: The Buyer shall take title subject to: Zoning, restrictions, prohibitions and other requirements imposed by governmental authority; Restrictions and matters appearing on the plat or otherwise common to the subdivision; Public utility easements of record, provided said easements are located on the side or rear lines of the property and are not more than ten feet in width as to the rear line and seven and one half feet in width as to the side line, unless otherwise specified herein; Taxes for year of closing and subsequent years; assumed mortgages and purchase money mortgages, if any; Other _____and restrictions in deed recorded in Deed Book 65, page 235____ provided, however, that none of the foregoing shall prevent use of the property for the purpose of _____a residence_____

VII. POSSESSION: Seller covenants and warrants that there are no parties in possession other than the Seller; and if the property is rented, the tenant(s) disclosed pursuant to Standard "G" on reverse side. Seller agrees to deliver possession of said property at time of closing unless otherwise specified below. If possession is to be delivered prior to closing, Buyer assumes all risk of loss to the property from date of possession, shall be responsible and liable for maintenance thereof from date of possession, and shall be deemed to have accepted the property, real and personal, in its existing condition as of time of taking possession

VIII. ASSIGNABILITY: (CHECK ONE) Buyer ☒ may assign ☐ may not assign this contract

IX. TYPEWRITTEN OR HANDWRITTEN PROVISIONS: Typewritten or handwritten provisions inserted in this form or attached hereto as Addenda shall control all printed provision in conflict therewith

X. FINANCING: If the purchase price or any part thereof is to be financed by a third party loan, this Contract is conditioned upon the Buyer obtaining a firm commitment for said loan within _____ days from date hereof, at an interest rate not to exceed _____%, term of _____ years, and in the principal amount of $_____ Buyer agrees to use reasonable diligence to obtain said loan and failing the obtaining of the same within said time period, either party hereto may cancel this Contract

XI. SPECIAL CLAUSES:

WITNESS: (Two are required)   Executed by Buyer on __August 15, 1974__

I. Witness _____   s/ __Tom Buyer_____ (SEAL)

U. Witness _____   s/ __Tess Buyer_____ (SEAL)

WITNESS: (Two are required)   Executed by Seller on __August 31, 1974__

H. Witness _____   s/ __John Seller_____ (SEAL)

S. Witness _____   s/ __Jane Seller_____ (SEAL)

Deposit received on __August 15, 1974__ to be held subject to this Contract; if check, subject to clearance

                                                   By __Real Tor_____ (SEAL)
                                                        Escrow Agent

broker is still entitled to a commission. However, if Parker sells the property without the assistance of the broker, she need not pay the commission. Finally, Parker can give the broker an *exclusive right to sell*. In this situation, the broker is entitled to a commission no matter who sells the real estate—Parker, this broker, or another broker. An exclusive right to sell usual-

BROKER'S COMPENSATION: Seller agrees to pay the real estate broker named below, at time of closing, from the disbursements of the proceeds of sale, compensation in the amount of __5__ % of gross purchase price for his services in effecting the sale. In the event Buyer fails to perform and deposit is retained, 50% thereof, but not exceeding the broker's compensation as above computed, shall be paid to the broker, as full consideration for broker's services including costs expended by broker, and the balance shall be applied first in payment of attorney's fees and other expenses incurred on behalf of Seller, and the remainder shall be paid to Seller. If the transaction shall not be closed because of refusal of Seller to perform, the Seller shall pay said commission in full to broker on demand.

s/ **Real Tor** _____ (SEAL)   s/ **John Seller** _____ (SEAL)
             Broker   Seller

By _____   s/ **Jane Seller** _____ (SEAL)

This form has been approved by _____

and _____

STANDARDS FOR REAL ESTATE TRANSACTIONS

A. EVIDENCE OF TITLE (1) A base contract of title prepared or brought current by a reputable and existing abstract firm (if not existing then certified as correct by an existing firm) purporting to be an accurate synopsis of the instrument affecting the title to subject real property recorded in public records of the county wherein the land is situated, through date of this Contract. For purposes of this Contract a "base abstract" shall mean an abstract commencing with the earliest public records, or such later date as may be customary in the county wherein the land is situate, which has been last certified to a date within 35 years immediately preceding the date of this Contract. Seller shall convey a marketable title in accordance with the Standards adopted from time to time by The Florida Bar, subject only to liens, encumbrances, exceptions or qualifications set forth in this Contract and those which shall be discharged by Seller at or before closing. Upon closing of this transaction such abstract shall become the property of Buyer, subject to the right of retention thereof by first mortgagee until fully paid; or (2) A title guarantee commitment issued by a qualified title insuror agreeing to issue to Buyer, upon recording of the deed hereafter mentioned, an Owner's Guarantee in the amount of the purchase price, insuring title of the Buyer to the real property, subject only to liens, encumbrances, exceptions or qualifications set forth in this Contract and those which shall be discharged by Seller at or before closing. Buyer shall have thirty (30) days, if abstract, or five (5) days, if title guarantee, from date of receiving evidence of title, to examine same. If title is found defective, Buyer shall, within three (3) days thereafter, notify Seller in writing specifying defect(s). If said defects render title unmarketable, Seller shall have 120 days from receipt of notice within which to remove said defect(s), and if Seller is unsuccessful in removing them within said time, Buyer shall have the option of either (1) accepting the title as it then is, or (2) demanding a refund of all monies paid hereunder which shall forthwith be returned to Buyer and thereupon Buyer and Seller shall be released of all further obligations under the Contract; however, Seller agrees that he will, if title is found to be unmarketable, use diligent effort to correct the defects in title within the time limit provided therefor, including the bringing of necessary suits.

B. EXISTING MORTGAGES The Seller shall obtain and furnish a statement from the mortgagee(s) setting forth principal balance, method of payment, interest rate, and whether the mortgage(s) is in good standing. In the event a mortgage requires acceptance or approval of Buyer by the mortgagee in order to avoid default, and mortgage does not approve the Buyer, then Buyer, at his option, may rescind the contract and receive a return of all deposits made hereunder.

C. PURCHASE MONEY MORTGAGES The purchase money note and mortgage, if any, shall provide for a thirty (30) day grace period in the event of default; if it is a first mortgage and a 15 day grace period if a second mortgage, shall provide for right of prepayment in whole or in part without penalty; shall not provide for acceleration in event of resale of the property; and shall be otherwise in form and content required by Seller's attorney; provided, however, Seller shall not require clauses not customarily found in mortgages and mortgage notes generally utilized by savings and loan institutions in the county wherein the property is located. Said mortgage shall require the owner of the property encumbered to keep all prior liens and encumbrances in good standing and forbid the owner of the property from accepting modifications of or future advances under prior mortgage(s).

D. SURVEY The Buyer, within time and examination thereof, may have the property surveyed at his expense. If the survey, certified by a registered Florida surveyor shows any encroachment on said property or that improvements intended to be located on the subject property in fact encroach on lands of others, or violate any of the Contract covenants, the same shall be treated as a title defect. Any survey prepared in connection with or as a consequence of this transaction may include a description of the property under the Florida Coordinate System as defined in Chapter 177, Florida Statutes.

E. TERMITE INSPECTION Within ten (10) days from date of this Contract Buyer may have the improvements inspected at Buyer's expense by a licensed and bonded exterminator to determine whether there is any active terminate infestation or existing substantial damage from prior terminate infestation in the improvements. The consequence of said infestation or damage shall be that Seller shall pay all costs of treatment required to remedy such infestation or damage, including cost of repairing or replacing all portions of said improvement which are infested or damaged. However, in the event costs to be incurred are more than three percent (3%) of assessed valuation of improvements to the real property, based upon the most recent assessment by the County Tax Assessor, then Buyer shall have the option of cancelling this Contract within ten (10) days after receipt of the termite inspection report by giving written notice to Seller, or Buyer may elect to proceed with the transaction, in which event Buyer shall receive a credit at closing of an amount equal to three (3%) percent of said assessed valuation. "Termite" shall be deemed to include all wood destroying organisms.

F. INGRESS AND EGRESS Seller covenants and warrants that there is ingress and egress to said property.

G. LEASES Seller shall, not less than fifteen (15) days prior to closing, furnish to Buyer copies of all written leases and estoppel letters from each tenant specifying the nature and duration of said tenant's occupancy, rental rates and advanced rent and security deposits paid by tenant. In the event Seller is unable to obtain such letters from tenants, the same information shall be furnished by Seller to Buyer within said time period in the form of a Seller's affidavit, and Buyer may thereafter contact tenants to confirm such information. Seller shall deliver and assign all original leases to Buyer at closing.

H. LIENS Seller shall, both as to the realty and personalty being sold hereunder, furnish to Buyer at time of closing an affidavit attesting to the absence, unless otherwise provided for herein, of any financing statements, claims of lien or potential lienors known to Seller and further attesting that there have been no improvements to the property for 90 days immediately preceding date of closing. If the property has been improved within said time, Seller shall deliver releases or waivers of all mechanic's liens, executed by general contractors, subcontractors, suppliers, and materialmen, in addition to Seller's lien affidavit, setting forth the names of all such general contractors, subcontractors, suppliers and materialmen and further reciting that in fact all bills for work to the subject property which could serve as a basis for a mechanic's lien have been paid or will be paid at closing.

I. PLACE OF CLOSING Closing shall be held at office of Seller's attorney, if said office is located in the county wherein subject property is located; if not, then as otherwise agreed upon.

J. TIME Time is of the essence of this Contract. Any reference herein to time periods of less than 6 days shall in the computation thereof exclude Saturdays, Sundays and legal holidays, and any time period provided for herein which shall end on a Saturday, Sunday or legal holiday shall extend to 5:00 p.m. of the next full business day.

K. DOCUMENTS FOR CLOSING Seller's attorney shall prepare deed, mechanic's lien affidavit and any corrective instruments that may be required in connection with perfecting the title; Buyer's attorney will prepare closing statement, mortgage, mortgage note, and financing statements.

L. EXPENSES State surtax and documentary stamps which are required to be affixed to the instrument of conveyance and cost of recording any corrective instruments shall be paid by Seller. Documentary stamps to be affixed to the note or notes secured by the purchase money mortgage, intangible tax on mortgage and cost of recording the deed, purchase money mortgage and financing statement shall be paid by Buyer.

M. PRORATION OF TAXES (REAL AND PERSONAL) Taxes shall be prorated based on the current year's tax with due allowance made for maximum allowable discount and homestead or other exemptions if allowed for said year. If closing occurs at a date when the current year's taxes are not fixed, and current year's assessment is available, taxes will be prorated based upon such assessment, and the prior year's millage. If current year's assessment is not available, then taxes will be prorated on the prior year's tax; provided, however, if there are completed improvements on the property by January 1st of year of closing, which improvements were not in existence on January 1st of the prior year, then taxes shall be prorated to date of closing based upon the prior year's millage and at an equitable assessment to be agreed upon between the parties, failing which, request will be made to the county tax assessor for an informal assessment taking into consideration homestead exemption, if any. However, any tax proration based on an estimate may at request of either party to the transaction, be subsequently readjusted upon receipt of tax bill and a statement to that effect is to be set forth in the closing statement.

N. SPECIAL ASSESSMENT LIENS Certified, confirmed and ratified special assessment liens as of date of closing (and not as of date of Contract) are to be paid by Seller. Pending liens as of date of closing shall be assumed by Buyer, provided, however, that where the improvement has been substantially completed as of the date of Contract, such pending lien shall be considered as certified, confirmed or ratified and Seller shall, at closing, be charged an amount equal to the last estimate by the public body of the assessment for the improvement.

O. PERSONAL PROPERTY The Seller represents and warrants that all major appliances, plumbing, electrical installations and machinery included in the sale shall be in working order and repair as of date of closing. Buyer may at his sole expense and on reasonable notice, cause an inspection to be made by a licensed firm or firms dealing in the repair and maintenance of such items with said inspections taking place within the period allowed for examination of the evidence of title or the taking of possession of subject property by Buyer, whichever event occurs first. Failure to object in writing to Seller within said time period shall be deemed a waiver of such right. Valid objections shall be resolved at cost of Seller with funds therefor being escrowed at closing. If a purchase money mortgage is taken by Seller, all personal property being conveyed will, at option of Seller, be subject to the lien of the mortgage note and evidenced by a recorded financing statement.

P. RISK OF LOSS If the improvements are damaged by fire or other casualty prior to closing, and cost of restoring same does not exceed three percent (3%) of the assessed valuation of the improvements so damaged, cost of such restoration shall be an obligation of the Seller and closing shall proceed pursuant to the terms of the Contract. In the event the cost of repair of restoration shall be an amount equal to three (3%) percent or more of the assessed valuation of improvements so damaged, Buyer shall have the option of either taking the property as is, together with any insurance proceeds payable by virtue of such loss or damage, or of cancelling this Contract and receiving return of all deposits made hereunder.

Q. MAINTENANCE Between date of contract and date of closing the property, including lawn, shrubbery and pool, if any shall be maintained by Seller in the condition as it existed as of date of Contract, ordinary wear and tear excepted.

R. PROCEEDS OF SALE AND CLOSING PROCEDURE The deed shall be recorded and evidence of title continued at Buyer's expense, to show title in Buyer, without any encumbrance or change from the date of the last evidence which would render Seller's title unmarketable, and the cash proceeds of sale shall be held in escrow by Seller's attorney or by such other escrow agent as may be mutually agreed upon for a period of not longer than five (5) days. If Seller's title is rendered unmarketable, Buyer's attorney shall within said five (5) day period, notify Seller's attorney in writing of the defect and Seller shall have thirty (30) days from date of receipt of such notification to cure said defect. In the event Buyer fails to make timely demand for refund, he shall take title as is, waiving all rights against Seller as to such intervening defect except as may be available to Buyer by virtue of warranties, if any, contained in deed. In the event a portion of the purchase price is to be derived from institutional financing or re-financing, the requirements of the lending institution as to place, time and procedures for closing, and for disbursement of mortgage proceeds, shall control, anything in this Contract to the contrary notwithstanding.

ly lasts for a specified period of time; after that time, Parker is free to make arrangements with another broker if the property has not yet been sold.

CONTRACT OF SALE Once a buyer is located, a contract for the sale of the land must be negotiated. See Exhibit 52-2 for a typical contract. Here Parker must decide, inter alia, the cost of title examination and insurance, how to allocate property taxes, and what the actual purchase price will be. The contract for the sale of real estate must be in writing to be enforceable. The writing need not specify all the details of the transaction, but it should contain the essential terms of the bargain and be signed by the parties. The essential terms are: (1) an identification of the parties, (2) the description of the land to be conveyed, (3) the purchase price, and (4) the signature. In most cases, after the details of the transaction have been negotiated, an attorney will draw up a long, formal document that will be signed by both the seller and the buyer.

TITLE EXAMINATION   After the sales contract has been negotiated, the buyer will begin the *title examination*. Essentially, a title examination is the examination of all past transfers and sales of the piece of property in question. Every county has a filing system where deeds, plats, and other instruments are recorded. A skilled examiner can determine from these records whether there are any liens, easements, profits, or other encumbrances on the land. These records, known as the chain of title, go back to the original grant or deed from the United States or the particular state where the land is located.[13] Usually, private abstract companies prepare what is known as an *abstract*. This document lists all of the records relating to a particular parcel of land. The attorney and title examiner do not have to search through the records themselves. The examiner then gives an opinion as to the validity of the title. Often, the sales contract requires a buyer to purchase *title insurance*—an insurance that protects both the seller and the buyer in the event that someone is shown to have a better title. Title insurance companies have their own

staffs of attorneys and abstractors who examine titles on a full-time basis. Once a title insurance company's staff approves a title, the company will issue insurance on the property.

Along with the title examination, the sales contract may require the seller to make a survey of the land to check the exact boundaries and to make sure they coincide with the legal description contained in the deed and the county records. In addition, the survey makes sure no neighboring buildings or structures overlap onto the property.

OBTAINING A MORTGAGE   Ordinarily most buyers do not have enough cash to buy real estate outright, so they arrange for a loan. To obtain the loan, the purchaser must put the property up as collateral. *Mortgages* are essentially liens against the property that enable the lender to foreclose and sell the real estate if the borrower fails to make timely payments. In most cases, a bank or savings and loan association is contacted for financing. In some cases, the seller may agree to loan the buyer the purchase price in exchange for the buyer's promissory note and mortgage. Either type of mortgage is known as a *(first) purchase money mortgage* because the seller or lender supplies the buyer with the *money* to *purchase* the house.

CLOSING   The final stage of the sale is called the *closing*. The transaction is closed by the buyer paying the purchase price and the seller delivering the deed to the buyer. The closing is usually attended by the buyer, the seller, their attorneys, and the lender. When the property is being mortgaged, the lender ordinarily closes the mortgage deal, paying the seller for the property and receiving a lien (mortgage) on the property at the same time.

Transfer by Will or Inheritance

Property that is transferred on an owner's death is passed either by *will* or by *inheritance*. If the owner of land dies with a will, the land that the owner had prior to death passes according to the

---

13.   Today the title search need not go back all the way to the grant from the government. Nearly every state has a marketable record title act that provides that the roots of title older than thirty or forty years are conclusively presumed to be valid. In other words, if the chain of title can be traced back thirty or forty years with no defects, no further search need be made.

terms of the will. If the owner dies without a will, state statutes prescribe how and to whom the property will pass. Ordinarily, when the owner dies without a will, the property passes to the deceased's living heirs. This topic is discussed in Chapter 55.

Eminent Domain

Eminent domain (condemnation) is the power of the government to take land for public use. When a new public highway or railroad is to be built, the government must decide where to build it and how much land to condemn. The government then starts a condemnation proceeding in which the owner can show why the land should not be appropriated for public use and the government or agency involved can show why the public needs this particular parcel of land. Once the government determines that the land is to be condemned or taken for public use, another proceeding is held to determine the fair value of the land, which is usually approximately equal to its market value. The fair value is paid to the property owner as compensation for the taking of the property. Under federal and state constitutions, government is not allowed to take property without paying just compensation for it. A condemnation transfers title from the owner to the government. Then the government is considered the true owner and can use the land for whatever purpose was originally contemplated.

Adverse Possession

Adverse possession is a means of obtaining title to land without a deed being delivered. Essentially, when one person possesses the property of another for a certain statutory period of time, usually twenty or twenty-one years, that person (called the adverse possessor) acquires title to the land and cannot be removed from the land by the original owner. The adverse possessor is vested with a perfect title just as if there had been a conveyance by deed. Once title to the property has been obtained, if the new owner abandons the premises, title will not pass to the original owner. It will *escheat* to the state according to state law.

In order to hold property adversely, four elements must be satisfied. First, possession must be actual and exclusive; that is, the possessor must take sole physical occupancy of the property. Second, the possession must be open, visible, and notorious, not secret or clandestine. The possessor must occupy the land for all the world to see. Third, possession must be continuous and peaceable for the required period of time. This means that the possessor must not be interrupted in the occupancy by the true owner or by the courts. Being evicted or being served with an eviction notice will stop the statute of limitations from running and likewise stop the adverse possession. Finally, possession must be hostile and adverse. In other words, the possessor must claim the property as against the whole world. He or she cannot live on the property with the permission of the owner. Thus, a tenant who holds over is not holding adversely to the landlord, since the law presumes that the landlord is permitting the tenant to stay. Until the tenant repudiates the landlord-tenant relationship, he or she is not occupying the premises with hostility and adversity. An adverse possessor cannot claim more land than he or she has continuously occupied (as by fencing in an area). Thus, someone living in a small shack on a thousand acre cattle farm cannot claim the whole thousand acres unless he or she has regularly and continuously used it.

QUESTIONS AND CASE PROBLEMS

1.   Pabst Brewing Company purchased two adjoining lots from Jones. A brewery was located on one lot, and a very expensive residence was on the other lot. At the time of the purchase, Jones was the fee simple owner of the brewery, but unknown to either party, he owned only a life estate in the residence. After the purchase, the character of the real estate in the area changed. Factories and other breweries with railroad tracks made the area undesirable for a residence, and

the house could not be rented profitably. Pabst removed the residence and graded down the property to fit it to commercial purposes, which greatly enhanced the property's value. Subsequently, Melms, who owned the remaining interest in the house sold by Jones, brought suit against Pabst to have himself declared owner of the property on which the residence stood and to recover damages for waste by Pabst. The waste claimed was the destruction of the residence and the grading down of the land to street level. Can Melms recover? [Melms v. Pabst Brewing Co., 104 Wis. 7, 79 N.W. 738 (1899)]

2. Waltz leased certain premises to Fetting Manufacturing Jewelry Company for five years at various annual rentals payable in monthly installments. Near the end of the term, the parties attempted to negotiate a new lease, but they could not agree on terms. Fetting gave timely notice to Waltz that he was preparing to move, but he asked Waltz to extend the lease for a month or two. Although the parties were unable to agree on terms for an extension of the lease, Fetting continued to occupy the premises for one month after the expiration of the lease, without Waltz's consent. Then Fetting vacated the premises and refused to pay any further rent. Waltz sued, contending that the unauthorized holding over obligated Fetting to pay for another year. Can Waltz recover? [Fetting Mfg. Jewelry Co. v. Waltz, 160 Md. 50, 152 A. 434 (1930)]

3. United Homes Corporation owned and managed an apartment complex in the state of Washington. McCutcheon, one of United Homes's tenants, was injured when he fell down an unlighted interior stairway. The stairway was unlighted because United Homes had negligently failed to change the overhead lightbulbs. The stairway on which McCutcheon sustained his injury was located at the end of the hallway and was used by all the tenants in the apartment building. Will United Homes Corporation be liable for McCutcheon's injury? Explain. Would the answer be different if the lease signed by McCutcheon contained a clause stating that the lessor could not be held liable for injuries that the lessee sustained while entering or leaving the building? [McCutcheon v. United Homes Corp., 2 Wash.App. 618, 469 P.2d 997 (1970)]

4. Wilmore, the owner of a tract of land known as Robinson's Beach, periodically rented parcels of the land to various persons who built bungalows on them. The bungalows, built without the consent or interference of Wilmore, were placed on cinder blocks that in turn rested on top of the ground. Water and electrical

hookups were made in a way that they could be readily removed. The bungalows were easily removable without injury either to them or to the land. Subsequently, Sigrol Realty Corporation purchased the land from Wilmore, but the purchase contract made no mention of the bungalows. Upon learning of the purchase, Valcich, the owner of several of the bungalows, began to remove them. Sigrol Realty brought an action to enjoin removal of the bungalows, claiming it purchased them as part of the realty. Should the injunction be issued? [Sigrol Realty Corp. v. Valcich, 12 App.Div.2d 430, 212 N.Y.S.2d 224 (1961)]

5. Piper and Mowris owned adjacent tracts of land. Mowris had purchased his land from Thomas and Beatrice Carr in 1925. At the time the Carrs sold the land to Mowris, they owned an easement across Piper's land. When they sold their land to Mowris, they also sold him their easement. Over the next thirty years, Mowris seldom used the right of way over Piper's land, and it became overgrown "like a wilderness." Does Mowris still own an easement over Piper's land? Assume that, thirty years ago, Piper had built a fence along the boundary line dividing his and Mowris's property and that this fence obstructed Mowris's right of way. Has Mowris lost his easement? [Piper v. Mowris, 466 Pa. 89, 351 A.2d 635 (1976)]

6. The owners of the Seven Palms Motor Inn decided that their motel was in need of renovation. Accordingly, they ordered a large quantity of bedspreads, curtain rods, and drapes from Sears, Roebuck and Company. Thereafter, Seven Palms Motor Inn failed to pay its bill, which amounted to approximately $8,000, including installation. Under Missouri law, a supplier of fixtures can establish a lien on the land and building to which the fixtures become attached. Sears sought to establish such a lien to make it easier to recover the debt that Seven Palms owed it. Which, if any, of the above-named items will Sears be able to argue are fixtures? [Sears, Roebuck & Co. v. Seven Palms Motor Inn, 530 S.W.2d 695 (Mo.1975)]

7. X conveyed a life estate in certain land to her son, S, with the remainder to T. The deed was properly executed, signed by X, and delivered to S, but it was never recorded. X died one year later, leaving S her sole heir. Eighteen months later, S sold the land to P. The title records showed that the land was owned by X; therefore, P ascertained that S was X's sole heir. After the sale, T, who then occupied the land refused to relinquish possession to P. Who is entitled to the land? [Earle v. Fiske, 103 Mass. 491 (1870)]

8. Grow Investment and Mortgage Company con-

veyed to Larry Jones, by warranty deed, a residential lot located in Utah County. Among other things, the deed provided that the lot was subject to all "easements of record." Before Jones purchased the land, he inspected it and found an open irrigation ditch running down the east side and partly along the south side of the lot. It appeared to Jones that the ditch had at one time been used by the lot adjacent and to the north of the one that Jones was inspecting; it no longer seemed to be in use because it contained tree limbs, building refuse, weeds, and trash. After his inspection, Jones purchased the land from Grow Investment and later attempted to fill the ditch. The owners of the land in the lot adjacent and to the north of Jones's lot were able to stop Jones from filling the ditch since they had a legally valid easement by prescription in the ditch. What can Jones do? [Jones v. Grow Investment and Mortgage Co., 11 Utah 2d 326, 358 P.2d 909 (1961)]

9.   Morton was a construction contractor of residential properties. One of the houses that Morton built was sold by his agent to a purchaser named Humber. The house was new when Humber purchased it. Shortly after the purchase, Humber lit a fire in the fireplace, and, because of a crack in the hearth, the house caught fire, and was damaged extensively. It was unclear whether the crack was the result of Morton's negligence, but Humber sought to recover from Morton under the theory that when Morton sold the house to Humber, he warranted that it was reasonably fit for human habitation. Morton argued that that was not the law and that the common law rule of *caveat emptor* ("let the buyer beware") governed the sale of realty. Who is correct? [Humber v. Morton, 426 S.W.2d 554 (Tex.1968)]

10.   Smyth was the owner of a one-ninth interest in land. The other owners, who were cotenants, owned a combined eight-ninths interest in the property. Smyth and the other owners were tenants in common. The land was of considerable value, since large quantities of rock asphalt were just below its surface. Smyth mined one-ninth of the rock asphalt, sold it, and personally retained the profits. The other cotenants of the property sued Smyth, seeking a division of his profits from the mining operations among all the cotenants. Smyth claimed that since he took only one-ninth of the rock, which was his ownership share, he should not be divested of the profits. What result? [White v. Smyth, 147 Tex. 272, 214 S.W.2d 967 (1948)]

53

Future Interests, Nonpossessory Interests, and Land Use Control

The last chapter defined real property and then discussed the nature of an estate and how estates are acquired. Generally, the estates that were discussed were those in which the person having the estate (ownership interest) was also in *present* possession of the land. This chapter discusses estates and other types of interests in land that do not involve present possession by the owner. The last part of the chapter discusses encumbrances on land that affect the way land can be used.

FUTURE INTERESTS

A person can convey an estate that is limited by a specified period of time; the life of the grantor, grantee, or other person; or by an occurrence. The person to whom such an estate is conveyed has a *present possessory interest*. Life estates, terms for years, and fee simple determinable estates are examples of estates that carry present possessory interests, and which include a residuary interest that may or may not have been disposed of by the grantor. This residuary interest is a *future interest*, and it can take several forms. If it remains in the grantor, it is called a *reversion*, a *possibility of reverter*, or a *power of termination*. The first two are by far the more common residuary interests that a grantor retains. If the future interest is not retained by the grantor, then it is called either a *remainder* or an *executory interest*. Remainders can be either *vested* or *contingent*, depending upon the terms of the conveyance.

630

Reversionary Interests and Powers of Termination

When a grantor owns a fee simple estate in land and conveys an estate to another with a duration that is less than the duration of the estate that the grantor owns, there is an undisposed residue remaining in the grantor. That undisposed residue is called a **reversion**. For example, X owns a fee simple estate and conveys a life estate in Blackacre to A. X has not disposed of the interest in the land that remains after A's life. Therefore, X has automatically retained a reversion, and the reversion is a future interest. It is preceded by A's life estate, which is an estate in possession. X's reversion is created by operation of law. X does not have a present possessory interest in Blackacre but has a *vested* future interest—that is, an absolute right to possession of Blackacre at some point in the future, a right that X can convey in the present.

If X conveys Blackacre "to A and her heirs," he conveys a fee simple absolute. There is no future interest in Blackacre, since X has conveyed the entire estate to A. But what if X conveys a fee simple determinable, which is slightly less than a fee simple absolute? What has X retained? Suppose X conveys Blackacre "to A and her heirs as long as it is used for educational purposes." X has conveyed a fee simple determinable and, by operation of law, has retained a **possibility of reverter**—a future interest in favor of the grantor that is contingent on the happening of the event named in the conveyance. The conveyance of a determinable fee that gives rise to a possibility of reverter usually includes the words *so long as, until, while,* or *during.*

Powers of termination are also future interests retained by a grantor who is conveying an estate subject to a condition. Powers of termination are similar to possibilities of reverter except that future possession by the grantor requires an affirmative act. (That is, it does not occur automatically.) For example, suppose X conveys Blackacre "to A and her heirs, but if liquor is sold on the premises, the right to enter and terminate the estate is re-served." X has retained a power of termination and has the right to repossess the land in the future if liquor is sold on the premises and if X acts affirmatively to retake possession of Blackacre.

Remainders and Executory Interests

If the owner of real property conveys an estate that is less than a fee simple absolute and does not retain the residuary interest, then that interest will take the form of either a **remainder** or an **executory interest**. As mentioned above, a remainder can be either vested or contingent. Both are future interests, but the holder of a vested remainder has an absolute right to possession at the end of the prior estate. The owner of a contingent remainder has only a conditional right to possession when the prior estate ends. Both are estates in land in favor of persons other than the grantor, and both can be transferred to other persons (that is, purchased and sold, inherited, devised or bequeathed). Suppose X, the owner of Blackacre, transfers it "to A for ninety-nine years remainder to D." A has a present possessory interest in Blackacre in the form of a ninety-nine-year term. D has a future possessory interest in Blackacre, which is presently vested and which takes effect instantly at the end of ninety-nine years. Note the difference between D's vested remainder in this example and E's contingent remainder in the following example. X conveys Blackacre "to C for life remainder to E if and only if E marries within C's life." In this example, C has a present possessory interest in the form of a life estate, and E has a contingent remainder—a future possessory interest that is not vested at present. Its vesting is *contingent* upon E's marrying within C's lifetime. If E does not marry within C's lifetime, then the remainder that E would have taken *reverts* to X, who, by operation of law, retains a possibility of reverter at the time of the conveyance. If E does marry during C's lifetime, then E's future possessory interest *vests* immediately, but E still cannot take possession of Blackacre until the end of C's life estate.

Executory interests are future possessory interests in real property that are conveyed to persons other than the grantor at the time of a conveyance. These interests were not recognized at common law but are recognized in all states today. Executory interests are similar to vested and contingent remainders, with one important difference. Executory interests do not occur instantly at the end of a prior estate. In the examples of vested and contingent remainders above, note that D's and E's remainder interests become possessory interests as soon as the preceding estates terminate naturally. Executory interests take effect either before or after the natural termination of a preceding estate. To illustrate, X conveys Blackacre "to A for twenty years, but if A should divorce, then Blackacre is to pass immediately to C." C has a future interest in Blackacre that will become a present possessory interest if A becomes divorced. C's future interest, which can *cut short* A's interest, is known as a *shifting* executory interest. If X conveys Blackacre "to B for life and one year after B's death to D," B has a life estate, and D has an executory interest that will not arise until one year after the termination of B's life estate. Such an executory interest is known as a *springing* executory interest. By operation of law, X retains a reversion in Blackacre of one year, and D's executory interest then *springs* from X.

Rule Against Perpetuities

The purpose of the Rule Against Perpetuities is to prevent the tying up of property ownership. The Rule achieves this purpose by preventing *remoteness in vesting*. In its simplest form, the Rule is: No interest is good unless it must vest, if at all, not later than twenty-one years after some life in being at the creation of the interest (excluding periods of gestation). The Rule is not a perfect solution to the problem of tying up title, but it is stated in such precise terms that *any* conveyance that ties up title for a long period of time will be voided by the Rule. Unfortunately, some conveyances that do not tie up title are also voided by the rule. Before looking at any examples of the Rule in operation, the student should note that interests in land can be created either by deed (*inter vivos*) or by will (at the grantor's death). This is important in determining the identity of the life in being to which the rule refers.

The first example is of a conveyance that is not voided by the Rule Against Perpetuities. Suppose X conveys Blackacre by deed "to B for life, then to C for life, then to D for life remainder to D's children." B, C, and D all have life estates, and D's children have a vested remainder in Blackacre. The Rule Against Perpetuities does not void the vested remainder of D's children, since their identity will be known at D's death (or within the period of gestation thereafter). Since X specifically names D in the conveyance, D must be alive at the creation of his or her interest and therefore is a life in being. The interests of D's children will vest, if at all, within twenty-one years of D's death, since their identities must be determined no later than nine months (the gestation period) after D's death. If D has no children, this will be known at D's death, and ownership of Blackacre will revert to X or X's heirs.

If X conveys Blackacre *by will* "to the first of my grandchildren to reach the age of twenty-one," this conveyance does not violate the Rule Against Perpetuities. Since the conveyance was by will, the interest in the first of X's grandchildren to reach twenty-one is not created until X's death. X's *children* will be deemed the "lives in being" under the Rule, since X can have no more children after death. Within twenty-one years of the death of any of X's children (the "lives in being"), the interest in X's *grandchildren* must vest, since no grandchild of X's can possibly reach the age of twenty-one more than twenty-one years after the death of the last of X's children (excluding periods of gestation). If X's will leaves Blackacre "to the first of my grandchildren to reach age thirty," the Rule Against Perpetuities will void any possible interest in X's grandchildren unless, at the time of X's death, one of the grandchildren is at least thirty years old. Even if, at X's death, X's oldest grandchild is five days short of thirty and in perfect health, he or she cannot obtain ownership of Blackacre under this latter version of X's will, since it is possible that he or she might die before age thirty and that none of X's other grandchildren will reach age thirty within twenty-one years of the death of X's last child. The Rule Against Perpetuities does not take into consideration probabilities of vesting; it considers only possible remoteness of vesting.

X may convey Blackacre *by deed* "to the first of my grandchildren to reach twenty-one." If, at the time of the conveyance, which is by deed, none of X's grandchildren is at least twenty-one years of age, then this conveyance will fail under the Rule Against Perpetuities. Again, even if several of X's grandchildren are between twenty and twenty-one years of age at the time of the conveyance (that is, at the time their contingent interest is created), there remains the possibility, however remote, that all of them will die, that X will then die, and that none of X's future grandchildren will reach twenty-one within twenty-one years of X's death. Note that in this example the "life in being" is not X's children but X. This is because the conveyance is by deed and because there is a period of time (twenty-one years) before the interest created by X might vest, during which X could outlive all of his or her children. Once again, the Rule Against Perpetuities is con-

cerned not with the probability but with the possibility of this happening.

Suppose X conveys Blackacre *by will* "to the first baby born in Southern Methodist Hospital after my death." Even if two dozen babies are delivered each day at Southern Methodist Hospital, this conveyance by X is void, since it violates the Rule Against Perpetuities. Since the conveyance is by will, and the takers under the will are not X's descendants, it is impossible to determine a life in being. X could not serve as the life in being because X will be dead at the time his or her will takes effect. Since there is a possibility that no baby will be born at Southern Methodist Hospital within twenty-one years after X's death, the conveyance violates the Rule. X could have achieved the desired result and avoided the Rule by drafting the provision to read: "To the first baby born at Southern Methodist Hospital; but if none is born within twenty-one years of my death, then to my heirs."

It is most important to determine who the "life in being" is when deciding whether the Rule Against Perpetuities has been violated. The person whose life serves as the measuring rod need not be mentioned in the document creating the property interest at issue and need not take any interest in the property. Furthermore, the person need not be connected in any way with the property or the persons designated to take it.

BACKGROUND AND FACTS *In her will, Philomena Lux provided that some of her real estate was to be held in trust for her grandchildren. The property was to be sold later, and the proceeds distributed when the youngest of her grandchildren reached 21 years of age. Philomena was survived by one son, age 30, and by five grandchildren ranging in age from 2 to 8. Philomena's surviving son was not named as a beneficiary to any part of the property that went to the grandchildren. A residuary beneficiary of the will objected to the devise of real estate on the ground that it violated the Rule Against Perpetuities.*

DECISION AND RATIONALE *Philomena Lux's gift of real estate did not violate the Rule Against Perpetuities. A devise will contravene the*

LUX v. LUX

Supreme Court of Rhode Island, 1972.
109 R.I. 592, 288 A.2d 701.

rule if it is at all possible that the interests of any beneficiary (Philomena's grandchildren here) will vest more that 21 years after some life in being at the time of the devisee's death. Since no grandchildren will be born to Philomena after Philomena's only son dies, and since any grandchildren living at her son's death must reach age 21 within 21 years, the proceeds from the property will vest within "some life in being plus 21 years."

Philomena's son serves as the "life in being" even though he is not mentioned as a beneficiary to the will. "The person whose life serves as the measuring rod need not be mentioned in the will, nor need he take any interest in the property. He need not be connected in any way with the property or the persons designated to take it."

The Rule Against Perpetuities is in a state of transition. Because of the sometimes anomalous results obtained by a strict application of the rule, some jurisdictions have made slight modifications. The most notable of these are the *wait and see doctrine* and the *cy pres* doctrine. Under the wait and see doctrine, a period of time set by statute must pass before a conveyance is voided by the Rule. The example in which X conveyed Blackacre by will "to the first child born at Southern Methodist Hospital after my death" would likely be saved in a jurisdiction with a wait and see statute, since a child would surely be born at the hospital shortly after X's death. Literally translated, *cy pres* means "as nearly as possible." Under the *cy pres* doctrine, a conveyance that would violate the Rule Against Perpetuities in its original form will be redrafted to conform to the intent of the grantor as nearly as possible without violating the rule. For example, if X conveys Blackacre by will "to the first of my grandchildren to reach twenty-five years of age," the age designated by the grantor will be reduced to twenty-one so that the conveyance will not be voided by the Rule.

NONPOSSESSORY INTERESTS

Ownership of land (freehold interests and interests less than freehold) is usually characterized by the owner's *possession* of the land. An owner of an interest in land can have a present right to possession, or, as in the case of future interests, can have a future right to possession. Some interests in land do not include any rights of possession. These interests, known as nonpossessory interests, include easements, profits, and licenses. Because easements and profits are similar, and the same rules apply to both, they will be discussed together.

Easements and Profits

An **easement** is the right of a person to make limited use of another person's property without taking anything from the property. For example, an easement can be the right to walk across another's property. A **profit** is the right to go onto land in possession of another and take away some part of the land itself or some product of the land. For example, R, the owner of Sandy View, gives A the right to go there and remove all the sand and gravel that A needs for her cement business. A has a profit. The difference between an easement and a profit is that an easement merely allows a person to use land without taking anything from it while a profit allows a person to take something from the land. Easements and profits can be classified as either *appurtenant* or *in gross*.

EASEMENT (OR PROFIT) APPURTENANT An easement or profit appurtenant arises where the owner of one piece of land has a right to go onto (or remove things from) an adjacent piece of land owned by another. Suppose W, the owner of Whiteacre, has a right to drive his or her car across G's land, Greenacre, which is adjacent to

Whiteacre. This right of way over Greenacre is an easement appurtenant to Whiteacre and can be used only by the owner of Whiteacre. W can convey the easement when he or she conveys Whiteacre.

The outstanding feature of an easement appurtenant is that it involves two pieces of land owned by two different persons. The parcels of land and the persons who own them are known respectively as the *dominant tenement*, the *servient tenement*, the *dominant tenant*, and the *servient tenant*. In the example above, Whiteacre is the dominant tenement, since it is benefited by the easement, and Greenacre is the servient tenement, since it is burdened by the easement. In addition, W is the dominant tenant, since he or she is the owner of White-acre, and G is the servient tenant.

EASEMENT (OR PROFIT) IN GROSS An easement or profit in gross exists when the right to use or take things from another's land is not dependent upon the owner of the easement or profit also owning an adjacent tract of land. Suppose Z owns a parcel of land with a marble quarry. Z conveys to the XYZ Corporation, which owns no land, the right to come onto Z's land and remove up to five hundred pounds of marble per day. XYZ Corporation owns a profit in gross. An easement or profit in gross requires the existence of only one piece of land that must be owned by someone other than the owner of the easement or profit in gross.

Effect of Sale of Property

Whenever a parcel of land that is benefited by an easement or profit appurtenant is sold, the property carries the easement or profit along with it. Thus, if W sells Whiteacre to T and includes the appurtenant right-of-way across Greenacre in the deed to T, T will own both the property and the easement that benefits it.

When a piece of land that has the burden of an easement or profit appurtenant is sold, the new owner must recognize its existence only if he or she knew or should have known of it or if it was recorded in the appropriate office of the county. Thus, if W records his easement across Greenacre in the appropriate county office before G conveys the land, the new owner of Greenacre will have to allow W, or any subsequent owner of Whiteacre, to continue to use the path across Greenacre.

Creation of an Easement (or Profit)

Profits and easements can be created by *deed* or *will* or by *implication, necessity,* or *prescription.* Creation by deed or will simply involves delivery of a deed or disposition in a will by the owner of an easement stating that the grantee (the person receiving the profit or easement) is granted the rights in the easement or profit that the grantor had. An easement or profit is created by *implication* when the circumstances surrounding the division of a piece of property imply its creation. For example, suppose B divides a parcel of land that has only one well for drinking water and conveys the half without a well to D. Here, a profit by implication arises, since D needs drinking water. An easement by *necessity* does not require division of property for its existence. A person who rents an apartment by necessity has an easement in the private road leading up to it.

Easements and profits *by prescription* arise when one person uses another person's land for a period of time equal to the statute of limitations for recovery of property. If the owner of the land does not object to the use of the land for the required period of time, the person using the land has an easement or profit by prescription. Suppose Alfred Carin owns a plot of land with an old coal mine on it. Carin's neighbor, Max Beta, goes onto Carin's land every Sunday, Monday, and Tuesday and removes several wheelbarrows of coal for a period of seven years. The applicable statute of limitations for recovery of real property is five years. In this situation, Beta has a profit by prescription since he has openly taken coal for the limitations period without any objection from Carin, and Carin can no longer object. Beta owns the profit and can continue taking the coal as long as he wants. Of course, Beta cannot take substantially more coal than he took in the past. Thus, if he started a regular mining operation, Carin could stop him.

TERMINATION An easement or profit is terminated or extinguished in several ways. The simplest means of extinguishing it is deeding it back to the owner of the land that is burdened by it. Second, the owner of an easement or profit can abandon it and create evidence of his or her intent to relinquish the right to use it. Mere nonuse will not extinguish an easement or profit *unless it is accompanied by an intent to abandon*. Third, when the owner of an easement or profit becomes the owner of the property burdened by it, then it is merged into the property. Essentially, the individual now owns both the easement or profit and the land, so there is no need for the easement or profit to continue. The individual can simply use the land as owner in fee simple.

Licenses

A license is the revocable right of a person to come onto another person's land. It is a personal privilege that arises from the consent of the owner of the land and that can be revoked by the owner. Therefore, unlike easements or profits, a license cannot arise by prescription, since a prescriptive claim is, by definition, adverse to the rights of the property owner.

An example of a license is a ticket to attend a movie at a theater. A theater owner issues the ticket, which entitles the holder to enter onto the property of the owner. Another example of a license arises when a landowner sells personal property that is located on the land. For example, Ferguson purchases a tractor owned by Wilson that Wilson has left in the middle of his cornfield. Ferguson's purchase gives him the license to enter onto the cornfield to remove the tractor. A person who has property rights in the nature of a license can also have contractual rights. Since the rights of a licensee are revocable at the will of the licensor, a person should

always look to the possible existence of an underlying contract to bolster his or her rights against the licensor.

LAND USE CONTROL

Land use control deals with the *limitations* placed upon property owners that either arise by agreement (covenants running with the land, equitable servitudes) or are imposed by the government (zoning).

Covenants Running with the Land

A **covenant running with the land** is an agreement under which a landowner either acquires certain rights or is under certain obligations merely because he or she owns the land that is bound by the covenant. A covenant running with the land lies somewhere between a contract and an easement or profit appurtenant. Instead of binding person to person (as a contract does) or land to land (as an easement does), a covenant running with the land binds a person to land. Consider an example. Y is the owner of Grasslands, a twenty-acre estate whose northern half contains a small reservoir. Y wishes to convey the northern half to Arid City, but before she does, she digs an irrigation ditch connecting the reservoir with the lower ten acres that she uses as farmland. When Y conveys the northern ten acres to Arid City, she enters into an agreement with the city. The agreement, which is contained in the deed, states, "Arid City, its heirs and assigns, promise not to remove more than five thousand gallons of water per day from the Grasslands reservoir." Y has created a covenant running with the land under which Arid City and all future owners of the northern ten acres of Grasslands are limited to the amount of water they can draw from its reservoir.

Four requirements must be met for a covenant running with the land to be enforceable. If they are not met, a simple contract is created between the two original parties only.

1.   The covenant running with the land must be created in a written agreement (covenant). It is usually contained in the document that conveys the land (deed or will).

2.   The parties must intend that the covenant *run with the land.* In other words, the instrument that contains the covenant must state not only that the promissor is bound by the terms of the covenant but that all the promissor's "successors, heirs, or assigns" will be bound.

3.   The covenant must *touch and concern* the land. The limitations on the activities of the owner of the burdened land must have some connection with the land. For example, a purchaser of land cannot be bound by a covenant requiring him or her to drive only Ford pickups, since such a restriction has no relation to the land purchased.

4.   The original parties to the covenant must be in *privity of estate* at the time the covenant is created. This means that the relationship between them must be landlord-tenant, vendor-purchaser, testator-devisee, and so forth. Note that this is unlike an easement appurtenant, which can be created by two parties who merely own adjoining land and are not in privity of estate.

Equitable Servitudes

Because of the confusion over the meaning and application of the privity of estate requirement, covenants running with the land have not been a very effective device for guiding the development of residential and commercial land. Therefore, courts of equity have created an alternative means of private land use control known as **equitable servitudes**. Covenants running with the land and equitable servitudes are similar in their application and effect, but the requirements for enforcing an equitable servitude are somewhat less stringent. An equitable servitude is created by an instrument that complies with the Statute of Frauds, an intention that the use of land be restricted, and *notice* of the restriction to the person acquiring the burdened land. For example, A owns two adjacent lots, Brownacre and Redacre. A con-

veys Redacre to the city of Pleasantville, stipulating in the deed that it be utilized only as a wildlife sanctuary and that no buildings be built on it. A also records the restriction in the county land records office. Thereafter, when the Ace Construction Company purchases Redacre from Pleasantville with the intention of building office buildings on it, it is bound by the restrictions that A placed on the land even if the restrictions are not contained in the deed by which it obtains the land from Pleasantville. Because the restrictions are recorded in the appropriate county office, Ace Construction Company is deemed to be on *constructive notice* of the restrictions.

Developers generally utilize equitable servitudes when developing a large parcel of land and subdividing it into residences. The developer will file a **plat** in the county records office that describes the land being developed and the restrictions under which each subdivided lot is sold.[1]

Equitable servitudes and covenants running with the land have also been used to perpetuate neighborhood segregation. For example, property owners in entire neighborhoods sometimes joined together and conveyed their homes to a straw man (usually a lawyer) who wrote in a restrictive covenant proscribing resale to minority groups. The straw man would then reconvey the property to the initial owners. In the Supreme Court case of Shelley v. Kraemer, such restrictive covenants were declared unconstitutional and could no longer be enforced in a court of law.[2] In addition, the Civil Rights Act of 1968 (also known as the Fair Housing Act) prohibits all discrimination based on race, color, religion, or national origin in the sale and leasing of housing.

Zoning

The government is by far the most potent force in guiding the development and use of land.

1.   A plat, also called a plot, is a map or representation on paper of a piece of land subdivided into lots, with streets, alleys, and so forth usually drawn to scale. When filed with the appropriate records office, the plat contains the restrictions under which the subdivided lots have been sold.
2.   334 U.S. 1, 68 S.Ct. 836 (1948).

State and local governments have far greater resources and enforcement powers than private individuals to control land use. Moreover, since, ideally, the government represents majority interests, it is in the best position to determine land uses that reflect the needs of society as a whole.

The state's power to control the use of land is derived from two sources: eminent domain and police power. Through eminent domain, the government can take land for public use, but it must pay just compensation, so this is an expensive method of land use control. Under its police power, however, the state can pass laws aimed at protecting public health, safety, morals, and general welfare. These laws can affect owners' rights and uses of land, but the state does not have to compensate the landowner. If the state's legislation restricts the landowner's property rights too much, the state's *regulation* will be deemed a *confiscation* and subject to the eminent domain requirements that just compensation be paid. For example, suppose Jones owns a large tract of land that she purchased with the intent to subdivide and develop into residential properties. At the time of the purchase, there were no zoning regulations restricting use of the land. If the state attempts to zone Jones's entire tract of land as "parkland only" and prohibits her from developing any part of it, the action will be deemed confiscatory, since the government will be denying her the ability to use her property for any purpose for which it is reasonably suited. The state will have to compensate Jones, since it has effectively confiscated her land. However, if the state zones Jones's parcel of land as "three-fourths residential, one-fourth park area" after her purchase, this zoning regulation is not confiscatory since she will be able to use most of the property for building residences.

The state's power to regulate the use of land is limited in two other ways, both of which arise from the Fourteenth Amendment. First, the state cannot regulate the use of land arbitrarily or unreasonably, since this would be a denial of property without due process. There must be a *rational basis* for the classifications that the state imposes on the property. Note, however, that this limitation is not very stringent. Any act that is reasonably related to the health or general welfare of the public has a rational basis. Second, a state's regulation of land use control cannot be discriminatory. The state is prohibited from discriminating against any race, religion, or nationality. The state is also generally prohibited from discriminating against any other group as well. Discrimination on the basis of race, religion, or national origin is never justifiable. However, discrimination based on other factors (for example, low income versus high income groups) may be upheld if there is a rational basis for the discrimination.

Nonconforming Use

The problems associated with zoning are often the result of normal growing pains experienced by expanding suburban areas that once were rural in nature. John Gordon, a chicken farmer, has lived with his family in Charlesville and has been a chicken farmer all his life. Since Charlesville is located only eighty miles from Megalopolis, a booming sunbelt town, it is being invaded by suburbanites. Charlesville had never heard of zoning until the late 1960s, when its newly-elected zoning board decided that the 125 acres surrounding Gordon's 2 acre chicken farm were best suited for suburban residents. Gordon appealed to the zoning board, claiming that his chicken farm, originally owned by his father, was located on the same 2 acres for seventy-five years. After hearing Gordon's plea, the zoning board gave him two years to close down and move his business. Gordon's chicken farm, which was in operation long before his area was zoned, is known as a **nonconforming use.** If the zoning ordinance called for Gordon's immediate removal, this would be confiscatory, and the government body promulgating the ordinance would have to pay just compensation for taking the farm. But as long as the nonconforming use is permitted to continue for a reasonable period of time, it is not deemed a taking of property, and therefore no compensation is necessary.

Floating Zones

Generally, the state agency charged with the responsibility of land use planning can take one of two approaches. The first is to designate, all at once, use restrictions on each parcel of land located within the entire area to be zoned (usually a city or town). Alternatively, the state agency can use "floating zones," deciding initially how much land should be designated for each of a variety of particular uses (commercial, residential, park, farming) and later assigning such designations at the request of landowners. Under the "floating zone" concept, the amount of land to be used for any one purpose is determined at the outset, but it is not assigned in what otherwise might be an arbitrary manner. This allows for flexibility in zoning.

Variance

A landowner whose land has been limited by a zoning ordinance to a particular use cannot make an alternative use of the land unless he or she first obtains a zoning variance. A landowner must meet three criteria to be entitled to a variance:

1. The landowner must find it impossible to realize a reasonable return on the land as zoned.
2. The adverse effect of the zoning ordinance must be particular to the person seeking the variance and not one that has a similar effect on the other landowners within the same zone.
3. A granting of the variance must not alter the essential character of the zoned area substantially.

By far the most important criterion used in granting a variance is whether it will alter the character of the neighborhood substantially. Courts tend to be rather lenient about the first two requirements. As the following case shows, courts also tend to defer to the discretion of zoning boards unless they have abused it.

BACKGROUND AND FACTS   *The city of Moline planned to build a new firehouse. The plans called for one slightly larger than present zoning ordinances allowed. Also, the new building was to be set back about four feet farther than the zoning allowed. The city sought a zoning variance, and Alfred and Marie Conner, who owned the property adjacent to and facing the site of the new construction, objected to the variance. When the variance was granted, the Conners appealed the zoning board's ruling to the courts.*

DECISION AND RATIONALE   *The variance granted by the zoning board was approved. The zoning board's primary function is to see to it that zoning ordinances are strictly followed. But, on occasion, due to changing community needs or simply to the irregular shape of a particular lot, the board must consider and weigh the propriety of granting a variance. The board should grant a variance only if it has heard substantial evidence that the variance would not seriously affect any adjoining property or the general welfare of the community. "Neither this court nor the trial court can substitute its judgment on the evidence for that of the Board. We may only determine whether the Board could reach the conclusion it did upon the evidence before it. We hold it could. *** The Board could find here that in the absence of a variance Moline would be confronted with substantial additional expense, interruption of fire protection service during the period of construction, and unnecessary inconvenience if not outright danger to the residents of the district."*

CONNER v. HERD
Court of Appeals of Missouri,
1970. 452 S.W.2d 272.

QUESTIONS AND CASE PROBLEMS

1. Susan Barnard died in 1899. Her will created a trust for her son, Charles Barnard, and transferred certain assets that she owned at her death to a trustee. Her will further provided that the trustee "hold, manage, and keep invested one-third of the assets for and during the life of my son Charles Inman Barnard: to pay the net income of such one-third in trust to my son Charles Inman Barnard for and during his life." The will went on to provide that the trust assets were to be transferred to Charles' issue (children), and "in default of such issue then to transfer said share to my granddaughter, Mary Curtis." Charles Barnard received the income from the trust during his life, but he died without marrying or having any children. Mary Curtis died before him. At the time the trust was created, what interest did Charles Barnard have? What interest, if any, did Mary Curtis have? Does Mary Curtis's untimely death affect her interest? [Williams v. Welch, 358 Mass. 514, 265 N.E.2d 854 (1970)]

2. Dixie Gardens, Inc. was a developer in Pasco County, Florida. Henry Sloane purchased a lot and residence from a Dixie Gardens development. The deed read in part as follows: "If the developer or the Crestridge Utilities Corporation causes garbage collection service bi-weekly to be made available, the owner of each lot shall pay the developer or its assigns, the sum of $1.75 per month therefor." Sloane wished to employ another contractor for garbage collection, but Dixie Gardens argued that Sloane was bound by the provision quoted above, which amounted to a covenant running with the land. Is Dixie Gardens correct? [Sloane v. Dixie Gardens, Inc., 278 So.2d 309 (Fla.App.1973)]

3. In 1961, Mary Schaefers divided her real property and conveyed it to her children, William, Elfreda, Julienne, and Rosemary. The deed from Mary Schaefers to her daughter Rosemary contained the following language: "It is further mutually agreed by and between the grantor and the grantee that as part of the consideration set out above, the grantee agrees to provide a permanent home for my daughter, Elfreda, should she desire or request one, and for my son, William Schaefers, should he desire or request one. Failure to perform the above will be considered a material breach of the consideration set out herein."

In 1974, Rosemary conveyed her portion of her mother's property to Edward and Arthur Apel. Subsequently, William Schaefers attempted to prevent the sale to the Apels from taking place by telling them that the house was encumbered by a covenant running with the land and that if they purchased the house, they would be bound to provide a home for William and Elfreda Schaefers. Is Rosemary's promise to provide a home for William and Elfreda (should they demand one) a covenant running with the land? [Schaefers v. Apel, 295 Ala. 277, 328 So.2d 274 (1976)]

4. Charles W. Parker died leaving a valid will that placed his property in trust and paid the income from the trust to his wife, Emma, for the remainder of her life. The will provided that at Emma's death the trust assets were to be taken out of trust and given "to William H. Parker [Charles's brother]; but if William H. Parker is not living at the death of my wife, Emma, then his share should vest in the Presbyterian Church of Carlyle." What is the nature of Emma's interest? Of William H Parker's interest? Of the Presbyterian Church of Carlyle's interest? [Presbyterian Church of Carlyle v. St. Louis Union Trust Co., 18 Ill.App.3d 713, 310 N.E.2d 412 (1974)]

5. Plastics Company, Inc. was the lessor of certain premises in New Jersey that it used to store goods designated for shipment. Attached to the leased buildings was a loading platform, and in front of the loading platform was a short driveway leading to the street. After loading merchandise onto one of its trucks, Plastics Company left the truck in the driveway overnight and the next morning found that the goods had been stolen. Plastics Company sought to recover under its insurance policy with Travelers Indemnity Company. The insurance policy, however, applied only to goods in transit. The policy explicitly provided: "This policy does not insure property while it is located in or on premises, owned, leased, or occupied by the assured." The court determined that if the driveway on which the truck was parked at the time of the theft could be deemed an easement, then the truck would be deemed to be on "leased premises," and the insurance policy would not cover the theft. How could the lawyer for the Travelers Indemnity Company argue that the driveway constituted an easement? [Den Gre Plastics Co. v. Travelers Indem. Co., 107 N.J.Super. 535, 259 A.2d 485 (1969)]

6. Columbus Cosmetic Corporation and Shoppers Fair of South Bend, Inc. entered into an agreement whereby Shoppers Fair granted Columbus "an exclusive license to occupy 1,500 square feet of space

in Shoppers Fair of South Bend for the purpose of selling drugs, cosmetics, etc." The agreement became effective in February 1960 and was to extend for a period of five years. Columbus had the right to renew for an additional five years provided it gave a one-year written notice. Shoppers Fair had the right to terminate the agreement after one year by giving written notice to Columbus at least sixty days before April in any year of the agreement, "but only if Columbus's sales during any lease year immediately preceding such notice are not more than 4 percent of the gross sales of the Shoppers Fair store." The agreement further provided that Columbus would pay Shoppers Fair 7 percent of its gross receipts or $9,600 each year, whichever was greater. Does Columbus's right to occupy floor space at Shoppers Fair constitute a license, or is it something more? [Columbus Cosmetic Corp. v. Shoppers Fair of South Bend, 26 App.Div.2d 391, 275 N.Y.S.2d 135 (1966)]

7. On November 21, 1967, North Clearlake Development Corporation entered into a contract with Clearlake Utilities Company that provided that "Clearlake Utilities Company shall have and is hereby granted the exclusive right to furnish water and sewer service" to the approximately eighty acres of land that North Clearlake Development Corporation had developed and to "all owners and occupants of any part thereof for and during the entire term of this contract." At the time of the contract, North Clearlake Development Corporation owned a large tract of land that it had just begun developing. Will the contract between Clearlake Utilities and North Clearlake Development constitute a covenant running with the land, binding all persons who thereafter purchase lots and homes in the development? [Clearlake Apartments, Inc. v. Clearlake Utilities Co., 537 S.W.2d 48 (Tex.Civ.App. 1976)]

8. In his will, Fletcher devised land to his granddaughter for life, then to the heirs of her body, if any, and if not, then to Fletcher's son, his heirs, and assigns. Assuming that at the time Fletcher dies, his only granddaughter is seven years old, what is the nature of her interest? What interest, if any, do the "heirs of her body" have? [Fletcher v. Hurdle, 259 Ark. 640, 536 S.W.2d 109 (1976)]

9. Under a zoning ordinance enacted on November 14, 1960, and effective January 1, 1961, a 460-acre parcel of land in Ulster County was designated an "agricultural zone." Shortly before the effective date of the ordinance, Kart Wheelers Raceway, Inc. began construction of a two-acre go-cart raceway on a tract of land located on part of the area that was zoned for agriculture. Prior to the enactment of the ordinance, Kart Wheelers had expended the sum of $487 for work performed on the premises for the purpose of readying it for the raceway. The facilities were completed in August 1961 at a total cost of $33,000. The town of Lloyd then attempted to enforce the zoning ordinance against Kart Wheelers Raceway, seeking to have it remove the go-cart raceway *immediately*. Kart Wheelers claimed that the town could not force it to remove the raceway since the raceway constituted a "nonconforming use." Is Kart Wheelers correct in its assertion? [Town of Lloyd v. Kart Wheelers Raceway, 28 App.Div.2d 1015, 283 N.Y.S.2d 756 (1967)]

10. Wilson owned a single-family home in a residentially zoned district in Harrison, Arkansas. Under local zoning ordinances, such a residence could be used for a home occupation, which the ordinance defined as one carried on solely by the inhabitants of the dwelling. Wilson sought permission from the Harrison zoning board to employ an outsider. The board granted the permission. The City of Harrison, however, appealed the board's decision on the ground that the board had authority only to grant a variance and that it had exceeded its power in authorizing a "nonconforming use." In addition, the city argued that, under the circumstances, the board should not have authorized Wilson to employ an outsider regardless of whether it had the authority to do so. Discuss the merits of the board's action and of the city's appeal. [City of Harrison v. Wilson, 248 Ark. 736, 453 S.W.2d 730 (1970)]

54

Insurance

THE NATURE OF INSURANCE

Insurance is a contract by which the insurance company (insurer) promises to pay a sum of money or give something of value to another (either the insured or the beneficiary) in the event that the insured is injured or sustains damage as the result of particular stated contingencies. Basically, insurance is an arrangement for *transferring and allocating risk*. In many cases, **risk** can be described as a prediction concerning potential loss, based on known and unknown factors. However, insurance involves much more than a game of chance, and insurers have an interest in seeing that risk is minimized. Many familiar safety devices are now commonplace because of insurance laws—automobile seat belts, fire escapes, train whistles, railroad crossing lights, reflecting road signs, and break-away highway lightposts, among others.

The Concept of Risk Pooling

All types of insurance use the principle of pooling of risk; that is, they spread the risk among a large number of people—the pool—to make the premiums small compared to the coverage offered. Consider life insurance. For any particular age group, only a small number of individuals will die in any one year. If a large percentage of this age group pays premiums to a life insurance company in exchange for a benefit payment in case of premature death, there will be a sufficient amount of money to pay the beneficiaries of the policyholders who do die. Given a long enough time for correction of data about the group and the particular disaster—in this case premature death—insurance companies can predict the total number of premature deaths in any one year with great accuracy. Thus, they can estimate the total amount they will have to pay if they insure the group, and they can predict the rates they will have to charge each member of the group in order to make the necessary payments and make a profit for the company.

Classification of Insurance

Insurance is classified according to the nature of the risk involved. For example, there is fire insurance, casualty insurance, life insurance, title insurance, and so forth. The persons and interests protected under each of these types of insurance policies differ. This is reasonable because, depending upon the nature of the activity, certain types of losses are expected, certain types are foreseeable, and certain others are unforeseeable.

Terminology

An insurance contract is called a **policy**; the consideration paid to the insurer is called a **premium**; and the insurance company is sometimes called an underwriter.

PARTIES   The *parties* to an insurance policy are the insurer (the insurance company) and the insured (the person obtaining the insurance policy and covered by its provisions). Insurance contracts are usually obtained through an *agent*, who ordinarily works for the insurance company, or a *broker*, who is ordinarily an independent contractor. When a broker deals with an applicant for insurance, the broker is, in effect, the applicant's agent. By contrast, an insurance agent is an agent of the insurance company. Thus, an insurance agent's relationship with the applicant for insurance is controlled by ordinary rules of agency law (see Chapter 34). As a general rule, the insurance company is bound by the acts of its agents when they act within the agency relationship. On the other hand, a broker has no relationship with the insurance company and is an agent of the applicant for insurance. The status of agent or broker can be extremely important in determining liability. In most situations, state law determines the status of all parties writing or obtaining insurance. In some states, the broker and agent are treated identically, but in others they are not.

INSURABLE INTEREST   A person can insure anything in which he or she has an *insurable interest.* A person has an insurable interest in property if damage to or destruction of the property will cause that person a *direct pecuniary or monetary loss.* For example, a person has an insurable interest in his or her own health or life and in the health or life of his or her spouse. But a person cannot obtain fire insurance on the White House or auto insurance on A. J. Foyt's race cars. It is immaterial whether a person is a legal or equitable owner of the property being insured. If the person is in possession of the property, then he or she has an insurable interest. Thus, if A. J. Foyt lends someone one of his race cars for the weekend, that person has an insurable interest in the car for that period of time. (See the discussion of bailments in Chapter 16.)

An insurable interest must exist at the time the loss occurs but not necessarily at the time the policy or contract of insurance is entered into, unless state statute provides otherwise. For example, B purchases an automobile, taking title in her name but intending the vehicle to be used by T. The insurance company issues a policy naming T as the insured. T uses the car for a period of time, decides to leave the state, and returns the car to B with no intention of ever using it again. Sometime later, B decides to sell the car. A potential buyer tests it and is involved in an accident. The insurance company can successfully defend against paying for the prospective buyer's accident. When T voluntarily abandoned the use of the vehicle, T's insurable interest ceased to exist.[1]

Insurable interest applying to life insur-

1.   See Universal C.I.T. v. Foundation Reserve Ins. Co., 79 N.M. 785, 450 P.2d 194 (1969).

ance is somewhat different. Every person has an insurable interest in his or her own life and can therefore insure it, naming anyone as beneficiary.

A person has an insurable interest in the life of another person if the person expects to receive some pecuniary gain from the fact that the other person's life continues or expects to suffer financial loss if the other person dies. Hence, a creditor can have an insurable interest in the life of a debtor because the death of the debtor may mean that the creditor will not be paid. In some instances, creditors do take out insurance policies on the life of debtors. However, if the creditor's insurance policy is unreasonably large—that is, substantially greater in amount than the debt—the policy may be void.

Consider two examples that illustrate the concept of insurable interest more clearly. James Jones insures his life for $100,000 with Continental Insurance Company, naming Henry Mason as beneficiary of the policy. When Jones dies, Continental Insurance cannot refuse to pay Mason merely because he had no insurable interest in the life of Jones. The beneficiary of a life insurance policy need not have an insurable interest in the insured. Jones was actually insuring his own life for the benefit of Mason. Obviously, Jones has an insurable interest in his own life. On the other hand, if Jones bought a policy with Continental Insurance to insure the life of his next door neighbor, Robert Samuel, Continental Insurance could refuse to pay the face value of the policy upon Samuel's death because Jones had no insurable interest in Samuel's life.

The existence of an insurable interest is a primary concern when determining liability under an insurance policy. In the following case, the insurance company claimed that the policyholders had lost their insurable interest in certain real property by leasing the premises to a third party. Moreover, since the plaintiffs (the policyholders) had not demonstrated any actual loss, they had no interest in the property and, hence, no insurable interest. At trial, the judge agreed with the insurance company's argument.

GENDRON v. PAWTUCKET MUT. INS. CO.
Supreme Judicial Court of Maine, 1978.
384 A.2d 694.

BACKGROUND AND FACTS *In 1969 the owner of a gas station purchased insurance against fire loss. Shortly thereafter, the owner leased the service station to Shell Oil Company. The lease agreement provided that Shell could demolish the existing building and construct a new ranch-style service station and that Shell was obligated to insure (and was exclusively entitled to insure) the premises. The existing gas station was scheduled for demolition but was still being used when it was destroyed by fire. The insurance company refused to pay claiming that the lease provision destroyed the owner's insurable interest.*

DECISION AND RATIONALE *The lease did not destroy the owner's insurable interest. First, the mere leasing of the property was not enough of an alienation to destroy the owner's insurable interest. Second, the insurance company could not assert that Shell's exclusive right to insure the premise indicated that the plaintiffs had surrendered their insurable interest in the property. "The insurer simply cannot thus benefit from collateral contractual relations between the insured and a third person so long as the insured retains legal title to the property."*

KEY MAN INSURANCE Key man insurance involves an organization insuring the life of a person who is important to the organization. Typically, a partnership will insure the life of each partner because the death of any one partner will legally dissolve the firm and cause some degree of loss to the partnership. So, too, a corporation has an insurable interest in the life expectancy of a key executive whose death would result in financial loss to the company.

WHEN MUST AN INSURABLE INTEREST EXIST? The insurable interest in life insurance must exist *at the time the policy is obtained.* This is exactly the opposite of property insurance, where the insurable interest must exist at the time the loss occurs and not necessarily when the policy is purchased. Because of this rule involving life insurance, in most states a divorce will not affect a policy. If the divorced spouse is named as beneficiary, the divorce action will not automatically divest that spouse's right to the proceeds or to an insurable interest.

An insured can assign the proceeds of his or her life insurance policy to a third person (beneficiary) who has no insurable interest, but the reverse is not true. Only those who have an insurable interest in the other person's life, such as a close relative, creditor, business associate, or employer, can take out a life insurance policy.

INDEMNITY

In fire insurance policies, insurance coverage is usually an *indemnity;* that is, the insurance pays only for what is actually lost. This is usually the replacement value of the property minus any depreciation. In addition, once payment is made, the insurance company is entitled to "stand in the shoes" of the insured in pursuing any lawsuits arising from the incident. This is called the right of subrogation.

THE RIGHT OF SUBROGATION

The right of subrogation allows the insured's insurance company to request reimbursement from the person who caused the loss or from that person's insurance company. Suppose that Sarah Washington's car is completely wrecked in an accident and that the issue of negligence is not clear-cut. Washington's insurance company might pay to have the car fixed or replaced, but under the right of subrogation, it can attempt to collect from the other person's insurance company if negligence is proven. Once Washington receives payment from her insurance company, the company is subrogated to any claim she may have against the wrongdoer. In other words, Washington cannot collect once from her own insurance company and once from the other person's insurance company.

OTHER INSURANCE CLAUSES

Suppose in the example above that Washington has both medical insurance on her automobile policy and Blue Cross health insurance through her employer, General Motors. Suppose also that she is injured in the auto accident, and her total medical bills amount to $2,000. Washington cannot be reimbursed simultaneously by her General Motors Blue Cross group health insurance policy and by her automobile insurance policy. Most group insurance policies have a so-called "other insurance" or coordination of benefits clause stating that any person with more than one insurance policy on property or health cannot collect more than the total financial losses sustained. Consider another example. Edward Johnson takes out fire insurance on his house from two different companies, with each policy having a face value of $50,000. If Johnson's house burns down he will not be paid $100,000 if the replacement value of the house is only $50,000. Each insurance company will pay Johnson a pro rata share of the loss—in this case, 50 percent.

STATE REGULATION OF INSURANCE

Each state has its own laws regulating domestic insurance companies. Statutes provide the method of incorporation, licensing, supervision, liquidation of insurers, and the licensing and supervision of agents and brokers. State law also regulates foreign insurance companies that conduct business within the state.

THE INSURANCE CONTRACT

An insurance contract is governed by the general principles of contract law. The application for insurance is usually attached to the policy and made part of the insurance contract. An insurance applicant is bound by any false statements that appear in the application (subject to certain exceptions). Because the insurance company evaluates the risk factors based on the information included in the insurance application, misstatements or misrepresentations can void a policy, especially if the insurance company can show that it would not have extended insurance if it had known the facts.

Timing

When an insurance contract comes into effect is important. In some instances, the insurance applicant is not protected until a formal written policy is issued. In other situations, the applicant is protected between the time the application is received and the time the insurance company either accepts or rejects it. Four situations should be kept in mind:

1. A broker is merely the agent of an applicant. Therefore, if the broker fails to procure a policy, the customer is not insured. According to general principles of agency law, if the broker fails to obtain policy coverage and the applicant is damaged as a result, then the broker is liable to the damaged applicant/principal for the loss.

2. A person who seeks insurance from an insurance company's agent will usually be protected from the moment the application is made, provided some form of premium has been paid. Between the time the application is received and either rejected or accepted, the applicant is covered (possibly subject to certain conditions, such as successfully passing a medical examination). Usually the agent will write a memorandum or **binder** indicating that a policy is forthcoming and stating its essential terms.

3. If the parties agree that the policy will be issued and delivered at a later time, the contract is not effective until the policy is issued and delivered or sent to the applicant, depending upon the agreement. Thus, any loss sustained between the time of application and the delivery of the policy is not covered.

4. Parties can agree that a life insurance policy will be binding at the time the insured pays the first premium. The policy, however, can be *expressly contingent* upon the applicant's passing a physical examination. If the applicant pays the premium and passes the examination, then the policy coverage is continuously in effect. If the applicant pays the premium but dies before having the physical examination, then the applicant's estate must show that the applicant would have passed the examination had he or she not died.

Coverage on an insurance policy can begin when the policy is issued or, depending upon the terms of the contract, after a certain period of time has elapsed.

Interpreting Provisions of an Insurance Contract

The words used in an insurance contract have their ordinary meaning and are interpreted in light of the nature of the coverage involved. Where there is an ambiguity in the policy, the provision is interpreted against the insurance company. When it is unclear whether an insurance contract actually exists because the written policy has not been delivered, the uncertainty will be determined against the insurance company. The court will presume that the policy is in effect unless the company can show otherwise.

KEDDIE v. BENEFICIAL INS. INC.
Supreme Court of Nevada, 1978.
94 Nev. 418, 580 P.2d 955.

BACKGROUND AND FACTS *Keddie owned a thirty-two foot boat that he used solely for commercial fishing. He contacted MacDonald, an insurance agent, about buying insurance for it. He did not request commercial fishing coverage, nor did he advise MacDonald that the vessel was a commercial fishing boat. Keddie filled out an application for* yacht insurance (applicable only to vessels not used for commercial purposes). The application did not include certain items of equipment that would have indicated the commercial use of the vessel. Subsequently, Keddie asked MacDonald to obtain a six-month quote, but the insurance company later informed MacDonald that it would not write a six-month policy. While the correspondence among Keddie, MacDonald, and the insurance company was going on, the vessel was destroyed by fire. The insurance company refused to pay.

DECISION AND RATIONALE   *Keddie could not recover from the insurance company. His claim that the insurance company's agent was negligent in failing to process and procure insurance before fire destroyed the boat was not adequate. Even if the agent had been negligent, the type of insurance that Keddie had requested would not have covered the fire loss to his vessel. "Once an agreement to procure insurance has been reached the insurance agent is obliged to use reasonable diligence to place the insurance and seasonably [within a reasonable amount of time] to notify the client if he is unable to do so. The agreement to procure, however, must be one for a policy of insurance which would have covered the loss incurred. Had an insurance policy been issued pursuant to Keddie's application for Yacht Insurance, such policy would not have covered the loss incurred. Consequently, there is no basis for liability."*

INTERPRETATION

The courts are increasingly cognizant of the fact that most people have no special training and therefore do not understand the intricate terminology used in insurance policies. The following case illustrates this problem.

BACKGROUND AND FACTS   *The insured (the plaintiff) was covered by an accidental death and dismemberment policy that provided full coverage in the event of "total and irrecoverable loss of entire sight of an eye." The plaintiff was in an accident and had a traumatic cataract surgically removed from his eye. After surgery, the plaintiff was fitted with a contact lens in his right eye. He had some amount of vision with the contact lens but could not tolerate wearing it. In effect, his eye was of little functional value, and there was no medical assurance that his eyesight could ever be regained. The insurance company (defendant) denied coverage under the policy.*

ROY v. ALLSTATE INS. CO.

Superior Court of Connecticut, Appellate Session, 1978.
34 Conn.Sup. 650, 383 A.2d 637.

DECISION AND RATIONALE   *The insured had suffered an "irrecoverable loss of sight" within the meaning of the insurance policy. The meaning of the phrase "irrecoverable loss of sight" must be ascertained by examining what the insured reasonably expected when he contracted for the insurance. Intent can be discerned by looking at the language used* *in the policy, taking the words to have their ordinary meaning, unless otherwise indicated. Generally, irrecoverable loss of sight means loss of the practical use of an eye and never regaining it. The court concluded: "Any view that the loss was recoverable would necessarily rest upon the assumption that the plaintiff would continue to be able to wear the contact lens indefinitely ***. It is clear that the average man purchasing a policy similar to the one in this case would reasonably expect to be insured for an injury to his eye of the type involved in this case where, within the period of coverage, vision could be restored only to the limited extent it was restored here."*

CANCELLATION OF INSURANCE POLICIES

Under most state laws, once the initial premium on a policy has been paid, the policy does not automatically lapse if the next premium is not paid on the due date. Most policies allow a **grace period** of thirty or thirty-one days.

However, once there is a default in the payment of a premium, the insurer may be required to take certain steps before cancelling the policy. A default in the payment of a life insurance premium may require the insurer to issue a paid-up policy in a smaller amount than originally contracted, to provide extended insurance for a period of time, or to pay the cash surrender value of the policy. These are alternatives to cancellation. When the insurance contract expressly declares that the insurance company cannot cancel the policy, these alternatives are important. When the insurance company can cancel the policy, contract provisions or state statutes usually require that the insurer give advance written notice of cancellation. Of course, an insurer cannot cancel a policy (or refuse to write a renewal policy) because of the national origin or the race of an applicant. Moreover, an insurance company cannot cancel a policy in order to penalize an insured who has just appeared as a witness in a case against the company.

DEFENSES AGAINST PAYMENT TO THE INSURED

An insurance company can raise any of the defenses that would be valid in any ordinary action on a contract and some defenses that do not apply in ordinary contract actions. If the insurance company can show that the policy was procured by fraud, misrepresentation, or violation of warranties, it may have a valid defense for its nonpayment on a claim. (The insurance company may also have the right to disaffirm or rescind the insurance contract.) Improper actions, such as those that are against public policy or are otherwise illegal, can give the insurance company a defense against payment of a claim or allow it to rescind the contract.

The following case involved the issue of liability for fire damage resulting from the actions of one of the insured persons under a contract of insurance. Because the insureds were married, the company claimed that the wrongful act of one spouse was attributable to the other, thereby preventing either from recovering fire insurance proceeds.

STEIGLER v. INS. CO. OF NORTH AMERICA Supreme Court of Delaware, 1977. 384 A.2d 398.	**BACKGROUND AND FACTS** *Mr. and Mrs. Steigler owned property as tenants by the entirety and insured it under an Insurance Company of North America (INA) policy. The husband deliberately set fire to the property. The wife was not involved in the act in any way and claimed that she should not have been barred from recovering under the policy as*

an innocent cotenant. She claimed only her pro rata share of the fire insurance proceeds. INA defended against payment relying on the general rule that an innocent spouse cannot recover under a fire insurance policy for damages if the other spouse deliberately burns their jointly owned property.

DECISION AND RATIONALE *Although the prevailing rule is that a spouse, no matter how innocent, cannot recover under a policy for damages resulting from the deliberate acts of the other spouse, this particular case was an exception to the rule. Herbert Steigler was convicted of assault with intent to murder his wife through the fire that was the basis of the insurance claim in this action. "If a wife were barred from recovery for such an act then, in reality, she will have been held responsible for the crime of her husband. And such a result is clearly repugnant to the general rule of law that, a wife is not vicariously liable for the criminal acts of her husband merely because of the existence of the marital relationship."*

REBUTTAL OF THE DEFENSES OF THE INSURANCE COMPANY

There are certain ways in which the insurance company can be prevented from asserting some defenses that are normally available. State statutes and case law provide for such estoppel. For example, if a company tells an insured that information requested on a form is optional, and the insured provides it anyway, the company cannot use the information to avoid its contractual obligation under the insurance contract. In the life insurance field, certain clauses become incontestable after a stated period of time. For example, statements as to the age of the insured, even though incorrect, normally do not allow the insurance company to escape payment upon the death of the insured. Typically, the time period after which estoppel for such defenses occurs is two years.

TYPES OF INSURANCE

Insurance policies are often classified by the type of risk they insure—for example, dental insurance, automobile liability coverage, theft insurance, flood insurance. The remainder of this chapter will discuss the general aspects of four types of insurance: (1) life insurance, (2) fire and homeowner's insurance, (3) automobile insurance, and (4) accident and health insurance.

TWO BASIC TYPES OF LIFE INSURANCE

There are basically two types of life insurance—term and whole life. **Term** offers "pure" protection. **Whole life**—also called straight life, ordinary life, or cash-value insurance—combines protection with a cash surrender value or saving fund. Exhibit 54-1 (panels a and b) illustrates the difference between term insurance and whole life insurance.

The Different Types of Term Insurance

There are three types of term insurance: (1) level, (2) decreasing, and (3) mortgage.

LEVEL TERM Premiums for level term insurance commonly increase at the end of each term, such as every five years, if the insured wishes to keep the same face value on the insurance policy. The increased premium reflects the rising probability of death as age increases.

EXHIBIT 54-1
SUMMARY OF
INSURANCE
PLANS

DECREASING TERM Decreasing term insurance has a level premium but a decreasing face value, as illustrated in panel c of Exhibit 54-1.

MORTGAGE TERM Mortgage term insurance, or home protection plan, declines in face value an amount equal to the mortgage left to be paid. The idea is that if the insured dies, the home can be paid off with the proceeds. A mortgage term insurance policy decreases in uneven dollar amounts. (This type of insurance can insure other consumer debt also.)

Renewability and Convertibility

Term insurance policies often have other features. A term policy is called renewable if the coverage can be continued at the end of each period merely by paying the increased premium and without having a medical examination.

Some policies are guaranteed renewable until the policyholder reaches retirement age.

Riders are often attached to term policies to permit the insured to convert the policy into whole life, for example, without having a medical examination. This convertibility feature of a term policy is often required by statute.

Whole Life Insurance

Whole life insurance premiums generally remain at the same level throughout the life of a policy. As a result, the policyholder pays more than is necessary to cover the insurance company's risk in the early years and less than is necessary to cover the company's risk in later years. Compared with term insurance, whole life is relatively more costly because it is a form of financial investment as well as insurance protection. The investment feature of the policy is known as its cash value.

LIVING BENEFITS Living benefits of a whole life policy include converting it into some sort of lump sum payment or stream of retirement income. When the insured reaches retirement age, premium payments on whole life can be discontinued and one of the following living benefit programs can be started:

1. Protection for the rest of the insured's life but at a lower face value.
2. Full protection but for a definite number of years in the future (extended term insurance).
3. A cash settlement that returns whatever savings and dividends have not been used to pay off the insurance company for excessive costs incurred for the particular age group of the insured (the cash surrender fund).
4. Conversion of a whole life policy into an annuity whereby the insured receives a specified amount of income each year for a certain number of years or for the rest of the insured's life.

BORROWING ON THE CASH VALUE OF THE POLICY One feature of a whole life insurance policy is that the insured can borrow on its cash value whenever needed. The interest rates on such loans are relatively favorable, as they should be, since the insured is in a sense borrowing his or her own money. Rates depend on the contract and the age of the policy. However, if the insured dies while the loan is outstanding, the sum paid to the beneficiary is reduced by the amount of the loan plus interest. In any event, this borrowing power can be considered as a cushion against financial emergencies.

DEATH BENEFITS In most life insurance policies, the insured specifies a beneficiary, who receives the death benefits of that policy. If Ken Kerr buys a $10,000 ordinary life policy and does not borrow any money on it, his beneficiary will receive $10,000 when he dies. However, there are certain options for settling a life insurance policy. The first plan involves a lump sum payment. In the second plan, the face value of the insurance policy is retained by the insurance company, but a small interest payment is made to the beneficiary for a certain number of years or for life. At the end of the specified period, the principal (face value) is then paid according to the terms in the contract. In the third plan, the face value is paid to the beneficiary in the form of annual, semiannual, quarterly, or monthly installments. The company makes regular payments of equal amounts until the fund is depleted. The insurance company guarantees a specific number of payments or payments that will total the face value of the policy. If, however, the beneficiary dies before the guaranteed payments have been made, the remainder goes to the estate of the beneficiary or as otherwise directed in the contract. This is sometimes called an annuity plan.

Other Types of Life Insurance Policies

There are numerous other types of life insurance policies. **Limited payment whole life** is a policy payable at the death of the insured, with little cash and surrender values. The premiums are paid for a stated number of years or until the insured reaches a certain age, such as sixty or sixty-five. An **endowment policy** offers a combination of temporary life insurance and a rapidly increasing cash surrender fund. It can be considered both a term insurance policy and a growing savings account. Exhibit 54-1, panel e, illustrates the main features of an endowment policy. A retirement endowment policy is one in which the insured continues paying until the cash surrender has exceeded the face value of the policy. This can be seen in panel f of Exhibit 54-1.

AUTOMOBILE INSURANCE

There are basically two kinds of automobile insurance: liability insurance and comprehensive and collision insurance.

Property Damage and Bodily Injury Liability

One kind of automobile insurance covers bodily injury and property damage liability. Liability limits are usually described by a series of three numbers, such as 25/50/5. This means that the policy will pay a maximum of $25,000 for bodily injury to one person, $50,000 to more than one person, and a maximum of $5,000 for property damage in one accident. Most insurance companies offer liability up to $300,000 and sometimes $500,000.

Individuals who are dissatisfied with the maximum liability limits offered by regular automobile insurance coverage can purchase a separate amount of coverage under an "umbrella policy". Umbrella limits sometimes go as high as $5 million. They also cover personal liability in excess of homeowner's liability limits.

Physical Damage Coverage

Another kind of automobile insurance covers damage to the insured's car in any type of collision. Usually, it is not advisable to purchase full collision coverage (otherwise known as zero deductible). The price per year is quite high because it is likely that small but costly repair jobs will be required each year. Most people take out $50 or $100 deductible coverage, which costs about one-fourth the price of zero deductible.

COMPREHENSIVE Comprehensive insurance covers loss, damage, and destruction by fire, hurricane, hail, and vandalism. It is separate from collision insurance. Full comprehensive insurance is quite expensive. Again, $50 or $100 deductible is usually preferable.

Uninsured Motorist Coverage

Uninsured motorist coverage insures the driver and passengers against injury caused by any driver without insurance or by a hit-and-run driver. Certain states require that it be included in all insurance policies sold to drivers.

Accidental Death Benefits

Sometimes called double indemnity, accidental death benefits provide a lump sum to named beneficiaries if the policyholder dies in an automobile accident. It generally costs very little, but it may not be necessary if the insured has a sufficient amount of life insurance.

Medical Payment Coverage

Medical payments provided for in an auto insurance policy cover hospital and other medical bills and sometimes funeral expenses. This insurance protects all the passengers in the insured's car when the insured is driving.

No-Fault Auto Insurance

In May 1974, President Nixon wired the National Governors Conference that no-fault auto insurance was "an idea whose time has come." The president added, though, that the place for no-fault action was at the state, not the federal, level. Labor and consumer groups, however, were dissatisfied with the pace of state action and the lobbying tactics of no-fault opponents. Therefore, pressure was brought upon Congress to institute a federal plan. Supporters of the plan indicate that eventually it will save motorists $1 billion a year in auto insurance premiums.

Under a no-fault insurance system, the insured's insurance company does not have to decide whose fault the accident was before payments are made for medical expenses resulting from the accident. In a traditional liability-based fault system, it must be determined who caused the accident. The insurer of the party deemed "at fault" then pays the bills—medical, lost earnings, pain and suffering, and automobile repairs—of the injured party.

No-fault insurance is not a new idea. Almost all other types of insurance are no-fault already. For example, life insurance companies pay without asking about fault (unless death is caused by suicide). The same is true of fire, homeowner's, and health and accident insurance. If a person breaks an ankle and is covered under a medical plan, the insurer does not ask whose fault it is before the medical bills are paid.

Original proponents of no-fault auto insurance believed it soon would be adopted by all states in the union. However, by 1977, only sixteen states had converted to pure no-fault.[2]

Another eight states have passed some modified form of no-fault automobile insurance. In most no-fault states, the laws apply only to bodily injuries. Property damage claims are still settled by standard liability and collision sections of automobile insurance policies.

In no-fault states, the other party in an

2. The states are Colorado, Connecticut, Florida, Georgia, Hawaii, Kansas, Kentucky, Massachusetts, Michigan, Minnesota, Nevada, New Jersey, New York, North Dakota, Pennsylvania, and Utah.

automobile accident can still be sued. Generally, certain "threshold" criteria must be satisfied before suit is allowed for pain and suffering, inconvenience, lost wages, and deprivation of the company of a spouse. The medical threshold level ranges from a few hundred dollars up to two thousand dollars in the sixteen no-fault states. In other states, serious injury or permanent disfigurement must be suffered before suits will be allowed.

Worker's Compensation

Worker's compensation insurance is a type of accident, health, and disability insurance that has been made mandatory by statutes in all states. It provides a system of compensation for workers who suffer losses in the course of their employment. It usually covers losses due to physical injury. Some states have enacted statutes that provide coverage for losses due to disease and illness. The geographical location and the type of industry in a particular jurisdiction dictate which type of disease losses are covered. For example, such statutes provide coverage for lung diseases in areas where coal mining is the major occupation.

The amount of compensation to be paid to the injured or ill worker is determined by a fixed schedule of payment benefits, based on three basic factors: (1) the wages that the injured party was earning, (2) the seriousness of the injury, and (3) the permanence of the injury. Suppose that Deel had an injury and was 10 percent permanently disabled. In such a case, if Deel was earning $200 per week, he would receive 10 percent of this figure, or $20 per week, for a predetermined time, according to the benefit schedule then in effect.

QUESTIONS AND CASE PROBLEMS

1. Thompson contracted with Occidental Life Insurance Company of California for an insurance policy on his life. The beneficiary of the policy was his wife. Before Occidental issued the policy to

Thompson, Thompson filled out an application in which he was asked several questions regarding his health. One of the questions asked if Thompson had ever had pressure in his chest. Another asked if he had any disorder with his blood or blood vessels. Thompson entered negative answers to each of these questions since, earlier that morning, one of Occidental's physicians had asked him about these conditions.

At that time, he had explained to the physician that two months earlier he had been treated for phlebitis (vein inflammation) and, at about the same time, had experienced minor chest pains. Thompson died in an accident shortly thereafter, and Occidental refused to pay on this life insurance policy, claiming that Thompson misrepresented facts on the application. Under these circumstances, is Thompson's wife entitled to Thompson's life insurance benefits? [Thompson v. Occidental Life Ins. Co., 109 Cal.Rptr. 473, 513 P.2d 353 (1973)]

2. Donald R. Noah was the beneficiary of three life insurance policies that insured the life of William L. Noah, Donald's brother. The insurer was Mutual Savings Life Insurance Company. While the policies were in force, William Noah drowned in Galveston, Texas. Mutual Savings Life refused to pay Donald Noah on the ground that he did not have an insurable interest in his brother's life. Donald Noah sued the company. Is Donald Noah entitled to collect under the policies? Would the answer be the same if William Noah had been Donald's cousin? What if he had been Donald's nephew? [Mutual Sav. Life Ins. Co. v. Noah, 291 Ala. 444, 282 So.2d 271 (1973)]

3. Cahn, Inc., an insurance brokerage firm, procured a homeowner's liability policy from the Michigan Millers Mutual Insurance Company at the request of Effye Lewis. The policy covered property owned by her and located on Dixwell Avenue in New Haven, Connecticut. In October, four years later, Lewis purchased other property on Read Street and obtained a liability insurance policy on this property from another insurer. About two months later, she moved from her Dixwell Avenue property to her Read Street property. In April of the following year, Lewis mailed Cahn a premium payment on the policy covering the Dixwell Avenue property. With the payment she enclosed a note requesting that her mail be sent to her Read Street property. Cahn interpreted the note to mean not only that she had moved but that she desired to have her liability insurance coverage transferred to the Read Street property. With this in mind, Cahn requested and received an indorsement from the Michigan Millers Insurance Company transferring the insurance coverage to the Read Street property. Nine months later, a neighbor was injured on Lewis's Dixwell Avenue property. She requested Michigan Millers to defend the suit as required under the policy, but the insurance company declined, claiming that the Dixwell Avenue property was no longer insured. With a sharp attorney, Lewis was able to recover from Michigan Millers Insurance

Company even though the injury occurred on uninsured property. How did Lewis's attorney manage to recover? [Lewis v. Michigan Millers Mut. Ins. Co., 154 Conn. 660, 228 A.2d 803 (1967)]

4. On January 24, 1961, Vulcan and Borden entered into an agreement whereby Vulcan agreed to render certain engineering and procurement services for Borden's chemical plant in Geismar, Louisiana. Part of the agreement provided: "All disputes shall be submitted to arbitration upon the demand of either party to the dispute." In 1962, several accidents occurred at the Borden plant, causing substantial damage. They were Vulcan's fault. Borden and its insurance company, Lumbermens Mutual Casualty, conducted lengthy negotiations regarding the extent to which Lumbermens would pay for the damages. After Borden and Lumbermens reached a settlement, Lumbermens brought suit against Vulcan to recover for the damage that Vulcan had caused. Vulcan objected to Lumbermens lawsuit on the ground that no disputes between Vulcan and Borden could be brought before a court before they were submitted to arbitration. Must Lumbermens Mutual submit to arbitration with Vulcan? [Lumbermens Mut. Cas. Co. v. Borden Co., 268 F.Supp. 303 (S.D.N.Y.1967)]

5. In February 1967, Gentry agreed orally to purchase a house and property owned by Irwin. The next day Gentry procured fire insurance from the Hanover Insurance Company for the home. On March 14, 1967, before the purchase transaction was completed, the house was destroyed by fire. Gentry sought to recover under the insurance policy from Hanover Insurance Company. Hanover refused to pay. Should Gentry be able to recover? [Gentry v. Hanover Ins. Co., 284 F.Supp. 626 (W.D.Ark.1968)]

6. Charles and Norma Watson asked the Dillingham Company, Ltd., to write an automobile insurance policy to cover the use of a 1965 Volkswagen by their minor son, Mark. The car was owned by Mark's mother. Since Mark had been involved in several accidents, Dillingham decided that it could obtain insurance only through the Automobile Assigned Risk Plan. Mark went to Dillingham's offices to apply for the Plan, partially filled out an application form, and signed the form and a blank duplicate. The application form provided in part that the insurance agent processing an assigned risk application was not the agent of the insurance company to which the application would be assigned. A Dillingham employee completed Mark's application form but expressly requested issuance of a "nonowner policy" even though Mark had indicated in the application

that he was a seventeen-year-old living with his parents. The completed application was sent to the Plan's office. Subsequently, Mark was assigned to the United States Fidelity and Guaranty Company, to which he forwarded his first premium payment. The company issued a policy including an indorsement entitled "nonowner policy," which provided that the policy did not apply to "any automobile owned by the named insured or a member of the same household." Mark was involved in an accident while driving his mother's automobile. Is the United States Fidelity and Guaranty Company obligated to pay under the policy? [Watson v. United States Fidelity and Guaranty Co., 427 F.2d 1355 (9th Cir. 1970)]

7.   Bunge Corporation was one of the holders of warehouse receipts on vegetable oils stored in the tanks of a warehousing subsidiary of the American Express Company. In late 1963, it was discovered that a massive fraud had been perpetrated by Tino de Angelis, president of a vegetable oil concern, and that there was little or no oil in the tanks. This scandal was popularly known as the "salad oil swindle." Bunge brought suit on a contract of insurance against its insurance company, London and Overseas Insurance, to recover its losses. Thereafter, Bunge entered into a settlement agreement with American Express, giving it a release from liability; that is, Bunge agreed not to sue American Express. London refused to pay anything to Bunge Corporation but proceeded to institute an action against American Express on the theory that its negligence was the cause of Bunge's loss. The court promptly threw out London's lawsuit, and the judge cited two reasons why London had no right to sue. What were they? [Bunge Corp. v. London and Overseas Ins. Co., 394 F.2d 496 (2d Cir. 1968)]

8.   In June 1961, Groban contracted to purchase an inventory of Caterpillar tractor parts from SLDC. Before that purchase was concluded, Groban contracted to resell the inventory to Union. At Union's request, Groban agreed to obtain marine war risk insurance on the shipment at Union's expense. Groban subsequently purchased two contracts of insurance, one naming itself as beneficiary and the second naming Union as beneficiary. The goods were destroyed during shipment. If Groban attempts to recover under the insurance policy, will it have an insurable interest? If Union attempts to recover, will it have an insurable interest? [Groban v. S. S. Pegu, 331 F.Supp. 883 (S.D.N.Y.1971)]

9.   On June 8, 1966, a convent that had been constructed in 1877 burned to the ground. It was insured by Royal Insurance Company. At the time of the fire, the previous residents of the convent, the Sisters of Presentation, had abandoned the old building and moved into a new one. Under an agreement with the bishop, they had obligated themselves to surrender the old convent for demolition. They had already received new land and a new building in exchange for their contractual agreement that the old land would be occupied by an expanding high school. The Sisters of Presentation demanded recovery from Royal Insurance Company, but Royal refused to pay on the ground that the Sisters of Presentation had no insurable interest in the building. The Sisters of Presentation argued that, had their new building been destroyed by fire, they might have been forced to reoccupy the old convent even though it would not be habitable without an expenditure of approximately $120,000. Do the Sisters of Presentation have an insurable interest in the old convent? [Royal Ins. Co. v. Sisters of Presentation, 430 F.2d 759 (9th Cir. 1970)]

10.   In 1950, Youse purchased a fire insurance policy from Employers Fire Insurance Company. The policy covered most of Youse's personal property and provided that the company would pay for "all direct loss or damage by fire." Youse accidentally lost his ring in a pile of trash near a trash burner. Youse later recovered it, but only after the trash had been burned. The ring was extensively damaged. Should Youse recover? Was this the type of fire that Employers Fire Insurance Company had in mind when it provided coverage for Youse's property? Should this matter? [Youse v. Employers Fire Ins. Co., 172 Kan. 111, 238 P.2d 472 (1951)]

55

Wills, Trusts, and Estates

The laws of succession of property are a necessary corollary to the concept of private ownership of property. The law requires that upon death, title to the decedent's property must vest somewhere. The decedent can direct the passage of property after death by *will*, subject to certain limitations imposed by the state. If no valid will has been executed, the person is said to have died *intestate*, and state law prescribes the distribution of the property among heirs or next of kin. If no heirs or kin can be found, the property escheats (title is transferred) to the state.

In addition, a person can transfer property through a *trust*.[1] The owner (settlor) transfers legal title to the property to a *trustee*, who has a duty imposed by law to hold the property for the use or benefit of another (the beneficiary).

The following sections will describe how testamentary dispositions are made by *will*, by *statutes of descent and distribution*, or with *trusts*.

ORIGINS OF INHERITANCE LAWS

Under the common law, persons had no power to control the distribution of their property after death. This power is derived solely from statutes

---

1. Note that a "trust" can be set up by the property owner *during his or her life* (by a deed accompanied by a trust document) or *at his or her death* (by a will accompanied by a trust document). This chapter discusses both.

originating in feudal England, where the transfer of property at death was strictly controlled. The heir (the one who inherited) was required to pay the feudal lord a sum of money[2] for the privilege of succeeding to his or her ancestor's lands. When a tenant died without heirs, the land escheated (title passed) to the feudal lord of the manor.[3] Sweeping land reforms in England during the 1920s replaced inheritance payments and escheat to the feudal lord with the right of the crown to receive inheritance taxes and to take property of an intestate without heirs. Modern legislation has changed the terminology but not the result. In all states, title to land of persons dying intestate and without heirs vests in the state; the right to make a will and the way to make one are determined by state laws. Wills must follow rigid technical statutory requirements. Furthermore, taxes are imposed upon the transfer of property at death by the state and federal governments.

PURPOSES OF INHERITANCE LAWS

State regulation of inheritance has developed in response to certain desirable social and political goals. Four principles underlie U.S. inheritance and succession laws.[4]

1. *The concept of private property.* Any system of laws to regulate the passage of a decedent's estate must do so in the context of a firmly rooted tradition of private ownership of property.
2. *Effectuating the individual's testamentary intent.* The right to direct the distribution of one's own property to whomever one chooses (subject to the rights of the surviving spouse and

minor children) is a basic tenet of U.S. jurisprudence. Many formalities surround the court's duty to insure that when a will is offered for authentication, it is in fact the genuine and final expression of the decedent's wishes. The seriousness of this function is reflected in the highly publicized controversy over the numerous proffers of "authentic" wills belonging to billionaire Howard Hughes. The freedom of an individual to have his or her intentions satisfied after death is subject to limitations imposed by law.

3. *The policy favoring family.* Protection of the family has been a cornerstone of inheritance laws throughout history. As noted earlier, intestate succession is inheritance by heirs of the deceased. In contemporary law, this goal is reinforced by state statutes guaranteeing that an absolute portion of the decedent's estate will be allotted to the surviving spouse and minor children. Although laws differ from state to state, most provide a *homestead exemption* from taxation and creditors, a family allowance to provide funds to meet daily expenses until the estate is settled, and an exemption for household and personal effects.

4. *Reflection of societal interests.* State succession laws perpetuate certain social and political goals by: (1) protecting a decedent's family from absolute poverty against creditors' claims (and preventing the family's dependency on the state), (2) obtaining money through escheat (transfer of abandoned property to the state), (3) channeling the efficient and economic use of property by prohibiting wasteful bequests (devises), (4) encouraging educational and scientific research and other civic programs through estate tax exemptions or deductions, and (5) maintaining social stability and confidence in the legal system by adhering to traditional principles of law.

WILLS
Concept of a Will

A **will** is the final declaration of the disposition that a person desires to have made of his or her property after death. It is a formal instrument

---

2. The sum, called a relief, was usually equivalent to one year's rent.
3. It was not until 1925 that escheat for failure of heirs was abolished. C. J. Moynihan, *Introduction to the Law of Real Property* (St. Paul, Minn. West Publishing, 1962), p. 22.
4. For a discussion of the goals of succession laws and the need for increasing flexibility in applying these laws, see John T. Gaubatz, "Notes toward a Truly Modern Wills Act," *University of Miami Law Review* 31 (Spring 1977): 497.

that must follow the *exact* requirements of the Statute of Wills in order to be effective. The reasoning behind such a strict requirement is obvious. A will becomes effective only after death. No attempts to modify it after the death of the maker are allowed because the court cannot ask the maker to confirm the attempted modifications.

A will is *revocable* at any time before death. For example, Walt Harrison has a valid will. He decides to add a bequest to his niece. If he dies on the way to the lawyer's office, the current will takes effect without the intended gift to the niece. Although Harrison's will was not binding during his lifetime, it becomes binding upon his death.

VOCABULARY OF WILLS AND TRUSTS Every area of law has its own special vocabulary, and wills and trusts are no exception. A man who makes out a will is known as a **testator**, and a woman who makes out a will is called a **testatrix.** The court responsible for administering any legal problems surrounding a will is called a **probate court.** When a person dies, a *personal representative* settles the affairs of the deceased. An **executor** or **executrix** is a personal representative named in the will; an **administrator** or **administratrix** is a personal representative appointed by the court for a decedent who dies without a will or who fails to name an executor in the will. A gift of real estate by will is generally called a **devise**, and a gift of personal property under a will is called a **bequest.**

TYPES OF GIFTS Gifts by will can be *specific, general,* or *residuary.* A *specific* devise or bequest describes particular property that can be distinguished from all the rest of the testator's property. For example, Johnson's will provides, "I give my nephew, Tom, my gold pocket watch with initials MTJ." A *general* gift does not single out any particular item of property, and any property of comparable nature will satisfy the gift. For example, "I give Dana $10,000." A specified sum of money is almost always a *general* gift. Sometimes a will provides that any assets remaining after specific gifts are made and debts are paid will be distributed through a residuary clause. A residuary provision is used because the exact amount to be distributed cannot be determined until all other gifts and payouts are made. A residuary estate can pose problems, however, when the will directs that only a portion of the money or assets be divided among named beneficiaries, leaving some assets still remaining. In such a case, if the court cannot determine the testator's intent, the remainder of the residuary passes according to laws of intestacy.

In the following case, the lower court tried to apply a distribution formula not actually provided by the terms of the will's "general residuary clause."

KORTZ v. AMERICAN NAT. BANK OF CHEYENNE
Supreme Court of Wyoming, 1977.
571 P.2d 985.

BACKGROUND AND FACTS *Johnson died leaving a will that contained the following residuary clause: "I hereby give bequeath and devise one-quarter of the balance of my money and estate of which I may die seised and possessed, both real, personal and mixed, of every kind, character and description whatsoever and wheresoever situate to THE CANCER SOCIETY to be theirs absolutely and forever. I hereby give, bequeath and devise one-half (1/2) of the balance of my money to LILLIAN BUTLER to be hers absolutely and forever." The trial court interpreted the clause to mean that one-third of the residuary was intended for the American Cancer Society and two-thirds for Lillian Butler. Johnson's daughter and heir by intestacy objected.*

DECISION AND RATIONALE   *One-quarter of Johnson's estate went to the Cancer Society, one-half to Lillian Butler, and the remaining quarter, by intestacy, passed to Johnson's daughter. The fact that the residuary clause at issue did not expressly dispose of all of Johnson's residuary estate did not mean that the lower court could rewrite Johnson's will. "We hold that the language of the Johnson will is clear and unambiguous. As a result, the testator intended a portion of his residuary estate to pass by intestacy."*

OTHER PURPOSES OF A WILL   A will can serve many purposes besides the distribution of property. It can appoint a guardian for minor children or incapacitated adults. It can appoint a personal representative to settle the affairs of the deceased. State laws vary in the types of powers and functions that they grant to personal representatives under the supervision of the probate court.

The Uniform Probate Code

Probate laws vary from state to state. In 1969, the American Bar Association and the National Conference of Commissions on Uniform State Laws approved the Uniform Probate Code (UPC). The UPC codifies general principles and procedures for the resolution of conflicts in settling estates and relaxes some of the requirements of a valid will found under earlier state laws. References to UPC provisions will be included where general practice in most states is consistent. However, since succession and inheritance laws vary widely among different states, one should always check the particular laws of the state involved.[5]

Testamentary Capacity

Not everyone who owns property necessarily qualifies to make a valid disposition of that property by will. *Testamentary capacity*

_____
5.   For example, California law differs *substantially* from the UPC.

requires the testator to be of *legal age* and *sound mind* at the time the will is made. The *legal age for executing* a will varies, but in most states and under the UPC, the minimum age is eighteen years. [UPC Sec. 2-501] Thus, a will of a twenty-one-year-old decedent written when the person was twelve is *invalid*.

The concept of "being in sound mind" refers to the testator's ability to formulate and comprehend a personal plan for the disposition of property. Further, a testator must intend the document to be his or her will.

Courts have grappled with the requirement of *sound mind* for a long time and not always with consistent results. Mental incapacity is a highly subjective matter that is not easily measured. The general test for testamentary capacity has the following provisions:

1.   The testator must comprehend and remember the "natural objects of his or her bounty" (usually family members, but including persons for whom the testator has affection).
2.   The testator must comprehend the kind and character of the property being distributed.
3.   The testator must understand and formulate a plan for disposing of the property to family members and friends.

Less mental ability is required to make a will than to manage one's own business affairs or to enter into a contract. Thus, a testator may be feeble, aged, eccentric, or offensive and still possess testamentary capacity. Moreover, a person can be judged insane or have insane delusions about certain subjects yet, during lucid moments, still be of *sound mind* to make a valid will.

    In the following case, testamentary capacity appeared to be present even though the testator was diagnosed schizophrenic. The will was valid because, according to clear and convincing proof on the court record, it was executed during a lucid interval.

ESTATE OF GENTRY
Court of Appeals of Oregon,
1976.
32 Or.App. 45, 573 P.2d 322.

BACKGROUND AND FACTS *After his discharge from the army, Gentry was confined in the psychiatric ward at a veterans administration hospital. He was adjudicated incompetent and was placed under guardianship with Pioneer Trust Company. During the course of his confinement, Gentry executed a will. The will named his mother as sole beneficiary and disinherited his daughter. After Gentry died, his daughter came forward to contest the will and to assert her right by virtue of intestate succession. The ward physician, Gentry's attorney, and various other persons presented evidence at the trial that Gentry was lucid at the time he made the will.*

DECISION AND RATIONALE *Gentry was sufficiently competent to make a will, and the will was therefore valid. Mental competency to make a will is determined at the time the will is actually made. The will of an insane person may be valid if it is made during a lucid interval. The court upheld Johnson's will, stating the following: "Where a testator is under guardianship at the time of the execution of the will and the guardianship was established because of the ward's mental incompetency, a presumption of mental incompetency arises. However, merely because the testator was under guardianship at the time of execution of the will is not conclusive of his mental incompetency at the time if the evidence shows that the testator possessed the requisite testamentary capacity at the time of the execution of the will."*

FORMAL
REQUIREMENTS OF A WILL

A will must comply with strict formalities designed to insure that the testator or testatrix understood his or her actions and to help prevent fraud. Unless statutory requirements are met, the will is declared void and the decedent's property is distributed according to the laws of intestacy of that state. The requirements are not uniform among the jurisdictions. However, most states uphold the following basic requirements for executing a will.

1. *A will must be in writing.* A written document is generally required, although in some cases oral wills are found valid.[6] [UPC Sec. 2-502] The writing itself can be informal as long as it substantially complies with the statutory requirements. In some states a will can be handwritten in crayon or ink. It can be written on a sheet or scrap of paper, on a paper bag, or on a piece of cloth. A will in the handwriting of the testator is called **holographic** (or olographic). A will also can refer to a written memorandum that itself is not a will but that contains information necessary to carry out the will. For example, T's will provides that a certain sum of money be divided among a group

---

6. *Nuncupative* is the legal name for an oral will. An oral will made by a soldier on active service or a sailor at sea is recognized as valid in many states for distributing *personal* property, but it will not transfer title to real property.

of charities designated on a particular list T gave to the trustee *the same day the will was signed.* The written list will be "incorporated by reference" into the will only if it was in existence when the will was executed (signed) and if it is sufficiently described so that it can be identified.

2. *A will must be signed by the testator.* It is a fundamental requirement in almost all jurisdictions that the testator or testatrix's signature appear, generally at the end of the will. Each jurisdiction dictates by statute and court decision what constitutes a signature. Initials, an "X" or other mark, and words like *Mom* have all been upheld as valid when it was shown that the testator intended them to be a signature.

3. *A will must be witnessed.* A will must be attested by two and sometimes three witnesses. The number of witnesses, their qualifications, and the manner in which the witnessing must be done are generally set out in a statute.

A witness can be required to be disinterested—that is, not a beneficiary under the will. By contrast, the UPC provides that a will is valid even if it is attested by an interested witness. [UPC Sec. 2-505] There are no age requirements for witnesses, but they must be competent.

Witnesses function to verify that the testator actually executed (signed) the will and had the requisite intent and capacity at the time. A witness does not have to read the contents of the will. Usually, the testator and witnesses must all sign in sight of one another, but the UPC deems it sufficient if the testator acknowledges his or her signature to the witnesses. [UPC Sec. 2-502] The UPC does not require all parties to sign in the presence of one another.

4. *A will can be "published."* Publication is an oral declaration by the maker to the witnesses that the document they are about to sign is his or her "last will and testament." Publication is becoming an unnecessary formality in most states, and it is not required under the UPC.

Holographic Wills

Generally, strict compliance with the formalities listed above is required before a document is accepted as the decedent's will. The holographic will presents one of the few exceptions. A holographic will is one that is completely in the handwriting of the decedent. For a holographic will to be probated (validated), it must also be dated and signed by the decedent.

FRAUD, UNDUE INFLUENCE, AND MISTAKE

A valid will must represent the maker's intention to create a will that transfers and distributes his or her property. When it can be shown that the decedent's plan of distribution was the result of fraud or improper pressure brought by another person, the will is declared invalid.

Undue influence may be a factor if the testator or testatrix ignores blood relatives and names as beneficiary a nonrelative who is in constant close contact and in a position to influence the making of the will. For example, a nurse or friend caring for the deceased before death named as the beneficiary to the exclusion of all family members might well be challenged for undue influence.

Fraud will invalidate a will. Assume X dies leaving his property to B. B had convinced X that he was X's long lost son, but in fact he is not. The will is invalid.

REVOCATION OF WILLS

An executed will is revocable by the maker at any time during the maker's lifetime. Wills can also be revoked by operation of law. Revocation can be partial or complete, and it must follow certain strict formalities.

Act of the Maker

REVOCATION BY PHYSICAL ACT The testator or testatrix may revoke a will by intentionally burning, tearing, cancelling, obliterating, or destroying it, or by having someone else do so in the presence of and at the maker's direction.[7] In some states, partial revocation by physical act of

---

7. The destruction cannot be inadvertent. It must show the maker's intent to revoke.

the maker is recognized. Thus, those portions of a will lined out or torn away are dropped, and the remaining parts of the will are valid. In no case, however, can a provision be crossed out and an additional or substitute provision written in. Such altered portions require reexecution (resigning) and reattestation (rewitnessing). This is commonly done by **codicil.**

To revoke a will by physical act, it is necessary to follow the mandates of a state statute exactly. Where a state statute prescribes the exact methods for revoking a will by physical act, those are the only methods that will revoke the will.

ESTATE OF EGLEE
Supreme Court of Rhode Island, 1978.
__R.I.__, 383 A.2d 586.

BACKGROUND AND FACTS   *Eglee died in November of 1973. Her stepson filed a petition requesting that a written instrument that she had executed and dated be admitted to probate as her will. The document complied with state laws, but Eglee had made red pencil lines through every word and through the signature. In addition, diagonally across each clause were the decedent's initials, the word "obliterated," and the date. The entire document, however, remained legible despite the defacement.*

DECISION AND RATIONALE   *Although the decendent had demonstrated an intention to revoke her will, she had not complied with the precise methods of revocation required by state law. Therefore, her will was valid despite her intent to revoke. Under state statute, revocation could only be effected by intent to revoke coupled with the act of "burning, tearing or otherwise destroying" the will. "The plaintiff contends that the phrase "otherwise destroying" in [the state's statute] should be construed so as to include the acts of cancelling and obliterating. However, in interpreting such provisions our duty is very narrowly described. We must construe statutes, not redraft them. *** The rationale for making statutory formalities governing revocation of a will mandatory is to prevent mistake, misrepresentation, and fraud."*

REVOCATION IN ANOTHER WRITING   A **codicil** is simply a separate written instrument that amends or revokes provisions in a will. It eliminates the necessity of redrafting the entire will merely to add to it or amend it. A codicil can also be used to revoke an entire will and must be executed with the same formalities required for a will. It must refer expressly to the will. In effect, it updates a will because the will is "incorporated by reference" into the codicil.

A *second will* can be executed that may or may not revoke the first or a prior will, depending upon the language used. The second will must specifically use words like, "This will hereby revokes all prior wills." If the second will is otherwise valid and properly executed, it will revoke all prior wills. If the express *declaration of revocation* is missing, then both wills are read together. If any of the dispositions made in the second will are inconsistent with the prior will, the second will controls.

Revocation by Operation of Law

MARRIAGE   In general, a will written and executed before marriage will be revoked by the fact of marriage. Public policy provides that a person's new marital obligations change any prior decisions concerning the disposition of property. Under the Uniform Probate Code

(UPC), a subsequent marriage *does not revoke* a will. [UPC Sec. 2-508] The new spouse is entitled to whatever share of the estate the law provides for testators who die without a will. The rest is passed under the will. [UPC Sec. 2-301]

DIVORCE OR ANNULMENT   Under common law and the UPC, divorce does not necessarily revoke the entire will. A divorce or an annulment occurring after a will has been executed will revoke those dispositions of property made under the will to the former spouse.

CHILDREN BORN AFTER A WILL IS EXECUTED   If a child is born after a will has been executed and if it appears that the testator would have made a provision for the child, then the child is entitled to receive whatever portion of the estate he or she is allowed under state intestate laws. Most state laws allow a child to receive some portion of the estate if no provision is made in a will, unless it appears from the terms of the will that the testator intended to disinherit the child. Under the UPC, the rule is the same. [UPC Sec. 2-302]

RIGHTS UNDER A WILL

The law imposes certain limitations on the way a person can dispose of property in a will. For example, a married person who makes a will cannot deny leaving a certain portion of the estate to the surviving spouse. In most states this is called a "forced share," and it is often one-third.

Beneficiaries under a will have rights as well. A beneficiary can renounce his or her share of the property given under a will.[8] Further, a surviving spouse can renounce the amount given under a will and elect to take the "forced share" if the forced share is larger than the amount of the gift. State statutes provide the methods by which a surviving spouse accomplishes renunciation. The purpose of these

_____

8. Usually done for tax reasons or because the recipient would fare better by taking his or her elective share.

statutes is to allow the spouse to obtain whichever distribution would be most advantageous.

STATUTES OF DESCENT AND DISTRIBUTION

The rules of descent are statutory. That means each state can regulate how property shall be distributed when a person dies without a will. State laws attempt to carry out what would have been the wishes of the decedent.

The rules of descent vary widely from state to state. However, there is usually a special statutory provision for the rights of the surviving spouse and minor children. In addition, the law provides that the debts of the decedent must first be satisfied out of his or her estate. The remaining assets then pass to the surviving spouse and to the children. For example, A dies intestate and is survived by his wife, B, and his children, C and D. A's property passes according to **intestacy laws.** After A's outstanding debts are paid, B will receive the real estate (either in fee simple or as a life estate) and ordinarily a one-third to one-half interest in the property. B will probably also be entitled to one-half of A's personal property. The remaining real and personal property will pass to C and D in equal portions.

Distribution

State statutes of descent and distribution specify the order in which other descendants of an intestate share in the estate. When there are no surviving spouse or children, then grandchildren, brothers and sisters, and, in some states, parents of the decedent are the next in line to share. These relatives are usually called *lineal descendants.* If there are no lineal descendants, then *collateral heirs* are the next group to share. Collateral heirs include nieces, nephews, aunts, and uncles of the decedent. If there are still no survivors in any of those groups of people related to the decedent, most statutes provide that the property shall be distributed among the next of kin of any of the collateral heirs. Stepchildren are not considered kin. However, legally adopted children are recognized as lawful heirs of their adoptive parents. Because state statutes differ so widely, very few generalizations can be made about the laws of descent and distribution. It is extremely important to refer to the exact terms of the applicable state statutes when addressing any problem of intestacy distribution.

Under the UPC, the surviving spouse is entitled to take an elective share of one-third of the decedent's estate. [UPC Sec. 2-201] In addition, the UPC provides that the surviving spouse is entitled to:

1. A homestead allowance of $5,000.
2. A household and personal effects exemption to a value not to exceed $3,500.
3. A family allowance for a period of up to one year after the death occurs to provide for daily expenses before the estate is settled, up to the amount of $6,000. [UPC Secs. 2-401, 402, 403, and 404]

THE PATTERN OF INTESTACY DISTRIBUTION When a person dies intestate, the statute of the state where the decedent died will govern descent and distribution except for real estate, which is governed by the laws of the state where the real property is located.

When there is a surviving spouse, that spouse usually receives a share of the estate— half if there is also a surviving child and one-third if there are two or more children. Only where no children or grandchildren survive the decedent will a surviving spouse succeed to the _entire_ estate.

When an intestate is survived by descendants of deceased children, the question arises as to what share the descendants (that is, grandchildren of the intestate) will receive. **Per stirpes** is a method of dividing an intestate share where a class or group of distributees (for example, grandchildren) take the share that their deceased parent _would have been_ entitled to inherit. This is best explained by an example: Smith has three children, #1, #2, and #3. Child #1 has one child, D. Child #2 has two children,

E and F. Child #3 has no children. Child #1 and child #2 die before Smith (their father). Child #3 is still living when Smith dies. (Smith's wife is also dead.) Had all children been living, child #1, child #2, and child #3 would each be entitled to one-third of Smith's estate. In a _per stirpes_ distribution, the lineal descendants of the deceased children will inherit whatever share was owed to their parents. Thus, grandchild D will inherit the one-third share that would have gone to D's parent, Smith's child #1. Grandchildren E and F must divide the one-third share that would have gone to their parent, Smith's child #2. Thus, E and F each receive a sixth. Child #3, who is still alive, gets one-third. If child #3 had had children, it would not have affected the distribution.

Another type of distribution of an estate is on a **per capita** basis. This means simply that each person takes an equal share of the estate. Thus, according to the above example, D, E, F, and child #3 would each have received a per capita share of one-quarter.

In most states and under the Uniform Probate Code, inlaws do not share in an estate. If a child dies before his or her parents, the child's spouse will not receive an inheritance. Thus, the surviving spouses of child #1 and child #2 of Smith in the example above are not entitled to any share of the estate. Only the grandchildren (D, E, and F) are entitled to share.

Whether or not an illegitimate child inherits depends on state statute. In all states, intestate succession between the mother and the child exists. In some states, intestate succession between the father and the child can occur only where the child is "legitimized" by ceremony or the child has been "acknowledged" by the father. The constitutionality of these illegitimacy statutes has recently been upheld by the Supreme Court.

TRUSTS

A trust involves real property or personal property. The _legal_ title to the property is transferred to the trustee, who is charged with certain duties of dealing with the property for the benefit of another person, the beneficiary. If Sanford conveys his farm to South Miami First National Bank, to be held for the benefit of Sanford's daughters, Sanford has created a trust. Sanford is the settlor, South Miami First National Bank is the trustee, and Sanford's daughters are the beneficiaries.

Express Trusts

An express trust is one created by a written instrument. Two types of trusts will be discussed: *inter vivos* trusts and testamentary trusts.

INTER VIVOS TRUSTS   An **inter vivos trust** is a trust executed by a grantor during his or her lifetime. The grantor executes a "trust deed," and legal title to the trust property passes to the trustee. The trustee has a duty to administer the property as directed by the grantor for the benefit and in the interest of the beneficiaries. The trustee must preserve the trust property, make it productive, and, if required by the terms of the trust deed, pay income to the beneficiaries, all in accordance with the terms of the trust. Once the *inter vivos* trust is created, the grantor has, in effect, given over the property for the benefit of beneficiaries. There can be favorable tax-related considerations to setting up an *inter vivos* trust.

TESTAMENTARY TRUSTS   A **testamentary trust** is a trust created by will to come into existence upon the settlor's death. Although a testamentary trust has a trustee who maintains legal title to the trust property, actions of the trustee are subject to judicial approval. The trustee of a testamentary trust can be named in the will or be appointed by the court. Unlike the *inter vivos* trust, a testamentary trust will not fail because a trustee has not been named in the will. The legal responsibilities of the trustees are the same in both kinds of trust. If the will setting up a testamentary trust is invalid, then the trust will also be invalid. The property that was supposed to be in the trust will then pass according to intestacy laws, not according to the terms of the trust.

BACKGROUND AND FACTS   *By the terms of his will, Claflin left all of his personal property to a trustee "to sell and dispose of the same and to pay the proceeds to my son Albert in the following manner: $10,000 when he is of the age of 21 years, $10,000 when he is the age of 24 years and the balance when he is of the age of 30 years." Albert was not quite twenty-one when his father died. When he reached twenty-one he received $10,000. Prior to reaching twenty-five, Albert brought an action against the trustee to compel the payment of the remainder of the trust fund.*

DECISION AND RATIONALE   *Albert was not entitled to immediate payment of the trust property. Although it was undisputable that his interest in the trust property was vested and absolute and that no other person was entitled to it, distribution of the trust assets before Albert reached thirty years of age would have been contrary to the trust provision. It is clear from the will that Albert's father did not intend Albert to have the remaining trust property until his thirtieth birthday. Even though Albert can sell his interest in the trust, and it can be reached*

CLAFLIN v. CLAFLIN
Supreme Court of
Massachusetts, 1889.
149 Mass. 19, 20 N.E. 454.

> *by his creditors, the restrictions are not altogether useless. As the court explained, "there is not the same danger that he will spend the property while it is in the hands of the trustees as there would be if it were in his own."*

ORAL TRUSTS An oral *inter vivos* trust is recognized in law. Of course, the property involved must be such that the Statute of Frauds will not prevent its transfer. In other words, the subject matter of an oral trust should not involve the transfer of realty, because the Statute of Frauds requires that any contract concerning the transfer of realty must be in writing. However, oral trusts can be used to transfer personal property. For example, Appelton, a grantor, hands certain jewelry over to Tyms and says, "Keep this jewelry for my daughter and give it to her when she reaches twenty-one." Appelton has created a valid oral trust with Tyms as the trustee. Appelton's daughter is the beneficiary. Tyms is under a duty to hand the property over to the daughter when she reaches twenty-one.

Implied Trusts

If property has been transferred through an oral trust and the trustee does not perform his or her duties, a court of equity can impose trust obligations on the trustee. This is especially true when the trustee uses fraud, duress, or undue influence or abuses a confidential relationship in order to come into the trustee position. If a beneficiary can prove that an oral trust was created, then a court of equity will either require the trustee to act on behalf of the beneficiary or declare that no trust exists. In that case, the property must be returned to the general estate of the decedent, and it then passes to the beneficiaries.

ESTATE ADMINISTRATION

The orderly procedure used to collect assets, settle debts, and distribute the remaining assets when a person dies is the subject matter of estate administration. This section will look at the duties of the personal representative of the deceased.

Principle Duties of the Personal Representative

The rules and procedures for managing the estate of a deceased are controlled by statute. Thus, they vary from state to state. In every state, there is a special court, often called a "probate court," which oversees the management of estates of decedents.

The first step after a person dies is usually to determine whether or not the decedent left a will. Sometimes the decedent's attorney will have that information or at least know if a will was ever executed. Sometimes it is not known for some time whether a valid will exists. The personal papers of the deceased must be reviewed. If a will exists, it probably names a personal representative to administer the estate. If there is no will, or if the will fails to name a personal representative, then the court must appoint one. Under the UPC, the term *personal representative* includes the executor (person named in the will) and administrator (person appointed by the court). [UPC Sec. 1-201(30)]

The first duty of the personal representative is to inventory and collect the assets of the decedent. If necessary, the assets must be appraised to determine their value. Both the rights of creditors and the rights of beneficiaries must be protected during the estate administration proceedings. In addition, the personal representative is responsible for managing the assets of the estate during the administration period and not allowing them to be wasted or depleted unnecessarily. A decedent's property often seems to "disappear" shortly after his or her death—usually into the hands of friends and relatives.

The personal representative receives and pays valid claims of creditors and arranges for the estate to pay federal and state income taxes and estate taxes (or inheritance taxes, depending on the state). A personal representative is required to post a bond to insure honest and faithful performance. Usually the bond exceeds the estimated value of the personal estate of the decedent. In some cases, the will can specify that the personal representative need not post a bond.

Each step in the administration of the estate is determined by state statute. When the ultimate distribution of assets to beneficiaries is determined, the personal representative is responsible for distributing the estate pursuant to court order. Once the assets have been distributed, the estate is closed, and the personal representative is relieved of any further responsibility or liability for the estate. Exhibit 55-1 lists the duties of the personal representative.

EXHIBIT 55-1   THE DUTIES OF THE PERSONAL REPRESENTATIVE

It would be impossible to indicate all the duties the executor must perform, but here are some.

1. Managing the estate until it is settled, including
   a. Collecting debts due the estate.
   b. Managing real estate; arranging for maintenance and repairs.
   c. Registering securities in the name of the estate.
   d. Collecting insurance proceeds.
   e. Running family business, if necessary.
   f. Arranging for the family's support during probate.
   g. Properly insuring assets.

2. Collecting all assets and necessary records, including
   a. Locating the will, insurance policies, real estate papers, car registrations, and birth certificates.
   b. Filing claims for pension, Social Security, profit sharing and veterans benefits.
   c. Taking possession of bank accounts, real estate, personal effects, and safe deposit boxes.
   d. Obtaining names, addresses, and Social Security numbers of all heirs.
   e. Making an inventory of all assets.
   f. Setting up records and books.

3. Determining the estate's obligations, including
   a. Determining which claims are legally due.
   b. Obtaining receipts for all claims paid.
   c. Checking on mortgages and other loans.

4. Computing and then paying all death taxes due, which requires
   a. Selecting the most beneficial tax alternatives.
   b. Deciding which assets to sell to provide necessary funds.
   c. Paying taxes on time to avoid penalties.
   d. Opposing what you think are unfair evaluations established by governmental taxing authorities.

5. Computing beneficiaries' shares and then distributing the estate, which includes
   a. Determining who gets particular items and settling family disputes.
   b. Transferring title to real estate and other property.
   c. Selling off assets to pay cash legacies.
   d. Paying final estate costs.
   e. Preparing accountings for the court's approval.

Reprinted by permission from *Personal Finance Today*, p. 519. Copyright © Roger LeRoy Miller Inc., (West Publishing Co.: St. Paul) 1979.

Probate versus Nonprobate

To probate a will means to determine whether or not it is valid. The process of probate is time-consuming and costly, and the court is involved in every step of the proceedings. Attorneys and personal representatives often become involved in probate.

Many states have statutes that allow for the distribution of assets without probate proceedings. Faster and less expensive methods are then used. For example, property can be transferred by affidavit, and problems or questions can be handled during an administrative hearing. In addition, some state statutes provide that title to cars, savings and checking accounts, and certain other property can be passed merely by filling out forms.

SUMMARY PROCEDURES   The use of summary procedures in estate administration can save time and money. The expense of a personal representative's commission, attorneys' fees, appraisers' fees, and so forth can be eliminated or at least minimized if the parties utilize summary administration procedures. But in situations—for example, where a guardian for minor children or an incompetent person must be appointed and a trust has been created to protect the minor or incompetent—probate procedures cannot be avoided. In the ordinary situation, a person can employ various will substitutes to avoid the cost of probate—for example, *inter vivos* trusts, life insurance policies with named beneficiaries, or joint tenancy arrangements. Not all methods are suitable for every estate, but there are alternatives to a complete probate administration.

THE TAXATION OF ESTATES*

In the past, gift taxes (those imposed on the grantor of the gift) were less than estate taxes.

*The following material is adapted with permission from *Personal Finance Today*, pp. 514-517. Copyright© Roger LeRoy Miller Inc., (West Publishing Co.: St. Paul) 1979.

Thus, it was beneficial for older individuals to make parts of their estates gifts to their future heirs to reduce the total taxes on the estates. This is often not the case now. The Tax Reform Act of 1976 virtually rewrote the estate and gift tax code. Specifically, the deductions and credits granted in the 1976 Tax Reform Act exempt all but the extremely rich from federal estate taxes. Thus, one basic reason for setting up trusts has been eliminated for almost all individuals in the United States. The tax rate, which is the same for gifts and estates, is given in the unified rate schedule in Exhibit 55-2.

Comparing the Old Law with the New

It is interesting to compare the old federal estate tax law with the new one. Under the old law, half the estate could be left to a spouse, tax-free; then an additional $60,000 was exempt from taxes. Now, half the estate *or* up to $250,000 (whichever is *greater*) can be left to a spouse, tax-free. The $60,000 additional exemption is increased by means of a tax credit to $175,000 by 1981. Exhibit 55-3 shows the taxes due at the first partner's death, including the marital deduction. These figures are for 1981 and beyond; the taxes due were slightly more in 1979 and 1980. Taxes due on the estate of a single person are also shown.

THE NUMBERS ARE SMALL

In 1981, 98 percent of all estates will pay no federal estate tax. Estates up to $425,000 can be passed on to heirs free of any estate and gift taxes. For a person who has yet to accumulate significant wealth, it hardly pays to try to grasp the intricacies of estate taxation.

STATE INHERITANCE AND ESTATE TAXES

An **inheritance tax** is paid by those who receive the property; an estate tax is paid by the estate. Most states impose an inheritance tax, but some impose an estate tax instead. Others impose both. The state inheritance tax (or estate tax, if that is the case) usually is set at a lower rate than the federal estate tax, but state exemptions usually are smaller than federal exemptions. Thus, the actual state tax due can be, and often is, considerably higher than the federal tax due.

State inheritance taxes are based on the value of the assets inherited by the individual. They are owed to the state in which the inherited assets are located rather than the state in which the person inheriting them lives. In many cases, the state tax rate varies not only with the value of the assets but also with the relationship

---

EXHIBIT 55-2   UNIFIED RATE SCHEDULE

If the amount with respect to which the tentative tax is to be computed is:

The tentative tax is:

If the amount with respect to which the tentative tax is to be computed is:	The tentative tax is:
Not over $10,000	18% of such amount.
Over $10,000 but not over $20,000	$1,800, plus 20% of the excess of such amount over $10,000.
Over $20,000 but not over $40,000	$3,800, plus 22% of the excess of such amount over $20,000.
Over $40,000 but not over $60,000	$8,200, plus 24% of the excess of such amount over $40,000.
Over $60,000 but not over $80,000	$13,000, plus 26% of the excess of such amount over $60,000.
Over $80,000 but not over $100,000	$18,200, plus 28% of the excess of such amount over $80,000.
Over $100,000 but not over $150,000	$23,800, plus 30% of the excess of such amount over $100,000.
Over $150,000 but not over $250,000	$38,800, plus 32% of the excess of such amount over $150,000.
Over $250,000 but not over $500,000	$70,800, plus 34% of the excess of such amount over $250,000.
Over $500,000 but not over $750,000	$155,800, plus 37% of the excess of such amount over $500,000.
Over $750,000 but not over $1,000,000	$248,300, plus 39% of the excess of such amount over $750,000.
Over $1,000,000 but not over $1,250,000	$345,800, plus 41% of the excess of such amount over $1,000,000.
Over $1,250,000 but not over $1,500,000	$448,300, plus 43% of the excess of such amount over $1,250,000.
Over $1,500,000 but not over $2,000,000	$555,800, plus 45% of the excess of such amount over $1,500,000.
Over $2,000,000 but not over $2,500,000	$780,800, plus 49% of the excess of such amount over $2,000,000.
Over $2,500,000 but not over $3,000,000	$1,025,800, plus 53% of the excess of such amount over $2,500,000.
Over $3,000,000 but not over $3,500,000	$1,290,800, plus 57% of the excess of such amount over $3,000,000.
Over $3,500,000 but not over $4,000,000	$1,575,800, plus 61% of the excess of such amount over $3,500,000.
Over $4,000,000 but not over $4,500,000	$1,880,800, plus 65% of the excess of such amount over $4,000,000.
Over $4,500,000 but not over $5,000,000	$2,205,800, plus 69% of the excess of such amount over $4,500,000.
Over $5,000,000	$2,550,800, plus 70% of the excess of such amount over $5,000,000.

EXHIBIT 55-3   FEDERAL ESTATE TAXES IN 1981 AND AFTER

Adjusted Gross Estate (after subtracting debts, funeral expenses, administrative costs, etc.)	Taxes Due at First Partner's Death (includes marital deduction)	Taxes Due at Death (single persons)
$ 60,000	$ 0	$ 0
80,000	0	0
100,000	0	0
200,000	0	6,600
300,000	0	37,200
400,000	0	68,000
500,000	21,400	98,900
1,000,000	98,800	265,600

of the recipient to the deceased. Exhibit 55-4 lists state inheritance taxes.

The Pick Up Tax

Most states have an added estate tax, which is usually called a pick up tax. This tax is designed to insure that an amount at least equal to the maximum allowable federal estate tax credit is charged. Some states, such as Florida, establish an estate tax exactly equal to the maximum federal credit allowed for state estate taxes paid. This makes it attractive for people to move to these states when they retire. This tax does not, however, increase the *total* death taxes paid; it applies only when the amount due from other state death taxes is less than the allowable federal estate credit.

EXHIBIT 55-4   STATE INHERITANCE TAX RATES

Source: Commerce Clearing House.

Selected Categories of Heirs as of September 1, 1976

	Rate (percent)			
State	Spouse, child or parent	Brother or sister	Other than relative	Maximum rate applies above (thousands)
California	3—14	6—20	10—24	$ 400
Colorado	2—8	3—10	10—19	500
Connecticut	2—8	4—10	8—14	1,000
Delaware	1—6	5—10	10—16	200
Hawaii	1.5—7.5	3.5—9	3.5—9	250
Idaho	2—15	4—20	8—30	500
Illinois	2—14	2—14	10—30	500
Indiana	1—10	5—15	7—20	1,500
Iowa	1—8	5—10	10—15	150
Kansas	.5—5	3—12.5	10—15	500
Kentucky	2—10	4—16	6—16	500
Louisiana	2—3	5—7	5—10	25
Maine	5—10	8—14	14—18	250
Maryland	1	10	10	
Massachusetts	1.8—11.8	5.5—19.3	8—19.3	1,000
Michigan	2—8	2—8	10—15	750
Minnesota	1.5—10	6—25	8—30	1,000
Missouri	1—6	3—18	5—30	400
Montana	2—8	4—16	8—32	100
Nebraska	1	1	6—18	60
New Hampshire		15	15	
New Jersey	1—16	11—16	15—16	3,200
North Carolina	1—12	4—16	8—17	3,000
Oregon	3—12	3—12	3—12	500
Pennsylvania	6	15	15	
Rhode Island	2—9	3—10	8—15	1,000
South Dakota		4—16	6—24	100
Tennessee	5.5—9.5	6.5—20	6.5—20	500
Texas	1—6	3—10	5—20	1,000
Virginia	1—5	2—10	5—15	1,000
Washington	1—10	3—20	10—25	500
West Virginia	3—13	4—18	10—30	1,000
Wisconsin	1.25—12.5	5—25	10—30	500
Wyoming	2	2	6	
District of Columbia	1—8	5—23	5—23	1,000

QUESTIONS AND CASE PROBLEMS

1. In December 1927, Brainard decided to trade on the stock market during 1928. He consulted a lawyer and was advised that it was possible for him to trade in trust for his children and other members of his family. Brainard discussed the matter with his wife and mother and stated to them that he declared a trust of his stock trading during 1928 "for the benefit of my family—my wife, mother, and my two children." During 1928, Brainard traded on the stock market, and, by the end of the year, he determined his compensation at slightly less than $10,000. Is there a valid trust? [Brainard v. Commissioner, 91 F.2d 880 (7th Cir. 1937)]

2. On August 3, 1942, Albert Gordon delivered fifteen policies of insurance on his own life to the Portland Trust Bank pursuant to the terms of a written trust agreement. The trust instrument, executed on the same date, stated that the bank as trustee would be the beneficiary of the life insurance policies and would have the duty to collect the proceeds at Gordon's death. The trust instrument further provided that the bank as trustee would distribute the income earned from the proceeds in monthly installments to Gordon's wife. Was there a valid trust? Who is the settlor? The trustee? The beneficiary? Does the fact that Gordon can revoke the life insurance policies at any time prior to his death affect the answer? [Gordon v. Portland Trust Bank, 201 Or. 648, 271 P.2d 653 (1954)]

3. Harris executed a written instrument in which he named Bishop as trustee of $17,000 in bonds, notes, mortgages, and money. The instrument declared that Harris was hereby transferring these assets to Bishop in trust for the benefit of the public library in Alexandria, Ohio. Thereafter, however, Harris received interest on some of the notes and still had access to the money and instruments that were the subject of the trust. Has Harris created a valid trust? Consider the requirements of making a valid gift. [Whitehead v. Bishop, 23 Ohio App. 315, 155 N.E. 565 (1925)]

4. In 1925, Campbell died, leaving a will whose ninth clause read as follows: "My good friends Clark and Smith I appoint as my trustees. Each of my trustees is competent by reason of familiarity with the property, my wishes and friendships, to wisely distribute some portion at least of said property. I therefore give and bequeath to my trustees all my property in trust to make disposal by the way of a momento from myself, of such articles to such of my friends as they, my trustees, shall select. All of said property, not so disposed of by them, my trustees are directed to sell and the proceeds of such sale or sales to become and be disposed of as a part of the residue of my estate." Valid trust? [Clark v. Campbell, 82 N.H. 281, 133 A. 166 (1926)]

5. Edwin L. Bunker died intestate. He was survived by the following persons: his son, James Bunker; his uncle Cyrus's legally adopted son, Walter Bunker; his aunt's illegitimate daughter; James M. Steele, a son of a half-brother of the intestate's mother; and three living children of another half-brother of the intestate's mother. There was $1 million in Edwin's estate when he died. Under the rules of intestacy, who takes what? What will the answer be if James Bunker is not living at the time of his father's death? [Estate of Bunker, 106 N.H. 391, 211 A.2d 902 (1965)]

6. H. W. Wolfe died at the age of sixty-seven, leaving personal property worth about $4,000 and more than five hundred acres of land. Just before he died on July 31, 1911, he properly executed a will that contained the following provision: "I, H. W. Wolfe, will and bequeath to Miss Mary Lilly Luffman, a tract of land near Roaring Gap Post Office, on State Road and South Fork, adjoining the lands of J. M. Royal and others, the land bought by me from H. D. Woodruff. Witness my hand and seal, this thirty first day of July, 1911." On August 14, 1911, Wolfe wrote another will that provided in part: "I, H. W. Wolfe, do make and declare this to be my last will and testament. I will and bequeath all my effects to my brothers and sisters, to be divided equally among them. Witness my hand and seal, this the fourteenth day of August, 1911." Both wills were properly signed and attested. Who is entitled to what under these wills? [In re Wolfe's Will, 185 N.C. 563, 117 S.E. 804 (1923)]

7. The will of Grace Bradley Walters was properly executed and was witnessed by Margaret Weldon and Richard Coleman Bradley, both of whom were also legatees. However, only Richard Coleman Bradley would take if the will was not probated because he was next of kin. Will Margaret Weldon be able to share in Grace Bradley Walters's estate? [In re Walters' Estate, 285 N.Y. 158, 33 N.E.2d 72 (1941)]

8. Neptune Center Associates was a limited partnership engaged mainly in the business of making investments. Office Buildings of America, Inc., was a

corporation engaged in the business of purchasing commercial buildings, acting primarily as a broker. The investing members of Neptune Center Associates decided to purchase the Neptune City shopping center. A representative of the association contacted Office Buildings of America to arrange the deal. Thereafter, Neptune Associates gave Office Buildings of America approximately $400,000 "to be utilized for the specific purpose of purchasing Neptune City shopping center." Office Buildings of America was not to make the purchase for a number of weeks. In the meantime, it used the money given it by Neptune Associates to pay some of its general business expenses. Has a trust been created here? If so, have any duties of the trust relationship been broken? [McGlynn v. Schultz, 95 N.J. Super. 412, 231 A.2d 386 (1967)]

9. F. V. Richardson was the owner and operator of a service station in Franklin County, Florida. On May 1, 1968, Ken Watson drove his car into Richardson's service station, filled it up with gas, then told Richard-son that he wanted someone to witness his will. Richardson, in the presence of Watson, asked Barbara Shiver, a customer, to witness the will also. She signed the will as a witness in the presence of Richardson and Watson. Richardson then signed the will as a witness and asked W. W. Cooper to sign it also. All this time, Watson stood very close by, watching each of the witnesses sign the will. Each of the witnesses was aware that this was Watson's will. Is Watson's will valid? [In re Estate of Watson, 226 So.2d 249 (Fla. App. 1969)]

10. Jesse Butterfield Morris died on February 11, 1967. On April 6, 1967, the Security First National Bank offered a document for probate as Morris's holographic will. The document was entirely in Morris's handwriting, but it contained no signatures of witnesses. The document was dated (November 1, 1965), was addressed to the Security First National Bank, and contained the initials J. B. M. at the end. Should Morris's will be probated? [In re Estate of Morris, 268 Cal. App.2d 638, 74 Cal.Rptr. 32 (1969)]

APPENDIX A
The Uniform
Commercial Code
1977 Official Text

(Adopted in 52 jurisdictions; all 50 States, although Louisiana has adopted only Articles 1, 3, 4, and 5; the District of Columbia, and the Virgin Islands.)

The Code consists of 10 Articles as follows:

Art.

1. GENERAL PROVISIONS

2. Sales

3. Commercial Paper

4. Bank Deposits and Collections

5. Letters of Credit

6. Bulk Transfers

7. Warehouse Receipts, Bills of Lading and Other Documents of Title

8. Investment Securities

9. Secured Transactions: Sales of Accounts, Contract Rights and Chattel Paper

10. Effective Date and Repealer

Article 1
GENERAL PROVISIONS

Part 1 Short Title, Construction, Application and Subject Matter of the Act

§ 1—101. Short Title.

This Act shall be known and may be cited as Uniform Commercial Code.

§ 1—102. Purposes; Rules of Construction; Variation by Agreement.

(1) This Act shall be liberally construed and applied to promote its underlying purposes and policies.

(2) Underlying purposes and policies of this Act are

(a) to simplify, clarify and modernize the law governing commercial transactions;

(b) to permit the continued expansion of commercial practices through custom, usage and agreement of the parties;

(c) to make uniform the law among the various jurisdictions.

(3) The effect of provisions of this Act may be varied by agreement, except as otherwise provided in this Act and except that the obligations of good faith, diligence, reasonableness and care prescribed by this Act may not be disclaimed by agreement but the parties may by agreement determine the standards by which the performance of such obligations is to be measured if such standards are not manifestly unreasonable.

(4) The presence in certain provisions of this Act of the words "unless otherwise agreed" or words of similar import does not imply that the effect of other provisions may not be varied by agreement under subsection (3).

(5) In this Act unless the context otherwise requires

(a) words in the singular number include the plural, and in the plural include the singular;

(b) words of the masculine gender include the feminine and the neuter, and when the sense so indicates words of the neuter gender may refer to any gender.

§ 1—103. Supplementary General Principles of Law Applicable.

Unless displaced by the particular provisions of this Act, the principles of law and equity, including the law merchant and the law relative to capacity to contract, principal and agent, estoppel, fraud, misrepresentation, duress, coercion, mistake, bankruptcy, or other validating or invalidating cause shall supplement its provisions.

§ 1—104. Construction Against Implicit Repeal.

This Act being a general act intended as a unified coverage of its subject matter, no part of it shall be deemed to be impliedly repealed by subsequent legislation if such construction can reasonably be avoided.

§ 1—105. Territorial Application of the Act; Parties' Power to Choose Applicable Law.

(1) Except as provided hereafter in this section, when a transaction bears a reasonable relation to this state and also to another state or nation the parties may agree that the law either of this state or of such other state or nation shall govern their rights and duties. Failing such agreement this Act applies to transactions bearing an appropriate relation to this state.

(2) Where one of the following provisions of this Act specifies the applicable law, that provision governs and a contrary agreement is effective only to the

extent permitted by the law (including the conflict of laws rules) so specified:

Rights of creditors against sold goods. Section 2—402.

Applicability of the Article on Bank Deposits and Collections. Section 4—102.

Bulk transfers subject to the Article on Bulk Transfers. Section 6—102.

Applicability of the Article on Investment Securities. Section 8—106.

Perfection provisions of the Article on Secured Transactions. Section 9—103.

§ 1—106. Remedies to Be Liberally Administered.

(1) The remedies provided by this Act shall be liberally administered to the end that the aggrieved party may be put in as good a position as if the other party had fully performed but neither consequential or special nor penal damages may be had except as specifically provided in this Act or by other rule of law.

(2) Any right or obligation declared by this Act is enforceable by action unless the provision declaring it specifies a different and limited effect.

§ 1—107. Waiver or Renunciation of Claim or Right After Breach.

Any claim or right arising out of an alleged breach can be discharged in whole or in part without consideration by a written waiver or renunciation signed and delivered by the aggrieved party.

§ 1—108. Severability.

If any provision or clause of this Act or application thereof to any person or circumstances is held invalid, such invalidity shall not affect other provisions or applications of the Act which can be given effect without the invalid provision or application, and to this end the provisions of this Act are declared to be severable.

§ 1—109. Section Captions.

Section captions are parts of this Act.

Part 2 General Definitions and Principles of Interpretation

§ 1—201. General Definitions

Subject to additional definitions contained in the subsequent Articles of this Act which are applicable to specific Articles or Parts thereof, and unless the context otherwise requires, in this Act:

(1) "Action" in the sense of a judicial proceeding includes recoupment, counterclaim, set-off, suit in equity and any other proceedings in which rights are determined.

(2) "Aggrieved party" means a party entitled to resort to a remedy.

(3) "Agreement" means the bargain of the parties in fact as found in their language or by implication from other circumstances including course of dealing or usage of trade or course of performance as provided in this Act (Sections 1—205 and 2—208). Whether an agreement has legal consequences is determined by the provisions of this Act, if applicable; otherwise by the law of contracts (Section 1—103). (Compare "Contract".)

(4) "Bank" means any person engaged in the business of banking.

(5) "Bearer" means the person in possession of an instrument, document of title, or certificated security payable to bearer or indorsed in blank.

(6) "Bill of lading" means a document evidencing the receipt of goods for shipment issued by a person engaged in the business of transporting or forwarding goods, and includes an airbill. "Airbill" means a document serving for air transportation as a bill of lading does for marine or rail transportation, and includes an air consignment note or air waybill.

(7) "Branch" includes a separately incorporated foreign branch of a bank.

(8) "Burden of establishing" a fact means the burden of persuading the triers of fact that the existence of the fact is more probable than its non-existence.

(9) "Buyer in ordinary course of business" means a person who in good faith and without knowledge that the sale to him is in violation of the ownership rights or security interest of a third party in the goods buys in ordinary course from a person in the business of selling goods of that kind but does not include a pawnbroker. All persons who sell minerals or the like (including oil and gas) at wellhead or minehead shall be deemed to be persons in the business of selling goods of that kind. "Buying" may be for cash or by exchange of other property or on secured or un-

secured credit and includes receiving goods or documents of title under a pre-existing contract for sale but does not include a transfer in bulk or as security for or in total or partial satisfaction of a money debt.

(10) "Conspicuous": A term or clause is conspicuous when it is so written that a reasonable person against whom it is to operate ought to have noticed it. A printed heading in capitals (as: NON-NEGOTIABLE BILL OF LADING) is conspicuous. Language in the body of a form is "conspicuous" if it is in larger or other contrasting type or color. But in a telegram any stated term is "conspicuous". Whether a term or clause is "conspicuous" or not is for decision by the court.

(11) "Contract" means the total legal obligation which results from the parties' agreement as affected by this Act and any other applicable rules of law. (Compare "Agreement".)

(12) "Creditor" includes a general creditor, a secured creditor, a lien creditor and any representative of creditors, including an assignee for the benefit of creditors, a trustee in bankruptcy, a receiver in equity and an executor or administrator of an insolvent debtor's or assignor's estate.

(13) "Defendant" includes a person in the position of defendant in a cross-action or counterclaim.

(14) "Delivery" with respect to instruments, documents of title, chattel paper, or certificated securities means voluntary transfer of possession.

(15) "Document of title" includes bill of lading, dock warrant, dock receipt, warehouse receipt or order for the delivery of goods, and also any other document which in the regular course of business or financing is treated as adequately evidencing that the person in possession of it is entitled to receive, hold and dispose of the document and the goods it covers. To be a document of title a document must purport to be issued by or addressed to a bailee and purport to cover goods in the bailee's possession which are either identified or are fungible portions of an identified mass.

(16) "Fault" means wrongful act, omission or breach.

(17) "Fungible" with respect to goods or securities means goods or securities of which any unit is, by nature or usage of trade, the equivalent of any other like unit. Goods which are not fungible shall be deemed fungible for the purposes of this Act to the extent that under a particular agreement or document unlike units are treated as equivalents.

(18) "Genuine" means free of forgery or counterfeiting.

(19) "Good faith" means honesty in fact in the conduct or transaction concerned.

(20) "Holder" means a person who is in possession of a document of title or an instrument or a certificated investment security drawn, issued, or indorsed to him or his order or to bearer or in blank.

(21) To "honor" is to pay or to accept and pay, or where a credit so engages to purchase or discount a draft complying with the terms of the credit.

(22) "Insolvency proceedings" includes any assignment for the benefit of creditors or other proceedings intended to liquidate or rehabilitate the estate of the person involved.

(23) A person is "insolvent" who either has ceased to pay his debts in the ordinary course of business or cannot pay his debts as they become due or is insolvent within the meaning of the federal bankruptcy law.

(24) "Money" means a medium of exchange authorized or adopted by a domestic or foreign government as a part of its currency.

(25) A person has "notice" of a fact when

(a) he has actual knowledge of it; or

(b) he has received a notice or notification of it; or

(c) from all the facts and circumstances known to him at the time in question he has reason to know that it exists.

A person "knows" or has "knowledge" of a fact when he has actual knowledge of it. "Discover" or "learn" or a word or phrase of similar import refers to knowledge rather than to reason to know. The time and circumstances under which a notice or notification may cease to be effective are not determined by this Act.

(26) A person "notifies" or "gives" a notice or notification to another by taking such steps as may be reasonably required to inform the other in ordinary

course whether or not such other actually comes to know of it. A person "receives" a notice or notification when

(a) it comes to his attention; or

(b) it is duly delivered at the place of business through which the contract was made or at any other place held out by him as the place for receipt of such communications.

(27) Notice, knowledge or a notice or notification received by an organization is effective for a particular transaction from the time when it is brought to the attention of the individual conducting that transaction, and in any event from the time when it would have been brought to his attention if the organization had exercised due diligence. An organization exercises due diligence if it maintains reasonable routines for communicating significant information to the person conducting the transaction and there is reasonable compliance with the routines. Due diligence does not require an individual acting for the organization to communicate information unless such communication is part of his regular duties or unless he has reason to know of the transaction and that the transaction would be materially affected by the information.

(28) "Organization" includes a corporation, government or governmental subdivision or agency, business trust, estate, trust, partnership or association, two or more persons having a joint or common interest, or any other legal or commercial entity.

(29) "Party", as distinct from "third party", means a person who has engaged in a transaction or made an agreement within this Act.

(30) "Person" includes an individual or an organization (See Section 1—102).

(31) "Presumption" or "presumed" means that the trier of fact must find the existence of the fact presumed unless and until evidence is introduced which would support a finding of its non-existence.

(32) "Purchase" includes taking by sale, discount, negotiation, mortgage, pledge, lien, issue or re-issue, gift or any other voluntary transaction creating an interest in property.

(33) "Purchaser" means a person who takes by purchase.

(34) "Remedy" means any remedial right to which an aggrieved party is entitled with or without resort to a tribunal.

(35) "Representative" includes an agent, an officer of a corporation or association, and a trustee, executor or administrator of an estate, or any other person empowered to act for another.

(36) "Rights" includes remedies.

(37) "Security interest" means an interest in personal property or fixtures which secures payment or performance of an obligation. The retention or reservation of title by a seller of goods notwithstanding shipment or delivery to the buyer (Section 2—401) is limited in effect to a reservation of a "security interest". The term also includes any interest of a buyer of accounts or chattel paper which is subject to Article 9. The special property interest of a buyer of goods on identification of such goods to a contract for sale under Section 2—401 is not a "security interest", but a buyer may also acquire a "security interest" by complying with Article 9. Unless a lease or consignment is intended as security, reservation of title thereunder is not a "security interest" but a consignment is in any event subject to the provisions on consignment sales (Section 2—326). Whether a lease is intended as security is to be determined by the facts of each case; however, (a) the inclusion of an option to purchase does not of itself make the lease one intended for security, and (b) an agreement that upon compliance with the terms of the lease the lessee shall become or has the option to become the owner of the property for no additional consideration or for a nominal consideration does make the lease one intended for security.

(38) "Send" in connection with any writing or notice means to deposit in the mail or deliver for transmission by any other usual means of communication with postage or cost of transmission provided for and properly addressed and in the case of an instrument to an address specified thereon or otherwise agreed, or if there be none to any address reasonable under the circumstances. The receipt of any writing or notice within the time at which it would have arrived if properly sent has the effect of a proper sending.

(39) "Signed" includes any symbol executed or adopted by a party with present intention to authenticate a writing.

(40) "Surety" includes guarantor.

(41) "Telegram" includes a message transmitted by radio, teletype, cable, any mechanical method of transmission, or the like.

(42) "Term" means that portion of an agreement which relates to a particular matter.

(43) "Unauthorized" signature or indorsement means one made without actual, implied or apparent authority and includes a forgery.

(44) "Value". Except as otherwise provided with respect to negotiable instruments and bank collections (Sections 3—303, 4—208 and 4—209) a person gives "value" for rights if he acquires them

>   (a) in return for a binding commitment to extend credit or for the extension of immediately available credit whether or not drawn upon and whether or not a chargeback is provided for in the event of difficulties in collection; or

>   (b) as security for or in total or partial satisfaction of a pre-existing claim; or

>   (c) by accepting delivery pursuant to a pre-existing contract for purchase; or

>   (d) generally, in return for any consideration sufficient to support a simple contract.

(45) "Warehouse receipt" means a receipt issued by a person engaged in the business of storing goods for hire.

(46) "Written" or "writing" includes printing, typewriting or any other intentional reduction to tangible form.
Amended in 1962, 1972 and 1977.

§ 1—202. Prima Facie Evidence by Third Party Documents.

A document in due form purporting to be a bill of lading, policy or certificate of insurance, official weigher's or inspector's certificate, consular invoice, or any other document authorized or required by the contract to be issued by a third party shall be prima facie evidence of its own authenticity and genuineness and of the facts stated in the document by the third party.

§ 1—203. Obligation of Good Faith.

Every contract or duty within this Act imposes an obligation of good faith in its performance or enforcement.

§ 1—204. Time; Reasonable Time; "Seasonably".

(1) Whenever this Act requires any action to be taken within a reasonable time, any time which is not manifestly unreasonable may be fixed by agreement.

(2) What is a reasonable time for taking any action depends on the nature, purpose and circumstances of such action.

(3) An action is taken "seasonably" when it is taken at or within the time agreed or if no time is agreed at or within a reasonable time.

§ 1—205. Course of Dealing and Usage of Trade.

(1) A course of dealing is a sequence of previous conduct between the parties to a particular transaction which is fairly to be regarded as establishing a common basis of understanding for interpreting their expressions and other conduct.

(2) A usage of trade is any practice or method of dealing having such regularity of observance in a place, vocation or trade as to justify an expectation that it will be observed with respect to the transaction in question. The existence and scope of such a usage are to be proved as facts. If it is established that such a usage is embodied in a written trade code or similar writing the interpretation of the writing is for the court.

(3) A course of dealing between parties and any usage of trade in the vocation or trade in which they are engaged or of which they are or should be aware give particular meaning to and supplement or qualify terms of an agreement.

(4) The express terms of an agreement and an applicable course of dealing or usage of trade shall be construed wherever reasonable as consistent with each other; but when such construction is unreasonable express terms control both course of dealing and usage of trade and course of dealing controls usage of trade.

(5) An applicable usage of trade in the place where any part of performance is to occur shall be used in interpreting the agreement as to that part of the performance.

(6) Evidence of a relevant usage of trade offered by one party is not admissible unless and until he has given the other party such notice as the court finds sufficient to prevent unfair surprise to the latter.

§ 1—206. **Statute of Frauds for Kinds of Personal Property Not Otherwise Covered.**

(1) Except in the cases described in subsection (2) of this section a contract for the sale of personal property is not enforceable by way of action or defense beyond five thousand dollars in amount or value of remedy unless there is some writing which indicates that a contract for sale has been made between the parties at a defined or stated price, reasonably identifies the subject matter, and is signed by the party against whom enforcement is sought or by his authorized agent.

(2) Subsection (1) of this section does not apply to contracts for the sale of goods (Section 2—201) nor of securities (Section 8—319) nor to security agreements (Section 9—203).

§ 1—207. **Performance or Acceptance Under Reservation of Rights.**

A party who with explicit reservation of rights performs or promises performance or assents to performance in a manner demanded or offered by the other party does not thereby prejudice the rights reserved. Such words as "without prejudice", "under protest" or the like are sufficient.

§ 1—208. **Option to Accelerate at Will.**

A term providing that one party or his successor in interest may accelerate payment or performance or require collateral or additional collateral "at will" or "when he deems himself insecure" or in words of similar import shall be construed to mean that he shall have power to do so only if he in good faith believes that the prospect of payment or performance is impaired. The burden of establishing lack of good faith is on the party against whom the power has been exercised.

§ 1—209. **Subordinated Obligations**

An obligation may be issued as subordinated to payment of another obligation of the person obligated, or a creditor may subordinate his right to payment of an obligation by agreement with either the person

obligated or another creditor of the person obligated. Such a subordination does not create a security interest as against either the common debtor or a subordinated creditor. This section shall be construed as declaring the law as it existed prior to the enactment of this section and not as modifying it. Added 1966.

Note: *This new section is proposed as an optional provision to make it clear that a subordination agreement does not create a security interest unless so intended.*

Article 2
SALES

Part 1
Short Title, Construction and Subject Matter

§ 2—101. **Short Title.**

This Article shall be known and may be cited as Uniform Commercial Code—Sales.

§ 2—102. **Scope; Certain Security and Other Transactions Excluded From This Article.**

Unless the context otherwise requires, this Article applies to transactions in goods; it does not apply to any transaction which although in the form of an unconditional contract to sell or present sale is intended to operate only as a security transaction nor does this Article impair or repeal any statute regulating sales to consumers, farmers or other specified classes of buyers.

§ 2—103. **Definitions and Index of Definitions.**

(1) In this Article unless the context otherwise requires

    (a) "Buyer" means a person who buys or contracts to buy goods.

    (b) "Good faith" in the case of a merchant means honesty in fact and the observance of reasonable commercial standards of fair dealing in the trade.

    (c) "Receipt" of goods means taking physical possession of them.

    (d) "Seller" means a person who sells or contracts to sell goods.

(2) Other definitions applying to this Article or to

specified Parts thereof, and the sections in which they appear are:

"Acceptance". Section 2—606.

"Banker's credit". Section 2—325.

"Between merchants". Section 2—104.

"Cancellation". Section 2—106(4).

"Commercial unit". Section 2—105.

"Confirmed credit". Section 2—325.

"Conforming to contract". Section 2—106.

"Contract for sale". Section 2—106.

"Cover". Section 2—712.

"Entrusting". Section 2—403.

"Financing agency". Section 2—104.

"Future goods". Section 2—105.

"Goods". Section 2—105.

"Identification". Section 2—501.

"Installment contract". Section 2—612.

"Letter of Credit". Section 2—325.

"Lot". Section 2—105.

"Merchant". Section 2—104.

"Overseas". Section 2—323.

"Person in position of seller". Section 2—707.

"Present sale". Section 2—106.

"Sale". Section 2—106.

"Sale on approval". Section 2—326.

"Sale or return". Section 2—326.

"Termination". Section 2—106.

(3) The following definitions in other Articles apply to this Article:

"Check". Section 3—104.

"Consignee". Section 7—102.

"Consignor". Section 7—102.

"Consumer goods". Section 9—109.

"Dishonor". Section 3—507.

"Draft". Section 3—104.

(4) In addition Article 1 contains general definitions and principles of construction and interpretation applicable throughout this Article.

§ 2—104. **Definitions: "Merchant"; "Between Merchants"; "Financing Agency".**

(1) "Merchant" means a person who deals in goods of the kind or otherwise by his occupation holds himself out as having knowledge or skill peculiar to the practices or goods involved in the transaction or to whom such knowledge or skill may be attributed by his employment of an agent or broker or other intermediary who by his occupation holds himself out as having such knowledge or skill.

(2) "Financing agency" means a bank, finance company or other person who in the ordinary course of business makes advances against goods or documents of title or who by arrangement with either the seller or the buyer intervenes in ordinary course to make or collect payment due or claimed under the contract for sale, as by purchasing or paying the seller's draft or making advances against it or by merely taking it for collection whether or not documents of title accompany the draft. "Financing agency" includes also a bank or other person who similarly intervenes between persons who are in the position of seller and buyer in respect to the goods (Section 2—707).

(3) "Between merchants" means in any transaction with respect to which both parties are chargeable with the knowledge or skill of merchants.

§ 2—105. **Definitions: Transferability; "Goods"; "Future" Goods; "Lot"; "Commercial Unit".**

(1) "Goods" means all things (including specially manufactured goods) which are movable at the time of identification to the contract for sale other than the money in which the price is to be paid, investment securities (Article 8) and things in action. "Goods" also includes the unborn young of animals and growing crops and other identified things attached to realty as described in the section on goods to be severed from realty (Section 2—107).

(2) Goods must be both existing and identified before any interest in them can pass. Goods which are not both existing and identified are "future" goods. A purported present sale of future goods or of any interest therein operates as a contract to sell.

(3) There may be a sale of a part interest in existing identified goods.

(4) An undivided share in an identified bulk of fungible goods is sufficiently identified to be sold although the quantity of the bulk is not determined. Any agreed proportion of such a bulk or any quantity thereof agreed upon by number, weight or other measure may to the extent of the seller's interest in the bulk be sold to the buyer who then becomes an owner in common.

(5) "Lot" means a parcel or a single article which is the subject matter of a separate sale or delivery, whether or not it is sufficient to perform the contract.

(6) "Commercial unit" means such a unit of goods as by commercial usage is a single whole for purposes of sale and division of which materially impairs its character or value on the market or in use. A commercial unit may be a single article (as a machine) or a set of articles (as a suite of furniture or an assortment of sizes) or a quantity (as a bale, gross, or carload) or any other unit treated in use or in the relevant market as a single whole.

§ 2—106. **Definitions: "Contract"; "Agreement"; "Contract for Sale"; "Sale"; "Present Sale"; "Conforming" to Contract; "Termination"; "Cancellation".**

(1) In this Article unless the context otherwise requires "contract" and "agreement" are limited to those relating to the present or future sale of goods. "Contract for sale" includes both a present sale of goods and a contract to sell goods at a future time. A "sale" consists in the passing of title from the seller to the buyer for a price (Section 2—401). A "present sale" means a sale which is accomplished by the making of the contract.

(2) Goods or conduct including any part of a performance are "conforming" or conform to the contract when they are in accordance with the obligations under the contract.

(3) "Termination" occurs when either party pursuant to a power created by agreement or law puts an end to the contract otherwise than for its breach. On "termination" all obligations which are still executory on both sides are discharged but any right based on prior breach or performance survives.

(4) "Cancellation" occurs when either party puts an end to the contract for breach by the other and its effect is the same as that of "termination" except that the cancelling party also retains any remedy for breach of the whole contract or any unperformed balance.

§ 2—107. **Goods to Be Severed From Realty: Recording.**

(1) A contract for the sale of minerals or the like (including oil and gas) or a structure or its materials to be removed from realty is a contract for the sale of goods within this Article if they are to be severed by the seller but until severance a purported present sale thereof which is not effective as a transfer of an interest in land is effective only as a contract to sell.

(2) A contract for the sale apart from the land of growing crops or other things attached to realty and capable of severance without material harm thereto but not described in subsection (1) or of timber to be cut is a contract for the sale of goods within this Article whether the subject matter is to be severed by the buyer or by the seller even though it forms part of the realty at the time of contracting, and the parties can by identification effect a present sale before severance.

(3) The provisions of this section are subject to any third party rights provided by the law relating to realty records, and the contract for sale may be executed and recorded as a document transferring an interest in land and shall then constitute notice to third parties of the buyer's rights under the contract for sale.

Part 2 **Form, Formation and Readjustment of Contract**

§ 2—201. **Formal Requirements; Statute of Frauds.**

(1) Except as otherwise provided in this section a contract for the sale of goods for the price of $500 or more is not enforceable by way of action or defense unless there is some writing sufficient to indicate that a contract for sale has been made between the parties and signed by the party against whom enforcement is sought or by his authorized agent or broker. A writing is not insufficient because it omits or incorrectly states a term agreed upon but the contract is not enforceable under this paragraph beyond the quantity of goods shown in such writing.

(2) Between merchants if within a reasonable time a writing in confirmation of the contract and sufficient against the sender is received and the party receiving it has reason to know its contents, it satisfies the requirements of subsection (1) against such party unless written notice of objection to its contents is given within ten days after it is received.

(3) A contract which does not satisfy the requirements of subsection (1) but which is valid in other respects is enforceable

(a) if the goods are to be specially manufactured for the buyer and are not suitable for sale to others in the ordinary course of the seller's business and the seller, before notice of repudiation is received and under circumstances which reasonably indicate that the goods are for the buyer, has made either a substantial beginning of their manufacture or commitments for their procurement; or

(b) if the party against whom enforcement is sought admits in his pleading, testimony or otherwise in court that a contract for sale was made, but the contract is not enforceable under this provision beyond the quantity of goods admitted; or

(c) with respect to goods for which payment has been made and accepted or which have been received and accepted (Sec. 2—606).

§ 2—202. **Final Written Expression: Parol or Extrinsic Evidence.**

Terms with respect to which the confirmatory memoranda of the parties agree or which are otherwise set forth in a writing intended by the parties as a final expression of their agreement with respect to such terms as are included therein may not be contradicted by evidence of any prior agreement or of a contemporaneous oral agreement but may be explained or supplemented

(a) by course of dealing or usage of trade (Section 1—205) or by course of performance (Section 2—208); and

(b) by evidence of consistent additional terms unless the court finds the writing to have been intended also as a complete and exclusive statement of the terms of the agreement.

§ 2—203. **Seals Inoperative.**

The affixing of a seal to a writing evidencing a contract for sale or an offer to buy or sell goods does not constitute the writing a sealed instrument and the law with respect to sealed instruments does not apply to such a contract or offer.

§ 2—204. **Formation in General.**

(1) A contract for sale of goods may be made in any

manner sufficient to show agreement, including conduct by both parties which recognizes the existence of such a contract.

(2) An agreement sufficient to constitute a contract for sale may be found even though the moment of its making is undetermined.

(3) Even though one or more terms are left open a contract for sale does not fail for indefiniteness if the parties have intended to make a contract and there is a reasonably certain basis for giving an appropriate remedy.

§ 2—205. **Firm Offers.**

An offer by a merchant to buy or sell goods in a signed writing which by its terms gives assurance that it will be held open is not revocable, for lack of consideration, during the time stated or if no time is stated for a reasonable time, but in no event may such period of irrevocability exceed three months; but any such term of assurance on a form supplied by the offeree must be separately signed by the offeror.

§ 2—206. **Offer and Acceptance in Formation of Contract.**

(1) Unless other unambiguously indicated by the language or circumstances

(a) an offer to make a contract shall be construed as inviting acceptance in any manner and by any medium reasonable in the circumstances;

(b) an order or other offer to buy goods for prompt or current shipment shall be construed as inviting acceptance either by a prompt promise to ship or by the prompt or current shipment of conforming or nonconforming goods, but such a shipment of non-conforming goods does not constitute an acceptance if the seller seasonably notifies the buyer that the shipment is offered only as an accommodation to the buyer.

(2) Where the beginning of a requested performance is a reasonable mode of acceptance an offeror who is not notified of acceptance within a reasonable time may treat the offer as having lapsed before acceptance.

§ 2—207. **Additional Terms in Acceptance or Confirmation.**

(1) A definite and seasonable expression of accep-

tance or a written confirmation which is sent within a reasonable time operates as an acceptance even though it states terms additional to or different from those offered or agreed upon, unless acceptance is expressly made conditional on assent to the additional or different terms.

(2) The additional terms are to be construed as proposals for addition to the contract. Between merchants such terms become part of the contract unless:

    (a) the offer expressly limits acceptance to the terms of the offer;

    (b) they materially alter it; or

    (c) notification of objection to them has already been given or is given within a reasonable time after notice of them is received.

(3) Conduct by both parties which recognizes the existence of a contract is sufficient to establish a contract for sale although the writings of the parties do not otherwise establish a contract. In such case the terms of the particular contract consist of those terms on which the writings of the parties agree, together with any supplementary terms incorporated under any other provisions of this Act.

§ 2—208. Course of Performance or Practical Construction.

(1) Where the contract for sale involves repeated occasions for performance by either party with knowledge of the nature of the performance and opportunity for objection to it by the other, any course of performance accepted or acquiesced in without objection shall be relevant to determine the meaning of the agreement.

(2) The express terms of the agreement and any such course of performance, as well as any course of dealing and usage of trade, shall be construed whenever reasonable as consistent with each other; but when such construction is unreasonable, express terms shall control course of performance and course of performance shall control both course of dealing and usage of trade (Section 1—205).

(3) Subject to the provisions of the next section on modification and waiver, such course of performance shall be relevant to show a waiver or modification of

any term inconsistent with such course of performance.

§ 2—209. Modification, Rescission and Waiver.

(1) An agreement modifying a contract within this Article needs no consideration to be binding.

(2) A signed agreement which excludes modification or rescission except by a signed writing cannot be otherwise modified or rescinded, but except as between merchants such a requirement on a form supplied by the merchant must be separately signed by the other party.

(3) The requirements of the statute of frauds section of this Article (Section 2—201) must be satisfied if the contract as modifed is within its provisions.

(4) Although an attempt at modification or rescission does not satisfy the requirements of subsection (2) or (3) it can operate as a waiver.

(5) A party who has made a waiver affecting an executory portion of the contract may retract the waiver by reasonable notification received by the other party that strict performance will be required of any term waived, unless the retraction would be unjust in view of a material change of position in reliance on the waiver.

§ 2—210. Delegation of Performance; Assignment of Rights.

(1) A party may perform his duty through a delegate unless otherwise agreed or unless the other party has a substantial interest in having his original promisor perform or control the acts required by the contract. No delegation of performance relieves the party delegating of any duty to perform or any liability for breach.

(2) Unless otherwise agreed all rights of either seller or buyer can be assigned except where the assignment would materially change the duty of the other party, or increase materially the burden or risk imposed on him by his contract, or impair materially his chance of obtaining return performance. A right to damages for breach of the whole contract or a right arising out of the assignor's due performance of his entire obligation can be assigned despite agreement otherwise.

(3) Unless the circumstances indicate the contrary a

prohibition of assignment of "the contract" is to be construed as barring only the delegation to the assignee of the assignor's performance.

(4) An assignment of "the contract" or of "all my rights under the contract" or an assignment in similar general terms is an assignment of rights and unless the language or the circumstances (as in an assignment for security) indicate the contrary, it is a delegation of performance of the duties of the assignor and its acceptance by the assignee constitutes a promise by him to perform those duties. This promise is enforceable by either the assignor or the other party to the original contract.

(5) The other party may treat any assignment which delegates performance as creating reasonable grounds for insecurity and may without prejudice to his rights against the assignor demand assurances from the assignee (Section 2—609).

Part 3 General Obligation and Construction of Contract

§ 2—301. General Obligations of Parties.

The obligation of the seller is to transfer and deliver and that of the buyer is to accept and pay in accordance with the contract.

§ 2—302. Unconscionable Contract or Clause.

(1) If the court as a matter of law finds the contract or any clause of the contract to have been unconscionable at the time it was made the court may refuse to enforce the contract, or it may enforce the remainder of the contract without the unconscionable clause, or it may so limit the application of any unconscionable clause as to avoid any unconscionable result.

(2) When it is claimed or appears to the court that the contract or any clause thereof may be unconscionable the parties shall be afforded a reasonable opportunity to present evidence as to its commercial setting, purpose and effect to aid the court in making the determination.

§ 2—303. Allocation or Division of Risks.

Where this Article allocates a risk or a burden as between the parties "unless otherwise agreed", the agreement may not only shift the allocation but may also divide the risk or burden.

§ 2—304. Price Payable in Money, Goods, Realty, or Otherwise.

(1) The price can be made payable in money or otherwise. If it is payable in whole or in part in goods each party is a seller of the goods which he is to transfer.

(2) Even though all or part of the price is payable in an interest in realty the transfer of the goods and the seller's obligations with reference to them are subject to this Article, but not the transfer of the interest in realty or the transferor's obligations in connection therewith.

§ 2—305. Open Price Term.

(1) The parties if they so intend can conclude a contract for sale even though the price is not settled. In such a case the price is a reasonable price at the time for delivery if

(a) nothing is said as to price; or

(b) the price is left to be agreed by the parties and they fail to agree; or

(c) the price is to be fixed in terms of some agreed market or other standard as set or recorded by a third person or agency and it is not so set or recorded.

(2) A price to be fixed by the seller or by the buyer means a price for him to fix in good faith.

(3) When a price left to be fixed otherwise than by agreement of the parties fails to be fixed through fault of one party the other may at his option treat the contract as cancelled or himself fix a reasonable price.

(4) Where, however, the parties intend not to be bound unless the price be fixed or agreed and it is not fixed or agreed there is no contract. In such a case the buyer must return any goods already received or if unable so to do must pay their reasonable value at the time of delivery and the seller must return any portion of the price paid on account.

§ 2—306. Output, Requirements and Exclusive Dealings.

(1) A term which measures the quantity by the output of the seller or the requirements of the buyer means such actual output or requirements as may occur in good faith, except that no quantity unreasonably

disproportionate to any stated estimate or in the absence of a stated estimate to any normal or otherwise comparable prior output or requirements may be tendered or demanded.

(2) A lawful agreement by either the seller or the buyer for exclusive dealing in the kind of goods concerned imposes unless otherwise agreed an obligation by the seller to use best efforts to supply the goods and by the buyer to use best efforts to promote their sale.

§ 2—307. **Delivery in Single Lot or Several Lots.**

Unless otherwise agreed all goods called for by a contract for sale must be tendered in a single delivery and payment is due only on such tender but where the circumstances give either party the right to make or demand delivery in lots the price if it can be apportioned may be demanded for each lot.

§ 2—308. **Absence of Specified Place for Delivery.**

Unless otherwise agreed

(a) the place for delivery of goods is the seller's place of business or if he has none his residence; but

(b) in a contract for sale of identified goods which to the knowledge of the parties at the time of contracting are in some other place, that place is the place for their delivery; and

(c) documents of title may be delivered through customary banking channels.

§ 2—309. **Absence of Specific Time Provisions; Notice of Termination.**

(1) The time for shipment or delivery or any other action under a contract if not provided in this Article or agreed upon shall be a reasonable time.

(2) Where the contract provides for successive performances but is indefinite in duration it is valid for a reasonable time but unless otherwise agreed may be terminated at any time by either party.

(3) Termination of a contract by one party except on the happening of an agreed event requires that reasonable notification be received by the other party and an agreement dispensing with notification is invalid if its operation would be unconscionable.

§ 2—310. **Open Time for Payment or Running of Credit; Authority to Ship Under Reservation.**

Unless otherwise agreed

(a) payment is due at the time and place at which the buyer is to receive the goods even though the place of shipment is the place of delivery; and

(b) if the seller is authorized to send the goods he may ship them under reservation, and may tender the documents of title, but the buyer may inspect the goods after their arrival before payment is due unless such inspection is inconsistent with the terms of the contract (Section 2—513); and

(c) if delivery is authorized and made by way of documents of title otherwise than by subsection (b) then payment is due at the time and place at which the buyer is to receive the documents regardless of where the goods are to be received; and

(d) where the seller is required or authorized to ship the goods on credit the credit period runs from the time of shipment but post-dating the invoice or delaying its dispatch will correspondingly delay the starting of the credit period.

§ 2—311. **Options and Cooperation Respecting Performance.**

(1) An agreement for sale which is otherwise sufficiently definite (subsection (3) of Section 2—204) to be a contract is not made invalid by the fact that it leaves particulars of performance to be specified by one of the parties. Any such specification must be made in good faith and within limits set by commercial reasonableness.

(2) Unless otherwise agreed specifications relating to assortment of the goods are at the buyer's option and except as otherwise provided in subsections (1)(c) and (3) of Section 2—319 specifications or arrangements relating to shipment are at the seller's option.

(3) Where such specification would materially affect the other party's performance but is not seasonally made or where one party's cooperation is necessary to the agreed performance of the other but is not seasonably forthcoming, the other party in addition to all other remedies

(a) is excused for any resulting delay in his own performance; and

(b) may also either proceed to perform in any reasonable manner or after the time for a material part of his own performance treat the failure to specify or to cooperate as a breach by failure to deliver or accept the goods.

§ 2—312. **Warranty of Title and Against Infringement; Buyer's Obligation Against Infringement.**

(1) Subject to subsection (2) there is in a contract for sale a warranty by the seller that

(a) the title conveyed shall be good, and its transfer rightful; and

(b) the goods shall be delivered free from any security interest or other lien or encumbrance of which the buyer at the time of contracting has no knowledge.

(2) A warranty under subsection (1) will be excluded or modified only by specific language or by circumstances which give the buyer reason to know that the person selling does not claim title in himself or that he is purporting to sell only such right or title as he or a third person may have.

(3) Unless otherwise agreed a seller who is a merchant regularly dealing in goods of the kind warrants that the goods shall be delivered free of the rightful claim of any third person by way of infringement or the like but a buyer who furnishes specifications to the seller must hold the seller harmless against any such claim which arises out of compliance with the specifications.

§ 2—313. **Express Warranties by Affirmation, Promise, Description, Sample.**

(1) Express warranties by the seller are created as follows:

(a) Any affirmation of fact or promise made by the seller to the buyer which relates to the goods and becomes part of the basis of the bargain creates an express warranty that the goods shall conform to the affirmation or promise.

(b) Any description of the goods which is made part of the basis of the bargain creates an express warranty that the goods shall conform to the description.

(c) Any sample or model which is made part of the basis of the bargain creates an express warranty that the whole of the goods shall conform to the sample or model.

(2) It is not necessary to the creation of an express warranty that the seller use formal words such as "warrant" or "guarantee" or that he have a specific intention to make a warranty, but an affirmation merely of the value of the goods or a statement purporting to be merely the seller's opinion or commendation of the goods does not create a warranty.

§ 2—314. **Implied Warranty: Merchantability; Usage of Trade.**

(1) Unless excluded or modified (Section 2—316), a warranty that the goods shall be merchantable is implied in a contract for their sale if the seller is a merchant with respect to goods of that kind. Under this section the serving for value of food or drink to be consumed either on the premises or elsewhere is a sale.

(2) Goods to be merchantable must be at least such as

(a) pass without objection in the trade under the contract description; and

(b) in the case of fungible goods, are of fair average quality within the description; and

(c) are fit for the ordinary purposes for which such goods are used; and

(d) run, within the variations permitted by the agreement, of even kind, quality and quantity within each unit and among all units involved; and

(e) are adequately contained, packaged, and labeled as the agreement may require; and

(f) conform to the promises or affirmations of fact made on the container or label if any.

(3) Unless excluded or modified (Section 2—316) other implied warranties may arise from course of dealing or usage of trade.

§ 2—315. **Implied Warranty: Fitness for Particular Purpose.**

Where the seller at the time of contracting has reason to know any particular purpose for which the goods are required and that the buyer is relying on the seller's skill or judgment to select or furnish suitable goods, there is unless excluded or modified under the next section an implied warranty that the goods shall be fit for such purpose.

§ 2—316. **Exclusion or Modification of Warranties.**

(1) Words or conduct relevant to the creation of an express warranty and words or conduct tending to negate or limit warranty shall be construed wherever reasonable as consistent with each other; but subject to the provisions of this Article on parol or extrinsic evidence (Section 2—202) negation or limitation is inoperative to the extent that such construction is unreasonable.

(2) Subject to subsection (3), to exclude or modify the implied warranty of merchantability or any part of it the language must mention merchantability and in case of a writing must be conspicuous, and to exclude or modify any implied warranty of fitness the exclusion must be by a writing and conspicuous. Language to exclude all implied warranties of fitness is sufficient if it states, for example, that "There are no warranties which extend beyond the description on the face hereof."

(3) Notwithstanding subsection (2)

(a) unless the circumstances indicate otherwise, all implied warranties are excluded by expressions like "as is", "with all faults" or other language which in common understanding calls the buyer's attention to the exclusion of warranties and makes plain that there is no implied warranty; and

(b) when the buyer before entering into the contract has examined the goods or the sample or model as fully as he desired or has refused to examine the goods there is no implied warranty with regard to defects which an examination ought in the circumstances to have revealed to him; and

(c) an implied warranty can also be excluded or modified by course of dealing or course of performance or usage of trade.

(4) Remedies for breach of warranty can be limited in accordance with the provisions of this Article on liquidation or limitation of damages and on contractual modification of remedy (Sections 2—718 and 2—719).

§ 2—317. **Cumulation and Conflict of Warranties Express or Implied.**

Warranties whether express or implied shall be construed as consistent with each other and as cumulative, but if such construction is unreasonable the intention of the parties shall determine which warranty is dominant. In ascertaining that intention the following rules apply:

(a) Exact or technical specifications displace an inconsistent sample or model or general language of description.

(b) A sample from an existing bulk displaces inconsistent general language of description.

(c) Express warranties displace inconsistent implied warranties other than an implied warranty of fitness for a particular purpose.

§ 2—318. **Third Party Beneficiaries of Warranties Express or Implied.**

Note: If this Act is introduced in the Congress of the United States this section should be omitted. (States to select one alternative.)

Alternative A

A seller's warranty whether express or implied extends to any natural person who is in the family or household of his buyer or who is a guest in his home if it is reasonable to expect that such person may use, consume or be affected by the goods and who is injured in person by breach of the warranty. A seller may not exclude or limit the operation of this section.

Alternative B

A seller's warranty whether express or implied extends to any natural person who may reasonably be expected to use, consume or be affected by the goods and who is injured in person by breach of the warranty. A seller may not exclude or limit the operation of this section.

Alternative C

A seller's warranty whether express or implied extends to any person who may reasonably be expected to use, consume or be affected by the goods and who is injured by breach of the warranty. A seller may not exclude or limit the operation of this section with respect to injury to the person of an individual to whom the warranty extends. As amended 1966.

§ 2—319. **F.O.B. and F.A.S. Terms.**

(1) Unless otherwise agreed the term F.O.B. (which means "free on board") at a named place, even though used only in connection with the stated price, is a delivery term under which

(a) when the term is F.O.B. the place of shipment, the seller must at that place ship the goods in the manner provided in this Article (Section 2—504) and bear the expense and risk of putting them into the possession of the carrier; or

(b) when the term is F.O.B. the place of destination, the seller must at his own expense and risk transport the goods to that place and there tender delivery of them in the manner provided in this Article (Section 2—503);

(c) when under either (a) or (b) the term is also F.O.B. vessel, car or other vehicle, the seller must in addition at his own expense and risk load the goods on board. If the term is F.O.B. vessel the buyer must name the vessel and in an appropriate case the seller must comply with the provisions of this Article on the form of bill of lading (Section 2—323).

(2) Unless otherwise agreed the term F.A.S. vessel (which means "free alongside") at a named port, even though used only in connection with the stated price, is a delivery term under which the seller must

(a) at his own expense and risk deliver the goods alongside the vessel in the manner usual in that port or on a dock designated and provided by the buyer; and

(b) obtain and tender a receipt for the goods in exchange for which the carrier is under a duty to issue a bill of lading.

(3) Unless otherwise agreed in any case falling within subsection (1) (a) or (c) or subsection (2) the buyer must seasonably give any needed instructions for making delivery, including when the term is F.A.S. or F.O.B. the loading berth of the vessel and in an appropriate case its name and sailing date. The seller may treat the failure of needed instructions as a failure of cooperation under this Article (Section 2—311). He may also at his option move the goods in any reasonable manner preparatory to delivery or shipment.

(4) Under the term F.O.B. vessel or F.A.S. unless otherwise agreed the buyer must make payment against tender of the required documents and the seller may not tender nor the buyer demand delivery of the goods in substitution for the documents.

§ 2—320. **C.I.F. and C. & F. Terms.**

(1) The term C.I.F. means that the price includes in a lump sum the cost of the goods and the insurance and freight to the named destination. The term C. & F. or C.F. means that the price so includes cost and freight to the named destination.

(2) Unless otherwise agreed and even though used only in connection with the stated price and destination, the term C.I.F. destination or its equivalent requires the seller at his own expense and risk to

(a) put the goods into the possession of a carrier at the port for shipment and obtain a negotiable bill or bills of lading covering the entire transportation to the named destination; and

(b) load the goods and obtain a receipt from the carrier (which may be contained in the bill of lading) showing that the freight has been paid or provided for; and

(c) obtain a policy or certificate of insurance, including any war risk insurance, of a kind and on terms then current at the port of shipment in the usual amount, in the currency of the contract, shown to cover the same goods covered by the bill of lading and providing for payment of loss to the order of the buyer or for the account of whom it may concern; but the seller may add to the price the amount of the premium for any such war risk insurance; and

(d) prepare an invoice of the goods and procure any other documents required to effect shipment or to comply with the contract; and

(e) forward and tender with commercial promptness all the documents in due form and with any indorsement necessary to perfect the buyer's rights.

(3) Unless otherwise agreed the term C. & F. or its equivalent has the same effect and imposes upon the seller the same obligations and risks as a C.I.F. term except the obligation as to insurance.

(4) Under the term C.I.F. or C. & F. unless otherwise agreed the buyer must make payment against tender

of the required documents and the seller may not tender nor the buyer demand delivery of the goods in substitution for the documents.

§ 2—321. **C.I.F. or C. & F.: "Net Landed Weights"; "Payment on Arrival"; Warranty of Condition on Arrival.**

Under a contract containing a term C.I.F. or C. & F.

(1) Where the price is based on or is to be adjusted according to "net landed weights", "delivered weights", "out turn" quantity or quality or the like, unless otherwise agreed the seller must reasonably estimate the price. The payment due on tender of the documents called for by the contract is the amount so estimated, but after final adjustment of the price a settlement must be made with commercial promptness.

(2) An agreement described in subsection (1) or any warranty of quality or condition of the goods on arrival places upon the seller the risk of ordinary deterioration, shrinkage and the like in transportation but has no effect on the place or time of identification to the contract for sale or delivery or on the passing of the risk of loss.

(3) Unless otherwise agreed where the contract provides for payment on or after arrival of the goods the seller must before payment allow such preliminary inspection as is feasible; but if the goods are lost delivery of the documents and payment are due when the goods should have arrived.

§ 2—322. **Delivery "Ex-Ship".**

(1) Unless otherwise agreed a term for delivery of goods "ex-ship" (which means from the carrying vessel) or in equivalent language is not restricted to a particular ship and requires delivery from a ship which has reached a place at the named port of destination where goods of the kind are usually discharged.

(2) Under such a term unless otherwise agreed

(a) the seller must discharge all liens arising out of the carriage and furnish the buyer with a direction which puts the carrier under a duty to deliver the goods; and

(b) the risk of loss does not pass to the buyer until the goods leave the ship's tackle or are otherwise properly unloaded.

§ 2—323. **Form of Bill of Lading Required in Overseas Shipment; "Overseas".**

(1) Where the contract contemplates overseas shipment and contains a term C.I.F. or C. & F. or F.O.B. vessel, the seller unless otherwise agreed must obtain a negotiable bill of lading stating that the goods have been loaded on board or, in the case of a term C.I.F. or C. & F., received for shipment.

(2) Where in a case within subsection (1) a bill of lading has been issued in a set of parts, unless otherwise agreed if the documents are not to be sent from abroad the buyer may demand tender of the full set; otherwise only one part of the bill of lading need be tendered. Even if the agreement expressly requires a full set

(a) due tender of a single part is acceptable within the provisions of this Article on cure of improper delivery (subsection (1) of Section 2—508); and

(b) even though the full set is demanded, if the documents are sent from abroad the person tendering an incomplete set may nevertheless require payment upon furnishing an indemnity which the buyer in good faith deems adequate.

(3) A shipment by water or by air or a contract contemplating such shipment is "overseas" insofar as by usage of trade or agreement it is subject to the commercial, financing or shipping practices characteristic of international deep water commerce.

§ 2—324. **"No Arrival, No Sale" Term.**

Under a term "no arrival, no sale" or terms of like meaning, unless otherwise agreed,

(a) the seller must properly ship conforming goods and if they arrive by any means he must tender them on arrival but he assumes no obligation that the goods will arrive unless he has caused the non-arrival; and

(b) where without fault of the seller the goods are in part lost or have so deteriorated as no longer to conform to the contract or arrive after the contract time, the buyer may proceed as if there had been casualty to identified goods (Section 2—613).

§ 2—325. **"Letter of Credit" Term; "Confirmed Credit".**

(1) Failure of the buyer seasonably to furnish an agreed letter of credit is a breach of the contract for sale.

(2) The delivery to seller of a proper letter of credit suspends the buyer's obligation to pay. If the letter of credit is dishonored, the seller may on seasonable notification to the buyer require payment directly from him.

(3) Unless otherwise agreed the term "letter of credit" or "banker's credit" in a contract for sale means an irrevocable credit issued by a financing agency of good repute and, where the shipment is overseas, of good international repute. The term "confirmed credit" means that the credit must also carry the direct obligation of such an agency which does business in the seller's financial market.

§ 2—326. **Sale on Approval and Sale or Return; Consignment Sales and Rights of Creditors.**

(1) Unless otherwise agreed, if delivered goods may be returned by the buyer even though they conform to the contract, the transaction is

(a) a "sale on approval" if the goods are delivered primarily for use, and

(b) a "sale or return" if the goods are delivered primarily for resale.

(2) Except as provided in subsection (3), goods held on approval are not subject to the claims of the buyer's creditors until acceptance; goods held on sale or return are subject to such claims while in the buyer's possession.

(3) Where goods are delivered to a person for sale and such person maintains a place of business at which he deals in goods of the kind involved, under a name other than the name of the person making delivery, then with respect to claims of creditors of the person conducting the business the goods are deemed to be on sale or return. The provisions of this subsection are applicable even though an agreement purports to reserve title to the person making delivery until payment or resale or uses such words as "on consignment" or "on memorandum". However, this subsection is not applicable if the person making delivery

(a) complies with an applicable law providing for a consignor's interest or the like to be evidenced by a sign, or

(b) establishes that the person conducting the business is generally known by his creditors to be substantially engaged in selling the goods of others, or

(c) complies with the filing provisions of the Article on Secured Transactions (Article 9).

(4) Any "or return" term of a contract for sale is to be treated as a separate contract for sale within the statute of frauds section of this Article (Section 2—201) and as contradicting the sale aspect of the contract within the provisions of this Article on parol or extrinsic evidence (Section 2—202).

§ 2—327. **Special Incidents of Sale on Approval and Sale or Return.**

(1) Under a sale on approval unless otherwise agreed

(a) although the goods are identified to the contract the risk of loss and the title do not pass to the buyer until acceptance; and

(b) use of the goods consistent with the purpose of trial is not acceptance but failure seasonably to notify the seller of election to return the goods is acceptance, and if the goods conform to the contract acceptance of any part is acceptance of the whole; and

(c) after due notification of election to return, the return is at the seller's risk and expense but a merchant buyer must follow any reasonable instructions.

(2) Under a sale or return unless otherwise agreed

(a) the option to return extends to the whole or any commercial unit of the goods while in substantially their original condition, but must be exercised seasonably; and

(b) the return is at the buyer's risk and expense.

§ 2—328. **Sale by Auction.**

(1) In a sale by auction if goods are put up in lots each lot is the subject of a separate sale.

(2) A sale by auction is complete when the auctioneer so announces by the fall of the hammer or in other customary manner. Where a bid is made while the hammer is falling in acceptance of a prior bid the auctioneer may in his discretion reopen the bidding or declare the goods sold under the bid on which the hammer was falling.

(3) Such a sale is with reserve unless the goods are in explicit terms put up without reserve. In an auction with reserve the auctioneer may withdraw the goods at any time until he announces completion of the sale. In an auction without reserve, after the auctioneer calls for bids on an article or lot, that article or lot cannot be withdrawn unless no bid is made within a reasonable time. In either case a bidder may retract his bid until the auctioneer's announcement of completion of the sale, but a bidder's retraction does not revive any previous bid.

(4) If the auctioneer knowingly receives a bid on the seller's behalf or the seller makes or procures such a bid, and notice has not been given that liberty for such bidding is reserved, the buyer may at his option avoid the sale or take the goods at the price of the last good faith bid prior to the completion of the sale. This subsection shall not apply to any bid at a forced sale.

Part 4 Title, Creditors and Good Faith Purchasers

§ 2—401. Passing of Title; Reservation for Security; Limited Application of This Section.

Each provision of this Article with regard to the rights, obligations and remedies of the seller, the buyer, purchasers or other third parties applies irrespective of title to the goods except where the provision refers to such title. Insofar as situations are not covered by the other provisions of this Article and matters concerning title became material the following rules apply:

(1) Title to goods cannot pass under a contract for sale prior to their identification to the contract (Section 2—501), and unless otherwise explicitly agreed the buyer acquires by their identification a special property as limited by this Act. Any retention or reservation by the seller of the title (property) in goods shipped or delivered to the buyer is limited in effect to a reservation of a security interest. Subject to these provisions and to the provisions of the Article on Secured Transactions (Article 9), title to goods passes from the seller to the buyer in any manner and on any conditions explicitly agreed on by the parties.

(2) Unless otherwise explicitly agreed title passes to the buyer at the time and place at which the seller completes his performance with reference to the physical delivery of the goods, despite any reservation of a security interest and even though a document of title is to be delivered at a different time or place; and in particular and despite any reservation of a security interest by the bill of lading

(a) if the contract requires or authorizes the seller to send the goods to the buyer but does not require him to deliver them at destination, title passes to the buyer at the time and place of shipment; but

(b) if the contract requires delivery at destination, title passes on tender there.

(3) Unless otherwise explicitly agreed where delivery is to be made without moving the goods,

(a) if the seller is to deliver a document of title, title passes at the time when and the place where he delivers such documents; or

(b) if the goods are at the time of contracting already identified and no documents are to be delivered, title passes at the time and place of contracting.

(4) A rejection or other refusal by the buyer to receive or retain the goods, whether or not justified, or a justified revocation of acceptance revests title to the goods in the seller. Such revesting occurs by operation of law and is not a "sale".

§ 2—402. Rights of Seller's Creditors Against Sold Goods.

(1) Except as provided in subsections (2) and (3), rights of unsecured creditors of the seller with respect to goods which have been identified to a contract for sale are subject to the buyer's rights to recover the goods under this Article (Sections 2—502 and 2—716).

(2) A creditor of the seller may treat a sale or an identification of goods to a contract for sale as void if as against him a retention of possession by the seller is fraudulent under any rule of law of the state where the goods are situated, except that retention of possession in good faith and current course of trade by a merchant-seller for a commercially reasonable time after a sale or identification is not fraudulent.

(3) Nothing in this Article shall be deemed to impair the rights of creditors of the seller

(a) under the provisions of the Article on Secured Transactions (Article 9); or

(b) where identification to the contract or delivery is made not in current course of trade but in satisfaction of or as security for a pre-existing claim for money, security or the like and is made under circumstances which under any rule of law of the state where the goods are situated would apart from this Article constitute the transaction a fraudulent transfer or voidable preference.

§ 2—403. **Power to Transfer; Good Faith Purchase of Goods; "Entrusting".**

(1) A purchaser of goods acquires all title which his transferor had or had power to transfer except that a purchaser of a limited interest acquires rights only to the extent of the interest purchased. A person with voidable title has power to transfer a good title to a good faith purchaser for value. When goods have been delivered under a transaction of purchase the purchaser has such power even though

(a) the transferor was deceived as to the identity of the purchaser, or

(b) the delivery was in exchange for a check which is later dishonored, or

(c) it was agreed that the transaction was to be a "cash sale", or

(d) the delivery was procured through fraud punishable as larcenous under the criminal law.

(2) Any entrusting of possession of goods to a merchant who deals in goods of that kind gives him power to transfer all rights of the entruster to a buyer in ordinary course of business.

(3) "Entrusting" includes any delivery and any acquiescence in retention of possession regardless of any condition expressed between the parties to the delivery or acquiescence and regardless of whether the procurement of the entrusting or the possessor's disposition of the goods have been such as to be larcenous under the criminal law.

(4) The rights of other purchasers of goods and of lien creditors are governed by the Articles on Secured Transactions (Article 9), Bulk Transfers (Article 6) and Documents of Title (Article 7).

Part 5 Performance

§ 2—501. **Insurable Interest in Goods; Manner of Identification of Goods.**

(1) The buyer obtains a special property and an insurable interest in goods by identification of existing goods as goods to which the contract refers even though the goods so identified are nonconforming and he has an option to return or reject them. Such identification can be made at any time and in any manner explicitly agreed to by the parties. In the absence of explicit agreement identification occurs

(a) when the contract is made if it is for the sale of goods already existing and identified;

(b) if the contract is for the sale of future goods other than those described in paragraph (c), when goods are shipped, marked or otherwise designated by the seller as goods to which the contract refers;

(c) when the crops are planted or otherwise become growing crops or the young are conceived if the contract is for the sale of unborn young to be born within twelve months after contracting or for the sale of crops to be harvested within twelve months or the next normal harvest season after contracting whichever is longer.

(2) The seller retains an insurable interest in goods so long as title to or any security interest in the goods remains in him and where the identification is by the seller alone he may until default or insolvency or notification to the buyer that the identification is final substitute other goods for those identified.

(3) Nothing in this section impairs any insurable interest recognized under any other statute or rule of law.

§ 2—502. **Buyer's Right to Goods on Seller's Insolvency.**

(1) Subject to subsection (2) and even though the goods have not been shipped a buyer who has paid a part or all of the price of goods in which he has a special property under the provisions of the immediately preceding section may on making and keeping good a tender of any unpaid portion of their price recover them from the seller if the seller becomes insolvent within ten days after receipt of the first installment on their price.

(2) If the identification creating his special property has been made by the buyer he acquires the right to recover the goods only if they conform to the contract for sale.

§ 2—503. **Manner of Seller's Tender of Delivery.**

(1) Tender of delivery requires that the seller put and hold conforming goods at the buyer's disposition and give the buyer any notification reasonably necessary to enable him to take delivery. The manner, time and place for tender are determined by the agreement and this Article, and in particular

    (a) tender must be at a reasonable hour, and if it is of goods they must be kept available for the period reasonably necessary to enable the buyer to take possession; but

    (b) unless otherwise agreed the buyer must furnish facilities reasonably suited to the receipt of the goods.

(2) Where the case is within the next section respecting shipment tender requires that the seller comply with its provisions.

(3) Where the seller is required to deliver at a particular destination tender requires that he comply with subsection (1) and also in any appropriate case tender documents as described in subsections (4) and (5) of this section.

(4) Where goods are in the possession of a bailee and are to be delivered without being moved

    (a) tender requires that the seller either tender a negotiable document of title covering such goods or procure acknowledgment by the bailee of the buyer's right to possession of the goods; but

    (b) tender to the buyer of a non-negotiable document of title or of a written direction to the bailee to deliver is sufficient tender unless the buyer seasonably objects, and receipt by the bailee of notification of the buyer's rights fixes those rights as against the bailee and all third persons; but risk of loss of the goods and of any failure by the bailee to honor the non-negotiable document of title or to obey the direction remains on the seller until the buyer has had a reasonable time to present the document or direction, and a refusal by the bailee to honor the document or to obey the direction defeats the tender.

(5) Where the contract requires the seller to deliver documents

    (a) he must tender all such documents in correct form, except as provided in this Article with respect to bills of lading in a set (subsection (2) of Section 2—323); and

    (b) tender through customary banking channels is sufficient and dishonor of a draft accompanying the documents constitutes non-acceptance or rejection.

§ 2—504. **Shipment by Seller.**

Where the seller is required or authorized to send the goods to the buyer and the contract does not require him to deliver them at a particular destination, then unless otherwise agreed he must

(a) put the goods in the possession of such a carrier and make such a contract for their transportation as may be reasonable having regard to the nature of the goods and other circumstances of the case; and

(b) obtain and promptly deliver or tender in due form any document necessary to enable the buyer to obtain possession of the goods or otherwise required by the agreement or by usage of trade; and

(c) promptly notify the buyer of the shipment.

Failure to notify the buyer under paragraph (c) or to make a proper contract under paragraph (a) is a ground for rejection only if material delay or loss ensues.

§ 2—505. **Seller's Shipment Under Reservation.**

(1) Where the seller has identified goods to the contract by or before shipment:

    (a) his procurement of a negotiable bill of lading to his own order or otherwise reserves in him a security interest in the goods. His procurement of the bill to the order of a financing agency or of the buyer indicates in addition only the seller's expectation of transferring that interest to the person named.

    (b) a non-negotiable bill of lading to himself or his nominee reserves possession of the goods as security but except in a case of conditional delivery (subsection (2) of Section 2—507) a non-negotiable bill of lading naming the buyer as consignee reserves no security interest even though the seller retains possession of the bill of lading.

(2) When shipment by the seller with reservation of a security interest is in violation of the contract for sale it constitutes an improper contract for transportation

within the preceding section but impairs neither the rights given to the buyer by shipment and identification of the goods to the contract nor the seller's powers as a holder of a negotiable document.

§ 2—506. Rights of Financing Agency.

(1) A financing agency by paying or purchasing for value a draft which relates to a shipment of goods acquires to the extent of the payment or purchase and in addition to its own rights under the draft and any document of title securing it any rights of the shipper in the goods including the right to stop delivery and the shipper's right to have the draft honored by the buyer.

(2) The right to reimbursement of a financing agency which has in good faith honored or purchased the draft under commitment to or authority from the buyer is not impaired by subsequent discovery of defects with reference to any relevant document which was apparently regular on its face.

§ 2—507. Effect of Seller's Tender; Delivery on Condition.

(1) Tender of delivery is a condition to the buyer's duty to accept the goods and, unless otherwise agreed, to his duty to pay for them. Tender entitles the seller to acceptance of the goods and to payment according to the contract.

(2) Where payment is due and demanded on the delivery to the buyer of goods or documents of title, his right as against the seller to retain or dispose of them is conditional upon his making the payment due.

§ 2—508. Cure by Seller of Improper Tender or Delivery; Replacement.

(1) Where any tender or delivery by the seller is rejected because non-conforming and the time for performance has not yet expired, the seller may seasonably notify the buyer of his intention to cure and may then within the contract time make a conforming delivery.

(2) Where the buyer rejects a non-conforming tender which the seller had reasonable grounds to believe would be acceptable with or without money allowance the seller may if he seasonably notifies the buyer have a further reasonable time to substitute a conforming tender.

§ 2—509. Risk of Loss in the Absence of Breach.

(1) Where the contract requires or authorizes the seller to ship the goods by carrier

(a) if it does not require him to deliver them at a particular destination, the risk of loss passes to the buyer when the goods are duly delivered to the carrier even though the shipment is under reservation (Section 2—505); but

(b) if it does require him to deliver them at a particular destination and the goods are there duly tendered while in the possession of the carrier, the risk of loss passes to the buyer when the goods are there duly so tendered as to enable the buyer to take delivery.

(2) Where the goods are held by a bailee to be delivered without being moved, the risk of loss passes to the buyer

(a) on his receipt of a negotiable document of title covering the goods; or

(b) on acknowledgment by the bailee of the buyer's right to possession of the goods; or

(c) after his receipt of a non-negotiable document of title or other written direction to deliver, as provided in subsection (4)(b) of Section 2—503.

(3) In any case not within subsection (1) or (2), the risk of loss passes to the buyer on his receipt of the goods if the seller is a merchant; otherwise, the risk passes to the buyer on tender of delivery.

(4) The provisions of this section are subject to contrary agreement of the parties and to the provisions of this Article on sale on approval (Section 2—327) and on effect of breach on risk of loss (Section 2—510).

§ 2—510. Effect of Breach on Risk of Loss.

(1) Where a tender or delivery of goods so fails to conform to the contract as to give a right of rejection the risk of their loss remains on the seller until cure or acceptance.

(2) Where the buyer rightfully revokes acceptance he may to the extent of any deficiency in his effective insurance coverage treat the risk of loss as having rested on the seller from the beginning.

(3) Where the buyer as to conforming goods already identified to the contract for sale repudiates or is

otherwise in breach before risk of their loss has passed to him, the seller may to the extent of any deficiency in his effective insurance coverage treat the risk of loss as resting on the buyer for a commercially reasonable time.

§ 2—511. **Tender of Payment by Buyer; Payment by Check.**

(1) Unless otherwise agreed tender of payment is a condition to the seller's duty to tender and complete any delivery.

(2) Tender of payment is sufficient when made by any means or in any manner current in the ordinary course of business unless the seller demands payment in legal tender and gives any extension of time reasonably necessary to procure it.

(3) Subject to the provisions of this Act on the effect of an instrument on an obligation (Section 3—802), payment by check is conditional and is defeated as between the parties by dishonor of the check on due presentment.

§ 2—512. **Payment by Buyer Before Inspection.**

(1) Where the contract requires payment before inspection non-conformity of the goods does not excuse the buyer from so making payment unless

(a) the non-conformity appears without inspection; or

(b) despite tender of the required documents the circumstances would justify injunction against honor under the provisions of this Act (Section 5—114).

(2) Payment pursuant to subsection (1) does not constitute an acceptance of goods or impair the buyer's right to inspect or any of his remedies.

§ 2—513. **Buyer's Right to Inspection of Goods.**

(1) Unless otherwise agreed and subject to subsection (3), where goods are tendered or delivered or identified to the contract for sale, the buyer has a right before payment or acceptance to inspect them at any reasonable place and time and in any reasonable manner. When the seller is required or authorized to send the goods to the buyer, the inspection may be after their arrival.

(2) Expenses of inspection must be borne by the buyer but may be recovered from the seller if the goods do not conform and are rejected.

(3) Unless otherwise agreed and subject to the provisions of this Article on C.I.F. contracts (subsection (3) of Section 2—321), the buyer is not entitled to inspect the goods before payment of the price when the contract provides

(a) for delivery "C.O.D." or on other like terms; or

(b) for payment against documents of title, except where such payment is due only after the goods are to become available for inspection.

(4) A place or method of inspection fixed by the parties is presumed to be exclusive but unless otherwise expressly agreed it does not postpone identification or shift the place for delivery or for passing the risk of loss. If compliance becomes impossible, inspection shall be as provided in this section unless the place or method fixed was clearly intended as an indispensable condition failure of which avoids the contract.

§ 2—514. **When Documents Deliverable on Acceptance; When on Payment.**

Unless otherwise agreed documents against which a draft is drawn are to be delivered to the drawee on acceptance of the draft if it is payable more than three days after presentment; otherwise, only on payment.

§ 2—515. **Preserving Evidence of Goods in Dispute.**

In furtherance of the adjustment of any claim or dispute

(a) either party on reasonable notification to the other and for the purpose of ascertaining the facts and preserving evidence has the right to inspect, test and sample the goods including such of them as may be in the possession or control of the other; and

(b) the parties may agree to a third party inspection or survey to determine the conformity or condition of the goods and may agree that the findings shall be binding upon them in any subsequent litigation or adjustment.

Part 6 **Breach, Repudiation and Excuse**

§ 2—601. **Buyer's Rights on Improper Delivery.**

Subject to the provisions of this Article on breach in

installment contracts (Section 2—612) and unless otherwise agreed under the sections on contractual limitations of remedy (Sections 2—718 and 2—719), if the goods or the tender of delivery fail in any respect to conform to the contract, the buyer may

(a) reject the whole; or

(b) accept the whole; or

(c) accept any commercial unit or units and reject the rest.

§ 2—602. **Manner and Effect of Rightful Rejection.**

(1) Rejection of goods must be within a reasonable time after their delivery or tender. It is ineffective unless the buyer seasonably notifies the seller.

(2) Subject to the provisions of the two following sections on rejected goods (Sections 2—603 and 2—604),

(a) after rejection any exercise of ownership by the buyer with respect to any commercial unit is wrongful as against the seller; and

(b) if the buyer has before rejection taken physical possession of goods in which he does not have a security interest under the provisions of this Article (subsection (3) of Section 2—711), he is under a duty after rejection to hold them with reasonable care at the seller's disposition for a time sufficient to permit the seller to remove them; but

(c) the buyer has no further obligations with regard to goods rightfully rejected.

(3) The seller's rights with respect to goods wrongfully rejected are governed by the provisions of this Article on seller's remedies in general (Section 2—703).

§ 2—603. **Merchant Buyer's Duties as to Rightfully Rejected Goods.**

(1) Subject to any security interest in the buyer (subsection (3) of Section 2—711), when the seller has no agent or place of business at the market of rejection a merchant buyer is under a duty after rejection of goods in his possession or control to follow any reasonable instructions received from the seller with respect to the goods and in the absence of such instructions to make reasonable efforts to sell them for the seller's account if they are perishable or threaten to decline in value speedily. Instructions are

not reasonable if on demand indemnity for expenses is not forthcoming.

(2) When the buyer sells goods under subsection (1), he is entitled to reimbursement from the seller or out of the proceeds for reasonable expenses of caring for and selling them, and if the expenses include no selling commission then to such commission as is usual in the trade or if there is none to a reasonable sum not exceeding ten per cent on the gross proceeds.

(3) In complying with this section the buyer is held only to good faith and good faith conduct hereunder is neither acceptance nor conversion nor the basis of an action for damages.

§ 2—604. **Buyer's Options as to Salvage of Rightfully Rejected Goods.**

Subject to the provisions of the immediately preceding section on perishables if the seller gives no instructions within a reasonable time after notification of rejection the buyer may store the rejected goods for the seller's account or reship them to him or resell them for the seller's account with reimbursement as provided in the preceding section. Such action is not acceptance or conversion.

§ 2—605. **Waiver of Buyer's Objections by Failure to Particularize.**

(1) The buyer's failure to state in connection with rejection a particular defect which is ascertainable by reasonable inspection precludes him from relying on the unstated defect to justify rejection or to establish breach

(a) where the seller could have cured it if stated seasonably; or

(b) between merchants when the seller has after rejection made a request in writing for a full and final written statement of all defects on which the buyer proposes to rely.

(2) Payment against documents made without reservation of rights precludes recovery of the payment for defects apparent on the face of the documents.

§ 2—606. **What Constitutes Acceptance of Goods.**

(1) Acceptance of goods occurs when the buyer

(a) after a reasonable opportunity to inspect the goods signifies to the seller that the goods are conforming or that he will take or retain them in spite of their nonconformity; or

(b) fails to make an effective rejection (subsection (1) of Section 2—602), but such acceptance does not occur until the buyer has had a reasonable opportunity to inspect them; or

(c) does any act inconsistent with the seller's ownership; but if such act is wrongful as against the seller it is an acceptance only if ratified by him.

(2) Acceptance of a part of any commercial unit is acceptance of that entire unit.

§ 2—607. Effect of Acceptance; Notice of Breach; Burden of Establishing Breach After Acceptance; Notice of Claim or Litigation to Person Answerable Over.

(1) The buyer must pay at the contract rate for any goods accepted.

(2) Acceptance of goods by the buyer precludes rejection of the goods accepted and if made with knowledge of a non-conformity cannot be revoked because of it unless the acceptance was on the reasonable assumption that the non-conformity would be seasonably cured but acceptance does not of itself impair any other remedy provided by this Article for non-conformity.

(3) Where a tender has been accepted

(a) the buyer must within a reasonable time after he discovers or should have discovered any breach notify the seller of breach or be barred from any remedy; and

(b) if the claim is one for infringement or the like (subsection (3) of Section 2—312) and the buyer is sued as a result of such a breach he must so notify the seller within a reasonable time after he receives notice of the litigation or be barred from any remedy over for liability established by the litigation.

(4) The burden is on the buyer to establish any breach with respect to the goods accepted.

(5) Where the buyer is sued for breach of a warranty or other obligation for which his seller is answerable over

(a) he may give his seller written notice of the litigation. If the notice states that the seller may come in and defend and that if the seller does not do so he will be bound in any action against him by his buyer by any determination of fact common to the two litigations, then unless the seller after seasonable receipt of the notice does come in and defend he is so bound.

(b) if the claim is one for infringement or the like (subsection (3) of Section 2—312) the original seller may demand in writing that his buyer turn over to him control of the litigation including settlement or else be barred from any remedy over and if he also agrees to bear all expense and to satisfy any adverse judgment, then unless the buyer after seasonable receipt of the demand does turn over control the buyer is so barred.

(6) The provisions of subsections (3), (4) and (5) apply to any obligation of a buyer to hold the seller harmless against infringement or the like (subsection (3) of Section 2—312).

§ 2—608. Revocation of Acceptance in Whole or in Part.

(1) The buyer may revoke his acceptance of a lot or commercial unit whose non-conformity substantially impairs its value to him if he has accepted it

(a) on the reasonable assumption that its non-conformity would be cured and it has not been seasonably cured; or

(b) without discovery of such non-conformity if his acceptance was reasonably induced either by the difficulty of discovery before acceptance or by the seller's assurances.

(2) Revocation of acceptance must occur within a reasonable time after the buyer discovers or should have discovered the ground for it and before any substantial change in condition of the goods which is not caused by their own defects. It is not effective until the buyer notifies the seller of it.

(3) A buyer who so revokes has the same rights and duties with regard to the goods involved as if he had rejected them.

§ 2—609. Right to Adequate Assurance of Performance.

(1) A contract for sale imposes an obligation on each party that the other's expectation of receiving due performance will not be impaired. When reasonable grounds for insecurity arise with respect to the performance of either party the other may in writing demand adequate assurance of due performance and

until he receives such assurance may if commercially reasonable suspend any performance for which he has not already received the agreed return.

(2) Between merchants the reasonableness of grounds for insecurity and the adequacy of any assurance offered shall be determined according to commercial standards.

(3) Acceptance of any improper delivery or payment does not prejudice the aggrieved party's right to demand adequate assurance of future performance.

(4) After receipt of a justified demand failure to provide within a reasonable time not exceeding thirty days such assurance of due performance as is adequate under the circumstances of the particular case is a repudiation of the contract.

§ 2—610. **Anticipatory Repudiation.**

When either party repudiates the contract with respect to a performance not yet due the loss of which will substantially impair the value of the contract to the other, the aggrieved party may

(a) for a commercially reasonable time await performance by the repudiating party; or

(b) resort to any remedy for breach (Section 2—703 or Section 2—711), even though he has notified the repudiating party that he would await the latter's performance and has urged retraction; and

(c) in either case suspend his own performance or proceed in accordance with the provisions of this Article on the seller's right to identify goods to the contract notwithstanding breach or to salvage unfinished goods (Section 2—704).

§ 2—611. **Retraction of Anticipatory Repudiation.**

(1) Until the repudiating party's next performance is due he can retract his repudiation unless the aggrieved party has since the repudiation cancelled or materially changed his position or otherwise indicated that he considers the repudiation final.

(2) Retraction may be by any method which clearly indicates to the aggrieved party that the repudiating party intends to perform, but must include any assurance justifiably demanded under the provisions of this Article (Section 2—609).

(3) Retraction reinstates the repudiating party's rights under the contract with due excuse and allowance to the aggrieved party for any delay occasioned by the repudiation.

§ 2—612. **"Installment Contract"; Breach.**

(1) An "installment contract" is one which requires or authorizes the delivery of goods in separate lots to be separately accepted, even though the contract contains a clause "each delivery is a separate contract" or its equivalent.

(2) The buyer may reject any installment which is non-conforming if the non-conformity substantially impairs the value of that installment and cannot be cured or if the non-conformity is a defect in the required documents; but if the non-conformity does not fall within subsection (3) and the seller gives adequate assurance of its cure the buyer must accept that installment.

(3) Whenever non-conformity or default with respect to one or more installments substantially impairs the value of the whole contract there is a breach of the whole. But the aggrieved party reinstates the contract if he accepts a non-conforming installment without seasonably notifying of cancellation or if he brings an action with respect only to past installments or demands performance as to future installments.

§ 2—613. **Casualty to Identified Goods.**

Where the contract requires for its performance goods identified when the contract is made, and the goods suffer casualty without fault of either party before the risk of loss passes to the buyer, or in a proper case under a "no arrival, no sale" term (Section 2—324) then

(a) if the loss is total the contract is avoided; and

(b) if the loss is partial or the goods have so deteriorated as no longer to conform to the contract the buyer may nevertheless demand inspection and at his option either treat the contract as avoided or accept the goods with due allowance from the contract price for the deterioration or the deficiency in quantity but without further right against the seller.

§ 2—614. **Substituted Performance.**

(1) Where without fault of either party the agreed berthing, loading, or unloading facilities fail or an agreed type of carrier becomes unavailable or the agreed manner of delivery otherwise becomes com-

mercially impracticable but a commercially reasonable substitute is available, such substitute performance must be tendered and accepted.

(2) If the agreed means or manner of payment fails because of domestic or foreign governmental regulation, the seller may withhold or stop delivery unless the buyer provides a means or manner of payment which is commercially a substantial equivalent. If delivery has already been taken, payment by the means or in the manner provided by the regulation discharges the buyer's obligation unless the regulation is discriminatory, oppressive or predatory.

§ 2—615. **Excuse by Failure of Presupposed Conditions.**

Except so far as a seller may have assumed a greater obligation and subject to the preceding section on substituted performance:

(a) Delay in delivery or non-delivery in whole or in part by a seller who complies with paragraphs (b) and (c) is not a breach of his duty under a contract for sale if performance as agreed has been made impracticable by the occurrence of a contingency the non-occurrence of which was a basic assumption on which the contract was made or by compliance in good faith with any applicable foreign or domestic governmental regulation or order whether or not it later proves to be invalid.

(b) Where the causes mentioned in paragraph (a) affect only a part of the seller's capacity to perform, he must allocate production and deliveries among his customers but may at his option include regular customers not then under contract as well as his own requirements for further manufacture. He may so allocate in any manner which is fair and reasonable.

(c) The seller must notify the buyer seasonably that there will be delay or non-delivery and, when allocation is required under paragraph (b), of the estimated quota thus made available for the buyer.

§ 2—616. **Procedure on Notice Claiming Excuse.**

(1) Where the buyer receives notification of a material or indefinite delay or an allocation justified under the preceding section he may by written notification to the seller as to any delivery concerned, and where the prospective deficiency substantially impairs the value of the whole contract under the provisions of this Article relating to breach of installment contracts (Section 2—612), then also as to the whole,

(a) terminate and thereby discharge any unexecuted portion of the contract; or

(b) modify the contract by agreeing to take his available quota in substitution.

(2) If after receipt of such notification from the seller the buyer fails so to modify the contract within a reasonable time not exceeding thirty days the contract lapses with respect to any deliveries affected.

(3) The provisions of this section may not be negated by agreement except in so far as the seller has assumed a greater obligation under the preceding section.

Part 7 **Remedies**

§ 2—701. **Remedies for Breach of Collateral Contracts Not Impaired.**

Remedies for breach of any obligation or promise collateral or ancillary to a contract for sale are not impaired by the provisions of this Article.

§ 2—702. **Seller's Remedies on Discovery of Buyer's Insolvency.**

(1) Where the seller discovers the buyer to be insolvent he may refuse delivery except for cash including payment for all goods theretofore delivered under the contract, and stop delivery under this Article (Section 2—705).

(2) Where the seller discovers that the buyer has received goods on credit while insolvent he may reclaim the goods upon demand made within ten days after the receipt, but if misrepresentation of solvency has been made to the particular seller in writing within three months before delivery the ten day limitation does not apply. Except as provided in this subsection the seller may not base a right to reclaim goods on the buyer's fraudulent or innocent misrepresentation of solvency or of intent to pay.

(3) The seller's right to reclaim under subsection (2) is subject to the rights of a buyer in ordinary course or other good faith purchaser under this Article (Section 2—403). Successful reclamation of goods excludes all other remedies with respect to them.

§ 2—703. **Seller's Remedies in General.**

Where the buyer wrongfully rejects or revokes acceptance of goods or fails to make a payment due on or before delivery or repudiates with respect to a part or the whole, then with respect to any goods directly affected and, if the breach is of the whole contract (Section 2—612), then also with respect to the whole undelivered balance, the aggrieved seller may

(a) withhold delivery of such goods;

(b) stop delivery by any bailee as hereafter provided (Section 2—705);

(c) proceed under the next section respecting goods still unidentified to the contract;

(d) resell and recover damages as hereafter provided (Section 2—706);

(e) recover damages for non-acceptance (Section 2—708) or in a proper case the price (Section 2—709);

(f) cancel.

§ 2—704. **Seller's Right to Identify Goods to the Contract Notwithstanding Breach or to Salvage Unfinished Goods.**

(1) An aggrieved seller under the preceding section may

(a) identify to the contract conforming goods not already identified if at the time he learned of the breach they are in his possession or control;

(b) treat as the subject of resale goods which have demonstrably been intended for the particular contract even though those goods are unfinished.

(2) Where the goods are unfinished an aggrieved seller may in the exercise of reasonable commercial judgment for the purposes of avoiding loss and of effective realization either complete the manufacture and wholly identify the goods to the contract or cease manufacture and resell for scrap or salvage value or proceed in any other reasonable manner.

§ 2—705. **Seller's Stoppage of Delivery in Transit or Otherwise.**

(1) The seller may stop delivery of goods in the possession of a carrier or other bailee when he discovers the buyer to be insolvent (Section 2—702) and may stop delivery of carload, truckload, plane-load or larger shipments of express or freight when the buyer repudiates or fails to make a payment due before delivery or if for any other reason the seller has a right to withhold or reclaim the goods.

(2) As against such buyer the seller may stop delivery until

(a) receipt of the goods by the buyer; or

(b) acknowledgment to the buyer by any bailee of the goods except a carrier that the bailee holds the goods for the buyer; or

(c) such acknowledgment to the buyer by a carrier by reshipment or as warehouseman; or

(d) negotiation to the buyer of any negotiable document of title covering the goods.

(3) (a) To stop delivery the seller must so notify as to enable the bailee by reasonable diligence to prevent delivery of the goods.

(b) After such notification the bailee must hold and deliver the goods according to the directions of the seller but the seller is liable to the bailee for any ensuing charges or damages.

(c) If a negotiable document of title has been issued for goods the bailee is not obliged to obey a notification to stop unitl surrender of the document.

(d) A carrier who has issued a non-negotiable bill of lading is not obliged to obey a notification to stop received from a person other than the con-signor.

§ 2—706. **Seller's Resale Including Contract for Resale.**

(1) Under the conditions stated in Section 2—703 on seller's remedies, the seller may resell the goods concerned or the undelivered balance thereof. Where the resale is made in good faith and in a commercially reasonable manner the seller may recover the difference between the resale price and the contract price together with any incidental damages allowed under the provisions of this Article (Section 2—710), but less expenses saved in consequence of the buyer's breach.

(2) Except as otherwise provided in subsection (3) or unless otherwise agreed resale may be at public or private sale including sale by way of one or more contracts to sell or of identification to an existing contract of the seller. Sale may be as a unit or in parcels and at any time and place and on any terms but every aspect of the sale including the method, manner, time, place and terms must be commercially

reasonable. The resale must be reasonably identified as referring to the broken contract, but it is not necessary that the goods be in existence or that any or all of them have been identified to the contract before the breach.

(3) Where the resale is at private sale the seller must give the buyer reasonable notification of his intention to resell.

(4) Where the resale is at public sale

(a) only identified goods can be sold except where there is a recognized market for a public sale of futures in goods of the kind; and

(b) it must be made at a usual place or market for public sale if one is reasonably available and except in the case of goods which are perishable or threaten to decline in value speedily the seller must give the buyer reasonable notice of the time and place of the resale; and

(c) if the goods are not to be within the view of those attending the sale the notification of sale must state the place where the goods are located and provide for their reasonable inspection by prospective bidders; and

(d) the seller may buy.

(5) A purchaser who buys in good faith at a resale takes the goods free of any rights of the original buyer even though the seller fails to comply with one or more of the requirements of this section.

(6) The seller is not accountable to the buyer for any profit made on any resale. A person in the position of a seller (Section 2—707) or a buyer who has rightfully rejected or justifiably revoked acceptance must account for any excess over the amount of his security interest, as hereinafter defined (subsection (3) of Section 2—711).

§ 2—707. **"Person in the Position of a Seller".**

(1) A "person in the position of a seller" includes as against a principal an agent who has paid or become responsible for the price of goods on behalf of his principal or anyone who otherwise holds a security interest or other right in goods similar to that of a seller.

(2) A person in the position of a seller may as provided in this Article withhold or stop delivery (Section 2—705) and resell (Section 2—706) and recover incidental damages (Section 2—710).

§ 2—708. **Seller's Damages for Non-Acceptance or Repudiation.**

(1) Subject to subsection (2) and to the provisions of this Article with respect to proof of market price (Section 2—723), the measure of damages for non-acceptance or repudiation by the buyer is the difference between the market price at the time and place for tender and the unpaid contract price together with any incidental damages provided in this Article (Section 2—710), but less expenses saved in consequence of the buyer's breach.

(2) If the measure of damages provided in subsection (1) is inadequate to put the seller in as good a position as performance would have done then the measure of damages is the profit (including reasonable overhead) which the seller would have made from full performance by the buyer, together with any incidental damages provided in this Article (Section 2—710), due allowance for costs reasonably incurred and due credit for payments or proceeds of resale.

§ 2—709. **Action for the Price.**

(1) When the buyer fails to pay the price as it becomes due the seller may recover, together with any incidental damages under the next section, the price

(a) of goods accepted or of conforming goods lost or damaged within a commercially reasonable time after risk of their loss has passed to the buyer; and

(b) of goods identified to the contract if the seller is unable after reasonable effort to resell them at a reasonable price or the circumstances reasonably indicate that such effort will be unavailing.

(2) Where the seller sues for the price he must hold for the buyer any goods which have been identified to the contract and are still in his control except that if resale becomes possible he may resell them at any time prior to the collection of the judgment. The net proceeds of any such resale must be credited to the buyer and payment of the judgment entitles him to any goods not resold.

(3) After the buyer has wrongfully rejected or revoked acceptance of the goods or has failed to make a payment due or has repudiated (Section 2—610), a

seller who is held not entitled to the price under this section shall nevertheless be awarded damages for non-acceptance under the preceding section.

§ 2—710. Seller's Incidental Damages.

Incidental damages to an aggrieved seller include any commercially reasonable charges, expenses or commissions incurred in stopping delivery, in the transportation, care and custody of goods after the buyer's breach, in connection with return or resale of the goods or otherwise resulting from the breach.

§ 2—711. Buyer's Remedies in General; Buyer's Security Interest in Rejected Goods.

(1) Where the seller fails to make delivery or repudiates or the buyer rightfully rejects or justifiably revokes acceptance then with respect to any goods involved, and with respect to the whole if the breach goes to the whole contract (Section 2—612), the buyer may cancel and whether or not he has done so may in addition to recovering so much of the price as has been paid

>   (a) "cover" and have damages under the next section as to all the goods affected whether or not they have been identified to the contract; or

>   (b) recover damages for non-delivery as provided in this Article (Section 2—713).

(2) Where the seller fails to deliver or repudiates the buyer may also

>   (a) if the goods have been identified recover them as provided in this Article (Section 2—502); or

>   (b) in a proper case obtain specific performance or replevy the goods as provided in this Article (Section 2—716).

(3) On rightful rejection or justifiable revocation of acceptance a buyer has a security interest in goods in his possession or control for any payments made on their price and any expenses reasonably incurred in their inspection, receipt, transportation, care and custody and may hold such goods and resell them in like manner as an aggrieved seller (Section 2—706).

§ 2—712. "Cover"; Buyer's Procurement of Substitute Goods.

(1) After a breach within the preceding section the buyer may "cover" by making in good faith and without unreasonable delay any reasonable purchase of or contract to purchase goods in substitution for those due from the seller.

(2) The buyer may recover from the seller as damages the difference between the cost of cover and the contract price together with any incidental or consequential damages as hereinafter defined (Section 2—715), but less expenses saved in consequence of the seller's breach.

(3) Failure of the buyer to effect cover within this section does not bar him from any other remedy.

§ 2—713. Buyer's Damages for Non-Delivery or Repudiation.

(1) Subject to the provisions of this Article with respect to proof of market price (Section 2—723), the measure of damages for non-delivery or repudiation by the seller is the difference between the market price at the time when the buyer learned of the breach and the contract price together with any incidental and consequential damages provided in this Article (Section 2—715), but less expenses saved in consequence of the seller's breach.

(2) Market price is to be determined as of the place for tender or, in cases of rejection after arrival or revocation of acceptance, as of the place of arrival.

§ 2—714. Buyer's Damages for Breach in Regard to Accepted Goods.

(1) Where the buyer has accepted goods and given notification (subsection (3) of Section 2—607) he may recover as damages for any non-conformity of tender the loss resulting in the ordinary course of events from the seller's breach as determined in any manner which is reasonable.

(2) The measure of damages for breach of warranty is the difference at the time and place of acceptance between the value of the goods accepted and the value they would have had if they had been as warranted, unless special circumstances show proximate damages of a different amount.

(3) In a proper case any incidental and consequential damages under the next section may also be recovered.

§ 2—715. Buyer's Incidental and Consequential Damages.

(1) Incidental damages resulting from the seller's

breach include expenses reasonably incurred in inspection, receipt, transportation and care and custody of goods rightfully rejected, any commercially reasonable charges, expenses or commissions in connection with effecting cover and any other reasonable expense incident to the delay or other breach.

(2) Consequential damages resulting from the seller's breach include

(a) any loss resulting from general or particular requirements and needs of which the seller at the time of contracting had reason to know and which could not reasonably be prevented by cover or otherwise; and

(b) injury to person or property proximately resulting from any breach of warranty.

§ 2—716 **Buyer's Right to Specific Performance or Replevin.**

(1) Specific performance may be decreed where the goods are unique or in other proper circumstances.

(2) The decree for specific performance may include such terms and conditions as to payment of the price, damages, or other relief as the court may deem just.

(3) The buyer has a right of replevin for goods identified to the contract if after reasonable effort he is unable to effect cover for such goods or the circumstances reasonably indicate that such effort will be unavailing or if the goods have been shipped under reservation and satisfaction of the security interest in them has been made or tendered.

§ 2—717. **Deduction of Damages From the Price.**

The buyer on notifying the seller of his intention to do so may deduct all or any part of the damages resulting from any breach of the contract from any part of the price still due under the same contract.

§ 2—718. **Liquidation or Limitation of Damages; Deposits.**

(1) Damages for breach by either party may be liquidated in the agreement but only at an amount which is reasonable in the light of the anticipated or actual harm caused by the breach, the difficulties of proof of loss, and the inconvenience or nonfeasibility of otherwise obtaining an adequate remedy. A term

fixing unreasonably large liquidated damages is void as a penalty.

(2) Where the seller justifiably withholds delivery of goods because of the buyer's breach, the buyer is entitled to restitution of any amount by which the sum of his payments exceeds

(a) the amount to which the seller is entitled by virtue of terms liquidating the seller's damages in accordance with subsection (1), or

(b) in the absence of such terms, twenty per cent of the value of the total performance for which the buyer is obligated under the contract or $500, whichever is smaller.

(3) The buyer's right to restitution under subsection (2) is subject to offset to the extent that the seller establishes

(a) a right to recover damages under the provisions of this Article other than subsection (1), and

(b) the amount or value of any benefits received by the buyer directly or indirectly by reason of the contract.

(4) Where a seller has received payment in goods their reasonable value or the proceeds of their resale shall be treated as payments for the purposes of subsection (2); but if the seller has notice of the buyer's breach before reselling goods received in part performance, his resale is subject to the conditions laid down in this Article on resale by an aggrieved seller (Section 2—706).

§ 2—719. **Contractual Modification or Limitation of Remedy.**

(1) Subject to the provisions of subsections (2) and (3) of this section and of the preceding section on liquidation and limitation of damages,

(a) the agreement may provide for remedies in addition to or in substitution for those provided in this Article and may limit or alter the measure of damages recoverable under this Article, as by limiting the buyer's remedies to return of the goods and repayment of the price or to repair and replacement of non-conforming goods or parts; and

(b) resort to a remedy as provided is optional unless the remedy is expressly agreed to be exclusive, in which case it is the sole remedy.

(2) Where circumstances cause an exclusive or limited remedy to fail of its essential purpose, remedy may be had as provided in this Act.

(3) Consequential damages may be limited or excluded unless the limitation or exclusion is unconscionable. Limitation of consequential damages for injury to the person in the case of consumer goods is prima facie unconscionable but limitation of damages where the loss is commercial is not.

§ 2—720. **Effect of "Cancellation" or "Rescission" on Claims for Antecedent Breach.**

Unless the contrary intention clearly appears, expressions of "cancellation" or "rescission" of the contract or the like shall not be construed as a renunciation or discharge of any claim in damages for an antecedent breach.

§ 2—721. **Remedies for Fraud.**

Remedies for material misrepresentation or fraud include all remedies available under this Article for non-fraudulent breach. Neither rescission or a claim for rescission of the contract for sale nor rejection or return of the goods shall bar or be deemed inconsistent with a claim for damages or other remedy.

§ 2—722. **Who Can Sue Third Parties for Injury to Goods.**

Where a third party so deals with goods which have been identified to a contract for sale as to cause actionable injury to a party to that contract

(a) a right of action against the third party is in either party to the contract for sale who has title to or a security interest or a special property or an insurable interest in the goods; and if the goods have been destroyed or converted a right of action is also in the party who either bore the risk of loss under the contract for sale or has since the injury assumed that risk as against the other;

(b) if at the time of the injury the party plaintiff did not bear the risk of loss as against the other party to the contract for sale and there is no arrangement between them for disposition of the recovery, his suit or settlement is, subject to his own interest, as a fiduciary for the other party to the contract;

(c) either party may with the consent of the other sue for the benefit of whom it may concern.

§ 2—723. **Proof of Market Price: Time and Place.**

(1) If an action based on anticipatory repudiation comes to trial before the time for performance with respect to some or all of the goods, any damages based on market price (Section 2—708 or Section 2—713) shall be determined according to the price of such goods prevailing at the time when the aggrieved party learned of the repudiation.

(2) If evidence of a price prevailing at the times or places described in this Article is not readily available the price prevailing within any reasonable time before or after the time described or at any other place which in commercial judgment or under usage of trade would serve as a reasonable substitute for the one described may be used, making any proper allowance for the cost of transporting the goods to or from such other place.

(3) Evidence of a relevant price prevailing at a time or place other than the one described in this Article offered by one party is not admissible unless and until he has given the other party such notice as the court finds sufficient to prevent unfair surprise.

§ 2—724. **Admissibility of Market Quotations.**

Whenever the prevailing price or value of any goods regularly bought and sold in any established commodity market is in issue, reports in official publications or trade journals or in newspapers or periodicals of general circulation published as the reports of such market shall be admissible in evidence. The circumstances of the preparation of such a report may be shown to affect its weight but not its admissibility.

§ 2—725. **Statute of Limitations in Contracts for Sale.**

(1) An action for breach of any contract for sale must be commenced within four years after the cause of action has accrued. By the original agreement the parties may reduce the period of limitation to not less than one year but may not extend it.

(2) A cause of action accrues when the breach occurs, regardless of the aggrieved party's lack of knowledge of the breach. A breach of warranty occurs when tender of delivery is made, except that where a warranty explicitly extends to future performance of the goods and discovery of the breach must await the time of such performance the cause of action accrues

when the breach is or should have been discovered.

(3) Where an action commenced within the time limited by subsection (1) is so terminated as to leave available a remedy by another action for the same breach such other action may be commenced after the expiration of the time limited and within six months after the termination of the first action unless the termination resulted from voluntary discontinuance or from dismissal for failure or neglect to prosecute.

(4) This section does not alter the law on tolling of the statute of limitations nor does it apply to causes of action which have accrued before this Act becomes effective.

Article 3
COMMERCIAL PAPER

Part 1 Short Title, Form and Interpretation

§ 3—101. **Short Title.**

This Article shall be known and may be cited as Uniform Commercial Code—Commercial Paper.

§ 3—102. **Definitions and Index of Definitions.**

(1) In this Article unless the context otherwise requires

(a) "Issue" means the first delivery of an instrument to a holder or a remitter.

(b) An "order" is a direction to pay and must be more than an authorization or request. It must identify the person to pay with reasonable certainty. It may be addressed to one or more such persons jointly or in the alternative but not in succession.

(c) A "promise" is an undertaking to pay and must be more than an acknowledgment of an obligation.

(d) "Secondary party" means a drawer or endorser.

(e) "Instrument" means a negotiable instrument.

(2) Other definitions applying to this Article and the sections in which they appear are:
"Acceptance". Section 3—410.

"Accommodation party". Section 3—415.
"Alteration". Section 3—407.
"Certificate of deposit". Section 3—104.
"Certification". Section 3—411.
"Check". Section 3—104.
"Definite time". Section 3—109.
"Dishonor". Section 3—507.
"Draft". Section 3—104.
"Holder in due course". Section 3—302.
"Negotiation". Section 3—202.
"Note". Section 3—104.
"Notice of dishonor". Section 3—508.
"On demand". Section 3—108.
"Presentment". Section 3—504.
"Protest". Section 3—509.
"Restrictive Indorsement". Section 3—205.
"Signature". Section 3—401.

(3) The following definitions in other Articles apply to this Article:
"Account". Section 4—104.
"Banking Day". Section 4—104.
"Clearing House". Section 4—104.
"Collecting Bank". Section 4—105.
"Customer". Section 4—104.
"Depositary Bank". Section 4—105.
"Documentary Draft". Section 4—104.
"Intermediary Bank". Section 4—105.
"Item". Section 4—104.
"Midnight deadline". Section 4—104.
"Payor Bank". Section 4—105.

(4) In addition Article 1 contains general definitions and principles of construction and interpretation applicable throughout this Article.

§ 3—103. **Limitations on Scope of Article.**

(1) This Article does not apply to money, documents of title or investment securities.

(2) The provisions of this Article are subject to the provisions of the Article on Bank Deposits and Collections (Article 4) and Secured Transactions (Article 9).

§ 3—104. **Form of Negotiable Instruments; "Draft"; "Check"; "Certificate of Deposit"; "Note".**

(1) Any writing to be a negotiable instrument within this Article must

(a) be signed by the maker or drawer; and

(b) contain an unconditional promise or order to pay a sum certain in money and no other promise, order, obligation or power given by the maker or drawer except as authorized by this Article; and

(c) be payable on demand or at a definite time; and

(d) be payable to order or to bearer.

(2) A writing which complies with the requirements of this section is

(a) a "draft" ("bill of exchange") if it is an order;

(b) a "check" if it is a draft drawn on a bank and payable on demand;

(c) a "certificate of deposit" if it is an acknowledgment by a bank of receipt of money with an engagement to repay it;

(d) a "note" if it is a promise other than a certificate of deposit.

(3) As used in other Articles of this Act, and as the context may require, the terms "draft", "check", "certificate of deposit" and "note" may refer to instruments which are not negotiable within this Article as well as to instruments which are so negotiable.

§ 3—105. **When Promise or Order Unconditional.**

(1) A promise or order otherwise unconditional is not made conditional by the fact that the instrument

(a) is subject to implied or constructive conditions; or

(b) states its consideration, whether performed or promised, or the transaction which gave rise to the instrument, or that the promise or order is made or the instrument matures in accordance with or "as per" such transaction; or

(c) refers to or states that it arises out of a separate agreement or refers to a separate agreement for rights as to prepayment or acceleration; or

(d) states that it is drawn under a letter of credit; or

(e) states that it is secured, whether by mortgage, reservation of title or otherwise; or

(f) indicates a particular account to be debited or any other fund or source from which reimbursement is expected; or

(g) is limited to payment out of a particular fund or the proceeds of a particular source, if the instrument is issued by a government or governmental agency or unit; or

(h) is limited to payment out of the entire assets of a partnership, unincorporated association, trust or estate by or on behalf of which the instrument is issued.

(2) A promise or order is not unconditional if the instrument

(a) states that it is subject to or governed by any other agreement; or

(b) states that it is to be paid only out of a particular fund or source except as provided in this section.

§ 3—106. **Sum Certain.**

(1) The sum payable is a sum certain even though it is to be paid

(a) with stated interest or by stated installments; or

(b) with stated different rates of interest before and after default or a specified date; or

(c) with a stated discount or addition if paid before or after the date fixed for payment; or

(d) with exchange or less exchange, whether at a fixed rate or at the current rate; or

(e) with costs of collection or an attorney's fee or both upon default.

(2) Nothing in this section shall validate any term which is otherwise illegal.

§ 3—107. **Money.**

(1) An instrument is payable in money if the medium of exchange in which it is payable is money at the time the instrument is made. An instrument payable in "currency" or "current funds" is payable in money.

(2) A promise or order to pay a sum stated in a foreign currency is for a sum certain in money and, unless a different medium of payment is specified in the instrument, may be satisfied by payment of that number of dollars which the stated foreign currency will purchase at the buying sight rate for that currency on the day on which the instrument is payable or, if

payable on demand, on the day of demand. If such an instrument specifies a foreign currency as the medium of payment the instrument is payable in that currency.

§ 3—108. **Payable on Demand.**

Instruments payable on demand include those payable at sight or on presentation and those in which no time for payment is stated.

§ 3—109. **Definite Time.**

(1) An instrument is payable at a definite time if by its terms it is payable

(a) on or before a stated date or at a fixed period after a stated date; or

(b) at a fixed period after sight; or

(c) at a definite time subject to any acceleration; or

(d) at a definite time subject to extension at the option of the holder, or to extension to a further definite time at the option of the maker or acceptor or automatically upon or after a specified act or event.

(2) An instrument which by its terms is otherwise payable only upon an act or event uncertain as to time of occurrence is not payable at a definite time even though the act or event has occurred.

§ 3—110. **Payable to Order.**

(1) An instrument is payable to order when by its terms it is payable to the order or assigns of any person therein specified with reasonable certainty, or to him or his order, or when it is conspicuously designated on its face as "exchange" or the like and names a payee. It may be payable to the order of

(a) the maker or drawer; or

(b) the drawee; or

(c) a payee who is not maker, drawer or drawee; or

(d) two or more payees together or in the alternative; or

(e) an estate, trust or fund, in which case it is payable to the order of the representative of such estate, trust or fund or his successors; or

(f) an office, or an officer by his title as such in which case it is payable to the principal but the incumbent of the office or his successors may act as if he or they were the holder; or

(g) a partnership or unincorporated association, in which case it is payable to the partnership or association and may be indorsed or transferred by any person thereto authorized.

(2) An instrument not payable to order is not made so payable by such words as "payable upon return of this instrument properly indorsed."

(3) An instrument made payable both to order and to bearer is payable to order unless the bearer words are handwritten or typewritten.

§ 3—111. **Payable to Bearer.**

An instrument is payable to bearer when by its terms it is payable to

(a) bearer or the order of bearer; or

(b) a specified person or bearer; or

(c) "cash" or the order of "cash", or any other indication which does not purport to designate a specific payee.

§ 3—112. **Terms and Omissions Not Affecting Negotiability.**

(1) The negotiability of an instrument is not affected by

(a) the omission of a statement of any consideration or of the place where the instrument is drawn or payable; or

(b) a statement that collateral has been given to secure obligations either on the instrument or otherwise of an obligor on the instrument or that in case of default on those obligations the holder may realize on or dispose of the collateral; or

(c) a promise or power to maintain or protect collateral or to give additional collateral; or

(d) a term authorizing a confession of judgment on the instrument if it is not paid when due; or

(e) a term purporting to waive the benefit of any law intended for the advantage or protection of any obligor; or

(f) a term in a draft providing that the payee by indorsing or cashing it acknowledges full satisfaction of an obligation of the drawer; or

(g) a statement in a draft drawn in a set of parts (Section 3—801) to the effect that the order is effective only if no other part has been honored.

(2) Nothing in this section shall validate any term which is otherwise illegal.

§ 3—113. **Seal.**

An instrument otherwise negotiable is within this Article even though it is under a seal.

§ 3—114. **Date, Antedating, Postdating.**

(1) The negotiability of an instrument is not affected by the fact that it is undated, antedated or postdated.

(2) Where an instrument is antedated or postdated the time when it is payable is determined by the stated date if the instrument is payable on demand or at a fixed period after date.

(3) Where the instrument or any signature thereon is dated, the date is presumed to be correct.

§ 3—115. **Incomplete Instruments.**

(1) When a paper whose contents at the time of signing show that it is intended to become an instrument is signed while still incomplete in any necessary respect it cannot be enforced until completed, but when it is completed in accordance with authority given it is effective as completed.

(2) If the completion is unauthorized the rules as to material alteration apply (Section 3—407), even though the paper was not delivered by the maker or drawer; but the burden of establishing that any completion is unauthorized is on the party so asserting.

§ 3—116. **Instruments Payable to Two or More Persons.**

An instrument payable to the order of two or more persons

(a) if in the alternative is payable to any one of them and may be negotiated, discharged or enforced by any of them who has possession of it;

(b) if not in the alternative is payable to all of them and may be negotiated, discharged or enforced only by all of them.

§ 3—117. **Instruments Payable With Words of Description.**

An instrument made payable to a named person with the addition of words describing him

(a) as agent or officer of a specified person is payable to his principal but the agent or officer may act as if he were the holder;

(b) as any other fiduciary for a specified person or purpose is payable to the payee and may be negotiated, discharged or enforced by him;

(c) in any other manner is payable to the payee unconditionally and the additional words are without effect on subsequent parties.

§ 3—118. **Ambiguous Terms and Rules of Construction.**

The following rules apply to every instrument:

(a) Where there is doubt whether the instrument is a draft or a note the holder may treat it as either. A draft drawn on the drawer is effective as a note.

(b) Handwritten terms control typewritten and printed terms, and typewritten control printed.

(c) Words control figures except that if the words are ambiguous figures control.

(d) Unless otherwise specified a provision for interest means interest at the judgment rate at the place of payment from the date of the instrument, or if it is undated from the date of issue.

(e) Unless the instrument otherwise specifies two or more persons who sign as maker, acceptor or drawer or indorser and as a part of the same transaction are jointly and severally liable even though the instrument contains such words as "I promise to pay."

(f) Unless otherwise specified consent to extension authorizes a single extension for not longer than the original period. A consent to extension, expressed in the instrument, is binding on secondary parties and accommodation makers. A holder may not exercise his option to extend an instrument over the objection of a maker or acceptor or other party who in accordance with Section 3—604 tenders full payment when the instrument is due.

§ 3—119. **Other Writings Affecting Instrument.**

(1) As between the obligor and his immediate obligee or any transferee the terms of an instrument may be modified or affected by any other written agreement executed as a part of the same transaction, except that a holder in due course in not affected by any limitation of his rights arising out of the separate written agreement if he had no notice of the limitation when he took the instrument.

(2) A separate agreement does not affect the negotiability of an instrument.

§ 3—120. Instruments "Payable Through" Bank.

An instrument which states that it is "payable through" a bank or the like designates that bank as a collecting bank to make presentment but does not of itself authorize the bank to pay the instrument.

§ 3—121. Instruments Payable at Bank.

Note: If this Act is introduced in the Congress of the United States this section should be omitted.
(States to select either alternative)

Alternative A—

A note or acceptance which states that it is payable at a bank is the equivalent of a draft drawn on the bank payable when it falls due out of any funds of the maker or acceptor in current account or otherwise available for such payment.

Alternative B—

A note or acceptance which states that it is payable at a bank is not of itself an order or authorization to the bank to pay it.

§ 3—122. Accrual of Cause of Action.

(1) A cause of action against a maker or an acceptor accrues

    (a) in the case of a time instrument on the day after maturity;

    (b) in the case of a demand instrument upon its date or, if no date is stated, on the date of issue.

(2) A cause of action against the obligor of a demand or time certificate of deposit accrues upon demand, but demand on a time certificate may not be made until on or after the date of maturity.

(3) A cause of action against a drawer of a draft or an indorser of any instrument accrues upon demand following dishonor of the instrument. Notice of dishonor is a demand.

(4) Unless an instrument provides otherwise, interest runs at the rate provided by law for a judgment

    (a) in the case of a maker, acceptor or other primary obligor of a demand instrument, from the date of demand;

    (b) in all other cases from the date of accrual of the cause of action.

Part 2 Transfer and Negotiation

§ 3—201. Transfer: Right to Indorsement.

(1) Transfer of an instrument vests in the transferee such rights as the transferor has therein, except that a transferee who has himself been a party to any fraud or illegality affecting the instrument or who as a prior holder had notice of a defense or claim against it cannot improve his position by taking from a later holder in due course.

(2) A transfer of a security interest in an instrument vests the foregoing rights in the transferee to the extent of the interest transferred.

(3) Unless otherwise agreed any transfer for value of an instrument not then payable to bearer gives the transferee the specifically enforceable right to have the unqualified indorsement of the transferor. Negotiation takes effect only when the indorsement is made and until that time there is no presumption that the transferee is the owner.

§ 3—202. Negotiation.

(1) Negotiation is the transfer of an instrument in such form that the transferee becomes a holder. If the instrument is payable to order it is negotiated by delivery with any necessary indorsement; if payable to bearer it is negotiated by delivery.

(2) An indorsement must be written by or on behalf of the holder and on the instrument or on a paper so firmly affixed thereto as to become a part thereof.

(3) An indorsement is effective for negotiation only when it conveys the entire instrument or any unpaid residue. If it purports to be of less it operates only as a partial assignment.

(4) Words of assignment, condition, waiver, guaranty, limitation or disclaimer of liability and the like accompanying an indorsement do not affect its character as an indorsement.

§ 3—203. Wrong or Misspelled Name.

Where an instrument is made payable to a person under a misspelled name or one other than his own he may indorse in that name or his own or both; but signature in both names may be required by a person paying or giving value for the instrument.

§ 3—204. Special Indorsement; Blank Indorsement.

(1) A special indorsement specifies the person to

whom or to whose order it makes the instrument payable. Any instrument specially indorsed becomes payable to the order of the special indorsee and may be further negotiated only by his indorsement.

(2) An indorsement in blank specifies no particular indorsee and may consist of a mere signature. An instrument payable to order and indorsed in blank becomes payable to bearer and may be negotiated by delivery alone until specially indorsed.

(3) The holder may convert a blank indorsement into a special indorsement by writing over the signature of the indorser in blank any contract consistent with the character of the indorsement.

§ 3—205. **Restrictive Indorsements.**

An indorsement is restrictive which either

(a) is conditional; or

(b) purports to prohibit further transfer of the instrument; or

(c) includes the words "for collection", "for deposit", "pay any bank", or like terms signifying a purpose of deposit or collection; or

(d) otherwise states that it is for the benefit or use of the indorser or of another person.

§ 3—206. **Effect of Restrictive Indorsement.**

(1) No restrictive indorsement prevents further transfer or negotiation of the instrument.

(2) An intermediary bank, or a payor bank which is not the depositary bank, is neither given notice nor otherwise affected by a restrictive indorsement of any person except the bank's immediate transferor or the person presenting for payment.

(3) Except for an intermediary bank, any transferee under an indorsement which is conditional or includes the words "for collection", "for deposit", "pay any bank", or like terms (subparagraphs (a) and (c) of Section 3—205) must pay or apply any value given by him for or on the security of the instrument consistently with the indorsement and to the extent that he does so he becomes a holder for value. In addition such transferee is a holder in due course if he otherwise complies with the requirements of Section 3—302 on what constitutes a holder in due course.

(4) The first taker under an indorsement for the benefit of the indorser or another person (subparagraph (d) of Section 3—205) must pay or apply any value given by him for or on the security of the instrument consistently with the indorsement and to the extent that he does so he becomes a holder for value. In addition such taker is a holder in due course if he otherwise complies with the requirements of Section 3—302 on what constitutes a holder in due course. A later holder for value is neither given notice nor otherwise affected by such restrictive indorsement unless he has knowledge that a fiduciary or other person has negotiated the instrument in any transaction for his own benefit or otherwise in breach of duty (subsection (2) of Section 3—304).

§ 3—207. **Negotiation Effective Although It May Be Rescinded.**

(1) Negotiation is effective to transfer the instrument although the negotiation is

(a) made by an infant, a corporation exceeding its powers, or any other person without capacity; or

(b) obtained by fraud, duress or mistake of any kind; or

(c) part of an illegal transaction; or

(d) made in breach of duty.

(2) Except as against a subsequent holder in due course such negotiation is in an appropriate case subject to rescission, the declaration of a constructive trust or any other remedy permitted by law.

§ 3—208. **Reacquisition.**

Where an instrument is returned to or reacquired by a prior party he may cancel any indorsement which is not necessary to his title and reissue or further negotiate the instrument, but any intervening party is discharged as against the reacquiring party and subsequent holders not in due course and if his indorsement has been cancelled is discharged as against subsequent holders in due course as well.

Part 3 Rights of a Holder

§ 3—301. **Rights of a Holder.**

The holder of an instrument whether or not he is the owner may transfer or negotiate it and, except as otherwise provided in Section 3—603 on payment or satisfaction, discharge it or enforce payment in his own name.

§ 3—302. **Holder in Due Course.**

(1) A holder in due course is a holder who takes the instrument

    (a) for value; and

    (b) in good faith; and

    (c) without notice that it is overdue or has been dishonored or of any defense against or claim to it on the part of any person.

(2) A payee may be a holder in due course.

(3) A holder does not become a holder in due course of an instrument:

    (a) by purchase of it at judicial sale or by taking it under legal process; or

    (b) by acquiring it in taking over an estate; or

    (c) by purchasing it as part of a bulk transaction not in regular course of business of the transferor.

(4) A purchaser of a limited interest can be a holder in due course only to the extent of the interest purchased.

§ 3—303. **Taking for Value.**

A holder takes the instrument for value

(a) to the extent that the agreed consideration has been performed or that he acquires a security interest in or a lien on the instrument otherwise than by legal process; or

(b) when he takes the instrument in payment of or as security for an antecedent claim against any person whether or not the claim is due; or

(c) when he gives a negotiable instrument for it or makes an irrevocable commitment to a third person.

§ 3—304. **Notice to Purchaser.**

(1) The purchaser has notice of a claim or defense if

    (a) the instrument is so incomplete, bears such visible evidence of forgery or alteration, or is otherwise so irregular as to call into question its validity, terms or ownership or to create an ambiguity as to the party to pay; or

    (b) the purchaser has notice that the obligation of any party is voidable in whole or in part, or that all parties have been discharged.

(2) The purchaser has notice of a claim against the instrument when he has knowledge that a fiduciary has negotiated the instrument in payment of or as security for his own debt or in any transaction for his own benefit or otherwise in breach of duty.

(3) The purchaser has notice that an instrument is overdue if he has reason to know

    (a) that any part of the principal amount is overdue or that there is an uncured default in payment of another instrument of the same series; or

    (b) that acceleration of the instrument has been made; or

    (c) that he is taking a demand instrument after demand has been made or more than a reasonable length of time after its issue. A reasonable time for a check drawn and payable within the states and territories of the United States and the District of Columbia is presumed to be thirty days.

(4) Knowledge of the following facts does not of itself give the purchaser notice of a defense or claim

    (a) that the instrument is antedated or postdated;

    (b) that it was issued or negotiated in return for an executory promise or accompanied by a separate agreement, unless the purchaser has notice that a defense or claim has arisen from the terms thereof;

    (c) that any party has signed for accommodation;

    (d) that an incomplete instrument has been completed, unless the purchaser has notice of any improper completion;

    (e) that any person negotiating the instrument is or was a fiduciary;

    (f) that there has been default in payment of interest on the instrument or in payment of any other instrument, except one of the same series.

(5) The filing or recording of a document does not of itself constitute notice within the provisions of this Article to a person who would otherwise be a holder in due course.

(6) To be effective notice must be received at such time and in such manner as to give a reasonable opportunity to act on it.

§ 3—305. **Rights of a Holder in Due Course.**

To the extent that a holder is a holder in due course he takes the instrument free from

(1) all claims to it on the part of any person; and

(2) all defenses of any party to the instrument with whom the holder has not dealt except

(a) infancy, to the extent that it is a defense to a simple contract; and

(b) such other incapacity, or duress, or illegality of the transaction, as renders the obligation of the party a nullity; and

(c) such misrepresentation as has induced the party to sign the instrument with neither knowledge nor reasonable opportunity to obtain knowledge of its character or its essential terms; and

(d) discharge in insolvency proceedings; and

(e) any other discharge of which the holder has notice when he takes the instrument.

§ 3—306. Rights of One Not Holder in Due Course.

Unless he has the rights of a holder in due course any person takes the instrument subject to

(a) all valid claims to it on the part of any person; and

(b) all defenses of any party which would be available in an action on a simple contract; and

(c) the defenses of want or failure of consideration, nonperformance of any condition precedent, non-delivery, or delivery for a special purpose (Section 3—408); and

(d) the defense that he or a person through whom he holds the instrument acquired it by theft, or that payment or satisfaction to such holder would be inconsistent with the terms of a restrictive indorsement. The claim of any third person to the instrument is not otherwise available as a defense to any party liable thereon unless the third person himself defends the action for such party.

§ 3—307. Burden of Establishing Signatures, Defenses and Due Course.

(1) Unless specifically denied in the pleadings each signature on an instrument is admitted. When the effectiveness of a signature is put in issue

(a) the burden of establishing it is on the party claiming under the signature; but

(b) the signature is presumed to be genuine or authorized except where the action is to enforce the obligation of a purported signer who has died or become incompetent before proof is required.

(2) When signatures are admitted or established, production of the instrument entitles a holder to recover on it unless the defendant establishes a defense.

(3) After it is shown that a defense exists a person claiming the rights of a holder in due course has the burden of establishing that he or some person under whom he claims is in all respects a holder in due course.

Part 4 Liability of Parties

§ 3—401. Signature.

(1) No person is liable on an instrument unless his signature appears thereon.

(2) A signature is made by use of any name, including any trade or assumed name, upon an instrument, or by any word or mark used in lieu of a written signature.

§ 3—402. Signature in Ambiguous Capacity.

Unless the instrument clearly indicates that a signature is made in some other capacity it is an indorsement.

§ 3—403. Signature by Authorized Representative.

(1) A signature may be made by an agent or other representative, and his authority to make it may be established as in other cases of representation. No particular form of appointment is necessary to establish such authority.

(2) An authorized representative who signs his own name to an instrument

(a) is personally obligated if the instrument neither names the person represented nor shows that the representative signed in a representative capacity;

(b) except as otherwise established between the immediate parties, is personally obligated if the instrument names the person represented but does not show that the representative signed in a representative capacity, or if the instrument does not name the person represented but does show that the representative signed in a representative capacity.

(3) Except as otherwise established the name of an organization preceded or followed by the name and office of an authorized individual is a signature made in a representative capacity.

§ 3—404. Unauthorized Signatures.

(1) Any unauthorized signature is wholly inoperative

as that of the person whose name is signed unless he ratifies it or is precluded from denying it; but it operates as the signature of the unauthorized signer in favor of any person who in good faith pays the instrument or takes it for value.

(2) Any unauthorized signature may be ratified for all purposes of this Article. Such ratification does not of itself affect any rights of the person ratifying against the actual signer.

§ 3—405. **Impostors; Signature in Name of Payee.**

(1) An indorsement by any person in the name of a named payee is effective if

(a) an impostor by use of the mails or otherwise has induced the maker or drawer to issue the instrument to him or his confederate in the name of the payee; or

(b) a person signing as or on behalf of a maker or drawer intends the payee to have no interest in the instrument; or

(c) an agent or employee of the maker or drawer has supplied him with the name of the payee intending the latter to have no such interest.

(2) Nothing in this section shall affect the criminal or civil liability of the person so indorsing.

§ 3—406. **Negligence Contributing to Alteration or Unauthorized Signature.**

Any person who by his negligence substantially contributes to a material alteration of the instrument or to the making of an unauthorized signature is precluded from asserting the alteration or lack of authority against a holder in due course or against a drawee or other payor who pays the instrument in good faith and in accordance with the reasonable commercial standards of the drawee's or payor's business.

§ 3—407. **Alteration.**

(1) Any alteration of an instrument is material which changes the contract of any party thereto in any respect, including any such change in

(a) the number or relations of the parties; or

(b) an incomplete instrument, by completing it otherwise than as authorized; or

(c) the writing as signed, by adding to it or by removing any part of it.

(2) As against any person other than a subsequent holder in due course

(a) alteration by the holder which is both fraudulent and material discharges any party whose contract is thereby changed unless that party assents or is precluded from asserting the defense;

(b) no other alteration discharges any party and the instrument may be enforced according to its original tenor, or as to incomplete instruments according to the authority given.

(3) A subsequent holder in due course may in all cases enforce the instrument according to its original tenor, and when an incomplete instrument has been completed, he may enforce it as completed.

§ 3—408. **Consideration.**

Want or failure of consideration is a defense as against any person not having the rights of a holder in due course (Section 3—305), except that no consideration is necessary for an instrument or obligation thereon given in payment of or as security for an antecedent obligation of any kind. Nothing in this section shall be taken to displace any statute outside this Act under which a promise is enforceable notwithstanding lack or failure of consideration. Partial failure of consideration is a defense pro tanto whether or not the failure is in an ascertained or liquidated amount.

§ 3—409. **Draft Not an Assignment.**

(1) A check or other draft does not of itself operate as an assignment of any funds in the hands of the drawee available for its payment, and the drawee is not liable on the instrument until he accepts it.

(2) Nothing in this section shall affect any liability in contract, tort or otherwise arising from any letter of credit or other obligation or representation which is not an acceptance.

§ 3—410. **Definition and Operation of Acceptance.**

(1) Acceptance is the drawee's signed engagement to honor the draft as presented. It must be written on the draft, and may consist of his signature alone. It becomes operative when completed by delivery or notification.

(2) A draft may be accepted although it has not been

signed by the drawer or is otherwise incomplete or is overdue or has been dishonored.

(3) Where the draft is payable at a fixed period after sight and the acceptor fails to date his acceptance the holder may complete it by supplying a date in good faith.

§ 3—411. Certification of a Check.

(1) Certification of a check is acceptance. Where a holder procures certification the drawer and all prior indorsers are discharged.

(2) Unless otherwise agreed a bank has no obligation to certify a check.

(3) A bank may certify a check before returning it for lack of proper indorsement. If it does so the drawer is discharged.

§ 3—412. Acceptance Varying Draft.

(1) Where the drawee's proffered acceptance in any manner varies the draft as presented the holder may refuse the acceptance and treat the draft as dishonored in which case the drawee is entitled to have his acceptance cancelled.

(2) The terms of the draft are not varied by an acceptance to pay at any particular bank or place in the United States, unless the acceptance states that the draft is to be paid only at such bank or place.

(3) Where the holder assents to an acceptance varying the terms of the draft each drawer and indorser who does not affirmatively assent is discharged.

§ 3—413. Contract of Maker, Drawer and Acceptor.

(1) The maker or acceptor engages that he will pay the instrument according to its tenor at the time of his engagement or as completed pursuant to Section 3—115 on incomplete instruments.

(2) The drawer engages that upon dishonor of the draft and any necessary notice of dishonor or protest he will pay the amount of the draft to the holder or to any indorser who takes it up. The drawer may disclaim this liability by drawing without recourse.

(3) By making, drawing or accepting the party admits as against all subsequent parties including the drawee the existence of the payee and his then capacity to indorse.

§ 3—414. Contract of Indorser; Order of Liability.

(1) Unless the indorsement otherwise specifies (as by such words as "without recourse") every indorser engages that upon dishonor and any necessary notice of dishonor and protest he will pay the instrument according to its tenor at the time of his indorsement to the holder or to any subsequent indorser who takes it up, even though the indorser who takes it up was not obligated to do so.

(2) Unless they otherwise agree indorsers are liable to one another in the order in which they indorse, which is presumed to be the order in which their signatures appear on the instrument.

§ 3—415. Contract of Accommodation Party.

(1) An accommodation party is one who signs the instrument in any capacity for the purpose of lending his name to another party to it.

(2) When the instrument has been taken for value before it is due the accommodation party is liable in the capacity in which he has signed even though the taker knows of the accommodation.

(3) As against a holder in due course and without notice of the accommodation oral proof of the accommodation is not admissible to give the accommodation party the benefit of discharges dependent on his character as such. In other cases the accommodation character may be shown by oral proof.

(4) An indorsement which shows that it is not in the chain of title is notice of its accommodation character.

(5) An accommodation party is not liable to the party accommodated, and if he pays the instrument has a right of recourse on the instrument against such party.

§ 3—416. Contract of Guarantor.

(1) "Payment guaranteed" or equivalent words added to a signature mean that the signer engages that if the instrument is not paid when due he will pay it according to its tenor without resort by the holder to any other party.

(2) "Collection guaranteed" or equivalent words added to a signature mean that the signer engages that if the instrument is not paid when due he will pay it according to its tenor, but only after the holder has reduced his claim against the maker or acceptor to judgment and execution has been returned unsatis-

fied, or after the maker or acceptor has become insolvent or it is otherwise apparent that it is useless to proceed against him.

(3) Words of guaranty which do not otherwise specify guarantee payment.

(4) No words of guaranty added to the signature of a sole maker or acceptor affect his liability on the instrument. Such words added to the signature of one of two or more makers or acceptors create a presumption that the signature is for the accommodation of the others.

(5) When words of guaranty are used presentment, notice of dishonor and protest are not necessary to charge the user.

(6) Any guaranty written on the instrument is enforcible notwithstanding any statute of frauds.

§ 3—417. **Warranties on Presentment and Transfer.**

(1) Any person who obtains payment or acceptance and any prior transferor warrants to a person who in good faith pays or accepts that

(a) he has a good title to the instrument or is authorized to obtain payment or acceptance on behalf of one who has a good title; and

(b) he has no knowledge that the signature of the maker or drawer is unauthorized, except that this warranty is not given by a holder in due course acting in good faith

(i) to a maker with respect to the maker's own signature; or

(ii) to a drawer with respect to the drawer's own signature, whether or not the drawer is also the drawee; or

(iii) to an acceptor of a draft if the holder in due course took the draft after the acceptance or obtained the acceptance without knowledge that the drawer's signature was unauthorized; and

(c) the instrument has not been materially altered, except that this warranty is not given by a holder in due course acting in good faith

(i) to the maker of a note; or

(ii) to the drawer of a draft whether or not the

drawer is also the drawee; or

(iii) to the acceptor of a draft with respect to an alteration made prior to the acceptance if the holder in due course took the draft after the acceptance, even though the acceptance provided "payable as originally drawn" or equivalent terms; or

(iv) to the acceptor of a draft with respect to an alteration made after the acceptance.

(2) Any person who transfers an instrument and receives consideration warrants to his transferee and if the transfer is by indorsement to any subsequent holder who takes the instrument in good faith that

(a) he has a good title to the instrument or is authorized to obtain payment or acceptance on behalf of one who has a good title and the transfer is otherwise rightful; and

(b) all signatures are genuine or authorized; and

(c) the instrument has not been materially altered; and

(d) no defense of any party is good against him; and

(e) he has no knowledge of any insolvency proceeding instituted with respect to the maker or acceptor or the drawer of an unaccepted instrument.

(3) By transferring "without recourse" the transferor limits the obligation stated in subsection (2) (d) to a warranty that he has no knowledge of such a defense.

(4) A selling agent or broker who does not disclose the fact that he is acting only as such gives the warranties provided in this section, but if he makes such disclosure warrants only his good faith and authority.

§ 3—418. **Finality of Payment or Acceptance.**

Except for recovery of bank payments as provided in the Article on Bank Deposits and Collections (Article 4) and except for liability for breach of warranty on presentment under the preceding section, payment or acceptance of any instrument is final in favor of a holder in due course, or a person who has in good faith changed his position in reliance on the payment.

§ 3—419. **Conversion of Instrument; Innocent Representative.**

(1) An instrument is converted when

(a) a drawee to whom it is delivered for acceptance refuses to return it on demand; or

(b) any person to whom it is delivered for payment refuses on demand either to pay or to return it; or

(c) it is paid on a forged indorsement.

(2) In an action against a drawee under subsection (1) the measure of the drawee's liability is the face amount of the instrument. In any other action under subsection (1) the measure of liability is presumed to be the face amount of the instrument.

(3) Subject to the provisions of this Act concerning restrictive indorsements a representative, including a depositary or collecting bank, who has in good faith and in accordance with the reasonable commercial standards applicable to the business of such representative dealt with an instrument or its proceeds on behalf of one who was not the true owner is not liable in conversion or otherwise to the true owner beyond the amount of any proceeds remaining in his hands.

(4) An intermediary bank or payor bank which is not a depositary bank is not liable in conversion solely by reason of the fact that proceeds of an item indorsed restrictively (Sections 3—205 and 3—206) are not paid or applied consistently with the restrictive indorsement of an indorser other than its immediate transferor.

Part 5 **Presentment, Notice of Dishonor and Protest**

§ 3—501. **When Presentment, Notice of Dishonor, and Protest Necessary or Permissible.**

(1) Unless excused (Section 3—511) presentment is necessary to charge secondary parties as follows:

(a) presentment for acceptance is necessary to charge the drawer and indorsers of a draft where the draft so provides, or is payable elsewhere than at the residence or place of business of the drawee, or its date of payment depends upon such presentment. The holder may at his option present for acceptance any other draft payable at a stated date;

(b) presentment for payment is necessary to charge any indorser;

(c) in the case of any drawer, the acceptor of a draft payable at a bank or the maker of a note payable at a bank, presentment for payment is necessary, but failure to make presentment discharges such drawer, acceptor or maker only as stated in Section 3—502(1)(b).

(2) Unless excused (Section 3—511)

(a) notice of any dishonor is necessary to charge any indorser;

(b) in the case of any drawer, the acceptor of a draft payable at a bank or the maker of a note payable at a bank, notice of any dishonor is necessary, but failure to give such notice discharges such drawer, acceptor or maker only as stated in Section 3—502(1)(b).

(3) Unless excused (Section 3—511) protest of any dishonor is necessary to charge the drawer and indorsers of any draft which on its face appears to be drawn or payable outside of the states, territories, dependencies, and possessions of the United States, the District of Columbia and the Commonwealth of Puerto Rico. The holder may at his option make protest of any dishonor of any other instrument and in the case of a foreign draft may on insolvency of the acceptor before maturity make protest for better security.

(4) Notwithstanding any provision of this section, neither presentment nor notice of dishonor nor protest is necessary to charge an indorser who has indorsed an instrument after maturity.

§ 3—502. **Unexcused Delay; Discharge.**

(1) Where without excuse any necessary presentment or notice of dishonor is delayed beyond the time when it is due

(a) any indorser is discharged; and

(b) any drawer or the acceptor of a draft payable at a bank or the maker of a note payable at a bank who because the drawee or payor bank becomes insolvent during the delay is deprived of funds maintained with the drawee or payor bank to cover the instrument may discharge his liability by written assignment to the holder of his rights against the drawee or payor bank in respect of such funds, but such drawer, acceptor or maker is not otherwise discharged.

(2) Where without excuse a necessary protest is delayed beyond the time when it is due any drawer or indorser is discharged.

§ 3—503. **Time of Presentment.**

(1) Unless a different time is expressed in the instrument the time for any presentment is determined as follows:

(a) where an instrument is payable at or a fixed period after a stated date any presentment for acceptance must be made on or before the date it is payable;

(b) where an instrument is payable after sight it must either be presented for acceptance or negotiated within a reasonable time after date or issue whichever is later;

(c) where an instrument shows the date on which it is payable presentment for payment is due on that date;

(d) where an instrument is accelerated presentment for payment is due within a reasonable time after the acceleration;

(e) with respect to the liability of any secondary party presentment for acceptance or payment of any other instrument is due within a reasonable time after such party becomes liable thereon.

(2) A reasonable time for presentment is determined by the nature of the instrument, any usage of banking or trade and the facts of the particular case. In the case of an uncertified check which is drawn and payable within the United States and which is not a draft drawn by a bank the following are presumed to be reasonable periods within which to present for payment or to initiate bank collection:

(a) with respect to the liability of the drawer, thirty days after date or issue whichever is later; and

(b) with respect to the liability of an indorser, seven days after his indorsement.

(3) Where any presentment is due on a day which is not a full business day for either the person making presentment or the party to pay or accept, present-

ment is due on the next following day which is a full business day for both parties.

(4) Presentment to be sufficient must be made at a reasonable hour, and if at a bank during its banking day.

§ 3—504. **How Presentment Made.**

(1) Presentment is a demand for acceptance or payment made upon the maker, acceptor, drawee or other payor by or on behalf of the holder.

(2) Presentment may be made

(a) by mail, in which event the time of presentment is determined by the time of receipt of the mail; or

(b) through a clearing house; or

(c) at the place of acceptance or payment specified in the instrument or if there be none at the place of business or residence of the party to accept or pay. If neither the party to accept or pay nor anyone authorized to act for him is present or accessible at such place presentment is excused.

(3) It may be made

(a) to any one of two or more makers, acceptors, drawees or other payors; or

(b) to any person who has authority to make or refuse the acceptance or payment.

(4) A draft accepted or a note made payable at a bank in the United States must be presented at such bank.

(5) In the cases described in Section 4—210 presentment may be made in the manner and with the result stated in that section.

§ 3—505. **Rights of Party to Whom Presentment Is Made.**

(1) The party to whom presentment is made may without dishonor require

(a) exhibition of the instrument; and

(b) reasonable identification of the person making presentment and evidence of his authority to make it if made for another; and

(c) that the instrument be produced for acceptance or payment at a place specified in it, or if there be none at any place reasonable in the circumstances; and

(d) a signed receipt on the instrument for any

partial or full payment and its surrender upon full payment.

(2) Failure to comply with any such requirement invalidates the presentment but the person presenting has a reasonable time in which to comply and the time for acceptance or payment runs from the time of compliance.

§ 3—506. **Time Allowed for Acceptance or Payment.**

(1) Acceptance may be deferred without dishonor until the close of the next business day following presentment. The holder may also in a good faith effort to obtain acceptance and without either dishonor of the instrument or discharge of secondary parties allow postponement of acceptance for an additional business day.

(2) Except as a longer time is allowed in the case of documentary drafts drawn under a letter of credit, and unless an earlier time is agreed to by the party to pay, payment of an instrument may be deferred without dishonor pending reasonable examination to determine whether it is properly payable, but payment must be made in any event before the close of business on the day of presentment.

§ 3—507. **Dishonor; Holder's Right of Recourse; Term Allowing Re-Presentment.**

(1) An instrument is dishonored when

(a) a necessary or optional presentment is duly made and due acceptance or payment is refused or cannot be obtained within the prescribed time or in case of bank collections the instrument is seasonably returned by the midnight deadline (Section 4—301); or

(b) presentment is excused and the instrument is not duly accepted or paid.

(2) Subject to any necessary notice of dishonor and protest, the holder has upon dishonor an immediate right of recourse against the drawers and indorsers.

(3) Return of an instrument for lack of proper indorsement is not dishonor.

(4) A term in a draft or an indorsement thereof allowing a stated time for re-presentment in the event of any dishonor of the draft by nonacceptance if a time draft or by nonpayment if a sight draft gives the holder as against any secondary party bound by the term an option to waive the dishonor without affecting the liability of the secondary party and he may present again up to the end of the stated time.

§ 3—508. **Notice of Dishonor.**

(1) Notice of dishonor may be given to any person who may be liable on the instrument by or on behalf of the holder or any party who has himself received notice, or any other party who can be compelled to pay the instrument. In addition an agent or bank in whose hands the instrument is dishonored may give notice to his principal or customer or to another agent or bank from which the instrument was received.

(2) Any necessary notice must be given by a bank before its midnight deadline and by any other person before midnight of the third business day after dishonor or receipt of notice of dishonor.

(3) Notice may be given in any reasonable manner. It may be oral or written and in any terms which identify the instrument and state that it has been dishonored. A misdescription which does not mislead the party notified does not vitiate the notice. Sending the instrument bearing a stamp, ticket or writing stating that acceptance or payment has been refused or sending a notice of debit with respect to the instrument is sufficient.

(4) Written notice is given when sent although it is not received.

(5) Notice to one partner is notice to each although the firm has been dissolved.

(6) When any party is in insolvency proceedings instituted after the issue of the instrument notice may be given either to the party or to the representative of his estate.

(7) When any party is dead or incompetent notice may be sent to his last known address or given to his personal representative.

(8) Notice operates for the benefit of all parties who have rights on the instrument against the party notified.

§ 3—509. **Protest; Noting for Protest.**

(1) A protest is a certificate of dishonor made under the hand and seal of a United States consul or vice consul or a notary public or other person authorized to certify dishonor by the law of the place where

dishonor occurs. It may be made upon information satisfactory to such person.

(2) The protest must identify the instrument and certify either that due presentment has been made or the reason why it is excused and that the instrument has been dishonored by nonacceptance or nonpayment.

(3) The protest may also certify that notice of dishonor has been given to all parties or to specified parties.

(4) Subject to subsection (5) any necessary protest is due by the time that notice of dishonor is due.

(5) If, before protest is due, an instrument has been noted for protest by the officer to make protest, the protest may be made at any time thereafter as of the date of the noting.

§ 3—510. **Evidence of Dishonor and Notice of Dishonor.**

The following are admissible as evidence and create a presumption of dishonor and of any notice of dishonor therein shown:

(a) a document regular in form as provided in the preceding section which purports to be a protest;

(b) the purported stamp or writing of the drawee, payor bank or presenting bank on the instrument or accompanying it stating that acceptance or payment has been refused for reasons conconsistent with dishonor;

(c) any book or record of the drawee, payor bank, or any collecting bank kept in the usual course of business which shows dishonor, even though there is no evidence of who made the entry.

§ 3—511. **Waived or Excused Presentment, Protest or Notice of Dishonor or Delay Therein.**

(1) Delay in presentment, protest or notice of dishonor is excused when the party is without notice that it is due or when the delay is caused by circumstances beyond his control and he exercises reasonable diligence after the cause of the delay ceases to operate.

(2) Presentment or notice or protest as the case may be is entirely excused when

(a) the party to be charged has waived it expressly or by implication either before or after it is due; or

(b) such party has himself dishonored the in-

strument or has countermanded payment or otherwise has no reason to expect or right to require that the instrument be accepted or paid; or

(c) by reasonable diligence the presentment or protest cannot be made or the notice given.

(3) Presentment is also entirely excused when

(a) the maker, acceptor or drawee of any instrument except a documentary draft is dead or in insolvency proceedings instituted after the issue of the instrument; or

(b) acceptance or payment is refused but not for want of proper presentment.

(4) Where a draft has been dishonored by nonacceptance a later presentment for payment and any notice of dishonor and protest for nonpayment are excused unless in the meantime the instrument has been accepted.

(5) A waiver of protest is also a waiver of presentment and of notice of dishonor even though protest is not required.

(6) Where a waiver of presentment or notice or protest is embodied in the instrument itself it is binding upon all parties; but where it is written above the signature of an indorser it binds him only.

Part 6 Discharge

§ 3—601. **Discharge of Parties.**

(1) The extent of the discharge of any party from liability on an instrument is governed by the sections on

(a) payment or satisfaction (Section 3—603); or

(b) tender of payment (Section 3—604); or

(c) cancellation or renunciation (Section 3—605); or

(d) impairment of right of recourse or of collateral (Section 3—606); or

(e) reacquisition of the instrument by a prior party (Section 3—208); or

(f) fraudulent and material alteration (Section 3—407); or

(g) certification of a check (Section 3—411); or

(h) acceptance varying a draft (Section 3—412); or

(i) unexcused delay in presentment or notice of dishonor or protest (Section 3—502).

(2) Any party is also discharged from his liability on an instrument to another party by any other act or agreement with such party which would discharge his simple contract for the payment of money.

(3) The liability of all parties is discharged when any party who has himself no right of action or recourse on the instrument

(a) reacquires the instrument in his own right; or

(b) is discharged under any provision of this Article, except as otherwise provided with respect to discharge for impairment of recourse or of collateral (Section 3—606).

§ 3—602. **Effect of Discharge Against Holder in Due Course.**

No discharge of any party provided by this Article is effective against a subsequent holder in due course unless he has notice thereof when he takes the instrument.

§ 3—603. **Payment or Satisfaction.**

(1) The liability of any party is discharged to the extent of his payment or satisfaction to the holder even though it is made with knowledge of a claim of another person to the instrument unless prior to such payment or satisfaction the person making the claim either supplies indemnity deemed adequate by the party seeking the discharge or enjoins payment or satisfaction by order of a court of competent jurisdiction in an action in which the adverse claimant and the holder are parties. This subsection does not, however, result in the discharge of the liability

(a) of a party who in bad faith pays or satisfies a holder who acquired the instrument by theft or who (unless having the rights of a holder in due course) holds through one who so acquired it; or

(b) of a party (other than an intermediary bank or a payor bank which is not a depositary bank) who pays or satisfies the holder of an instrument which has been restrictively indorsed in a manner not consistent with the terms of such restrictive indorsement.

(2) Payment or satisfaction may be made with the consent of the holder by any person including a stranger to the instrument. Surrender of the instrument to such a person gives him the rights of a transferee (Section 3—201).

§ 3—604. **Tender of Payment.**

(1) Any party making tender of full payment to a holder when or after it is due is discharged to the extent of all subsequent liability for interest, costs and attorney's fees.

(2) The holder's refusal of such tender wholly discharges any party who has a right of recourse against the party making the tender.

(3) Where the maker or acceptor of an instrument payable otherwise than on demand is able and ready to pay at every place of payment specified in the instrument when it is due, it is equivalent to tender.

§ 3—605. **Cancellation and Renunciation.**

(1) The holder of an instrument may even without consideration discharge any party

(a) in any manner apparent on the face of the instrument or the indorsement, as by intentionally cancelling the instrument or the party's signature by destruction or mutilation, or by striking out the party's signature; or

(b) by renouncing his rights by a writing signed and delivered or by surrender of the instrument to the party to be discharged.

(2) Neither cancellation nor renunciation without surrender of the instrument affects the title thereto.

§ 3—606. **Impairment of Recourse or of Collateral.**

(1) The holder discharges any party to the instrument to the extent that without such party's consent the holder

(a) without express reservation of rights releases or agrees not to sue any person against whom the party has to the knowledge of the holder a right of recourse or agrees to suspend the right to enforce against such person the instrument or collateral or otherwise discharges such person, except that failure or delay in effecting any required presentment, protest or notice of dishonor with respect to any such person does not discharge any party as to whom presentment, protest or notice of dishonor is effective or unnecessary; or

(b) unjustifiably impairs any collateral for the instrument given by or on behalf of the party or any person against whom he has a right of recourse.

(2) By express reservation of rights against a party with a right of recourse the holder preserves

(a) all his rights against such party as of the time when the instrument was originally due; and

(b) the right of the party to pay the instrument as of that time; and

(c) all rights of such party to recourse against others.

Part 7 Advice of International Sight Draft

§ 3—701. **Letter of Advice of International Sight Draft.**

(1) A "letter of advice" is a drawer's communication to the drawee that a described draft has been drawn.

(2) Unless otherwise agreed when a bank receives from another bank a letter of advice of an international sight draft the drawee bank may immediately debit the drawer's account and stop the running of interest pro tanto. Such a debit and any resulting credit to any account covering outstanding drafts leaves in the drawer full power to stop payment or otherwise dispose of the amount and creates no trust or interest in favor of the holder.

(3) Unless otherwise agreed and except where a draft is drawn under a credit issued by the drawee, the drawee of an international sight draft owes the drawer no duty to pay an unadvised draft but if it does so and the draft is genuine, may appropriately debit the drawer's account.

Part 8
Miscellaneous

§ 3—801. **Drafts in a Set.**

(1) Where a draft is drawn in a set of parts, each of which is numbered and expressed to be an order only if no other part has been honored, the whole of the parts constitutes one draft but a taker of any part may become a holder in due course of the draft.

(2) Any person who negotiates, indorses or accepts a single part of a draft drawn in a set thereby becomes liable to any holder in due course of that part as if it were the whole set, but as between different holders in due course to whom different parts have been

negotiated the holder whose title first accrues has all rights to the draft and its proceeds.

(3) As against the drawee the first presented part of a draft drawn in a set is the part entitled to payment, or if a time draft to acceptance and payment. Acceptance of any subsequently presented part renders the drawee liable thereon under subsection (2). With respect both to a holder and to the drawer payment of a subsequently presented part of a draft payable at sight has the same effect as payment of a check notwithstanding an effective stop order (Section 4—407).

(4) Except as otherwise provided in this section, where any part of a draft in a set is discharged by payment or otherwise the whole draft is discharged.

§ 3—802. **Effect of Instrument on Obligation for Which It Is Given.**

(1) Unless otherwise agreed where an instrument is taken for an underlying obligation

(a) the obligation is pro tanto discharged if a bank is drawer, maker or acceptor of the instrument and there is no recourse on the instrument against the underlying obligor; and

(b) in any other case the obligation is suspended pro tanto until the instrument is due or if it is payable on demand until its presentment. If the instrument is dishonored action may be maintained on either the instrument or the obligation; discharge of the underlying obligor on the instrument also discharges him on the obligation.

(2) The taking in good faith of a check which is not postdated does not of itself so extend the time on the original obligation as to discharge a surety.

§ 3—803. **Notice to Third Party.**

Where a defendant is sued for breach of an obligation for which a third person is answerable over under this Article he may give the third person written notice of the litigation, and the person notified may then give similar notice to any other person who is answerable over to him under this Article. If the notice states that the person notified may come in and defend and that if the person notified does not do so he will in any action against him by the person giving the notice be bound by any determination of fact common to the two litigations, then unless after seasonable receipt of the notice the person notified does come in and defend he is so bound.

§ 3—804. Lost, Destroyed or Stolen Instruments.

The owner of an instrument which is lost, whether by destruction, theft or otherwise, may maintain an action in his own name and recover from any party liable thereon upon due proof of his ownership, the facts which prevent his production of the instrument and its terms. The court may require security indemnifying the defendant against loss by reason of further claims on the instrument.

§ 3—805. Instruments Not Payable to Order or to Bearer.

This Article applies to any instrument whose terms do not preclude transfer and which is otherwise negotiable within this Article but which is not payable to order or to bearer, except that there can be no holder in due course of such an instrument.

Article 4
BANK DEPOSITS AND COLLECTIONS

Part 1 General Provisions and Definitions

§ 4—101. Short Title.

This Article shall be known and may be cited as Uniform Commercial Code—Bank Deposits and Collections.

§ 4—102. Applicability.

(1) To the extent that items within this Article are also within the scope of Articles 3 and 8, they are subject to the provisions of those Articles. In the event of conflict the provisions of this Article govern those of Article 3 but the provisions of Article 8 govern those of this Article.

(2) The liability of a bank for action or non-action with respect to any item handled by it for purposes of presentment, payment or collection is governed by the law of the place where the bank is located. In the case of action or non-action by or at a branch or separate office of a bank, its liability is governed by the law of the place where the branch or separate office is located.

§ 4—103. Variation by Agreement; Measure of Damages; Certain Action Constituting Ordinary Care.

(1) The effect of the provisions of this Article may be varied by agreement except that no agreement can disclaim a bank's responsibility for its own lack of good faith or failure to exercise ordinary care or can limit the measure of damages for such lack or failure; but the parties may by agreement determine the standards by which such responsibility is to be measured if such standards are not manifestly unreasonable.

(2) Federal Reserve regulations and operating letters, clearing house rules, and the like, have the effect of agreements under subsection (1), whether or not specifically assented to by all parties interested in items handled.

(3) Action or non-action approved by this Article or pursuant to Federal Reserve regulations or operating letters constitutes the exercise of ordinary care and, in the absence of special instructions, action or non-action consistent with clearing house rules and the like or with a general banking usage not disapproved by this Article, prima facie constitutes the exercise of ordinary care.

(4) The specification or approval of certain procedures by this Article does not constitute disapproval of other procedures which may be reasonable under the circumstances.

(5) The measure of damages for failure to exercise ordinary care in handling an item is the amount of the item reduced by an amount which could not have been realized by the use of ordinary care, and where there is bad faith it includes other damages, if any, suffered by the party as a proximate consequence.

§ 4—104. Definitions and Index of Definitions.

(1) In this Article unless the context otherwise requires

    (a) "Account" means any account with a bank and includes a checking, time, interest or savings account;

    (b) "Afternoon" means the period of a day between noon and midnight;

    (c) "Banking day" means that part of any day on which a bank is open to the public for carrying on substantially all of its banking functions;

(d) "Clearing house" means any association of banks or other payors regularly clearing items;

(e) "Customer" means any person having an account with a bank or for whom a bank has agreed to collect items and includes a bank carrying an account with another bank;

(f) "Documentary draft" means any negotiable or nonnegotiable draft with accompanying documents, securities or other papers to be delivered against honor of the draft;

(g) "Item" means any instrument for the payment of money even though it is not negotiable but does not include money;

(h) "Midnight deadline" with respect to a bank is midnight on its next banking day following the banking day on which it receives the relevant item or notice or from which the time for taking action commences to run, whichever is later;

(i) "Properly payable" includes the availability of funds for payment at the time of decision to pay or dishonor;

(j) "Settle" means to pay in cash, by clearing house settlement, in a charge or credit or by remittance, or otherwise as instructed. A settlement may be either provisional or final;

(k) "Suspends payments" with respect to a bank means that it has been closed by order of the supervisory authorities, that a public officer has been appointed to take it over or that it ceases or refuses to make payments in the ordinary course of business.

(2) Other definitions applying to this Article and the sections in which they appear are:
"Collecting bank" Section 4—105.
"Depositary bank" Section 4—105.
"Intermediary bank" Section 4—105.
"Payor bank" Section 4—105.
"Presenting bank" Section 4—105.
"Remitting bank" Section 4—105.

(3) The following definitions in other Articles apply to this Article:
"Acceptance" Section 3—410.
"Certificate of deposit" Section 3—104.
"Certification" Section 3—411.
"Check" Section 3—104.
"Draft" Section 3—104.

"Holder in due course" Section 3—302.
"Notice of dishonor" Section 3—508.
"Presentment" Section 3—504.
"Protest" Section 3—509.
"Secondary party" Section 3—102.

(4) In addition Article 1 contains general definitions and principles of construction and interpretation applicable throughout this Article.

§ 4—105. **"Depositary Bank"; "Intermediary Bank"; "Collecting Bank"; "Payor Bank"; "Presenting Bank"; "Remitting Bank".**

In this Article unless the context otherwise requires:

(a) "Depositary bank" means the first bank to which an item is transferred for collection even though it is also the payor bank;

(b) "Payor bank" means a bank by which an item is payable as drawn or accepted;

(c) "Intermediary bank" means any bank to which an item is transferred in course of collection except the depositary or payor bank;

(d) "Collecting bank" means any bank handling the item for collection except the payor bank;

(e) "Presenting bank" means any bank presenting an item except a payor bank;

(f) "Remitting bank" means any payor or intermediary bank remitting for an item.

§ 4—106. **Separate Office of a Bank.**

A branch or separate office of a bank [maintaining its own deposit ledgers] is a separate bank for the purpose of computing the time within which and determining the place at or to which action may be taken or notices or orders shall be given under this Article and under Article 3.

Note: The brackets are to make it optional with the several states whether to require a branch to maintain its own deposit ledgers in order to be considered to be a separate bank for certain purposes under Article 4. In some states "maintaining its own deposit ledgers" is a satisfactory test. In others branch banking practices are such that this test would not be suitable.

§ 4—107. **Time of Receipt of Items.**

(1) For the purpose of allowing time to process items, prove balances and make the necessary entries on its books to determine its position for the day, a bank may fix an afternoon hour of two P.M. or later as a

cut-off hour for the handling of money and items and the making of entries on its books.

(2) Any item or deposit of money received on any day after a cut-off hour so fixed or after the close of the banking day may be treated as being received at the opening of the next banking day.

§ 4—108. **Delays.**

(1) Unless otherwise instructed, a collecting bank in a good faith effort to secure payment may, in the case of specific items and with or without the approval of any person involved, waive, modify or extend time limits imposed or permitted by this Act for a period not in excess of an additional banking day without discharge of secondary parties and without liability to its transferor or any prior party.

(2) Delay by a collecting bank or payor bank beyond time limits prescribed or permitted by this Act or by instructions is excused if caused by interruption of communication facilities, suspension of payments by another bank, war, emergency conditions or other circumstances beyond the control of the bank provided it exercises such diligence as the circumstances require.

§ 4—109. **Process of Posting.**

The "process of posting" means the usual procedure followed by a payor bank in determining to pay an item and in recording the payment including one or more of the following or other steps as determined by the bank:

(a) verification of any signature;

(b) ascertaining that sufficient funds are available;

(c) affixing a "paid" or other stamp;

(d) entering a charge or entry to a customer's account;

(e) correcting or reversing an entry or erroneous action with respect to the item.

Part 2 Collection of Items: Depositary and Collecting Banks

§ 4—201. **Presumption and Duration of Agency Status of Collecting Banks and Provisional Status of Credits; Applicability of Article; Item Indorsed "Pay Any Bank".**

(1) Unless a contrary intent clearly appears and prior to the time that a settlement given by a collecting bank for an item is or becomes final (subsection (3) of Section 4—211 and Sections 4—212 and 4—213) the bank is an agent or sub-agent of the owner of the item and any settlement given for the item is provisional. This provision applies regardless of the form of indorsement or lack of indorsement and even though credit given for the item is subject to immediate withdrawal as of right or is in fact withdrawn; but the continuance of ownership of an item by its owner and any rights of the owner to proceeds of the item are subject to rights of a collecting bank such as those resulting from outstanding advances on the item and valid rights of setoff. When an item is handled by banks for purposes of presentment, payment and collection, the relevant provisions of this Article apply even though action of parties clearly establishes that a particular bank has purchased the item and is the owner of it.

(2) After an item has been indorsed with the words "pay any bank" or the like, only a bank may acquire the rights of a holder

(a) until the item has been returned to the customer initiating collection; or

(b) until the item has been specially indorsed by a bank to a person who is not a bank.

§ 4—202. **Responsibility for Collection; When Action Seasonable.**

(1) A collecting bank must use ordinary care in

(a) presenting an item or sending it for presentment; and

(b) sending notice of dishonor or non-payment or returning an item other than a documentary draft to the bank's transferor [or directly to the depositary bank under subsection (2) of Section 4—212] (see note to Section 4—212) after learning that the item has not been paid or accepted as the case may be; and

(c) settling for an item when the bank receives final settlement; and

(d) making or providing for any necessary protest; and

(e) notifying its transferor of any loss or delay in transit within a reasonable time after discovery thereof.

(2) A collecting bank taking proper action before its midnight deadline following receipt of an item, notice or payment acts seasonally; taking proper action within a reasonably longer time may be seasonable but the bank has the burden of so establishing.

(3) Subject to subsection (1)(a), a bank is not liable for the insolvency, neglect, misconduct, mistake or default of another bank or person or for loss or destruction of an item in transit or in the possession of others.

§ 4—203. **Effect of Instructions.**

Subject to the provisions of Article 3 concerning conversion of instruments (Section 3—419) and the provisions of both Article 3 and this Article concerning restrictive indorsements only a collecting bank's transferor can give instructions which affect the bank or constitute notice to it and a collecting bank is not liable to prior parties for any action taken pursuant to such instructions or in accordance with any agreement with its transferor.

§ 4—204. **Methods of Sending and Presenting; Sending Direct to Payor Bank.**

(1) A collecting bank must send items by reasonably prompt method taking into consideration any relevant instructions, the nature of the item, the number of such items on hand, and the cost of collection involved and the method generally used by it or others to present such items.

(2) A collecting bank may send

(a) any item direct to the payor bank;

(b) any item to any non-bank payor if authorized by its transferor; and

(c) any item other than documentary drafts to any non-bank payor, if authorized by Federal Reserve regulation or operating letter, clearing house rule or the like.

(3) Presentment may be made by a presenting bank at a place where the payor bank has requested that presentment be made.

§ 4—205. **Supplying Missing Indorsement; No Notice from Prior Indorsement.**

(1) A depositary bank which has taken an item for collection may supply any indorsement of the customer which is necessary to title unless the item contains the words "payee's indorsement required" or the like. In the absence of such a requirement a statement placed on the item by the depositary bank to the effect that the item was deposited by a customer or credited to his account is effective as the customer's indorsement.

(2) An intermediary bank, or payor bank which is not a depositary bank, is neither given notice nor otherwise affected by a restrictive indorsement of any person except the bank's immediate transferor.

§ 4—206. **Transfer Between Banks.**

Any agreed method which identifies the transferor bank is sufficient for the item's further transfer to another bank.

§ 4—207. **Warranties of Customer and Collecting Bank on Transfer or Presentment of Items; Time for Claims.**

(1) Each customer or collecting bank who obtains payment or acceptance of an item and each prior customer and collecting bank warrants to the payor bank or other payor who in good faith pays or accepts the item that

(a) he has a good title to the item or is authorized to obtain payment or acceptance on behalf of one who has a good title; and

(b) he has no knowledge that the signature of the maker or drawer is unauthorized, except that this warranty is not given by any customer or collecting bank that is a holder in due course and acts in good faith

(i) to a maker with respect to the maker's own signature; or

(ii) to a drawer with respect to the drawer's own signature, whether or not the drawer is also the drawee; or

(iii) to an acceptor of an item if the holder in due course took the item after the acceptance or obtained the acceptance without knowledge that the drawer's signature was unauthorized; and

(c) the item has not been materially altered, except that this warranty is not given by any customer or collecting bank that is a holder in due course and acts in good faith

(i) to the maker of a note; or

(ii) to the drawer of a draft whether or not the drawer is also the drawee; or

(iii) to the acceptor of an item with respect to an alteration made prior to the acceptance if the holder in due course took the item after the acceptance, even though the acceptance provided "payable as originally drawn" or equivalent terms; or

(iv) to the acceptor of an item with respect to an alteration made after the acceptance.

(2) Each customer and collecting bank who transfers an item and receives a settlement or other consideration for it warrants to his transferee and to any subequent collecting bank who takes the item in good faith that

(a) he has a good title to the item or is authorized to obtain payment or acceptance on behalf of one who has a good title and the transfer is otherwise rightful; and

(b) all signatures are genuine or authorized; and

(c) the item has not been materially altered; and

(d) no defense of any party is good against him; and

(e) he has no knowledge of any insolvency proceeding instituted with respect to the maker or acceptor or the drawer of an unaccepted item.

In addition each customer and collecting bank so transferring an item and receiving a settlement or other consideration engages that upon dishonor and any necessary notice of dishonor and protest he will take up the item.

(3) The warranties and the engagement to honor set forth in the two preceding subsections arise notwithstanding the absence of indorsement or words of guaranty or warranty in the transfer or presentment and a collecting bank remains liable for their breach despite remittance to its transferor. Damages for breach of such warranties or engagement to honor shall not exceed the consideration received by the customer or collecting bank responsible plus finance charges and expenses related to the item, if any.

(4) Unless a claim for breach of warranty under this section is made within a reasonable time after the person claiming learns of the breach, the person

liable is discharged to the extent of any loss caused by the delay in making claim.

§ 4—208. **Security Interest of Collecting Bank in Items, Accompanying Documents and Proceeds.**

(1) A bank has a security interest in an item and any accompanying documents or the proceeds of either

(a) in case of an item deposited in an account to the extent to which credit given for the item has been withdrawn or applied;

(b) in case of an item for which it has given credit available for withdrawal as of right, to the extent of the credit given whether or not the credit is drawn upon and whether or not there is a right of charge-back; or

(c) if it makes an advance on or against the item.

(2) When credit which has been given for several items received at one time or pursuant to a single agreement is withdrawn or applied in part the security interest remains upon all the items, any accompanying documents or the proceeds of either. For the purpose of this section, credits first given are first withdrawn.

(3) Receipt by a collecting bank of a final settlement for an item is a realization on its security interest in the item, accompanying documents and proceeds. To the extent and so long as the bank does not receive final settlement for the item or give up possession of the item or accompanying documents for purposes other than collection, the security interest continues and is subject to the provisions of Article 9 except that

(a) no security agreement is necessary to make the security interest enforceable (subsection (1) (b) of Section 9—203); and

(b) no filing is required to perfect the security interest; and

(c) the security interest has priority over conflicting perfected security interests in the item, accompanying documents or proceeds.

§ 4—209. **When Bank Gives Value for Purposes of Holder in Due Course.**

For purposes of determining its status as a holder in due course, the bank has given value to the extent that it has a security interest in an item provided that the bank otherwise complies with the requirements of Section 3—302 on what constitutes a holder in due course.

§ 4—210. **Presentment by Notice of Item Not Payable by, Through or at a Bank; Liability of Secondary Parties.**

(1) Unless otherwise instructed, a collecting bank may present an item not payable by, through or at a bank by sending to the party to accept or pay a written notice that the bank holds the item for acceptance or payment. The notice must be sent in time to be received on or before the day when presentment is due and the bank must meet any requirement of the party to accept or pay under Section 3—505 by the close of the bank's next banking day after it knows of the requirement.

(2) Where presentment is made by notice and neither honor nor request for compliance with a requirement under Section 3—505 is received by the close of business on the day after maturity or in the case of demand items by the close of business on the third banking day after notice was sent, the presenting bank may treat the item as dishonored and charge any secondary party by sending him notice of the facts.

§ 4—211. **Media of Remittance; Provisional and Final Settlement in Remittance Cases.**

(1) A collecting bank may take in settlement of an item

(a) a check of the remitting bank or of another bank on any bank except the remitting bank; or

(b) a cashier's check or similar primary obligation of a remitting bank which is a member of or clears through a member of the same clearing house or group as the collecting bank; or

(c) appropriate authority to charge an account of the remitting bank or of another bank with the collecting bank; or

(d) if the item is drawn upon or payable by a person other than a bank, a cashier's check, certified check or other bank check or obligation.

(2) If before its midnight deadline the collecting bank properly dishonors a remittance check or authorization to charge on itself or presents or forwards for collection a remittance instrument of or on another bank which is of a kind approved by subsection (1) or

has not been authorized by it, the collecting bank is not liable to prior parties in the event of the dishonor of such check, instrument or authorization.

(3) A settlement for an item by means of a remittance instrument or authorization to charge is or becomes a final settlement as to both the person making and the person receiving the settlement

(a) if the remittance instrument or authorization to charge is of a kind approved by subsection (1) or has not been authorized by the person receiving the settlement and in either case the person receiving the settlement acts seasonably before its midnight deadline in presenting, forwarding for collection or paying the instrument or authorization,—at the time the remittance instrument or authorization is finally paid by the payor by which it is payable;

(b) if the person receiving the settlement has authorized remittance by a non-bank check or obligation or by a cashier's check or similar primary obligation of or a check upon the payor or other remitting bank which is not of a kind approved by subsection (1) (b),—at the time of the receipt of such remittance check or obligation; or

(c) if in a case not covered by sub-paragraphs (a) or (b) the person receiving the settlement fails to seasonably present, forward for collection, pay or return a remittance instrument or authorization to it to charge before its midnight deadline,—at such midnight deadline.

§ 4—212. **Right of Charge-Back or Refund.**

(1) If a collecting bank has made provisional settlement with its customer for an item and itself fails by reason of dishonor, suspension of payments by a bank or otherwise to receive a settlement for the item which is or becomes final, the bank may revoke the settlement given by it, charge back the amount of any credit given for the item to its customer's account or obtain refund from its customer whether or not it is able to return the items if by its midnight deadline or within a longer reasonable time after it learns the facts it returns the item or sends notification of the facts. These rights to revoke, charge-back and obtain refund terminate if and when a settlement for the item received by the bank is or becomes final (subsec-

tion (3) of Section 4—211 and subsections (2) and (3) of Section 4—213).

[(2) Within the time and manner prescribed by this section and Section 4—301, an intermediary or payor bank, as the case may be, may return an unpaid item directly to the depositary bank and may send for collection a draft on the depositary bank and obtain reimbursement. In such case, if the depositary bank has received provisional settlement for the item, it must reimburse the bank drawing the draft and any provisional credits for the item between banks shall become and remain final.]

Note: Direct returns is recognized as an innovation that is not yet established bank practice, and therefore, Paragraph 2 has been bracketed. Some lawyers have doubts whether it should be included in legislation or left to development by agreement.

(3) A depositary bank which is also the payor may charge-back the amount of an item to its customer's account or obtain refund in accordance with the section governing return of an item received by a payor bank for credit on its books (Section 4—301).

(4) The right to charge-back is not affected by

(a) prior use of the credit given for the item; or

(b) failure by any bank to exercise ordinary care with respect to the item but any bank so failing remains liable.

(5) A failure to charge-back or claim refund does not affect other rights of the bank against the customer or any other party.

(6) If credit is given in dollars as the equivalent of the value of an item payable in a foreign currency the dollar amount of any charge-back or refund shall be calculated on the basis of the buying sight rate for the foreign currency prevailing on the day when the person entitled to the charge-back or refund learns that it will not receive payment in ordinary course.

§ 4—213. **Final Payment of Item by Payor Bank; When Provisional Debits and Credits Become Final; When Certain Credits Become Available for Withdrawal.**

(1) An item is finally paid by a payor bank when the bank has done any of the following, whichever happens first:

(a) paid the item in cash; or

(b) settled for the item without reserving a right to revoke the settlement and without having such right under statute, clearing house rule or agreement; or

(c) completed the process of posting the item to the indicated account of the drawer, maker or other person to be charged therewith; or

(d) made a provisional settlement for the item and failed to revoke the settlement in the time and manner permitted by statute, clearing house rule or agreement.

Upon a final payment under subparagraphs (b), (c) or (d) the payor bank shall be accountable for the amount of the item.

(2) If provisional settlement for an item between the presenting and payor banks is made through a clearing house or by debits or credits in an account between them, then to the extent that provisional debits or credits for the item are entered in accounts between the presenting and payor banks or between the presenting and successive prior collecting banks seriatim, they become final upon final payment of the item by the payor bank.

(3) If a collecting bank receives a settlement for an item which is or becomes final (subsection (3) of Section 4—211, subsection (2) of Section 4—213) the bank is accountable to its customer for the amount of the item and any provisional credit given for the item in an account with its customer becomes final.

(4) Subject to any right of the bank to apply the credit to an obligation of the customer, credit given by a bank for an item in an account with its customer becomes available for withdrawal as of right

(a) in any case where the bank has received a provisional settlement for the item,—when such settlement becomes final and the bank has had a reasonable time to learn that the settlement is final;

(b) in any case where the bank is both a depositary bank and a payor bank and the item is finally paid,—at the opening of the bank's second banking day following receipt of the item.

(5) A deposit of money in a bank is final when made but, subject to any right of the bank to apply the deposit to an obligation of the customer, the deposit

becomes available for withdrawal as of right at the opening of the bank's next banking day following receipt of the deposit.

§ 4—214. **Insolvency and Preference.**

(1) Any item in or coming into the possession of a payor or collecting bank which suspends payment and which item is not finally paid shall be returned by the receiver, trustee or agent in charge of the closed bank to the presenting bank or the closed bank's customer.

(2) If a payor bank finally pays an item and suspends payments without making a settlement for the item with its customer or the presenting bank which settlement is or becomes final, the owner of the item has a preferred claim against the payor bank.

(3) If a payor bank gives or a collecting bank gives or receives a provisional settlement for an item and thereafter suspends payments, the suspension does not prevent or interfere with the settlement becoming final if such finality occurs automatically upon the lapse of certain time or the happening of certain events (subsection (3) of Section 4—211, subsections (1)(d), (2) and (3) of Section 4—213).

(4) If a collecting bank receives from subsequent parties settlement for an item which settlement is or becomes final and suspends payments without making a settlement for the item with its customer which is or becomes final, the owner of the item has a preferred claim against such collecting bank.

Part 3 Collection of Items: Payor Banks

§ 4—301. **Deferred Posting; Recovery of Payment by Return of Items; Time of Dishonor.**

(1) Where an authorized settlement for a demand item (other than a documentary draft) received by a payor bank otherwise than for immediate payment over the counter has been made before midnight of the banking day of receipt the payor bank may revoke the settlement and recover any payment if before it has made final payment (subsection (1) of Section 4—213) and before its midnight deadline it

(a) returns the item; or

(b) sends written notice of dishonor or nonpayment if the item is held for protest or is otherwise unavailable for return.

(2) If a demand item is received by a payor bank for credit on its books it may return such item or send notice of dishonor and may revoke any credit given or recover the amount thereof withdrawn by its customer, if it acts within the time limit and in the manner specified in the preceding subsection.

(3) Unless previous notice of dishonor has been sent an item is dishonored at the time when for purposes of dishonor it is returned or notice sent in accordance with this section.

(4) An item is returned:

(a) as to an item received through a clearing house, when it is delivered to the presenting or last collecting bank or to the clearing house or is sent or delivered in accordance with its rules; or

(b) in all other cases, when it is sent or delivered to the bank's customer or transferor or pursuant to his instructions.

§ 4—302. **Payor Bank's Responsibility for Late Return of Item.**

In the absence of a valid defense such as breach of a presentment warranty (subsection (1) of Section 4—207), settlement effected or the like, if an item is presented on and received by a payor bank the bank is accountable for the amount of

(a) a demand item other than a documentary draft whether properly payable or not if the bank, in any case where it is not also the depositary bank, retains the item beyond midnight of the banking day of receipt without settling for it or, regardless of whether it is also the depositary bank, does not pay or return the item or send notice of dishonor until after its midnight deadline; or

(b) any other properly payable item unless within the time allowed for acceptance or payment of that item the bank either accepts or pays the item or returns it and accompanying documents.

§ 4—303. **When Items Subject to Notice, Stop-Order, Legal Process or Setoff; Order in Which Items May Be Charged or Certified.**

(1) Any knowledge, notice or stop-order received by, legal process served upon or setoff exercised by a payor bank, whether or not effective under other rules of law to terminate, suspend or modify the

bank's right or duty to pay an item or to charge its customer's account for the item, comes too late to so terminate, suspend or modify such right or duty if the knowledge, notice, stop-order or legal process is received or served and a reasonable time for the bank to act thereon expires or the setoff is exercised after the bank has done any of the following:

(a) accepted or certified the item;

(b) paid the item in cash;

(c) settled for the item without reserving a right to revoke the settlement and without having such right under statute, clearing house rule or agreement;

(d) completed the process of posting the item to the indicated account of the drawer, maker or other person to be charged therewith or otherwise has evidenced by examination of such indicated account and by action its decision to pay the item; or

(e) become accountable for the amount of the item under subsection (1) (d) of Section 4—213 and Section 4—302 dealing with the payor bank's responsibility for late return of items.

(2) Subject to the provisions of subsection (1) items may be accepted, paid, certified or charged to the indicated account of its customer in any order convenient to the bank.

Part 4 Relationship Between Payor Bank and Its Customer

§ 4—401. When Bank May Charge Customer's Account.

(1) As against its customer, a bank may charge against his account any item which is otherwise properly payable from that account even though the charge creates an overdraft.

(2) A bank which in good faith makes payment to a holder may charge the indicated account of its customer according to

(a) the original tenor of his altered item; or

(b) the tenor of his completed item, even though the bank knows the item has been completed unless the bank has notice that the completion was improper.

§ 4—402. Bank's Liability to Customer for Wrongful Dishonor.

A payor bank is liable to its customer for damages proximately caused by the wrongful dishonor of an item. When the dishonor occurs through mistake liability is limited to actual damages proved. If so proximately caused and proved damages may include damages for an arrest or prosecution of the customer or other consequential damages. Whether any consequential damages are proximately caused by the wrongful dishonor is a question of fact to be determined in each case.

§ 4—403. Customer's Right to Stop Payment; Burden of Proof of Loss.

(1) A customer may by order to his bank stop payment of any item payable for his account but the order must be received at such time and in such manner as to afford the bank a reasonable opportunity to act on it prior to any action by the bank with respect to the item described in Section 4—303.

(2) An oral order is binding upon the bank only for fourteen calendar days unless confirmed in writing within that period. A written order is effective for only six months unless renewed in writing.

(3) The burden of establishing the fact and amount of loss resulting from the payment of an item contrary to a binding stop payment order is on the customer.

§ 4—404. Bank Not Obligated to Pay Check More Than Six Months Old.

A bank is under no obligation to a customer having a checking account to pay a check, other than a certified check, which is presented more than six months after its date, but it may charge its customer's account for a payment made thereafter in good faith.

§ 4—405. Death or Incompetence of Customer.

(1) A payor or collecting bank's authority to accept, pay or collect an item or to account for proceeds of its collection if otherwise effective is not rendered ineffective by incompetence of a customer of either bank existing at the time the item is issued or its collection is undertaken if the bank does not know of an adjudication of incompetence. Neither death nor incompetence of a customer revokes such authority to accept, pay, collect or account until the bank knows of

the fact of death or of an adjudication of incompetence and has reasonable opportunity to act on it.

(2) Even with knowledge a bank may for ten days after the date of death pay or certify checks drawn on or prior to that date unless ordered to stop payment by a person claiming an interest in the account.

§ 4—406. Customer's Duty to Discover and Report Unauthorized Signature or Alteration.

(1) When a bank sends to its customer a statement of account accompanied by items paid in good faith in support of the debit entries or holds the statement and items pursuant to a request or instructions of its customer or otherwise in a reasonable manner makes the statement and items available to the customer, the customer must exercise reasonable care and promptness to examine the statement and items to discover his unauthorized signature or any alteration on an item and must notify the bank promptly after discovery thereof.

(2) If the bank establishes that the customer failed with respect to an item to comply with the duties imposed on the customer by subsection (1) the customer is precluded from asserting against the bank

(a) his unauthorized signature or any alteration on the item if the bank also establishes that it suffered a loss by reason of such failure; and

(b) an unauthorized signature or alteration by the same wrongdoer on any other item paid in good faith by the bank after the first item and statement was available to the customer for a reasonable period not exceeding fourteen calendar days and before the bank receives notification from the customer of any such unauthorized signature or alteration.

(3) The preclusion under subsection (2) does not apply if the customer establishes lack of ordinary care on the part of the bank in paying the item(s).

(4) Without regard to care or lack of care of either the customer or the bank a customer who does not within one year from the time the statement and items are made available to the customer (subsection (1)) discover and report his unauthorized signature or any alteration on the face or back of the item or does not within three years from that time discover and report any unauthorized indorsement is precluded from

asserting against the bank such unauthorized signature or indorsement or such alteration.

(5) If under this section a payor bank has a valid defense against a claim of a customer upon or resulting from payment of an item and waives or fails upon request to assert the defense the bank may not assert against any collecting bank or other prior party presenting or transferring the item a claim based upon the unauthorized signature or alteration giving rise to the customer's claim.

§ 4—407. Payor Bank's Right to Subrogation on Improper Payment.

If a payor bank has paid an item over the stop payment order of the drawer or maker or otherwise under circumstances giving a basis for objection by the drawer or maker, to prevent unjust enrichment and only to the extent necessary to prevent loss to the bank by reason of its payment of the item, the payor bank shall be subrogated to the rights

(a) of any holder in due course on the item against the drawer or maker; and

(b) of the payee or any other holder of the item against the drawer or maker either on the item or under the transaction out of which the item arose; and

(c) of the drawer or maker against the payee or any other holder of the item with respect to the transaction out of which the item arose.

Part 5 Collection of Documentary Drafts

§ 4—501. Handling of Documentary Drafts; Duty to Send for Presentment and to Notify Customer of Dishonor.

A bank which takes a documentary draft for collection must present or send the draft and accompanying documents for presentment and upon learning that the draft has not been paid or accepted in due course must seasonably notify its customer of such fact even though it may have discounted or bought the draft or extended credit available for withdrawal as of right.

§ 4—502. Presentment of "On Arrival" Drafts.

When a draft or the relevant instructions require presentment "on arrival", "when goods arrive" or the like, the collecting bank need not present until in its judgment a reasonable time for arrival of the goods has expired. Refusal to pay or accept because the goods have not arrived is not dishonor; the bank must notify its transferor of such refusal but need not present the draft again until it is instructed to do so or learns of the arrival of the goods.

§ 4—503. Responsibility of Presenting Bank for Documents and Goods; Report of Reasons for Dishonor; Referee in Case of Need.

Unless otherwise instructed and except as provided in Article 5 a bank presenting a documentary draft

(a) must deliver the documents to the drawee on acceptance of the draft if it is payable more than three days after presentment; otherwise, only on payment; and

(b) upon dishonor, either in the case of presentment for acceptance or presentment for payment, may seek and follow instructions from any referee in case of need designated in the draft or if the presenting bank does not choose to utilize his services it must use diligence and good faith to ascertain the reason for dishonor, must notify its transferor of the dishonor and of the results of its effort to ascertain the reasons therefor and must request instructions.

But the presenting bank is under no obligation with respect to goods represented by the documents except to follow any reasonable instructions seasonably received; it has a right to reimbursement for any expense incurred in following instructions and to prepayment of or indemnity for such expenses.

§ 4—504. Privilege of Presenting Bank to Deal With Goods; Security Interest for Expenses.

(1) A presenting bank which, following the dishonor of a documentary draft, has seasonably requested instructions but does not receive them within a reasonable time may store, sell, or otherwise deal with the goods in any reasonable manner.

(2) For its reasonable expenses incurred by action under subsection (1) the presenting bank has a lien upon the goods or their proceeds, which may be foreclosed in the same manner as an unpaid seller's lien.

Article 5
LETTERS OF CREDIT

§ 5—101. Short Title.

This Article shall be known and may be cited as Uniform Commercial Code—Letters of Credit.

§ 5—102. Scope.

(1) This Article applies

(a) to a credit issued by a bank if the credit requires a documentary draft or a documentary demand for payment; and

(b) to a credit issued by a person other than a bank if the credit requires that the draft or demand for payment be accompanied by a document of title; and

(c) to a credit issued by a bank or other person if the credit is not within subparagraphs (a) or (b) but conspicuously states that it is a letter of credit or is conspicuously so entitled.

(2) Unless the engagement meets the requirements of subsection (1), this Article does not apply to engagements to make advances or to honor drafts or demands for payment, to authorities to pay or purchase, to guarantees or to general agreements.

(3) This Article deals with some but not all of the rules and concepts of letters of credit as such rules or concepts have developed prior to this act or may hereafter develop. The fact that this Article states a rule does not by itself require, imply or negate application of the same or a converse rule to a situation not provided for or to a person not specified by this Article.

§ 5—103. Definitions.

(1) In this Article unless the context otherwise requires

(a) "Credit" or "letter of credit" means an engagement by a bank or other person made at the request of a customer and of a kind within the scope of this Article (Section 5—102) that the issuer will honor drafts or other demands for payment upon compliance with the conditions specified in the credit. A credit may be either revocable or irrevocable. The engagement may be either an agreement to honor or a statement that the bank or other person is authorized to honor.

(b) A "documentary draft" or a "documentary demand for payment" is one honor of which is conditioned upon the presentation of a document or documents. "Document" means any paper including document of title, security, invoice, certificate, notice of default and the like.

(c) An "issuer" is a bank or other person issuing a credit.

(d) A "beneficiary" of a credit is a person who is entitled under its terms to draw or demand payment.

(e) An "advising bank" is a bank which gives notification of the issuance of a credit by another bank.

(f) A "confirming bank" is a bank which engages either that it will itself honor a credit already issued by another bank or that such a credit will be honored by the issuer or a third bank.

(g) A "customer" is a buyer or other person who causes an issuer to issue a credit. The term also includes a bank which procures issuance or confirmation on behalf of that bank's customer.

(2) Other definitions applying to this Article and the sections in which they appear are:

"Notation of Credit". Section 5—108.

"Presenter". Section 5—112(3).

(3) Definitions in other Articles applying to this Article and the sections in which they appear are:

"Accept" or "Acceptance". Section 3—410.

"Contract for sale". Section 2—106.

"Draft". Section 3—104.

"Holder in due course". Section 3—302.

"Midnight deadline". Section 4—104.

"Security". Section 8—102.

(4) In addition, Article 1 contains general definitions and principles of construction and interpretation applicable throughout this Article.

§ 5—104. **Formal Requirements; Signing.**

(1) Except as otherwise required in subsection (1) (c)

of Section 5—102 on scope, no particular form of phrasing is required for a credit. A credit must be in writing and signed by the issuer and a confirmation must be in writing and signed by the confirming bank. A modification of the terms of a credit or confirmation must be signed by the issuer or confirming bank.

(2) A telegram may be a sufficient signed writing if it identifies its sender by an authorized authentication. The authentication may be in code and the authorized naming of the issuer in an advice of credit is a sufficient signing.

§ 5—105. **Consideration.**

No consideration is necessary to establish a credit or to enlarge or otherwise modify its terms.

§ 5—106. **Time and Effect of Establishment of Credit.**

(1) Unless otherwise agreed a credit is established

(a) as regards the customer as soon as a letter of credit is sent to him or the letter of credit or an authorized written advice of its issuance is sent to the beneficiary; and

(b) as regards the beneficiary when he receives a letter of credit or an authorized written advice of its issuance.

(2) Unless otherwise agreed once an irrevocable credit is established as regards the customer it can be modified or revoked only with the consent of the customer and once it is established as regards the beneficiary it can be modified or revoked only with his consent.

(3) Unless otherwise agreed after a revocable credit is established it may be modified or revoked by the issuer without notice to or consent from the customer or beneficiary.

(4) Notwithstanding any modification or revocation of a revocable credit any person authorized to honor or negotiate under the terms of the original credit is entitled to reimbursement for or honor of any draft or demand for payment duty honored or negotiated

before receipt of notice of the modification or revocation and the issuer in turn is entitled to reimbursement from its customer.

§ 5—107. Advice of Credit; Confirmation; Error in Statement of Terms.

(1) Unless otherwise specified an advising bank by advising a credit issued by another bank does not assume any obligation to honor drafts drawn or demands for payment made under the credit but it does assume obligation for the accuracy of its own statement.

(2) A confirming bank by confirming a credit becomes directly obligated on the credit to the extent of its confirmation as though it were its issuer and acquires the rights of an issuer.

(3) Even though an advising bank incorrectly advises the terms of a credit it has been authorized to advise the credit is established as against the issuer to the extent of its original terms.

(4) Unless otherwise specified the customer bears as against the issuer all risks of transmission and reasonable translation or interpretation of any message relating to a credit.

§ 5—108. "Notation Credit"; Exhaustion of Credit.

(1) A credit which specifies that any person purchasing or paying drafts drawn or demands for payment made under it must note the amount of the draft or demand on the letter or advice of credit is a "notation credit".

(2) Under a notation credit

(a) a person paying the beneficiary or purchasing a draft or demand for payment from him acquires a right to honor only if the appropriate notation is made and by transferring or forwarding for honor the documents under the credit such a person warrants to the issuer that the notation has been made; and

(b) unless the credit or a signed statement that an appropriate notation has been made accompanies the draft or demand for payment the issuer may

delay honor until evidence of notation has been procured which is satisfactory to it but its obligation and that of its customer continue for a reasonable time not exceeding thirty days to obtain such evidence.

(3) If the credit is not a notation credit

(a) the issuer may honor complying drafts or demands for payment presented to it in the order in which they are presented and is discharged pro tanto by honor of any such draft or demand;

(b) as between competing good faith purchasers of complying drafts or demands the person first purchasing has priority over a subsequent purchaser even though the later purchased draft or demand has been first honored.

§ 5—109. Issuer's Obligation to Its Customer.

(1) An issuer's obligation to its customer includes good faith and observance of any general banking usage but unless otherwise agreed does not include liability or responsibility

(a) for performance of the underlying contract for sale or other transaction between the customer and the beneficiary; or

(b) for any act or omission of any person other than itself or its own branch or for loss or destruction of a draft, demand or document in transit or in the possession of others; or

(c) based on knowledge or lack of knowledge of any usage of any particular trade.

(2) An issuer must examine documents with care so as to ascertain that on their face they appear to comply with the terms of the credit but unless otherwise agreed assumes no liability or responsibility for the genuineness, falsification or effect of any document which appears on such examination to be regular on its face.

(3) A non-bank issuer is not bound by any banking usage of which it has no knowledge.

§ 5—110. Availability of Credit in Portions; Presenter's Reservation of Lien or Claim.

(1) Unless otherwise specified a credit may be used

in portions in the discretion of the beneficiary.

(2) Unless otherwise specified a person by presenting a documentary draft or demand for payment under a credit relinquishes upon its honor all claims to the documents and a person by transferring such draft or demand or causing such presentment authorizes such relinquishment. An explicit reservation of claim makes the draft or demand non-complying.

§ 5—111. Warranties on Transfer and Presentment.

(1) Unless otherwise agreed the beneficiary by transferring or presenting a documentary draft or demand for payment warrants to all interested parties that the necessary conditions of the credit have been complied with. This is in addition to any warranties arising under Articles 3, 4, 7 and 8.

(2) Unless otherwise agreed a negotiating, advising, confirming, collecting or issuing bank presenting or transferring a draft or demand for payment under a credit warrants only the matters warranted by a collecting bank under Article 4 and any such bank transferring a document warrants only the matters warranted by an intermediary under Articles 7 and 8.

§ 5—112. Time Allowed for Honor or Rejection; Withholding Honor or Rejection by Consent; "Presenter".

(1) A bank to which a documentary draft or demand for payment is presented under a credit may without dishonor of the draft, demand or credit

(a) defer honor until the close of the third banking day following receipt of the documents; and

(b) further defer honor if the presenter has expressly or impliedly consented thereto.

Failure to honor within the time here specified constitutes dishonor of the draft or demand and of the credit [except as otherwise provided in subsection (4) of Section 5—114 on conditional payment].

Note: The bracketed language in the last sentence of subsection (1) should be included only if the optional provisions of Section 5—114(4) and (5) are included.

(2) Upon dishonor the bank may unless otherwise instructed fulfill its duty to return the draft or demand and the documents by holding them at the disposal of the presenter and sending him an advice to that effect.

(3) "Presenter" means any person presenting a draft or demand for payment for honor under a credit even though that person is a confirming bank or other correspondent which is acting under an issuer's authorization.

§ 5—113. Indemnities.

(1) A bank seeking to obtain (whether for itself or another) honor, negotiation or reimbursement under a credit may give an indemnity to induce such honor, negotiation or reimbursement.

(2) An indemnity agreement inducing honor, negotiation or reimbursement

(a) unless otherwise explicitly agreed applies to defects in the documents but not in the goods; and

(b) unless a longer time is explicitly agreed expires at the end of ten business days following receipt of the documents by, the ultimate customer unless notice of objection is sent before such expiration date. The ultimate customer may send notice of objection to the person from whom he received the documents and any bank receiving such notice is under a duty to send notice to its transferor before its midnight deadline.

§ 5—114. Issuer's Duty and Privilege to Honor; Right to Reimbursement.

(1) An issuer must honor a draft or demand for payment which complies with the terms of the relevant credit regardless of whether the goods or documents conform to the underlying contract for sale or other contract between the customer and the beneficiary. The issuer is not excused from honor of such a draft or demand by reason of an additional general term that all documents must be satisfactory to the issuer, but an issuer may require that specified documents must be satisfactory to it.

(2) Unless otherwise agreed when documents appear

on their face to comply with the terms of a credit but a required document does not in fact conform to the warranties made on negotiation or transfer of a document of title (Section 7—507) or of a certificated security (Section 8—306) or is forged or fraudulent or there is fraud in the transaction:

(a) the issuer must honor the draft or demand for payment if honor is demanded by a negotiating bank or other holder of the draft or demand which has taken the draft or demand under the credit and under circumstances which would make it a holder in due course (Section 3—302) and in an appropriate case would make it a person to whom a document of title has been duly negotiated (Section 7—502) or a bona fide purchaser of a certificated security (Section 8—302); and

(b) in all other cases as against its customer, an issuer acting in good faith may honor the draft or demand for payment despite notification from the customer of fraud, forgery or other defect not apparent on the face of the documents but a court of appropriate jurisdiction may enjoin such honor.

(3) Unless otherwise agreed an issuer which has duly honored a draft or demand for payment is entitled to immediate reimbursement of any payment made under the credit and to be put in effectively available funds not later than the day before maturity of any acceptance made under the credit.

[(4) When a credit provides for payment by the issuer on receipt of notice that the required documents are in the possession of a correspondent or other agent of the issuer

(a) any payment made on receipt of such notice is conditional; and

(b) the issuer may reject documents which do not comply with the credit if it does so within three banking days following its receipt of the documents; and

(c) in the event of such rejection, the issuer is entitled by charge back or otherwise to return of the payment made.]

[(5) In the case covered by subsection (4) failure to reject documents within the time specified in sub-paragraph (b) constitutes acceptance of the documents and makes the payment final in favor of the beneficiary.]

Amended in 1977.

Note: *Subsections (4) and (5) are bracketed as optional. If they are included the bracketed language in the last sentence of Section 5—112(1) should also be included.*

§ 5—115. **Remedy for Improper Dishonor or Anticipatory Repudiation.**

(1) When an issuer wrongfully dishonors a draft or demand for payment presented under a credit the person entitled to honor has with respect to any documents the rights of a person in the position of a seller (Section 2—707) and may recover from the issuer the face amount of the draft or demand together with incidental damages under Section 2—710 on seller's incidental damages and interest but less any amount realized by resale or other use or disposition of the subject matter of the transaction. In the event no resale or other utilization is made the documents, goods or other subject matter involved in the transaction must be turned over to the issuer on payment of judgment.

(2) When an issuer wrongfully cancels or otherwise repudiates a credit before presentment of a draft or demand for payment drawn under it the beneficiary has the rights of a seller after anticipatory repudiation by the buyer under Section 2—610 if he learns of the repudiation in time reasonably to avoid procurement of the required documents. Otherwise the beneficiary has an immediate right of action for wrongful dishonor.

§ 5—116. **Transfer and Assignment.**

(1) The right to draw under a credit can be transferred or assigned only when the credit is expressly designated as transferable or assignable.

(2) Even though the credit specifically states that it is nontransferable or nonassignable the beneficiary may before performance of the conditions of the credit assign his right to proceeds. Such an assignment is an assignment of an account under Article 9 on Secured Transactions and is governed by that Article except that

(a) the assignment is ineffective until the letter of credit or advice of credit is delivered to the assignee which delivery constitutes perfection of the security interest under Article 9; and

(b) the issuer may honor drafts or demands for

payment drawn under the credit until it receives a notification of the assignment signed by the beneficiary which reasonably identifies the credit involved in the assignment and contains a request to pay the assignee; and

(c) after what reasonably appears to be such a notification has been received the issuer may without dishonor refuse to accept or pay even to a person otherwise entitled to honor until the letter of credit or advice of credit is exhibited to the issuer.

(3) Except where the beneficiary has effectively assigned his right to draw or his right to proceeds, nothing in this section limits his right to transfer or negotiate drafts or demands drawn under the credit.

§ 5—117. **Insolvency of Bank Holding Funds for Documentary Credit.**

(1) Where an issuer or an advising or confirming bank or a bank which has for a customer procured issuance of a credit by another bank becomes insolvent before final payment under the credit and the credit is one to which this Article is made applicable by paragraphs (a) or (b) of Section 5—102(1) on scope, the receipt or allocation of funds or collateral to secure or meet obligations under the credit shall have the following results:

(a) to the extent of any funds or collateral turned over after or before the insolvency as indemnity against or specifically for the purpose of payment of drafts or demands for payment drawn under the designated credit, the drafts or demands are entitled to payment in preference over depositors or other general creditors of the issuer or bank; and

(b) on expiration of the credit or surrender of the beneficiary's rights under it unused any person who has given such funds or collateral is similarly entitled to return thereof; and

(c) a charge to a general or current account with a bank if specifically consented to for the purpose of indemnity against or payment of drafts or demands for payment drawn under the designated credit falls under the same rules as if the funds had been drawn out in cash and then turned over with specific instructions.

(2) After honor or reimbursement under this section the customer or other person for whose account the insolvent bank has acted is entitled to receive the documents involved.

Article 6
BULK TRANSFERS

§ 6—101. **Short Title.**

This Article shall be known and may be cited as Uniform Commercial Code—Bulk Transfers.

§ 6—102. **"Bulk Transfer"; Transfers of Equipment; Enterprises Subject to This Article; Bulk Transfers Subject to This Article.**

(1) A "bulk transfer" is any transfer in bulk and not in the ordinary course of the transferor's business of a major part of the materials, supplies, merchandise or other inventory (Section 9—109) of an enterprise subject to this Article.

(2) A transfer of a substantial part of the equipment (Section 9—109) of such an enterprise is a bulk transfer if it is made in connection with a bulk transfer of inventory, but not otherwise.

(3) The enterprises subject to this Article are all those whose principal business is the sale of merchandise from stock, including those who manufacture what they sell.

(4) Except as limited by the following section all bulk transfers of goods located within this state are subject to this Article.

§ 6—103. **Transfers Excepted From This Article.**

The following transfers are not subject to this Article:

(1) Those made to give security for the performance of an obligation;

(2) General assignments for the benefit of all the creditors of the transferor, and subsequent transfers by the assignee thereunder;

(3) Transfers in settlement or realization of a lien or other security interest;

(4) Sales by executors, administrators, receivers,

trustees in bankruptcy, or any public officer under judicial process;

(5) Sales made in the course of judicial or administrative proceedings for the dissolution or reorganization of a corporation and of which notice is sent to the creditors of the corporation pursuant to order of the court or administrative agency;

(6) Transfers to a person maintaining a known place of business in this State who becomes bound to pay the debts of the transferor in full and gives public notice of that fact, and who is solvent after becoming so bound;

(7) A transfer to a new business enterprise organized to take over and continue the business, if public notice of the transaction is given and the new enterprise assumes the debts of the transferor and he receives nothing from the transaction except an interest in the new enterprise junior to the claims of creditors;

(8) Transfers of property which is exempt from execution.

Public notice under subsection (6) or subsection (7) may be given by publishing once a week for two consecutive weeks in a newspaper of general circulation where the transferor had its principal place of business in this state an advertisement including the names and addresses of the transferor and transferee and the effective date of the transfer.

§ 6—104. **Schedule of Property, List of Creditors.**

(1) Except as provided with respect to auction sales (Section 6—108), a bulk transfer subject to this Article is ineffective against any creditor of the transferor unless:

   (a) The transferee requires the transferor to furnish a list of his existing creditors prepared as stated in this section; and

   (b) The parties prepare a schedule of the property transferred sufficient to identify it; and

   (c) The transferee preserves the list and schedule for six months next following the transfer and permits inspection of either or both and copying therefrom at all reasonable hours by any creditor of the transferor, or files the list and schedule in (a public office to be here identified).

(2) The list of creditors must be signed and sworn to or affirmed by the transferor or his agent. It must contain the names and business addresses of all creditors of the transferor, with the amounts when known, and also the names of all persons who are known to the transferor to assert claims against him even though such claims are disputed. If the transferor is the obligor of an outstanding issue of bonds, debentures or the like as to which there is an indenture trustee, the list of creditors need include only the name and address of the indenture trustee and the aggregate outstanding principal amount of the issue.

(3) Responsibility for the completeness and accuracy of the list of creditors rests on the transferor, and the transfer is not rendered ineffective by errors or omissions therein unless the transferee is shown to have had knowledge.

§ 6—105. **Notice to Creditors.**

In addition to the requirements of the preceding section, any bulk transfer subject to this Article except one made by auction sale (Section 6—108) is ineffective against any creditor of the transferor unless at least ten days before he takes possession of the goods or pays for them, whichever happens first, the transferee gives notice of the transfer in the manner and to the persons hereafter provided (Section 6—107).

[§ 6—106. **Application of the Proceeds.**

In addition to the requirements of the two preceding sections:

(1) Upon every bulk transfer subject to this Article for which new consideration becomes payable except those made by sale at auction it is the duty of the transferee to assure that such consideration is applied so far as necessary to pay those debts of the transferor which are either shown on the list furnished by the transferor (Section 6—104) or filed in writing in the place stated in the notice (Section 6—107) within thirty days after the mailing of such notice. This duty of the transferee runs to all the holders of such debts, and may be enforced by any of them for the benefit of all.

(2) If any of said debts are in dispute the necessary sum may be withheld from distribution until the dispute is settled or adjudicated.

(3) If the consideration payable is not enough to pay all of the said debts in full distribution shall be made pro rata.]

Note: *This section is bracketed to indicate division of opinion as to whether or not it is a wise provision, and to suggest that this is a point on which State enactments may differ without serious damage to the principle of uniformity. In any State where this section is omitted, the following parts of sections, also bracketed in the text, should also be omitted, namely:*

Section 6—107(2)(c).
    6—108(3)(c).
    6—109(2).

In any State where this section is enacted, these other provisions should be also.

Optional Subsection (4)

[(4) The transferee may within ten days after he takes possession of the goods pay the consideration into the (specify court) in the county where the transferor had its principal place of business in this state and thereafter may discharge his duty under this section by giving notice by registered or certified mail to all the persons to whom the duty runs that the consideration has been paid into that court and that they should file their claims there. On motion of any interested party, the court may order the distribution of the consideration to the persons entitled to it.]

Note: *Optional subsection (4) is recommended for those states which do not have a general statute providing for payment of money into court.*

§ 6—107. **The Notice.**

(1) The notice to creditors (Section 6—105) shall state:

    (a) that a bulk transfer is about to be made; and

    (b) the names and business addresses of the transferor and transferee, and all other business names and addresses used by the transferor within three years last past so far as known to the transferee; and

    (c) whether or not all the debts of the transferor are to be paid in full as they fall due as a result of the transaction, and if so, the address to which creditors should send their bills.

(2) If the debts of the transferor are not to be paid in full as they fall due or if the transferee is in doubt on that point then the notice shall state further:

    (a) the location and general description of the property to be transferred and the estimated total of the transferor's debts;

    (b) the address where the schedule of property and list of creditors (Section 6—104) may be inspected;

    (c) whether the transfer is to pay existing debts and if so the amount of such debts and to whom owing;

    (d) whether the transfer is for new consideration and if so the amount of such consideration and the time and place of payment; [and]

    [(e) if for new consideration the time and place where creditors of the transferor are to file their claims.]

(3) The notice in any case shall be delivered personally or sent by registered or certified mail to all the persons shown on the list of creditors furnished by the transferor (Section 6—104) and to all other persons who are known to the transferee to hold or assert claims against the transferor.

§ 6—108. **Auction Sales; "Auctioneer".**

(1) A bulk transfer is subject to this Article even though it is by sale at auction, but only in the manner and with the results stated in this section.

(2) The transferor shall furnish a list of his creditors and assist in the preparation of a schedule of the property to be sold, both prepared as before stated (Section 6—104).

(3) The person or persons other than the transferor who direct, control or are responsible for the auction are collectively called the "auctioneer". The auctioneer shall:

    (a) receive and retain the list of creditors and prepare and retain the schedule of property for the period stated in this Article (Section 6—104);

    (b) give notice of the auction personally or by registered or certified mail at least ten days before it occurs to all persons shown on the list of creditors and to all other persons who are known to him to hold or assert claims against the transferor; [and]

    [(c) assure that the net proceeds of the auction are applied as provided in this Article (Section 6—106).]

(4) Failure of the auctioneer to perform any of these duties does not affect the validity of the sale or the title of the purchasers, but if the auctioneer knows that the auction constitutes a bulk transfer such failure renders the auctioneer liable to the creditors of the transferor as a class for the sums owing to them from the transferor up to but not exceeding the net proceeds of the auction. If the auctioneer consists of several persons their liability is joint and several.

§ 6—109. **What Creditors Protected; [Credit for Payment to Particular Creditors].**

(1) The creditors of the transferor mentioned in this Article are those holding claims based on transactions or events occurring before the bulk transfer, but creditors who become such after notice to creditors is given (Sections 6—105 and 6—107) are not entitled to notice.

[(2) Against the aggregate obligation imposed by the provisions of this Article concerning the application of the proceeds (Section 6—106 and subsection (3) (c) of 6—108) the transferee or auctioneer is entitled to credit for sums paid to particular creditors of the transferor, not exceeding the sums believed in good faith at the time of the payment to be properly payable to such creditors.]

§ 6—110. **Subsequent Transfers.**

When the title of a transferee to property is subject to a defect by reason of his non-compliance with the requirements of this Article, then:

(1) a purchaser of any of such property from such transferee who pays no value or who takes with notice of such non-compliance takes subject to such defect, but

(2) a purchaser for value in good faith and without such notice takes free of such defect.

§ 6—111. **Limitation of Actions and Levies.**

No action under this Article shall be brought nor levy made more than six months after the date on which the transferee took possession of the goods unless the transfer has been concealed. If the transfer has been concealed, actions may be brought or levies made within six months after its discovery.

Note to Article 6: *Section 6—106 is bracketed to indicate division of opinion as to whether or not it is a wise provision,* and to suggest that this is a point on which State enactments may differ without serious damage to the principle of uniformity.

In any State where Section 6—106 is not enacted, the following parts of sections, also bracketed in the text, should also be omitted, namely:

Sec. 6—107(2)(e).
   6—108(3)(c).
   6—109(2).

In any State where Section 6—106 is enacted, these other provisions should be also.

Article 7
Warehouse Receipts, Bills of Lading and Other Documents of Title

Part 1 General

§ 7—101. **Short Title.**

This Article shall be known and may be cited as Uniform Commercial Code—Documents of Title.

§ 7—102. **Definitions and Index of Definitions.**

(1) In this Article, unless the context otherwise requires:

(a) "Bailee" means the person who by a warehouse receipt, bill of lading or other document of title acknowledges possession of goods and contracts to deliver them.

(b) "Consignee" means the person named in a bill to whom or to whose order the bill promises delivery.

(c) "Consignor" means the person named in a bill as the person from whom the goods have been received for shipment.

(d) "Delivery order" means a written order to deliver goods directed to a warehouseman, carrier or other person who in the ordinary course of business issues warehouse receipts or bills of lading.

(e) "Document" means document of title as defined in the general definitions in Article 1 (Section 1—201).

(f) "Goods" means all things which are treated as

movable for the purposes of a contract of storage or transportation.

(g) "Issuer" means a bailee who issues a document except that in relation to an unaccepted delivery order it means the person who orders the possessor of goods to deliver. Issuer includes any person for whom an agent or employee purports to act in issuing a document if the agent or employee has real or apparent authority to issue documents, notwithstanding that the issuer received no goods or that the goods were misdescribed or that in any other respect the agent or employee violated his instructions.

(h) "Warehouseman" is a person engaged in the business of storing goods for hire.

(2) Other definitions applying to this Article or to specified Parts thereof, and the sections in which they appear are:

"Duly negotiate". Section 7—501.

"Person entitled under the document". Section 7—403(4).

(3) Definitions in other Articles applying to this Article and the sections in which they appear are:

"Contract for sale". Section 2—106.

"Overseas". Section 2—323.

"Receipt" of goods. Section 2—103.

(4) In addition Article 1 contains general definitions and principles of construction and interpretation applicable throughout this Article.

§ 7—103. Relation of Article to Treaty, Statute, Tariff, Classification or Regulation.

To the extent that any treaty or statute of the United States, regulatory statute of this State or tariff, classification or regulation filed or issued pursuant thereto is applicable, the provisions of this Article are subject thereto.

§ 7—104. Negotiable and Non-Negotiable Warehouse Receipt, Bill of Lading or Other Document of Title.

(1) A warehouse receipt, bill of lading or other document of title is negotiable

(a) if by its terms the goods are to be delivered to bearer or to the order of a named person; or

(b) where recognized in overseas trade, if it runs to a named person or assigns.

(2) Any other document is non-negotiable. A bill of lading in which it is stated that the goods are consigned to a named person is not made negotiable by a provision that the goods are to be delivered only against a written order signed by the same or another named person.

§ 7—105. Construction Against Negative Implication.

The omission from either Part 2 or Part 3 of this Article of a provision corresponding to a provision made in the other Part does not imply that a corresponding rule of law is not applicable.

Part 2 Warehouse Receipts: Special Provisions

§ 7—201. Who May Issue a Warehouse Receipt; Storage Under Government Bond.

(1) A warehouse receipt may be issued by any warehouseman.

(2) Where goods including distilled spirits and agricultural commodities are stored under a statute requiring a bond against withdrawal or a license for the issuance of receipts in the nature of warehouse receipts, a receipt issued for the goods has like effect as a warehouse receipt even though issued by a person who is the owner of the goods and is not a warehouseman.

§ 7—202. Form of Warehouse Receipt; Essential Terms; Optional Terms.

(1) A warehouse receipt need not be in any particular form.

(2) Unless a warehouse receipt embodies within its written or printed terms each of the following, the warehouseman is liable for damages caused by the omission to a person injured thereby:

(a) the location of the warehouse where the goods are stored;

(b) the date of issue of the receipt;

(c) the consecutive number of the receipt;

(d) a statement whether the goods received will be delivered to the bearer, to a specified person, or to a specified person or his order;

(e) the rate of storage and handling charges, except that where goods are stored under a field warehousing arrangement a statement of that fact is sufficient on a non-negotiable receipt;

(f) a description of the goods or of the packages containing them;

(g) the signature of the warehouseman, which may be made by his authorized agent;

(h) if the receipt is issued for goods of which the warehouseman is owner, either solely or jointly or in common with others, the fact of such ownership; and

(i) a statement of the amount of advances made and of liabilities incurred for which the warehouseman claims a lien or security interest (Section 7—209). If the precise amount of such advances made or of such liabilities incurred is, at the time of the issue of the receipt, unknown to the warehouseman or to his agent who issues it, a statement of the fact that advances have been made or liabilities incurred and the purpose thereof is sufficient.

(3) A warehouseman may insert in his receipt any other terms which are not contrary to the provisions of this Act and do not impair his obligation of delivery (Section 7—403) or his duty of care (Section 7—204). Any contrary provisions shall be ineffective.

§ 7—203. Liability for Non-Receipt or Misdescription.

A party to or purchaser for value in good faith of a document of title other than a bill of lading relying in either case upon the description therein of the goods may recover from the issuer damages caused by the non-receipt or misdescription of the goods, except to the extent that the document conspicuously indicates that the issuer does not know whether any part or all of the goods in fact were received or conform to the description, as where the description is in terms of marks or labels or kind, quantity or condition, or the receipt or description is qualified by "contents, condition and quality unknown", "said to contain" or the like, if such indication be true, or the party or purchaser otherwise has notice.

§ 7—204. Duty of Care; Contractual Limitation of Warehouseman's Liability.

(1) A warehouseman is liable for damages for loss of or injury to the goods caused by his failure to exercise such care in regard to them as a reasonably careful man would exercise under like circumstances but unless otherwise agreed he is not liable for damages which could not have been avoided by the exercise of such care.

(2) Damages may be limited by a term in the warehouse receipt or storage agreement limiting the amount of liability in case of loss or damage, and setting forth a specific liability per article or item, or value per unit of weight, beyond which the warehouseman shall not be liable; provided, however, that such liability may on written request of the bailor at the time of signing such storage agreement or within a reasonable time after receipt of the warehouse receipt be increased on part or all of the goods thereunder, in which event increased rates may be charged based on such increased valuation, but that no such increase shall be permitted contrary to a lawful limitation of liability contained in the warehouseman's tariff, if any. No such limitation is effective with respect to the warehouseman's liability for conversion to his own use.

(3) Reasonable provisions as to the time and manner of presenting claims and instituting actions based on the bailment may be included in the warehouse receipt or tariff.

(4) This section does not impair or repeal . . .

Note: *Insert in subsection (4) a reference to any statute which imposes a higher responsibility upon the warehouseman or invalidates contractual limitations which would be permissible under this Article.*

§ 7—205. Title Under Warehouse Receipt Defeated in Certain Cases.

A buyer in the ordinary course of business of fungible goods sold and delivered by a warehouseman who is also in the business of buying and selling such goods takes free of any claim under a warehouse receipt even though it has been duly negotiated.

§ 7—206. Termination of Storage at Warehouseman's Option.

(1) A warehouseman may on notifying the person on whose account the goods are held and any other person known to claim an interest in the goods require payment of any charges and removal of the goods from the warehouse at the termination of the period of storage fixed by the document, or, if no

period is fixed, within a stated period not less than thirty days after the notification. If the goods are not removed before the date specified in the notification, the warehouseman may sell them in accordance with the provisions of the section on enforcement of a warehouseman's lien (Section 7—210).

(2) If a warehouseman in good faith believes that the goods are about to deteriorate or decline in value to less than the amount of his lien within the time prescribed in subsection (1) for notification, advertisement and sale, the warehouseman may specify in the notification any reasonable shorter time for removal of the goods and in case the goods are not removed, may sell them at public sale held not less than one week after a single advertisement or posting.

(3) If as a result of a quality or condition of the goods of which the warehouseman had no notice at the time of deposit the goods are a hazard to other property or to the warehouse or to persons, the warehouseman may sell the goods at public or private sale without advertisement on reasonable notification to all persons known to claim an interest in the goods. If the warehouseman after a reasonable effort is unable to sell the goods he may dispose of them in any lawful manner and shall incur no liability by reason of such disposition.

(4) The warehouseman must deliver the goods to any person entitled to them under this Article upon due demand made at any time prior to sale or other disposition under this section.

(5) The warehouseman may satisfy his lien from the proceeds of any sale or disposition under this section but must hold the balance for delivery on the demand of any person to whom he would have been bound to deliver the goods.

§ 7—207. **Goods Must Be Kept Separate; Fungible Goods.**

(1) Unless the warehouse receipt otherwise provides, a warehouseman must keep separate the goods covered by each receipt so as to permit at all times identification and delivery of those goods except that different lots of fungible goods may be commingled.

(2) Fungible goods so commingled are owned in common by the persons entitled thereto and the warehouseman is severally liable to each owner for

that owner's share. Where because of overissue a mass of fungible goods is insufficient to meet all the receipts which the warehouseman has issued against it, the persons entitled include all holders to whom overissued receipts have been duly negotiated.

§ 7—208. **Altered Warehouse Receipts.**

Where a blank in a negotiable warehouse receipt has been filled in without authority, a purchaser for value and without notice of the want of authority may treat the insertion as authorized. Any other unauthorized alteration leaves any receipt enforceable against the issuer according to its original tenor.

§ 7—209. **Lien of Warehouseman.**

(1) A warehouseman has a lien against the bailor on the goods covered by a warehouse receipt or on the proceeds thereof in his possession for charges for storage or transportation (including demurrage and terminal charges), insurance, labor, or charges present or future in relation to the goods, and for expenses necessary for preservation of the goods or reasonably incurred in their sale pursuant to law. If the person on whose account the goods are held is liable for like charges or expenses in relation to other goods whenever deposited and it is stated in the receipt that a lien is claimed for charges and expenses in relation to other goods, the warehouseman also has a lien against him for such charges and expenses whether or not the other goods have been delivered by the warehouseman. But against a person to whom a negotiable warehouse receipt is duly negotiated a warehouseman's lien is limited to charges in an amount or at a rate specified on the receipt or if no charges are so specified then to a reasonable charge for storage of the goods covered by the receipt subsequent to the date of the receipt.

(2) The warehouseman may also reserve a security interest against the bailor for a maximum amount specified on the receipt for charges other than those specified in subsection (1), such as for money advanced and interest. Such a security interest is governed by the Article on Secured Transactions (Article 9).

(3) (a) A warehouseman's lien for charges and expenses under subsection (1) or a security interest under subsection (2) is also effective against any person who so entrusted the bailor with possession of

the goods that a pledge of them by him to a good faith purchaser for value would have been valid but is not effective against a person as to whom the document confers no right in the goods covered by it under Section 7—503.

(b) A warehouseman's lien on household goods for charges and expenses in relation to the goods under subsection (1) is also effective against all persons if the depositor was the legal possessor of the goods at the time of deposit. "Household goods" means furniture, furnishings and personal effects used by the depositor in a dwelling.

(4) A warehouseman loses his lien on any goods which he voluntarily delivers or which he unjustifiably refuses to deliver.

§ 7—210. Enforcement of Warehouseman's Lien.

(1) Except as provided in subsection (2), a warehouseman's lien may be enforced by public or private sale of the goods in bloc or in parcels, at any time or place and on any terms which are commercially reasonable, after notifying all persons known to claim an interest in the goods. Such notification must include a statement of the amount due, the nature of the proposed sale and the time and place of any public sale. The fact that a better price could have been obtained by a sale at a different time or in a different method from that selected by the warehouseman is not of itself sufficient to establish that the sale was not made in a commercially reasonable manner. If the warehouseman either sells the goods in the usual manner in any recognized market therefor, or if he sells at the price current in such market at the time of his sale, or if he has otherwise sold in conformity with commercially reasonable practices among dealers in the type of goods sold, he has sold in a commercially reasonable manner. A sale of more goods than apparently necessary to be offered to insure satisfaction of the obligation is not commercially reasonable except in cases covered by the preceding sentence.

(2) A warehouseman's lien on goods other than goods stored by a merchant in the course of his business may be enforced only as follows:

(a) All persons known to claim an interest in the goods must be notified.

(b) The notification must be delivered in person

or sent by registered or certified letter to the last known address of any person to be notified.

(c) The notification must include an itemized statement of the claim, a description of the goods subject to the lien, a demand for payment within a specified time not less than ten days after receipt of the notification, and a conspicuous statement that unless the claim is paid within the time the goods will be advertised for sale and sold by auction at a specified time and place.

(d) The sale must conform to the terms of the notification.

(e) The sale must be held at the nearest suitable place to that where the goods are held or stored.

(f) After the expiration of the time given in the notification, an advertisement of the sale must be published once a week for two weeks consecutively in a newspaper of general circulation where the sale is to be held. The advertisement must include a description of the goods, the name of the person on whose account they are being held, and the time and place of the sale. The sale must take place at least fifteen days after the first publication. If there is no newspaper of general circulation where the sale is to be held, the advertisement must be posted at least ten days before the sale in not less than six conspicuous places in the neighborhood of the proposed sale.

(3) Before any sale pursuant to this section any person claiming a right in the goods may pay the amount necessary to satisfy the lien and the reasonable expenses incurred under this section. In that event the goods must not be sold, but must be retained by the warehouseman subject to the terms of the receipt and this Article.

(4) The warehouseman may buy at any public sale pursuant to this section.

(5) A purchaser in good faith of goods sold to enforce a warehouseman's lien takes the goods free of any rights of persons against whom the lien was valid, despite noncompliance by the warehouseman with the requirements of this section.

(6) The warehouseman may satisfy his lien from the proceeds of any sale pursuant to this section but must hold the balance, if any, for delivery on demand to

any person to whom he would have been bound to deliver the goods.

(7) The rights provided by this section shall be in addition to all other rights allowed by law to a creditor against his debtor.

(8) Where a lien is on goods stored by a merchant in the course of his business the lien may be enforced in accordance with either subsection (1) or (2).

(9) The warehouseman is liable for damages caused by failure to comply with the requirements for sale under this section and in case of willful violation is liable for conversion.

Part 3 Bills of Lading: Special Provisions

§ 7—301. **Liability for Non-Receipt or Misdescription; "Said to Contain"; "Shipper's Load and Count"; Improper Handling.**

(1) A consignee of a non-negotiable bill who has given value in good faith or a holder to whom a negotiable bill has been duly negotiated relying in either case upon the description therein of the goods, or upon the date therein shown, may recover from the issuer damages caused by the misdating of the bill or the non-receipt or misdescription of the goods, except to the extent that the document indicates that the issuer does not know whether any part of all of the goods in fact were received or conform to the description, as where the description is in terms of marks or labels or kind, quantity, or condition or the receipt or description is qualified by "contents or condition of contents of packages unknown", "said to contain", "shipper's weight, load and count" or the like, if such indication be true.

(2) When goods are loaded by an issuer who is a common carrier, the issuer must count the packages of goods if package freight and ascertain the kind and quantity if bulk freight. In such cases "shipper's weight, load and count" or other words indicating that the description was made by the shipper are ineffective except as to freight concealed by packages.

(3) When bulk freight is loaded by a shipper who makes available to the issuer adequate facilities for weighing such freight, an issuer who is a common carrier must ascertain the kind and quantity within a

reasonable time after receiving the written request of the shipper to do so. In such cases "shipper's weight" or other words of like purport are ineffective.

(4) The issuer may by inserting in the bill the words "shipper's weight, load and count" or other words of like purport indicate that the goods were loaded by the shipper; and if such statement be true the issuer shall not be liable for damages caused by the improper loading. But their omission does not imply liability for such damages.

(5) The shipper shall be deemed to have guaranteed to the issuer the accuracy at the time of shipment of the description, marks, labels, number, kind, quantity, condition and weight, as furnished by him; and the shipper shall indemnify the issuer against damage caused by inaccuracies in such particulars. The right of the issuer to such indemnity shall in no way limit his responsibility and liability under the contract of carriage to any person other than the shipper.

§ 7—302. **Through Bills of Lading and Similar Documents.**

(1) The issuer of a through bill of lading or other document embodying an undertaking to be performed in part by persons acting as its agents or by connecting carriers is liable to anyone entitled to recover on the document for any breach by such other persons or by a connecting carrier of its obligation under the document but to the extent that the bill covers an undertaking to be performed overseas or in territory not contiguous to the continental United States or an undertaking including matters other than transportation this liability may be varied by agreement of the parties.

(2) Where goods covered by a through bill of lading or other document embodying an undertaking to be performed in part by persons other than the issuer are received by any such person, he is subject with respect to his own performance while the goods are in his possession to the obligation of the issuer. His obligation is discharged by delivery of the goods to another such person pursuant to the document, and does not include liability for breach by any other such persons or by the issuer.

(3) The issuer of such through bill of lading or other document shall be entitled to recover from the

connecting carrier or such other person in possession of the goods when the breach of the obligation under the document occurred, the amount it may be required to pay to anyone entitled to recover on the document therefor, as may be evidenced by any receipt, judgment, or transcript thereof, and the amount of any expense reasonably incurred by it in defending any action brought by anyone entitled to recover on the document therefor.

§ 7—303. **Diversion; Reconsignment; Change of Instructions.**

(1) Unless the bill of lading otherwise provides, the carrier may deliver the goods to a person or destination other than that stated in the bill or may otherwise dispose of the goods on instructions from

(a) the holder of a negotiable bill; or

(b) the consignor on a non-negotiable bill notwithstanding contrary instructions from the consignee; or

(c) the consignee on a non-negotiable bill in the absence of contrary instructions from the consignor, if the goods have arrived at the billed destination or if the consignee is in possession of the bill; or

(d) the consignee on a non-negotiable bill if he is entitled as against the consignor to dispose of them.

(2) Unless such instructions are noted on a negotiable bill of lading, a person to whom the bill is duly negotiated can hold the bailee according to the original terms.

§ 7—304. **Bills of Lading in a Set.**

(1) Except where customary in overseas transportation, a bill of lading must not be issued in a set of parts. The issuer is liable for damages caused by violation of this subsection.

(2) Where a bill of lading is lawfully drawn in a set of parts, each of which is numbered and expressed to be valid only if the goods have not been delivered against any other part, the whole of the parts constitute one bill.

(3) Where a bill of lading is lawfully issued in a set of parts and different parts are negotiated to different persons, the title of the holder to whom the first due negotiation is made prevails as to both the document

and the goods even though any later holder may have received the goods from the carrier in good faith and discharged the carrier's obligation by surrender of his part.

(4) Any person who negotiates or transfers a single part of a bill of lading drawn in a set is liable to holders of that part as if it were the whole set.

(5) The bailee is obliged to deliver in accordance with Part 4 of this Article against the first presented part of a bill of lading lawfully drawn in a set. Such delivery discharges the bailee's obligation on the whole bill.

§ 7—305. **Destination Bills.**

(1) Instead of issuing a bill of lading to the consignor at the place of shipment a carrier may at the request of the consignor procure the bill to be issued at destination or at any other place designated in the request.

(2) Upon request of anyone entitled as against the carrier to control the goods while in transit and on surrender of any outstanding bill of lading or other receipt covering such goods, the issuer may procure a substitute bill to be issued at any place designated in the request.

§ 7—306. **Altered Bills of Lading.**

An unauthorized alteration or filling in of a blank in a bill of lading leaves the bill enforceable according to its original tenor.

§ 7—307. **Lien of Carrier.**

(1) A carrier has a lien on the goods covered by a bill of lading for charges subsequent to the date of its receipt of the goods for storage or transportation (including demurrage and terminal charges) and for expenses necessary for preservation of the goods incident to their transportation or reasonably incurred in their sale pursuant to law. But against a purchaser for value of a negotiable bill of lading a carrier's lien is limited to charges stated in the bill or the applicable tariffs, or if no charges are stated then to a reasonable charge.

(2) A lien for charges and expenses under subsection (1) on goods which the carrier was required by law to receive for transportation is effective against the consignor or any person entitled to the goods unless the carrier had notice that the consignor lacked

authority to subject the goods to such charges and expenses. Any other lien under subsection (1) is effective against the consignor and any person who permitted the bailor to have control or possession of the goods unless the carrier had notice that the bailor lacked such authority.

(3) A carrier loses his lien on any goods which he voluntarily delivers or which he unjustifiably refuses to deliver.

§ 7—308. **Enforcement of Carrier's Lien.**

(1) A carrier's lien may be enforced by public or private sale of the goods, in bloc or in parcels, at any time or place and on any terms which are commercially reasonable, after notifying all persons known to claim an interest in the goods. Such notification must include a statement of the amount due, the nature of the proposed sale and the time and place of any public sale. The fact that a better price could have been obtained by a sale at a different time or in a different method from that selected by the carrier is not of itself sufficient to establish that the sale was not made in a commercially reasonable manner. If the carrier either sells the goods in the usual manner in any recognized market therefor or if he sells at the price current in such market at the time of his sale or if he has otherwise sold in conformity with commercially reasonable practices among dealers in the type of goods sold he has sold in a commercially reasonable manner. A sale of more goods than apparently necessary to be offered to ensure satisfaction of the obligation is not commercially reasonable except in cases covered by the preceding sentence.

(2) Before any sale pursuant to this section any person claiming a right in the goods may pay the amount necessary to satisfy the lien and the reasonable expenses incurred under this section. In that event the goods must not be sold, but must be retained by the carrier subject to the terms of the bill and this Article.

(3) The carrier may buy at any public sale pursuant to this section.

(4) A purchaser in good faith of goods sold to enforce a carrier's lien takes the goods free of any rights of persons against whom the lien was valid, despite noncompliance by the carrier with the requirements of this section.

(5) The carrier may satisfy his lien from the proceeds of any sale pursuant to this section but must hold the balance, if any, for delivery on demand to any person to whom he would have been bound to deliver the goods.

(6) The rights provided by this section shall be in addition to all other rights allowed by law to a creditor against his debtor.

(7) A carrier's lien may be enforced in accordance with either subsection (1) or the procedure set forth in subsection (2) of Section 7—210.

(8) The carrier is liable for damages caused by failure to comply with the requirements for sale under this section and in case of willful violation is liable for conversion.

§ 7—309. **Duty of Care; Contractual Limitation of Carrier's Liability.**

(1) A carrier who issues a bill of lading whether negotiable or non-negotiable must exercise the degree of care in relation to the goods which a reasonably careful man would exercise under like circumstances. This subsection does not repeal or change any law or rule of law which imposes liability upon a common carrier for damages not caused by its negligence.

(2) Damages may be limited by a provision that the carrier's liability shall not exceed a value stated in the document if the carrier's rates are dependent upon value and the consignor by the carrier's tariff is afforded an opportunity to declare a higher value or a value as lawfully provided in the tariff, or where no tariff is filed he is otherwise advised of such opportunity; but no such limitation is effective with respect to the carrier's liability for conversion to its own use.

(3) Reasonable provisions as to the time and manner of presenting claims and instituting actions based on the shipment may be included in a bill of lading or tariff.

Part 4 Warehouse Receipts and Bills of Lading: General Obligations

§ 7—401. **Irregularities in Issue of Receipt or Bill or Conduct of Issuer.**

The obligations imposed by this Article on an issuer

apply to a document of title regardless of the fact that

(a) the document may not comply with the requirements of this Article or of any other law or regulation regarding its issue, form or content; or

(b) the issuer may have violated laws regulating the conduct of his business; or

(c) the goods covered by the document were owned by the bailee at the time the document was issued; or

(d) the person issuing the document does not come within the definition of warehouseman if it purports to be a warehouse receipt.

§ 7—402. **Duplicate Receipt or Bill; Overissue.**

Neither a duplicate nor any other document of title purporting to cover goods already represented by an outstanding document of the same issuer confers any right in the goods, except as provided in the case of bills in a set, overissue of documents for fungible goods and substitutes for lost, stolen or destroyed documents. But the issuer is liable for damages caused by his overissue or failure to identify a duplicate document as such by conspicuous notation on its face.

§ 7—403. **Obligation of Warehouseman or Carrier to Deliver; Excuse.**

(1) The bailee must deliver the goods to a person entitled under the document who complies with subsections (2) and (3), unless and to the extent that the bailee establishes any of the following:

  (a) delivery of the goods to a person whose receipt was rightful as against the claimant;

  (b) damage to or delay, loss or destruction of the goods for which the bailee is not liable [, but the burden of establishing negligence in such cases is on the person entitled under the document];

Note: The brackets in (1)(b) indicate that State enactments may differ on this point without serious damage to the principle of uniformity.

  (c) previous sale or other disposition of the goods in lawful enforcement of a lien or on warehouseman's lawful termination of storage;

  (d) the exercise by a seller of his right to stop delivery pursuant to the provisions of the Article on Sales (Section 2—705);

  (e) a diversion, reconsignment or other disposition pursuant to the provisions of this Article (Section 7—303) or tariff regulating such right;

  (f) release, satisfaction or any other fact affording a personal defense against the claimant;

  (g) any other lawful excuse.

(2) A person claiming goods covered by a document of title must satisfy the bailee's lien where the bailee so requests or where the bailee is prohibited by law from delivering the goods until the charges are paid.

(3) Unless the person claiming is one against whom the document confers no right under Sec. 7—503(1), he must surrender for cancellation or notation of partial deliveries any outstanding negotiable document covering the goods, and the bailee must cancel the document or conspicuously note the partial delivery thereon or be liable to any person to whom the document is duly negotiated.

(4) "Person entitled under the document" means holder in the case of a negotiable document, or the person to whom delivery is to be made by the terms of or pursuant to written instructions under a non-negotiable document.

§ 7—404. **No Liability for Good Faith Delivery Pursuant to Receipt or Bill.**

A bailee who in good faith including observance of reasonable commercial standards has received goods and delivered or otherwise disposed of them according to the terms of the document of title or pursuant to this Article is not liable therefor. This rule applies even though the person from whom he received the goods had no authority to procure the document or to dispose of the goods and even though the person to whom he delivered the goods had no authority to receive them.

Part 5 Warehouse Receipts and Bills of Lading: Negotiation and Transfer

§ 7—501. **Form of Negotiation and Requirements of "Due Negotiation".**

(1) A negotiable document of title running to the order of a named person is negotiated by his indorsement and delivery. After his indorsement in blank or

to bearer any person can negotiate it by delivery alone.

(2) (a) A negotiable document of title is also negotiated by delivery alone when by its original terms it runs to bearer.

(b) When a document running to the order of a named person is delivered to him the effect is the same as if the document had been negotiated.

(3) Negotiation of a negotiable document of title after it has been indorsed to a specified person requires indorsement by the special indorsee as well as delivery.

(4) A negotiable document of title is "duly negotiated" when it is negotiated in the manner stated in this section to a holder who purchases it in good faith without notice of any defense against or claim to it on the part of any person and for value, unless it is established that the negotiation is not in the regular course of business or financing or involves receiving the document in settlement or payment of a money obligation.

(5) Indorsement of a non-negotiable document neither makes it negotiable nor adds to the transferee's rights.

(6) The naming in a negotiable bill of a person to be notified of the arrival of the goods does not limit the negotiability of the bill nor constitute notice to a purchaser thereof of any interest of such person in the goods.

§ 7—502. **Rights Acquired by Due Negotiation.**

(1) Subject to the following section and to the provisions of Section 7—205 on fungible goods, a holder to whom a negotiable document of title has been duly negotiated acquires thereby:

(a) title to the document;

(b) title to the goods;

(c) all rights accruing under the law of agency or estoppel, including rights to goods delivered to the bailee after the document was issued; and

(d) the direct obligation of the issuer to hold or deliver the goods according to the terms of the document free of any defense or claim by him except those arising under the terms of the docu-

ment or under this Article. In the case of a delivery order the bailee's obligation accrues only upon acceptance and the obligation acquired by the holder is that the issuer and any indorser will procure the acceptance of the bailee.

(2) Subject to the following section, title and rights so acquired are not defeated by any stoppage of the goods represented by the document or by surrender of such goods by the bailee, and are not impaired even though the negotiation or any prior negotiation constituted a breach of duty or even though any person has been deprived of possession of the document by misrepresentation, fraud, accident, mistake, duress, loss, theft or conversion, or even though a previous sale or other transfer of the goods or document has been made to a third person.

§ 7—503. **Document of Title to Goods Defeated in Certain Cases.**

(1) A document of title confers no right in goods against a person who before issuance of the document had a legal interest or a perfected security interest in them and who neither

(a) delivered or entrusted them or any document of title covering them to the bailor or his nominee with actual or apparent authority to ship, store or sell or with power to obtain delivery under this Article (Section 7—403) or with power of disposition under this Act (Sections 2—403 and 9—307) or other statute or rule of law; nor

(b) acquiesced in the procurement by the bailor or his nominee of any document of title.

(2) Title to goods based upon an unaccepted delivery order is subject to the rights of anyone to whom a negotiable warehouse receipt or bill of lading covering the goods has been duly negotiated. Such a title may be defeated under the next section to the same extent as the rights of the issuer or a transferee from the issuer.

(3) Title to goods based upon a bill of lading issued to a freight forwarder is subject to the rights of anyone to whom a bill issued by the freight forwarder is duly negotiated; but delivery by the carrier in accordance with Part 4 of this Article pursuant to its own bill of lading discharges the carrier's obligation to deliver.

§ 7—504. **Rights Acquired in the Absence of Due Negotiation; Effect of Diversion; Seller's Stoppage of Delivery.**

(1) A transferee of a document, whether negotiable or non-negotiable, to whom the document has been delivered but not duly negotiated, acquires the title and rights which his transferor had or had actual authority to convey.

(2) In the case of a non-negotiable document, until but not after the bailee receives notification of the transfer, the rights of the transferee may be defeated

(a) by those creditors of the transferor who could treat the sale as void under Section 2—402; or

(b) by a buyer from the transferor in ordinary course of business if the bailee has delivered the goods to the buyer or received notification of his rights; or

(c) as against the bailee by good faith dealings of the bailee with the transferor.

(3) A diversion or other change of shipping instructions by the consignor in a non-negotiable bill of lading which causes the bailee not to deliver to the consignee defeats the consignee's title to the goods if they have been delivered to a buyer in ordinary course of business and in any event defeats the consignee's rights against the bailee.

(4) Delivery pursuant to a non-negotiable document may be stopped by a seller under Section 2—705, and subject to the requirement of due notification there provided. A bailee honoring the seller's instructions is entitled to be indemnified by the seller against any resulting loss or expense.

§ 7—505. **Indorser Not a Guarantor for Other Parties.**

The indorsement of a document of title issued by a bailee does not make the indorser liable for any default by the bailee or by previous indorsers.

§ 7—506. **Delivery Without Indorsement: Right to Compel Indorsement.**

The transferee of a negotiable document of title has a specifically enforceable right to have his transferor supply any necessary indorsement but the transfer becomes a negotiation only as of the time the indorsement is supplied.

§ 7—507. **Warranties on Negotiation or Transfer of Receipt or Bill.**

Where a person negotiates or transfers a document of title for value otherwise than as a mere intermediary under the next following section, then unless otherwise agreed he warrants to his immediate purchaser only in addition to any warranty made in selling the goods

(a) that the document is genuine; and

(b) that he has no knowledge of any fact which would impair its validity or worth; and

(c) that his negotiation or transfer is rightful and fully effective with respect to the title to the document and the goods it represents.

§ 7—508. **Warranties of Collecting Bank as to Documents.**

A collecting bank or other intermediary known to be entrusted with documents on behalf of another or with collection of a draft or other claim against delivery of documents warrants by such delivery of the documents only its own good faith and authority. This rule applies even though the intermediary has purchased or made advances against the claim or draft to be collected.

§ 7—509. **Receipt or Bill: When Adequate Compliance With Commercial Contract.**

The question whether a document is adequate to fulfill the obligations of a contract for sale or the conditions of a credit is governed by the Articles on Sales (Article 2) and on Letters of Credit (Article 5).

Part 6 **Warehouse Receipts and Bills of Lading: Miscellaneous Provisions**

§ 7—601. **Lost and Missing Documents.**

(1) If a document has been lost, stolen or destroyed, a

court may order delivery of the goods or issuance of a substitute document and the bailee may without liability to any person comply with such order. If the document was negotiable the claimant must post security approved by the court to indemnify any person who may suffer loss as a result of non-surrender of the document. If the document was not negotiable, such security may be required at the discretion of the court. The court may also in its discretion order payment of the bailee's reasonable costs and counsel fees.

(2) A bailee who without court order delivers goods to a person claiming under a missing negotiable document is liable to any person injured thereby, and if the delivery is not in good faith becomes liable for conversion. Delivery in good faith is not conversion if made in accordance with a filed classification or tariff or, where no classification or tariff is filed, if the claimant posts security with the bailee in an amount at least double the value of the goods at the time of posting to indemnify any person injured by the delivery who files a notice of claim within one year after the delivery.

§ 7—602. **Attachment of Goods Covered by a Negotiable Document.**

Except where the document was originally issued upon delivery of the goods by a person who had no power to dispose of them, no lien attaches by virtue of any judicial process to goods in the possession of a bailee for which a negotiable document of title is outstanding unless the document be first surrendered to the bailee or its negotiation enjoined, and the bailee shall not be compelled to deliver the goods pursuant to process until the document is surrendered to him or impounded by the court. One who purchases the document for value without notice of the process or injunction takes free of the lien imposed by judicial process.

§ 7—603. **Conflicting Claims; Interpleader.**

If more than one person claims title or possession of the goods, the bailee is excused from delivery until he has had a reasonable time to ascertain the validity of the adverse claims or to bring an action to compel all claimants to interplead and may compel such interpleader, either in defending an action for non-delivery of the goods, or by original action, whichever is appropriate.

Article 8
INVESTMENT SECURITIES

Part 1 **Short Title and General Matters**

§ 8—101. **Short Title.**

This Article shall be known and may be cited as Uniform Commercial Code—Investment Securities.

§ 8—102. **Definitions and Index of Definitions.**

(1) In this Article, unless the context otherwise requires:

(a) A "certificated security" is a share, participation, or other interest in property of or an enterprise of the issuer or an obligation of the issuer which is

(i) represented by an instrument issued in bearer or registered form;

(ii) of a type commonly dealt in on securities exchanges or markets or commonly recognized in any area in which it is issued or dealt in as a medium for investment; and

(iii) either one of a class or series or by its terms divisible into a class or series of shares, participations, interests, or obligations.

(b) An "uncertificated security" is a share, participation, or other interest in property or an enterprise of the issuer or an obligation of the issuer which is

(i) not represented by an instrument and the transfer of which is registered upon books maintained for that purpose by or on behalf of the issuer;

(ii) of a type commonly dealt in on securities exchanges or markets; and

(iii) either one of a class or series or by its terms divisible into a class or series of shares, participations, interests, or obligations.

(c) A "security" is either a certificated or an uncertificated security. If a security is certificated, the terms "security" and "certificated security" may mean either the intangible interest, the instrument representing that interest, or both, as the context requires. A writing that is a certificated security is governed by this Article and not by Article 3, even though it also meets the requirements of that Article. This Article does not apply to money. If a certificated security has been retained by or surrendered to the issuer or its transfer agent for reasons other than registration of transfer, other temporary purpose, payment, exchange, or acquisition by the issuer, that security shall be treated as an uncertificated security for purposes of this Article.

(d) A certificated security is in "registered form" if

(i) it specifies a person entitled to the security or the rights it represents; and

(ii) its transfer may be registered upon books maintained for that purpose by or on behalf of the issuer, or the security so states.

(e) A certificated security is in "bearer form" if it runs to bearer according to its terms and not by reason of any indorsement.

(2) A "subsequent purchaser" is a person who takes other than by original issue.

(3) A "clearing corporation" is a corporation registered as a "clearing agency" under the federal securities laws or a corporation:

(a) at least 90 percent of whose capital stock is held by or for one or more organizations, none of which, other than a national securities exchange or association, holds in excess of 20 percent of the capital stock of the corporation, and each of which is

(i) subject to supervision or regulation pursuant to the provisions of federal or state banking laws or state insurance laws,

(ii) a broker or dealer or investment company registered under the federal securities laws, or

(iii) a national securities exchange or association registered under the federal securities laws; and

(b) any remaining capital stock of which is held by individuals who have purchased it at or prior to the time of their taking office as directors of the corporation and who have purchased only so much of the capital stock as is necessary to permit them to qualify as directors.

(4) A "custodian bank" is a bank or trust company that is supervised and examined by state or federal authority having supervision over banks and is acting as custodian for a clearing corporation.

(5) Other definitions applying to this Article or to specified Parts thereof and the sections in which they appear are:

"Adverse claim". Section 8—302.
"Bona fide purchaser". Section 8—302.
"Broker". Section 8—303.
"Debtor". Section 9—105.
"Financial intermediary". Section 8—313.
"Guarantee of the signature". Section 8—402.
"Initial transaction statement". Section 8—408.
"Instruction". Section 8—308.
"Intermediary bank". Section 4—105.
"Issuer". Section 8—201.
"Overissue". Section 8—104.
"Secured Party". Section 9—105.
"Security Agreement". Section 9—105.

(6) In addition, Article 1 contains general definitions and principles of construction and interpretation applicable throughout this Article.

Amended in 1962, 1973 and 1977.

§ 8—103. Issuer's Lien.

A lien upon a security in favor of an issuer thereof is valid against a purchaser only if:

(a) the security is certificated and the right of the issuer to the lien is noted conspicuously thereon; or

(b) the security is uncertificated and a notation of the right of the issuer to the lien is contained in the initial transaction statement sent to the purchaser or, if his interest is transferred to him other than by registration of transfer, pledge, or release, the initial transaction statement sent to the registered owner or the registered pledgee.

Amended in 1977.

§ 8—104. **Effect of Overissue; "Overissue".**

(1) The provisions of this Article which validate a security or compel its issue or reissue do not apply to the extent that validation, issue, or reissue would result in overissue; but if:

(a) an identical security which does not constitute an overissue is reasonably available for purchase, the person entitled to issue or validation may compel the issuer to purchase the security for him and either to deliver a certificated security or to register the transfer of an uncertificated security to him, against surrender of any certificated security he holds; or

(b) a security is not so available for purchase, the person entitled to issue or validation may recover from the issuer the price he or the last purchaser for value paid for it with interest from the date of his demand.

(2) "Overissue" means the issue of securities in excess of the amount the issuer has corporate power to issue.

Amended in 1977.

§ 8—105. **Certificated Securities Negotiable; Statements and Instructions Not Negotiable; Presumptions.**

(1) Certificated securities governed by this Article are negotiable instruments.

(2) Statements (Section 8—408), notices, or the like, sent by the issuer of uncertificated securities and instructions (Section 8—308) are neither negotiable instruments nor certificated securities.

(3) In any action on a security:

(a) unless specifically denied in the pleadings, each signature on a certificated security, in a necessary indorsement, on an initial transaction statement, or on an instruction, is admitted;

(b) if the effectiveness of a signature is put in issue, the burden of establishing it is on the party claiming under the signature, but the signature is presumed to be genuine or authorized;

(c) if signatures on a certificated security are admitted or established, production of the security entitles a holder to recover on it unless the defendant establishes a defense or a defect going to the validity of the security;

(d) if signatures on an initial transaction statement are admitted or established, the facts stated in the statement are presumed to be true as of the time of its issuance; and

(e) after it is shown that a defense or defect exists, the plaintiff has the burden of establishing that he or some person under whom he claims is a person against whom the defense or defect is ineffective (Section 8—202).

Amended in 1977.

§ 8—106. **Applicability.**

The law (including the conflict of laws rules) of the jurisdiction of organization of the issuer governs the validity of a security, the effectiveness of registration by the issuer, and the rights and duties of the issuer with respect to:

(a) registration of transfer of a certificated security;

(b) registration of transfer, pledge, or release of an uncertificated security; and

(c) sending of statements of uncertificated securities.

Amended in 1977.

§ 8—107. **Securities Transferable; Action for Price.**

(1) Unless otherwise agreed and subject to any applicable law or regulation respecting short sales, a person obligated to transfer securities may transfer any certificated security of the specified issue in bearer form or registered in the name of the transferee, or indorsed to him or in blank, or he may transfer an equivalent uncertificated security to the transferee or a person designated by the transferee.

(2) If the buyer fails to pay the price as it comes due under a contract of sale, the seller may recover the price of:

(a) certificated securities accepted by the buyer;

(b) uncertificated securities that have been transferred to the buyer or a person designated by the buyer; and

(c) other securities if efforts at their resale would be unduly burdensome or if there is no readily available market for their resale.

Amended in 1977.

§ 8—108. **Registration of Pledge and Release of Uncertificated Securities.**

A security interest in an uncertificated security may be evidenced by the registration of pledge to the secured party or a person designated by him. There can be no more than one registered pledge of an uncertificated security at any time. The registered owner of an uncertificated security is the person in whose name the security is registered, even if the security is subject to a registered pledge. The rights of a registered pledgee of an uncertificated security under this Article are terminated by the registration of release.

Added in 1977.

Part 2 Issue—Issuer

§ 8—201. **"Issuer"**

(1) With respect to obligations on or defenses to a security, "issuer" includes a person who:

(a) places or authorizes the placing of his name on a certificated security (otherwise than as authenticating trustee, registrar, transfer agent, or the like) to evidence that it represents a share, participation, or other interest in his property or in an enterprise, or to evidence his duty to perform an obligation represented by the certificated security;

(b) creates shares, participations, or other interests in his property or in an enterprise or undertakes obligations, which shares, participations, interests, or obligations are uncertificated securities;

(c) directly or indirectly creates fractional interests in his rights or property, which fractional interests are represented by certificated securities; or

(d) becomes responsible for or in place of any other person described as an issuer in this section.

(2) With respect to obligations on or defenses to a security, a guarantor is an issuer to the extent of his guaranty, whether or not his obligation is noted on a certificated security or on statements of uncertificated securities sent pursuant to Section 8—408.

(3) With respect to registration of transfer, pledge, or release (Part 4 of this Article), "issuer" means a person on whose behalf transfer books are maintained.

Amended in 1977.

§ 8—202. **Issuer's Responsibility and Defenses; Notice of Defect or Defense.**

(1) Even against a purchaser for value and without notice, the terms of a security include:

(a) if the security is certificated, those stated on the security;

(b) if the security is uncertificated, those contained in the initial transaction statement sent to such purchaser or, if his interest is transferred to him other than by registration of transfer, pledge, or release, the initial transaction statement sent to the registered owner or registered pledgee; and

(c) those made part of the security by reference, on the certificated security or in the initial transaction statement, to another instrument, indenture, or document or to a constitution, statute, ordinance, rule, regulation, order or the like, to the extent that the terms referred to do not conflict with the terms stated on the certificated security or contained in the statement. A reference under this paragraph does not of itself charge a purchaser for value with notice of a defect going to the validity of the security, even though the certificated security or statement expressly states that a person accepting it admits notice.

(2) A certificated security in the hands of a purchaser for value or an uncertificated security as to which an initial transaction statement has been sent to a purchaser for value, other than a security issued by a government or governmental agency or unit, even though issued with a defect going to its validity, is valid with respect to the purchaser if he is without notice of the particular defect unless the defect involves a violation of constitutional provisions, in which case the security is valid with respect to a subsequent purchaser for value and without notice of

the defect. This subsection applies to an issuer that is a government or governmental agency or unit only if either there has been substantial compliance with the legal requirements governing the issue or the issuer has received a substantial consideration for the issue as a whole or for the particular security and a stated purpose of the issue is one for which the issuer has power to borrow money or issue the security.

(3) Except as provided in the case of certain unauthorized signatures (Section 8—205), lack of genuineness of a certificated security or an initial transaction statement is a complete defense, even against a purchaser for value and without notice.

(4) All other defenses of the issuer of a certificated or uncertificated security, including nondelivery and conditional delivery of a certificated security, are ineffective against a purchaser for value who has taken without notice of the particular defense.

(5) Nothing in this section shall be construed to affect the right of a party to a "when, as and if issued" or a "when distributed" contract to cancel the contract in the event of a material change in the character of the security that is the subject of the contract or in the plan or arrangement pursuant to which the security is to be issued or distributed.

Amended in 1977.

§ 8—203. **Staleness as Notice of Defects or Defenses.**

(1) After an act or event creating a right to immediate performance of the principal obligation represented by a certificated security or that sets a date on or after which the security is to be presented or surrendered for redemption or exchange, a purchaser is charged with notice of any defect in its issue or defense of the issuer if:

(a) the act or event is one requiring the payment of money, the delivery of certificated securities, the registration of transfer of uncertificated securities, or any of these on presentation or surrender of the certificated security, the funds or securities are available on the date set for payment or exchange, and he takes the security more than one year after that date; and

(b) the act or event is not covered by paragraph (a) and he takes the security more than 2 years after the date set for surrender or presentation or the date on which performance became due.

(2) A call that has been revoked is not within subsection (1).

Amended in 1977.

§ 8—204. **Effect of Issuer's Restrictions on Transfer.**

A restriction on transfer of a security imposed by the issuer, even if otherwise lawful, is ineffective against any person without actual knowledge of it unless:

(a) the security is certificated and the restriction is noted conspicuously thereon; or

(b) the security is uncertificated and a notation of the restriction is contained in the initial transaction statement sent to the person or, if his interest is transferred to him other than by registration of transfer, pledge, or release, the initial transaction statement sent to the registered owner or the registered pledgee.

Amended in 1977.

§ 8—205. **Effect of Unauthorized Signature on Certificated Security or Initial Transaction Statement.**

An unauthorized signature placed on a certificated security prior to or in the course of issue or placed on an initial transaction statement is ineffective, but the signature is effective in favor of a purchaser for value of the certificated security or a purchaser for value of an uncertificated security to whom the initial transaction statement has been sent, if the purchaser is without notice of the lack of authority and the signing has been done by:

(a) an authenticating trustee, registrar, transfer agent, or other person entrusted by the issuer with the signing of the security, of similar securities, or of initial transaction statements or the immediate preparation for signing of any of them; or

(b) an employee of the issuer, or of any of the foregoing, entrusted with responsible handling of the security or initial transaction statement.

Amended in 1977.

§ 8—206. **Completion or Alteration of Certificated Security or Initial Transaction Statement.**

(1) If a certificated security contains the signatures necessary to its issue or transfer but is incomplete in any other respect:

(a) any person may complete it by filling in the blanks as authorized; and

(b) even though the blanks are incorrectly filled in, the security as completed is enforceable by a purchaser who took it for value and without notice of the incorrectness.

(2) A complete certificated security that has been improperly altered, even though fraudulently, remains enforceable, but only according to its original terms.

(3) If an initial transaction statement contains the signatures necessary to its validity, but is incomplete in any other respect:

(a) any person may complete it by filling in the blanks as authorized; and

(b) even though the blanks are incorrectly filled in, the statement as completed is effective in favor of the person to whom it is sent if he purchased the security referred to therein for value and without notice of the incorrectness.

(4) A complete initial transaction statement that has been improperly altered, even though fraudulently, is effective in favor of a purchaser to whom it has been sent, but only according to its original terms.

Amended in 1977.

§ 8—207. **Rights and Duties of Issuer With Respect to Registered Owners and Registered Pledgees.**

(1) Prior to due presentment for registration of transfer of a certificated security in registered form, the issuer or indenture trustee may treat the registered owner as the person exclusively entitled to vote, to receive notifications, and otherwise to exercise all the rights and powers of an owner.

(2) Subject to the provisions of subsections (3), (4), and (6), the issuer or indenture trustee may treat the registered owner of an uncertificated security as the person exclusively entitled to vote, to receive notifications, and otherwise to exercise all the rights and powers of an owner.

(3) The registered owner of an uncertificated security that is subject to a registered pledge is not entitled to registration of transfer prior to the due presentment to the issuer of a release instruction. The exercise of conversion rights with respect to a convertible uncertificated security is a transfer within the meaning of this section.

(4) Upon due presentment of a transfer instruction from the registered pledgee of an uncertificated security, the issuer shall:

(a) register the transfer of the security to the new owner free of pledge, if the instruction specifies a new owner (who may be the registered pledgee) and does not specify a pledgee;

(b) register the transfer of the security to the new owner subject to the interest of the existing pledgee, if the instruction specifies a new owner and the existing pledgee; or

(c) register the release of the security from the existing pledge and register the pledge of the security to the other pledgee, if the instruction specifies the existing owner and another pledgee.

(5) Continuity of perfection of a security interest is not broken by registration of transfer under subsection (4)(b) or by registration of release and pledge under subsection (4)(c), if the security interest is assigned.

(6) If an uncertificated security is subject to a registered pledge:

(a) any uncertificated securities issued in exchange for or distributed with respect to the pledged security shall be registered subject to the pledge;

(b) any certificated securities issued in exchange for or distributed with respect to the pledged security shall be delivered to the registered pledgee; and

(c) any money paid in exchange for or in redemption of part or all of the security shall be paid to the registered pledgee.

(7) Nothing in this Article shall be construed to affect the liability of the registered owner of a security for calls, assessments, or the like.

Amended in 1977.

§ 8—208. **Effect of Signature of Authenticating Trustee, Registrar, or Transfer Agent.**

(1) A person placing his signature upon a certificated

security or an initial transaction statement as authenticating trustee, registrar, transfer agent, or the like, warrants to a purchaser for value of the certificated security or a purchaser for value of an uncertificated security to whom the initial transaction statement has been sent, if the purchaser is without notice of the particular defect, that:

(a) the certificated security or initial transaction statement is genuine;

(b) his own participation in the issue or registration of the transfer, pledge, or release of the security is within his capacity and within the scope of the authority received by him from the issuer; and

(c) he has reasonable grounds to believe the security is in the form and within the amount the issuer is authorized to issue.

(2) Unless otherwise agreed, a person by so placing his signature does not assume responsibility for the validity of the security in other respects.

Amended in 1962 and 1977.

Part 3 Transfer

§ 8—301. **Rights Acquired by Purchaser.**

(1) Upon transfer of a security to a purchaser (Section 8—313), the purchaser acquires the rights in the security which his transferor had or had actual authority to convey unless the purchaser's rights are limited by Section 8—302(4).

(2) A transferee of a limited interest acquires rights only to the extent of the interest transferred. The creation or release of a security interest in a security is the transfer of a limited interest in that security.

Amended in 1977.

§ 8—302. **"Bona Fide Purchaser"; "Adverse Claim"; Title Acquired by Bona Fide Purchaser.**

(1) A "bona fide purchaser" is a purchaser for value in good faith and without notice of any adverse claim:

(a) who takes delivery of a certificated security in

bearer form or in registered form, issued or indorsed to him or in blank;

(b) to whom the transfer, pledge, or release of an uncertificated security is registered on the books of the issuer; or

(c) to whom a security is transferred under the provisions of paragraph (c), (d)(i), or (g) of Section 8—313(1).

Amended in 1977.

§ 8—303. **"Broker".**

"Broker" means a person engaged for all or part of his time in the business of buying and selling securities, who in the transaction concerned acts for, buys a security from, or sells a security to, a customer. Nothing in this Article determines the capacity in which a person acts for purposes of any other statute or rule to which the person is subject.

§ 8—304. **Notice to Purchaser of Adverse Claims.**

(1) A purchaser (including a broker for the seller or buyer, but excluding an intermediary bank) of a certificated security is charged with notice of adverse claims if:

(a) the security, whether in bearer or registered form, has been indorsed "for collection" or "for surrender" or for some other purpose not involving transfer; or

(b) the security is in bearer form and has on it an unambiguous statement that it is the property of a person other than the transferor. The mere writing of a name on a security is not such a statement.

(2) A purchaser (including a broker for the seller or buyer, but excluding an intermediary bank) to whom the transfer, pledge, or release of an uncertificated security is registered is charged with notice of adverse claims as to which the issuer has a duty under Section 8—403(4) at the time of registration and which are noted in the initial transaction statement sent to the purchaser or, if his interest is transferred to him other than by registration of transfer, pledge, or release, the initial transaction statement sent to the registered owner or the registered pledgee.

(3) The fact that the purchaser (including a broker for

the seller or buyer) of a certificated or uncertificated security has notice that the security is held for a third person or is registered in the name of or indorsed by a fiduciary does not create a duty of inquiry into the rightfulness of the transfer or constitute constructive notice of adverse claims. However, if the purchaser (excluding an intermediary bank) has knowledge that the proceeds are being used or the transaction is for the individual benefit of the fiduciary or otherwise in breach of duty, the purchaser is charged with notice of adverse claims.

Amended in 1977.

§ 8—305. **Staleness as Notice of Adverse Claims.**

An act or event that creates a right to immediate performance of the principal obligation represented by a certificated security or sets a date on or after which a certificated security is to be presented or surrendered for redemption or exchange does not itself constitute any notice of adverse claims except in the case of a transfer:

(a) after one year from any date set for presentment or surrender for redemption or exchange; or

(b) after 6 months from any date set for payment of money against presentation or surrender of the security if funds are available for payment on that date.

Amended in 1977.

§ 8—306. **Warranties on Presentment and Transfer of Certificated Securities; Warranties of Originators of Instructions.**

(1) A person who presents a certificated security for registration of transfer or for payment or exchange warrants to the issuer that he is entitled to the registration, payment, or exchange. But, a purchaser for value and without notice of adverse claims who receives a new, reissued, or re-registered certificated security on registration of transfer or receives an initial transaction statement confirming the registration of transfer of an equivalent uncertificated security to him warrants only that he has no knowledge of any unauthorized signature (Section 8—311) in a necessary indorsement.

(2) A person by transferring a certificated security to a purchaser for value warrants only that:

(a) his transfer is effective and rightful;

(b) the security is genuine and has not been materially altered; and

(c) he knows of no fact which might impair the validity of the security.

(3) If a certificated security is delivered by an intermediary known to be entrusted with delivery of the security on behalf of another or with collection of a draft or other claim against delivery, the intermediary by delivery warrants only his own good faith and authority, even though he has purchased or made advances against the claim to be collected against the delivery.

(4) A pledgee or other holder for security who redelivers a certificated security received, or after payment and on order of the debtor delivers that security to a third person, makes only the warranties of an intermediary under subsection (3).

(5) A person who originates an instruction warrants to the issuer that:

(a) he is an appropriate person to originate the instruction; and

(b) at the time the instruction is presented to the issuer he will be entitled to the registration of transfer, pledge, or release.

(6) A person who originates an instruction warrants to any person specially guaranteeing his signature (subsection 8—312(3)) that:

(a) he is an appropriate person to originate the instruction; and

(b) at the time the instruction is presented to the issuer

(i) he will be entitled to the registration of transfer, pledge, or release; and

(ii) the transfer, pledge, or release requested in the instruction will be registered by the issuer free from all liens, security interests, restrictions, and claims other than those specified in the instruction.

(7) A person who originates an instruction warrants to a purchaser for value and to any person guaranteeing the instruction (Section 8—312(6)) that:

(a) he is an appropriate person to originate the instruction;

(b) the uncertificated security referred to therein is valid; and

(c) at the time the instruction is presented to the issuer

(i) the transferor will be entitled to the registration of transfer, pledge, or release;

(ii) the transfer, pledge, or release requested in the instruction will be registered by the issuer free from all liens, security interests, restrictions, and claims other than those specified in the instruction; and

(iii) the requested transfer, pledge, or release will be rightful.

(8) If a secured party is the registered pledgee or the registered owner of an uncertificated security, a person who originates an instruction of release or transfer to the debtor or, after payment and on order of the debtor, a transfer instruction to a third person, warrants to the debtor or the third person only that he is an appropriate person to originate the instruction and, at the time the instruction is presented to the issuer, the transferor will be entitled to the registration of release or transfer. If a transfer instruction to a third person who is a purchaser for value is originated on order of the debtor, the debtor makes to the purchaser the warranties of paragraphs (b), (c)(ii) and (c)(iii) of subsection (7).

(9) A person who transfers an uncertificated security to a purchaser for value and does not originate an instruction in connection with the transfer warrants only that:

(a) his transfer is effective and rightful; and

(b) the uncertificated security is valid.

(10) A broker gives to his customer and to the issuer and a purchaser the applicable warranties provided in this section and has the rights and privileges of a purchaser under this section. The warranties of and in favor of the broker, acting as an agent are in addition to applicable warranties given by and in favor of his customer.

Amended in 1962 and 1977.

§ 8—307. **Effect of Delivery Without Indorsement; Right to Compel Indorsement.**

If a certificated security in registered form has been delivered to a purchaser without a necessary indorsement he may become a bona fide purchaser only as of the time the indorsement is supplied; but against the

transferor, the transfer is complete upon delivery and the purchaser has a specifically enforceable right to have any necessary indorsement supplied.
Amended in 1977.

§ 8—308. **Indorsements; Instructions.**

(1) An indorsement of a certificated security in registered form is made when an appropriate person signs on it or on a separate document an assignment or transfer of the security or a power to assign or transfer it or his signature is written without more upon the back of the security.

(2) An indorsement may be in blank or special. An indorsement in blank includes an indorsement to bearer. A special indorsement specifies to whom the security is to be transferred, or who has power to transfer it. A holder may convert a blank indorsement into a special indorsement.

(3) An indorsement purporting to be only of part of a certificated security representing units intended by the issuer to be separately transferable is effective to the extent of the indorsement.

(4) An "instruction" is an order to the issuer of an uncertificated security requesting that the transfer, pledge, or release from pledge of the uncertificated security specified therein be registered.

(5) An instruction originated by an appropriate person is:

(a) a writing signed by an appropriate person; or

(b) a communication to the issuer in any form agreed upon in a writing signed by the issuer and an appropriate person.

If an instruction has been originated by an appropriate person but is incomplete in any other respect, any person may complete it as authorized and the issuer may rely on it as completed even though it has been completed incorrectly.

(6) "An appropriate person" in subsection (1) means the person specified by the certificated security or by special indorsement to be entitled to the security.

(7) "An appropriate person" in subsection (5) means:

(a) for an instruction to transfer or pledge an uncertificated security which is then not subject to a registered pledge, the registered owner; or

(b) for an instruction to transfer or release an

uncertificated security which is then subject to a registered pledge, the registered pledgee.

(8) In addition to the persons designated in subsections (6) and (7), "an appropriate person" in subsections (1) and (5) includes:

(a) if the person designated is described as a fiduciary but is no longer serving in the described capacity, either that person or his successor;

(b) if the persons designated are descirbed as more than one person as fiduciaries and one or more are no longer serving in the described capacity, the remaining fiduciary or fiduciaries, whether or not a successor has been appointed or qualified;

(c) if the person designated is an individual and is without capacity to act by virtue of death, incompetence, infancy, or otherwise, his executor, administrator, guardian, or like fiduciary;

(d) if the persons designated are described as more than one person as tenants by the entirety or with right of survivorship and by reason of death all cannot sign, the survivor or survivors;

(e) a person having power to sign under applicable law or controlling instrument; and

(f) to the extent that the person designated or any of the foregoing persons may act through an agent, his authorized agent.

(9) Unless otherwise agreed, the indorser of a certificated security by his indorsement or the originator of an instruction by his origination assumes no obligation that the security will be honored by the issuer but only the obligations provided in Section 8—306.

(10) Whether the person signing is appropriate is determined as of the date of signing and an indorsement made by or an instruction originated by him does not become unauthorized for the purposes of this Article by virtue of any subsequent change of circumstances.

(11) Failure of a fiduciary to comply with a controlling instrument or with the law of the state having jurisdiction of the fiduciary relationship, including any law requiring the fiduciary to obtain court approval of the transfer, pledge, or release, does not render his indorsement or an instruction originated by him unauthorized for the purposes of this Article.
Amended in 1962 and 1977.

§ 8—309. **Effect of Indorsement Without Delivery.**

An indorsement of a certificated security, whether special or in blank, does not constitute a transfer until delivery of the certificated security on which it appears or, if the indorsement is on a separate document, until delivery of both the document and the certificated security.
Amended in 1977.

§ 8—310. **Indorsement of Certificated Security in Bearer Form.**

An indorsement of a certificated security in bearer form may give notice of adverse claims (Section 8—304) but does not otherwise affect any right to registration the holder possesses.
Amended in 1977.

§ 8—311. **Effect of Unauthorized Indorsement or Instruction.**

Unless the owner or pledgee has ratified an unauthorized indorsement or instruction or is otherwise precluded from asserting its ineffectiveness:

(a) he may assert its ineffectiveness against the issuer or any purchaser, other than a purchaser for value and without notice of adverse claims, who has in good faith received a new, reissued, or re-registered certificated security on registration of transfer or received an initial transaction statement confirming the registration of transfer, pledge, or release of an equivalent uncertificated security to him; and

(b) an issuer who registers the transfer of a certificated security upon the unauthorized indorsement or who registers the transfer, pledge, or release of an uncertificated security upon the unauthorized instruction is subject to liability for improper registration (Section 8—404).
Amended in 1977.

§ 8—312. **Effect of Guaranteeing Signature, Indorsement or Instruction.**

(1) Any person guaranteeing a signature of an indorser of a certificated security warrants that at the time of signing:

(a) the signature was genuine;

(b) the signer was an appropriate person to indorse (Section 8—308); and

(c) the signer had legal capacity to sign.

(2) Any person guaranteeing a signature of the originator of an instruction warrants that at the time of signing:

(a) the signature was genuine;

(b) the signer was an appropriate person to originate the instruction (Section 8—308) if the person specified in the instruction as the registered owner or registered pledgee of the uncertificated security was, in fact, the registered owner or registered pledgee of the security, as to which fact the signature guarantor makes no warranty;

(c) the signer had legal capacity to sign; and

(d) the taxpayer identification number, if any, appearing on the instruction as that of the registered owner or registered pledgee was the taxpayer identification number of the signer or of the owner or pledgee for whom the signer was acting.

(3) Any person specially guaranteeing the signature of the originator of an instruction makes not only the warranties of a signature guarantor (subsection (2)) but also warrants that at the time the instruction is presented to the issuer:

(a) the person specified in the instruction as the registered owner or registered pledgee of the uncertificated security will be the registered owner or registered pledgee; and

(b) the transfer, pledge, or release of the uncertificated security requested in the instruction will be registered by the issuer free from all liens, security interests, restrictions, and claims other than those specified in the instruction.

(4) The guarantor under subsections (1) and (2) or the special guarantor under subsection (3) does not otherwise warrant the rightfulness of the particular transfer, pledge, or release.

(5) Any person guaranteeing an indorsement of a certificated security makes not only the warranties of a signature guarantor under subsection (1) but also warrants the rightfulness of the particular transfer in all respects.

(6) Any person guaranteeing an instruction request-

ing the transfer, pledge, or release of an uncertificated security makes not only the warranties of a special signature guarantor under subsection (3) but also warrants the rightfulness of the particular transfer, pledge, or release in all respects.

(7) No issuer may require a special guarantee of signature (subsection (3)), a guarantee of indorsement (subsection (5)), or a guarantee of instruction (subsection (6)) as a condition to registration of transfer, pledge, or release.

(8) The foregoing warranties are made to any person taking or dealing with the security in reliance on the guarantee, and the guarantor is liable to the person for any loss resulting from breach of the warranties. Amended in 1977.

§ 8—313. **When Transfer to Purchaser Occurs; Financial Intermediary as Bona Fide Purchaser; "Financial Intermediary".**

(1) Transfer of a security or a limited interest (including a security interest) therein to a purchaser occurs only:

(a) at the time he or a person designated by him acquires possession of a certificated security;

(b) at the time the transfer, pledge, or release of an uncertificated security is registered to him or a person designated by him;

(c) at the time his financial intermediary acquires possession of a certificated security specially indorsed to or issued in the name of the purchaser;

(d) at the time a financial intermediary, not a clearing corporation, sends him confirmation of the purchase and also by book entry or otherwise identifies as belonging to the purchaser

(i) a specific certificated security in the financial intermediary's possession;

(ii) a quantity of securities that constitute or are part of a fungible bulk of certificated securities in the financial intermediary's possession or of uncertificated securities registered in the name of the financial intermediary; or

(iii) a quantity of securities that constitute or are part of a fungible bulk of securities shown on the account of the financial intermediary on the books of another financial intermediary;

(e) with respect to an identified certificated security to be delivered while still in the possession of a third person, not a financial intermediary, at the time that person acknowledges that he holds for the purchaser;

(f) with respect to a specific uncertificated security the pledge or transfer of which has been registered to a third person, not a financial intermediary, at the time that person acknowledges that he holds for the purchaser;

(g) at the time appropriate entries to the account of the purchaser or a person designated by him on the books of a clearing corporation are made under Section 8—320;

(h) with respect to the transfer of a security interest where the debtor has signed a security agreement containing a description of the security, at the time a written notification, which, in the case of the creation of the security interest, is signed by the debtor (which may be a copy of the security agreement) or which, in the case of the release or assignment of the security interest created pursuant to this paragraph, is signed by the secured party, is received by

(i) a financial intermediary on whose books the interest of the transferor in the security appears;

(ii) a third person, not a financial intermediary, in possession of the security, if it is certificated;

(iii) a third person, not a financial intermediary, who is the registered owner of the security, if it is uncertificated and not subject to a registered pledge; or

(iv) a third person, not a financial intermediary, who is the registered pledgee of the security, if it is uncertificated and subject to a registered pledge;

(i) with respect to the transfer of a security interest where the transferor has signed a security agreement containing a description of the security, at the time new value is given by the secured party; or

(j) with respect to the transfer of a security interest where the secured party is a financial intermediary and the security has already been transferred to the financial intermediary under paragraphs (a), (b), (c), (d), or (g), at the time the transferor has signed a security agreement containing a description of the security and value is given by the secured party.

(2) The purchaser is the owner of a security held for him by a financial intermediary, but cannot be a bona fide purchaser of a security so held except in the circumstances specified in paragraphs (c), (d)(i), and (g) of subsection (1). If a security so held is part of a fungible bulk, as in the circumstances specified in paragraphs (d)(ii) and (d)(iii) of subsection (1), the purchaser is the owner of a proportionate property interest in the fungible bulk.

(3) Notice of an adverse claim received by the financial intermediary or by the purchaser after the financial intermediary takes delivery of a certificated security as a holder for value or after the transfer, pledge, or release of an uncertificated security has been registered free of the claim to a financial intermediary who has given value is not effective either as to the financial intermediary or as to the purchaser. However, as between the financial intermediary and the purchaser the purchaser may demand transfer of an equivalent security as to which no notice of adverse claim has been received.

(4) A "financial intermediary" is a bank, broker, clearing corporation, or other person (or the nominee of any of them) which in the ordinary course of its business maintains security accounts for its customers and is acting in that capacity. A financial intermediary may have a security interest in securities held in account for its customer.

Amended in 1962 and 1977.

§ 8—314. **Duty to Transfer, When Completed**

(1) Unless otherwise agreed, if a sale of a security is made on an exchange or otherwise through brokers:

(a) the selling customer fulfills his duty to transfer at the time he:

(i) places a certificated security in the possession of the selling broker or a person designated by the broker;

(ii) causes an uncertificated security to be registered in the name of the selling broker or a person designated by the broker;

(iii) if requested, causes an acknowledgment to be made to the selling broker that a certificated or uncertificated security is held for the broker; or

(iv) places in the possession of the selling broker or of a person designated by the broker a transfer instruction for an uncertificated security, providing the issuer does not refuse to register the requested transfer if the instruction is presented to the issuer for registration within 30 days thereafter; and

(b) the selling broker, including a correspondent broker acting for a selling customer, fulfills his duty to transfer at the time he:

(i) places a certificated security in the possession of the buying broker or a person designated by the buying broker;

(ii) causes an uncertificated security to be registered in the name of the buying broker or a person designated by the buying broker;

(iii) places in the possession of the buying broker or of a person designated by the buying broker a transfer instruction for an uncertificated security, providing the issuer does not refuse to register the requested transfer if the instruction is presented to the issuer for registration within 30 days thereafter; or

(iv) effects clearance of the sale in accordance with the rules of the exchange on which the transaction took place.

(2) Except as provided in this section or unless otherwise agreed, a transferor's duty to transfer a security under a contract of purchase is not fulfilled until he:

(a) places a certificated security in form to be negotiated by the purchaser in the possession of the purchaser or of a person designated by the purchaser;

(b) causes an uncertificated security to be registered in the name of the purchaser or a person designated by the purchaser; or

(c) if the purchaser requests, causes an acknowledgment to be made to the purchaser that a certificated or uncertificated security is held for the purchaser.

(3) Unless made on an exchange, a sale to a broker purchasing for his own account is within subsection (2) and not within subsection (1).

Amended in 1977.

§ 8—315. **Action Against Transferee Based Upon Wrongful Transfer**

(1) Any person against whom the transfer of a security is wrongful for any reason, including his incapacity, as against anyone except a bona fide purchaser, may:

(a) reclaim possession of the certificated security wrongfully transferred;

(b) obtain possession of any new certificated security representing all or part of the same rights;

(c) compel the origination of an instruction to transfer to him or a person designated by him an uncertificated security constituting all or part of the same rights; or

(d) have damages.

(2) If the transfer is wrongful because of an unauthorized indorsement of a certificated security, the owner may also reclaim or obtain possession of the security or a new certificated security, even from a bona fide purchaser, if the ineffectiveness of the purported indorsement can be asserted against him under the provisions of this Article on unauthorized indorsements (Section 8—311).

(3) The right to obtain or reclaim possession of a certificated security or to compel the origination of a transfer instruction may be specifically enforced and the transfer of a certificated or uncertificated security enjoined and a certificated security impounded pending the litigation.

Amended in 1977.

§ 8—316. **Purchaser's Right to Requisites for Registration of Transfer, Pledge, or Release on Books**

Unless otherwise agreed, the transferor of a certificated security or the transferor, pledgor, or pledgee of an uncertificated security on due demand must supply his purchaser with any proof of his authority to transfer, pledge, or release or with any other requisite necessary to obtain registration of the

transfer, pledge, or release of the security; but if the transfer, pledge, or release is not for value, a transferor, pledgor, or pledgee need not do so unless the purchaser furnishes the necessary expenses. Failure within a reasonable time to comply with a demand made gives the purchaser the right to reject or rescind the transfer, pledge, or release.
Amended in 1977.

§ 8—317. **Creditors' Rights**

(1) Subject to the exceptions in subsections (3) and (4), no attachment or levy upon a certificated security or any share or other interest represented thereby which is outstanding is valid until the security is actually seized by the officer making the attachment or levy, but a certificated security which has been surrendered to the issuer may be reached by a creditor by legal process at the issuer's chief executive office in the United States.

(2) An uncertificated security registered in the name of the debtor may not be reached by a creditor except by legal process at the issuer's chief executive office in the United States.

(3) The interest of a debtor in a certificated security that is in the possession of a secured party not a financial intermediary or in an uncertificated security registered in the name of a secured party not a financial intermediary (or in the name of a nominee of the secured party) may be reached by a creditor by legal process upon the secured party.

(4) The interest of a debtor in a certificated security that is in the possession of or registered in the name of a financial intermediary or in an uncertificated security registered in the name of a financial intermediary may be reached by a creditor by legal process upon the financial intermediary on whose books the interest of the debtor appears.

(5) Unless otherwise provided by law, a creditor's lien upon the interest of a debtor in a security obtained pursuant to subsection (3) or (4) is not a restraint on the transfer of the security, free of the lien, to a third party for new value; but in the event of a transfer, the lien applies to the proceeds of the transfer in the hands of the secured party or financial intermediary, subject to any claims having priority.

(6) A creditor whose debtor is the owner of a security is entitled to aid from courts of appropriate jurisdiction, by injunction or otherwise, in reaching the security or in satisfying the claim by means allowed at law or in equity in regard to property that cannot readily be reached by ordinary legal process.
Amended in 1977.

§ 8—318. **No Conversion by Good Faith Conduct**

An agent or bailee who in good faith (including observance of reasonable commercial standards if he is in the business of buying, selling, or otherwise dealing with securities) has received certificated securities and sold, pledged, or delivered them or has sold or caused the transfer or pledge of uncertificated securities over which he had control according to the instructions of his principal, is not liable for conversion or for participation in breach of fiduciary duty although the principal had no right so to deal with the securities.
Amended in 1977.

§ 8—319. **Statute of Frauds**

A contract for the sale of securities is not enforceable by way of action or defense unless:

(a) there is some writing signed by the party against whom enforcement is sought or by his authorized agent or broker, sufficient to indicate that a contract has been made for sale of a stated quantity of described securities at a defined or stated price;

(b) delivery of a certificated security or transfer instruction has been accepted, or transfer of an uncertificated security has been registered and the transferee has failed to send written objection to the issuer within 10 days after receipt of the initial transaction statement confirming the registration, or payment has been made, but the contract is enforceable under this provision only to the extent of the delivery, registration, or payment;

(c) within a reasonable time a writing in confirmation of the sale or purchase and sufficient against the sender under paragraph (a) has been received by the party against whom enforcement is sought and he has failed to send written objection to its contents within 10 days after its receipt; or

(d) the party against whom enforcement is sought admits in his pleading, testimony, or otherwise in court that a contract was made for the sale of a stated quantity of described securities at a defined or stated price.
Amended in 1977.

§ 8—320. **Transfer or Pledge Within Central Depository System**

(1) In addition to other methods, a transfer, pledge, or release of a security or any interest therein may be effected by the making of appropriate entries on the books of a clearing corporation reducing the account of the transferor, pledgor, or pledgee and increasing the account of the transferee, pledgee, or pledgor by the amount of the obligation or the number of shares or rights transferred, pledged, or released, if the security is shown on the account of a transferor, pledgor, or pledgee on the books of the clearing corporation; is subject to the control of the clearing corporation; and

    (a) if certificated,

        (i) is in the custody of the clearing corporation, another clearing corporation, a custodian bank, or a nominee of any of them; and

        (ii) is in bearer form or indorsed in blank by an appropriate person or registered in the name of the clearing corporation, a custodian bank, or a nominee of any of them; or

    (b) if uncertificated, is registered in the name of the clearing corporation, another clearing corporation, a custodian bank, or a nominee of any of them.

(2) Under this section entries may be made with respect to like securities or interests therein as a part of a fungible bulk and may refer merely to a quantity of a particular security without reference to the name of the registered owner, certificate or bond number, or the like, and, in appropriate cases, may be on a net basis taking into account other transfers, pledges, or releases of the same security.

(3) A transfer under this section is effective (Section 8—313) and the purchaser acquires the rights of the transferor (Section 8—301). A pledge or release under this section is the transfer of a limited interest. If a pledge or the creation of a security interest is intended, the security interest is perfected at the time when both value is given by the pledgee and the appropriate entries are made (Section 8—321). A transferee or pledgee under this section may be a bona fide purchaser (Section 8—302).

(4) A transfer or pledge under this section is not a registration of transfer under Part 4.

(5) That entries made on the books of the clearing

corporation as provided in subsection (1) are not appropriate does not affect the validity or effect of the entries or the liabilities or obligations of the clearing corporation to any person adversely affected thereby.

Added in 1962; amended in 1977.

§ 8—321. **Enforceability, Attachment, Perfection and Termination of Security Interests**

(1) A security interest in a security is enforceable and can attach only if it is transferred to the secured party or a person designated by him pursuant to a provision of Section 8—313(1).

(2) A security interest so transferred pursuant to agreement by a transferor who has rights in the security to a transferee who has given value is a perfected security interest, but a security interest that has been transferred solely under paragraph (i) of Section 8—313(1) becomes unperfected after 21 days unless, within that time, the requirements for transfer under any other provision of Section 8—313(1) are satisfied.

(3) A security interest in a security is subject to the provisions of Article 9, but:

    (a) no filing is required to perfect the security interest; and

    (b) no written security agreement signed by the debtor is necessary to make the security interest enforceable, except as provided in paragraph (h), (i), or (j) of Section 8—313(1). The secured party has the rights and duties provided under Section 9—207, to the extent they are applicable, whether or not the security is certificated, and, if certificated, whether or not it is in his possession.

(4) Unless otherwise agreed, a security interest in a security is terminated by transfer to the debtor or a person designated by him pursuant to a provision of Section 8—313(1). If a security is thus transferred, the security interest, if not terminated, becomes unperfected unless the security is certificated and is delivered to the debtor for the purpose of ultimate sale or exchange or presentation, collection, renewal, or registration of transfer. In that case, the security interest becomes unperfected after 21 days unless, within that time, the security (or securities for which it has been exchanged) is transferred to the secured

party or a person designated by him pursuant to a provision of Section 8—313(1).

Added in 1977.

Part 4 Registration

§ 8—401. **Duty of Issuer to Register Transfer, Pledge, or Release**

(1) If a certificated security in registered form is presented to the issuer with a request to register transfer or an instruction is presented to the issuer with a request to register transfer, pledge, or release, the issuer shall register the transfer, pledge, or release as requested if:

(a) the security is indorsed or the instruction was originated by the appropriate person or persons (Section 8—308);

(b) reasonable assurance is given that those indorsements or instructions are genuine and effective (Section 8—402);

(c) the issuer has no duty as to adverse claims or has discharged the duty (Section 8—403);

(d) any applicable law relating to the collection of taxes has been complied with; and

(e) the transfer, pledge, or release is in fact rightful or is to a bona fide purchaser.

(2) If an issuer is under a duty to register a transfer, pledge, or release of a security, the issuer is also liable to the person presenting a certificated security or an instruction for registration or his principal for loss resulting from any unreasonable delay in registration or from failure or refusal to register the transfer, pledge, or release.

Amended in 1977.

§ 8—402. **Assurance that Indorsements and Instructions Are Effective**

(1) The issuer may require the following assurance that each necessary indorsement of a certificated security or each instruction (Section 8—308) is genuine and effective:

(a) in all cases, a guarantee of the signature (Section 8—312(1) or (2)) of the person indorsing a certificated security or originating an instruction including, in the case of an instruction, a warranty of the taxpayer identification number or, in the

absence thereof, other reasonable assurance of identity;

(b) if the indorsement is made or the instruction is originated by an agent, appropriate assurance of authority to sign;

(c) if the indorsement is made or the instruction is originated by a fiduciary, appropriate evidence of appointment or incumbency;

(d) if there is more than one fiduciary, reasonable assurance that all who are required to sign have done so; and

(e) if the indorsement is made or the instruction is originated by a person not covered by any of the foregoing, assurance appropriate to the case corresponding as nearly as may be to the foregoing.

(2) A "guarantee of the signature" in subsection (1) means a guarantee signed by or on behalf of a person reasonably believed by the issuer to be responsible. The issuer may adopt standards with respect to responsibility if they are not manifestly unreasonable.

(3) "Appropriate evidence of appointment or incumbency" in subsection (1) means:

(a) in the case of a fiduciary appointed or qualified by a court, a certificate issued by or under the direction or supervision of that court or an officer thereof and dated within 60 days before the date of presentation for transfer, pledge, or release; or

(b) in any other case, a copy of a document showing the appointment or a certificate issued by or on behalf of a person reasonably believed by the issuer to be responsible or, in the absence of that document or certificate, other evidence reasonably deemed by the issuer to be appropriate. The issuer may adopt standards with respect to the evidence if they are not manifestly unreasonable. The issuer is not charged with notice of the contents of any document obtained pursuant to this paragraph (b) except to the extent that the contents relate directly to the appointment or incumbency.

(4) The issuer may elect to require reasonable assurance beyond that specified in this section, but if it does so and, for a purpose other than that specified in

subsection (3)(b), both requires and obtains a copy of a will, trust, indenture, articles of co-partnership, by-laws, or other controlling instrument, it is charged with notice of all matters contained therein affecting the transfer, pledge, or release.

Amended in 1977.

§ 8—403. Issuer's Duty as to Adverse Claims

(1) An issuer to whom a certificated security is presented for registration shall inquire into adverse claims if:

(a) a written notification of an adverse claim is received at a time and in a manner affording the issuer a reasonable opportunity to act on it prior to the issuance of a new, reissued, or re-registered certificated security, and the notification identifies the claimant, the registered owner, and the issue of which the security is a part, and provides an address for communications directed to the claimant; or

(b) the issuer is charged with notice of an adverse claim from a controlling instrument it has elected to require under Section 8—402(4).

(2) The issuer may discharge any duty of inquiry by any reasonable means, including notifying an adverse claimant by registered or certified mail at the address furnished by him or, if there be no such address, at his residence or regular place of business that the certificated security has been presented for registration of transfer by a named person, and that the transfer will be registered unless within 30 days from the date of mailing the notification, either:

(a) an appropriate restraining order, injunction, or other process issues from a court of competent jurisdiction; or

(b) there is filed with the issuer an indemnity bond, sufficient in the issuer's judgment to protect the issuer and any transfer agent, registrar, or other agent of the issuer involved from any loss it or they may suffer by complying with the adverse claim.

(3) Unless an issuer is charged with notice of an adverse claim from a controlling instrument which it has elected to require under Section 8—402(4) or receives notification of an adverse claim under subsection (1), if a certificated security presented for registration is indorsed by the appropriate person or persons the issuer is under no duty to inquire into adverse claims. In particular:

(a) an issuer registering a certificated security in the name of a person who is a fiduciary or who is described as a fiduciary is not bound to inquire into the existence, extent, or correct description of the fiduciary relationship; and thereafter the issuer may assume without inquiry that the newly registered owner continues to be the fiduciary until the issuer receives written notice that the fiduciary is no longer acting as such with respect to the particular security;

(b) an issuer registering transfer on an indorsement by a fiduciary is not bound to inquire whether the transfer is made in compliance with a controlling instrument or with the law of the state having jurisdiction of the fiduciary relationship, including any law requiring the fiduciary to obtain court approval of the transfer; and

(c) the issuer is not charged with notice of the contents of any court record or file or other recorded or unrecorded document even though the document is in its possession and even though the transfer is made on the indorsement of a fiduciary to the fiduciary himself or to his nominee.

(4) An issuer is under no duty as to adverse claims with respect to an uncertificated security except:

(a) claims embodied in a restraining order, injunction, or other legal process served upon the issuer if the process was served at a time and in a manner affording the issuer a reasonable opportunity to act on it in accordance with the requirements of subsection (5);

(b) claims of which the issuer has received a written notification from the registered owner or the registered pledgee if the notification was received at a time and in a manner affording the issuer a reasonable opportunity to act on it in accordance with the requirements of subsection (5);

(c) claims (including restrictions on transfer not imposed by the issuer) to which the registration of transfer to the present registered owner was subject and were so noted in the initial transaction statement sent to him; and

(d) claims as to which an issuer is charged with notice from a controlling instrument it has elected to require under Section 8—402(4).

(5) If the issuer of an uncertificated security is under a duty as to an adverse claim, he discharges that duty by:

(a) including a notation of the claim in any statements sent with respect to the security under Sections 8—408(3), (6), and (7); and

(b) refusing to register the transfer or pledge of the security unless the nature of the claim does not preclude transfer or pledge subject thereto.

(6) If the transfer or pledge of the security is registered subject to an adverse claim, a notation of the claim must be included in the initial transaction statement and all subsequent statements sent to the transferee and pledgee under Section 8—408.

(7) Notwithstanding subsections (4) and (5), if an uncertificated security was subject to a registered pledge at the time the issuer first came under a duty as to a particular adverse claim, the issuer has no duty as to that claim if transfer of the security is requested by the registered pledgee or an appropriate person acting for the registered pledgee unless:

(a) the claim was embodied in legal process which expressly provides otherwise;

(b) the claim was asserted in a written notification from the registered pledgee;

(c) the claim was one as to which the issuer was charged with notice from a controlling instrument it required under Section 8—402(4) in connection with the pledgee's request for transfer; or

(d) the transfer requested is to the registered owner.

Amended in 1977.

§ 8—404. **Liability and Non-Liability for Registration**

(1) Except as provided in any law relating to the collection of taxes, the issuer is not liable to the owner, pledgee, or any other person suffering loss as a result of the registration of a transfer, pledge, or release of a security if:

(a) there were on or with a certificated security the necessary indorsements or the issuer had received an instruction originated by an appropriate person (Section 8—308); and

(b) the issuer had no duty as to adverse claims or has discharged the duty (Section 8—403).

(2) If an issuer has registered a transfer of a certificated security to a person not entitled to it, the issuer on demand shall deliver a like security to the true owner unless:

(a) the registration was pursuant to subsection (1);

(b) the owner is precluded from asserting any claim for registering the transfer under Section 8—405(1); or

(c) the delivery would result in overissue, in which case the issuer's liability is governed by Section 8—104.

(3) If an issuer has improperly registered a transfer, pledge, or release of an uncertificated security, the issuer on demand from the injured party shall restore the records as to the injured party to the condition that would have obtained if the improper registration had not been made unless:

(a) the registration was pursuant to subsection (1); or

(b) the registration would result in overissue, in which case the issuer's liability is governed by Section 8—104.

Amended in 1977.

§ 8—405. **Lost, Destroyed, and Stolen Certificated Securities**

(1) If a certificated security has been lost, apparently destroyed, or wrongfully taken, and the owner fails to notify the issuer of that fact within a reasonable time after he has notice of it and the issuer registers a transfer of the security before receiving notification, the owner is precluded from asserting against the issuer any claim for registering the transfer under Section 8—404 or any claim to a new security under this section.

(2) If the owner of a certificated security claims that the security has been lost, destroyed, or wrongfully taken, the issuer shall issue a new certificated security or, at the option of the issuer, an equivalent

uncertificated security in place of the original security if the owner:

(a) so requests before the issuer has notice that the security has been acquired by a bona fide purchaser;

(b) files with the issuer a sufficient indemnity bond; and

(c) satisfies any other reasonable requirements imposed by the issuer.

(3) If, after the issue of a new certificated or uncertificated security, a bona fide purchaser of the original certificated security presents it for registration of transfer, the issuer shall register the transfer unless registration would result in overissue, in which event the issuer's liability is governed by Section 8—104. In addition to any rights on the indemnity bond, the issuer may recover the new certificated security from the person to whom it was issued or any person taking under him except a bona fide purchaser or may cancel the uncertificated security unless a bona fide purchaser or any person taking under a bona fide purchaser is then the registered owner or registered pledgee thereof.

Amended in 1977.

§ 8—406. Duty of Authenticating Trustee, Transfer Agent, or Registrar

(1) If a person acts as authenticating trustee, transfer agent, registrar, or other agent for an issuer in the registration of transfers of its certificated securities or in the registration of transfers, pledges, and releases of its uncertificated securities, in the issue of new securities, or in the cancellation of surrendered securities:

(a) he is under a duty to the issuer to exercise good faith and due diligence in performing his functions; and

(b) with regard to the particular functions he performs, he has the same obligation to the holder or owner of a certificated security or to the owner or pledgee of an uncertificated security and has the same rights and privileges as the issuer has in regard to those functions.

(2) Notice to an authenticating trustee, transfer agent, registrar or other agent is notice to the issuer with respect to the functions performed by the agent.

Amended in 1977.

§ 8—407. Exchangeability of Securities

(1) No issuer is subject to the requirements of this section unless it regularly maintains a system for issuing the class of securities involved under which both certificated and uncertificated securities are regularly issued to the category of owners, which includes the person in whose name the new security is to be registered.

(2) Upon surrender of a certificated security with all necessary indorsements and presentation of a written request by the person surrendering the security, the issuer, if he has no duty as to adverse claims or has discharged the duty (Section 8—403), shall issue to the person or a person designated by him an equivalent uncertificated security subject to all liens, restrictions, and claims that were noted on the certificated security.

(3) Upon receipt of a transfer instruction originated by an appropriate person who so requests, the issuer of an uncertificated security shall cancel the uncertificated security and issue an equivalent certificated security on which must be noted conspicuously any liens and restrictions of the issuer and any adverse claims (as to which the issuer has a duty under Section 8—403(4)) to which the uncertificated security was subject. The certificated security shall be registered in the name of and delivered to:

(a) the registered owner, if the uncertificated security was not subject to a registered pledge; or

(b) the registered pledgee, if the uncertificated security was subject to a registered pledge.

Added in 1977.

§ 8—408. Statements of Uncertificated Securities

(1) Within 2 business days after the transfer of an uncertificated security has been registered, the issuer shall send to the new registered owner and, if the security has been transferred subject to a registered pledge, to the registered pledgee a written statement containing:

(a) a description of the issue of which the uncertificated security is a part;

(b) the number of shares or units transferred;

(c) the name and address and any taxpayer identification number of the new registered owner and, if the security has been transferred subject to a registered pledge, the name and address and any taxpayer identification number of the registered pledgee;

(d) a notation of any liens and restrictions of the issuer and any adverse claims (as to which the issuer has a duty under Section 8—403(4)) to which the uncertificated security is or may be subject at the time of registration or a statement that there are none of those liens, restrictions, or adverse claims; and

(e) the date the transfer was registered.

(2) Within 2 business days after the pledge of an uncertificated security has been registered, the issuer shall send to the registered owner and the registered pledgee a written statement containing:

(a) a description of the issue of which the uncertificated security is a part;

(b) the number of shares or units pledged;

(c) the name and address and any taxpayer identification number of the registered owner and the registered pledgee;

(d) a notation of any liens and restrictions of the issuer and any adverse claims (as to which the issuer has a duty under Section 8—403(4)) to which the uncertificated security is or may be subject at the time of registration or a statement that there are none of those liens, restrictions, or adverse claims; and

(e) the date the pledge was registered.

(3) Within 2 business days after the release from pledge of an uncertificated security has been registered, the issuer shall send to the registered owner and the pledgee whose interest was released a written statement containing:

(a) a description of the issue of which the uncertificated security is a part;

(b) the number of shares or units released from pledge;

(c) the name and address and any taxpayer identification number of the registered owner and the pledgee whose interest was released;

(d) a notation of any liens and restrictions of the issuer and any adverse claims (as to which the issuer has a duty under Section 8—403(4)) to which the uncertificated security is or may be subject at the time of registration or a statement that there are none of those liens, restrictions, or adverse claims; and

(e) the date the release was registered.

(4) An "initial transaction statement" is the statement sent to:

(a) the new registered owner and, if applicable, to the registered pledgee pursuant to subsection (1);

(b) the registered pledgee pursuant to subsection (2); or

(c) the registered owner pursuant to subsection (3).

Each initial transaction statement shall be signed by or on behalf of the issuer and must be identified as "Initial Transaction Statement".

(5) Within 2 business days after the transfer of an uncertificated security has been registered, the issuer shall send to the former registered owner and the former registered pledgee, if any, a written statement containing:

(a) a description of the issue of which the uncertificated security is a part;

(b) the number of shares or units transferred;

(c) the name and address and any taxpayer identification number of the former registered owner and of any former registered pledgee; and

(d) the date the transfer was registered.

(6) At periodic intervals no less frequent than annually and at any time upon the reasonable written request of the registered owner, the issuer shall send to the registered owner of each uncertificated security a dated written statement containing:

(a) a description of the issue of which the uncertificated security is a part;

(b) the name and address and any taxpayer identification number of the registered owner;

(c) the number of shares or units of the uncertificated security registered in the name of the registered owner on the date of the statement;

(d) the name and address and any taxpayer identification number of any registered pledgee and the number of shares or units subject to the pledge; and

(e) a notation of any liens and restrictions of the issuer and any adverse claims (as to which the issuer has a duty under Section 8—403(4)) to which the uncertificated security is or may be subject or a statement that there are none of those liens, restrictions, or adverse claims.

(7) At periodic intervals no less frequent than annually and at any time upon the reasonable written request of the registered pledgee, the issuer shall send to the registered pledgee of each uncertificated security a dated written statement containing:

(a) a description of the issue of which the uncertificated security is a part;

(b) the name and address and any taxpayer identification number of the registered owner;

(c) the name and address and any taxpayer identification number of the registered pledgee;

(d) the number of shares or units subject to the pledge; and

(e) a notation of any liens and restrictions of the issuer and any adverse claims (as to which the issuer has a duty under Section 8—403(4)) to which the uncertificated security is or may be subject or a statement that there are none of those liens, restrictions, or adverse claims.

(8) If the issuer sends the statements described in subsections (6) and (7) at periodic intervals no less frequent than quarterly, the issuer is not obliged to send additional statements upon request unless the owner or pledgee requesting them pays to the issuer the reasonable cost of furnishing them.

(9) Each statement sent pursuant to this section must bear a conspicuous legend reading substantially as follows: "This statement is merely a record of the rights of the addressee as of the time of its issuance. Delivery of this statement, of itself, confers no rights on the recipient. This statement is neither a negotiable instrument nor a security."

Added in 1977.

Article 9
Secured Transactions; Sales of Accounts and Chattel Paper

Note: *The adoption of this Article should be accompanied by the repeal of existing statutes dealing with conditional sales, trust receipts, factor's liens where the factor is given a non-possessory lien, chattel mortgages, crop mortgages, mortgages on railroad equipment, assignment of accounts and generally statutes regulating security interests in personal property.*

Where the state has a retail installment selling act or small loan act, that legislation should be carefully examined to determine what changes in those acts are needed to conform them to this Article. This Article primarily sets out rules defining rights of a secured party against persons dealing with the debtor; it does not prescribe regulations and controls which may be necessary to curb abuses arising in the small loan business or in the financing of consumer purchases on credit. Accordingly there is no intention to repeal existing regulatory acts in those fields by enactment or re-enactment of Article 9. See Section 9—203(4) and the Note thereto.

Part 1 Short Title, Applicability and Definitions

§ 9—101. **Short Title.**

This Article shall be known and may be cited as Uniform Commercial Code—Secured Transactions.

§ 9—102. **Policy and Subject Matter of Article.**

(1) Except as otherwise provided in Section 9—104 on excluded transactions, this Article applies

(a) to any transaction (regardless of its form) which is intended to create a security interest in personal property or fixtures including goods, documents, instruments, general intangibles, chattel paper or accounts; and also

(b) to any sale of accounts or chattel paper.

(2) This Article applies to security interests created by contract including pledge, assignment, chattel mortgage, chattel trust, trust deed, factor's lien, equipment trust, conditional sale, trust receipt, other lien or title retention contract and lease or consignment intended as security. This Article does not apply to statutory liens except as provided in Section 9—310.

(3) The application of this Article to a security interest in a secured obligation is not affected by the fact that

the obligation is itself secured by a transaction or interest to which this Article does not apply. Amended in 1972.

§ 9—103. **Perfection of Security Interest in Multiple State Transactions**

(1) Documents, instruments and ordinary goods.

(a) This subsection applies to documents and instruments and to goods other than those covered by a certificate of title described in subsection (2), mobile goods described in subsection (3), and minerals described in subsection (5).

(b) Except as otherwise provided in this subsection, perfection and the effect of perfection or non-perfection of a security interest in collateral are governed by the law of the jurisdiction where the collateral is when the last event occurs on which is based the assertion that the security interest is perfected or unperfected.

(c) If the parties to a transaction creating a purchase money security interest in goods in one jurisdiction understand at the time that the security interest attaches that the goods will be kept in another jurisdiction, then the law of the other jurisdiction governs the perfection and the effect of perfection or non-perfection of the security interest from the time it attaches until thirty days after the debtor receives possession of the goods and thereafter if the goods are taken to the other jurisdiction before the end of the thirty-day period.

(d) When collateral is brought into and kept in this state while subject to a security interest perfected under the law of the jurisdiction from which the collateral was removed, the security interest remains perfected, but if action is required by Part 3 of this Article to perfect the security interest,

(i) if the action is not taken before the expiration of the period of perfection in the other jurisdiction or the end of four months after the collateral is brought into this state, whichever period first expires, the security interest becomes unperfected at the end of that period and is thereafter deemed to have been unperfected as against a person who became a purchaser after removal;

(ii) if the action is taken before the expiration of the period specified in subparagraph (i), the security interest continues perfected thereafter;

(iii) for the purpose of priority over a buyer of consumer goods (subsection (2) of Section 9—307), the period of the effectiveness of a filing in the jurisdiction from which the collateral is removed is governed by the rules with respect to perfection in subparagraphs (i) and (ii).

(2) Certificate of title.

(a) This subsection applies to goods covered by a certificate of title issued under a statute of this state or of another jurisdiction under the law of which indication of a security interest on the certificate is required as a condition of perfection.

(b) Except as otherwise provided in this subsection, perfection and the effect of perfection or non-perfection of the security interest are governed by the law (including the conflict of laws rules) of the jurisdiction issuing the certificate until four months after the goods are removed from that jurisdiction and thereafter until the goods are registered in another jurisdiction, but in any event not beyond surrender of the certificate. After the expiration of that period, the goods are not covered by the certificate of title within the meaning of this section.

(c) Except with respect to the rights of a buyer described in the next paragraph, a security interest, perfected in another jurisdiction otherwise than by notation on a certificate of title, in goods brought into this state and thereafter covered by a certificate of title issued by this state is subject to the rules stated in paragraph (d) of subsection (1).

(d) If goods are brought into this state while a security interest therein is perfected in any manner under the law of the jurisdiction from which the goods are removed and a certificate of title is issued by this state and the certificate does not show that the goods are subject to the security interest or that they may be subject to security interests not shown on the certificate, the security interest is subordinate to the rights of a buyer of the goods who is not in the business of selling goods of that kind to the extent that he gives value and receives delivery of the goods after issuance of the certificate and without knowledge of the security interest.

(3) Accounts, general intangibles and mobile goods.

(a) This subsection applies to accounts (other than an account described in subsection (5) on minerals) and general intangibles (other than uncertificated securities) and to goods which are mobile and which are of a type normally used in more than one jurisdiction, such as motor vehicles, trailers, rolling stock, airplanes, shipping containers, road building and construction machinery and commercial harvesting machinery and the like, if the goods are equipment or are inventory leased or held for lease by the debtor to others, and are not covered by a certificate of title described in subsection (2).

(b) The law (including the conflict of laws rules) of the jurisdiction in which the debtor is located governs the perfection and the effect of perfection or non-perfection of the security interest.

(c) If, however, the debtor is located in a jurisdiction which is not a part of the United States, and which does not provide for perfection of the security interest by filing or recording in that jurisdiction, the law of the jurisdiction in the United States in which the debtor has its major executive office in the United States governs the perfection and the effect of perfection or non-perfection of the security interest through filing. In the alternative, if the debtor is located in a jurisdiction which is not a part of the United States or Canada and the collateral is accounts or general intangibles for money due or to become due, the security interest may be perfected by notification to the account debtor. As used in this paragraph, "United States" includes its territories and possessions and the Commonwealth of Puerto Rico.

(d) A debtor shall be deemed located at his place of business if he has one, at his chief executive office if he has more than one place of business, otherwise at his residence. If, however, the debtor is a foreign air carrier under the Federal Aviation Act of 1958, as amended, it shall be deemed located at the designated office of the agent upon whom service of process may be made on behalf of the foreign air carrier.

(e) A security interest perfected under the law of the jurisdiction of the location of the debtor is perfected until the expiration of four months after a change of the debtor's location to another jurisdiction, or until perfection would have ceased by the law of the first jurisdiction, whichever period first expires. Unless perfected in the new jurisdiction before the end of that period, it becomes unperfected thereafter and is deemed to have been unperfected as against a person who became a purchaser after the change.

(4) Chattel paper.

The rules stated for goods in subsection (1) apply to a possessory security interest in chattel paper. The rules stated for accounts in subsection (3) apply to a non-possessory security interest in chattel paper, but the security interest may not be perfected by notification to the account debtor.

(5) Minerals.

Perfection and the effect of perfection or non-perfection of a security interest which is created by a debtor who has an interest in minerals or the like (including oil and gas) before extraction and which attaches thereto as extracted, or which attaches to an account resulting from the sale thereof at the wellhead or minehead are governed by the law (including the conflict of laws rules) of the jurisdiction wherein the wellhead or minehead is located.

(6) Uncertificated securities.

The law (including the conflict of laws rules) of the jurisdiction of organization of the issuer governs the perfection and the effect of perfection or non-perfection of a security interest in uncertificated securities.

Amended in 1972 and 1977.

§ 9—104. **Transactions Excluded From Article.**

This Article does not apply

(a) to a security interest subject to any statute of the United States, to the extent that such statute governs the rights of parties to and third parties affected by transactions in particular types of property; or

(b) to a landlord's lien; or

(c) to a lien given by statute or other rule of law for services or materials except as provided in Section 9—310 on priority of such liens; or

(d) to a transfer of a claim for wages, salary or other compensation of an employee; or

(e) to a transfer by a government or governmental subdivision or agency; or

(f) to a sale of accounts or chattel paper as part of a sale of the business out of which they arose, or an assignment of accounts or chattel paper which is for the purpose of collection only, or a transfer of a right to payment under a contract to an assignee who is also to do the performance under the contract or a transfer of a single account to an assignee in whole or partial satisfaction of a preexisting indebtedness; or

(g) to a transfer of an interest in or claim in or under any policy of insurance, except as provided with respect to proceeds (Section 9—306) and priorities in proceeds (Section 9—312); or

(h) to a right represented by a judgment (other than a judgment taken on a right to payment which was collateral); or

(i) to any right of set-off; or

(j) except to the extent that provision is made for fixtures in Section 9—313, to the creation or transfer of an interest in or lien on real estate, including a lease or rents thereunder; or

(k) to a transfer in whole or in part of any claim arising out of tort; or

(l) to a transfer of an interest in any deposit account (subsection (1) of Section 9—105), except as provided with respect to proceeds (Section 9—306) and priorities in proceeds (Section 9—312).

Amended in 1972.

§ 9—105. Definitions and Index of Definitions

(1) In this Article unless the context otherwise requires:

(a) "Account debtor" means the person who is obligated on an account, chattel paper or general intangible;

(b) "Chattel paper" means a writing or writings which evidence both a monetary obligation and a security interest in or a lease of specific goods, but a charter or other contract involving the use or hire of a vessel is not chattel paper. When a transaction is evidenced both by such a security agreement or a lease and by an instrument or a series of instruments, the group of writings taken together constitutes chattel paper;

(c) "Collateral" means the property subject to a security interest, and includes accounts and chattel paper which have been sold;

(d) "Debtor" means the person who owes payment or other performance of the obligation secured, whether or not he owns or has rights in the collateral, and includes the seller of accounts or chattel paper. Where the debtor and the owner of the collateral are not the same person, the term "debtor" means the owner of the collateral in any provision of the Article dealing with the collateral, the obligor in any provision dealing with the obligation, and may include both where the context so requires;

(e) "Deposit account" means a demand, time, savings, passbook or like account maintained with a bank, savings and loan association, credit union or like organization, other than an account evidenced by a certificate of deposit;

(f) "Document" means document of title as defined in the general definitions of Article 1 (Section 1—201), and a receipt of the kind described in subsection (2) of Section 7—201;

(g) "Encumbrance" includes real estate mortgages and other liens on real estate and all other rights in real estate that are not ownership interests;

(h) "Goods" includes all things which are movable at the time the security interest attaches or which are fixtures (Section 9—313), but does not include money, documents, instruments, accounts, chattel paper, general intangibles, or minerals or the like (including oil and gas) before extraction. "Goods" also includes standing timber which is to be cut and removed under a conveyance or contract for sale, the unborn young of animals, and growing crops;

(i) "Instrument" means a negotiable instrument (defined in Section 3—104), or a certificated security (defined in Section 8—102) or any other writing which evidences a right to the payment of money and is not itself a security agreement or lease and is of a type which is in ordinary course of business transferred by delivery with any necessary indorsement or assignment;

(j) "Mortgage" means a consensual interest created by a real estate mortgage, a trust deed on real estate, or the like;

(k) An advance is made "pursuant to commitment" if the secured party has bound himself to make it, whether or not a subsequent event of default or other event not within his control has relieved or may relieve him from his obligation;

(l) "Security agreement" means an agreement which creates or provides for a security interest;

(m) "Secured party" means a lender, seller or other person in whose favor there is a security interest, including a person to whom accounts or chattel paper have been sold. When the holders of obligations issued under an indenture of trust, equipment trust agreement or the like are represented by a trustee or other person, the representative is the secured party;

(n) "Transmitting utility" means any person primarily engaged in the railroad, street railway or trolley bus business, the electric or electronics communications transmission business, the transmission of goods by pipeline, or the transmission or the production and transmission of electricity, steam, gas or water, or the provision of sewer service.

(2) Other definitions applying to this Article and the sections in which they appear are:

"Account". Section 9—106.
"Attach". Section 9—203.
"Construction mortgage". Section 9—313(1).
"Consumer goods". Section 9—109(1).
"Equipment". Section 9—109(2).
"Farm products". Section 9—109(3).
"Fixture". Section 9—313(1).
"Fixture filing". Section 9—313(1).
"General intangibles". Section 9—106.
"Inventory". Section 9—109(4).
"Lien creditor". Section 9—301(3).
"Proceeds". Section 9—306(1).
"Purchase money security interest". Section 9—107.
"United States". Section 9—103.

(3) The following definitions in other Articles apply to this Article:

"Check". Section 3—104.
"Contract for sale". Section 2—106.
"Holder in due course". Section 3—302.
"Note". Section 3—104.
"Sale". Section 2—106.

(4) In addition Article 1 contains general definitions and principles of construction and interpretation applicable throughout this Article.

Amended in 1966, 1972 and 1977.

§ 9—106. **Definitions: "Account"; "General Intangibles".**

"Account" means any right to payment for goods sold or leased or for services rendered which is not evidenced by an instrument or chattel paper, whether or not it has been earned by performance. "General intangibles" means any personal property (including things in action) other than goods, accounts, chattel paper, documents, instruments, and money. All rights to payment earned or unearned under a charter or other contract involving the use or hire of a vessel and all rights incident to the charter or contract are accounts. Amended in 1966, 1972.

§ 9—107. **Definitions: "Purchase Money Security Interest".**

A security interest is a "purchase money security interest" to the extent that it is

(a) taken or retained by the seller of the collateral to secure all or part of its price; or

(b) taken by a person who by making advances or incurring an obligation gives value to enable the debtor to acquire rights in or the use of collateral if such value is in fact so used.

§ 9—108. **When After-Acquired Collateral Not Security for Antecedent Debt.**

Where a secured party makes an advance, incurs an obligation, releases a perfected security interest, or otherwise gives new value which is to be secured in whole or in part by after-acquired property his security interest in the after-acquired collateral shall be deemed to be taken for new value and not as security for an antecedent debt if the debtor acquires his rights in such collateral either in the ordinary course of his business or under a contract of purchase made pursuant to the security agreement within a reasonable time after new value is given.

§ 9—109. Classification of Goods; "Consumer Goods"; "Equipment"; "Farm Products"; "Inventory".

Goods are

(1) "consumer goods" if they are used or bought for use primarily for personal, family or household purposes;

(2) "equipment" if they are used or bought for use primarily in business (including farming or a profession) or by a debtor who is a non-profit organization or a governmental subdivision or agency or if the goods are not included in the definitions of inventory, farm products or consumer goods;

(3) "farm products" if they are crops or livestock or supplies used or produced in farming operations or if they are products of crops or livestock in their unmanufactured states (such as ginned cotton, wool-clip, maple syrup, milk and eggs), and if they are in the possession of a debtor engaged in raising, fattening, grazing or other farming operations. If goods are farm products they are neither equipment nor inventory;

(4) "inventory" if they are held by a person who holds them for sale or lease or to be furnished under contracts of service or if he has so furnished them, or if they are raw materials, work in process or materials used or consumed in a business. Inventory of a person is not to be classified as his equipment.

§ 9—110. Sufficiency of Description.

For purposes of this Article any description of personal property or real estate is sufficient whether or not it is specific if it reasonably identifies what is described.

§ 9—111. Applicability of Bulk Transfer Laws.

The creation of a security interest is not a bulk transfer under Article 6 (see Section 6—103).

§ 9—112. Where Collateral Is Not Owned by Debtor.

Unless otherwise agreed, when a secured party knows that collateral is owned by a person who is not the debtor, the owner of the collateral is entitled to

receive from the secured party any surplus under Section 9—502(2) or under Section 9—504(1), and is not liable for the debt or for any deficiency after resale, and he has the same right as the debtor

(a) to receive statements under Section 9—208;

(b) to receive notice of and to object to a secured party's proposal to retain the collateral in satisfaction of the indebtedness under Section 9—505;

(c) to redeem the collateral under Section 9—506;

(d) to obtain injunctive or other relief under Section 9—507(1); and

(e) to recover losses caused to him under Section 9—208(2).

§ 9—113. Security Interests Arising Under Article on Sales.

A security interest arising solely under the Article on Sales (Article 2) is subject to the provisions of this Article except that to the extent that and so long as the debtor does not have or does not lawfully obtain possession of the goods

(a) no security agreement is necessary to make the security interest enforceable; and

(b) no filing is required to perfect the security interest; and

(c) the rights of the secured party on default by the debtor are governed by the Article on Sales (Article 2).

§ 9—114. Consignment.

(1) A person who delivers goods under a consignment which is not a security interest and who would be required to file under this Article by paragraph (3) (c) of Section 2—326 has priority over a secured party who is or becomes a creditor of the consignee and who would have a perfected security interest in the goods if they were the property of the consignee, and also has priority with respect to identifiable cash proceeds received on or before delivery of the goods to a buyer, if

    (a) the consignor complies with the filing provision of the Article on Sales with respect to consignments (paragraph (3) (c) of Section 2—326) before the consignee receives possession of the goods; and

    (b) the consignor gives notification in writing to

the holder of the security interest if the holder has filed a financing statement covering the same types of goods before the date of the filing made by the consignor; and

(c) the holder of the security interest receives the notification within five years before the consignee receives possession of the goods; and

(d) the notification states that the consignor expects to deliver goods on consignment to the consignee, describing the goods by item or type.

(2) In the case of a consignment which is not a security interest and in which the requirements of the preceding subsection have not been met, a person who delivers goods to another is subordinate to a person who would have a perfected security interest in the goods if they were the property of the debtor. Added in 1972.

Part 2 Validity of Security Agreement and Rights of Parties Thereto

§ 9—201. General Validity of Security Agreement.

Except as otherwise provided by this Act a security agreement is effective according to its terms between the parties, against purchasers of the collateral and against creditors. Nothing in this Article validates any charge or practice illegal under any statute or regulation thereunder governing usury, small loans, retail installment sales, or the like, or extends the application of any such statute or regulation to any transaction not otherwise subject thereto.

§ 9—202. Title to Collateral Immaterial.

Each provision of this Article with regard to rights, obligations and remedies applies whether title to collateral is in the secured party or in the debtor.

§ 9—203. Attachment and Enforceability of Security Interest; Proceeds; Formal Requisites

(1) Subject to the provisions of Section 4—208 on the security interest of a collecting bank, Section 8—321 on security interests in securities and Section 9—113 on a security interest arising under the Article on Sales, a security interest is not enforceable against the debtor or third parties with respect to the collateral and does not attach unless:

(a) the collateral is in the possession of the secured party pursuant to agreement, or the debtor has signed a security agreement which contains a description of the collateral and in addition, when the security interest covers crops growing or to be grown or timber to be cut, a description of the land concerned;

(b) value has been given; and

(c) the debtor has rights in the collateral.

(2) A security interest attaches when it becomes enforceable against the debtor with respect to the collateral. Attachment occurs as soon as all of the events specified in subsection (1) have taken place unless explicit agreement postpones the time of attaching.

(3) Unless otherwise agreed a security agreement gives the secured party the rights to proceeds provided by Section 9—306.

(4) A transaction, although subject to this Article, is also subject to .... *, and in the case of conflict between the provisions of this Article and any such statute, the provisions of such statute control. Failure to comply with any applicable statute has only the effect which is specified therein.

Amended in 1972 and 1977.

Note: *At * in subsection (4) insert reference to any local statute regulating small loans, retail installment sales and the like.*

The foregoing subsection (4) is designed to make it clear that certain transactions, although subject to this Article, must also comply with other applicable legislation.

This Article is designed to regulate all the "security" aspects of transactions within its scope. There is, however, much regulatory legislation, particularly in the consumer field, which supplements this Article and should not be repealed by its enactment. Examples are small loan acts, retail installment selling acts and the like. Such acts may provide for licensing and rate regulation and may prescribe particular forms of contract. Such provisions should remain in force despite the enactment of this Article. On the other hand if a retail installment selling act contains provisions on filing, rights on default, etc., such provisions should be repealed as inconsistent with this Article except that inconsistent provisions as to deficiencies, penalties, etc., in the Uniform Consumer Credit Code and other recent related legislation should remain because those statutes were drafted after the substantial enactment of the Article and with the intention of modifying certain provisions of this Article as to consumer credit.

§ 9—204. After-Acquired Property; Future Advances.

(1) Except as provided in subsection (2), a security agreement may provide that any or all obligations covered by the security agreement are to be secured by after-acquired collateral.

(2) No security interest attaches under an after-acquired property clause to consumer goods other than accessions (Section 9—314) when given as additional security unless the debtor acquires rights in them within ten days after the secured party gives value.

(3) Obligations covered by a security agreement may include future advances or other value whether or not the advances or value are given pursuant to commitment (subsection (1) of Section 9—105). Amended in 1972.

§ 9—205. Use or Disposition of Collateral Without Accounting Permissible.

A security interest is not invalid or fraudulent against creditors by reason of liberty in the debtor to use, commingle or dispose of all or part of the collateral (including returned or repossessed goods) or to collect or compromise accounts or chattel paper, or to accept the return of goods or make repossessions, or to use, commingle or dispose of proceeds, or by reason of the failure of the secured party to require the debtor to account for proceeds or replace collateral. This section does not relax the requirements of possession where perfection of a security interest depends upon possession of the collateral by the secured party or by a bailee. Amended in 1972.

§ 9—206. Agreement Not to Assert Defenses Against Assignee; Modification of Sales Warranties Where Security Agreement Exists.

(1) Subject to any statute or decision which establishes a different rule for buyers or lessees of consumer goods, an agreement by a buyer or lessee that he will not assert against an assignee any claim or defense which he may have against the seller or lessor is enforceable by an assignee who takes his assignment for value, in good faith and without notice of a claim or defense, except as to defenses of a type which may be asserted against a holder in due course of a negotiable instrument under the Article on Commercial Paper (Article 3). A buyer who as part of

one transaction signs both a negotiable instrument and a security agreement makes such an agreement.

(2) When a seller retains a purchase money security interest in goods the Article on Sales (Article 2) governs the sale and any disclaimer, limitation or modification of the seller's warranties. Amended in 1962.

§ 9—207. Rights and Duties When Collateral is in Secured Party's Possession.

(1) A secured party must use reasonable care in the custody and preservation of collateral in his possession. In the case of an instrument or chattel paper reasonable care includes taking necessary steps to preserve rights against prior parties unless otherwise agreed.

(2) Unless otherwise agreed, when collateral is in the secured party's possession

(a) reasonable expenses (including the cost of any insurance and payment of taxes or other charges) incurred in the custody, preservation, use or operation of the collateral are chargeable to the debtor and are secured by the collateral;

(b) the risk of accidental loss or damage is on the debtor to the extent of any deficiency in any effective insurance coverage;

(c) the secured party may hold as additional security any increase or profits (except money) received from the collateral, but money so received, unless remitted to the debtor, shall be applied in reduction of the secured obligation;

(d) the secured party must keep the collateral identifiable but fungible collateral may be commingled;

(e) the secured party may repledge the collateral upon terms which do not impair the debtor's right to redeem it.

(3) A secured party is liable for any loss caused by his failure to meet any obligation imposed by the preceding subsections but does not lose his security interest.

(4) A secured party may use or operate the collateral for the purpose of preserving the collateral or its value or pursuant to the order of a court of appropriate jurisdiction or, except in the case of consumer goods, in the manner and to the extent provided in the security agreement.

§ 9—208. Request for Statement of Account or List of Collateral.

(1) A debtor may sign a statement indicating what he believes to be the aggregate amount of unpaid indebtedness as of a specified date and may send it to the secured party with a request that the statement be approved or corrected and returned to the debtor. When the security agreement or any other record kept by the secured party identifies the collateral a debtor may similarly request the secured party to approve or correct a list of the collateral.

(2) The secured party must comply with such a request within two weeks after receipt by sending a written correction or approval. If the secured party claims a security interest in all of a particular type of collateral owned by the debtor he may indicate that fact in his reply and need not approve or correct an itemized list of such collateral. If the secured party without reasonable excuse fails to comply he is liable for any loss caused to the debtor thereby; and if the debtor has properly included in his request a good faith statement of the obligation or a list of the collateral or both the secured party may claim a security interest only as shown in the statement against persons misled by his failure to comply. If he no longer has an interest in the obligation or collateral at the time the request is received he must disclose the name and address of any successor in interest known to him and he is liable for any loss caused to the debtor as a result of failure to disclose. A successor in interest is not subject to this section until a request is received by him.

(3) A debtor is entitled to such a statement once every six months without charge. The secured party may require payment of a charge not exceeding $10 for each additional statement furnished.

Part 3 Rights of Third Parties; Perfected and Unperfected Security Interests; Rules of Priority

§ 9—301. Persons Who Take Priority Over Unperfected Security Interests; Rights of "Lien Creditor".

(1) Except as otherwise provided in subsection (2), an unperfected security interest is subordinate to the rights of

(a) persons entitled to priority under Section 9—312;

(b) a person who becomes a lien creditor before the security interest is perfected;

(c) in the case of goods, instruments, documents, and chattel paper, a person who is not a secured party and who is a transferee in bulk or other buyer not in ordinary course of business or is a buyer of farm products in ordinary course of business, to the extent that he gives value and receives delivery of the collateral without knowledge of the security interest and before it is perfected;

(d) in the case of accounts and general intangibles, a person who is not a secured party and who is a transferee to the extent that he gives value without knowledge of the security interest and before it is perfected.

(2) If the secured party files with respect to a purchase money security interest before or within ten days after the debtor receives possession of the collateral, he takes priority over the rights of a transferee in bulk or of a lien creditor which arise between the time the security interest attaches and the time of filing.

(3) A "lien creditor" means a creditor who has acquired a lien on the property involved by attachment, levy or the like and includes an assignee for benefit of creditors from the time of assignment, and a trustee in bankruptcy from the date of the filing of the petition or a receiver in equity from the time of appointment.

(4) A person who becomes a lien creditor while a security interest is perfected takes subject to the security interest only to the extent that it secures advances made before he becomes a lien creditor or within 45 days thereafter or made without knowledge of the lien or pursuant to a commitment entered into without knowledge of the lien. Amended in 1972.

§ 9—302. When Filing Is Required to Perfect Security Interest; Security Interests to Which Filing Provisions of This Article Do Not Apply

(1) A financing statement must be filed to perfect all security interests except the following:

(a) a security interest in collateral in possession of the secured party under Section 9—305;

(b) a security interest temporarily perfected in instruments or documents without delivery under Section 9—304 or in proceeds for a 10 day period under Section 9—306;

(c) a security interest created by an assignment of a beneficial interest in a trust or a decedent's estate;

(d) a purchase money security interest in consumer goods; but filing is required for a motor vehicle required to be registered; and fixture filing is required for priority over conflicting interests in fixtures to the extent provided in Section 9—313;

(e) an assignment of accounts which does not alone or in conjunction with other assignments to the same assignee transfer a significant part of the outstanding accounts of the assignor;

(f) a security interest of a collecting bank (Section 4—208) or in securities (Section 8—321) or arising under the Article on Sales (see Section 9—113) or covered in subsection (3) of this section;

(g) an assignment for the benefit of all the creditors of the transferor, and subsequent transfers by the assignee thereunder.

(2) If a secured party assigns a perfected security interest, no filing under this Article is required in order to continue the perfected status of the security interest against creditors of and transferees from the original debtor.

(3) The filing of a financing statement otherwise required by this Article is not necessary or effective to perfect a security interest in property subject to

(a) a statute or treaty of the United States which provides for a national or international registration or a national or international certificate of title or which specifies a place of filing different from that specified in this Article for filing of the security interest; or

(b) the following statutes of this state; [list any certificate of title statute covering automobiles, trailers, mobile homes, boats, farm tractors, or the like, and any central filing statute.]; but during any period in which collateral is inventory held for sale by a person who is in the business of selling goods of that kind, the filing provisions of this Article (Part 4) apply to a security interest in that collateral created by him as debtor; or

(c) a certificate of title statute of another jurisdiction under the law of which indication of a security interest on the certificate is required as a condition of perfection (subsection (2) of Section 9—103).

(4) Compliance with a statute or treaty described in subsection (3) is equivalent to the filing of a financing statement under this Article, and a security interest in property subject to the statute or treaty can be perfected only by compliance therewith except as provided in Section 9—103 on multiple state transactions. Duration and renewal of perfection of a security interest perfected by compliance with the statute or treaty are governed by the provisions of the statute or treaty; in other respects the security interest is subject to this Article.

Amended in 1972 and 1977.

§ 9—303. **When Security Interest Is Perfected; Continuity of Perfection.**

(1) A security interest is perfected when it has attached and when all of the applicable steps required for perfection have been taken. Such steps are specified in Sections 9—302, 9—304, 9—305 and 9—306. If such steps are taken before the security interest attaches, it is perfected at the time when it attaches.

(2) If a security interest is originally perfected in any way permitted under this Article and is subsequently perfected in some other way under this Article, without an intermediate period when it was unperfected, the security interest shall be deemed to be perfected continuously for the purposes of this Article.

§ 9—304. **Perfection of Security Interest in Instruments, Documents, and Goods Covered by Documents; Perfection by Permissive Filing; Temporary Perfection Without Filing or Transfer of Possession**

(1) A security interest in chattel paper or negotiable documents may be perfected by filing. A security interest in money or instruments (other than certificated securities or instruments which constitute part of chattel paper) can be perfected only by the secured party's taking possession, except as provided

in subsections (4) and (5) of this section and subsections (2) and (3) of Section 9—306 on proceeds.

(2) During the period that goods are in the possession of the issuer of a negotiable document therefor, a security interest in the goods is perfected by perfecting a security interest in the document, and any security interest in the goods otherwise perfected during such period is subject thereto.

(3) A security interest in goods in the possession of a bailee other than one who has issued a negotiable document therefor is perfected by issuance of a document in the name of the secured party or by the bailee's receipt of notification of the secured party's interest or by filing as to the goods.

(4) A security interest in instruments (other than certificated securities) or negotiable documents is perfected without filing or the taking of possession for a period of 21 days from the time it attaches to the extent that it arises for new value given under a written security agreement.

(5) A security interest remains perfected for a period of 21 days without filing where a secured party having a perfected security interest in an instrument (other than a certificated security), a negotiable document or goods in possession of a bailee other than one who has issued a negotiable document therefor

  (a) makes available to the debtor the goods or documents representing the goods for the purpose of ultimate sale or exchange or for the purpose of loading, unloading, storing, shipping, transshipping, manufacturing, processing or otherwise dealing with them in a manner preliminary to their sale or exchange, but priority between conflicting security interests in the goods is subject to subsection (3) of Section 9—312; or

  (b) delivers the instrument to the debtor for the purpose of ultimate sale or exchange or of presentation, collection, renewal or registration of transfer.

(6) After the 21 day period in subsections (4) and (5) perfection depends upon compliance with applicable provisions of this Article.

Amended in 1972 and 1977.

§ 9—305. **When Possession by Secured Party Perfects Security Interest Without Filing**

A security interest in letters of credit and advices of credit (subsection (2) (a) of Section 5—116), goods, instruments (other than certificated securities), money, negotiable documents, or chattel paper may be perfected by the secured party's taking possession of the collateral. If such collateral other than goods covered by a negotiable document is held by a bailee, the secured party is deemed to have possession from the time the bailee receives notification of the secured party's interest. A security interest is perfected by possession from the time possession is taken without a relation back and continues only so long as possession is retained, unless otherwise specified in this Article. The security interest may be otherwise perfected as provided in this Article before or after the period of possession by the secured party.

Amended in 1972 and 1977.

§ 9—306. **"Proceeds"; Secured Party's Rights on Disposition of Collateral.**

(1) "Proceeds" includes whatever is received upon the sale, exchange, collection or other disposition of collateral or proceeds. Insurance payable by reason of loss or damage to the collateral is proceeds, except to the extent that it is payable to a person other than a party to the security agreement. Money, checks, deposit accounts, and the like are "cash proceeds". All other proceeds are "non-cash proceeds".

(2) Except where this Article otherwise provides, a security interest continues in collateral notwithstanding sale, exchange or other disposition thereof unless the disposition was authorized by the secured party in the security agreement or otherwise, and also continues in any identifiable proceeds including collections received by the debtor.

(3) The security interest in proceeds is a continuously perfected security interest if the interest in the original collateral was perfected but it ceases to be a perfected security interest and becomes unperfected ten days after receipt of the proceeds by the debtor unless

  (a) a filed financing statement covers the original collateral and the proceeds are collateral in which a security interest may be perfected by filing in the office or offices where the financing statement has been filed and, if the proceeds are acquired with cash proceeds, the description of collateral in the financing statement indicates the types of property constituting the proceeds; or

(b) a filed financing statement covers the original collateral and the proceeds are identifiable cash proceeds; or

(c) the security interest in the proceeds is perfected before the expiration of the ten day period.

Except as provided in this section, a security interest in proceeds can be perfected only by the methods or under the circumstances permitted in this Article for original collateral of the same type.

(4) In the event of insolvency proceedings instituted by or against a debtor, a secured party with a perfected security interest in proceeds has a perfected security interest only in the following proceeds:

(a) in identifiable non-cash proceeds and in separate deposit accounts containing only proceeds;

(b) in identifiable cash proceeds in the form of money which is neither commingled with other money nor deposited in a deposit account prior to the insolvency proceedings;

(c) in identifiable cash proceeds in the form of checks and the like which are not deposited in a deposit account prior to the insolvency proceedings; and

(d) in all cash and deposit accounts of the debtor in which proceeds have been commingled with other funds, but the perfected security interest under this paragraph (d) is

(i) subject to any right to set-off; and

(ii) limited to an amount not greater than the amount of any cash proceeds received by the debtor within ten days before the institution of the insolvency proceedings less the sum of (I) the payments to the secured party on account of cash proceeds received by the debtor during such period and (II) the cash proceeds received by the debtor during such period to which the secured party is entitled under paragraphs (a) through (c) of this subsection (4).

(5) If a sale of goods results in an account or chattel paper which is transferred by the seller to a secured party, and if the goods are returned to or are repossessed by the seller or the secured party, the following rules determine priorities:

(a) If the goods were collateral at the time of sale,

for an indebtedness of the seller which is still unpaid, the original security interest attaches again to the goods and continues as a perfected security interest if it was perfected at the time when the goods were sold. If the security interest was originally perfected by a filing which is still effective, nothing further is required to continue the perfected status; in any other case, the secured party must take possession of the returned or repossessed goods or must file.

(b) An unpaid transferee of the chattel paper has a security interest in the goods against the transferor. Such security interest is prior to a security interest asserted under paragraph (a) to the extent that the transferee of the chattel paper was entitled to priority under Section 9—308.

(c) An unpaid transferee of the account has a security interest in the goods against the transferor. Such security interest is subordinate to a security interest asserted under paragraph (a).

(d) A security interest of an unpaid transferee asserted under paragraph (b) or (c) must be perfected for protection against creditors of the transferor and purchasers of the returned or repossessed goods.

Amended in 1972.

§ 9—307. **Protection of Buyers of Goods.**

(1) A buyer in ordinary course of business (subsection (9) of Section 1—201) other than a person buying farm products from a person engaged in farming operations takes free of a security interest created by his seller even though the security interest is perfected and even though the buyer knows of its existence.

(2) In the case of consumer goods, a buyer takes free of a security interest even though perfected if he buys without knowledge of the security interest, for value and for his own personal, family or household purposes unless prior to the purchase the secured party has filed a financing statement covering such goods.

(3) A buyer other than a buyer in ordinary course of business (subsection (1) of this section) takes free of a security interest to the extent that it secures future advances made after the secured party acquires knowledge of the purchase, or more than 45 days

after the purchase, whichever first occurs, unless made pursuant to a commitment entered into without knowledge of the purchase and before the expiration of the 45 day period. Amended in 1972.

§ 9—308. **Purchase of Chattel Paper and Instruments.**

A purchaser of chattel paper or an instrument who gives new value and takes possession of it in the ordinary course of his business has priority over a security interest in the chattel paper or instrument

(a) which is perfected under Section 9—304 (permissive filing and temporary perfection) or under Section 9—306 (perfection as to proceeds) if he acts without knowledge that the specific paper or instrument is subject to a security interest; or

(b) which is claimed merely as proceeds of inventory subject to a security interest (Section 9—306) even though he knows that the specific paper or instrument is subject to the security interest.

Amended in 1972.

§ 9—309. **Protection of Purchasers of Instruments, Documents and Securities**

Nothing in this Article limits the rights of a holder in due course of a negotiable instrument (Section 3—302) or a holder to whom a negotiable document of title has been duly negotiated (Section 7—501) or a bona fide purchaser of a security (Section 8—302) and the holders or purchasers take priority over an earlier security interest even though perfected. Filing under this Article does not constitute notice of the security interest to such holders or purchasers.
Amended in 1977.

§ 9—310. **Priority of Certain Liens Arising by Operation of Law.**

When a person in the ordinary course of his business furnishes services or materials with respect to goods subject to a security interest, a lien upon goods in the possession of such person given by statute or rule of law for such materials or services takes priority over a perfected security interest unless the lien is statutory and the statute expressly provides otherwise.

§ 9—311. **Alienability of Debtor's Rights: Judicial Process.**

The debtor's rights in collateral may be voluntarily or involuntarily transferred (by way of sale, creation of a security interest, attachment, levy, garnishment or other judicial process) notwithstanding a provision in the security agreement prohibiting any transfer or making the transfer constitute a default.

§ 9—312. **Priorities Among Conflicting Security Interests in the Same Collateral**

(1) The rules of priority stated in other sections of this Part and in the following sections shall govern when applicable: Section 4—208 with respect to the security interests of collecting banks in items being collected, accompanying documents and proceeds; Section 9—103 on security interests related to other jurisdictions; Section 9—114 on consignments.

(2) A perfected security interest in crops for new value given to enable the debtor to produce the crops during the production season and given not more than three months before the crops become growing crops by planting or otherwise takes priority over an earlier perfected security interest to the extent that such earlier interest secures obligations due more than six months before the crops become growing crops by planting or otherwise, even though the person giving new value had knowledge of the earlier security interest.

(3) A perfected purchase money security interest in inventory has priority over a conflicting security interest in the same inventory and also has priority in identifiable cash proceeds received on or before the delivery of the inventory to a buyer if

(a) the purchase money security interest is perfected at the time the debtor receives possession of the inventory; and

(b) the purchase money secured party gives notification in writing to the holder of the conflicting security interest if the holder had filed a financing statement covering the same types of inventory (i) before the date of the filing made by the purchase money secured party, or (ii) before the beginning of the 21 day period where the purchase money security interest is temporarily perfected without filing or possession (subsection (5) of Section 9—304); and

(c) the holder of the conflicting security interest receives the notification within five years before the debtor receives possession of the inventory; and

(d) the notification states that the person giving the notice has or expects to acquire a purchase money security interest in inventory of the debtor, describing such inventory by item or type.

(4) A purchase money security interest in collateral other than inventory has priority over a conflicting security interest in the same collateral or its proceeds if the purchase money security interest is perfected at the time the debtor receives possession of the collateral or within ten days thereafter.

(5) In all cases not governed by other rules stated in this section (including cases of purchase money security interests which do not qualify for the special priorities set forth in subsections (3) and (4) of this section), priority between conflicting security interests in the same collateral shall be determined according to the following rules:

(a) Conflicting security interests rank according to priority in time of filing or perfection. Priority dates from the time a filing is first made covering the collateral or the time the security interest is first perfected, whichever is earlier, provided that there is no period thereafter when there is neither filing nor perfection.

(b) So long as conflicting security interests are unperfected, the first to attach has priority.

(6) For the purposes of subsection (5) a date of filing or perfection as to collateral is also a date of filing or perfection as to proceeds.

(7) If future advances are made while a security interest is perfected by filing, the taking of possession, or under Section 8—321 on securities, the security interest has the same priority for the purposes of subsection (5) with respect to the future advances as it does with respect to the first advance. If a commitment is made before or while the security interest is so perfected, the security interest has the same priority with respect to advances made pursuant thereto. In other cases a perfected security interest has priority from the date the advance is made.

Amended in 1972 and 1977.

§ 9—313. **Priority of Security Interests in Fixtures.**

(1) In this section and in the provisions of Part 4 of this Article referring to fixture filing, unless the context otherwise requires

(a) goods are "fixtures" when they become so related to particular real estate that an interest in them arises under real estate law

(b) a "fixture filing" is the filing in the office where a mortgage on the real estate would be filed or recorded of a financing statement covering goods which are or are to become fixtures and conforming to the requirements of subsection (5) of Section 9—402

(c) a mortgage is a "construction mortgage" to the extent that it secures an obligation incurred for the construction of an improvement on land including the acquisition cost of the land, if the recorded writing so indicates.

(2) A security interest under this Article may be created in goods which are fixtures or may continue in goods which become fixtures, but no security interest exists under this Article in ordinary building materials incorporated into an improvement on land.

(3) This Article does not prevent creation of an encumbrance upon fixtures pursuant to real estate law.

(4) A perfected security interest in fixtures has priority over the conflicting interest of an encumbrancer or owner of the real estate where

(a) the security interest is a purchase money security interest, the interest of the encumbrancer or owner arises before the goods become fixtures, the security interest is perfected by a fixture filing before the goods become fixtures or within ten days thereafter, and the debtor has an interest of record in the real estate or is in possession of the real estate; or

(b) the security interest is perfected by a fixture filing before the interest of the encumbrancer or owner is of record, the security interest has priority over any conflicting interest of a predecessor in title of the encumbrancer or owner, and the debtor has an interest of record in the real estate or is in possession of the real estate; or

(c) the fixtures are readily removable factory or office machines or readily removable replacements of domestic applicances which are consumer goods, and before the goods become fixtures the security interest is perfected by any method permitted by this Article; or

(d) the conflicting interest is a lien on the real estate obtained by legal or equitable proceedings after the security interest was perfected by any method permitted by this Article.

(5) A security interest in fixtures, whether or not perfected, has priority over the conflicting interest of an encumbrancer or owner of the real estate where

(a) the encumbrancer or owner has consented in writing to the security interest or has disclaimed an interest in the goods as fixtures; or

(b) the debtor has a right to remove the goods as against the encumbrancer or owner. If the debtor's right terminates, the priority of the security interest continues for a reasonable time.

(6) Notwithstanding paragraph (a) of subsection (4) but otherwise subject to subsections (4) and (5), a security interest in fixtures is subordinate to a construction mortgage recorded before the goods become fixtures if the goods become fixtures before the completion of the construction. To the extent that it is given to refinance a construction mortgage, a mortgage has this priority to the same extent as the construction mortgage.

(7) In cases not within the preceding subsections, a security interest in fixtures is subordinate to the conflicting interest of an encumbrancer or owner of the related real estate who is not the debtor.

(8) When the secured party has priority over all owners and encumbrancers of the real estate, he may, on default, subject to the provisions of Part 5, remove his collateral from the real estate but he must reimburse any encumbrancer or owner of the real estate who is not the debtor and who has not otherwise agreed for the cost of repair of any physical injury, but not for any diminution in value of the real estate caused by the absence of the goods removed or by any necessity of replacing them. A person entitled to reimbursement may refuse permission to remove until the secured party gives adequate security for the performance of this obligation. Amended in 1972.

§ 9—314. **Accessions.**

(1) A security interest in goods which attaches before they are installed in or affixed to other goods takes priority as to the goods installed or affixed (called in this section "accessions") over the claims of all persons to the whole except as stated in subsection (3) and subject to Section 9—315(1).

(2) A security interest which attaches to goods after they become part of a whole is valid against all persons subsequently acquiring interests in the whole except as stated in subsection (3) but is invalid against any person with an interest in the whole at the time the security interest attaches to the goods who has not in writing consented to the security interest or disclaimed an interest in the goods as part of the whole.

(3) The security interests described in subsections (1) and (2) do not take priority over

(a) a subsequent purchaser for value of any interest in the whole; or

(b) a creditor with a lien on the whole subsequently obtained by judicial proceedings; or

(c) a creditor with a prior perfected security interest in the whole to the extent that he makes subsequent advances

if the subsequent purchase is made, the lien by judicial proceedings obtained or the subsequent advance under the prior perfected security interest is made or contracted for without knowledge of the security interest and before it is perfected. A purchaser of the whole at a foreclosure sale other than the holder of a perfected security interest purchasing at his own foreclosure sale is a subsequent purchaser within this section.

(4) When under subsections (1) or (2) and (3) a secured party has an interest in accessions which has priority over the claims of all persons who have interests in the whole, he may on default subject to the provisions of Part 5 remove his collateral from the whole but he must reimburse any encumbrancer or owner of the whole who is not the debtor and who has not otherwise agreed for the cost of repair of any physical injury but not for any diminution in value of the whole caused by the absence of the goods removed or by any necessity for replacing them. A person entitled to reimbursement may refuse permission to remove until the secured party gives adequate security for the performance of this obligation.

§ 9—315. **Priority When Goods Are Commingled or Processed.**

(1) If a security interest in goods was perfected and subsequently the goods or a part thereof have become part of a product or mass, the security interest continues in the product or mass if

(a) the goods are so manufactured, processed, assembled or commingled that their identity is lost in the product or mass; or

(b) a financing statement covering the original goods also covers the product into which the goods have been manufactured, processed or assembled.

In a case to which paragraph (b) applies, no separate security interest in that part of the original goods which has been manufactured, processed or assembled into the product may be claimed under Section 9—314.

(2) When under subsection (1) more than one security interest attaches to the product or mass, they rank equally according to the ratio that the cost of the goods to which each interest originally attached bears to the cost of the total product or mass.

§ 9—316. **Priority Subject to Subordination.**

Nothing in this Article prevents subordination by agreement by any person entitled to priority.

§ 9—317. **Secured Party Not Obligated on Contract of Debtor.**

The mere existence of a security interest or authority given to the debtor to dispose of or use collateral does not impose contract or tort liability upon the secured party for the debtor's acts or omissions.

§ 9—318. **Defenses Against Assignee; Modification of Contract After Notification of Assignment; Term Prohibiting Assignment Ineffective; Identification and Proof of Assignment.**

(1) Unless an account debtor has made an enforceable agreement not to assert defenses or claims arising out of a sale as provided in Section 9—206 the rights of an assignee are subject to

(a) all the terms of the contract between the account debtor and assignor and any defense or claim arising therefrom; and

(b) any other defense or claim of the account debtor against the assignor which accrues before the account debtor receives notification of the assignment.

(2) So far as the right to payment or a part thereof under an assigned contract has not been fully earned by performance, and notwithstanding notification of the assignment, any modification of or substitution for the contract made in good faith and in accordance with reasonable commercial standards is effective against an assignee unless the account debtor has otherwise agreed but the assignee acquires corresponding rights under the modified or substituted contract. The assignment may provide that such modification or substitution is a breach by the assignor.

(3) The account debtor is authorized to pay the assignor until the account debtor receives notification that the amount due or to become due has been assigned and that payment is to be made to the assignee. A notification which does not reasonably identify the rights assigned is ineffective. If requested by the account debtor, the assignee must seasonably furnish reasonable proof that the assignment has been made and unless he does so the account debtor may pay the assignor.

(4) A term in any contract between an account debtor and an assignor is ineffective if it prohibits assignment of an account or prohibits creation of a security interest in a general intangible for money due or to become due or requires the account debtor's consent to such assignment or security interest. Amended in 1972.

Part 4 Filing

§ 9—401. **Place of Filing; Erroneous Filing; Removal of Collateral.**

First Alternative Subsection (1)

(1) The proper place to file in order to perfect a security interest is as follows:

(a) when the collateral is timber to be cut or is minerals or the like (including oil and gas) or accounts subject to subsection (5) of Section 9—103, or when the financing statement is filed as a fixture filing (Section 9—313) and the collateral is goods which are or are to become fixtures, then in the office where a mortgage on the real estate would be filed or recorded;

(b) in all other cases, in the office of the [Secretary of State].

Second Alternative Subsection (1)

(1) The proper place to file in order to perfect a security interest is as follows:

(a) when the collateral is equipment used in farming operations, or farm products, or accounts or general intangibles arising from or relating to the sale of farm products by a farmer, or consumer goods, then in the office of the . . . . in the county of the debtor's residence or if the debtor is not a resident of this state then in the office of the . . . . in the county where the goods are kept, and in addition when the collateral is crops growing or to be grown in the office of the . . . . in the county where the land is located;

(b) when the collateral is timber to be cut or is minerals or the like (including oil and gas) or accounts subject to subsection (5) of Section 9—103, or when the financing statement is filed as a fixture filing (Section 9—313) and the collateral is goods which are or are to become fixtures, then in the office where a mortgage on the real estate would be filed or recorded;

(c) in all other cases, in the office of the [Secretary of State].

Third Alternative Subsection (1)

(1) The proper place to file in order to perfect a security interest is as follows:

(a) when the collateral is equipment used in farming operations, or farm products, or accounts or general intangibles arising from or relating to the sale of farm products by a farmer, or consumer goods, then in the office of the . . . . in the county of the debtor's residence or if the debtor is not a resident of this state then in the office of the . . . . in the county where the goods are kept, and in addition when the collateral is crops growing or to be grown in the office of the . . . . in the county where the land is located;

(b) when the collateral is timber to be cut or is minerals or the like (including oil and gas) or accounts subject to subsection (5) of Section 9—103, or when the financing statement is filed as a fixture filing (Section 9—313) and the collateral is goods which are or are to become fixtures, then

in the office where a mortgage on the real estate would be filed or recorded;

(c) in all other cases, in the office of the [Secretary of State] and in addition, if the debtor has a place of business in only one county of this state, also in the office of . . . . of such county, or, if the debtor has no place of business in this state, but resides in the state, also in the office of . . . . of the county in which he resides.

Note: *One of the three alternatives should be selected as subsection (1).*

(2) A filing which is made in good faith in an improper place or not in all of the places required by this section is nevertheless effective with regard to any collateral as to which the filing complied with the requirements of this Article and is also effective with regard to collateral covered by the financing statement against any person who has knowledge of the contents of such financing statement.

(3) A filing which is made in the proper place in this state continues effective even though the debtor's residence or place of business or the location of the collateral or its use, whichever controlled the original filing, is thereafter changed.

Alternative Subsection (3)

[(3) A filing which is made in the proper county continues effective for four months after a change to another county of the debtor's residence or place of business or the location of the collateral, whichever controlled the original filing. It becomes ineffective thereafter unless a copy of the financing statement signed by the secured party is filed in the new county within said period. The security interest may also be perfected in the new county after the expiration of the four-month period; in such case perfection dates from the time of perfection in the new county. A change in the use of the collateral does not impair the effectiveness of the original filing.]

(4) The rules stated in Section 9—103 determine whether filing is necessary in this state.

(5) Notwithstanding the preceding subsections, and subject to subsection (3) of Section 9—302, the proper place to file in order to perfect a security interest in collateral, including fixtures, of a transmitting utility is the office of the [Secretary of State]. This filing constitutes a fixture filing (Section 9—313) as to the

collateral described therein which is or is to become fixtures.

(6) For the purposes of this section, the residence of an organization is its place of business if it has one or its chief executive office if it has more than one place of business. Amended in 1962 and 1972.

Note: *Subsection (6) should be used only if the state chooses the Second or Third Alternative Subsection (1).*

§ 9—402. **Formal Requisites of Financing Statement; Amendments; Mortgage as Financing Statement.**

(1) A financing statement is sufficient if it gives the names of the debtor and the secured party, is signed by the debtor, gives an address of the secured party from which information concerning the security interest may be obtained, gives a mailing address of the debtor and contains a statement indicating the types, or describing the items, of collateral. A financing statement may be filed before a security agreement is made or a security interest otherwise attaches. When the financing statement covers crops growing or to be grown, the statement must also contain a description of the real estate concerned. When the financing statement covers timber to be cut or covers minerals or the like (including oil and gas) or accounts subject to subsection (5) of Section 9—103, or when the financing statement is filed as a fixture filing (Section 9—313) and the collateral is goods which are or are to become fixtures, the statement must also comply with subsection (5). A copy of the security agreement is sufficient as a financing statement if it contains the above information and is signed by the debtor. A carbon, photographic or other reproduction of a security agreement or a financing statement is sufficient as a financing statement if the security agreement so provides or if the original has been filed in this state.

(2) A financing statement which otherwise complies with subsection (1) is sufficient when it is signed by the secured party instead of the debtor if it is filed to perfect a security interest in

> (a) collateral already subject to a security interest in another jurisdiction when it is brought into this state, or when the debtor's location is changed to this state. Such a financing statement must state that the collateral was brought into this state or

that the debtor's location was changed to this state under such circumstances; or

(b) proceeds under Section 9—306 if the security interest in the original collateral was perfected. Such a financing statement must describe the original collateral; or

(c) collateral as to which the filing has lapsed; or

(d) collateral acquired after a change of name, identity or corporate structure of the debtor (subsection (7)).

(3) A form substantially as follows is sufficient to comply with subsection (1):

Name of debtor (or assignor).....................................
Address..
Name of secured party (or assignee).......................
Address..
1. This financing statement covers the following types (or items) of property:
     (Describe)..
2. (If collateral is crops) The above described crops are growing or are to be grown on:
     (Describe Real Estate).......................................
3. (If applicable) The above goods are to become fixtures on *
*Where appropriate substitute either "The above timber is standing on . . . . " or "The above minerals or the like (including oil and gas) or accounts will be financed at the wellhead or minehead of the well or mine located on . . . . ."
     (Describe Real Estate)..
and this financing statement is to be filed [for record] in the real estate records. (If the debtor does not have an interest of record) The name of a record owner is...
4. (If products of collateral are claimed) Products of the collateral are also covered.

(use   ....
whichever   Signature of Debtor (or Assignor)

is   ....
applicable)   Signature of Secured Party
                         (or Assignee)

(4) A financing statement may be amended by filing a writing signed by both the debtor and the secured

party. An amendment does not extend the period of effectiveness of a financing statement. If any amendment adds collateral, it is effective as to the added collateral only from the filing date of the amendment. In this Article, unless the context otherwise requires, the term "financing statement" means the original financing statement and any amendments.

(5) A financing statement covering timber to be cut or covering minerals or the like (including oil and gas) or accounts subject to subsection (5) of Section 9—103, or a financing statement filed as a fixture filing (Section 9—313) where the debtor is not a transmitting utility, must show that it covers this type of collateral, must recite that it is to be filed [for record] in the real estate records, and the financing statement must contain a description of the real estate [sufficient if it were contained in a mortgage of the real estate to give constructive notice of the mortgage under the law of this state]. If the debtor does not have an interest of record in the real estate, the financing statement must show the name of a record owner.

(6) A mortgage is effective as a financing statement filed as a fixture filing from the date of its recording if

(a) the goods are described in the mortgage by item or type; and

(b) the goods are or are to become fixtures related to the real estate described in the mortgage; and

(b) the mortgage complies with the requirements for a financing statement in this section other than a recital that it is to be filed in the real estate records; and

(d) the mortgage is duly recorded.

No fee with reference to the financing statement is required other than the regular recording and satisfaction fees with respect to the mortgage.

(7) A financing statement sufficiently shows the name of the debtor if it gives the individual, partnership or corporate name of the debtor, whether or not it adds other trade names or names of partners. Where the debtor so changes his name or in the case of an organization its name, identity or corporate structure that a filed financing statement becomes seriously misleading, the filing is not effective to perfect a security interest in collateral acquired by the

debtor more than four months after the change, unless a new appropriate financing statement is filed before the expiration of that time. A filed financing statement remains effective with respect to collateral transferred by the debtor even though the secured party knows of or consents to the transfer.

(8) A financing statement substantially complying with the requirements of this section is effective even though it contains minor errors which are not seriously misleading. Amended in 1972.

Note: *Language in brackets is optional.*

Note: *Where the state has any special recording system for real estate other than the usual grantor-grantee index (as, for instance, a tract system or a title registration or Torrens system) local adaptations of subsection (5) and Section 9—403(7) may be necessary. See Mass.Gen.Laws Chapter 106, Section 9—409.*

§ 9—403. **What Constitutes Filing; Duration of Filing; Effect of Lapsed Filing; Duties of Filing Officer.**

(1) Presentation for filing of a financing statement and tender of the filing fee or acceptance of the statement by the filing officer constitutes filing under this Article.

(2) Except as provided in subsection (6) a filed financing statement is effective for a period of five years from the date of filing. The effectiveness of a filed financing statement lapses on the expiration of the five year period unless a continuation statement is filed prior to the lapse. If a security interest perfected by filing exists at the time insolvency proceedings are commenced by or against the debtor, the security interest remains perfected until termination of the insolvency proceedings and thereafter for a period of sixty days or until expiration of the five year period, whichever occurs later. Upon lapse the security interest becomes unperfected, unless it is perfected without filing. If the security interest becomes unperfected upon lapse, it is deemed to have been unperfected as against a person who became a purchaser or lien creditor before lapse.

(3) A continuation statement may be filed by the secured party within six months prior to the expiration of the five year period specified in subsection (2). Any such continuation statement must be signed by the secured party, identify the original statement by

file number and state that the original statement is still effective. A continuation statement signed by a person other than the secured party of record must be accompanied by a separate written statement of assignment signed by the secured party of record and complying with subsection (2) of Section 9—405, including payment of the required fee. Upon timely filing of the continuation statement, the effectiveness of the original statement is continued for five years after the last date to which the filing was effective whereupon it lapses in the same manner as provided in subsection (2) unless another continuation statement is filed prior to such lapse. Succeeding continuation statements may be filed in the same manner to continue the effectiveness of the original statement. Unless a statute on disposition of public records provides otherwise, the filing officer may remove a lapsed statement from the files and destroy it immediately if he has retained a microfilm or other photographic record, or in other cases after one year after the lapse. The filing officer shall so arrange matters by physical annexation of financing statements to continuation statements or other related filings, or by other means, that if he physically destroys the financing statements of a period more than five years past, those which have been continued by a continuation statement or which are still effective under subsection (6) shall be retained.

(4) Except as provided in subsection (7) a filing officer shall mark each statement with a file number and with the date and hour of filing and shall hold the statement or a microfilm or other photographic copy thereof for public inspection. In addition the filing officer shall index the statement according to the name of the debtor and shall note in the index the file number and the address of the debtor given in the statement.

(5) The uniform fee for filing and indexing and for stamping a copy furnished by the secured party to show the date and place of filing for an original financing statement or for a continuation statement shall be $.......... if the statement is in the standard form prescribed by the [Secretary of State] and otherwise shall be $.........., plus in each case, if the financing statement is subject to subsection (5) of Section 9—402, $........... The uniform fee for each name more than one required to be indexed shall be

$........... The secured party may at his option show a trade name for any person and an extra uniform indexing fee of $.......... shall be paid with respect thereto.

(6) If the debtor is a transmitting utility (subsection (5) of Section 9—401) and a filed financing statement so states, it is effective until a termination statement is filed. A real estate mortgage which is effective as a fixture filing under subsection (6) of Section 9—402 remains effective as a fixture filing until the mortgage is released or satisfied of record or its effectiveness otherwise terminates as to the real estate.

(7) When a financing statement covers timber to be cut or covers minerals or the like (including oil and gas) or accounts subject to subsection (5) of Section 9—103, or is filed as a fixture filing, [it shall be filed for record and] the filing officer shall index it under the names of the debtor and any owner of record shown on the financing statement in the same fashion as if they were the mortgagors in a mortgage of the real estate described, and, to the extent that the law of this state provides for indexing of mortgages under the name of the mortgagee, under the name of the secured party as if he were the mortgagee thereunder, or where indexing is by description in the same fashion as if the financing statement were a mortgage of the real estate described. Amended in 1972.

Note: *In states in which writings will not appear in the real estate records and indices unless actually recorded the bracketed language in subsection (7) should be used.*

§ 9—404. **Termination Statement.**

(1) If a financing statement covering consumer goods is filed on or after ...., then within one month or within ten days following written demand by the debtor after there is no outstanding secured obligation and no commitment to make advances, incur obligations or otherwise give value, the secured party must file with each filing officer with whom the financing statement was filed, a termination statement to the effect that he no longer claims a security interest under the financing statement, which shall be identified by file number. In other cases whenever there is no outstanding secured obligation and no commitment to make advances, incur obligations or otherwise give value, the secured party must on written demand by the debtor send the debtor, for

each filing officer with whom the financing statement was filed, a termination statement to the effect that he no longer claims a security interest under the financing statement, which shall be identified by file number. A termination statement signed by a person other than the secured party of record must be accompanied by a separate written statement of assignment signed by the secured party of record complying with subsection (2) of Section 9—405, including payment of the required fee. If the affected secured party fails to file such a termination statement as required by this subsection, or to send such a termination statement within ten days after proper demand therefor, he shall be liable to the debtor for one hundred dollars, and in addition for any loss caused to the debtor by such failure.

(2) On presentation to the filing officer of such a termination statement he must note it in the index. If he has received the termination statement in duplicate, he shall return one copy of the termination statement to the secured party stamped to show the time of receipt thereof. If the filing officer has a microfilm or other photographic record of the financing statement, and of any related continuation statement, statement of assignment and statement of release, he may remove the originals from the files at any time after receipt of the termination statement, or if he has no such record, he may remove them from the files at any time after one year after receipt of the termination statement.

(3) If the termination statement is in the standard form prescribed by the [Secretary of State], the uniform fee for filing and indexing the termination statement shall be $......, and otherwise shall be $......, plus in each case an additional fee of $...... for each name more than one against which the termination statement is required to be indexed. Amended in 1972.

Note: *The date to be inserted should be the effective date of the revised Article 9.*

§ 9—405. **Assignment of Security Interest; Duties of Filing Officer; Fees.**

(1) A financing statement may disclose an assignment of a security interest in the collateral described in the financing statement by indication in the financing statement of the name and address of the assignee or by an assignment itself or a copy thereof on the face or back of the statement. On presentation to the filing officer of such a financing statement the filing officer shall mark the same as provided in Section 9—403(4). The uniform fee for filing, indexing and furnishing filing data for a financing statement so indicating an assignment shall be $...... if the statement is in the standard form prescribed by the [Secretary of State] and otherwise shall be $......, plus in each case an additional fee of $...... for each name more than one against which the financing statement is required to be indexed.

(2) A secured party may assign of record all or part of his rights under a financing statement by the filing in the place where the original financing statement was filed of a separate written statement of assignment signed by the secured party of record and setting forth the name of the secured party of record and the debtor, the file number and the date of filing of the financing statement and the name and address of the assignee and containing a description of the collateral assigned. A copy of the assignment is sufficient as a separate statement if it complies with the preceding sentence. On presentation to the filing officer of such a separate statement, the filing officer shall mark such separate statement with the date and hour of the filing. He shall note the assignment on the index of the financing statement, or in the case of a fixture filing, or a filing covering timber to be cut, or covering minerals or the like (including oil and gas) or accounts subject to subsection (5) of Section 9—103, he shall index the assignment under the name of the assignor as grantor and, to the extent that the law of this state provides for indexing the assignment of a mortgage under the name of the assignee, he shall index the assignment of the financing statement under the name of the assignee. The uniform fee for filing, indexing and furnishing filing data about such a separate statement of assignment shall be $...... if the statement is in the standard form prescribed by the [Secretary of State] and otherwise shall be $......, plus in each case an additional fee of $...... for each name more than one against which the statement of assignment is required to be indexed. Notwithstanding the provisions of this subsection, an assignment of record of a security interest in a fixture contained in a mortgage effective as a fixture filing (subsection (6) of

Section 9—402) may be made only by an assignment of the mortgage in the manner provided by the law of this state other than this Act.

(3) After the disclosure or filing of an assignment under this section, the assignee is the secured party of record. Amended in 1972.

§ 9—406. **Release of Collateral; Duties of Filing Officer; Fees.**

A secured party of record may by his signed statement release all or a part of any collateral described in a filed financing statement. The statement of release is sufficient if it contains a description of the collateral being released, the name and address of the debtor, the name and address of the secured party, and the file number of the financing statement. A statement of release signed by a person other than the secured party of record must be accompanied by a separate written statement of assignment signed by the secured party of record and complying with subsection (2) of Section 9—405, including payment of the required fee. Upon presentation of such a statement of release to the filing officer he shall mark the statement with the hour and date of filing and shall note the same upon the margin of the index of the filing of the financing statement. The uniform fee for filing and noting such a statement of release shall be $...... if the statement is in the standard form prescribed by the [Secretary of State] and otherwise shall be $......, plus in each case an additional fee of $...... for each name more than one against which the statement of release is required to be indexed. Amended in 1972.

[§ 9—407. **Information From Filing Officer**].

[(1) If the person filing any financing statement, termination statement, statement of assignment, or statement of release, furnishes the filing officer a copy thereof, the filing officer shall upon request note upon the copy the file number and date and hour of the filing of the original and deliver or send the copy to such person.]

[(2) Upon request of any person, the filing officer shall issue his certificate showing whether there is on file on the date and hour stated therein, any presently effective financing statement naming a particular debtor and any statement of assignment thereof and if there is, giving the date and hour of filing of each such

statement and the names and addresses of each secured party therein. The uniform fee for such a certificate shall be $...... if the request for the certificate is in the standard form prescribed by the [Secretary of State] and otherwise shall be $....... Upon request the filing officer shall furnish a copy of any filed financing statement or statement of assignment for a uniform fee of $...... per page.] Amended in 1972.

Note: *This section is proposed as an optional provision to require filing officers to furnish certificates. Local law and practices should be consulted with regard to the advisability of adoption.*

§ 9—408. **Financing Statements Covering Consigned or Leased Goods.**

A consignor or lessor of goods may file a financing statement using the terms "consignor," "consignee," "lessor," "lessee" or the like instead of the terms specified in Section 9—402. The provisions of this Part shall apply as appropriate to such a financing statement but its filing shall not of itself be a factor in determining whether or not the consignment or lease is intended as security (Section 1—201(37)). However, if it is determined for other reasons that the consignment or lease is so intended, a security interest of the consignor or lessor which attaches to the consigned or leased goods is perfected by such filing. Added in 1972.

Part 5 **Default**

§ 9—501. **Default; Procedure When Security Agreement Covers Both Real and Personal Property.**

(1) When a debtor is in default under a security agreement, a secured party has the rights and remedies provided in this Part and except as limited by subsection (3) those provided in the security agreement. He may reduce his claim to judgment, foreclose or otherwise enforce the security interest by any available judicial procedure. If the collateral is documents the secured party may proceed either as to the documents or as to the goods covered thereby. A secured party in possession has the rights, remedies and duties provided in Section 9—207. The rights and remedies referred to in this subsection are cumulative.

(2) After default, the debtor has the rights and remedies provided in this Part, those provided in the security agreement and those provided in Section 9—207.

(3) To the extent that they give rights to the debtor and impose duties on the secured party, the rules stated in the subsections referred to below may not be waived or varied except as provided with respect to compulsory disposition of collateral (subsection (3) of Section 9—504 and Section 9—505) and with respect to redemption of collateral (Section 9—506) but the parties may by agreement determine the standards by which the fulfillment of these rights and duties is to be measured if such standards are not manifestly unreasonable:

(a) subsection (2) of Section 9—502 and subsection (2) of Section 9—504 insofar as they require accounting for surplus proceeds of collateral;

(b) subsection (3) of Section 9—504 and subsection (1) of Section 9—505 which deal with disposition of collateral;

(c) subsection (2) of Section 9—505 which deals with acceptance of collateral as discharge of obligation;

(d) Section 9—506 which deals with redemption of collateral; and

(e) subsection (1) of Section 9—507 which deals with the secured party's liability for failure to comply with this Part.

(4) If the security agreement covers both real and personal property, the secured party may proceed under this Part as to the personal property or he may proceed as to both the real and the personal property in accordance with his rights and remedies in respect of the real property in which case the provisions of this Part do not apply.

(5) When a secured party has reduced his claim to judgment the lien of any levy which may be made upon his collateral by virtue of any execution based upon the judgment shall relate back to the date of the perfection of the security interest in such collateral. A judicial sale, pursuant to such execution, is a foreclosure of the security interest by judicial procedure within the meaning of this section, and the secured party may purchase at the sale and thereafter hold the collateral free of any other requirements of this Article. Amended in 1972.

§ 9—502. **Collection Rights of Secured Party.**

(1) When so agreed and in any event on default the secured party is entitled to notify an account debtor or the obligor on an instrument to make payment to him whether or not the assignor was theretofore making collections on the collateral, and also to take control of any proceeds to which he is entitled under Section 9—306.

(2) A secured party who by agreement is entitled to charge back uncollected collateral or otherwise to full or limited recourse against the debtor and who undertakes to collect from the account debtors or obligors must proceed in a commercially reasonable manner and may deduct his reasonable expenses of realization from the collections. If the security agreement secures an indebtedness, the secured party must account to the debtor for any surplus, and unless otherwise agreed, the debtor is liable for any deficiency. But, if the underlying transaction was a sale of accounts or chattel paper, the debtor is entitled to any surplus or is liable for any deficiency only if the security agreement so provides. Amended in 1972.

§ 9—503. **Secured Party's Right to Take Possession After Default.**

Unless otherwise agreed a secured party has on default the right to take possession of the collateral. In taking possession a secured party may proceed without judicial process if this can be done without breach of the peace or may proceed by action. If the security agreement so provides the secured party may require the debtor to assemble the collateral and make it available to the secured party at a place to be designated by the secured party which is reasonably convenient to both parties. Without removal a secured party may render equipment unusable, and may dispose of collateral on the debtor's premises under Section 9—504.

§ 9—504. **Secured Party's Right to Dispose of Collateral After Default; Effect of Disposition.**

(1) A secured party after default may sell, lease or otherwise dispose of any or all of the collateral in its then condition or following any commercially reasonable preparation or processing. Any sale of goods is

subject to the Article on Sales (Article 2). The proceeds of disposition shall be applied in the order following to

    (a) the reasonable expenses of retaking, holding, preparing for sale or lease, selling, leasing and the like and, to the extent provided for in the agreement and not prohibited by law, the reasonable attorneys' fees and legal expenses incurred by the secured party;

    (b) the satisfaction of indebtedness secured by the security interest under which the disposition is made;

    (c) the satisfaction of indebtedness secured by any subordinate security interest in the collateral if written notification of demand therefor is received before distribution of the proceeds is completed. If requested by the secured party, the holder of a subordinate security interest must seasonably furnish reasonable proof of his interest, and unless he does so, the secured party need not comply with his demand.

(2) If the security interest secures an indebtedness, the secured party must account to the debtor for any surplus, and, unless otherwise agreed, the debtor is liable for any deficiency. But if the underlying transaction was a sale of accounts or chattel paper, the debtor is entitled to any surplus or is liable for any deficiency only if the security agreement so provides.

(3) Disposition of the collateral may be by public or private proceedings and may be made by way of one or more contracts. Sale or other disposition may be as a unit or in parcels and at any time and place and on any terms but every aspect of the disposition including the method, manner, time, place and terms must be commercially reasonable. Unless collateral is perishable or threatens to decline speedily in value or is of a type customarily sold on a recognized market, reasonable notification of the time and place of any public sale or reasonable notification of the time after which any private sale or other intended disposition is to be made shall be sent by the secured party to the debtor, if he has not signed after default a statement renouncing or modifying his right to notification of sale. In the case of consumer goods no other notification need be sent. In other cases notification shall be sent to any other secured party from whom the secured party has received (before sending his notification to the debtor or before the debtor's renunciation of his rights) written notice of a claim of an interest in the collateral. The secured party may buy at any public sale and if the collateral is of a type customarily sold in a recognized market or is of a type which is the subject of widely distributed standard price quotations he may buy at private sale.

(4) When collateral is disposed of by a secured party after default, the disposition transfers to a purchaser for value all of the debtor's rights therein, discharges the security interest under which it is made and any security interest or lien subordinate thereto. The purchaser takes free of all such rights and interests even though the secured party fails to comply with the requirements of this Part or of any judicial proceedings

    (a) in the case of a public sale, if the purchaser has no knowledge of any defects in the sale and if he does not buy in collusion with the secured party, other bidders or the person conducting the sale; or

    (b) in any other case, if the purchaser acts in good faith.

(5) A person who is liable to a secured party under a guaranty, indorsement, repurchase agreement or the like and who receives a transfer of collateral from the secured party or is subrogated to his rights has thereafter the rights and duties of the secured party. Such a transfer of collateral is not a sale or disposition of the collateral under this Article. Amended in 1972.

§ 9—505. Compulsory Disposition of Collateral; Acceptance of the Collateral as Discharge of Obligation.

(1) If the debtor has paid sixty per cent of the cash price in the case of a purchase money security interest in consumer goods or sixty per cent of the loan in the case of another security interest in consumer goods, and has not signed after default a statement renouncing or modifying his rights under this Part a secured party who has taken possession of collateral must dispose of it under Section 9—504 and if he fails to do so within ninety days after he takes possession the debtor at his option may recover in conversion or under Section 9—507(1) on secured party's liability.

(2) In any other case involving consumer goods or

any other collateral a secured party in possession may, after default, propose to retain the collateral in satisfaction of the obligation. Written notice of such proposal shall be sent to the debtor if he has not signed after default a statement renouncing or modifying his rights under this subsection. In the case of consumer goods no other notice need be given. In other cases notice shall be sent to any other secured party from whom the secured party has received (before sending his notice to the debtor or before the debtor's renunciation of his rights) written notice of a claim of an interest in the collateral. If the secured party receives objection in writing from a person entitled to receive notification within twenty-one days after the notice was sent, the secured party must dispose of the collateral under Section 9—504. In the absence of such written objection the secured party may retain the collateral in satisfaction of the debtor's obligation. Amended in 1972.

§ 9—506. **Debtor's Right to Redeem Collateral.**

At any time before the secured party has disposed of collateral or entered into a contract for its disposition under Section 9—504 or before the obligation has been discharged under Section 9—505(2) the debtor or any other secured party may unless otherwise agreed in writing after default redeem the collateral by tendering fulfillment of all obligations secured by the collateral as well as the expenses reasonably incurred by the secured party in retaking, holding and preparing the collateral for disposition, in arranging for the sale, and to the extent provided in the agreement and not prohibited by law, his reasonable attorneys' fees and legal expenses.

§ 9—507. **Secured Party's Liability for Failure to Comply With This Part.**

(1) If it is established that the secured party is not proceeding in accordance with the provisions of this Part disposition may be ordered or restrained on appropriate terms and conditions. If the disposition has occurred the debtor or any person entitled to notification or whose security interest has been made known to the secured party prior to the disposition has a right to recover from the secured party any loss caused by a failure to comply with the provisions of this Part. If the collateral is consumer goods, the debtor has a right to recover in any event an amount

not less than the credit service charge plus ten per cent of the principal amount of the debt or the time price differential plus 10 per cent of the cash price.

(2) The fact that a better price could have been obtained by a sale at a different time or in a different method from that selected by the secured party is not of itself sufficient to establish that the sale was not made in a commercially reasonable manner. If the secured party either sells the collateral in the usual manner in any recognized market therefor or if he sells at the price current in such market at the time of his sale or if he has otherwise sold in conformity with reasonable commercial practices among dealers in the type of property sold he has sold in a commercially reasonable manner. The principles stated in the two preceding sentences with respect to sales also apply as may be appropriate to other types of disposition. A disposition which has been approved in any judicial proceeding or by any bona fide creditors' committee or representative of creditors shall conclusively be deemed to be commercially reasonable, but this sentence does not indicate that any such approval must be obtained in any case nor does it indicate that any disposition not so approved is not commercially reasonable.

Article 10
EFFECTIVE DATE AND REPEALER

§ 10—101. **Effective Date.**

This Act shall become effective at midnight on December 31st following its enactment. It applies to transactions entered into and events occurring after that date.

§ 10—102. **Specific Repealer; Provision for Transition.**

(1) The following acts and all other acts and parts of acts inconsistent herewith are hereby repealed:
(Here should follow the acts to be specifically repealed including the following:

    Uniform Negotiable Instruments Act
    Uniform Warehouse Receipts Act
    Uniform Sales Act
    Uniform Bills of Lading Act
    Uniform Stock Transfer Act

Uniform Conditional Sales Act

Uniform Trust Receipts Act

Also any acts regulating:

Bank collections

Bulk sales

Chattel mortgages

Conditional sales

Factor's lien acts

Farm storage of grain and similar acts

Assignment of accounts receivable)

(2) Transactions validly entered into before the effective date specified in Section 10—101 and the rights, duties and interests flowing from them remain valid thereafter and may be terminated, completed, consummated or enforced as required or permitted by any statute or other law amended or repealed by this Act as though such repeal or amendment had not occurred.

Note Subsection (1) should be separately prepared for each state. The foregoing is a list of statutes to be checked.

§ 10—103. **General Repealer.**

Except as provided in the following section, all acts and parts of acts inconsistent with this Act are hereby repealed.

§ 10—104. **Laws Not Repealed.**

(1) The Article on Documents of Title (Article 7) does not repeal or modify any laws prescribing the form or contents of documents of title or the services or facilities to be afforded by bailees, or otherwise regulating bailees' businesses in respects not specifically dealt with herein; but the fact that such laws are violated does not affect the status of a document of title which otherwise complies with the definition of a document of title (Section 1—201).

[(2) This Act does not repeal................*, cited as the Uniform Act for the Simplification of Fiduciary Security Transfers, and if in any respect there is any inconsistency between that Act and the Article of this Act on investment securities (Article 8) the provisions of the former Act shall control.]

Note: At * in subsection (2) insert the statutory reference to the Uniform Act for the Simplification of Fiduciary Security Transfers if such Act has previously been enacted. If it has not been enacted, omit subsection (2).

Article 11
(REPORTERS' DRAFT)
EFFECTIVE DATE AND
TRANSITION PROVISIONS

This material has been numbered Article 11 to distinguish it from Article 10, the transition provision of the 1962 Code, which may still remain in effect in some states to cover transition problems from pre-Code law to the original Uniform Commercial Code. Adaptation may be necessary in particular states. The terms "[old Code]" and "[new Code]" and "[old U.C.C.]" and "[new U.C.C.]" are used herein, and should be suitably changed in each state.

Note: This draft was prepared by the Reporters and has not been passed upon by the Review Committee, the Permanent Editorial Board, the American Law Institute, or the National Conference of Commissioners on Uniform State Laws. It is submitted as a working draft which may be adapted as appropriate in each state.

§ 11—101. **Effective Date.**

This Act shall become effective at 12:01 A.M. on ———, 19——.

§ 11—102. **Preservation of Old Transition Provision.**

The provisions of [here insert reference to the original transition provision in the particular state] shall continue to apply to [the new U.C.C.] and for this purpose the [old U.C.C. and new U.C.C.] shall be considered one continuous statute.

§ 11—103. **Transition to [New Code]—General Rule.**

Transactions validly entered into after [effective date of old U.C.C.] and before [effective date of new U.C.C.], and which were subject to the provisions of [old U.C.C.] and which would be subject to this Act as amended if they had been entered into after the effective date of [new U.C.C.] and the rights, duties and interests flowing from such transactions remain valid after the latter date and may be terminated, completed, consummated or enforced as required or permitted by the [new U.C.C.]. Security interests arising out of such transactions which are perfected when [new U.C.C.] becomes effective shall remain perfected until they lapse as provided in [new

U.C.C.], and may be continued as permitted by [new U.C.C.], except as stated in Section 11—105.

§ 11—104. **Transition Provision on Change of Requirement of Filing.**

A security interest for the perfection of which filing or the taking of possession was required under [old U.C.C.] and which attached prior to the effective date of [new U.C.C.] but was not perfected shall be deemed perfected on the effective date of [new U.C.C.] if [new U.C.C.] permits perfection without filing or authorizes filing in the office or offices where a prior ineffective filing was made.

§ 11—105. **Transition Provision on Change of Place of Filing.**

(1) A financing statement or continuation statement filed prior to [effective date of new U.C.C.] which shall not have lapsed prior to [the effective date of new U.C.C.] shall remain effective for the period provided in the [old Code], but not less than five years after the filing.

(2) With respect to any collateral acquired by the debtor subsequent to the effective date of [new U.C.C.], any effective financing statement or continuation statement described in this section shall apply only if the filing or filings are in the office or offices that would be appropriate to perfect the security interests in the new collateral under [new U.C.C.].

(3) The effectiveness of any financing statement or continuation statement filed prior to [effective date of new U.C.C.] may be continued by a continuation statement as permitted by [new U.C.C.], except that if [new U.C.C.] requires a filing in an office where there was no previous financing statement, a new financing statement conforming to Section 11—106 shall be filed in that office.

(4) If the record of a mortgage of real estate would have been effective as a fixture filing of goods described therein if [new U.C.C.] had been in effect on the date of recording the mortgage, the mortgage shall be deemed effective as a fixture filing as to such goods under subsection (6) of Section 9—402 of the [new U.C.C.] on the effective date of [new U.C.C.].

§ 11—106. **Required Refilings.**

(1) If a security interest is perfected or has priority

when this Act takes effect as to all persons or as to certain persons without any filing or recording, and if the filing of a financing statement would be required for the perfection or priority of the security interest against those persons under [new U.C.C.], the perfection and priority rights of the security interest continue until 3 years after the effective date of [new U.C.C.]. The perfection will then lapse unless a financing statement is filed as provided in subsection (4) or unless the security interest is perfected otherwise than by filing.

(2) If a security interest is perfected when [new U.C.C.] takes effect under a law other than [U.C.C.] which requires no further filing, refiling or recording to continue its perfection, perfection continues until and will lapse 3 years after [new U.C.C.] takes effect, unless a financing statement is filed as provided in subsection (4) or unless the security interest is perfected otherwise than by filing, or unless under subsection (3) of Section 9—302 the other law continues to govern filing.

(3) If a security interest is perfected by a filing, refiling or recording under a law repealed by this Act which required further filing, refiling or recording to continue its perfection, perfection continues and will lapse on the date provided by the law so repealed for such further filing, refiling or recording unless a financing statement is filed as provided in subsection (4) or unless the security interest is perfected otherwise than by filing.

(4) A financing statement may be filed within six months before the perfection of a security interest would otherwise lapse. Any such financing statement may be signed by either the debtor or the secured party. It must identify the security agreement, statement or notice (however denominated in any statute or other law repealed or modified by this Act), state the office where and the date when the last filing, refiling or recording, if any, was made with respect thereto, and the filing number, if any, or book and page, if any, of recording and further state that the security agreement, statement or notice, however denominated, in another filing office under the [U.C.C.] or under any statute or other law repealed or modified by this Act is still effective. Section 9—401 and Section 9—103 determine the proper place to file

such a financing statement. Except as specified in this subsection, the provisions of Section 9—403(3) for continuation statements apply to such a financing statement.

§ 11—107. **Transition Provisions as to Priorities.**

Except as otherwise provided in [Article 11], [old U.C.C.] shall apply to any questions of priority if the positions of the parties were fixed prior to the effective date of [new U.C.C.]. In other cases questions of priority shall be determined by [new U.C.C.].

§ 11—108. **Presumption that Rule of Law Continues Unchanged.**

Unless a change in law has clearly been made, the provisions of [new U.C.C.] shall be deemed declaratory of the meaning of the [old U.C.C.]

GLOSSARY

A

abandoned property   Property which the owner has parted with no intention of recovering it.

abuse of discretion   Clearly erroneous judgment; usually used in reference to action taken by an administrative agency which has no foundation in fact or in law.

acceleration clause   Clauses in contracts for rent, or for installment payments, which provide that all future payments will become due immediately upon the failure to tender timely payment on any one installment. (see *installment contracts, tender, severable contracts*.)

acceptance   The offeree's notification to the offeror that he agrees to be bound by the terms of the offeror's proposal. Although, historically acceptance had to be in the exact manner specified by the offeror, the trend is to allow acceptance by any means which will reasonably notify the offeror of the acceptance.

accession   1) The changing (through manufacturing) of one good into a new good (*i.e.*, flour into bread). 2) The right to all that which one's property produces (*i.e.*, fruit from trees) or to that which becomes added to or incorporated to that property (*i.e.*, buildings on one's land). 3) The right, upon payment for the original materials, to keep an article manufactured out of goods which were innocently converted. (see *conversion*)

accommodation party   A person who indorses a note, but is to receive no payment from it, nor consideration for his indorsement. Unless he uses a qualified indorsement, he is liable as a surety (secondarily liable) on the note.

accord An agreement between two persons, one of whom has a right of action against the other, to settle the dispute.

accord and satisfaction An agreement and payment between two parties, one of whom has a right of action against the other. After the agreement has been made, and payment has been tendered the "accord and satisfaction" is complete.

account 1) An intangible concept of individualized funds maintained by banks for each depositor. 2) A legal action, asking for a setting out of revenues, expenses, etc.

actual authority Power of an agent to bind its principal where such power derives either from express or implied agreement between principal and agent.

actus reus The "guilty act." As opposed to the mens rea, the *actus reus* is the physical aspect of a crime whereas the mens rea involves the psychological or intent factor.

adhesion contracts Standard "form" contracts, such as those between a large retailer and a consumer.

administrative law The rules under which administrative agencies such as the SEC and FTC carry out their duties and responsibilities. This law can initially be enforced by these agencies, outside the judicial process.

administrative process Methods prescribed by the Legislature which govern an agency's powers and procedure in enforcement of administrative law.

administrator (trix) One who is appointed by a court to handle the probate (disposition) of a person's estate if that person dies intestate. (see *estate, will, intestacy laws*)

adverse possession The acquisition of title to real property by occupying it, with the knowledge of the owner, for a period of time specified by state statutes.

affirmative defense A response to a plaintiff's claim which attacks the plaintiff's *legal* right to bring an action as opposed to attacking the truth of the claim. Running of the statute of limitations is an example of an affirmative defense.

agency A relationship between two persons whereby agreement or otherwise, one is bound by the words and acts of the other. The former is a *principal*; the latter is an *agent*.

agreement Synonym for contract.

allonge A piece of paper attached to a negotiable instrument, upon which transferees can make indorsements if there is no room left on the instrument itself.

answer The defendant's response to the complaint. Filing of the complaint and answer are governed by rules of procedure.

anticipatory breach or **anticipatory repudiation** The assertion by a party that he will not perform an obligation which he is contractually obligated to perform at a future time.

apparent authority Such authority as a reasonable person would assume an agent has in light of the conduct of the principal. Apparent authority cannot be established solely by the conduct of the agent and must be chargeable to the principal.

appellant The party who invokes the appellate jurisdiction of a superior court, after that party has lost in the inferior court. May be either the plaintiff or defendant.

appellee The party who won in the inferior court; the party against whom the appeal is taken.

arbitrary and capricious Without basis in fact or law. Without a rational basis.

arbitration The settling of a dispute by submitting it to a disinterested third party other than a court.

arbitration clauses Clauses in a contract which provide that in case of dispute the parties will determine their rights by means of compromise *outside* the judicial system.

arson The malicious burning of another's dwelling. Some statutes have expanded this to include any building, and to destruction by other means, *i.e.*, exploding.

articles of incorporation The instrument under which a corporation is formed which serves as a request to the state to be treated as a corporation under its laws.

articles of partnership The written contract by which parties enter into a partnership, to be governed by the terms set forth in the contract.

artisan's lien A possessory lien given to a person who has made improvements and added value to another person's personal property. This is given a security for services performed.

assault Any word or action intended to cause the

person to whom it is directed to be in fear of immediate physical harm; a reasonably believable threat. (see *battery*)

assault and battery   An intentional threat of bodily harm and the carrying out of the threat.

assignment   The act of transferring to another all or part of one's property, interest, or rights. In contract, one can assign to another his right to receive the performance of the other obligated party.

assignment of rights   See *assignment*.

assumption of risk   The bargained for transfer of any underlying risks in a contract (e.g., theft losses) from the party who otherwise would naturally or legally bear the losses flowing from such risks to the other party.

attachment   In a secured transaction, the process by which a security interest in the property of another becomes enforceable. Attachment may occur upon the taking possession of the property or upon the signing of a security agreement by the person pledging the property as collateral.

B

bailee   One to whom goods are entrusted by a bailor, for the bailor's benefit.

bailment   Agreement to entrust goods of one person (bailor) to another (bailee).

bailor   One who entrusts his goods to another, for his (bailor's) benefit.

bankruptcy   Proceedings under law, initiated either by an "insolvent" person or business entity or by its creditors seeking to have the court adjudge it a *bankrupt*. Bankruptcy also includes the process of administering the bankrupt's assets and/or dividing its assets among its creditors.

battery   The unprivileged intentional touching of another. (see *assault*)

bearer paper   In the law of commercial paper, any instrument which runs to the bearer. It includes instruments payable to the bearer or to "cash."

beneficiary   One who holds equitable title to property being held in trust, such property being cared for by the trustee. (see *fiduciary duty*)

bequest   A gift by will of personal property. (verb—to bequeath)

bilateral contract   A contract which includes the exchange of a promise for a promise. (as opposed to unilateral contract)

bill of lading   A document which serves both to evidence the receipt of goods for shipment and to pass title of the goods.

binder   A written, temporary insurance policy. (see *policy*)

"Blue Sky" laws   Another name for state laws which regulate the offer and sale of securities.

bond   An instrument which evidences a corporate debt. It is a security which involves no ownership interest in the issuing corporation.

bond indenture   An instrument of indebtedness issued by a corporation.

breach   See breach of contract.

breach of contract   Failure of a promisor to substantially perform the obligations of a contract.

burglary   The unlawful entry, at night, into a building with the intent to commit theft. Some state statutes expand this to include the intent to commit any felony. (see *felony*)

bylaws   The rules which a business firm adopts in order to control the conduct of its internal affairs.

C

capital stock   The amount of money or property contributed by shareholders to be used as a corporation's financial foundation. The total amount of stock to be issued in return for capital contributions is limited by the corporation's charter. (see *charter*)

cashier's check   A negotiable instrument drawn by a bank on itself.

causa mortis gifts   A gift made because the giver (donor) contemplates his imminent death. If the donor does not die of that ailment, the gift is revoked, because the intent was to give it upon death. No title transfers until the donor's death.

cause of action   A legal right of redress against another; it includes both the right to sue and the right to recover in a court of law.

caveat emptor (Latin)   Literally, "let the buyer beware."

cease and desist order   Administrative or judicial order commanding a business firm to cease conducting the activities which the agency or court has deemed "unfair or deceptive trade practices."

certified check   A check drawn by an individual on his own account but bearing a guarantee by a bank that the bank will pay the check regardless of whether the drawer's account contains adequate funds at the time the check is presented.

charter   The basic document under which a corporation is organized, setting forth the corporation's and shareholders' rights and duties.

chattel   Tangible personal property.

chattel paper   Any instrument which evidences both a security interest in collateral and a money obligation with respect to the collateral.

check   An unconditional order to pay a sum certain to bearer or to whom the check is made out. The check is drawn on a bank, signed by the drawer, and payable on demand.

civil law   1) That branch of law which deals with the definition and enforcement of all private or public rights, as opposed to criminal matters. 2) The law compiled by the early Roman jurists, which is still in force in many Western European states, and is the foundation for the law in Louisiana.

class action suit   A legal action in which a group of persons (usually more than thirty) are represented by one or a few persons. The class can be either a plaintiff or a defendant.

close corporation   A corporation whose shareholders are limited to a small group of persons, often including only family members. Shareholders of a close corporation usually reserve *preemptive* rights with respect to the shares of all other shareholders.

codicil   A written supplement or modification of a will. Codicils must be executed with the same formalities as a will.

collateral   Those goods which the secured party has an interest in, as security in case of nonpayment by the debtor.

collecting bank   Any bank handling an item for collection, except the payor bank.

commercial paper   Negotiable instruments, which are signed writings by which the maker promises (unconditionally) to pay a certain amount of money to the bearer of the paper (*i.e.,* checks, promissory notes).

common law   That body of law developed in English and American courts, not attributable to a legislature.

common stock   Shares of ownership in a corporation which are lowest in priority with respect to payment of dividends and distribution of the corporation's assets upon dissolution.

comparative negligence   Concept in tort law whereby liability for injuries resulting from negligent acts is shared by all persons who were guilty of negligence, including the injured party, on a basis proportionate to each person's carelessness.

compensatory damages   Money damages equivalent to the actual value of the performance promised to defendant/breaching party by plaintiff, or the loss sustained by plaintiff.

complaint   The charge made by a plaintiff or by the state to a judicial officer alleging wrongdoing on the part of the defendant. Thus, the plaintiff is also referred to as the complainant.

concurrent conditions   Conditions which must occur or be performed at the same time; they are mutually dependent. No obligations arise until the simultaneous performance of these conditions.

concurrent estates   Estates in land of equal quantity and quality held by two or more persons simultaneously.

condition   A qualification on a contractual agreement. The obligation to perform can be varied, depending on whether the conditions are met or not.

condition precedent   A qualification on a contractual agreement which must be met before the other party's obligations arise. If the condition is not met, the (conditional) obligation never arises. There can be no breach until the condition is met.

condition subsequent   A qualification on a contract which, if met, discharges the (conditional) obligation of the other party. If the condition never arises, the other party's obligation is absolute.

confusion   The mixing together of two or more goods so that the independent goods cannot be identified.

conglomerate mergers   Mergers between firms which do not compete with each other because they are in different industries as opposed to horizontal and vertical mergers.

consent decree   A judgment entered, by a court, by the consent of the parties. In a consent decree neither party admits guilt or wrongdoing.

consequential damages   Special damages, which compensate for loss that is indirect or mediate (*i.e.,* lost profits). The special damages must have been reasonably foreseeable at the time the breach or injury occurred, in order for the plaintiff to collect them.

consideration That which motivates the exchange of promises in a contractual agreement. The consideration, which must be present to make the contract legally binding, must be lawful in itself. It is a flexible term, and can refer to anything of value. (see *contract*)

consolidation A contractual and statutory process whereby two or more corporations join to become a completely new corporation. The original corporations cease to exist, and the new corporation acquires all their assets and liabilities (*i.e.*, A + B = C).

constructive delivery The recognition of the act of intending that title to property be transferred to someone else, even though actual, physical delivery of the property is not made (because of difficulty, impossibility) (*i.e.*, the transfer of a key to a safe constructively delivers the contents of the safe).

constructive/implied conditions Conditions or qualifications to a promise which arise from the very nature of the promise and which the law recognizes as conditioning the promise even though not expressly stated.

consumer goods Goods which are purchased primarily for personal use.

contract A set of promises constituting an agreement between parties, giving each a legal duty to the other and also the right to seek a remedy for the breach of the promises/duties owed to each. (see *specific performance, injunction*) The elements of an enforceable contract are competent parties, a proper subject matter, consideration (an exchange of promises/duties), and mutuality of agreement and of obligation. (see *consideration*)

contracts implied-in-law Promises which the law imposes upon contracting parties in general, as opposed to contracts implied-in-fact which have as their basis the underlying facts and circumstances of a particular contractual situation.

contracts under seal Formal agreements in which the seal is a substitute for *consideration*. A court will not invalidate a contract under seal for lack of consideration.

contractual capacity The threshold mental capacity required by the law for a party who enters into a contract to be bound by that contract. Contractual capacity will not be found where one is forced to sign a contract under duress or is insane.

contributory negligence Any wrongful or negligent act by a complaining party which contributed to or enhanced the complaining party's injuries. Contributory negligence is an absolute bar to recovery in some jurisdictions. (see *negligence, affirmative defense*)

conversion The wrongful taking or retaining possession of property which belongs to another.

corporation An association of persons, usually entered into to carry out business endeavors. The law treats the corporation itself as a person which can sue and be sued. The corporation is distinct from the individuals who compose it (shareholders). The corporation survives the death of its investors, as the shares can usually be transferred. Created under state corporation statutes.

counterclaim A pleading by a defendant against the plaintiff in which the defendant states a claim for damages resulting from allegedly wrongful acts of the plaintiff. The counterclaim need not arise out of the same facts and circumstances as the plaintiff's claim.

counter-offer An offeree's response to an offeror in which the offeree proposes different or additional terms than were contained in the original offer. Acceptance of a counter-offer constitutes a contract, and a counter-offer itself constitutes a rejection of the original offer.

course of dealing The understandings which arise between two parties with respect to time and quality of performance expected and which develop over a period of time and number of transactions between the two parties.

course of performance The understandings and standards of time and quality of performance which develop between two parties during the performance of an executory contract.

covenant of quiet enjoyment A promise by the landlord to the tenant, implied in law, that the landlord will not cause the tenant to be evicted.

covenant running with the land An executory promise made between a promisor and promisee but which binds them as landowners and binds subsequent owners of the land bound by the covenant.

creditor beneficiary A third person, who is not a

party to a contract to whom one of the parties owes a prior obligation. As a part of the contract, the other party obligates himself to honor the prior debt to the beneficiary. The beneficiary can enforce the debt against either party.

crime A broad term for violations of law which are punishable by the state or nation. Crimes are codified by legislatures and their objective is the protection of the public. (see *civil law, criminal law*)

crimes mala in se Acts which are morally wrong/wrong in themselves whether prohibited by human laws or not. (see *crimes mala prohibita*)

crimes mala prohibita Acts which are prohibited by human law, but are not necessarily wrong in themselves. (see *crimes mala in se*)

criminal law Governs and defines those actions which subject the convicted offender to punishment imposed by the state.

cure The right of a party who tenders non-conforming performance to reform his performance within a reasonable time.

cy pres Doctrine in the law of trusts and wills under which a grantor's (or testator's) wishes will be carried out "as nearly as possible" even though the grant (bequest or devise) is illegal in its original form.

D

damages Money sought as a remedy for a breach of contract action or for tortious acts.

debt securities Securities which are of such duration that they evidence an obligation of the corporation to repay the holder, rather than evidencing an investment by the holder in exchange for stock.

debtor A person who owes a sum of money or other obligations to another.

deceit A false representation of facts made recklessly, maliciously, or with knowledge of its falsity, with the intent to cause the injured person to rely on the misrepresentation. (see *fraud*)

deed A document by which title to property (usually real property) is passed.

de facto corporation A business which holds itself out as a corporation but which has not been organized in substantial compliance with state corporation law.

defamation Anything published or publicly spoken which causes injury to another's good name, reputation or character. (see *slander, libel*)

defendant The party against whom the action is brought.

defense of property The legally recognized privilege of a person to do limited harm to another in defending his or her property. One may only use the amount of force necessary to protect his or her property, as the use of even slightly greater force will be deemed wrongful.

de jure corporation A corporation which has been organized substantially in compliance with state corporation laws.

delegation The act of transferring to another all or part of one's duties arising under a contract.

demurrer A pleading in which a defendant admits to the facts as alleged by the plaintiff but asserts that the plaintiff's claim fails to state a cause of action (i.e., has no basis in law).

depositary bank The first bank to which an item is transferred for collection even though it may also be the payor bank.

devise To make a gift of real property by will.

disaffirmance The repudiation of an obligation.

discharge Termination of one's obligation. In contract law, discharge occurs when the promisor has fully performed his or her promised performance or when a party to a contract has substantially breached the contract (then the other party is discharged).

discharge in bankruptcy The release of a bankrupt from all debts which are provable, except those specifically excepted from discharge by statute.

discovery A method by which opposing parties may obtain information from each other, to narrow down the issues to be presented at trial. Generally governed by rules of procedure, but may be controlled by the court.

dishonor The refusal to pay or accept an instrument which has been properly presented.

dissolution The formal disbanding of a partnership. Can take place by agreement of the parties, death of a partner, or court order. (see *partnership for term, partnership at will*)

dividend (a) A distribution of profits to corporate shareholders, disbursed in proportion to the number of shares held.

dividend (b) Share of the proceeds of a bankrupt's estate received by a general creditor.

documents of title Documents exchanged in the regular course of business which evidence the right to possession of goods (e.g., bills of lading, warehouse receipts, etc.).

domestic corporation In any given state, a corporation which is doing business and is organized under the laws of the state.

donee beneficiary   A person not a party to a contract but to whom the benefits of a contract flow as a result of the promisee's intention to make a gift to that person.

draft   Any negotiable instrument drawn on any person (including a bank) which orders that person to pay a certain sum of money.

drawee   The person who is ordered to pay on an instrument. With a check, the bank is always the drawee.

drawer   A person who initiates a draft (including a check) thereby ordering the drawee to pay.

due process   An individual's right not to be deprived of life, liberty, or property without a hearing.

duress   Any unlawful threat or coercion used by a person to induce another to act or refrain from acting in a manner he or she otherwise would.

E

easement   The right to use another's property in a manner established either by express or implied agreement.

easement appurtenant   An easement on a "servient estate," which serves a "dominant estate."

easement in gross   The right to use another's land which is not dependent upon ownership of land by the holder of the easement.

embezzlement   The fraudulent appropriation of money or other property by a person to whom the money or property has been entrusted.

eminent domain   The power of a government to take land from private citizens for a fair compensation.

endowment policy   In life insurance, a policy which is payable when the insured reaches a given age, or upon his death, if that occurs earlier.

equitable servitude   A restriction on the use of land enforceable in a court of equity.

equity   The system of remedial justice, separate from the common law, based upon settled rules of fairness, justice and honesty.

equity of redemption   The right of mortgager to redeem or purchase property which the mortgagor forfeited by breaching the mortgage agreement.

equity securities   Securities with no repayment terms or with repayment terms of such long duration

that they represent an ownership interest in a corporation rather than debt.

estate   Full ownership interest in land.

estray statutes   State laws dealing with person's rights in property whose ownership is unknown.

exclusive dealing contract   An agreement under which a producer of goods agrees to sell its goods exclusively through one distributor.

exculpatory contract or clause   A contract or contract clause which releases one of the parties from liability for his or her negligent acts.

executed contract   An agreement which has been substantially (or completely) performed by both parties.

executor (trix)   A person either expressly or by implication appointed by a testator to see that his will is administered appropriately. (see *will, testator*)

executory contract   A contract calling for continual performance by one or both of the parties.

executory interest   A future interest not held by the grantor which either cuts short (shifting) or begins some time after (springing) the natural termination of the preceding estate.

express condition   A qualification or condition upon which a promise is based and which is stated in the body of the contract.

express contract   A contract which is either oral or written. (As opposed to *implied contract*.)

express warranty   A promise, ancillary to an underlying sales agreement which is included in the written or oral terms of the sales agreement and under which the promisor assures the quality of the goods.

ex-ship   Words in a contract denoting that the seller may choose the shipper, and that risk of loss shall pass to the buyer upon the goods leaving the ship. Buyer is also responsible for any subsequent landing charges.

F

F.A.S.   "Free alongside ship"; delivery term under which the seller is obligated to deliver goods to a specified loading dock and bears all risk of loss up to that point.

factual causation   In tort law, the physical connection between a person's act or failure to act and the resulting injury to another or damage to property.

fee simple absolute   An estate or interest in land with no time or use limitations whatsoever.

fee simple defeasible   An estate which can be taken

away (by the prior grantor) upon the occurrence or non-occurrence of a specified event.

felony Crime which carries the most severe sanctions, usually ranging from one year in prison to the forfeiture of one's life (*i.e.*, arson, murder, rape, robbery).

fiduciary duty A duty to act for someone else's benefit, while subordinating one's personal interests to that of the other person. It is the highest standard of duty implied by law (*i.e.*, trustee, guardian).

financing statement A document setting out a lienholder's security interest in goods. When the document is filed with the appropriate government agency, all potential lenders are put on constructive notice of the security interest.

firm offers A signed writing which promises to keep an offer open for a specified time. Unlike an option, no consideration need by given to make the offer non-revocable. (see *merchant's firm offer*)

fixture A thing which was once personal property, but has become attached to real property in such a way that it takes on the characteristics of real property and becomes part of that real property. (see *chattel, personal property, real property*)

floating lien A security interest in varying assets (e.g., inventory).

floating zone A concept in zoning whereby land use is predetermined by assigning specified portions of an entire area to particular uses while not immediately assigning particular parcels to a certain use.

F.O.B. "Free on board"; the seller in a commercial contract which contains the term F.O.B. has the duty to load the goods for shipment without expense to the buyer. Once loaded properly, the buyer assumes the risk of loss in case the goods are damaged.

forebearance Refraining from doing something that one has a legal right to do.

foreclosure A proceeding in equity whereby a mortgagee either takes title to or forces the sale of the mortgagor's property in satisfaction of a debt.

foreign corporation In any given state, a corporation which does business in the state without being incorporated therein.

forgery The false or unauthorized signature of a document, or the false making of a document, with the intent to defraud. (see *fraud*)

form An agreement which places the risks and burdens normally associated with the underlying exchange on one of the parties and which leaves no room for bargaining over these terms.

formal contract An agreement which the law requires be executed under seal or in the presence of witnesses or both.

fraud Any misrepresentation either by misstatement or omission knowingly made with the intention of defrauding another and on which a reasonable person would and does rely to his detriment.

frustration of purpose doctrine Court created doctrine under which a party to a contract will be relieved of his or her duty to perform when the objective purpose for performance no longer exists (due to reasons beyond that party's control).

fungible goods Goods which cannot be distinguished from other goods of the same type (*i.e.*, bushels of wheat, apples of the same brand).

future interest A present interest in land in which the right of enjoyment or possession is in the future.

G

garnishment A process whereby a creditor legally appropriates the debtor's property or wages which are in the hands of a third party.

gift Any transfer of property to another which is without consideration, past or present.

gift causa mortis See causa mortis gift.

good faith Honesty in fact as well as honesty in the conduct or transaction concerned.

goods Any tangible personal property which can be traded in the marketplace.

grace period A span of time, after insurance policy premium (payment) was due, during which the policy remains in effect. (see *policy*)

grand jury A body of people (usually 23) selected to conduct fact finding hearings for the purpose of issuing true bills for criminal offenses. The grand jury does not adjudicate, it only accuses. The grand jurors need only find probable cause to indict someone, as opposed to the exclusion of reasonable doubt standard which is necessary to convict someone of a crime. In certain situations, the state or U.S. prosecutor can issue an information, rather than seek a grand-jury indictment. (see *information, true bill*)

grantor One who transfers real property by deed.

guaranty An agreement in which the guarantor agrees to satisfy the debt of another (the debtor). The guarantor is responsible only if and when the debtor fails to repay; he is secondarily liable.

H

holder   A person who is in possession of a document or negotiable instrument which runs to him.

holder in due course   A person who is a holder of an instrument and who took it in good faith, for value, and without notice that the instrument is overdue or has been dishonored or that any defense or claim exists against it.

holder through a holder in due course   One who acquires the rights of a holder in due course by taking the instrument through him in good faith.

holographic document   A document written entirely in the signer's handwriting.

homestead exemption   Law allowing a householder/head of a family to designate his house and adjoining land a homestead, and exempting it from liability for his general debts.

horizontal merger   A merger between two companies which compete in the marketplace.

I

identification   Proof that a thing is what it is purported or represented to be.

implied authority   The power of an agent to act on behalf of his principal which is inferred from the responsibilities imposed on the agent in his employment.

implied-in-fact contract   A promise which the law deems as part of an overall agreement because the underlying facts and circumstances logically infer the existence of such a promise.

implied warranty   A guarantee which the law implies either through the situation of the parties or the nature of the transaction. (see *usage of trade, course of dealing*)

implied warranty of merchantability   See warranty of merchantability.

impossibility of performance   Doctrine under which a party to a contract is relieved of his or her duty to perform since performance has become impossible or totally impracticable (through no fault of the party).

impracticability   (commercial   impracticability)   Broadened interpretation of the doctrine of impossibility which holds that a party to a business related contract will be relieved of his or her duty to perform when premise (e.g., existence of certain goods) on which the contract was based no longer exists due to unforeseeable events.

incidental beneficiary   A person who indirectly receives, or will receive, a benefit as the result of a contract entered into by other parties. Since the incidental beneficiary is neither a donee beneficiary nor a creditor beneficiary he has no right to enforce the contract.

indemnification   The right of an employer/principal to recover (be indemnified) from an employee/agent anything paid out to satisfy claims arising from the employee/agent's negligence within the scope of his employment/agency. (see *respondeat superior, power of attorney*)

indictment   A charge by a grand jury that a named person has committed an unlawful act.

indorsement   A signature placed on an instrument or a document of title for the purpose of transferring one's ownership in the instrument or document of title.

informal contract   An agreement which is valid regardless of whether it is witnessed or sealed.

information   A formal accusation or complaint issued in certain types of actions by a prosecuting attorney or other law officer. The types of actions are set forth in the rules of states or the Federal Rules of Criminal Procedure. (see *grand jury, true bill*)

injunction   An order by a court requiring a person to act or refrain from acting in a certain manner.

insolvency   The financial state of a person when his liabilities exceed the value of his assets *or* when, due to the non-liquidity of his assets he is unable or unwilling to pay his debts as they come due.

installment contract   An executory agreement whereby either property purchased or payments due, or both, are made periodically.

insurable interest   An interest either in a person's life or well-being or in property which is sufficiently substantial that insuring against injury to the person or damage to the property will not amount to a mere wagering contract.

intangible property   A property right, usually represented by a document or certificate which has no intrinsic value but which evidences a valuable ownership interest.

intermediary bank   Any bank to which an item is

transferred in the course of collection, except the depositary or payor bank.

inter vivos gift   A gift made by a living person which is not in contemplation of death.

inter vivos trust   A trust in which the grantor (settlor) is a living person. (*i.e.*, a trust not established by a will)

intestacy laws   State laws determining the way in which an intestate's (one who dies with no will) estate is divided.

intestate   (Dying) without a valid will.

inventory   Goods held for sale or lease or to be furnished under contracts of service, including work in process and materials used or consumed in a business. Inventory of a person is not to be classified as his equipment.

invitee   Person who, either expressly or impliedly, is privileged to enter upon another's land. The inviter owes the invitee the duty to exercise reasonable care to protect an individual from harm (*i.e.*, a customer in a store, the postman).

involuntary bankruptcy   A proceeding against an insolvent debtor which is initiated by the debtor's creditors.

issue   The first delivery of an instrument to a holder or a remitter.

J

joint and several liability   Liability of a group of persons for the same act (or failure to act) whereby a claimant may sue one or more of the parties separately or all of them together at his option.

joint liability   Liability of a group of persons for the same wrongful act (or failure to act) whereby when one is sued, he can insist that the others be sued with him.

joint tenancy   The ownership interest of two or more co-owners of property whereby each owns an undivided portion of the property. The key feature of joint tenancy is the "right of survivorship" whereby, upon the death of one of the joint tenants, his interest automatically passes to the others and cannot be transferred in his will.

judgment creditor   A person in whose favor a money judgment has been entered by a court of law and who has not yet been paid.

judgment debt   A monetary obligation which is either evidenced by a written record, or brought about by legal action against the debtor.

jurisdiction   The authority of a court to hear and decide a specific action.

jurisprudence   The science of philosophy of law.

L

laissez-faire   Doctrine advocating government restraint in regulation of business.

larceny   Act of taking another's personal property unlawfully. Burglary carried to its logical conclusion. Some states classify larceny as either Grand or Petit, depending on the property's value. (see *burglary*)

law   Rules of social conduct to be followed by citizens of a society, as pronounced by that society's government.

law merchant   Relates chiefly to the transactions of merchants, mariners, and other commercial traders. Consists chiefly of the general customs of the trades, which remain law unless displaced by specific statutes (see *Uniform Commercial Code*).

lease   A transfer by the landlord/lessor of real or personal property to the tenant/lessee for a period of time, for a consideration (usually the payment of rent). At the end of the period, the land reverts to the lessor.

legality   Lawfulness.

legally sufficient consideration   That type of consideration which the law recognizes as *legally* adequate to support a contract. Legal sufficiency does not deal with monetary value of consideration (e.g., "love and affection" is not legally sufficient consideration).

lessee   A person who pays for the use or possession of another's property.

lessor   A property owner who allows others to use his property in exchange for payment of rent.

letters of credit   A written instrument, usually issued by a bank on behalf of a buyer, in which the issuer promises to pay the bearer of the instrument (seller) upon proper delivery of goods, or at a specified time thereafter.

libel   A written defamation. The press is, to a certain degree, protected from libel actions by the First Amendment.

license   A revocable privilege to enter on the land of another.

lien   An encumbrance upon a property, to satisfy or protect a claim for payment of a debt.

life estate   An interest in land which exists only for

the duration of the life of some person, usually the holder of the estate.

limited liability   Concept in corporation law whereby shareholders' liability for debts incurred by the corporation are limited to the money which the shareholders invested in their stock.

limited partnership   A partnership consisting of one or more general partners, who carry on the business as well as contribute assets and are liable to the full extent of their personal assets for debts of the partnership, and one or more limited partners, who just contribute assets and are liable only up to the amount contributed by them. (see *partnership by contract*)

liquidated damages   An amount, stipulated in the contract, which the parties believe to be a reasonable estimation of the damages which will occur in the event of a breach.

liquidated debt   A debt which is for a known or ascertainable sum of money, the amount of which cannot be disputed by either the debtor or creditor.

liquidation   Sale of the assets of a corporation for cash and distribution of the cash received to creditors and then to shareholders.

lost property   Property which the owner has involuntarily parted with and does not know where to find or recover it.

M

maker   One who issues a promissory note (*i.e.,* one who promises to pay a certain sum to the holder of the note which he executes).

mechanic's lien   A lien which a creditor has in property which is in his possession and which has been increased in value by the creditor through the application of his labor and materials.

merchant   A person who deals in goods of the kind or holds himself out as having knowledge or skills peculiar to the trade or goods involved, or to whom such skills can be attributed because of the nature of his employment.

merchant's firm offer   A signed, written offer to buy or sell goods, which by its terms will be held open for a certain time, without requiring consideration. The U.C.C. limits merchant's firm offers to a maximum of three months. (see *firm offer,* U.C.C.)

merger   A statutory and contractual process by which one corporation (surviving corporation) acquires all the assets and liabilities of another corpora-

tion (merged corporation). The shareholders of the merged corporation receive either payment for their shares or shares in the surviving corporation (*i.e.,* A + B = A).

misdemeanors   Lessor crime, punishable by more severe sanctions than a disturbance of the peace, but not as severe as felonies.

mislaid property   Property which the owner has voluntarily parted with, with the intention of retrieving later, but which cannot now be found. Does not include intentionally hidden property.

mortgage   A written instrument giving some person (the mortgagee), usually a creditor, an interest (lien) in the debtor's (mortgagor's) property as security for a debt.

mortgagee   The person who takes the security interest under the mortgage agreement.

mortgagor   The person who pledges collateral in a mortgage agreement.

mutual assent   Agreement by both parties to a contract to any particular term.

N

necessaries   Goods and services, such as food, shelter, clothing and employment, which are deemed necessary or essential for a person's well being.

negative easement   A burden on land whereby the landowner is restricted under an easement agreement not to use his property in a certain way. (e.g., not to build a building higher than four stories so as to preserve an adjacent landholder's view.)

negligence   Conduct which falls below that standard of care which would be exercised by the "reasonable man," in relation to the protection of others. A legal duty is inherent in negligence. (see *tort*) Negligence is a lesser disregard of duty than recklessness or willfulness.

negotiable instruments   A written and signed unconditional promise to pay a specified sum of money at a specified time. (see *commercial paper*)

negotiation   The transferring of an instrument to another in a manner that will vest the transferee with the right to enforce the instrument.

nominal damages   An award of damages whereby a court recognizes that there has been a technical breach of duty but has found that no financial loss or injury has resulted from the breach of duty.

note   Same as *promissory note.*

novation   The release of an old debt or debtor with the substitution of a new one in its/his place.

nuisance   An act which interferes with a person's possession or ability to use his or her property.

O

objective theory of contracts   The view taken by American law that contracting parties shall only be bound by terms which can be objectively inferred from promises made. Contract law does not examine a contracting party's subjective intent or underlying motive.

offer   A proposal to do something by an offeree which creates in the offeror a legal power to bind the offeree to the terms of his proposal by accepting the offer.

offeree   One to whom an offer is made.

offeror   Person who makes an offer.

option contract   A contract whereby the offeror cannot revoke his offer for a stipulated time period, and the offeree can accept or reject during this period without fear of the offer being put to another person. Here, the offeree must give consideration for the option (the non-revocable offer), as well as for the further contractual promises, if he accepts.

order paper   An instrument which is payable to the payee or to any person the payee by his indorsement designates.

ordinary bailment   A transfer of goods to the bailee in trust for the bailor, with benefits going to both parties. In exchange for a fee, the bailee agrees to safely keep the property until the bailor recovers it. The bailee is responsible for exercising due care toward the goods.

output contract   A binding agreement where one party agrees to deliver/sell his entire output of a good (an unspecified amount at the time of agreement) to another party, and the other agrees to accept all of the goods supplied.

P

pari delicto   At equal fault.

parol evidence rule   Substantive rule of contracts under which a court will not receive into evidence oral or written statements made prior to or contemporaneous with a written agreement where the court finds that the written agreement was intended by the parties to be a final and complete expression of their agreement.

partnership   Two or more persons associated for the purpose of carrying on a business for profit.

partnership at will   A partnership which, by the terms of the Articles of Partnership, may be dissolved at any time by any of the partners.

partnership by estoppel   Two or more persons which associate in a cooperative business enterprise and hold themselves out as partners.

payee   Person to whom a negotiable instrument is made payable.

payor bank   A bank by which an item is payable as drawn (or is payable as accepted).

penalties   Amounts stipulated to in the contract, but either not being a reasonable estimation of the damages, or motivated solely by a desire to deter a breach. The agreement as to the amount will not be enforced, and recovery will be limited to actual damages.

per capita   The manner of distribution of property whereby the heirs to an intestate's estate share and share alike. As opposed to *per stirpes*.

perfect tender rule   Strict doctrine, whereby tender of performance/goods which does not exactly conform to the contract can properly be rejected. (see *tender, substantial performance*)

perfection   The method by which a secured party obtains a guarantee that his security interest cannot be challenged by a subsequent secured party. Usually accomplished by filing a financing statement at a location set out in the state statute. (see *secured party, security interest, financing statement*)

periodic tendency   Interest in land created by the payment of rent at a fixed interval.

personal property   Property which is movable; any property which is not real property. (see *real property*)

per stirpes   Manner of distribution of property whereby a class or group of distributees take the share which their deceased would have been entitled to (e.g., A dies leaving one son, B, and two grandchildren of deceased daughter C. B takes one-half and the two grandchildren each take one-quarter).

piercing the corporate veil   A court's act of ignoring the separate legal existence of the corporation and thereby holding the corporation's officers personally liable for their wrongdoings.

plaintiff   The party bringing an action.

plat   A chart or map, usually filed with a municipal

or county agency, which delineates the parcels into which a large tract of land has been subdivided.

pleadings Statements by the plaintiff and the defendant which detail the facts, charges, and defenses. Modern rules simplify common law pleading, often requiring only the complaint, answer, and sometimes a reply to the answer.

pledge That which is offered as security for the payment of a debt.

policy The contract encompassing an insurance agreement.

pooling agreement A procedure whereby shareholders can increase their voting power, which is directly related to the number of shares held.

possibility of reverter A future interest in land which a grantor retains after conveying property subject to a condition subsequent. (see *future interest*)

power of attorney A writing authorizing another to act as one's agent or attorney.

power of termination A future interest in land which results when a grantor conveys land subject to a condition subsequent but also conditions the reversion of the land on the affirmative retaking of possession either by himself or his heirs.

precedent A case which furnishes an example or authority for deciding subsequent cases in which identical or similar facts are presented.

preemptive right A shareholder's right to purchase newly issued stock of a corporation, before it is offered to any outside buyers, on a pro rata basis, thereby allowing the shareholder to maintain his proportionate share and voice in the corporation.

preferential transfer A transfer by one who is insolvent to one or more of his creditors within 90 days of bankruptcy whereby the creditor to whom the property was transferred is put in a better position than other creditors with respect to their priority claims to the assets of the insolvent.

preferred stock Classes of stock which have priority over common stock both as to payment of dividends and distribution of assets upon the corporation's dissolution.

prenuptial agreement An agreement made by the parties to a marriage prior to the marriage. If the consideration for the agreement is the forthcoming marriage, there must be a signed writing to make the agreement enforceable. (see *Statute of Frauds*)

prescription The acquiring of an easement (or profit) by continuous and open use of land owned by another for a prescribed statutory period.

presentment Demand by a holder of commercial paper for payment (or acceptance).

presentment warranty A guarantee that, when presented by a holder for payment, the instrument will be honored.

prima facie (Latin) "at first sight." Something that is considered true because, on the face of it, it appears to be true.

principal A person who, by agreement or otherwise, authorizes an agent to act on his behalf such that acts of the agent become binding on the principal.

privilege In tort law, the ability to act contrary to another person's right without that person having legal redress for such acts. Privilege is usually raised as a defense, such as where A attacks B, B has a privilege to fight back to reasonably protect himself; but for A's assault in battery, B's battery would contravene A's rights.

privity of contract The relationship which exists between the promisor and promisee of a contract.

probable cause Reasonable ground to believe the existence of facts warranting acts such as search or arrest of a person.

probate The process of proving and validating a will.

probate court A special court, in some jurisdictions, having jurisdiction of proceedings concerning the settlement of a person's estate. (see *jurisdiction, estate*)

procedure The manner by which parties and courts must act when bringing an action, whether civil, criminal, or administrative. Includes pleading, process, evidence, and practice.

procedural law That law which deals with the manner of bringing an action.

profit The right to enter upon and remove things from the property of another. (e.g., the right to enter onto a person's land and remove sand and gravel therefrom.)

promisee Person to whom a contractual duty is owed.

promisor Person who is under a contractual duty to another.

promissory estoppel A legal principle whereby a party is not allowed (estopped) to deny certain relevant facts, because of statements they made, or because they made procedural errors. (*i.e.*, a defendant who does not plead an affirmative defense is estopped from doing so at trial.) (see *affirmative defense*)

promissory note   A written instrument signed by a maker promising to pay a sum certain in money to a payee or a holder on a specified date.

promoter   An entrepreneur who, utilizing his own capital, purchases or leases facilities and equipment for, and participates in the organization of a newly formed corporation. Promoters generally assume substantial risks in organizing new corporations, but also stand to realize significant profits from their efforts.

property   Anything subject to being used, possessed, and disposed of; need not be tangible ("rights" are property).

proximate cause   The "next" or "substantial" cause; in tort law, a concept used to determine whether a plaintiff's injury was the result of a defendant's negligent act. If the negligent act of a defendant was the sole cause or was a substantial cause of injuries to a plaintiff, the defendant will be liable to the plaintiff.

proxy   An agreement between a stockholder and another under which the stockholder authorizes the other to vote the stockholder's shares in a certain manner.

punitive damages   Compensation in excess of actual or consequential damages. They are awarded in order to punish the wrongdoer, and will be awarded only in cases involving willful or malicious misconduct. Also called "smart money."

purchase money security interest   A security interest which the seller of goods retains when it "lends" the purchase price to the purchaser of the goods. Such a security interest is automatically perfected.

Q

qualified indorsement   An indorsement on a negotiable instrument under which the indorser disclaims secondary liability on the instrument; under a qualified indorsement, however, an indorser still gives warranties of title. The most common qualified indorsement is "without recourse."

quasi-contracts   A quasi-contract is not a contract at all, but a *remedy* afforded to a person who renders services or delivers goods to another who accepts the goods or services without payment for them.

quasi-judicial power   The power of an administra-

tive agency to adjudicate the rights of individuals before it.

quasi-legislative   The power of an administrative agency to engage in rule-making.

quitclaim deed   A deed conveying title to real property, but guaranteeing nothing, not even the transferor's title, to the purchaser.

quorum   The number of persons who must be present at a meeting of a corporation's stockholders in order for action taken at the meeting to be valid.

R

rate making power   Government power to determine and set rates for business (*i.e.*, wage rate, prices).

ratification   In contract, the act of adopting or confirming an act which does not meet the contractual obligation, or carried out by one without the authority to do so (or was incompetent at the time the contract was made). The act of ratification causes the ratifier to give up his right to sue for a performance which does not otherwise conform with the contract.

real property   Property consisting of land and building thereupon, which are stationary, as opposed to personal property, which can be moved. Real property includes things growing on land before they are severed (such as timber) as well as fixtures.

reality of assent   Consideration of whether a person to a contract *actually* or only *impliedly* "accepts" each and every proposed term.

reasonable doubt   The standard used to determine the guilt or innocence of a person criminally charged. To be guilty of a crime, one must be proved guilty "beyond and to the exclusion of every reasonable doubt."

reciprocal contract   A bilateral contract.

recognizance   An obligation to return or reappear before a court.

reformation   A court ordered correction of a written instrument, to cause it to reflect the true intentions of the parties.

rejection   An offeree's communication to the offeror that the offeree does not accept the terms of the proposal made by the offeror.

remainder   A future interest in property held by a person other than a grantor which occurs at the natural termination of the preceding estate. A remainder is a present right to future possession and can either be vested or contingent.

remand The act of an appellate court sending a case back to the trial court ordering it to conduct either limited new hearings or an entire new trial.

replevin An action in equity brought to recover possession of goods unlawfully taken by another; as opposed to recovering the value of the goods. (see *conversion*)

reply Procedurally, a plaintiff's response to a defendant's answer.

repudiation Rejection of a contract involving the unconditional refusal by one of the parties to perform.

requirements contracts An agreement under which a promisor promises to supply the promisee with all the goods and/or services the promisee might require from period to period. While such contracts were at one time void for indefiniteness of amount, they are now universally valid.

res judicata A rule that prohibits the same factual dispute between two parties to be retried by a court after final judgment has been entered by a trial court and all appeals have been exhausted (or the time for appeal has passed).

rescission A remedy whereby the contract is cancelled and the parties are returned to the positions they occupied before the contract was made. May be done through mutual consent of the parties, by their conduct, or by the decree of a court of equity.

respondeat superior A principle of law which says that an employer is liable for the negligent acts of his employees while they are working within the scope of their employment.

restitution An equitable remedy under which a person who has rendered services to another, but where no valid contract between the two exists, will be reimbursed for the costs of his acts but will not be awarded profits; as opposed to an action for breach of contract.

restrictive indorsement Any indorsement of a negotiable instrument which purports to prohibit further transfer of the instrument. As against banks, such indorsements are usually ineffective.

reversion A future interest under which a grantor retains a present right to future interest of property which he conveys to another; usually the residue of a life estate, the reversion is always a vested property interest.

robbery Theft from a person, accompanied by assault and/or battery. (see *assault, battery*)

rule against perpetuities Rule against remoteness in vesting which states: "no interest in property is good unless it must vest, if at all, not later than 21 years, plus a period of gestation, after some life or lives in being at the time of creation of the interest."

S

sale The passing of title from the seller to the buyer for a price.

satisfaction The tender of substitute performance in return for the relinquishment of the right of action on a prior obligation. (see *accord and satisfaction*)

scope of employment The activities in which an employee engages in the carrying out of his employer's business which are reasonably foreseeable by the employer.

secured party Anyone who has an interest in a good, which they can exercise upon the occurrence or nonoccurrence of an event, and receive possession of the good.

secured transaction Any transaction, regardless of its form, which is intended to create a security interest in personal property or fixtures including goods, documents, and other intangibles.

securities Stock certificates or bonds given as evidence of a contribution to the assets of a corporation under which the security holder receives either an ownership interest in the corporation or a promise of repayment by the corporation.

security agreement An agreement which creates or provides for a security interest.

security interest An interest in personal property or fixtures which secures payment or performance of an obligation.

self-defense The legally recognized privilege to protect one's self or one's property against injury by another. The privilege of self-defense only protects acts which are reasonably necessary to protect one's self or one's property.

severable contract A contract which includes two or more promises which can be acted on separately such that the failure to perform one promise does not necessarily put the promisor in breach of the entire agreement.

shareholder The holder of an ownership interest in a corporation.

shipment contract Any agreement for the sale of goods under which the seller is authorized or required only to bear the expense of putting the goods in the hands of a common carrier and bears the risk of loss only up to that point. A contract for the sale of goods which is silent on a delivery term is presumed to be a shipment contract.

shop right doctrine   An employer's privilege to use an invention developed by an employee, without compensating that employee.

short-swing profits   Profits made on the purchase and sale of stock of a corporation within a six-month period.

sight draft   A draft which is payable upon proper presentment.

signature   The name or mark of a person, written by himself, or at his direction. In commercial law, any word or mark used with the intention of indorsing an instrument constitutes a signature. (see *indorsement*)

slander   An oral defamation.

sole proprietorship   A business which is owned and operated by a single person (or his or her immediate family) which is not incorporated under the laws of the domiciliary state.

special bailment   Any of a number of relationships, including gratuitous bailments, for the benefit of the bailor only; involuntary bailments, which arise by the accidental leaving of property with another (the bailee need exercise only "ordinary care"); and constructive bailments, where one person holds another's goods in such a manner that the law imposes a bailment situation.

special indorsement   An indorsement (signature of the transferor in a negotiation) specifying to whom the instrument is payable.

specific performance   An equitable remedy, whereby the court orders one of the parties to a contract to perform his duties under the contract. Usually granted when money damages would be an inadequate remedy (e.g., purchase and sale of real property).

stale check   A check, other than a certified check, which is presented more than six months after its date.

stare decisis   A flexible doctrine of the courts, recognizing the value of following prior decisions (precedent) in cases similar to the one now before the court—the practice of a court's being consistent with prior decisions based on similar facts.

Statute of Frauds   Statutory requirement (based on English common law) requiring that certain types of contracts be written to be enforceable. (e.g., contracts for the sale of goods over $500; contracts for the sale of land; contracts which cannot, by their terms, be performed within a year.)

statute of limitations   Statutes of the federal government and the various states setting maximum time periods during which certain actions can be tried. After the time period set out in the applicable statute of limitations has run, no legal action can be brought regardless of whether any cause of action ever existed.

statutory law   Laws which are enacted by a legislative body. (As opposed to constitutional law, administrative law or case law.)

stop payment order   An order by a drawer of a check directing his bank not to pay a check.

strict liability   Liability regardless of fault. Under tort law, strict liability is imposed on any person who introduces into commerce any good which is unreasonably dangerous when in a defective condition.

Subchapter S corporation   A corporation which, because it has filed as a Subchapter S and because it has met certain requirements as set out by the internal revenue code qualifies for special income tax treatment. Essentially, a Subchapter S corporation is taxed the same as a partnership while at the same time allowing the corporation's owners to enjoy the privilege of limited liability.

sublease   A lease executed by the lessee of land to a third person, conveying the same interest which the lessee enjoys, but for a shorter term than that for which the lessee holds.

subrogation   The substitution of one person in the place of another giving the former the same legal rights which the latter had. Subrogation appears most frequently in construction contracts, insurance contracts and in negotiable instrument law.

substantial performance   A doctrine of commercial reasonableness which recognizes that the rendering of a performance which does not exactly meet the terms of the agreement will be looked upon as fulfillment of the obligation less the damages which result from any deviation from the promised performance.

substantive law   Laws which define the rights and duties of individuals with respect to each other, as opposed to procedural law which defines the manner in which these rights and duties may be enforced.

substituted agreement A contract whereby the parties to an already existing contract agree that the existing contract is no longer binding and that a new contract or agreement will take its place.

summary judgment A judgment entered by a trial court which is based upon the valid assertion by a defendant that the plaintiff does not have a cause of action.

surety One who agrees to pay the debt of another. The surety is liable to the debtor even if the creditor does not seek to collect from the principal (original debtor) first. (see *suretyship*)

suretyship The relationship among three parties whereby one person (the surety) guarantees payment of a debtor's debt for performance of an obligor's duties to a creditor or obligee.

surviving corporation The corporation which, through a merger, acquires the assets and liabilities of another corporation.

T

tangible personal property Property, which can be moved, which has physical substance and can be distinguished by the five senses; corporeal property.

tenancy at sufferance Maintenance of occupancy by someone who has no estate in the land. He occupies only because the person entitled to eject him has not; he has no estate or title.

tenancy at will The right of a tenant to remain in possession of land until either he or the landlord chooses to terminate the tenancy.

tenancy by the entirety The joint ownership of property by husband and wife. Five "unities" must be present: time, title, interest, possession, and person (under common law, husband and wife were one person). Neither party can alienate or encumber the property, it is inherited by the survivor of the two, and dissolution of marriage transforms it to tenancy in common.

tenancy for years A non-freehold estate/lease for a specified number of years, at which time the interest reverts to the grantor. The lease can be renewed or not at the end of the term of years.

tenancy from period to period (periodic tenancy) A non-freehold estate/lease which exists for a period of one year or less, and can be renewed or not at the end of each period (*i.e.*, monthly).

tenancy in common Co-ownership of property whereby each tenant owns an undivided fractional part of the property, and none owns the whole as in joint tenancy.

tender A timely offer, or expression of willingness, to pay a debt or perform an obligation.

testamentary trust A trust which is created by will, and therefore does not take effect until the death of the testator.

testate Leaving a valid will; when a person dies leaving a valid will he dies testate.

testator (trix) One who makes and executes a will. (see *will*)

title The right to full ownership of property.

title insurance An insurance policy which insures against defects in the title of property (usually real property).

tort Civil wrongs (as opposed to criminal) not arising from a breach of contract; a breach of a legal duty owed by the defendant to the plaintiff. That breach must be the proximate cause of the harm done to plaintiff. (see *proximate cause, negligence*)

tortfeasor One who commits a personal wrong (or a tort).

trade acceptance A bill of exchange/draft drawn by the seller of goods on the purchaser, and accepted by such purchaser. It represents the purchaser's promise to pay.

trade fixture Articles placed in or attached to buildings by the tenant, to carry on the tenant's business. They are generally removable without material harm to the real property.

trademark A word or symbol which has become sufficiently associated with a good (common law) or has been registered with a government agency; once established, the person using the trademark has the right to bring a legal action against those who infringe upon the protection given the trademark. The remedy may be criminal, money damages, or an injunction against the defendant. (see *injunction*)

trespass Any transgression or offense against the property of another.

trespass to land The mere intentional or unintentional passing over another person's land uninvited, regardless whether any physical damage was done to the land.

trespass to personalty Same as trespass.

traveler's check A check drawn by the issuing bank upon itself which is accepted by the act of issuance.

Like a cashier's check, the bank is secondarily liable as drawee; additionally, it is primarily liable as acceptor.

true bill   Often called an indictment, the true bill is issued by the grand jury after a finding of probable cause to accuse a person of a criminal offense. (see *information, grand jury*)

trustee   One who holds legal title to property "in trust" for the benefit of another person (beneficiary), and who must carry out specific duties with regard to the property. The trustee owes a fiduciary duty to the beneficiary. (see *fiduciary duty*)

trustee in bankruptcy   The person appointed to oversee the estate of a bankrupt.

tying agreement   A requirement in a contract between a buyer and seller whereby the buyer of a specific good is obligated to purchase additional connected products.

U

ultra vires   Activities of a corporation's managers which are outside the scope of the power granted them by the corporation.

unconscionable contracts   A contract which is void as against public policy because one party, as a result of his disproportionate bargaining power, is forced to accept terms which are unfairly burdensome to him and which unfairly benefit the dominating party.

undue influence   Abuse of one's position of influence or relationship with another person to persuade that person to act or refrain from acting in a certain manner; usually involves breach of a fiduciary duty.

unilateral contract   A contract under which promise of payment or performance is given in exchange for performance by the other party (as opposed to a promise to perform by the other party).

unliquidated debt   An obligation which has not been reduced to a specific money amount; also, there may be a dispute between the parties as to this undetermined amount.

usage of trade   The prevailing, accepted customs within a particular trade or industry. It is implied that merchants are cognizant of the usage of their trade.

usury   Charging interest on a debt above the statutory maximum, as defined by various state statutes. A contract which includes a usurious interest rate is illegal, and therefore unenforceable.

venue   The geographical district in which the action is tried and from which the jury is selected. (see *jurisdiction*)

vertical merger   A combining of two firms, one of which purchases goods for resale from the other. If a producer or wholesaler acquires a retailer it is a *forward* merger. If a retailer or distributor acquires its producer it is a *backward* merger. (see *merger*)

vertical price-fixing contract   An agreement to maintain prices between producers and wholesalers or distributors, between producers and retailers, or between wholesalers or distributors and retailers.

vicarious liability   Responsibility for someone else's actions, arising out of some legal relationship. (see *respondeat superior, power of attorney*)

void   Having no legal force or binding effect.

voidable   That which may be legally annulled at the option of one of the parties.

voluntary bankruptcy   A bankruptcy proceeding which is initiated by the debtor.

voting trust   The entrusting of shares of a corporation to a trustee who is authorized to vote the shares so that certain persons remain directors, and thus in control of the corporation.

W

waiver   An intentional, knowing relinquishment of a legal right. (see *accord, satisfaction, novation*)

warehouseman   A person engaged in the business of storing goods for hire.

warehouse receipt   A receipt issued by a person engaged in the business of storing goods for hire; it is a document of title.

warranty   A guarantee by one party to the other that certain facts or conditions actually exist as represented, thus relieving the promisee of a duty to ascertain those facts himself. Under the U.C.C., three types of warranty exist. (see *promisee*)

warranty deed   A deed under which the grantor guarantees to the grantee that he (the grantor) has title to the property conveyed in the deed and that there are no encumbrances on the property other than what the grantor has represented.

warranty of merchantability   A promise by the seller of goods that they are reasonably fit for the general purpose for which they are sold.

watered stock   Stock issued by a corporation as fully

paid for, when in fact the entire par value has not been paid.

whole life A life insurance policy in which the insured pays a level premium for his or her entire life and in which there is a constantly accumulating cash value which the insured can withdraw or borrow against.

will An instrument directing what is to be done with a person's property upon his death, made by that person and revocable during his lifetime. No interests pass until the testator dies. (see *testator*)

winding up The settling of accounts and liquidation of assets or a partnership or corporation just prior to dissolution.

writ A written court order or a judicial process, directing that a sheriff, judge, or other judicial officer do what is commanded by the writ. Thus, a "writ of certiorari" commands the inferior court to send the record of the case to the issuing court, which will take appellate jurisdiction.

writ of certiorari Court order giving jurisdiction to an appellate court, on that court's discretion after a review of the petition, which is submitted by a party to the action. Many cases reach the U.S. Supreme Court this way, since there is no absolute right to Supreme Court review. (see *writ*)

writ of execution A writ which puts in force a court's decree.

Z

zoning The division of the land of an entire city or county by a legislature whereby the legislature prescribes certain general or particular uses for various segments of the land.

INDEX

†